'... when it comes to helping wine drinkers make sense of the now thousands of wines being produced in this country, (Halliday) is in a class of his own.'
— *Sunday Herald Sun*

'An annual "must have" for those racing to keep up with the hurly-burly of the Australian wine industry, and it's easy to see why.'
— *The Age*

'Halliday has refined the art of tucking diverse information ... into a readable and compact package.'
— *Melbourne Times*

'Halliday brings a vast knowledge to the subject, so even a few words carry a weight unmatched by lesser mortals.'
— *Gold Coast Bulletin*

'(Wine) buyers will find his assessments expert and informative, and those with cellars, however modest, will be helped by his assessment of past vintages.'
— *Herald Sun*

james halliday

australia & new zealand

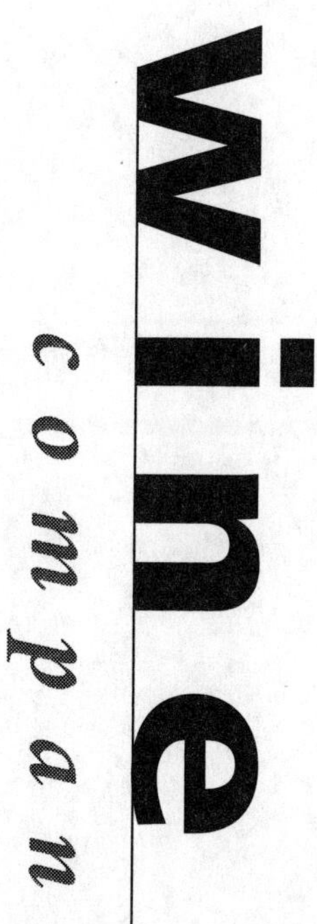

2002 EDITION

james halliday

australia & new zealand

wine companion

2002 EDITION

HarperCollinsPublishers

HarperCollins*Publishers*

First published as *Australia and New Zealand Wine Companion* in Australia in 1997
This edition published in 2001
by HarperCollins*Publishers* Pty Limited
ABN 36 009 913 517
A member of HarperCollins*Publishers* (Australia) Pty Limited Group
www.harpercollins.com.au

HarperCollins*Publishers*
25 Ryde Road, Pymble, Sydney, NSW 2073, Australia
31 View Road, Glenfield, Auckland 10, New Zealand
77–85 Fulham Palace Road, London W6 8JB, United Kingdom
Hazelton Lanes, 55 Avenue Road, Suite 2900, Toronto, Ontario M5R 3L2
and 1995 Markham Road, Scarborough, Ontario M1B 5M8, Canada
10 East 53rd Street, New York NY 10022, USA

ISBN 0 7322 7037 5
ISSN 1445-5447

Cover inset photograph by Kevin Judd

Typeset in Bembo 8/9.5 by HarperCollins Design Studio

Printed and bound in Australia by Griffin Press on 65gsm Bulky Paperback

5 4 3 2 1 01 02 03 04

about the author

James Halliday is Australia's most respected wine writer. Over the past thirty years he has worn many hats: lawyer, winemaker and grape grower, wine judge, wine consultant, journalist and author. He has now discarded his legal hat, but actively continues in his other roles, incessantly travelling, researching and tasting wines in all the major wine-producing countries. He judges regularly at wine shows in Australia, the UK, the US, South Africa and New Zealand.

James Halliday has written or contributed to over 40 books on wine since he began writing in 1979 (notable contributions include the *Oxford Companion* and *Larousse Encylopedia of Wine*). Various of his books have been translated into Japanese, French and German, and have been published in the UK and the US as well as Australia.

His most recent works include *Classic Wines of Australia*, *An Introduction to Australian Wine*, *Wine Atlas of Australia and New Zealand* and *Collecting Wine: You and Your Cellar.*

Co-founder of the wine website, www.winepros.com.au, Halliday is proving to be as popular on the World Wide Web as he is in other mediums.

contents

how to use this book

The *Wine Companion* is arranged with wineries in alphabetical order, and the entries should be self-explanatory, but here I will briefly take you through the information for each entry.

winery entries

cape mentelle ★★★★★
Off Wallcliffe Road, Margaret River, WA 6285 **region** Margaret River
phone (08) 9757 3266 **fax** (08) 9757 3233 **open** 7 days 10–4.30
winemaker John Durham **production** 50 000 **est.** 1970
prod. range ($20–44 R) Chardonnay, Semillon Sauvignon Blanc, Cabernet Sauvignon, Cabernet Merlot, Shiraz, Zinfandel, Trinders Cabernet Merlot.
summary Notwithstanding majority ownership by Veuve Clicquot, David Hohnen remains very much in command of one of Australia's foremost medium-sized wineries. Exceptional marketing skills and wine of the highest quality, with the back-up of New Zealand's Cloudy Bay, are a potent combination. The Chardonnay and Semillon Sauvignon Blanc are among Australia's best, the potent Shiraz usually superb, and the berry/spicy Zinfandel makes one wonder why this grape is not as widespread in Australia as it is in California.

winery name Cape Mentelle

Although it might seem that stating the winery name is straightforward, this is not necessarily so. To avoid confusion, wherever possible I use the name that appears most prominently on the wine label and do not refer to any associated trading name.

ratings ★★★★★

The winery star system may be interpreted as follows:

★★★★★ Outstanding winery regularly producing exemplary wines.
★★★★☆ Extremely good; virtually on a par with a five-star winery.
★★★★ Consistently produces high-quality wines.
★★★☆ A solid, reliable producer of good wine.
★★★ Typically good, but may have a few lesser wines.
★★☆ Adequate.
★★ Hard to recommend.

If the ratings seem generous, so be it. The fact is that Australia is blessed with a marvellous climate for growing grapes, a high degree of technological skill, and a remarkable degree of enthusiasm and dedication on the part of its winemakers. Across the price spectrum, Australian wines stand tall in the markets of the world. I see no reason, therefore, to shrink from recognising excellence. NR = not rated, either because the winery is new or because I have not tasted enough of its wines.

address Off Wallcliffe Road, Margaret River, WA 6285
phone (08) 9757 3266 **fax** (08) 9757 3233

The details are usually those of the winery and cellar door but in a few instances may simply be of the winery; this occurs when the wine is made at another winery under contract and is sold only through retail.

region Margaret River

The mapping of Australia into Zones and Regions with legally defined boundaries is now well underway. This edition sees radical changes (and additions) to the regional names and boundaries. Wherever possible the official 'Geographic Indication' name has been adopted, and where the registration process is incomplete, I have used the most likely name.

cellar door sales hours **open** 7 days 10–4.30

Although a winery might be listed as not open or only open on weekends, some may in fact be prepared to open by appointment. Many will, some won't; a telephone call will establish whether it is possible or not. Also, virtually every winery that is shown as being open only for weekends is in fact open for public holidays as well. Once again, a telephone call will confirm this.

winemaker John Durham

In the large companies the winemaker is simply the head of a team; there may be many executive winemakers actually responsible for specific wines.

production 50 000

This figure given (representing the number of cases produced each year) is merely an indication of the size of the operation. Some wineries (principally but not exclusively the large companies) regard this information as confidential; in that event, NFP (not for publication) will appear. NA = information was not available.

year of establishment **est.** 1970

A more or less self-explanatory item, but keep in mind that some makers consider the year in which they purchased the land to be the year of establishment, others the year in which they first planted grapes, others the year they first made wine, others the year they first offered wine for sale, and so on. There may also be minor complications where there has been a change of ownership or a break in production.

price range and prod. range ($20–44 R) Chardonnay, Semillon Sauvignon Blanc, Cabernet Sauvignon, Cabernet Merlot, Shiraz, Zinfandel, Trinders Cabernet Merlot.

The **price range** given covers the least expensive through to the most expensive wines usually made by the winery in question (where the information was available). Hence there may be a significant spread. That spread, however, may not fully cover fluctuations that occur in retail pricing, particularly with the larger companies. Erratic and often savage discounting remains a feature of the wine industry, and prices must therefore be seen as approximate.

For Australia, this spread has been compounded by the introduction on July 1 2000 of the Goods and Services Tax (GST) of 10 per cent and the special and uniquely discriminatory Wine Equalisation Tax (WET) of 29 per cent imposed on top of one another in a tax-on-tax pyramid.

Notwithstanding Federal Government assurances that the price of wine would not increase by more than 1.5 per cent, and notwithstanding the fierce scrutiny of Professor Allan Fels and the ACCC, most prices will have risen by 3-5 per cent since this book went to print.The Australian winery prices are for purchase in Australia, in Australian dollars; those for New Zealand are for purchase in New Zealand, in New Zealand dollars.

I have indicated whether the price is cellar door (CD), mailing list (ML) or retail (R). By and large, the choice has been determined by which of the three methods of sale is most important to the winery. The price of Australian and New Zealand wines in other countries is affected by a number of factors, including excise and customs duty, distribution mark-up and currency fluctuations. Contact the winery for details.

product range Particularly with the larger companies, it is not possible to give a complete list of the wines. The saving grace is that these days most of the wines are simply identified on their label by their varietal composition.

summary Notwithstanding majority ownership by Veuve Clicquot, David Hohnen remains very much in command of one of Australia's foremost medium-sized wineries. Exceptional marketing skills and wine of the highest quality, with the back-up of New Zealand's Cloudy Bay, are a potent combination. The Chardonnay and Semillon Sauvignon Blanc are among Australia's best, the potent Shiraz usually superb, and the berry/spicy Zinfandel makes one wonder why this grape is not as widespread in Australia as it is in California.

My summary of the winery. Little needs to be said, except that I have tried to vary the subjects I discuss in this part of the winery entry.

The vine leaf symbol indicates wineries that are new entries in this year's listing.

tasting notes

The major difference between the 2002 Companion and prior years is the deletion of background information on each wine for which a tasting note is provided. This decision has been taken purely for reasons of space. With the marked increase of the number of wineries, the only alternative would have been the omission of over 800 wine entries.

Cape Mentelle Cabernet Sauvignon
🍷🍷🍷🍷🍸 **1995** Medium to full red-purple; a bouquet with uncommon depth and complexity, and a range of secondary earthy/cedary/berry characters already starting to appear. A wine with similarly good structure and depth to the palate although the flavours are tending more towards the savoury end of the spectrum than the opulently fruity. **rating:** 90

best drinking 2000–2010 **best vintages** '76, '78, '82, '83, '86, '90, '91, '93, '94, '95 **drink with** Loin of lamb • $43.20

wine name Cape Mentelle Cabernet Sauvignon

In most instances, the wine's name will be prefaced by the name of the winery.

ratings 🍷🍷🍷🍷🍸

Two ratings are given for each wine; the ratings apply to the vintage reviewed, and may vary from one year to the next.

Points scale	Glass symbol	
98–100	–	Perfection which exists only as an idea.
94–97	🍷🍷🍷🍷🍷	As close to perfection as the real world will allow.
90–93	🍷🍷🍷🍷🍸	Excellent wine full of character; of gold medal standard.
85–89	🍷🍷🍷🍷	Very good wine; clear varietal definition/style; silver verging on gold medal standard.
80–84	🍷🍷🍷🍸	Good fault-free, flavoursome; high bronze to silver medal standard.

You will see that most of the wines reviewed in this book rate 84 points (3½ glasses) or better. This is not wanton generosity on my part. It simply reflects the fact that the 2000 or so wines selected for specific review are the tip of more than 6000 tasting notes accumulated over the past year. In other words, the wines described are among Australia's top 20 per cent. NR = not rated.

🍷🍷🍷🍷🍷 **1995** Medium to full red-purple; a bouquet with uncommon depth and complexity, and a range of secondary earthy/cedary/berry characters already starting to appear. A wine with similarly good structure and depth to the palate although the flavours are tending more towards the savoury end of the spectrum than the opulently fruity. **rating:** 90

The tasting note opens with the vintage of the wine tasted. With the exception of a very occasional classic wine, this tasting note will have been made within the 12 months prior to publication. Even that is a long time, and during the life of this book the wine will almost certainly change. More than this, remember that tasting is a highly subjective and imperfect art. NV = non-vintage.

best drinking 2000–2010

I will usually give a range of years or a more specific comment (such as 'quick-developing style'), but whatever my best drinking recommendation, always consider it with extreme caution and as an approximate guide at best. When to drink a given wine is an intensely personal decision, which only you can make.

best vintages '76, '78, '82, '83, '86, '90, '91, '93, '94, '95

Self-explanatory information, but a note of caution: wines do change in the bottle, and it may be that were I to taste all of the best vintages listed, I would demote some and elevate some not mentioned.

drink with Loin of lamb

Again, merely a suggestion – a subliminal guide to the style of wine.

price • $43.20

This is a guide only.

$NA = information not available.

Abbreviation: mlf = malolactic fermentation.

key to regions

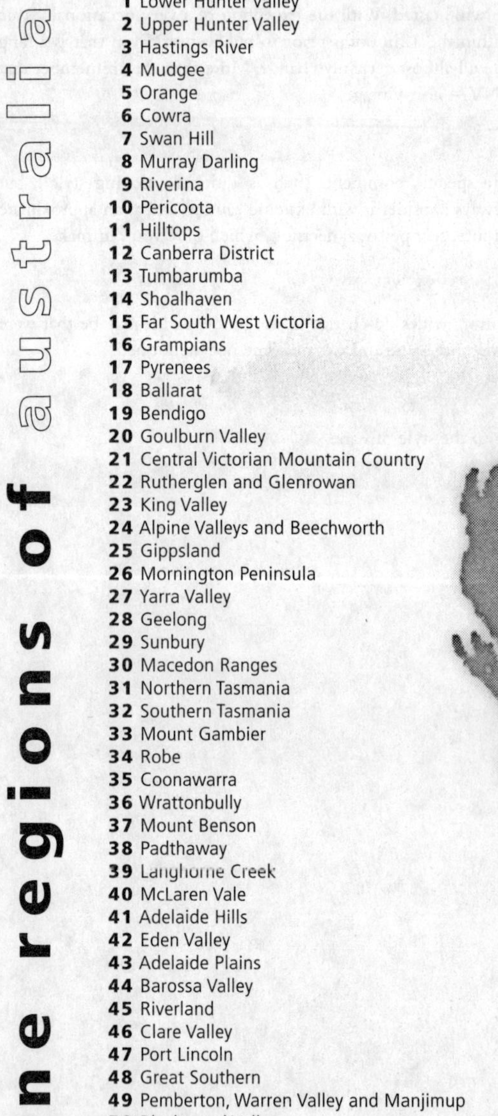

1 Lower Hunter Valley
2 Upper Hunter Valley
3 Hastings River
4 Mudgee
5 Orange
6 Cowra
7 Swan Hill
8 Murray Darling
9 Riverina
10 Pericoota
11 Hilltops
12 Canberra District
13 Tumbarumba
14 Shoalhaven
15 Far South West Victoria
16 Grampians
17 Pyrenees
18 Ballarat
19 Bendigo
20 Goulburn Valley
21 Central Victorian Mountain Country
22 Rutherglen and Glenrowan
23 King Valley
24 Alpine Valleys and Beechworth
25 Gippsland
26 Mornington Peninsula
27 Yarra Valley
28 Geelong
29 Sunbury
30 Macedon Ranges
31 Northern Tasmania
32 Southern Tasmania
33 Mount Gambier
34 Robe
35 Coonawarra
36 Wrattonbully
37 Mount Benson
38 Padthaway
39 Langhorne Creek
40 McLaren Vale
41 Adelaide Hills
42 Eden Valley
43 Adelaide Plains
44 Barossa Valley
45 Riverland
46 Clare Valley
47 Port Lincoln
48 Great Southern
49 Pemberton, Warren Valley and Manjimup
50 Blackwood Valley
51 Margaret River
52 Geographe
53 South-west Coast
54 Perth Hills
55 Swan District
56 South Burnett
57 Granite Belt

Northern Territory
Queensland
South Australia
New South Wales
ACT
Victoria
Tasmania
brisbane
sydney
adelaide
melbourne
launceston
hobart
56
57
1
2
3
4
5
6
7
8
9
10
11
12
13
14
15
16
17
18
19
20
21
22
23
24
25
26
27
28
29
30
31
32
33
34
35
36
37
38
39
40
41
42
43
44
45
46
47

wine regions of new zealand

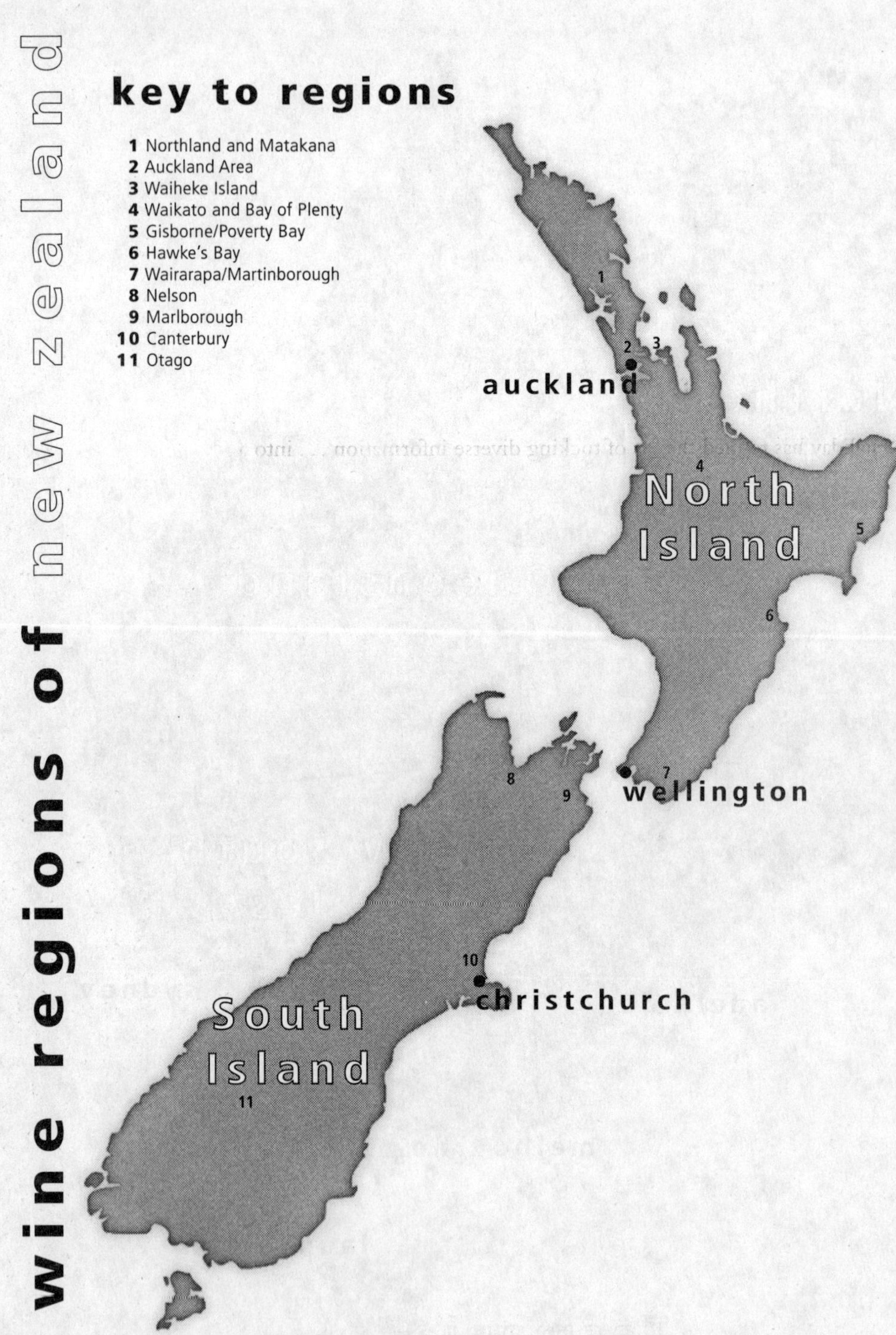

the best of the best by variety

This year follows in the tradition of last year by listing the top wines from well over 5000 tasting notes made between April 2000 and March 2001. As I have said before, the lists brutally expose the imperfections of assigning numbers (or points) to wines and giving those points the appearance of immutable validity. The reality is they are part of a series of snapshots, as accurate as I could make them at the time and in the varying circumstances of the particular tasting.

There are some notable omissions, most frequently because the wine in question did not cross my tasting table in the year. There are also some surprising inclusions: I have resisted the temptation to edit the lists in any way.

Finally, for obvious reasons, I have listed Australian and New Zealand wines separately.

australia

riesling

On a scale of points per dollar, Riesling stands supreme in the Australian market, and while there are signs of the long-awaited renaissance finally arriving, the demand is largely confined to the domestic market. Australian Riesling marches to the tune of its own drum, which will always, it seems, limit its international appeal; hence the levers which have been pulled to up the price of other categories don't operate here.

Wine	Points
2000 Crawford River Reserve Riesling	97
1999 Tamar Ridge Josef Chromy Selection Riesling	97
2000 Gilberts Riesling	96
2000 Knight Granite Hills Riesling	96
2000 Leasingham Bin 7 Riesling	96
2000 Crawford River Riesling	95
2000 East Arm Riesling	95
1995 Pewsey Vale The Contour Riesling	95
1998 Tamar Ridge Riesling	95
2000 Craigow Riesling	94
2000 Dal Zotto Riesling	94
1999 Elsewhere Vineyard Riesling	94
2000 Freycinet Riesling	94
2000 Grant Burge Thorn Vineyard Riesling	94
2000 Grosset Polish Hill Riesling	94
2000 Orlando Jacob's Creek Riesling	94
1996 Peter Lehmann Eden Valley Reserve Riesling	94
2000 Tamar Ridge Riesling	94
2000 Wolf Blass Gold Label Riesling	94

semillon

I seem to have been somewhat economical with my points for Semillon this year, surprising given my personal predilection for the wine. However, as I have commented in previous editions, appreciation of young Semillon requires both experience and a degree of faith in the future — or alternatively, residence in Sydney, where most of the wine is sold and consumed.

Wine	Points
2000 Keith Tulloch Semillon	94
2000 Lamont Barrel Fermented Semillon	94
2000 Lenswood Vineyards Semillon	94
1995 McWilliam's Mount Pleasant Lovedale Semillon	94
2000 Tyrrell's Lost Block Semillon	94
2000 Annie's Lane Semillon	93
2000 Brokenwood Semillon	93

1997 McWilliam's Mount Pleasant Elizabeth	93
1997 Tyrrell's Stevens Reserve Semillon	93
1999 Alkoomi Wandoo	92
2000 Henry Lawson Semillon	92
1990 Maling Family Waverley Estate Semillon	92
2000 Chain of Ponds Semillon	91
2000 Crawford River Semillon	91
2000 Kulkunbulla The Glandore Semillon	91
2000 Molly Morgan Joe's Block Semillon	91
1994 Penfolds Trial Bin Adelaide Hills McLaren Vale Semillon	91
2000 Reynolds Hunter Valley Semillon	91

sauvignon blanc and sauvignon blanc semillon blends — and a few others

Recent vintages haven't been particularly kind for Sauvignon Blanc, which doesn't like hot weather. The relatively small group provided the opportunity to tack on three puppy-dogs' tails which otherwise wouldn't have been recognised.

2000 Grosset Semillon Sauvignon Blanc	94
1999 Petaluma Viognier	94
2000 Trevelen Farm Sauvignon Blanc	94
2000 Alkoomi Sauvignon Blanc	93
2000 Clonakilla Viognier	93
2000 Island Brook Estate Verdelho	93
1999 Leeuwin Estate Art Series Sauvignon Blanc	93
2000 Shaw & Smith Sauvignon Blanc	93
2000 Willow Bridge Estate Sauvignon Blanc Semillon	93
2000 Deep Woods Estate Semillon Sauvignon Blanc	92
2000 Diamond Valley Vineyards Yarra Valley Sauvignon Blanc	92
2000 Knappstein Semillon Sauvignon Blanc	92
1998 Suckfizzle Augusta Semillon Sauvignon Blanc	92
2000 Cape Mentelle Semillon Sauvignon Blanc	91
2000 Geoff Weaver Sauvignon Blanc	91
2000 Phillip Island Sauvignon Blanc	91
2000 Pierro Fire Gully Semillon Sauvignon Blanc	91

chardonnay

Nineteen wines scoring 94 points or more, or 28 scoring 93 points and over? Either way, the group emphasises that however vocal the ABC (Anything But Chardonnay) club may be, Chardonnays make by far the largest contribution to the top end of the white wine sector of the Australian market.

1997 Penfolds Yattarna Chardonnay	97
1999 Cullen Chardonnay	96
1999 Grosset Piccadilly Chardonnay	96

1999 Pipers Brook Vineyard Estate Chardonnay	95
1999 Tyrrell's Vat 47 Pinot Chardonnay	95
1999 Wellington Chardonnay	95
1999 Cape Mentelle Chardonnay	94
1998 Capel Vale Frederick Chardonnay	94
2000 Derwent Estate Chardonnay	94
1999 Dromana Estate Reserve Chardonnay	94
1999 Hardys Eileen Hardy Chardonnay	94
1999 Lake's Folly Chardonnay	94
1998 Leeuwin Estate Art Series Chardonnay	94
1999 Miceli Olivia's Chardonnay	94
1997 Petaluma Tiers Chardonnay	94
2000 Providence Chardonnay	94
1999 Vasse Felix Chardonnay	94
1999 Voyager Estate Chardonnay	94
1999 Wells Parish Chardonnay	94

sweet white wines

A distinctly eclectic group, covering a range of varieties and styles from all over Australia. Due to the reluctance of restaurants to pursue a more active by-the-glass programme for 'stickies', it is a limited market, and the quantities made (other than perhaps Noble One) are small, the wines often difficult to track down.

1999 De Bortoli Noble One Botrytis Semillon	94
1999 Kulkunbulla Botrytis Semillon	94
1999 Heggies Botrytis Riesling 375 ml	93
2000 Holm Oak Botrytis Riesling	93
1999 Crawford River Nektar	92
2000 Mariners Rest Autumn Gold	92
1999 Xanadu Noble Semillon	92
1998 Yalumba Noble Pick Viognier	92
1999 Miranda Golden Botrytis	91
1999 Neagles Rock Vineyards Sweet Dorothy Botrytis Riesling	91
2000 Bloodwood Noble Riesling	90
1998 Charles Melton Sotto di Ferro	90
1999 Lowe Family Botrytis Semillon	90
2000 Mount Horrocks Cordon Cut Riesling	90
1999 Westend 3 Bridges Golden Mist Botrytis Semillon	90
1999 Yalumba Noble Pick Riesling	90

sparkling wines

The usual suspects are all here; to add a touch of spice, however, the 1995 Hardys Arras which heads this year's list is not the same wine as that which headed up last year's (rather shorter) list.

1995 Hardys Arras Pinot Chardonnay	96
1996 Pipers Brook Pirie Cuvée	95
1995 Seppelt M2 Chardonnay Pinot Noir	95
NV Rockford Black Shiraz	94
1990 Seppelt Great Western Vineyard Sparkling Shiraz	94
1994 Seppelt Salinger Méthode Champenoise	94
1995 Tamar Ridge RV	94
1997 Yarrabank Brut Cuvée	94
1996 Brown Brothers Whitlands Pinot Chardonnay	93
NV Hanging Rock Macedon Cuvée	93
1993 Seppelt M2 Sparkling Show Shiraz	93
1997 Domaine Chandon Brut	92
1997 Domaine Chandon Brut Rosé	92
1996 Freycinet Radenti	92
1996 Jansz	92

pinot noir

If nothing else, the list proves I do not have a home-town bias: only two Yarra Valley Pinots feature on the list, including a relative newcomer to the Valley, Wedgetail Estate. Once again, Tasmania fares best, and in the next edition will almost certainly be cashing in on the 2000 vintage, one of its best ever.

1999 Providence Miguet Reserve Pinot Noir	97
1999 Ashton Hills Pinot Noir	95
1999 Lark Hill Pinot Noir	95
1999 Lenswood Vineyards Pinot Noir	95
1999 Bannockburn by Farr Pinot Noir	94
1999 Moorilla Estate Reserve Pinot Noir	94
1998 Pembroke Pinot Noir	94
1999 Wedgetail Estate Reserve Pinot Noir	94
1999 Winstead Pinot Noir	94
1999 Main Ridge Half Acre Pinot Noir	93
1999 Paringa Estate Pinot Noir	93
1999 Redgate Pinot Noir	93
1999 Stefano Lubiana Pinot Noir	93
1999 Dalrymple Special Bin Pinot Noir	92
1999 Diamond Valley Estate Pinot Noir	92
1999 Holm Oak Pinot Noir	92
2000 Prince Albert Pinot Noir	92
1999 Salitage Pinot Noir	92

shiraz

This group suggests that Shiraz is in even better shape than Chardonnay, but take a look at the preponderance of 1996 and 1998 vintage wines.

You simply won't find so many treasures (particularly from South Australia) when the 1999 and 2000 vintages come on stream, although there are some hot spots elsewhere in Australia in those years.

1998 Best's Thomson Family Shiraz	97
1996 Penfolds Grange	97
1996 Annie's Lane Copper Trail Shiraz	96
1998 Brokenwood Graveyard Shiraz	96
1999 Vasse Felix Shiraz	96
1998 Baileys of Glenrowan 1904 Block Shiraz	95
1998 Brand's of Coonawarra Stentiford's Reserve Shiraz	95
1999 Clos Clare Shiraz	95
1998 Dalwhinnie Eagle Series Pyrenees Shiraz	95
1999 Dalwhinnie Moonambel Shiraz	95
1998 Hamilton Centurion 100 Year Old Shiraz	95
1998 Jim Barry The Armagh	95
1998 Mount Langi Ghiran Langi Shiraz	95
1996 Penfolds St Henri Shiraz	95
1998 Plantagenet Mount Barker Shiraz	95
1998 Ravenswood Lane Reunion Shiraz	95
1996 Seppelt Great Western Shiraz	95
1998 Clarendon Hills Piggot Range Shiraz	94
1999 Clonakilla Shiraz Viognier	94
1997 Coriole Lloyd Reserve Shiraz	94
1998 Driftwood Estate Shiraz	94
1998 Edwards & Chaffey Section 353 Shiraz	94
1998 Hewitson L'Oizeau Shiraz	94
1998 Ingoldby Reserve Shiraz	94
1999 Keith Tulloch Kester Shiraz	94
1998 Keith Tulloch Kester Shiraz	94
1998 Langmeil The Freedom Shiraz	94
1997 Leasingham Classic Clare Shiraz	94
1998 Leasingham Classic Clare Shiraz	94
1999 Merum Shiraz	94
1999 Mitchell Peppertree Vineyard Shiraz	94
1998 Mount Ida Shiraz	94
1997 Penfolds RWT Shiraz	94
1996 Peter Lehmann Stonewell Shiraz	94
1998 The Fleurieu Shiraz	94
1998 Torbreck The Factor	94
1999 Voyager Estate Shiraz	94
1998 Waninga Shiraz	94
1998 Wirra Wirra RSW Shiraz	94
1998 Wynns Coonawarra Estate Michael Shiraz	94
1998 Yaldara The Farms Barossa Valley Shiraz	94
1998 Yering Station Reserve Shiraz	94

shiraz blends

Should there be more wines in this group, and will its composition change in the future? The answer is yes; Cabernet Sauvignon is increasingly being blended with Merlot et al, while the Rhone Valley-inspired Shiraz blends (witness the three Torbreck wines) point the direction for the future.

1998 Torbreck The RunRig	95
1998 Wendouree Shiraz Malbec	95
1998 Chapel Hill The Vicar Cabernet Shiraz	94
1999 Gralyn Estate Shiraz Cabernet	94
1998 McWilliam's Winemaker's Reserve Cabernet Shiraz	94
1998 Penfolds Bin 389 Cabernet Shiraz	94
1998 Wolf Blass Black Label Cabernet Sauvignon Shiraz	94
1998 Henschke Keyneton Estate Shiraz Cabernet Malbec	93
1997 Torbreck The RunRig	92
1999 Torbreck The Steading	92
1998 Virgin Hills	92
1997 Wolf Blass Black Label Cabernet Sauvignon Shiraz	92

merlot

I don't claim to understand every facet of Merlot, but I'm equally sure no one else does either. By and large I have given high points to wines which do show varietal character (either flavour or structure, preferably both) but there are one or two inclusions on the list which might equally well be labelled Cabernet Sauvignon.

1999 Chestnut Grove Merlot	94
1998 Haan Merlot Prestige	94
1999 Taylors Merlot	94
1998 Wirra Wirra Merlot	94
1999 Blue Wren Merlot	93
1997 James Irvine Grand Merlot	93
1998 Kemblefield Estate Reserve Merlot	93
1999 Tatachilla McLaren Vale Merlot	93
1998 Capel Vale Howecroft Merlot	92
1999 Grey Sands Merlot	92
1997 Petaluma Merlot	92
1999 Symphonia King Valley Merlot	92
1999 Yarra Yering Merlot	92
1998 Hillstowe The Pinch Row Lenswood Merlot	91
1998 Xanadu Merlot	91
1998 Gapsted Ballerina Canopy Merlot	90
1998 Mountadam Merlot	90
1999 Tyrrell's Rufus Stone McLaren Vale Merlot	90

cabernet sauvignon

Twenty-three wines rated at 94 points or above tells its own story; this is a great group of wines in which Cabernet Sauvignon needs no blend mate (Merlot or Shiraz) to fill out the supposed hole in the middle. On the other hand, vintages such as 1998 do not come around with the frequency we would all like.

1998 Tatachilla McLaren Vale Cabernet Sauvignon	97
1998 Pepper Tree Reserve Coonawarra Cabernet Sauvignon	96
1996 Seppelt Dorrien Vineyard Cabernet Sauvignon	96
1998 Wynns Coonawarra Estate John Riddoch Cabernet Sauvignon	96
1998 Balnaves of Coonawarra Reserve Cabernet Sauvignon	95
1998 Wirra Wirra The Angelus Cabernet Sauvignon	95
1998 Zema Estate Cabernet Sauvignon	95
1996 Blass Barossa Cabernet Sauvignon	94
1998 Edwards & Chaffey Section 353 Cabernet Sauvignon	94
1998 Katnook Estate Cabernet Sauvignon	94
1996 Katnook Estate Odyssey Cabernet Sauvignon	94
1999 Killerby Cabernet Sauvignon	94
1998 Knappstein Enterprise Cabernet Sauvignon	94
1998 Lenton Brae Margaret River	94
1998 Lindemans St George	94
1998 Meadowbank Cabernet Sauvignon	94
1999 Meadowbank Cabernet Sauvignon	94
1998 Moss Wood Cabernet Sauvignon	94
1998 Normans Chais Clarendon Cabernet Sauvignon	94
1998 Orlando St Hugo Cabernet Sauvignon	94
1998 Penfolds Bin 407 Cabernet Sauvignon	94
1998 Starvedog Lane Cabernet Sauvignon	94
1998 Wynns Coonawarra Estate Black Label Cabernet Sauvignon	94

cabernet blends

The automatic inclusion of Cullen Cabernet Merlot at or near the top of the list failed only because of timing issues. In fact, the 1999 will likely head next year's list; since the database from which these lists come was closed off, the 1999 Cullen was tasted and accorded 97 points. It is remarkable how strongly Western Australia (particularly Margaret River) performs in this category.

1998 Grosset Gaia	96
1998 Voyager Estate Cabernet Sauvignon Merlot	96
1999 Black George Merlot Cabernet Franc	94
1999 Houghton Crofters Cabernet Merlot	94
1998 Howard Park Cabernet Sauvignon Merlot	94

1998 Lindemans Pyrus	94
1998 Moorilla Estate Reserve Cabernet Merlot	94
1998 Moss Brothers Cabernet Sauvignon Merlot	94
1998 Nepenthe Vineyards The Fugue	94
1998 Rosabrook Estate Cabernet Merlot	94
1998 Vasse Felix Heytesbury	94
1998 Wendouree Cabernet Malbec	94
1998 Blass Cabernet Merlot	93
1998 Brand's of Coonawarra Patron's Reserve	93
1998 Jamiesons Run Reserve Red	93
1998 Parker Coonawarra Estate First Growth	93
1997 Peter Lehmann The Mentor	93
1998 Pierro Cabernet Merlot	93
1997 Yalumba Signature Cabernet Shiraz	93
1999 Yarra Yering Dry Red No 1	93
1998 Zema Estate Cluny	93

fortified wines

A list of enduring classics which, by its very nature, changes little from one year to the next.

NV Seppelt Show Tawny Port DP90	97
NV Seppelt Show Fino Sherry DP117	96
NV Seppelt Show Reserve Muscat DP63	96
NV Bullers Calliope Rare Liqueur Tokay	95
NV Morris Old Premium Liqueur Muscat	95
NV Seppelt Show Oloroso Sherry DP38	95
NV All Saints Classic Release Tokay	94
NV Baileys Winemaker's Selection Old Liqueur Muscat	94
NV Baileys Winemaker's Selection Old Liqueur Tokay	94
NV Bullers Calliope Rare Liqueur Muscat	94
NV Campbells Merchant Prince Muscat	94
NV Campbells Rutherglen Tokay	94
NV De Bortoli Black Noble	94
NV Seppelt Amontillado Sherry DP116	94
NV Seppelt Para Liqueur Port	94
NV Seppelt Rutherglen Show Tokay DP57	94
1995 Stanton & Killeen Vintage Port	94
1999 Yarra Yering Portsorts	94
NV Campbells Isabella Tokay	93
NV Stanton & Killeen Tawny Port	93
NV Yaldara The Farms Show Liqueur Tawny Port	93

australian vintage charts

Each number represents a mark out of ten for the quality of vintages in each region.

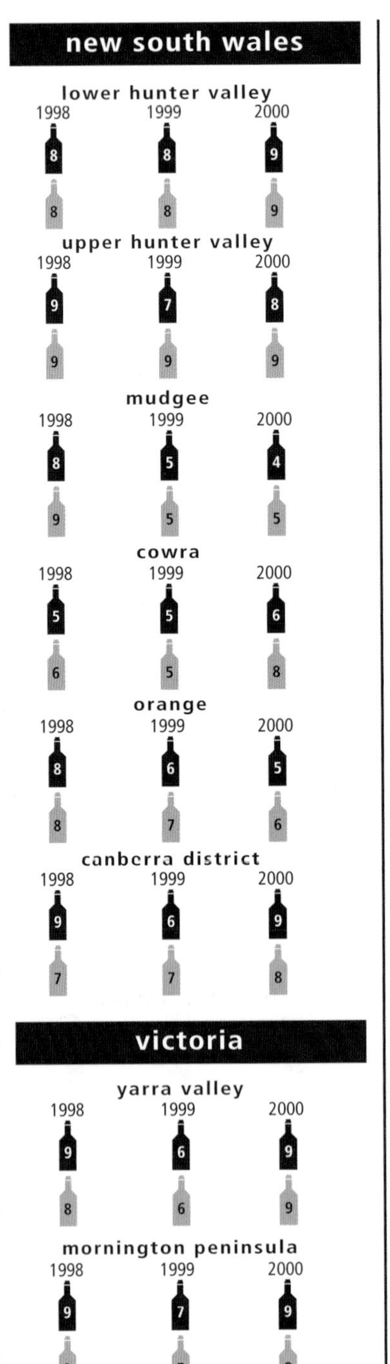

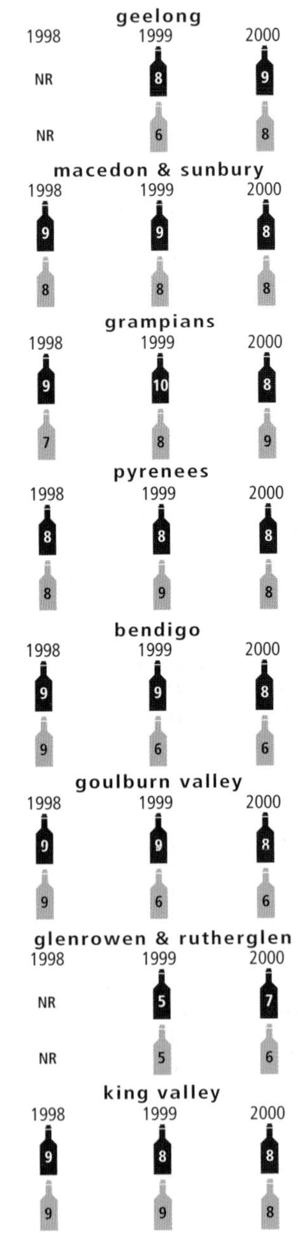

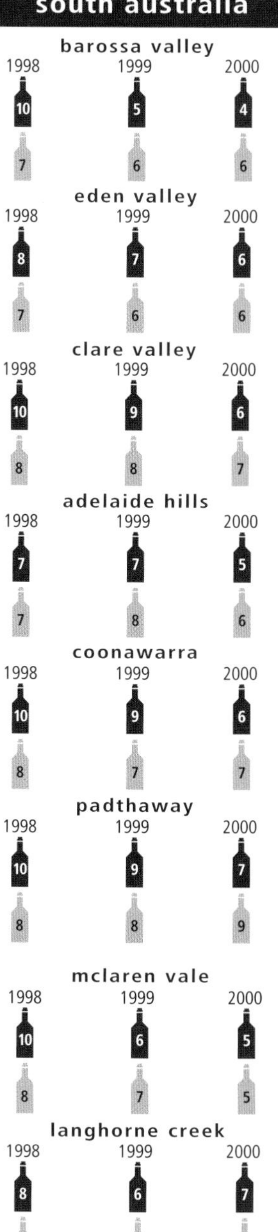

south australia

barossa valley

1998	1999	2000
10	5	4
7	6	6

eden valley

1998	1999	2000
8	7	6
7	6	6

clare valley

1998	1999	2000
10	9	6
8	8	7

adelaide hills

1998	1999	2000
7	7	5
7	8	6

coonawarra

1998	1999	2000
10	9	6
8	7	7

padthaway

1998	1999	2000
10	9	7
8	8	9

mclaren vale

1998	1999	2000
10	6	5
8	7	5

langhorne creek

1998	1999	2000
8	6	7
8	8	8

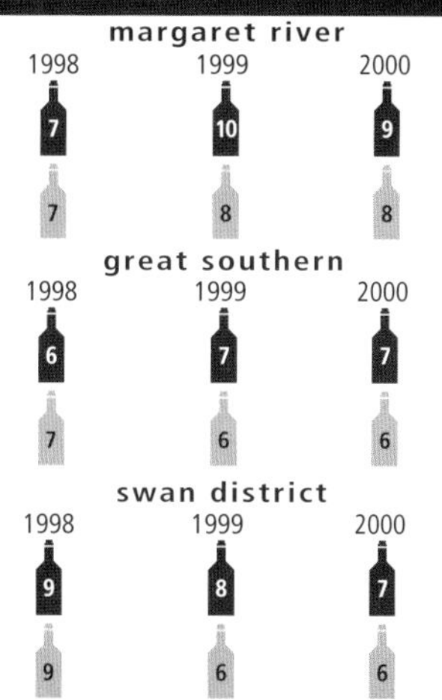

western australia

margaret river

1998	1999	2000
7	10	9
7	8	8

great southern

1998	1999	2000
6	7	7
7	6	6

swan district

1998	1999	2000
9	8	7
9	6	6

queensland

granite belt

1998	1999	2000
8	10	8
6	9	7

tasmania

northern tasmania

1998	1999	2000
10	9	9
9	9	9

southern tasmania

1998	1999	2000
9	8	10
8	7	9

new zealand

sauvignon blanc

Should it come as a surprise that there are only two more wines in this group than for the Chardonnays, each with the same cut-off point of 92 points? I don't know the answer: on the one hand, New Zealand's white wine specialty is Sauvignon Blanc; on the other Chardonnay is a more noble and more malleable variety.

Wine	Score
2000 Forrest Estate Sauvignon Blanc	96
2000 Selaks Premium Selection Sauvignon Blanc	95
2000 Brightwater Sauvignon Blanc	94
2000 Cloudy Bay Sauvignon Blanc	94
1997 Cloudy Bay Te Koko	94
2000 Drylands Estate Winemakers Reserve Sauvignon Blanc	94
2000 Hunter's Sauvignon Blanc	94
2000 Isabel Estate Marlborough Sauvignon Blanc	94
2000 Jackson Estate Sauvignon Blanc	94
2000 Mount Nelson Sauvignon Blanc	94
2000 Nobilo Icon Sauvignon Blanc	94
2000 Seresin Estate Sauvignon Blanc	94
2000 Villa Maria Private Bin Sauvignon Blanc	94
2000 Alexia Sauvignon Blanc	93
2000 Hunter's Single Vineyard Sauvignon Blanc	93
2000 Saint Clair Estate Wairau Reserve Sauvignon Blanc	93
2000 Clifford Bay Sauvignon Blanc	92
2000 Craggy Range Old Renwick Vineyard Sauvignon Blanc	92
2000 Firstland Marlborough Sauvignon Blanc	92
2000 Giesen Marlborough Sauvignon Blanc	92
2000 Hawkesbridge Willowbank Vineyard Sauvignon Blanc	92
2000 Kawarau Estate Sauvignon Blanc	92
2000 Lawson's Dry Hills Sauvignon Blanc	92
2000 Mount Riley Sauvignon Blanc	92
2000 Staete Landt Sauvignon Blanc	92
2000 West Brook Marlborough Sauvignon Blanc	92
2000 Whitehaven Single Vineyard Reserve Sauvignon Blanc	92

riesling

It has taken some time for Riesling to gain the recognition it deserves in New Zealand, but is now in third place in terms of plantings of white grapes, having overtaken the once ubiquitous muller thurgau. These fragrant, fruity wines, braced with high natural acidity, can be seen as a halfway house between Australian and German Rieslings in style. I have listed the sweet, botrytised versions separately.

2000 Felton Road Dry Riesling	96
2000 Drylands Estate Dry Riesling	94
2000 Kim Crawford Marlborough Dry Riesling	94
2000 Margrain Proprietor's Selection Riesling	94
1998 Montana Reserve Riesling	94
2000 Brightwater Neslon Riesling	93
2000 Framingham Dry Riesling	93
2000 Lawson's Dry Hills Riesling	93
2000 Neudorf Brightwater Riesling	93
2000 Isabel Estate Marlborough Riesling	92
2000 Neudorf Moutere Riesling	92
2000 Forrest Estate Dry Riesling	91
2000 Mt Difficulty Riesling	91
2000 Saint Clair Estate Fairhall Reserve Riesling	91
2000 Thainstone Cirrus Riesling	91
2000 Villa Maria Reserve Riesling	91

1998 Fromm La Strada Riesling Trockenbeerenauselese	98
2000 Margrain Botrytis Selection Riesling	96
1999 Villa Maria Reserve Noble Riesling	95
2000 Dry River Botrytis Selection Riesling	94
2000 Seifried Estate Ice Wine	94
2000 Waimea Estates Noble Riesling	94
2000 Forrest Estate Botrytis Riesling	93

chardonnay

There is no doubt New Zealand continues to refine and improve the style of its Chardonnays, both through better viticulture and clonal selection, and a softer, less intrusive hand in the winery.

1999 Vidal Reserve Chardonnay	95
1999 Church Road Reserve Chardonnay	94
2000 Craggy Range Seven Poplars Vineyard Chardonnay	94
1999 Foxes Island Chardonnay	94
1999 Grove Mill Marlborough Chardonnay	94
2000 Mission Chardonnay	94
1999 Neudorf Moutere Chardonnay	94
1999 Nga Waka Chardonnay	94
1999 Sacred Hill Rifleman's Chardonnay	94
2000 Saint Clair Estate Marlborough Chardonnay	94
1999 Clearview Estate Reserve Chardonnay	93
2000 Rimu Grove Chardonnay	93
2000 Sileni Chardonnay	93
1999 Villa Maria Reserve Marlborough Chardonnay	93
1999 Allan Scott Prestige Chardonnay	92
2000 Amor-Bendall Reserve Chardonnay	92

1999 Dry River Amaranth Chardonnay	92
1999 Felton Road Wines Barrel Fermented Chardonnay	92
1999 Lawson's Dry Hills Chardonnay	92
1999 Matariki Chardonnay	92
2000 Seresin Estate Chardonnay	92
2000 Te Mata Estate Chardonnay	92
1999 Te Mata Estate Elston Chardonnay	92
2000 Te Whau Chardonnay	92
2000 Villa Maria Keltern Chardonnay	92

other white wines

Something of a potpourri; to simplify the group a little I have grouped the wines by variety. Obviously, two wines stand out, and one of those (the 1998 Stonecroft Gewurztraminer) is a museum relic and no longer commercially available.

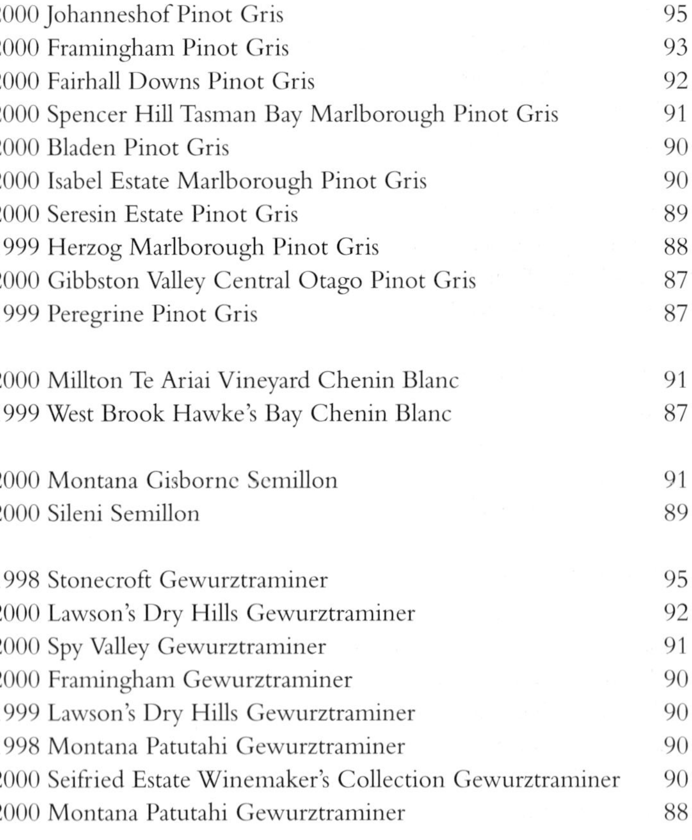

2000 Johanneshof Pinot Gris	95
2000 Framingham Pinot Gris	93
2000 Fairhall Downs Pinot Gris	92
2000 Spencer Hill Tasman Bay Marlborough Pinot Gris	91
2000 Bladen Pinot Gris	90
2000 Isabel Estate Marlborough Pinot Gris	90
2000 Seresin Estate Pinot Gris	89
1999 Herzog Marlborough Pinot Gris	88
2000 Gibbston Valley Central Otago Pinot Gris	87
1999 Peregrine Pinot Gris	87
2000 Millton Te Ariai Vineyard Chenin Blanc	91
1999 West Brook Hawke's Bay Chenin Blanc	87
2000 Montana Gisborne Semillon	91
2000 Sileni Semillon	89
1998 Stonecroft Gewurztraminer	95
2000 Lawson's Dry Hills Gewurztraminer	92
2000 Spy Valley Gewurztraminer	91
2000 Framingham Gewurztraminer	90
1999 Lawson's Dry Hills Gewurztraminer	90
1998 Montana Patutahi Gewurztraminer	90
2000 Seifried Estate Winemaker's Collection Gewurztraminer	90
2000 Montana Patutahi Gewurztraminer	88

pinot noir

I am acutely aware that the redoubtable Jancis Robinson in no way shares my enthusiasm for the present and future standing of New Zealand Pinot Noir. I have to respectfully disagree with her, and restate my belief that New Zealand has the potential to seriously challenge all but the greatest Burgundies by the end of this decade.

1999 Gibbston Valley Reserve Pinot Noir	96
1998 Martinborough Vineyard Reserve Pinot Noir	96
1999 Ata Rangi Pinot Noir	95
1999 Felton Road Pinot Noir Block 3	95
1999 Felton Road Pinot Noir Block 5	95
1999 Neudorf Moutere Reserve Pinot Noir	95
1999 Wither Hills Vineyards Pinot Noir	95
1999 Fromm La Strada Fromm Vineyard Pinot Noir	94
1999 Cloudy Bay Pinot Noir	94
1999 Giesen Canterbury Pinot Noir Reserve Barrel Selection	94
1999 Margrain Unfiltered Pinot Noir	94
1999 Mud House Black Swan Reserve Pinot Noir	94
1999 Quartz Reef Pinot Noir	94
1999 Seresin Estate Pinot Noir	94
2000 Spencer Hill Evan's Vineyard Moutere Pinot Noir	94
1999 Bell Hill Vineyard Old Weka Pass Road Pinot Noir	93
1999 Dry River Amaranth Pinot Noir	93
1999 Felton Road Pinot Noir	93
1999 Gibbston Valley Pinot Noir	93
1999 Neudorf Moutere Pinot Noir	93
1999 Pegasus Bay Prima Donna Pinot Noir	93
1999 Te Kairanga Reserve Pinot Noir	93
1999 Vidal Estate Pinot Noir	93
1999 Walnut Ridge Pinot Noir	93

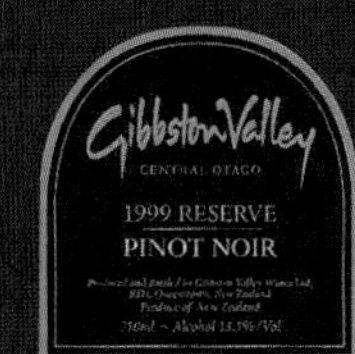

cabernet sauvignon and merlot

I have drawn attention time and again to the quality of the 1998 red wines from South Australia made from the Bordeaux varieties; exactly the same applies to New Zealand. It is a vintage that will almost certainly reshape New Zealand winemaker attitudes to ripeness and, in particular, tannin ripeness. It also lies at the core of the strong showing of the following wines.

1998 (Church Road) Tom	98
1998 Nautilus Riverbrook Reserve Cabernet Merlot	96
1999 Newton Forrest Cornerstone Cabernet Merlot	96
1999 Villa Maria Reserve Merlot Cabernet	96
1998 Te Awa Farm Zone 10 Cabernet Sauvignon	95
1998 Te Mata Estate Coleraine Cabernet Franc Merlot	95
1998 Kingsley Estate Gimblett Road Cabernet Sauvignon	94
1998 Nautilus Cabernet Merlot	94
1996 (Church Road) Tom	94
1999 Unison Selection	94
1998 Vidal Estate Reserve Cabernet Sauvignon	94
1999 Church Road Reserve Cabernet Sauvignon Merlot	93
1998 Mission Estate Reserve Cabernet Sauvignon Merlot	93

1998 Vidal Estate Reserve Cabernet Sauvignon Merlot	93
1998 Walnut Ridge Cabernet Sauvignon	93
1999 Wishart Estate Reserve Merlot Malbec Cabernet	93
1998 Chateau Waimarama Hawke's Bay Merlot Cabernet	92
1998 Newton Forrest Cornerstone Cabernet Sauvignon	92
1999 Ngatarawa Glazebrook Cabernet Merlot	92
1998 Te Mata Estate Awatea Cabernet Merlot	92
1999 Alpha Domus The Navigator Cabernet Merlot	91
1999 Vidal Estate Reserve Cabernet Sauvignon Merlot	91

australian wineries and wines

abbey vale ★★★★

Wildwood Road, Yallingup, WA 6282 **region** Margaret River
phone (08) 9755 2121 **fax** (08) 9755 2286 **open** 7 days 10–5
winemaker Dorham Mann, Kevin McKay **production** 42 000 **est.** 1986
product range ($14.50–49 CD) Semillon, Semillon Sauvignon Blanc, Verdelho, Sauvignon Blanc, Sunburst Verdelho, Contessa, Chardonnay, Monseigneur, Shiraz, Merlot, Merlot Shiraz, Cabernet Merlot, Reserve Cabernet Sauvignon, Port; Moonshine Ale brewed on the premises.
summary Abbey Vale has gone from strength to strength, vinifying an ever-increasing proportion of the production from its large 30-hectare vineyard (plus another 60 under contract), and winning a significant number of show awards. No doubt this success was what led to its acquisition by Swiss interests in 2000. The wines are exported to the US, the UK, France, Switzerland and Italy.

Abbey Vale Shiraz

🍷🍷🍷🍷 **1999** Medium to full red-purple; the bouquet is clean, with nicely ripened plum and black cherry fruits together with gentle oak. The palate has a similar array of flavours, with good weight and structure; soft tannins to close. **rating:** 88

best drinking 2004–2008 **best vintages** '99 **drink with** Diced lamb • $22

Abbey Vale Merlot

🍷🍷🍷🍷 **1998** Medium red-purple; the bouquet promises well with spicy/savoury aromatics and delivers on the palate where gentle red berry fruit has very nice, silky structure that basically catches you unawares and creeps up on you with each taste. **rating:** 87

best drinking 2002–2006 **best vintages** NA **drink with** Roast veal • $21

abercorn

Cassilis Road, Mudgee, NSW 2850 **region** Mudgee
phone (02) 6373 3106 **fax** (02) 6373 3108 **open** 7 days 10–4
winemaker Tim Stevens, Simon Gilbert (Contract) **production** 5000 **est.** 1996
product range ($14.95–34.95 R) Chardonnay, Reserve Chardonnay, Shiraz, Shiraz Cabernet; Barons Court is second label, comprising Chardonnay and Shiraz.
summary Tim and Connie Stevens acquired the 25-year-old Abercorn Vineyard in 1996 which, while admirably located next door to Huntington Estate, had become somewhat run down. Rejuvenation of the vineyard is well underway, and contract winemaking has moved to Simon Gilbert (with considerable involvement by Tim Stevens), with excellent results. The wine is starting to find retail distribution throughout Sydney in addition to its cellar-door and mail-order business.

Abercorn Reserve Chardonnay

🍷🍷🍷🍷 **1999** Light to medium green-yellow, very youthful. The bouquet is likewise relatively undeveloped, with the subtle interplay of fruit, barrel-ferment oak and what appears to be malolactic-fermentation influences. The palate is a replay of the bouquet, almost European in subtlety, and a very interesting wine. Only 200 cases were made. **rating:** 86

best drinking 2002–2006 **best vintages** NA **drink with** Milk-fed veal • $34.95

Abercorn Shiraz

🍷🍷🍷🍷 **1999** Dense red-purple; the bouquet offers complex, earthy shiraz plus scoops of oak, the latter which subsides on the powerful, complex black cherry-driven palate, with great structure and ample tannins. **rating:** 88

best drinking 2004–2009 **best vintages** '97, '98 **drink with** Rare roast beef • $24.95

ada river ★★★

2330 Main Road, Neerim South, Vic 3831 **region** Gippsland
phone (03) 5628 1661 **fax** (03) 5628 1661 **open** 10–6 weekends and public holidays
winemaker Peter Kelliher, Chris Kelliher **production** 1000 **est.** 1983
product range ($13–18 CD) From Gippsland-grown grapes Chardonnay, Pinot Noir, Cabernet Sauvignon; from Yarra Valley grapes Traminer, Chardonnay, Pinot Noir; Baw Baw Port.
summary The Kelliher family first planted vines on their dairy farm at Neerim South in 1983, extending the original Millstream Vineyard in 1989 and increasing plantings yet further by establishing the nearby Manilla Vineyard in 1994. The family also has the Goondalahg Vineyard at Steels Creek in the Yarra Valley under long-term lease, providing two distinct wine ranges. Production began in 1991, the first wines going on sale in 1995.

Ada River Yarra Valley Traminer

🍷🍷🍷🍷 **1999** Deep gold; powerful lychee and spice varietal character is followed by a very rich and soft palate. The grapes were harvested late, which has diminished the varietal character, although not the flavour. Good value at the price. **rating:** 83

best drinking Now–2003 **best vintages** NA **drink with** Asian prawns • $13

Ada River Yarra Valley Chardonnay

🍷🍷🍷🍷 **1997** Light green-yellow; smokehouse almond oak over lively grapefruit aromas are followed by an astonishingly youthful palate, with fresh and lively grapefruit and melon flavours. Like the Traminer, excellent value at the price. **rating:** 84

best drinking Now–2004 **best vintages** NA **drink with** Smoked fish • $14

affleck NR

154 Millynn Road, off Bungendore Road, Bungendore, NSW 2621 **region** Canberra District
phone (02) 6236 9276 **fax** (02) 6236 9090 **open** 7 days 9–5
winemaker Ian Hendry **production** 300 **est.** 1976
product range ($14–24 CD) Chardonnay, Semillon, Late Picked Sauvignon Blanc, Sweet White, Pinot Noir, Cabernet Shiraz, Muscat, Ruby Port.
summary The cellar-door and mail-order price list says the wines are 'grown, produced and bottled on the estate by Ian and Susie Hendry with much dedicated help from family and friends'. The original 2.5-hectare vineyard has been expanded to 7 hectares, and a new tasting room (offering light lunches) opened in 1999.

ainsworth estate NR

110 Ducks Lane, Seville, Vic 3139 **region** Yarra Valley
phone (03) 5964 4711 **fax** (03) 5964 4311 **open** 7 days 10.30–5
winemaker Denis Craig **production** 2500 **est.** 1994
product range ($17.95–25.65 CD) Unoaked Chardonnay, Chardonnay, Shiraz, Cabernet Sauvignon.
summary Denis Craig and wife Kerri planted their first 2 hectares of chardonnay and shiraz near Healesville in 1994. The grapes from this vineyard were sold until the 2000 vintage, when the first wines were made under the Ainsworth Estate label. In the intervening period they established a second vineyard at Ducks Lane, Seville, with another 2 hectares of vines, here planted to shiraz and pinot noir. They have also turned from selling to purchasing grapes with a total of just under 3 hectares of chardonnay, shiraz and cabernet sauvignon grown for them under contract. Their cellar door and barbecue area at Ducks Lane opened in March 2001; for the time being, at least, Denis Craig and Al Fencaros make the wines at Fencaros' Allinda winery in Dixons Creek.

Ainsworth Estate Unoaked Chardonnay

🍷🍷🍷🍷 **2000** Pale green straw; light citrus and melon aromas and flavours run through an exceedingly delicate wine which belies its 13.3° alcohol. A bronze-medal winner at the Southern Victorian Wines Show. **rating:** 81

best drinking Now **best vintages** NA **drink with** Light fish dishes • $17.95

aldinga bay winery NR

Main South Road, Aldinga, SA 5173 **region** McLaren Vale
phone (08) 8556 3179 **fax** (08) 8556 3350 **open** 7 days 10–5
winemaker Nick Girolamo **production** 8000 **est.** 1979
product range ($13–21 CD) Verdelho, Chardonnay, Shiraz, Sangiovese, Petit Verdot, Reserve Tawny Port.
summary The former Donolga Winery has had a name and image change since Nick Girolamo, the son of founders Don and Olga Girolamo, returned from Roseworthy College with a degree in oenology. Nick Girolamo has taken over both the winemaking and marketing; prices remain modest, though not as low as they once were, reflecting an increase in the quality and an upgrade in packaging. Aldinga Bay also has some very interesting varietal plantings, 16 varieties in all, including petit verdot, nebbiolo, barbera and sangiovese.

Aldinga Bay Shiraz

🍷🍷🍷🍷 **1999** Medium to full red-purple; solid dark berry and plum fruit together with vanilla oak on the bouquet flow into a medium bodied palate showing plum, a touch of mint and controlled oak. Nicely put together. **rating:** 85

best drinking 2003–2007 **best vintages** NA **drink with** Barbecued spare ribs • $14.80

alexandra bridge estate NR

Brockman Highway, Karridale, WA 6288 **region** Margaret River
phone (08) 9758 5000 **fax** (08) 9384 4811 **open** 7 days 10–4.30
winemaker Philip Tubb **production** 20 000 **est.** 1994
product range ($15–30 R) Semillon, Sauvignon Blanc, Chardonnay, Margaret River Classic, Shiraz, Cabernet Sauvignon.
summary Alexandra Bridge Estate is one of the fast-developing Margaret River ventures; 30 hectares of vines have been established since 1994, and production has risen from 3000 cases in 1999 to 20 000 cases in 2001 via an estate winery. Shortly prior to going to press, Possum Wines became the owner of the business.

alkoomi ★★★★★

Wingebellup Road, Frankland, WA 6396 **region** Great Southern
phone (08) 9855 2229 **fax** (08) 9855 2284 **open** 7 days 10.30–5
winemaker Michael Staniford, Merv Lange **production** 80 000 **est.** 1971
product range ($14–59 CD) Riesling, Wandoo (Semillon), Sauvignon Blanc, Unwooded Chardonnay, Chardonnay, Classic White, Classic Red, Shiraz, Cabernet Sauvignon, Blackbutt; Southlands Semillon Chenin Sauvignon Blanc, Shiraz Cabernet Merlot.
summary For those who see the wineries of Western Australia as suffering from the tyranny of distance, this most remote of them all shows there is no tyranny after all. It is a story of unqualified success due to sheer hard work, and no doubt to Merv and Judy Lange's aversion to borrowing a single dollar from the bank. The substantial production is entirely drawn from the ever-expanding estate vineyards, which by 2001 amounted to over 70 hectares. Wine quality across the range is impeccable, always with precisely defined varietal character. National retail distribution; exports to Hong Kong, Japan, Malaysia, the UK, Denmark and France.

Alkoomi Wandoo

▼▼▼▼▽ **1999** Light green-yellow; the bouquet has very good fruit definition and complexity, the palate likewise with a mix of citrus, lemon and lemon rind providing the anchor for a wine with well-above-average length and intensity. Very much in the Margaret River/Adelaide Hills rather than Hunter Valley style, but its price is a challenging one for a young Semillon, no matter how good. **rating:** 92

best drinking 2002–2007 **best vintages** '97, '98, '99 **drink with** Mussels • $34

Alkoomi Sauvignon Blanc

▼▼▼▼▽ **2000** The year 2000 may have been a difficult vintage for sauvignon blanc elsewhere, but not in the Great Southern. This is a gloriously fragrant wine, bursting with gooseberry and passionfruit aromas, the palate no less flavoursome and lively, with a touch of wild herb on the crisp finish. **rating:** 93

best drinking Now **best vintages** '95, '96, '97, '98, '00 **drink with** Ginger prawns • $19

Alkoomi Southlands Semillon Chenin Sauvignon Blanc

▼▼▼▼ **2000** Light green-yellow; a fresh and zesty bouquet has a mix of herbaceous and more tropical aromas; the palate is equally fresh and lively, although here the tropical characters are predominant. Well priced. **rating:** 85

best drinking Now **best vintages** NA **drink with** Seafood pasta • $14

Alkoomi Frankland River Chardonnay

▼▼▼▼▽ **1999** Medium yellow-green; a clean, fine and elegant bouquet with stonefruit and melon supported by subtle oak is replicated on the tight, elegant palate with gentle stonefruit, subtle oak and good length. **rating:** 93

best drinking Now–2006 **best vintages** '85, '88, '90, '92, '94, '97, '98, '99 **drink with** Stir-fried chicken with cashew nuts • $25

Alkoomi Frankland River Shiraz

▼▼▼▼ **1999** Dense red-purple; a concentrated and powerful bouquet crammed with blackberry and cherry leads into a potent, powerful black fruit palate with subliminal spice; it has gobbled up the oak in which it is matured, but is presently locked in on itself. May emerge as a spectacular wine in the years ahead. **rating:** 89

best drinking 2004–2009 **best vintages** '90, '93, '94, '97, '98, '99 **drink with** Lamb fillet • $23

Alkoomi Blackbutt

🍷🍷🍷🍷 **1998** Medium red-purple; the moderately intense but fragrant bouquet with spicy/cedary aromas leads into a palate with gentle, dark berry fruit and cedary flavours, finishing with fine, ripe, soft tannins. Very much in the Blackbutt style. **rating:** 90

🍷🍷🍷🍷 **1997** Medium red-purple; a very fragrant bouquet with a range of cedary/spicy/leafy aromas leads into an elegant palate with spicy, tangy berry fruit; fine, supple tannins and cedary oak round off a wine that is very much in the character of this medium bodied, cool-climate wine. **rating:** 92

best drinking Now–2010 **best vintages** '94, '95, '96, '97, '98 **drink with** Rare beef • $59

Alkoomi Frankland River Cabernet Sauvignon

🍷🍷🍷1998Medium red-purple; the bouquet is dull, suggesting some fruit oxidation, and the palate likewise misses the boat. Poor by the normally ultra-reliable Alkoomi standards. **rating:** 83

best drinking Now–2003 **best vintages** '83, '84, '86, '90, '93, '94, '95 **drink with** Rare rump steak • $27

allandale ★★★★

Lovedale Road, Lovedale, NSW 2320 **region** Lower Hunter Valley
phone (02) 4990 4526 **fax** (02) 4990 1714 **open** Mon–Sat 9–5, Sun 10–5
winemaker Bill Sneddon, Steve Langham **production** 20 000 **est.** 1978
product range ($15–24 CD) Hilltops Riesling, Semillon, Sauvignon Blanc, Chardonnay, Verdelho, Fleur (dessert wine), Lombardo (Pinot Noir Shiraz blend), Matthew Shiraz, McLaren Vale Shiraz, Mudgee Shiraz, Mudgee Cabernet Sauvignon, William Méthode Champenoise.
summary Without ostentation, this medium-sized winery has been under the control of winemaker Bill Sneddon for well over a decade. Allandale has developed something of a reputation as a Chardonnay specialist, but does offer a broad range of wines of good quality, with an increasing number of wines produced from grapes grown in the Hilltops region. The wines are exported to the UK and the US.

Allandale Verdelho

🍷🍷🍷 **2000** Pale straw-green; the bouquet is clean and light with faint tropical fruit salad aromas, the palate with more of the same, and a clean finish. **rating:** 82

best drinking Now **best vintages** NA **drink with** Smoked salmon pasta • $17

Allandale Hunter River Chardonnay

🍷🍷🍷🍷 **2000** Light to medium yellow-green; the clean, moderately intense bouquet shows sophisticated winemaking, with melon/nectarine/fig fruit married with well-balanced and integrated oak. A restrained palate, with melon and fig counterbalanced by touches of toast and cashew, and finishing with good acidity. **rating:** 89

best drinking Now–2003 **best vintages** '91, '94, '96, '98, '99, '00 **drink with** Smoked salmon • $18

allanmere NR

Allandale Road, Allandale, via Pokolbin, NSW 2321 **region** Lower Hunter Valley
phone (02) 4930 7387 **fax** (02) 4930 7900 **open** 7 days 9.30–5
winemaker Greg Silkman **production** 7000 **est.** 1984
product range ($15–20 CD) Gold Label Chardonnay, Semillon, Trinity White (Chardonnay, Semillon, Sauvignon Blanc), Cabernet Sauvignon, Trinity Red (Cabernet blend), Cabernet Shiraz. Durham Chardonnay is top-of-the-range Chardonnay.
summary Now owned by Monarch Winemaking Services. While it has a relatively low profile in conventional retail markets, cellar-door sales are flourishing in response to the ever-increasing tourist traffic in the Hunter Valley. No recent tastings. Exports to Japan, Switzerland, the US, Taiwan and the UK.

allinda NR

119 Lorimers Lane, Dixons Creek, Vic 3775 **region** Yarra Valley
phone (03) 5965 2450 **fax** (03) 5965 2467 **open** Weekends and public holidays 11–5
winemaker Al Fencaros **production** 2500 **est.** 1991
product range ($16.50–24.50 CD) Riesling, Sauvignon Blanc, Chardonnay, Late Harvest Riesling, Shiraz, Cabernets.

summary Winemaker Al Fencaros is a Bachelor of Wine Science (Charles Sturt University) and was formerly employed by De Bortoli in the Yarra Valley. All of the Allinda wines are produced on site; all except the Shiraz (from Heathcote) are estate-grown from a little over 3 hectares of vineyards. Limited retail distribution in Melbourne and Sydney.

all saints ★★★★

All Saints Road, Wahgunyah, Vic 3687 **region** Rutherglen
phone (02) 6033 1922 **fax** (02) 6033 3515 **open** Mon–Sat 9–5.30, Sun 10–5.30
winemaker Peter Brown **production** 30 000 **est.** 1864
product range ($9.80–395 CD) At the top of the table wines come Carlyle Chardonnay, Shiraz, Ruby Cabernet, Durif; then come All Saints Riesling, Marsanne, Merlot, Cabernet Sauvignon, Shiraz; at the bottom, Tokays and Muscats are headed by Museum Release, then Rare, then Grand, and finally Classic Rutherglen, in each case with a Muscat and a Tokay. Two sparklings also made.
summary The winery rating principally reflects the Show Reserve fortified wines, but the table wines are more than adequate. An excellent winery restaurant makes this a compulsory and most enjoyable stop for any visitor to the northeast. All Saints and St Leonards are now wholly owned by Peter Brown; the vast majority of the wines are sold through cellar door and by mailing list.

All Saints Shiraz

🍷🍷🍷🍷 **1998** Dense purple-red; the rich and concentrated bouquet is flooded with sweet, dark berry and plum fruit, the palate is ripe, full and smooth, moving more from plum to black cherry, supported by subtle oak. Winner of the Best Boutique Shiraz at the 2000 Boutique Wines of Australia Awards. **rating:** 87

best drinking 2003–2008 **best vintages** '92, '96, '98 **drink with** Venison • $17.60

All Saints Carlyle Durif

🍷🍷🍷🍷 **1998** Dense red-purple; very powerful bouquet with licorice, chocolate and earth aromas is followed by a commensurately massive and ripe palate with layers of inbuilt tannins. Approach with caution over the next ten years. Best Boutique Other Red Variety at the 2000 Boutique Wines of Australia Awards. **rating:** 89

best drinking 2008–2018 **best vintages** NA **drink with** Ox • $31.10

All Saints Carlyle Ruby Cabernet

🍷🍷🍷½ **1998** Dense red-purple; the bouquet offers a mix of chocolate, berry, vanilla and earth aromas and leads into a very concentrated and chewy palate. All in all, abrasive rather than appealing, but the wine certainly has plenty of presence. **rating:** 83

best drinking 2002–2008 **best vintages** NA **drink with** Marinated beef • $23.80

All Saints Cabernet Sauvignon

🍷🍷🍷🍷 **1998** Medium red-purple; smooth, gently ripe cabernet varietal fruit is augmented by American oak on the bouquet; a generously structured palate has plenty of flavour and tannin backbone, which will repay cellaring. **rating:** 86

best drinking 2003–2008 **best vintages** NA **drink with** Mature cheese • $17.60

All Saints Classic Release Tokay

🍷🍷🍷🍷🍷 **NV** Light golden-brown; rich and sweet malt and tea-leaf aromas with barely perceptible fortifying spirit. The palate is of medium to full weight, with malty/toffee/caramel/tea-leaf flavours, finishing with well-balanced acidity. **rating:** 94

best drinking Now **best vintages** NA **drink with** Try it as an aperitif • NA

All Saints Classic Release Muscat

🍷🍷🍷🍷½ **NV** Medium tawny with just a hint of brown on the rim; soft, raisiny varietal muscat with fractionally earthy spirit. The palate is quite luscious, with good raisined fruit, starting sweet and finishing with cleansing acidity. **rating:** 90

best drinking Now **best vintages** NA **drink with** Coffee and chocolates • NA

amberley estate ★★★★

Thornton Road, Yallingup, WA 6282 **region** Margaret River
phone (08) 9755 2288 **fax** (08) 9755 2171 **open** 7 days 10–4.30
winemaker Eddie Price, David Watson **production** 90 000 **est.** 1986

product range ($16–63 R) Semillon, Sauvignon Blanc, Semillon Sauvignon Blanc, Chenin Blanc, Chardonnay, Charlotte Street Chardonnay Semillon, Shiraz, Charlotte Street Shiraz Chardonnay Cabernet, Cabernet Merlot, Cabernet Sauvignon, Cabernet Reserve.
summary Its initial growth was based on its ultra-commercial, fairly sweet Chenin Blanc, which continues to provide the volume for the brand, selling out well prior to the following release. However, the quality of all of the other wines has risen markedly over recent years as the 31 hectares of estate plantings have become fully mature. In 2001 the capital-rich Palandri Wines acquired a 51 per cent shareholding, which will doubtless lead to increased exports to the UK, France, Germany, Singapore, Japan, Hong Kong and the US.

Amberley Estate Sauvignon Blanc

YYYY **2000** Light yellow-green; the bouquet is firm, with a mix of mineral, citrus and herb, the palate with plenty of weight, richness and structure; intriguingly, the fruit is ripe yet not tropical; relatively soft, subliminally sweet, finish. A success. **rating:** 89
best drinking Now **best vintages** '00 **drink with** Seafood pasta • $19

Amberley Estate Semillon Sauvignon Blanc

YYYY **1999** Light to medium green-yellow; a clean and quite ripe lemon/citrus bouquet is supported by subtle oak. The light to medium bodied palate is elegant, well composed and balanced, and has a clean finish. **rating:** 89
best drinking Now–2003 **best vintages** '95, '96, '97 **drink with** Richer Asian seafood dishes • $16.95

Amberley Estate Shiraz

YYYYY **1999** Medium red-purple; the bouquet is clean, firm and fresh with bright red cherry and plum fruit. The palate is powerful, with lots of ripe plum and cherry fruit, but has some elegance as well. **rating:** 91
best drinking 2004–2009 **best vintages** '94, '95, '96, '98, '99 **drink with** Moroccan lamb • $32

Amberley Estate Cabernet Merlot

YYYY **1998** Medium red-purple; the moderately intense bouquet is clean, with sweet, red berry fruit and a flick of oak. The palate is, as the bouquet promises, medium bodied, with a mix of sweet berry/olive/forest flavours giving a gently savoury cast; finishes with fine tannins. **rating:** 88
best drinking 2003–2008 **best vintages** '91, '92, '94, '97, '98 **drink with** Rack of lamb • $28

amietta vineyard and winery NR

30 Steddy Road, Lethbridge, Vic 3332 **region** Geelong
phone (03) 5281 7427 **fax** (03) 5281 7427 **open** By appointment
winemaker Nicholas Clark, Janet Cockbill **production** NA **est.** 1995
product range Riesling, Cabernet.
summary Janet Cockbill and Nicholas Clark are multitalented. Both are archaeologists, but Janet manages to combine part-time archaeology, part-time radiography (at Geelong Hospital) and part-time organic viticulture careers. Nicholas Clark is in his final (part-time) year of a viticulture degree at Charles Sturt University. When they purchased the property (which had half a hectare each of cabernet sauvignon and riesling already established) they decided to convert to a full-on organic vineyard regimen. Engagingly, Clark says, 'We are garagistes – literally. One day, when we grow up, we might even be wine producers.' They planted an additional 0.9 hectare of shiraz and 0.5 hectare of chardonnay in 2000, and their first Cabernet and Riesling will be available in September 2001.

anderson NR

Lot 12 Chiltern Road, Rutherglen, Vic 3685 **region** Rutherglen
phone (02) 6032 8111 **fax** (02) 6032 9028 **open** 7 days 10–5
winemaker Howard Anderson **production** 2000 **est.** 1993
product range ($12–25 CD) Semillon, Chenin Blanc, Doux Blanc, Chardonnay, Soft Cabernet, Shiraz, Merlot, Cabernet Sauvignon, Late Harvest Tokay, Méthode Champenoise range of Pinot Chardonnay, Chenin Blanc, Doux Blanc, Shiraz.
summary Having notched up a winemaking career spanning 30 years, including a stint at Seppelt Great Western, Howard Anderson and family have started their own winery, with a particular focus on sparkling wine made entirely on site.

Anderson Merlot

🍷🍷🍷🍷 **1999** Medium red-purple; the youthful and somewhat callow aromas offer a mix of earth and some red berry, but on the palate clever oak handling lifts the wine, contributing to a nice touch of subliminal sweetness, and finishing with moderately ripe tannins. **rating:** 83

best drinking Now–2004 **best vintages** NA **drink with** Light pasta • $19.50

andraos bros ★★★★

Winilba Vineyard, 150 Vineyard Road, Sunbury, Vic 3429 **region** Sunbury
phone (03) 9740 9703 **fax** (03) 9740 9795 **open** Fri–Sun and public holidays 11–5 or by appointment
winemaker Fred Andraos, Mario Marson (Consultant) **production** 2500 **est.** 1989
product range ($18-70 CD) Released under the Olde Winilba label are Riesling, Semillon, Semillon Sauvignon Blanc, Chardonnay, Pinot Shiraz, Pinot Noir, Shiraz, Cabernet Shiraz, Cabernet Sauvignon.
summary The original Winilba Vineyard was first planted in 1863, and remained in production until 1889. Exactly 100 years later the Andraos brothers commenced replanting the vineyard on the property they had purchased five years earlier. Over the following years they built a winery from the ruins of the original bluestone cellar, making the inaugural vintage in 1996. They have also established Estelle's Cellar Restaurant on the second floor of the building, which is open for dinner from Tuesday to Sunday and for lunch on Friday, Saturday, Sunday and public holidays.

Andraos Bros Olde Winilba Chardonnay

🍷🍷🍷🍷 **1998** Medium yellow-green; the clean, moderately intense bouquet has melon and grapefruit rather than oak as the dominant character; the light, fresh palate runs through melon to a hint of cashew; subtle oak, and ageing nicely. **rating:** 86

best drinking Now–2004 **best vintages** NA **drink with** Yarra Valley yabbies • $35

Andraos Bros Olde Winilba Grandfather's Shiraz

🍷🍷🍷🍷🍷 **1998** Medium to full purple-red, bright and strong; clean, ripe dark berry/plum/licorice-accent fruit on the bouquet is followed by a concentrated palate, with ripe cherry/plum/chocolate flavours supported by fine-grained tannins and subtle oak; has excellent mouthfeel. **rating:** 92

best drinking 2003–2010 **best vintages** '98 **drink with** Venison • $70

Andraos Bros Olde Winilba Cabernet Sauvignon

🍷🍷🍷🍷 **1998** Medium red, still tinged with purple; savoury/earthy/leafy/smoky overtones to the blackcurrant fruit of the bouquet are followed by a palate with good texture and structure, finishing with quite ripe, fine tannins. **rating:** 88

best drinking 2003–2008 **best vintages** '98 **drink with** Rack of lamb • $45

andrew garrett/ingoldby ★★★☆

Kangarilla Road, McLaren Vale, SA 5171 **region** McLaren Vale
phone (08) 8323 8853 **fax** (08) 8323 8271 **open** 7 days 10–4
winemaker Charles Hargrave **production** NFP **est.** 1983
product range ($9–25 R) Under the Andrew Garrett label are Semillon, Sauvignon Blanc, Chardonnay, Cabernet Merlot, Bold Shiraz, Vintage Pinot Chardonnay. Under Ingoldby label are Colombard, Riesling, Sauvignon Blanc, Chardonnay, Shiraz, Grenache, Tawny Port.
summary Andrew Garrett and Ingoldby are brands within the Beringer Blass wine group, with many of the wines now not having a sole McLaren Vale source but instead being drawn from regions across southeastern Australia. Over the past few years, winemaker Charles Hargrave has produced some excellent wines that provide great value for money.

Andrew Garrett Sauvignon Blanc

🍷🍷🍷🍷 **2000** Medium yellow-green; the bouquet is clean, but tending to plain, with subdued varietal character. The palate has authentic minerally/herbaceous characters and, best of all, is mercifully dry. Respectable value at the price. **rating:** 82

best drinking Now **best vintages** NA **drink with** Fish and chips • $9.50

Andrew Garrett Sauvignon Blanc Semillon

ŸŸŸŸ 2000 Light straw-green; the aromas are clean and direct, with more mineral than fruit characters evident. The palate, likewise, is crisp and minerally, with fairly high acidity. This wine will appeal to those with a European bent.
rating: 84

best drinking Now **best vintages** NA **drink with** Shellfish • $13

Andrew Garrett Sparkling Shiraz

ŸŸŸŸ 1998 Strong red-purple; clean, dark berry fruit on the bouquet flows through to fresh black cherry/berry fruit on the palate; mercifully, any oak is undetectable. A workmanlike wine for those who like young sparkling Shiraz.
rating: 83

best drinking Now–2003 **best vintages** NA **drink with** Game • $20

Andrew Garrett Bold Shiraz

ŸŸŸŸ 1999 Light to medium red-purple; the bouquet is clean, with a mix of berry, leaf and spice, but not particularly intense. Minimal oak input; the palate is similarly light to medium bodied, with pleasant red berry fruit, but not as rich or ripe as previous vintages.
rating: 84

best drinking Now–2004 **best vintages** '96, '98 **drink with** Wood-fired pizza • $14

Ingoldby Shiraz

ŸŸŸŸŸ 1999 Excellent bright purple-red; a moderately intense bouquet with clean, dark plum fruit and good oak balance and integration, thanks to the part-fermentation in that oak. A rich, full and concentrated palate with plum and blackberry fruit; good tannins to close. Gold medal in Hobart 2000.
rating: 90

best drinking 2004–2009 **best vintages** '99 **drink with** Steak and kidney pie • $16

Ingoldby Reserve Shiraz

ŸŸŸŸŸ 1998 Medium to full red-purple; rich, ripe dark berry and dark chocolate fruit on the bouquet is followed by a powerful, concentrated yet lively palate with delicious red berry and chocolate fruit the drivers. Oak, tannin and overall extract well controlled.
rating: 94

best drinking 2003–2013 **best vintages** '98 **drink with** Marinated venison • $25

Ingoldby Cabernet Sauvignon

Over the years Ingoldby has produced some quite wonderful Cabernet Sauvignon. It seems too much to hope that the best material will continue to come out under the Ingoldby label, but this has been a more than half decent wine. The wine is matured for 12 months in a mix of French and American oak.

ŸŸŸŸŸ 1999 Medium red-purple; the bouquet is quite savoury, with a mix of cedary/blackberry fruit and light oak. A strongly regional palate with chocolate and blackberry fruit in abundance; good tannins and oak.
rating: 91

best drinking 2003–2009 **best vintages** '90, '91, '94, '95, '98, '99 **drink with** Steak and kidney pie • $16

andrew garrett vineyard estates ★★★☆

134a The Parade, Norwood, SA 5067 **region** Warehouse
phone (08) 8379 0119 **fax** (08) 8379 7228 **open** Not
winemaker Andrew Garrett **production** NA **est.** 1986

product range ($10–52 R) There are three premium wine ranges. From the Yarra Valley in Victoria comes the Yarra Glen label, and from the Adelaide Hills in South Australia the Springwood Park label. In the lower price category come the Kelly's Promise (previously McLarens on the Lake) wines of Chardonnay, Shiraz, Cabernet Merlot and Brut Cuvée. Now also Martindale Hall from Clare Valley and Macedon Ridge from the Macedon Ranges.

summary The irrepressible Andrew Garrett has risen once again after 20 years in the wine industry as 'winemaker, innovator, entrepreneur, marketer and personality' (to use his own words). Andrew Garrett Vineyard Estates is now the umbrella for the Yarra Valley-based Yarra Glen label, the Adelaide Hills-based Springwood Park label, and for the Kelly's Promise range (previously known as McLarens on the Lake). Martindale Hall (Clare Valley) and Macedon Range are the most recent additions.

Yarra Glen Chardonnay

ŸŸŸŸ 1999 Medium yellow-green; there is quite ripe melon fruit to the solid bouquet, and the palate has good depth of flavour with an interplay of melon and nectarine.
rating: 84

best drinking Now–2003 **best vintages** NA **drink with** Poached chicken breast • NA

Andrew Garrett Vineyard Estates Kelly's Promise Grenache

YYYY 1998 Medium red-purple; the bouquet has light, juicy berry fruit but no obvious oak, the palate has simple but clean flavour in a medium-weight frame. **rating:** 83

best drinking Now–2003 **best vintages** NA **drink with** Takeaway • NA

Yarra Glen Cabernet Sauvignon

YYYY 1999 Medium red-purple; the bouquet has a mix of sweet berry and slightly more gamey notes, the palate has elegant red berry fruit, soft, fine tannins and gentle oak. Good outcome for the year. **rating:** 84

best drinking 2003–2007 **best vintages** NA **drink with** Roast beef • NA

andrew harris vineyards ★★★☆

Sydney Road, Mudgee, NSW 2850 **region** Mudgee
phone (02) 6373 1213 **fax** (02) 6373 1296 **open** Not
winemaker Frank Newman **production** 20 000 **est.** 1991
product range ($11.50–44.95 R) Premium Semillon, Verdelho, Chardonnay, Shiraz, Cabernet Sauvignon; Reserve Range of Chardonnay, Shiraz, Merlot, Cabernet Sauvignon; limited range of Double Vision (sparkling Shiraz) and The Vision (Shiraz Cabernet Sauvignon).
summary Andrew and Debbie Harris lost no time after purchasing a 300-hectare sheep station southeast of Mudgee in 1991. The first 6 hectares of vineyard were planted in that year and they have since been expanded to 101 hectares. A substantial portion of the production is sold to others, but right from the first vintage limited quantities of high-quality wines have been made under the Andrew Harris label, which deservedly enjoyed considerable show success with the first releases. Seems to have slipped a fraction in recent times.

Andrew Harris Semillon

YYYY 2000 Medium yellow-green; the bouquet is quite powerful, with spice, wild herbs and even lavender aromas; the palate has plenty of weight and presence, reflecting the interesting bouquet, but has a slightly grippy finish. **rating:** 85

best drinking Now–2003 **best vintages** NA **drink with** Asian fish • $15.95

Andrew Harris Reserve Chardonnay

YYYY 1999 Light to medium green-yellow; consistent with the winemaking techniques, there is subtle integration of the well-balanced oak with melon/citrus fruit on the bouquet, and the same successful and sophisticated interplay on the palate. A nice wine, the limitations, such as they are, lying more in the vineyard than in the winery. **rating:** 86

best drinking Now–2003 **best vintages** '95 **drink with** Roast pork • $27.95

Andrew Harris Reserve Shiraz

YYYY 1998 Medium red-purple; a fair whack of vanilla American oak hits the fruit on the bouquet, and likewise on the palate. However, red berry fruit does express itself, aided by nice, ripe tannins. A thoroughly traditional marriage, but not between equals. **rating:** 85

best drinking 2003–2007 **best vintages** '97 **drink with** Braised oxtail • $27.95

Andrew Harris The Vision

YYYYY 1997 Medium red-purple; a mix of ripe berry and more leathery/savoury notes sweetened by vanilla oak on the bouquet is followed by a palate with lots of sweet, plum and berry fruit; the oak is balanced and the tannins soft. Winner of two gold medals in 1999. **rating:** 90

best drinking Now–2007 **best vintages** '96, '97 **drink with** Steak and kidney pie • $44.95

Andrew Harris Reserve Merlot

YYYY 1998 Medium red-purple; the bouquet has quite pronounced varietal character with distinctly savoury/leaf/sweet leather aromas. The palate, likewise, has good varietal character with quite luscious spicy berry fruit, finishing with soft tannins and subtle oak. **rating:** 88

best drinking 2002–2007 **best vintages** NA **drink with** Marinated veal • $27.95

Andrew Harris Reserve Cabernet Sauvignon

YYYY 1998 Medium red-purple; earthy/leafy/berry aromas are softened by a touch of oak on the bouquet, but the palate stays in a fairly reserved, savoury earthy/herbal style, compatible with the French oak. **rating:** 85

best drinking 2002–2006 **best vintages** '94 **drink with** Sitr-fried beef • $27.95

andrew peace wines ★★★☆

PO Box 92 Piangil, Vic, 3597 **region** Swan Hill
phone (03) 5030 5291 **fax** (03) 5030 5605 **open** By appointment
winemaker Andrew Peace **production** 50 000 **est.** 1995
product range ($9.95–15.95 R) Sauvignon Blanc, Chardonnay, Colombard Chardonnay, Mourvedre Shiraz, Grenache Shiraz, Shiraz, Cabernet, Merlot.
summary The Peace family has been a major Swan Hill grape grower since 1980 and moved into winemaking with the opening of a $3 million winery in 1997. The modestly priced wines are aimed at supermarket-type outlets in Australia and, in particular, at the export market in the major destinations for Australian wine. The quality of the wines is consistently good.

angove's ★★★☆

Bookmark Avenue, Renmark, SA 5341 **region** Riverland
phone (08) 8580 3100 **fax** (08) 8580 3155 **open** Mon–Fri 9–5
winemaker Jane Gilham **production** 1 million **est.** 1886
product range ($3.15–45 CD) A range of new label designs and packaging for the five varietal ranges. At the top comes Sarnia Farm Chardonnay and Cabernet Sauvignon; then Mondiale White and Red (blends); then Classic Reserve, covering virtually all varieties; then Stonegate blended whites and reds; Butterfly Ridge wines; and bringing up the rear, Misty Vineyards.
summary Exemplifies the economies of scale achievable in the Australian Riverland without compromising potential quality. Very good technology provides wines that are never poor and that can sometimes exceed their theoretical station in life; the white varietals are best. Angove's expansion into Padthaway has resulted in estate-grown premium wines at the top of the range. As well as national distribution, Angove's is exported to virtually all the major markets in Europe, North America and Asia. For good measure, it also acts as a distributor of Perrier Jouet Champagne and several small Australian wineries.

annie's lane ★★★★★

Quelltaler Road, Watervale, SA 5452 **region** Clare Valley
phone (08) 8843 0003 **fax** (08) 8843 0096 **open** Mon–Fri 8.30–5, weekends 11–4
winemaker Wendy Stuckey, Nigel Dolan **production** NFP **est.** 1856
product range ($12–38 CD) Riesling, Semillon, Reserve Semillon, Shiraz, Copper Trail Shiraz, Old Vine Shiraz, Grenache Mourvedre, Clare/Barossa Cabernet Merlot.
summary The Clare Valley portfolio of Beringer Blass formerly made at Quelltaler is sold under the Annie's Lane label, the name coming from Annie Weyman, a turn-of-the-century local identity. Since 1996, a series of outstanding wines has appeared under the Annie's Lane label. The Quelltaler winery has been leased to some Clare Valley vignerons determined to keep it in going-concern condition.

Annie's Lane Semillon

🍷🍷🍷🍷🍷 **2000** Medium to full yellow-green; a clean, intense, ripe and rich bouquet in a style that is a cross between that of Adelaide Hills and Margaret River. The palate has excellent richness, body and intensity, with good balance if you accept the slightly grippy acid on the finish. **rating:** 93

best drinking Now–2007 **best vintages** '94, '96, '00 **drink with** Poached salmon • $16

Annie's Lane Shiraz

🍷🍷🍷🍷🍷 **1999** Medium to full purple-red; rich, luscious dark berry, chocolate and earth aromas are followed by a palate that is rich, full and luscious, yet not jammy; simply masses of enjoyable flavour. **rating:** 91

best drinking 2003–2013 **best vintages** '94, '96, '98, '99 **drink with** Pepper steak • $18

Annie's Lane Copper Trail Shiraz

🍷🍷🍷🍷🍷 **1997** Medium red-purple; the moderately fragrant bouquet has very good balance and integration of the plummy fruit and oak. The medium bodied palate likewise has it all together, with good structure and texture, ripe dark fruits, ripe tannins and good length. Not in the class of the multi-trophy-winning '96, but a well-above-average wine. **rating:** 92

🍷🍷🍷🍷🍷 **1996** The winner of six trophies at the 2000 Royal Adelaide Wine Show, including Best Red Wine of Show. Combines complexity with elegance at the start of bottle development; spicy berry fruit aromas lead into a long, harmonious and balanced palate with sweet berry, mint and licorice flavours, soft tannins and nice oak. **rating:** 96

best drinking 2003–2010 **best vintages** '96, '97 **drink with** Italian-style calf's liver • $38

Annie's Lane Old Vine Grenache Shiraz Mourvedre

🍷🍷🍷🍷🍷 **1998** The bouquet has quite intense savoury/blackberry/spicy/gamey aromas, leading into a succulent and supple palate with complex flavours in a ripe Rhône Valley style. Very nice mouthfeel. **rating:** 93

best drinking 2002–2010 **best vintages** '98 **drink with** Beef in red wine • $25

Annie's Lane Cabernet Merlot

🍷🍷🍷🍷🍷 **1999** Medium purple-red; the bouquet has smooth berry cassis fruit, the palate with rich, full chocolate and berry fruit flavours supported by ripe tannins and positive but not over-exuberant oak. **rating:** 90

best drinking 2002–2008 **best vintages** '94, '95, '97, '99 **drink with** Devilled kidneys • $18

antcliff's chase ★★★☆

RMB 4510, Caveat, via Seymour, Vic 3660 **region** Central Victorian Mountain Country
phone (03) 5790 4333 **fax** (03) 5790 4333 **open** Weekends 10–5
winemaker Chris Bennett, Ian Leamon **production** 800 **est.** 1982
product range ($14–30 CD) Riesling, Chardonnay, Pinot Noir, Ultra Pinot Noir, Cabernet Merlot.
summary A small family enterprise. They commenced planting the vineyards at an elevation of 600 metres in the Strathbogie Ranges in 1982; commenced wine production from the 4-hectare vineyard in the early 1990s. After an uncertain start, wine quality has picked up considerably.

Antcliff's Chase Riesling

🍷🍷🍷🍷 **2000** Medium to full yellow-green, deeper than the '98; the bouquet is full, slightly broad, with lots of ripe tropical fruit that carries through into the generously flavoured tropical/lime palate. There may have been some botrytis in the vineyard, although one would not have expected that from the 2000 vintage. **rating:** 85

best drinking Now–2004 **best vintages** NA **drink with** Smoked trout • $16

Antcliff's Chase Pinot Noir

🍷🍷🍷🍷 **1999** Medium red, with a slightly tawny rim; the light bouquet has a mix of foresty/earthy/spicy aromas, the light to medium bodied palate with some sweet fruit at the core and surrounded by more spicy/woodsy flavours. Moderate length; nice wine. **rating:** 86

best drinking Now–2003 **best vintages** NA **drink with** Asian stir-fry • $18

Antcliff's Chase Ultra Pinot Noir

🍷🍷🍷🍷 **1997** Medium red, with just a hint of gas around the rim; the bouquet is clean, not particularly aromatic, but the wine delivers on the palate with concentrated savoury/spicy characters, a touch of plum and a gentle but long finish. **rating:** 87

best drinking Now–2003 **best vintages** NA **drink with** Braised duck • $26

apsley gorge vineyard ★★★★

Rosedale Road, Bicheno, Tas 7215 **region** Southern Tasmania
phone (03) 6375 1221 **fax** (03) 6375 1589 **open** By appointment
winemaker Brian Franklin **production** 2000 **est.** 1988
product range ($21 CD) Chardonnay, Pinot Noir.
summary While nominally situated at Bicheno on the east coast, Apsley Gorge is in fact some distance inland, taking its name from a mountain pass. Clearly, it shares with the other east coast wineries the capacity to produce Chardonnay and Pinot Noir of excellent quality. Retail distribution in most states; exports to the UK.

Apsley Gorge Chardonnay

🍷🍷🍷🍷 **1999** Medium to full yellow-green; big, full, ripe fruit on the bouquet is precisely repeated on the palate in the rich, voluptuous 1999 vintage style. **rating:** 83

best drinking Now–2003 **best vintages** '96, '97, '98 **drink with** Sugar-cured tuna • $21

aquila estate ★★★

85 Carabooda Road, Carabooda, WA 6033 **region** Swan District
phone (08) 9561 8166 **fax** (08) 9561 8177 **open** By appointment
winemaker Andrew Spencer-Wright **production** 15 000 **est.** 1993

product range ($11.20–19.50 R) Sauvignon Blanc Semillon, Chenin Blanc, Chardonnay, Blackwood Valley Chardonnay, Chardonnay Semillon, Reflections (white blend), Shiraz, Merlot, Cabernet Sauvignon, Flame (red blend).
summary As Aquila Estate has matured, so have its grape sources centred on the Margaret River (principally) and Boyup Brook. The white wines are quite attractive; a tank-sample of the 1999 Shiraz showed promise. Exports to the UK, Singapore and Japan.

Aquila Estate Blackwood Valley Chardonnay

YYYY **1999** Light to medium yellow-green; the bouquet is predominantly fruit-driven, with melon and a touch of barrel-ferment oak; there isn't much depth to the palate, but what is there is attractive, with light citrussy fruit neatly balanced with gentle oak. **rating:** 84

best drinking Now–2003 **best vintages** NA **drink with** Light seafood • $14.25

Aquila Estate Cabernet Sauvignon

YYYY **1999** Medium red, seeming to show some premature development; a gentle savoury berry bouquet, then a palate with chocolate added to the savoury berry characters of the bouquet, finishing with fine tannins. Quick developing, but pleasant. **rating:** 84

best drinking Now–2004 **best vintages** NA **drink with** Beef in black bean sauce • $19.50

arakoon 

229 Main Road, McLaren Vale, SA 5171 **region** McLaren Vale
phone (08) 8323 7339 **fax** (02) 6566 6288 **open** Not
winemaker Patrik Jones, Raymond Jones **production** 1000 **est.** 1999
product range ($15–22 CD) Chardonnay, Pinot Black (Pinot Noir), Big, Fat and Gutsy (Shiraz Grenache), Dingabledinga Blend (Cabernet Shiraz).
summary Ray and Patrik Jones' first venture into wine came to nothing: a 1990 proposal for a film about the Australian wine industry with myself as anchorman. Five years too early, say Ray and Patrik. In 1991 they opened an agency for Australian wine in Stockholm and started exporting wine to that country, the UK, Germany and Switzerland in 1994. In 1999 they took the plunge into making their own wine and exporting it as well as the wines of others. Patrik is the winemaker, having completed a degree at the Waite Campus of the University of Adelaide. The graphic design of the labels, incidentally, is as outrageous as the names of the wines.

Arakoon Pinot Black

YYYY **1999** Quite deep red, with a touch of purple; a complex, dusty, foresty bouquet with plummy/spicy fruit is followed by a palate with plummy fruit on entry but which seems to dry out on the mid-palate. **rating:** 82

best drinking Now **best vintages** NA **drink with** Smoked duck • $22

Arakoon Big, Fat and Gutsy

YYYY **1999** Medium to full red-purple; the bouquet is rich and ripe with a mix of prune, mulberry and plum aromas; a powerful palate with a mix of gamey and more plummy flavours, with a somewhat hot finish, but well enough named. **rating:** 84

best drinking Now–2007 **best vintages** NA **drink with** Marinated game • $22

Arakoon Dingabledinga Blend

YYYY **1999** Medium red-purple; light, leafy cool-grown fruit on the bouquet is followed by a palate with an unusual mix of mint, red berry and spice in a slightly angular frame. **rating:** 81

best drinking Now–2003 **best vintages** NA **drink with** Yearling steak • $18

arlewood estate NR

Harmans Road South, Willyabrup, WA 6284 **region** Margaret River
phone (08) 9755 6267 **fax** (08) 9755 6267 **open** Weekends 11–5
winemaker Voyager Estate (Contract) **production** 2000 **est.** 1988
product range ($15–29 CD) Semillon, Unwooded Semillon, Sauvignon Blanc, Shiraz, Cabernet Sauvignon, Cabernet Merlot, Cabernet Reserve (Cabernet Sauvignon Merlot Cabernet Franc), Port.
summary Liz and John Wojturski have expanded their initial plantings of 2.5 hectares to over 9 hectares and now have limited distribution through agents in Sydney and Perth.

armstrong vineyards ★★★★

Lot 1 Military Road, Armstrong, Vic 3381 **region** Grampians
phone (08) 8277 6073 **fax** (08) 8277 6035 **open** Not
winemaker Tony Royal **production** 1000 **est.** 1989
product range ($47.95 R) Shiraz.
summary Armstrong Vineyards is the brain-child or love-child of Tony Royal. The former Seppelt Great Western winemaker now runs the Australian business of Seguin Moreau, the largest of the French coopers. Armstrong Vineyards has 6.5 hectares of shiraz, the first 2 hectares planted in 1989, the remainder in 1995–96. Low yields (4.5 to 5.5 tonnes per hectare) mean the wine will always be produced in limited quantities.

arranmore vineyard NR

Rangeview Road, Carey Gully, SA 5144 **region** Adelaide Hills
phone (08) 8390 3034 **fax** (08) 8390 0005 **open** By appointment
winemaker John Venus **production** 200 **est.** 1998
product range ($25.50 CD) Chardonnay, Black Pinot Noir, Cleggett's Block Shiraz Cabernet.
summary One of the tiny operations that are appearing all over the beautiful Adelaide Hills. The 2-hectare vineyard is planted to pinot noir, chardonnay and sauvignon blanc, and the wines are basically sold through word of mouth and mail order.

Arranmore Black Pinot Noir

1999 Medium red, with some purple; the bouquet has very ripe plum and spice aromas, the palate with abundant sweet, plummy fruit and lots of exotic spices. The wine has good texture and length, and the idiosyncratic oak handling has not detracted from it. **rating:** 88

best drinking 2002–2005 **best vintages** '99 **drink with** Coq au vin • $25.50

arrowfield 

Denman Road, Jerry's Plains, NSW 2330 **region** Upper Hunter Valley
phone (02) 6576 4041 **fax** (02) 6576 4144 **open** 7 days 10–5
winemaker Blair Duncan **production** 1 million **est.** 1968
product range ($12–21 R) Top-of-the-range Show Reserve range of Chardonnay, Semillon, Shiraz, Merlot, Cabernet Sauvignon, Late Harvest Botrytis Semillon; Hunter Valley Chardonnay, Semillon, Shiraz; Cowra Chardonnay, Merlot; Arrowfield varietals Chardonnay, Semillon Chardonnay, Sauvignon Blanc, Verdelho, Sauvignon Blanc, Shiraz, Cabernet Merlot.
summary After largely dropping the Arrowfield name in favour of Mountarrow and a plethora of other brands, this Japanese-owned company has come full circle, once again marketing the wines solely under the Arrowfield label. Its principal grape sources are Cowra and the Upper Hunter, but it does venture further afield from time to time. Exports to the US, the UK, New Zealand, Germany, Malaysia and Hong Kong.

Arrowfield Show Reserve Semillon

1998 Excellent bright, light green-yellow; the bouquet is complex, with the suggestion of the inclusion of a small percentage of barrel-fermented wine, but may simply represent good bottle development; the palate is fine, elegant and long, with a touch of lemon, and is developing slowly, an encouraging sign for the future. **rating:** 89

best drinking 2002–2008 **best vintages** '98 **drink with** Seafood risotto • $21

Arrowfield Hunter Valley Chardonnay

1999 Medium yellow-green; the bouquet is of light to medium intensity, with clean, nectarine peach fruit; the palate has pleasant flavour and, relatively speaking, is quite tight. Avoids the mawkish flavour of typical unoaked Chardonnay. **rating:** 85

best drinking Now–2003 **best vintages** NA **drink with** Takeaway • $15

Arrowfield Show Reserve Chardonnay

1999 Medium yellow-green; the peachy bouquet has subtle oak and lees influences, the light to medium bodied palate showing similar fruit character to the varietal release, with the addition of subtle oak. Not complex, but elegant. **rating:** 87

best drinking Now–2004 **best vintages** NA **drink with** Full-flavoured fish dishes • $21

Arrowfield Shiraz

YYYY 1999 Youthful purple-red; the moderately intense bouquet is clean, with some cherry fruit that flows through to the pleasant, medium-bodied but rather simple palate. Controlled use of oak (presumably oak chips).
rating: 83

best drinking Now **best vintages** NA **drink with** Red meats • $12

artamus NR

PO Box 489, Margaret River, WA 6285 **region** Margaret River
phone (08) 9757 8131 **fax** (08) 9757 8131 **open** Not
winemaker Michael Gadd **production** 250 **est.** 1994
product range ($15 R) Chardonnay.
summary Ann Dewar and Ian Parmenter (the celebrated television food presenter) planted a hectare of chardonnay cuttings (from Cape Mentelle) at their property on the north bank of the Margaret River. Their first wine was produced in 1998, made for them by Michael Gadd; 1999 is the second vintage.

Artamus Margaret River Chardonnay

YYYYY 1999 Light green-yellow; a quite fragrant bouquet with nectarine and some barrel-ferment characters lead into a wonderfully stylish and elegant palate with a mix of intense nectarine, cashew and smoky barrel-ferment characters; good acidity and length.
rating: 90

best drinking Now–2004 **best vintages** NA **drink with** Margaret River marron • $15

arthurs creek estate

Strathewen Road, Arthurs Creek, Vic 3099 **region** Yarra Valley
phone (03) 9714 8202 **fax** (03) 9824 0252 **open** Not
winemaker Tom Carson (Contract), Gary Baldwin (Consultant) **production** 1500 **est.** 1975
product range ($26–46 R) Chardonnay, Cabernet Sauvignon.
summary A latter-day folly of leading Melbourne QC S E K Hulme, who began the planting of 3 hectares of chardonnay, 4.3 hectares of cabernet sauvignon and 0.7 hectares of merlot at Arthurs Creek in the mid-1970s, and commenced to have wine made by various people for 15 years before deciding to sell any of it. A ruthless weeding-out process followed, with only the best of the older vintages offered. The Cabernets from the 1990s are absolutely outstanding, deeply fruited and marvellously structured. Exports to the UK, the US and Japan.

Arthurs Creek Chardonnay

YYYYY 1999 Medium to full yellow-green; sweet nectarine and melon fruit joins with spicy French oak to provide a complex bouquet; the palate is elegant and tight, with attractive melon and nectarine fruit; back to its top form, particularly given the indifferent vintage.
rating: 90

best drinking 2002–2007 **best vintages** '88, '90, '92, '93, '94, '95, '97, '99 **drink with** Veal fricassee • $26

Arthurs Creek Cabernet Sauvignon

YYYY 1996 Medium to full red-purple; the moderately intense bouquet has the typical cedary/leafy/savoury aromas of cool-grown cabernet sauvignon. These characters come through on the palate, accompanied by some plummy notes; finishes with fine tannins and pretty high acidity.
rating: 88

best drinking Now–2011 **best vintages** '82, '87, '89, '91, '92, '93, '94, '95, '96 **drink with** Lamb fillets • $43

ashbrook estate

Harmans Road South, Willyabrup, WA 6284 **region** Margaret River
phone (08) 9755 6262 **fax** (08) 9755 6290 **open** 7 days 11–5
winemaker Tony Devitt, Brian Devitt **production** 8000 **est.** 1975
product range ($14–26 CD) Gold Label Riesling, Black Label Riesling, Semillon, Sauvignon Blanc, Chardonnay, Verdelho, Cabernet Merlot.
summary A fastidious maker of consistently outstanding estate-grown table wines, Ashbrook Estate shuns publicity and the wine show system alike, however, and is less well-known than it deserves to be. It sells much of its wine through the cellar door and to an understandably very loyal mailing list clientele. All of the white wines are of the highest quality, year in, year out. Small quantities of the wines now find their way to Japan, Singapore and Hong Kong.

Ashbrook Estate Gold Label Riesling

▼▼▼▼ 2000 Light to medium yellow-green; the bouquet is clean, firm and solid, but not particularly aromatic. An immaculately made and balanced wine with plenty of length and mid-range lime/tropical flavours. **rating:** 88

best drinking Now–2004 **best vintages** '99 **drink with** Asparagus and salmon terrine • $16

Ashbrook Estate Semillon

▼▼▼▼▽ 2000 Light to medium yellow-green; the bouquet is fragrant, with sweet yet delicate blossom aromas; the palate has a range of blossom/honey/tropical flavours and no green or grassy characters. The fruit sweetness (the sweetness is from the fruit, not residual sugar) is neatly balanced by a tweak of acidity that runs through the finish and aftertaste. In typical Margaret River mould, has substance now, but will build even more with 3–5 years in bottle. **rating:** 90

best drinking Now–2006 **best vintages** '87, '92, '93, '94, '95, '97, '99 **drink with** Blanquette of veal • $14

Ashbrook Estate Verdelho

▼▼▼▼ 2000 Light to medium green-yellow; the spotlessly clean bouquet has pleasant, gentle fruit-salad aromas that give no hint of the vibrantly fresh-cut fruit-salad palate, with a squeeze of lemon, driven by amazing acidity and a jab of CO_2. **rating:** 88

best drinking Now–2004 **best vintages** NA **drink with** Chicken takeaway • $17

Ashbrook Estate Chardonnay

▼▼▼▼▽ 1999 Medium to full yellow-green; very strong, rich barrel-ferment characters allied with some bottle development invest the bouquet with considerable complexity; the palate is mouthfilling, rich and powerful, multiflavoured, and at the baroque end of the spectrum, particularly for Ashbrook Estate. **rating:** 91

best drinking Now–2004 **best vintages** '87, '92, '93, '94, '95, '98, '99 **drink with** Grilled spatchcock • $21

Ashbrook Estate Cabernet Merlot

▼▼▼▼ 1997 The colour is misleadingly developed, with brick tinges starting to appear; the bouquet also shows some aged, savoury Bordeaux-style aromas, but then the palate brings it all together with far sweeter than expected mocha/vanilla/gently earthy/berry fruit and a long, fine finish. **rating:** 87

best drinking Now–2004 **best vintages** NA **drink with** Braised beef • $24

asher NR

360 Goldsworthy Road, Lovely Banks, Geelong, Vic 3231 **region** Geelong
phone (03) 5276 1365 **open** Sat, public holidays 10–5, Sun 12–5
winemaker Brian Moten **production** Minuscule **est.** 1975
product range ($10 CD) Sauvignon Blanc, Cabernet Sauvignon, Malbec.
summary A tiny, semi home-winemaking operation situated at the picturesquely named town of Lovely Banks on the outskirts of Geelong.

ashton hills ★★★★★

Tregarthen Road, Ashton, SA 5137 **region** Adelaide Hills
phone (08) 8390 1243 **fax** (08) 8390 1243 **open** Weekends 11–5.30
winemaker Stephen George **production** 1500 **est.** 1982
product range ($17.50–42 CD) Chardonnay, Riesling, Salmon Brut, Blanc de Blanc, Pinot Noir, Piccadilly Valley Pinot Noir, Obliqua (Cabernet Merlot).
summary Stephen George wears three winemaker hats: one for Ashton Hills, drawing upon a 3.5-hectare estate vineyard high in the Adelaide Hills; one for Galah Wines; and one for Wendouree. It would be hard to imagine three wineries producing more diverse styles, with the elegance and finesse of Ashton Hills at one end of the spectrum and the awesome power of Wendouree at the other. The Riesling and Pinot Noir have moved into the highest echelon. Export markets have been developed in the UK, the US and Japan.

Ashton Hills Riesling

▼▼▼▼ 1999 Light green-yellow; the bouquet is still relatively closed, tight and youthful, with some herb/grass/mineral aromatics endeavouring to escape. The palate is still very light, but has lovely flowery touches of ripe apple. Be patient. **rating:** 89

best drinking 2002–2009 **best vintages** '89, '90, '91, '93, '94, '96, '97, '98 **drink with** Fresh asparagus • $19.60

Ashton Hills Chardonnay

ΨΨΨΨ♀ **1998** Medium yellow-green; a touch of French solids character adds complexity to both the bouquet and palate, with a mix of still-tight citrus and cashew aromas and flavours. Typically lean and slow developing. **rating:** 90

best drinking Now–2006 **best vintages** '95, '97, '98 **drink with** Bouillabaisse • $26.95

Ashton Hills Blanc de Blanc

ΨΨΨΨ♀ **1997** Medium straw-yellow; a nutty/creamy/bready bouquet is followed by a palate with ripe apple and spice flavours, finishing with the tight acidity one would expect of Ashton Hills. **rating:** 90

best drinking Now **best vintages** NA **drink with** Aperitif • $24.99

Ashton Hills Pinot Noir

ΨΨΨΨΨ **1999** A worthy successor to the superb 1997 Reserve from Ashton Hills. The aromas swirl from the glass, establishing the immediate presence of intense savoury/spicy/plummy fruit that runs through to the lingering palate with its mix of foresty/savoury and sweet plum fruit supported by leathery, fine tannins. **rating:** 95

best drinking Now–2006 **best vintages** '88, '91, '92, '93, '94, '97, '98, '99 **drink with** Smoked duck • $42

ashworths hill NR

Ashworths Road, Lancefield, Vic 3435 **region** Macedon Ranges
phone (03) 5429 1689 **fax** (03) 5429 1689 **open** 7 days 10–6
winemaker Anne Manning, John Ellis **production** 100 **est.** 1982
product range ($12–20 CD) Macedon Ranges Cabernet Sauvignon is the flagship; Victorian Riesling and Chardonnay also available.
summary Peg and Ken Reaburn offer light refreshments throughout the day; the property offers scenic views of the Macedon Ranges.

audrey wilkinson NR

Oakdale, DeBeyers Road, Pokolbin, NSW 2320 **region** Lower Hunter Valley
phone (02) 4998 7411 **fax** (02) 4998 7303 **open** Mon–Fri 9–5, weekends 9.30–5
winemaker Chris Cameron **production** 6000 **est.** 1999
product range ($19–27 CD) Semillon, Traminer, Chardonnay, Shiraz.
summary One of the most historic properties in the Hunter Valley, with a particularly beautiful location. The four wines come from the old plantings on the property, which has a very attractive cellar door. It is part of the James Fairfax wine group (headed by Pepper Tree) and will be involved in the planting of 100 hectares of vineyard in Coonawarra in 2001.

Audrey Wilkinson Semillon

ΨΨΨΨ **2000** Light green-yellow; a clean and fresh bouquet with pronounced herb and lemon varietal character, then a crisp, clean, bright and fresh palate with good balance and acidity; all the wine needs is time. **rating:** 87

best drinking 2004–2010 **best vintages** NA **drink with** Leave it in the cellar • $19

Audrey Wilkinson Shiraz

ΨΨΨ♀ **1998** Medium red-purple; the moderately intense bouquet has faintly gamey/regional overtones to the gently spicy fruit and oak. The palate is slightly unformed, quite gamey, but redeemed by more of those spice/nutmeg nuances evident in the bouquet. **rating:** 84

best drinking Now–2005 **best vintages** NA **drink with** Braised duck • $20

Audrey Wilkinson Reserve Cabernet Sauvignon

ΨΨΨΨ **1999** Medium to full red-purple; the solid, dark berry fruit with touches of chocolate on the bouquet is followed by a palate with loads of sweet oak coming over the top of the berry fruit; finishes with pleasantly soft tannins. **rating:** 85

best drinking 2002–2007 **best vintages** NA **drink with** Steak Diane • $27

auldstone ★★★

Booths Road, Taminick, via Glenrowan, Vic 3675 **region** Glenrowan
phone (03) 5766 2237 **fax** (03) 5766 2131 **open** Thur–Sat and school holidays 9–5, Sun 10–5
winemaker Michael Reid **production** 2000 **est.** 1987
product range ($10–24 CD) Riesling, Traminer Riesling, Chardonnay, Late Picked Riesling, Shiraz, Cabernet, Herceynia Tawny Port, Boweya Muscat, Sparkling Shiraz.
summary Michael and Nancy Reid have restored a century-old stone winery and have replanted the largely abandoned 24-hectare vineyard around it. Gourmet lunches are available on weekends.

austin's barrabool ★★★☆

50 Lemins Road, Waurn Ponds, Vic 3221 **region** Geelong
phone (03) 5241 8114 **fax** (03) 5241 8122 **open** By appointment
winemaker John Ellis (Contract), Pamela Austin **production** 2200 **est.** 1982
product range ($18–40 CD) Riesling, Chardonnay, Reserve Shiraz, Cabernet Sauvignon.
summary Pamela and Richard Austin have quietly built their business from a tiny base, but one that is now poised for much bigger things. The vineyard has been extended to 16.4 hectares, and instead of selling part of the production to others, they intend to significantly increase wine production under their own label — it doubled between 1998 and 1999. Wine quality, too, has risen, the wines being skilfully made by John Ellis at Hanging Rock.

Austin's Barrabool Riesling

ΥΥΥΥ **2000** Light straw-yellow; the bouquet is very light, with a mix of spice, mineral and a touch of herb, but no sweet fruit to be seen. The palate follows down the same track, somewhat unusual, and with a soft finish. May conceivably be going through a sulky phase. **rating:** 84
best drinking Now–2004 **best vintages** NA **drink with** Marinated scallops • $18

avalon vineyard ★★★

RMB 9556 Whitfield Road, Wangaratta, Vic 3678 **region** King Valley
phone (03) 5729 3629 **fax** (03) 5729 3635 **open** 7 days 10–5
winemaker Doug Groom **production** 1000 **est.** 1981
product range ($12–20 CD) Riesling, Chardonnay, Semillon Sauvignon Blanc, Late Harvest Semillon, Shiraz, Pinot Noir, Cabernet Sauvignon, Pinot Noir Méthode Champenoise.
summary Avalon Vineyard is situated in the King Valley, 4 kilometres north of Whitfield. Much of the production from the 10-hectare vineyard is sold to other makers, with limited quantities made by Doug Groom, a graduate of Roseworthy, and one of the owners of the property. Exports to the US.

Avalon Vineyard Chardonnay

ΥΥΥΥ **1999** Light to medium yellow-green; the bouquet is clean and fresh, with light melon fruit; the palate is light to medium bodied, simple but clean; melon and a touch of citrus run through to the finish. **rating:** 82
best drinking Now–2004 **best vintages** NA **drink with** Atlantic salmon • $15

Avalon Vineyard Pinot Noir

ΥΥΥΥ **1999** Developed tawny-red; the bouquet is of light to medium intensity, with a mix of foresty/briary/sappy aromas, the palate with a similar range of flavours and a faintly grippy finish. It would appear the shortcomings lie in the vineyard, not in the winery. **rating:** 80
best drinking Now **best vintages** NA **drink with** Chicken casserole • $18

avalon wines NR

1605 Bailey Road, Glen Forrest, WA 6071 **region** Perth Hills
phone (08) 9298 8049 **fax** (08) 9298 8049 **open** By appointment
winemaker Rob Marshall **production** 600 **est.** 1986
product range ($10–18 CD) Semillon, Chardonnay, Cane-Cut Semillon, Cabernet Merlot.
summary One of the newer wineries in the Perth Hills, it draws upon 0.75 hectare each of chardonnay, semillon and cabernet sauvignon.

bacchus estate NR

381 Milbrodale Road, Broke, NSW 2330 **region** Lower Hunter Valley
phone (02) 6579 1153 **fax** (02) 6579 1069 **open** By appointment
winemaker Andrew Margan (Contract) **production** 1000 **est.** 1993
product range ($14–20 CD) Chardonnay, Unwooded Chardonnay, Shiraz.
summary Another of the wineries springing up like mushrooms after spring rain in the Hunter Valley, in this instance at Broke. A little over 10 hectares of vineyard have been established, with a further 12 hectares to be planted in the near future. As the new plantings mature, production will increase significantly.

badger's brook NR

874 Maroondah Highway, Coldstream, Vic 3770 **region** Yarra Valley
phone (03) 5962 4130 **fax** (03) 5962 4238 **open** Weekends and public holidays 10–5
winemaker Contract **production** 5300 **est.** 1993
product range ($16–20 CD) Badger's Brook and Storm Ridge labels.
summary Situated prominently on the Maroondah Highway next door to the well-known Eyton-on-Yarra. Location is all, although not for the wines, which come from various sources.

Badger's Brook Chardonnay

YYYY **1999** Medium green-yellow; a clean, fresh, quite aromatic bouquet offers moderately intense melon and subtle oak; the light to medium bodied palate shows melon, a touch of cashew malolactic characters, finishing with subtle oak. **rating:** 85

best drinking Now–2004 **best vintages** NA **drink with** Yarra yabbies • $18

Badger's Brook Storm Ridge Chardonnay

YYYY **1999** Medium yellow-green; a complex, full peachy bouquet with slightly heavy oak is followed by a full palate, broken by a tweak of acidity on the finish. **rating:** 83

best drinking Now–2003 **best vintages** NA **drink with** Pasta • $17

Badger's Brook Storm Ridge Pinot Noir

YYYY **1999** Light to medium red; a fragrant, foresty, almost lemony, bouquet leads into a palate with a similar lemony twist to the savoury fruit. Unusual and interesting. **rating:** 83

best drinking Now–2004 **best vintages** NA **drink with** Smoked chicken • $18

bago vineyards ★★☆

Milligans Road, off Bago Road, Wauchope, NSW 2446 **region** Hastings River
phone (02) 6585 7099 **fax** (02) 6585 7099 **open** 7 days 11–5
winemaker John Steel, John Cassegrain (Contract) **production** 5000 **est.** 1985
product range ($10–21.50 CD) Chardonnay, Jazz White Classic, Verdelho, Chambourcin, Merlot Chambourcin, Jazz Red Classic, Sparkling Pinot Noir Chardonnay, Sparkling Chambourcin, Tawny Port.
summary Jim and Kay Mobs commenced planting the Broken Bago Vineyards in 1985 with 1 hectare of chardonnay and have now increased the total plantings to 12.5 hectares. Regional specialist John Cassegrain is the contract winemaker.

baileys of glenrowan ★★★★★

Cnr Taminick Gap and Upper Taminick Roads, Glenrowan, Vic 3675 **region** Glenrowan
phone (03) 5766 2392 **fax** (03) 5766 2596 **open** Mon–Fri 9–5, weekends 10–5
winemaker Nick Walker **production** 30 000 **est.** 1870
product range ($15–50 CD) Classic Chardonnay, Riesling, Touriga, Shiraz, 1904 Block Shiraz Cabernet Sauvignon and 1920's Block Shiraz are the principal wines; Warby Range, Founders and Winemaker's Selection Tokay and Muscat; Phantom's Lake Chardonnay and Shiraz were introduced in 1997 in fancy bottles.
summary Now part of the sprawling Beringer Blass empire, inherited via the Rothbury takeover. Has made some excellent Shiraz in recent years, but its greatest strength lies in its fortified wines. It is for these wines that the winery rating is given.

Baileys of Glenrowan Shiraz

🍷🍷🍷 1998 Dark red; the bouquet is sweet with a mix of slightly jammy, prune fruit and subtle oak; the palate is in the same sweet, slightly jammy spectrum, adding touches of chocolate; some hard edges to the finish need to soften. **rating:** 83

best drinking 2002–2008 **best vintages** NA **drink with** Lamb casserole • $17

Baileys of Glenrowan 1904 Block Shiraz

🍷🍷🍷🍷🍷 1998 Impenetrable red-purple; the bouquet is very concentrated, with a mix of prune and plum, the oak totally subservient. The palate is no less dense and concentrated, the tannins playing an important but not impressive role. A truly remarkable wine. **rating:** 95

best drinking 2008–2018 **best vintages** '98 **drink with** Leave it in the cellar • $45

Baileys 1920's Block Shiraz

🍷🍷🍷🍷 1998 Dense red-purple; the bouquet is quite complex, with a mix of cherry, licorice, spice and earth; the powerful palate has a mix of dark fruits and more earthy characters, with persistent and still quite grippy tannins. **rating:** 88

best drinking 2003–2013 **best vintages** '91, '92, '93, '96, '97 **drink with** Rare rump steak, venison • $25

Baileys of Glenrowan Cabernet Sauvignon

🍷🍷🍷🍷 1999 Medium red-purple; ripe blackcurrant, mulberry and prune aromas together with a hint of cedary oak lead into tangy, spicy, almost lemony, berry fruit on the palate, finishing with soft, slippery tannins. **rating:** 87

best drinking 2003–2009 **best vintages** NA **drink with** Lamb shanks • $17

Baileys Founder Liqueur Tokay

🍷🍷🍷🍷 NV Medium golden brown; full, complex, sweeter style of Tokay with clean spirit. The palate is rich, full and textured, with flavours of butterscotch and sweet biscuit and a chewy texture, but finishing long and clean. **rating:** 89

best drinking Now **best vintages** NA **drink with** Winter aperitif; summer after dinner • NA

Baileys Winemaker's Selection Old Liqueur Tokay

🍷🍷🍷🍷🍷 NV Deep brown; the bouquet shows obvious barrel-aged rancio characters: very complex but still retaining good varietal character. The wine has outstanding structure in the mouth, with complexity apparent immediately the wine is tasted. The flavours run in the cold tea/butterscotch/brandysnap spectrum, finishing with cleansing acidity. **rating:** 94

best drinking Now **best vintages** NA **drink with** After coffee; alternative to Cognac • NA

Baileys Founder Liqueur Muscat

🍷🍷🍷🍷 NV Medium red-brown; an arresting bouquet with hints of spice to the sweet, ripe, complex fruit. The same unusual spicy/cinnamon aspects are apparent on the rich and complex palate. **rating:** 88

best drinking Now **best vintages** NA **drink with** After coffee; alternative to Cognac • NA

Baileys Winemaker's Selection Old Liqueur Muscat

🍷🍷🍷🍷🍷 NV Dark brown, tending to olive on the rim; complex, faintly earthy/spirity aromas with an almost nutty edge to the raisined muscat fruit. A tremendously powerful and concentrated wine in the mouth, with excellent balance and a wonderful finish. Iron fist in a velvet glove. **rating:** 94

best drinking Now **best vintages** NA **drink with** After coffee; alternative to Cognac • NA

bainton family wines NR

390 Milbrodale Road, Fordwich, NSW 2330 **region** Lower Hunter Valley
phone (02) 9968 1764 **fax** (02) 9960 3454 **open** Not
winemaker Tony Bainton **production** 10 000 **est.** 1998
product range ($11–30 ML) Wollemi Semillon, Unwooded Chardonnay, Shiraz; Q Shiraz Chambourcin; Wollemi GOLD Botrytis Semillon, Wollemi GOLD Shiraz.
summary The Bainton family, headed by eminent Sydney QC Russell Bainton, has 48 hectares of vineyard. Currently selling most of the grapes but intending to steadily increase production in-house.

baldivis estate ★★☆

291 River Road, Serpentine, WA 6205 **region** South West Coast
phone (08) 9525 2066 **fax** (08) 9525 2411 **open** Mon–Fri 10–4; weekends, holidays 11–5
winemaker Mark Kailis, Sarah Siddons **production** 20 000 **est.** 1982
product range ($17–45 CD) Wooded and Unwooded Chardonnay, Sauvignon Blanc, Semillon Sauvignon Blanc, Pinot Noir Cabernet, Cabernet Merlot, Cabernet Sauvignon Reserve.
summary Acquired by Palandri Wines in 2000 and was, for a brief time, the improbable flagship for Palandri. There is ample viticultural and winemaking expertise, but although the wines are pleasant, soft and light bodied, they lack concentration.

Baldivis Estate Reserve Sauvignon Blanc

🍷🍷🍷🍷 **1998** Light to medium yellow-green; the bouquet is clean, not at all luscious, but with some distinctive herb and mineral varietal characters. The palate is light, the flavours running through herb, mineral and apple, and the finish clean. **rating:** 82

best drinking Now **best vintages** NA **drink with** Light seafood • NA

Baldivis Estate Semillon Sauvignon Blanc

🍷🍷🍷🍷 **1998** Light green-yellow; the bouquet is clean, of light to medium intensity, with a mix of mineral, herb and grass aromas. The palate is light but still retains crispness, the only drawback being a lack of concentration. **rating:** 83

best drinking Now **best vintages** NA **drink with** Shellfish • NA

bald mountain ★★★☆

Hickling Lane, Wallangarra, Qld 4383 **region** Granite Belt
phone (07) 4684 3186 **fax** (07) 4684 3433 **open** 7 days 10–5
winemaker Simon Gilbert (Contract) **production** 5000 **est.** 1985
product range ($11–19 CD) Classic Queenslander (in fact 100 per cent Sauvignon Blanc), Chardonnay, Late Harvest Sauvignon Blanc, Shiraz, Shiraz Cabernet.
summary Denis Parsons is a self-taught but exceptionally competent vigneron who has turned Bald Mountain into the viticultural showpiece of the Granite Belt. In various regional and national shows since 1988, Bald Mountain has won almost 70 show awards, placing it at the forefront of the Granite Belt wineries. The two Sauvignon Blanc-based wines, Classic Queenslander and the occasional non-vintage Late Harvest Sauvignon Blanc, are interesting alternatives to the mainstream wines. Future production will also see grapes coming from new vineyards near Tenterfield just across the border in New South Wales. No recent tastings. Significant exports to the Netherlands.

balgownie estate ★★★★

Hermitage Road, Maiden Gully, Vic 3551 **region** Bendigo
phone (03) 5449 6222 **fax** (03) 5449 6506 **open** Mon–Sat 10.30–5, Sun 12–4
winemaker Tobias Ansted **production** 12 000 **est.** 1969
product range ($14–26 CD) Estate-produced Chardonnay, Pinot Noir, Shiraz, Cabernet Sauvignon; Premier Cuvée (second, non-estate label); Maiden Gully Chardonnay, Cabernet Shiraz.
summary The sale of Balgownie foreshadowed in the previous edition of the *Wine Companion* has now eventuated, and major changes have followed. Vineyard plantings have been doubled to 36 hectares; Tobias Ansted has replaced Lindsay Ross as winemaker in the wake of a $3 million upgrade to the winery; and the Maiden Gully range has been introduced.

ballandean estate ★★★

Sundown Road, Ballandean, Qld 4382 **region** Granite Belt
phone (07) 4684 1226 **fax** (07) 4684 1288 **open** 7 days 9–5
winemaker Dylan Rhymer **production** 10 000 **est.** 1970
product range ($10–30 CD) Semillon, Semillon Sauvignon Blanc, Sauvignon Blanc, Black Label Sauvignon Blanc, Viognier, Chardonnay, Classic White, Sylvaner Late Harvest, Late Harvest Semillon, White Pearl (semi-sweet white), Lambrusco, Classic Red, Estate Shiraz, Black Label Shiraz, Black Label Merlot, Cabernet Sauvignon, Fortifieds, Sparkling.

summary The senior winery of the Granite Belt and by far the largest. The white wines are of diverse but interesting styles, the red wines smooth and usually well made. The estate specialty, Sylvaner Late Harvest, is a particularly interesting wine of good flavour. No recent tastings.

balnaves of coonawarra ★★★★☆

Main Road, Coonawarra, SA 5263 **region** Coonawarra
phone (08) 8737 2946 **fax** (08) 8737 2945 **open** Mon–Fri 9–5, weekends 10–5
winemaker Peter Bissell **production** 10 000 **est.** 1975
product range ($19–80 R) Chardonnay, The Blend (Merlot Cabernet Franc), Shiraz, Cabernet Merlot, Cabernet Sauvignon, Reserve Cabernet Sauvignon.
summary Former Hungerford Hill vineyard manager and now viticultural consultant-cum-grape-grower Doug Balnaves established his vineyard in 1975 but did not launch into winemaking until 1990, with colleague Ralph Fowler as contract winemaker in the early years. A striking new 300-tonne winery was built and was in operation for the 1996 vintage, with former Wynns Coonawarra Estate assistant winemaker, Peter Bissell, in charge. The expected leap in quality has indeed materialised with the 1996 and subsequent vintages. The wines are exported to the UK, Switzerland, Germany, the US, Japan and Hong Kong.

Balnaves Chardonnay

▼▼▼▼▽ **1999** Medium yellow-green; a powerful and complex bouquet with obvious barrel-ferment oak inputs is followed by a palate that tightens up and lengthens nicely. The citrus fruit has a real bite, and balances that oak. **rating:** 91

best drinking Now–2005 **best vintages** '92, '93, '94, '96, '98, '99 **drink with** Robe crayfish • $28

Balnaves Shiraz

▼▼▼▼▽ **1999** Inky red-purple; lots of dark fruit aromas with touches of spice are married with sweet oak on the bouquet; while it has surprising depth and concentration, the wine doesn't have quite the length of the '98s, but a very impressive wine nonetheless. Tasted as a tank sample immediately prior to bottling. **rating:** 90

best drinking 2004–2010 **best vintages** '93, '96, '97, '98, '99 **drink with** Cotechino sausages • $22

Balnaves The Blend

▼▼▼▼ **1999** Medium to full red-purple; dark, briary/berry/spicy aromas and gentle oak on the bouquet are followed by a well-structured palate, with sweet chocolate and berry fruit supported by soft tannins. Tasted as a tank sample shortly prior to bottling. **rating:** 88

best drinking 2003–2007 **best vintages** NA **drink with** Lamb loin • $19

Balnaves Cabernet Merlot

▼▼▼▼▽ **1999** Medium to full red-purple; the bouquet has ripe, dark berry fruit, a hint of chocolate and restrained oak. There is lots of cassis/blackberry fruit concentration and lingering tannins on the palate. Tasted as a tank sample shortly before bottling, and the points may prove conservative. **rating:** 90

best drinking 2004–2009 **best vintages** '90, '91, '92, '96, '99 **drink with** Calf's liver Italian style • $24

Balnaves Cabernet Sauvignon

▼▼▼▼▽ **1999** Full red-purple; full cassis/blackberry/mulberry aromas lead into a sweet, ripe and plush palate with nice chewy tannins and positive oak. Outstanding for the vintage. Tasted as a tank sample shortly before bottling. **rating:** 93

best drinking 2004–2012 **best vintages** '90, '91, '96, '98, '99 **drink with** Veal chops • $30

Balnaves of Coonawarra Reserve Cabernet Sauvignon

▼▼▼▼▼ **1998** Dense red-purple; the bouquet shows very concentrated, dark berry/cassis/blackberry fruit in Balnaves style, but with an extra degree of intensity. A very concentrated and powerful palate, with lush, ripe and dense fruit and appropriately balanced tannins and oak. A John Riddoch lookalike if ever there was one. **rating:** 95

best drinking 2005–2020 **best vintages** '98 **drink with** Salt bush lamb • $80

bannockburn by farr ★★★★☆

C/o Bannockburn, Midlands Highway, Bannockburn, Vic 3331 **region** Geelong
phone (03) 5281 1363 **fax** (03) 5281 1349 **open** Not
winemaker Gary Farr **production** 2000 **est.** 1999

product range ($45 R) Viognier, Chardonnay, Pinot Noir, Shiraz.
summary In 1994 Gary Farr and family planted just under 5 hectares of clonally-selected viognier, chardonnay, pinot noir and shiraz on a north-facing hill directly opposite the Bannockburn Winery, having acquired the land from the late Stuart Hooper (Bannockburn's then owner). For a multiplicity of reasons, in 1999 Farr decided to establish his own label for part of the grapes coming from the vineyard; the remainder goes to Bannockburn. The quality of the wines is exemplary, their character subtly different from those of Bannockburn itself. This is due, says Farr, to the interaction of the terroir of the hill and the clonal selection.

Bannockburn by Farr Viognier

YYYY **1999** Bright, light to medium green-yellow; the bouquet is clean and quite intense, yet no particular fruit character is dominant; the powerful, minerally palate could, in my view, be easily taken for Pinot Gris, but is certainly not short on power or presence. **rating:** 87

best drinking Now–2003 **best vintages** NA **drink with** Bouillabaisse • $45

Bannockburn by Farr Chardonnay

YYYYY **1999** Medium yellow-green; the complex bouquet has strong smoky barrel-ferment characters enveloping the citrus and melon fruit, the palate with powerful grip and flavour. Despite its 14°, it is austere rather than fleshy, but has a long finish. **rating:** 90

best drinking Now–2005 **best vintages** '99 **drink with** Pan-fried veal • $45

Bannockburn by Farr Pinot Noir

YYYYY **1999** Medium purple-red; a fragrant and stylish bouquet features abundant black cherry and strawberry fruit; the palate, with exemplary silky texture and structure, is complex and long, but not stalky. **rating:** 94

best drinking Now–2005 **best vintages** '99 **drink with** Barbecued quail • $45

Bannockburn by Farr Shiraz

YYYYY **1999** Medium to full purple-red; the complex aromas have true Rhône characteristics of the ripe black cherry, spice and licorice; the palate is bursting with youthful life, centred on juicy black cherry fruit and supported by controlled oak and tannins. Should develop marvellously well. **rating:** 92

best drinking 2003–2009 **best vintages** '99 **drink with** Coq au vin • $45

bannockburn vineyards ★★★★★

Midland Highway, Bannockburn, Vic 3331 **region** Geelong
phone (03) 5281 1363 **fax** (03) 5281 1349 **open** Not
winemaker Gary Farr **production** 9000 **est.** 1974
product range ($20–120 R) Riesling, Sauvignon Blanc, Chardonnay, SRH Chardonnay (named in honour of the late Stuart Reginald Hooper, founder of Bannockurn), Pinot Noir, Saignee (Rosé), Serré, Shiraz, Cabernet Merlot.
summary With the qualified exception of the Cabernet Merlot, which can be a little leafy and gamey, produces outstanding wines across the range, all with individuality, style, great complexity and depth of flavour. The low-yielding estate vineyards play their role, but so does the French-influenced winemaking of Gary Farr. Export markets have been established in the UK, the US, Hong Kong, New Zealand and Malaysia.

Bannockburn Vineyards Sauvignon Blanc

YYYY **1999** Light green-yellow; the bouquet is quite complex, with a mix of pea pod, lanolin and vanilla aromas; the palate is complex, and has grip, but I'm not sure this wine mightn't have been more attractive at 12 months of age. **rating:** 85

best drinking Now **best vintages** NA **drink with** Marinated calamari • $23

banrock station 

Holmes Road, off Sturt Highway, Kingston-on-Murray, SA 5331 **region** Riverland
phone (08) 8583 0299 **fax** (08) 8583 0288 **open** 7 days 10–4, except public holidays
winemaker Glenn James **production** NFP **est.** 1994
product range ($6.30–14.95 R) Semillon Chardonnay, Chardonnay, Shiraz Cabernet, Cabernet Merlot; Premium Range includes Wigley Reach Unwooded Chardonnay, Napper's Verdelho, Ball Island Shiraz, Cave Cliff Merlot and Sparkling Chardonnay and Shiraz.

summary The $1 million visitors centre at Banrock Station was opened in February 1999. Owned by BRL Hardy, the Banrock Station property covers over 1700 hectares, with 230 hectares of vineyard and the remainder being a major wildlife and wetland preservation area. The wines have consistently offered excellent value for money.

Banrock Station Ball Island Shiraz

🍷🍷🍷🍷 **1999** Medium red-purple; very ripe cherry with some prune and stewed plum fruit aromas get the wine off to a flying start. There is plenty of flavour on the palate, which is less ripe than the bouquet (and probably a good thing). Honest and full-flavoured, good value. **rating:** 82

best drinking Now **best vintages** '98 **drink with** Steak sandwich • $12.50

Banrock Station Cave Cliff Merlot

🍷🍷🍷🍷 **1999** Light to medium red-purple; there is some leafy/vegetal/spicy varietal character to the bouquet and the palate, but it trembles on the brink of being rather vegetal and gamey. **rating:** 80

best drinking Now **best vintages** '98 **drink with** Kransky sausages • $12.50

Banrock Station Cabernet Merlot

🍷🍷🍷🍷 **2000** Medium red-purple; fresh, juicy berry aromas are matched by similar flavours on the palate; has some mouthfeel and softness; excellent value at this price. **rating:** 83

best drinking Now **best vintages** NA **drink with** Takeaway • $7.99

barak estate NR

Barak Road, Moorooduc, Vic 3933 **region** Mornington Peninsula
phone (03) 5978 8439 **fax** (03) 5978 8439 **open** Weekends and public holidays 11–5
winemaker James Williamson **production** 500 **est.** 1996
product range ($17–20 CD) Chardonnay, Shiraz, Cabernet Sauvignon.
summary When James Williamson decided to plant vines on his 4-hectare Moorooduc property and establish a micro-winery, he already knew it was far cheaper to buy wine by the bottle than to make it. Undeterred, he ventured into grape-growing and winemaking, picking the first grapes in 1993 and opening Barak Estate in 1996. Old telegraph poles, railway sleepers, old palings and timber shingles have all been used in the construction of the picturesque winery.

barambah ridge NR

79 Goschnicks Road, Redgate, via Murgon, Qld 4605 **region** South Burnett
phone (07) 4168 4766 **fax** (07) 4168 4770 **open** 7 days 10–5
winemaker Charles Williams **production** 10 000 **est.** 1997
product range ($10.50–16.50 CD) Semillon, Ridge Semillon, Ridge White, Chardonnay, French Oaked Chardonnay, Ridge Red, Reserve Shiraz, Cabernet Sauvignon.
summary Barambah Ridge is owned by South Burnett Wines, an unlisted public company, and is a major new entrant on the Queensland wine scene. The winery constructed for the 1998 vintage has a crush of 150 tonnes. The 1997 wines were made by the omnipresent Bruce Humphery-Smith, winning an array of medals at the annual Sheraton/*Courier-Mail* Brisbane Queensland Wine Awards, including the trophy and gold medal for Best White Wine (with the 1997 unwooded Chardonnay). No recent tastings.

baratto's NR

Farm 678, Hanwood, NSW 2680 **region** Riverina
phone (02) 6963 0171 **fax** (02) 6963 0171 **open** 7 days 10–5
winemaker Peter Baratto **production** 6250 **est.** 1975
product range ($4–8 CD) Trebbiano Semillon, Chardonnay, Shiraz Barbera, Shiraz Cabernet, Cabernet Sauvignon.
summary Baratto's is in many ways a throwback to the old days. Peter Baratto has 15 hectares of vineyards and sells the wine in bulk or in 10- and 20-litre casks from the cellar door at old-time prices, from as little as $4 per litre. The 2000 Shiraz Cabernet at $7 and 80 points is a delightful, freshly fruited, no-frills glass.

barletta bros NR

95a Walkerville Terrace, Walkerville, SA 5081 **region** Clare Valley
phone (08) 8342 3395 **fax** (08) 8269 4008 **open** By appointment
winemaker Neil Pike (Polish Hill River Winery) **production** 3000 **est.** 1993
product range ($8–11 CD) Hand Picked Riesling, Shiraz, Dry Grown Grenache Shiraz.
summary There have been many twists since 1993 when Mario, Ben and Julio Barletta started an 'own brand' for their then-retail business, Walkerville Cellars. They no longer own Walkerville Cellars, and the winemaking business is now the sole business of Mario, who has an active involvement with contract winemaker Neil Pike. The Barletta tanks and barrels reside at Pikes, but Mario Barletta intends ultimately to establish his own independent vineyard, winery and operation. Retail distribution in South Australia and Melbourne; exports to the US and Germany.

Barletta Bros Hand Picked Riesling

🍷🍷🍷🍷 **1998** Medium yellow-green; the bouquet is still slightly hard, with strong mineral/slate aromas; the palate is similarly slow-developing in an intense mineral/acid style with the fruit still hidden. Could well surprise with more bottle age. **rating:** 84

best drinking 2002–2007 **best vintages** NA **drink with** Shellfish • $8

Barletta Bros Shiraz

🍷🍷🍷🍷 **1996** Medium to full red-purple, still youthful; abundant ripe, sweet berry and mint fruit is complexed by a touch of vanilla oak on the bouquet. The palate has plenty of concentration, with dark cherry fruit, both the oak and tannin levels being well controlled. On the other side, the wine gives the impression that it may have spent time in tank or been taken to bottle too soon, for it is still slightly callow and immature. **rating:** 84

best drinking Now–2006 **best vintages** NA **drink with** Grilled steak • NA

barnadown run ★★★

390 Cornella Road, Toolleen, Vic 3551 **region** Heathcote
phone (03) 5433 6376 **fax** (03) 5433 6386 **open** 7 days 10–5
winemaker Andrew Millis **production** 900 **est.** 1995
product range ($17–22 CD) Chardonnay, Reserve Chardonnay, Shiraz, Cabernet.
summary Named after the original pastoral lease, of which the vineyard is a part. Established on rich terra rossa soil, for which the best Heathcote vineyards are famous. Owner Andrew Millis carries out both the viticulture and winemaking at the 5-hectare vineyard. Exports to the US, the UK and Switzerland.

barossa ridge wine estate ★★★★

Light Pass Road, Tanunda, SA 5352 **region** Barossa Valley
phone (08) 8563 2811 **fax** (08) 8563 2811 **open** By appointment
winemaker Marco Litterini **production** 1700 **est.** 1987
product range ($20–23 CD) Valley of Vines Merlot Cabernet Franc Cabernet Sauvignon Petit Verdot, Old Creek Shiraz, Mardia's Vineyard Cabernet Franc, Bamboo Creek Merlot, Rocky Valley Cabernet Sauvignon.
summary A grape-grower turned winemaker with a small list of interesting red varietals, including the Valley of Vines blend of Merlot, Cabernet Franc, Cabernet Sauvignon and Petit Verdot (what a mouthful), the only such wine produced in the Barossa Valley. Production has doubled, and the wines have retail distribution in New South Wales. All of its wines are built in an impressively heroic style. Exports to Switzerland and Germany.

Barossa Ridge Old Creek Shiraz

🍷🍷🍷🍷🍷 **1999** Excellent red-purple; clean, rich blackberry and cherry fruit on the bouquet flows through into the palate, where it is joined by a touch of chocolate. While full bodied, the wine is not extractive, and the oak has been well judged. **rating:** 91

best drinking 2004–2009 **best vintages** '98, '99 **drink with** Ragout of venison • $23

Barossa Ridge Valley of Vines

🍷🍷🍷🍷 **1998** Medium to full red-purple; dark black fruit/blackberry/leathery aromas lead into a strong palate with blackberry, bitter chocolate, leather, subtle oak and ripe tannins. **rating:** 89

best drinking 2003–2008 **best vintages** NA **drink with** Rare rump steak • $20

Barossa Ridge Mardia's Vineyard Cabernet Franc

YYYY **1999** Medium red-purple; there is a spectrum of savoury/leathery/earthy characters on the bouquet, enriched by dark berry, spice and olive on the palate, which finishes with sweetly ripe tannins. Assured oak handling. **rating:** 88

best drinking 2003–2008 **best vintages** '98 **drink with** Beef in black bean sauce • $22

Barossa Ridge Rocky Valley Cabernet Sauvignon

YYYY **1999** Medium to full red-purple; very much in the vineyard style, with solid, dark berry/plum/ blackberry aromas and flavours. Here, too, the vanilla oak has been well balanced and integrated. **rating:** 87

best drinking 2003–2009 **best vintages** NA **drink with** Pot roast • $22

barossa settlers ★★★

Trial Hill Road, Lyndoch, SA 5351 **region** Barossa Valley
phone (08) 8524 4017 **fax** (08) 8524 4519 **open** Mon–Sat 10–4, Sun 11–4
winemaker Howard Haese **production** 800 **est.** 1983
product range ($12.50–32.50 CD) Gully Winds Riesling, Megan's Woolshed Flat Chardonnay, Joachim's Festive Champagne, Millowstowe Royale (Sparkling Red), Late Harvest Riesling, Joan's Block Grenache, Hoffnungsthal Settlement Shiraz, Howard's Bin 2000 Shiraz, Tom's Rostock Red (Shiraz), James Cabernet Sauvignon, Port, Sherry.
summary A superbly located cellar door is the only outlet (other than mail order) for the wines from this excellent vineyard owned by the Haese family. Production slowed in recent years, with the grapes from the 31-hectare vineyard being sold to others.

barossa valley estate ★★★☆

Heaslip Road, Angle Vale, SA 5117 **region** Adelaide Plains
phone (08) 8284 7000 **fax** (08) 8284 7219 **open** Mon–Fri 9–5, Sat 10–5
winemaker Natasha Mooney **production** 60 000 **est.** 1984
product range ($10–50 R) Spires Chardonnay Semillon, Shiraz Cabernet Sauvignon; Moculta Semillon, Chardonnay, Shiraz, Grenache, Cabernet Merlot; Ebenezer Chardonnay, Shiraz, Cabernet Sauvignon Merlot; and the premium E & E Sparkling Shiraz and Black Pepper Shiraz.
summary Barossa Valley Estate is now part-owned by BRL Hardy, marking the end of a period during which it was one of the last significant co-operative-owned wineries in Australia. Across the board, the wines are full-flavoured and honest. E & E Black Pepper Shiraz is an upmarket label with a strong reputation and following, the Ebenezer range likewise. Over-enthusiastic use of American oak (particularly with the red wines) has been the Achilles heel in the past. The wines are distributed in Australia and the UK by BRL Hardy, and by independent distributors in North America.

Barossa Valley Estate Moculta Shiraz

YYYY **1998** Dense red-purple; a concentrated bouquet with a mix of chocolate, cherry/berry and vanilla oak is followed by a rich, round and full-bodied wine replete with soft tannins. A traditional style, but as honest as the day is long, and representing great value at the price. **rating:** 86

best drinking Now–2008 **best vintages** '98 **drink with** Shepherd's pie • $15.99

Barossa Valley Estate Spires Shiraz Cabernet

YYYY **1999** Strong red-purple; the bouquet is quite complex, with a mix of slightly gamey and earthy aromas; the palate has above-average richness and weight for a wine in its price category, even if it is not quite in the class of the outstanding '98 wine. **rating:** 83

best drinking Now–2004 **best vintages** '98 **drink with** Pizza • $9.99

barratt ★★★★★

PO Box 204, Summertown, SA 5141 **region** Adelaide Hills
phone (08) 8390 1788 **fax** (08) 8390 1788 **open** By appointment
winemaker Jeffrey Grosset (Contract) **production** 1000 **est.** 1993
product range ($26.50–38.50 ML) Chardonnay, Pinot Noir.

summary Recently retired medical practitioner Lindsay Barratt and wife Carolyn own two vineyards at Summertown: the Uley Vineyard purchased from the late Ian Wilson in August 1990 and the Bonython Vineyard. They have 8.4 hectares of vines, some coming into production, and plan to add Sauvignon Blanc and Merlot to the wine range from 2002. Part of the production from the vineyards is sold to other makers, with Jeffrey Grosset the maker of the Chardonnay and Pinot Noir. Both wines are complex and of high quality. Limited quantities are sold in the UK, the US, Germany, Belgium and Singapore.

barretts wines NR

Portland–Nelson Highway, Portland, Vic 3305 **region** Henty
phone (03) 5526 5251 **open** 7 days 11–5
winemaker Rod Barrett **production** 1000 **est.** 1983
product range ($14–18 CD) Riesling, Traminer, Late Harvest Riesling, Pinot Noir, Cabernet Sauvignon, Port.
summary The second (and newer) winery in the Portland region. The initial releases were made at Best's, but since 1992 all wines have been made on the property by Rod Barrett.

barrington estate ★★★☆

Yarraman Road, Wybong, NSW 2333 **region** Upper Hunter Valley
phone (02) 6547 8118 **fax** (02) 6547 8039 **open** By appointment
winemaker Stephen Hagan (Contract) **production** 75 000 **est.** 1967
product range ($10.99–24 R) Top labels: Yarraman Road, Black Clay Chardonnay, Sandy Slopes Cabernet Shiraz; cheaper label: Barrington Estate; also Narrambla Verdelho and Chardonnay, The Banjo Shiraz.
summary Yarraman Road/Barrington Estate is the reincarnation of Penfolds Wybong Estate, into which Penfolds poured millions of dollars between 1960 and 1978, then sold the winery and surrounding vineyards to Rosemount Estate. Rosemount removed most of the unproductive vineyards and used the winery for red wine production until 1992, then converted it to pure storage area. In 1994 Gary and Karen Blom, after returning from the US, purchased the property from Rosemount. An Australian-born entrepreneur, Gary Blom had a highly successful career in the US. Their main investment here is the IMAX Theatre in Darling Harbour, but they intend to spend $3–4 million in redeveloping Barrington Estate. One physical sign was the purchase of Hay Shed Hill in November 2000.

barwang vineyard ★★★★☆

Barwang Road, Young, NSW 2594 **region** Hilltops
phone (02) 6382 3594 **fax** (02) 6382 2594 **open** Not
winemaker Jim Brayne, Russell Cody, Scott Zrna **production** NA **est.** 1969
product range ($15.95–23 R) Chardonnay, Semillon, Shiraz, Cabernet Sauvignon.
summary Peter Robertson pioneered viticulture in the Young region when he planted his first vines in 1975 as part of a diversification programme for his 400-hectare grazing property. When McWilliam's acquired Barwang in 1989, the vineyard amounted to 13 hectares; today the plantings exceed 100 hectares. Wine quality has been exemplary from the word go, always elegant, restrained and deliberately understated, and repaying extended cellaring. Interestingly, the name has been adopted for a large-volume, relatively low-priced range of wines for distribution in the US.

Barwang Chardonnay

ҮҮҮҮ **1999** Light green-yellow; fresh and lively nectarine/melon/peach fruit and a touch of oak on the bouquet; the fresh and lively palate has lighter than usual citrus/nectarine fruit, and there has been an intelligent downplay of oak to deal with the lighter fruit. **rating:** 88

best drinking Now–2004 **best vintages** '94, '98 **drink with** Calamari • $15.95

Barwang Shiraz

ҮҮҮҮ **1999** Medium to full red-purple; briary/savoury overtones to the berry and cherry of the bouquet manifest themselves again in providing a savoury frame to the palate, filled in to a degree with sweet, dark cherry fruit. Nowhere near the '98 vintage, the tannins and finish being slightly hard. Very much a product of the difficult vintage. **rating:** 86

best drinking 2003–2007 **best vintages** '90, '91, '92, '93, '94, '97, '98 **drink with** Parmesan cheese • $23

Barwang Cabernet Sauvignon

TTTT **1999** Medium to full red-purple; blackberry/foresty/savoury characters manifest themselves alongside riper fruit aromas on the bouquet; a big, powerful chunky wine, with strong, savoury, dark berry fruit. Decidedly more successful in a trying vintage than the Shiraz. **rating:** 89

best drinking 2004–2009 **best vintages** '89, '91, '92, '93, '96, '97, '98 **drink with** Beef Wellington • $19.95

basedow ★★★☆

161–165 Murray Street, Tanunda, SA 5352 **region** Barossa Valley
phone (08) 8563 3666 **fax** (08) 8563 3597 **open** Mon–Fri 10–5, weekends and public holidays 11–5
winemaker Craig Stansborough **production** 100 000 **est.** 1896
product range ($9.95–65 CD) Eden Valley Riesling, Barossa Valley Semillon (White Burgundy), Sauvignon Blanc Semillon, Barossa Chardonnay, Unwooded Chardonnay, Late Harvest, Oscar's Heritage, Grenache, Johannes Shiraz, Barossa Shiraz, Mistella, Old Tawny Port; Museum Release Watervale Riesling, Barossa Carbernet Sauvignon.
summary An old and proud label, particularly well known for its oak-matured Semillon (called White Burgundy on the Australian market), which underwent a number of changes of ownership during the 1990s. Overall, a reliable producer of solidly flavoured wines. Exports to the UK, the US, Canada, Hong Kong, the Netherlands, New Zealand, Singapore, Switzerland and Thailand.

Basedow Eden Valley Riesling

TTTT **1999** Light green-yellow; a quite potent mix of lime and herb aromas announces a very powerful wine, with well-above-average weight and grip. Has flavour to burn, even if it is a little short on finesse. Particularly good value. **rating:** 87

best drinking Now–2004 **best vintages** '99 **drink with** Rich fish dishes • $12

Basedow Barossa Shiraz

TTTY **1997** Medium red-purple; an old-fashioned, slightly leathery/earthy but far from unpleasant bouquet introduces a palate with sweeter fruit plus a touch of vanilla oak and soft tannins. **rating:** 83

best drinking Now–2004 **best vintages** NA **drink with** Steak and kidney pie • $16

basket range wines NR

c/o PO Basket Range, SA 5138 **region** Adelaide Hills
phone (08) 8390 1515 **fax** (08) 8390 0499 **open** Not
winemaker Phillip Broderick **production** 500 **est.** 1980
product range ($18 ML) A single Bordeaux-blend of Cabernet Sauvignon, Cabernet Franc, Merlot, Malbec drawn from 3 hectares of estate plantings.
summary A tiny operation known to very few, run by civil and Aboriginal rights lawyer Phillip Broderick, a most engaging man with a disarmingly laid-back manner.

bass fine wines NR

686 Richmond Road, Cambridge, Tas 7170 **region** Southern Tasmania
phone (03) 6231 6222 **fax** (03) 6231 6222 **open** Not
winemaker Various Contract **production** 890 **est.** 1999
product range ($17.50–23 R) Chardonnay, Pinot Noir, Cabernet Sauvignon, Strait Pinot Noir.
summary Bass Fine Wines runs entirely counter to the usual Tasmanian pattern of tiny, estate-based businesses. Guy Wagner has set up Bass as a classic negociant operation, working backwards from the marketplace. He is currently completing a wine-marketing degree at the University of Adelaide and intends to continue studies in oenology and viticulture while being involved in the making of the wines by contract makers Jim Chatto and Andrew Hood. The wines have been purchased from various vineyards in bottle and in barrel, but from the 2000 vintage also purchased as grapes. The winery has been set up as a Pinot Noir specialist with three levels of Pinot in the business plan, commencing with Strait Pinot in the fighting sector of the market, then Bass as a premium brand, and ultimately there will be a super-premium Pinot, possibly to come from 30-year-old plantings which have been contracted.

bass phillip ★★★★★

Tosch's Road, Leongatha South, Vic 3953 **region** Gippsland
phone (03) 5664 3341 **fax** (03) 5664 3209 **open** By appointment
winemaker Phillip Jones **production** 1500 **est.** 1979
product range ($27–145) Tiny quantities of Pinot Noir in three categories: standard, Premium and an occasional barrel of Reserve. A hatful of Chardonnay also made; plus Pinot Rosé and Gamay.
summary Phillip Jones has retired from the Melbourne rat-race to handcraft tiny quantities of superlative Pinot Noir which, at its best, has no equal in Australia. Painstaking site selection, ultra-close vine spacing and the very, very cool climate of South Gippsland are the keys to the magic of Bass Phillip and its eerily Burgundian Pinots.

batista ★★★★

Franklin Road, Middlesex, WA 6258 **region** Manjimup
phone (08) 9772 3530 **fax** (08) 9772 3530 **open** By appointment
winemaker Bob Peruch **production** 1200 **est.** 1993
product range ($19–28 CD) Pinot Noir, Shiraz, Shiraz Cabernet, Pinot Chardonnay Reserve Brut.
summary Batista is in fact the baptismal name of owner Bob Peruch, a Pinot Noir devotee whose father planted 1 hectare of vines back in the 1950s, although these have since gone. Between 1993 and 1996 Bob Peruch planted 1.5 hectare of pinot noir, 1.85 hectares of shiraz and the cabernet family, and 0.5 hectare of chardonnay destined for sparkling wine. The estate has two vineyards, one selected for pinot noir and chardonnay, and the other, 2 kilometres away, for shiraz, cabernet sauvignon, cabernet franc and merlot. The well-drained soils are of quartz and ironstone gravel; yields are restricted to around 7 tonnes per hectare.

Batista Shiraz

🍷🍷🍷🍷 **1999** Medium to full red-purple; the bouquet is extremely complex, with dark chocolate and spice aromas on one side and a salami-like character on the other, almost certainly oak-derived. The palate has firm, dark plum fruit supported by fine tannins and just a touch of oak. The ghost of possible bacterial activity lurks in the background.

rating: 86

best drinking Now–2004 **best vintages** NA **drink with** Game • $25

baxter stokes wines NR

65 Memorial Avenue, Baskerville, WA 6065 **region** Swan District
phone (08) 9296 4831 **fax** (08) 9296 4831 **open** 9.30–5 weekends and public holidays
winemaker Greg Stokes **production** 750 **est.** 1988
product range ($10–14 CD) Chardonnay, Verdelho, Shiraz Pinot Noir, Shiraz Cabernet Sauvignon.
summary A weekend and holiday operation for Greg and Lucy Stokes, with the production sold by mail order and through cellar door.

beckett's flat ★★★☆

Beckett Road, Metricup, WA 6280 **region** Margaret River
phone (08) 9755 7402 **fax** (08) 9755 7344 **open** 7 days 10–6
winemaker Belizar Ilic, Mark Lane (Consultant) **production** 4000 **est.** 1992
product range ($17–29 R) Sauvignon Blanc Semillon, Oak Matured Semillon Sauvignon Blanc, Verdelho, Chardonnay, Sparkling Shiraz, Shiraz, Reserve Merlot, Cabernet Sauvignon.
summary Bill and Noni Ilic opened Beckett's Flat in September 1997. Situated just off the Bussell Highway at Metricup, midway between Busselton and the Margaret River, it draws upon 8 hectares of estate vineyards, first planted in 1992. As from 1998 the wines have been made at the on-site winery. Accommodation is available. The wines are exported to the US.

Beckett's Flat Shiraz

🍷🍷🍷🍷 **1999** Youthful purple-red; clean, firm black cherry fruit with hints of earth and subtle oak on the bouquet is followed by a clean, firm palate with plenty of weight, but needing time to build texture and complexity.

rating: 84

best drinking 2002–2006 **best vintages** NA **drink with** Pizza • $23

Beckett's Flat Reserve Merlot

▼▼▼▼ **1999** Youthful purple-red; a clean bouquet with sweet red berry fruit and hints of vanilla is followed by a clean, smooth palate with supple tannins, subtle oak and gently sweet fruit. A pretty wine, but not particularly varietal. **rating:** 87

best drinking 2003–2008 **best vintages** NA **drink with** Roast veal • $29

Beckett's Flat Cabernet Sauvignon

▼▼▼▼ **1999** Youthful purple-red; a fresh, youthful and bright bouquet with light but clear cabernet varietal fruit leads into a medium-bodied palate with sweet berry fruit and soft tannins combining to provide pleasing mouthfeel. **rating:** 86

best drinking 2003–2007 **best vintages** '97 **drink with** Ox kidney • $23

belbourie 

Branxton Road, Rothbury, NSW 2330 **region** Lower Hunter Valley
phone (02) 4938 1556 **open** Weekends, holidays 10–sunset
winemaker Bob Davies **production** 2000 **est.** 1963
product range ($15–16 CD) Barramundi Chardonnay, Belah Semillon Chardonnay, Hermitage.
summary A winery with a rich, and at times highly controversial, history of wine and winemaking, but these days tending more to the conventional. It has always sought to encourage cellar-door and mailing list sales, focusing on monthly wine and food events, and has a loyal clientele.

belgenny vineyard ★★★☆

92 De Beyers Road, Pokolbin, NSW 2320 **region** Lower Hunter Valley
phone (02) 9247 5300 **fax** (02) 9247 7273 **open** Not
winemaker Monarch Winemaking Services (Contract) **production** 7000 **est.** 1990
product range ($15–23.50 R) Semillon, Unwooded Chardonnay, Chardonnay, Proprietor's Reserve Chardonnay, Merlot, Shiraz, Blanc de Blanc.
summary In 1999 partners Norman Seckold and Dudley Leitch realised a long-held ambition to establish a vineyard in the Hunter Valley with the acquisition of their 17-hectare site. Plantings have steadily increased and are presently chardonnay (5.7 hectares), shiraz (4.9 hectares), merlot (2 hectares) and semillon (1.2 hectares), and a carefully thought-out marketing strategy has been put in place.

Belgenny Vineyard Semillon

▼▼▼▼ **2000** Light green-yellow; a clean, smooth citrus/lemon/lemon zest bouquet is followed by a fine, delicate and crisp palate with lemon, mineral and grass flavours; has all the makings. **rating:** 85

best drinking 2003–2010 **best vintages** NA **drink with** Asparagus • $18

Belgenny Vineyard Chardonnay

▼▼▼▽ **2000** Light to medium green-yellow; a light-bodied, fruit-driven style, with melon and citrus fruit and very light oak impact, which is appropriate given the intensity of the fruit. Should develop nicely over the short term. **rating:** 84

▼▼▼▼ **1999** Medium yellow-green; the clean, moderately intense bouquet with gentle melon and nectarine fruit is replicated on the elegant, nectarine-accented palate. As with all the Belgenny wooded whites, the oak influence has been nicely restrained, and the wine has good length. Gold medal winner at the NSW Small Makers Competition, bronze medals elsewhere. **rating:** 88

best drinking Now–2003 **best vintages** NA **drink with** Grilled prawn salad • $22

Belgenny Vineyard Partner's Reserve Chardonnay

▼▼▼▼ **2000** Light green-yellow; a light, elegant bouquet is followed by a light but quite intense palate with lingering melon and citrus fruit flavours; the oak input, while evident, is restrained. **rating:** 86

best drinking 2002–2005 **best vintages** '99 **drink with** Milk-fed veal • $23

bellarine estate NR

2230 Portarlington Road, Bellarine, Vic 3222 **region** Geelong
phone (03) 5259 3310 **fax** (03) 5259 3393 **open** Weekends 10–5
winemaker Robin Brockett **production** 2500 **est.** 1995
product range ($20–25 R) Chardonnay, Shiraz.

summary A new arrival on the Bellarine Peninsula, but a substantial one, with 5 hectares of chardonnay, 4 hectares of pinot noir, 3 hectares of shiraz, 1.5 hectares of merlot and 0.5 hectare of sauvignon blanc. The wines are made by Robin Brockett at Scotchmans Hill.

bellingham vineyard ★★★

Pipers Brook, Tas 7254 **region** Northern Tasmania
phone (03) 6382 7149 **open** By appointment
winemaker Contract **production** 500 **est.** 1984
product range ($5.50–8 ML) Riesling, Chardonnay, Pinot Noir, Cabernet Sauvignon.
summary Dallas Targett, the long-term owner of Bellingham Vineyard, was in the course of selling both the vineyard and the vineyard name (though not the label design) as this book was going to press. No details available about the purchaser, but Dallas Targett has plans to start another vineyard close to Launceston.

belubula valley vineyards NR

Golden Gully, Mandurama, NSW 2798 **region** Orange
phone (02) 6367 5236 **fax** (02) 6362 4726 **open** Not
winemaker David Somervaille **production** 1000 **est.** 1986
product range Cabernet Sauvignon.
summary Belubula Valley is a foundation member of the Central Highlands Grapegrowers Association (now ORVA), centred on Orange. The vineyard is located on the Belubula River, near Carcoar, and the small amounts of wine made to date have not yet been commercially released. David Somervaille, incidentally, was the chairman of partners of the national law firm Blake Dawson Waldron.

beresford wines ★★★

49 Fraser Avenue, Happy Valley, SA 5159 **region** McLaren Vale
phone (08) 8322 3611 **fax** (08) 8322 3610 **open** Mon–Fri 9–5, weekends 11–5
winemaker Robert Dundon, Scott McIntosh **production** 250 000 **est.** 1985
product range ($8.50–21 CD) Beacon Hill Semillon Chardonnay, Shiraz Cabernet, Sparkling, Tawny Port; Highwood Sauvignon Blanc, Chardonnay, Shiraz; the Saints range of St Yvette Chardonnay, St Aline Cabernet Shiraz, St Monique Sparkling Brut; followed by the Belleville range of Chardonnay, Semillon Sauvignon Blanc, Shiraz and Cabernet Merlot.
summary The Beresford brand sits at the top of a range of labels primarily and successfully aimed at export markets in the UK, the US, Hong Kong and China. The accent is on price, and the wines do not aspire to great complexity. Quality, however, improved in the late 1990s. No tastings in 2000/2001.

berlingieri wines NR

28 Main Road, Charleston, SA 5244 **region** Adelaide Hills
phone (08) 8389 6118 **fax** (08) 8389 6929 **open** Tues–Sun 10–5
winemaker Vincenzo Berlingieri **production** 7000 **est.** 1992
product range ($9–20 ML) Chardonnay, Sparkling Shiraz, Pinot Noir Shiraz Cabernet, Cabernet Franc; under the Charleston label Semillon Riesling Chardonnay, Sparkling Chenin Blanc, Sparkling Shiraz, Shiraz Cabernet Merlot, Cabernet Shiraz, Liqueur Muscat, Tawny Liqueur Port.
summary Vincenzo Berlingieri, one of the great characters of the wine industry, arrived in Sydney with beard flowing and arms waving in the 1970s and successfully gained considerable publicity for his then McLaren Vale winery. Fortune did not follow marketing success for this research scientist who had arrived to work in plant genetics at Melbourne University's Botany Department in 1964, armed with a doctorate in agricultural science from Perugia University, Italy. However, after various moves, he is in business again with his children, Jason, John and Annika, for the time being sourcing most of the grapes from Langhorne Creek and McLaren Vale, but with Adelaide Hills wines in the planning pipeline. Most of the business is in unlabelled cleanskin form at yesterday's prices, sold only through a mailing list/direct order system.

Berlingieri Wines Lenswood Sanctuary Sparkling Shiraz

TTTT **NV** Vivid red-purple; the bouquet is rich, with obvious American oak in a somewhat leaden-footed mould. The bouquet may be big, but the palate is positively huge, with strong blackberry fruit and evident sweetness clearly pitched at the cellar-door trade; within its idiom, works quite well. **rating:** 83
best drinking Now–2004 **best vintages** NA **drink with** Your choice • $16

Berlingieri Cabernet Franc

▼▼▼▼ **1996** Medium red, the purple hue starting to disappear, as one might expect. The bouquet is clean and savoury, with a mix of spice and sweet tobacco leaf aromatics. The palate is well structured, with savoury/ tobacco-accented flavours, finishing with soft, fine tannins. Ready to roll right now. **rating:** 85

best drinking Now–2004 **best vintages** NA **drink with** Spaghetti bolognaise • $20

berri estates ★★

Sturt Highway, Glossop, SA 5344 **region** Riverland
phone (08) 8582 0300 **fax** (08) 8583 2224 **open** Mon–Sat 9–5, Sundays on long weekends 10–4
winemaker Paul Kasselbaum, Peter Hensel, Graham Buller **production** NFP **est.** 1916
product range Light Fruity Lexia, Fruity Gordo Moselle, Chablis, Claret, Rosé, White Lambrusco, all in cask form.
summary Strictly a producer of cask and bulk wine with no pretensions to grandeur and with a substantial part of the production exported in bulk. Part of the BRL Hardy Group.

berrys bridge ★★★★☆

Forsters Road, Carapooee, St Arnaud, Vic 3478 **region** Pyrenees
phone (03) 5496 3220 **fax** (03) 5496 3322 **open** By appointment
winemaker Jane Holt **production** 1500 **est.** 1990
product range ($28 CD) Shiraz, Cabernet Sauvignon.
summary While the date of establishment is 1990, Roger Milner purchased the property in 1975, intending to plant a vineyard having worked for three years at Reynell winery in South Australia. Four hectares of vines were planted (chiefly by his friends) but his then career in mineral exploration meant that the vines were neglected and ultimately ploughed in. In the mid-1980s he returned with Jane Holt, and together they began the construction of the stone house-cum-winery. Planting of the existing 7 hectares of vineyard commenced in 1990, around the time that Jane commenced her viticultural studies at Charles Sturt University (she completed the course in 1993, and has completed a subsequent wine science degree course in 2000). Until 1997 the grapes were sold to others, the first vintage (from 1997) being released in November 1998. The wines are distributed in Victoria through Winestock to a number of well-known retailers. Not surprisingly, the limited quantity sells out with great speed. Exports to the US.

Berrys Bridge Shiraz

▼▼▼▼ **1999** Inky red-purple; there is a massive concentration of fruit and oak on the bouquet and likewise on the palate; a huge, chunky wine, with the oak and tannins in the driving seat at the present moment. The 14.7° alcohol is no surprise. **rating:** 89

best drinking 2005–2015 **best vintages** '98 **drink with** Flame-grilled rump steak • $28

Berrys Bridge Cabernet Sauvignon

▼▼▼▼▽ **1999** Dense red-purple; masses of blackberry cassis fruit are married with powerful oak on the bouquet; a big, rich and concentrated palate, with better oak balance than the Shiraz, and showing some cedar/ cigar box characters that will build with age. **rating:** 92

best drinking 2005–2010 **best vintages** '98 **drink with** Garlic and herb-studded leg of lamb • $28

best's wines 

1 kilometre off Western Highway, Great Western, Vic 3377 **region** Grampians
phone (03) 5356 2250 **fax** (03) 5356 2430 **open** 7 days 10–5
winemaker Viv Thomson, Hamish Seabrook **production** 30 000 **est.** 1866
product range ($8–66 R) Great Western Chardonnay, Great Western Pinot Noir, Great Western Shiraz, Bin O Shiraz, Thomson Family Shiraz, Great Western Cabernet Sauvignon, together with a large range of fortified wines sourced from St Andrews at Lake Boga. Some of these wines are available only at cellar door.
summary An historic winery, owning some priceless vineyards planted as long ago as 1867 (other plantings are, of course, much more recent), which has consistently produced elegant, supple wines that deserve far greater recognition than they in fact receive. The Shiraz is a classic; the Thomson Family Shiraz magnificent. Exports to the UK, Canada, Holland, Belgium and Switzerland.

Best's Victoria Riesling

▼▼▼▽ **1999** Light green-yellow; the bouquet has light, citrus-tinged fruit and a whiff of sulphur dioxide. The palate is light-bodied with citrussy flavours and a fractionally hard finish that should soften over the next 12 months. **rating:** 80

best drinking Now **best vintages** NA **drink with** Summer salad • $10.50

Best's Concongella Vineyard Chardonnay

🍷🍷🍷🍷 **1998** Light green-yellow; a smooth, scented bouquet with just a whisper of oak is followed by a similarly smooth, nectarine and peach-flavoured palate, in easy drinking mode. **rating:** 84

best drinking Now–2003 **best vintages** NA **drink with** KFC • $28

Best's Pinot Noir

🍷🍷🍷🍷 **1999** Almost improbable purple-red; as the colour suggests, the bouquet is both powerful and youthful, with ripe cherry and plum fruit. The full-flavoured palate has the same fruit as the bouquet, together with substantial tannins. An unusual Pinot that needs at least five years. **rating:** 88

best drinking 2004–2009 **best vintages** NA **drink with** Game • $28

Best's Bin O Shiraz

🍷🍷🍷🍷🍷 **1998** Medium red-purple; the aromatic and intense bouquet has a mix of spice, leaf and red berry fruit; the palate is likewise in the cherry spectrum with sparkles of mint and spice. A typically elegant wine. **rating:** 90

best drinking 2002–2008 **best vintages** '78, '85, '88, '90, '91, '92, '94, '97, '98 **drink with** Roast veal, mature cheddar • $32

Best's Thomson Family Shiraz

🍷🍷🍷🍷🍷 **1998** Medium to full red-purple; a complex bouquet with sweet, dark cherry/plum fruit supported by excellent oak balance and integration; the palate is rich, intense and deep, yet elegant, and handles the alcohol with ease. 315 dozen made. **rating:** 97

best drinking 2005–2015 **best vintages** '95, '96, '97, '98 **drink with** Stir-fried beef • $60

Best's Victoria Shiraz

🍷🍷🍷🍷 **1998** Medium red-purple; the bouquet is moderately intense, clean and smooth, with cherry aromas and minimal oak. A pleasant, medium-bodied wine with sweet cherry fruit, uncomplicated by oak or tannins. All in all, well made and good value. **rating:** 83

best drinking Now–2003 **best vintages** NA **drink with** Pasta, light meat dishes • $12.50

Best's Cabernet Sauvignon

🍷🍷🍷🍷 **1998** Medium to full red-purple; there is positive, ripe varietal character to the bouquet which has scented, spicy berry and oak aromas intermingling; on the palate, lively berry flavours are underpinned by a touch of regional mint; silky texture. **rating:** 88

best drinking 2003–2008 **best vintages** '88, '91, '92, '93, '96 **drink with** Sirloin of beef • NA

Best's Victoria Cabernet Sauvignon

🍷🍷🍷🍷 **1998** Medium purple-red; the bouquet is light, fresh and simple, but the palate offers rather more, with nice blackcurrant/raspberry fruit and just a faint dusting of tannin. **rating:** 83

best drinking Now–2003 **best vintages** NA **drink with** Grilled meat • $12.50

bethany wines ★★★☆

Bethany Road, Bethany, via Tanunda, SA 5352 **region** Barossa Valley
phone (08) 8563 2086 **fax** (08) 8563 0046 **open** Mon–Sat 10–5, Sun 1–5
winemaker Geoff Schrapel, Robert Schrapel **production** 25 000 **est.** 1977
product range ($14–65 CD) Riesling (Reserve Dry, Special Select Late Harvest), Chardonnay, Wood Aged Semillon, The Manse (Semillon Riesling Chardonnay), Cabernet Merlot, Shiraz, Reserve Shiraz, Grenache, Shiraz Cabernet, Old Quarry Barossa Tawny Port, Old Quarry Barossa Fronti (White Port), Vintage Brut Chardonnay Blanc de Blanc.
summary The Schrapel family has been growing grapes in the Barossa Valley for over 140 years, but the winery has only been in operation since 1977. Nestling high on a hillside on the site of an old quarry, it is run by Geoff and Rob Schrapel, who produce a range of consistently well-made and attractively packaged wines. They have 36 hectares of vineyards in the Barossa Valley, 8 hectares in the Eden Valley and (recently and interestingly) 2 hectares of chardonnay and 2 hectares of cabernet sauvignon on Kangaroo Island. The wines have national distribution in Australia, and are exported to the UK, New Zealand, Europe, Taiwan and the US.

beyond broke vineyard NR

Cobcroft Road, Broke, NSW 2330 **region** Lower Hunter Valley
phone (02) 6026 2043 **fax** (02) 6026 2043 **open** Tastings available at Broke Village Store 10–4
winemaker Pete Howland (Contract) **production** 4000 **est.** 1996
product range ($14–22 R) Semillon, Verdelho, Chardonnay, Unwooded Chardonnay, Sparkling Semillon, Shiraz.
summary Beyond Broke Vineyard is the reincarnation of a former Lindemans vineyard purchased by Bob and Terry Kennedy in 1996. In a more than slightly ironical twist, the 1997 Beyond Broke Semillon won two trophies at the Hunter Valley Wine Show of that year, the first for the Best Current Vintage Semillon and the second the Henry John Lindeman Memorial Trophy for the Best Current Vintage Dry White Wine. Subsequent shows have been less spectacularly kind, but there is nothing surprising in that, and this winery's turn will come again when vintage conditions permit.

bianchet ★★★

Lot 3 Victoria Road, Lilydale, Vic 3140 **region** Yarra Valley
phone (03) 9739 1779 **fax** (03) 9739 1277 **open** Thurs–Mon 11–5
winemaker Keith Salter, Martin Williams (Consultant) **production** 2500 **est.** 1976
product range ($16–25 CD) Traminer, Semillon, Copestone Semillon Sauvignon Blanc, Chardonnay Cuvée, Verduzzo, Pinot Noir, Copestone Shiraz, Cabernets.
summary Recently sold by the founding Bianchet family to a small Melbourne-based syndicate, with Keith Salter and consultant Martin Williams taking on winemaking responsibilities. One of the most unusual wines from the winery is Verduzzo Gold, a late-harvest, sweet white wine made from the Italian grape variety. The wines are still basically sold through cellar door.

big hill vineyard NR

Cnr Calder Highway and Belvoir Park Road, Big Hill, Bendigo, Vic 3550 **region** Bendigo
phone (03) 5435 3366 **fax** (03) 5435 3311 **open** 7 days 10–5
winemaker John Ellis, Robert Fiumara (Contract) **production** 1000 **est.** 1998
product range ($11.60–25 CD) Granite White, Sauvignon Blanc, Chardonnay, Granite Botrytis, Granite Red, Shiraz, Big Hill Shiraz, Cabernet Sauvignon, Granite Port, Curly Port, Curly Muscat.
summary A partnership headed by Nick Cugura began the re-establishment of what is now called Big Hill Vineyard on a site that was first planted to grapes almost 150 years ago. That was in the height of the gold rush, when there was even a long-disappeared pub, the Granite Rock Hotel. The wheel has come full circle, for Big Hill Vineyard now has a café-restaurant overlooking the vineyard, with plans for bed and breakfast cottages. The restaurant specialises in wedding receptions, and provides limited conference facilities. The modern-day plantings began with 2 hectares of shiraz in 1998 (which provided the first wine in May 2000), followed by 1 hectare each of merlot and cabernet sauvignon.

bimbadgen estate ★★★★

Lot 21 McDonalds Road, Pokolbin, NSW 2321 **region** Lower Hunter Valley
phone (02) 4998 7585 **fax** (02) 4998 7732 **open** 7 days 9.30–5
winemaker Kees Van De Scheur, Simon Thistlewood **production** up to 100 000 **est.** 1968
product range ($12.50–35 R) Semillon, Chardonnay, Verdelho, Botrytis Semillon, Pinot Noir, Shiraz, Museum Release Shiraz, Cabernet Sauvignon, Port; Signature range is the super-premium range of Semillon, Chardonnay and Shiraz; Grand Ridge Estate is the lower-priced label with Semillon Chardonnay, Verdelho, Chardonnay, Sparkling Semillon, Shiraz and Shiraz Cabernet.
summary Established as McPherson Wines, then successively Tamalee, then Sobels, then Parker Wines and now Bimbadgen, this substantial winery has had what might politely be termed a turbulent history. It has the great advantage of having 45 hectares of estate plantings, mostly with now relatively old vines, supplemented by a separate estate vineyard at Yenda for the lower-priced Grand Ridge series. The restaurant is open seven days for lunch and from Wednesday to Saturday inclusive for dinner. Exports to Hong Kong, the UK and the US.

Bimbadgen Estate Semillon

YYYY **2000** Light to medium yellow-green; the bouquet is quite rich, with fruit spice aromatics. The palate has attractive lemon, grass and lemon leaf flavours, but is not flabby or phenolic. **rating:** 89
best drinking 2002–2007 **best vintages** '00 **drink with** Pasta • $17.50

Bimbadgen Estate Signature Semillon

▼▼▼▼ **1999** Light green-yellow; the bouquet is clean, moderately rich, with nicely focused lemon fruit; the palate, likewise, has positive lemon and mineral grip and flavour, promising to develop well over the next five years.
rating: 88

best drinking Now–2005 **best vintages** NA **drink with** Trout mousse • $22.50

Bimbadgen Estate Grand Ridge Verdelho

▼▼▼▽ **1999** Light green-yellow; both the bouquet and palate offer grip and concentration, though pinpointing any particular fruit characteristic beyond slightly lemony fruit salad is not easy. Whether you can expect more from Verdelho is more to the point. **rating:** 84

best drinking Now **best vintages** NA **drink with** Takeaway • $12.50

Bimbadgen Estate Chardonnay

▼▼▼▼ **1999** Full yellow-green; a typical Hunter regional bouquet, solid and smooth with ripe peach and melon fruit, is followed by a similarly rich and solid palate with peachy flavour in full-blown regional style. **rating:** 86

best drinking Now **best vintages** NA **drink with** Roast chicken • $17.50

Bimbadgen Estate Signature Shiraz

▼▼▼▼▽ **2000** Medium to full red-purple; youthful black cherry/berry fruit on the clean bouquet runs into a powerful, youthful, ripe structured palate that simply needs time. **rating:** 90

▼▼▼▼▽ **1999** Medium red-purple; the clean and smooth bouquet has abundant dark berry/cherry fruit; the palate is still in the primary phase of berry fruit, but is just starting to loosen up in terms of texture. **rating:** 90

best drinking 2005–2010 **best vintages** '98, '99, '00 **drink with** Game pie • $28

bindi wine growers ★★★★★

343 Melton Road, Gisborne, Vic 3437 **region** Macedon Ranges
phone (03) 5428 2564 **fax** (03) 5428 2564 **open** Not
winemaker Michael Dhillon, Stuart Anderson (Consultant) **production** 1000 **est.** 1988
product range ($33–50 ML) Chardonnay, Macedon Blanc de Blanc, Original Vineyard Pinot Noir, Block 5 Pinot Noir.
summary A relatively new arrival in the Macedon region, it has gone from strength to strength. The Chardonnay is top-shelf, the Pinot Noir as remarkable (albeit in a very different idiom) as Bass Phillip, Giaconda or any of the other tiny-production, icon wines. Notwithstanding the tiny production, the wines are exported (in small quantities, of course) to the UK, Italy, Singapore and the US.

birdwood estate 

Mannum Road, Birdwood, SA 5234 **region** Adelaide Hills
phone (08) 8263 0986 **fax** (08) 8263 0986 **open** Not
winemaker Oli Cucchiarelli **production** 700 **est.** 1990
product range ($14–23 ML) Chardonnay, Riesling, Merlot, Cabernet Sauvignon.
summary Birdwood Estate draws upon 5 hectares of estate vineyards progressively established since 1990. The quality of the white wines, and in particular the Chardonnay, has generally been good. The tiny production is principally sold through retail in Adelaide, with limited distribution in Sydney and Melbourne.

birnam wood wines 

Turanville Road, Scone, NSW 2337 **region** Upper Hunter Valley
phone (02) 6545 3286 **fax** (02) 6545 3431 **open** 7 days 11–4
winemaker Monarch Wines (Contract) **production** 25 000 **est.** 1994
product range ($9.95–16.50 R) Shakespeare Range: The Witches Brew Chardonnay, The Bards Tipple Semillon, The Kings Cup Shiraz. Family Range: Chardonnay, Verdelho. Reserve Chardonnay and Shiraz.
summary Former Sydney car dealer Mike Eagan and wife Min moved to Scone to establish a horse stud; the vineyard came later (in 1994) but is now a major part of the business, with over 30 hectares of vines. Most of the grapes are sold; a part only is vinified for Birnam Wood. Exports to Switzerland, Canada and China. Son Matthew has now joined the business after working for five years for Tyrrell's in its export department.

Birnam Wood Verdelho

ΨΨΨΨ 1999 Light to medium yellow-green; the bouquet is clean and quite rich, with tropical fruit salad aromatics. The palate has lots of flavour, ranging from ripe fruit salad to more grassy/citrussy nuances, augmented by good acidity. **rating:** 85

best drinking Now **best vintages** NA **drink with** Chicken pasta • $12.95

Birnam Wood Reserve Shiraz

ΨΨΨΨ 1999 Medium red-purple; an earthy/savoury/oaky bouquet precedes a palate with plenty of dark berry fruit, the oak and tannins not being over the top. **rating:** 85

best drinking 2003–2007 **best vintages** NA **drink with** Grilled calf's liver • $16.50

black george NR

Black Georges Road, Manjimup, WA 6258 **region** Pemberton
phone (08) 9772 3569 **fax** (08) 9772 3102 **open** 7 days 10.30–4.45
winemaker Dr Shelley E Wilson **production** 4000 **est.** 1991
product range ($17.50–32 CD) Unwooded Chardonnay, The Captains Reserve Chardonnay, Late Picked Verdelho, Classic White, Pinot Noir, Cabernet Franc Merlot.
summary A relatively recent arrival on the scene, with particular aspirations to make high-quality Pinot Noir. As with so much of the Pemberton region, it remains to be seen whether the combination of soil and climate will permit this; the quality of the Black George Merlot Cabernet Franc once again points in a different direction. Distributors have been appointed in New South Wales, Victoria and Queensland, with direct exports to the UK.

Black George Merlot Cabernet Franc

ΨΨΨΨΨ 1999 Medium red-purple; the bouquet is clean and smooth, with sweet berry fruit and a touch of spice; an elegant, balanced and harmonious palate ripples with gentle, red berry fruit supported by soft, ripe tannins and cedary oak. **rating:** 94

best drinking 2002–2010 **best vintages** '99 **drink with** Braised lamb • NA

blackjack vineyards ★★★☆

Cnr Blackjack Road and Calder Highway, Harcourt, Vic 3453 **region** Bendigo
phone (03) 5474 2355 **fax** (03) 5474 2355 **open** Weekends and public holidays 11–5, when stock available
winemaker Ian McKenzie, Ken Pollock **production** 2500 **est.** 1987
product range ($22 CD) Shiraz, Cabernet Merlot.
summary Established by the McKenzie and Pollock families on the site of an old apple and pear orchard in the Harcourt Valley. Best known for some very good Shirazes. Ian McKenzie, incidentally, is not to be confused with the Ian McKenzie of Seppelt Great Western. Exports to New Zealand.

blackwood crest wines 

RMB 404A, Boyup Brook, WA 6244 **region** Blackwood Valley
phone (08) 9767 3029 **fax** (08) 9767 3029 **open** 7 days 10–6
winemaker Max Fairbrass **production** 2000 **est.** 1976
product range ($13–21 CD) Rhine Riesling, Sauvignon Blanc, Semillon Sauvignon Blanc, Chardonnay, Shiraz, Cabernet Sauvignon, Ruby Port, Liqueur Muscat.
summary A small and remote winery that has produced one or two notable red wines full of flavour and character; worth watching, particularly now that it has added the striking Riesling to the mix.

Blackwood Crest Rhine Riesling

ΨΨΨΨ½ 1998 Medium yellow-green; the moderately intense bouquet has benefited from bottle-development in bolstering the lime and herb aromas. The palate has excellent intensity, with sweet lime juice flavours, and a long, lingering finish. By far the best wine in the portfolio. **rating:** 90

best drinking Now–2005 **best vintages** '98 **drink with** Salad • NA

blackwood wines NR

Kearney Street, Nannup, WA 6275 **region** Blackwood Valley
phone (08) 9756 0088 **fax** (08) 9756 0089 **open** Thur–Tues 10–4
winemaker Andrew Mountford (Contract) **production** 2500 **est.** 1998
product range ($17–24 CD) Blackwood White, Verdelho, Unwooded Chardonnay, Clay Pit Pinot Noir, Premium Red (Merlot Cabernet Shiraz), Blackwood Red (Merlot Malbec Cabernet Franc), Port.
summary Blackwood Wines draws upon 1 hectare each of chardonnay, merlot and chenin blanc, supplemented by contract-grown fruit which significantly broadens the product range. It also operates a Cellar Club with discounted prices for members, and a restaurant is open every day except Wednesdays.

Blackwood Wines Clay Pit Pinot Noir

1999 Light to medium purple-red; a clean, firm, straightforward cherry/strawberry bouquet and a light to medium-bodied palate with similar cherry and strawberry flavours, plus a light touch of oak. Simple now, but should develop over the next year or so. **rating:** 84

best drinking Now–2003 **best vintages** NA **drink with** Asian • NA

blanche barkly wines NR

Rheola Road, Kingower, Vic 3517 **region** Bendigo
phone (03) 5443 3664 **open** Weekends, public holidays 10–5
winemaker David Reimers **production** NFP **est.** 1972
product range ($10–16.50 CD) Shiraz, Cabernet Sauvignon.
summary Sporadic but small production and variable quality seem to be the order of the day; the potential has always been there. No recent tastings.

blaxlands wines NR

Broke Road, Pokolbin, NSW 2320 **region** Lower Hunter Valley
phone (02) 4998 7550 **fax** (02) 4998 7802 **open** 7 days 10.30–4.30
winemaker Trevor Drayton (Contract) **production** 1000 **est.** 1976
product range ($17–18 CD) Chardonnay, Chardonnay Semillon, Shiraz.
summary Chris Barnes is an industry veteran who ran Blaxlands Restaurant and Wine Centre in Pokolbin for almost 20 years before selling it to Len Evans in 1999. He is also the owner of 1.5 hectares each of chardonnay and semillon, the wines from which are included in the comprehensive range of Hunter Valley wines available from the Wine Centre (and the restaurant).

bleasdale vineyards ★★★★

Wellington Road, Langhorne Creek, SA 5255 **region** Langhorne Creek
phone (08) 8537 3001 **fax** (08) 8537 3224 **open** Mon–Sat 9–5, Sun 11–5
winemaker Michael Potts **production** 150 000 **est.** 1850
product range ($9–38 CD) Langhorne Crossing White and Dry Red; Verdelho, Chardonnay, Malbec, Generations Shiraz, Cabernet Shiraz, Mulberry Tree Cabernet Sauvignon, Bremerview Vineyard Shiraz, Frank Potts Cabernet Malbec Merlot Petit Verdot, Sparkling, Fortified.
summary One of the most historic wineries in Australia, drawing upon vineyards that are flooded every winter by diversion of the Bremer River, which provides moisture throughout the dry, cool, growing season. The wines offer excellent value for money, all showing the particular softness that is the hallmark of the Langhorne Creek region. Production has soared; export markets established in the UK, the US, Canada, New Zealand, Germany and Switzerland.

Bleasdale Vineyards Bremerview Vineyard Shiraz

1998 Strong, deep purple-red; rich, ripe, luscious black cherry fruit aromas introduce a big, strong, ripe blackberry-fruited palate; the oak is still integrating and the wine needs time. Will richly repay cellaring. **rating:** 87

best drinking 2003–2008 **best vintages** '98 **drink with** Char-grilled rump steak • $16.50

Bleasdale Vineyards Shiraz Cabernet

🍷🍷🍷🍷 **1997** Medium red, with just a touch of purple remaining. Bottle-developed, savoury fruit aromas are joined by a touch of charry American oak on the bouquet. The palate has a mix of plum, mint and more savoury flavours; the tannins are nicely balanced in a straightforward, easy-drinking red. **rating:** 83

best drinking Now–2004 **best vintages** NA **drink with** Braised rabbit • $13.50

Bleasdale Frank Potts

🍷🍷🍷🍷 **1997** Medium red-purple; the bouquet is quite sweet and ripe, with a spectrum of fruit aromas ranging from mint to slightly (and not unpleasantly) jammy; a big, luscious palate with dark berry flavours and soft, lingering tannins. A wine for now or later. **rating:** 89

best drinking Now–2007 **best vintages** '92, '94, '97 **drink with** Ragout of beef with olives • $24

Bleasdale Vineyards Mulberry Tree Cabernet Sauvignon

🍷🍷🍷🍷 **1999** Medium red-purple; the bouquet ranges through cedar, earth, plum and mint, moving more to ripe plum and mulberry on the palate, which is soft but ever-so-slightly spongy. Minimal oak input throughout. **rating:** 85

best drinking 2002–2006 **best vintages** '98 **drink with** Venison with juniper berry sauce • $16.50

Bleasdale Wood Matured Verdelho

🍷🍷🍷🍷 **NV** Light golden brown; the bouquet is clean and quite firm, with neutral spirit; the palate is quite gentle, with an appealing touch of honeysnap biscuit, and a cleansing, well-balanced finish. If drunk in summer, should be slightly chilled. **rating:** 88

best drinking Now–2005 **best vintages** NA **drink with** Aperitif • $13

bloodwood ★★★★

4 Griffin Road, Orange, NSW 2800 **region** Orange
phone (02) 6362 5631 **fax** (02) 6361 1173 **open** By appointment
winemaker Stephen Doyle, Jon Reynolds **production** 3000 **est.** 1983
product range ($11–25 ML) Riesling, Rosé of Malbec, Chardonnay, Schubert Chardonnay, Ice Riesling, Big Men in Tights (Rosé), Maurice (Bordeaux-blend), Cabernet, Merlot Noir, Chirac (Pinot Chardonnay).
summary Rhonda and Stephen Doyle are two of the pioneers of the burgeoning Orange district. The wines are sold mainly through cellar door and an energetically and informatively run mailing list; the principal retail outlet is Ian Cook's Fiveways Cellar, Paddington, Sydney. Bloodwood has done best with elegant but intense Chardonnay and the intermittent releases of super-late-harvest Ice Riesling.

Bloodwood Chardonnay

🍷🍷🍷🍷 **1999** Medium yellow-green; the bouquet is complex, with distinct toasty/nutty barrel-ferment characters woven around the melon fruit; the palate offers similar complex barrel-ferment/malolactic-ferment characters with a mix of cashew and melon. **rating:** 89

best drinking Now–2003 **best vintages** '99 **drink with** White-fleshed fish • $18

Bloodwood Noble Riesling

🍷🍷🍷🍷🍷 **2000** Light to medium yellow-green; the bouquet is clean and crisp, with a mix of citrus, lime and apricot aromas; the fruit tingle flavours on the palate are quite intense, although not overly complex, the wine being sustained by lively acidity. **rating:** 90

best drinking Now–2005 **best vintages** '94, '97, '99 **drink with** Any fruit-based dessert • $20

Bloodwood Big Men in Tights Rosé

🍷🍷🍷🍷 **2000** Light red, slightly deeper than rosé; spicy blackberry and plum aromas are followed by a plummy palate, with a touch of spice, and a markedly short finish that is, however, dry (or near-dry). **rating:** 82

best drinking Now **best vintages** NA **drink with** Cold meats; ham • $13

Bloodwood Maurice

🍷🍷🍷🍷 **1999** Medium red-purple; youthful, fresh leaf/mint/earth aromas lead into a palate with sweet minty berry fruit, minimal tannins and likewise oak. **rating:** 82

best drinking Now–2003 **best vintages** NA **drink with** Veal chops • $22.80

bluebush estate NR

Wilderness Road, Cessnock, NSW 2325 **region** Lower Hunter Valley
phone (02) 4930 7177 **fax** (02) 4930 7666 **open** Not
winemaker Contract **production** 200 **est.** 1991
product range ($15 R) Chardonnay.
summary Two hectares of vineyards (half chardonnay, half shiraz) have been established by David McGain; the Chardonnay is contract-made and sold by mail order.

blue pyrenees estate ★★★☆

Vinoca Road, Avoca, Vic 3467 **region** Pyrenees
phone (03) 5465 3202 **fax** (03) 5465 3529 **open** Mon–Fri 10–4.30, weekends and public holidays 10–5
winemaker Greg Dedman, Stuart Bourne **production** 125 000 **est.** 1963
product range ($7–60 CD) A three-tiered structure for the table wines sees Fiddlers Creek (sourced from southeast Australia) at the bottom; then Blue Pyrenees varietal range of Chardonnay, Shiraz and Cabernet Sauvignon in the middle; and at the top the Estate Reserve range of Chardonnay, Red (a Bordeaux-blend) and The Richardson Merlot. Alongside are the three sparkling wines of Reserve Brut, Midnight Brut and Midnight Cuvée.
summary Notwithstanding its distinguished French ownership, the perseverance of former winemaker Vincent Gere, a very well-equipped winery and lavish marketing expenditure, the former Chateau Remy has struggled. The 1996 renaming of the winery as Blue Pyrenees was a sign of that struggle, and also of a progressive shift in production towards still table wine (a sensible move). The third label, the multi-region-sourced Fiddlers Creek range, makes steady progress and offers real value for money at around $12; the varietal range (in fact sourced primarily from the estate) likewise at $14.95. Not surprisingly, the wines are exported throughout Asia (frequently through Remy subsidiaries), the UK and the US.

Blue Pyrenees Chardonnay

🍷🍷🍷🍷(½) **2000** Light green-yellow; the bouquet is clean, fairly neutral, of light to medium intensity, with some pleasant varietal melon fruit. Gentle melon and peach fruit is supported by almost subliminal oak on the palate; a no-frills, no pretensions style. **rating:** 84
best drinking Now–2003 **best vintages** NA **drink with** Veal scaloppine • $14.95

Blue Pyrenees Estate Reserve Chardonnay

🍷🍷🍷🍷 **1999** Medium to full yellow-green; the bouquet is solid, showing complex barrel ferment-derived characters, the palate similarly powerful and solid, perhaps a fraction heavy. **rating:** 87
best drinking Now–2003 **best vintages** NA **drink with** Veal fricassee • $26

Blue Pyrenees Shiraz

🍷🍷🍷(½) **1999** Medium red-purple; the bouquet has concentrated dark berry/earthy/leathery aromas which are quite attractive but muffled by slightly dusty oak. The palate has plenty of flavour, with more dark berry fruit flavours, but again an echo of that dusty, slightly coarse oak. Bronze medal winner Royal Melbourne Wine Show 2000. **rating:** 84
best drinking Now–2005 **best vintages** NA **drink with** Beef bordelaise • $14.95

Blue Pyrenees Victoria Shiraz

🍷🍷🍷🍷 **1999** Medium red-purple; there is plenty of depth to the earthy/savoury varietal shiraz fruit on the bouquet, and both here and on the palate there is good integration of the berry fruit, oak and tannins. **rating:** 85
best drinking 2003–2009 **best vintages** NA **drink with** Red-sauced pasta • $15

Blue Pyrenees Estate Reserve Red

🍷🍷🍷🍷(½) **1998** Medium to full red-purple; the bouquet is clean, with gently sweet berry plus some savoury overtones; the oak is surprisingly subtle. The palate has good balance, texture and weight, with attractive red berry fruit at its core, finishing with fine-grained tannins and the same high-quality oak evident on the bouquet. **rating:** 90
best drinking 2002–2008 **best vintages** '86, '89, '91, '94, '98 **drink with** Beef bordelaise • $29

Blue Pyrenees Estate The Richardson Merlot

🍷🍷🍷🍷 **1997** Medium red, with some purple remaining; the bouquet cascades through a range of savoury, spicy, earthy, minty, berry aromas. There is plenty of fruit on the palate, the best part being the warm tannins, part fruit- and part oak-derived. Whether this is the direction Merlot should be headed is another matter. **rating:** 88
best drinking 2002–2012 **best vintages** '97 **drink with** Game • $60

Blue Pyrenees Estate Cabernet Sauvignon

🍷🍷🍷🍷 **1999** Medium to full red-purple; the bouquet is clean and youthful, with pleasant berry varietal character. The medium-bodied palate has sweet minty berry fruit, soft tannins and subtle oak. **rating:** 84

best drinking Now–2005 **best vintages** NA **drink with** Hard cheese • $14.95

blue wren ★★★★

1 Cassilis Road, Mudgee, NSW 2850 **region** Mudgee
phone (02) 6372 6205 **fax** (02) 6372 6206 **open** Thurs–Mon 10.30–4.30
winemaker Simon Gilbert (Contract) **production** 3000 **est.** 1985
product range ($13–18 CD) Semillon, Chardonnay, Unwooded Chardonnay, Merlot, Cabernet Sauvignon Merlot, Chardonnay Port.

summary James and Diana Anderson have two vineyards. The first, Stoney Creek, situated 20 kilometres north of Mudgee, was planted in 1985 and acquired from the Britten family in early 1999. It has 2 hectares each of chardonnay and semillon, 1.5 hectares of cabernet and 0.5 hectare of merlot; the vines are dry-grown. The second vineyard has been planted to 2.4 hectares of shiraz and 1.4 hectares of verdelho, leaving more than 20 hectares as yet unplanted. The Bombira Vineyard, as it is known, is adjacent to the old Augustine vineyards owned by Mildara Blass. The early vintages have been most impressive, particularly the Merlot.

Blue Wren Semillon

🍷🍷🍷🍷 **2000** Light green-yellow; the clean, moderately intense bouquet has quite tight lemon/citrus aromas, the elegant palate with good intensity and length. **rating:** 87

best drinking Now–2007 **best vintages** NA **drink with** Calamari • $17

Blue Wren Merlot

🍷🍷🍷🍷🍷 **1999** Medium to full red-purple; a very seductive style with abundant sweet oak on both bouquet and palate. Fleshy and mouthfilling, with lots of flavour, although arguably showing relatively little varietal character. **rating:** 93

best drinking 2002–2007 **best vintages** '99 **drink with** Smoked lamb • $28

boireann NR

Donnellys Castle Road, The Summit, Qld 4377 **region** Granite Belt
phone (07) 4683 2194 **open** 7 days 10–4.30
winemaker Peter Stark **production** 350 **est.** 1998
product range ($14–22 CD) Shiraz Grenache Mourvedre, Merlot, Cabernet Merlot, Granite Belt Cabernet Sauvignon.

summary Peter and Therese Stark have a 10-hectare property set amongst the great granite boulders and trees that are so much part of the Granite Belt. Luxury accommodation is provided and supplements the winemaking activities. They have established a little over 1 hectare of vines planted to no less than seven varieties, including the four Bordeaux varieties that go to make a Bordeaux-blend; grenache and mourvedre provide a Rhône-blend, and there will also be a straight Merlot.

Boireann Grenache Shiraz Mourvedre

🍷🍷🍷🍷 **2000** Dense, deep purple, not unlike the colour of the Chambourcin; the bouquet is deep, dense and concentrated, a vinous black hole in space. A huge wine on the palate, still totally unresolved in every way; time in bottle may help but a much longer time in oak would have been even better. For all that, packed with interest and flavour. **rating:** 83

best drinking 2005–2010 **best vintages** NA **drink with** Barbecue • $22

boneo plains NR

RMB 1400, Browns Road, South Rosebud, Vic 3939 **region** Mornington Peninsula
phone (03) 5988 6208 **fax** (03) 5988 6208 **open** By appointment
winemaker R D Tallarida **production** 2500 **est.** 1988
product range ($10–22 CD) Chardonnay, Cabernet Sauvignon; Roch Unwooded Chardonnay, Roch Rosé.

summary A 9-hectare vineyard and winery established by the Tallarida family, well known as manufacturers and suppliers of winemaking equipment. The Chardonnay is the best of the wines so far released.

bonneyview NR

Sturt Highway, Barmera, SA 5345 **region** Riverland
phone (08) 8588 2279 **open** 7 days 9–5.30
winemaker Robert Minns **production** 5000 **est.** 1975
product range ($6–25 CD) Riesling, Chardonnay, Frontignan Blanc, Shiraz Petit Verdot, Cabernet Petit Verdot, Cabernet Blend, Fortifieds.
summary The smallest Riverland winery selling exclusively cellar door, with an ex-Kent cricketer and Oxford University graduate as its owner/winemaker. The Shiraz Petit Verdot (unique to Bonneyview) and Cabernet Petit Verdot add a particular dimension of interest to the wine portfolio.

booth's taminick cellars NR

Taminick, via Glenrowan, Vic 3675 **region** Glenrowan
phone (03) 5766 2282 **fax** (03) 5766 2151 **open** Mon–Sat 9–5, Sun 10–5
winemaker Peter Booth **production** 4000 **est.** 1904
product range ($6.50–12 CD) Trebbiano, Chardonnay, Late Harvest Trebbiano, Shiraz, Cabernet Merlot, Cabernet Sauvignon, Ports, Muscat.
summary Ultra-conservative producer of massively flavoured and concentrated red wines, usually with more than a few rough edges that time may or may not smooth over.

boston bay wines ★★★

Lincoln Highway, Port Lincoln, SA 5606 **region** The Peninsulas Zone
phone (08) 8684 3600 **fax** (08) 8684 3637 **open** Weekends, school/public holidays 11.30–4.30
winemaker David O'Leary (Contract) **production** 4000 **est.** 1984
product range ($11–17.50 CD) Riesling, Chardonnay, Shiraz, Merlot, Cabernet Sauvignon, Mistelle.
summary A strongly tourist-oriented operation which has extended the viticultural map in South Australia. It is situated at the same latitude as Adelaide, overlooking the Spencer Gulf at the southern tip of the Eyre Peninsula. Say proprietors Graham and Mary Ford: 'It is the only vineyard in the world to offer frequent sightings of whales at play in the waters at its foot.' No recent tastings.

botobolar ★★★☆

89 Botobolar Road, Mudgee, NSW 2850 **region** Mudgee
phone (02) 6373 3840 **fax** (02) 6373 3789 **open** Mon–Sat 10–5, Sun 10–3
winemaker Kevin Karstrom **production** 5000 **est.** 1971
product range ($7–24 CD) Sauvignon Blanc, Rain Goddess Dry White, Rain Goddess Sweet White, Marsanne, Chardonnay, Rain Goddess Red, Pinot Noir, Shiraz, Cabernet Sauvignon; The King, The Saviour (both Cabernet Shiraz blends); Low Preservative Chardonnay and Preservative Free Shiraz.
summary One of the first organic vineyards in Australia, with present owner Kevin Karstrom continuing the practices established by founder Gil Wahlquist. Preservative Free Dry White and Dry Red extend the organic practice of the vineyard to the winery. Shiraz is consistently the best wine to appear under the Botobolar label. Exports to the UK.

Botobolar The King

🍷🍷🍷🍷 **1999** Medium red-purple; the bouquet is clean, with ripe cassis berry fruit and subtle oak; as expected, the wine opens with the sweet fruit of the bouquet, but then mouth-ripping tannins take over. I wish I could say the tannins will soften before the fruit dies, but that would be gilding the lily, I'm afraid. **rating:** 84

best drinking 2003–2008 **best vintages** NA **drink with** Leave it in the cellar • $24

Botobolar The Saviour

🍷🍷🍷🍷 **1999** Medium red-purple; a moderately intense earthy/savoury bouquet leads into a light to medium bodied palate with predominantly savoury characters but some red fruits in the centre, and finishes with moderate tannins. **rating:** 83

best drinking 2002–2006 **best vintages** NA **drink with** Air-dried beef • $16

bowen estate 

Riddoch Highway, Coonawarra, SA 5263 **region** Coonawarra
phone (08) 8737 2229 **fax** (08) 8737 2173 **open** 7 days 10–5
winemaker Doug Bowen **production** 12 000 **est.** 1972
product range ($17.50–46 R) Chardonnay, Shiraz, The Blend, Cabernet Sauvignon, Ampelon.
summary One of the best-known names among the smaller Coonawarra wineries, with a great track record of red winemaking; Chardonnay and Sanderson Sparkling have joined the band, and the Riesling ended with the '93 vintage. Full-bodied reds at the top end of the ripeness spectrum are the winery trademarks, with a chewy richness uncommon in Coonawarra. Exports to Germany, Switzerland, Japan and New Zealand.

boynton's ★★★☆

Great Alpine Road, Porepunkah, Vic 3741 **region** Alpine Valleys
phone (03) 5756 2356 **fax** (03) 5756 2610 **open** 7 days 10–5
winemaker Kel Boynton, Eleana Anderson **production** 11 000 **est.** 1987
product range ($14–60 CD) Riesling, Sauvignon Blanc, Chardonnay, Boynton's Gold (Noble Riesling Chardonnay blend), Pinots (Pinot Meunier Pinot Noir), Shiraz, Merlot, Cabernet Sauvignon, Alluvium (Cabernet Sauvignon Merlot Petit Verdot), Vintage Brut.
summary The original 12.5-hectare vineyard, expanded to almost 16 hectares by 1996 plantings of pinot gris, durif and sauvignon blanc, is situated in the Ovens Valley north of the township of Bright, under the lee of Mount Buffalo. In the early years a substantial part of the crop was sold, but virtually all is now vinified at the winery. Overall, the red wines have always outshone the whites, initially with very strong American oak input, but in more recent years with better fruit/oak balance. Striking, indeed strident, new labelling has led to a minor name change by the dropping of the words 'of Bright'. The wines have distribution through the east coast of Australia; exports to Germany, Austria and the US.

Boynton's Alluvium

YYYY **1998** Medium red-purple; abundant oak makes its presence felt on the bouquet, although there is lots of dark berry fruit as well. The palate is complex, with a range of dark fruit flavours, and even more extract and tannin. While brawny, there is character to the wine that suggests it could develop into something special. **rating:** 89
best drinking 2003–2010 **best vintages** '98 **drink with** Beef in black bean sauce • $38

braewattie NR

Woodend Road, Rochford, Vic 3442 **region** Macedon Ranges
phone (03) 9818 5742 **fax** (03) 9818 8361 **open** By appointment
winemaker John Flynn, John Ellis **production** 250 **est.** 1993
product range ($18–25 R) Chardonnay, Pinot Noir.
summary A tiny operation, with the wines sold by mail order to friends and acquaintances.

brahams creek winery NR

Woods Point Road, East Warburton, Vic 3799 **region** Yarra Valley
phone (03) 9566 2802 **fax** (03) 9566 2802 **open** Weekends and public holidays 11–5
winemaker Geoff Richardson, Chris Young **production** 1200 **est.** 1990
product range ($11–13.50 CD) Sauvignon Blanc, Chardonnay, Pinot Noir, Merlot, Cabernet Sauvignon, Tawny Port.
summary Owner Geoff Richardson did not start marketing his wines until 1994; a string of older vintages are for sale at cellar door at an enticing price. Part of the grape production is sold to other Yarra Valley winemakers.

brand's of coonawarra 

Riddoch Highway, Coonawarra, SA 5263 **region** Coonawarra
phone (08) 8736 3260 **fax** (08) 8736 3208 **open** Mon–Fri 8–5, weekends 10–4
winemaker Jim Brand, Jim Brayne **production** NFP **est.** 1966
product range ($10.95–56 R) Riesling, Chardonnay, Sparkling Cabernet Sauvignon, Cabernet Merlot, Shiraz, Stentiford's Reserve Shiraz, Merlot, Cabernet Sauvignon, Patron's Reserve.

summary Part of a very substantial investment in Coonawarra by McWilliam's, which first acquired a 50 per cent interest from the founding Brand family then moved to 100 per cent, and followed this with the purchase of 100 hectares of additional vineyard land. Significantly increased production of the smooth wines for which Brand's is known will continue, has moved into top gear with the 1998 reds.

Brand's of Coonawarra Chardonnay

YYYY **1999** Medium yellow-green; a solid, almost beefy (muscular, not in flavour) bouquet with melon and fig leads into a similarly well-muscled palate, with plenty of fruit concentration and flavour. A fascinating contrast to the Barwang Chardonnay, which, like Brand's, is part of the McWilliam's winery portfolio. **rating:** 85

best drinking 2002–2005 **best vintages** '90, '92, '95, '96 **drink with** Pasta with salmon • $15.95

Brand's of Coonawarra Stentiford's Reserve Shiraz

YYYYY **1998** Deep, bright purple-red; the rich bouquet has abundant plum and spice balanced by quality oak; a high-class palate follows, with masses of controlled plum and spice flavours and excellent oak. The iron fist in a velvet glove. **rating:** 95

best drinking 2003–2013 **best vintages** '96, '97, '98 **drink with** Rack of lamb • $56

Brand's of Coonawarra Patron's Reserve

YYYYY **1998** Medium to full purple-red; a smooth bouquet with powerful cassis/berry fruit, which has soaked up the oak, is followed by a powerful palate with an abundance of fruit, extract and tannins, and still in the process of merging. I hold no fears for the future of this wine. **rating:** 93

best drinking 2004–2014 **best vintages** '98 **drink with** Osso bucco • $49.95

Brand's of Coonawarra Merlot

YYYY **1999** Medium to full red-purple; the bouquet is quite rich, with sweet cassis and redcurrant fruit; there is lots of depth to the structure, courtesy of oak and tannins. There is positive sweet fruit at the core of the wine, but is it varietal? **rating:** 85

best drinking 2004–2009 **best vintages** '97 **drink with** Veal chops • $27.95

brangayne of orange ★★★★☆

49 Pinnacle Road, Orange, NSW 2880 **region** Orange
phone (02) 6365 3229 **fax** (02) 6365 3170 **open** By appointment
winemaker Simon Gilbert (Contract) **production** 4200 **est.** 1994
product range ($15.50–26 CD) Sauvignon Blanc, Premium Chardonnay, Reserve Chardonnay, Orange Pinot Noir, Shiraz, The Tristan (Cabernet blend).

summary Orchardists Don and Pamela Hoskins decided to diversify into grape-growing in 1994 and have progressively established 25 hectares of high-quality vineyards. With viticultural consultancy advice from Dr Richard Smart and skilled contract-winemaking by Simon Gilbert, Brangayne has made an extraordinarily auspicious debut, emphatically underlining the potential of the Orange region. Exports to the UK.

Brangayne of Orange Sauvignon Blanc

YYYYY **2000** Light straw-green; an aromatic bouquet with tropical gooseberry and passionfruit aromas is followed by a crisp, clean and fresh palate; while the fruit is less pronounced than the bouquet suggests, this may not be a bad thing, for, overall, the wine has plenty of impact. **rating:** 90

best drinking Now **best vintages** NA **drink with** Caesar salad • $15.50

Brangayne Orange Pinot Noir

YYYY **1999** Medium red-purple; the bouquet has some lifted, slightly raisiny characters, the palate idiosyncratic but powerful, with dark plum fruit, and ample length and structure. Picked at 13° baumé on April 19, attesting to the cool growing conditions. **rating:** 85

best drinking 2002–2006 **best vintages** '98 **drink with** Jugged hare • $22

Brangayne of Orange The Tristan

YYYY **1999** Medium red-purple; the bouquet has solid, dark berry/briary fruit with gentle oak; the well-balanced palate has dark berry/currant/plum flavours with appropriate tannins. **rating:** 87

best drinking 2004–2010 **best vintages** '97, '98 **drink with** Grain-fed beef • $26

branson wines NR

Seppeltsfield Road, Greenock, SA 5360 **region** Barossa Valley
phone (08) 8562 8085 **fax** (08) 8562 8085 **open** Wed–Mon 10.30–5
winemaker Vicky Louise Bartier **production** 1000 **est.** 1997
product range ($10–35 CD) Semillon, Chardonnay, Spätlese, JB Brut Champagne, Highway Shiraz, Coach House Shiraz, Cabernet Sauvignon Merlot, Fine Old Tawny Port.
summary If you drive up the main highway from Adelaide to the Barossa Valley, the first large road sign you come across at the entrance to the Valley is one pointing the way to Seppeltsfield. Almost immediately after you leave the highway, and with Seppeltsfield only a couple of kilometres away, you will pass Branson Wines on the right-hand side. The property was acquired by James Branson in 1848; vines were first planted there in 1924, although somewhere along the way the vineyards were removed. Malcolm Aspden and his family bought the property in 1987 and three years later began a planting programme centred on shiraz; they now have 5 hectares of shiraz, and 1 hectare each of semillon, cabernet sauvignon and chardonnay. The cellar door was opened in 1997, and all wine produced is sold through the cellar door with the exception of small exports to New York.

bream creek

Marion Bay Road, Bream Creek, Tas 7175 **region** Southern Tasmania
phone (03) 6231 4646 **fax** (03) 6231 4646 **open** At Potters Croft, Dunally, tele**phone** (03) 6253 5469
winemaker Steve Lubiana (Contract) **production** 3000 **est.** 1975
product range ($17–22 CD) Riesling, Gewürztraminer, Schonburger, Chardonnay, Pinot Noir, Cabernet Sauvignon.
summary Until 1990 the Bream Creek fruit was sold to Moorilla Estate, but since that time the winery has been independently owned and managed under the control of Fred Peacock, legendary for the care he bestows on the vines under his direction. Peacock's skills have seen both an increase in production and also a vast lift in wine quality across the range, headed by the Pinot Noir. The 1996 acquisition of a second vineyard in the Tamar Valley has significantly strengthened the business base of the venture.

Bream Creek Riesling

YYYY **2000** Light to medium yellow-green; the bouquet is solid, with ripe lime aromas; the rich, distinctly sweet, fleshy palate borders on the edge of Spätlese, but reflecting the early-developing 2000 vintage. **rating:** 88
best drinking Now–2005 **best vintages** NA **drink with** Spring rolls • $17

Bream Creek Schonburger

YYYY **2000** Light green-yellow; scented pastille aromas are typically varietal. The clean and gentle palate, likewise, is totally true to variety with grapey pastille flavours balanced by brisk acidity. **rating:** 82
best drinking Now **best vintages** NA **drink with** Asian food • $17

Bream Creek Chardonnay

YYYY **1999** Medium to full yellow-green; strong, slightly pencilly/ropey oak on the bouquet doesn't appeal, but the palate has plenty of fruit flavour in a ripe melon and fig spectrum, more than compensating for the bouquet. **rating:** 83
best drinking Now–2004 **best vintages** NA **drink with** Crumbed brains • $18

Bream Creek Cabernet Sauvignon

YYYY **1999** Medium to full red-purple; the bouquet is rich, but also has cool-climate gamey canopy aromas; the palate, likewise, is an up-and-down ride, with sweet and sour aspects reflected in cassis and boot polish, but quite ripe tannins. It may all sound off-putting, but I like the wine more than most. **rating:** 85
best drinking 2004–2008 **best vintages** NA **drink with** Venison • $17

bremerton wines

Strathalbyn Road, Langhorne Creek, SA 5255 **region** Langhorne Creek
phone (08) 8537 3093 **fax** (08) 8537 3109 **open** 7 days 10–5
winemaker Rebecca Willson **production** 20 000 **est.** 1988
product range ($13.50–28 CD) Sauvignon Blanc, Verdelho, Young Vine Shiraz, Old Adam Shiraz, Bremerton Blend (red), Cabernet Sauvignon, Tamblyn (Cabernet Shiraz Merlot).

summary The Willsons have been grape-growers in the Langhorne Creek region for some considerable time but their dual business as grape-growers and winemakers has expanded significantly over the past few years. Their vineyards have more than doubled to over 100 hectares (predominantly cabernet sauvignon, shiraz and merlot), as has their production under the Bremerton label, no doubt in recognition of the quality of the wines. Wholesale distribution in all States of Australia; exports to the UK, the US, Canada, Hong Kong and Switzerland.

Bremerton Old Adam Shiraz

YYYYY **1998** Medium to full red-purple; a firm bouquet with predominantly earthy/savoury aromas and subdued sweetness is followed by a powerful palate, with those concentrated red berry/plum fruit characters one expects from 1998, the savoury characters merely acting to slightly restrain and give complexity. **rating:** 90

best drinking 2003–2008 **best vintages** '97, '98 **drink with** Parmesan cheese • $28

Bremerton Cabernet Sauvignon

YYYY **1998** Medium red-purple; the bouquet has abundant ripe cassis/berry/mulberry fruit and gentle oak, characters that flow through to the opening and mid-palate where first savoury characters and then slightly edgy tannins come in; nice, but doesn't quite follow through on the promise of the bouquet. **rating:** 85

best drinking 2002–2007 **best vintages** '91, '96, '97 **drink with** Braised beef in red wine • $26

brewery hill winery NR

Olivers Road, McLaren Vale, SA 5171 **region** McLaren Vale
phone (08) 8323 7344 **fax** (08) 8323 7355 **open** Mon–Fri 9–5, weekends 10–5
winemaker Warren Randall (Consultant) **production** 12 000 **est.** 1869
product range ($4–22.50 CD) Riesling, Semillon, Classic Spätlese, Chardonnay, Botrytis Riesling, Classic Dry Red, Merlot, Shiraz, Cabernet Sauvignon, Sparkling and Fortifieds.
summary A change of name and address for the former St Francis Winery, which has moved into the former Manning Park Winery and is now known as Brewery Hill Winery. Exports to Malaysia, Singapore and Fiji.

briagolong estate ★★☆

Valencia–Briagolong Road, Briagolong, Vic 3860 **region** Gippsland
phone (03) 5147 2322 **fax** (03) 5147 2400 **open** By appointment
winemaker Gordon McIntosh **production** 300 **est.** 1979
product range ($35 ML) Chardonnay, Pinot Noir.
summary This is very much a weekend hobby for medical practitioner Gordon McIntosh, who tries hard to invest his wines with Burgundian complexity, although with mixed success. He must have established an all-time record with the 15.4° alcohol in the '92 Pinot Noir.

brian barry wines ★★★☆

PO Box 128, Stepney, SA 5069 **region** Clare Valley
phone (08) 8363 6211 **fax** (08) 8362 0498 **open** Not
winemaker Brian Barry, Judson Barry **production** 10 000 **est.** 1977
product range ($19–35 R) Jud's Hill Handpicked Riesling, Chardonnay, Handpicked Merlot, Handpicked Cabernet Sauvignon; McLaren Vale Shiraz; Gleeson's Ridge Shiraz Merlot.
summary Brian Barry is an industry veteran with a wealth of winemaking and show-judging experience. His is nonetheless in reality a vineyard-only operation, with a substantial part of the output sold as grapes to other wineries and the wines made under contract at various wineries, albeit under Brian Barry's supervision. As one would expect, the quality is reliably good. Retail distribution through all States, and exports to the US, Canada, Taiwan, Switzerland and New Zealand.

Brian Barry Jud's Hill Handpicked Riesling

YYYY **2000** Medium to full yellow-green; a quite rich and complex bouquet with a very slight bready/yeasty overtone. The wine has plenty of power and length, with solidly ripe fruit and a faintly salty finish. **rating:** 87

best drinking Now–2004 **best vintages** '91, '92, '94, '95, '00 **drink with** Caesar salad • $18

Brian Barry Special Release Shiraz

YYYY **1999** Full red-purple; the bouquet shows very ripe sweet plum fruit intermingling with sweet oak; the powerful palate has spice, black pepper and plummy fruit balanced with plenty of oak and lingering tannins. **rating:** 89

best drinking 2004–2009 **best vintages** NA **drink with** Rare rump steak • $28

Brian Barry Jud's Hill Handpicked Merlot

🍷🍷🍷🍷 **1999** Medium to full red-purple; a very savoury/woodsy/sappy varietal bouquet with a vanilla oak background is a promising start; however, the oak comes thundering over the top of the palate, which is a pity. **rating:** 84

best drinking Now–2004 **best vintages** NA **drink with** Game stew • $35

Brian Barry Jud's Hill Handpicked Cabernet Sauvignon

🍷🍷🍷🍷 **1997** Bright, light to medium red, still with purple tinges; the bouquet is clean, and surprisingly fresh and light. A light to medium bodied palate, with redcurrant fruit at the core augmented by a touch of vanilla oak and finishing with faintly dusty tannins. **rating:** 84

best drinking Now–2004 **best vintages** '90, '92 **drink with** Rack of lamb • $25

briar ridge ★★★★☆

Mount View Road, Mount View, NSW 2325 **region** Lower Hunter Valley
phone (02) 4990 3670 **fax** (02) 4990 7802 **open** Mon–Sat 10–5, Sun 10–5
winemaker Neil McGuigan, Karl Stockhausen, Adrian Lockhart **production** 35 000 **est.** 1972
product range ($16.50–25.50 CD) Varietal Range of Methode Champenoise, Early Harvest Semillon, Hand Picked Chardonnay, Verdelho, Late Harvest Gewurztraminer, Botrytis Semillon, Old Vines Shiraz, Cabernet Sauvignon, Tawny Port; Signature Stockhausen Semillon, Hermitage and Cabernet Merlot; also Signature McGuigan Chardonnay and Signature Reserve Cabernet Merlot.
summary Semillon and Hermitage, each in various guises, have been the most consistent performers, underlying the suitability of these varieties to the Hunter Valley. The Semillon, in particular, invariably shows intense fruit and cellars well. Briar Ridge has been a model of stability with the winemaking duo of Neil McGuigan and Karl Stockhausen, and also has the comfort of over 48 hectares of estate vineyards, from which it is able to select the best grapes. Exports to the US and Switzerland.

Briar Ridge Early Harvest Semillon

🍷🍷🍷🍷🍷 **2000** Light green-yellow; crisp herb, mineral and lemon aromas are followed by an intense mix of lemon and mineral on the tightly constructed palate. The wine has a long finish, with good acidity and a touch of carbon dioxide, which will aid longevity. **rating:** 90

best drinking 2004–2010 **best vintages** NA **drink with** Crab or shellfish • $18.25

Briar Ridge Hand Picked Chardonnay

🍷🍷🍷🍷 **2000** Light green-yellow; the bouquet is light, with crisp citrus/melon fruit and barely detectable barrel-fermentation influences. The crisp, citrussy/melon palate is lively, halfway between Sauvignon Blanc and Chardonnay in terms of its flavour and feel. **rating:** 84

best drinking Now–2004 **best vintages** '87, '89, '91, '92, '97 **drink with** Light seafood • $18.25

Briar Ridge Neil McGuigan Chardonnay

🍷🍷🍷🍷 **1999** Glowing green-yellow; strong barrel-ferment oak aromas lead the bouquet, but there is attractive fruit there, too, which comes through quite strongly on the grapefruit and melon-flavoured palate. The finish is long, the barrel-ferment inputs not excessive. **rating:** 88

best drinking Now–2004 **best vintages** NA **drink with** Deep-fried stuffed zucchini flowers • $23.75

Briar Ridge Signature Reserve Cabernet Merlot

🍷🍷🍷🍷🍷 **1999** Medium purple-red; clean, sweet and ripe cassis/berry fruit on the bouquet is supported by subtle oak, the lively and tangy palate giving all of the indicators of cool-climate fruit; fine-grained tannins, subtle oak. **rating:** 92

best drinking 2003–2008 **best vintages** '99 **drink with** Roast loin of veal • $25.25

Briar Ridge Cabernet Sauvignon

🍷🍷🍷🍷🍷 **1999** Medium red, with a touch of purple on the rim; the bouquet is clean, with gently savoury overtones to the berry fruit, and a nice touch of oak. The medium-bodied palate is likewise very attractive, with sweet berry fruit and fine tannins. Not at all what you expect from the Hunter Valley. **rating:** 90

best drinking 2004–2009 **best vintages** NA **drink with** Braised lamb shanks • $19.25

bridgeman downs NR

Barambah Road, Moffatdale via Murgon, Qld 4605 **region** South Burnett
phone (07) 4168 4784 **fax** (07) 4168 4767 **open** By appointment
winemaker Bruce Humphery-Smith **production** NA **est.** NA
product range ($12–18.50 CD) Cellar White and Red; Chardonnay, Verdelho, Shiraz, Merlot Cabernet.
summary A substantial, albeit new, vineyard with 4 hectares of vines, the major plantings being of verdelho, chardonnay and shiraz, and lesser amounts of merlot and cabernet sauvignon. The perpetual-motion Bruce Humphery-Smith has been retained as consultant winemaker, which should ensure wine quality. The first wines were released from the 1998 vintage but were not tasted.

bridgewater mill ★★★★

Mount Barker Road, Bridgewater, SA 5155 **region** Adelaide Hills
phone (08) 8339 3422 **fax** (08) 8339 5311 **open** Mon–Fri 9.30–5, weekends 10–5
winemaker Brian Croser **production** 50 000 **est.** 1986
product range ($10–19 CD) 3 Districts Sauvignon Blanc, Chardonnay, Sparkling Riesling Brut, Sharefarmers Botrytis Semillon, Millstone Shiraz, Sharefarmers Red Blend (Malbec, Cabernet Sauvignon, Merlot, Cabernet Franc).
summary The second label of Petaluma, which consistently provides wines most makers would love to have as their top label. The fruit sources are diverse, with the majority of the sauvignon blanc and chardonnay coming from Petaluma-owned or managed vineyards, while the Shiraz is made from purchased grapes.

Bridgewater Mill 3 Districts Sauvignon Blanc

🍷🍷🍷🍷🍷(half) **2000** Light to medium yellow-green; a potent bouquet, redolent of gooseberry and passionfruit, is followed by a slightly less-confronting palate; the same flavours are present, but are lighter, and there is a cross-cut of acidity to freshen the finish. Without doubt, the best Bridgewater Mill Sauvignon Blanc to date. **rating:** 90
best drinking Now **best vintages** '92, '94, '95, '00 **drink with** Mousseline of scallops • $15.50

brinalon NR

18 Paringa Road, Red Hill South, Vic 3937 **region** Mornington Peninsula
phone (03) 5989 2105 **fax** (03) 5989 3159 **open** Weekends and public holidays 11–5, or by appointment
winemaker David Coy **production** 1500 **est.** 1995
product range ($17–24 CD) Sauvignon Blanc, Chardonnay, Pinot Noir, Shiraz.
summary In 1992 Jeff and Robin Seager selected a property at Red Hill South with the specific intention of establishing a vineyard. It nestles on the side of a valley, with the vines planted on a north-facing slope running down to a small creek that provides a natural dam site. A little under 4 hectares of vines were planted in 1995 (1.7 hectares of pinot noir, 1 hectare of chardonnay, 0.7 hectare of shiraz and 0.4 hectare of sauvignon blanc) and the Brinalon wines are made entirely from estate-grown grapes. Currently all wines are sold by mail order and through the cellar door, with the possibility of limited retail distribution down the track.

brindabella hills ★★★★

Woodgrove Close, via Hall, ACT 2618 **region** Canberra District
phone (02) 6230 2583 **fax** (02) 6230 2023 **open** Weekends, public holidays 10–5
winemaker Dr Roger Harris **production** 2500 **est.** 1989
product range ($16.50–25 CD) Riesling, Sauvignon Blanc Semillon, Chardonnay, Reserve Chardonnay, Shiraz, Tumbarumba Merlot, Cabernet, Reserve Cabernet.
summary Distinguished research scientist Dr Roger Harris presides over Brindabella Hills, which increasingly relies on estate-produced grapes; there are small plantings of cabernet sauvignon, cabernet franc, merlot, shiraz, chardonnay, sauvignon blanc, semillon and riesling. Wine quality has been consistently impressive. All of the wine is sold direct ex winery.

Brindabella Hills Sauvignon Blanc Semillon

🍷🍷🍷🍷 **2000** Light green-yellow; the moderately intense bouquet offers a pleasant interplay between gooseberry and melon on the one hand and more minerally/herbaceous characters on the other; the light to medium bodied palate shows all the signs of assured winemaking, following down the track of the bouquet. **rating:** 87
best drinking Now **best vintages** '00 **drink with** Gravlax • $18

Brindabella Hills Reserve Chardonnay

🍷🍷🍷🍷🍷 **1999** Medium yellow-green; complex barrel-ferment and lees aromas, coupled with some 'dirty French' solids characters provide a multi-layered bouquet. The palate is complex, with abundant structure, but does shorten off slightly on the finish. **rating:** 90

best drinking Now–2004 **best vintages** '96, '97, '99 **drink with** Pan-fried chicken breast • $25

Brindabella Hills Tumbarumba Merlot

🍷🍷🍷🍷 **2000** Light to medium red-purple; bright, lively, spicy aromatics lead into a light, bright and fresh palate, ideal for early drinking. **rating:** 83

best drinking Now **best vintages** NA **drink with** Asian • $18

Brindabella Hills Reserve Cabernet

🍷🍷🍷🍷 **1998** Medium red-purple; fresh blackberry and blackcurrant fruit, together with spicy notes, on the bouquet, is followed by smooth, sweet cassis berry fruit with attractive touches of cinnamon, spice and cedar. **rating:** 89

best drinking 2002–2007 **best vintages** '98 **drink with** Lamb shashlik • $25

Brindabella Hills Cabernet

🍷🍷🍷🍷 **1999** Medium red-purple; there are spicy, savoury overtones to the dark berry fruit aromas, the palate with a mix of spice, leaf and fragrant berry flavours; slightly green tannins on the finish are the only problem. **rating:** 84

best drinking 2002–2006 **best vintages** '90, '91, '93, '95, '96, '97 **drink with** Roast lamb • NA

britannia creek wines NR

75 Britannia Creek Road, Wesburn, Vic 3799 **region** Yarra Valley
phone (03) 5780 1426 **fax** (03) 5780 1426 **open** Weekends 10–6
winemaker Charlie Brydon **production** 1200 **est.** 1982
product range ($12–18 CD) Sauvignon Blanc, Semillon, Cabernets.
summary The wines from Britannia Creek Wines are made under the Britannia Falls label from 4 hectares of estate-grown grapes. A range of vintages are available from cellar door, with some interesting, full-flavoured Semillon.

broadview estate NR

Rowbottoms Road, Granton, Tas 7030 **region** Southern Tasmania
phone (03) 6263 6882 **fax** (03) 6263 6840 **open** Tues–Sun 10–5
winemaker Andrew Hood (Contract) **production** 250 **est.** 1996
product range ($16–18 CD) Stoney Ridge Riesling, Erin Vale Chardonnay.
summary David and Kaye O'Neil planted 0.5 hectare of chardonnay and 0.25 hectare each of riesling and pinot noir in the spring of 1996, producing limited quantities of Riesling and Chardonnay.

Broadview Estate Stoney Ridge Riesling

🍷🍷🍷🍷 **2000** Medium to full yellow-green; the bouquet is rich and ripe, with some toasty/herby characters evident; the palate veers more towards the herbaceous end of the spectrum, splitting the judges at the 2001 Tasmanian Wines Show. I was somewhere in the middle. **rating:** 85

best drinking Now–2005 **best vintages** NA **drink with** Smoked eel • $16

broke estate/ryan family wines ★★★

Wollombi Road, Broke, NSW 2330 **region** Lower Hunter Valley
phone (02) 9664 3000 **fax** (02) 9665 3303 **open** Weekends and public holidays 10–5, or by appointment
winemaker Matthew Ryan **production** 16 000 **est.** 1988
product range ($13–38 ML) Broke Estate is the premium label with Semillon, Chardonnay, Cabernets, Lacrima Angelorum (sweet white) and Sparkling Cabernets; the second label is Ryan Free Run Chardonnay and Single Vineyard Cabernets.
summary With high-profile consultant viticulturist Dr Richard Smart achieving some spectacular early results, Broke Estate has seldom been far from the headlines. Contrary to what one might expect, the opulent red wines (rather than the whites) have been the most successful.

brokenwood ★★★★☆

McDonalds Road, Pokolbin, NSW 2321 **region** Lower Hunter Valley
phone (02) 4998 7559 **fax** (02) 4998 7893 **open** 7 days 10–5
winemaker Iain Riggs **production** 70 000 **est.** 1970
product range ($10–80 R) Semillon, Cricket Pitch Sauvignon Blanc Semillon, ILR Semillon, Cricket Pitch Unwooded Chardonnay, Graveyard Chardonnay, Harlequin White, Jelka Riesling (dessert), Cricket Pitch Red, Harlequin Red, Cricket Pitch Cabernet Merlot, Shiraz, Pinot Noir, Cabernet Sauvignon, Rayner Vineyard Shiraz, Graveyard Shiraz, Mistress Block Shiraz.
summary Deservedly fashionable winery producing consistently excellent wines. Cricket Pitch Sauvignon Blanc Semillon has an especially strong following, as has Cabernet Sauvignon; the Graveyard Shiraz is one of the best Hunter reds available today, the unwooded Semillon a modern classic. In 1997 acquired a controlling interest in Seville Estate (Yarra Valley) and has also been involved in the establishment of substantial vineyards in Cowra. National distribution in Australia; exports to the US, the UK, Canada, Switzerland and Asia.

Brokenwood Semillon

▼▼▼▼▽ **2000** From a truly great (read dry) vintage, and tailor-made to give great enjoyment when young. Has developed nicely, if briskly, since July, starting to build an overlay of honey and toast on the herb/grass/lemon flavours of youth; plenty of mouthfeel and substance, balanced by lemony acidity on the finish. **rating:** 93

best drinking 2000–2005 **best vintages** '85, '86, '89, '92, '94, '95, '96, '97, '98, '99, '00 **drink with** Balmain bugs • $16

Brokenwood Cricket Pitch Sauvignon Blanc Semillon

▼▼▼▼ **2000** Light to medium straw-green; the bouquet is quite complex, with some minerally characters and the faintest hint of oak. There is plenty of flavour on the palate, with moderate length and grip and, again, subliminal oak. An easy-drinking style. **rating:** 85

best drinking Now **best vintages** NA **drink with** All seafood and white meat dishes • $14.95

Brokenwood Harlequin White

▼▼▼▽ **1999** Medium yellow-green; the bouquet is clean and soft, with some fruit-salad characters, the palate with more of the same. An adequate commercial wine without any pretence to complexity or character. **rating:** 81

best drinking Now **best vintages** NA **drink with** Takeaway • $16.50

Brokenwood Chardonnay

▼▼▼▼ **1999** Light green-yellow; a restrained melon and cashew bouquet is followed by a palate that is not particularly rich, but that is well balanced with melon and cashew flavours. The subliminal oak has as much to do with texture as flavour; a particular feature of the wine is the relatively leisurely pace of its development. **rating:** 87

best drinking Now–2004 **best vintages** NA **drink with** Quiche Lorraine • $19

Brokenwood Shiraz

▼▼▼▼ **1998** Medium red-purple; the bouquet is soft, moderately intense, with a mix of gamey/leather/ licorice aromas. The palate shows how to make a silk purse out of a sow's ear, with nice mouthfeel, aided by soft, persistent tannins. **rating:** 86

best drinking Now–2005 **best vintages** '91, '94, '95, '96 **drink with** Barbecued leg of lamb • $22.99

Brokenwood Graveyard Shiraz

▼▼▼▼▼ **1998** A very low-yielding 30-year-old estate vineyard and exemplary winemaking are producing a truly classic wine. Strong purple-red, it has pristine dark cherry varietal fruit, exemplary oak, and a hint of regional smoke on the bouquet. The palate has equal proportions of power, finesse and length; just be patient. **rating:** 96

best drinking 2005–2025 **best vintages** '85, '86, '87, '88, '89, '91, '93, '94, '95, '98 **drink with** Thick-cut rump steak • $80

Brokenwood Cricket Pitch Red

▼▼▼▼ **1998** Medium red-purple; the moderately intense bouquet is clean, with a mix of berry and faintly earthy notes. Sweet berry fruit and sweet vanilla oak intermingle on the palate, which has plenty of unpretentious flavour. **rating:** 86

best drinking Now–2003 **best vintages** NA **drink with** Any cheese or meat • $19

---

broke's promise wines ★★★☆

725 Milbrodale Road, Broke, NSW 2330 **region** Lower Hunter Valley
phone (02) 6579 1165 **fax** (02) 9438 4985 **open** By appointment
winemaker Andrew Margan (Contract) **production** 2000 **est.** 1996
product range ($15-18 R) The Dance of Anna Chardonnay, The Singing Chardonnay, Jesse's Eclipse Chardonnay, Hunter Valley Shiraz, Reserve Hunter Valley Shiraz.
summary Jane Marquard and Dennis Karp (and their young children) have established Broke's Promise on the banks of the Wollombi Brook adjacent to the Yengo National Park. They have followed tradition in planting shiraz, chardonnay and semillon, and broken with it by planting barbera and olive trees, the latter two inspired by a long stay in Italy. Exports to the UK, Vietnam and Hong Kong.

Broke's Promise The Dance of Anna Chardonnay

TTTT 1998 Medium yellow-green; a mix of scented oak and light nectarine fruit on the bouquet leads into a quite crisp palate, with gentle nectarine fruit and subtle oak. **rating:** 85

best drinking Now **best vintages** NA **drink with** Creamy pasta • $16

Broke's Promise The Singing Chardonnay

TTTY 1999 Medium to full yellow-green; the bouquet is quite rich, with peachy/buttery aromas and minimal oak influence. The palate is pleasant, with gently sweet fruit, but not a great deal of intensity. **rating:** 84

best drinking Now **best vintages** NA **drink with** Cold pork pie • $18

Broke's Promise Reserve Shiraz

TTTT 1999 Medium red-purple; the moderately intense bouquet is oak-dominated, although black cherry and plum fruit lurks in the forest. The medium-bodied palate has clean fruit, nice texture and is not over-extracted, with the fruit/oak balance under better control. **rating:** 85

best drinking 2002–2007 **best vintages** NA **drink with** Pizza • $17.85

---

brook eden vineyard NR

Adams Road, Lebrina, Tas 7254 **region** Northern Tasmania
phone (03) 6395 6244 **fax** (03) 6395 6211 **open** 7 days 10–5
winemaker Julian Alcorso (Contract) **production** 500 **est.** 1988
product range ($18 CD) Riesling, Chardonnay, Pinot Noir.
summary Sheila and the late Jan Bezemer established a 2.7-hectare vineyard on the 60-hectare Angus beef property they purchased in 1987. The vineyard site is beautiful; viticultural advice from the noted Fred Peacock.

brookland valley ★★★★☆

Caves Road, Willyabrup, WA 6284 **region** Margaret River
phone (08) 9755 6250 **fax** (08) 9755 6214 **open** Tues–Sun 11–4.30
winemaker Larry Cherubino **production** 8000 **est.** 1984
product range ($18–37 R) Sauvignon Blanc, Chardonnay, Merlot, Cabernet Merlot; Verse 1 Semillon Sauvignon Blanc, Chardonnay and Cabernet Sauvignon Merlot.
summary Brookland Valley has an idyllic setting, with its much enlarged Flutes Cafe one of the best winery restaurants in the Margaret River region. In 1997 BRL Hardy acquired a 50 per cent interest in the venture and took responsibility for viticulture and winemaking. The move towards richer and more complex red wines evident before the takeover has continued; the white wines have an extra degree of finesse and elegance.

Brookland Valley Sauvignon Blanc

TTTTY 2000 Light green-yellow; a clean, fresh, light and crisp bouquet offers asparagus, herbs and some citrus. The palate is clean, fresh and very correct, with some minerally characters to go with the fruity notes of the bouquet; nice balance and mouthfeel. **rating:** 90

best drinking Now–2003 **best vintages** '92, '93, '94, '95, '97, '99, '00 **drink with** Calamari • $24.99

Brookland Valley Chardonnay

TTTT 1999 Light green-yellow; clean, crisp grapefruit and melon fruit on the bouquet is followed by a light, lively fresh palate, an unwooded-with-a-twist style, relying principally on lees maturation. **rating:** 86

best drinking Now–2004 **best vintages** NA **drink with** Pan-fried veal • $31.99

Brookland Valley Verse 1 Chardonnay

ΥΥΥΥ **2000** Light green-yellow; the bouquet is quite fresh and tangy with a mix of citrus and melon fruit. The light to medium bodied palate is crisp, lively and fresh, repeating the citrus and melon fruit of the bouquet. **rating:** 86

best drinking Now–2003 **best vintages** '99 **drink with** Lemon chicken • $20

Brookland Valley Merlot

ΥΥΥΥ **1998** Medium red-purple; pronounced cedary oak dominates the bouquet, with earthy fruit and a dash of spice lurking underneath. The palate offers more of the same; a powerful wine, but oak-dominated. **rating:** 87

best drinking 2003–2008 **best vintages** NA **drink with** Devilled steak • $36.99

Brookland Valley Cabernet Sauvignon Merlot

ΥΥΥΥ **1998** Medium to full red-purple; a quite concentrated bouquet has appealing earthy berry fruit that justifies the strong oak. The palate is powerful and rich, with lots of berry fruit, but does dry slightly on the finish as the tannin and oak extract come into play. **rating:** 89

best drinking 2003–2008 **best vintages** '90, '91, '92, '93, '95, '97 **drink with** Char-grilled steak • $33.99

Brookland Valley Verse 1 Cabernet Sauvignon Merlot

ΥΥΥΥ **1999** Dense purple-red; very powerful, complex, ultra-ripe fruit, with a hint of game into the bargain, followed by a massively concentrated and rich palate. From a top vintage, and simply needs time to come to terms with itself (I hope). **rating:** 88

best drinking 2004–2009 **best vintages** '98 **drink with** Pasta • $21.99

brookside vineyard NR

5 Loaring Road, Bickley Valley, WA 6076 **region** Perth Hills
phone (08) 9291 8705 **fax** (08) 9291 5316 **open** Weekends and public holidays 10–5
winemaker Darlington Estate (Contract) **production** 450 **est.** 1984
product range ($10–19 CD) Classic White, Chardonnay, Cabernet Sauvignon, Methode Champenoise.
summary Brookside is one of the many doll's house-scale vineyard operations that dot the Perth Hills. It has 0.25 hectare each of chardonnay and cabernet sauvignon, basically selling the wine through a mailing list. It does, however, offer B&B accommodation at the house, with attractive views of the Bickley Valley.

brown brothers ★★★★

Snow Road, Milawa, Vic 3678 **region** King Valley
phone (03) 5720 5500 **fax** (03) 5720 5511 **open** 7 days 9–5
winemaker Terry Barnett, Wendy Cameron, Matt Fawcett **production** 770 000 **est.** 1885
product range ($11–45.50 R) A kaleidoscopic array of varietal wines, with a cross-hatch of appellations, the broadest being Victorian (e.g. Victorian Shiraz), more specific being King Valley (e.g. NV Brut and Pinot Chardonnay) and Milawa (e.g. Noble Riesling), then the Limited Release, Family Selection (e.g. Very Old Tokay and King Valley Chardonnay) and the Family Reserve ranges. Dinning's Shiraz is a cellar-door special; other wines also exclusive to the cellar door include Viognier, Tempranillo, Graciano and a range of Limited Release mainstream varietals.
summary Brown Brothers draws upon a considerable number of vineyards spread throughout a range of site climates, from very warm to very cool, with the climate varying according to altitude. It is also known for the diversity of varieties with which it works, and the wines always represent excellent value for money. Deservedly one of the most successful family wineries in Australia. The wines are exported to over 20 countries throughout Europe, the UK, Asia and the Far East. Conspicuously, Brown Brothers still remains outside the US market.

Brown Brothers King Valley Riesling

ΥΥΥΥ **2000** Fairly advanced colour, although the hue is correct enough; a rich, quite sweet, tropical-accented bouquet leads into a generously fleshy palate with ripe lime and pineapple flavours. A thoroughly user-friendly food style. **rating:** 89

best drinking Now–2004 **best vintages** NA **drink with** Asparagus salad • $13.75

Brown Brothers NV Pinot Chardonnay Brut

YYYY **NV** Medium yellow-green; the bouquet is quite complex, with a mix of bready yeast and more minerally aromas. The light to medium bodied palate has nice mouthfeel and above-average length, albeit with restrained fruit. **rating:** 88

best drinking Now **best vintages** NA **drink with** Aperitif • $18.50

Brown Brothers Whitlands Pinot Chardonnay

YYYYY **1996** Light green-yellow; the bouquet is clean, crisp and fresh, showing citrus and a touch of apple, the palate long, fine and elegant, with good structure and balance. **rating:** 93

best drinking Now **best vintages** '90, '91, '92, '93, '94, '96 **drink with** Shellfish • $39

Brown Brothers Dinning's Shiraz

YYYY **1998** Medium red-purple; the oak is less intrusive and overt than in previous years, but there is still every bit as much oak as there is fruit on the bouquet. A basically austere wine on the palate, with flashes of dark berry fruit in amongst the forest of oak and tannins. Cellaring will be worthwhile. **rating:** 86

best drinking 2003–2010 **best vintages** NA **drink with** Moroccan lamb • $39

Brown Brothers Limited Release Shiraz

YYYY **1998** Medium red-purple; the bouquet offers a powerful amalgam of oak (dominant) and black cherry fruit, the palate providing no surprises, simply adding heaps of tannin to the mix. This wine really does need time in bottle. **rating:** 85

best drinking 2005–2010 **best vintages** NA **drink with** Venison • $20

Brown Brothers Victorian Shiraz

YYYY **1998** Medium red-purple; the bouquet is clean and pleasant, with smooth plum and cherry fruit. The palate has much more structure, strength and tannins than is the norm with this wine, with plenty of plummy fruit and nicely integrated and balanced oak. **rating:** 87

best drinking Now–2010 **best vintages** '91, '92, '93, '94, '98 **drink with** Braised beef Chinese-style • $17.80

Brown Brothers Cellar Door Release Tempranillo

YYYY **1998** Medium to full red-purple, some gas evident on the rim; the bouquet is not aromatic, but does have touches of briar and spice, the wine opening up on its substantial palate with dark briary fruit and considerable tannins. Shows positive fruit character, and has soaked up the oak. Early days. **rating:** 85

best drinking 2003–2008 **best vintages** NA **drink with** Air-dried Spanish ham • $16.50

Brown Brothers Milawa Graciano

YYYY **1998** Excellent purple-red; the ripe and smooth bouquet has strong plum jam aromas, but in the best positive sense. The palate offers a well-balanced mix of ripe plum and more savoury fruit, the tannins soft, the oak negligible. **rating:** 88

best drinking 2002–2007 **best vintages** NA **drink with** Roast kid • $17.60

Brown Brothers Cabernet Sauvignon

YYYY **1998** Medium to full red-purple; the bouquet offers pleasant cassis and blackberry fruit supported by subtle oak, the palate continuing the theme of sweet blackberry fruit augmented by hints of chocolate and more savoury characters; good tannins to close. **rating:** 86

best drinking 2002–2008 **best vintages** NA **drink with** Beef • $17.80

Brown Brothers Victorian Cabernet Sauvignon

YYYY **1999** Medium to full red-purple; a quite full blackberry/blackcurrant bouquet with plenty of American oak is followed by a rich, big, full-on palate with fruit, oak and tannins all coming together quite well. **rating:** 86

best drinking 2003–2009 **best vintages** NA **drink with** Roast beef • $19

Brown Brothers Family Selection Very Old Tokay

YYYYY **NV** Medium to full tawny-red; very complex tea-leaf/plum-pudding/malty aromas. High-quality Tokay varietal character on the palate, which is lively and intense, with strong tea-leaf/malt/butterscotch flavours, and good balance and acidity. **rating:** 91

best drinking Now **best vintages** NA **drink with** After coffee • NA

browns of padthaway ★★☆

Keith Road, Padthaway, SA 5271 **region** Padthaway
phone (08) 8765 6063 **fax** (08) 8765 6083 **open** At Padthaway Estate
winemaker Contract **production** 35 000 **est.** 1993
product range ($10–20 R) Classic Diamond, Riesling, Sauvignon Blanc, Non Wooded Chardonnay, Verdelho, T-Trellis Shiraz, Redwood Cabernet Malbec, Myra Family Reserve Cabernet Sauvignon, Sparkling Shiraz.
summary The Brown family has for many years been the largest independent grape-grower in Padthaway, a district in which most of the vineyards were established and owned by Wynns, Seppelts, Lindemans and Hardys, respectively. A rapidly expanding range of wines is now appearing under the Browns of Padthaway label, the majority being pleasant but very light in body and flavour.

brush box vineyard NR

40 Rodd Street, Broke, NSW 2101 **region** Lower Hunter Valley
phone (02) 9913 1419 **fax** (02) 9913 1419 **open** Not
winemaker Peter Howland (Contract) **production** 600 **est.** 1997
product range ($13.50–16 CD) Verdelho, Chardonnay, Cabernet Merlot.
summary Paul and Suzanne Mackay have established their 6.5-hectare Brush Box Vineyard in a secluded part of the Fordwich Hills, with views across the Wollombi Valley to the northern perimeter ofYengo National Park. It is planted to chardonnay, verdelho, cabernet sauvignon and merlot, and so far sold by mail order only.

Brush Box Vineyard Chardonnay

▼▼▼▼ **2000** Medium yellow-green; smoky barrel-ferment aromas and melon fruit to the bouquet lead into an intense citrussy/tangy palate, with subtle barrel-ferment characters running through to a long finish. **rating:** 88
best drinking Now–2005 **best vintages** NA **drink with** Strong seafood • $16

bullers beverford

Murray Valley Highway, Beverford, Vic 3590 **region** Swan Hill
phone (03) 5037 6305 **fax** (03) 5037 6803 **open** Mon–Sat 9–5
winemaker Richard Buller (Jnr) **production** 50 000 **est.** 1952
product range ($9.50–39 CD) Victoria Chenin Blanc Colombard and Shiraz Grenache Malbec; The Magee Semillon Chardonnay and Cabernet Sauvignon Shiraz; White Label range of Semillon Chenin Blanc, Spätlese Lexia, Rosé, Shiraz, Cabernet Sauvignon; Victoria range of fortifieds including Port, Tokay and Muscat; also Sails Unwooded Chardonnay and Cabernet Shiraz Merlot.
summary Traditional wines that in the final analysis reflect both their Riverland origin and a fairly low-key approach to style in the winery. It is, however, one of the few remaining sources of reasonable-quality bulk fortified wine available to the public, provided in 22-litre Valorex barrels at $6.50 per litre. Some recent table wines have impressed.

Bullers Beverford Chenin Blanc

▼▼▼▽ **2000** Light to medium green-yellow; the bouquet is clean and light, with a touch of fruit salad; the palate in unashamedly commercial style, well made, with obvious residual sweetness. **rating:** 80
best drinking Now **best vintages** NA **drink with** Takeaway • $12

Bullers Beverford Magee Cabernet Shiraz

▼▼▼▼ **1998** Medium red-purple; the bouquet ranges through leaf, tobacco, briar, mint, spice and plum; a remarkably attractive wine in the mouth, with supple, sweet red and black berry fruit, an echo of the briar and leaf from the bouquet; subtle oak. Excellent value for money. **rating:** 85
best drinking Now–2004 **best vintages** '98 **drink with** Shepherd's pie • $12

bullers calliope ★★★★☆

Three Chain Road, Rutherglen, Vic 3685 **region** Rutherglen
phone (02) 6032 9660 **fax** (02) 6032 8005 **open** Mon–Sat 9–5, Sun 10–5
winemaker Andrew Buller **production** 5000 **est.** 1921
product range ($16–55 CD) Limited Release Shiraz, Mondeuse Shiraz, Grenache Cinsaut, Merlot Cabernet Sauvignon Cabernet Franc; Premium Black Label range and Museum Release range of old and rare material.
summary The rating is primarily for the fortified wines, and very much influenced by the superb Museum releases. Limited releases of Calliope Shiraz and Shiraz Mondeuse can also be very good.

Bullers Limited Release Merlot Cabernet Sauvignon Cabernet Franc

🍷🍷🍷🍷 **1997** Medium red-purple; the bouquet is quite fragrant, with leafy/earthy/berry aromas; the palate is attractive and remarkably elegant for a wine with such high alcohol (that acid has to be providing the essential balance) with red berry fruits, fine tannins and the barest suggestion of oak. **rating:** 86

best drinking 2002–2012 **best vintages** NA **drink with** Roast veal • $23

Bullers Calliope Rare Liqueur Tokay

🍷🍷🍷🍷🍷 **NV** Deep golden brown; a classic mix of sweet tea-leaf and crème brûlée aromas is followed by an outstanding palate showing the complexity that only age (and first-class base material) can bring; some nutty characters join the tea-leaf and crème brûlée of the bouquet. **rating:** 95

best drinking Now **best vintages** NA **drink with** Strictly unnecessary, a meal in itself • NA

Bullers Calliope Rare Liqueur Muscat

🍷🍷🍷🍷🍷 **NV** Deep brown with a touch of olive on the rim; full and deep, almost into chocolate, with intense raisined fruit; richly textured, with great structure to the raisined/plum-pudding fruit flavours, and obvious rancio age. **rating:** 94

best drinking Now **best vintages** NA **drink with** Strictly unnecessary, a meal in itself • NA

bungawarra NR

Bents Road, Ballandean, Qld 4382 **region** Granite Belt
phone (07) 4684 1128 **fax** (07) 4684 1128 **open** 7 days 10.30–4.30
winemaker Bruce Humphery-Smith, Jeff Harden **production** 1300 **est.** 1975
product range ($10–16 CD) Traminer, Thomas Semillon, Block Six Chardonnay, Foundation Chardonnay, Reserve Chardonnay, Bliss, Festival Red, Shiraz, Cabernet Sauvignon, Liquid Amber, Paragon Liqueur, Liqueur Muscat.
summary Now owned by Jeff Harden. It draws upon 5 hectares of mature vineyards which over the years have shown themselves capable of producing red wines of considerable character.

burge family winemakers 

Barossa Way, Lyndoch, SA 5351 **region** Barossa Valley
phone (08) 8524 4644 **fax** (08) 8524 4444 **open** 7 days 10–5
winemaker Rick Burge **production** 3000 **est.** 1928
product range ($15–25 CD) Olive Hill Riesling, Olive Hill Semillon, Chardonnay, Muscat Blanc Late Harvest, Clochmerle (Grenache), Olive Hill Grenache Shiraz, Olive Hill Shiraz Grenache Mourvedre, Draycott Shiraz Grenache, A Nice Red, Draycott Shiraz, Draycott Reserve Shiraz, Draycott Cabernet Merlot; Draycott Sparkling Red, Fortifieds.
summary Rick Burge came back to the family winery after a number of years successfully running St Leonards; there was much work to be done, but he has achieved much, using the base of very good fortified wines and markedly improving table-wine quality, with Draycott Shiraz (both standard and brilliant Reserve) leading the way. The wines are exported to the US, Singapore, Germany, Malaysia, the UK and Canada.

Burge Family Draycott Shiraz

🍷🍷🍷🍷 **1999** Medium purple-red; morello cherry, spice and mint aromas on the bouquet flow into an attractive palate, with distinctly sweet berry fruit (not residual sugar) on entry to the mid-palate, running through to an even finish. **rating:** 89

best drinking 2003–2007 **best vintages** '84, '88, '91, '94, '95, '98, '99 **drink with** Wild duck or, failing that, domestic duck • $24.80

Burge Family Olive Hill Shiraz Grenache Mourvedre

🍷🍷🍷🍷🍸 **1999** Medium red-purple; a smooth but complex bouquet with a range of dark berry and spice aromas is followed by a well-structured palate; here the flavours are of licorice, dark berry and small currant, with lingering, soft, ripe tannins. **rating:** 93

best drinking 2002–2010 **best vintages** NA **drink with** Game • $24.80

Burge Family A Nice Red

🍷🍷🍷🍷 **1998** Medium to full red-purple; very ripe, luscious and rich berry and mint aromas and flavours run through the bouquet and palate, finishing with soft tannins. **rating:** 85

best drinking Now–2006 **best vintages** NA **drink with** A nice hamburger • $14.80

Burge Family Clochemerle Grenache Cabernet

🍷🍷🍷🍷 **1999** Medium purple-red; mint, berry and spice aromas on the bouquet are followed by a plummy/blackberry palate with soft tannins and barely perceptible oak. **rating:** 86

best drinking 2002–2007 **best vintages** NA **drink with** Irish stew • $14.80

burnbrae NR

Hill End Road, Erudgere via Mudgee, NSW 2850 **region** Mudgee
phone (02) 6373 3504 **fax** (02) 6373 3601 **open** Wed–Mon 9–5
winemaker Alan Cox **production** NFP **est.** 1976
product range ($10–18 CD) Sauvignon Blanc, Chardonnay, Pinot Noir, Shiraz, Malbec, Cabernet Sauvignon, Vintage Port, Liqueur Muscat.
summary The founding Mace family sold Burnbrae to Alan Cox in 1996. It continues as an estate-based operation with 23 hectares of vineyards. No recent tastings.

burramurra 

Barwood Park, Nagambie, Vic 3608 **region** Goulburn Valley
phone (03) 5794 2181 **fax** (03) 5794 2755 **open** Not
winemaker Mitchelton (Contract) **production** 800 **est.** 1988
product range ($18 R) Cabernet Merlot.
summary Burramurra is the relatively low-profile vineyard operation of the Honourable Pat McNamara. Most of the grapes are sold to Mitchelton; a small amount is contract-made for the Burramurra label. Glowing reviews in the US have led to brisk export business with that country and to the selection of Burramurra by various international airlines.

Burramurra Cabernet Sauvignon Merlot

🍷🍷🍷🍷 **1997** Medium red-purple; has the greatest richness and intensity of the four wines so far released, with sweet, dark berry fruit on the bouquet, and an attractive amalgam of berry, cedar, chocolate and mocha on the palate; attractive savoury tannins add to the appeal. **rating:** 89

best drinking Now–2006 **best vintages** NA **drink with** Boned leg of lamb • NA

burrundulla NR

Sydney Road, Mudgee, NSW 2850 **region** Mudgee
phone (02) 6372 1620 **fax** (02) 6372 4058 **open** Not
winemaker Contract **production** NA **est.** 1996
product range NA
summary A very substantial venture still in its infancy; the Cox family (Chris, Michael and Ted) are in the course of establishing 54 hectares of vineyards planted to chardonnay, shiraz and cabernet sauvignon.

calais estates 

Palmers Lane, Pokolbin, NSW 2321 **region** Lower Hunter Valley
phone (02) 4998 7654 **fax** (02) 4998 7813 **open** Mon–Fri 9–5, weekends 10–5
winemaker Adrian Sheridan **production** 11 000 **est.** 1987
product range ($12–30 CD) Chenin Blanc, Semillon, Chardonnay, Reserve Chardonnay, Late Harvest Riesling, Sauterne, Shiraz Pinot, Shiraz, Reserve Shiraz, Cabernet Sauvignon.
summary A quite substantial operation but off the beaten track in Palmers Lane; at the time of writing an auction sale was scheduled, and it is likely it will emerge with new ownership.

cambewarra estate ★★★☆

520 Illaroo Road, Cambewarra, NSW 2540 **region** Shoalhaven
phone (02) 4446 0170 **fax** (02) 4446 0170 **open** Thur–Sun 10–5 and public holidays falling on a Monday.
winemaker Tamburlaine (Contract) **production** 3500 **est.** 1991
product range ($19–21 CD) Verdelho, Chambourcin, Cabernet Sauvignon, Vintage Port.
summary Geoffrey and Louise Cole founded Cambewarra Estate near the Shoalhaven River on the central southern coast of New South Wales. Contract-winemaking is competently carried out (a considerable distance away) at Tamburlaine Winery in the Hunter Valley. Cambewarra continues to produce attractive wines that have had significant success in wine shows.

Cambewarra Estate Chambourcin

🍷🍷🍷🍷 **2000** Vivid purple-red; a fresh and lively bouquet with juicy berry and spicy aromatics, and a palate that presents the same exuberant fruit in a highly appealing, early-drinking style. A particularly successful vintage. **rating:** 87

best drinking Now **best vintages** '94, '97, '98 **drink with** Italian cuisine • $21

campbells ★★★★

Murray Valley Highway, Rutherglen, Vic 3685 **region** Rutherglen
phone (02) 6032 9458 **fax** (02) 6032 9870 **open** Mon–Sat 9–5, Sun 10–5
winemaker Colin Campbell **production** 65 000 **est.** 1870
product range ($8–89 CD) Riesling, Gewurztraminer, Semillon, Chardonnay Semillon, Cellar White, Pedro Ximenez, Trebbiano, Bobbie Burns Chardonnay, Chardonnay, Autumn Harvest, Bobbie Burns Shiraz, Bobbie Burns Extended Maturation (Shiraz), Cellar Red, The Barkly Durif, Malbec, Shiraz Durif Cabernet, Cabernets, Cabernet Sauvignon, Rutherglen Tokay, Liquid Gold Tokay, Isabella Tokay, Rutherglen Muscat, Merchant Prince Muscat, Classic Muscat, Ports.
summary A winery with a wide range of table and fortified wines of ascending quality and price that are always honest; as so often happens in this part of the world, the fortified wines are the best, with the extremely elegant Isabella Tokay and Merchant Prince Muscat at the top of the tree. For all that, the table wines are impressive in a full-bodied style, and the winery rating is something of a compromise between that for the fortified wines and that for the table wines. A feature of the cellar door is an extensive range of back-vintage releases of small parcels of wine not available through any other outlet. National distribution through Red + White; exports to the UK, the US and Canada.

Campbells Shiraz Durif Cabernet Sauvignon

🍷🍷🍷🍷 **1998** Medium red-purple; the bouquet is potent, with lifted, earthy fruit aromas. The palate is sweeter than the bouquet suggests, with plum and licorice supported by balanced tannins. Little or no oak input. Could develop impressive complexity with bottle age while retaining its special character. **rating:** 85

best drinking 2002–2012 **best vintages** '98 **drink with** Strong meat dishes • $14.60

Campbells The Barkly Durif

🍷🍷🍷🍷 **1997** Medium red-purple; the bouquet is very ripe, with prune, raisin and sweet tea aromas. The palate is no less ripe with prune and chocolate flavours, finishing with ripe tannins and showing alcohol warmth throughout. **rating:** 86

best drinking Now–2004 **best vintages** NA **drink with** Jugged hare • $38.20

Campbells Isabella Tokay

🍷🍷🍷🍷🍷 **NV** Light tawny-gold; fragrant grapey, sweet tea-leaf aromas with clean spirit; the palate is luscious with sweet juicy berry and tea-leaf flavours, finishing with good acidity and a very clean aftertaste. **rating:** 93

best drinking Now **best vintages** NA **drink with** As fine an aperitif as it is a digestif • NA

Campbells Liquid Gold Tokay

🍷🍷🍷🍷🍷 **NV** Glowing golden-brown; totally delicious, sweet tea-leaf and caramel varietal aromas leap from the glass, with the flavour precisely tracking the bouquet. Clean spirit, sweet but not the least bit cloying. **rating:** 91

best drinking Now **best vintages** NA **drink with** Cake and coffee • NA

Campbells Rutherglen Tokay

TTTTT **NV** Bright golden-brown; lovely young cold-tea, tea-leaf varietal aromas flowing without a break into the palate, where the spirit is harmonious and does not threaten the wonderful tokay flavour. **rating:** 94

best drinking Now **best vintages** NA **drink with** As fine an aperitif as it is a digestif • NA

Campbells Liquid Gold Muscat

TTTTY **NV** Orange-brown; classic raisiny/grapey aromas lead into a young Muscat at its very best, with intense raisiny fruit, just a hint of nuttiness, and finishing with clean spirit. **rating:** 90

best drinking Now **best vintages** NA **drink with** Walnuts and almonds • NA

Campbells Merchant Prince Muscat

TTTTT **NV** Light to medium brown; intense but fragrant spice and raisin aromas with clean spirit. The palate is remarkably fresh and light given the age of the wine, with raisin, spice, malt and toffee flavours all intermingling, followed by cleansing acidity. **rating:** 94

best drinking Now **best vintages** NA **drink with** Coffee, high-quality biscuits • NA

Campbells Rutherglen Muscat

TTTTY **NV** Light tawny red; very youthful, raisiny fruit aromas, with the spirit fractionally jumpy (quite why, I am not sure). High-toned fruit on the palate adds a haunting edge to the flavour, almost floral. Intriguing and delicious. **rating:** 90

best drinking Now **best vintages** NA **drink with** Fruit cake • NA

candlebark hill NR

Fordes Lane, Kyneton, Vic 3444 **region** Macedon Ranges
phone (03) 9836 2712 **fax** (03) 9836 2712 **open** By appointment
winemaker David Forster, Llew Knight (Consultant) **production** 600 **est.** 1987
product range ($17–30 CD) Chardonnay, Pinot Noir, Cabernet Merlot, Cabernet Shiraz.
summary Candlebark Hill was established by David Forster on the northern end of the Macedon Ranges. It enjoys magnificent views over the central Victorian countryside north of the Great Dividing Range. The 3.5-hectare vineyard is planted to pinot noir (1.5 hectares) together with 1 hectare each of chardonnay and the three main Bordeaux varieties, complete with 0.5 hectare of shiraz and malbec. No recent tastings after a promising start.

canobolas-smith 

Boree Lane, off Cargo Road, Lidster, via Orange, NSW 2800 **region** Orange
phone (02) 6365 6113 **fax** (02) 6365 6113 **open** Weekends, public holidays 11–5
winemaker Murray Smith **production** 2000 **est.** 1986
product range ($24–30 CD) Chardonnay, Merlot, Alchemy (Cabernet blend).
summary Canobolas-Smith has established itself as one of the leading Orange district wineries with its distinctive blue wrap-around labels. Much of the wine is sold from the cellar door, which is well worth a visit. Exports to the US.

Canobolas-Smith Chardonnay

TTTT **1998** Medium to full yellow-green; overt, spicy barrel-ferment oak to the bouquet announces a big hitter, with ripe melon fruit, masses of oak and alcohol (15°). Very much the product of the hottest, earliest vintage on record. **rating:** 87

best drinking Now–2003 **best vintages** '94, '95, '96, '97 **drink with** Pasta • $25

Canobolas-Smith Alchemy

TTTT **1998** Medium red, with just a touch of purple remaining; a typical array of spicy/briary/leafy/berry aromas is supported by subtle oak on the bouquet. The palate has good mouthfeel and texture, with light, leafy, spicy flavours and appropriately under-done oak. **rating:** 86

best drinking 2002–2008 **best vintages** '98 **drink with** Milk-fed veal • $30

canungra valley vineyards NR

Lamington National Park Road, Canungra Valley, Qld 4275 **region** Queensland Zone
phone (07) 5543 4011 **fax** (07) 5543 4162 **open** 7 days 9–5
winemaker Andrew Hickenbotham, Mark Davidson (Contract) **production** NFP **est.** 1997
product range ($13.50–29 CD) Picnic range of White, Red, Semillon Chardonnay and Bubbles; Platypus range of Semillon Sauvignon Blanc, Chardonnay, Shiraz, Cabernet Merlot, Cabernet and Platypus Play Port; Preston Peak Cabernet Merlot; Molly O'Reilly Reserve Chardonnay, Golden Gleam, Vince Peter's Muscat, Argyle Blanc de Noirs.
summary Canungra Valley Vineyards has been established in the hinterland of the Gold Coast with a clear focus on broad-based tourism. Two hectares of vines have been established around the nineteenth-century homestead (relocated to the site from its original location in Warwick) but these provide only a small part of the wine offered for sale. In deference to the climate, 70 per cent of the estate plantings is chambourcin, the rain and mildew-resistent hybrid, the remainder being semillon. As the product range makes perfectly obvious, all the wine being offered at this early stage has been purchased from other winemakers. On the other hand, Canungra Valley offers a great deal of natural beauty for the general tourist.

Canungra Valley Platypus Semillon Sauvignon Blanc

🍷🍷🍷 **2000** Light green-yellow; the bouquet is soft and clean, moderately ripe, with some tropical fruit aromas; the palate is lighter, with a slightly fuzzy finish ex vanilla American oak. **rating:** 81
best drinking Now **best vintages** NA **drink with** Mud crab • $20

Canungra Valley Arglyle Blanc de Noirs

🍷🍷🍷 **2000** Pale bright pink; clean, fresh small berry fruit aromas, with just a hint of spicy/earthy character is followed by a palate that is not too sweet, and overall shows clever winemaking. **rating:** 84
best drinking Now **best vintages** NA **drink with** Antipasto • $25

cape bouvard NR

Mount John Road, Mandurah, WA 6210 **region** South West Coast
phone (08) 9739 1360 **fax** (08) 9739 1360 **open** 7 days 10–5
winemaker Gary Grierson **production** 2000 **est.** 1990
product range ($13–20 CD) Chenin Blanc, Dry White, Tuart Shiraz, Cabernet Sauvignon, Port.
summary Doggerel poet-cum-winemaker Gary Grierson draws upon 1 hectare of estate plantings but also buys grapes from other growers for this new label. The few wines tasted have been light but inoffensive.

cape clairault ★★★★

Henry Road, Willyabrup, WA 6280 **region** Margaret River
phone (08) 9755 6225 **fax** (08) 9755 6229 **open** 7 days 10–5
winemaker Ian Lewis, Peter Stark **production** 8000 **est.** 1976
product range ($13–22 CD) Under the Cape Clairault label: Sauvignon Blanc, Unwooded Chardonnay, Semillon Sauvignon Blanc, Riesling, Claireau (sweet white), Clairault (Cabernet blend); under the second Cape label: Cape White, Cape Rose, Cape Late Harvest and Cape Red.
summary Ian and Ani Lewis have been joined by two of their sons and, consequently, have not only decided not to sell the business but to double its size, with winery capacity being almost doubled from 85 tonnes to 150 tonnes. Notwithstanding increasing production, demand for the wines is so great that Cape Clairault has withdrawn from export to concentrate on the local market. A vineyard specialty is guinea fowl, not to be eaten (I think) but to control grasshopper plagues.

Cape Clairault Semillon Sauvignon Blanc

🍷🍷🍷🍷 **2000** Medium yellow-green; the bouquet is quite solid and ripe with pronounced gooseberry aromas; the palate is ripe and rich with lots of mouthfeel and a finish that shows a slight touch of oak. **rating:** 87
best drinking Now–2003 **best vintages** '88, '91, '92, '93, '95, '97 **drink with** Seafood salad • $20

cape horn vineyard NR

Echuca–Picola Road, Kanyapella, Vic 3564 **region** Goulburn Valley
phone (03) 5480 6013 **fax** (03) 5480 6013 **open** 7 days 10.30–5
winemaker John Ellis (Contract) **production** 1000 **est.** 1993

product range ($17–21 CD) Chardonnay, Sparkling Shiraz Durif, Shiraz, Durif, Cabernet Durif, Cabernet Sauvignon.

summary The unusual name comes from a bend in the Murray River that was considered by the riverboat owners of the 19th century to resemble Cape Horn, a resemblance now depicted on the wine label. The property was acquired by Echuca GP Dr Sue Harrison and her schoolteacher husband Ian in 1993 as a consequence of changes in secondary education. Ian Harrison set about planting 3 hectares each of chardonnay, shiraz and cabernet sauvignon, together with 1 hectare of durif; 2 hectares of marsanne followed in 1999, and 2 hectares of zinfandel in 2000. A new tasting-room facility and residence on the property are under construction, and accommodation units in the vineyard are planned.

Cape Horn Vineyard Chardonnay

YYYY **1999** Full straw-yellow colour; pronounced honey aromas, some peach and strong but pleasant oak on the bouquet are followed by a palate with curious milky overtones to the flavours of honey, peach and toast.

rating: 80

best drinking Now **best vintages** NA **drink with** Light pasta • NA

Cape Horn Vineyard Shiraz

YYYY **1999** Medium red-purple; the sweet red berry/plum/cherry fruit with vanilla oak on the bouquet is followed by a nearly identical palate in light to medium bodied mode. **rating:** 82

best drinking 2002–2006 **best vintages** NA **drink with** Braised lamb • NA

Cape Horn Vineyard Durif

YYYY **1998** Medium red-purple; a powerful bouquet with blackberry/gamey/leathery/vanilla aromas is followed by a substantial palate with a flavoursome mix of blackberry and oak; well made. **rating:** 85

best drinking Now–2007 **best vintages** NA **drink with** Barbecued meat • NA

cape jaffa wines ★★★★

Limestone Coast Road, Cape Jaffa, SA 5276 **region** Mount Benson and Robe
phone (08) 8768 5053 **fax** (08) 8768 5040 **open** 7 days 10–5
winemaker Derek Hooper **production** 10 000 **est.** 1993

product range ($16–35 CD) Unwooded Chardonnay (McLaren Vale), Semillon Sauvignon Blanc, Sauvignon Blanc, Barrel Fermented Chardonnay (Mount Benson and Padthaway), Shiraz (McLaren Vale), Siberia Shiraz, Cabernet Sauvignon (Mount Benson).

summary Cape Jaffa is the first of the Mount Benson wineries to come into production, albeit with most of the initial releases coming from other regions. Ultimately all of the wines will come from the substantial estate plantings of 25 hectares, which include the four major Bordeaux red varieties, shiraz, chardonnay, sauvignon blanc and semillon. It is a joint venture between the Hooper and Fowler families, and the winery (built of local paddock rock) has been designed to allow eventual expansion to 1000 tonnes, or 70 000 cases. Exports to the UK, the US and New Zealand.

Cape Jaffa Sauvignon Blanc

YYYY **2000** Light green-yellow; smoky barrel-fermented characters provide the initial impact on the bouquet, which then settles down with pleasant fruit. The palate has considerable length, aided by the barrel-ferment notes, but the fruit flavours are not particularly intense. A curious mix, but it does all work, and it is probable the wine will develop well over the next 12 months.

rating: 88

best drinking Now **best vintages** NA **drink with** Steamed mussels • $16

Cape Jaffa Semillon Sauvignon Blanc

YYYY **2000** Light green-yellow; charry/smoky oak is obvious on the bouquet in much the same fashion as the Sauvignon Blanc. The palate, too, is strikingly similar in character and style to the Sauvignon Blanc, having considerable length, and slightly muted fruit.

rating: 86

YYYY **1999** Medium to full yellow-green; the barrel-ferment component is quite evident on the bouquet, but works well in a complex and quite rich overall impact. The palate has plenty of flavour, but is not over the top, nor is it over-oaked.

rating: 88

best drinking Now **best vintages** NA **drink with** Robe crayfish • $16

Cape Jaffa Mount Benson Shiraz

🍷🍷🍷🍷 **1999** Medium purple-red; the bouquet is fresh, with light cherry aromas very reminiscent of the first vintage of the Chapoutier Shiraz from Mount Benson. The light to medium bodied palate has sweet cherry and mint fruit, supported by very fine, delicate tannins, and needs a touch more concentration and structure. **rating:** 85

best drinking Now–2004 **best vintages** NA **drink with** Spaghetti • $23

Cape Jaffa Siberia Shiraz

🍷🍷🍷🍷 **1999** Medium to full red-purple; the bouquet is complex, with aromatic cedar, spice and mulberry/ plum fruit; the smooth and clean palate has attractive plummy fruit well balanced with integrated oak. A wine that shows why Chapoutier has chosen this as one of its areas in Australia in which to grow shiraz. **rating:** 89

best drinking 2003–2008 **best vintages** NA **drink with** Osso bucco • $34.95

Cape Jaffa Mount Benson Cabernet Sauvignon

🍷🍷🍷🍷 **1999** Youthful red-purple; the bouquet is clean, fresh and quite aromatic, with redcurrant and raspberry fruit supported by subtle oak. A fresh, friendly, juicy/fruity style, with easy, soft tannins. **rating:** 87

🍷🍷🍷🍷½ **1998** Medium to full red-purple; the bouquet is quite pungent, with coffee bean, blackberry and dark chocolate fruit; there is lots going on here. The palate is rich, round and mouthfilling, with soft, ripe chocolate and blackberry flavours, and attractive, soft, rounded tannins. A really nice wine. **rating:** 93

best drinking 2002–2007 **best vintages** '98 **drink with** Rare roast beef • $20

capel vale ★★★★☆

Lot 5 Stirling Estate, Mallokup Road, Capel, WA 6271 **region** Geographe
phone (08) 9727 1986 **fax** (08) 9727 1904 **open** 7 days 10–4
winemaker Nicole Esdaile **production** 130 000 **est.** 1979
product range ($9.50–48 R) Layman's Hut range of Fronti, Tuart White, Jarrah Red; CV 'Bistro' range of Chenin, Unwooded Chardonnay, Sauvignon Blanc, Pinot Noir, Shiraz, Cabernet Merlot; Capel Vale 'Fine Dining' Riesling, Verdelho, Semillon, Sauvignon Blanc, Sauvignon Blanc Semillon, Chardonnay, Merlot, Shiraz, Cabernet Sauvignon, Late Harvest; 'Connoisseur' range of Whispering Hill Riesling, Seven Day Road Sauvignon Blanc, Frederick Chardonnay, Kinnaird Shiraz, Howecroft Merlot and Howecroft Cabernet Sauvignon Merlot; Sassy Sparkling Chardonnay, Tawny Port.
summary Capel Vale continues to expand its viticultural empire, its contract-grape sources and its marketing, the last through the recent introduction of a series of vineyard or similarly named super-premium wines. Against the run of play, as it were, the most successful of these super-premiums are the red wines, for it was the Riesling that first captured attention. The strong marketing focus the company has always had is driven by its indefatigable owner, Dr Peter Pratten, who has developed export markets throughout Europe and Asia.

Capel Vale Whispering Hill Riesling

🍷🍷🍷🍷 **2000** Light green-yellow; a fragrant bouquet with typical regional passionfruit overtones is followed by a palate with powerful flavour; faintly sweaty/reductive notes should dissipate with a little further bottle age. **rating:** 86

best drinking 2002–2007 **best vintages** '97, '98 **drink with** Thai cuisine • $22

Capel Vale Semillon Sauvignon Blanc

🍷🍷🍷½ **2000** Light green-yellow; a fresh and crisp bouquet has herb, apple and a faint hint of spice, the palate picking up on the spicy apple characters of the bouquet, but also showing too much carbon dioxide at this juncture. **rating:** 83

best drinking Now **best vintages** NA **drink with** Shellfish • $14.95

Capel Vale Frederick Chardonnay

🍷🍷🍷🍷🍷 **1998** Medium yellow-green; the bouquet is complex, with intense fruit and well-integrated barrel-ferment oak; there is lovely melon and stonefruit together with a hint of citrus on the long, lingering palate; once again, the oak has been impeccably handled. The best yet under the Frederick label. **rating:** 94

best drinking Now–2005 **best vintages** '98 **drink with** Marron (or yabbies) • $38

Capel Vale Shiraz

ΥΥΥΥ **1999** Medium red-purple; the bouquet is relatively light, but quite fragrant, with earthy cherry and some spice aromas. The bright and fresh palate is just a little simple, but pleasantly driven by sweet fruit, finishing with relatively brisk acidity. **rating:** 87

best drinking 2002–2006 **best vintages** NA **drink with** Designer pizza • NA

Capel Vale CV Shiraz

ΥΥΥΥ **1999** Light to medium purple-red; vibrant, spicy/leafy aromas proclaim the cool-climate origins for the wine. The palate is bright and zesty, with cherry, spice and mint fruit flavours, and minimal oak. **rating:** 85

best drinking Now **best vintages** NA **drink with** Oyster blade steak • $14.95

Capel Vale Merlot

ΥΥΥΥ **1999** Medium red, with a touch of purple; bright, spicy/savoury fruit has a hint of coffee, probably from the oak, on the bouquet. Fresh, red berry fruit comes through nicely on the palate, supported by gentle oak. **rating:** 87

best drinking 2002–2007 **best vintages** NA **drink with** Roast veal • $22

Capel Vale Howecroft Merlot

ΥΥΥΥ **1998** Medium red-purple; a fragrant and savoury bouquet has spicy olive aromas offset by a nice touch of sweet, cedary oak; the palate has appealing texture, structure and flavour, with long, fine tannins. A convincing example of the variety. **rating:** 92

best drinking 2002–2010 **best vintages** '95, '97, '98 **drink with** Rare eye fillet • $48

cape mentelle ★★★★★

Off Wallcliffe Road, Margaret River, WA 6285 **region** Margaret River
phone (08) 9757 3266 **fax** (08) 9757 3233 **open** 7 days 10–4.30
winemaker John Durham **production** 55 000 **est.** 1970
product range ($15.50–51.50 R) Chardonnay, Semillon Sauvignon Blanc, Sauvignon Blanc Semillon Wallcliffe Reserve, Georgiana, Marmaduke, Cabernet Sauvignon, Cabernet Merlot, Shiraz, Zinfandel.

summary Notwithstanding majority ownership by Veuve Clicquot, David Hohnen remains very much in command of one of Australia's foremost medium-sized wineries. Exceptional marketing skills and wine of the highest quality, with the back-up of New Zealand's Cloudy Bay, are a potent combination. The Chardonnay and Semillon Sauvignon Blanc are among Australia's best, the potent Shiraz usually superb, and the berry/spicy Zinfandel makes one wonder why this grape is not as widespread in Australia as it is in California. Enlarged its business by the slightly quixotic acquisition of Mountadam in September 2000. Exports to Asia and the US.

Cape Mentelle Wallcliffe Reserve Sauvignon Blanc Semillon

ΥΥΥΥ **1999** Medium yellow-green; the bouquet is solidly powerful and complex in a somewhat oaky Napa Valley-like style. There is more of the same on the strongly structured, powerful palate, which takes no prisoners and is classically described as a food style. **rating:** 86

best drinking Now **best vintages** NA **drink with** Sweetbreads • $31.50

Cape Mentelle Semillon Sauvignon Blanc

ΥΥΥΥ **2000** Light yellow-green; the bouquet is clean but relatively restrained, with some passionfruit and a touch of gooseberry coming through. The palate has good structure and length, with the faintest touch of spice and vanilla from the barrel-ferment component, finishing with bright acidity. Clever winemaking. **rating:** 91

best drinking Now–2004 **best vintages** '85, '88, '91, '93, '95, '96, '97, '98, '99, '00 **drink with** Fish, Asian cuisine • $21.60

Cape Mentelle Chardonnay

ΥΥΥΥΥ **1999** Although in the same sub-region as Leeuwin Estate and Devil's Lair, the style of this wine is distinctively different, with melon and stonefruit aromas and flavours rather than citrus. The sophisticated use of smoky/charry barrel-ferment oak inputs, together with controlled malolactic fermentation, results in subtle yet powerful wine. **rating:** 94

best drinking Now–2009 **best vintages** '90, '91, '92, '93, '94, '95, '96, '97, '98, '99 **drink with** Sweetbreads • $32.20

Cape Mentelle Shiraz

🍷🍷🍷🍷🍷 **1999** Medium to full red-purple; the complex bouquet ranges through licorice, plum and varietal game aromas, supported by subtle oak. The palate is still quite reserved, with fine-grained tannins. Will undoubtedly blossom over the years ahead, reflecting the great vintage. **rating:** 92

best drinking 2004–2009 **best vintages** '86, '88, '90, '91, '93, '94, '96, '97, '98, '99 **drink with** Stir-fried Asian beef • $28

Cape Mentelle Zinfandel

🍷🍷🍷🍷🍷 **1999** Medium red-purple; spicy chocolate, cedar and vanilla aromas are followed by a lively, fresh but smooth palate with spicy berry fruit and fine tannins; the oak is not overblown. **rating:** 92

best drinking 2003–2008 **best vintages** '86, '87, '91, '92, '93, '94, '95, '97, '98, '99 **drink with** Rare char-grilled rump steak • $32.50

Cape Mentelle Cabernet Sauvignon

🍷🍷🍷🍷 **1996** Medium red-purple; obvious bottle development has led to secondary aromas in a sweet yet savoury mix of chocolate, berry and vanilla. The palate flows directly from the bouquet; here, too, gently sweet oak helps. **rating:** 89

best drinking Now–2011 **best vintages** '76, '78, '82, '83, '86, '90, '91, '93, '94, '95 **drink with** Loin of lamb • $51.20

capercaillie ★★★☆

Londons Road, Lovedale, NSW 2325 **region** Lower Hunter Valley
phone (02) 4990 2904 **fax** (02) 4991 1886 **open** Mon–Sat 9–5, Sun 10–5
winemaker Alasdair Sutherland **production** 5000 **est.** 1995
product range ($17–40 CD) Watervale Riesling, Hunter Valley Gewurztraminer, Semillon, Chardonnay, Dessert Style Gewurztraminer, Hunter Valley Chambourcin, Ghillie Shiraz, Orange Highlands Merlot, Clan (Cabernet blend from Orange and Coonawarra), C Sparkling (Red).
summary The former Dawson Estate, now run by Hunter Valley veteran Alasdair Sutherland (no relation to Neil Sutherland of Sutherland Estate). The Capercaillie wines are usually full-flavoured and generous. Following the example of Brokenwood, its fruit sources are spread across southeastern Australia. The wines are exported to the UK.

Capercaillie Watervale Riesling

🍷🍷🍷🍷 **2000** Light to medium yellow-green; the bouquet is solid, with strong, slightly phenolic fruit aromas, the firm, powerful palate providing more of the same, and again showing a slightly phenolic character. **rating:** 84

best drinking Now–2004 **best vintages** NA **drink with** Vegetarian • $17

Capercaillie Hunter Valley Semillon

🍷🍷🍷🍷 **1998** Bright green-yellow; a complex bouquet with lemon/lemon rind aromas and a hint of honey leads into a palate with good presence and length, and undoubted medium-term development potential. **rating:** 88

best drinking Now–2005 **best vintages** '98 **drink with** Lemon chicken • $17

Capercaillie Hunter Valley Chardonnay

🍷🍷🍷🍷 **2000** Medium yellow-green; despite some reduced characters, the bouquet is quite intense, with citrussy fruit that flows through to the palate, augmented by subtle oak. Well out of the traditional regional style. **rating:** 83

best drinking Now–2004 **best vintages** NA **drink with** Rich fish dishes • $19

Capercaillie The Ghillie Shiraz

🍷🍷🍷🍷 **1999** Dense red-purple; the bouquet is powerful and concentrated, with lots of oak but also plenty of fruit. The palate is equivalently powerful, oaky and fairly extractive, and needs a great deal of patience, but will very likely get there in the end. Rated as it is today, and not what it may become. **rating:** 85

best drinking 2006–2012 **best vintages** NA **drink with** Marinated beef • $40

Capercaillie The Clan

🍷🍷🍷🍷 **1999** Medium red-purple; sweet spice/vanilla/leather/berry aromas lead into a thoroughly attractive wine on the palate, with lots of sweet berry fruit, sweet, ripe tannins and good acidity. The oak is not overly intrusive. **rating:** 86

best drinking 2002–2006 **best vintages** NA **drink with** Lasagne • $22

capogreco estate NR

Riverside Avenue, Mildura, Vic 3500 **region** Murray Darling
phone (03) 5023 3060 **open** Mon–Sat 10–6
winemaker Bruno Capogreco **production** NFP **est.** 1976
product range ($8–12 CD) Riesling, Moselle, Shiraz-Mataro, Cabernet Sauvignon, Claret, Rosé, Fortifieds.
summary Italian-owned and run, the wines are a blend of Italian and Australian Riverland influences; the herb-infused Rosso Dolce is a particularly good example of its kind.

captain's paddock NR

Booie–Crawford Road, Kingaroy, Qld 4610 **region** South Burnett
phone (07) 4162 4534 **fax** (07) 4162 4502 **open** Weekends 9–4
winemaker Charles Williams **production** 660 **est.** 1995
product range ($10–17 CD) Chardonnay, Captain's White, Shiraz, Captain's Red (semi-sweet).
summary Don and Judy McCallum planted the first hectare of vineyard in 1995, followed by a further 3 hectares in 1996, focusing on shiraz and chardonnay. It is a family affair; the mudbrick cellar-door building was made with bricks crafted by Don McCallum, Judy's screenprinting adorns the tables and chairs, and printed linen is for sale to the public. Their two children are both sculptors, with works on display at the winery. Captain's Paddock is fully licensed, offering either light platters or full dishes incorporating local produce. Meals are served either inside or alfresco in the courtyard with views over the Booie Ranges.

carabooda estate NR

297 Carabooda Road, Carabooda, WA 6033 **region** Swan District
phone (08) 9407 5283 **fax** (08) 9407 5283 **open** 7 days 10–6
winemaker Terry Ord **production** 2000 **est.** 1989
product range ($12.50–18 CD) Sauvignon Blanc, Chenin Blanc, Shiraz, Cabernet Shiraz, Cabernet Sauvignon.
summary 1989 is the year of establishment given by Terry Ord, but it might as well have been 1979 (when he made his first wine) or 1981 (when he and wife Simonne planted their first vines). But it has been a slowly, slowly exercise, with production from the 3 hectares of estate plantings now supplemented by purchased grapes, the first public release not being made until mid-1994. Red wines from the 1994 and 1995 vintages have been available ex cellar door since 1999, the whites since 1998. Since that time production has risen significantly.

carbunup estate ★★★

Bussel Highway, Carbunup, WA 6280 **region** Margaret River
phone (08) 9755 1111 **open** 7 days 10–5
winemaker Robert Credaro **production** NFP **est.** 1988
product range ($12–16 CD) Under the premium Vasse River Wines label: Chardonnay, Semillon, Sauvignon Blanc; under Carbunup Estate label: Verdelho, Shiraz.
summary A relative newcomer, selling part of the grapes produced from the 18 hectares of vineyards but keeping part for release under the Carbunup Estate and Vasse River labels (strikingly different in design, and giving no clue that they emanate from the same winery). It had early success with its white wines and in particular its Chardonnay and Semillon.

cargo road wines NR

Cargo Road, Orange, NSW 2800 **region** Orange
phone (02) 6365 6100 **open** Weekends 11–5
winemaker James Sweetapple **production** 1800 **est.** 1983
product range ($14–22.50 CD) Riesling, Gewürztraminer, Sauvignon Blanc, Merlot, Zinfandel, Cabernet Merlot.
summary This is one of the oldest vineyards in Orange, although it has been extended by recent plantings and now comprises zinfandel (3 hectares), sauvignon blanc (2.5 hectares), merlot (1.4 hectares), cabernet sauvignon (1.3 hectares), riesling (1.5 hectares) and gewurztraminer (0.4 hectare).

carilley estate NR

Lot 2 Hyem Road, Herne Hill, WA 6056 **region** Swan District
phone (08) 9296 1116 **fax** (08) 9296 1735 **open** By appointment
winemaker Rod Marshall **production** 1000 **est.** 1985

product range ($15–20 CD) Chenin Blanc, Chardonnay, Shiraz Merlot.
summary Doctors Laura and Isavel Carija have 2 hectares each of chenin blanc, shiraz and chardonnay, and 1 hectare of merlot. Most of the grapes are sold; only a small proportion is made under the Carilley Estate label, with very limited retail distribution or mail order. Carilley Estate is in the process of acquiring adjoining land and plans to build cellars which should open by 2002.

carindale wines NR

Palmers Lane, Pokolbin, NSW 2321 **region** Lower Hunter Valley
phone (02) 4998 7665 **fax** (02) 4998 7665 **open** Fri–Mon 10–4.30
winemaker Brian Walsh (Contract) **production** 1000 **est.** 1996
product range ($19.50–26.50 CD) Chardonnay, Blackthorn (Cabernet blend).
summary Carindale is still in its infancy, drawing upon 2 hectares of chardonnay, 1.2 hectares of cabernet franc and 0.2 hectare of merlot (together with a few muscat vines). At this juncture the wines are available only through cellar door and by mail order.

carlei estate NR

1 Albert Road, Upper Beaconsfield, Vic 3808 **region** Port Phillip Zone
phone (03) 5944 4599 **fax** (03) 5944 4599 **open** Weekends 11–5
winemaker Sergio Carlei **production** 400 **est.** 1998
product range ($25–55 CD) Chardonnay, Pinot Noir, Shiraz.
summary Sergio Carlei has established 3 hectares of vineyard using biodynamic and organic methods. The tiny production is sold through the cellar door and by mail order only.

carosa NR

310 Houston Street, Mount Helena, WA 6082 **region** Perth Hills
phone (08) 9572 1603 **fax** (08) 9572 1604 **open** Weekends, holidays 11–5 or by appointment
winemaker James Elson **production** 450 **est.** 1984
product range ($14–19 CD) Chardonnay, Summer White, Classic Dry White, Pinot Noir, Cabernet Merlot, Cabernet Sauvignon, Sparkling Pinot Noir, Pinot Noir, Old Tawny Port, White Port.
summary Very limited production and small-scale winemaking result in wines that can only be described as rustic, but that sell readily enough into the local market. Winemaker Jim Elson has extensive eastern Australia winemaking experience (with Seppelt) so should succeed. The wines are sold through cellar door and by mailing list.

Carosa Cabernet Merlot

🍷🍷🍷🍷 **1999** Medium red-purple; the moderately intense bouquet has some red fruit aromas with an earthy/savoury substrate; the palate offers rather more, with sweet, ripe plum and prune fruit providing plenty of flavour, finishing with soft tannins. **rating:** 83

best drinking 2002–2006 **best vintages** NA **drink with** Beef satay • $18

Carosa Cabernet Sauvignon

🍷🍷🍷🍷 **1999** Medium red-purple; the bouquet is clean, with moderately ripe sweet blackberry/currant fruit and a touch of earth; the palate is generously flavoured, with blackberry/blackcurrant fruit and subtle French oak influence. **rating:** 85

best drinking 2002–2007 **best vintages** NA **drink with** Barbecued meat • $18

---

casa fontana NR

4 Cook Street, Lutana, Tas 7009 **region** Southern Tasmania
phone (03) 6272 3180 **open** Not
winemaker Mark Fontana, Steve Lubiana (Contract) **production** 250 **est.** 1994
product range ($22 ML) Chardonnay, Pinot Noir.
summary Mark Fontana and his Japanese wife Shige planted their first pinot noir in 1994 and over the following two years expanded the vineyard to its present level of 2.6 hectares (1 hectare each of pinot noir and chardonnay, and 0.6 hectare of riesling). Mark Fontana is a metallurgist with Pasminco and came into grape-growing through his love of fine wine.

Casa Fontana Chardonnay

▼▼▼▼▽ **1999** Medium yellow-green; a complex bouquet offers tangy melon/citrus fruit and subtle oak; the palate is even more attractive; elegant, with a harmonious mouthfeel coming from a mix of creamy cashew and more fruit-driven characters. **rating:** 92

best drinking Now–2005 **best vintages** '99 **drink with** Veal sweetbreads • $22

cascabel ★★★★

Rogers Road, Willunga, SA 5172 **region** McLaren Vale
phone (08) 8557 4434 **fax** (08) 8557 4435 **open** By appointment
winemaker Susana Fernandez, Duncan Ferguson **production** 1500 **est.** 1997
product range ($16–28 R) Eden Valley Riesling, Fleurieu Sauvignon Blanc, Adelaide Hills Pinot Noir, Shiraz, McLaren Vale Grenache Shiraz, Sparkling Shiraz.
summary Cascabel's proprietors, Duncan Ferguson and Susana Fernandez, established Cascabel when they purchased a property at Willunga on the Fleurieu Peninsula and planted it to roussanne, tempranillo, graciano, monastrel, grenache, shiraz and viognier. The choice of grapes reflects the winemaking experience of the proprietors in Australia, the Rhône Valley, Bordeaux, Italy, Germany and New Zealand, and also Susana Fernandez's birthplace, Spain. Both are fully qualified and intend to move the production base steadily towards the style of the Rhône Valley, Rioja and other parts of Spain. In the meantime the 4000-case capacity winery they erected on site prior to the 1998 vintage is being kept busy with grapes sourced from areas throughout South Australia. The initial releases left no doubt that the proprietors know what they are doing, and it will be interesting to watch the development of the wines from the estate plantings. Exports to the US, Canada, the UK, New Zealand and Japan.

Cascabel Eden Valley Riesling

▼▼▼▼ **2000** Light green-yellow; the bouquet is of moderate to full intensity, with strong, ripe lime/tropical fruit and some mineral undertones. The palate is generous, with considerable weight and interesting texture, though overall the fruit is not particularly aromatic. Should develop reasonably quickly. **rating:** 89

best drinking Now–2004 **best vintages** '99 **drink with** Stir-fried prawns • $16

Cascabel Fleurieu Peninsula Shiraz

▼▼▼▼▽ **1999** Medium to full red-purple; the bouquet is solid, with dark berry and a mix of spice, prune and chocolate underlay. On the palate a savoury/spicy mix of dark plum, chocolate and licorice fruit is enhanced by excellent tannin and oak management. A particularly good achievement for the vintage. **rating:** 92

best drinking 2004–2014 **best vintages** '98, '99 **drink with** Ox cheek • $27

Cascabel Grenache et al

▼▼▼▽ **1999** Medium red-purple; the bouquet is complex, with gamey/savoury aromas that come through strongly on the palate, leaving me yearning for more sweet fruit. Perhaps I had an off day. **rating:** 82

best drinking Now–2003 **best vintages** NA **drink with** Beef stew • $18

casella 

Wakely Road, Yenda, NSW 2681 **region** Riverina
phone (02) 6968 1346 **fax** (02) 6968 1196 **open** Not
winemaker Alan Kennett **production** 1.2 million **est.** 1969
product range ($4.95–19.50 R) Chardonnay, Shiraz, Cabernet Sauvignon; under the Carramar Estate label: Semillon Sauvignon Blanc, Chardonnay, Unwooded Chardonnay, Botrytis Semillon, Merlot, Shiraz, Shiraz Cabernet, Cabernet Sauvignon; also Cottlers Bridge at significantly lower prices.
summary Casella is typical of the new wave sweeping through the Riverina. It draws upon 285 hectares of estate vineyards, selling much of its wine in bulk or as cleanskin bottled wine to other producers, but also marketing a range of varietals under the Carramar Estate label. Casella is part of the Semillon of the Riverina group (promoting dry Semillon), and overall its wines offer good value for money. Predictably, the Botrytis Semillon is the outstanding release. Retail distribution through the eastern States and South Australia; exports to the US, the UK, Japan and New Zealand.

cassegrain ★★★☆

Hastings River Winery, Fernbank Creek Road, Port Macquarie, NSW 2444 **region** Hastings River
phone (02) 6583 7777 **fax** (02) 6584 0354 **open** 7 days 9–5
winemaker John Cassegrain, Ben Wurst **production** 40 000 **est.** 1980
product range ($11.50–29 CD) Semillon, Sauvignon Blanc, Unwooded Chardonnay, Oaked Chardonnay, Verdelho, Traminer Riesling, Chambourcin, Pinot Noir, Cabernet Merlot, Merlot, Merlot Cabernet Franc; Five Mile Hollow Semillon Chardonnay, White, Classic Red; The Premiere Collection series of Fromenteau Reserve Chardonnay, Reserve Semillon, Reserve Chambourcin, Maximus; also a selection of sparkling, dessert and fortifieds.
summary A very substantial operation based in the Hastings Valley on the north coast of New South Wales. In earlier years it drew fruit from many parts of Australia but is now entirely supplied by the 154 hectares of estate plantings that offer 14 varieties, including the rare chambourcin, a French-bred cross. Exports to the UK, the US, Japan, Switzerland, Germany, the Netherlands, Canada and Asia.

Cassegrain Hastings River Semillon

YYYY **2000** Very pale straw-green; herb, mineral, grass and lemon tree leaves on the bouquet presage a palate with abundant flavour and length, with the flavour of sweet lemons (if that is possible). A nice, each-way proposition for drinking or cellaring. **rating:** 89
best drinking Now–2010 **best vintages** '97, '98, '00 **drink with** Oysters • $16.50

Cassegrain Hastings River Sauvignon Blanc

YYYY **2000** Water white; the bouquet is herbaceous and minerally, in a slightly old-fashioned style; the palate opens in the same fashion, but is neatly fleshed out on the finish by a fleck of residual sugar. **rating:** 86
best drinking Now **best vintages** NA **drink with** Pan-fried flathead • $15.50

Cassegrain Fromenteau Reserve Chardonnay

YYYY **1998** Glowing yellow-green; the bouquet has solid peach and honey fruit together with restrained oak; there is a rounded, smooth entry to the mouth and an attractive mid-palate of ripe honey and peach fruit, the oak again in the background. **rating:** 88
best drinking Now–2003 **best vintages** '89, '91, '93, '95, '96 **drink with** Rich chicken or veal • $23.95

Cassegrain BD Reserve Chambourcin

YYYY **1998** Medium red-purple; there is much less of the gamey varietal character than usual, instead offering cedar, red fruits and plum. There is a savoury mix of flavours on the palate, with a core of spicy plum, finishing with soft tannins. Ageing more attractively than anticipated. **rating:** 85
best drinking Now **best vintages** NA **drink with** Coq au vin • $22.95

castagna vineyard NR

Ressom Lane, Beechworth, Vic 3747 **region** North East Victoria
phone (03) 5728 2888 **fax** (03) 5728 2898 **open** By appointment
winemaker Julian Castagna **production** 2000 **est.** 1997
product range ($23–27 ML) Allegro Rosé, Genesis Syrah.
summary The elegantly labelled wines of Castagna will ultimately come from 4 hectares of estate shiraz and viognier in the course of establishment (the latter making up 15 per cent of the total). Winemaker Julian Castagna is intent on making wines that reflect the terroir as closely as possible, declining to use cultured yeast or filtration. The initial release of 1998 Genesis Syrah was in fact made from grapes purchased from a next-door neighbour, but all future wines will be estate-grown.

castle rock estate ★★★★

Porongurup Road, Porongurup, WA 6324 **region** Great Southern
phone (08) 9853 1035 **fax** (08) 9853 1010 **open** Mon–Fri 10–4, weekends and public holidays 10–5
winemaker Robert Diletti **production** 5000 **est.** 1983
product range ($14.50–22 CD) Riesling, Late Harvest Riesling, Great Southern White, Chardonnay, Pinot Noir, Cabernet Merlot, Merlot Cabernet Franc, Cabernet Sauvignon, Muscat Liqueur.

summary An exceptionally beautifully sited vineyard and cellar-door sales area with sweeping vistas from the Porongurups. Operated by the Diletti family, the standard of viticulture is very high, and the site itself ideally situated (quite apart from its beauty). The Rieslings have always been elegant and handsomely repaid time in bottle. In the most recent vintages the other wines of Castle Rock have improved considerably, with far greater weight and flavour than hitherto.

Castle Rock Estate Riesling

🍷🍷🍷🍷🍷 **2000** Very pale straw-green; clean, crisp mineral and apple aromas are joined by a touch of passionfruit, and lead into a delicate, crisp palate with apple, passionfruit and lime flavours; nice balance and length; good acidity. **rating:** 90

best drinking 2000–2007 **best vintages** '86, '89, '90, '91, '93, '94, '96, '97, '98, '00 **drink with** Seafood salad • $18.19

Castle Rock Estate Chardonnay

🍷🍷🍷🍷 **1999** Light green-yellow, fresh and bright; the bouquet is quite tight, with fresh melon fruit together with a light citrus dressing. The palate is still relatively light and undeveloped, but has some minerally length. A mini vertical tasting of prior vintages back to 1996 shows these wines develop well in bottle, the '96 in particular looking fresher and brighter than on any prior tasting, although there was something astray with the '98. **rating:** 82

best drinking Now–2005 **best vintages** NA **drink with** Marron or lobster • $21

cathcart ridge estate NR

Moyston Road, Cathcart, via Ararat, Vic 3377 **region** Grampians
phone (03) 5352 1997 **fax** (03) 5352 1558 **open** 7 days 10–5
winemaker David Farnhill, Simon Clayfield (Consultant) **production** 10 000 **est.** 1977
product range ($9.50–35 CD) Estate Reserve Range of Chardonnay, Shiraz, Merlot, Cabernet Sauvignon; Rhymney Reef Shiraz, Shiraz Cabernet, Merlot, Cabernet Merlot, Old Tawny Port; at the bottom of the price range: Mount Ararat Colombard, Shiraz.
summary In recent years Cathcart Ridge has raised capital to fund a significant expansion programme of both vineyards and the winery, but is still little known in the wider retail trade.

Cathcart Ridge Estate Chardonnay

🍷🍷🍷🍷 **1999** Medium to full red-purple; a complex, exotic bouquet with a mix of plum, spice, prune and citrus is followed by a similarly powerful and complex palate, providing all the flavours promised by the bouquet, rounded up with powerful tannins. Demands time and might well be given a higher rating when mature. **rating:** 86

best drinking 2004–2010 **best vintages** NA **drink with** Marinated beef • $30

Cathcart Ridge Estate Reserve Shiraz

🍷🍷🍷🍷 **1998** Medium red-purple; ripe plum, prune, mint and spice aromas are followed by a powerful palate, with savoury tannins running right through its length, and again that curious hint of lemon/citrus that shows in the varietal release. **rating:** 87

best drinking 2004–2012 **best vintages** NA **drink with** Lamb and rosemary • $30

catherine vale vineyard ★★★☆

656 Milbrodale Road, Bulga, NSW 2330 **region** Lower Hunter Valley
phone (02) 6579 1334 **fax** (02) 6579 1334 **open** Weekends and public holidays 10–5 or by appointment
winemaker John Hordern (Contract) **production** 1125 **est.** 1994
product range ($11–15.50 CD) Semillon, Chardonnay, Semillon Chardonnay.
summary Former schoolteachers Bill and Wendy Lawson have established Catherine Vale as a not-so-idle retirement venture. Both were involved in school athletics and sports programmes, handy training for do-it-yourself viticulturists. Most of the grapes from the 4.6-hectare vineyard are sold to contract-winemaker John Hordern; a small proportion is vinified for the Catherine Vale label.

Catherine Vale Semillon

🍷🍷🍷🍷 **1999** Light green-yellow; a crisp and quite fragrant bouquet with attractive lemon/lemon grass aromas leads into a fresh, crisp and youthful palate with slightly twitchy acid; demands time, and is developing slowly. **rating:** 85

best drinking 2002–2007 **best vintages** '98 **drink with** Shellfish • $12.80

catspaw farm NR

Texas Road, Stanthorpe, Qld 4380 **region** Granite Belt
phone (07) 4683 6229 **fax** (07) 4683 6386 **open** Thurs to Sun 10–5
winemaker Christopher Whitfort **production** 1000 **est.** 1989
product range ($12–21 CD) Sauvignon Blanc Semillon, Chardonnay, Sweet White, Golden Queen, Cabernet Shiraz, Liqueur Muscat, Liqueur Muscat Gold Label.
summary The foundations for Catspaw Farm were laid back in 1989 when planting of the vineyard began with chardonnay, riesling, cabernet franc, cabernet sauvignon, merlot, chambourcin and shiraz, totalling 4.6 hectares. More recently, Catspaw has moved with the times in planting rousanne, semillon, barbera and sangiovese, lifting total plantings to just under 8 hectares. The newer plantings are yet to come into bearing and the wines some time away from release. In the meantime a mixed bag of wines is available, some dating back to 1996. Catspaw, incidentally, also offers on-farm accommodation in a self-contained farmhouse (with disabled access) and picnic facilities.

celtic farm NR

39 Sweyn Street, North Balwyn, Vic 3104 **region** Warehouse
phone (03) 9836 2666 **fax** (03) 9836 2888 **open** Not
winemaker Gerry Taggert **production** 4000 **est.** 1997
product range ($18–30 R) South Block Riesling (Clare Valley), The Gridge Pinot Grigio (King Valley), Far Canal Shiraz (Coonawarra), Raisin Hell Rutherglen Muscat.
summary Yet another Warehouse winery, the brainchild of a marketing and sales team of Mark McKenzie and Gerry Taggert. The proprietors say, 'Celtic Farm is produced from classic varieties selected from Australia's premium wine regions and made with a total commitment to quality. While we have a desire to pay homage to our Celtic (drinking) heritage we are also acutely aware that wine should be about enjoyment, fun and not taking yourself too seriously.'

Celtic Farm Far Canal Coonawarra Shiraz

🍷🍷🍷🍷 **1998** Medium red-purple, slightly opaque; both the bouquet and palate show lots of oak, and even though it is French, at this juncture subjugates the lovely red berry fruit, which is, without question, at the core of the wine. Finishes with soft tannins, and the structural balance is good. I simply wish I could get away from that oak and give the wine the rating it deserves. **rating:** 85

best drinking 2003–2008 **best vintages** NA **drink with** Duck cassoulet • $30

Celtic Farm Raisin Hell Rutherglen Muscat

🍷🍷🍷🍷½ **NV** Medium tawny; the aromas are quite lovely, with intense grapey/raisiny fruit, the palate rich and concentrated, with classic raisin, Christmas-cake flavours. A powerful argument for the cause of younger rather than older Muscat. **rating:** 90

best drinking Now **best vintages** NA **drink with** Appropriate company • NA

chain of ponds ★★★★☆

Adelaide Road, Gumeracha, SA 5233 **region** Adelaide Hills
phone (08) 8389 1415 **fax** (08) 8389 1877 **open** 7 days 10.30–4.30
winemaker Caj Amadio (Contract) **production** 8000 **est.** 1993
product range ($10–33 CD) Riesling, Semillon, Sauvignon Blanc Semillon, Special Release Sauvignon Blanc, Chardonnay, Novello Rosso, Pinot Noir, Ledge Shiraz, Sangiovese, Amadeus Cabernet Sauvignon, Diva Pinot Chardonnay.
summary Caj and Genny Amadio are the largest growers in the Adelaide Hills, with 100 hectares of vineyards established on a Scott-Henry trellis producing 1000 tonnes of grapes a year, almost all sold to Penfolds, but with a small amount made into wine for sale under the Chain of Ponds label. The first vintage was 1993, and the wines first offered for sale in 1995. The full-flavoured white wines have enjoyed consistent show success, and the arrival of energetic Adelaide man-about-town Zar Brooks as general manager will doubtless ramp up the marketing of the brand. The Vineyard Balcony restaurant provides lunches on weekends and public holidays.

Chain of Ponds Semillon

🍷🍷🍷🍷½ **2000** Light to medium green-yellow; the bouquet is powerful, with strong herbal/grassy fruit and some mineral. The palate is tangy and crisp, with latent power, the flavours running through herb, grass and mineral. **rating:** 91

best drinking 2002–2006 **best vintages** '99, '00 **drink with** Sautéed calamari • $20

Chain of Ponds Sauvignon Blanc Semillon

YYYY½ **2000** Light green-yellow; a moderately aromatic bouquet has sweet citrus fruit waiting to be squeezed out of it; the palate has an attractive touch of stonefruit allied with more conventional citrus/lemon flavours; good length and style. **rating:** 90

best drinking Now–2005 **best vintages** '97, '98, '99 **drink with** Richer seafood dishes • $18

Chain of Ponds Chardonnay

YYYY **1999** Light to medium yellow-green; a stylish and subtle mix of fruit, oak and malolactic influences. On the palate nectarine fruit comes more to the fore together with touches of cashew and nicely controlled oak. **rating:** 89

best drinking Now–2004 **best vintages** '94, '97, '98 **drink with** Veal saltimbocca • $25

Chain of Ponds Ledge Shiraz

YYYY **1998** Medium red-purple; the powerful bouquet ranges through savoury, spicy and black cherry/berry aromas. The palate is finer and more restrained than the bouquet suggests it will be, with a hint of mint joining the fray, finishing with nicely balanced tannins. **rating:** 87

best drinking 2003–2008 **best vintages** NA **drink with** Duck and mushroom risotto • $33

Chain of Ponds Sangiovese

YYYY **1999** Light to medium red-purple; a clean, spicy, savoury bouquet leads into a palate with fine structure. Here, hints of cherry go alongside the brambly/savoury characters that are a varietal expression of the grape. **rating:** 86

best drinking 2002–2006 **best vintages** NA **drink with** Italian • $23

Chain of Ponds Amadeus Cabernet Sauvignon

YYYY **1998** Medium to full red-purple; a smooth and clean bouquet with a mix of red berry and redcurrant fruit, complexed with a touch of earth and dust. The palate is quite tight, with dark berry fruit flavours, still developing complexity, and supported by subtle oak. **rating:** 88

best drinking 2003–2008 **best vintages** '98 **drink with** Rib of beef • $25

chalk hill ★★★★

Field Street, McLaren Vale, SA 5171 **region** McLaren Vale
phone (08) 8556 2121 **fax** (08) 8556 2221 **open** Not
winemaker Contract **production** 2000 **est.** 1973
product range ($15–25 CD) Chardonnay, Shiraz, Cabernet Sauvignon.
summary Chalk Hill is in full flight again, drawing upon the 10 hectares of vineyards of grape-growing owners John and Di Harvey, who acquired Chalk Hill in 1996. Domestic distribution is solely through the cellar door and by mail order; a small portion is exported to the US.

Chalk Hill Shiraz

YYYY **1999** Medium purple-red; black cherry fruit and well-integrated and balanced vanilla oak aromas are followed by a palate with dark chocolate added to the mix, finishing with ripe tannins. **rating:** 88

best drinking 2003–2008 **best vintages** '97, '98 **drink with** Rich game dishes • $25

Chalk Hill Cabernet Sauvignon

YYYY½ **1999** Dense red-purple; deep, strong blackberry, olive, earth and vanilla aromas lead into a palate with sweet blackberry/blackcurrant fruit, soft tannins and controlled oak. **rating:** 90

best drinking 2004–2009 **best vintages** '99 **drink with** Leave it in the cellar • $25

chambers rosewood ★★★★☆

Barkley Street, Rutherglen, Vic 3685 **region** Rutherglen
phone (02) 6032 8641 **fax** (02) 6032 8101 **open** Mon–Sat 9–5, Sun 11–5
winemaker Bill Chambers **production** 10 000 **est.** 1858
product range ($8–150 CD) A wide range of table wines, including such rarities as a Riesling and Gouias blend, Blue Imperial (which is in fact Cinsaut) and a wide range of fortified wines. The supremely great wines are

the Rare Tokay and Rare Muscat, and the very good Special Muscat and Special Tokay. These are now offered in 375 ml bottles at prices that are starting to reflect their intrinsic value, and are rather higher than the prices for the same wines when last offered in 750 ml bottles.

summary The winery rating is given for the Muscats and Tokays and is in fact a compromise between the Special Muscat and Tokay (rated 'grand' under the Rutherglen Classification system) and the Rare wines, which are on a level all of their own, somewhere higher than five stars. The chief virtue of the table wines is that they are cheap. Exports to the US, the UK and Belgium.

Chambers Rosewood Botrytis Tokay

YYYY 2000 Medium to full yellow-gold; a complex bouquet with cumquat and some gingerbread aromas leads into a cumquat, peach and gingerbread palate finishing with good acidity. **rating:** 86

best drinking Now–2005 **best vintages** NA **drink with** Fruit tart • $19

Chambers Rosewood Rutherglen Tokay

YYYY NV Golden-brown. The bouquet is fresh, but there is a slight cosmetic edge, verging on dishwashing soap. The palate is better, with tea-leaf/fish-oil varietal character. **rating:** 83

best drinking Now **best vintages** NA **drink with** After-dinner biscuits • $12.50

chapel hill ★★★★☆

Chapel Hill Road, McLaren Vale, SA 5171 **region** McLaren Vale

phone (08) 8323 8429 **fax** (08) 8323 9245 **open** 7 days 12–5

winemaker Pam Dunsford (Consultant), Angela Meaney **production** 60 000 **est.** 1979

product range ($14–40 CD) Unwooded Chardonnay, Reserve Chardonnay, Verdelho, McLaren Vale Shiraz, The Vicar (Cabernet Shiraz), Reserve Cabernet Shiraz, McLaren Vale/Coonawarra Cabernet Sauvignon, Tawny Port.

summary A leading medium-sized winery in the region, due in part to capital provided by Adelaide-based Gerard Industries and, even more, to the skills of consultant winemaker Pam Dunsford. In the second half of 2000 Chapel Hill was sold to the diversified Swiss Thomas Schmidheiny group which owns the respected Cuvaison winery in California, as well as vineyards in Switzerland and Argentina. From my knowledge of Cuvaison stretching back 15 years or so, I am confident Chapel Hill is in safe hands.

Chapel Hill Reserve Chardonnay

YYYY 1999 Medium straw-yellow; the bouquet is solid, with ripe peach fruit, the palate similarly flavoursome, but somewhat unfocused. **rating:** 86

best drinking Now **best vintages** '91, '92, '93, '94, '97, '98 **drink with** Slow-cooked fresh salmon • $25

Chapel Hill Shiraz

YYYY 1998 Inky, dense colour; the bouquet is very concentrated, with fruit and oak vying for supremacy. The palate is typical of many of the highest-rated wines out of McLaren Vale, with an amazing depth of flavour that seems to have strong aphrodisiac qualities for American wine writers. For their effete Australian counterparts, cellaring for a minimum of five and preferably ten years seems sensible. **rating:** 89

best drinking 2005–2015 **best vintages** '91, '94, '95, '96 **drink with** Grilled calf's liver • $28

Chapel Hill The Vicar Cabernet Shiraz

YYYYY 1998 Medium red-purple; the bouquet is solid, with dark plum, berry and cassis fruit doing the work; a softly succulent palate follows, with more of that sweet plum, dark berry and chocolate fruit, with complementary oak and soft, ripe tannins. **rating:** 94

best drinking 2003–2013 **best vintages** '94, '96, '98 **drink with** Entrecôte of beef • $35

Chapel Hill McLaren Vale/Coonawarra Cabernet Sauvignon

YYYYY 1998 Medium to full red-purple; the bouquet has a mix of powerful savoury/earthy cabernet fruit together with a sweeter, more chocolatey component contributed by the McLaren Vale material. The palate is concentrated and weighty, with a mix of blackberry, currant and chocolate flavours; an excellent balance has been achieved between fruit and oak, and the wine can be approached without undue caution. **rating:** 90

best drinking 2005–2010 **best vintages** '88, '90, '91, '92, '95, '98 **drink with** Marinated beef • $25

chapman's creek vineyard NR

RMS 447 Yelverton Road, Willyabrup, WA 6280 **region** Margaret River
phone (08) 9755 7545 **fax** (08) 9755 7571 **open** 7 days 10.30–4.30
winemaker Various Contract **production** 5000 **est.** 1989
product range ($15–26 R) Chenin Blanc, Unoaked Chardonnay, Chardonnay, Merlot, Cabernet Merlot, Tawny Port.
summary Tony Lord is an extremely experienced wine journalist who for many years was editor and part-owner of *Decanter* magazine in the UK, one of the leaders in the field. He still writes for Australian magazines and newspapers and knows the industry extremely well. Notwithstanding this, he has been positively reclusive about Chapman's Creek Vineyard, which he owns. The few wines I have tasted have been excellent, fully reflecting the outstanding quality of the Willyabrup subregion of the Margaret River.

charles cimicky ★★★☆

Gomersal Road, Lyndoch, SA 5351 **region** Barossa Valley
phone (08) 8524 4025 **fax** (08) 8524 4772 **open** Tues–Sat 10.30–4.30
winemaker Charles Cimicky **production** 15 000 **est.** 1972
product range ($15–25 CD) Sauvignon Blanc, Chardonnay, Cabernet Franc, Classic Merlot, Cabernet Sauvignon, Signature Shiraz, Old Fireside Tawny Port.
summary These wines are of very good quality, thanks to the lavish (and sophisticated) use of new French oak in tandem with high-quality grapes. The intense, long-flavoured Sauvignon Blanc has been a particularly consistent performer, as has the rich, voluptuous American-oaked Signature Shiraz. Limited retail distribution in South Australia, Victoria, New South Wales and Western Australia, with exports to the UK, the US, Switzerland, Canada, Malaysia and Hong Kong.

charles melton ★★★★★

Krondorf Road, Tanunda, SA 5352 **region** Barossa Valley
phone (08) 8563 3606 **fax** (08) 8563 3422 **open** 7 days 11–5
winemaker Charlie Melton **production** 10 000 **est.** 1984
product range ($16.90–46.80 R) Rosé of Virginia, Grenache, Shiraz, Nine Popes (Shiraz Grenache Mourvedre), Cabernet Sauvignon, Sparkling Red, Sotto di Ferro (sweet white).
summary Charlie Melton, one of the Barossa Valley's great characters, with wife Virginia by his side, makes some of the most eagerly sought à la mode wines in Australia. Inevitably, the Melton empire grew in response to the insatiable demand, with a doubling of estate vineyards to 13 hectares (and the exclusive management and offtake of a further 10 hectares) and the erection of a new barrel store in 1996. The expanded volume has had no adverse effect on the wonderfully rich, sweet and well-made wines. Exports to the UK, Ireland, Switzerland, France, the US and Southeast Asia.

Charles Melton Sparkling Red

🍷🍷🍷🍷 **NV** Medium to full red-purple; a rich, complex bouquet with some licorice notes to the fruit, and also oak in a baroque style, is followed by a massively flavoured palate, which simply needs ten years on cork to loosen up and show its best. **rating:** 88

best drinking 2005–2010 **best vintages** NA **drink with** Borscht • $46.80

Charles Melton Sotto di Ferro

🍷🍷🍷🍷½ **1998** Full gold; a clean honey/honeycomb bouquet leads into a rich and intense palate with nuts, dried fruits and honey in a sumptuous cradle, finishing with appropriate acidity. **rating:** 90

best drinking Now **best vintages** NA **drink with** Cake and coffee • NA

Charles Melton Rosé of Virginia

🍷🍷🍷🍷½ **2000** If I was a dictator, I would punish those who don't buy this lovely wine by making them drink that ghastly Californian Blush. Vivid fuschia-purple, an aromatic mix of cherry and strawberry on the bouquet is followed by a lively palate with sweet, fresh red cherry-accented fruit before moving into a crisp, cleansing dry finish. **rating:** 93

best drinking Now **best vintages** '97, '98, '00 **drink with** Summer lunch of any kind • $16.80

charles reuben estate NR

777 Middle Tea Tree Road, Tea Tree, Tas 7017 **region** Southern Tasmania
phone (03) 6268 1702 **fax** (03) 6231 3571 **open** Wed–Sun 10–5
winemaker Tim Krushka **production** 350 **est.** 1990
product range ($15–22 CD) Riesling, Chardonnay, Unwooded Chardonnay, Pinot Noir.
summary Charles Reuben Estate has 1.5 hectares of pinot noir, 0.5 hectare of chardonnay and a few rows of riesling in production. It has also planted 1.2 hectares of the four Bordeaux varieties, headed by cabernet sauvignon with a little cabernet franc, merlot and petit verdot, and 0.6 hectare of sauvignon blanc accompanied by a few rows of semillon. The principal wines will be Pinot Noir, Chardonnay, a Bordeaux-blend red and a Sauvignon Blanc Semillon, although there is an element of trial in the plantings to establish which varieties succeed best on the estate.

charles sturt university winery ★★★☆

Boorooma Street, North Wagga Wagga, NSW 2650 **region** Southern New South Wales Zone
phone (02) 6933 2435 **fax** (02) 6933 4072 **open** Mon–Fri 11–5, weekends 11–4
winemaker Greg Gallagher **production** 15 000 **est.** 1977
product range ($10–22 R) The precise composition varies from one release to the next, but is divided into two sections: the top-of-the-range Limited Release Series (e.g. Cabernet Sauvignon Shiraz, Cowra Chardonnay, Méthode Champenoise, Cabernet Sauvignon, Botrytis Semillon, Liqueur Port and Liqueur Muscat); and a basic range of lower-priced varietals including Chardonnay, Traminer Riesling, Sauvignon Blanc Semillon and Cabernet Sauvignon Shiraz.
summary Between 1990 and 1996 winemaking at Charles Sturt University was carried out under the direction of Rodney Hooper, who managed to resolve the dual roles of producing commercial wines and teaching students with consummate skill. Subsequent vintages are not in the same class as those made by Hooper, although they do offer quite good value at their price points. The wines are exported to the US.

charley brothers 

The Ruins Way, Inneslake, Port Macquarie, NSW 2444 **region** Hastings River
phone (02) 6581 1332 **fax** (02) 6581 0391 **open** Mon–Fri 1–5, weekends 10–5
winemaker John Cassegrain (Contract), Nick Charley **production** 1000 **est.** 1988
product range ($11–16 CD) Semillon, Chardonnay, Summer White, Pinot Noir, Shiraz, Cabernet Merlot, Cabernet Sauvignon, Inneslake Mist.
summary The property upon which the Charley Brothers vineyard is established has been in the family's ownership since the early 1900s but in fact had been planted to vines by a Major Innes in the 1840s. After carrying on logging and fruit-growing at various times, the Charley family planted vines in 1988 with the encouragement of John Cassegrain. Around 7.5 hectares of vines have been established.

charlotte plains NR

RMB 3180, Dooleys Road, Maryborough, Vic 3465 **region** Bendigo
phone (03) 5361 3137 **open** By appointment
winemaker Roland Kaval **production** 80 **est.** 1990
product range ($16 ML) Shiraz.
summary Charlotte Plains is a classic example of miniaturism. Production comes from a close-planted vineyard that is only one-third of a hectare, a quarter being shiraz, the remainder sauvignon blanc. The minuscule production is sold solely through the mailing list and by phone.

chateau doré NR

Mandurang Road, via Bendigo, Vic 3551 **region** Bendigo
phone (03) 5439 5278 **open** Tues–Sun 10–6
winemaker Ivan Gross **production** 1000 **est.** 1860
product range ($9–14 CD) Riesling, Shiraz, Cabernet Sauvignon, Tawny Port.
summary Has been in the ownership of the Gross family since 1860, with the winery buildings dating back respectively to 1860 and 1893. All wine is sold through cellar door.

chateau dorrien NR

Cnr Seppeltsfield Road and Barossa Valley Way, Dorrien, SA 5352 **region** Barossa Valley
phone (08) 8562 2850 **fax** (08) 8562 1416 **open** 7 days 10–5
winemaker Fernando Martin **production** 2000 **est.** 1983
product range ($10–18 CD) Riesling, Semillon Chardonnay, Traminer, Frontignac Traminer, Frontignac Spaetlese, Late Harvest Frontignac, Semillon Chardonnay Sparkling Brut, Prima Vera (light red), Limited Release Grenache, Shiraz, Cabernet Sauvignon, Tawny Port.
summary Unashamedly and successfully directed at the tourist trade.

chateau francois ★★★

Broke Road, Pokolbin, NSW 2321 **region** Lower Hunter Valley
phone (02) 4998 7548 **fax** (02) 4998 7805 **open** Weekends 9–5 or by appointment
winemaker Don Francois **production** 700 **est.** 1969
product range ($11 ML) Pokolbin Mallee Semillon, Chardonnay, Shiraz Pinot Noir.
summary The retirement hobby of former NSW Director of Fisheries, Don Francois. Soft-flavoured and structured wines that frequently show regional characters but which are modestly priced and are all sold through the cellar door and mailing list to a loyal following. The tasting room is available for private dinners for 12–16 people. Don Francois sailed through a quadruple-bypass followed by a mild stroke with his sense of humour intact, if not enhanced. A subsequent newsletter said (inter alia) '… my brush with destiny has changed my grizzly personality and I am now sweetness and light … Can you believe? Well, almost!' He even promises comfortable tasting facilities.

chateau hornsby NR

Petrick Road, Alice Springs, NT 0870 **region** Alice Springs
phone (08) 8955 5133 **fax** (08) 8955 5133 **open** 7 days 11–4
winemaker Gordon Cook **production** 1000 **est.** 1976
product range ($12–17 CD) Riesling, Semillon, Chardonnay, Shiraz, Cabernet Sauvignon.
summary Draws in part upon 3 hectares of estate plantings, and in part from grapes and wines purchased from other regions. Very much a tourist-oriented operation, with numerous allied entertainments on offer.

chateau leamon ★★★☆

5528 Calder Highway, Bendigo, Vic 3550 **region** Bendigo
phone (03) 5447 7995 **fax** (03) 5447 0855 **open** Wed–Mon 10–5
winemaker Ian Leamon **production** 2000 **est.** 1973
product range ($15–30 CD) Riesling, Semillon, Chardonnay, Shiraz, Reserve Shiraz, Cabernet Merlot.
summary After a period of uncertainty, Chateau Leamon is (a little tentatively) returning to some of its former glory. Ian Leamon is using locally grown grapes but is also looking to the Strathbogie Ranges for grapes for other wines, including Pinot Noir. Limited retail distribution in Victoria and Queensland; exports to Asia and the US.

Chateau Leamon Semillon

TTTT **2000** Medium yellow-green; the bouquet is slightly broad, but quite complex, and the oak is not too obtrusive. The palate has plenty of presence and grip, with lemony fruit supported by a touch of spicy oak.
rating: 86

best drinking Now–2005 **best vintages** NA **drink with** Calamari • NA

Chateau Leamon Reserve Shiraz

TTTY **1999** Medium to full red-purple; the bouquet is complex, but strongly driven by lemon and vanilla oak, the palate even more subjugated by the oak. Made in the same style as the '98, so one can only assume it is receiving strong market acceptance. I just wish there were more wines like the lovely '97. **rating:** 84

best drinking 2004–2009 **best vintages** '97 **drink with** Rich game • NA

Chateau Leamon Reserve Cabernet Sauvignon

TTTT **1999** Medium red-purple; the moderately sweet bouquet has a mix of mint and dark berry fruit aromas, the palate a ripe mix of dark chocolate and berry fruit; the tannins are soft, and, happily, the oak subtle. **rating:** 87

best drinking 2004–2009 **best vintages** NA **drink with** Leg of lamb • NA

chateau pato ★★★★☆

Thompson's Road, Pokolbin, NSW 2321 **region** Lower Hunter Valley
phone (02) 4998 7634 **fax** (02) 4998 7860 **open** By appointment
winemaker Nicholas Paterson **production** 300 **est.** 1980
product range ($18–25CD) Pinot Noir, Shiraz.
summary Nicholas and Roger Paterson took over responsibility for this tiny winery following the death of their father, David Paterson, during the 1993 vintage. Two and a half hectares of shiraz, 1 hectare of chardonnay and 0.5 hectare of pinot noir; most of the grapes are sold, with a tiny quantitiy of shiraz being made into a marvellous wine. On all the evidence, David Paterson's inheritance is being handsomely guarded.

Chateau Pato Shiraz

1999 Full red-purple; the clean bouquet has solid, deep dark fruit aromas supported by a touch of oak; the palate has an abundance of rich, sweet plummy fruit, but is not the least extractive, thanks to good tannin and oak management. **rating:** 93

best drinking 2004–2009 **best vintages** '86, '87, '90, '91, '94, '98, '99 **drink with** Barbecued beef • NA

chateau tanunda NR

9 Basedow Road, Tanunda, SA 5352 **region** Barossa Valley
phone (08) 8563 3888 **fax** (08) 8563 1422 **open** 7 days 10–5
winemaker Simon Gilbert, Ralph Fowler (Contract) **production** 8000 **est.** 1890
product range ($14–36 CD) The Chateau Riesling, Chardonnay, Shiraz and Cabernet Sauvignon; Chateau Cadet Frontignac, Chardonnay, Cabernet Rose, Shiraz, Merlot, Cabernet Sauvignon Shiraz, Shiraz, Cabernet Sauvignon.
summary This is one of the most imposing winery buildings in the Barossa Valley, built from stone quarried at nearby Bethany in the late 1880s. It started life as a winery, then became a specialist brandy distillery until the death of the Australian brandy industry, whereafter it was simply used as storage cellars. It has now been completely restored, and converted into a major convention facility catering for groups up to 400. The large complex also houses a cellar door where the Chateau Tanunda wines are sold; Chateau Bistro, gardens and a croquet lawn; the Barossa Small Winemakers Centre offering wines made by small independent winemakers in the region; and, finally, specialist support services for tour operators.

chatsfield ★★★★

O'Neil Road, Mount Barker, WA 6324 **region** Great Southern
phone (08) 9851 1704 **fax** (08) 9851 1704 **open** Tues–Sun, public holidays 10.30–4.30
winemaker Rob Lee, John Wade (Consultant) **production** 6000 **est.** 1976
product range ($14–19 CD) Mount Barker Riesling, Gewurztraminer, Chardonnay, Cabernet Franc, Shiraz.
summary Irish-born medical practitioner Ken Lynch can be proud of his achievements at Chatsfield, as can most of the various contract-winemakers who have taken the high-quality estate-grown material and made some impressive wines, notably the Riesling, vibrant Cabernet Franc (as an unwooded nouveau style) and spicy licorice Shiraz. It has to be said, however, there is an element of the unpredictable in some of the wines. Exports to Ireland, the UK, the US, Canada, Japan, Hong Kong and Singapore.

Chatsfield Mount Barker Riesling

1998 Medium yellow-green; the bouquet is highly aromatic, with a mix of toast and lime aromas. The palate is as intense as the bouquet promises, with lime on toast flavours, and a long, crisp acid finish. **rating:** 89

best drinking 2000–2005 **best vintages** '85, '87, '89, '90, '93, '94, '96 **drink with** Spring salads • $18.99

Chatsfield Chardonnay

2000 Light to medium yellow-green; fresh, light melon and nectarine aromas on the bouquet lead into an appealing, light to medium bodied palate with identical fruit flavours, and surprisingly little impact from the oak. **rating:** 85

best drinking Now **best vintages** '87, '89, '90, '93, '97 **drink with** Grilled scampi • NA

Chatsfield Shiraz

TTTT **1999** Medium purple-red; bright, spicy/earthy/berry/cherry fruit on the bouquet changes course slightly on the palate, with predominantly cherry-flavoured fruit joined by touches of mint and leaf. A nice, cool-climate style, with subtle oak. **rating:** 87

TTTTY **1998** Medium to full red-purple; complex, ripe plum/licorice/berry aromas and flavours, with slightly savoury undertones, run through the bouquet and palate. Fully representative of a successful vintage in the region. **rating:** 92

best drinking 2003–2007 **best vintages** '88, '89, '90, '94, '95, '98 **drink with** Mature cheddar, finer red meat dishes • NA

chepstowe vineyard NR

Fitzpatricks Lane, Carngham, Vic 3351 **region** Ballarat
phone (03) 5344 9412 **fax** (03) 5344 9403 **open** 7 days 10–5
winemaker John Ellis (Contract) **production** 700 **est.** 1994
product range ($25–30 CD) Chardonnay, Pinot Noir.
summary Way back in 1983 Bill Wallace asked the then Yellowglen winemaker Dominique Landragin what he thought about the suitability of a block of steeply sloping grazing land on the side of the Chepstowe Hill, looking northeast across to the Grampians and its various mountains, including Mount Misery. Landragin replied, 'It might be possible to grow grapes there', and Wallace subsequently acquired the property. It was not until November 1994 that 1 hectare each of pinot noir and chardonnay was planted, followed by an additional hectare of pinot noir in 1996. In the warmest of vintages it is possible to obtain full ripeness for table wines, but in normal years I suspect sparkling wine (of potentially high quality) might be the best option.

Chepstowe Vineyard Pinot Noir

TTTT **1999** Dark red; deep, dark plum and spice aromas on the bouquet lead into a rich, plummy and ripe palate with spicy tones, good acidity and appropriately fine tannins. A landmark vintage for Chepstowe. **rating:** 87

best drinking Now–2005 **best vintages** '99 **drink with** Teriyaki chicken • $30

chestnut grove ★★★★

Chestnut Grove Road, Manjimup, WA 6258 **region** Manjimup
phone (08) 9772 4345 **fax** (08) 9772 4543 **open** Mon–Sat 10–4, Sunday by appointment
winemaker Kim Horton **production** 9000 **est.** 1988
product range ($15–37 CD) Chardonnay, Reserve Chardonnay, Sauvignon Blanc, Verdelho, Pinot Noir, Cabernet Merlot, Merlot, Vermilion, Platinum.
summary A substantial vineyard that is now reaching maturity and the erection of an on-site winery are the most obvious signs of change, but ownership, too, has been passed on by founder Vic Kordic to his sons Paul (a Perth lawyer) and Mark (who is the general manager of the wine business).

Chestnut Grove Verdelho

TTTT **2000** Light straw-green; light, soft, ripe fruit salad fruit is offset by a touch of mineral on the bouquet; there is more of the same soft, sweet, ripe fruit salad varietal fruit flavour on the easygoing palate. **rating:** 88

best drinking Now **best vintages** '97 **drink with** Asian seafood • $18

Chestnut Grove Reserve Chardonnay

TTTY **1999** Light straw-green; the bouquet has a light charry/smoky edge to the grapefruit and melon aromas; the palate has some length and concentration, but is still on the delicate side. **rating:** 84

best drinking Now–2003 **best vintages** NA **drink with** Light seafood • $21.60

Chestnut Grove Pinot Noir

TTTT **1999** Medium red; the bouquet is clean, with a slightly foresty/earthy edge to the cherry and plum fruit; the palate opens with plenty of solid plum fruit, but does tail away slightly on the finish. Pretty pricey. **rating:** 85

best drinking Now–2003 **best vintages** NA **drink with** Pot-roasted quail • $37

Chestnut Grove Merlot

TTTTT **1999** Medium red-purple; the fragrant bouquet announces an unusually fine example of the variety, with olive, spice and cedar flavours running through a long, intense palate. The oak is well balanced, and there is no lack of concentration. **rating:** 94

best drinking 2002–2008 **best vintages** '99 **drink with** Milk-fed veal • NA

Chestnut Grove Cabernet Merlot

🍷🍷🍷🍷 **1999** Medium red-purple; a mix of berry, mint, leaf and spice on the bouquet is followed by a quite potent palate with minty/berry/leafy flavours together with a touch of bitter chocolate. **rating:** 83

best drinking 2002–2005 **best vintages** '95 **drink with** Lamb's fry • $20.10

chestnut hill vineyard NR

1280 Pakenham Road, Mount Burnett, Vic 3781 **region** Gippsland
phone (03) 5942 7314 **fax** (03) 5942 7314 **open** Weekends and public holidays 10.30–5.30, or by appointment
winemaker Charlie Javor **production** 1100 **est.** 1995
product range ($15–18 CD) Chardonnay, Sauvignon Blanc, Shiraz.
summary Charlie and Ivka Javor started Chestnut Hill with small plantings of chardonnay and shiraz in 1985 and have slowly increased the vineyards to their present total of a little over 3 hectares. The first wines were made in 1995, and all distribution is through the cellar door and direct to a few restaurants. Situated less than one hour's drive from Melbourne, the picturesque vineyard is situated among the rolling hills in the southeast of the Dandenongs near Mount Burnett. The wines reflect the cool climate.

chislett's lachlan valley wines NR

Wandary Lane, Forbes, NSW 2871 **region** Lachlan Valley
phone (02) 6852 3983 **open** By appointment
winemaker Frank Chislett **production** NA **est.** 1920
product range Chardonnay, Riesling, Semillon, Shiraz, Pinot Noir, Cabernet Sauvignon.
summary The Chislett family (Frank, Les and Annette) have been quietly making wines in a century-old winery since the 1920s, but the wines are seldom, if ever, seen outside cellar door.

chittering estate NR

Chittering Valley Road, Lower Chittering, WA 6084 **region** Greater Perth Zone
phone (08) 9273 6255 **fax** (08) 9273 6101 **open** Weekends and public holidays 11–4.30 (Apr–Dec)
winemaker Francois Jacquard **production** 12 000 **est.** 1982
product range ($14.90–21 R) Chardonnay, Hill Top Reserve Chardonnay, Semillon Sauvignon Blanc, Pinot Noir, Cabernet Merlot, Hill Top Reserve Cabernet Sauvignon.
summary Chittering Estate was sold in late 1997, and no information has been forthcoming about its new owner's intentions.

ciavarella ★★★

Evans Lane, Oxley, Vic 3678 **region** King Valley
phone (03) 5727 3384 **fax** (03) 5727 3384 **open** Mon–Sat 9–6, Sun 10–6
winemaker Cyril Ciavarella **production** 3000 **est.** 1978
product range ($13–18 CD) Semillon, Verdelho, Chardonnay, Sweet White, Rosé, Durif, Dolcino (medium-bodied sweet red), Shiraz, Cabernet Sauvignon.
summary Cyril and Jan Ciavarella both entered the wine industry from other professions and have been producing wine since 1992. The vineyard was planted in 1978, with plantings and varieties being extended over the years. One variety, aucerot (first release in 375 ml bottles late 2001) was produced by Maurice O'Shea of McWilliam's Mount Pleasant in the Hunter Valley 50 or more years ago; the Ciavarella vines have been grown from cuttings collected from an old Glenrowan vineyard before the parent plants were removed in the mid-1980s.

Ciavarella Cabernet Sauvignon

🍷🍷🍷🍷 **1999** Medium red-purple; there is an array of leafy/earthy/foresty overtones to the berry fruit; the light to medium bodied palate has modest berry fruit and a mildly astringent finish. Overall, there seemed to be some shaded canopy/yield issues. **rating:** 82

best drinking 2002–2004 **best vintages** NA **drink with** Roast lamb • $17

clarendon hills ★★★★☆

Brookmans Road, Blewitt Springs, SA 5171 **region** McLaren Vale
phone (08) 8364 1484 **fax** (08) 8364 1484 **open** By appointment
winemaker Roman Bratasiuk **production** 18 000 **est.** 1989
product range ($60–175 R) Hickinbotham Vineyard Semillon, Chardonnay (from the Norton Summit, Kangarilla and Hickinbotham Vineyards), Hickinbotham Vineyard Pinot Noir, Old Vine Grenache (from the Kangarilla, Blewitt Springs Hickinbotham, Romas Vineyards), Shiraz (Hickinbotham, Piggott Range, Liandra, Brookman, Moritz Vineyards), Astralis, Merlot from the Brookman and Hickinbotham Vineyards and Cabernet Sauvignon from the Brookman, Sandown and Hickinbotham Vineyards.
summary Clarendon Hills produces some of the most startlingly concentrated, rich and full-bodied red wines to be found in Australia, rivalled in this respect only by Wendouree. Roman Bratasiuk is a larger-than-life figure who makes larger-than-life wines. Technocrats may quibble about this or that aspect, but influential judges such as Robert Parker have neither reservations about nor problems with the immense, brooding red wines that Bratasiuk regularly produces from the small patches of old, low-yielding vines that he ferrets out. Moreover, even the technocrats were silenced by the technical excellence of the 1998 vintage wines, all of which were matured in new oak. Exports to New Zealand, the US, Canada, Germany, Switzerland, Belgium, the Netherlands, Sweden, the UK and Japan.

Clarendon Hills Piggott Range Shiraz

YYYYY **1998** Medium to full purple-red; a complex bouquet with a mix of berry, spice and game has Rhône overtones, and also potent oak. The bouquet is flooded with rich, complex, luscious berry fruit that easily sustains the new oak; still a baby. **rating:** 94
best drinking 2003–2013 **best vintages** '98 **drink with** Seared beef • $120

Clarendon Hills Hickinbotham Cabernet Sauvignon

YYYY **1998** Medium to full red-purple; lusciously sweet dark berry/cassis/plum fruit with a touch of spice and gentle oak on the bouquet is followed by a palate with abundant sweet berry fruit on entry, then pronounced savoury tannins on the finish. **rating:** 92
best drinking 2003–2013 **best vintages** '98 **drink with** Kangaroo fillet • $90

clearview estate mudgee NR

Cnr Sydney and Rocky Water Hole Roads, Mudgee, NSW 2850 **region** Mudgee
phone (02) 6372 4546 **fax** (02) 6372 7577 **open** Fri–Mon 10–4, or by appointment
winemaker Joe Lesnik **production** 2200 **est.** 1995
product range ($14–19 CD) Church Creek Chardonnay (oaked and unoaked); Rocky Waterhole Red Shiraz and Cabernet Sauvignon.
summary No relationship with the famous Hawke's Bay winery, but doubtless John E Hickey would be delighted to achieve the same quality. They have progressively planted 4.16 hectares of shiraz, 2.16 hectares each of chardonnay and cabernet sauvignon, 1.5 hectares of merlot, and small amounts of cabernet franc, semillon, pinot grigio, barbera and sangiovese (yet to come into bearing) since 1995, and send the grapes to the Hunter Valley for contract-making. An 'Aussie Farm'-style cellar door, with a timber deck looking out over the vineyard and surrounding vista, was opened in September 2000. Exports to the US.

clemens hill NR

686 Richmond Road, Cambridge, Tas 7170 **region** Southern Tasmania
phone (03) 6248 5985 **fax** (03) 6231 6222 **open** By appointment
winemaker Andrew Hood (Contract) **production** 500 **est.** 1994
product range ($16 CD) Sauvignon Blanc, Chardonnay, Pinot Noir.
summary Owned by Kevin and Jacqueline Wagner, whose son Ben Wagner is one of Tasmania's foremost viticulturists. 1998 was the first vintage, and both it and 1999 have produced wines of show-medal quality. It has 0.5 hectare each of sauvignon blanc and pinot noir and 0.2 hectare of chardonnay.

Clemens Hill Sauvignon Blanc

YYY **2000** Medium yellow-green; as is usual, the influence of the oak has been kept nicely in check; a slightly herbaceous bouquet leads into a smooth, medium-bodied, moderately intense palate with touches of gooseberry and herb; well balanced. **rating:** 84
best drinking Now **best vintages** NA **drink with** Shellfish • $16

cleveland ★★★☆

Shannons Road, Lancefield, Vic 3435 **region** Macedon Ranges
phone (03) 5429 1449 **fax** (03) 5429 2017 **open** 7 days 9–5
winemaker Keith Brien **production** 2500 **est.** 1985
product range ($10–45 CD) Macedon Brut, Brut Rose, Chardonnay, Pinot Noir, Heathcote Shiraz, Cabernet Merlot; Brien Family Chardonnay Gordo and Muscat Gordo Blanco.
summary The Cleveland homestead was built in 1889 in the style of a Gothic Revival manor house but had been abandoned for 40 years when purchased by the Briens in 1983. It has since been painstakingly restored, and 3.8 hectares of surrounding vineyard established. Cleveland has done best with Pinot Noir and Chardonnay, but the occasional Cabernet Sauvignon attests to an unusually favourable vineyard site in a very cool region. Exports to the UK.

Cleveland Macedon Chardonnay

🍷🍷🍷🍸 **1998** Light to medium yellow-green; the bouquet is still youthful and tight, with slightly grassy edges to the aroma; the palate has light citrussy/melon fruit, the wine suggesting it will be long-lived but may never really evolve. **rating:** 84
best drinking Now–2008 **best vintages** NA **drink with** Light seafood • $24

Cleveland Macedon Brut

🍷🍷🍷🍷 **1996** Excellent appearance; light green-yellow with a fine mousse. The clean and fresh bouquet has a mix of citrus, mineral and apple aromas, the palate similarly clean, fresh and lively, with excellent length. The acidity is just a fraction high, which seems to cut back the complexity. **rating:** 88
best drinking Now–2005 **best vintages** NA **drink with** Oysters • $35

Cleveland Heathcote Shiraz

🍷🍷🍷🍷 **1999** Dense purple-red; the bouquet is rich, dense, ripe and luscious, oozing sweet plum fruit. The palate is massively concentrated and, not surprisingly, the tannins are slightly extractive, but should settle down with enough bottle age. **rating:** 89
best drinking 2004–2014 **best vintages** '99 **drink with** Barbecued rump steak • $24

cliff house

57 Camms Road, Kayena, Tas 7270 **region** Northern Tasmania
phone (03) 6394 7454 **fax** (03) 6394 7454 **open** By appointment
winemaker Julian Alcorso (Contract) **production** 2500 **est.** 1983
product range ($18–20 R) Riesling, Chardonnay, Pinot Noir, Devil's Elbow (Pinot Cabernet blend), Cabernet Sauvignon.
summary Cliff House has undergone a metamorphosis. In 1999 Geoff and Cheryl Hewitt sold the 4-hectare vineyard they established in the Tamar Valley area in 1983. They have now turned a two-hole golf course around their house into a second, new vineyard, planted to riesling and pinot noir. Until this comes into production they will sell their remaining stocks of wine contract-made from the old plantings.

clonakilla

Crisps Lane, Murrumbateman, NSW 2582 **region** Canberra District
phone (02) 6227 5877 **fax** (02) 6227 5871 **open** 7 days 11–5
winemaker Tim Kirk **production** 3500 **est.** 1971
product range ($16–36 CD) Riesling, Chardonnay, Semillon Sauvignon Blanc, Viognier, Shiraz Viognier, Cabernet Merlot.
summary The indefatigable Tim Kirk, who has many of the same personality characteristics as Frank Tate (of Evans & Tate), has taken over the management of Clonakilla from father and scientist Dr John Kirk. The quality of the wines is excellent, none more so than the highly regarded Shiraz Viognier, which sells out quickly every year. Exports to the US, the UK, Canada and Asia.

Clonakilla Riesling

🍷🍷🍷🍷 **2000** Light to medium yellow-green; the bouquet is fragrant, with aromatic lime and herb notes; there is markedly sweet fruit on the mid-palate, veering towards tropical and passionfruit; good length. **rating:** 89
best drinking Now–2005 **best vintages** '91, '93, '94, '95, '97, '00 **drink with** Spiced Asian dishes • $18

Clonakilla Viognier

ΨΨΨΨΨ **2000** Vibrant, light to medium green-yellow; the bouquet has quite distinctive fruit varietal character, with a mix of lychee and mandarin blossom, aromas that carry on to an equally distinctive palate with mandarin/lychee flavours; well balanced. **rating:** 93

best drinking Now–2003 **best vintages** '00 **drink with** Carpaccio of salmon • $30

Clonakilla Shiraz Viognier

ΨΨΨΨΨ **1999** Medium red-purple; a fragrant, spicy and elegant bouquet with a nice touch of French oak is followed by a palate with more depth and richness, with concentrated black cherry and spice, and nicely judged oak. Due to the frost, only 1 tonne to the acre, but the wine retains elegance and style. **rating:** 94

best drinking 2003–2009 **best vintages** '90, '92, '93, '94, '95, '97, '98, '99 **drink with** Jugged hare • $36

Clonakilla Cabernet Merlot

ΨΨΨΨ **1999** Medium red-purple; the bouquet offers a mix of ripe and more savoury notes, but smooth right out on the palate where sweet, polished red berry and plum fruit is supported by soft, ripe tannins. **rating:** 88

best drinking 2002–2007 **best vintages** '97 **drink with** Tea-smoked lamb • $24

clos clare NR

Government Road, Watervale, SA 5452 **region** Clare Valley
phone (08) 8843 0161 **fax** (08) 8843 0161 **open** Weekends and public holidays 10–5
winemaker Various Contract **production** 1000 **est.** 1993
product range ($15–23.50 CD) Riesling, Shiraz.
summary Clos Clare is based on a small (1.5-hectare) unirrigated section of the original Florita Vineyard once owned by Leo Buring and which produces Riesling of extraordinary concentration and power. Exports to the US and Canada.

Clos Clare Riesling

ΨΨΨΨ **2000** Light to medium yellow-green; quite intense herb and mineral fruit aromas are accompanied by a slightly bready/yeasty character that seems to be part and parcel of many of the Clare Valley Rieslings of the 2000 vintage. The palate is very flavoursome, with plenty of fruit, and just an echo of the yeast character of the bouquet. **rating:** 84

best drinking 2002–2005 **best vintages** NA **drink with** Thai cuisine • $16.50

Clos Clare Shiraz

ΨΨΨΨΨ **1999** Dense purple-red; a big, powerful, concentrated bouquet in an earthy/oaky style is followed by a sumptuously rich, essencey, berry and dark chocolate-flavoured palate that is not too tannic or extractive. **rating:** 95

best drinking 2002–2012 **best vintages** '99 **drink with** Vension ragout • $23.50

clovely estate NR

Steinhardts Road, Moffatdale, via Murgon, Qld 4605 **region** South Burnett
phone (07) 3876 5200 **fax** (07) 3876 5200 **open** 7 days 10–5
winemaker David Lowe, Adam Chapman (Contract) **production** 15 000 **est.** 1998
product range ($12.95–14.95 CD) Left Field Semillon Chardonnay, Chardonnay, Shiraz; Fifth Row Chardonnay, Shiraz Cabernet.
summary Although newly born, Clovely Estate has the largest vineyards in Queensland, having established 174 hectares of vines at two locations just to the east of Murgon in the Burnett Valley. There are 127 hectares of red grapes (including 74 hectares of shiraz) and 47 hectares of white grapes. The attractively packaged wines are sold in four tiers: Clovely Estate at the top end, and which will not be produced every year; Left Field, strongly fruity and designed to age; Fifth Row, for early drinking; and Outback, primarily designed for the export market.

clover hill ★★★★☆

Clover Hill Road, Lebrina, Tas 7254 **region** Northern Tasmania
phone (03) 6395 6114 **fax** (03) 6395 6257 **open** 7 days 10–5, by appointment in winter
winemaker Shane Clohesy, Chris Markell **production** 4000 **est.** 1986
product range ($33 R) Clover Hill (Sparkling).

summary Clover Hill was established by Taltarni in 1986 for the sole purpose of making a premium sparkling wine. Its 20 hectares of vineyards, comprising 12 hectares of chardonnay, 6.5 hectares of pinot noir and 1.5 hectares of pinot meunier, are still coming into bearing, and production is steadily increasing. Wine quality is excellent, combining finesse with power and length.

Clover Hill

🍷🍷🍷🍷🍷 **1997** Light straw-green; a complex, tight bouquet with spicy touches, almost clove-like; a tight, citrussy, long, lively and lingering palate follows. **rating:** 90

best drinking Now–2004 **best vintages** '90, '91, '92, '95, '96 **drink with** Caviar, shellfish • NA

coalville vineyard ★★★

RMB 4750 Moe South Road, Moe South, Vic 3825 **region** Gippsland
phone (03) 5127 4229 **fax** (03) 5127 2148 **open** 7 days 10–5
winemaker Peter Beasley **production** 250 **est.** 1985
product range ($15 ML) A single wine, predominantly Cabernet Sauvignon with a little Cabernet Franc, Malbec and Merlot, labelled Coalville Red.
summary This is the new name for Mair's Coalville, following the sale of the property by Dr Stewart Mair to Peter Beasley. I am unaware of any other changes.

cobanov NR

Stock Road, Herne Hill, WA 6056 **region** Swan District
phone (08) 9296 4210 **open** Wed–Sun 9–5.30
winemaker Steve Cobanov **production** 10 000 **est.** 1960
product range ($6–10 CD) Chenin Blanc, Chardonnay, Sauvignon Blanc, Verdelho, Shiraz, Grenache, Cabernet Sauvignon.
summary A substantial family-owned operation producing a mix of bulk and bottled wine from 21 hectares of estate grapes. Part of the annual production is sold as grapes to other producers, including Houghton; part is sold in bulk; part is sold in 2-litre flagons, and the remainder in modestly priced bottles.

cobaw ridge ★★★★☆

31 Perc Boyer's Lane, East Pastoria via Kyneton, Vic 3444 **region** Macedon Ranges
phone (03) 5423 5227 **fax** (03) 5423 5227 **open** 7 days 10–5
winemaker Alan Cooper **production** 1400 **est.** 1985
product range ($28–45 CD) Chardonnay, Lagrein, Shiraz, Shiraz Viognier.
summary Nelly and Alan Cooper have established Cobaw Ridge's 6-hectare vineyard at an altitude of 610 metres in the hills above Kyneton complete with self-constructed pole-framed mudbrick house and winery. The plantings of cabernet sauvignon have been removed and partially replaced by lagrein, a variety that sent me scuttling to Jancis Robinson's seminal book on grape varieties, from which I learned it is a northeast Italian variety typically used to make delicate Rosé, but at Cobaw Ridge it is made into an impressive full-bodied dry red.

Cobaw Ridge Chardonnay

🍷🍷🍷🍷 **1999** Medium yellow-green; the bouquet offers fine but positive melon fruit, backed with subtle oak. There is nicely ripened melon and peach providing a positively sweet mid-palate (fruit, not sugar, sweet) and a gentle, nutty finish. **rating:** 88

best drinking Now–2004 **best vintages** '99 **drink with** Honey chicken • $28

Cobaw Ridge Shiraz

🍷🍷🍷🍷 **1999** Medium purple-red; clean, fresh cherry, spice and earth aromas lead into a lively palate, with similar flavours to the bouquet, and an attractive filigreed texture. Subtle oak. **rating:** 89

best drinking 2002–2008 **best vintages** '97, '99 **drink with** Rare beef • $31

Cobaw Ridge Lagrein

🍷🍷🍷🍷🍷 **1999** Full red-purple; the bouquet offers intriguing, warm, spicy characters allied with a touch of chocolate; there is sweet, small berry fruit, spice and chocolate intermingling on the palate with supple tannins. Not surprising the wine was so successful. **rating:** 90

best drinking 2002–2006 **best vintages** '99 **drink with** Braised ox cheek • $45

cobbitty wines NR

Cobbitty Road, Cobbitty, NSW 2570 **region** South Coast Zone
phone (02) 4651 2281 **fax** (02) 4651 2671 **open** Mon–Sat 10–5, Sun 12–6
winemaker Giovanni Cogno **production** 5000 **est.** 1964
product range ($5–14 CD) A full range of generic table, fortified and sparkling wines under the Cobbitty Wines label; also cocktail wines.
summary Draws upon 10 hectares of estate plantings of muscat, barbera, grenache and trebbiano, relying very much on local and ethnic custom.

cockfighter's ghost vineyard ★★★☆

Lot 251 Milbrodale Road, Broke, NSW 2330 **region** Lower Hunter Valley
phone (02) 9667 1622 **fax** (02) 9667 1442 **open** Not
winemaker Various Contract **production** 15 000 **est.** 1994
product range ($16.50–28.50 R) Semillon, Verdelho, Unwooded Chardonnay, Chardonnay, Pinot Noir, Shiraz, Coonawarra Premium Reserve Cabernet Sauvignon.
summary Like Poole's Rock Vineyard, owned by eminent Sydney merchant banker David Clarke but run and marketed as a separate venture, with lower wine prices. The wine has retail distribution throughout Australia, and is exported to the UK and the US.

Cockfighter's Ghost Semillon

ΥΥΥΥ **1999** Medium yellow-green; there are the first signs of toasty notes starting to appear on the lifted bouquet, and there is plenty happening through the fresh, lime/lemon/herb palate, which is in the transition phase between young and mature Semillon. **rating:** 86

best drinking 2003–2008 **best vintages** '96, '98 **drink with** Fresh asparagus • $16.50

Cockfighter's Ghost Vineyard Coonawarra Premium Reserve Cabernet Sauvignon

ΥΥΥΥ **1998** Medium to full red-purple; the bouquet has positive earthy/berry varietal character, supported by nicely judged oak. The medium-bodied palate is clean and direct, with no frills, but has length and development potential. **rating:** 85

best drinking 2003–2010 **best vintages** '98 **drink with** Seared beef • $28.50

cofield wines ★★★☆

Distillery Road, Wahgunyah, Vic 3687 **region** Rutherglen
phone (02) 6033 3798 **fax** (02) 6033 0798 **open** Mon–Sat 9–5, Sun 10–5
winemaker Max Cofield, Damien Cofield **production** 7000 **est.** 1990
product range ($12–25 CD) Riesling, Chenin Blanc, Semillon, Semillon Chardonnay, Chardonnay, Late Harvest Muscadelle, Shiraz, Merlot, Cabernet Sauvignon, Cabernet Merlot, Sparkling, Fortified.
summary District veteran Max Cofield, together with wife Karen and sons Damien, Ben and Andrew, is developing a strong cellar-door sales base by staging in-winery functions with guest chefs, and also providing a large barbecue and picnic area. (The Pickled Sisters Cafe is open for lunch Wed–Mon; telephone (02) 6033 2377.) The quality of the red wines, in particular, is good and improving all the time. Limited retail distribution in Melbourne and Tasmania.

Cofield Rutherglen Merlot

ΥΥΥΥ **1999** Medium red-purple; the bouquet offers quite pronounced varietal character with a mix of olive/savoury/spicy notes that carry through onto the palate; despite the egg-white fining, the tannins are a touch abrasive on the finish. **rating:** 84

best drinking 2004–2009 **best vintages** NA **drink with** Veal piccata • $18

Cofield Cabernet Merlot

ΥΥΥΥ **1997** Medium red; the bouquet is clean, with the fruit having the slightly savoury edges one expects from this blend. The palate is enhanced by gently sweet, cedary oak merging into sweet, leathery fruit with soft, fine tannins. There are no green characters lurking in the background. **rating:** 85

best drinking Now–2004 **best vintages** NA **drink with** Veal cutlets • $16

Cofield Cabernet Sauvignon

TTTT **1999** Medium red-purple; the moderately intense bouquet offers blackberry fruit with some sweet earthy characters which are strongly varietal; a powerful wine on the palate, with blackberry, blackcurrant and earth flavours filling out the mid-palate in particular. Will be long lived. **rating:** 86

best drinking 2003–2010 **best vintages** NA **drink with** Venison • $16

coldstream hills NR

31 Maddens Lane, Coldstream, Vic 3770 **region** Yarra Valley
phone (03) 5964 9388 **fax** (03) 5964 9389 **open** 7 days 10–5
winemaker James Halliday, Paul Lapsley **production** 50 000 **est.** 1985
product range ($20–54 CD) Pinot Gris, Sauvignon Blanc, Chardonnay, Reserve Chardonnay, Pinot Noir, Reserve Pinot Noir, Merlot, Reserve Merlot, Briarston (Cabernet Merlot), Reserve Cabernet Sauvignon; Limited Release Shiraz, Blanc de Noirs and Botrytis Chardonnay.
summary Founded by the author, who continues to be involved with the winemaking with Paul Lapsley, but acquired by Southcorp in mid-1996. Expansion plans already then underway have been maintained, with well in excess of 100 hectares of owned or managed estate vineyards as the base. Chardonnay and Pinot Noir continue to be the principal focus; Merlot came on-stream from the 1997 vintage. Vintage conditions permitting, these three wines are made in both varietal and Reserve form, the latter in restricted quantities.

Coldstream Hills Chardonnay

1999 Medium yellow-green; the bouquet offers quite complex melon aromatics underpinned by soft, gently spicy oak. The palate is in the mainstream of Coldstream Hills style, with sweet melon and stonefruit flavours again supported by gentle French oak.

best drinking 2002–2007 **best vintages** '86, '88, '91, '92, '93, '94, '96, '97 **drink with** Oven-roasted blue eye cod • NA

Coldstream Hills Reserve Chardonnay

1999 Light to medium yellow-green; the bouquet is stylish and more reserved than the varietal release, with gentle barrel-ferment and cashew mlf characters. The fine and elegant palate has excellent structure, with melon and cashew blending with balanced and integrated oak through to a long finish. Not for the first time, Chardonnay has come through a difficult vintage in surprisingly good form.

best drinking 2003–2009 **best vintages** '88, '91, '92, '93, '94, '96, '97 **drink with** Veal, chicken • NA

Coldstream Hills Shiraz

1999 Quite full medium red-purple; dark cherry/berry/spice aromatics and subtle French oak on the bouquet lead into a medium-bodied palate with quite complex dark cherry/plum and spice flavours, finishing with lively acidity. Seems to have picked up weight since bottling.

best drinking 2002–2006 **best vintages** NA **drink with** Spiced lamb • NA

Coldstream Hills Briarston

1999 Medium red-purple; a spotlessly clean bouquet offers a seamless marriage of dark berry fruit and oak. The palate is equally attractive, with blackberry, raspberry and a touch of chocolate, together with perceptible French oak. The tannins are fine in the usual Coldstream style. No Reserve Cabernet Sauvignon was made in 1999, the Cabernet from the best estate block which usually provides the release is being incorporated in Briarston.

best drinking 2003–2009 **best vintages** '88, '90, '91, '92, '94, '97, '98, '99 **drink with** Lamb with redcurrant sauce • NA

collina wines NR

Princes Highway, Mogo, NSW 2536 **region** South Coast Zone
phone (02) 4474 0005 **open** 7 days 10–5
winemaker Nicola Collins **production** NA **est.** 1999
product range ($15–22 CD) Chardonnay, Classic White, Gewurztraminer, Late Harvest Riesling Traminer, South Coast Cabernets, Rougon (semi-sweet red).
summary In the spring of 1980, Jim Collins planted the first vines on the south coast at Bega's Grevillea Estate. His daughter Nicola was winemaker from the outset and, having completed 16 vintages, encouraged her father to build a second winery at Mogo in the Eurobodalla region. The winery does not have vineyards of its own, sourcing grapes in part from Grevillea Estate and from the growing number of south coast vineyards. As with Grevillea Estate, the operation is aimed at the general tourist rather than the wine connoisseur.

colmaur NR

447 Native Corners Road, Campania, Tas 7026 **region** Southern Tasmania
phone (03) 6260 4312 **fax** (03) 6260 4580 **open** By appointment
winemaker Michael Vishacki (Contract) **production** 100 **est.** 1994
product range ($20 R) Chardonnay, Pinot Noir.
summary Colmaur is sufficiently small for the vines to be counted: presently 1100 chardonnay and 1700 pinot noir in production. In 2000/2001 a further 600 chardonnay, 1350 pinot noir and 250 cabernet sauvignon were planted, and that will be the total extent of the vineyard. Likewise, production will be limited to the five new French oak barrels purchased in 2000, producing 100 to 120 cases of wine per year; any surplus grapes will be sold. Likewise, there are 700 olive trees in production, and Colmaur has its own oil press, producing 26 litres in 2000 but with more expected in the future.

Colmaur Pinot Noir

YYYY **1999** Medium to full red, with just a touch of purple; the bouquet offers a range of spice, fresh earth and plum, the palate ripe plummy fruit yet with a quite silky texture. **rating:** 86
best drinking Now–2006 **best vintages** NA **drink with** Coq au vin • $20

connor park winery NR

59 Connors Road, Leichardt, Vic 3516 **region** Bendigo
phone (03) 5437 5234 **fax** (03) 5437 5204 **open** 7 days 10–6
winemaker Ross Lougoon **production** 2000 **est.** 1994
product range ($12–28 CD) Riesling, Semillon, Sparkling Shiraz, Merlot, Shiraz, Cabernet, Port, Muscat.
summary The original planting of 2 hectares of vineyard dates back to the mid-1960s and to the uncle of the present owners, who had plans for designing an automatic grape harvester. The plans came to nothing, and when the present owners purchased the property in 1985 the vineyard had run wild. They resuscitated the vineyard (which formed part of a much larger mixed farming operation) and until 1994 were content to sell the grapes to other winemakers. Since then the vineyard has been expanded to 10 hectares, and while part of the grapes is sold to others, significant quantities are made under the Connor Park label and sold through cellar door and by mail order.

constable & hershon ★★★☆

1 Gillards Road, Pokolbin, NSW 2320 **region** Lower Hunter Valley
phone (02) 4998 7887 **fax** (02) 4998 7887 **open** 7 days 10–5
winemaker Neil McGuigan (Contract) **production** 5000 **est.** 1981
product range ($20–24 CD) Semillon, Chardonnay, Unwooded Chardonnay, Vintage Collection Chardonnay, Shiraz, Merlot.
summary Features four spectacular formal gardens: the Rose, Knot and Herb, Secret and Sculpture; a free garden tour is conducted every Monday to Friday at 10.30 am lasting 30 minutes. The 9.75-hectare vineyard is itself spectacularly situated under the backdrop of the Brokenback Range. Typically offers a range of several vintages of each variety ex cellar door or by mailing list. The quality is good, sometimes very good.

constables ★★★

Graphite Road, West Manjimup, WA 6258 **region** Pemberton
phone (08) 9772 1375 **open** 7 days 9–5
winemaker Houghton (Contract) **production** NFP **est.** 1988
product range ($10–15 CD) Riesling, Sauvignon Blanc, Chardonnay, Cabernet Sauvignon.
summary Father John and son Michael, together with other members of the Constable family, have established an 11-hectare vineyard at Manjimup. Most of the grapes are sold to Houghton under a long-term contract, and limited quantities are made for the Constable label by Houghton under contract.

coolangatta estate ★★★☆

1335 Bolong Road, Shoalhaven Heads, NSW 2535 **region** Shoalhaven
phone (02) 4448 7131 **fax** (02) 4448 7997 **open** 7 days 10–5

winemaker Tyrrell's (Contract) **production** 5000 **est.** 1988
product range ($17.50–23 CD) Sauvignon Blanc Chardonnay, Unwooded Chardonnay, Alexander Berry Chardonnay, Verdelho, Chardonnay Brut, Chambourcin, Cabernet Shiraz, Merlot, Merlot Shiraz, Cabernet Sauvignon, Vintage Port.
summary Coolangatta Estate is part of a 150-hectare resort with accommodation, restaurants, golf course, etc, with some of the oldest buildings convict-built in 1822. It might be thought that the wines are tailored purely for the tourist market, but in fact the standard of viticulture is exceptionally high (immaculate Scott-Henry trellising), and the winemaking is wholly professional (contract by Tyrrell's).

Coolangatta Estate Semillon

YYYY **2000** Light, bright straw-green, exactly as the colour should be; the bouquet offers strong herb and fresh cut grass aromas that lead into a lively, lemony palate with quite high acidity. All in all, a classic Semillon that cries out to be cellared. **rating:** 86
best drinking 2003–2008 **best vintages** '98 **drink with** Grilled fish • $18.50

Coolangatta Estate Sauvignon Blanc Chardonnay

YYYY **2000** Light straw-green; the bouquet is clean, fresh and crisp, with minerally aromas. The palate has some nice fruit, with a hint of white peach, but it does raise the question as to why the Sauvignon Blanc is blended with the Chardonnay rather than the Semillon. **rating:** 85
best drinking Now **best vintages** '91, '94, '98 **drink with** Whitebait • $15.50

Coolangatta Estate Verdelho

YYYY **2000** Light to medium green-yellow; the bouquet has exemplary fruit salad varietal character, clean and fresh. The palate is lively, once again showing authentic varietal character; skilled winemaking has invested the wine with perfectly judged acid/fruit/residual sugar balance. **rating:** 86
best drinking Now **best vintages** 2000 **drink with** Pasta • $17.50

Coolangatta Estate Alexander Berry Chardonnay

YYYY **2000** Light green-yellow; the bouquet is clean, light and fresh, with the lightest touch of French oak. The palate is, similarly, spotlessly clean, fresh and correct, but by no means overpowering, finishing with a nice citrussy touch. I finally hit upon 88 points after much humming and haa-ing with myself. **rating:** 88
best drinking Now–2003 **best vintages** '91, '94, '96, '97, '00 **drink with** Avocado and seafood • $22

Coolangatta Estate Eileen Chambourcin

YYYY **2000** Dense, inky purple-red; the bouquet is redolent of dark plum, with some gamey varietal character. The palate, similarly, is ultra-typical, with that volume of flavour filling the forepalate, and then falling off abruptly on the finish. **rating:** 85
best drinking Now **best vintages** '99 **drink with** Pizza • $19

coombend estate ★★★★☆

Coombend, via Swansea, Tas 7190 **region** Southern Tasmania
phone (03) 6257 8881 **fax** (03) 6257 8484 **open** 7 days 9–6
winemaker Andrew Hood (Contract) **production** 2000 **est.** 1985
product range ($19–26 CD) Riesling, Sauvignon Blanc, Cabernet Sauvignon.
summary John Fenn Smith originally established 1.75 hectares of cabernet sauvignon, 2.25 hectares of sauvignon blanc and 0.3 hectare of riesling (together with a little cabernet franc) on his 2600-hectare sheep station, choosing that part of his property which is immediately adjacent to Freycinet. This slightly quixotic choice of variety has been justified by the success of the wine in limited show entries. In December 1998 Coombend opened a brand-new, purpose-built cellar-door sales area and has also significantly expanded its plantings to include riesling and sauvignon blanc.

Coombend Estate Sauvignon Blanc

YYYY **2000** Medium to full yellow-green; a powerful, solid bouquet with subtle oak but not a great deal of fruit aromatics leads into a well-structured palate that in other respects is a replay of the bouquet. **rating:** 83
best drinking Now–2003 **best vintages** NA **drink with** Sugar-cured tuna • $19

cooperage estate NR

15 Markovitch Lane, Junortoun, Vic 3551 **region** Bendigo
phone 0418 544 743 **open** Not
winemaker Graham Gregurek **production** NA **est.** 1995
product range NA
summary The Gregurek family has established 2.2 hectares of shiraz and cabernet sauvignon at their vineyard on the southern outskirts of the town of Bendigo. As the name suggests, there is also a cooperage on site.

coorinja ★★☆

Toodyay Road, Toodyay, WA 6566 **region** Greater Perth Zone
phone (08) 9574 2280 **open** Mon–Sat 10–5
winemaker Michael Wood **production** 3200 **est.** 1870
product range ($8–10.50 CD) Dry White, Claret, Hermitage, Burgundy, Fortifieds; the latter account for 50 per cent of Coorinja's production.
summary This evocative and historic winery, nestling in a small gully, seems to be in a time-warp, begging to be used as a set for a film. A recent revamp of the packaging accompanied a more than respectable Hermitage with lots of dark chocolate and sweet berry flavour, finishing with soft tannins.

cope-williams ★★★☆

Glenfern Road, Romsey, Vic 3434 **region** Macedon Ranges
phone (03) 5429 5428 **fax** (03) 5429 5655 **open** 7 days 11–5
winemaker David Cowburn **production** 7000 **est.** 1977
product range ($14–25 R) Chardonnay, Cabernet Merlot; d'Vine is second label: Riesling, Chardonnay and Cabernet Sauvignon; winery specialty: sparkling wine, Macedon R.O.M.S.E.Y.
summary One of the high-country Macedon pioneers, specialising in sparkling wines that are full flavoured but also producing excellent Chardonnay and Pinot Noir table wines in the warmer vintages. A traditional 'English Green'-type cricket ground is available for hire and booked out most days of the week from spring through till autumn.

Cope-Williams Chardonnay

🍷🍷🍷 **1998** Light to medium yellow-green; the bouquet is clean, not particularly aromatic in fruit terms, but with some minerally notes and subtle oak. The slow-developing palate is fresh, clean and light, with pleasant citrus/mineral flavours. **rating:** 84
best drinking Now–2006 **best vintages** NA **drink with** Shellfish • $19

Cope-Williams Pinot Noir

🍷🍷🍷🍷 **1997** Light to medium red; a lively, tangy, sappy/minty bouquet is precisely repeated on the long, sappy palate, with its typical ultra-cool-grown fruit style. Like the Chardonnay, showing longevity. **rating:** 86
best drinking Now–2004 **best vintages** NA **drink with** Smoked quail • $24

coriole ★★★★☆

Chaffeys Road, McLaren Vale, SA 5171 **region** McLaren Vale
phone (08) 8323 8305 **fax** (08) 8323 9136 **open** Mon–Fri 10–5, weekends and public holidays 11–5
winemaker Grant Harrison **production** 30 000 **est.** 1967
product range ($14–55 R) Lalla Rookh Semillon, Semillon Sauvignon Blanc, Chenin Blanc, Botrytis Chenin Blanc, Sangiovese, Nebbiolo, Shiraz, Redstone (Shiraz Cabernet Grenache), Diva (Sangiovese blend), Cabernet Sauvignon; Mary Kathleen (Cabernet blend), Lloyd Reserve Shiraz, Lalla Rookh Grenache Shiraz, Lloyd Sangiovese Cabernet.
summary Justifiably best known for its Shiraz, which, both in the rare Lloyd Reserve and standard forms, is extremely impressive. It has spread its wings in recent years, being one of the first wineries to catch onto the Italian fashion with its Sangiovese, but its white varietal wines lose nothing by comparison. It is also a producer of high-quality olive oil, which is distributed commercially throughout Australia. The wines are exported to the UK, the US, Canada, Switzerland, Germany, the Netherlands, Taiwan, Japan, Singapore and New Zealand.

Coriole Semillon Sauvignon Blanc

YYYY **2000** Light green-yellow; an attractively pungent and crisp herb/grass/lemon bouquet leads into a light, fresh palate with some pleasing minerally edges to the texture. **rating:** 85

best drinking Now **best vintages** NA **drink with** Battered fish • $15

Coriole Shiraz

YYYYY **1998** Dense red-purple; very powerful, concentrated earthy/chocolatey varietal fruit is supported by subtle oak on the bouquet. The palate is similarly powerful, with savoury licorice, chocolate and cherry fruit, not at all jammy, although it does weigh in at 14° alcohol. Finishes with lingering tannins. **rating:** 93

best drinking 2003–2013 **best vintages** '90, '91, '96, '98 **drink with** Steak and kidney pie • $26

Coriole Lloyd Reserve Shiraz

YYYYY **1997** Medium to full red; the bouquet is sweet and smooth, with delicious dark berry/cherry fruit, some spice and subtle oak. An elegantly framed and built palate, with a mix of dark cherry and more savoury flavours, finishes with fine-grained tannins. It carries its 14° alcohol easily. **rating:** 94

best drinking 2002–2012 **best vintages** '70, '74, '84, '88, '89, '90, '91, '92, '94, '95, '96, '97 **drink with** Ragout of lamb • $55

Coriole Redstone

YYYY **1998** Medium to full red-purple; a most unusual bouquet with a mix of savoury/spicy/lemony aromas is followed by a powerful palate with a mix of earthy/lemony flavours, finishing with chewy tannins. **rating:** 84

best drinking 2002–2007 **best vintages** NA **drink with** Lamb's fry • $19.95

Coriole Mary Kathleen Cabernet Merlot

YYYYY **1996** Reserve. Medium to full red-purple; the bouquet is clean, with a mix of leaf, cassis and earth aromas. A powerful wine in the mouth, with regional chocolate adding to the berry/earth characters of the bouquet. Strongly varietal, with an edge of austerity. **rating:** 90

best drinking Now–2006 **best vintages** '90, '91, '92, '94, '95, '96, '97 **drink with** Mature cheddar • $37.50

cosham NR

101 Union Road, Carmel, via Kalamunda, WA 6076 **region** Perth Hills
phone (08) 9293 5424 **fax** (08) 9293 5062 **open** Weekends and public holidays 10–5
winemaker Julie White **production** 1000 **est.** 1989
product range ($16 CD) Chardonnay, Pinot Noir, Cabernet Merlot, Methode Champenoise Brut.
summary The newest of the Perth Hills ventures, with a microscopic amount of wine available. Both the Chardonnay and Pinot Noir spend two years in French oak barriques before bottling – a long time by any standards. Improbable though it may seem, exports to the US.

cowra estate ★★★

Boorowa Road, Cowra, NSW 2794 **region** Cowra
phone (02) 6342 1136 **fax** (02) 6342 4286 **open** 7 days 9–6
winemaker Simon Gilbert (Contract) **production** 15 000 **est.** 1973
product range ($9.50–14.95 CD) Sauvignon Blanc, Chardonnay, Unwooded Chardonnay, Verdelho, Cool Classic Sparkling Blanc de Blanc, Cabernet Rosé, Cabernet Sauvignon Shiraz, Cabernets. The Classic Bat series of Chardonnay, Pinot Noir and Cabernet Merlot is now at the head of the range.
summary Cowra Estate was purchased from the family of founder Tony Gray by South African-born food and beverage entrepreneur John Geber in 1995. A vigorous promotional campaign has gained a higher domestic profile for the once export-oriented brand. John Geber is actively involved in the promotional effort and rightly proud of the excellent value for money that the wines represent. The Quarry Wine Cellars and Restaurant offer visitors a full range of all of the Cowra Estate's wines, and also wines from the other producers in the region, including Richmond Grove, Hungerford Hill, Arrowfield, Mulyan and Chiverton.

Cowra Estate Cabernet Rosé

YYYY **2000** Fresh, bright pink; the bouquet is fresh and lively, with a mix of raspberry and more earthy fruit; the palate is crisp, clean and well made, with a touch of subliminal sweetness. Another success for this very reliable wine. **rating:** 82

best drinking Now **best vintages** NA **drink with** Summer lunch • $14.95

crabtree of watervale ★★★☆

North Terrace, Watervale SA 5452 **region** Clare Valley
phone (08) 8843 0069 **fax** (08) 8843 0144 **open** 7 days 11–5
winemaker Robert Crabtree **production** 5000 **est.** 1979
product range ($15–20 CD) Riesling, Semillon, Grenache, Bay of Biscay, Shiraz, Shiraz Cabernet Sauvignon, Cabernet Sauvignon, Muscat, Windmill Tawny.
summary The gently eccentric Robert Crabtree and wife Elizabeth are once again very much part of the business, making full-flavoured, classic Clare Valley styles.

Crabtree of Watervale Riesling

▼▼▼▽ **2000** Medium to full yellow-green; a slightly aggressive, strong bouquet with rather green, herbaceous aromas. The palate shows similar citrus/lemon flavours, in quasi-Sauvignon Blanc mode. **rating:** 83
best drinking Now–2004 **best vintages** '99 **drink with** Ginger prawns • $18

Crabtree of Watervale Grenache

▼▼▼▼▽ **2000** Medium red-purple; the bouquet is fresh, with pleasing spicy fruit characters, the palate clean and fresh with pleasant cherry and spice fruit before tailing away fractionally on the finish. Good early-drinking style. **rating:** 90
best drinking Now **best vintages** NA **drink with** Cold meat salad • $15

Crabtree of Watervale Bay of Biscay Grenache

▼▼▼▼ **2000** Fresh, lively strawberry/cherry fruit aromas are followed by a charming summer-style rosé with cherry and raspberry fruit, and the amount of sweetness that causes a wine such as this to walk out of the cellar door by the truckload. **rating:** 87
best drinking Now **best vintages** NA **drink with** An ice block • $15

craig avon vineyard ★★★☆

Craig Avon Lane, Merricks North, Vic 3926 **region** Mornington Peninsula
phone (03) 5989 7465 **fax** (03) 5989 7615 **open** Weekends and public holidays 12–5
winemaker Ken Lang **production** 1000 **est.** 1986
product range ($29–33 CD) Chardonnay, Pinot Noir, Cabernet.
summary All of the wines are sold cellar door and by mailing list. The wines are competently made, clean and with a pleasant fruit flavour.

craigie knowe 

Glen Gala Road, Cranbrook, Tas 7190 **region** Southern Tasmania
phone (03) 6223 5620 **fax** (03) 6223 5009 **open** Weekends or by appointment
winemaker Dr John Austwick **production** 500 **est.** 1979
product range ($20–23 ML) Cabernet Sauvignon, Pinot Noir.
summary John Austwick makes a small quantity of full-flavoured, robust Cabernet Sauvignon in a tiny winery as a weekend relief from a busy metropolitan dental practice. The Pinot Noir is made in a style that will appeal to confirmed Cabernet Sauvignon drinkers, and John Austwick had a couple of barrels of 1998 Cabernet Sauvignon that, if bottled separately, would have appealed to everyone who has ever lifted a wine glass.

craiglee 

Sunbury Road, Sunbury, Vic 3429 **region** Sunbury
phone (03) 9744 4489 **fax** (03) 9744 4489 **open** Sun, public holidays 10–5, or by appointment
winemaker Patrick Carmody **production** 2000 **est.** 1976
product range ($17–34 CD) Chardonnay, Pinot Noir, Shiraz, Cabernet Sauvignon.
summary An historic winery with a proud nineteenth-century record, it recommenced winemaking in 1976 after a prolonged hiatus. Produces one of the finest cool-climate Shirazes in Australia, redolent of cherry, licorice and spice in the better (i.e. warmer) vintages, lighter-bodied in the cooler ones. Maturing vines and improved viticulture have made the wines more consistent (and even better) over the past ten years or so.

craigow ★★★★

528 Richmond Road, Cambridge, Tas 7170 **region** Southern Tasmania
phone (03) 6248 5379 **fax** (03) 6248 5482 **open** Fri–Sun 10–5, or by appointment
winemaker Julian Alcorso (Contract) **production** 500 **est.** 1989
product range ($18.50–25 CD) Riesling, Gewurztraminer, Chardonnay, Pinot Noir.
summary Craigow has substantial vineyards, with 5 hectares of pinot noir and another 5 hectares divided between riesling, chardonnay and gewurztraminer. Barry and Cathy have moved from being grape-growers with only one wine made for sale to a portfolio of four wines, while continuing to sell most of their grapes. Their cellar door opened in December 1999.

Craigow Riesling

🍷🍷🍷🍷🍷 **2000** Light to medium green-yellow; the bouquet offers a mix of mineral (dominant) and citrus/lime, the latter characters, however, coming through on the intense, lively and long palate with rich tropical/lime in the middle, and tingling acidity on the finish. **rating:** 94

best drinking 2002–2009 **best vintages** '00 **drink with** Fish terrine • $18.50

Craigow Gewurztraminer

🍷🍷🍷🍷 **2000** Light green-yellow; spicy overtones to more lime-accented fruit on the bouquet lead into a wine with far more power than one normally encounters in Tasmania. As an example of gewurztraminer varietal character, not outstanding, but as a spicy white wine, very good. **rating:** 86

best drinking Now–2003 **best vintages** NA **drink with** Asian • $24

Craigow Pinot Noir

🍷🍷🍷🍷 **1999** Very good and bright light to medium red-purple; the moderately intense bouquet is fragrant, with slightly earthy/stemmy overtones to the strong plummy fruit. The palate has good length and persistence, with savoury/stemmy/earthy overtones to the plummy fruit. The only criticism is a slight lack of density. Provoked a wide range of opinion from the judges at the 2001 Tasmanian Wines Show (and retasted by me thereafter). **rating:** 87

best drinking 2002–2006 **best vintages** NA **drink with** Duck casserole • $25

craneford ★★★☆

Moorundie Street, Truro, SA 5356 **region** Barossa Valley
phone (08) 8564 0003 **fax** (08) 8564 0008 **open** Wed–Mon 11–5
winemaker John Zilm **production** 3000 **est.** 1978
product range ($9–25 CD) Eden Valley Riesling, Barossa Valley Chardonnay, Barossa Valley Unwooded Chardonnay, Barossa Valley Semillon, Frontignac, Shiraz, Quartet, Grenache, Fortified and Sparkling.
summary The purchase of Craneford by owner/winemaker John Zilm has wrought many changes. It has moved to a new winery (and café) and is supported by 15 hectares of Barossa Valley shiraz. Wine quality, too, has leapt. Retail distribution in Sydney and Melbourne, and exports to Japan through Australian Prestige Wines.

crane winery NR

Haydens Road, Kingaroy, Qld 4610 **region** South Burnett
phone (07) 4162 7647 **fax** (07) 4162 8381 **open** 7 days 9–4
winemaker John Crane **production** 4000 **est.** 1996
product range ($10–23 ML) Moscato, Verdelho, Semillon, Unwooded Chardonnay, Chardonnay, Late Harvest Frontignac, Hillside White and Red, Ruby Cabernet, Merlot, Shiraz, Shiraz Cabernet Sauvignon, Cabernet Sauvignon, Sparkling Burgundy, Pinot Semillon Chardonnay Sparkling, Estate Sparkling Cuvée, Vintage Liqueur Shiraz, Liqueur Muscat.
summary Established by John and Sue Crane, Crane Winery is one of several in the burgeoning Kingaroy (or South Burnett) region in Queensland. It draws upon 4 hectares of estate plantings but also purchases grapes from 20 other growers in the region. Interestingly, Sue Crane's great-grandfather established a vineyard planted to shiraz 100 years ago (in 1898) and which remained in production until 1970.

cranswick estate ★★★

Walla Avenue, Griffith, NSW 2680 **region** Riverina
phone (02) 6962 4133 **fax** (02) 6962 2888 **open** 7 days 10–4
winemaker Andrew Schulz, Tim Pearce **production** 1.2 million **est.** 1976
product range ($6–20 ML) There are several ranges; at the top: the Premium and Regional Selection ranges (with Autumn Gold Botrytis Semillon off to one side and higher priced again) comprising Barrel Fermented Semillon, Young Vine Chardonnay, Cocoparra Marsanne, Cocoparra Vineyard Shiraz, Cocoparra Merlot, Cocoparra Cabernet Sauvignon; the volume-selling Vignette Range of Fruition (White Frontignac), Semillon, Chardonnay, Pinot Chardonnay, Shiraz, Cabernet Merlot, Unoaked Botrytis Semillon; Aldridge Sparkling Brut; also lower-priced ranges: Kidman Way, Cedar Creek and Barramundi Varietal.
summary Taking full advantage of the buoyant share market and the continuing export success of Australian wines, Cranswick Estate made a highly successful entry to the lists of the Australian Associated Stock Exchanges in 1997. The substantial capital raised has seen the further expansion of the business, firmly aimed at the export market in the UK, Europe, the US, Japan, Iceland, and Southeast Asia.

Cranswick Estate Vignette Botrytis Semillon

🍷🍷🍷🍷 **1999** Glowing yellow-green; high-toned aromas of honey, mead and cashew lead into a palate with lots of honey and peach fruit flavour, but which seems unbalanced by the high acidity that jags somewhat on the finish. A ripe dessert will undoubtedly smooth out the bumps. **rating:** 83

best drinking Now **best vintages** '99 **drink with** Rich, sweet desserts • $9.99

Cranswick Estate Cocoparra Vineyard Shiraz

🍷🍷🍷🍷 **1998** Medium red-purple; a flood of vanilla-accented American oak overwhelms the bouquet and the palate. There is no question some nice fruit flavour lurks underneath the oak, but less (oak) would have been so much better. **rating:** 82

best drinking Now–2003 **best vintages** '97 **drink with** Steak and kidney pie • $18

---

crawford river wines ★★★★★

Hotspur Upper Road, Condah, Vic 3303 **region** Henty
phone (03) 5578 2267 **fax** (03) 5578 2240 **open** 7 days 10–4
winemaker John Thomson **production** 3600 **est.** 1975
product range ($18–30 CD) Riesling, Reserve Riesling, Semillon Sauvignon Blanc, Chardonnay, Cabernet Merlot, Cabernet Sauvignon, Nektar.
summary Exemplary wines right across the range are made by part-time winemaker John Thomson, who clearly has the winemaker's equivalent of the gardener's green thumb. The Riesling is consistently outstanding, the Cabernet-based wines excellent in warmer vintages. Exports to the UK, Germany, Singapore and Austria.

Crawford River Riesling

🍷🍷🍷🍷🍷 **2000** Less fashionable than the Clare Valley Riesling icons, perhaps, but every bit as consistently outstanding year in, year out. A fragrant and very pure mix of lime and a dash of passionfruit fills the bouquet, followed by a palate of piercing delicacy, with apple added to the mix. **rating:** 95

best drinking Now–2010 **best vintages** '86, '88, '89, '91, '94, '96, '97, '98, '99, '00 **drink with** Tempura oysters • $26.50

Crawford River Reserve Riesling

🍷🍷🍷🍷🍷 **2000** Very light green-yellow; intense lime and herb aromatics lead into a similarly intense yet fine and very long palate, which is beautifully poised and balanced. How John Thomson achieves this with such a high level of alcohol is beyond my comprehension. **rating:** 97

best drinking 2004–2014 **best vintages** '99, '00 **drink with** Richer fish dishes • NA

Crawford River Semillon

🍷🍷🍷🍷 **2000** Very light straw-green; a clean, crisp, fine grassy bouquet is followed by a similarly crisp and clean palate with excellent structure, texture and length, finishing with minerally acidity. Simply needs time. **rating:** 91

best drinking 2003–2010 **best vintages** '00 **drink with** Crab • $22

Crawford River Semillon Sauvignon Blanc

🍷🍷🍷🍷 **2000** Light straw-green; a clean, crisp and minerally bouquet has touches of both grass and lemon, the fine and fresh palate picking up intensity with lemony/mineral acidity on the finish. **rating:** 88

best drinking Now–2005 **best vintages** '96, '97 **drink with** Crab or shellfish • $20

Crawford River Nektar

🍷🍷🍷🍷Y **1999** Glowing yellow-green; the bouquet has intense lime and apple aromas, spotlessly clean in typical Crawford River style. The excellently balanced palate has a long and lingering finish; great with fresh fruit. **rating:** 92

best drinking Now–2006 **best vintages** '99 **drink with** Any rich dessert • $24

crisford winery NR

556 Hermitage Road, Pokolbin, NSW 2022 **region** Lower Hunter Valley
phone (02) 9387 1100 **fax** (02) 9387 6688 **open** Not
winemaker David Hook (Contract) **production** NA **est.** 1990
product range A single wine, Synergy (Merlot Cabernet Franc blend).
summary Carol and Neal Crisford have established 2.6 hectares of merlot and cabernet franc which go to produce Synergy (a name that I fancy has been trademarked by Hamilton).

crosswinds vineyard ★★★★

10 Vineyard Drive, Tea Tree, Tas 7017 **region** Southern Tasmania
phone (03) 6268 1091 **fax** (03) 6268 1091 **open** Mon–Fri 10–5, weekends by appointment
winemaker Andrew Vasiljuk **production** 1500 **est.** 1990
product range ($16–20 ML) Riesling, Unwooded Chardonnay, Chardonnay, Pinot Noir, Cabernet Sauvignon.
summary Crosswinds has two vineyards: the 1-hectare Tea Tree Vineyard and the 2-hectare Margate Vineyard. As well as cellar-door sales, has retail distribution in Melbourne and small exports to the UK and Southeast Asia. Both Chardonnay and Pinot Noir have excelled in recent years.

Crosswinds Non-Wooded Pinot Noir

🍷🍷🍷Y **2000** Excellent purple-red hue; plum and cherry fruit on both bouquet and a rich, flavoursome palate does all the work. Inevitably lacks complexity, but bottle age could well produce some interesting characters. **rating:** 84

best drinking Now–2004 **best vintages** '98 **drink with** Braised duck • $18

cruickshank callatoota estate ★★☆

2656 Wybong Road, Wybong, NSW 2333 **region** Upper Hunter Valley
phone (02) 6547 8149 **fax** (02) 6547 8144 **open** 7 days 9–5
winemaker John Cruickshank, Andrew Thomas (Consultant) **production** 7000 **est.** 1973
product range ($9–15 CD) Cabernet Rosé, Two Cabernets, Cabernet Franc, Cabernet Sauvignon (Cask 12, Show Reserve and Pressings), Old Tawny Port.
summary Owned by Sydney management consultant John Cruickshank and family. Wine quality definitely improved in the 1990s, although the wines still show strong regional and rather earthy characters; the label itself likewise doggedly remains old-fashioned. The 2000 Cabernet Rosé is delicate, clean and crisp (82 points) and the most appealing of the range. The other six wines from the 1996 and 1998 vintages tasted in March 2001 all had harsh and often earthy tannins, the one exception being 1996 Cabernet Franc (81 points).

cubbaroo cellars NR

Cubbaroo Station, Wee Waa, NSW 2388 **region** Western Plains Zone
phone (02) 6796 1741 **fax** (02) 6796 1751 **open** Thurs–Sun 12–10
winemaker Simon Gilbert (Contract) **production** NA **est.** 1972
product range ($10–15 CD) Shiraz, Port.
summary Cubbaroo Cellars has led a shadowy existence in the heart of the Namoi Valley cotton country since the early 1970s. For a while it seemed that it had ceased production under the Cubbaroo Cellars label, selling its grapes to wineries in the Hunter Valley. However, the 10.8 hectares of shiraz planted long ago has now been supplemented by 4 hectares of cabernet sauvignon (not yet producing), so its fortunes may be on the rise. The two wines presently available are sold only through the cellar door.

cullen wines ★★★★★

Caves Road, Cowaramup, WA 6284 **region** Margaret River
phone (08) 9755 5277 **fax** (08) 9755 5550 **open** 7 days 10–4
winemaker Vanya Cullen, Trevor Kent **production** 18 000 **est.** 1971
product range ($25–70 CD) Flagship wines: Chardonnay, Sauvignon Blanc, Pinot Noir, Semillon Sauvignon Blanc, Reserve Cabernet Sauvignon Merlot; premium wines: Classic Dry White, Blanc de Noir, Velvet Red, Autumn Harvest.
summary One of the pioneers of Margaret River, it has always produced long-lived wines of highly individual style from the substantial and mature estate vineyards. Winemaking is now in the hands of Vanya Cullen, daughter of the founders; and she is possessed of an extraordinarily good palate. The Chardonnay is superb, while the Cabernet Merlot goes from strength to strength; indeed, I would rate it Australia's best. The wines are distributed throughout Australia and also make their way to significant export markets in the UK, the US, Europe and Asia.

Cullen Chardonnay

🍷🍷🍷🍷🍷 **1999** Estate-grown on 30-year-old vines and hand-crafted by Vanya Cullen, who is equally at home with Montrachet. A mix of melon, fig and stonefruit combines with subtle, gently smoky oak on the bouquet; the palate has some similarities to the Cape Mentelle, but the fruit is even more vibrant. **rating:** 96
best drinking Now–2009 **best vintages** '93, '94, '96, '98, '99 **drink with** Marron • $46

---

curlewis winery NR

55 Navarre Road, Curlewis, Vic 3222 **region** Geelong
phone (03) 5250 4567 **fax** (03) 5250 4567 **open** By appointment
winemaker Rainer Breit **production** 800 **est.** 1998
product range ($29.50 R) Pinot Noir.
summary Rainer Breit and partner Wendy Oliver have achieved a great deal in a remarkably short period of time. In 1996 they purchased their property at Curlewis with 1.6 hectares of what were then 11-year-old pinot noir vines; previously, and until 1998, the grapes had been sold to Scotchman's Hill. They set to and established an on-site winery, making 800 cases of very good Pinot Noir in their first vintage of 1998. Rainer Breit is a self-taught winemaker, but the full bag of pinot noir winemaking tricks was used in 1998: cold-soaking, hot-fermentation, post-ferment maceration, part inoculated and partly wild yeast use, prolonged lees contact, and bottling the wine neither fined nor filtered. While Breit and Oliver are self-confessed 'pinotphiles', they have planted a little chardonnay and buy a little locally grown shiraz and chardonnay, but do not yet make these wines on a commercial scale.

Curlewis Pinot Noir

🍷🍷🍷🍷 **1998** Medium red, with just a hint of purple remaining; a strongly authentic bouquet with a mix of savoury/spicy/foresty aromas picks up even more depth and interest on the palate, where plummy/spicy fruit joins the foresty character of the bouquet. Has good length and balance. 150 cases made. **rating:** 88
best drinking Now–2004 **best vintages** '98 **drink with** Tea-smoked duck • $30

---

currency creek wines ★★★☆

Winery Road, Currency Creek, SA 5214 **region** Currency Creek
phone (08) 8555 4069 **fax** (08) 8555 4100 **open** 7 days 10–5
winemaker Warren Randall (Contract) **production** 8000 **est.** 1969
product range ($9–26 CD) Dry White (Semillon Chardonnay), Sauvignon Blanc, Chardonnay, Late Harvest (White Frontignac Riesling), Princess Alexandrina Noble Riesling, Harmony (Cabernet Shiraz), Ostrich Hill Shiraz, Cabernet Sauvignon, Sparkling, Fortifieds.
summary Constant name changes early in the piece (Santa Rosa, Tonkins have also been tried) did not help the quest for identity or recognition in the marketplace, but the winery has nonetheless produced some outstanding wood-matured whites and pleasant soft reds that sell at attractive prices.

Currency Creek Wines Ostrich Hill Shiraz

🍷🍷🍷🍷½ **1998** Bright purple-red; the moderately intense bouquet is driven by cherry and a little plum, the oak subtle. Gently ripe, sweet cherry and plum fruit ripple along the smooth palate, supported by fine, soft tannins. Excellent mouthfeel, carrying its alcohol with ease. **rating:** 91
best drinking 2003–2010 **best vintages** '98 **drink with** Rack of lamb • $16.95

curtis NR

Foggo Road, McLaren Vale, SA 5171 **region** McLaren Vale
phone (08) 8323 8389 **open** Weekends 11–4.30
winemaker P Curtis **production** 1500 **est.** 1988
product range ($4–5.50 CD) Riesling, Moselle, Claret, Shiraz Grenache, Ruby Port, Tawny Port.
summary A small and relatively new producer in McLaren Vale, whose wines I have not tasted.

dalfarras ★★★★

PO Box 123, Nagambie, Vic 3608 **region** Goulburn Valley
phone (03) 5794 2637 **fax** (03) 5794 2360 **open** Not
winemaker Alister Purbrick, Alan George **production** 30 000 **est.** 1991
product range ($12.95–49.95 R) Unwooded Chardonnay, Barrel Fermented Chardonnay, Sauvignon Blanc, Marsanne, Shiraz, Cabernet Sauvignon, Reserve Cabernet Sauvignon.
summary The personal project of Alister Purbrick and artist-wife Rosa (née) Dalfarra, whose paintings adorn the labels of the wines. Alister, of course, is best known as winemaker at Chateau Tahbilk, the family winery and home, but this range of wines is intended to (in Alister's words) 'allow me to expand my winemaking horizons and mould wines in styles different to Chateau Tahbilk'. It now draws upon 37 hectares of its own plantings in the Goulburn Valley, and the business continues to grow year by year. In the 1998 show season the Dalfarras wines had outstanding success, with the 1991 Reserve Cabernet Sauvignon winning two trophies, a gold, two silver and seven bronze medals, backed up by the 1998 Sauvignon Blanc and 1997 Marsanne, both of which won gold medals and a number of silver and bronze awards. Exports to the UK.

Dalfarras Marsanne

YYYY½ **1998** Light to medium green-yellow; the bouquet is fresh and tangy, with lemon and vanilla complemented by subtle oak. The palate is lively and fresh, with tangy, crisp fruit giving excellent mouthfeel; the fruit has gobbled up the oak, and provides considerable length and grip. A cellaring special. **rating:** 90
best drinking Now–2008 **best vintages** '98 **drink with** Brains in black butter • $14.95

dalrymple ★★★★

1337 Pipers Brook Road, Pipers Brook, Tas 7254 **region** Northern Tasmania
phone (03) 6382 7222 **fax** (03) 6382 7222 **open** 7 days 10–5
winemaker Bertel Sundstrup **production** 3800 **est.** 1987
product range ($16–35 CD) Chardonnay, Unwooded Chardonnay, Sauvignon Blanc, Pinot Noir, Pinot Noir Special Bin, Fume Blanc.
summary A partnership between Jill Mitchell and her sister and brother-in-law, Anne and Bertel Sundstrup, inspired by father Bill Mitchell's establishment of the Tamarway Vineyard in the late 1960s. In 1991 Tamarway reverted to the Sundstrup and Mitchell families and it, too, will be producing wine in the future, probably under its own label but sold ex the Dalrymple cellar door. As production has grown (significantly), so has that of wine quality across the board, often led by its Sauvignon Blanc.

Dalrymple Sauvignon Blanc

YYYY½ **2000** Light green-yellow; extremely potent passionfruit and gooseberry aromas and flavours speak of a long, cold, slow (too slow?) ferment. The intensity of the varietal character is admirable, but there was much discussion at the 2001 Tasmanian Wines Show before its gold medal was awarded. **rating:** 90
best drinking Now–2003 **best vintages** '94, '96, '00 **drink with** Tartare of Atlantic salmon • NA

Dalrymple Chardonnay

YYYY **1999** Medium green-yellow; super-intense grapefruit and melon aromas flow through into a tangy, grapefruit-flavoured palate; subtle oak. Once upon a time this style would have been an automatic gold medal, but no more. However, the style is very true to Dalrymple. **rating:** 85
best drinking Now–2004 **best vintages** '91, '92, '94, '97 **drink with** Braised pork neck • NA

Dalrymple Pinot Noir

YYY½ **1999** Medium to full red-purple; the bouquet is firm and savoury/stemmy/foresty; however, the palate is distinctly sweeter and riper than the bouquet, with attractive plum and just a touch of forest. Almost certainly has its best years in front of it. **rating:** 82
best drinking Now–2004 **best vintages** '98 **drink with** Chinese barbecued pork • NA

Dalrymple Special Bin Pinot Noir

YYYYY **1999** Medium red-purple; the bouquet is clean and fragrant, with a mix of strawberry and plum, with a substrate of more tangy/stemmy character. The medium-bodied palate follows down the same track, opening with ripe, plummy/spicy fruit then intersected with a tangy, herbal cut. I like the style a lot; others have been less enthusiastic.

rating: 92

best drinking 2002–2007 **best vintages** '99 **drink with** Breast of duck • NA

dalwhinnie ★★★★★

Taltarni Road, RMB 4378, Moonambel, Vic 3478 **region** Pyrenees
phone (03) 5467 2388 **fax** (03) 5467 2237 **open** 7 days 10–5
winemaker David Jones, Rick Kinzbrunner (Contract) **production** 5500 **est.** 1976
product range ($26–120 CD) Dalwhinnie Chardonnay and Pinot Noir, Moonambel Shiraz and Cabernet, Eagle Series Shiraz.

summary David and Jenny Jones have acquired full ownership of Dalwhinnie from Ewan Jones, and have three children of their own to ensure the future succession. In the meantime, Dalwhinnie goes from strength to strength, making outstanding wines right across the board. The wines all show tremendous depth of fruit flavour, reflecting the relatively low-yielding but very well-maintained vineyards. It is hard to say whether the Chardonnay or the Shiraz is the more distinguished; the Pinot Noir (made with assistance from Rick Kinzbrunner) was a startling arrival from out of nowhere. A further 8 hectares of shiraz (with a little viognier) were planted in the spring of 1999 on a newly acquired block on Taltarni Road, permitting the further development of export markets already established in the UK, Asia, Germany and the US.

Dalwhinnie Chardonnay

YYYYY **1999** Light to medium yellow-green; the bouquet is typically clean and smooth, with stonefruit, cashew and oak perfectly balanced and integrated. The palate is stylish and well balanced, offering a mix of cashew, melon, fig and gentle oak. Eerily close to the '98.

rating: 91

best drinking 2002–2007 **best vintages** '87, '88, '90, '92, '93, '94, '96, '98, '99 **drink with** Turkey • $26

Dalwhinnie Pinot Noir

YYYY **1999** Quite developed colour; the bouquet is right in the Dalwhinnie slot: spicy, savoury, stemmy and stylish; the light to medium bodied palate has a touch of mint (not really desirable), but quite magical texture and style.

rating: 88

best drinking Now **best vintages** NA **drink with** Game • $32

Dalwhinnie Eagle Series Pyrenees Shiraz

YYYYY **1998** Medium red-purple; the bouquet is extremely aromatic and complex, with spicy, cedary carbonic characters flowing through to an equivalently complex palate that has an utterly different fruit register and an equally different silky/foresty tannin structure.

rating: 95

best drinking 2002–2010 **best vintages** '98 **drink with** Game • $120

Dalwhinnie Moonambel Shiraz

YYYYY **1999** Medium to full red-purple; luscious dark cherry and plum with hints of spice from the fruit and oak on the bouquet, then a richly structured palate with full dark cherry and plum fruit. There are no jammy or porty characters at all, the wine flowing through to marvellously ripe but soft tannins on the finish.

rating: 95

best drinking 2004–2014 **best vintages** '86, '88, '90, '91, '92, '94, '95, '97, '98, '99 **drink with** Potent cheeses, strong red meats • $45

Dalwhinnie Moonambel Cabernet Sauvignon

YYYY **1999** Medium red-purple; the bouquet is quite scented, with sweet cassis/currant/blackberry fruit. The palate opens with abundant dark berry fruit, but then moves through to all-pervasive tannins that need to settle and soften, and there has to be a question about the long-term balance of the wine.

rating: 87

best drinking 2004–2014 **best vintages** '92, '93 **drink with** Rare char-grilled rump steak • $40

dalyup river estate NR

Murrays Road, Esperance, WA 6450 **region** South West Australia Zone
phone (08) 9076 5027 **fax** (08) 9076 5027 **open** Weekends 10–4

winemaker Tom Murray **production** 700 **est.** 1987
product range ($12–15 CD) Hellfire White, Esperance Sauvignon Blanc, Esperance Shiraz, Esperance Cabernet Sauvignon, Port.
summary Arguably the most remote winery in Australia other than Chateau Hornsby in Alice Springs. The quantities are as small as the cellar-door prices are modest; this apart, the light but fragrant wines show the cool climate of this ocean-side vineyard. Came from out of the clouds to win the trophy for Best Wine of Show at the West Australian Show in 1999 with its Shiraz.

dal zotto wines ★★★★

Edi Road, Cheshunt, Vic 3678 **region** King Valley
phone (03) 5729 8321 **fax** (03) 5729 8490 **open** Thurs–Mon 10–5
winemaker Otto Dal Zotto, Warren Proft **production** 5000 **est.** 1987
product range ($12–24 CD) Riesling, Chardonnay, Shiraz, Merlot, Cabernet Merlot, Cabernet Sauvignon.
summary Dal Zotto Wines remains primarily a contract grape-grower, with almost 26 hectares of vineyards (predominantly chardonnay, cabernet sauvignon and merlot, but with trial plantings of sangiovese, barbera and marzemino), but does make a small amount of wine for local sale and by mail order. As the tasting notes indicate, the wines deserve a far wider audience.

Dal Zotto Riesling

🍷🍷🍷🍷🍷 **2000** Light straw-green; the bouquet is light, clean and crisp, with some floral lime aromatics, but also a strong minerally content. The palate has very considerable intensity and length, with a spread of ripe lime, tropical and apple flavours, closing with brisk acidity. **rating:** 94
best drinking Now–2005 **best vintages** '00 **drink with** Tempura prawns • $14

Dal Zotto Chardonnay

🍷🍷🍷🍷 **1999** Medium to full yellow-green; obvious, smoky barrel-ferment aromas mingle with peach and melon on the bouquet; there is attractive peachy fruit to the weighty palate, augmented by well-balanced oak. **rating:** 88
best drinking Now **best vintages** NA **drink with** Grilled spatchcock • $18

Dal Zotto Shiraz

🍷🍷🍷🍷 **1998** Excellent red-purple; the bouquet is clean and quite rich, with an attractive mix of savoury berry fruit and gentle oak. The palate is well above the average King Valley wine, with plenty of fruit structure and concentration; sweet but not jammy; nice length and subtle oak. **rating:** 89
best drinking 2002–2007 **best vintages** NA **drink with** Beef shish kebabs • $24

danbury estate NR

Billimari, NSW 2794 (PO Box 605, Cowra, NSW 2794) **region** Cowra
phone (02) 6341 2204 **fax** (02) 6341 4690 **open** Tues–Sun 10–4
winemaker Peter Howland (Contract) **production** 4000 **est.** 1996
product range ($12.95–15.30 CD) Chardonnay, Cabernet Merlot.
summary A specialist Chardonnay producer established by Jonathon Middleton, with 8 hectares in production and the wines made under contract. The Quarry Restaurant is open the same hours as the winery.

Danbury Estate Chardonnay

🍷🍷🍷½ **1999** Medium yellow-green; a clean, gentle bouquet of melon, fig and mineral, supported by gentle oak, leads into a crisp, clean Chablis-style palate with minerally characters; ageing quite nicely. **rating:** 83
best drinking Now–2003 **best vintages** NA **drink with** White fish • NA

d'arenberg ★★★★☆

Osborn Road, McLaren Vale, SA 5171 **region** McLaren Vale
phone (08) 8323 8206 **fax** (08) 8323 8423 **open** 7 days 10–5
winemaker Chester Osborn, Phillip Dean **production** 150 000 **est.** 1912
product range ($10–60 R) Dry Dam Riesling, Dryland Sauvignon Blanc, Broken Fishplate Sauvignon Blanc, Last Ditch Viognier, Olive Grove Chardonnay, Other Side Chardonnay, White Ochre, Noble Riesling, Noble Semillon, Peppermint Paddock Sparkling Chambourcin, Twenty Eight Road Mourvedre, d'Arry's Original Shiraz

Grenache, Custodian Grenache, Peppermint Paddock Chambourcin, Dead Arm Shiraz, Footbolt Old Vine Shiraz, Red Ochre, Ironstone Pressings, High Trellis Cabernet Sauvignon, The Coppermine Road Cabernet Sauvignon; Vintage Fortified Shiraz, Nostalgia Rare Tawny.

summary Originally a conservative, traditional (albeit successful) business, d'Arenberg adopted a much higher profile in the second half of the 1990s, with a cascade of volubly worded labels and the opening of a spectacularly situated and high-quality restaurant, d'Arry's Verandah. Happily, wine quality has more than kept pace with the label uplifts. An incredible number of export markets spread across Europe, North America and Asia, with all of the major countries represented.

d'Arenberg The Broken Fishplate Sauvignon Blanc

YYYY **2000** Light green-yellow; the bouquet is firm, ranging through mineral and more grassy/herbaceous aromas. The palate is firm, clean and correct, not intense, and of moderate length. **rating:** 86

best drinking Now **best vintages** NA **drink with** Steamed fish • $19

d'Arenberg The Other Side Chardonnay

YYYY **1999** Medium yellow-straw; the bouquet is clean and solid, but not particularly aromatic; the palate, however, opens up with clean, smooth, ripe peach flavours, subtle oak and nice length. **rating:** 88

best drinking Now–2003 **best vintages** NA **drink with** Roast turkey • $35

d'Arenberg Noble Semillon

YYYY **1999** Golden-brown, really too advanced for its age; a caramelised toffee bouquet leads into a liquid toffee and honeysnap palate, held together by balanced acidity. Fairly extreme, but lots of flavour impact if consumed sooner rather than later. **rating:** 86

best drinking Now **best vintages** NA **drink with** Pecan pie • $32.95

d'Arenberg The Footbolt Old Vine Shiraz

YYYY **1999** Medium to full red-purple; there is lots of dark, spicy fruit on the bouquet, the oak evident but controlled. The palate shows full, sweet berry fruit, closing with oak and balanced tannins. Simply doesn't have the fruit persistence of the '98s. **rating:** 88

best drinking 2002–2007 **best vintages** '82, '88, '90, '91, '94, '95, '96, '97 **drink with** Smoked lamb with redcurrant sauce • $21.50

d'Arenberg d'Arry's Original Shiraz Grenache

YYYYY **1999** Medium purple-red; a very fresh and youthful bouquet with bright cherry jam varietal character is followed by a palate with excellent mouthfeel and balance; still a baby, but will make it. **rating:** 90

best drinking 2004–2010 **best vintages** '63, '76, '86, '87, '88, '91, '95, '96, '97 **drink with** Jugged hare • $21.50

d'Arenberg Twenty Eight Road Mourvedre

YYYY **1999** Medium to full red-purple; dark, spicy blackberry aromas with a touch of licorice lead into a powerful dark-fruited palate with abundant varietal tannins and a lingering aftertaste. **rating:** 89

best drinking 2004–2009 **best vintages** '95, '96 **drink with** Thick, rare rump • $32.95

d'Arenberg The Custodian Grenache

YYYY **1999** Light to medium red-purple; sweet varietal jammy/berry fruit with a touch of spice on the bouquet is largely repeated on the spicy dried berry palate. **rating:** 86

best drinking 2002–2007 **best vintages** '91, '92, '94, '95, '96, '98 **drink with** Ragout of venison • $27.50

d'Arenberg The High Trellis Cabernet Sauvignon

YYYY **1999** Medium to full red-purple; very ripe and full blackcurrant/blackberry/prune aromas are replicated on the palate with addition of chewy tannins. All in all, a very big, powerful wine. **rating:** 89

best drinking 2004–2009 **best vintages** '98 **drink with** Rack of lamb • $18.50

dargo valley winery NR

Lower Dargo Road, Dargo, Vic 3682 **region** Gippsland

phone (03) 5140 1228 **fax** (03) 5140 1388 **open** Mon–Thur 12–8; weekends, holidays 10–8 (closed Fridays)

winemaker Hermann Bila **production** 200 **est.** 1985

product range ($12–14 CD) Traminer, Rhine Riesling, Sauvignon Blanc, Chardonnay, Pinot Noir, Cabernet Sauvignon, Port, Muscat.

summary Two and a half hectares are situated in mountain country north of Maffra and looking towards the Bogong National Park. Hermann Bila comes from a family of European winemakers; there is an on site restaurant, and Devonshire teas and ploughman's lunches are provided, which is very useful given the remote locality. The white wines tend to be rustic, the sappy/earthy/cherry Pinot Noir the pick of the red wines.

darling estate ★★★

Whitfield Road, Cheshunt, Vic 3678 **region** King Valley
phone (03) 5729 8396 **fax** (03) 5729 8396 **open** By appointment
winemaker Guy Darling, Rick Kinzbrunner (Consultant) **production** 200 **est.** 1990
product range ($6.25–18.75 ML) Koombahla Riesling, Nambucca Chenin Blanc, Koombahla Chardonnay, Koombahla Pinot Noir, Nambucca Gamay, Koombahla Shiraz, Koombahla Cabernet Franc, Koombahla Cabernet Sauvignon.
summary Guy Darling was one of the pioneers of the King Valley when he planted his first vines in 1970. For many years the entire production was purchased by Brown Brothers, providing their well-known Koombahla Estate label. Much of the production from the 23 hectares is still sold to Brown Brothers (and others), but since 1991 Guy Darling has had a fully functional winery established on the vineyard, making a small portion of the production into wine (which was, in fact, his original motivation for planting the first vines). All the wines on sale have considerable bottle age.

darling park ★★★★

Red Hill Road, Red Hill, Vic 3937 **region** Mornington Peninsula
phone (03) 5989 2732 **fax** (03) 5989 2254 **open** Weekends and public holidays 11–5 and any time the vineyard gates are open
winemaker John Sargeant, John Brooks **production** 1700 **est.** 1986
product range ($16–30 CD) Chardonnay, Pinot Gris, Querida (Rosé), Tempranillo, Decadence, Pinot Noir, Pinot Noir Reserve, Shiraz, Merlot, Cabernet Merlot, Halcyon Cabernet.
summary The labels are the most gloriously baroque of any to be found in Australia and would give the American Bureau of Alcohol, Tobacco and Firearms (which governs such matters in the US) total cardiac arrest. At the ripe young age of 70 John Sargeant took over the winemaking of the red wines as from the 1996 vintage, and John and Delys Sargeant have now opened a cellar door-cum-restaurant.

Darling Park Pinot Noir

🍷🍷🍷🍷🍷 **2000** Medium red-purple; a complex and strongly varietal bouquet with spicy/foresty/savoury overtones to the cherry and plum fruit. The palate is in the same mode, with spicy, plummy fruit; nice balance, weight and length. The best from Darling Park to date, fully reflecting the excellent vintage. **rating:** 90
best drinking 2002–2005 **best vintages** '00 **drink with** Roast squab • $25

darlington estate ★★★☆

Lot 39 Nelson Road, Darlington, WA 6070 **region** Perth Hills
phone (08) 9299 6268 **fax** (08) 9299 7107 **open** Thurs–Sun and holidays 12–5
winemaker John Griffiths **production** 2000 **est.** 1983
product range ($13–30 CD) Sonata (Sauvignon Blanc), Semillon, Chardonnay, Symphony (Verdelho), Serenade (Chardonnay), Shiraz, Cabernet Sauvignon, Brut, Ruby Port; Darling Red (Grenache), Darling White (Unwooded Chardonnay), Darling Rose (Grenache).
summary By far the largest producer in the Perth Hills region, and the best. Winemaking responsibilities passed to Caspar van der Meer, Balt's son, who graduated from Roseworthy in 1995 and, after a vintage at Chateau de Landiras in Bordeaux, joined the family business in 1996, returning to Languedoc in 1997 to make a large quantity of wine for the US market. He has now left to pursue further overseas winemaking opportunities with winemaking passing to John Griffiths, who is possessed of an excellent palate.

david hook wines NR

Carramar, Belford, NSW 2335 **region** Lower Hunter Valley
phone (02) 6574 7164 **fax** (02) 6574 7209 **open** By appointment
winemaker David Hook **production** 2000 **est.** 1984
product range ($14–16 R) Chardonnay, Semillon, Pinot Noir, Adina Pinot Grigio; The Gorge range of Unwooded Chardonnay, Classic Dry White, Chardonnay, Verdelho, Semillon, Pinot Noir and Shiraz.

summary Principally sold through Pokolbin Estate and by mailing list; the Chardonnay is a soft, buttery/toasty wine in mainstream Hunter Valley style. The choice of three names, Hook's Pothana Vineyard, The Gorge and David Hook Wines, does no one any favours.

The Gorge Semillon

TTTT **1999** Light to medium green-yellow; a clean, smooth and quite rich bouquet with quite lemony fruit leads into a full-flavoured palate with lemon and even a hint of stonefruit; slightly broad, and relatively quick-developing. **rating:** 85

best drinking Now–2004 **best vintages** NA **drink with** Stuffed crab claw • $14.07

The Gorge Semillon Sauvignon Blanc

TTTY **1999** Light to medium yellow-green; the bouquet is soft, with a suggestion of the barest hint of oak, though none is mentioned either on the label or on other background material provided by Pothana. The palate is in easy-drinking mode, but does shorten significantly on the finish. **rating:** 83

best drinking Now **best vintages** NA **drink with** Light seafood • $14.07

The Gorge Shiraz

TTTY **1999** Medium to full red-purple; there are overtones of mint and vanilla and a substrate of earth to the berry fruit of the bouquet, which smooths out on the light to medium-bodied red berry palate, finishing with soft tannins and subtle oak. **rating:** 84

best drinking 2002–2006 **best vintages** NA **drink with** Rack of lamb • $15.73

david traeger ★★★☆

139 High Street, Nagambie, Vic 3608 **region** Goulburn Valley
phone (03) 5794 2514 **fax** (03) 5794 1776 **open** 7 days 10–5
winemaker David Traeger **production** 10 000 **est.** 1986
product range ($11–29.50 R) Verdelho, Shiraz, Cabernet; Helvetia (available from cellar door only), Classic Dry (Riesling Semillon), Late Harvest (Riesling Verdelho), Cabernet Dolce, Cabernet Shiraz Merlot, Tawny Port.
summary David Traeger learned much during his years as assistant winemaker at Mitchelton, and knows central Victoria well. The red wines are solidly crafted, the Verdelho interesting but more variable in quality. Reasonably active retail distribution through Victoria, New South Wales and Queensland, with exports to the UK, the US, Japan and Singapore.

David Traeger Verdelho

TTTT **2000** Light to medium green-yellow; the bouquet is clean, with positive, tropical fruit salad aromas, clear and uncluttered. The palate has good mouthfeel, with tropical fruit on the mid-palate and neatly balanced acidity on the finish. More than workmanlike. **rating:** 85

best drinking Now–2003 **best vintages** '91, '94, '95, '97 **drink with** Sweet and sour pork • $17.50

David Traeger Shiraz

TTTT **1998** Strong red-purple; ripe dark berry/black cherry fruit has touches of mint and chocolate on the bouquet. These flavours come through strongly on the palate, supported by positive vanilla American oak and soft tannins on the finish. Traditional, perhaps, but well balanced and flavoursome. **rating:** 88

best drinking 2003–2008 **best vintages** '88, '92, '97, '98 **drink with** Wild duck • $29.50

deakin estate 

Kulkyne Way, via Red Cliffs, Vic 3496 **region** Murray Darling
phone (03) 5029 1666 **fax** (03) 5024 3316 **open** Not
winemaker Mark Zeppel **production** 200 000 **est.** 1980
product range ($9.99–12.99 R) Colombard, Sauvignon Blanc, Chardonnay, Shiraz, Cabernet Sauvignon, Brut; Alfred Chardonnay and Alfred Shiraz were flagbearers, replaced by the Select range in November 2000.
summary Effectively replaces the Sunnycliff label in the Yunghanns-owned Katnook Estate, Riddoch and (now) Deakin Estate triumvirate, which constitutes the Wingara Wine Group. Sunnycliff is still used for export purposes but does not appear on the domestic market any more. Deakin Estate draws on 346 hectares of its own vineyards, making it largely self-sufficient, and produces competitively priced wines of consistent quality and impressive value, getting better year by year. Exports to the UK, the US, Canada, Switzerland, Hong Kong and the Philippines.

Deakin Estate Sauvignon Blanc

🍷🍷🍷🍷 **2000** Pale straw-green; the bouquet is light, but has rather more varietal character than one might expect, with touches of fresh gooseberry. The palate is light, but clean and crisp, with hints of herbaceous and gooseberry varietal fruit. More than useful at the price. **rating:** 82

best drinking Now **best vintages** NA **drink with** Vegetarian • $10

de bortoli ★★★★

De Bortoli Road, Bilbul, NSW 2680 **region** Riverina
phone (02) 6964 9444 **fax** (02) 6964 9400 **open** Mon–Sat 9–5.30, Sun 9–4
winemaker Nick Guy, Ralph Graham **production** 3 million **est.** 1928
product range ($4.90–42.50 CD) Noble One Botrytis Semillon is the flagship wine; Premium varietals under Deen De Bortoli label; a low-priced range of varietal and generic wines under the Sacred Hill label; Sparkling, Fortified. Substantial exports in bulk; Montage Semillon Sauvignon Blanc, Chardonnay Semillon, Cabernet Merlot.
summary Famous among the cognoscenti for its superb Botrytis Semillon, which in fact accounts for only a minute part of its total production, this winery turns around low-priced varietal and generic wines that are invariably competently made and equally invariably provide value for money. Exports include Canada, Singapore, Japan, Hong Kong, Sweden and Thailand.

De Bortoli Vat 2 Sauvignon Blanc

🍷🍷🍷🍷 **2000** Very light straw-green; the bouquet is clean and light, with a mix of grassy varietal fruit and just a hint of pineapple. The palate follows down the same track, the wine simply lacking intensity but, by the same token, providing easy drinking. **rating:** 80

best drinking Now **best vintages** NA **drink with** Tom yum soup • $12

De Bortoli Vat 5 Late Semillon

🍷🍷🍷🍷 **1996** Glowing, golden; rich cumquat, lime and toffee aromas are followed by a palate that is tangy and lively, but is nowhere near as intense or as sweet as Noble One. Compared with any other yardstick, certainly has character. **rating:** 87

best drinking Now **best vintages** NA **drink with** Fresh or poached fruit • $10

De Bortoli Noble One Botrytis Semillon

🍷🍷🍷🍷🍷 **1999** Glowing green-yellow; the complex, intense and layered bouquet ranges through lime, marmalade and cumquat; the palate is very intense and very well balanced, the lingering acidity stretching the acidity on and on. **rating:** 94

best drinking 2002–2008 **best vintages** '82, '84, '87, '90, '91, '94, '95, '96, '97, '98, '99 **drink with** Crème brûlée • $22

Deen De Bortoli Shiraz

🍷🍷🍷🍷🍷 **1999** This wine eloquently attests to the transformation over recent years of the quality of red wines from the irrigation areas. A decidedly complex and rich bouquet with a touch of licorice and attractive oak introduces a palate with richness and texture to the dark berry, licorice and spice flavours; good tannins, too. **rating:** 90

best drinking Now–2003 **best vintages** '99 **drink with** Meat pie, designer or not • $11

De Bortoli Vat 8 Shiraz

🍷🍷🍷🍷 **1999** Medium red-purple; the bouquet is clean, quite smooth, with plum and a touch of blackberry; the palate is soft, clean and surprisingly rich, with well-handled vanilla (American) oak. 14.5° alcohol. A trophy and gold medal winner. **rating:** 86

best drinking Now–2004 **best vintages** NA **drink with** Barbecued pork ribs • $10

De Bortoli Deen De Bortoli Vat 1 Durif

🍷🍷🍷🍷 **1999** Light to medium red-purple; clean, fresh berry aromas are not particularly distinctive; there is rather more to the palate, with dark berry/chocolate/licorice fruit, the touch of tannins speaking of the variety as much as anything else. Simply good value at the price, with a little flick of interest from the varietal composition. **rating:** 83

best drinking Now **best vintages** NA **drink with** Takeway • $10

De Bortoli Show Liqueur Muscat

🍷🍷🍷🍷 **NV** Dark red; a complex raisin and fruit cake bouquet leads into a luscious, rich and complex palate with excellent concentration and a strong grapey/raisiny expression of varietal character. **rating:** 88

best drinking Now **best vintages** NA **drink with** Coffee and cake • $14.50

De Bortoli Black Noble

YYYYY **NV** Mahogany brown with no red tints; you can literally see the raisins and the plum pudding swirling through the intense bouquet and through the classic plum pudding and spice-flavoured palate. Great length and balance, and not too heavy.

rating: 94

best drinking Now **best vintages** NA **drink with** On its own as an aperitif or with coffee • NA

de bortoli (victoria) ★★★★★

Pinnacle Lane, Dixons Creek, Vic 3775 **region** Yarra Valley
phone (03) 5965 2271 **fax** (03) 5965 2442 **open** 7 days 10–5
winemaker Stephen Webber, David Slingsby-Smith, David Bicknell **production** 170 000 **est.** 1987
product range ($12–36 R) At the top comes the premium Melba (Cabernet blend), followed by Yarra Valley Gewurztraminer, Chardonnay, Pinot Noir, Shiraz, Cabernet Franc, Merlot, Cabernet Sauvignon; then comes the intermediate Gulf Station range of Riesling, Semillon Sauvignon Blanc, Unwooded Chardonnay, Chardonnay, Pinot Noir, Shiraz and Cabernet Sauvignon; the Windy Peak range of Riesling, Spätlese Riesling, Chardonnay, Pinot Noir, Cabernet Shiraz Merlot, Prestige Cuvée.
summary The quality arm of the bustling De Bortoli group, run by Leanne De Bortoli and husband Stephen Webber, ex-Lindeman winemaker. The top label (De Bortoli), the second (Gulf Station) and the third label (Windy Peak) offer wines of consistently good quality and excellent value; the complex Chardonnay is of outstanding quality. Shares the same amazing split of export markets with its parent. Exports to the UK, Europe, Asia and the US.

De Bortoli Gulf Station Riesling

YYYY **2000** Light green-yellow; plenty of fruit aromas ranging from sweet lime through to a touch of herb introduce a wine with good structure and intensity on the palate; dissolved carbon dioxide (and sulphur dioxide) needs time to settle down, which will happen.

rating: 89

best drinking Now–2006 **best vintages** NA **drink with** Artichoke with hollandaise sauce • $16

De Bortoli Yarra Valley Gewurztraminer

YYYY **1999** Light green-yellow; the bouquet offers delicate rose-petal and spice aromas, the palate crisp, clean, bone-dry and finishing with crisp acidity that masks any suggestion of sweetness. Has won one gold, two silver and three bronze medals; no mean feat for a variety that by and large finds little favour with show judges.

rating: 89

best drinking Now **best vintages** '99 **drink with** Chinese Szechuan-style food • $24

De Bortoli Gulf Station Semillon Sauvignon Blanc

YYYY **2000** Light green-yellow; the fresh bouquet has crisp, lemony fruit with a hint of gooseberry. The palate is similarly lively, fresh and crisp, with citrussy flavours and lively acidity in classic summer seafood style.

rating: 88

best drinking Now **best vintages** NA **drink with** Summer seafood • $16

De Bortoli Gulf Station Unwooded Chardonnay

YYYY **2000** Light to medium yellow-green; there is quite firm melon and citrus fruit to the bouquet, the palate likewise with crisp, tangy fruit, good acidity and above-average length and presence.

rating: 88

best drinking Now–2003 **best vintages** NA **drink with** Yabbies • $16

De Bortoli Windy Peak Chardonnay

YYYY **2000** Light straw-green; the moderately intense bouquet shows an obvious but clever touch of toasty oak alongside melon fruit. The palate is lively, fresh and elegant, not exhibiting a great volume of fruit, but certainly indicative of clever winemaking. A gold and trophy winner at the 2000 Melbourne Wine Show, gold medal at 2000 Brisbane Wine Show.

rating: 88

best drinking Now **best vintages** '90, '92, '93, '94, '97, '00 **drink with** Sashimi • $13

De Bortoli Yarra Valley Chardonnay

YYYYY **1999** A trophy and multi gold-medal winner from what is euphemistically called a difficult vintage. Glowing yellow-green, the complex bouquet offers perfectly balanced and integrated oak with ripe melon fruit, the seamless and equally well-balanced palate sustained by natural acidity running through the long finish.

rating: 93

best drinking Now–2004 **best vintages** '90, '92, '93, '94, '96, '97, '98, '99 **drink with** Braised pork neck • $23

De Bortoli Gulf Station Pinot Noir

YYYY **2000** Medium red-purple; the bouquet offers clean, smooth, plummy fruit that is not especially complex, but the underlying power is immediately evident on the palate, which has an abundance of plummy fruit and likely to develop very well. As it is, one of the top three or four competitively-priced Pinots in Australia. **rating:** 88

best drinking 2002–2006 **best vintages** '00 **drink with** Roast pigeon • $15

De Bortoli Gulf Station Shiraz

YYYY **1999** Excellent bright red-purple; the moderately intense bouquet is clean, with plum, cherry and spicy fruit aromas supported by subtle oak. The palate has good balance and weight, with more of the plum, spice and savoury flavours promised by the bouquet. A particularly good outcome for a difficult vintage. **rating:** 87

best drinking 2002–2006 **best vintages** '99 **drink with** Stir-fried beef • $16

De Bortoli Yarra Valley Shiraz

YYYY **1999** Medium red-purple; a spicy, leafy, briary mix on the bouquet is offset by a touch of vanilla oak; the light to medium bodied palate brings dark cherry into the mix, finishing with light tannins. A good outcome for the vintage. **rating:** 87

best drinking 2002–2006 **best vintages** '88, '90, '91, '92, '94, '97, '98 **drink with** Grilled calf's liver • $29

De Bortoli Yarra Valley Cabernet Sauvignon

YYYY **1999** Medium to full red-purple; the bouquet is clean, with ripe blackberry/earth varietal character; the palate is similar, with slightly austere blackberry fruit, the cedary oak well balanced and integrated. **rating:** 88

best drinking 2003–2008 **best vintages** '88, '90, '91, '92, '94, '95, '97, '98 **drink with** Beef casserole • $29

deep dene vineyard NR

36 Glenisla Road, Bickley, WA 6076 **region** Perth Hills
phone (08) 9293 0077 **fax** (08) 9293 0077 **open** By appointment
winemaker Celine Rousseau (Contract) **production** 4000 **est.** 1994
product range ($25–28 R) Pinot Noir, Shiraz.
summary The largest of the Perth Hills vineyards, with French-born and trained Celine Rousseau as winemaker. It draws upon 4 hectares of pinot noir and 0.5 hectare of shiraz, continuing the near-obsession of the Perth Hills vignerons with pinot noir in a climate that, to put it mildly, is difficult for the variety.

deep woods estate NR

Lot 10 Commonage Road, Yallingup, WA 6282 **region** Margaret River
phone (08) 9756 6066 **fax** (08) 9756 6066 **open** Tues–Sun 11–5, 7 days during holidays
winemaker Bruce Dukes, Ben Gould **production** 12 000 **est.** 1987
product range ($16–24 CD) Semillon, Verdelho, Late Harvest (Verdelho), Eden (Botrytis Semillon), Deep Red Shiraz, Cabernet Sauvignon, Reserve Cabernet Sauvignon.
summary The substantial-sized Deep Woods Estate has a convoluted history, with a number of changes of ownership since the first vines were planted in 1987. It is now owned by Malcolm and Margaret Gould who, with assistance from their children, are running both Deep Woods Estate and the Margaret River Marron Farm. In all, there are 24 hectares of vineyard planted to 14 different varieties, with a winery erected in 1998.

Deep Woods Estate Semillon Sauvignon Blanc

YYYYY **2000** Light green-yellow; the bouquet has a nice mix of a gentle touch of tropical fruit with more grassy/lemony notes; the palate has excellent mouthfeel with the fruit flavours of passionfruit, gooseberry, lemon and grass flowing throughout the length, without dipping. A crisp, clean finish rounds it off. **rating:** 92

best drinking Now **best vintages** '00 **drink with** Margaret River abalone • $18.95

Deep Woods Estate Cabernet Sauvignon

YYYYY **1999** Medium to full red-purple; sweet, dark berry/cassis aromas drive the bouquet, and there is abundant soft, sweet, ripe dark berry/cassis fruit on the palate, supported by subtle oak and soft, ripe tannins. **rating:** 90

best drinking 2003–2009 **best vintages** '99 **drink with** Venison with juniper berry sauce • $21.95

de iuliis ★★★☆

Lot 1 Lovedale Road, Keinbah, NSW 2321 **region** Lower Hunter Valley
phone (02) 4930 7403 **fax** (02) 4968 8192 **open** By appointment
winemaker David Hook, Michael De Iuliis **production** 5000 **est.** 1990
product range ($11–17 CD) Semillon, Verdelho, Chardonnay, Shiraz, Cabernet Merlot, Sparkling Pinot Chardonnay.
summary Three generations of the De Iuliis family have been involved in the establishment of their 19.5-hectare vineyard at Keinbah in the Lower Hunter Valley. The family acquired the property in 1986 and planted the first vines in 1990, selling the grapes from the first few vintages to Tyrrell's but retaining small amounts of grapes for release under the De Iuliis label. Michael De Iuliis, the third-generation family member involved, is completing postgraduate studies in oenology at the Roseworthy Campus of Adelaide University and assists David Hook (a long-term Hunter winemaker) in making the wine. The overall quality of the wines is good; at this juncture, they are only available by mail order or from cellar door.

delacolline estate ★★★

Whillas Road, Port Lincoln, SA 5606 **region** The Peninsulas Zone
phone (08) 8682 5277 **fax** (08) 8682 4455 **open** Weekends 9–5
winemaker Andrew Mitchell (Contract) **production** 650 **est.** 1984
product range ($10–15 R) Riesling, Fumé Blanc, Cabernet Sauvignon.
summary Joins Boston Bay as the second Port Lincoln producer; the white wines are made under contract in the Clare Valley. The 3-hectare vineyard, run under the direction of Tony Bassett, reflects the cool maritime influence: ocean currents sweep up from the Antarctic.

delamere ★★★

Bridport Road, Pipers Brook, Tas 7254 **region** Northern Tasmania
phone (03) 6382 7190 **fax** (03) 6382 7250 **open** 7 days 10–5
winemaker Richard Richardson **production** 2000 **est.** 1983
product range ($16–24 CD) Chardonnay, Chardonnay Reserve, White Pinot Noir, Pinot Noir (Standard, Dry Red and Reserve), Sparkling.
summary Richie Richardson produces elegant, rather light-bodied wines that have a strong following. The Chardonnay has been most successful: a textured, complex, malolactic-influenced wine with great creamy feel in the mouth. The Pinots typically show pleasant varietal fruit, but seem to suffer from handling problems with oak and a touch of oxidation. Retail distribution through fine wine outlets in Tasmania, Melbourne, Sydney and Brisbane.

delaney's creek winery NR

70 Hennessey Road, Delaney's Creek, Qld 4514 **region** Queensland Zone
phone (07) 5496 4925 **fax** (07) 5496 4926 **open** Mon–Fri 10–4, weekends and public holidays 10–5
winemaker Brian Wilson **production** 3000 **est.** 1997
product range ($9.50–14.50 CD) Verdelho, Marsanne Blanc, Muscat Rosé, Cabernet Franc, Shiraz Cabernet Franc, Fortifieds.
summary Tom Weidmann established this winery in 1997 and by doing so has expanded the vineyard map of Queensland even further. Delaney's Creek is situated near the town of Woodford, itself not far northwest of Caboolture. In 1998 Weidmann planted an exotic mix of 1 hectare each of shiraz, chardonnay, sangiovese, touriga nacional and verdelho. In the meantime he is obtaining his grapes from 4 hectares of contract-grown fruit, including cabernet sauvignon, cabernet franc, merlot, shiraz, chardonnay, marsanne and verdelho.

delatite ★★★★

Stoneys Road, Mansfield, Vic 3722 **region** Central Victorian Mountain Country
phone (03) 5775 2922 **fax** (03) 5775 2911 **open** 7 days 10–4
winemaker Rosalind Ritchie **production** 14 000 **est.** 1982
product range ($15–35 CD) Riesling, Dead Man's Hill Gewürztraminer, Sauvignon Blanc, Unoaked Chardonnay, Chardonnay, Late Picked Riesling, Delmelza Pinot Chardonnay, Pinot Noir, Shiraz, Merlot, Malbec,

Dungeon Gully, Devil's River (Cabernet Sauvignon Malbec Shiraz), Fortifieds; V.S. Limited Edition Riesling, R.J. Limited Edition (Cabernet blend).

summary With its sweeping views across to the snow-clad alps, this is uncompromising cool-climate viticulture, and the wines naturally reflect the climate. Light but intense Riesling and spicy Traminer flower with a year or two in bottle, and in the warmer vintages the red wines achieve flavour and mouthfeel, albeit with a distinctive mintiness. Exports to the UK, Switzerland, Malaysia and Singapore.

Delatite Riesling

YYYY 2000 Very light yellow-straw; light, floral spice and herb aromas are in the mainstream of the Delatite style, the palate almost painfully shy and delicate in the manner of a young Semillon. History puts the development potential beyond doubt; the rating is that of today, not tomorrow. **rating:** 85

best drinking 2003–2009 **best vintages** '82, '86, '87, '93, '97, '99 **drink with** Grilled fish • $18

Delatite V.S. Limited Edition Riesling

YYYYY 1999 Light green-yellow; the bouquet is clean and fresh, with sweet lime juice and hints of toast and mineral. The palate has excellent structure and intensity, with a distinctly minerally grip. An elegant wine. **rating:** 91

best drinking 2002–2009 **best vintages** '99 **drink with** Shellfish • $23

Delatite Dead Man's Hill Gewürztraminer

YYYY 2000 Very light straw; perfumed, spicy, floral aromatics and flavours are absolutely indicative of the very cool climate. Like the Riesling, a certainty to age well. **rating:** 84

best drinking 2003–2008 **best vintages** '82, '86, '87, '93, '94, '97, '99 **drink with** Smoked trout • $23

Delatite Shiraz

YYYY 1998 Medium red-purple; a fine, spicy/leafy/savoury bouquet is followed by a light to medium bodied palate reflecting the characters of the bouquet, and adding a touch of mint. **rating:** 84

best drinking Now–2005 **best vintages** '94 **drink with** Leg of lamb • $23

Delatite Devil's River

YYYY 1998 Light to medium red-purple; as ever, the bouquet offers a mix of mint, leaf and spice, the palate likewise, picked up slightly by a touch of sweet oak on the finish. **rating:** 83

best drinking 2002–2005 **best vintages** '82, '86, '88, '90 **drink with** Leg of lamb • $23

Delatite Dungeon Gully

YYYY 2000 Medium red-purple; a lively, predominantly spicy bouquet with some leaf and red berry characters is followed by an interesting palate, with pronounced cinnamon spice to the red berry fruit and fine tannins. A most appealing early-drinking style. **rating:** 87

best drinking Now **best vintages** NA **drink with** Italian • $18

Delatite R.J. Limited Edition

YYYY 1998 Medium red-purple; as ever, a mix of very fragrant leafy/spicy/savoury but, above all, minty fruit. The palate provides the same in spades, shrieking of the site climate. **rating:** 85

best drinking 2002–2007 **best vintages** NA **drink with** Lamb with mint sauce • $35

del rios vineyard NR

2320 Ballan Road, Anakie, Vic 3221 **region** Geelong

phone (03) 9497 4644 **fax** (03) 9497 4644 **open** By appointment

winemaker Contract **production** 1300 **est.** 1996

product range ($18–23 ML) Sauvignon Blanc Mt Anakie, Sauvignon Blanc Crisp, Chardonnay, Marsanne, Pinot Noir, Shiraz, Cabernet Sauvignon.

summary German del Rio was born in northern Spain (in 1920) where his family owned vineyards. After three generations in Australia, his family has established 16 hectares of vines on their 104-hectare property on the slopes of Mount Anakie, the principal focus being chardonnay, pinot noir and cabernet sauvignon (4 hectares each) then marsanne, sauvignon blanc, merlot and shiraz (1 hectare each). Planting commenced in 1996, and vintage 2000 was the first commercial release.

demondrille vineyards NR

RMB 97, Prunevale Road, Kingsvale, NSW 2587 **region** Hilltops
phone (02) 6384 4272 **fax** (02) 6384 4272 **open** Weekends 10.30–5 or by appointment
winemaker Tambourlaine (Contract) **production** 1000 **est.** 1979
product range ($12–18 CD) The Dove (Sauvignon Blanc Semillon), Purgatory (Pinot Noir), Bloodline (Pinot Noir), The Raven (Shiraz) and Black Rose (Cabernet Sauvignon Merlot Franc), together with lesser quantities of cellar-door-only wines (from the 'Tin Shed' range).
summary Pamela Gillespie and Robert Provan purchased the former Hercynia Vineyard and winery in 1995. Pam Gillespie has an Associate Diploma in Winemaking and Marketing from Adelaide University, Roseworthy, and has been in the hospitality industry since 1989. Her partner has had a remarkable career and is now part-way through a Bachelor of Science degree at Sydney University, majoring in agriculture. Most of the wines from Demondrille are made at Charles Sturt University, with smaller quantities made on site. Purgatory, though far from a great wine, is not so bad as to deserve its (bizarre) name. Specially created food platters featuring local produce are available at the winery each weekend.

dennis 

Kangarilla Road, McLaren Vale, SA 5171 **region** McLaren Vale
phone (08) 8323 8665 **fax** (08) 8323 9121 **open** Mon–Fri 10–5, weekends and holidays 11–5
winemaker Peter Dennis **production** 10 000 **est.** 1970
product range ($14–40 CD) Sauvignon Blanc, Chardonnay, Shiraz, Cabernet Sauvignon, Grenache, Merlot, Egerton Vintage Port, Old Tawny Port.
summary A low-profile winery that has from time to time made some excellent wines, most notably the typically full-blown, buttery/peachy Chardonnay; in 1998, however, the pendulum swung towards the Shiraz and Cabernet Sauvignon.

d'entrecasteaux NR

Boorara Road, Northcliffe, WA 6262 **region** Pemberton
phone (08) 9776 7232 **open** By appointment
winemaker Alkoomi (Contract) **production** 600 **est.** 1988
product range Chardonnay, Sauvignon Blanc, Pinot Noir, Cabernet Sauvignon.
summary Not to be confused with the now moribund Tasmanian winery of the same name but likewise taking its name from the French explorer Admiral Bruni D'Entrecasteaux, who visited both Tasmania and the southwest coast of Western Australia. Four hectares of estate vineyards, planted on rich Karri loam, produce grapes for the wines that are contract-made at Alkoomi.

derwent estate 

329 Lyell Highway, Granton, Tas 7070 **region** Southern Tasmania
phone (03) 6248 5073 **fax** (03) 6248 5073 **open** Not
winemaker Stefano Lubiana (Contract) **production** 300 **est.** 1993
product range ($17.50 ML) Riesling, Chardonnay, Pinot Noir.
summary The Hanigan family has established Derwent Estate as part of a diversification programme for their 400-hectare mixed farming property. Five hectares of vineyard have been progressively planted since 1993, initially to riesling, followed by chardonnay and pinot noir.

Derwent Estate Chardonnay

YYYYY **2000** Light to medium green-yellow; clean, citrus and herb aromas are balanced by very subtle oak on the bouquet; an elegant and harmonious palate with considerable length is again supported, rather than threatened, by oak. **rating:** 94

best drinking Now–2005 **best vintages** '00 **drink with** Slow-cooked Atlantic salmon • NA

Derwent Estate Pinot Noir

YYYYY **1999** Strong red-purple, bright and clear; the bouquet has distinct stemmy/foresty characters, but there is attractive fresh fruit underneath that hint of stemminess, and the wine has great length and intensity on the palate. An abundance of new oak adds another dimension to the curate's egg. **rating:** 91

best drinking 2002–2007 **best vintages** NA **drink with** Jugged hare • NA

devil's lair ★★★★☆

Rocky Road, Forest Grove, via Margaret River, WA 6286 **region** Margaret River
phone (08) 9757 7573 **fax** (08) 9757 7533 **open** By appointment
winemaker Stuart Pym **production** 14 000 **est.** 1985
product range ($19–42 R) Chardonnay, Margaret River (Cabernet blend); Fifth Leg Dry White and Dry Red.
summary Having rapidly carved out a high reputation for itself through a combination of clever packaging and marketing allied with impressive wine quality, Devil's Lair was acquired by Southcorp Wine Group (Penfolds, etc) in 1996, and production was projected to increase to over 50 000 cases. I ceased to have any involvement with Devil's Lair in May 2000, and hence now rate it and its wines.

Devil's Lair Chardonnay

1999 Light to medium green-yellow; the bouquet is spotlessly clean, of moderate to full intensity, fruit-driven, with nectarine, melon and a touch of citrus. The palate is lively, intense, tangy and fresh, and the wine will undoubtedly be long lived. However, it seems a fairly radical departure in style from prior vintages, and it will be interesting to see how diehard Devil's Lair supporters view the wine. Incidentally, I was briefly involved in the styling of the wine, and have to take some of the responsibility for the change. That said, I have no present or future role in Devil's Lair. **rating:** 92

best drinking 2002–2009 **best vintages** '92, '94, '96, '97, '99 **drink with** Rich white meat • $38

Devil's Lair Fifth Leg Dry Red

1999 Medium to full red-purple; a ripe, complex bouquet with blackberry, blackcurrant and spice aromas is followed by a full palate, offering by far the ripest and most complex fruit flavours to date, the tannins being relatively restrained. Fully reflects an excellent vintage. **rating:** 90

best drinking 2003–2009 **best vintages** '99 **drink with** Devilled kidneys • NA

Devil's Lair Margaret River

1998 Medium to full red-purple; the smooth bouquet shows very good fruit and oak balance and integration, with predominantly blackberry/earthy aromas. As ever, a powerful palate, with lots of dark currant and dark berry fruit, then pervasive, lingering tannins. Leave it, if you possibly can, in the lair for another five years. **rating:** 91

best drinking 2005–2012 **best vintages** '97, '98 **drink with** Char-grilled rump • $40

diamond valley vineyards ★★★★☆

2130 Kinglake Road, St Andrews, Vic 3761 **region** Yarra Valley
phone (03) 9710 1484 **fax** (03) 9710 1369 **open** Not
winemaker David Lance, James Lance **production** 6000 **est.** 1976
product range ($17.50–50.99 R) Chardonnay, Pinot Noir, Cabernet; Yarra Valley (formerly Blue Label) Sauvignon Blanc, Chardonnay, Pinot Noir, Cabernet Merlot; Close Planted Pinot Noir.
summary One of the Yarra Valley's finest producers of Pinot Noir and an early pacesetter for the variety, making wines of tremendous style and crystal-clear varietal character. They are not Cabernet Sauvignon look-alikes but true Pinot Noir, fragrant and intense. Much of the wine is sold through a well-presented mailing list, supplemented by national distribution through Red + White. Deserves five stars for its Pinot Noirs.

Diamond Valley Vineyards Yarra Valley Sauvignon Blanc

2000 Light green-yellow; the bouquet is delicate, but with fragrant passionfruit and blossom aromas. The palate, too, is delicate and fine, but crisp, with a mix of herb, asparagus and passionfruit. All together, an elegant and charming wine. **rating:** 92

best drinking Now–2003 **best vintages** '00 **drink with** Mussels • $16.99

Diamond Valley Estate Pinot Noir

1999 Medium red-purple; a complex and intense bouquet with obvious oak input alongside the sappy/foresty overlay to the fine plum/cherry fruit of the palate, which has good intensity and length. Less evolved than its sister wine, the Yarra Valley (formerly Blue Label). **rating:** 92

best drinking 2002–2005 **best vintages** '86, '90, '91, '92, '93, '94, '96, '98, '99 **drink with** Wild duck • $50.99

Diamond Valley Yarra Valley Cabernet Merlot

1999 Medium red, with just a touch of purple; the bouquet is typically light, ranging through earth, leaf and cassis, with the fragrance progressively swelling; the wine has attractive raspberry/blackberry flavours, but seems to lack finish and texture. **rating:** 84

best drinking Now–2004 **best vintages** NA **drink with** Yearling steak • $20.50

diggers rest NR

205 Old Vineyard Road, Sunbury, Vic 3429 **region** Sunbury
phone (03) 9740 1660 **fax** (03) 9740 1660 **open** By appointment
winemaker Peter Dredge **production** 1000 **est.** 1987
product range ($15–20 CD) Chardonnay, Pinot Noir, Shiraz, Cabernet Sauvignon.
summary Diggers Rest was purchased from the founders Frank and Judith Hogan in July 1998; the new owners, Elias and Joseph Obeid, intend to expand the vineyard resources and significantly increase production.

djinta djinta winery NR

10 Stevens Road, Kardella South, Vic 3950 **region** Gippsland
phone (03) 5658 1163 **fax** (03) 5658 1863 **open** Weekends and public holidays 10–5 or by appointment
winemaker Peter Harley **production** 170 **est.** 1991
product range ($15–21 CD) Semillon, Sauvignon Blanc, Marsanne, Cabernets Merlot, Cabernet Sauvignon.
summary One of a group of wineries situated between Leongatha and Korumburra, the most famous being Bass Phillip. Vines were first planted in 1986 but were largely neglected until Peter and Helen Harley acquired the property in 1991 and set about reviving the 2 hectares of sauvignon blanc and a little cabernet sauvignon, and planted an additional 3 hectares (in total) of merlot, cabernet franc, cabernet sauvignon, semillon, marsanne, roussane and viognier. The first vintage was 1995, during the time that Peter Harley was completing a Bachelor of Applied Science (Wine Science) at Charles Sturt University. They are deliberately adopting a low-technology approach to both vineyard and winery practices, using organic methods wherever possible. They hoped to finish the winery building and a 40-seat restaurant at some stage during 2000.

Djinta Djinta Marsanne Roussanne Viognier

🍷🍷🍷🍸 **2000** Light straw-green; the bouquet is minerally, but slightly muffled. The palate is clean, with good mouthfeel and weight but, as with the bouquet, the fruit doesn't sing, the varietal expression like a Salvadore Dali face. **rating:** 82

best drinking Now–2004 **best vintages** NA **drink with** Understanding • NA

Djinta Djinta Cabernets Merlot

🍷🍷🍷🍸 **1998** Medium red with a touch of purple; a leafy/briary/stemmy/berry bouquet leads into a light to medium bodied palate with some elegance, but drawing most of its character from the savoury end of the spectrum and quite ripe tannins. **rating:** 83

best drinking 2002–2006 **best vintages** NA **drink with** Rack of lamb • NA

domaine a NR

Campania, Tas 7026 **region** Southern Tasmania
phone (03) 6260 4174 **fax** (03) 6260 4390 **open** Mon–Fri 9–4, weekends by appointment
winemaker Peter Althaus **production** 5000 **est.** 1973
product range ($18–60 CD) Top label, Domaine A with Cabernet Sauvignon and Pinot Noir; second label, Stoney Vineyard with Aurora (wood-matured Sylvaner), Sauvignon Blanc, Pinot Noir, Cabernet Sauvignon.
summary The striking black label of the premium Stoney Vineyard wine, dominated by the single multicoloured 'A', signified the change of ownership from George Park to Swiss businessman Peter Althaus. The NR rating for the winery is given in deference to Peter Althaus, who has no faith whatsoever in Australian wine judges or critics, and profoundly disagrees with their ratings. Exports to Switzerland, the US, Singapore, Japan and Hong Kong.

domaine chandon ★★★★★

Green Point, Maroondah Highway, Coldstream, Vic 3770 **region** Yarra Valley
phone (03) 9739 1110 **fax** (03) 9739 1095 **open** 7 days 10.30–4.30
winemaker Dr Tony Jordan, Neville Rowe, James Gosper **production** 90 000 **est.** 1986
product range ($12.50–52 CD) Sparkling (Méthode Champenoise) specialist with five sparkling wines: Brut, Blanc de Blancs, Blanc de Noirs, Rosé, Yarra Valley Cuvée Riche; Green Point is the export label for sparkling wines, also used in all markets for the table wines in varietal and Estate versions; Colonnades is the third label, for table wines.

summary Wholly owned by Moet et Chandon, and the most important wine facility in the Yarra Valley, superbly located with luxurious tasting facilities (a small tasting charge is levied). The wines are exemplary, thought by many to be the best produced by Moet et Chandon in any of its overseas subsidiary operations, a complex blend of French and Australian style. Exports to the UK, Asia and Japan.

Domaine Chandon Green Point Estate Chardonnay

🍷🍷🍷🍷🍸 **1998** Medium yellow-green; the bouquet is quite complex and rich, with fullish melon fruit and nice oak, the palate smooth and well composed with melon, ripe stonefruit and fig flavours supported by high-quality oak through to a long finish. **rating:** 93

best drinking Now–2003 **best vintages** '98 **drink with** Salmon roe • $28

Domaine Chandon Blanc de Blancs

🍷🍷🍷🍷🍸 **1997** Glowing yellow-green; complex bready/autolysis/creamy aromas combine with the fruit, which expresses itself on the palate in a citrus/grapefruit/melon spectrum. Bready characters here reinforce the balance and length of the wine. **rating:** 90

best drinking Now–2003 **best vintages** '90, '92, '93, '95, '97 **drink with** Light seafood • $33

Domaine Chandon Blanc de Noirs

🍷🍷🍷🍷🍸 **1996** Salmon-bronze; a rich, spicy/bready bouquet is followed by a powerful yet not aggressive palate with rounded bready/biscuity/spicy flavours. **rating:** 91

best drinking Now **best vintages** '90, '92, '94, '96 **drink with** Gougères • $33

Domaine Chandon Brut

🍷🍷🍷🍷🍸 **1997** Included because it offers a stark contrast in style, being powerful, rich and concentrated. Bronze-tinged (though not as deeply as the 1996); the bouquet is complex and bready, with touches of spice and straw, the palate with abundant, rounded mouthfeel and flavour, all reflecting the concentration of the 1997 vintage. **rating:** 92

best drinking Now **best vintages** '88, '90, '91, '92, '93, '94, '95, '97 **drink with** Ideal aperitif • $33

Domaine Chandon Brut

🍷🍷🍷🍷 **NV** Salmon-bronze; the solid biscuity/bready bouquet has lots of character, the palate being big, soft and rich, with ripe biscuity flavours with a touch of strawberry; has obvious flavour appeal. **rating:** 86

best drinking Now **best vintages** NA **drink with** Whatever • $20

Domaine Chandon Cuvée Riche

🍷🍷🍷🍷 **NV** Salmon-pink; a big, spicy, rich strawberry-accented bouquet is followed by a palate with full-on flavour and appreciable, though not overwhelming, sweetness; true dessert style. **rating:** 88

best drinking Now **best vintages** NA **drink with** Cakes, fresh fruit • $33

Domaine Chandon Brut Rosé

🍷🍷🍷🍷🍸 **1997** Vibrant salmon; the moderately intense, clean bouquet has aromas of spice and bread, the palate showing surprising delicacy; the best of the '97 vintage, with citrus, strawberry and spice flavours. **rating:** 92

best drinking Now–2003 **best vintages** '90, '92, '93, '94, '97 **drink with** Poached salmon, Asian cuisine • $33

Domaine Chandon Green Point Estate Pinot Noir

🍷🍷🍷🍷 **1998** Medium purple-red; the bouquet is quite intense and complex, with a range of savoury/earthy/foresty characters coupled with obvious oak. The palate is big, very ripe, with savoury plummy fruit; considerable extract and tannin. In the Tarrawarra style. **rating:** 89

best drinking Now–2004 **best vintages** NA **drink with** Venison • $28

Domaine Chandon Green Point McLaren Vale Shiraz

🍷🍷🍷🍷🍸 **1998** Dense red-purple; a full, voluptuous black cherry, plum and licorice bouquet is followed by a rich, ripe plummy palate with excellent oak integration and balance, finishing with sweet, ripe tannins. Has the statutory 14.5° alcohol. **rating:** 90

best drinking 2002–2010 **best vintages** '98 **drink with** Rich game dishes • $25

dominion wines NR

Upton Road, Strathbogie Ranges, via Avenel, Vic 3664 **region** Strathbogie Ranges
phone (03) 5796 2718 **fax** (03) 5796 2719 **open** 7 days 10–5
winemaker Rob Dolan, Travis Bush **production** 32 000 **est.** 1999
product range ($10–18 CD) The cheaper Vinus range of Muscat Gordo, Riesling, Chardonnay, Shiraz Cabernet, Sparkling Shiraz; followed by the Alexander Park label offering Riesling, Sauvignon Blanc, Unwooded Chardonnay, Chardonnay, Pinot Noir, Shiraz, Cabernet Sauvignon.
summary Dominion is a major newcomer in the wine industry. Between December 1996 and September 1999, 91 hectares of vines were planted at Alexander Park with sauvignon blanc, chardonnay, pinot noir, shiraz and cabernet sauvignon the principal varieties, and smaller amounts of riesling, verdelho and merlot. Prior to the 2000 vintage a winery designed by award-winning architect Scott Shelton was erected at Alexander Park; at full capacity it will be able to process up to 7500 tonnes of fruit. It will have two functions: firstly, the production of the company's own brands of Dominion Estate, Alexander Park, Vinus and Saddle Mountain; secondly, contract winemaking services for other major Australian wine companies.

Dominion Alexander Park Riesling

YYYY **2000** Medium to full yellow-green, deep for a young Riesling; the bouquet is full and soft with a mix of tropical, citrus and even apricot aromas. The palate is soft, easy, flavoursome and ready to go, but not particularly intense and will develop quickly. **rating:** 84
best drinking Now **best vintages** NA **drink with** Rich seafood • $18

Dominion Alexander Park Chardonnay

YYYY **2000** Light green-yellow; the bouquet is fresh, with citrus and melon fruit intermingling, together with just a hint of spicy oak. The palate is likewise led by citrus and melon fruit in typical cool-climate mode; not particularly intense, but very smooth, and the oak has been well handled. **rating:** 86
best drinking Now–2003 **best vintages** NA **drink with** Deep-fried calamari • $18

Dominion Alexander Park Shiraz

YYYY **1999** Medium red-purple; the bouquet is intense and fragrant, with a mix of cinnamon spice and vanilla over soft red fruit, the medium-bodied palate showing the seductive use of American oak that is well balanced and integrated with the sweet red fruit flavours. A user-friendly wine. **rating:** 88
best drinking Now–2005 **best vintages** NA **drink with** Steak and kidney pie • $18

dominique portet NR

c/o Yering Station, 38 Melba Highway, Yering, Vic 3775 **region** Yarra Valley
phone (03) 9882 3547 **fax** (03) 9882 0997 **open** Not
winemaker Dominique Portet **production** 4000 **est.** 2000
product range ($11 R) Sauvignon Blanc, Cabernet Sauvignon.
summary Dominique Portet was bred in the purple. He spent his early years at Chateau Lafite (where his father was regisseur) and was one of the very first flying winemakers, commuting to Clos du Val in the Napa Valley, where his brother is winemaker, and helping with the initial vintages. Since 1976 he has lived in Australia, spending more than 20 years as managing director of Taltarni; he also developed the Clover Hill Vineyard in Tasmania. After retiring from Taltarni, he spent six months in Provence with his family, making wine and setting up an international distribution network, but always intended to return to Australia and set up in the Yarra Valley, a region he has been closely observing since the mid-1980s. For the time being, he is renting space at Yering Station until he finds the perfect site to locate his winery, 'which is not so easy', he says.

Dominique Portet Yarra Sauvignon Blanc

YYYY **2000** Very pale straw-green; the bouquet is crisp and clean, relatively light, with mineral and grass aromas. Shortly after bottling, the wine was crisp, clean and correct, but has yet to start to really express itself. **rating:** 85
best drinking Now–2004 **best vintages** NA **drink with** Shellfish • $11

donnelly river wines ★★★

Lot 159 Vasse Highway, Pemberton, WA 6260 **region** Pemberton
phone (08) 9776 2052 **fax** (08) 9776 2053 **open** 7 days 9.30–4.30
winemaker Blair Mieklejohn **production** 4000 **est.** 1986

product range ($15–19 CD) Chardonnay, Mist (white blend), Sauvignon Blanc, Pinot Noir, Cabernet Sauvignon, Port.

summary Donnelly River Wines draws upon 16 hectares of estate vineyards, planted in 1986 and which produced the first wines in 1990. It has performed consistently well with its Chardonnay.

Donnelly River Chardonnay

1999 Light to medium green-yellow; a clean, relatively light bouquet offers melon and stonefruit supported by subtle, barrel-ferment oak inputs. The palate is in precisely the same mode, light and elegant, the fruit and oak subtle rather than overt. **rating:** 84

best drinking Now–2004 **best vintages** '91, '93, '94 **drink with** Light Italian • NA

Donnelly River Cabernet Sauvignon

1999 Medium red; vanilla/cedar oak aromas marry with spice and redcurrant on both the bouquet and palate, where the sweet berry fruit leads the way, soft tannins bringing up the rear. **rating:** 85

best drinking 2003–2007 **best vintages** NA **drink with** Veal goulash • NA

donovan wines

RMB 2017 Pomonal Road, Stawell, Vic 3380 **region** Grampians

phone (03) 5358 2727 **fax** (03) 5358 2727 **open** By appointment

winemaker Chris Peters **production** 2000 **est.** 1977

product range ($14–28 ML) Chardonnay, Shiraz, Cabernet Sauvignon, Sparkling.

summary Donovan quietly makes some concentrated, powerful Shiraz, with several vintages of the latter typically on offer. Limited wholesale distribution in Melbourne through Dilettare; otherwise most of the wine is sold via mail order with some bottle age.

Donovan Shiraz

1998 Medium to full red, with a slightly blackish edge to the colour. Ripe, dusty plum and prune aromas on the bouquet flow into a palate where ripe, prune flavours dominate. The suggestion throughout is of a fairly high pH level, which does make the wine very soft. **rating:** 84

best drinking Now–2004 **best vintages** '98 **drink with** Venison • $28

doonkuna estate

Barton Highway, Murrumbateman, NSW 2582 **region** Canberra District

phone (02) 6227 5811 **fax** (02) 6227 5085 **open** 7 days 11–4

winemaker Malcolm Burdett **production** 3000 **est.** 1973

product range ($11–25 CD) Riesling, Gewurztraminer, Sauvignon Blanc, Sauvignon Blanc Semillon, Chardonnay, Rose, Pinot Noir, Shiraz, Cabernet Sauvignon Merlot, Cian (Pinot Noir Chardonnay), Late Harvest Riesling, Cabernet Merlot; also Rising Ground range of Chardonnay, Shiraz and Cabernet Sauvignon Merlot.

summary Following the acquisition of Doonkuna by Barry and Maureen Moran in late 1996, the plantings have been increased from a little under 4 hectares to 20 hectares (in 1998). The cellar-door prices remain modest, and increased production will follow in the wake of the new plantings.

Doonkuna Estate Riesling

2000 Very light straw-green; the bouquet is firm and crisp, with notes of mineral and dry herb, but not particularly aromatic. There is rather more fruit weight to the palate, which highlights the lime and herb flavours, and respectable length. **rating:** 84

best drinking 2002–2007 **best vintages** '88, '90, '91, '92, '95, '97 **drink with** Antipasto • $12

Doonkuna Estate Sauvignon Blanc Semillon

2000 Light green-yellow; the bouquet is clean and crisp, and while not particularly aromatic, has a nice edge to it. The same characters come into play on the clean and crisp palate with a mix of mineral, grass and lemon flavours; good length and finish. **rating:** 87

best drinking Now **best vintages** NA **drink with** Thai • $16

Doonkuna Estate Shiraz

1999 Medium to full red-purple; there is a strong minty overlay in typical Doonkuna style to both the bouquet and palate. Some cherry fruit on the palate, but others like this minty character much more than I do. **rating:** 83

best drinking 2003–2007 **best vintages** '92, '96, '97 **drink with** Rack of lamb • $25

dorrien estate NR

Cnr Barossa Valley Way and Siegersdorf Road, Tanunda, SA 5352 **region** Barossa Valley
phone (08) 8561 2200 **fax** (08) 8561 2299 **open** Not
winemaker Simon Adams, Wayne Dutschke, Steve Chapman, Nick Badrice, John Schwartzkopff, Sally Blackwell, Mark Starick **production** NFP **est.** 1982
product range ($10.50–35.50 CD) Produces a substantial number of wines under proprietary labels (Dorrien Estate, Rare Print, New Eden, Avon Brae) for the Cellarmaster Group; notable are Storton Hill, Di Fabio, Black Wattle Mount Benson, Wright's Bay, Addison Selection 49, Bosworth Edge, Vasarelli and others.
summary The Cellarmaster Group was acquired by Beringer Blass in 1997. Dorrien Estate is the physical base of the vast Cellarmaster network which, wearing its retailer's hat, is by far the largest direct-sale outlet in Australia. It buys substantial quantities of wine from other makers either in bulk or as cleanskin (i.e. unlabelled bottles), or with recognisable but subtly different labels of the producers concerned. It is also making increasing quantities of wine on its own account at Dorrien Estate, many of which are quite excellent and of trophy quality. The labelling of these wines is becoming increasingly sophisticated, giving little or no clue to the Cellarmaster link.

Black Wattle Cabernet Sauvignon

🍷🍷🍷🍷🍷 **1998** Medium to full red-purple; the bouquet is rich, with masses of berry, savoury chocolate and vanilla oak inputs. The palate shows excellent cassis fruit supported by sweet but fine tannins and well-chosen and neatly balanced oak. **rating:** 93
best drinking 2003–2013 **best vintages** '98 **drink with** Mature cheddar • $35.49

dowie doole ★★★☆

182 Main Road, McLaren Vale, SA 5171 **region** McLaren Vale
phone (08) 8323 7535 **fax** (08) 8323 7536 **open** At Ingleburne, Willunga Road, 10–5 weekdays, 11–5 weekends and public holidays
winemaker Brian Light (Contract) **production** 6000 **est.** 1996
product range ($15.50–21.50 R) Chenin Blanc, Semillon Sauvignon Blanc, Merlot, Shiraz, Cabernet Sauvignon.
summary The imaginatively packaged and interestingly named Dowie Doole was a joint venture between two McLaren Vale grape-growers: architect Drew Dowie and one-time international banker Norm Doole. Between them they have over 40 hectares of vineyards, and only a small proportion of their grapes are used to produce the Dowie Doole wines. In 1999 the partnership was expanded to include industry marketing veteran Leigh Gilligan, who returned to his native McLaren Vale after five years in Coonawarra (Gilligan is also involved with Boar's Rock). The wines have retail distribution in South Australia and the eastern States, and are exported to Canada, Germany and Fiji.

Dowie Doole Shiraz

🍷🍷🍷🍷 **1999** Full red-purple; dense, very ripe plum, prune and chocolate aromas lead into a palate with lusciously sweet fruit and carrying the mandatory 14.5° alcohol for McLaren Vale, before moving into lingering tannins on the finish. The parts do need some time to come together, but will do so. **rating:** 86
best drinking 2003–2009 **best vintages** NA **drink with** Beef in black bean sauce • NA

Dowie Doole Cabernet Sauvignon

🍷🍷🍷🍷 **1999** Medium red-purple; the fragrant bouquet has a mix of berry, earth and leaf, the palate sweetening up with chocolate and vanilla oak accompanying dark berry fruit and soft tannins. **rating:** 85
best drinking 2002–2007 **best vintages** NA **drink with** Kangaroo fillet • NA

drayton's family wines ★★★☆

Oakey Creek Road, Cessnock, NSW 2321 **region** Lower Hunter Valley
phone (02) 4998 7513 **fax** (02) 4998 7743 **open** Mon–Fri 8–5, weekends and public holidays 10–5
winemaker Trevor Drayton **production** 90 000 **est.** 1853
product range ($7–70 CD) Several label ranges including budget-priced Oakey Creek, New Generation and Hunter Valley; Vineyard Reserve Chardonnay, Semillon, Pinot Noir, Shiraz, Merlot; Sparkling and Fortifieds; top-of-the-range Limited Release Chardonnay, Shiraz, Susanne Semillon, William Shiraz, Joseph Shiraz, Bin 5555 Shiraz, Botrytis Semillon, Old Vineyard Sherry and Liqueur Muscat.
summary A family-owned and run stalwart of the Valley, producing honest, full-flavoured wines that sometimes excel themselves and are invariably modestly priced. The size of the production will come as a surprise to many

but it is a clear indication of the good standing of the brand, notwithstanding the low profile of recent years. It is not to be confused with Reg Drayton Wines. National retail distribution with exports to New Zealand, the US, Japan, Singapore, Taiwan, Samoa and Switzerland.

drews creek wines NR

558 Wollombi Road, Broke, NSW 2330 **region** Lower Hunter Valley
phone (02) 6579 1062 **fax** (02) 6579 1062 **open** By appointment
winemaker David Lowe (Contract) **production** 300 **est.** 1993
product range ($10–16 R) Chardonnay, Unoaked Chardonnay, Merlot.
summary Graeme Gibson and his partners are developing Drews Creek step by step. The initial planting of 2 hectares of chardonnay and 3 hectares of merlot was made in 1991, and the first grapes produced in 1993. A further 2.5 hectares of sangiovese were planted in September 1999. Most of the grapes have been sold to contract-winemaker David Lowe, but a small quantity of wine has been made for sale to friends and through the mailing list. The cellar door opened in 2000, and ultimately several holiday cabins overlooking the vineyard and Wollombi Brook will be opened.

driftwood estate ★★★★

Lot 13 Caves Road, Yallingup, WA 6282 **region** Margaret River
phone (08) 9755 6323 **fax** (08) 9755 6343 **open** 7 days 11–4.30
winemaker Barney Mitchell, Severine Madoux **production** 15 000 **est.** 1989
product range ($13.50–29 CD) Classic White, Meadow Wood Dry White, Semillon, Sauvignon Blanc Semillon, Chardonnay, Cane Cut Semillon (dessert style), Shiraz, Merlot, Cabernet Sauvignon, Sparkling, Tawny Port.
summary Driftwood Estate is yet another remarkable new entrant onto the vibrant Margaret River scene. Quite apart from offering a brasserie restaurant capable of seating 200 people (open seven days for lunch and dinner) and a mock-Greek open-air theatre, its wines feature striking and stylish packaging (even if strongly reminiscent of that of Devil's Lair) and opulently flavoured wines. The winery architecture is, it must be said, opulent but not stylish. The wines are exported to Japan, the UK and Malaysia.

Driftwood Estate Shiraz

🍷🍷🍷🍷🍷 **1998** Medium to full purple-red; a complex and powerful bouquet with licorice and sundry ripe dark berry aromas is followed by an ultra-complex palate with black cherry, blackberry, spice and savoury flavours; great structure, aided by supple, sweet tannins on the finish. **rating:** 94
best drinking 2003–2013 **best vintages** '98 **drink with** Lamb kebabs • $29

dromana estate ★★★★

Cnr Harrison's Road and Bittern–Dromana Road, Dromana, Vic 3936 **region** Mornington Peninsula
phone (03) 5987 3800 **fax** (03) 5981 0714 **open** 7 days 11–4
winemaker Garry Crittenden **production** 20 000 **est.** 1982
product range ($15–45 CD) Dromana Estate Sauvignon Blanc, Chardonnay, Reserve Chardonnay, Pinot Noir, Reserve Pinot Noir, Shiraz, Reserve Merlot, Cabernet Merlot; second label Schinus range of Riesling, Chenin Blanc, Sauvignon Blanc, Chardonnay, Melia, Merlot, Longest Lunch Brut, Rosé, Pinot Noir; and a newly packaged range of Italian generics, Arneis, Barbera, Dolcetto, Sangiovese, Granaccia, Riserva, Nebbiolo and Rosato under the Garry Crittenden i label.
summary Since it was first established, Dromana Estate has never been far from the headlines. The energetic marketing genius of Garry Crittenden has driven it hither and thither, launching a brief but highly successful foray into the UK market, and since then concentrating much of its efforts on a no less successful restaurant and cellar door with a kaleidoscopic array of wines: first under the Dromana Estate label, then under the Schinus label and, in late 1995, a strikingly revamped range of Italian-accented wines, the i wines. In late 2000 became the head of an expanded empire, yet another winery to raise significant working capital via listing on the Stock Exchange. Exports to the UK, the US and Asia.

Dromana Estate Schinus Sauvignon Blanc

🍷🍷🍷🍷 **2000** Very pale green-yellow; the bouquet is light, clean, crisp and correct with a mix of herb, blossom and gooseberry aromas. The palate is fresh, lively and light, with a gentle mix of gooseberry and passionfruit, and neatly balanced acidity. **rating:** 87
best drinking Now **best vintages** NA **drink with** Shellfish • $15

Garry Crittenden i Arneis

YYYY 2000 Light green-yellow; the bouquet is clean and quite intense, with pear and apple aromas. The palate has length and intensity, yet retains delicacy; pear and apple fruit is highlighted by excellent acidity. **rating:** 88

best drinking Now–2004 **best vintages** '00 **drink with** Vegetable terrine • $22

Dromana Estate Chardonnay

YYYYY 2000 Light to medium yellow-green; the bouquet offers the usual subtle yet complex interplay between barrel-ferment, lees and malolactic-ferment inputs. The fine and delicate palate produces more of the same, with melon, a touch of cashew and appropriately restrained oak. **rating:** 91

YYYYY 1999 Light to medium yellow-green; the subtle and elegant bouquet has a mix of nutty malolactic characters together with a touch of 'French' mineral character; the refined, indeed understated, palate flows logically on from the bouquet, with its mix of melon, mineral and more nutty flavours all supported by subtle oak. Four trophies at the 2000 Cool Climate Wine Show. **rating:** 93

best drinking 2002–2005 **best vintages** '91, '92, '97, '98, '99, '00 **drink with** Crab • $30

Dromana Estate Reserve Chardonnay

YYYYY 1999 Light to medium green-yellow; the bouquet is clean, still remarkably fine and youthful, with the hallmark cashew mlf and subtle inputs. The palate follows down precisely the same track, with citrus and melon providing a gently sweet core around which the rest of the structure is built. **rating:** 94

best drinking Now–2005 **best vintages** '91, '94, '96, '97, '99 **drink with** Kassler • $42

Dromana Estate Mornington Estate Pinot Noir

YYYY 1999 Light red; the clean but very light bouquet has faint cherry aromas, the palate with cherry/cherry pip, but not a lot of power or concentration. **rating:** 83

best drinking Now **best vintages** NA **drink with** Light Asian dishes • $20

Dromana Estate Shiraz

YYYY 1999 Medium to full red-purple; quite ripe black cherry fruit is the primary aroma, with some savoury/ forest notes. The palate offers tangy, cool-grown cherry fruit flavours, with lively acidity and subtle oak. **rating:** 88

best drinking 2002–2006 **best vintages** '97 **drink with** Beef stroganoff • $26.80

Garry Crittenden i R osato

YYYY 1999 Light salmon; the bouquet is clean and light, with a mix of strawberry, cherry and rose-petal aromas. The palate is well balanced, with quite good flavour levels, finishing dry and with appropriate acidity. **rating:** 85

best drinking Now **best vintages** NA **drink with** Brasserie food • $17

Garry Crittenden i Barbera

YYYY 1999 Medium red-purple; the bouquet is aromatic and potent, with savoury/briary aromas that follow into a savoury palate with a mix of dark plum, a touch of mint, and cedary notes more likely coming from the fruit than the oak. Nice wine. **rating:** 87

best drinking Now–2004 **best vintages** '99 **drink with** Osso bucco • $22

Garry Crittenden i Dolcetto

YYYY 1999 Bright purple-red; the moderately intense bouquet offers spice, cinnamon and some plum; a smooth and juicy palate likewise has plum and some spice flavours; a very soft finish with low tannins. **rating:** 85

best drinking Now **best vintages** NA **drink with** Pizza • $22

Garry Crittenden i Sangiovese

YYYYY 1999 Garry Crittenden has been the champion of the Italian cause in Australia for a number of years with his striking i range. This is the most convincing yet, with lots of dark berry/spicy/woodsy aromas and flavour; there is depth and texture to the structure, and good length on the palate. **rating:** 91

best drinking Now–2005 **best vintages** '99 **drink with** Osso bucco • $22

Dromana Estate Cabern et Merlot

YYYY 1999 Youthful purple-red; the bouquet is fragrant, with spicy/earthy fruit and a hint of salami, probably from the oak. The palate has nice texture and mouthfeel, with ripe berry fruit and soft tannins; gets it all together, and doesn't have any overhang from the oak notes of the bouquet. Particularly impressive given the vintage. **rating:** 88

best drinking 2002–2007 **best vintages** '91, '93, '97, '98 **drink with** Beef in red wine sauce • $26.80

dulcinea ★★★★

Jubilee Road, Sulky, Ballarat, Vic 3352 **region** Ballarat
phone (03) 5334 6440 **fax** (03) 5334 6828 **open** 7 days 9–5
winemaker Rod Stott **production** 800 **est.** 1983
product range ($14–18 CD) Chardonnay, Sauvignon Blanc, Pinot Noir, Shiraz, Cabernet Sauvignon.
summary Rod Stott is a part-time but passionate grape-grower and winemaker who chose the name Dulcinea from *The Man of La Mancha*, where only a fool fights windmills. With winemaking help from various sources, there are some interesting and often complex wines, including some exceptionally impressive recent releases.

dusty hill vineyard NR

Barambah Road, Moffatdale, via Murgon, Qld 4605 **region** South Burnett
phone (07) 4168 4700 **fax** (07) 4169 5983 **open** 7 days 10–5
winemaker Andrew Hickinbotham (Contract) Mike Hayes (Viticultural Consultant) **production** 2000 **est.** 1996
product range ($15–25 R) Dusty Rosé.
summary Joe Prendergast and family have established 2 hectares each of shiraz and cabernet sauvignon, 1 hectare each of merlot and verdelho, 0.75 hectare of semillon and 0.5 hectare of black muscat. The vines are crop-thinned to obtain maximum ripeness in the fruit and to maximise tannin extract, although the winery's specialty is the Dusty Rosé, continuing a long tradition of rosé/Beaujolais-style wines from Queensland. The 2000 vintage of this wine came equal top at the 2000 Melbourne Royal Wine Show with a bronze medal.

dutschke wines NR

Lyndoch Valley Road, Lyndoch, SA 5351 **region** Barossa Valley
phone (08) 8265 6567 **fax** (08) 8265 2635 **open** Not
winemaker Wayne Dutschke **production** 2500 **est.** 1990
product range ($25–45 R) Oscar Semmler Shiraz, St Jakobi Shiraz, Willowbend Merlot Shiraz Cabernet.
summary Wayne Dutschke has had ten years of winemaking experience with major wine companies in South Australia, Victoria and New South Wales but has returned to South Australia to join his uncle, Ken Semmler, a leading grape-grower in the Barossa Valley and now in the Adelaide Hills. No recent tastings, simply because Willow Bend sells out of wine in less than six months each year. Annual release in August; there is limited retail distribution in Sydney and Melbourne.

dyson wines NR

Sherriff Road, Maslin Beach, SA 5170 **region** McLaren Vale
phone (08) 8386 1092 **fax** (08) 8327 0066 **open** 7 days 10–5
winemaker Allan Dyson **production** 2000 **est.** 1976
product range ($15–18 CD) Chardonnay, Viognier, Cabernet Sauvignon.
summary Allan Dyson, who describes himself as 'a young man of 50 years' has recently established 1.5 hectares of viognier and has absolutely no thoughts of slowing down or retiring.

east arm vineyard ★★★★☆

111 Archers Road, Hillwood, Tas 7250 **region** Northern Tasmania
phone (03) 6334 0266 **fax** (03) 6334 1405 **open** By appointment
winemaker Andrew Hood, Bert Sundstrup, Nicholas Butler (Contract) **production** 1000 **est.** 1993
product range ($14–21 ML) Riesling, Chardonnay, Pinot Noir.
summary East Arm Vineyard was established by Launceston gastroenterologist Dr John Wettenhall and partner Anita James, who also happens to have completed the Charles Sturt University Diploma in Applied Science (wine-growing). The 2 hectares of vineyard that came into full production in 1998 is more or less equally divided between riesling, chardonnay and pinot noir. It is established on an historic block, part of a grant made to retired British soldiers of the Georgetown garrison in 1821, and slopes down to the Tamar River. The property is 25 hectares, and there are plans for further planting and, somewhere down the track, a winery.

East Arm Riesling

🍷🍷🍷🍷🍷 **2000** Light green-yellow; a clean bouquet with the gentle tropical/lime aromas indicative of the 2000 vintage is followed by a lively palate with a mix of lime and more minerally flavours, with crisp acidity on a long, lingering, stylish finish. **rating:** 95

best drinking 2002–2010 **best vintages** '98, '99, '00 **drink with** Scallops • $18

eastbrook estate NR

Lot 3 Vasse Highway, Eastbrook, WA 6260 **region** Pemberton
phone (08) 9776 1251 **fax** (08) 9776 1251 **open** Fri–Sun, public holidays 11–4
winemaker Kim Skipworth **production** 2000 **est.** 1990
product range ($10–17 CD) Chardonnay, Pinot Noir, Cabernet Sauvignon, Port.
summary Established on part of the same former grazing property that also accommodates Salitage, Phoenicia, and Dr Bill Pannell's vineyard. A jarrah pole, limestone and cedar weatherboard winery and restaurant have been built on the site by former Perth real estate agent Kim Skipworth, who is also a shareholder in one of the major Margaret River cheese factories. The wines come from 7 hectares of estate plantings of pinot noir, chardonnay, sauvignon blanc and shiraz.

eastern peake NR

Clunes Road, Coghills Creek, Vic 3364 **region** Ballarat
phone (03) 5343 4245 **fax** (03) 5343 4365 **open** 7 days 10–5
winemaker Norman Latta **production** 1500 **est.** 1983
product range ($15–20 CD) Chardonnay, Alba, Persuasion (Pinot Rosé), Pinot Noir.
summary Norm Latta and Di Pym commenced the establishment of Eastern Peake, situated 25 kilometres northeast of Ballarat on a high plateau overlooking the Creswick Valley, almost 15 years ago. In the early years the grapes were sold to Trevor Mast of Mount Chalambar and Mount Langi Ghiran, but the 4.5 hectares of vines are now dedicated to the production of Eastern Peake wines. The Pinot Noir is on the minerally/stemmy side; earlier bottling might preserve more of the sweet fruit.

eden valley wines NR

Main Street, Eden Valley, SA 5235 **region** Eden Valley
phone (08) 8564 1111 **fax** (08) 8564 1110 **open** 7 days 10–5
winemaker Peter Thompson **production** 4000 **est.** 1994
product range ($10–20 CD) Riesling, Old Butts Riesling, Chardonnay, Shiraz, Cabernet Sauvignon, White Port, Tawny Port.
summary Eden Valley Wines has waxed and waned over the years but seems now in the ascendant. The venture now has 30 hectares each of recently planted riesling, cabernet sauvignon and shiraz, with 5 hectares of much older mourvedre. A major part of the production is sold as grapes to others; the wines currently on sale have varied (non-estate) backgrounds.

edwards & chaffey ★★★★☆

Chaffey's Road, McLaren Vale, SA 5171 **region** McLaren Vale
phone (08) 8323 8250 **fax** (08) 8323 9308 **open** Mon–Sat 10–5, Sun 11–4
winemaker Fiona Donald **production** NFP **est.** 1850
product range ($15–32 R) Under the varietal range, E&C Chardonnay, Shiraz and Cabernet Sauvignon; under the premium Edwards & Chaffey Section 353 label, a similar range; also Edwards & Chaffey sparkling; the Seaview range of Riesling, Verdelho, Chardonnay and Shiraz Grenache and Seaview sparkling range of Brut, Brut de Brut, Chardonnay, Blanc de Blancs, Grand Cuvée, Gull Rock, Pinot Noir Chardonnay Brut continues in existence, but is not produced from McLaren Vale grapes.
summary In an endeavour to reposition the brand and obtain recognition (in terms of price) for the quality, Seaview has all but been phased out, and henceforth the winery (and the leading brands) will travel under the Edwards & Chaffey label; a nice twist given that these are the names of the partners who developed the business prior to its (indirect) acquisition by Southcorp.

Seaview Blanc de Blancs

🍷🍷🍷🍷 **1996** Light green-yellow; the bouquet is clean and crisp, with citrussy fruit and a delicate hint of bready yeast; the moderately intense palate is crisp and elegant, with convincing length to the finish. **rating:** 88
best drinking Now **best vintages** NA **drink with** Antipasto • $18

Seaview Pinot Chardonnay Brut Reserve

🍷🍷🍷🍷 **1997** Medium to full straw-yellow; a quite rich and ripe bouquet with a mix of honeyed/toasty/bready aromas is followed by a medium-weight palate with nice mouthfeel, but which is not particularly intense or long. **rating:** 85
best drinking Now–2003 **best vintages** NA **drink with** Seafood • $18

Edwards & Chaffey Section 353 Pinot Chardonnay

🍷🍷🍷🍷🍷 **1995** Medium to full straw-yellow; a big, slightly broad, but powerful and complex yeasty/bready/ gently aldehydic bouquet leads into a complex and powerful palate that does, however, lighten up on the finish, which is no bad thing. **rating:** 90

best drinking Now–2003 **best vintages** NA **drink with** Trout mousse • $24

Edwards & Chaffey Section 353 Shiraz

🍷🍷🍷🍷🍷 **1998** Medium to full red-purple; a complex, rich and deep bouquet with a multitude of berry, chocolate and earth aromas, is followed by a powerful and complex wine with masses of dark berry/cherry fruit flowing in layers, and closing with perfect tannins. **rating:** 94

best drinking 2003–2013 **best vintages** '92, '94, '95, '96, '97, '98 **drink with** Aged fillet steak • NA

Edwards & Chaffey Section 353 Cabernet Sauvignon

🍷🍷🍷🍷🍷 **1998** Medium to full red-purple; a complex and sophisticated bouquet has ripe spicy/berry fruit in abundance; the palate, likewise, has compelling texture, structure and mouthfeel, featuring well-balanced and integrated oak with dark berry fruit. **rating:** 94

best drinking 2003–2013 **best vintages** '92, '94, '96, '97, '98 **drink with** Char-grilled rump • NA

edwards vineyard NR

Cnr Caves and Ellensbrook Roads, Cowaramup, WA 6284 **region** Margaret River
phone (08) 9755 5125 **fax** (08) 9755 5120 **open** Fri–Sun and public holidays 10.30–5
winemaker Michael Edwards, Stuart Pym (Contract) **production** 5000 **est.** 1994
product range ($19–23 CD) Sauvignon Blanc, Semillon Sauvignon Blanc, Shiraz.
summary This is very much a family affair. Michael Edwards is employed as a winemaker at Voyager Estate; Chris Edwards is vineyard manager, while Fiona and Bianca Edwards are involved in sales and marketing. They have a substantial vineyard, planted to chardonnay (3 hectares), semillon (2.5 hectares), sauvignon blanc (2.1 hectares), shiraz (4.8 hectares) and cabernet sauvignon (7.6 hectares) and have plans to build a winery in time for the 2004 vintage.

Edwards Vineyard Sauvignon Blanc

🍷🍷🍷🍷🍷 **2000** Pale green-yellow; the bouquet is clean, firm and quite intense, in a herbal/minerally mould. The palate is clean, firm, and with the influence of a well-handled but delicate touch of oak. **rating:** 90

best drinking Now **best vintages** NA **drink with** Scallop terrine • $19

Edwards Vineyard Shiraz

🍷🍷🍷🍷 **1999** Medium to full red-purple; there is a mix of gamey/earthy/spicy overtones to berry fruit on the bouquet; a very powerful wine on the palate with over-extracted tannins. A lighter touch or more fining might have helped, for the underlying fruit is good. **rating:** 83

best drinking 2003–2008 **best vintages** NA **drink with** Leave it in the cellar • $23

elan vineyard NR

17 Turners Road, Bittern, Vic 3918 **region** Mornington Peninsula
phone (03) 5983 1858 **fax** (03) 5983 2821 **open** First weekend of month and public holidays 11–5 or by appointment
winemaker Selma Lowther **production** 600 **est.** 1980
product range ($13–16 CD) Olive's Paddock Riesling, Chardonnay, Shiraz, Gamay, Cabernet Merlot.
summary Selma Lowther, fresh from Charles Sturt University (as a mature-age student), made an impressive debut with her spicy, fresh, crisp Chardonnay. Most of the grapes from the 2.5 hectares of estate vineyards are sold; production remains minuscule.

elderton ★★★★

3 Tanunda Road, Nuriootpa, SA 5355 **region** Barossa Valley
phone (08) 8562 1058 **fax** (08) 8562 2844 **open** Mon–Fri 8.30–5, weekends and holidays 11–4
winemaker James Irvine **production** 32 000 **est.** 1984
product range ($9.95–65 CD) Riesling, Chardonnay, Golden Riesling, Golden Semillon, Pinot Chardonnay, Merlot, Shiraz, Cabernet Sauvignon; Tantalus White and Red; Command Shiraz is the flagbearer.

summary The wines are based on some old, high-quality Barossa floor estate vineyards, and all are driven to a lesser or greater degree by lashings of American oak; the Command Shiraz is at the baroque end of the spectrum and has to be given considerable respect within the parameters of its style. National retail distribution, with exports to the UK, the US, Europe and Asia.

Elderton Chardonnay

YYYY 1999 Light to medium yellow-green; the bouquet is clean, neutral and with relatively subtle oak input. The palate is solid, unobjectionable, but devoid of any interest in terms of varietal fruit flavour; at least the oak is subtle, and the overall effect is inoffensive. **rating:** 80

best drinking Now **best vintages** NA **drink with** KFC • $17

Elderton Shiraz

YYYY 1998 Deep red-purple; the bouquet is very rich, with sweet chocolate, vanilla and cherry aromas. The palate has plenty of luscious fruit and even more vanilla American oak. **rating:** 86

best drinking Now–2007 **best vintages** '86, '88, '90, '91, '92, '94 **drink with** Steak and kidney pie • $26

Elderton Command Shiraz

YYYY 1996 Medium red, starting to show some development. The bouquet is scented, with plush leathery, oaky aromas. The palate is complex, with that ultra-ripe, ultra-minty fruit that is undoubtedly one of the regional characteristics of ripe Barossa Shiraz, and which seems to be intensified by the vanilla oak. **rating:** 89

best drinking Now–2006 **best vintages** NA **drink with** Kangaroo • $65

Elderton Merlot

YYYY 1997 Medium red, tinged with purple; the aromas are in an intermediate savoury/earthy/leafy spectrum, varietally correct. The wine has very good mouthfeel and structure, silky and fine. **rating:** 88

best drinking Now–2005 **best vintages** NA **drink with** Rib of veal • $30

Elderton Cabernet Sauvignon

YYYY 1998 Medium red-purple; there is some berry fruit on the bouquet but even more oak; the palate has masses of vanilla and chocolate flavours, with ripe cabernet fruit lurking somewhere in the oak forest; soft tannins. **rating:** 84

best drinking Now–2006 **best vintages** NA **drink with** Barbecued T-bone • $21

eldredge ★★★☆

Spring Gully Road, Clare, SA 5453 **region** Clare Valley
phone (08) 8842 3086 **fax** (08) 8842 3086 **open** 7 days 11–5
winemaker Leigh Eldredge, Tim Adams (Consultant) **production** 6500 **est.** 1993
product range ($13–22 CD) Watervale Riesling, Semillon Sauvignon Blanc, Late Harvest Riesling, New Age Grenache, Blue Chip Shiraz, Cabernet Sauvignon, Sparkling, Port.
summary Leigh and Karen Eldredge have established their winery and cellar-door sales area in the Sevenhill Ranges at an altitude of 500 metres, above the town of Watervale. The wines are distributed in Victoria and exported to Southeast Asia and Japan through Australian Prestige Wines, and through the remainder of the Australian States by Normans. Also exports to the UK.

Eldredge Watervale Riesling

YYYY 2000 Medium yellow-green; the bouquet is solid, falling on the richer, fuller style of the divide, which marked the 2000 vintage in the Clare Valley. The palate, likewise, is full and perhaps a little heavy, but is certainly stacked with flavour. Silver medal winner at the 2000 Clare Valley Wine Show. **rating:** 84

best drinking Now–2004 **best vintages** '98 **drink with** Bruschetta • $16

Eldredge Semillon Sauvignon Blanc

YYYY 1999 Medium to full yellow-green; a solid, clean bouquet with a mix of mineral and hay/straw aromas. The palate has flavour, but not a great deal of mid-palate vinosity, picking up again to a degree on the finish. **rating:** 81

best drinking Now–2003 **best vintages** NA **drink with** Fish cakes • $16

Eldredge Cabernet Sauvignon

TTTTY **1998** Medium to full red-purple; clean, supple, dark berry fruit with some chocolatey notes on the bouquet lead into an elegant palate with sweet berry and chocolate fruit; the pleasing mouthfeel is in large part due to silky tannins. I seemed to like this wine more than some other judges at the 2000 Clare Valley Wine Show. **rating:** 93

best drinking 2003–2013 **best vintages** '95, '98 **drink with** Barbecued lamb • $22

eldridge estate ★★★☆

Red Hill Road, Red Hill, Vic 3937 **region** Mornington Peninsula
phone (03) 5989 2644 **fax** (03) 5989 2644 **open** Weekends, public holidays and January 1–26 11–5
winemaker David Lloyd **production** 800 **est.** 1985
product range ($18–30 CD) Semillon Sauvignon Blanc, Chardonnay, Gamay, Pinot Noir, Cabernet Merlot, Sparkling.
summary The Eldridge Estate vineyard, with seven varieties included in its 3.5 hectares, was purchased by Wendy and David Lloyd in 1995. Major retrellising work has been undertaken, changing to Scott-Henry, and all of the wines will now be estate-grown and made. The wines are available at the Victorian Wine Centre and Tastings, Armadale, in Melbourne, and a few leading restaurants in Melbourne and Sydney.

Eldridge Estate Chardonnay

TTTTY **1999** Medium yellow-green; the bouquet is complex, with strong barrel-ferment and malolactic-ferment influences, but the fruit shines through; the palate has good length and acidity, the grapefruit, melon and cashew flavours of the fruit supported by well-integrated oak. To my mind, better than the more fashionable '98 vintage. **rating:** 91

best drinking Now–2005 **best vintages** '99 **drink with** Poached fish • $30

Eldridge Estate Pinot Noir

TTTY **1999** Light to medium red-purple; an earthy/savoury/foresty/cherry bouquet flows through into a fresh, lively and crisp palate that has the flavours promised by the bouquet, but which needs a year or so for the acid to (appear to) soften. **rating:** 84

best drinking 2002–2005 **best vintages** NA **drink with** Braised duck • $30

Eldridge Estate Gamay

TTTT **2000** Medium purple-red; the bouquet is clean, with plum and spice aromas, the palate smooth and fresh, offering plum with a twist of lemon; not only a good wine, but an interesting one, with strong varietal character. Chill it slightly if the day is warm. **rating:** 88

best drinking Now **best vintages** NA **drink with** Cold meats • $20

elgee park ★★★☆

Wallaces Road, Merricks North, Vic 3926 **region** Mornington Peninsula
phone (03) 5989 7338 **fax** (03) 5989 7338 **open** The Sunday of the Queen's Birthday weekend
winemaker Stonier, T'Gallant (Contract) **production** 1500 **est.** 1972
product range ($14–25 R) Excellence (Riesling), Chardonnay, Pinot Gris, Pinot Noir, Cabernet, Cuvée Brut; Baillieu Myer Family Reserve Riesling, Viognier, Chardonnay, Pinot Noir and Cabernet Merlot.
summary The pioneer of the Mornington Peninsula in its twentieth-century rebirth, owned by Baillieu Myer and family. The wines are now made at Stonier's and T'Gallant, Elgee Park's own winery having been closed, and the overall level of activity decreased. Melbourne retail distribution through Flinders Wholesale.

Elgee Park Family Reserve Riesling

TTTT **2000** Light straw-green; there is plenty of action on the aromatic, flowery lime/tropical bouquet; the palate is fresh, lively and attractive, finishing with well-balanced acidity. **rating:** 89

best drinking Now–2004 **best vintages** NA **drink with** Light seafood • $14

Elgee Park Family Reserve Viognier

TTTT **1999** Medium yellow-green; the bouquet is quite rich, with some honeyed/baked apple/honeysuckle aromas that follow through into the rich, glossy, mouthfilling texture of the palate. The texture is correct, the flavour (in varietal terms) not so precise. However, has development potential. **rating:** 86

best drinking Now–2006 **best vintages** NA **drink with** Chinese prawns • $25

Elgee Park Family Reserve Chardonnay

TTTT **1999** Medium to full yellow-green; there are complex, toasty bottle-developed barrel-ferment aromas leading into a soft cashew, hazelnut, toast and melon-flavoured palate. **rating:** 85

best drinking Now **best vintages** NA **drink with** Seafood risotto • $24

Elgee Park Family Reserve Pinot Noir

TTTT **1999** Light to medium red-purple; the moderately intense bouquet has foresty/savoury aromas that mark the opening of the light to medium bodied palate, with plum, strawberry and violets then appearing and running through to the long finish. Light-bodied, but stylish. **rating:** 87

best drinking Now–2003 **best vintages** '97 **drink with** Quail • $25

Elgee Park Family Reserve Merlot

TTTT **1998** Medium red-purple; earthy/dusty/savoury overtones to the dark berry fruit of the bouquet are reflected in the concentrated, savoury palate, which shows the benefit of some oak sweetening. **rating:** 86

best drinking 2002–2007 **best vintages** NA **drink with** Braised lamb • $22

Elgee Park Family Reserve Cabernet Sauvignon

TTTT **1998** Light to medium red-purple; the bouquet is quite fragrant, with a hint of herbaceousness from the cabernet component, and olive tones from the merlot. The palate is elegant and long, with some of those herb and olive flavours coming through from the bouquet, finishing with fine tannins. **rating:** 85

best drinking 2002–2006 **best vintages** NA **drink with** Soft, triple-cream cheese • $22

eling forest winery ★★★

Hume Highway, Sutton Forest, NSW 2577 **region** Southern New South Wales Zone
phone (02) 4878 9499 **fax** (02) 4878 9499 **open** 7 days 10–5
winemaker Leslie Fritz, Michelle Crockett **production** 3500 **est.** 1987
product range ($8–45 CD) Riesling, Tramini (Traminer), Furmint, Linden Leaf Harslevelu, Chardonnay, Lunel, Catherine Hill, Botrytis Riesling, Rose, Carla (Red), Cabernet Sauvignon, Peach Brandy, Peach Ambrosia, Cherry Port.

summary Eling Forest's mentally agile and innovative founder Leslie Fritz celebrated his 80th birthday not long after he planted the first vines at his Sutton Forest vineyard in 1987. He proceeded to celebrate his 88th birthday by expanding the vineyards from 3 to 4 hectares, primarily with additional plantings of the Hungarian varieties. He has also developed a Cherry Port and is using the spinning cone technology to produce various peach-based liqueurs, utilising second-class peach waste. Right across the extensive range, the wines are increasingly technically well made, even if far more European than Australian in terms of fruit weight.

Eling Forest Furmint

TTTY **1999** Pale straw-green; the bouquet is clean, with a touch of herb and grass, not unlike Semillon; the palate is clean, crisp and restrained, with no particular fruit flavour but showing the good acidity and length its Hungarian ancestry would suggest. **rating:** 82

best drinking Now–2006 **best vintages** NA **drink with** Summer salads • $16.50

Eling Forest Linden Leaf Harslevelu

TTTY **2000** Very pale straw-green; there are herb, apple and spice aromatics that distinguish this wine from the more neutral tones of the Furmint bouquet. The light to medium bodied palate is fresh and clean, seemingly fairly low in alcohol, but technically spot-on. **rating:** 82

best drinking Now–2004 **best vintages** NA **drink with** Shellfish, light seafood • NA

elmslie ★★☆

Upper McEwans Road, Legana, Tas 7277 **region** Northern Tasmania
phone (03) 6330 1225 **fax** (03) 6330 2161 **open** By appointment
winemaker Ralph Power **production** 600 **est.** 1972
product range ($18 ML) Pinot Noir, Cabernet Sauvignon.

summary A small, specialist red winemaker, who from time to time blends Pinot Noir with Cabernet. The fruit from the now fully mature vineyard (0.5 hectare of pinot noir and 1.5 hectares of cabernet sauvignon) has depth and character, but operational constraints mean that the style of the wine is often somewhat rustic.

elmswood estate NR

75 Monbulk–Seville Road, Wandin East, Vic 3139 **region** Yarra Valley
phone (03) 5964 3015 **fax** (03) 5964 3405 **open** Weekends 10–5 and by appointment
winemaker Contract **production** 2000 **est.** 1981
product range ($20–30 ML) Chardonnay, Unoaked Chardonnay, Cabernet Merlot, Cabernet Sauvignon.
summary Rod and Dianne Keller purchased their 4-hectare vineyard in June 1999; it had been planted in 1981 on the red volcanic soils of the far-southern side of the valley that stretches from Wandin to Warburton. Previously, the grapes had been sold to other Yarra Valley winemakers, but the Kellers immediately set about having their own wine made from the estate. The cellar door offers spectacular views across the Upper Yarra Valley to Mount Donna Buang and Warburton, and B&B accommodation planned for 2001. The wines are sold chiefly through cellar door and mailing list, with limited restaurant listings.

Elmswood Estate Unoaked Chardonnay

ΥΥΥΥ **2000** Light green-yellow; light, crisp melon and citrus aromas have a slight herbal twang, the palate quite distinctly citrussy and lively. Well made. **rating:** 82
best drinking Now **best vintages** NA **drink with** Light fish • NA

Elmswood Estate Chardonnay

ΥΥΥΥ **2000** Light to medium yellow-green; quite subtle smoky barrel-ferment aromas join the citrus and melon of the bouquet, with a similar play on the palate, the problem being with the overall sweetness, possibly suggesting an incomplete fermentation. **rating:** 83
best drinking Now **best vintages** NA **drink with** Grilled chicken • NA

elsewhere vineyard ★★★★☆

42 Dillons Hill Road, Glaziers Bay, Tas 7109 **region** Southern Tasmania
phone (03) 6295 1228 **fax** (03) 6295 1591 **open** Not
winemaker Andrew Hood (Contract), Steve Lubiana (Contract) **production** 4000 **est.** 1984
product range ($20–30 ML) Riesling, Chardonnay, Pinot Noir, Methode Champenoise.
summary Kylie and Andrew Cameron's evocatively named Elsewhere Vineyard used to jostle for space with a commercial flower farm. It is a mark of the success of the wines that in 1993 some of the long-established flowers made way for additional chardonnay and riesling, although it is Elsewhere's long-lived Pinot Noirs that are so stunning. The estate-produced range comes from the 6 hectares of pinot noir, 3 hectares of chardonnay and 1 hectare of riesling that constitute the immaculately tended vineyard.

Elsewhere Vineyard Riesling

ΥΥΥΥΥ **1999** Medium yellow-green; a strong, Alsace-like bouquet with fruit, petrol and lime is repeated on the powerful dry palate, again showing Alsace characters, finishing with firm acidity. Striking and unusual. **rating:** 94
best drinking Now–2008 **best vintages** '99 **drink with** Seafood bisque • NA

Elsewhere Vineyard Unwooded Chardonnay

ΥΥΥΥ **1999** Light green-yellow; the bouquet offers intense citrus/melon/grapefruit aromas leaning even towards lime juice on the palate; a powerful wine, even if fractionally reductive. **rating:** 86
best drinking Now–2004 **best vintages** NA **drink with** Marinated scallops • $20

Elsewhere Vineyard Pinot Noir

ΥΥΥΥΥ **1999** Medium red; potent spice/briar/forest/slippery/tangy fruit aromas, all coalescing, then a long, stylish palate in which spice, strawberry and plum come to the fore, supported by gentle oak. An impressive follow-on to the '98. **rating:** 91
best drinking Now–2004 **best vintages** '89, '91, '93, '95, '98, '99 **drink with** Breast of duck with demi glaze • $30

elsmore's caprera grove NR

657 Milbrodale Road, Broke, NSW 2330 **region** Lower Hunter Valley
phone (02) 6579 1344 **fax** (02) 6579 1355 **open** By appointment
winemaker Jim Chatto, Gary Reid (Contract) **production** 500 **est.** 1995

product range ($15–20 CD) Wooded Chardonnay, Chardonnay, Peregrinus Methode Champenoise, Bartolomeo Botrytis Chardonnay.

summary Bindy and Chris Elsmore purchased their 16-hectare property at Broke in 1995, subsequently establishing 4 hectares of chardonnay, verdelho and shiraz, with chardonnay taking the lion's share of the plantings. Their interest in wine came not from their professional lives (Chris is a retired commodore of the Royal Australian Navy and Bindy had a career in advertising, marketing and personnel) but from numerous trips to the wine regions of France, Italy and Spain.

eltham vineyards ★★★

225 Shaws Road, Arthurs Creek, Vic 3099 **region** Yarra Valley
phone (03) 9439 4688 **fax** (03) 9439 5121 **open** By appointment
winemaker George Apted, John Graves **production** 850 **est.** 1990
product range ($14.95–18.95 ML) Chardonnay, Pinot Noir, Cabernet Sauvignon.
summary Drawing upon vineyards at Arthurs Creek and Eltham, John Graves (brother of David Graves of the illustrious Californian Pinot producer Saintsbury) produces tiny quantities of quite stylish Chardonnay and Pinot Noir, the former showing nice barrel-ferment characters.

elysium vineyard NR

393 Milbrodale Road, Broke, NSW 2330 **region** Lower Hunter Valley
phone (02) 9664 2368 **fax** (02) 9664 2368 **open** By appointment
winemaker Tyrrell's (Contract) **production** 300 **est.** 1990
product range ($19.95 R) Verdelho.
summary Elysium was once part of a much larger vineyard established by John Tulloch (not part of the Tulloch operation owned by Southcorp), who continues to look after the viticulture, with the 1 hectare of verdelho being vinified at Tyrrell's. The Elysium Vineyard cottage, large enough to accommodate six people, has won a number of tourism awards, and proprietor Victoria Foster conducts wine-education weekends on request, with meals prepared by a chef brought in for the occasion. As at last advice, the cost per person for a gourmet weekend was $300.

emerald estate NR

Main North Road, Stanley Flat, SA 5453 **region** Clare Valley
phone (08) 8842 3296 **fax** (08) 8842 2220 **open** Mon, Tues, Thurs, Fri 11–5, weekends 10–5
winemaker Tim Adams (Consultant), Frank Sheppard **production** 1670 **est.** 1990
product range ($9–15 CD) Riesling, Unwooded Chardonnay, Classic Dry White, Shiraz, Cabernet Sauvignon.
summary Don and Gwen Carroll purchased a 33-hectare property at Stanley Flat in 1990. A small existing vineyard was pulled out, and since 1990 20 hectares of vines have been established. Most of the production is sold to leading wineries in the region, a portion being retained for the Emerald Estate wine range, with limited retail distribution in Melbourne.

ensay winery NR

Great Alpine Road, Ensay, Vic 3895 **region** Gippsland
phone (03) 5157 3203 **fax** (03) 5157 3372 **open** Weekends, public and school holidays 11–5 or by appointment
winemaker David Coy **production** 1500 **est.** 1992
product range ($17–20 R) Chardonnay, Pinot Noir, Shiraz, Cabernet Sauvignon.
summary A weekend and holiday business for the Coy family, headed by David Coy, with 2.5 hectares of chardonnay, pinot noir, merlot, shiraz and cabernet sauvignon.

eppalock ridge NR

633 North Redesdale Road, Redesdale, Vic 3444 **region** Heathcote
phone (03) 5425 3135 **fax** (03) 5425 3135 **open** 7 days 10–6 by appointment
winemaker Rod Hourigan **production** 1500 **est.** 1979
product range ($25 CD) Shiraz, Cabernet Merlot.
summary A low-key operation now focusing mainly on Shiraz produced from the 4 hectares of this variety; the other wine in the portfolio comes from the 2.7 hectares of cabernet sauvignon, merlot and cabernet franc.

ermes estate NR

2 Godings Road, Moorooduc, Vic 3933 **region** Mornington Peninsula
phone (03) 5978 8376 **open** Weekends and public holidays 11–5
winemaker Ermes Zucchet **production** 500 **est.** 1989
product range ($10–15 CD) Riesling Malvasia, Chardonnay Pinot Grigio, Cabernet Merlot.
summary Ermes and Denise Zucchet commenced planting of the 2-hectare estate in 1989 with chardonnay, riesling, cabernet sauvignon and merlot, adding pinot gris in 1991. In 1994 an existing piggery on the property was converted to a winery and cellar-door area (in the Zucchets' words, the pigs having been evicted), and the modestly priced wines are on sale during the weekends. No recent tastings.

ese vineyards NR

1013 Tea Tree Road, Tea Tree, Tas 7017 **region** Southern Tasmania
phone 0417 319 875 **fax** (03) 6272 5398 **open** 7 days 10–5
winemaker Michael Vishacki (Contract) **production** 420 **est.** 1994
product range ($20–24 CD) Chardonnay, Pinot Noir.
summary Elvio and Natalie Brianese are an architect and graphic designer couple whose extended family have centuries-old viticultural roots in the Veneto region of northern Italy. Their winery has 2.5 hectares of vineyard and got off to a flying start with a gold and silver medal for its 1997 Pinot Noir. Subsequent vintages have been less exhilarating, but there is no question the potential is there.

eumundi winery NR

2 Bruce Highway, Eumundi, Qld 4562 **region** Queensland Zone
phone (07) 5442 7444 **fax** (07) 5442 7455 **open** Not
winemaker Andrew Hickinbotham (Contract), Mike Hayes (Viticultural Consultant) **production** 1000 **est.** 1996
product range ($14–20 R) Semillon, Chardonnay, Taminga, Shiraz, Tempranillo, Durif, Merlot, Chambourcin, Cabernet Sauvignon.
summary Eumundi Vineyard is set on 21 hectares of riverfront land in the beautiful Eumundi Valley, 12 kilometres inland from Noosa Heads. The climate is hot, wet, humid and maritime, the only saving grace being the regular afternoon northeast sea breeze. It is a challenging environment in which to grow grapes, and over five years the owners, Robyn and Gerry Humphrey, have trialled 14 different varieties and three different trellis systems. Currently they have 3 hectares of tempranillo, 1 hectare each of shiraz and chambourcin, 0.8 hectare of petit verdot, durif and mourvedre, and a touch of verdelho. Plantings planned for 2000–2001 included refosco, tannat, lambrusca, albarino and torrontes, which gives some idea of their eclectic approach.

evans & tate 

Metricup Road, Willyabrup, WA 6280 **region** Margaret River
phone (08) 9755 6244 **fax** (08) 9755 6346 **open** 7 days 10.30–4.30
winemaker Steve Warne **production** 220 000 **est.** 1970
product range ($13–50 R) Gnangara Chardonnay and Shiraz; the Margaret River range of Margaret River Classic, Verdelho, Semillon, Sauvignon Blanc Semillon, Two Vineyards Chardonnay, Sparkling, Barrique 61 Cabernet Merlot, Merlot and Cabernet Sauvignon; followed by Redbrook Semillon and Chardonnay.
summary Single-handedly changed perceptions of the Swan Valley red wines in the 1970s before opening its highly successful Margaret River operation, which goes from strength to strength. The most recent expansion has been the establishment of a large vineyard in the new Jindong subregion of the Margaret River, precipitating a flood of other arrivals in that area. The continuing rapid growth of the business has taken the edge off the wines which, while immaculately crafted and ever-reliable, lack the concentration and complexity of the very best wines of the region. National distribution; exports to Canada, the UK, France, Switzerland and Hong Kong.

Evans & Tate Margaret River Semillon

2000 Light green-yellow; light, classic lemony citrus aromas, spotlessly clean, introduce a crisp, delicate and lively palate, finishing with brisk acidity. **rating:** 89

best drinking Now–2003 **best vintages** '91, '92, '93, '94, '95, '00 **drink with** Marron, yabbies • $19.85

Evans & Tate Margaret River Sauvignon Blanc Semillon

2000 Light green-yellow; a crisp and clean bouquet with predominantly mineral and a touch of herb is followed by a delicate palate, with slightly more tropical/gooseberry/passionfruit flavours, moving through to a crisp, clean finish. **rating:** 85

best drinking Now **best vintages** NA **drink with** Shellfish • $19.85

Evans & Tate Two Vineyards Chardonnay

🍷🍷🍷🍷 **2000** Light to medium yellow-green; charry barrel-ferment aromas come in over a base of grapefruit/melon fruit; the palate offers a similar play and, while far from big, is quite elegant. **rating:** 86

best drinking Now–2004 **best vintages** '91, '92, '93, '94, '95, '98 **drink with** Sugar-cured tuna • $19.85

Evans & Tate Margaret River Shiraz

🍷🍷🍷🍷 **1999** Vivid purple-red; the bouquet is of light to medium intensity, with fresh, earthy berry fruit; slightly simple overall. The palate has more weight than the bouquet suggests, with cherry and some earthy fruit. Subtle oak. **rating:** 85

best drinking Now–2005 **best vintages** '86, '88, '90, '91, '92, '93, '95, '96 **drink with** Strong red-meat dishes • $26.50

Evans & Tate Barrique 61 Cabernet Merlot

🍷🍷🍷🍷 **1999** Excellent medium to full red-purple; the bouquet has more weight and richness than previous vintages of this wine, with cassis and blackberry fruit together with touches of chocolate. The palate follows on directly, with plenty of depth and character, fully reflecting an outstanding vintage. Good oak handling. Much more weight and structure than normal. **rating:** 89

best drinking 2003–2010 **best vintages** '99 **drink with** Gourmet sausages • $20

evans family ★★★★☆

Palmers Lane, Pokolbin, NSW 2321 **region** Lower Hunter Valley
phone (02) 4998 7333 **fax** (02) 4998 7798 **open** By appointment
winemaker Contract **production** 3000 **est.** 1979
product range ($15.50–22.50 ML) Pinchem Chardonnay, Howards Chardonnay, Statue Vineyard Sparkling Pinot, Chapel Gamay, Hillside Pinot Noir.
summary In the wake of the acquisition of Rothbury by Mildara Blass, Len Evans' wine interests now focus on Evans Family (estate-grown and produced from vineyards around the family home), the Evans Wine Company (a quite different, part-maker, part-negociant business) and, most recently, Tower Estate. Len Evans continues to persist with the notion that the Hunter Valley can produce Gamay and Pinot Noir of quality and, irritatingly, occasionally produces evidence to suggest he may be half right. There is, of course, no such reservation with the Semillon or the Chardonnay.

Evans Family Semillon

🍷🍷🍷🍷🍷 **1997** Glowing yellow-green; the bouquet has abundant toast, mineral and honey aromas, the palate following down the same track and starting to develop nicely. Despite the generosity of the flavour, has elegance, thanks to the good balance and acidity. **rating:** 90

best drinking Now–2007 **best vintages** NA **drink with** Richer fish dishes • $15.50

evelyn county estate ★★★★

55 Eltham–Yarra Glen Road, Kangaroo Ground, Vic 3097 **region** Yarra Valley
phone (03) 9437 1668 **fax** (03) 9437 1232 **open** 7 days 9–5
winemaker David Lance (Contract) **production** 1500 **est.** 1994
product range ($17.50–30 CD) Black Paddock range of Sauvignon Blanc, Chardonnay, Merlot, Cabernet Sauvignon.
summary The 7-hectare Evelyn County Estate was established by former Coopers & Lybrand managing partner Roger Male and his wife Robyn, who is currently completing a degree in Applied Science (Wine Science) at Charles Sturt University. David Lance (of Diamond Valley) is currently making the wines, and an architect-designed cellar-door sales area, gallery and restaurant opened in April 2001. As one would expect, the quality of the wines is good.

Evelyn County Estate Black Paddock Sauvignon Blanc

🍷🍷🍷🍷 **2000** Light green-yellow; an attractive and moderately intense bouquet offers passionfruit, gooseberry and touches of herb; the palate has less fruit than the bouquet promises, tending to be crisp and minerally, but well handled. **rating:** 86

best drinking Now **best vintages** NA **drink with** White-fleshed fish • $17.50

Evelyn County Estate Black Paddock Chardonnay

ΨΨΨΨ **1999** Light to medium yellow-green; the bouquet is clean, of light to moderate intensity, with subtle barrel-ferment oak inputs. The palate offers more of the same, but at the extreme end of the elegance and subtlety scale. Retasted November 2000; the wine retains the elegance it showed when young but has picked up complexity. **rating:** 88

best drinking Now **best vintages** NA **drink with** Yarra Valley trout • $20

Evelyn County Estate Black Paddock Merlot

ΨΨΨΨ **1999** Medium purple-red; strong, spicy/smoky French oak wafts over scented, sweet berry fruit on the bouquet. Raspberry and redcurrant fruit flavours come through well on the palate, which is quite silky in texture, finishing with fine tannins. A thoroughly nice wine. **rating:** 87

best drinking 2002–2007 **best vintages** '99 **drink with** Yearling steak • $30

Evelyn County Estate Cabernet Sauvignon

ΨΨΨΨY **1998** Medium to full red-purple; the bouquet is ripe, with juicy berry/ribena aromas, and a slightly edgy/earthy background; sweet, juicy berry fruit flows along the tongue, with soft tannins and gentle oak. Shows its cool-climate origins from start to finish. **rating:** 90

best drinking 2003–2008 **best vintages** NA **drink with** Roast veal • $25

excelsior peak NR

22 Wrights Road, Drummoyne, NSW 2047 (postal address) **region** Tumbarumba
phone (02) 6948 5102 **fax** (02) 6948 5102 **open** Not
winemaker Charles Sturt University (Contract) **production** 1150 **est.** 1980
product range ($18–22 ML) Chardonnay, Pinot Noir, Méthode Champenoise.
summary Excelsior Peak proprietor Juliet Cullen established the first vineyard in Tumbarumba in 1980. That vineyard was thereafter sold to Southcorp, and Juliet Cullen subsequently established another vineyard, now releasing wines under the Excelsior Peak label. Plantings total 9 hectares, with 6.5 hectares in production.

eyton-on-yarra ★★★★

Cnr Maroondah Highway and Hill Road, Coldstream, Vic 3370 **region** Yarra Valley
phone (03) 5962 2119 **fax** (03) 5962 5319 **open** 7 days 10–5
winemaker Matthew Aldridge **production** 13 000 **est.** 1993
product range ($22–40 R) There are now three labels in the range: at the top NDC Reserve, a tribute to the late Newell Cowan, who effectively founded Eyton-on-Yarra; the main varietal range under the Eyton label; and the third label range of Dalry Road, the name of the second vineyard owned by Eyton.
summary Now owned and run by the energetic and innovative Deidre Cowan, overseeing an excellent and capacious restaurant, a sound shell for concerts of every shape and hue, and, of course, the winemaking side of a substantial business that is able to draw on over 50 hectares of estate vineyards. Retail distribution through Victoria, New South Wales and the ACT.

Eyton-on-Yarra Pinot Chardonnay

ΨΨΨY **1997** Light green-yellow; the bouquet is quite complex, with some aldehydic characters which are, however, within the acceptable limits of the style. The palate is quite fine and long, with some echoes of the aldehydes of the bouquet, but a crisp finish. Stylised as much as stylish. **rating:** 84

best drinking Now–2003 **best vintages** NA **drink with** Hors d'oeuvres • $30

Eyton-on-Yarra Shiraz

ΨΨΨY **1998** Medium red-purple; spice and cedar are joined by hints of vanilla and sweet earth on the bouquet, the palate with bright but very firm and slightly sharp-edged fruit. Nearly there, and might soften and open up with a few more years in bottle. **rating:** 84

best drinking 2002–2006 **best vintages** NA **drink with** Rack of lamb • $24.50

fairfield vineyard NR

Murray Valley Highway, Browns Plains, via Rutherglen, Vic 3685 **region** Rutherglen
phone (02) 6032 9381 **open** Mon–Sat 10–5, some Sun 12–5
winemaker Andrew Sutherland-Smith **production** 4200 **est.** 1959

product range ($8.50–15 CD) White Hermitage, Riesling, Moselle, Rosé, Light Red, Shiraz, Durif, Cabernet Sauvignon, Fortified.

summary Specialist in red and fortified wines made with nineteenth-century equipment housed in the grounds of the historic Fairfield Mansion, built by G F Morris. A tourist must. Offers a wide range of back-vintages.

faisan estate NR

Amaroo Road, Borenore, NSW 2800 **region** Orange
phone (02) 6365 2380 **open** Not
winemaker Col Walker **production** 500 **est.** 1992
product range ($8–13 ML) Chardonnay, Canobolas Classic White, Pinot Noir, Britton's Block Cabernet Sauvignon, Old Block Cabernet Sauvignon.

summary Faisan Estate, within sight of Mount Canobolas and 20 kilometres west of the city of Orange, has been established by Trish and Col Walker. They now have almost 7 hectares of vineyards coming into bearing and have purchased grapes from other growers in the region in the interim.

farrell's limestone creek

Mount View Road, Mount View, NSW 2325 **region** Lower Hunter Valley
phone (02) 4991 2808 **fax** (02) 4991 3414 **open** Weekends, public holidays 10–5
winemaker Neil McGuigan (Consultant) **production** 3500 **est.** 1980
product range ($17–20 CD) Semillon, Chardonnay, Shiraz, Merlot, Cabernet Sauvignon Merlot.

summary The Farrell family purchased 20 hectares on Mount View in 1980 and gradually established 7.3 hectares of vineyards planted to semillon, verdelho, chardonnay, shiraz, cabernet sauvignon and merlot. Most of the grapes are sold to McWilliam's, which contract-makes a small amount for cellar-door sales. The quality of the wines is as good as one would expect, with a range of back-vintages available at cellar door.

felsberg winery

Townsends Road, Glen Aplin, Qld 4381 **region** Granite Belt
phone (07) 4683 4332 **fax** (07) 4683 4377 **open** 7 days 9–5
winemaker Otto Haag **production** 2700 **est.** 1983
product range ($12–16 CD) Rhine Riesling, Traminer, White Classic, Chardonnay, Merlot, Shiraz, Cabernet Sauvignon, Mead, Ruby Mead.

summary Felsberg has been offering wine for sale via cellar door made by former master brewer Otto Haag. I had problems with the first few vintages but, after a gap in tasting of several years, I have renewed my acquaintance with Felsberg through the vintages since 1997.

Felsberg Merlot

YYYY **1999** Medium red-purple; the bouquet is clean, of light to medium intensity, with earthy/berry/spicy aromas, backed by subtle oak; the clean, light to medium bodied palate has pleasant fruit, but not a great deal of length or intensity. **rating:** 82

best drinking Now–2003 **best vintages** NA **drink with** Veal ragout • $16

Felsberg Cabernet Shiraz

YYYY **1999** Medium to full red-purple; chunky, dark blackberry fruit and subtle oak on the bouquet are followed by a concentrated savoury/earthy/blackberry palate with very powerful tannins. Approach with caution. **rating:** 84

best drinking 2004–2009 **best vintages** NA **drink with** Leave it in the cellar • NA

ferguson falls estate NR

Pile Road, Dardanup, WA 6236 **region** Geographe
phone (08) 9728 1083 **fax** (08) 9728 1616 **open** By appointment
winemaker James Pennington (Contract) **production** 1000 **est.** 1983
product range ($15–21.50 CD) Chardonnay, Cabernet Sauvignon.

summary Peter Giumelli and family are dairy farmers in the lush Ferguson Valley, 180 kilometres south of Perth. In 1983 they planted 3 hectares of cabernet sauvignon, chardonnay and merlot, making their first wines for commercial release from the 1995 and 1996 vintages, which confirmed the suitability of the region for the production of premium wine.

Ferguson Falls Estate Cabernet Sauvignon

🍷🍷🍷🍷 **1999** Medium red-purple; unusual spicy/meaty/leafy/roast meat/jammy aromas follow through into a high-flavoured palate with echoes of the bouquet. Highly pointed at the 2000 Western Australia Wine Show; other judges were even more enamoured of the wine than I was. **rating:** 87

best drinking 2002–2007 **best vintages** NA **drink with** Marinated beef • $21.50

fergusson ★★★★

Wills Road, Yarra Glen, Vic 3775 **region** Yarra Valley
phone (03) 5965 2237 **fax** (03) 5965 2405 **open** 7 days 11–5
winemaker Christopher Keyes, Peter Fergusson **production** 10 000 **est.** 1968
product range ($16–50 CD) Two basic ranges: the lower-priced Tartan Range is sourced from grapes grown outside the Yarra Valley, with Chardonnay, Semillon Sauvignon Blanc, Shiraz, Cabernet Sauvignon and Fine Old Tawny Port; and the Estate Range of Victoria Chardonnay, Victoria Reserve Chardonnay, Blanc de Blanc, LJK Pinot Noir, Jeremy Shiraz, Benjamyn Cabernet Sauvignon and Benjamyn Reserve Cabernet Sauvignon.
summary Best known as a favoured tourist destination, particularly for tourist coaches, and offering hearty fare in comfortable surroundings accompanied by wines of non-Yarra Valley origin. For this reason the limited quantities of its estate wines are often ignored, but should not be.

Fergusson LJK Pinot Noir

🍷🍷🍷🍷 **1998** Medium red, with just a tinge of purple; the bouquet has quite solid briary/plummy fruit, the palate ripe, perhaps tending a little to dry red, but quite a good outcome for a vintage that favoured the Bordeaux varieties more than pinot noir. **rating:** 83

best drinking Now–2004 **best vintages** NA **drink with** Deep-fried quail • $25

fermoy estate NR

Metricup Road, Willyabrup, WA 6280 **region** Margaret River
phone (08) 9755 6285 **fax** (08) 9755 6251 **open** 7 days 11–4.30
winemaker Michael Kelly **production** 15 000 **est.** 1985
product range ($12–28 CD) Sauvignon Blanc, Sentinel (Sauvignon Blanc Semillon), Semillon, Chenin Blanc, Chardonnay, Reserve Chardonnay, Cabernet Sauvignon, Reserve Cabernet.
summary Consistently produces wines with a particular character and style, with the focus away from primary fruit and into secondary flavours, with strong structure; the Americans would call them 'food styles'. Quite deliberately out of the mainstream, but seeking to rejoin it in the wake of a change of ownership.

fern hill estate 

Ingoldby Road, McLaren Flat, SA 5171 **region** McLaren Vale
phone (08) 8383 0167 **fax** (08) 8383 0107 **open** Mon–Fri 10–5, weekends 10–5
winemaker Grant Burge (Contract) **production** 5000 **est.** 1975
product range ($14.95–17.95 CD) Semillon, Chardonnay, Shiraz, Cabernet Sauvignon.
summary One suspects there have been significant changes since Wayne Thomas sold Fern Hill to the Hill International Group, and not all for the better. The wines are now exported to the UK, the US, Canada, Japan, New Zealand, Singapore and Switzerland.

five oaks vineyard 

60 Aitken Road, Seville, Vic 3139 **region** Yarra Valley
phone (03) 5964 3704 **fax** (03) 5964 3064 **open** Weekends and public holidays 10–5 and by appointment
winemaker Wally Zuk **production** 2000 **est.** 1997
product range ($15–25 CD) Riesling, Chardonnay, Merlot, Cabernet Merlot, Cabernet Sauvignon.
summary Wally and Judy Zuk purchased the Five Oaks Vineyard in Seville from Oakridge Estate, which has moved to its new premises on the other side of the Yarra Valley. Wally Zuk, with a background in nuclear physics, has completed his Wine Science degree at Charles Sturt University. He has now retired from the nuclear science world and is devoting himself (with help from Michael Zitzlaff of Oakridge and his wife Judy) to running Five Oaks. The winery rating is given for the red wines; the white wines are less successful.

Five Oaks Vineyard Cabernet Sauvignon

YYYY **1999** Medium to full red-purple; strong, charry/toasty barrel-ferment oak characters accompany blackcurrant and earth fruit on both the bouquet and powerful palate; fruit and oak tannins are fairly assertive on the finish. **rating:** 87

best drinking 2003–2009 **best vintages** NA **drink with** Roast beef • $23

572 richmond road NR

572 Richmond Road, Cambridge, Tas 7170 (postal 44 Lambert Street, Kangaroo Point, Qld 4169)
region Southern Tasmania
phone 0419 878 023 **fax** (07) 3391 4565 **open** At Craigow Fri–Sun 10–5
winemaker Andrew Hood, Julian Alcorso (Contract) **production** 200 **est.** 1994
product range ($20.50–23.50 ML) Riesling, Gewurztraminer, Chardonnay.
summary It hardly needs be said 572 Richmond Road is both the address and the name of the vineyard. It is owned by medical professionals John and Sue Carney, and is situated adjacent to Andrew Hood's winery, hence becoming part of a spectacular vineyard development with various ownerships all situated close to the winery.

572 Richmond Road Riesling

YYYY **2000** Light to medium yellow-green; in typical vintage style, ripe and rich, the palate very firm and powerful, with the tropical lime flavours of the year balanced (perhaps too pointedly) by acidity. **rating:** 85

best drinking Now–2005 **best vintages** NA **drink with** Mussels • $20.50

572 Richmond Road Gewurztraminer

YYYYY **2000** Light green-yellow; a light, fragrant bouquet with some lime blossom and spice that leads into an elegant, intense and long palate, with lime blossom, apple and spice rippling along. **rating:** 90

best drinking Now–2004 **best vintages** '00 **drink with** Chinese crystal prawns • $23.50

flinders bay NR

Davis Road, Witchcliffe, WA 6286 **region** Margaret River
phone (08) 9757 6281 **fax** (08) 9757 6353 **open** Not
winemaker Clive Otto, Will Shields (Contract) **production** 15 000 **est.** 1995
product range ($15–25 R) Sauvignon Blanc Semillon, Pericles Sauvignon Blanc Semillon, Verdelho, Chardonnay, Shiraz, Merlot, Agincourt Cabernet Sauvignon Malbec Merlot.
summary Flinders Bay is a joint venture between the Gillespie and Ireland families. The Gillespies have been grape-growers and viticultural contractors in the Margaret River region for over 20 years, while Bill and Noel Ireland were prominent retailers in Sydney from 1979 to 1996. All in all, a potent and synergistic combination. Fifty hectares of vines were planted between 1995 and 1998 at Karridale, an extremely cool subregion (possibly the coolest in Western Australia) with the climate influenced by both the Indian and Southern Oceans. The wines presently being produced are blends of grapes from the northern and central parts of the Margaret River with estate-grown grapes. Ultimately, all of the wines will be estate-produced. They are contract-made at Vasse Felix, which also provides the cellar-door facility for Flinders Bay. Exports to the UK and the US.

Flinders Bay Shiraz

YYYY **1999** Medium red-purple; the moderately intense bouquet is clean, with nicely focused berry, plum and spice fruit aromas. The palate provides more of the same, with sweet cherry/berry fruit, and well-balanced and controlled oak and tannins. **rating:** 89

best drinking 2002–2007 **best vintages** '99 **drink with** Baby lamb • $25

Flinders Bay Agincourt Cabernet Sauvignon Malbec Merlot

YYYYY **1999** Medium to full red-purple; strong briary/savoury overtones to dark berry fruit on the bouquet are followed by a palate with abundant, ripe cassis fruit running from the entry to the mid-palate, then nicely offset by savoury tannins through to the finish. Gold medal at the Perth Wine Show 2000. **rating:** 90

best drinking 2004–2009 **best vintages** '99 **drink with** Ragout of beef • $25

fonty's pool ★★★☆

c/o Cape Mentelle Vineyards, PO Box 11, Margaret River, WA 6285 **region** Manjimup
phone (08) 9757 3266 **fax** (08) 9757 3233 **open** Not
winemaker Eloise Jarvis (Cape Mentelle) **production** 2000 **est.** 1998

product range ($21–25 R) Chardonnay, Pinot Noir, Shiraz.
summary Fonty's Pool is a joint venture between Cape Mentelle and Fonty's Pool Farms. The Fonty's Pool vineyards are part of the original farm owned by pioneer settler Archie Fontanini, who was granted land by the government in 1907. In the early 1920s a large dam was created to provide water for the intensive vegetable farming that was part of the farming activities. The dam became known as Fonty's Pool and to this day remains a famous local landmark and recreational facility. The first grapes were planted in 1989, and the vineyard is now one of the region's largest, supplying grapes to a number of leading West Australian wineries. Only a small part of the production is used for Fonty's Pool; the wines are made at Cape Mentelle by Eloise Jarvis, who is part of the Cape Mentelle winemaking team.

Fonty's Pool Chardonnay

YYYY 1999 Light to medium green-yellow; a complex and sophisticated bouquet with a subtle mix of melon, cashew and oak is followed by a similarly sophisticated palate, with cashew/nutty/creamy flavours and texture. **rating:** 89

best drinking 2002–2006 **best vintages** NA **drink with** Oyster soup • $21

Fonty's Pool Pinot Noir

YYYY 1999 Medium red-purple; strongly savoury/foresty/briary aromas on the bouquet are followed by a palate with some plummy fruit, providing more sweetness. Even more would have been better still, but the wine has style. **rating:** 85

best drinking Now–2004 **best vintages** NA **drink with** Coq au vin • $25

Fonty's Pool Shiraz

YYYY 1999 Light to medium red-purple; the moderately intense bouquet is predominantly spicy, with some briary/savoury notes underlying the spice. The bright, indeed, slightly pointed, fruit and acidity on the palate need time to come together, when the spicy characters will add complexity. **rating:** 86

best drinking 2003–2007 **best vintages** NA **drink with** Cassoulet • $21

forest hill vineyard ★★★☆

Muirs Highway, Mount Barker, WA 6324 **region** Great Southern
phone (08) 9851 2096 **fax** (08) 9851 1486 **open** By appointment
winemaker Clive Otto, Will Shields **production** 10 000 **est.** 1966
product range ($15–20 CD) Riesling, Sauvignon Blanc Semillon, Chardonnay, Shiraz, Cabernet Sauvignon.
summary This is one of the oldest 'new' winemaking operations in West Australia, and was the site for the first grape plantings for the Great Southern regions in 1966 on a farming property owned by the Pearce family. The Forest Hill brand became well known, aided by the fact that a 1975 Riesling made by Sandalford from Forest Hill grapes won nine trophies in national wine shows. In 1989 the property was acquired by Heytesbury Holdings (Janet Holmes à Court) as part of the Vasse Felix operation, and most of the grapes were used in the Vasse Felix wines. The only Forest Hill wines were a Riesling and a Cabernet Sauvignon, produced in small quantities and largely sold locally. In 1997 the property was acquired by interests associated with Perth stockbroker Tim Lyons, and a programme of renovation and expansion of the vineyards commenced. It is likely that a winery and new cellar door will be constructed on site; in the meantime the wines continue to be made at Vasse Felix, which also buys part of the grape production from the 80 hectares of vines.

Forest Hill Vineyard Riesling

YYYY 2000 Light green-yellow; fragrant, spices, herbs and flowers intermingle with more classic lime and mineral characters on the bouquet. The palate is quite delicate, with an interplay between minerally acidity and a subliminal hint of residual sweetness. Less fruit intensity than anticipated. **rating:** 86

best drinking Now–2004 **best vintages** NA **drink with** Summer salad • $15

Forest Hill Vineyard Chardonnay

YYYY 1999 Light green-yellow; the bouquet is light and quite crisp, with melon fruit and subtle oak. The palate, likewise, has delicate melon citrus fruit in a light-bodied frame, but has surprising length and intensity. Once again, exemplary oak handling. Great value. **rating:** 88

best drinking Now–2004 **best vintages** '99 **drink with** Grilled marron • $15

Forest Hill Vineyard Shiraz

🍷🍷🍷🍷 **1998** Medium red-purple; the bouquet is solid, with quite ripe, sweet leathery/spicy aromas, aromas that flow through into the medium-bodied palate; needs a little more texture for top points. **rating:** 82

best drinking 2002–2007 **best vintages** NA **drink with** Veal chops • $20

fox creek wines ★★★★

Malpas Road, Willunga, SA 5172 **region** McLaren Vale
phone (08) 8556 2403 **fax** (08) 8556 2104 **open** 7 days 11–5
winemaker Daniel Hills, Tony Walker **production** 35 000 **est.** 1995
product range ($15.50–36 CD) Verdelho, Semillon Sauvignon Blanc, Sauvignon Blanc, Chardonnay, Vixen Sparkling Shiraz Cabernet Franc, Grenache Shiraz, Short Row Shiraz, Reserve Shiraz, JSM Shiraz Cabernets, Merlot, Reserve Cabernet Sauvignon.
summary Fox Creek has made a major impact since coming on-stream late in 1995. It is the venture of a group of distinguished Adelaide doctors (three of them professors), with particular input from the Watts family, which established the vineyard back in 1985. The Reserve red wines, and especially the Reserve Shiraz, are outstanding and have enjoyed considerable show success. As well as comprehensive distribution throughout Australia, the wines are exported to the UK, the US, Canada, Germany, Switzerland, Belgium, New Zealand, Thailand and Hong Kong.

Fox Creek JSM Shiraz Cabernets

🍷🍷🍷🍷 **1999** Medium to full red-purple; the moderately intense bouquet has clean, pleasantly ripe dark berry fruit, the palate with plenty of youthful juicy berry fruit and controlled oak. Trophy winner for Best Consumer Red Wine Blend at the 2000 Adelaide Wine Show. **rating:** 89

best drinking 2002–2006 **best vintages** '99 **drink with** Rib of beef • $22

Fox Creek Reserve Cabernet Sauvignon

🍷🍷🍷🍷 **1998** Dense red-purple; very ripe blackberry and cassis fruit is the primary driver of the bouquet, with oak a secondary but nonetheless obvious influence. As ever, the palate has huge extract and tannins to frame the fruit; a Henry VIII style, probably better appreciated with rich meat. **rating:** 86

best drinking 2003–2013 **best vintages** '96, '97 **drink with** Game pie • NA

frankland estate ★★★☆

Frankland Road, Frankland, WA 6396 **region** Great Southern
phone (08) 9855 1544 **fax** (08) 9855 1549 **open** By appointment
winemaker Barrie Smith, Judi Cullam **production** 12 000 **est.** 1988
product range ($18–34 R) Under the Isolation Ridge label are Riesling, Chardonnay, Shiraz, Cabernet Sauvignon; Olmo's Reward (Bordeaux-blend) is the flagbearer.
summary A rapidly growing Frankland River operation, situated on a large sheep property owned by Barrie Smith and Judi Cullam. The 29-hectare vineyard has been established progressively since 1988, and a winery was built on the site for the 1993 vintage. The Riesling, Isolation Ridge and Olmo's Reward are consistent in style, and all the wines are energetically promoted and marketed by Judi Cullam. Exports to the US, the UK, Japan, Belgium, Switzerland, Denmark and Singapore.

Frankland Estate Isolation Ridge Riesling

🍷🍷🍷🍷 **2000** Medium straw-yellow; there are some lime/pastille aromas to the bouquet, but the palate seems hard and somewhat stripped. The finger of suspicion points at problems during the bottling leading to a degree of oxidation. **rating:** 83

best drinking Now **best vintages** '92, '93, '94, '96, '98 **drink with** Antipasto • $21.50

Frankland Estate Isolation Ridge

🍷🍷🍷🍷 **1998** Medium red-purple; the bouquet is in a leathery, savoury, spicy mode, the palate in much the same bracket, firm and with predominantly earthy/savoury feel and flavour. The wine seems to need either a dash of fresher oak or some extra retention of sweet fruit unless, of course, you are of the school that prefers secondary to primary flavours. **rating:** 83

best drinking Now–2004 **best vintages** '92, '93, '97 **drink with** Braised lamb shanks • $23.99

Frankland Estate Olmo's Reward

YYYY **1997** Medium red; soft, earthy/savoury bottle-developed aromas lead into a palate that is absolutely in the usual Olmo's Reward style, with savoury/earthy characters reminiscent of medium-year Bordeauxs. A continuing need for better oak is evident. **rating:** 86

best drinking Now–2006 **best vintages** NA **drink with** Veal chops • $32

freycinet ★★★★★

15919 Tasman Highway, via Bicheno, Tas 7215 **region** Southern Tasmania
phone (03) 6257 8574 **fax** (03) 6257 8454 **open** Mon–Fri 9–5, weekends 10–5
winemaker Claudio Radenti, Lindy Bull **production** 6000 **est.** 1980
product range ($15–38 CD) Riesling, Riesling Muller Thurgau, Chardonnay, Pinot Noir, Cabernet Merlot, Radenti (Methode Champenoise), Cabernet Sauvignon.
summary The 9-hectare Freycinet vineyards are beautifully situated on the sloping hillsides of a small valley. The soils are podsol and decaying granite with a friable clay subsoil, and the combination of aspect, slope, soil and heat summation produce red grapes of unusual depth of colour and ripe flavours. One of Australia's foremost producers of Pinot Noir, with a wholly enviable track record of consistency, which is rare with such a temperamental variety. Exports to the UK, Hong Kong and Japan.

Freycinet Riesling

YYYYY **2000** Light green-yellow; fragrant, tangy lime blossom, lemon, herb and spice aromas are followed by a crisp, long palate with the intensity of flavour building on the mid- to back-palate; well-balanced acidity accents the finish. Will be long lived. **rating:** 94

best drinking Now–2010 **best vintages** '00 **drink with** Seared scallops • $21

Freycinet Chardonnay

YYYYY **1999** Light to medium green-yellow; the bouquet is less powerful than the usual Freycinet style, with fragrant citrus and melon, the palate likewise with lively melon and citrus; however, the Freycinet thumbprint does come on with the quite strong cashew malolactic-fermentation characters which underlie both bouquet and palate. **rating:** 90

best drinking Now–2006 **best vintages** '93, '94, '95, '96, '98, '99 **drink with** Abalone • $25

Freycinet Radenti

YYYYY **1996** Medium green-yellow; a fine, clean, tangy citrus and lemon bouquet is followed by a palate that is elegant, fine and delicate, yet has structural complexity, and impressive length and balance. **rating:** 92

best drinking Now–2004 **best vintages** '96 **drink with** Oysters • $35

Freycinet Cabernet Sauvignon Merlot

YYYYY **1998** Medium red-purple; light berry fruit on the bouquet has touches of spice and earth, moving into a more glossy/minty palate that is quite sweet overall, but which does finish with a lot of tannin (and subtle oak). **rating:** 90

best drinking 2003–2010 **best vintages** '98 **drink with** Braised lamb • $31

frog rock ★★★☆

Cassilis Road, Mudgee, NSW 2850 **region** Mudgee
phone (02) 6372 2408 **fax** (02) 6372 6924 **open** Weekends 11–4 or by appointment
winemaker Simon Gilbert (Contract), David Lowe (Contract) **production** 6000 **est.** 1973
product range ($20–25 ML) Chardonnay, Shiraz, Premium Shiraz Cabernet, Chambourcin, Merlot, Cabernet Sauvignon.
summary Frog Rock is the former Tallara Vineyard, established almost 30 years ago by leading Sydney chartered accountant Rick Turner. There are now 60 hectares of vineyard, with 25 hectares each of shiraz and cabernet sauvignon, and much smaller plantings of chardonnay, semillon, merlot, petit verdot and chambourcin. The wines are exported to the UK and the US; Australian sales by mail order/direct.

Frog Rock Premium Shiraz Cabernet Sauvignon

YYYY **1998** Medium red-purple; the smooth, moderately intense bouquet has an attractive range of berry and chocolate aromas supported by subtle oak. The palate has plenty of weight and concentration, in a savoury/ berry, rather than lush, mode, with soft tannins and well-balanced oak. **rating:** 87

best drinking 2002–2008 **best vintages** '98 **drink with** T-bone • $25

Frog Rock Chambourcin

1999 Bright purple-red; an intriguing bouquet with some earth and multiple spice aromas overlying sweet fruit. The palate has typically sweet, slightly jammy fruit flavour, the varietal hollow mid-palate, and soft tannins to close. **rating:** 82

best drinking Now **best vintages** NA **drink with** Takeaway • $20

Frog Rock Cabernet Sauvignon

1998 Medium to full red-purple; the bouquet is flooded with sweet cassis, chocolate and mint fruit aromas supported by attractive oak. A youthful, powerful palate with exemplary ripe varietal fruit flavour and good structure. Good now, but its best years are in front of it. **rating:** 91

best drinking 2003–2013 **best vintages** NA **drink with** Marinated beef • NA

fyffe field NR

RMB 4243 Murray Valley Highway, Yarrawonga, Vic 3730 **region** Goulburn Valley
phone (03) 5748 4282 **fax** (03) 5748 4284 **open** 7 days 10–5
winemaker David Traeger (Contract) **production** 1300 **est.** 1993
product range ($9–20 CD) Diamond White, Byramine White, Verdelho, Big Rivers Rose, Byramine Dry Red, Shiraz, Shiraz Petit Verdot, Touriga, Cabernet Sauvignon Petit Verdot, Tokay, Muscat, Tawny Snort.
summary Fyffe Field has been established by Graeme and Liz Diamond near the Murray River between Cobram and Yarrawonga. The mudbrick and leadlight tasting room is opposite an historic homestead. A highlight is the ornamental pig collection, a display set up long before Babe was born.

galafrey 

Quangellup Road, Mount Barker, WA 6324 **region** Great Southern
phone (08) 9851 2022 **fax** (08) 9851 2324 **open** 7 days 10–5
winemaker Ian Tyrer **production** 9000 **est.** 1977
product range ($12–50 CD) Riesling, Muller, Semillon Sauvignon Blanc, Chardonnay, Unoaked Chardonnay, Classic Reserve, Art Label White, Late Harvest, Reserve Botrytis Riesling, Pinot Noir, Shiraz, Cabernet Sauvignon, Reserve Cabernet Sauvignon, Art Label Premium Dry Red, Tawny Port.
summary Relocated to a new purpose-built but utilitarian winery after previously inhabiting the exotic surrounds of the old Albany wool store, Galafrey makes wines with plenty of robust, if not rustic, character, drawing grapes in the main from 12 hectares of estate plantings at Mount Barker. Exports to the Netherlands, Switzerland and Japan. Quality is on the rise again after a period of uncertainty.

Galafrey Riesling

1999 Light yellow-green; a crisp, tight and powerful bouquet offers predominantly mineral and lime aromas, with just a hint of toast. The palate is fresh and pure, with powerful lime/mineral fruit, good acidity and good length. A radical change from the far sweeter wines made until 1996. **rating:** 93

best drinking Now–2010 **best vintages** '90, '91, '99 **drink with** Sweet and sour pork • $14

galah wine 

Tregarthen Road, Ashton, SA 5137 **region** Adelaide Hills
phone (08) 8390 1243 **fax** (08) 8390 1243 **open** Available at Ashton Hills
winemaker Stephen George **production** 1000 **est.** 1986
product range ($7.50–20 ML) SE Aust Semillon Chardonnay, Brut, Sparkling Red, McLaren Vale Cabernet Shiraz, Clare Valley Cabernet Malbec Shiraz, Clare Valley Shiraz.
summary Over the years, Stephen George has built up a network of contacts across South Australia from which he gains some very high-quality small parcels of grapes or wine for the Galah label. These are all sold direct at extremely low prices for the quality. Exports to the UK and the US.

gallagher estate 

Dog Trap Road, Murrumbateman, NSW 2582 **region** Canberra District
phone (02) 6254 9957 **fax** (02) 6254 9957 **open** Not
winemaker Greg Gallagher **production** 2500 **est.** 1995
product range ($14–20 R) Chardonnay, Shiraz.

summary Greg Gallagher was senior winemaker at Taltarni for 20 years, where he worked with Dominique Portet. He began planning a change of career at much the same time as did Dominique, and began the establishment of a small vineyard at Murrumbateman in 1995, planting a little over 1 hectare each of chardonnay and shiraz. He has now moved to the region with his family, his major job at the present time being winemaker at the Charles Sturt University Winery, playing a central role in training the winemakers of tomorrow. The wines are available by mail order and through Oak Barrel Wines at Fyshwick, Canberra.

Gallagher Estate Chardonnay

ΨΨΨΨ **2000** Light green-yellow; the bouquet is clean, distinctly light in intensity, but with an attractive tangy edge to the fruit uncompromised by oak; the palate is light, clean, fresh and citrussy, the oak input again minimal. A nice, no-frills wine which has been well handled. **rating:** 85

best drinking Now–2003 **best vintages** NA **drink with** Light seafood • NA

Gallagher Estate Bin 16 Shiraz

ΨΨΨΨ **1999** Medium to full red-purple; the moderately intense bouquet is clean, offering a mix of berry, earth and oak; the palate has good richness, with dark cherry touched by mint; subtle oak and soft tannins. **rating:** 87

best drinking 2002–2007 **best vintages** NA **drink with** Shoulder of lamb • NA

gapsted wines ★★★★

Great Alpine Road, Gapsted, Vic 3737 **region** King Valley
phone (03) 5751 1383 **fax** (03) 5751 1368 **open** 7 days 11–5
winemaker Michael Cope-Williams, Shayne Cunningham **production** 3000 **est.** 1997
product range ($20–30 R) Ballerina Canopy range of Chardonnay, Shiraz, Durif, Merlot, Cabernet Franc, Cabernet Sauvignon.
summary Gapsted is the premier brand of the Victorian Alps Wine Co, the latter primarily a contract-crush facility that processes grapes for 48 growers in the King and Alpine Valleys. The estate plantings total a little over 9 hectares of shiraz, cabernet sauvignon, petit verdot and merlot, but the Gapsted wines come both from these estate plantings and from contract-grown fruit. All incorporate the 'ballerina canopy' tag, a reference to the open nature of this particular training method which is ideally suited to these regions. The wines have had outstanding success in both national shows and the 2001 Winewise Small Vigneron Awards.

Gapsted Ballerina Canopy Chardonnay

ΨΨΨΨ **1999** Light green-yellow; fragrant melon fruit aromas have gentle oak and mlf cashew overtones. The palate is fresh and youthful, the winemaking inputs having been very successfully managed and balanced; finishes with pleasantly brisk acidity. Topped the Chardonnay class at the 2001 Winewise Small Vigneron Awards, also winning five bronze medals in shows. **rating:** 88

best drinking Now **best vintages** '98, '99 **drink with** Fettuccine a la pana • $20

Gapsted Ballerina Canopy Shiraz

ΨΨΨΨ **1997** Medium red-purple; the aromas of the bouquet range through berry, earth, leather and vanilla, while on the palate sweet berry and chocolate fruit flavours are supported by good extract and tannins, and the wholly appropriate use of oak. **rating:** 86

best drinking 2002–2007 **best vintages** NA **drink with** Beef spare ribs • $20

Gapsted Ballerina Canopy Durif

ΨΨΨΨ **1998** Medium red-purple; ripe, savoury/chocolate aromas are offset against prune and spice on the bouquet. The palate has potent, chocolate, blackberry and prune fruit, with tannins on the cusp of acceptability. Whatever else, will be long lived. **rating:** 88

best drinking 2005–2013 **best vintages** '98 **drink with** Braised ox cheek • $30

Gapsted Ballerina Canopy Cabernet Franc

ΨΨΨΨ **1997** Holding red hue pretty well; the bouquet is quite fragrant, with red berry fruit and touches of leaf and spice. The medium-weight red berry fruit, spice and vanilla oak on the palate come as no surprise, but the tannins do, giving the wine more structure than expected. **rating:** 85

best drinking 2002–2006 **best vintages** NA **drink with** Roast veal • $20

Gapsted Ballerina Canopy Merlot

YYYYY 1998 Medium red-purple; a clean, smooth and ripe bouquet with small red berry fruit aromas and subtle oak is followed by an attractively ripe palate with red berry fruit and gentle tannins. I'm not entirely convinced on the varietal character issue, but it's a very nice wine. **rating:** 90

best drinking 2003–2008 **best vintages** '98 **drink with** Grilled marinated lamb fillets • $20

Gapsted Ballerina Canopy Cabernet Sauvignon

YYYY 1998 Medium red-purple; quite strong oak merges with blackcurrant fruit on the bouquet; sweet blackcurrant/cassis fruit is again swathed in oak on the palate, which finishes with lingering tannins. **rating:** 87

best drinking 2003–2008 **best vintages** NA **drink with** Braised beef • $20

garbin estate NR

209 Toodyay Road, Middle Swan, WA 6056 **region** Swan District

phone (08) 9274 1747 **fax** (08) 9274 1747 **open** 7 days 10.30–5.30

winemaker Peter Garbin **production** 2000 **est.** 1956

product range ($14–18 CD) Chenin Blanc, Chardonnay, Shiraz, Cabernet Merlot, Dessert Wine, Ruby Port.

summary Peter Garbin, winemaker by weekend and design draftsman by week, decided in 1990 that he would significantly upgrade the bulk fortified winemaking business started by his father in 1956. The vineyards have been replanted, the winery re-equipped, and the first of the new-generation wines produced in 1994. The wines have since received significant critical acclaim, both locally and nationally, none more so than the 1999 Cabernet Merlot.

Garbin Estate Shiraz

YYYY 1999 Slightly questionable colour introduces a lighter style; clean, with some fragrance to the bouquet. The palate is fresh, bright and lively, but with faintly olivaceous/green/leafy undertones. **rating:** 84

best drinking 2002–2007 **best vintages** NA **drink with** Vegetarian • NA

garden gully vineyards ★★★★

Western Highway, Great Western, Vic 3377 **region** Grampians

phone (03) 5356 2400 **fax** (03) 5356 2400 **open** Mon–Fri 10.30–5.30, weekends 10–5.30

winemaker Brian Fletcher, Warren Randall **production** 2000 **est.** 1987

product range ($13–27 CD) Riesling, Shiraz, Sparkling Shiraz, Tokay.

summary Given the skills and local knowledge of the syndicate that owns Garden Gully, it is not surprising that the wines are typically good: an attractive stone cellar-door sales area is an additional reason to stop and pay a visit. Shiraz produced from the 100-year-old vines adjoining the cellar door is especially good. The 4 hectares of shiraz is complemented by 3 hectares of riesling, providing another good wine.

Garden Gully Riesling

YYYY 2000 Light to medium yellow-green; the bouquet is clean, with gentle lime and touches of ripe apple, showing more overt fruit than some of its predecessors. The palate has good structure, even if it is ever-so-slightly soft; the fruit flows evenly through to a long finish. Great value. **rating:** 88

best drinking 2002–2008 **best vintages** '98, '00 **drink with** Light seafood • $13

Garden Gully Shiraz

YYYYY 1999 Excellent purple-red; a powerful dark cherry/dark plum bouquet that has lots of American oak. The conjunction of sweet berry/cherry fruit and sweet vanilla oak works particularly well on the palate, soft tannins adding to the appeal. **rating:** 91

best drinking 2004–2014 **best vintages** '91, '93, '95, '98, '99 **drink with** Barbecued lamb • $21

garlands NR

Marmion Street, off Mount Barker Hill Road, Mount Barker, WA 6324 **region** Great Southern

phone (08) 9851 2737 **fax** (08) 9851 2686 **open** Thurs–Sun and public holidays 10–4 or by appointment

winemaker Michael Garland **production** 3500 **est.** 1996

product range ($12–25 CD) Sauvignon Blanc, Chardonnay, Barker Hill White, Cabernet Franc.

summary Garlands is a partnership between Michael and Julie Garland and their vigneron neighbours Craig and Caroline Drummond. Michael Garland has come to grape-growing and winemaking with a varied background in biological research, computer sales and retail clothing; he is now enrolled at Charles Sturt University for his degree in oenology, but already has significant practical experience behind him. A tiny but highly functional winery was erected prior to the 2000 vintage, the earlier wines being made elsewhere. The winery has a capacity of 150 tonnes, and will continue contract-making for other small producers in the region as well as making the wine from the 6 hectares of estate vineyards planted to cabernet franc, sauvignon blanc, chardonnay, riesling, shiraz and cabernet sauvignon.

Garlands Cabernet Franc

ΨΨΨΨΨ **1998** Medium red-purple; a clean, fruit-driven bouquet with subtle oak leads into a sweet, ripe palate with a mix of raspberry, redcurrant and blackcurrant fruit. Soft tannins to close. **rating:** 90

best drinking 2002–2007 **best vintages** '96, '98 **drink with** Venison pie • NA

gartelmann hunter estate ★★★☆

Lovedale Road, Lovedale, NSW 2321 **region** Lower Hunter Valley
phone (02) 4930 7113 **fax** (02) 4930 7114 **open** 7 days 10–5
winemaker Jane Wilson, David Lowe, Monarch Winemaking Services (Contract) **production** 7000 **est.** 1970
product range ($11–25 R) Semillon, Chenin Blanc, Chardonnay, Moritz (Chardonnay Semillon Chenin Blanc), Dry White, Shiraz, Diedrich Shiraz, Sparkling.
summary In 1996 Jan and Jorg Gartelmann purchased what was previously the George Hunter Estate, established by Sydney restaurateur Oliver Shaul in 1970. They acquired 16 hectares of mature vineyards, producing a limited amount of wine under the Gartelmann label in 1997 and moving to full production in 1998. Exports to Germany.

Gartelmann Hunter Estate Semillon

ΨΨΨΨ **2000** Medium yellow-green, quite full for a one-year-old Semillon. The bouquet is big and forward, with citrus, grass and herb, even a touch of white peach; the palate is in a full, early-developing style. All in all, the obverse of the '99. **rating:** 84

best drinking Now–2003 **best vintages** '99 **drink with** Shellfish • $19

Gartelmann Hunter Estate Shiraz

ΨΨΨΨ **1999** Medium red-purple; the bouquet is savoury, with a range of sweet, earthy/leathery aromas showing distinctive regional varietal character. The medium-bodied palate replays the flavours of the bouquet; it is quite long, but the tannins are slightly dry. **rating:** 86

best drinking 2002–2007 **best vintages** NA **drink with** Braised beef • $22

Gartelmann Hunter Estate Diedrich Shiraz

ΨΨΨΨ **1999** Medium red-purple; the savoury bouquet has slightly denser fruit than the standard varietal wine, and the oak, while evident, is not overplayed. The palate has a nice core of gently sweet cherry and plum fruit, backed with touches of vanilla; well-handled extract and tannins. **rating:** 89

best drinking 2004–2009 **best vintages** '99 **drink with** Smoked lamb • $25

gecko valley NR

Bailiff Road, via 700 Glenlyon Road, Gladstone, Qld 4680 **region** Queensland Zone
phone (07) 4979 0400 **fax** (07) 4979 0500 **open** 7 days 10–5
winemaker Bruce Humphery-Smith (Contract) **production** 1500 **est.** 1997
product range ($12.50–18.50 CD) Lightly Oaked Chardonnay, Special Reserve Chardonnay, Special Reserve Verdelho, Lazy Lizard White, Lazy Lizard Red, Special Reserve Shiraz, Liqueur Shiraz, Liqueur Mead.
summary Gecko Valley extends the viticultural map of Queensland yet further, situated little more than 50 kilometres off the Tropic of Capricorn in an area better known for sugar-cane farming and mineral activities. The 3-hectare vineyard (1 hectare each of chardonnay, verdelho and shiraz) provides the base for the table wines made by the omnipresent Bruce Humphery-Smith, supplemented by a range of liqueurs, ports and muscats made several thousand kilometres further south. As one would expect, the facility caters for the general tourist, with a café and a gift shop with a wide range of merchandise.

geebin wines NR

3729 Channel Highway, Birchs Bay, Tas 7162 **region** Southern Tasmania
phone (03) 6267 4750 **fax** (03) 6267 5090 **open** 7 days 10–5
winemaker Andrew Hood (Contract) **production** 50 **est.** 1983
product range ($17 CD) Riesling, Cabernet Sauvignon.

summary Although production is minuscule, quality has been consistently high. The Riesling is well made, but the interesting wine from this far southern vineyard is Cabernet Sauvignon; clearly, the vineyard enjoys favourable ripening conditions. With 0.7 hectare of vineyards (including 0.3 hectare of chardonnay yet to come into bearing) Geebin claims to be the smallest commercial producer in Australia, but isn't: Scarp Valley and (temporarily) Jollymont are smaller.

gehrig estate ★★★

Cnr Murray Valley Highway and Howlong Road, Barnawartha, Vic 3688 **region** Rutherglen
phone (02) 6026 7296 **fax** (02) 6026 7424 **open** Mon–Sat 9–5, Sun 10–5
winemaker Brian Gehrig **production** 5000 **est.** 1858
product range ($8.50–29 CD) Chenin Blanc, Riesling, Chardonnay, Trebbiano, Autumn Riesling, Late Harvest Tokay, Pinot Noir, Shiraz, Cabernet Sauvignon, Fortifieds.
summary An historic winery and adjacent house are superb legacies of the nineteenth century. Progressive modernisation of the winemaking facilities and operations has seen the quality of the white wines improve significantly, while the red wines now receive a percentage of new oak. Another recent innovation has been the introduction of the Gourmet Courtyard, serving lunch on weekends, public holidays and Victorian school holidays. A wide-ranging tasting of dry white, red and fortified wines in March 1999 showed Brian Gehrig to be equally at home with all three styles, the wines very reasonably priced for their quality.

Gehrig Estate Old Tawny Port

🍷🍷🍷🍷 **NV** The colour is dark, with a few red hues still there indicating intermediate age. The bouquet is solid, with sweet fruit and some rancio; a big, rich Rutherglen style on the palate which, like the bouquet, does not show any signs of staleness. **rating:** 86
best drinking Now **best vintages** NA **drink with** Coffee • NA

gembrook hill ★★★★

Launching Place Road, Gembrook, Vic 3783 **region** Yarra Valley
phone (03) 5968 1622 **fax** (03) 5968 1699 **open** By appointment
winemaker Timo Mayer **production** 2000 **est.** 1983
product range ($30–40 R) Sauvignon Blanc, Chardonnay, Pinot Noir.
summary The 6-hectare Gembrook Hill Vineyard is situated on rich, red volcanic soils 2 kilometres north of Gembrook in the coolest part of the Yarra Valley. The vines are not irrigated, with consequent natural vigour control. The Sauvignon Blanc is invariably good, sometimes outstanding.

Gembrook Hill Chardonnay

🍷🍷🍷 **1999** Light green-yellow; a light, fresh, clean and citrussy bouquet leads into a palate of almost fairy-like delicacy, with just the faintest touch of oak. The good thing is that the wine retains balance, and has not been forced to be something it is not. **rating:** 83
best drinking Now **best vintages** '90, '91, '93, '94, '97 **drink with** Crab, prawns • $30

gemtree vineyards ★★★★

Kangarilla Road, McLaren Flat, SA 5171 **region** McLaren Vale
phone (08) 8383 0403 **fax** (08) 8383 0506 **open** Not
winemaker Mike Brown **production** 1900 **est.** 1992
product range ($25 R) McLaren Vale Shiraz, Cabernet Sauvignon Merlot Petit Verdot.
summary The Buttery family, headed by Paul and Jill and with Melissa as viticulturist for Gemtree Vineyards, has been actively involved in grape-growing in McLaren Vale since 1980, when they purchased their first vineyard. Today the family owns a little over 110 hectares of vines, the oldest block of 25 hectares on Tatachilla Road at McLaren Vale, planted in 1970. Exports to the US and Switzerland.

Gemtree McLaren Vale Shiraz

🍷🍷🍷🍷 **1999** Medium purple-red; the bouquet offers a mix of blackberry, anise, licorice and vanilla, the palate with attractive fruit flavour and weight. The gentle oak and tannin extract add yet further appeal. **rating:** 88
best drinking 2003–2009 **best vintages** '98 **drink with** Rich casseroles • $25

geoff hardy wines ★★★★

c/o Pertaringa Wines, cnr Hunt and Rifle Range Roads, McLaren Vale, SA 5171 **region** McLaren Vale
phone (08) 8323 8125 **fax** (08) 8323 7766 **open** At Pertaringa
winemaker Geoff Hardy, Ben Riggs **production** 5000 **est.** 1996
product range ($15–36 CD) Kuitpo Sauvignon Blanc, Shiraz, Cabernet; Wirrega Vineyard Petit Verdot.
summary Geoff Hardy wines come from 30 hectares of vines, with a large percentage of the grape production being sold to other makers. Retail distribution through South Australia, New South Wales, Victoria and Queensland; exports to the UK, the US, Canada, Hong Kong and New Zealand.

Geoff Hardy Kuitpo Sauvignon Blanc

YYYY **2000** Light green-yellow; the bouquet offers a fragrant mix of gooseberry, herb and asparagus aromas, the palate crisp and pungent, with herbal/asparagus flavours that are on the green end of the spectrum, but without compromising the pleasant mouthfeel and balance. **rating:** 89
best drinking Now **best vintages** NA **drink with** Sushi • $19

Geoff Hardy Kuitpo Shiraz

YYYY **1998** Medium red-purple; the bouquet has pronounced fragrance, with a mix of spice, leaf, cherry and earth aromas, the oak subtle. Nicely weighted, fine tannins run through the palate giving structure to the flavours of cherry and mint. **rating:** 89
best drinking 2003–2008 **best vintages** '93, '98 **drink with** Rich red-meat dishes • $32

Geoff Hardy Wirrega Vineyard Petit Verdot

YYYY **1999** Medium red-purple; a very fragrant but most unusual bouquet with a mix of thyme, mint and spice is followed by a palate with a potent mix of thyme, mint and berry; shows most unusual fruit characters. **rating:** 84
best drinking Now–2003 **best vintages** NA **drink with** Designer sausages • $15

geoff merrill ★★★★

291 Pimpala Road, Woodcroft, SA 5162 **region** McLaren Vale
phone (08) 8381 6877 **fax** (08) 8322 2244 **open** Mon–Fri 10–5, Sun 12–5
winemaker Geoff Merrill, Goe DiFabio, Scott Heidrich **production** 120 000 **est.** 1980
product range ($9.95–40 R) A change in brand structure has resulted in the Geoff Merrill range becoming Geoff Merrill Reserve, representing the ultra-premium wines; the former Premium range is now released under the Geoff Merill label; Who Cares The Whites and Who Cares The Reds; Mount Hurtle wines are sold exclusively through Vintage Cellars/Liquorland.
summary If Geoff Merrill ever loses his impish sense of humour or his zest for life, high and not-so-high, we shall all be the poorer. He is seeking to lift the profile of his wines on the domestic market; in 1998 the product range was rearranged into two tiers: premium (in fact simply varietal) and reserve, the latter being the older (and best) wines, reflecting the desire for elegance and subtlety of this otherwise exuberant winemaker. As well as national retail distribution, significant exports to the UK, Europe, the US and Asia.

Geoff Merrill Grenache Rosé

YYYY **2000** Bright, light red-purple; the bouquet is bright and fresh, with a mix of strawberry and more earthy aromas, the palate crisp, fresh and zesty, almost lemony. **rating:** 89
best drinking Now **best vintages** NA **drink with** Terrine, pâté • $13

Geoff Merrill Shiraz

YYYY **1998** Medium red-purple; clean, red berry fruit aromas are supported by gentle oak and a touch of varietal earth; the light to medium bodied palate is smooth, quite fresh, and pleasantly balanced. **rating:** 85
best drinking 2002–2007 **best vintages** '97 **drink with** Ragout of veal • $21

Geoff Merrill Cabernet Merlot

YYYY **1998** Medium red-purple; the clean, moderately intense bouquet offers direct red berry fruit and a flick of oak. The fresh, clean, medium-bodied, no-frills palate is similarly direct and well balanced. Ready to roll. **rating:** 86
best drinking Now–2004 **best vintages** NA **drink with** Veal goulash • $21

Geoff Merrill Reserve Cabernet Sauvignon

YYYYY 1996 Medium red, with some purple remaining. A quite fragrant bouquet offers gentle cedar and spice over cassis fruit, the palate very refined, with gentle cassis/cedar/vanilla flavours and fine tannins. A lovely wine showing its ripeness (13.5°). **rating:** 92

best drinking Now–2010 **best vintages** '96 **drink with** Rack of lamb • $40

geoff weaver ★★★★★

2 Gilpin Lane, Mitcham, SA 5062 **region** Adelaide Hills
phone (08) 8272 2105 **fax** (08) 8271 0177 **open** Not
winemaker Geoff Weaver **production** 4500 **est.** 1982
product range ($17–42 ML) Riesling, Sauvignon Blanc, Chardonnay, Pinot Noir, Cabernet Merlot.
summary This is now the full-time business of former Hardy Group chief winemaker Geoff Weaver. He draws upon a little over 11 hectares of vineyard established between 1982 and 1988; for the time being, at least, the physical winemaking is carried out by Geoff Weaver at Petaluma. He produces invariably immaculate Riesling and Sauvignon Blanc, and one of the longest-lived Chardonnays to be found in Australia, which has intense grapefruit and melon flavour. The beauty of the labels ranks supreme with that of Pipers Brook. The wines are exported to the US and the UK.

Geoff Weaver Sauvignon Blanc

YYYYY 2000 Light green-yellow; the bouquet is quite powerful, with a mix of citrus, gooseberry and more herbaceous fruit. The palate veers back more to the delicacy and elegance which is Weaver's trademark, with good mouthfeel, length and acidity to close. **rating:** 91

best drinking Now–2003 **best vintages** '00 **drink with** Blue swimmer crab • $21

Geoff Weaver Pinot Noir

YYYY 1997 Medium to full red-purple; a complex, powerful bouquet with a mix of dark plum, spice and forest underlay is followed by a very powerful and concentrated palate, with awesome tannins for a Pinot Noir. The low crop and small berry size in the vintage is presumably part of the reason for those tannins. Less would have been better. **rating:** 89

best drinking Now–2006 **best vintages** NA **drink with** Rich game • $42

giaconda ★★★★★

McClay Road, Beechworth, Vic 3747 **region** Beechworth
phone (03) 5727 0246 **fax** (03) 5727 0246 **open** By appointment
winemaker Rick Kinzbrunner **production** 2000 **est.** 1985
product range ($40–75 R) Chardonnay, Pinot Noir, Cabernet Sauvignon.
summary Wines that have a super-cult status and that, given the tiny production, are extremely difficult to find, sold chiefly through restaurants and mail order. All have a cosmopolitan edge befitting Rick Kinzbrunner's international winemaking experience. The Chardonnay and Pinot Noir are made in contrasting styles: the Chardonnay tight and reserved, the Pinot Noir usually opulent and ripe.

gidgee estate wines NR

441 Weeroona Drive, Wamboin, NSW 2621 **region** Canberra District
phone (02) 6236 9506 **fax** (02) 6236 9070 **open** First weekend of each month or by appointment
winemaker David Madew, Andrew McEwin (Contract) **production** 300 **est.** 1996
product range ($13–16 CD) Riesling, Chardonnay, Ensemble (Cabernet blend).
summary Brett and Cheryl Lane purchased the 1-hectare vineyard in 1996; it had been planted to riesling, chardonnay, cabernet sauvignon, cabernet franc and merlot over a ten-year period prior to its acquisition, but had been allowed to run down and needed to be rehabilitated. The Lanes intend to double the vineyard size over the next two years and have retained David Madew and Andrew McEwen as contract winemakers. The 1998 Chardonnay was a full-bodied buttery/peachy style with balancing acidity (83 points); the Bordeaux-blend Ensemble lay at the other extreme, with leafy/minty green fruit characters.

gilberts ★★★★☆

RMB 438 Albany Highway, Kendenup, via Mount Barker, WA 6323 **region** Great Southern
phone (08) 9851 4028 **fax** (08) 9851 4021 **open** Wed–Mon 10–5
winemaker Plantagenet (Contract) **production** 3000 **est.** 1980
product range ($14–25 CD) Riesling, Alira (medium sweet), Chardonnay, Shiraz, Cabernet Shiraz, Old Tawny.
summary A part-time occupation for sheep and beef farmers Jim and Beverly Gilbert, but a very successful one. The now mature vineyard, coupled with contract-winemaking at Plantagenet, has produced small quantities of high-quality Riesling and Chardonnay; the small production sells out quickly each year, with retail distribution through New South Wales, Victoria and Western Australia, and exports to Canada and Asia through Inland Trading, and the UK via Pearson-French.

Gilberts Riesling

🍷🍷🍷🍷🍷 **2000** Light green-yellow; a remarkable bouquet, intense yet fine, with exemplary lime-accented fruit varietal aroma balanced by a slatey cut. The palate lives up to the bouquet, beautifully balanced, with plenty of intensity and structure to the subtle, limey fruit; will age well. Multiple trophy winner, including Best Wine of Show, Wine Show of Western Australia 2000. **rating:** 96
best drinking Now–2010 **best vintages** '91, '92, '94, '95, '96, '97, '00 **drink with** Asparagus with prosciutto • $20

gilgai winery NR

Tingha Road, Gilgai, NSW 2360 **region** Northern Slopes Zone
phone (02) 6723 1204 **open** 7 days 10–6
winemaker Keith Whish **production** 400 **est.** 1968
product range Semillon, Shiraz Cabernet, Chandelier (Fortified White), Port.
summary Inverell medical practitioner Dr Keith Whish has been quietly producing wines from his 6-hectare vineyard for almost 30 years. All of the production is sold through cellar door.

glaetzer wines NR

34 Barossa Valley Way, Tanunda, SA 5352 **region** Barossa Valley
phone (08) 8563 0288 **fax** (08) 8563 0218 **open** Mon–Sat 10.30–4.30, Sun and public holidays 1–4.30
winemaker Colin Glaetzer, Ben Glaetzer **production** 3000 **est.** 1995
product range ($16–45 CD) Bush Vine Semillon, Semillon Ratafia, Grenache Mourvedre; Sparkling Pinot Noir, Bishop Shiraz, Malbec Cabernet Sauvignon, Shiraz, Sparkling Shiraz.
summary Colin and Ben Glaetzer are almost as well known in South Australian wine circles as Wolf Blass winemaker John Glaetzer, and, needless to say, they are all related. Glaetzer Wines purchases its grapes from Barossa Valley growers and makes an array of traditional Barossa styles. National retail distribution; exports to the US, Germany, the UK, Belgium, Italy, the Netherlands and Canada.

glenalbyn NR

84 Halls Road, Kingower, Vic 3517 **region** Bendigo
phone (03) 5438 8255 **fax** (03) 5438 8255 **open** 10.30–5 or by appointment
winemaker Lee (Leila) Gillespie **production** 500 **est.** 1997
product range ($18–25 CD) Pinot Noir, Cabernet Sauvignon.
summary When Leila Gillespie's great-grandfather applied for his land title in 1856, he had already established a vineyard on the property. A survey plan of 1857 shows the cultivation paddocks, one marked the Grape Paddock, and a few of the original grape vines have survived in the garden, which abuts the National Trust and Heritage homestead. In 1986 Leila and John Gillespie decided on a modest diversification of their sheep, wool and cereal crop farm, and began the establishment of 4 hectares of vineyards. Since 1997 Leila Gillespie has made the wine on a self-taught basis, with Cabernet Sauvignon from 1997, 1998 and 1999 joined by Pinot Noir in the latter year.

Glenalbyn Cabernet Sauvignon

🍷🍷🍷🍷 **1998** Excellent red-purple colour; the bouquet is clean, with a good balance and dark berry fruit and oak, and just a few errant hay/straw aromas. The bouquet gives no clue to the massively concentrated and tannic palate, with abundant dark berry fruit underneath those tannins. Demands and should repay extended cellaring. **rating:** 84
best drinking 2005–2010 **best vintages** NA **drink with** Marinated beef • $25

glenara wines ★★★☆

126 Range Road North, Upper Hermitage, SA 5131 **region** Adelaide Hills
phone (08) 8380 5277 **fax** (08) 8380 5056 **open** Mon–Fri 11–5 (closed public holidays)
winemaker Trevor Jones **production** 5000 **est.** 1971
product range ($15–24 CD) Riesling, Sauvignon Blanc, Sauvignon Blanc Semillon, Unwooded Chardonnay, Pinot Noir, Shiraz, Cabernet Rosé, Merlot, Cabernet Merlot, Cabernet Sauvignon, White Quartz (Sparkling), Old Tawny Port.
summary Glenara has been owned by the Verrall family since 1924; the first vines were planted in 1971, the first wine made in 1975, and the winery built in 1988. Has proceeded to produce many good wines, particularly the full-flavoured Rieslings, but also with creditable full-bodied reds. The wines have limited retail distribution in all States, and are exported to Hong Kong, Japan, Malaysia, the Philippines, Singapore, the US, Canada, Germany, the Netherlands and the UK.

glenayr ★★★★

Back Tea Tree Road, Richmond, Tas 7025 **region** Southern Tasmania
phone (03) 6260 2388 **fax** (03) 6260 2691 **open** Mon–Fri 8–5
winemaker Andrew Hood **production** 500 **est.** 1975
product range ($18–20 CD) Riesling, Chardonnay, Pinot Noir, Cabernet Shiraz Merlot; Tolpuddle Vineyards Chardonnay and Pinot Noir.
summary The principal occupation of Chris Harrington is as viticultural manager of the substantial Tolpuddle Vineyard, the grapes of which are sold to Domaine Chandon. Tiny quantities of wine are made from an adjacent 1-hectare vineyard for mailing list sales under the GlenAyr label; chardonnay and pinot noir grapes are also purchased from Tolpuddle Vineyards.

GlenAyr Chardonnay

🍷🍷🍷🍷🍷 **1999** Medium yellow-green; the bouquet is complex, with obvious barrel-ferment oak characters, but the powerful palate is more driven by its intense citrus and melon fruit, the oak subtle and well balanced. **rating:** 90
best drinking Now–2005 **best vintages** '98, '99 **drink with** Milk-fed veal • $19

glen erin vineyard retreat NR

Rochford Road, Lancefield, Vic 3435 **region** Macedon Ranges
phone (03) 5429 1041 **fax** (03) 5429 2053 **open** Weekends, public holidays 10–6
winemaker Brian Scales, John Ellis **production** 200 **est.** 1993
product range ($17–30 CD) Gewurztraminer, Chardonnay, Pinot Noir, Mystic Park Macedon Sparkling.
summary Brian Scales acquired the former Lancefield Winery and renamed it Glen Erin. Wines are contract-made from Macedon grapes and elsewhere, and sold only through cellar door; the conference and function facilities are supported by 24 accommodation rooms.

glenfinlass NR

Elysian Farm, Parkes Road, Wellington, NSW 2820 **region** Central Ranges Zone
phone (02) 6845 2011 **fax** (02) 6845 3329 **open** Sat 9–5 or by appointment
winemaker Brian G Holmes **production** 500 **est.** 1971
product range ($15–25 CD) Sauvignon Blanc, Drought Drop (Shiraz, Cabernet Sauvignon, Sauvignon Blanc).
summary The weekend and holiday hobby of Wellington solicitor Brian Holmes, who has wisely decided to leave it at that. I have not tasted the wines for many years, but the last wines I did taste were competently made. Wines are in short supply owing to drought (1998), frost (1999) and flooding (2000). It is a sign of his resilience (and sense of humour) that the 1998 Drought Drop is currently on sale, a blend of 50 per cent Shiraz, 25 per cent Cabernet Sauvignon and 25 per cent Sauvignon Blanc.

glenguin ★★★☆

River Oaks Vineyard, Lot 8 Milbrodale Road, Broke, NSW 2330 **region** Lower Hunter Valley
phone (02) 6579 1009 **fax** (02) 6579 1009 **open** At Boutique Wine Centre, Broke Road, Pokolbin
winemaker Robin Tedder MW **production** 15 000 **est.** 1993
product range ($17.50–30 R) Individual Vineyard series of The Old Broke Block Semillon, Unwooded Chardonnay, Shiraz, Merlot, Cabernet Sauvignon.

summary Glenguin's vineyard has been established along the banks of the Wollombi Brook by Robin, Rita and Andrew Tedder, Robin and Andrew being the grandsons of Air Chief Marshal Tedder, made Baron of Glenguin by King George VI in recognition of his wartime deeds. (Glenguin is also the name of a Scottish distillery that continues to produce a single malt but which is otherwise unconnected.) Glenguin has 15 hectares of vineyard at Broke and another 4 hectares at Orange (cabernet and merlot). An extensive range of samples arrived for tasting just as this (2002) edition was going to press. Exports to Europe and Asia.

gloucester ridge vineyard ★★★☆

Lot 7489 Burma Road, Pemberton, WA 6260 **region** Pemberton
phone (08) 9776 1035 **fax** (08) 9776 1390 **open** 7 days 10–5 (until late Saturday)
winemaker Brenden Smith **production** 12 500 **est.** 1985
product range ($17–30 CD) Semillon, Sauvignon Blanc, Sauvignon Blanc Semillon, Unwooded Chardonnay, Chardonnay, Reserve Chardonnay, Late Harvest Riesling, Premium Reserve Pinot Noir, Cabernets, Cabernet Sauvignon, Pemberton Red and Port.
summary Gloucester Ridge is the only vineyard located within the Pemberton town boundary, within easy walking distance. It is owned and operated by Don and Sue Hancock; the current releases are impressive. Retail distribution in Queensland, New South Wales and Victoria; exports to Hong Kong and the Netherlands.

Gloucester Ridge Vineyard Unwooded Chardonnay

🍷🍷🍷🍷 **2000** Light green-yellow; a highly fragrant bouquet with extreme passionfruit and more herbaceous notes is replicated on the palate; a dead-set cross between Chardonnay and Sauvignon Blanc, but at least it has character and life. **rating:** 89

best drinking Now–2003 **best vintages** NA **drink with** Fish consommé • $17

Gloucester Ridge Chardonnay

🍷🍷🍷🍷🍷 (4½) **1999** Medium yellow-green; the moderately intense bouquet is clean, with tangy nectarine fruit and a splash of oak; the gentle, quite stylish palate is light bodied, but the melon and nectarine fruit is supported, rather than challenged by, the oak. **rating:** 90

best drinking Now–2003 **best vintages** '99 **drink with** Eel pâté • $20

Gloucester Ridge Cabernet Sauvignon

🍷🍷🍷🍷 **1998** Medium red-purple; the bouquet is clean, quite savoury and with the earthy notes that cabernet can produce; the palate has long, intense, dark berry fruit with slightly sharp savoury edges. I wish I were more certain what is going on here. **rating:** 86

best drinking 2003–2007 **best vintages** NA **drink with** Barbecued lamb chops • $30

gnadenfrei estate NR

Seppeltsfield Road, Marananga, via Nuriootpa, SA 5355 **region** Barossa Valley
phone (08) 8562 2522 **fax** (08) 8562 3470 **open** Tues–Sun 10–5.30
winemaker Malcolm Seppelt **production** 1500 **est.** 1979
product range ($12–20 CD) Riesling, Semillon, Traminer Riesling, Shiraz Grenache, Tawny Port, Sparkling.
summary A strictly cellar-door operation, which relies on a variety of sources for its wines but has a core of 2 hectares of estate shiraz and 1 hectare of grenache. A restaurant presided over by Joylene Seppelt is open for morning teas, lunches and afternoon teas. Small quantities of the wines make their way to Pennsylvania, USA.

golden grape estate NR

Oakey Creek Road, Pokolbin, NSW 2321 **region** Lower Hunter Valley
phone (02) 4998 7588 **fax** (02) 4998 7730 **open** 7 days 10–5
winemaker Neil McGuigan (Consultant) **production** NFP **est.** 1985
product range ($14.95–29.90 CD) Premier Semillon, Gewurztraminer, Sauvignon Blanc, Semillon Verdelho, Happy Valley Chardonnay, Five Star (light fruity), Frizzante Rosé, Mount Leonard (Cabernet Sauvignon), Domaine Springton (Shiraz), Classic Red, Fortifieds.
summary German-owned and unashamedly directed at the tourist, with a restaurant, barbecue and picnic areas, wine museum and separate tasting room for bus tours. The substantial range of wines is of diverse origin and style. The operation now has over 42 hectares of Hunter Valley plantings.

golden grove estate ★★★☆

Sundown Road, Ballandean, Qld 4382 **region** Granite Belt
phone (07) 4684 1291 **fax** (07) 4684 1247 **open** 7 days 9–5
winemaker Sam Costanzo **production** 10 000 **est.** 1993
product range ($10–15 CD) Accommodation Creek Classic White and Classic Dry Red, Muscadean, Rosé, Shiraz, Cabernet Merlot, Liqueur Muscat.
summary Golden Grove Estate was established by Mario and Sebastiana Costanzo in 1946, producing stonefruit and table grapes for the fresh-fruit market. The first wine grapes (shiraz) were planted in 1972, but it was not until 1985, when ownership passed to son Sam Costanzo and wife Grace, that the use of the property started to change. In 1993 chardonnay and merlot joined the shiraz, followed by cabernet sauvignon, sauvignon blanc and semillon. Wine quality has steadily improved, with many medals in regional shows awarded up to 2000, leading to national (though limited) retail distribution.

golden gully wines NR

5900 Midwestern Highway, Mandurama, NSW 2792 **region** Orange
phone (02) 6367 5148 **fax** (02) 6367 4148 **open** Not
winemaker Jon Reynolds (Contract) **production** 1300 **est.** 1994
product range ($17 R) Shiraz, Cabernet Sauvignon.
summary Still very much in the development phase, production rising to 60 cases in 1999 from 21 cases in 1998. Family and friends stuff, indeed. However, Kevin and Julie Bate have established over 5 hectares of vineyard (2 hectares of cabernet sauvignon, 1.6 hectares of shiraz, 0.5 hectare of merlot and 0.5 hectare each of semillon and sauvignon blanc planted in 1999), and rose to fully commercial levels in 2001.

golders vineyard ★★★☆

Bridport Road, Pipers Brook, Tas 7254 **region** Northern Tasmania
phone (03) 6395 4142 **fax** (03) 6395 4142 **open** By appointment
winemaker Richard Crabtree **production** 400 **est.** 1991
product range ($18 R) Pinot Noir.
summary The initial plantings of 1.5 hectares of pinot noir have been supplemented by 1.5 hectares of chardonnay. The quality of the Pinot Noir has been good from the initial vintage in 1995.

goona warra vineyard ★★★☆

Sunbury Road, Sunbury, Vic 3429 **region** Sunbury
phone (03) 9740 7766 **fax** (03) 9744 7648 **open** 7 days 10–5
winemaker John Barnier, Nick Bickford **production** 2500 **est.** 1863
product range ($14–28 CD) Semillon Sauvignon Blanc, Chardonnay, Black Cygnet Chardonnay, Roussane, Pinot Noir, Cabernets, Black Cygnet Cabernet Shiraz, Black Widow Brut, Black Cygnet Tawny Port.
summary An historic stone winery, established under this name by a nineteenth-century Victorian premier. A capital infusion by a Melbourne-based venture-capital group in early 2001 will result in a doubling of production. Excellent tasting facilities; an outstanding venue for weddings and receptions; Sunday lunch also served. Situated 30 minutes drive from Melbourne (10 minutes north of Tullamarine Airport). Berry Bros & Rudd import the wines into the UK.

goundrey ★★★★

Muir Highway, Mount Barker, WA 6324 **region** Great Southern
phone (08) 9851 1777 **fax** (08) 9851 1997 **open** Mon–Sat 10–4.30, Sun 11–4.30
winemaker David Martin, Cyril Ashman **production** 151 000 **est.** 1976
product range ($15.50–40 R) Chenin Blanc, Classic White, Unwooded Chardonnay, Late Picked Riesling, Shiraz Grenache, Cabernet Merlot; Reserve range of Riesling, Sauvignon Blanc, Chardonnay, Pinot Noir, Shiraz, Merlot, Cabernet Sauvignon, Noble Botrytis; second label is Fox River.
summary Under the ownership of Perth businessman Jack Bendat, not to mention the injection of many millions of dollars into vineyard and winery expansion, Goundrey grows apace. There seems to be a widening gap between the quality of the Reserve wines (usually, but not invariably, good) and the varietal range (workmanlike). This may be no bad thing from a commercial viewpoint, particularly if the differential is reflected in the price, but does make an overall rating difficult, a difficulty compounded by the recent surge in quality in the second label of Fox River. National distribution; exports to the US, Asia, the UK and Europe.

Goundrey Reserve Riesling

🍷🍷🍷🍷 **1999** Medium yellow-green; the bouquet is quite powerful, with traditional kerosene, mineral and talc aromas, more in the style of the Clare Valley than Great Southern. The palate is similar, needing bottle age to soften the mouthfeel and (hopefully) fill out the back-palate, which seems to dip significantly. **rating:** 85

best drinking 2002–2007 **best vintages** NA **drink with** Fresh asparagus • $20.30

Goundrey Classic White

🍷🍷🍷🍷½ **2000** Light green-yellow; the bouquet is fresh and fragrant, with a mix of lime, citrus and passionfruit; the palate is delicate, clean and crisp, rather than powerful, but has good length aided by nice acidity. **rating:** 90

best drinking Now **best vintages** '00 **drink with** Steamed Chinese fish • $16.10

Goundrey Reserve Chardonnay

🍷🍷🍷½ **1999** Medium to full yellow-green; strong barrel-ferment oak characters sit on top of the fruit on the bouquet, and similarly dominate the palate. Pay your money and take your choice: either over-oaked, or under-fruited. **rating:** 83

best drinking Now–2003 **best vintages** '91, '94, '95 **drink with** Coquilles St Jacques • $34

Fox River Shiraz

🍷🍷🍷🍷 **1999** Medium red-purple; the bouquet is quite rich, with plum and earth varietal fruit to the fore; the palate has abundant, ripe plum, spice and earth flavours with nicely balanced tannins, and oak merely in the background. **rating:** 87

best drinking 2002–2005 **best vintages** NA **drink with** Corned beef • $15.30

Fox River Shiraz Cabernet

🍷🍷🍷🍷 **1999** Medium red-purple; the moderately intense bouquet offers ripe plum and cherry fruit; a pleasant, fresh, medium-bodied palate, nicely balanced by a soft touch of vanilla oak. With 30 per cent South Australian content, doubtful that it should have been entered in the West Australian Wine Show. **rating:** 89

best drinking Now–2005 **best vintages** NA **drink with** Takeaway • $14.45

Goundrey Cabernet Merlot

🍷🍷🍷🍷 **1999** Medium red-purple; mint, berry and a touch of leaf on the bouquet are followed by a sweet, minty berry flavoured palate with quite nice mouthfeel. Gentle oak handling is a plus. **rating:** 89

best drinking 2002–2007 **best vintages** '99 **drink with** Smoked beef • $17

governor's choice winery NR

Berghofer Road, Westbrook, via Toowoomba, Qld 4350 **region** Queensland Zone
phone (07) 4630 6101 **fax** (07) 4630 6701 **open** Weekends 9–5 or by appointment
winemaker James Yates **production** 1000 **est.** 1999
product range ($15 CD) Semillon, Chardonnay, Shiraz, Cabernet Sauvignon.
summary This is a part-winery, part-premium-guest house accommodation venture situated 18 kilometres from the town of Toowoomba. Three hectares of estate plantings produce chardonnay, shiraz, verdelho, cabernet sauvignon and malbec, made on site and sold through cellar door on weekends or to guests.

gralyn estate ★★★★☆

Caves Road, Willyabrup, WA 6280 **region** Margaret River
phone (08) 9755 6245 **fax** (08) 9755 6245 **open** 7 days 10.30–4.30
winemaker Graham Hutton, Merilyn Hutton **production** 2500 **est.** 1975
product range ($16–90 CD) Reserve Riesling, Late Harvest Riesling, Old Vine Shiraz, Late Harvest Cabernet, Cabernet Nouveau, Shiraz Cabernet, Cabernet Sauvignon, and an extensive range of Fortifieds including White Port, Vintage Port and Tawny Port.
summary The move from primarily fortified-wine to table-wine production continues, and does so with considerable success. The red wines are made in a distinctively different style from most of those from the Margaret River region, with a softness and sweetness (in part from American oak) reminiscent of some of the better-made wines from the eastern States. With one exception, it has reached new heights with the quality of its 1999 vintage red wines.

Gralyn Estate Old Vine Shiraz

🍷🍷🍷 1999 Medium red-purple; the bouquet is quite powerful, with earthy berry fruit and obvious vanilla oak. That vanilla oak comes to dominate the palate to a distracting degree. A pity. **rating:** 84

best drinking 2002–2007 **best vintages** '94, '95, '96 **drink with** Strong red-meat dishes • $50

Gralyn Estate Shiraz Cabernet

🍷🍷🍷🍷🍷 1999 Medium to full red-purple; the bouquet is rich and full, flooded with dark plum, cherry, chocolate and vanilla aromas, the full-bodied palate, rich and ripe (but not overripe); sure handling of oak and tannins produces a long, impressive wine (at an impressive price). **rating:** 94

best drinking 2004–2014 **best vintages** '95, '99 **drink with** Smoked lamb • $90

Gralyn Estate Cabernet Sauvignon

🍷🍷🍷🍷 1999 Medium to full red-purple; the bouquet is rich and ripe, with abundant, sweet blackcurrant fruit and lashings of vanilla oak. There are rich, ripe, fleshy, mouthfilling blackcurrant, chocolate and vanilla flavours on the palate, replete with soft tannins. A gold-medal winner at the 2000 Sheraton Wine Awards, and silver medals at important national wine shows. **rating:** 93

best drinking 2004–2010 **best vintages** '99 **drink with** Marinated beef • $75

Gralyn Estate Vintage Port

🍷🍷🍷🍷 2000 Dense red-purple; clean spirit runs through nice fruit, the palate as well balanced as always. One cannot help but think the base material would be better in dry table wine. **rating:** 89

best drinking 2002–2010 **best vintages** '99 **drink with** Coffee • $50

grampians estate NR

Mafeking Road, Willaura, Vic 3379 **region** Grampians
phone (03) 5354 6245 **fax** (03) 5354 6257 **open** By appointment
winemaker Simon Clayfield **production** 700 **est.** 1989
product range ($15–18 CD) Mafeking Unwooded Chardonnay, Mafeking Gold Chardonnay, Mafeking Shiraz.
summary Ten years ago local farmers and graziers Sarah and Tom Guthrie decided to diversify their activities while continuing their fat lamb and wool production. So they planted a little over 1.5 hectares each of shiraz and chardonnay, and opened the Thermopylae Host Farm business. This offers two farm-stay buildings, a five-bedroom shearer's cottage that sleeps 12, and a five-room miner's cottage that sleeps ten. They also secured the services of immensely experienced local winemaker Simon Clayfield to produce the Grampians Estate wines. These are sold to those who stay on the farm, which offers an unusually wide range of activities; the wines are also available by direct mail order and at one or two local hotels, including the Kookaburra Rest at Halls Gap.

granite ridge wines NR

Sundown Road, Ballandean, Qld 4382 **region** Granite Belt
phone (07) 4684 1263 **fax** (07) 4684 1250 **open** 7 days 9–5
winemaker Dennis Ferguson, Juliane Ferguson **production** 1200 **est.** 1995
product range ($11–28 CD) Crystals Semillon Chardonnay, Goldies Unwooded Chardonnay, First Oak Oaked Chardonnay, Granite Rock Shiraz, Fergies Hill Merlot, Millennium Cabernet Merlot, Granite Grange Cabernet Sauvignon, Granite Garnet (Medium Sweet Red), Liqueur Muscat.
summary Formerly known as Denlana Ferguson Estate Wines, Granite Ridge has had considerable success, with both the 1995 and 1996 Cabernet Sauvignon being judged Queensland's Best Cabernet (though quite by whom I am not sure); continues to be run by Dennis Ferguson.

grant burge ★★★★☆

Jacobs Creek, Tanunda, SA 5352 **region** Barossa Valley
phone (08) 8563 3700 **fax** (08) 8563 2807 **open** 7 days 10–5
winemaker Grant Burge **production** 108 000 **est.** 1988
product range ($9.95–79.95 R) Has recently moved to a series of vineyard-designated varietal wines including Thorn Vineyard Riesling, Kraft Vineyard Sauvignon Blanc, Zerk Vineyard Semillon, Barossa Ranges Chardonnay, Lily Farm Frontignac, Filsell Shiraz, Hillcott Merlot, and Cameron Vale Cabernet Sauvignon. Top-of-the-range reds are Meshach Shiraz, The Holy Trinity (Grenache Shiraz Mourvedre) and Shadrach Cabernet Sauvignon; also Rubycind and Virtuoso; RBS1 Semillon, RBS2 Semillon, MSJ1 Shiraz Cabernet. The budget-priced Barossa Vines range joined the band in late 1999.

summary As one might expect, this very experienced industry veteran makes consistently good full-flavoured and smooth wines chosen from the pick of the crop of his extensive vineyard holdings, which total an impressive 200 hectares; the immaculately restored/rebuilt stone cellar-door sales buildings are another attraction. The provocatively named The Holy Trinity (a Grenache Shiraz Mourvedre blend) joins Shadrach and Meshach at the top of the range. In late 1999 Grant Burge repurchased the farm from Mildara Blass by acquiring the Krondorf winery (not the brand) in which he made his first fortune. He has renamed it Barossa Vines. The wines are exported to the UK, Europe, the US, Canada and Asia.

Grant Burge Thorn Vineyard Riesling

🍷🍷🍷🍷🍷 **2000** Light green-yellow; the bouquet is clean, quite fragrant, with a mix of lime and passionfruit. The palate is crisp, clean and quite intense, in a linear style, with lime, apple and passionfruit flavours; grip and length. Gold medal at the Royal Adelaide Wine Show 2000. **rating:** 94

best drinking Now–2006 **best vintages** '88, '90, '92, '93, '94, '96, '98, '00 **drink with** Smoked trout mousse • $16

Grant Burge Lily Farm Frontignac

🍷🍷🍷🍷 **2000** Light to medium green-yellow; the bouquet is not as aromatic as one might expect, but the palate is intense, in a lime-juicy mode, more than simply grapey. A good example of the style, with a lingering finish, and excellent value. **rating:** 85

best drinking Now **best vintages** NA **drink with** A summer's morning • $9.95

Grant Burge Barossa Vines Chardonnay

🍷🍷🍷🍷 **2000** Medium to full yellow-green; oaky scents are the first impression, followed by the ripe, yellow peach and pineapple fruit. The palate is soft, quite generous, but slightly phenolic towards the finish. **rating:** 83

best drinking Now **best vintages** NA **drink with** KFC • $12

Grant Burge Age Unknown Liqueur Muscat

🍷🍷🍷🍷 **NV** Medium red-brown; the bouquet has strong, youthful muscat varietal character, the palate likewise showing positive muscat varietal character, but is not particularly complex nor rich. **rating:** 84

best drinking Now **best vintages** NA **drink with** Chocolate • $28

Grant Burge 20 Year Old Tawny Port

🍷🍷🍷🍷🍷 **NV** Light to medium tawny-red; the bouquet is quite stylish, with obvious age and rancio cut. The palate offers more of the same, with intensity and complexity, plenty of rancio character, and a pleasingly dry finish. **rating:** 92

best drinking Now–2007 **best vintages** NA **drink with** Walnuts • $28

great lakes wines NR

Herivals Road, Wootton, NSW 2423 **region** Hastings River
phone (02) 4997 7255 **fax** (02) 4997 7450 **open** 7 days 11–5
winemaker Steve Aitkins, David Hooke **production** 1200 **est.** 1990
product range ($9–16 CD) Semillon Chardonnay, Chardonnay, Shiraz, Chambourcin, Mellow Red.
summary John Webber and family began planting their vineyard on the mid-north coast of New South Wales in 1990. There is a 4-hectare vineyard planted to chambourcin, shiraz, cabernet sauvignon, chardonnay, semillon and verdelho, and the Webbers are proud of the fact that (to use their words) 'we are a fair dinkum winery where we "grow the grapes" and "we make the wine"'.

greenock creek wines NR

Radford Road, Seppeltsfield, SA 5360 **region** Barossa Valley
phone (08) 8562 8103 **fax** (08) 8562 8259 **open** Wed–Mon 11–5
winemaker Michael Waugh **production** 2500 **est.** 1978
product range ($24–125 CD) Cornerstone Grenache, Apricot Block Shiraz, Seven Acre Shiraz, Creek Block Shiraz, Roennfeldt Road Shiraz, Cabernet Sauvignon, Roennfeldt Road Cabernet Sauvignon.
summary Michael and Annabelle Waugh are disciples of Rocky O'Callaghan of Rockford Wines and have deliberately accumulated a series of old dryland, low-yielding Barossa vineyards, aiming to produce wines of unusual depth of flavour and character. They have handsomely succeeded in this aim. They also offer superior accommodation in the ancient but beautifully restored two-bedroom cottage 'Miriam's'; Michael Waugh is a highly skilled stonemason. Exports to the UK, the US and Switzerland.

green valley vineyard NR

3137 Sebbes Road, Forest Grove, WA 6286 **region** Margaret River
phone (08) 9384 3131 **open** 7 days 10–5
winemaker Keith Mugford (Contract) **production** 3000 **est.** 1980
product range ($15–27.50 CD) Riesling, Chardonnay, Premium Dry White, Cabernet Sauvignon.
summary Ed and Eleanore Green commenced the development of Green Valley Vineyard in 1980. It is still a part-time operation, with the wines made by contract, but production has grown steadily from the 7.7 hectares of vines, and the Cabernet Sauvignon has been a consistent medal-winner. Exports to Singapore and the US.

grevillea estate NR

Buckajo Road, Bega, NSW 2550 **region** South Coast Zone
phone (02) 6492 3006 **fax** (02) 6492 5330 **open** 7 days 9–5
winemaker Nicola Collins **production** 2900 **est.** 1980
product range ($10–18 CD) Daisy Hill Riesling, Lunatic Hill Sauvignon Blanc, Unoaked Chardonnay, Peak Hill Chardonnay, Gewurztraminer, Traminer Riesling, Rougon, Grosse's Creek Merlot, Edmund Kirby Cabernet Sauvignon, Old Tawny Port.
summary A tourist-oriented winery that successfully sells all of its surprisingly large production through cellar door and to local restaurants. The wines have attractive labels, but it has to be said wine quality is not good.

grey sands ★★★★

Frankford Highway, Glengarry, Tas 7275 **region** Northern Tasmania
phone (03) 6396 1167 **fax** (03) 6396 1153 **open** By appointment
winemaker Bob Richter **production** 350 **est.** 1989
product range ($19–26 CD) Pinot Gris, Merlot.
summary Bob and Rita Richter began the slow establishment of Grey Sands in 1988, slowly increasing the plantings over the ensuing ten years to the present total of 2.5 hectares. The ultra-high density of 8900 vines per hectare partially reflects the experience gained by the Richters during a three-year stay in England, during which time they visited many vineyards across Europe, and partially Bob Richter's graduate diploma in wine from Roseworthy Agricultural College (1985/86).

Grey Sands Pinot Gris

TTTT **1999** Light green-yellow; the bouquet is clean, with a mix of predominantly mineral and slight honeysuckle fruit. The same flavours come through on the palate, but it is the mouthfeel that gives the wine most distinction. Definitely made more in a Pinot Gris (in other words Alsatian) than Grigio (Italian) style. Retasted January 2001 and has developed attractively, with an almost honeyed mouthfeel. **rating:** 83

best drinking Now **best vintages** NA **drink with** Bocconcini • $16

Grey Sands Merlot

TTTTT **1999** Medium red-purple; the bouquet is complex, with sweet berry fruit, the barest touch of game, and subtle oak. The palate has attractive sweet fruit, a hint of chocolate, and gentle, ripe tannins. A well-made wine in true Merlot style. **rating:** 92

best drinking 2003–2009 **best vintages** '99 **drink with** Braised lamb • $26

grosset ★★★★★

King Street, Auburn, SA 5451 **region** Clare Valley
phone (08) 8849 2175 **fax** (08) 8849 2292 **open** Wed–Sun 10–5 from first week of September for approx. six weeks
winemaker Jeffrey Grosset **production** 8500 **est.** 1981
product range ($23.95–54 R) Watervale Riesling, Polish Hill Riesling, Semillon Sauvignon Blanc, Piccadilly Chardonnay, Gaia (a Cabernet blend), Noble Riesling, Reserve Pinot Noir.
summary Jeffrey Grosset served part of his apprenticeship at the vast Lindeman Karadoc winery, moving from the largest to one of the smallest when he established Grosset Wines in its old stone winery. He now crafts the wines with the utmost care from grapes grown to the most exacting standards; all need a certain amount of time in bottle to achieve their ultimate potential, not the least the Rieslings and Gaia, among Australia's best examples of their kind. At a Riesling Summit held in Hamburg in the latter part of 1998, Grosset was voted Riesling Winemaker of the Year. Exports to the UK, the US, Japan, Belgium and Germany mean a continuous shortage of the wines in all markets.

Grosset Polish Hill Riesling

🍷🍷🍷🍷🍷 **2000** Light to medium yellow-green; the bouquet is quite rich, with more overt fruit than the wine often displays when young; the palate, likewise, is powerful, with considerable depth and length, the aftertaste full of authority, yet not aggressive. **rating:** 94

best drinking Now–2011 **best vintages** '87, '90, '93, '94, '96, '97, '98, '99, '00 **drink with** Grilled South Australian whiting • $35

Grosset Watervale Riesling

🍷🍷🍷🍷🍷 **2000** Light to medium yellow-green; full, lime, mineral and a spicy grip to the powerful bouquet is followed by a generous, relatively open palate, again with a characteristic spicy edge. **rating:** 93

best drinking 2002–2010 **best vintages** '81, '86, '90, '93, '94, '95, '96, '97, '98, '99, '00 **drink with** Thai soup • $30

Grosset Semillon Sauvignon Blanc

🍷🍷🍷🍷🍷 **2000** Why ignore Jeffrey Grossett's other white wines just because his two Rieslings are so good, particularly when this wine is the epitome of the unwooded style. Crisp, clean and lively lemon, grass and herb aromas are followed by an intense, high-flavoured, lively palate with great length and persistence. **rating:** 94

best drinking Now–2004 **best vintages** '93, '94, '95, '96, '97, '99, '00 **drink with** Antipasto • $28.50

Grosset Piccadilly Chardonnay

🍷🍷🍷🍷🍷 **1999** Another demonstration of Jeffrey Grosset's virtuosity as a winemaker, and of his unrelenting attention to detail. The bouquet is rich and scented, with ripe stonefruit and ripe pear aromas, the palate offering abundant fruit flavour in the same vein, yet retaining delicacy. And yes, there is French oak in the background. **rating:** 96

best drinking Now–2009 **best vintages** '96, '97, '99 **drink with** Milk-fed veal • $43

Grosset Gaia

🍷🍷🍷🍷🍷 **1998** Three Grosset wines selected, but no Riesling; oh, well. A blend of 75 per cent Cabernet, the remainder Franc and Merlot. The promise of the vivid colour is reflected in the spotlessly clean, ripe cassis and blackberry bouquet and the concentrated and luscious palate, backed by persistent tannins; an extra dimension of elegance and intensity. **rating:** 96

best drinking 2003–2018 **best vintages** '90, '91, '92, '94, '95, '96, '98 **drink with** Clare hare pie • $54

grove estate ★★★☆

Murringo Road, Young, NSW 2594 **region** Hilltops
phone (02) 6382 6999 **fax** (02) 6382 4527 **open** Weekends 10–5 or by appointment
winemaker Jenny Bright, Monarch Winemaking Services (Contract) **production** 2000 **est.** 1989
product range ($14–21 CD) Hilltops Semillon, Murringo Way Chardonnay, The Cellar Block Shiraz, Hilltops Zinfandel, The Partners Cabernet Sauvignon.
summary A partnership headed by Brian Mullany has established a 30-hectare vineyard planted to semillon, chardonnay, merlot, shiraz, cabernet sauvignon and zinfandel. Most of the grapes are sold (principally to Southcorp), but a limited amount of wine is contract-made by Monarch Winemaking Services for the Grove Estate label.

Grove Estate Murringo Way Chardonnay

🍷🍷🍷🍷 **1999** Medium yellow-green; the melon fruit of the bouquet has slightly singed yeast fermentation characters that happily do not persist on the palate, which is quite elegant, with crisp melon and mineral flavours. **rating:** 82

best drinking Now–2003 **best vintages** NA **drink with** Seafood consommé • $16.50

Grove Estate Zinfandel

🍷🍷🍷🍷 **2000** Medium red-purple; the fragrant bouquet has the aroma of small berries (blueberries) with touches of spice in a convincingly varietal mode. There is intense and quite distinctive fruit flavour on the sweet mid-palate; the texture is silky, and the wine finishes with good acidity. **rating:** 87

best drinking Now–2006 **best vintages** '00 **drink with** Designer pizza • $21

Grove Estate The Partners Cabernet Sauvignon

TTTT **1999** Medium to full red-purple; there are distinctive peppermint toothpaste aromas plus red berry fruit on the bouquet, the wine settling down on the palate with abundant red berry fruit running through to a long finish augmented by lingering tannins; the oak influence is subtle throughout. **rating:** 88

best drinking 2002–2008 **best vintages** '99 **drink with** Beef Bordelaise • $30

grove hill NR

120 Old Norton Summit Road, Norton Summit, SA 5136 **region** Adelaide Hills
phone (08) 8390 1437 **fax** (08) 8390 1437 **open** Sunday 11–5
winemaker David Powell (Contract) **production** 500 **est.** 1978
product range ($22–35 ML) Riesling, Chardonnay, Marguerite Pinot Chardonnay.
summary Grove Hill is a heritage property established in 1846 with the original homestead and outbuildings and held by the same family since then. Not entered in the Adelaide Hills Wines Show and no recent tastings.

haan wines ★★★★☆

Siegersdorf Road, Tanunda, SA 5352 **region** Barossa Valley
phone (08) 8562 4590 **fax** (08) 8562 4590 **open** Not
winemaker James Irvine (Contract) **production** 4000 **est.** 1993
product range ($18–35 ML) Viognier, Chanticleer Sparkling Rosé, Wilhelmus (red blend), Shiraz Prestige, Merlot Prestige.
summary Hans and Fransien Haan established their business in 1993 when they acquired a 16-hectare vineyard near Tanunda. The primary focus is on Merlot and in particular on the luxury Merlot Prestige, and they understandably chose James Irvine as their contract-winemaker. There are no cellar-door sales; the wines are sold through distributors in the eastern States; Australian Prestige Wines also acts as export distributor.

Haan Viognier

TTTTY **2000** Glowing yellow-green; rich honeysuckle, fruit pastille and apricot aromas are followed by a palate with masses of ripe, gently spiced fruit flavours that follow logically on from the bouquet. **rating:** 90

best drinking Now–2004 **best vintages** '99, '00 **drink with** Rich fish dishes • $18.50

Haan Shiraz Prestige

TTTT **1998** Medium red-purple; firm, savoury/leafy/earthy/spicy fruit aromas are followed by a quite lively palate, with some mint and leaf flavours joining the band, but not as luscious as most '98 Shiraz, which for some may be no bad thing. **rating:** 89

best drinking 2003–2008 **best vintages** NA **drink with** Rump of lamb • $35

Haan Merlot Prestige

TTTTT **1998** Packaged in one of the aggravatingly tall bottles, but never mind, it has excellent bloodlines and, better still, pronounced varietal character. Earthy overtones to the fruit and a nice touch of oak on the bouquet are followed by an intense, slippery palate with a core of sweet berry fruit; fine tannins. **rating:** 94

best drinking 2003–2010 **best vintages** '96, '97, '98 **drink with** Game pie • $35

haig NR

Square Mile Road, Mount Gambier, SA 5290 **region** Mount Gambier
phone (08) 8725 5414 **fax** (08) 8725 5414 **open** 7 days 11–5
winemaker Katnook (Contract) **production** 1000 **est.** 1982
product range ($16–19 CD) Chardonnay, Late Harvest Chardonnay, Botrytis Chardonnay, Pinot Noir, Cabernet Sauvignon.
summary The 4 hectares of estate vineyards are planted on the rich volcanic soils near the slopes of the famous Blue Lake of Mount Gambier. I have neither seen nor tasted the wines.

hainault ★★★

255 Walnut Road, Bickley, WA 6076 **region** Perth Hills
phone (08) 9328 6728 **fax** (08) 9328 6895 **open** Weekends 10–5
winemaker Celine Rousseau, Gary Dixon **production** 2300 **est.** 1980

product range ($14–21 CD) The Terroir Range of Gewurztraminer, Pinot Noir, Merlot, Shiraz; Barking Owl Sauvignon Blanc Semillon, Chardonnay, Fruity Muscat, Old Vine Red, Cabernets, Vineyard Port; and Talus Sparkling.
summary Under the energetic ownership of public-affairs consultant and businessman Bill Mackey and wife Vicki, the changes have come thick and fast at Hainault. Plantings have increased to 11 hectares; Celine Rousseau, a highly qualified French-born and trained oenologist, has been installed as winemaker; and the Barking Owl range, attractively packaged, and sourced from Pemberton, the Bickley and Swan Valleys, has been introduced to sit under the Hainault Terroir range. Limited distribution in Victoria and the ACT.

halcyon daze ★★★

19 Uplands Road, Lilydale, Vic 3140 **region** Yarra Valley
phone (03) 9726 7111 **fax** (03) 9726 7111 **open** By appointment
winemaker Richard Rackley **production** 500 **est.** 1982
product range ($28–30 ML) Merlot, Cabernet Franc Merlot.
summary One of the lower-profile wineries with a small, estate-grown production which in fact sells the major part of its output of grapes from its 6.5 hectares of vines to others. Immaculate viticulture ensures that the grapes have a strong market. At the time of going to print expressions of interest were being sought for the sale of the property.

hamelin bay ★★★★

Brockman Highway, Karridale, WA 6288 **region** Margaret River
phone (08) 9758 5555 **fax** (08) 9389 6020 **open** Mon–Fri 10–5 (by appointment)
winemaker Philip Tubb **production** 15 000 **est.** 1992
product range ($16–25 R) Sauvignon Blanc, Semillon Sauvignon Blanc, Chardonnay, Classic Rampant White, Classic Rampant Red, Cabernet Sauvignon.
summary The 25-hectare Hamelin Bay vineyard, established by the Drake-Brockman family, has enjoyed outstanding success with its first wine releases from the 1996 and 1997 vintages. The initial releases were contract-made, but a winery with cellar-door sales facility was opened in the year 2000. In the meantime, production has increased from 5000 to 15 000 cases. Exports to the UK and the US.

Hamelin Bay Sauvignon Blanc

🍷🍷🍷🍷 **2000** Very pale straw-green; the bouquet has some mineral and herb aromas, but does not stray into the tropical end of the spectrum. The palate follows down the same track, with good length and persistence on the finish, thanks to lemony acidity. **rating:** 85
best drinking Now **best vintages** NA **drink with** Char-grilled octopus • $18.10

Hamelin Bay Semillon Sauvignon Blanc

🍷🍷🍷🍷 **2000** Very light green-yellow; the bouquet has a mix of grass, herb and mineral, the palate picking up with slightly sweeter mid-palate fruit with a hint of passionfruit that contributes to pleasing mouthfeel. **rating:** 86
best drinking Now **best vintages** NA **drink with** Tempura • $18.10

Hamelin Bay Classic Rampant Red

🍷🍷🍷½ **1999** Very deep and youthful purple, almost as if it had come direct from the fermenter. The bouquet is as dense as the colour suggests, but very closed. A massively concentrated and rich wine that would have been a great blend component, but which on its own is altogether in your face. 14.5° alcohol is part of the explanation. **rating:** 84
best drinking 2004–2009 **best vintages** NA **drink with** Barbecued bangers • $18.10

Hamelin Bay Cabernet Sauvignon

🍷🍷🍷🍷½ **1999** Medium purple-red; there are nice spicy, aromatic edges to the cassis/redcurrant fruit of the bouquet, moving into a lively palate with cassis/berry flavours, fine tannins and well-integrated oak. 400 cases made **rating:** 90
best drinking 2003–2009 **best vintages** NA **drink with** Butterfly leg of lamb • $24.85

hamilton ★★★★

Main Road, Willunga, SA 5172 **region** McLaren Vale
phone (08) 8556 2288 **fax** (08) 8556 2868 **open** Mon–Fri 10–5, weekends 11–5
winemaker Phillipa Treadwell **production** 25 000 **est.** 1837
product range ($13–50 R) Synergy Dry White, Chardonnay, Pinot Noir, Shiraz; Hamilton Almond Grove Chardonnay, Ayliffe's Orchard Sauvignon Blanc, Slate Quarry Riesling, The Chook Sauvignon Blanc, Chenin Blanc, Noble Semillon Sauvignon Blanc, Lot 148 Merlot, Gumprs' Block Shiraz, Hut Block Cabernet Sauvignon; Hamilton Reserve wines are Richard Hamilton Signature Chardonnay, Marion Vineyard Grenache Shiraz, Old Vines Shiraz, Egremont Reserve Merlot, Burton's Vineyard Grenache Shiraz; also The Hills Adelaide Hills Chardonnay and Pinot Noir.
summary The quality and character of the Richard Hamilton wines have been consolidated over the past five years or so, no doubt due to the skills of winemaker Phillipa Treadwell and former winemaker Ralph Fowler, with support from owner Dr Richard Hamilton. The wines are boldly styled, and full of flavour and character. Exports to Singapore, Thailand, Malaysia, New Zealand, the US, the UK, Denmark, Switzerland, Belgium and the Netherlands.

Hamilton The Chook Chenin Blanc

YYYY **1999** Medium yellow-green; gentle creamy/nutty oak works well with the gentle fruit without suppressing it. The palate is similarly altogether surprising, with restrained nutty/creamy flavours and a bone-dry finish. Clever winemaking, appalling marketing. **rating:** 86

best drinking Now **best vintages** NA **drink with** Poached chicken • $14.95

Hamilton The Hills Chardonnay

YYYY **1999** Medium yellow-green; quite potent, tangy melon fruit with subtle oak on the bouquet leads into a full, quite strongly fruited palate with melon and stonefruit flavours; a slightly grippy finish detracts somewhat from an otherwise good wine. **rating:** 85

best drinking Now–2003 **best vintages** NA **drink with** White-fleshed fish • $20.95

Hamilton Centurion 100 Year Old Shiraz

YYYYY **1998** The vines were planted in 1892, hence the name. Particularly by the standards of McLaren Vale, a stylish, albeit powerful, example of old vine Shiraz. Concentrated dark plum, blackberry and earth fruit on the bouquet is replicated by the concentrated savoury/black-fruited palate, finishing with fine but persistent tannins. **rating:** 95

best drinking 2003–2020 **best vintages** '98 **drink with** Braised ox cheek • $49.95

Hamilton Gumprs' Block Shiraz

YYYY **1999** Dark red-purple; ripe, savoury, spicy licorice and plum fruit on the bouquet leads into a ripe black cherry and plum-flavoured palate with quite persistent tannins and a lick of vanilla oak. **rating:** 87

best drinking 2004–2009 **best vintages** NA **drink with** Kebabs • $21

Hamilton Marion Vineyard Grenache Shiraz

YYYY **1998** Medium red-purple; the bouquet is at the extreme edge of vegetal/spice/earth varietal character, the light to medium bodied palate likewise way left of centre. This is a character I have seen from time to time with Hamilton wines from McLaren Vale; sometimes it works, sometimes it doesn't. **rating:** 84

best drinking Now–2003 **best vintages** NA **drink with** Spiced beef • $29.95

Hamilton Egremont Reserve Merlot

YYYY **1997** Dense red, with some purple on the rim. The bouquet is clean, with quite sweet dark chocolate, cedar and spice aromas. A powerful wine on the palate, again showing that distinctive McLaren Vale chocolate, backed by abundant dark fruit flavours. The hint of cedar will become more evident as the wine ages, and it does need time to reach its full potential. **rating:** 89

best drinking 2005–2012 **best vintages** '97 **drink with** Stuffed shoulder of lamb • $45.95

Hamilton Hut Block Cabernets

YYYY **1998** Dense purple-red; concentrated, ripe blackberry and blackcurrant fruit melds with vanilla oak on the bouquet. The palate is chewy, concentrated and dense, with abundant fruit and slightly furry tannins. There are no green edges, which sometimes appear in these Hamilton wines, and it is probable the wine will merit higher points in the future. **rating:** 85

best drinking 2003–2008 **best vintages** NA **drink with** Venison ragout • $22.95

Hamilton Hut Block Cabernet Sauvignon

🍷🍷🍷🍷 **1999** Medium purple-red; dark berry fruit on the bouquet has some varietal savoury cut supported by appropriate oak. The palate has quite good structure and texture, although the fruit is essentially fragile, notwithstanding the old-vine origin, presumably a reflection of the vintage. **rating:** 85

best drinking 2003–2008 **best vintages** '86, '90, '91, '93 **drink with** Beef Provençale • $21

hamiltons bluff NR

Longs Corner Road, Canowindra, NSW 2804 **region** Cowra

phone (02) 6344 2079 **fax** (02) 6344 2165 **open** Weekends and holidays 10–4, Mon–Fri by appointment

winemaker Andrew Margan **production** 5000 **est.** 1995

product range ($14.50–22 CD) Canowindra Grossi range of Unwooded Chardonnay, Cabernet Sauvignon; Cowra Chardonnay, Chairman's Reserve Chardonnay, Sangiovese, Methode Champenoise, Devonian Red NV.

summary Hamiltons Bluff is owned and operated by the Andrews family, who planted 45 hectares of vines in 1995. The first crop was produced in 1998, and three different Chardonnays were contract-made by Andrew Margan. The Cowra Chardonnay and Canowindra Grossi Chardonnay received medals at the 1998 Cowra Wine Show. Cellar-door sales opened in 1999, heralding a new stage of development for the Cowra region.

hamilton's ewell vineyards ★★★★

Siegersdorf Vineyard, Barossa Valley Way, Tanunda, SA 5352 **region** Barossa Valley

phone (08) 8231 0088 **fax** (08) 8231 0355 **open** Mon–Fri 10–5, weekends 11–5

winemaker Robert Hamilton **production** 3000 **est.** 1837

product range ($13.50–26 CD) Riesling, Unwooded Chardonnay, Railway Chardonnay, Stonegarden Grenache, Railway Shiraz, Fuller's Barn Shiraz.

summary Mark Hamilton, an Adelaide lawyer, is a sixth-generation direct descendent of Richard Hamilton, who arrived in South Australia in 1838 (a year after the State was proclaimed) and made his first wine in 1841. Hamilton's Ewell Vineyards remained in the family until 1979, when it was acquired by Mildara Wines, much to Mark Hamilton's dismay. Since 1991 he has set about building yet another Hamilton wine business by a series of astute vineyard acquisitions, and buying back the name Hamilton's Ewell from Mildara Blass. Most of the grapes are sold, but there is scope to very significantly increase production in the years ahead.

Hamilton's Ewell Vineyards Fuller's Barn Shiraz

🍷🍷🍷🍷🍷 **1998** Medium to full red-purple; the bouquet is solid and dense, with dark berry, chocolate and earth aromas, the palate massively concentrated, with rich fruit, subtle oak, and quite pronounced and very attractive bitter dark chocolate flavours. A towering 15.5° alcohol, but carries it well. **rating:** 90

best drinking 2003–2013 **best vintages** '98 **drink with** Kangaroo fillet • $26

Hamilton's Ewell Vineyards Railway Shiraz

🍷🍷🍷🍷 **1998** Medium to full red-purple; there is noticeably sweet berry fruit and quite pronounced American oak, both in a different register from the Fuller's Barn Shiraz. A rich, concentrated palate with lots of fruit and oak extract promises a long life in a high-alcohol style. **rating:** 88

best drinking 2003–2010 **best vintages** NA **drink with** Braised game • $26

hanging rock winery ★★★★

The Jim Jim, Jim Road, Newham, Vic 3442 **region** Macedon Ranges

phone (03) 5427 0542 **fax** (03) 5427 0310 **open** 7 days 10–5

winemaker John Ellis **production** 30 000 **est.** 1982

product range ($12–48 CD) Macedon Cuvée VII, Rock Riesling, The Jim Jim Sauvignon Blanc, Victoria Semillon Sauvignon Blanc, Victoria Chardonnay, Rock White (Chardonnay), Late Harvest Riesling, Late Harvest Gewurztraminer, Macedon Rosé, Central Highlands Pinot Noir, Victoria Cabernet Merlot, Gralaine Merlot, Victoria Shiraz, Rock Red (Shiraz, Grenache Pinot Noir), Picnic Red, White and Brut, 'S' (sticky).

summary The Macedon area has proved very marginal in spots, and the Hanging Rock vineyards, with their lovely vista towards the Rock, are no exception. John Ellis has thus elected to source additional grapes from various parts of Victoria to produce an interesting and diverse style of wines. The low-priced Picnic White and Picnic Red, with the striking label, have been particularly successful. Exports to the UK, Canada, Hong Kong, Taiwan and Japan.

Hanging Rock Gewurztraminer

🍷🍷🍷🍷🍸 **1999** Light straw-green; the aromas are not powerful, but run in a perfect spice/lychee varietal spectrum. The palate has the same flavours, fleshed out with the clever attention of just a touch of residual sugar. **rating:** 90

best drinking Now–2003 **best vintages** NA **drink with** Asian • NA

Hanging Rock The Jim Jim Sauvignon Blanc

🍷🍷🍷🍷 **2000** Pale green-straw; a fresh, crisp, very delicate and fine bouquet and palate are in the mainstream of this ultra-cool vineyard style. There is a subliminal hint of gooseberry running throughout and, wisely, the wine has not been forced during the winemaking process. **rating:** 88

best drinking Now–2003 **best vintages** '93, '95, '96, '99, '00 **drink with** Oysters • $22

Hanging Rock Macedon Cuvée

🍷🍷🍷🍷🍸 **NV VIII** Medium to full yellow-green; the complex and full bouquet has lots of bready/nutty autolysis characters, but no aldehydes; a complex, rich and full palate, quite dry, and with good acidity. **rating:** 93

best drinking Now–2004 **best vintages** V, VI, VIII **drink with** Oysters Kilpatrick • $48

Hanging Rock Winery Heathcote Shiraz

🍷🍷🍷🍷🍸 **1999** Medium to full red-purple; the bouquet is powerful and rich, with high-toned berry fruit and vanilla oak; concentrated berry fruit provides lots of flavour and extract on the palate, my only wish being there was rather less American and more French oak. **rating:** 92

best drinking 2004–2009 **best vintages** '97, '98, '99 **drink with** Roast venison • $20

hankin estate NR

Johnsons Lane, Northwood, via Seymour, Vic 3660 **region** Goulburn Valley
phone (03) 5792 2396 **fax** (03) 9353 2927 **open** Weekends 10–5
winemaker Dr Max Hankin **production** 600 **est.** 1975
product range ($7–22 CD) Semillon, Sauvignon Blanc, Premium Dry White, Rosé, Shiraz, Shiraz Cabernet Malbec, Cabernet Sauvignon.
summary Hankin Estate is now the principal occupation of Dr Max Hankin, who has retired from full-time medical practice. He has to contend with phylloxera, which decimated the original plantings, with the replanting process still underway.

hanns creek estate NR

Kentucky Road, Merricks North, Vic 3926 **region** Mornington Peninsula
phone (03) 5989 7266 **fax** (03) 5989 7500 **open** 7 days 11–5
winemaker Tony Aubrey-Slocock **production** 1500 **est.** 1987
product range ($18–25 CD) Chardonnay, Rosé, Pinot Noir, Cabernet Shiraz, Cabernet Sauvignon.
summary Denise and Tony Aubrey-Slocock have established a 3-hectare vineyard on the slopes of Merricks North. After an uncertain start, with contract-winemaking moving around, Kevin McCarthy took control and wine style steadied.

hansen hilltops ★★★★

Barwang Ridge, 1 Barwang Road, via Young, NSW 2594 **region** Hilltops
phone (02) 6382 6363 **fax** (02) 6382 6363 **open** Fri-Mon 10–6
winemaker Charles Sturt University (Contract) **production** 2100 **est.** 1979
product range ($15.50–18 CD) Riesling, Chardonnay Semillon, Cabernet Sauvignon.
summary The vineyard has 5 hectares of vines, 1 hectare each of riesling, chardonnay, shiraz, cabernet sauvignon, and a further hectare roughly split between semillon, merlot and malbec. The plantings date back to 1979, but the first wines were not made until the late 1990s. Peter Hansen points out there are only two vineyards at Barwang, both part of the original Barwang sheep station, McWilliam's and his. Perhaps a little cheekily, he goes on to point out that the difference is that his wines are produced solely from non-irrigated vines that are hand-picked and hand-pruned, and, into the bargain, are ten years older than the McWilliam's.

Hansen Hilltops Riesling

ᴛᴛᴛᴛ♀ **1999** Light green-yellow; a highly aromatic bouquet with flowery, spicy, lime aromas leaping from the glass is followed by a very intense, lime juice-charged, long and striking palate. **rating:** 92

best drinking Now–2007 **best vintages** '99 **drink with** Antipasto • $18

Hansen Hilltops Cabernet Sauvignon

ᴛᴛᴛᴛ♀ **1999** Medium to full red-purple; clean, smooth blackberry/blackcurrant fruit is woven through French oak; a concentrated and powerful palate with dark berry fruit flavours, lingering tannins and fine oak. **rating:** 91

best drinking 2003–2010 **best vintages** '99 **drink with** Ragout of lamb • $18

hanson-tarrahill vineyard ★★★

(postal) 49 Cleveland Avenue, Lower Plenty, Vic 3093 **region** Yarra Valley
phone (03) 9439 7425 **fax** (03) 9439 4217 **open** Not
winemaker Dr Ian Hanson **production** 800 **est.** 1983
product range ($20–30 R) Pinot Noir, Cabernets, Arundel (Cabernet blend), Tarra's Block Cabernet Franc, Cabernet Sauvignon.
summary Dental surgeon Ian Hanson planted his first vines in the late 1960s, close to the junction of the Yarra and Plenty Rivers; in 1983 those plantings were extended (with 3000 vines), and in 1988 the Tarrahill property at Yarra Glen was established with 4 further hectares. Hanson is the name that appears most prominently on the newly designed labels; Tarrahill Vineyard is in much smaller type.

Hanson-Tarrahill Vineyard Pinot Noir

ᴛᴛᴛ♀ **1999** Medium red; the bouquet is quite complex, with savoury/foresty aromas that come through on the palate together with dark plum and what appear to be green, stem tannins. Despite the relatively high acidity, the wine is a little short, but not a bad outcome for the vintage. **rating:** 84

best drinking Now–2003 **best vintages** NA **drink with** Coq au vin • $22

Hanson-Tarrahill Vineyard Arundel

ᴛᴛᴛ♀ **1998** The colour is quite developed; complex cedar/cigar box/savoury aromas on the bouquet translate into a complex, savoury/cedary palate with strong tannin grip. Little or no primary fruit flavour is left; may appeal to some for this very reason. **rating:** 84

best drinking Now–2004 **best vintages** NA **drink with** Mushroom risotto • $30

Hanson-Tarrahill Vineyard Tarra's Block Cabernets

ᴛᴛᴛ♀ **1999** Medium red; a light, leafy/cedary bouquet is followed by a palate with similar cedary/leafy flavours running through to a long finish sustained by good acidity. Nonetheless, the wine looks far older than it is, and will have a short plateau. Once again, might have been bottled earlier. **rating:** 83

best drinking Now–2003 **best vintages** NA **drink with** Marinated lamb • $22

happs ★★★☆

Commonage Road, Dunsborough, WA 6281 **region** Margaret River
phone (08) 9755 3300 **fax** (08) 9755 3846 **open** 7 days 10–5
winemaker Erl Happ, Mark Aitken **production** 18 000 **est.** 1978
product range ($13–22 CD) Dry table wines are Anne Coralie Semillon, Semillon Verdelho, Marrimee (Semillon Chenin Blanc), Viognier, Marsanne, PF White (Preservative Free), Chardonnay, PF Red (Preservative Free), Shiraz, Merlot and Cabernet Merlot; sweet table wines are Fuschia, Topaz and Late Picked Verdelho; fortifieds are Fortis (Vintage Port), 10 Year Fortis (Tawny), Fortissimo, Garnet (from Muscat à Petit Grains) and Pale Gold (White Port).
summary Former schoolteacher turned potter and winemaker Erl Happ is an iconoclast and compulsive experimenter. Many of the styles he makes are very unconventional, and in the future are likely to be even more so: the Karridale vineyard planted in 1994 has no less than 28 different varieties established. Merlot has been a winery specialty for a decade. Limited retail distribution through New South Wales, Victoria and Queensland and, more recently, exports to Europe.

Happs Semillon Verdelho

🍷🍷🍷🍷 **2000** Light green-yellow; the bouquet is clean and quite ripe, with pleasant fruit-salad aromatics. The palate is fresh and tangy, in a clearly defined drink-now mode. **rating:** 84

best drinking Now **best vintages** NA **drink with** Seafood • $16.50

Happs Viognier

🍷🍷🍷🍷🍷 **2000** Light green-yellow; a highly aromatic bouquet with fruit pastille and orange blossom varietal aromas is followed by a lively, fresh palate, again with those pastille/blossom flavours. The mouthfeel and texture doesn't quite show the high alcohol, which is all the more interesting. **rating:** 90

best drinking Now–2003 **best vintages** '00 **drink with** Chinese sweet and sour • $20

Happs Marsanne

🍷🍷🍷🍷 **2000** Pale straw-green; the bouquet has mineral, talc and lemon aromas; the crisp and still reserved palate provides a replay of the bouquet, with talc, mineral and lemon flavours, but should develop even more character over the next few years. **rating:** 85

best drinking 2002–2005 **best vintages** NA **drink with** Thai soup • $16

Happs PF Red

🍷🍷🍷🍷 **2000** Medium red-purple; a soft, gently earthy/spicy bouquet is followed by a palate that, as at the end of February 2001, was still fresh, and has quite good tannin structure which will, by rights, retain its freshness for a little while yet. **rating:** 84

best drinking Now **best vintages** NA **drink with** Anything that takes your fancy • $15

harcourt valley vineyards NR

Calder Highway, Harcourt, Vic 3453 **region** Bendigo
phone (03) 5474 2223 **fax** (03) 5474 2293 **open** 7 days 11–6
winemaker John Livingstone **production** 2500 **est.** 1976
product range ($14–20CD) Chardonnay, Riesling, Barbara's Shiraz, Cabernet Sauvignon.
summary Traditional producer of rich, full-bodied red wines typical of the district, but sporadic and largely outdated tastings since ownership changed preclude evaluation.

hardys ★★★★☆

Reynell Road, Reynella, SA 5161 **region** McLaren Vale
phone (08) 8392 2222 **fax** (08) 8392 2202 **open** 7 days 10–4, except public holidays
winemaker Peter Dawson, Stephen Pannell, Tom Newton, Ed Carr **production** NFP **est.** 1853
product range ($8–65 R) At the bottom comes the R&R range of Riesling Traminer, Colombard Chardonnay, Chardonnay, Shiraz, Merlot, Cabernet Sauvignon, Classic Cuvée; then Nottage Hill Riesling, Chardonnay, Shiraz, Cabernet Sauvignon Shiraz; Siegersdorf Riesling and Chardonnay; No Preservative Added range of Chardonnay, Shiraz and Cabernet Sauvignon; Insignia Chardonnay Sauvignon Blanc, Chardonnay and Cabernet Sauvignon Shiraz; Tintara Cellars Chardonnay, Shiraz and Cabernet Sauvignon; Sir James sparkling; super-premium Tintara Grenache and Shiraz, Eileen Hardy Chardonnay, Shiraz and Thomas Hardy Cabernet Sauvignon, Arras Pinot Noir Chardonnay; also superior-quality Brandies and Ports including Australia's finest Vintage Port.
summary Since the 1992 merger of Thomas Hardy and the Berri Renmano group, the business has flourished, and the shareholders have profited greatly. The merged group has confounded expectations by aggressively, and very successfully, pushing the premium end of the business, making a number of acquisitions and investments across the length and breadth of Australia, all aimed at the upper end of the market. A high level of winemaking expertise and commitment have been essential to this success. It is basically for these wines that the winery rating is given.

Hardys Padthaway Unwooded Chardonnay

🍷🍷🍷🍷🍷 **2000** I am no friend of unwooded Chardonnay in general; most is bland, neither fish nor fowl, and likely considered not worth putting in oak. This wine has a tangy presence and personality, with fresh, fragrant grapefruit and nectarine fruit in a highly fragrant and flavoursome mould; refreshing, and inviting the second glass. **rating:** 90

best drinking Now **best vintages** '00 **drink with** Designer fish and chips • $15.99

Hardys Eileen Hardy Chardonnay

🍷🍷🍷🍷🍷 **1999** Glowing yellow-green; complex, toasty/charry barrel-ferment characters are the first impression on the bouquet, with an array of intense melon, stonefruit and grapefruit aromas following. The wine has intense and potent melon and grapefruit flavour, with good acidity contributing to the considerable length. The oak inputs do need to come together with further time in bottle but, on the other hand, the wine was tasted prior to release. **rating:** 94

🍷🍷🍷🍷½ **1998** Medium yellow-green; the bouquet is complex, with melon and cashew fruit balanced by spicy nutmeg oak; on the palate, there is a similar mix of tangy fruit and cashew overtones, but the spicy oak is a tad too assertive at this point. **rating:** 91

best drinking 2002–2007 **best vintages** '85, '87, '90, '91, '93, '94, '96, '99 **drink with** Fresh Atlantic salmon • $35

Hardys Arras

🍷🍷🍷🍷🍷 **1995** Pinot Chardonnay. Confusingly, this is not the same wine as the 1995 Arras released last year, which was chardonnay-dominant. Nonetheless, has a similar show record with five trophies and 16 gold medals. Spotlessly clean and with quite brilliant intensity, I would never pick the high percentage of pinot noir (79 per cent) in the lingering, citrus-tinged but ripe palate. **rating:** 96

best drinking Now **best vintages** '95 **drink with** Aperitif • $54.99

Hardys Omni

🍷🍷🍷🍷 **NV** What seemed to have a strange name and packaging has proved an enduring, best-selling, bottle-fermented sparkler, thanks in no small measure to winemaker Ed Carr's blending skills. Abundant, ripe peachy fruit on both bouquet and palate is balanced by quite good acidity and appropriate dosage sweetness. Easy and appealing. **rating:** 85

best drinking Now **best vintages** NA **drink with** Aperitif • $9.99

Hardys Sir James Brut de Brut

🍷🍷🍷🍷 **NV** Medium to full straw-yellow; the bouquet is quite complex, with nutty/bready overtones to the fruit; the palate is fresh, clean, lively and remarkably fine for a wine of its price, providing the flavours promised by the bouquet. **rating:** 89

best drinking Now **best vintages** NA **drink with** Hors d'oeuvres • $14.99

Hardys Sir James Vintage Brut

🍷🍷🍷🍷 **1995** Medium to full straw-yellow; the bouquet has obvious complexity, with bready/yeasty aromas; the palate is very intense, high-flavoured and long, bordering on going over the top. **rating:** 87

best drinking Now **best vintages** '94 **drink with** Chinese dumplings • $25.99

Hardys Sir James Sparkling Shiraz

🍷🍷🍷🍷 **1995** Medium to full red-purple; the bouquet is earthy and potent, with spicy tones adding complexity, the palate with powerful, juicy berry fruit, and relatively high dosage to balance the phenolics. **rating:** 89

best drinking Now–2005 **best vintages** NA **drink with** Quail • $25.99

Hardys Eileen Hardy Shiraz

🍷🍷🍷🍷½ **1998** Dense red-purple; there is the predictably dense and brooding dark cherry/dark plum fruit on the bouquet, the oak positive but not excessive. The palate is rich, full and savoury, with berry fruit still fleshing out on the back palate; continues the trend of recent years to refine the role of oak in the wine. **rating:** 93

🍷🍷🍷🍷½ **1997** Full purple-red; the bouquet abounds with rich, red berry fruit allied with smoky, spicy oak. The palate is dense, packed with the flavour of black cherry, blackberry and mulberry and oak, which will ultimately give cedary characters to the wine. All in all, a brooding giant that absolutely demands prolonged cellaring. **rating:** 92

best drinking 2003–2013 **best vintages** '70, '88, '91, '93, '95, '96, '97, '98 **drink with** Game pie • $65

Tintara Cellars Shiraz

🍷🍷🍷🍷 **1998** Medium to full red-purple; the moderately intense bouquet is quite sweet, with plum and spice, together with an appropriate touch of oak. The palate is likewise medium bodied, with nice plum and spice flavour, a touch of oak, and representing good value at the price. **rating:** 85

best drinking Now–2004 **best vintages** NA **drink with** Grilled chops • $15

Hardys Tintara Limited Release Shiraz

1999 Medium to full purple-red; the concentrated bouquet offers a complex array of dark plum, dark berry and well-balanced oak aromas. As ever, a powerful palate, with ripe, chunky, chewy fruit, oak and tannin. Unquestionably a wine for the long term. **rating:** 90

best drinking 2004–2014 **best vintages** '95, '96, '97 **drink with** Beef in black bean sauce • $35

Hardys Tintara Limited Release Grenache

1999 Medium to full red, with a touch of purple on the rim; the bouquet has complex, spicy overtones to the dark berry fruit and underlying oak. The palate reveals the most powerful and concentrated Grenache on the market today, with masses of dark fruit and savoury tannins. **rating:** 90

best drinking 2003–2013 **best vintages** '95, '97, '99 **drink with** Very rich meat dishes • $29

harewood estate ★★★☆

Scotsdale Road, Denmark, WA 6333 **region** Great Southern
phone (08) 9840 9078 **fax** (08) 9840 9053 **open** By appointment
winemaker Michael Kerrigan **production** 700 **est.** 1988
product range ($29–30 R) Chardonnay, Pinot Noir.
summary Keith and Margie Graham have established a showpiece vineyard at Binalong. The majority of the grapes are sold to Howard Park and Domaine Chandon, but gradually increasing amounts of wine are being made under the Harewood Estate label. The wines have retail distribution in Perth and are exported to the UK but are otherwise only available by mail order.

Harewood Estate Chardonnay

1999 Medium yellow-green; the attractive melon and nectarine fruit is slightly hampered by oak on the bouquet, but the wine sorts itself out on the fresh, youthful, tight palate, where grapefruit, melon and nectarine run through to a long finish. **rating:** 86

best drinking Now–2004 **best vintages** '97, '98 **drink with** Seafood risotto • $30

Harewood Estate Pinot Noir

1998 Light to medium red, with just a touch of purple; the bouquet is clean, with savoury/foresty aromas, but fairly light fruit; the palate likewise is quite savoury, with some tannins, but the fruit either wasn't there or, more likely was, but has started to dip slightly. **rating:** 84

best drinking Now **best vintages** NA **drink with** Hare, of course • $29

hartzview wine centre 

RSD 1034 Off Cross Road, Gardners Bay, Tas 7112 **region** Southern Tasmania
phone (03) 6295 1623 **open** 7 days 9–5
winemaker Andrew Hood (Contract), Robert Patterson **production** NFP **est.** 1988
product range ($18 CD) Chardonnay, Pinot Noir; also a range of Pig and Whistle Hill fruit wines.
summary A combined wine centre, offering wines from a number of local Huon Valley wineries, and also newly erected and very comfortable accommodation for six people in a separate, self-contained house. Hartzview table wines (produced from 3 hectares of estate plantings) are much to be preferred to the self-produced Pig and Whistle Hill fruit wines.

Hartzview Pinot Noir

1999 Medium red-purple; fragrant spice, cherry and stem aromas precede a powerhouse, tangy strawberry/cherry-flavoured palate, finishing with acidity that some found unmanageable. I like the wine, particularly for its fantastic bouquet. **rating:** 89

best drinking 2002–2006 **best vintages** NA **drink with** Peking duck • NA

haselgrove ★★★★

Foggo Road, McLaren Vale, SA 5171 **region** McLaren Vale
phone (08) 8323 8706 **fax** (08) 8323 8049 **open** Mon–Fri 9–5, weekends 10–5
winemaker Nick Haselgrove **production** 216 000 **est.** 1981

product range ($10–50 R) Lost Sheep range of Chardonnay, Shiraz and Cabernet Sauvignon, McLaren Vale Pictures Series Sauvignon Blanc, Chardonnay, Grenache, Shiraz, Cabernet Sauvignon; Futures Shiraz; Bentwing Chardonnay, Shiraz, Cabernet Sauvignon; premium releases under 'H' Reserve label and Limelight McLaren Vale Syrah; Sparkling, Port; lesser priced varietals under Sovereign Series.

summary Haselgrove Wines became a wholly owned subsidiary of the publicly listed Cranswick Premium Wines Limited in mid-1997. Under Nick Haselgrove's direction, the premium red wines, and in particular the 'H' Reserve range, have gone from strength to strength. Exports to the UK, New Zealand and the US.

Haselgrove 'H' Viognier

▼▼▼▼ **2000** Medium to full yellow-green; the bouquet is rich and ripe, with tropical honeysuckle and spice aromas. The mouthfilling and round palate reflects the varietal background in its texture (14° alcohol) rather more than in its flavour, but does work. **rating:** 86

best drinking Now–2004 **best vintages** NA **drink with** Braised rabbit • NA

Haselgrove Bentwing Chardonnay

▼▼▼▼ **2000** Light to medium yellow-green; the bouquet is clean, quite fragrant, with melon and citrus fruit; the palate, similarly, is clean and fresh, with direct citrus/melon fruit and just a twitch of oak. **rating:** 85

best drinking Now–2003 **best vintages** NA **drink with** Fried calamari • $22

Haselgrove 'H' Reserve Chardonnay

▼▼▼▼ **1999** Light green-yellow; a smooth bouquet has melon fruit complexed by subtle barrel-fermentation characters, a lively tasting palate has attractive melon and nectarine fruit together with remarkably subtle oak (and moderate length). **rating:** 87

best drinking Now–2004 **best vintages** NA **drink with** Avocado and prawn salad • NA

Haselgrove Limelight Syrah

▼▼▼▼ **1998** Medium to full red-purple; the bouquet is solid, ripeish, but not particularly effusive. There is solid, smooth, sweet berry fruit attesting to the quality of the base material on the palate, but the tannins and oak extract seem faintly dusty. **rating:** 88

best drinking 2003–2008 **best vintages** NA **drink with** Steak and kidney pie • $45

Haselgrove 'H' Shiraz

▼▼▼▼▽ **1998** Dense red-purple; a concentrated, inky/savoury bouquet threatens to overwhelm you, the palate succeeding in so doing with huge oak, fruit and extract. The points are as much for intimidation as anything else. **rating:** 90

best drinking 2008–2013 **best vintages** '91, '94, '96, '97 **drink with** Eye fillet • $50

Haselgrove Lost Sheep Shiraz

▼▼▼▽ **1999** Medium red-purple; the bouquet is quite fragrant, with sweet cherry and touches of strawberry fruit; the palate moves through cherry, plum and mint in a light to medium bodied frame; a fun summer red. **rating:** 84

best drinking Now–2003 **best vintages** NA **drink with** Lamb chops, of course • $15

Haselgrove Picture Series Shiraz

▼▼▼▼▽ **1999** Bright red-purple; the bouquet is clean and smooth, with ripe red berry fruits and some vanilla spice oak. A rich, ripe and generous palate has red and dark berry fruit, supple texture and subtle oak. An impressive 1999 vintage red at the price. **rating:** 90

best drinking 2003–2008 **best vintages** '99 **drink with** Spiced beef • $18

Haselgrove Bentwing Cabernet Sauvignon

▼▼▼▽ **1998** Medium red; the bouquet is earthy, slightly dull and lacks freshness, but the palate picks up markedly with quite sweet berry and chocolate fruit, finishing with soft tannins. **rating:** 84

best drinking Now–2005 **best vintages** NA **drink with** Braised beef • $22

Haselgrove 'H' Cabernet Sauvignon

▼▼▼▼ **1998** Medium red-purple; the moderately intense bouquet has fresh red berry fruit with a touch of lift, the medium-bodied palate adding a few savoury notes to the fruit, supported by sweet oak. **rating:** 87

best drinking 2002–2007 **best vintages** '94 **drink with** Char-grilled rump • $50

hastwell & lightfoot ★★★☆

Foggo Road, McLaren Vale, SA 5171 **region** McLaren Vale
phone (08) 8323 8692 **fax** (08) 8323 8098 **open** Not
winemaker Nick Haselgrove (Contract) **production** 1200 **est.** 1990
product range ($16.50 ML) Shiraz, Cabernet.
summary Hastwell & Lightfoot is an offshoot of a rather larger grape-growing business, with the majority of the grapes from the 15 hectares of vineyard being sold to others; the vineyard was planted in 1988 and the first grapes produced in 1990. Until the advent of GST, the wines were under the small business sales tax exemption, hence the mouthwateringly low prices. Incidentally, the labels are once seen, never forgotten. Exports to Germany, the US and New Zealand.

Hastwell & Lightfoot Shiraz

🍷🍷🍷🍷 **1999** Medium to full red-purple; the bouquet has a savoury, spicy opening, then some earthy notes to black cherry fruit; the palate reverses the order, with dark cherry fruit followed by persistent, savoury tannins. Lacks the lusciousness of the '98. **rating:** 86

best drinking 2003–2007 **best vintages** '98 **drink with** Ravioli • $16.50

hawley vineyard ★★★☆

Hawley Beach, Hawley, Tas 7307 **region** Northern Tasmania
phone (03) 6428 6221 **fax** (03) 6428 6844 **open** 7 days
winemaker Andrew Pirie (Contract) **production** 1000 **est.** 1988
product range ($18–25 R) Rubicon Chardonnay, Unwooded Chardonnay, Rubicon Pinot Noir.
summary Hawley Vineyard overlooks Hawley Beach and thence northeast to Bass Strait. It is established on an historic 200-hectare farming property, with Hawley House offering dining and accommodation in a grand style. There are no other vineyards in what is a unique winegrowing region, and few hoteliers-cum-viticulturists as flamboyant as owner Simon Hawley. Limited distribution in Sydney.

Hawley Vineyard Pinot Noir

🍷🍷🍷🍸 **1999** Medium red-purple; the bouquet is briary/foresty, and not particularly intense, but picks up on the gentle spicy/plummy palate; sympathetic oak handling produces an easy-drinking style. **rating:** 84

best drinking Now–2004 **best vintages** '97 **drink with** Coq au vin • NA

hay shed hill estate

RMB 398, Harman's Mill Road, Willyabrup, WA 6280 **region** Margaret River
phone (08) 9755 6234 **fax** (08) 9755 6305 **open** 7 days 10.30–5
winemaker Peter Stanlake **production** 25 000 **est.** 1987
product range ($13–35 CD) Semillon, Sauvignon Blanc, Chardonnay, Pinot Noir, Cabernet Franc, Cabernet Sauvignon (light, unwooded), Cabernet Sauvignon; Pitchfork Pink (Rosé), Pitchfork White, Pitchfork Red.
summary A landmark on the Margaret River scene, with a striking 200-tonne winery, acquired in 2000 by Barrington Estate. Wine quality has been a touch inconsistent, but the 'sold-out' sign so often displayed speaks for itself. At their best, tangy and incisive. The wines are distributed through retail outlets in Perth, Melbourne and Sydney, and are exported to the UK.

hayward's whitehead creek

Lot 18A Hall Lane, Seymour, Vic 3660 **region** Goulburn Valley
phone (03) 5792 3050 **open** Mon–Sat 9–6, Sun 10–6
winemaker Sid Hayward, David Hayward **production** 1000 **est.** 1975
product range ($9.50–14.50 CD) Riesling, Shiraz, Cabernet Sauvignon.
summary The 4.5 hectares of low-yielding, 25-year-old vines make powerful wines in a somewhat rustic mode, perhaps, but at low prices by the standards of today.

Hayward's Whitehead Creek Riesling

🍷🍷🍷🍸 **2000** Light to medium yellow-green; the bouquet is firm, minerally and not particularly aromatic, the palate similarly firm, solid and honest; even if it is slightly phenolic, it comes at a very good price. **rating:** 83

best drinking Now–2005 **best vintages** NA **drink with** Fish and chips • $9.50

Hayward's Whitehead Creek Cabernet Sauvignon

YYYY **1998** Medium to full red, with just a hint of purple remaining; a solid, earthy/blackberry bouquet is followed by a palate with very ripe, faintly jammy blackberry/blackcurrant flavours; massive extract and tannins; rustic and potentially long lived. **rating:** 83

best drinking 2003–2010 **best vintages** NA **drink with** Barbecued sausages • $14.50

heathcote winery ★★★☆

183–185 High Street, Heathcote, Vic 3523 **region** Heathcote
phone (03) 5433 2595 **fax** (03) 5433 3081 **open** Thurs–Sun 11–5
winemaker Mark Kelly, Jonathan Mepham **production** 4000 **est.** 1978
product range ($12.50–41 CD) Cellar Door range of Thomas Craven Viognier, Thomas Craven Chardonnay and Thomas Craven Shiraz; Premium Range of Chardonnay and Mail Coach Shiraz; Super Premium Range of Curagee Viognier and Curagee Shiraz.
summary The Heathcote Winery is back in business with a vengeance. The wines are being produced predominantly from the 26 hectares of estate vineyard, and some from local and other growers under long-term contracts. The tasting room facilities have been restored and upgraded.

Heathcote Curagee Viognier

YYYY **2000** Light yellow-green; the bouquet opens with gentle barrel-ferment oak, which is pleasant, but seems to sit on rather than augment the varietal character. The palate provides the same in spades; a nice wine, but you would have to work hard to unearth the varietal character if tasted blind. **rating:** 84

best drinking Now–2004 **best vintages** NA **drink with** Chicken sausage • $35

Heathcote Curagee Shiraz

YYYYY **1998** Medium red-purple; a complex bouquet, with touches of game surrounding the dark plum and gentle oak, is followed by a rich palate with plum, cherry and hints of exotic spices. The wine has good structure, tannins and length. **rating:** 90

best drinking 2003–2010 **best vintages** NA **drink with** Venison • $40.50

Heathcote Winery Mail Coach Shiraz

YYYY **1998** Medium red-purple; the bouquet is ripe, quite complex, with a mix of plum, spice, sweet leather and game. The palate replicates the bouquet, with good mouthfeel to the dark berry/gamey/briary fruit. **rating:** 89

best drinking 2003–2008 **best vintages** '98 **drink with** Barbecued meat • $24.95

Heathcote Thomas Craven Shiraz

YYYY **1999** Dense red-purple; solid, ripe dark berry/cherry fruit on the bouquet is followed by a palate with plenty of dark berry and chocolate flavour; the tannins are a tad abrasive, but there is lots going on here. **rating:** 85

best drinking 2003–2008 **best vintages** NA **drink with** Rare beef • $14.50

Heathcote Shiraz Viognier

YYYY **1998** Dense red-purple; powerful black fruits and lots of vanilla oak surge from the glass, the palate with more of the same. It is a pity there is so much oak, for it is reasonably certain there are some interesting fruit dynamics going on here. Perhaps time will let the fruit express itself, perhaps not. **rating:** 83

best drinking 2003–2007 **best vintages** NA **drink with** Devilled kidneys • NA

heathfield ridge wines ★★★★

Cnr Caves Road and Penola Highway, Naracoorte, SA 5271 **region** Wrattonbully
phone (08) 8762 4133 **fax** (08) 8762 0141 **open** Mon–Sat 11–5, Sun 11–4
winemaker Pat Tocaciu, Neil Doddridge **production** 50 000 **est.** 1998
product range ($10.50–44 CD) Wonambi Range of Chardonnay Sauvignon Blanc, Shiraz and Chardonnay Pinot Noir (Sparkling); Sauvignon Blanc, Reserve Chardonnay, Jennifer Padthaway Shiraz, Shiraz, Merlot, Cabernet Sauvignon, Patrick Coonawarra Cabernet Sauvignon.
summary Heathfield Ridge Wines is the major winery in the Wrattonbully region. Opened in time for the 1998 vintage, its major function is a contract crush facility but it offers full winemaking facilities for others, and also releases wines under the Heathfield Ridge label, partly utilising over 100 hectares of estate vineyards. The cellar-door sales area was duly opened at the end of 1999. Exports to the UK, the US and Malaysia.

heathvale ★★★☆

Saw Pit Gully Road, via Keyneton, SA 5353 **region** Eden Valley
phone (08) 8564 8248 **fax** (08) 8564 8248 **open** Not
winemaker Paul Bailey (Contract) **production** 500 **est.** 1987
product range ($18–22 R) Chardonnay, Shiraz.
summary The origins of Heathvale go back to 1865, when William Heath purchased a 60-hectare property, establishing a fruit orchard and 8 hectares of vineyard. The wine was made in the cellar of the house that stands on the property today, occupied by current owners Trevor and Faye March. Heath's vines disappeared in the early 1900s, but the Marches now have 3 hectares each of shiraz and cabernet sauvignon, and 2 hectares each of chardonnay and riesling in production. Trevor March is a trained viticulturist and is completing his studies for a Master of Viticulture degree at the Waite Campus of the University of Adelaide, with a double life as a lecturer in viticulture at the Barossa Valley Campus of the Murray Institute of TAFE and as a vineyard consultant.

Heathvale Chardonnay

ΥΥΥΥ **2000** Light green-yellow; the bouquet is clean, with gentle melon and a subtle nutty/creamy oak influence. The palate is similarly clean, quite long, with sophisticated use of lees and oak to add texture and style. **rating:** 89
best drinking Now–2004 **best vintages** NA **drink with** Light risotto • $20

Heathvale Shiraz

ΥΥΥ **1998** Medium red-purple; a clean, moderately intense bouquet, predominantly cherry and plum, but also with a faint touch of mint, is followed by a light to medium bodied palate with minty berry fruit; neither particularly complex nor intense, but pleasant enough. **rating:** 83
best drinking Now–2005 **best vintages** NA **drink with** Chinese pork • $22

heggies vineyard ★★★★

Heggies Range Road, Eden Valley, SA 5235 **region** Eden Valley
phone (08) 8565 3203 **fax** (08) 8565 3380 **open** At Yalumba
winemaker Hugh Reimers **production** 12 000 **est.** 1971
product range ($17–26 R) Riesling, Viognier, Chardonnay, Botrytis Riesling, Merlot.
summary Heggies was the second of the high-altitude (570 metres) vineyards established by S Smith & Sons (Yalumba), with plantings on the 120-hectare former grazing property commencing in 1973. The once simple view of Heggies as a better white than red wine producer has become more complicated, with the pendulum swinging backwards and forwards according to vintage. Exports to all major markets.

Heggies Riesling

ΥΥΥΥ **2000** Light green-yellow; the clean and crisp bouquet offers a mix of mineral, apple and lime aromas, the palate firm, lively and fresh, with mineral and apple fruit. **rating:** 86
best drinking Now–2007 **best vintages** '95, '96, '98, '99 **drink with** Seafood salad • $15.99

Heggies Chardonnay

ΥΥΥΥ **1999** Medium yellow-green; in the groove of the Heggies style, with a solid, ripe citrus and melon bouquet and controlled oak. The medium- to full-bodied palate replicates the fruit characters of the bouquet, sturdily structured. **rating:** 86
best drinking Now–2004 **best vintages** '86, '91, '93, '97 **drink with** Veal, turkey • $26

Heggies Botrytis Riesling 375 ml

ΥΥΥΥΥ **1999** Excellent green-yellow; intense lime and cumquat fruit aromas on the bouquet lead into a palate with abundant lime juice flavour, and excellent balance, length and intensity. Wines such as this deserve a far wider audience. **rating:** 93
best drinking Now–2005 **best vintages** '92, '94, '97, '99 **drink with** Poached fruit or fruit tart • $17

Heggies Pinot Noir

ΥΥΥΥ **1998** Medium red; the bouquet offers a mix of plum jam, hay and spice, all adding up to positive varietal character. The palate, likewise, has strong varietal character in a very ripe style; well made and a surprise packet until one sees the clonal origin. In cooler vintages could be truly exciting. **rating:** 86
best drinking Now–2003 **best vintages** NA **drink with** Barossa quail • $26

Heggies Merlot

ΥΥΥΥ **1997** Medium red-purple; a pleasant, complex, bottle-developed bouquet with quite sweet savoury aromas is followed by a palate in which tannins run throughout and threaten the fruit somewhat, but, all in all, not a bad follow-on from the '96 vintage. **rating:** 86

best drinking Now–2004 **best vintages** '93, '95, '96 **drink with** Rack of veal • $23.95

helm ★★★☆

Butt's Road, Murrumbateman, NSW 2582 **region** Canberra District
phone (02) 6227 5953 **fax** (02) 6227 0207 **open** Thur–Mon 10–5
winemaker Ken Helm **production** 3000 **est.** 1973
product range ($16–30 CD) Riesling Classic Dry, Chardonnay (Non Oaked), Merlot, Cabernet Merlot, Cabernet Sauvignon, Helm (Cabernet blend).
summary Ken Helm is well known as one of the more stormy petrels of the wine industry and is an energetic promoter of his wines and of the Canberra district generally. His wines have been consistent bronze-medal winners, with silvers and the occasional gold dotted here and there, such as the gold medal to the 1997 Cabernet Merlot at the 1999 Sydney Royal Wine Show. The wines have limited retail distribution in New South Wales, the ACT and Victoria.

Helm Riesling

ΥΥΥΥY **2000** Very light green-yellow; the bouquet is crisp and lively with passionfruit, lime and mineral aromas. The palate provides more of the same, with the flavours merging in a wine of moderate intensity and excellent balance. **rating:** 90

best drinking Now–2004 **best vintages** '00 **drink with** Asparagus terrine • $20

henke ★★☆

175 Henke Lane, Yarck, Vic 3719 **region** Central Victorian Mountain Country
phone (03) 5797 6277 **fax** (03) 5797 6277 **open** By appointment
winemaker Tim Miller, Caroline Miller **production** 250 **est.** 1974
product range ($20 CD) Shiraz, Shiraz Cabernet.
summary Produces tiny quantities of deep-coloured, full-flavoured, minty red wines known only to a chosen few. Typically, a range of back-vintages up to five years of age is available at cellar door.

henkell wines NR

Melba Highway, Dixons Creek, Vic 3775 **region** Yarra Valley
phone (03) 9417 4144 **open** Weekends 11–5
winemaker Contract **production** 500 **est.** 1988
product range ($13–29.50 CD) Under the Henkell label are Trocken, Trocken Piccolo, Rose, Rose Piccolo, Brut, Adam Henkell; under Henkell Southeastern Australia are Riverland Riesling Spätlese, Riverland Chablis, Riverland Cabernet Grenache, Port; under Henkell Yarra Valley are Sauvignon Blanc, Chardonnay, Pinot Noir and Cabernet Sauvignon.
summary Hans Henkell started with a 57-variety Heinz mix in the vineyard, but has now rationalised it to a total of 17.7 hectares of sauvignon blanc, chardonnay, pinot noir and cabernet sauvignon. Most of the grapes are sold, with small amounts contract-made each year. And, yes, Hans Henkell is part of the family.

henley park wines NR

149 Swan Street, West Swan, WA 6055 **region** Swan District
phone (08) 9296 4328 **fax** (08) 9296 1313 **open** Tues–Sun 10–5
winemaker Claus Petersen, Lisbet Petersen **production** 3500 **est.** 1935
product range ($9.95–15.95 CD) Semillon, Chenin Blanc, Classic White, Muscat Gordo Blanco (late picked), Autumn Harvest (Sauternes style), Mousse Rosé Brut (Méthode Champenoise), Shiraz, Cabernet Sauvignon, Shiraz Cabernet Merlot, Tawny Port.
summary Henley Park, like so many Swan Valley wineries, was founded by a Yugoslav family, but it is now jointly owned by Danish and Malaysian interests, a multicultural mix if ever there was one. Majority owner and winemaker Claus Petersen arrived in 1986 and had his moment of glory in 1990 when Henley Park was the Most Successful Exhibitor at the Mount Barker Wine Show. Much of the production is sold through cellar door (and exported to Denmark and Malaysia).

henschke ★★★★★

Henschke Road, Keyneton, SA 5353 **region** Eden Valley
phone (08) 8564 8223 **fax** (08) 8564 8294 **open** Mon–Fri 9–4.30, Sat 9–12, public holidays 10–3
winemaker Stephen Henschke **production** 40 000 **est.** 1868
product range ($19–243 CD) From the Henschke Eden Valley sources, Sauvignon Blanc, Sauvignon Blanc Semillon, Cranes Eden Valley Chardonnay, Chenin Blanc, Dry White Frontignac, Joseph Hill Gewurztraminer, Louis Semillon, Tilly's Vineyard, Julius Riesling, Noble Rot Riesling, Johann's Garden Grenache Shiraz Mourvedre, Keyneton Estate, Mount Edelstone, Cyril Henschke Cabernet Sauvignon, Hill of Grace. From the Lenswood Vineyard in the Adelaide Hills, Green's Hill Riesling, Croft Chardonnay, Giles Pinot Noir, Abbott's Prayer Cabernet Merlot.
summary Unchallenged as the best medium-sized red-wine producer in Australia and has gone from strength to strength over the past 16 years or so under the guidance of Stephen and Prue Henschke. The red wines fully capitalise on the very old, low-yielding, high-quality vines and are superbly made with sensitive but positive use of new small oak: Hill of Grace is second only to Penfolds Grange as Australia's red wine icon. Exports to the UK, Switzerland, Italy, Germany, Austria, France, Hong Kong, Malaysia, Taiwan, Fiji, Singapore and Japan.

Henschke Lenswood Croft Chardonnay

🍷🍷🍷🍷 **1999** Medium to full yellow, very advanced for its age; the bouquet, too, while offering ripe peach and attractive spicy oak, is also quite advanced, and it comes as no surprise to find the palate softening off. Possibly an instance of the dreaded random oxidation at work. **rating:** 87

best drinking Now **best vintages** NA **drink with** Gravlax • $34.50

Henschke Mount Edelstone

🍷🍷🍷🍷▽ **1998** Medium red-purple; a fragrant and aromatic bouquet with spicy overtones to the berry and leaf fruit leads into a palate where spice, berry, cherry, leaf and mint are all present in abundance. The oak has been perfectly controlled throughout, and the wine finishes with excellent, fine tannins. **rating:** 93

best drinking 2003–2013 **best vintages** '52, '56, '61, '66, '67, '78, '82, '86, '88, '90, '92, '93, '94, '95, '96, '98 **drink with** Beef bourguignon • $67

Henschke Keyneton Estate Shiraz Cabernet Malbec

🍷🍷🍷🍷▽ **1998** Clear and bright red-purple; a fresh, lively berry-accented bouquet of light to moderate intensity is followed by a sophisticated palate in which everything flows seductively through sweet berry fruit, gently sweet/spicy vanilla oak and soft tannins. **rating:** 93

best drinking 2002–2008 **best vintages** '82, '84, '86, '88, '90, '92, '93, '94, '96, '97, '98 **drink with** Veal chops • $29.99

Henschke Johann's Garden Grenache Shiraz Mourvedre

🍷🍷🍷🍷🍷 **1999** A bargain for Henschke devotees, the bouquet is as redolent as any garden with luscious, juicy plum, prune, berry and licorice fruit, the palate oozing sweet yet not jammy, fruit and has structure. **rating:** 94

best drinking Now–2005 **best vintages** '98, '99 **drink with** Coq au vin • $30

Henschke Abbott's Prayer Cabernet Merlot

🍷🍷🍷🍷 **1998** Medium red-purple; a fragrant leafy/cedary bouquet proclaiming its cool-climate origins and supported by subtle oak leads into some odd green mint flavours on entry to the mouth, but the ship then rights itself with nice structure and fine tannins. **rating:** 88

best drinking 2002–2007 **best vintages** '89, '90, '91, '92, '93, '94, '96, '97, '98 **drink with** Guinea fowl in red wine sauce • $67

Henschke Cyril Henschke Cabernet

🍷🍷🍷🍷 **1997** Medium red-purple; the bouquet has a mix of very ripe, opulent cassis and blackberry fruit together with more fragrant cedary/foresty notes, promising much for the palate. Here, however, cedary, dusty tannins, part oak-derived, part from the fruit, disrupt the flow. **rating:** 87

best drinking 2002–2007 **best vintages** '78, '80, '85, '86, '88, '90, '91, '92, '93, '94, '96 **drink with** Roast lamb • $87.50

henty brook estate NR

Box 49, Dardanup, WA 6236 **region** Geographe
phone (08) 9728 1459 **fax** (08) 9728 1459 **open** By appointment
winemaker James Pennington (Contract) **production** 350 **est.** 1994

product range ($12–16 CD) Sauvignon Blanc Semillon, Shiraz.
summary One hectare each of shiraz and sauvignon blanc and 0.5 hectare of semillon were planted in the spring of 1994 and are still coming into bearing. James Pennington is the contract-winemaker; the first releases now on the market.

heritage estate NR

Granite Belt Drive, Cottonvale, Qld 4375 **region** Granite Belt
phone (07) 4685 2197 **fax** (07) 4685 2112 **open** 7 days 9–5
winemaker Jim Barnes **production** 5000 **est.** 1992
product range ($9.50–35 CD) Semillon, Dry White, Semillon Chardonnay, Harvest Blend, Chardonnay, Club Red, Shiraz, Roswal Shiraz, Merlot, Cabernet Merlot, Fortified and flavoured wines.
summary A very successful winery, with many awards in recent years. Showcases its wines through its winery and cellar door, situated in a refurbished apple cold-store dating from the 1920s. The estate plantings comprise chardonnay (2 hectares), merlot (2 hectares), shiraz (1 hectare) and cabernet sauvignon (1 hectare).

Heritage Estate Cabernet Franc

ΥΥΥΥ **1999** Light to medium red-purple; there is a quite fragrant mix of earthy/dusty/spicy fruit and vanilla oak on the bouquet, the palate adding some reasonably varietal green-leaf characters to the mix. **rating:** 84
best drinking 2002–2006 **best vintages** NA **drink with** Braised rabbit • $19.50

heritage farm wines NR

RMB 1005 Murray Valley Highway, Cobram, Vic 3655 **region** Goulburn Valley
phone (03) 5872 2376 **fax** (03) 5872 2376 **open** 7 days 9–5
winemaker Roy Armfield **production** 2000 **est.** 1987
product range ($5–12 CD) Riesling, Traminer Riesling, Moselle, Chardonnay are varietal releases; there are a considerable number of generic releases and fortified wines on sale at the cellar door.
summary Heritage Farm claims to be the only vineyard and orchard in Australia still using horsepower, with Clydesdales used for most of the general farmwork. The winery and cellar-door area also boasts restored horse-drawn farm machinery and a bottle collection. All wines are sold by mailing list and from the cellar door.

heritage wines ★★★★☆

106a Seppeltsfield Road, Marananga, SA 5355 **region** Barossa Valley
phone (08) 8562 2880 **fax** (08) 8562 2692 **open** 7 days 11–5
winemaker Stephen Hoff **production** 6000 **est.** 1984
product range ($13–22 CD) Riesling, Semillon, Shiraz, Cabernet Malbec, Cabernet Sauvignon, Barossa Shiraz, Rossco's Shiraz.
summary A little-known winery that deserves a far wider audience, for Stephen Hoff is apt to produce some startlingly good wines. At various times the Chardonnay, Riesling (from old Clare Valley vines) and Rossco's Shiraz (now the flagbearer) have all excelled, at other times not. The red wines were emphatically on song in the 1998 vintage. Limited exports to the UK through Australian Wine Agencies.

Heritage Wines Cabernet Sauvignon

ΥΥΥΥΥ **1999** Medium to full red-purple; the bouquet is clean and rich, with full dark berry/currant fruit, the palate following on logically with plush, rich, ripe fruit exactly reproducing the flavours of the bouquet. A particularly good outcome for the vintage. **rating:** 91
best drinking 2004–2010 **best vintages** '98, '99 **drink with** Barbecued beef • $22

hermes morrison wines NR

253 Swan Ponds Road, Woodstock, NSW 2793 **region** Central Ranges Zone
phone (02) 6345 0153 **fax** (02) 6345 0153 **open** 7 days 10–5 summer, winter weekends and public holidays
winemaker Jill Lindsay (Contract) **production** 600 **est.** 1990
product range ($12–15 CD) Riesling, Semillon, Sauvignon Blanc, Chardonnay, Pinot Noir, Shiraz Cabernet.
summary The Morrison family established their Hermes Poll Dorset Stud in 1972, which has now been joined by Hermes Morrison wines. The cellar door stands by the side of a large lake fed by cold, clear water welling up from subterranean caves, and a 10-minute walk takes you to the summit of Mount Palatine, one of the highest peaks in the shire and with a spectacular view of the Canobolas Mountains 80 kilometres away.

herons rise vineyard NR

Saddle Road, Kettering, Tas 7155 **region** Southern Tasmania
phone (03) 6267 4339 **fax** (03) 6267 4245 **open** By appointment
winemaker Andrew Hood **production** 300 **est.** 1984
product range ($14–16.50 CD) Muller Thurgau, Dry White, Pinot Noir.
summary Sue and Gerry White run a small stone country guesthouse in the D'Entrecasteaux Channel area and basically sell the wines produced from the surrounding hectare of vineyard to those staying at the two self-contained cottages. The postal address for bookings is PO Box 271, Kettering, Tas 7155.

Herons Rise Muller Thurgau Riesling

🍷🍷🍷 2000 Medium yellow-green; the bouquet is quite rich, with notes of lime and tropical fruit; the palate is solid, slightly off-dry, and does cloy a little, but no doubt is just what Herons Rise needs. **rating:** 83
best drinking Now **best vintages** NA **drink with** Shellfish • $14

Herons Rise Pinot Noir

🍷🍷🍷 1999 Medium red-purple; a slightly stalky/earthy bouquet is followed by a quintessentially long and slippery palate, with those savoury/stemmy flavours that can work with Pinot Noir like no other red variety. **rating:** 84
best drinking Now–2005 **best vintages** NA **drink with** Roast veal • $16.50

hesperos wines NR

36 Elva Street, Margaret River, WA 6285 **region** Margaret River
phone (08) 9757 3302 **fax** (08) 9757 3302 **open** By appointment
winemaker Jürg Muggli **production** 1250 **est.** 1993
product range ($18.50–30 CD) Sauvignon Blanc, Shiraz.
summary Hesperos is the venture of Jürg Muggli and Sandra Hancock. It supplies Jürg Muggli's winemaking skills to Xanadu, where he has been resident winemaker for many years. It also has a 30-hectare property near Witchcliffe between Cape Mentelle and Devil's Lair, with the potential of 15 hectares of vineyard; planting started in the winter of 1999. In the meantime the Hesperos wines are made from purchased grapes; the first wine produced under the Hesperos label was a 1993 Shiraz, followed by a 1995 Sauvignon Blanc. Shiraz and Sauvignon Blanc have been produced in each successive vintage. Exports to Japan, Switzerland and Germany.

hewitson ★★★★☆

16 McGowan Avenue, Unley, SA 5061 **region** Warehouse
phone (08) 8271 5755 **fax** (08) 8271 5570 **open** Not
winemaker Dean Hewitson **production** 4500 **est.** 1996
product range ($18–37 R) La Source Eden Valley Riesling, L'Oizeau Shiraz, Old Garden Mourvedre, Barossa Shiraz, Barossa Valley Grenache.
summary Dean Hewitson was a Petaluma winemaker for ten years, and during that time managed to do three vintages in France and one in Oregon as well as undertaking his Masters at UC Davis, California. It is hardly surprising that the Hewitson wines are immaculately made from a technical viewpoint. However, he has also managed to source 30-year-old riesling from the Eden Valley and 70-year-old shiraz from McLaren Vale for his first two releases, following on with a Barossa Valley Mourvedre produced from 145-year-old vines at Rowland Flat, and a Barossa Valley Shiraz and Grenache coming from 60-year-old vines at Tanunda. The vineyards are now under long-term contracts to Ian Hewitson. Exports to New Zealand, China, Japan, Malaysia, Singapore, the US, Canada, Finland, the Netherlands, Norway, Germany and the UK.

Hewitson Barossa Shiraz

🍷🍷🍷🍷 1999 Medium to full purple-red; the moderately intense bouquet is clean, with firm berry/cherry fruit at the wheel. The palate has sweet plum and cherry fruit, with appealing soft tannins running right through the length of the palate; well-controlled oak. Impressive outcome for an ordinary vintage. **rating:** 90
best drinking 2002–2009 **best vintages** '98, '99 **drink with** Kangaroo fillet • $37

Hewitson L'Oizeau Shiraz

🍷🍷🍷🍷🍷 1998 Medium to full red-purple; the bouquet is sweet, rich and ripe, with a dazzling array of licorice, vanilla and dark berry aromas. The palate is powerful, with plum, black cherry, licorice and more savoury touches, all supported by perfectly judged and integrated oak. **rating:** 94
best drinking 2003–2013 **best vintages** '97, '98 **drink with** Hearty red-meat dishes • $37

Hewitson Old Garden Mourvedre

YYYY **1999** Medium red-purple; clean, soft and sweet raspberry fruit on the bouquet is repeated on the sweet, soft raspberry and plum palate, with judiciously controlled tannins and oak. **rating:** 87

best drinking Now–2005 **best vintages** NA **drink with** Devilled kidneys • $37

Hewitson Grenache

YYY **1999** Medium red-purple; the bouquet is clean, with juicy/minty fruit aromas, the palate offering similar juicy/minty/jammy berry fruit which, despite all the flavour, lacks complexity in structural terms. **rating:** 84

best drinking Now–2004 **best vintages** NA **drink with** Italian • $24

hickinbotham NR

Nepean Highway (near Wallaces Road), Dromana, Vic 3936 **region** Mornington Peninsula
phone (03) 5981 0355 **fax** (03) 5981 0355 **open** 7 days
winemaker Andrew Hickinbotham **production** 3000 **est.** 1981
product range ($14–28 CD) Chardonnay, MP Chardonnay with Aligote, Taminga, Sparkling (Strawberry Kiss), Family Reserve Pinot Noir, Jackal's Run Shiraz Cabernet Grenache, MP Merlot, MP Shiraz, MP Cabernet Merlot.
summary After a peripatetic period and a hiatus in winemaking, Hickinbotham established a permanent vineyard and winery base at Dromana. It now makes only Mornington Peninsula wines, drawing in part on 5 hectares of estate vineyards, and in part on contract-grown fruit. The wines are principally sold through cellar door and mail order.

Hickinbotham Family Reserve Pinot Noir

YYYY **1998** Medium red-purple; the bouquet opens with solid, sweet plummy fruit, then shows some more foresty characters before the palate switches back to very sweet, almost jammy, plummy fruit with a good sprinkling of spice. An unusual wine in many ways. **rating:** 86

best drinking Now–2003 **best vintages** NA **drink with** Asian game or bird dishes • $28

hidden creek 

Eukey Road, Ballandean, Qld 4382 **region** Granite Belt
phone (07) 4684 1383 **fax** (07) 4684 1355 **open** Mon–Fri 12–3, weekends 10–4
winemaker Adrien Kuffer **production** 1400 **est.** 1998
product range ($13.50–18 CD) Semillon, Chardonnay, Mountain Muscat, Shiraz, First Block Shiraz, Merlot.
summary A beautifully located vineyard and winery on a ridge overlooking the Ballandean township and the Severn River Valley, separated from Girraween National Park by Doctors Creek. The granite boulder-strewn hills mean that the 70-hectare property will only provide a little over 6 hectares of vineyard, in turn divided into six different blocks. The two wines tasted to date were of modest but acceptable quality.

hidden river estate NR

Mullineaux Road, Pemberton, WA 6260 **region** Pemberton
phone (08) 9776 1437 **fax** (08) 9776 0189 **open** 7 days 9–4
winemaker Brenden Smith **production** 1500 **est.** 1994
product range ($14.50–24 ML) Three Feathers Blend Semillon Sauvignon Blanc Chardonnay, Unwooded Chardonnay, Wooded Chardonnay, Late Picked Riesling, Authentic Basket Press Shiraz, Cabernet Sauvignon, Aged Cell Door Tawny Port.
summary Phil and Sandy Goldring spent ten years operating farm chalets in the Pemberton area before selling the business and retiring to become grape-growers, with the intention of selling the grapes to others. However, they found old habits hard to kick, so opened a cellar-door sales and café/restaurant, and planned to establish a boutique brewery on site in 2001. It is a business with a very strong marketing push, a 1901 Kalgoorlie tram having been purchased, renovated and installed on site to provide more seating for the restaurant. I hope the Goldrings did not pay much for the tram.

highbank NR

Riddoch Highway, Coonawarra, SA 5263 **region** Coonawarra
phone (08) 8736 3311 **fax** (08) 8736 3122 **open** By appointment
winemaker Dennis Vice, Trevor Mast **production** 1000 **est.** 1986
product range ($40 CD) Chardonnay, Basket Pressed Cabernet Blend, Basket Pressed Cabernet Sauvignon.

summary Mount Gambier lecturer in viticulture Dennis Vice makes a tiny quantity of smooth, melon-accented Chardonnay and stylish Coonawarra Cabernet Blend of good quality that is sold through local restaurants and cellar door, with limited Melbourne distribution. Intermittent exports to various countries.

highland heritage estate ★★★☆

Mitchell Highway, Orange, NSW 2800 **region** Orange
phone (02) 6361 3612 **fax** (02) 6361 3613 **open** Mon–Fri 9–3, weekends 9–5
winemaker John Hordern, Rex D'Aquino **production** 3500 **est.** 1984
product range ($10–30 CD) Under the Mount Canobolas label: Chardonnay, Sauvignon Blanc, Pinot Noir; Gosling Creek Chardonnay; and the newly released Wellwood Estate label.
summary The estate plantings have increased from 4 hectares to over 15 hectares, with new plantings in 1995 and 1997 to come into full production by 2001. The tasting facility is unusual: a converted railway carriage overlooking the vineyard.

highway wines NR

612 Great Northern Highway, Herne Hill, WA 6056 **region** Swan District
phone (08) 9296 4354 **open** Mon–Sat 8.30–6
winemaker Tony Bakranich **production** 4000 **est.** 1954
product range ($5–14.50 CD) Exclusively Fortified wines, of which 20 are available, including six different styles of Sherry, six Muscats, three Ports, and so forth.
summary A survivor of another era, when literally dozens of such wineries plied their business in the Swan Valley. It still enjoys a strong local trade, selling much of its wine in fill-your-own-containers and 2-litre flagons, with lesser quantities sold by the bottle.

hill-smith estate 

PO Box 10, Angaston, SA 5353 **region** Eden Valley
phone (08) 8561 3200 **fax** (08) 8561 3393 **open** At Yalumba
winemaker Robert Hill-Smith, Hugh Reimers **production** 3500 **est.** 1973
product range ($18 R) Sauvignon Blanc, Chardonnay.
summary Part of the Yalumba stable, drawing upon its own estate plantings comprising 23 hectares of chardonnay and sauvignon blanc. Over the years has produced some excellent wines, but quality does seem to vary significantly with vintage, and the winery rating is a compromise between the best and the least. Exports to all major markets.

Hill-Smith Estate Sauvignon Blanc

YYYY **2000** Light green-yellow; the bouquet is clean and soft, with some tropical and gooseberry fruit, the medium-bodied palate moving more into the herbaceous/mineral spectrum, but then closing with a slightly spongy finish. **rating:** 85
best drinking Now **best vintages** '86, '92, '93, '94, '95, '96, '99 **drink with** Fresh mussels • $17.99

hills of plenty NR

370 Yan Yean Road, Yarrambat, Vic 3091 **region** Port Phillip Zone
phone (03) 9436 2264 **fax** (03) 9436 2264 **open** Last Sun of each month 12–5, or by appointment
winemaker Karen Coulston **production** 400 **est.** 1998
product range ($14–20 ML) Riesling, Sauvignon Blanc, Chardonnay, Pinot Noir, Cabernet Sauvignon.
summary Hills of Plenty has been established just outside the Melbourne metropolitan area, a few minutes' drive north of Greensborough. There is a tiny 0.2-hectare vineyard of riesling, chardonnay and cabernet sauvignon around the winery, but most of the fruit is purchased from other regions, notably Geelong, Gippsland and Swan Hill. The tiny production means that the cellar door only opens once a month, but it is turned into a festive occasion with live music, and picnics or barbecues welcome.

hillstowe 

104 Main Road, Hahndorf, SA 5245 **region** Adelaide Hills
phone (08) 8388 1400 **fax** (08) 8388 1411 **open** 7 days 10–5
winemaker Chris Laurie **production** 14 000 **est.** 1980

product range ($15.95–45 R) A range of vineyard and varietal-designated wines of ascending price and quality, being Buxton Sauvignon Blanc, Chardonnay, Buxton Shiraz, Buxton Cabernet Merlot; and at the top end, Adelaide Hills Udy's Mill Chardonnay, Udy's Mill Pinot Noir, Mary's Hundred Shiraz, The Pinch Row Lenswood Merlot.

summary Founded by renowned viticulturist David Paxton and Chris Laurie, but now owned by the latter and his family. Its principal vineyard, Udy's Mill, at Lenswood has 17 hectares planted, supplementing McLaren Vale grapes coming from the Buxton Vineyard. The wines are exported to the UK, Canada, the US, Europe and Asia.

Hillstowe Lenswood Pinot Gris

🍷🍷🍷🍷🍷 **2000** Pale pink tones to the colour are acceptable within the context of the variety. The bouquet is clean, with spice, mineral and a hint of pear followed by a palate in which the flavours are hard to define, other than being vaguely flowery, allied with a touch of the pear of the bouquet. Good length. **rating:** 90

best drinking Now–2004 **best vintages** NA **drink with** Blue swimmer crab • $28

Hillstowe The Pinch Row Lenswood Merlot

🍷🍷🍷🍷🍷 **1998** Bright purple-red; the bouquet is clean, with moderately sweet, small berry fruit and subtle oak. The palate vibrates with layer upon layer of fresh, juicy, red berry fruit, so much so, indeed, that it gives the impression of being slightly callow. Time in bottle should sort this out. **rating:** 91

best drinking 2003–2008 **best vintages** '98 **drink with** Osso bucco • $45

hills view vineyards NR

11 Main Avenue, Frewville, SA 5063 **region** McLaren Vale
phone (08) 8338 0666 **fax** (08) 8338 0666 **open** Not
winemaker Brett Howard **production** 12 000 **est.** 1998

product range ($10–30 R) Three ranges of wines produced: Blewitt Springs Semillon, Chardonnay, Shiraz and Cabernet Sauvignon; Howard Fleurieu Semillon and Coonawarra Shiraz; Hills View Chardonnay Verdelho, Shiraz Cabernet and Cabernet Merlot.

summary District veteran Brett Howard, with 20 years winemaking experience, is now the winemaker for Hills View Vineyards, producing the Hills View Vineyards range of wines, the Blewitt Springs range and the single wine under the Howard label. The latter is a Coonawarra Shiraz released only in the best vintages.

Blewitt Springs Shiraz

🍷🍷🍷🍷 **1999** Medium purple-red; there is a mix of ripe cherry/berry fruit allied with more minty/leafy aromas on the bouquet. The light- to medium-bodied palate is still coming together, with cherry, plum and a touch of earth; the oak influence throughout is minimal. **rating:** 84

🍷🍷🍷🍷🍷 **1998** Medium to full red-purple; the bouquet is clean, rich and with classic cherry, plum and vanilla aromas. The palate is extremely rich, yet not over the top, with sweet, ripe cherry and plum fruit, the oak nicely controlled, and the tannins soft. **rating:** 91

best drinking 2004–2009 **best vintages** '98 **drink with** Home-made steak and mushroom pie • $16.95

Blewitt Springs Cabernet Sauvignon

🍷🍷🍷🍷 **1998** Medium red-purple; the bouquet is quite light and clean, with fresh, red berry fruit. The palate is in similar style, fresh, fruit-driven and not aspiring to complexity. **rating:** 84

best drinking 2000–2005 **best vintages** '98 **drink with** Veal chops • $15.95

hjt vineyards NR

Keenan Road, Glenrowan, Vic 3675 **region** Glenrowan
phone (03) 5766 2252 **fax** (03) 5765 3260 **open** Fri, Sat 10–5 and Sunday during school holidays
winemaker Wendy Tinson **production** 1200 **est.** 1979

product range ($11.50–17.50 CD) A varietal range, with occasional use of bin numbers denoting winemaking approaches, Bin 4 being more delicate, Bin 19 fuller-bodied. Wines include Riesling Bins 4 and 19, Chardonnay, Chenin Blanc Bin 19, Late Picked Riesling, Pinot Noir, Cabernet Pinot, Shiraz, Cabernet Sauvignon, Merlot, Tawny Port.

summary Founded by the late Harry Tinson after he left Baileys following a long and illustrious stewardship, and now run by his daughter Wendy Tinson, with tiny production all sold from the cellar door. No recent tastings, alas.

hoffmann's NR

Ingoldby Road, McLaren Flat, SA 5171 **region** McLaren Vale
phone (08) 8383 0232 **fax** (08) 8383 0232 **open** 7 days 11–5
winemaker Nick Holmes (Consultant) **production** 1000 **est.** 1996
product range ($14–18 CD) Chardonnay, Shiraz, Cabernet Sauvignon.
summary Peter and Anthea Hoffmann have been growing grapes at their property in Ingoldby Road since 1978, and Peter Hoffmann has worked at various wineries in McLaren Vale since 1979. Both he and Anthea have undertaken courses at the Regency TAFE Institute in Adelaide, and (in Peter Hoffmann's words) 'in 1996 we decided that we knew a little about winemaking and opened a small cellar door'.

hollick ★★★★

Riddoch Highway, Coonawarra, SA 5263 **region** Coonawarra
phone (08) 8737 2318 **fax** (08) 8737 2952 **open** 7 days 9–5
winemaker Ian Hollick, David Norman **production** 30 000 **est.** 1983
product range ($15–60 R) A very disciplined array of products with Riesling, Sauvignon Blanc Semillon, Unoaked Chardonnay, Pinot Noir and Shiraz Cabernet Sauvignon at the lower end of the price range; Reserve Chardonnay, Cabernet Sauvignon Merlot and The Nectar (sweet) in the middle, along with Sparkling Merlot; Ravenswood, the deluxe Cabernet Sauvignon and Wilgha Shiraz at the top end. Also small range of limited cellar-door releases.
summary Hollick has, if it were possible, added to the reputation of Coonawarra since it released its first wines in the mid-1980s. Winner of many trophies (including the most famous of all, the Jimmy Watson), its wines are well crafted and competitively priced, although sometimes a little on the light side. National distribution in all States; exports to the UK, the US, New Zealand, Canada, Hong Kong, Singapore, Malaysia, New Zealand, Denmark, Belgium, Holland and Switzerland.

Hollick Riesling

ΥΥΥΥ **2000** Light straw-green; crisp mineral/talc/slate aromas join with lime on the bouquet. An attractively fresh mix of lime and mineral follows on the palate, which has good length. **rating:** 87
best drinking Now–2006 **best vintages** '99 **drink with** Light seafood • $16.80

Hollick Neilson's Block Merlot

ΥΥΥΥ **1999** Medium red-purple; bright, clean, soft berry fruit seems to have soaked up the oak on both the bouquet and palate. The latter is elegant, with more texture and structure than the bouquet, the sweet oak coming to the fore along with silky/soft tannins on the finish. Carries a pretty hefty price tag. **rating:** 87
best drinking 2003–2008 **best vintages** NA **drink with** Cassoulet • $55

Hollick Ravenswood

ΥΥΥΥ **1998** Medium red, with some purple, and not 100 per cent bright; the savoury, earthy, blackberry fruit with well-integrated oak on the bouquet is followed by a savoury, reserved palate that doesn't have the ripe berry fruit of many '98s, but is well constructed, and will have particular appeal to those who don't like what they call 'lollipop' wines. **rating:** 88
best drinking 2003–2010 **best vintages** '88, '90, '91, '93, '94 **drink with** Scotch fillet • $60

hollyclare NR

940 Milbrodale Road, Broke, NSW 2330 **region** Lower Hunter Valley
phone (02) 6579 1193 **fax** (02) 6579 1269 **open** Weekends 10–5 by appointment
winemaker Tamburlaine (Contract) **production** 2000 **est.** 1987
product range ($15–20 CD) Semillon, Unwooded Semillon, Chardonnay, Chardonnay Semillon, Shiraz.
summary John Holdsworth established the Hollyclare Vineyard (now totalling 3 hectares of chardonnay, semillon and shiraz) ten years ago, but the Hollyclare label is a relatively new one on the market. While the wines are made under contract at Tamburlaine, Hollyclare has its own dedicated wine tanks and all of the wines are estate-grown.

holly folly NR

649 Campersic Road, Baskerville, WA 6056 **region** Swan District
phone (08) 9296 2043 **fax** (08) 9296 2043 **open** Not
winemaker Peter Hollingworth **production** 400 **est.** 1995

product range ($8.50–12.50 ML) Dry White, Chenin Blanc, Verdelho (both Barrel Fermented and Barrel Aged), Marsanne, Chardonnay, Merlot, Petit Verdot, Grenache, Light Red, Sparkling.

summary Peter Hollingworth clearly has a sense of humour and a sense of perspective. He began the establishment of the 11.5 hectares of vineyards (planted to chenin blanc, chardonnay, viognier, marsanne, verdelho, petit verdot, grenache and merlot) in 1995, but it was not until 2000 that the necessary producer's licence was obtained, and in October of that year he embarked upon the limited release of the 400-case production, destined mainly for friends and acquaintances. Given the size of the plantings, production will no doubt increase in the years ahead, although part of the grape supply is sold to others in the valley.

holm oak ★★★★

RSD 256 Rowella, West Tamar, Tas 7270 **region** Northern Tasmania
phone (03) 6394 7577 **fax** (03) 6394 7350 **open** 7 days 10–5
winemaker Nick Butler, Julian Alcorso **production** 3000 **est.** 1983
product range ($16–25 R) Riesling, Chardonnay, Reserve Chardonnay, Tyrian Rosé, Pinot Noir, Cabernet Sauvignon.

summary The Butler family produces tremendously rich and strongly flavoured red wines from the vineyard situated on the banks of the Tamar River, and which takes its name from the grove of oak trees planted about the turn of the century and originally intended for the making of tennis racquets. Together with Marion's Vineyard, it suggests that this section of the Tamar Valley may even be too warm for pinot noir in some vintages; certainly it is well suited to cabernet sauvignon and chardonnay.

Holm Oak Riesling

2000 Medium green-yellow; a highly aromatic bouquet with passionfruit and pineapple is followed by a palate with intense flavours identical to those of the bouquet; it might be argued some of these characters are a sign of slight reduction. **rating:** 91

best drinking 2003–2008 **best vintages** '99, '00 **drink with** Sweet and sour pork • NA

Holm Oak Chardonnay

1999 Medium to full yellow-green; the bouquet is big and slightly broad, with peach and nectarine aromas, and full, rich, ripe fruit on the palate providing masses of flavour. **rating:** 84

best drinking Now–2003 **best vintages** NA **drink with** Fish and chips • NA

Holm Oak Botrytis Riesling

2000 Medium yellow-green; intense botrytis lime aromas lead into an intense, long, lingering palate with the varietal character preserved rather than obliterated by botrytis, finishing with crisp, lingering acidity. **rating:** 93

best drinking Now–2006 **best vintages** '00 **drink with** Fresh fruit • NA

Holm Oak Pinot Noir

1999 Dark red-purple; ripe, dark plum aromas are, perhaps surprisingly, without any pruney overtones. The palate follows down the same track, with thick, ripe plummy fruit tightening up and lengthening on the finish. Even better than the '98. **rating:** 92

best drinking 2002–2008 **best vintages** '98, '99 **drink with** Quail • NA

Holm Oak Cabernet Sauvignon

1999 Medium red-purple; the bouquet has cassis and some greener notes, the palate likewise running through cassis, leaf and mint, finishing with soft tannins. **rating:** 86

best drinking 2003–2008 **best vintages** NA **drink with** Sirloin • NA

home hill NR

73 Nairn Street, Ranelagh, Tas 7109 **region** Southern Tasmania
phone (03) 6264 1028 **fax** (03) 6264 1069 **open** 7 days 10–5
winemaker Michael Vishacki, Stefano Lubiana (Contract), Jim Chatto (Contract) **production** 1900 **est.** 1994
product range ($12–21.50 ML) Chardonnay, Kelly's Reserve Chardonnay, Dry White, Pinot Noir.

summary Terry and Rosemary Bennett planted their first half-hectare of vines in 1994 on gentle slopes in the beautiful Huon Valley. The plantings were quickly extended to 3 hectares, with another hectare planted in 1999. Production has increased to the point where a cellar door, winery and restaurant are planned to open by the end of 2001.

Home Hill Pinot Noir

🍷🍷🍷🍷 **1999** Light to medium red-purple; a stylish, spicy/stemmy bouquet leads into a no less stylish, although somewhat advanced, palate, where spicy/foresty overtones to the small berry fruit give length to the finish.

rating: 85

best drinking Now–2004 **best vintages** NA **drink with** Smoked quail • $18

honeytree estate NR

16 Gillards Road, Pokolbin, NSW 2321 **region** Lower Hunter Valley
phone (02) 4998 7693 **fax** (02) 4998 7693 **open** Wed–Thurs 11–4, Fri–Sun 10–5
winemaker Contract **production** 3600 **est.** 1970
product range ($10–25 CD) Semillon, Traminer, Clairette, Old Vine Shiraz, Cabernet Sauvignon, Port.
summary The Honeytree Estate vineyard was first planted in 1970, and for a period of time wines were produced under the Honeytree Estate label. It then disappeared, but has since been revived. Its 10 hectares of vines are of shiraz, cabernet sauvignon, semillon and a little clairette, known in the Hunter Valley as blanquette, and a variety which has been in existence there for well over a century. Jancis Robinson comments that the wine 'tends to be very high in alcohol, a little low in acid and to oxidise dangerously fast', but in a sign of the times the first Honeytree Clairette sold out so quickly (in four weeks) that 2.2 hectares of vineyard has been grafted over to additional clairette.

Honeytree Estate Shiraz

🍷🍷🍷½ **1999** Medium red-purple; there are slight leafy/earthy edges to the berry fruit of the bouquet, but rather more sweet, dark cherry fruit on the medium-bodied palate. Finishes with fine, grainy tannins, and should improve with time in bottle.

rating: 84

best drinking 2004–2008 **best vintages** NA **drink with** Shepherd's pie • $20

hope estate ★★★★

Cobcroft Road, Broke, NSW 2330 **region** Lower Hunter Valley
phone (02) 6579 1161 **fax** (02) 6579 1373 **open** 7 days 10–4
winemaker Peter Howland **production** 30 000 **est.** 1996
product range ($15–20 CD) Semillon, Verdelho, Unwooded Chardonnay, Chardonnay, Botrytised Semillon, Blanc de Noir, Shiraz, Merlot, Cabernet Merlot, Cabernet Sauvignon.
summary Pharmacist Michael Hope has come a long way since acquiring his first vineyard in the Hunter Valley in 1994. The Hunter Valley empire now encompasses three substantial vineyards and the former Saxonvale Winery, acquired in 1996, renamed Hope Estate, and refurbished at a cost of over $1 million. That, however, proved to be only the first step, for Hope has acquired most of the assets of the former public-listed Vincorp, including its Donnybrook Vineyard in Western Australia, and a $6 million acquisition of the Virgin Hills brand, its original 14-hectare vineyard, another nearby 32-hectare vineyard at Glenhope, a lease of the historic winery, and the acquisition of all Virgin Hills stocks. In the middle of all this Hope Estate has managed to produce some excellent wines thanks to the skills of winemaker Peter Howland. The wines are exported to the US, the UK, Germany and New Zealand.

Hope Estate Semillon

🍷🍷🍷🍷 **2000** Light straw-green; the bouquet ranges through herb, spice and capsicum, the palate retaining grip and freshness notwithstanding the alcohol, replaying the capsicum and herb flavours promised by the bouquet. Well balanced.

rating: 89

best drinking 2003–2008 **best vintages** NA **drink with** Balmain bugs • $15.90

Hope Estate Verdelho

🍷🍷🍷½ **1999** Light to medium green-yellow; while no particular character dominates the bouquet, it has distinctly greater complexity than most Verdelhos. The palate provides the same structure, with gently ripe fruit and subliminal hints of vanilla.

rating: 84

best drinking Now–2003 **best vintages** NA **drink with** Chicken • NA

Hope Estate Chardonnay

🍷🍷🍷🍷½ **1999** Medium to full yellow-green; the bouquet is truly complex, with barrel-ferment, cashew, fig and peach aromas. There is an abundance of presence and flavour to the palate, with a hint of sweetness that may be fruit, glycerol, alcohol or residual sugar, but not so high as to rob the wine of its undoubted character. It was the only gold medal at the 2000 Sydney Wine Show in Class 28, Dry White Table Wine Full-Bodied.

rating: 90

best drinking Now–2003 **best vintages** '99 **drink with** Roast turkey • $17.80

Hope Estate Shiraz

1999 Medium to full purple-red; smooth, ripe plummy fruit with well-integrated oak on the bouquet is followed by a palate with rich, ripe dark fruit flavours; it is the texture and structure of the wine, however, that really grabs the attention, with particularly good oak and tannin management. **rating:** 91

best drinking 2004–2009 **best vintages** '99 **drink with** Venison • $19.80

Hope Estate Merlot

1999 Medium red-purple; very lemony/olivaceous/savoury/earthy aromas are reflected in the savoury palate. Here the strength is the fine structure and feel to the tannins, wholly appropriate to Merlot. It is simply that the fruit has its limitations. **rating:** 85

best drinking 2002–2006 **best vintages** NA **drink with** Braised veal • $19.80

hoppers hill vineyards NR

Googodery Road, Cumnock, NSW 2867 **region** Central Ranges Zone
phone (02) 6367 7270 **open** Weekends 11–5
winemaker Robert Gilmore **production** NFP **est.** 1990
product range ($10–12 CD) Chardonnay, Sauvignon Blanc, Dry White, Cabernet Franc Merlot, Cabernet Sauvignon.
summary The Gilmores planted their vineyard in 1980, using organic growing methods and using no preservatives or filtration in the winery, which was established in 1990. Not surprisingly, the wines cannot be judged or assessed against normal standards, but may have appeal in a niche market.

horndale NR

Fraser Avenue, Happy Valley, SA 5159 **region** McLaren Vale
phone (08) 8387 0033 **fax** (08) 8387 0033 **open** Mon–Sat 9–6, Sun and public holidays 10–5.30
winemaker Phil Albrecht **production** NFP **est.** 1896
product range ($8.90–17.90 CD) Riesling, Colombard Semillon Chardonnay, Semillon Chardonnay, Chardonnay, Shiraz Cabernet, Cabernet Merlot, Shiraz Grenache, Cabernet Sauvignon Cabernet Franc, Cabernet Sauvignon; a wide range of dessert and fortified wines.
summary Established in 1896 and has remained continuously in production in one way or another since that time, but there have been a number of changes of ownership and direction, and the wines are only available from the cellar door and mail order. A personal connection is the Horndale Brandy my father used to buy 50 years ago, although it no longer appears on the extensive price list.

horseshoe vineyard NR

Horseshoe Road, Horseshoe Valley, via Denman, NSW 2328 **region** Upper Hunter Valley
phone (02) 6547 3528 **open** Weekends 9–5
winemaker John Hordern **production** NFP **est.** 1986
product range ($13–18 CD) Classic Hunter Semillon, Chardonnay Semillon, Chardonnay, Pinot Noir.
summary Fell by the wayside after its wonderful start in 1986, with rich, full-flavoured, barrel-fermented Semillons and Chardonnays. The '87 Semillon was exhibited in the Museum Class at the 1996 Hunter Valley Wine Show and was still drinking beautifully, winning a strong silver medal. Younger vintages do not have the same magic.

hotham wines 

South Wandering Road, Wandering, WA 6308 **region** Margaret River
phone (08) 9884 1525 **open** By appointment
winemaker James Pennington, Gary Baldwin (Consultant) **production** 5000 **est.** 1987
product range ($14.50–39 CD) Semillon, Semillon Sauvignon Blanc, Chenin Blanc, Dryandra White, Chardonnay, Cabernet Merlot, Sandalwood Red, Classic Dry White, Cabernets.

summary Situated in a region of its own making, 120 kilometres southeast of Perth, it has a continental climate with cold winters and hot summer days but cool nights, tempered by the altitude of 350 metres. Some exceptionally good wines have been made by former science teacher and now Charles Sturt University graduate James Pennington, on whose family property Hotham Valley Estate is established, albeit by way of a subdivision with outside investment. A state-of-the-art winery was built in 1993. Further details for the Hotham empire appear under the Wildwood (Margaret River) entry. James Pennington has also created considerable interest with a patented development of oak treatment using sandalwood. Exports to the UK.

Hotham Cabernet Sauvignon

YYYY **1999** Medium red-purple; the ripe, ribena berry aromas verge on the stewed, with more very ripe berry/chocolatey fruit running through the palate. Gives the impression of having been picked a little too late. **rating:** 85

best drinking 2002–2007 **best vintages** NA **drink with** Lamb casserole • $39

houghton ★★★★★

Dale Road, Middle Swan, WA 6056 **region** Swan District

phone (08) 9274 5100 **fax** (08) 9274 5372 **open** 7 days 10–5, except Christmas Day and Good Friday

winemaker Larry Cherubino **production** 300 000 **est.** 1836

product range ($9.90–65 R) Semillon Sauvignon Blanc, Chardonnay Verdelho, White Burgundy, Show Reserve White Burgundy, Chardonnay, Late Picked Verdelho, Cabernet Shiraz Merlot; Crofters Semillon Sauvignon Blanc, Chardonnay, Cabernet Merlot; finally, the super-premium Jack Mann (Cabernet blend).

summary The five-star rating may seem extreme but is very deliberate, and is in no small measure justified by Houghton White Burgundy, one of Australia's largest-selling white wines (and which is almost entirely consumed within days of purchase, but which is superlative with seven or so years' bottle age). To borrow a phrase of the late Jack Mann, 'There are no bad wines here.' Former winemaker Paul Lapsley's abundant winemaking skills brought the Jack Mann red and the Houghton Reserve Shiraz to the very forefront of Australian wine quality.

Houghton Chardonnay Verdelho

YYYY **2000** Light green-yellow; a fragrant, passionfruit-accented bouquet in inimitable style, with a near repetition on the palate. Lively nectarine and citrus flavours have a strikingly different fruit register to east coast flavours. **rating:** 85

best drinking Now **best vintages** NA **drink with** Asian seafood • $11.99

Houghton Crofters Semillon Sauvignon Blanc

YYYY **2000** Light green-yellow; intense herbaceous fruit leaps from the glass, with no sign of the reduction that sometimes seems endemic to this blend in Western Australia. The palate softens slightly, which is no bad thing, resulting in pleasant mouthfeel and balance, yet retaining the positive fruit of the bouquet. **rating:** 87

best drinking Now–2003 **best vintages** '96 **drink with** Lemon chicken • NA

Houghton White Burgundy

YYYY **2000** Arguably an article of faith, for it is more to do with five years time than today. Most will never know, happy to enjoy the gentle, passionfruit and tropical fruit aroma and flavour of today and eschew the rich, honeyed complexity of maturity. **rating:** 87

best drinking Now–2006 **best vintages** '83, '87, '89, '91, '93, '95, '99, '00 **drink with** Trout mousse • $11.99

Houghton Crofters Chardonnay

YYYYY **2000** Light green-yellow; charry barrel-ferment oak makes the first statement on the bouquet, followed by tight grapefruit aromas. Grapefruit and melon come through on the palate, and then the barrel-ferment characters. Needs 12 months to sort itself out, but did win a gold medal at the 2001 Royal Sydney Wine Show in the premium classes. **rating:** 91

YYYYY **1999** Medium yellow-green; a complex and stylish bouquet with grapefruit and melon, and perfectly integrated barrel-ferment oak. An elegant, lingering and fine palate with identical grapefruit and melon flavours, and the same subtle oak. Two well-deserved gold medals to its credit. **rating:** 93

best drinking 2002–2006 **best vintages** '97, '98, '99, '00 **drink with** Crumbed brains • NA

Houghton Cabernet Shiraz Merlot

YYYYY **1999** This was a pretty snappy vintage for much of the west, and it shows in this wine. Good colour; ripe, blackberry/blackcurrant fruit on the bouquet is followed by an ample, fruit-driven palate with abundant fruit flavour and extract, finishing with nicely rounded tannins. **rating:** 90

best drinking Now–2005 **best vintages** '99 **drink with** Barbecued meat • $11.99

Houghton Crofters Cabernet Merlot

▼▼▼▼▼ **1999** Dense purple-red; intense, concentrated dark berry/blackberry fruit has soaked up the oak in which it was matured, powering both the bouquet and palate. Lingering and powerful tannins on the palate guarantee what the colour and fruit have already suggested: a long life. **rating:** 94

best drinking 2004–2014 **best vintages** '94, '95, '97, '98, '99 **drink with** Kangaroo • $22.99

howard park ★★★★★

Miamup Road, Cowaramup, WA 6284 **region** Great Southern
phone (08) 9755 9988 **fax** (08) 9755 9048 **open** 7 days 10–5
winemaker Michael Kerrigan, James Kellie **production** 100 000 **est.** 1986
product range ($17–75 R) Madfish Premium Dry White and Red provide low-priced volume; limited quantities of Howard Park Riesling, Chardonnay, Botrytis Semillon, Leston Shiraz, Cabernet Merlot, Scotsdale Cabernet Merlot, Scotsdale Cabernet Sauvignon.
summary In the wake of its acquisition by the Birch family, the emphasis has switched from the Great Southern; a splendid new winery has been constructed in the Margaret River region (incorporating Feng Shui principles) to complement the (near new) Denmark winery. Michael Kerrigan has become chief winemaker, and it seems new wines have joined the product range. Howard Park has 230 hectares of estate and selected long-term contract vineyards in all of the best regions for cool-climate fruit production in southern Western Australia. The philosophy is to source fruit from the region best suited to a particular variety, thus flagship Howard Park Cabernet Merlot has Cabernet Sauvignon from Margaret River and Mount Barker with Cabernet Franc from the Frankland River and Merlot from Pemberton. Exports to the US, Canada, New Zealand, the UK, Belgium, Switzerland, Malaysia, Singapore, Hong Kong and Japan.

Howard Park Riesling

▼▼▼▼▽ **2000** Light to medium yellow-green; the bouquet is typically clean, crisp and fresh, with a range of mineral, herb, citrus and apple aromas. The palate is very tight and crisp, with powerful, minerally acid; an austere wine which really needs to be left alone for a while. **rating:** 90

best drinking 2003–2010 **best vintages** '91, '93, '94, '95, '96, '97, '98, '99 **drink with** Fresh asparagus, Asian seafood • $22.34

Howard Park Madfish Premium Dry White

▼▼▼▼ **2000** Light green-yellow; the moderately intense bouquet has an appealing mix of stonefruit, citrus and gooseberry aromas, the palate with gently ripe fruit in a stonefruit and citrus spectrum, flowing smoothly across the tongue and into the finish. **rating:** 89

best drinking Now **best vintages** '00 **drink with** Chicken • $17

Howard Park Chardonnay

▼▼▼▼▽ **1999** Light to medium green-yellow; a spotlessly clean and fresh bouquet with nectarine and nicely tuned oak is followed by a fine, elegant citrus/nectarine palate, perhaps a tad too fine for some. Sheraton gold medal winner 2000. **rating:** 92

best drinking Now–2004 **best vintages** '93, '94, '95, '96, '97, '99 **drink with** Pan-fried veal • $35.74

Howard Park Leston Shiraz

▼▼▼▼▽ **1999** Medium to full red-purple; there is a sophisticated fusion of fruit and French oak on the spicy, savoury bouquet, with the smooth, ripe cherry fruit coming to the fore on the palate. Nicely controlled spicy oak puts the seal on some smart winemaking. **rating:** 93

best drinking 2003–2009 **best vintages** '99 **drink with** Spiced lamb with couscous • $33

Howard Park Cabernet Sauvignon Merlot

▼▼▼▼▼ **1998** Medium to full red-purple; sweet berry fruit and sweet, spicy French oak support a bouquet showing good ripeness and no volatile acidity problems whatsoever. The palate confirms the convincing return to form, notwithstanding the challenges of the growing season. The wine has a seductive structure, and soft, persistent tannins. **rating:** 94

best drinking 2003–2010 **best vintages** '86, '88, '89, '90, '92, '93, '94, '96, '98 **drink with** Lamb fillets, mature cheddar • $74.50

Howard Park Scotsdale Cabernet Sauvignon

▼▼▼▼▽ **1999** Medium red-purple; the moderately intense and spotlessly clean bouquet has cassis and red berry fruit with evident but controlled French oak; the palate is very attractive, with sweet berry fruit shot through with tannins that run through the length of the palate. The slightly assertive oak will undoubtedly soften and integrate with a few more years in bottle. **rating:** 92

best drinking 2004–2009 **best vintages** '99 **drink with** Rare fillet steak • $33

howards way vineyard NR

Cobcroft Road, Broke, NSW 2330 **region** Lower Hunter Valley
phone (02) 4998 1336 **fax** (02) 4938 3775 **open** Not
winemaker Andrew Margan (Contract) **production** 3500 **est.** NA
product range ($15–20 ML) Semillon, Pinot Noir, Shiraz.
summary Yet another of the dozens of new vineyards and labels that have appeared in the Hunter Valley in the latter part of the 1990s. Eight hectares of shiraz, 3 hectares of pinot noir and 2 hectares of semillon provide a substantial base, and retail distribution began in 1999.

howarth's pycnantha hill NR

Benbournie Road, Clare, SA 5453 **region** Clare Valley
phone (08) 8842 2137 **fax** (08) 8842 2137 **open** Not
winemaker Jim Howarth **production** 800 **est.** 1997
product range ($11–15 R) Riesling, Chardonnay, Shiraz, Cabernet Sauvignon.
summary The Howarth family progressively established 2.4 hectares of vineyard from 1987, making its first commercial vintage ten years later in 1997. *Acacia pycnantha* is the botanic name for the golden wattle that grows wild over the hills of the Howarth farm, and they say it was 'a natural choice to name our vineyards Pycnantha Hill'. I am not too sure that marketing gurus would agree, but there we go.

Howarth's Pycnantha Hill Chardonnay

▼▼▼▼ **1999** Medium to full yellow-green; the bouquet is complex and quite powerful, with grapefruit and melon together with abundant oak. A big wine in the mouth, but quite well balanced, with peachy/honey fruit and oak well balanced and integrated; good acidity to close. **rating:** 85

best drinking Now **best vintages** NA **drink with** Milk-fed veal • $13

hugh hamilton ★★★

McMurtrie Road, McLaren Vale, SA 5171 **region** McLaren Vale
phone (08) 8323 8689 **fax** (08) 8323 9488 **open** Mon–Fri 10–5, weekends and public holidays 11–5
winemaker Hugh Hamilton **production** 8500 **est.** 1992
product range ($14.50–19.50 R) Chenin Blanc, Unwooded Chardonnay, Shiraz, Merlot, Cabernet Sauvignon, Sparkling Shiraz.
summary Hugh Hamilton is a member of the famous Hamilton winemaking family, there being an intensely (and well-known) competitive spirit existing between those various members – notably between Richard and Hugh – which can only be good for the consumer.

hugo 

Elliott Road, McLaren Flat, SA 5171 **region** McLaren Vale
phone (08) 8383 0098 **fax** (08) 8383 0446 **open** Sun–Fri 10.30–5, Sat 12–5
winemaker John Hugo **production** 9000 **est.** 1982
product range ($15.50–30 R) Sauvignon Blanc, Unwooded Chardonnay, Grenache, Reserve Shiraz, Shiraz, Cabernet Sauvignon, Port.
summary A winery that came from relative obscurity to prominence in the late 1980s with some lovely ripe, sweet reds which, while strongly American-oak-influenced, were quite outstanding. Subsequent red releases have continued in the same style, albeit slightly less exciting. There are 32 hectares of estate plantings, with part of the grape production sold to others. The wines are exported to the US, Canada and Singapore.

Hugo Unwooded Chardonnay

🍷🍷🍷🍷 **2000** Light to medium yellow-green; the moderately intense bouquet has melon and nectarine fruit, the palate with similar flavours, but above-average length and intensity; good acidity. **rating:** 85

best drinking Now **best vintages** NA **drink with** KFC • $15.50

Hugo Shiraz

🍷🍷🍷 **1999** Medium red-purple; berry, chocolate and earth aromas, with the addition of some vanilla on the bouquet lead into a chewy, chocolate and black cherry-flavoured palate; a touch of vanilla oak appears before persistent tannins take over on the finish. **rating:** 84

best drinking 2003–2007 **best vintages** '86, '88, '90, '92, '94, '98 **drink with** Irish stew • $20.50

Hugo Reserve Shiraz

🍷🍷🍷🍷 **1998** Dense red-purple; a massive and concentrated bouquet with blackberry/cherry fruit and lots of vanilla from new American oak is followed by similarly awesome, rich and concentrated palate in Henry VIII style, and a mere 14.5° alcohol. **rating:** 90

best drinking 2008–2015 **best vintages** '98 **drink with** A haunch of beef • $30

Hugo Dry Grown Grenache

🍷🍷🍷🍷 **1998** Medium red, showing some development; a mix of berry, spice and earth on the bouquet leads into a medium-bodied palate ranging through spicy berry and more savoury flavours; the tannins, happily, fall in the middle. **rating:** 85

best drinking 2002–2005 **best vintages** NA **drink with** Steak and kidney pie • $18.50

Hugo Cabernet Sauvignon

🍷🍷🍷🍷 **1998** Medium to full red-purple; concentrated blackberry/blackcurrant fruit is surrounded by lots of McLaren Vale chocolate, and supported by attractive oak handling. A powerful wine on the palate, with plenty of extract and richness; the tannins are likewise good. **rating:** 87

best drinking 2003–2013 **best vintages** '90, '92, '94, '98 **drink with** Rump steak • $19

hungerford hill ★★★☆

McDonalds Road, Pokolbin, NSW 2321 **region** Lower Hunter Valley

phone 1300 651 650 **fax** (02) 4998 7682 **open** Mon–Fri 9–4.30, weekends 10–4.30

winemaker Ian Walsh (former) **production** 30 000 **est.** 1967

product range ($13–18 R) Tumbarumba Chardonnay, Sauvignon Blanc, Pinot Gris and Pinot Noir; Cowra Chardonnay, Cowra Verdelho, Young Chardonnay, Young Semillon, Late Picked Semillon, Late Picked Riesling, Griffith Botrytis Semillon, Cabernet Merlot, Hunter Shiraz, Hilltops Shiraz, Hilltops Cabernet Sauvignon, Adelaide Hills–McLaren Vale Cabernet.

summary Now purely a brand owned by Southcorp, with the wines being made at Tulloch. However, eye-catching labels and a range of regionally sourced wines substantially elevated the status of the brand on the ever-parochial Sydney market, and raised wine quality to a significant degree.

Hungerford Hill Tumbarumba Sauvignon Blanc

🍷🍷🍷🍷 **1999** Light green-yellow; the moderately intense and smooth bouquet has a mix of gooseberry and citrus aromas; the palate is tight, indeed taut, and holding well, with slatey/mineral characters and nice, bright acidity. **rating:** 89

best drinking Now–2003 **best vintages** NA **drink with** Seafood risotto • $18

Hungerford Hill Cowra Chardonnay

🍷🍷🍷🍷 **1999** Light to medium yellow-green; a pleasant and clean bouquet with sweet melon fruit and subtle oak is replicated on the palate, which has good balance and mouthfeel, melon fruit supported by gentle oak. A better example of Cowra Chardonnay. **rating:** 86

best drinking Now **best vintages** NA **drink with** Chicken pasta • $14

Hungerford Hill Tumbarumba Pinot Noir

🍷🍷🍷🍷 **2000** Medium red-purple; the plummy bouquet, complete with hints of forest floor, is clearly varietal, a soft, smooth, supple palate adding to the appeal. **rating:** 87

best drinking Now–2004 **best vintages** NA **drink with** Chicken yakitori • NA

Hungerford Hill Hilltops Cabernet Sauvignon

YYYY **1998** Medium to full red-purple; solid dark berry fruit and positive oak on the bouquet flow through to the palate, which has far more depth and structure than anticipated, with surprising strength and tannins.

rating: 88

best drinking 2003–2008 **best vintages** '98 **drink with** Designer meat pie • NA

hunter ridge NR

Hermitage Road, Pokolbin, NSW 2320 **region** Lower Hunter Valley
phone (02) 4998 7500 **fax** (02) 4998 7211 **open** 7 days 10–5
winemaker Stephen Pannell **production** NFP **est.** 1996
product range ($12.50–22 R) Semillon, Verdelho, Chardonnay, Shiraz, Cabernet Merlot Reserve, Cabernet Sauvignon.
summary Hunter Ridge is effectively a joint venture between BRL Hardy and McGuigan Wines Limited. The grapes come from the vineyards surrounding the Hunter Ridge cellar door and which are owned by McGuigan Wines. The wines are fermented and partially matured in the Hunter Valley but are finally blended, finished and bottled by BRL Hardy in South Australia. The winery is also home to Keith Tulloch Wines and Evans Family Wines.

huntington estate ★★★★☆

Cassilis Road, Mudgee, NSW 2850 **region** Mudgee
phone (02) 6373 3825 **fax** (02) 6373 3730 **open** Mon–Fri 9–5, Sat 10–5, Sun 10–3
winemaker Susie Roberts **production** 20 000 **est.** 1969
product range ($13.50–30.50 CD) Semillon, Semillon Chardonnay, Chardonnay Barrel Fermented, Rosé, sundry sweet whites; red wines are released under bin numbers (FB = full-bodied, MB = medium-bodied) comprising Shiraz, Shiraz Special Reserve, Shiraz Cabernet Merlot, Cabernet Shiraz, Cabernet Merlot, Cabernet Sauvignon, Cabernet Sauvignon Special Reserve.
summary The remarkable Roberts family members have a passion for wine that is equalled only by their passion for music, with the Huntington Music Festival a major annual event. The red wines of Huntington Estate are outstanding and sell for absurdly low prices. The wines are not exported; almost all are sold via cellar door and mailing list.

Huntington Estate Shiraz

YYYY **1998** Bin FB19. Light to medium red-purple; the bouquet is relatively light, with aromas of spice, leaf and mint, the flavoursome palate in the same spectrum, all suggesting the wine will mature relatively quickly for a Huntington wine. I am also slightly puzzled as to why this should be characterised as full-bodied. **rating:** 86

best drinking 2002–2007 **best vintages** '74, '75, '78, '79, '84, '90, '91, '93, '94, '95, '97 **drink with** Kangaroo fillet • $16.50

Huntington Estate Cabernet Sauvignon

YYYY **1998** Bin FB16. Medium red-purple; cedary/dusty/earthy cabernet varietal aromas are followed by a palate with sweet berry at the core, finishing with quite pronounced tannins. A vintage slashed by hail just before veraison. Only 300 cases made. **rating:** 85

best drinking 2003–2008 **best vintages** '74, '79, '81, '84, '89, '90, '94, '95, '97 **drink with** Grilled rump steak • NA

huntleigh vineyards NR

Tunnecliffes Lane, Heathcote, Vic 3523 **region** Heathcote
phone (03) 5433 2795 **fax** (03) 5433 2795 **open** 7 days 10–5.30
winemaker Leigh Hunt **production** 500 **est.** 1975
product range ($13–20 CD) Riesling, Traminer, Shiraz, Cabernet Sauvignon; Leckie Shiraz.
summary The wines are all made at the winery by former stockbroker Leigh Hunt from estate-grown grapes.

Huntleigh Vineyards Cabernet Sauvignon

YYYY 1998 Excellent purple-red; clean, ripe cassis/berry cabernet varietal fruit on the bouquet shows even more attractively on the clean and rich palate. A fruit-driven wine with good structure and just a hint of oak.

rating: 90

best drinking 2003–2008 **best vintages** '98 **drink with** Rib of beef • NA

hunt's foxhaven estate NR

Canal Rocks Road, Yallingup, WA 6282 **region** Margaret River
phone (08) 9755 2232 **fax** (08) 9255 2249 **open** Weekends, holidays 11–5 or by appointment
winemaker David Hunt **production** 1000 **est.** 1978
product range ($12–15 CD) Riesling (dry and sweet), Semillon, Canal Rocks White, Yallingup Classic, Noble Riesling, Hunting Pink, Cabernet Sauvignon.
summary Draws upon 4 hectares of vines progressively established, the oldest being 25-year-old riesling. All of the wine is sold through cellar door and by mail order.

hurley vineyard NR

101 Balnarring Road, Balnarring, Vic 3926 **region** Mornington Peninsula
phone (03) 9608 8220 **fax** (03) 9608 7293 **open** Not
winemaker Contract **production** NA **est.** 1998
product range Pinot Noir.
summary Hurley Vineyard has been established by Melbourne Queen's Counsel, Kevin Bell. Four hectares of pinot noir were planted in 1998; no tastings to date.

hutton vale vineyard NR

Hutton Vale, Stone Jar Road, Angaston, SA 5353 **region** Eden Valley
phone (08) 8564 8270 **fax** (08) 8564 8385 **open** By appointment
winemaker David Powell, Chris Ringland, Caroline Dunn **production** 200 **est.** 1999
product range ($18–39 ML) Riesling, Shiraz, Grenache Mataro.
summary John Howard Angas (who arrived in South Australia in 1843, aged 19, charged with the responsibility of looking after the affairs of his father, George Fife Angas) named part of the family estate Hutton Vale. It is here that John Angas, John Howard's great-great-grandson, and wife Jan tend a little over 26 hectares of vines and produce (or, at least, Jan does) a range of jams, chutneys and preserves. Almost all of the grapes are sold, a tiny quantity being made by the Who's Who of the Barossa Valley: David Powell of Torbreck, Chris Ringland of Rockford and Caroline Dunn of Mildara Blass. Most of the wine is sold by mail order, and what is left is exported. I haven't tasted the wines, but I'm prepared to wager they are of outstanding quality.

ibis wines ★★★

239 Kearneys Drive, Orange, NSW 2800 **region** Orange
phone (02) 6362 3257 **fax** (02) 6362 5779 **open** Weekends and public holidays 11–5 or by appointment
winemaker Phil Stevenson **production** 300 **est.** 1988
product range ($16–22 CD) Riesling, Chardonnay, Reserve Chardonnay, Pinot Noir, Kanjara Shiraz, Cabernet Sauvignon, Cabernet Franc; Habitat Sauvignon Blanc, Pinot Noir, Merlot.
summary Ibis Wines is located just north of Orange (near the botanic gardens) on what was once a family orchard. Planting of the vineyard commenced in 1988, and after interim winemaking arrangements a new winery was completed on the property in 1998. The grapes are sourced from the home vineyards at an altitude of 800 metres, from the Habitat Vineyard at 1100 metres on Mount Canobolas (pinot noir and merlot) and from the Kanjara Vineyard (shiraz). Wine quality has shown steady improvement over the past couple of years.

Habitat Sauvignon Blanc

YYY 2000 Medium yellow-green; the bouquet is clean, well made, with light but perceptible varietal fruit aromas; the bouquet is likewise clean, quite ripe, with some gooseberry flavours on the mid-palate, and pleasing minerally acidity on the finish.

rating: 84

best drinking Now **best vintages** NA **drink with** Vegetarian • $18

Ibis Wines Kanjara Shiraz

YYYY 1999 Medium to full red-purple; the bouquet is very ripe, with plum and prune aromas; the fruit-driven palate offers similarly ripe plum, prune and chocolate flavours, closing with gentle tannins. **rating:** 83

best drinking 2002–2007 **best vintages** NA **drink with** Rich meat dishes • $20

Habitat Merlot

YYYY 1999 Medium red; the bouquet is very ripe, with dried-fruit aromas, suggesting some berry shrivel prior to picking. The palate is similarly ripe, but does have a distinctive savoury/olive varietal cut, and the texture is quite good. **rating:** 82

best drinking Now–2004 **best vintages** NA **drink with** Something feathered • $20

inchiquin wines NR

PO Box 865, Clare, SA 5453 **region** Clare Valley
phone (08) 8843 4210 **open** Not
winemaker Stephen McInerney **production** 500 **est.** 1998
product range ($13–20 ML) Riesling, Cabernet Shiraz.
summary Stephen McInerney learned his trade on the winery floor in various parts of the world: his first experience came in 1985 at Jim Barry Wines where he spent a number of years before moving to Pikes. In the intervening period he worked as a flying winemaker in France, Oregon, Spain and Argentina. He is now assistant winemaker at the new and large Kirribilly Winery in the Clare Valley. He established Inchiquin Wines with his partner Kate Strachan, herself with great industry credentials, primarily as the viticulturist for Taylor's (previously Southcorp), which has the largest vineyards in the Clare Valley. The wines, incidentally, are made by Stephen McInerney at Pikes.

Inchiquin Cabernet Shiraz

YYYY 1999 Medium purple-red; the bouquet is powerful and youthful, with earthy characters that are, however, clean. The palate is very powerful and concentrated, with a high level of extract; the points are, to a degree, an article of faith in the long-term future of the wine. Very consistently pointed at silver medal level at the 2000 Clare Valley Wine Show. **rating:** 89

best drinking 2004–2014 **best vintages** NA **drink with** Leave it in the cellar • $20

indigo ridge ★★★

Icely Road, Orange, NSW 2800 **region** Orange
phone (02) 6362 1851 **fax** (02) 6362 1851 **open** By appointment
winemaker Jon Reynolds (Contract) **production** 750 **est.** 1995
product range ($16–28 ML) Sauvignon Blanc, Cabernet Sauvignon, Ophir Gold.
summary Indigo Ridge has 4 hectares each of sauvignon blanc and cabernet sauvignon; production is still very small, and all of the wines are sold by cellar door and mail order.

Indigo Ridge Sauvignon Blanc

YYYY 2000 Light green-yellow; a clean and crisp grassy/minerally bouquet is followed by a clean, fresh, crisp palate with grassy/asparagus/lemon flavours and brisk acidity on the finish. **rating:** 84

best drinking Now **best vintages** NA **drink with** Shellfish • $20

Indigo Ridge Cabernet Sauvignon

YYYY 1999 Dark red, with a slightly suspect edge; a solid, briary/savoury/blackberry bouquet is replicated on the palate, with a similar mix of flavours. The finish is assertive, and slightly tough. **rating:** 83

best drinking 2002–2007 **best vintages** NA **drink with** Barbecued meat • $28

inglewood vineyards ★★★

Yarrawa Road, Denman, NSW 2328 **region** Upper Hunter Valley
phone (02) 6547 2556 **fax** (02) 6547 2546 **open** Not
winemaker Gary Reed (Contract) **production** 25 000 **est.** 1988
product range ($7.50–20 R) Atmosphere Coastal White and Inland Red; Two Rivers Stone's Throw Semillon, Wild Fire Unwooded Chardonnay, Hidden Hive Verdelho, Rocky Crossing Cabernet Sauvignon, Back Track

Cabernets; Reserve Hunter Semillon, Hunter Chardonnay, Hunter Shiraz and McLaren Vale/Hunter Cabernet Sauvignon.
summary A significant addition to the viticultural scene in the Upper Hunter Valley, with almost 170 hectares of vineyards established, involving a total investment of around $7 million. Much of the fruit is sold to Southcorp under long-term contracts, but part is made under contract for the expanding winemaking and marketing operations of Inglewood. The emphasis is on Chardonnay and Semillon, and the wines have been medal winners in the wine show circuit.

inigo wines NR

Lot 2 New England Highway, Glen Aplin, Qld 4382 **region** Granite Belt
phone (07) 3397 6425 **fax** (07) 3397 5280 **open** Fri 12–3, weekends 10–5 or by appointment
winemaker Janis Carter **production** 450 **est.** 1996
product range ($16–18 CD) Sauvignon Blanc, Semillon Sauvignon Blanc, Verdelho, Cabernet Shiraz Merlot, Cabernet Merlot.
summary The property and winery operate as a kind of home-stay operation, and anyone staying at the Chateau Bernard and St Ignatius Vineyard Retreat (Inigo's home) can help in the winery.

innisfail vineyards NR

Cross Street, Batesford, Vic 3221 **region** Geelong
phone (03) 5276 1258 **fax** (03) 5276 1258 **open** By appointment
winemaker Ron Griffiths **production** 2000 **est.** 1980
product range ($14–24 ML) Riesling, Chardonnay, Pinot Noir, Cabernet Sauvignon Merlot.
summary This 6-hectare vineyard released its first wines in 1988, made in a small but modern winery on site, with a chewy, complex Chardonnay from both 1989 and 1990 attesting to the quality of the vineyard. No tastings for many years, however.

ironbark ridge vineyard NR

Middle Road Mail Service 825, Purga, Qld 4306 **region** Queensland Zone
phone (07) 5464 6787 **fax** (07) 5464 6858 **open** By appointment
winemaker Mark Ravenscroft (Contract) **production** 250 **est.** 1984
product range ($15–28 ML) Chardonnay, Reserve Chardonnay, Shiraz, Vintage Port.
summary Ipswich is situated on the coastal side of the Great Dividing Range, and the high summer humidity and rainfall will inevitably provide challenges for viticulture here. On the evidence of the '98 Chardonnay, Ironbark Ridge is capable of producing Chardonnay equal to the best from Queensland.

iron pot bay wines ★★★☆

West Bay Road, Rowella, Tas 7270 **region** Northern Tasmania
phone (03) 6394 7320 **fax** (03) 6394 7346 **open** By appointment
winemaker Andrew Hood, Jim Chatto (Contract) **production** 2000 **est.** 1988
product range ($20 R) Unwooded Chardonnay, Semillon Sauvignon Blanc, Pinot Grigio.
summary Iron Pot Bay is now part of the syndicate that has established Rosevears Estate, with its large, state-of-the-art winery erected on the banks of the Tamar. The vineyard takes its name from a bay on the Tamar River and is strongly maritime-influenced, producing delicate but intensely flavoured unwooded white wines.

Iron Pot Bay Pinot Grigio

🍷🍷🍷🍷 **2000** Light green-yellow; a floral bouquet with a mix of herb and wildflower aromas leads into a brightly profiled palate, with herb, apple and spice flavours, finishing with brisk acidity. **rating:** 88
best drinking Now–2004 **best vintages** '95, '96, '00 **drink with** Antipasto • NA

ironwood estate NR

RMB 1288 Porongurup, WA 6234 **region** Great Southern
phone (08) 9853 1126 **fax** (08) 9853 1172 **open** By appointment
winemaker Robert Lee, John Wade (Consultant) **production** 1000 **est.** 1996
product range ($14–21 CD) Riesling, Chardonnay, Shiraz, Cabernet Sauvignon.

summary Ironwood Estate was established in 1996 when the first wines were made from purchased grapes. In the same year chardonnay, shiraz and cabernet sauvignon were planted on a northern slope of the Porongurup Range. The twin peaks of the Porongurups rise above the vineyard and provide the basis for the label design. The first estate-grown grapes were vinified at the new Porongurup Winery, erected for the 1999 vintage and jointly owned by Jingalla and Chatsfield Wines.

irvine ★★★★

Roeslers Road, Eden Valley, SA 5235 **region** Eden Valley
phone (08) 8564 1046 **fax** (08) 8564 1314 **open** Not
winemaker James Irvine **production** 4850 **est.** 1980
product range ($15–95 R) Under the cheaper Eden Crest label: Unwooded Chardonnay, Pinot Gris, Merlot, Merlot Cabernet, Zinfandel Merlot, Meslier Brut, Pinot Chardonnay Brut; under the premium James Irvine label: Brut Royale, Merlot Brut and (at the top of the tree) Grand Merlot.
summary Industry veteran Jim Irvine, who has successfully guided the destiny of so many South Australian wineries, quietly introduced his own label in 1991, although the vineyard from which the wines are sourced was commenced in 1980 and now comprises 1 hectare each of merlot and pinot gris, 0.73 hectare of zinfandel, 3.8 hectares of chardonnay and 4.9 hectares of merlot. Much of the production is exported to Germany, Switzerland, the US, Japan, Taiwan, New Zealand, Hong Kong and Singapore.

Irvine Brut Royale

YYYY **1988** Glowing yellow-green; the bouquet is quite intense, with some of the toasty characters one would expect from prolonged ageing on lees and then cork, yet still retains freshness. There is similar fruit intensity on entry to the mouth, with good acid balance on the finish. The mid-palate does dip slightly, but that is verging on the hypercritical. **rating:** 87

best drinking Now–2003 **best vintages** '88 **drink with** Antipasto • $36

Irvine Meslier Brut

YYYY **1999** Light green-yellow; fresh, floral/citrus/leaf/blossom aromas are followed by a lemony, crisp and relatively straightforward palate. **rating:** 85

best drinking Now–2003 **best vintages** NA **drink with** Aperitif • $16

Irvine Eden Crest Merlot

YYYY **1999** Medium red-purple; gently sweet berry fruit aromas, with touches of fruit and oak spice are followed by a palate with attractive plum and berry fruit in an easy, appealing drink-now style. Fine tannins and the barest touch of oak; supple and sweet. **rating:** 86

best drinking Now–2005 **best vintages** '97, '98 **drink with** Barossa sausage • $28

James Irvine Grand Merlot

YYYYY **1997** Medium to full red-purple; very ripe spicy/plummy fruit is surrounded by well-integrated oak on the bouquet. A powerful and complex palate has a mix of plum, spice and olive flavours. Excellent concentration and texture, without sacrificing finesse. Particularly impressive for the vintage, which has a lesser reputation than '96. **rating:** 93

best drinking 2002–2013 **best vintages** '96, '97 **drink with** Venison • $95

Irvine Eden Crest Merlot Cabernet

YYYY **1999** Medium red, with just a touch of purple; the bouquet has a mix of olive, herb, berry, spice and biscuit aromas, the medium-bodied palate with berry, a touch of chocolate, herb and spice, lifted by a touch of sweet oak and soft tannins. Once again, a success. **rating:** 86

best drinking 2003–2008 **best vintages** '97 **drink with** Rabbit in herbs and red wine • $28

island brook estate NR

817 Bussell Highway, Metricup, WA 6280 **region** Margaret River
phone (08) 9755 7501 **fax** (08) 9755 7008 **open** By appointment
winemaker Contract **production** NA **est.** 1985
product range Chardonnay, Verdelho, Cabernet Sauvignon.

summary Linda and Peter Jenkins purchased Island Brook from Ken and Judy Brook in early 2001, and are currently renovating both the winery and vineyard. They planned to re-open the cellar-door sales area in October/November 2001.

Island Brook Estate Verdelho

🍷🍷🍷🍷🍷 **2000** Light straw-green; the bouquet is quite aromatic, with a dash of crisp, lemon juice poured over the fruit salad. The palate is delicate, well balanced, and quite long in the mouth, with a particularly good finish; Verdelho starts sweet and finishes with acidity. This gold medal-winning wine has captured both ends of the spectrum. **rating:** 93

best drinking Now–2003 **best vintages** '00 **drink with** Summer salad • NA

ivanhoe wines NR

Marrowbone Road, Pokolbin, NSW 2320 **region** Lower Hunter Valley
phone (02) 4998 7325 **fax** (02) 4998 7848 **open** 7 days 10–5
winemaker Stephen Drayton, Tracy Drayton **production** 7000 **est.** 1995
product range ($15–27 CD) Various varietal wines under the Ivanhoe and Stephen Drayton Signature Series, including Semillon, Verdelho, Gewurztraminer, Chardonnay, Chambourcin, Shiraz, Cabernet Sauvignon and sparkling.
summary Stephen Drayton is the son of the late Reg Drayton and, with wife Tracy, is the third branch of the family to be actively involved in winemaking in the Hunter Valley. The property on which the vineyard is situated has been called Ivanhoe for over 140 years, and 25 hectares of 30-year-old vines provide high-quality fruit for the label. The plans are to build a replica of the old homestead (burnt down, along with much of the winery, in the 1968 bushfires) to operate as a sales area.

jackson's hill NR

Mount View Road, Mount View, NSW 2321 **region** Lower Hunter Valley
phone (02) 4990 1273 **fax** (02) 4991 3233 **open** 7 days 10–5
winemaker Mike Winborne **production** 1200 **est.** 1984
product range ($14–20 CD) Semillon, Vin en Rose, Cabernet Franc, Cabernet Sauvignon.
summary One of the newer arrivals on the spectacularly scenic Mount View Road, making tiny quantities of wine sold exclusively through the cellar door and specialising in Cabernet Franc. No recent tastings, but Jackson's Hill does produce marvellous home-made chocolates.

jadran NR

445 Reservoir Road, Orange Grove, WA 6109 **region** Perth Hills
phone (08) 9459 1110 **open** Mon–Sat 10–8, Sun 11–5
winemaker Steve Radojkovich **production** NFP. **est.** 1967
product range ($6–12 CD) Riesling, Hermitage, generic red and white table wines, Sparkling, Fortifieds.
summary A quite substantial operation which basically services local clientele, occasionally producing wines of quite surprising quality from a variety of fruit sources.

james estate ★★★☆

Mudgee Road, Baerami, via Denman, NSW 2333 **region** Upper Hunter Valley
phone (02) 6547 5168 **fax** (02) 6547 5164 **open** 7 days 10–4.30
winemaker Peter Orr **production** 75 000 **est.** 1971
product range ($8–20 R) Café Range Chardonnay, Shiraz Cabernet, Cabernet Merlot; Sundara range of Chardonnay Semillon, Chardonnay, Shiraz Cabernet, Cabernet Merlot; Compass Range Semillon, Chardonnay, White Sylvaner, Verdelho, Merlot, Shiraz, Cabernet Sauvignon; Reserve Chardonnay, Botrytis Semillon, Shiraz; Methode Champenoise, Grand Cuvée.
summary A substantial viticultural enterprise with 98 hectares of vineyards planted to ten varieties. Since a change of ownership in 1997 there have been many innovations, including the appointment of Peter Orr as winemaker after a winemaking career with McWilliam's Mount Pleasant and thereafter Allandale Wines, and the complete revamping and repackaging of the wines. In December 2000 the company issued a prospectus seeking to raise just under $5 million to fund the development of over 80 hectares of new vineyards, which will substantially increase winery production.

James Estate Reserve Chardonnay

TTTT **1999** Light to medium green-yellow; nectarine, melon and fig fruit aromas are complexed by a touch of barrel fermentation on the bouquet; the palate is gentle and understated, with fig, melon and cashew flavours, and an attractive creamy texture. **rating:** 87

best drinking Now–2004 **best vintages** NA **drink with** Grilled spatchcock • $20

James Estate Sundara Chardonnay

TTTY **1999** Medium yellow-green; the bouquet is quite fragrant with citrus and melon fruit aromas, and the 'subtle oak' specified on the label hard to see. The clean and fresh palate has plenty of flavour, with tropical overtones to citrussy fruit. **rating:** 84

best drinking Now **best vintages** NA **drink with** Creamy pasta • $10

James Estate Reserve Shiraz

TTTT **1999** Medium red-purple; the moderately intense bouquet is clean, with a mix of sweet cherry and chocolate fruit aromas. The palate is nicely balanced, with sweet cherry fruit, chocolate and a touch of vanilla oak; well-balanced tannins to close. **rating:** 85

best drinking 2002–2007 **best vintages** '99 **drink with** Lamb shanks • $20

jamiesons run/mildara ★★★★

Penola–Naracoorte Road, Coonawarra, SA 5263 **region** Coonawarra

phone (08) 8736 3380 **fax** (08) 8736 3307 **open** Mon–Fri 9–4.30, weekends 10–4

winemaker David O'Leary, Scott Rawlinson **production** NFP **est.** 1955

product range ($10–40 R) Jamiesons Run Sauvignon Blanc, Chardonnay, Pinot Noir, Red, Merlot, Reserve, Alexander Block, McShane's Block. Also made are Mildara Coonawarra Cabernet Sauvignon and Robertson's Well Shiraz and Cabernet Sauvignon.

summary The quality jewel in the crown of the Beringer Blass wine empire but a jewel that has always been put to industrial use, with the near-exclusive emphasis on the ever-expanding Jamiesons Run. For all that, it has to be said the quality of Jamiesons Run has been zealously protected, notwithstanding the growth in volume of its production and brand extension. Worldwide distribution.

Jamiesons Run Pinot Noir

TTTT **1999** Light to medium red; while not power-packed, the bouquet has slippery/savoury varietal character and spice, the palate with a mix of savoury, spicy cherry and plum, and an entirely appropriate texture and weight. **rating:** 85

best drinking Now–2003 **best vintages** NA **drink with** Risotto • NA

Mildara Robertson's Well Shiraz

TTTT **1999** Medium to full red-purple; a dense and rich berry, chocolate and spice bouquet, the palate a carbon copy, showing good extract and tannin management, and subtle oak. **rating:** 88

best drinking 2004–2009 **best vintages** NA **drink with** Braised oxtail • NA

Jamiesons Run McShane's Block

TTTTY **1998** Strong red-purple; vanilla and spice oak are immediately obvious on the bouquet, but there is dark plum fruit to justify that oak. The palate is rich, with sweet, ripe plum and prune fruit, obvious but not excessive oak, and good tannins. **rating:** 90

best drinking 2003–2010 **best vintages** NA **drink with** Beef Bordelaise • NA

Jamiesons Run Reserve Red

TTTTY **1998** Medium to full red-purple; the bouquet has more charry/toasty oak than the standard wine, and deeper, more powerful fruit. A complex, rich and powerful palate ranges through blackberry and blackcurrant fruit plus sustained tannins. The best Reserve so far. **rating:** 93

best drinking 2003–2013 **best vintages** '95, '96, '98 **drink with** Porterhouse steak • $40

Jamiesons Run Coonawarra Merlot

TTTT **1999** Medium to full red-purple; a mix of leafy berry and fresh, sweet juicy fruit, combined with gentle oak, leads into a palate with strong, sweet mid-palate berry fruit, finishing with fine tannins. **rating:** 86

best drinking 2003–2007 **best vintages** NA **drink with** Fillet of lamb • NA

Jamiesons Run Coonawarra Red

ΥΥΥΥΥ **1998** Medium red-purple; the moderately intense bouquet is quite fragrant, with sweet blackberry and mulberry fruit. Most attractive sweet berry, cassis, plum and blackberry fruit flavours are supported by a nice touch of oak and fine tannins. Has evolved very well since being bottled. **rating:** 90

best drinking 2003–2008 **best vintages** '86, '88, '90, '91, '93, '96, '98 **drink with** Mediterranean, Italian cuisine • $16.50

Mildara Coonawarra Cabernet Sauvignon

ΥΥΥΥΥ **1998** Medium to full red-purple; clean, ripe cassis/berry fruit, the mark of the vintage, is married with positive French oak on the bouquet. The palate has smooth and sweet cassis and blackcurrant fruit, again with a nice touch of French oak, finishing with soft but persistent tannins. Adelaide-Hyatt Wine of the Year in 2000. **rating:** 91

best drinking 2003–2010 **best vintages** '63, '86, '88, '90, '91, '98 **drink with** Beef casserole • $21

Jamiesons Run Alexander Block Cabernet

ΥΥΥΥΥ **1998** Medium to full red-purple; rich blackberry and mulberry fruit, together with a splash of oak on the bouquet, flow into a ripe and rich palate with a mix of cassis, blackberry and chocolate. Sure oak handling and good tannins round off a thoroughly impressive wine. **rating:** 94

best drinking 2003–2013 **best vintages** '98 **drink with** Lamb • NA

jane brook estate ★★★

229 Toodyay Road, Middle Swan, WA 6056 **region** Swan District
phone (08) 9274 1432 **fax** (08) 9274 1211 **open** Mon–Fri 10–5, weekends and public holidays 12–5
winemaker Julie White, David Atkinson **production** 15 000 **est.** 1972
product range ($10.50–45 CD) Sauvignon Blanc, James Vineyard Verdelho, James Vineyard Chardonnay, Back Block Shiraz, Mountjoy Cabernet Merlot, Benjamin David and Elizabeth Jane Methode Champenoise; also Plain Jane and Atkinson labels.
summary An attractive winery that relies in part on substantial cellar-door trade and in part on varying export markets, with much work having been invested in the Japanese market in recent years. It has established a vineyard in the Margaret River and also is now sourcing fruit from Pemberton, Ferguson Valley and Arthur River. Exports to the UK, Japan, Malaysia and Singapore, with significant markets in Sydney and throughout New South Wales.

Jane Brook James Vineyard Verdelho

ΥΥΥΥ **2000** Medium yellow-green; the bouquet has distinctive fruit-salad/honeysuckle aromas; the light to medium bodied palate follows down the same track, with plenty of soft fruit. The limitations in the wine stem from the variety, not the winery. **rating:** 84

best drinking Now **best vintages** NA **drink with** Takeaway chicken • NA

jardee NR

Old School House, Jardee, WA 6258 **region** Pemberton
phone (08) 9777 1552 **fax** (08) 9777 1552 **open** Not
winemaker Barrie Smith **production** 510 **est.** 1994
product range ($18–22 R) Chardonnay, Pinot Noir.
summary Jardee is a pioneering mill town; the wines are in fact made in tiny quantities from purchased fruit, the operation being a part-time interest for proprietor Steve Miolin.

jasper hill ★★★★★

Drummonds Lane, Heathcote, Vic 3523 **region** Heathcote
phone (03) 5433 2528 **fax** (03) 5433 3143 **open** By appointment
winemaker Ron Laughton **production** 3000 **est.** 1975
product range ($17–66 R) Georgia's Paddock Riesling, Georgia's Paddock Shiraz, Emily's Paddock Shiraz Cabernet Franc.
summary The red wines of Jasper Hill are highly regarded and much sought after, invariably selling out at cellar door and through the mailing list within a short time of release. These are wonderful wines in admittedly Leviathan mould, reflecting the very low yields and the care and attention given to them by Ron Laughton. The oak is not overdone, the fruit flavours showing Central Victoria at its best.

jasper valley NR

RMB 880 Croziers Road, Berry, NSW 2535 **region** Shoalhaven
phone (02) 4464 1596 **fax** (02) 4464 1596 **open** 7 days 9.30–5.30
winemaker Contract **production** 1100 **est.** 1976
product range ($4.20–12 CD) White Burgundy, Riesling, Traminer Riesling, Moselle, Summer Red, Cabernet Sauvignon, Port; also non-alcoholic fruit wines.
summary A strongly tourist-oriented winery with most of its wine purchased as cleanskins from other makers. Features about 1 hectare of lawns, barbecue facilities, and sweeping views.

jeanneret wines ★★★☆

Jeanneret Road, Sevenhill, SA 5453 **region** Clare Valley
phone (08) 8843 4308 **fax** (08) 8843 4251 **open** Mon–Fri 11–5, weekends and public holidays 10–5
winemaker Ben Jeanneret **production** 3500 **est.** 1992
product range ($15–22 CD) Riesling, Semillon, Sparkling Grenache, Grenache Shiraz, Shiraz, Cabernet Sauvignon.
summary Jeanneret's fully self-contained winery has a most attractive outdoor tasting area and equally attractive picnic facilities situated on the edge of a small lake surrounded by bushland. While it did not open the business until October 1994, its first wine was in fact made in 1992 (Shiraz) and it has already established a loyal following. National wholesale distribution; export markets have been established in Canada and the UK.

Jeanneret Riesling

TTTT **2000** Medium yellow-green; the bouquet is direct and quite powerful, with a mix of mineral, lime and passionfruit aromas. The palate has good balance, length and intensity in a powerful but not phenolic frame.
rating: 89
best drinking 2002–2010 **best vintages** NA **drink with** Shellfish • $15

Jeanneret Shiraz

TTTT **1999** Medium purple-red; the moderately intense and fresh bouquet has earthy/spicy fruit aromas, followed by a quite elegant, unforced and smooth palate, with clean, berry fruit. Very much an alternative style to the power-hitters of the Valley.
rating: 88
best drinking 2002–2007 **best vintages** NA **drink with** Beef stew with olives • $20

jeir creek ★★★

Gooda Creek Road, Murrumbateman, NSW 2582 **region** Canberra District
phone (02) 6227 5999 **fax** (02) 6227 5900 **open** Fri–Sun, holidays 10–5
winemaker Rob Howell **production** 4000 **est.** 1984
product range ($16–20 CD) Riesling, Reserve Riesling, Botrytis Semillon Sauvignon Blanc, Sauvignon Blanc, Chardonnay, Pinot Noir, Cabernet Merlot.
summary Rob Howell came to part-time winemaking through a love of drinking fine wine and is intent on improving both the quality and consistency of his wines. It is now a substantial (and still growing) business, with the vineyard plantings increased to 11 hectares (with more cabernet sauvignon, shiraz and merlot).

jenke vineyards ★★★☆

Barossa Valley Way, Rowland Flat, SA 5352 **region** Barossa Valley
phone (08) 8524 4154 **fax** (08) 8524 5044 **open** 7 days 11–5
winemaker Kym Jenke **production** 8000 **est.** 1989
product range ($13.50–30 CD) Riesling, Semillon, Chardonnay, Grenache, Mourvedre, Merlot, Cabernet Franc, Cabernet Sauvignon, Shiraz, Sparkling Shiraz.
summary The Jenkes have been vignerons in the Barossa since 1854 and have over 45 hectares of vineyards; a small part of the production is now made and marketed through a charming restored stone cottage cellar door. Wholesale distribution in Victoria and New South Wales; exports to the UK, the US, Switzerland and Germany.

Jenke Shiraz

TTTT **1998** Medium red-purple, with just a touch of carbon dioxide showing on the rim; the moderately intense bouquet has a mix of berry, earth and chocolate that leads into a palate with sweet plum and touches of raspberry and chocolate; good extract and length.
rating: 87
best drinking 2003–2008 **best vintages** '90, '91, '96, '98 **drink with** Barbecued rump • $25

Jenke Cabernet Franc

ŸŸŸY **1998** Medium red; some distinctive leafy/spicy aromatics are followed by a much sweeter palate with more berry, chocolate and vanilla flavours, finishing with soft tannins. **rating:** 84

best drinking Now–2005 **best vintages** NA **drink with** Chinese barbecued pork • $15

jester hill wines NR

Mount Stirling Road, Glen Aplin, Qld 4381 **region** Granite Belt
phone (07) 4683 4380 **fax** (02) 6622 3190 **open** Fri–Sun 10–4
winemaker Mark Ravenscroft **production** 830 **est.** 1993
product range ($12.50–16 CD) Sauvignon Blanc, Chardonnay, Shiraz, Cabernet Sauvignon Shiraz, Dysons Flat Fortified Shiraz.

summary A family-run vineyard situated in the pretty valley of Glen Aplin in the Granite Belt. The owners, John and Genevieve Ashwell, aim to concentrate on small quantities of premium-quality wines reflecting the full-bodied style of the region. Believing that good wine is made in the vineyard, John and Genevieve have spent the first seven years establishing healthy, strong vines on well-drained soil.

jim barry wines ★★★★☆

Main North Road, Clare, SA 5453 **region** Clare Valley
phone (08) 8842 2261 **fax** (08) 8842 3752 **open** Mon–Fri 9–5, weekends, holidays 9–4
winemaker Mark Barry **production** 40 000 **est.** 1959
product range ($10–140 ML) Watervale Riesling, Clare Valley Chardonnay, Unwooded Chardonnay, Lavendar Hill, Noble Riesling, McCrae Wood Shiraz, The Armagh (Shiraz), McCrae Wood Cabernet Sauvignon, Clare Valley Cabernet Sauvignon, Cabernet Sauvignon Shiraz, McCrae Wood Cabernet Malbec, Fortifieds.

summary The Armagh and the McCrae Wood range continue to stand out as the very best wines from Jim Barry, exceptionally concentrated and full-flavoured. The remainder are seldom less than adequate but do vary somewhat from one vintage to the next. Has an exceptional viticultural resource base of 247 hectares of mature Clare Valley vineyards. Exports to the UK, much of Europe, North America, Japan and Southeast Asia.

Jim Barry Watervale Riesling

ŸŸŸŸ **2000** Medium yellow-green; the bouquet has quite ripe fruit, with a mix of lime and more tropical aromas. The palate, likewise, has lots of lime and passionfruit flavour, with good length and intensity. Probably quick developing. **rating:** 89

best drinking Now–2005 **best vintages** '83, '86, '89, '91, '94, '95, '99 **drink with** Ginger pork • $14.95

Jim Barry McCrae Wood Shiraz

ŸŸŸŸY **1998** Medium to full red-purple; a typically fragrant and lush bouquet with a mix of berry, mint, cedar, tobacco and spice, followed by a plush palate ranging through all of the flavours of the bouquet with chocolate and mint to the fore; the oak is controlled, as are the tannins. **rating:** 91

best drinking 2003–2013 **best vintages** '92, '93, '94, '95, '97, '98 **drink with** Jugged hare • $39.95

Jim Barry The Armagh

ŸŸŸŸŸ **1998** Dense red-purple; rich, luscious dark berry, chocolate and earth aromas, perfectly ripened, with the oak in the back seat where it should be. The palate is rich and luscious, with layer-upon-layer of minty berry fruit and tannins to sustain it for the long haul. **rating:** 95

best drinking 2003–2018 **best vintages** '89, '90, '91, '92, '93, '95, '96, '98 **drink with** The richest game dish possible • $140

Jim Barry Cabernet Sauvignon Shiraz

ŸŸŸŸ **1999** Very ripe fruit on the bouquet, runs from plum into prune, but the generously endowed palate doesn't go over the top: good depth and structure with ripe plum/blackberry/prune fruit, sweet oak and soft tannins. **rating:** 89

best drinking Now–2007 **best vintages** '99 **drink with** Irish stew • $14.95

Jim Barry Clare Valley Cabernet Sauvignon

ŸŸŸŸ **1999** Medium to full red-purple; dark, savoury berry fruit is offset by slightly smoky bacon oak on the bouquet, while the palate is very ripe and plummy/pruney in hallmark 1999 vintage style. **rating:** 86

best drinking 2003–2007 **best vintages** '79, '85, '87, '89, '90, '94, '98 **drink with** Spiced beef • $21.95

jindalee estate ★★★☆

265 Ballan Road, Moorabool, North Geelong, Vic 3215 **region** Geelong
phone (03) 5277 2836 **fax** (03) 5277 2840 **open** 7 days 10–5
winemaker Scott Ireland **production** 150 000 **est.** 1997
product range ($10–20 R) Geelong Fettlers Rest Gewurztraminer, Chardonnay, Shiraz, Merlot, Geelong Fettlers Rest Shiraz, Cabernet Sauvignon, Geelong Fettlers Rest Cabernet Shiraz.
summary Jindalee Wines made its debut with the 1997 vintage. It is part of the Littore Group, which currently has 450 hectares of premium-wine grapes in wine production and under development in the Riverland. Corporate offices are now at the former Idyll Vineyard, acquired by Jindalee in late 1997. Here 15 hectares of estate vineyards are being re-trellised and upgraded, and a premium Jindalee Estate range is now made. Retail distribution through Red + White and Options Wines (SA); exports to the UK, the US and Canada.

Jindalee Estate Geelong Fettler's Rest Gewurztraminer

🍷🍷🍷🍷 **2000** Light green-yellow; the bouquet is delicate and light, with spicy fruit and the faintest hint of salami. The palate is crisp and clean, with touches of spice, but overall surprisingly light-on. **rating:** 84
best drinking Now–2004 **best vintages** NA **drink with** Lightly spiced Asian • $18

Jindalee Estate Geelong Fettler's Rest Shiraz

🍷🍷🍷🍷 **1999** Medium red-purple; a clean, bright, fresh cherry and spice-accented bouquet with subtle oak is followed by a light to medium bodied palate with attractive, sweet black cherry and plum fruit, fine tannins and subtle oak. Well wrought. **rating:** 89
best drinking 2003–2009 **best vintages** '99 **drink with** Yearling steak • $20

jindi creek NR

426 Turner Road, Denmark, WA 6333 **region** Great Southern
phone (08) 9848 1113 **fax** (08) 9848 1844 **open** Thurs–Mon 11–4.30 Nov–June
winemaker Brenden Smith **production** 700 **est.** 1996
product range ($15–22 CD) Semillon Sauvignon Blanc, Semillon Wooded Chardonnay, Unwooded Chardonnay, Pinot Noir, Shiraz, Cabernet.
summary The Ponsfords (Nick, Rosemary and son Andrew) used to run a stock-fencing contract business, and Rosemary always had an interest in cooking and hospitality. They decided that moving into winemaking and running a restaurant would be an easier life, and now wryly admit, 'How wrong can you be!?' They have planted 5.5 hectares of chardonnay, semillon, sauvignon blanc, pinot noir, merlot and cabernet sauvignon, with a few rows of verdelho and marsanne, but up to this point have been selling part of the crop to other wineries. They hope in the future a newly formed co-operative will allow all of the estate production to be vinified, and may then need to look beyond the cellar door and restaurant, through which all of the present output is sold.

jingalla ★★★★

RMB 1316 Bolganup Dam Road, Porongurup, WA 6324 **region** Great Southern
phone (08) 9853 1023 **fax** (08) 9853 1023 **open** 7 days 10.30–5
winemaker John Wade, Robert Lee (Consultant) **production** 3500 **est.** 1979
product range ($11–23 CD) Great Southern White and Red, Riesling, Semillon, Verdelho, Late Harvest, Botrytis Riesling Verdelho, Shiraz Reserve, Cabernet Rouge, Cabernet Sauvignon, Late Harvest Semillon, Tawny Port, Liqueur Muscat.
summary Jingalla is a family-run business, owned and run by Geoff and Nita Clarke and Barry and Shelley Coad, the latter the ever-energetic wine marketer of the business. The 8 hectares of hillside vineyards are low-yielding, with the white wines succeeding best. Consistently competent contract-winemaking has resulted in a range of very reliable, positively flavoured wines. While best known for its wooded and unwooded whites, it also produces some lovely red wines. National distribution; exports to Japan, Germany and Taiwan.

jinks creek winery NR

Tonimbuk Road, Tonimbuk, Vic 3815 **region** Gippsland
phone (03) 5629 8502 **fax** (03) 5629 8551 **open** By appointment
winemaker Andrew Clarke **production** 700 **est.** 1981
product range ($18–22 CD) Sauvignon Blanc, Pinot Noir, Shiraz.

summary Jinks Creek Winery is situated between Gembrook and Bunyip, bordering the evocatively named Bunyip State Park. While the winery was not built until 1992, planting of the 2.5-hectare vineyard started back in 1981 and all of the wines are estate-grown. The 'sold out' sign goes up each year.

Jinks Creek Sauvignon Blanc

🍷🍷🍷🍷 **1999** Light straw-green; the bouquet is clean, with light herbal/herbaceous/asparagus aromas that are repeated on the moderately long palate; does flatten out slightly on the finish. **rating:** 84

best drinking Now **best vintages** NA **drink with** Salads • $18

joadja vineyards NR

Joadja Road, Berrima, NSW 2577 **region** South Coast Zone
phone (02) 4878 5236 **fax** (02) 4878 5236 **open** 7 days 10–5
winemaker Kim Moginie **production** 2000 **est.** 1983
product range ($13–21 CD) Classic Dry White, Sauvignon Blanc, Chardonnay, Botrytis Autumn Riesling, Sauternes, Classic Dry Red, Cabernet Malbec, Christopher Tawny Port.
summary The strikingly labelled Joadja Vineyards wines, first made in 1990, are principally drawn from 7 hectares of estate vineyards situated in the cool hills adjacent to Berrima. Both the red and whites have a consistent eucalypt/peppermint character which is clearly a product of the climate and (possibly) soil.

john gehrig wines ★★☆

Oxley–Milawa Road, Oxley, Vic 3678 **region** King Valley
phone (03) 5727 3395 **fax** (03) 5727 3699 **open** 7 days 9–5
winemaker John Gehrig **production** 5600 **est.** 1976
product range ($9–25 CD) Oxley Dry White, Riesling, Chardonnay, Late Harvest Riesling, Sparkling, Oxley Rose, Pinot Noir, King River Red, Merlot, Cabernet Merlot, Fortifieds.
summary Honest, if seldom exciting, wines; the occasional Chardonnay, Pinot Noir, Merlot and Cabernet Merlot have, however, risen above their station.

jollymont NR

145 Pullens Road, Woodbridge, Tas 7162 **region** Southern Tasmania
phone (03) 6267 4594 **fax** (03) 6267 4594 **open** Not
winemaker Andrew Hood (Contract) **production** 20 **est.** 1990
product range ($20–25 R) Chardonnay, Pinot Noir.
summary However briefly, Jollymont displaced Scarp Valley as the smallest producer in Australia, its 1998 vintage (the first) producing ten cases, the next, 20. The vines are not irrigated, nor will they be, and Peter and Heather Kreet do not intend to sell any wine younger than three to four years old. Their aim is to produce wines of maximum intensity and complexity.

jones winery NR

Jones Road, Rutherglen, Vic 3685 **region** Rutherglen
phone (02) 6032 8496 **fax** (02) 6032 8495 **open** Fri–Sun and public holidays 10–5
winemaker Mandy Jones **production** 600 **est.** 1864
product range ($12–40 CD) Annie's Classique Dry White, Classique Dry Red, LJ Shiraz, Fortified.
summary Late in 1998 the winery was purchased from Les Jones by Leanne Schoen and Mandy and Arthur Jones (nieces and nephew of Les). They are planning to refurbish the winery, and to concentrate on Shiraz and the styles of wine that the winery is known for. All wine is sold through the cellar door.

Jones LJ Shiraz

🍷🍷🍷🍷 **1999** So dark is the red-purple colour that it stains the glass; strong berry fruit on the bouquet can't totally disguise some fairly rough American oak, but there are no problems with the palate. Potent, dark berry fruit floods the mid-palate, with chocolatey overtones and ample ripe tannins. A mere 14.8° alcohol. **rating:** 88

best drinking 2004–2014 **best vintages** '99 **drink with** Char-grilled rump • $35

juniper estate NR

Harmans Road South, Cowaramup, WA 6284 **region** Margaret River
phone (08) 9755 9000 **fax** (08) 9755 9100 **open** 7 days 10–5
winemaker Mark Messenger **production** 7000 **est.** 1998
product range ($14–35 ML) Under the Juniper Crossing label are Riesling, Semillon Sauvignon Blanc, Chenin Blanc, Chardonnay, Late Harvest Riesling, Shiraz; Juniper Estate Semillon, Cabernet Sauvignon.
summary This is the reincarnation of Wrights, which was sold by founders Henry and Maureen Wright in 1998. The 10-hectare vineyard has been re-trellised, and the last 1.5 hectares of plantable land has seen the key plantings of shiraz and cabernet sauvignon increase a little. A major building programme was completed in February 2000, giving Juniper Estate a new 250-tonne capacity winery, barrel hall and cellar-door facility. The Juniper family is a famous one in the Margaret River region, its strong artistic bent evident in the immaculate packaging and background material. Juniper Crossing wines use a mix of estate-grown and contract-purchased grapes from other Margaret River vineyards. The Juniper Estate releases are made only from the 25-year-old estate plantings.

jyt wines NR

De Beyers Road, Pokolbin, NSW 2320 **region** Lower Hunter Valley
phone (02) 4998 7528 **fax** (02) 4998 7370 **open** Thurs–Tues 10–5
winemaker Jay Tulloch, Julie Tulloch **production** 1750 **est.** 1996
product range ($16–20 CD) Semillon, Verdelho, Chardonnay.
summary When Jay Tulloch left in 1996, it marked the end of a 100-year, multi-generational association with JY Tulloch and Sons (part of the Southcorp Wine Group). However, it did not mark the end of the Tulloch family's involvement with the wine industry, for he and wife Julie have established a 3-hectare hillside vineyard on the picturesque De Beyers Road which (appropriately) overlooks the old Tulloch winery. Here they have planted 0.6 hectare each of semillon, chardonnay, verdelho, shiraz and sangiovese.

kaesler wines & vineyard ★★★★

Barossa Valley Way, Nuriootpa, SA 5355 **region** Barossa Valley
phone (08) 8562 4488 **fax** (08) 8562 4499 **open** 7 days 10–5
winemaker Reid Bosward **production** 14 000 **est.** 1990
product range ($10–36 CD) Home Block Semillon, Old Vine Semillon, Prestige Semillon, Late Harvest Semillon, Bush Vine Grenache, Old Vine Grenache, Single Wire Merlot, Old Vine Shiraz, Stonehouse Shiraz, Reid's Rasp (Shiraz, Cabernet Sauvignon Merlot), Beerenauslese, Fortifieds.
summary Toby and Treena Hueppauff purchased Kaesler Farm, with its 12 hectares of vines (since doubled to over 24 hectares), in 1985 and since 1990 have been producing wine under the Kaesler label. The winery has an à la carte restaurant offering both indoor and outdoor dining; there is also accommodation. The wines are exported to California.

Kaesler Old Vine Shiraz

YYYYY **1998** Medium red-purple; the moderately intense bouquet is clean, with red cherry fruit, subtle oak and a touch of spice. The palate shows all the best features of the '98 vintage, with an extra degree of weight and depth to the mix of cherry, berry and bitter chocolate supported by fine, ripe tannins and unobtrusive oak.

rating: 92

best drinking 2003–2013 **best vintages** '98 **drink with** Buffalo steak • $36

Kaesler Reid's Rasp

YYYY **1998** Excellent red-purple colour; the bouquet has clean, red and blackcurrant/blackberry fruit and subtle oak. The palate has an interesting array of ripe berry fruit flavours which do, however, dip fractionally towards the finish.

rating: 88

best drinking 2002–2007 **best vintages** NA **drink with** Moroccan lamb • $20

kaiser stuhl

Tanunda Road, Nuriootpa, SA 5355 **region** Barossa Valley
phone (08) 8560 9389 **fax** (08) 8568 9489 **open** Mon–Sat 10–5, Sun 11–5
winemaker Nigel Logos **production** 1.3 million **est.** 1931

product range ($4–16 R) Black Forest, generic whites under bin numbers, Claret Bin 33, Bin 44 Riesling, Bin 55 Moselle, Bin 66 Burgundy, Bin 77 Chablis, Sparkling; also extensive cask and flagon range.
summary Part of the Southcorp Wines empire but a shadow of its former self, with its once-famous Green Ribbon Riesling and Red Ribbon Shiraz no more. Essentially provides flagon-quality wines in bottles at competitive prices.

kalari vineyards NR

120 Carro Park Road, Cowra, NSW 2794 **region** Cowra
phone (02) 6342 1465 **fax** (02) 6342 1465 **open** Fri–Mon 10–4
winemaker Jill Lindsay, Jon Reynold (Contract) **production** 2000 **est.** 1995
product range ($14–18 ML) Verdelho, Late Picked Verdelho, Chardonnay, Unwooded Chardonnay, Shiraz.
summary Kalari Vineyards is yet another of the new brands to appear in the Cowra region, with 15.5 hectares of vines established. A Verdelho, Chardonnay and Shiraz are being included in the initial release.

kangarilla road vineyard & winery ★★★★

Kangarilla Road, McLaren Vale, SA 5171 **region** McLaren Vale
phone (08) 8383 0533 **fax** (08) 8383 0044 **open** Mon–Fri 9–5, weekends 11–5
winemaker Kevin O'Brien **production** 20 000 **est.** 1975
product range ($12–30 CD) Chardonnay, Zinfandel, Shiraz, Cabernet Sauvignon, Tawny Port, Vintage Port.
summary Kangarilla Road Vineyard & Winery was formerly known as Stevens Cambrai. Long-time industry identity Kevin O'Brien and wife Helen purchased the property in July 1997, and have now fully established the strikingly labelled Kangarilla Road brand in place of Cambrai. Exports to the US and the UK.

Kangarilla Road Zinfandel

TTTT 1999 Medium purple-red; clean, ripe plum and blackberry fruit merges with surprisingly gentle vanilla oak; on the palate, juicy/spicy plum and blackberry fruit is at the core of a wine with controlled oak, extract and tannins. A reward for a lot of work done in the vineyard, including crop-thinning and bunch-thinning. Only 350 dozen made. **rating:** 89

best drinking 2002–2007 **best vintages** '96, '99 **drink with** Spiced Moroccan lamb • $30

Kangarilla Road Cabernet Sauvignon

TTTT 1999 Medium to full red-purple; the moderately intense bouquet has an attractive array of red berry fruit, touches of earth and oak. The palate is sweet, and quite lush, with blackcurrant/blackberry fruit, supported by nicely balanced tannins and oak. **rating:** 87

best drinking 2003–2008 **best vintages** '99 **drink with** Ox tongue • $19

kangaroo island vines NR

c/o 413 Payneham Road, Felixstow, SA 5070 **region** Fleurieu Zone
phone (08) 8365 3411 **fax** (08) 8336 2462 **open** Not
winemaker Caj Amadio **production** 600 **est.** 1990
product range ($20–25 ML) Island Sting, Kate's Block Shiraz, Florance Cabernet Merlot, Special Reserve Cabernet Merlot.
summary Kangaroo Island is another venture of Caj and Genny Amadio, with the wines being sold through the Chain of Ponds cellar door. The Amadios have been the focal point of the development of vineyards on Kangaroo Island, producing the wines not only from their own tiny planting of 450 vines on quarter of an acre, but buying grapes from other vignerons on the island. The tiny quantities of wine so far produced strongly support the notion that Kangaroo Island has an excellent climate for Bordeaux-style reds, particularly the excellent Special Reserve Cabernet Merlot.

Kangaroo Island Vines Kate's Block Shiraz

TTTT 1999 Medium to full red-purple; there is plenty happening on the complex bouquet, with spicy/earthy fruit and vanilla oak. The palate has abundant black cherry, chocolate and earth fruit, with firm but not bitter tannins, the oak well judged. **rating:** 89

best drinking 2004–2009 **best vintages** '99 **drink with** Bratwurst sausages • $25

Kangaroo Island Vines Florance Cabernet Merlot

YYYY **1999** Medium to full red-purple; very ripe plum/prune fruit is joined by positive oak on the bouquet. The palate really needs time to settle down, with a mix of ripe fruit, mint and then fairly tough tannins. **rating:** 84

best drinking 2004–2009 **best vintages** '97 **drink with** Braised lamb • $25

kangderaar vineyard NR

Melvilles Caves Road, Rheola, Vic 3517 **region** Bendigo
phone (03) 5438 8292 **fax** (03) 5438 8292 **open** Mon–Sat 9–5, Sun 10–5
winemaker James Nealy **production** 500 **est.** 1980
product range ($12–15 CD) Chardonnay, Vintage Reserve Chardonnay, Cabernet Sauvignon.
summary The 4.5-hectare vineyard is situated at Rheola, near the Melville Caves, said to have been the hideout of the bushranger Captain Melville in the 1850s, and surrounded by the Kooyoora State Park. It is owned by James and Christine Nealy.

kanjara NR

Cargo Road, Orange, NSW 2800 **region** Orange
phone (02) 6365 6148 **fax** (02) 6362 0593 **open** Not
winemaker Jan Carter, Mark Davidson (Contract) **production** 300 **est.** 1994
product range Riesling, Shiraz, Cabernet Sauvignon.
summary Since 1994 Jan Carter has progressively established a small vineyard with shiraz (1.04 hectares), riesling (0.57 hectare), cabernet sauvignon (0.74 hectare), sauvignon blanc (0.34 hectare) and merlot (0.11 hectare). Grapes have been produced on a commercial basis for three years, but the first wines (Riesling, Shiraz and Cabernet Sauvignon) will not be released until the end of 2001.

kara kara vineyard 

Sunraysia Highway, St Arnaud, Vic 3478 (10 km south of St Arnaud) **region** Pyrenees
phone (03) 5496 3294 **fax** (03) 5496 3294 **open** Mon–Fri 10.30–6, weekends 9–6
winemaker John Ellis, Steve Zsigmond **production** 2000 **est.** 1977
product range ($18–27 CD) Semillon Chardonnay, Sauvignon Blanc, Chardonnay, Shiraz Cabernet, Cabernet Sauvignon Shiraz.
summary Hungarian-born Steve Zsigmond comes from a long line of vignerons and sees Kara Kara as the eventual retirement occupation for himself and wife Marlene. Steve Zsigmond is a graduate of the Adelaide University Roseworthy campus wine-marketing course, and worked for Yalumba and Negociants as a sales manager in Adelaide and Perth. He looks after sales and marketing from the Melbourne premises of Kara Kara, and the wine is contract-made by John Ellis, with consistent results. Draws upon 9 hectares of estate plantings.

Kara Kara Semillon Chardonnay

YYYY **2000** Light green-yellow; the bouquet has light, lemony fruit with a touch of nectarine, the palate a replay, with fresh, light lemon/nectarine fruit. **rating:** 82

best drinking Now **best vintages** NA **drink with** Lightly smoked fish • $18

Kara Kara Chardonnay

YYYY **1999** Medium yellow-green; clean, moderately ripe fruit on the bouquet has slightly subdued varietal character, perhaps due to the oak. The palate is unpretentious, with modest fruit flavour, but quite well balanced. **rating:** 83

best drinking Now **best vintages** NA **drink with** Pasta • $20

karina vineyard ★★★★

35 Harrisons Road, Dromana, Vic 3936 **region** Mornington Peninsula
phone (03) 5981 0137 **fax** (03) 5981 0137 **open** Weekends 11–5, 7 days in January
winemaker Gerard Terpstra **production** 1500 **est.** 1984
product range ($13–19 CD) Riesling, Sauvignon Blanc, Chardonnay, Cabernet Merlot, Bald Hill Creek (Cabernet Sauvignon).

summary A typical Mornington Peninsula vineyard, situated in the Dromana/Redhill area on rising, north-facing slopes, just 3 kilometres from the shores of Port Phillip Bay. Immaculately tended and with picturesque garden surrounds. Fragrant Riesling and cashew-accented Chardonnay are usually its best wines.

Karina Cabernet Merlot

ŸŸŸŸ **1998** Medium red-purple; the bouquet is fragrant, quite light, with leafy/minty/berry aromas that are repeated on the palate. Here there is fairly brisk acidity, particularly for a '98 vintage wine. **rating:** 84

best drinking 2002–2006 **best vintages** '92, '93 **drink with** Calf's liver • $18

karl seppelt ★★★☆

Ross Dewells Road, Springton, SA 5235 **region** Eden Valley
phone (08) 8568 2378 **fax** (08) 8568 2799 **open** 7 days 10–5
winemaker Karl Seppelt, Petaluma (Contract) **production** 5000 **est.** 1981
product range ($14–24 CD) Riesling, Springton Chardonnay, Langhorne Creek Shiraz, Merlot, Springton Cabernet Sauvignon, Chardonnay Brut, Sparkling Shiraz, Brut Sauvage, Fino Sherry, Liqueur Muscat, Vintage Port, Tawny Port.
summary After experimenting with various label designs and names, Karl Seppelt (former marketing director of Seppelt) has decided to discontinue the brand name Grand Cru (although retaining it as a business name) and henceforth market the wines from his estate vineyards under his own name. The quality is highly consistent across the range, and the wines are exported to Canada, Germany and Japan.

karrivale 

Woodlands Road, Porongurup, WA 6324 **region** Great Southern
phone (08) 9853 1009 **fax** (08) 9853 1129 **open** Wed–Sun 10–5
winemaker Gavin Berry (Contract) **production** 1170 **est.** 1979
product range ($12–18 CD) Riesling, Chardonnay.
summary A tiny Riesling specialist in the wilds of the Porongurups, forced to change its name from Narang because Lindemans felt it could be confused with its (now defunct) Nyrang Shiraz brand; truly a strange world. This beautifully sited vineyard and its long-lived Riesling were acquired by Dr Peter Honey prior to the 2001 vintage.

karriview 

RMB 913 Roberts Road, Denmark, WA 6333 **region** Great Southern
phone (08) 9840 9381 **fax** (08) 9840 9381 **open** Summer school holidays 7 days 11–4, Feb–Dec Fri–Tues 11–4
winemaker Michael Kerrigan (Contract) **production** 800 **est.** 1986
product range ($23–28 CD) Chardonnay, Pinot Noir.
summary One hectare each of immaculately tended pinot noir and chardonnay on ultra-close spacing produce tiny quantities of two wines of remarkable intensity, quality and style. Available only from the winery, but worth the effort. There is some vintage variation; the winery rating is based upon the successes, not the disappointments. Typically, back-vintages are available; with age, the Pinot Noir acquires strong foresty characters which are quite Burgundian.

katnook estate 

Riddoch Highway, Coonawarra, SA 5263 **region** Coonawarra
phone (08) 8737 2394 **fax** (08) 8737 2397 **open** Mon–Fri 9–4.30, weekends 10–4.30
winemaker Wayne Stehbens **production** 70 000 **est.** 1979
product range ($8.50–80 R) Under the premium Katnook label: Riesling, Sauvignon Blanc, Chardonnay, Botrytis Riesling, Chardonnay Brut, Sparkling Shiraz, Cabernet Sauvignon, Merlot, Odyssey (super-premium Cabernet) and Prodigy (super-premium Shiraz); under the Riddoch label: Chardonnay, Sauvignon Blanc, Shiraz and Cabernet Shiraz Merlot; also Woolshed Chardonnay and Cabernet Shiraz Merlot.
summary Still the largest contract grape-grower and supplier in Coonawarra, selling 60 per cent of its grape production to others. The historic stone woolshed, in which the second vintage in Coonawarra (1896) was made and which has served Katnook since 1980, is being restored. The 1997 launch of the flagship Odyssey and the 2000 follow-up with Prodigy Shiraz point the way for a higher profile for the winemaking side of the venture. Exports to the UK, Northern Ireland, the US, Canada, Switzerland, Hong Kong and the Philippines.

Katnook Estate Riesling

YYYYy **2000** Light green-yellow; attractive lime and lemon aromas are conventional, the hint of stonefruit less so, but without in any way detracting from the appeal. The light to medium bodied palate has lively flavours and good fruit intensity, and likewise good length. **rating:** 90

best drinking Now–2006 **best vintages** '00 **drink with** Vegetable terrine • $18.99

Katnook Estate Sauvignon Blanc

YYYY **2000** Medium yellow-green; the bouquet is quite powerful, dominated by gooseberry, together with a hint of passionfruit; the palate is solid, with plenty of flavour, needing only a touch more acidity on the finish. **rating:** 88

best drinking Now **best vintages** '84, '86, '90, '92, '94, '95, '96, '98 **drink with** Oysters • $25

Katnook Estate Chardonnay

YYYY **1998** Developed yellow; a soft, nutty, moderately complex bouquet is low in fruit aromatics, the palate with gentle peach fruit and nutty oak; medium weight and medium length. Maybe in a dull phase, or perhaps a dodgy bottle. **rating:** 86

best drinking Now–2003 **best vintages** '84, '86, '90, '92, '94, '96, '97 **drink with** Poached salmon • $30

Katnook Estate Chardonnay Brut

YYYY **1995** Light green-yellow; a crisp, floral bouquet with citrus, apple and melon aromas leads into a very delicate, almost fairy floss-like palate; crisp, clean and dry. **rating:** 87

best drinking Now–2005 **best vintages** NA **drink with** Aperitif • NA

Katnook Estate Botrytis Semillon

YYYY **1995** Glowing yellow-green; moderately complex cumquat and mandarin aromas are followed by a palate with lots of sweet, honeyed flavour and subtle oak, but which is not especially complex. **rating:** 86

best drinking Now **best vintages** NA **drink with** Fruit tart • $20

Katnook Estate Shiraz

YYYYy **1998** Medium red-purple; the bouquet is moderately intense but very fragrant, opening with earthy aromas, then moving into a more complex game/licorice spectrum. The savoury characters of the bouquet are sweetened up by the clever use of the high-quality oak on the palate, and the wine finishes with fine, soft tannins. **rating:** 92

best drinking 2003–2010 **best vintages** '98 **drink with** Rack of veal • $40

Katnook Estate Prodigy Shiraz

YYYYy **1997** Medium to full red-purple; the bouquet is ultra-rich and ultra-ripe, ranging through plum, licorice, black cherry, prune and chocolate. The warmth of the alcohol greets the entrance of the wine into the mouth, followed by a complex, slightly gamey/savoury fruit then powerful, slightly dry, tannins. A Leviathan prodigy indeed. **rating:** 90

best drinking Now–2010 **best vintages** '97 **drink with** Wild game • $80

Katnook Estate Cabernet Sauvignon

YYYYY **1998** Medium red-purple; a classic bouquet reflecting more or less equally the climate/terroir of Coonawarra and the character of cabernet sauvignon as it manifests itself in Coonawarra, the aromas a mix of berry, briar, earth in a savoury spectrum. The palate is perfectly weighted and structured, the wine polished yet substantial; particularly sweet tannins on the finish give the wine special character. **rating:** 94

best drinking 2003–2013 **best vintages** '90, '91, '92, '94, '97, '98 **drink with** Prime rib of beef • $40

Katnook Estate Odyssey Cabernet Sauvignon

YYYYY **1996** Dark red-purple; the bouquet is particularly complex, with briary/dusty/earthy overtones to the fruit and oak. The palate has a mix of cedar, blackberry and sweet savoury/earthy flavours; fine-grained tannins round off a wine with very good balance and length. **rating:** 94

best drinking Now–2011 **best vintages** '91, '92, '94, '96 **drink with** Yearling beef • $80

kay bros amery ★★★☆

Kay Road, McLaren Vale, SA 5171 **region** McLaren Vale

phone (08) 8323 8211 **fax** (08) 8323 9199 **open** Mon–Fri 9–5, weekends and public holidays 12–5

winemaker Colin Kay **production** 6500 **est.** 1890

product range ($15–30 CD) Late Harvest Sauvignon Blanc, Pinot Noir, Shiraz, Block 6 Shiraz, Hillside Shiraz, Grenache, Merlot, Cabernet Sauvignon; Port Liqueur, Muscat.

summary A traditional winery with a rich history and 17 hectares of priceless old vines; while the white wines have been variable, the red wines and fortified wines can be very good. Of particular interest is Block 6 Shiraz, made from 100-year-old vines; both vines and wine are going from strength to strength. Exports to New Zealand, Singapore, the US and Canada.

Kay Bros Amery Shiraz

ΥΥΥΥ **1998** Medium to full red-purple; dark blackberry, prune and plum aromas lead into a palate with good weight, concentration and extract, the earthy varietal fruit supported by lingering tannins. **rating:** 89

best drinking 2003–2008 **best vintages** '98 **drink with** Prime rib • $20

Kay Bros Amery Hillside Shiraz

ΥΥΥΥY **1998** Medium to full red-purple; very ripe, rich and concentrated blackberry, plum and earth aromas foreshadow a palate with seductively sweet dark berry and dark chocolate flavours surrounded by supple tannins. Minimal oak input throughout.

best drinking 2003–2013 **best vintages** '98 **drink with** Braised beef • $30

Kay Bros Amery Cabernet Sauvignon

ΥΥΥΥY **1998** Dense purple-red; ripe blackcurrant, prune and chocolate aromas lead into a very rich and dense palate with a similar range of chocolate, Rhône and blackcurrant fruit, with all the tannins needed for a long life. **rating:** 90

best drinking 2003–2013 **best vintages** '98 **drink with** Stir-fried beef • $20

keith tulloch wine ★★★★★

Lilywood Farm, O'Connors Road, Pokolbin, NSW 2325 **region** Lower Hunter Valley

phone (02) 4990 7867 **fax** (02) 4990 7171 **open** Not

winemaker Keith Tulloch **production** 5500 **est.** 1997

product range ($14–42 R) Under the Keith Tulloch label: Semillon, Chardonnay, Kester Shiraz, Merlot; Perdiem label: Verdelho, Chardonnay, Shiraz, Cabernet Sauvignon.

summary Keith Tulloch is, of course, a member of the Tulloch family who have played such a leading role in the Hunter Valley for over a century. Formerly a winemaker at Lindemans and then Rothbury Estate, he is responsible for the production of Evans Family Wines as well as developing his own label since 1997. Moves are currently underway to centralise all of the winemaking at Hunter Ridge Winery, where he will be based permanently. I cannot remember being more impressed with an initial release of wines than those under the Keith Tulloch label. The only problem is the small scale of their production, like that of Jeffrey Grosset in his early days. There is the same almost obsessive attention to detail, the same almost ascetic intellectual approach, the same refusal to accept anything but the best.

Keith Tulloch Semillon

ΥΥΥΥΥ **2000** Light green-yellow; the bouquet has gentle citrus/lemon/grass aromas surrounded by subtle but immaculately handled oak. The palate is very long and impressive, the flavour linear and persistent, not compromising the varietal character, yet giving this young wine rarely encountered texture. I think it will age beautifully, but who cares. **rating:** 94

best drinking Now–2010 **best vintages** '00 **drink with** Lobster • $26

Keith Tulloch Chardonnay

ΥΥΥΥY **1998** Light to medium yellow-green; a spotlessly clean bouquet with fig and melon aromas woven through the gentle oak; then a light to medium bodied palate with a mix of cashew, melon and pear finishing with excellent acidity. Elegant and stylish. 100 cases made. **rating:** 91

best drinking Now–2004 **best vintages** '98 **drink with** Blue-eye cod • NA

Keith Tulloch Kester Shiraz

ΥΥΥΥΥ **1999** Medium to full red-purple; the French oak makes a positive contribution to the fragrant bouquet, but is seamlessly integrated with the fruit; the palate, with its mix of intense but elegant plum and cherry fruit, cedary oak, and fine, lingering tannins, is totally impressive. 500 cases made. **rating:** 94

ΥΥΥΥΥ **1998** Medium to full red-purple; the complex bouquet has a wonderful combination of leathery/spicy overtones to the plummy fruit; incredibly, does have northern Rhône Valley overtones. The palate is velvety and rich, with plum and spice fruit, great oak and tremendous length. The wine is powerful, but carries its high alcohol with style. 500 cases made. **rating:** 94

best drinking 2004–2014 **best vintages** '98, '99 **drink with** Rare fillet of beef • $42

Keith Tulloch Merlot

ΥΥΥΥ **1999** Medium red-purple; a quite fragrant and savoury bouquet with spice and olive aromas is followed by a finely focused palate with the red fruit that many see as the mark of Merlot, supported by relatively subtle oak and soft tannins. **rating:** 89

best drinking 2002–2007 **best vintages** NA **drink with** Rabbit or hare • $26

kellermeister ★★★

Barossa Valley Highway, Lyndoch, SA 5351 **region** Barossa Valley
phone (08) 8524 4303 **fax** (08) 8524 4880 **open** 7 days 9–6
winemaker Trevor Jones **production** 8000 **est.** 1970
product range ($8.50–26.50 CD) High Country Riesling, Show Reserve Riesling, Abendlese, Frontignan Spätlese and Auslese, Late Harvest Sylvaner, Cabernet Rosé, Black Sash Shiraz, Cabernet Sauvignon, Cabernet Shiraz, Sparkling and Fortifieds; also the Trevor Jones range (under his own label) of Virgin Chardonnay, Riesling, Cabernet Merlot and Dry Grown Barossa Shiraz.
summary Specialises in older vintage wines made in traditional fashion, an extraordinary array of which are on offer at enticing prices. There is always a range of vintages available; the wines are soft and generous, if very traditional in style.

kellybrook ★★★☆

Fulford Road, Wonga Park, Vic 3115 **region** Yarra Valley
phone (03) 9722 1304 **fax** (03) 9722 2092 **open** Mon–Sat 9–6, Sun 11–6
winemaker Darren Kelly, Philip Kelly **production** 3000 **est.** 1960
product range ($14–26 CD) Riesling, Gewürztraminer, Chardonnay, Enfield Chardonnay, Pinot Noir, Shiraz, Merlot, Cabernet Merlot, Cabernet Shiraz, Brut Pinot Noir Chardonnay, Champagne Cider, Apple Brandy, Liqueur Muscat, Old Vintage Tawny Port.
summary The 8-hectare vineyard is situated at Wonga Park at the entrance to the principal winegrowing areas of the Yarra Valley, replete with picnic area and a full-scale restaurant. As well as table wine, a very competent producer of both cider and apple brandy (in Calvados style). Retail distribution through Victoria, New South Wales, Queensland and South Australia.

Kellybrook Chardonnay

ΥΥΥΥ **2000** Medium yellow-green; the bouquet is precisely as one would expect, showing melon and hints of citrus; the palate has plenty of weight in a ripe melon, fig and nectarine spectrum, supported by judicious oak. **rating:** 85

best drinking Now–2005 **best vintages** NA **drink with** Yarra Valley yabbies • $18

Kellybrook Cabernet Merlot

ΥΥΥΥΥ **2000** Full red-purple; ripe cassis berry fruit leads the bouquet and literally floods the palate. A lovely wine, with oak very much in the background. Tasted as a tank sample, but sufficiently impressive to warrant its inclusion, and on the basis that it was a final blend. **rating:** 90

ΥΥΥΥ **1998** Medium red tinged with purple. Berry, mint and leaf aromas are clean and light. Pleasant, gentle red berry flavours define a straightforward wine from a particularly good vintage that eliminated the green edges one sometimes sees in cool-grown cabernet merlot. **rating:** 83

best drinking 2004–2010 **best vintages** '00 **drink with** Beef in red wine sauce • $22

kelly's creek ★★★★☆

RSD 226a Lower Whitehills Road, Relbia, Tas 7258 **region** Northern Tasmania
phone (03) 6234 9696 **fax** (03) 6231 6222 **open** Not
winemaker Andrew Hood (Contract) **production** 650 **est.** 1992
product range ($15–17 R) Riesling, Chardonnay, Pinot Noir, Cabernet Sauvignon.

summary Kelly's Creek draws on 1 hectare of riesling and 0.2 hectare each of chardonnay, pinot noir and cabernet sauvignon. Its majority owner is Darryl Johnson, who runs the vineyard with help from Guy Wagner, who describes himself as 'merely a marketing minion'. Small quantities of Riesling are made for Kelly's Creek, all vintages having had notable success at the Tasmanian Wines Show.

kelman vineyards ★★★☆

Cnr Oakey Creek Road and Mount View Road, Pokolbin, NSW 2320 **region** Lower Hunter Valley
phone (02) 4991 5456 **fax** (02) 4991 7555 **open** 7 days 10–5
winemaker Simon Gilbert (Contract) **production** 3000 **est.** 1999
product range ($14.50–20 CD) Semillon, Pond Block Chardonnay, Shiraz.
summary The Kelman Estate is a California-type development on the outskirts of Cessnock. A 40-hectare property has been subdivided into 80 residential development lots, but with 8 hectares of vines wending between the lots under common ownership. In a sign of the times, part of the chardonnay has already been grafted across to shiraz before coming into full production, and the vineyard has the potential to ultimately produce 8000 cases a year. In the meantime, each owner will receive 12 cases a year of the wines produced by the vineyard, with the balance being available for sale via mail order (phone (02) 4991 5456 for details) and through a single Sydney retail outlet. The Chardonnay is a nice, fresh wine, with light melon fruit, free of the dreaded oak chips.

Kelman Estate Semillon

YYYY **2000** Light straw-green; a classic, crisp and restrained bouquet with notes of mineral and dried herb is followed by a lively, crisp and fresh palate with the whole of its life in front of it. **rating:** 87
best drinking 2003–2008 **best vintages** NA **drink with** Leave it in the cellar • $17.50

kenilworth bluff wines NR

Lot 13 Bluff Road, Kenilworth, Qld 4574 **region** Queensland Coastal
phone (07) 5472 3723 **open** Fri–Sun 10–4 and by appointment
winemaker Bruce Humphery-Smith (Contract) **production** NA **est.** 1993
product range ($13–16 CD) Semillon, Chardonnay, Shiraz, Merlot, Cabernet Sauvignon.
summary Brian and Colleen Marsh modestly describe themselves as 'little more than hobbyists at this point in time' but also admit that 'our wines show tremendous promise'. They began planting the vineyards in 1993 in a hidden valley at the foot of Kenilworth Bluff, and now have 4 hectares (shiraz, cabernet sauvignon, merlot, semillon, chardonnay) coming into bearing. Presently the wines are made off site by Bruce Humphery-Smith, but one day the Marshes hope it will be feasible to establish an on-site winery.

kennedys keilor valley NR

Lot 3 Overnewton Road, Keilor, Vic 3036 **region** Sunbury
phone (03) 9311 6246 **fax** (03) 9331 6246 **open** By appointment
winemaker Peter Dredge **production** 300 **est.** 1994
product range ($16 CD) Chardonnay.
summary A newly established estate-based Chardonnay specialist, producing its only wine from 1.8 hectares of relatively newly established vineyards.

kevin sobels wines NR

Cnr Broke and Halls Roads, Pokolbin, NSW 2321 **region** Lower Hunter Valley
phone (02) 4998 7766 **fax** (02) 4998 7475 **open** 7 days 10–5
winemaker Kevin Sobels **production** 5000 **est.** 1992
product range ($12–18 CD) Chardonnay, Semillon, Traminer, Pinot Noir.
summary Veteran winemaker Kevin Sobels has found yet another home, drawing upon 8 hectares of vineyards (originally planted by the Ross Jones family) to produce wines sold almost entirely through cellar door and mail order, with limited retail representation. The cellar door offers light meals and picnic and barbecue facilities.

kies family wines NR

Barossa Valley Way, Lyndoch, SA 5381 **region** Barossa Valley
phone (08) 8524 4110 **fax** (08) 8524 4110 **open** 7 days 10–4.30
winemaker Jim Irvine **production** 2500 **est.** 1969
product range ($7–18 CD) Eden Valley Riesling, Classic Dry White, Sauvignon Blanc Semillon, Oak Matured

Semillon, Chardonnay, Sparkling, Sparkling Heysen Gold, Lambrusco, White Barossa, Heysen Gold, Grenache, Old Vineyard Shiraz, Cabernet Sauvignon, Tawny Port.
summary The Kies family has been resident in the Barossa Valley since 1857, with the present generation of winemakers being the fifth, and their children the sixth. Until 1969 the family sold almost all the grapes to others, but in that year launched their own brand, Karrawirra. The co-existence of Killawarra forced a name change in 1983 to Redgum Vineyard, and this business was in turn subsequently sold. Later still, Kies Family Wines opened for business, drawing upon vineyards up to 100 years old which had remained in the family throughout the changes, offering a wide range of wines through the 1880 vintage cellar door.

kilgour estate NR

85 McAdams Lane, Bellarine, Vic 3223 **region** Geelong
phone (03) 5251 2223 **fax** (03) 5251 2223 **open** Wed–Sun 10.30–6, 7 days in Jan
winemaker John Ellis (Consultant) **production** 2000 **est.** 1989
product range Chardonnay, Pinot Noir.
summary Kilgour Estate has 7 hectares of vines, and the wines are contract-made by John Ellis at Hanging Rock. Fruit-driven Pinot Noir and Chardonnay are winery specialties, the Pinot Noir having won at least one gold medal.

kilikanoon ★★★★

Penna Lane, Penwortham, SA 5453 **region** Clare Valley
phone (08) 8843 4377 **fax** (08) 8843 4377 **open** Weekends and public holidays 11–5
winemaker Kevin Mitchell **production** 5000 **est.** 1997
product range ($15–25 CD) Morts Block Riesling, Semillon, Adelaide Hills Sauvignon Blanc, Prodigal Grenache, Oracle Shiraz, Siblings (Grenache, Shiraz, Cabernet Sauvignon), Cabernet Sauvignon.
summary Kilikanoon has 11 hectares of estate vineyards at Leasingham and Penwortham. Wholesale distribution in South Australia, Victoria and Western Australia; exports to the US, Canada, the UK, Germany, Switzerland and Hong Kong.

Kilikanoon Morts Block Riesling

🍷🍷🍷🍷 **2000** Light green-yellow; the bouquet shows strong regional character with its mix of slate, talc, mineral and herb; the full flavour of the palate follows down the track of the bouquet in a generous, relatively early-developing style. **rating:** 88
best drinking Now–2004 **best vintages** NA **drink with** Sushi • $15

Kilikanoon Semillon

🍷🍷🍷½ **2000** Medium yellow-green; spicy nutmeg oak drives the bouquet, but there is plenty of total flavour in both fruit and oak terms on the palate; the real criticism is that, almost inevitably, it is a head and shoulders style that slides away on the finish after a powerful opening. **rating:** 84
best drinking Now–2004 **best vintages** NA **drink with** Vichyssoise • $16

Kilikanoon Adelaide Hills Sauvignon Blanc

🍷🍷🍷½ **1999** Light green-yellow; the clean and crisp bouquet is of light to medium intensity, exhibiting grass and mineral aromas; a clean, well-made wine with good structure and balance, but lacks varietal fruit intensity. **rating:** 84
best drinking Now **best vintages** NA **drink with** Shellfish • $16

Kilikanoon Oracle Shiraz

🍷🍷🍷🍷½ **1999** Medium to full red-purple; the bouquet offers abundant dark plum, blackberry and cherry fruit with just a touch of vanilla oak. The palate has good fruit intensity, not over-extracted, and with a sensitive use of oak. A very good outcome for the vintage. **rating:** 90
best drinking 2003–2009 **best vintages** '98 **drink with** Roast shoulder of lamb • $25

Kilikanoon Siblings

🍷🍷🍷½ **1998** Medium red-purple; the lifted bouquet shows sweet, jammy grenache varietal character, the palate abundant, sweet plum jam flavours, low tannins and minimal oak. Ready now. **rating:** 83
best drinking Now **best vintages** NA **drink with** Pizza • $15

Kilikanoon Prodigal Grenache

▼▼▼▼ **1999** Medium to full red-purple; rich, dense prune and sweet, dark berry fruit aromas on the bouquet are followed by a chewy, rich and jammy/juicy palate which is strongly varietal, the fruit sweetness coming on the tip of the tongue as the wine enters the mouth. **rating:** 86

best drinking Now–2004 **best vintages** NA **drink with** Braised oxtail • $18

killawarra ★★★☆

Tanunda Road, Nuriootpa, SA 5355 **region** Barossa Valley
phone (08) 8560 9389 **fax** (08) 8562 1669 **open** See Penfolds
winemaker Steve Goodwin **production** 205 000 **est.** 1975
product range ($9–15 R) Only Sparkling wines: Non Vintage Brut, Vintage Brut, Brut Cremant, Premier Brut and Reserve Brut; also Non Vintage Sparkling Burgundy, Killawarra 'K' series Vintage Pinot Noir Chardonnay and Sparkling Shiraz Cabernet.
summary Purely a Southcorp brand, without any particular presence in terms of either vineyards or winery, but increasingly styled in a mode different from the Seaview or Seppelt wines. As one would expect, the wines are competitively priced, and what is more, perform well in national wine shows.

killerby ★★★★

Caves Road, Willyabrup, WA 6280 **region** Margaret River
phone 1800 655 722 **fax** 1800 679 578 **open** 7 days 10–4.30
winemaker Paul Boulden **production** 14 000 **est.** 1973
product range ($16.50–32.50 R) Semillon, Semillon Sauvignon Blanc, Selection Sauvignon Blanc, Chardonnay, Shiraz, Cabernet Sauvignon and budget-priced April Classic White (Traminer Semillon Chardonnay blend) and April Classic Red (Shiraz Pinot Cabernet blend).
summary The members of the Killerby family are long-term residents of the southwest; Ben Killerby is the fourth generation. The estate vineyards of 29 hectares have been progressively established since 1973, most now fully mature. The Chardonnay, in particular, is very highly rated by some critics, but I would like to see a little more succulence and concentration. Australian distribution through Lionel Samson and The Main Domain Wine Company; exports to the US.

Killerby Semillon Sauvignon Blanc

▼▼▼▼▽ **2000** Light to medium green-yellow; the bouquet is at once complex yet restrained, the accent being on things other than primary fruit; however on the palate nice, ripe gooseberry fruit comes through, the oak component adding more to texture and structure than to flavour. It all works well. **rating:** 90

best drinking Now–2004 **best vintages** '00 **drink with** Grilled fish • $24

Killerby Shiraz

▼▼▼▼ **1999** Strong red-purple; the aromas are ripe, sweet and solid, with some earthy overtones. A big, rich, complex palate, but slightly chewy oak and tannins make the finish a little tough and bitter at this point. Does appear to have sufficient fruit to come into balance with further bottle age. **rating:** 89

best drinking 2004–2010 **best vintages** '91, '92, '94, '98, '99 **drink with** Game pie • $25

Killerby Cabernet Sauvignon

▼▼▼▼▼ **1999** Strong, deep colour; the bouquet is flooded with sweet blackberry/blackcurrant/cassis fruit, fruit which powers a rich, complex, multilayered and excellently textured palate. Gold medal at the 2000 Wine Show of Western Australia. **rating:** 94

best drinking 2003–2013 **best vintages** '87, '89, '92, '93, '94, '96, '99 **drink with** Mature cheddar • $25

kimbarra wines NR

422 Barkly Street, Ararat, Vic 3377 **region** Grampians
phone (03) 5352 2238 **open** Mon–Fri 9–5
winemaker Peter Leeke **production** 3500 **est.** 1990
product range NA
summary Peter and David Leeke have established 14 hectares of riesling, shiraz and cabernet sauvignon, the three varieties overall that have proved best suited to the Grampians region.

king river estate NR

RMB 9300, Wangaratta, Vic 3677 **region** King Valley
phone (03) 5729 3689 **fax** (03) 5729 3688 **open** By appointment
winemaker Trevor Knaggs **production** 1500 **est.** 1996
product range ($18–20 CD) Chardonnay, Shiraz, Merlot, Cabernet Sauvignon.
summary Trevor Knaggs, with the assistance of his father Collin, began the establishment of King River Estate in 1990, making the first wines in 1996. The initial plantings were of 3.3 hectares each of chardonnay and cabernet sauvignon, followed by 8 hectares of merlot and 3 hectares of shiraz. More recent plantings have extended the varietal range with verdelho, viognier, barbera and sangiovese, lifting the total plantings to a substantial 20 hectares. Home-stay accommodation is available in the farm-style guest house. Needless to say, bookings are essential.

kings creek winery ★★★★

237 Myers Road, Bittern, Vic 3918 **region** Mornington Peninsula
phone (03) 5983 2102 **fax** (03) 5983 5153 **open** 7 days 11–5
winemaker Brien Cole, Ian Wood **production** 4000 **est.** 1981
product range ($16–25 R) Sauvignon Blanc, Chardonnay, Reserve Chardonnay, Pinot Noir, Reserve Pinot Noir; White Label Pinot Gris, Unwooded Chardonnay, Sauvignon Blanc, Pinot Noir.
summary Kings Creek was originally operated by the Bell, Glover and Perraton families, ownership now resting with Kings Creek Winery Pty Ltd. Planting commenced in 1981, and the vines are now fully mature. Since 1990 the quality of the wines, particularly of the Pinot Noir and Chardonnay, has provided excellent value for money. Limited retail distribution in New South Wales and Victoria, exports to the US.

Kings Creek Sauvignon Blanc

YYYY **2000** Light to medium yellow-green; the bouquet is quite potent with herbal/herbaceous aromas set against riper fruit characters; the medium-bodied palate has some of the lychee flavours claimed on the back label, with a relatively soft finish. An alternative style. **rating:** 85

best drinking Now **best vintages** NA **drink with** Fish terrine • $16

Kings Creek Pinot Gris

YYYY **1998** The colour has a straw edge, which is quite acceptable for the variety. The bouquet is very rich, with ripe, tropical varietal fruit aromas. It seems to break up somewhat on the palate, with some Alsace-like characters, which are appealing, but there is also a slightly hot alcohol finish. Needs food. **rating:** 83

best drinking Now–2003 **best vintages** NA **drink with** Braised pork neck • $16

Kings Creek Unwooded Chardonnay

YYYY **1998** Light to medium yellow-green; the bouquet is clean, light and undeveloped, the palate fresh, with light melon and citrus fruit. An attractive unwooded Chardonnay which, while relatively simple in terms of structure, has good balance and the capacity to age. **rating:** 84

best drinking Now–2003 **best vintages** NA **drink with** Salad • $16

Kings Creek Chardonnay

YYYY **2000** Light green-yellow; light melon fruit on the bouquet is not helped by what seems to be slightly indifferent oak; the palate is light, straightforward, with gentle melon fruit. Not as good as previous years. **rating:** 83

best drinking Now–2003 **best vintages** '88, '91, '93, '94 **drink with** Stir-fried chicken • $16

Kings Creek Pinot Noir

YYYY **2000** Light to medium purple-red; the bouquet is clean, with gentle plummy varietal fruit with a hint of soft, French oak. The palate has ripe, plummy fruit, and while it may lack intensity, provides authentic pinot varietal character at a price matched by few other wines of this variety. **rating:** 84

best drinking Now–2004 **best vintages** '88, '89, '91, '92, '94, '95, '97, '98 **drink with** Chinese duck with mushrooms • $16

kingsley ★★★

6 Kingsley Court, Portland, Vic 3305 **region** Henty
phone (03) 5523 1864 **fax** (03) 5523 1644 **open** 7 days 1–4

winemaker Contract **production** 1200 **est.** 1983
product range ($13–21 CD) Riesling, Botrytis Riesling, Late Harvest Riesling, Chardonnay, Cabernet Sauvignon.
summary Only a small part of the 10 hectares is made into wine under contract, the remainder being sold as grapes. Older vintages are usually available at cellar door.

kingston estate ★★★☆

PO Box 67, Kingston-on-Murray, SA 5331 **region** Riverland
phone (08) 8583 0500 **fax** (08) 8583 0505 **open** By appointment
winemaker Bill Moularadellis, Rod Chapman **production** 100 000 **est.** 1979
product range ($10–33 R) Verdelho, Chardonnay, Semillon Sauvignon Blanc, Shiraz, Cabernet Sauvignon, Merlot; Tessera (Cabernet blend), Sarantos Soft Press Chardonnay; Special Releases of Saprian NV, Durif, Zinfandel and Viognier; Reserve range of Chardonnay, Shiraz, Merlot and Petit Verdot.
summary Kingston Estate is a substantial and successful Riverland winery, crushing 10 000 tonnes a year and exporting 80 per cent of its production. It is only in recent years that it has turned its attention to the domestic market with national distribution. It has also set up long-term purchase contracts with growers in the Clare Valley, Adelaide Hills, Langhorne Creek and Mount Benson, and embarked on a programme of expanding its varietal range, and seems to have seized the opportunity of significantly increasing its prices.

Kingston Estate Chardonnay

ΥΥΥΥ **1999** Medium green-yellow; the moderately intense bouquet has ripe fruit, with a touch of charry/ smoky oak, moving through to a soft, round palate with pleasant peach and nectarine fruit; subliminal oak.
rating: 84

best drinking Now **best vintages** '91, '92, '94, '96 **drink with** Veal in white sauce • NA

Kingston Estate Sarantos Soft Press Chardonnay

ΥΥΥΥ **1998** Light green-yellow; a light, fresh, melon-accent bouquet, without the use of chippy oak, is replicated on the palate with crisp, light melon fruit. **rating:** 84

best drinking Now **best vintages** NA **drink with** Takeaway • NA

Kingston Estate Reserve Shiraz

ΥΥΥΥ **1998** Medium red-purple; the first impression from the bouquet is obvious, dusty, vanilla American oak, and while the palate opens with sweet plummy fruit, oak flavour and extract really hits the finish. **rating:** 83

best drinking Now–2004 **best vintages** '97 **drink with** Hamburger • NA

Kingston Estate Reserve Petit Verdot

ΥΥΥΥ **1998** Medium red-purple; spicy oak aromatics sit on top of the varietal character on the bouquet, but not so much on the palate, where very ripe chocolate/blackberry fruit manifests itself, finishing with nice tannins. However, I doubt whether a winemaker from Bordeaux would recognise the variety. **rating:** 84

best drinking 2002–2005 **best vintages** NA **drink with** Marinated lamb • NA

kingtree wines NR

Kingtree Road, Wellington Mills, via Dardanup, WA 6326 **region** Geographe
phone (08) 9728 3050 **fax** (08) 9728 3113 **open** 7 days 12–5.30
winemaker Contract **production** 1000 **est.** 1991
product range ($16–20 CD) Riesling, Sauvignon Blanc, Gerrasse White, Cabernet Merlot.
summary Kingtree Wines, with 2.5 hectares of estate plantings, is part of the Kingtree Lodge development, a four and a half-star luxury retreat in dense jarrah forest.

kinvarra estate NR

RMB 5141, New Norfolk, Tas 7140 **region** Southern Tasmania
phone (03) 6286 1333 **fax** (03) 6286 2026 **open** Not
winemaker Andrew Hood **production** 90 **est.** 1990
product range ($13.50–15 ML) Riesling, Pinot Noir.
summary Kinvarra is the part-time occupation of David and Sue Bevan, with their wonderful 1827 homestead depicted on the label. There is only 1 hectare of vines, half riesling and half pinot noir, and most of the crop is sold to Wellington Wines.

kirkham estate NR

3 Argyle Street, Camden, NSW 2570 **region** South Coast Zone
phone (02) 4655 7722 **fax** (02) 4655 7722 **open** 7 days 11–5
winemaker Stan Aliprandi **production** 3000 **est.** 1993
product range ($9.50–15.50 CD) Traminer Riesling, Semillon, Semillon Chardonnay, Chardonnay, Botrytis Semillon, Pinot Noir, Lambrusco, Merlot, Cabernet Sauvignon, Tawny Port.
summary Kirkham Estate is one of six or so wine producers near Camden, a far cry from the 18 producers of the mid-nineteenth century but still indicative of the growth of vineyards and winemakers everywhere. It is the venture of Stan Aliprandi, a former Riverina winemaker with an interesting career going back over 30 years. It draws upon 9 hectares of vineyards, planted to chardonnay, semillon, verdelho, petit verdot, shiraz, merlot, pinot noir and cabernet sauvignon, supplemented, it would seem, by grapes (and wines) purchased elsewhere.

kirwan's bridge wines NR

Cnr of Lobb's Lane and Kirwan's Bridge Road, Nagambie, Vic 3608 **region** Goulburn Valley
phone (03) 5794 1777 **fax** (03) 5794 1993 **open** Not
winemaker Anna Hubbard **production** 1500 **est.** 1997
product range ($15–35 ML) Riesling, Marsanne, Shiraz, Merlot.
summary A major development, with over 35 hectares planted to a major emphasis on the Rhône varietals (7.9 hectares of marsanne, 2.7 hectares of viognier, with 1.3 hectares of roussane to be planted 2001; and 11.2 hectares of shiraz, 2.7 hectares of mourvedre and 2.5 hectares of grenache). A side bet on 4.8 hectares of cabernet sauvignon, 2.4 hectares of merlot and 1.3 hectares of riesling rounds off the planting. The wines are available by mailing list, and the cellar door will open in 2002, when an ecotourist island accessed by canoe or aluminium boat will be offered, with bird-watching opportunities.

knappstein lenswood vineyards ★★★★★

Crofts Road, Lenswood, SA 5240 **region** Adelaide Hills
phone (08) 8389 8111 **fax** (08) 8389 8555 **open** By appointment
winemaker Tim Knappstein **production** 10 000 **est.** 1981
product range ($22–53 R) Semillon, Sauvignon Blanc, Chardonnay, Pinot Noir, The Palatine, Cabernets.
summary Knappstein Lenswood Vineyards is now the sole (and full-time) occupation of Tim and Annie Knappstein, Tim Knappstein having retired from the winery which bears his name in the Clare Valley, and having sold most of the Clare vineyards to Petaluma (along with the wine business). With 25.5 hectares of close-planted, vertically trained vineyards maintained to the exacting standards of Tim Knappstein, the business will undoubtedly add to the reputation of the Adelaide Hills as an ultra-premium area. Complex Chardonnay, intense Sauvignon Blanc and broodingly powerful yet stylish Pinot Noir are trailblazers. The wines are exported to the UK, the US, Canada, Japan, Belgium, Switzerland, Germany, Fiji and Singapore.

Lenswood Vineyards Semillon

YYYYY **2000** Light to medium green-yellow; an elegant and complex bouquet with a perceptible but well-integrated touch of oak; the palate is likewise elegant and long, fruit-driven, but with the masterly use of oak and malolactic fermentation. Despite the winemaker inputs, still has varietal grass and citrus focus. **rating:** 94
best drinking 2002–2006 **best vintages** '98, '99, '00 **drink with** Victor Harbour whiting • $25

Lenswood Vineyards Sauvignon Blanc

YYYY **2000** Light green-yellow; a powerful, concentrated bouquet with mineral/grass aromas leads into a powerful, concentrated and somewhat grippy palate, which certainly has presence, but lacks that touch of mid-palate vinosity needed for higher points, and which it achieves in most vintages. **rating:** 87
best drinking Now **best vintages** '94, '95, '97, '98 **drink with** Shellfish • $17.99

Lenswood Vineyards Chardonnay

YYYYY **1999** Medium to full yellow-green; a complex, multi-layered bouquet with quite pronounced fig and cashew aromas is followed by an intense palate, where melon and grapefruit join the fig and cashew of the bouquet. The oak influence is positive but, as usual, well balanced. **rating:** 92
best drinking 2002–2007 **best vintages** '93, '94, '95, '96, '97, '98, '99 **drink with** Terrine of smoked salmon • $30.50

Lenswood Vineyards Pinot Noir

🍷🍷🍷🍷🍷 **1999** Medium red-purple; an intense mix of plum, cherry and spice on the bouquet foreshadows a complex but tight palate which is real evolution in style, sustained by a long, velvety finish. Needs several years to unlock its undoubted complexity. **rating:** 95

best drinking 2003–2008 **best vintages** '91, '93, '94, '95, '96, '97, '98, '99 **drink with** Quail, hare • $45.50

Lenswood Vineyards The Palatine

🍷🍷🍷🍷 **1998** Medium purple-red; the bouquet is potent, earthy, and with some astringent edges to the dark berry fruit. The palate is austere, but powerful, very much in a cool-climate/Bordeaux style. Will particularly appeal to those with European palates. **rating:** 89

best drinking 2003–2012 **best vintages** '97, '98 **drink with** Roast venison • $53

knappstein wines ★★★★☆

2 Pioneer Avenue, Clare, SA 5453 **region** Clare Valley

phone (08) 8842 2600 **fax** (08) 8842 3831 **open** Mon–Fri 9–5, Sat 11–5, Sun and public holidays 11–4

winemaker Andrew Hardy **production** 40 000 **est.** 1976

product range ($19–39 R) Riesling, Cellar Release Riesling, Gewurztraminer, Chardonnay, Semillon Sauvignon Blanc, Botrytis Riesling, Shiraz, Enterprise Shiraz, Cabernet Merlot, Enterprise Cabernet Sauvignon.

summary Very much part of the Petaluma empire, with Andrew Hardy now a veteran of the region. The 100 hectares of mature estate vineyards in prime locations supply grapes both for the Knappstein brand and for wider Petaluma use. The current releases are particularly impressive. The wines are exported to the UK and much of Europe and much of Asia.

Knappstein Cellar Release Riesling

🍷🍷🍷🍷½ **1995** Bright green-gold; the bouquet has a mix of ripe lime and toasty bottle-developed characters, the palate with weight and flavour ranging from sweet lime through to honey and just a hint of toast. Excellent acidity provides a long, clean finish. **rating:** 92

best drinking Now–2006 **best vintages** '95 **drink with** Rich seafood • $27.50

Knappstein Hand Picked Riesling

🍷🍷🍷🍷 **2000** Light green-yellow; there are distinct herb and spice overtones to the lime fruit of the bouquet; a young, intense, powerful spicy/chalky palate begs for time. **rating:** 88

best drinking 2003–2010 **best vintages** '77, '78, '79, '80, '83, '86, '90, '93, '94, '96, '97 **drink with** Salads of all kinds • $15

Knappstein Semillon Sauvignon Blanc

🍷🍷🍷🍷½ **2000** Light to medium yellow-green; the bouquet is quite ripe and complex, with subtle, spicy oak, the palate offering the same interplay of fruit and oak in a complex white Bordeaux style with good mouthfeel. Sophisticated winemaking. **rating:** 92

best drinking Now–2003 **best vintages** '98 **drink with** Rich fish dishes • NA

Knappstein Clare Valley Chardonnay

🍷🍷🍷🍷 **2000** Bright green-yellow; strong barrel-ferment and malolactic-ferment characters open the bouquet, with citrus and melon fruit trailing along thereafter. The palate is a fully structured barrel-fermented style, with all the hallmarks of skilled winemaking, the problem lying purely in the refusal of chardonnay to yield up its true quality. **rating:** 85

best drinking 2002–2006 **best vintages** NA **drink with** Takeaway • $22

Knappstein Wines Clare Valley Shiraz

🍷🍷🍷🍷 **1999** Medium red-purple; a clean, moderately intense bouquet has scented earthy/berry varietal fruit supported by subtle oak. As always, the palate is well constructed, with abundant varietal fruit, and well-balanced tannins flowing through to the finish. **rating:** 88

🍷🍷🍷🍷½ **1998** Medium purple-red; the bouquet is quite complex with a mix of dark cherry, black plum, mint, leaf and earth; sweet berry fruit with splashes of spice and licorice are supported by fine tannins and oak. Lighter than some of the powerhouses from the Clare Valley in 1998, and easy to overlook the long, silky finish. **rating:** 91

best drinking 2003–2008 **best vintages** '98 **drink with** Moroccan lamb • $22

Knappstein Enterprise Shiraz

▼▼▼▼▽ **1998** Medium to full red-purple; the fragrant bouquet has cherry/berry fruit, lightly touched with spice and earth; the palate moves up several degrees, with rich, dark cherry/berry fruit, and lingering tannins building from the mid-palate onwards through to the long finish. **rating:** 92

best drinking 2003–2013 **best vintages** '94, '96, '97, '98 **drink with** Rich red-meat dishes • $39

Knappstein Enterprise Cabernet Sauvignon

▼▼▼▼▼ **1998** Dense red-purple; a concentrated, ripe blackcurrant and cassis bouquet is followed by a big, dense, powerful palate with the same ripe currant/cassis flavours, a touch of chocolate and lots of built-in tannins and oak. A wine in heroic style. **rating:** 94

best drinking 2003–2013 **best vintages** '96, '98 **drink with** Thick-cut lamb loin chops • $39

knight granite hills 

1481 Burke and Wills Track, Baynton, Kyneton, Vic 3444 **region** Macedon Ranges
phone (03) 5423 7264 **fax** (03) 5423 7288 **open** Mon–Sat 10–6, Sun 12–6
winemaker Llew Knight **production** 7000 **est.** 1970
product range ($13.90–40 R) Riesling, Chardonnay, Pinot Noir, Shiraz, Cabernet Sauvignon, Sparkling; also MICA Riesling, Pinot Noir and Cabernet Shiraz, Reserve Cabernet, Méthode Champenoise.
summary Knight Granite Hills was one of the early pacesetters, indeed the first pacesetter, for cool-climate, spicy Shiraz and intense Riesling. Revived marketing in a buoyant market and the introduction of the lesser-priced MICA range have resulted in greater activity; plantings remain the same at 9 hectares of mature, low-yielding vineyards.

Knight Granite Hills Riesling

▼▼▼▼▼ **2000** Light to medium green-yellow; fine, intense and fragrant lime, citrus and apple aromas are replicated on the delicate yet intense palate with its mix of lime and passionfruit, a twist of mineral; moves from a sweet mid-palate to a crisp, dry, lingering finish. **rating:** 96

best drinking Now–2010 **best vintages** '86, '90, '93, '94, '98, '00 **drink with** Sugar-cured tuna • $19

Knight Granite Hills Méthode Champenoise

▼▼▼▼▽ **1996** Medium straw-yellow; the moderately intense bouquet takes some time to open up and show the underlying complexity. The palate has particularly attractive mouthfeel, with a touch of creaminess, good length and a dry but not overly acidic finish. **rating:** 90

best drinking Now–2003 **best vintages** '94, '96 **drink with** Poached fish • $40

knights eurunderee flats NR

655 Henry Lawson Drive, Mudgee, NSW 2850 **region** Mudgee
phone (02) 6373 3954 **fax** (02) 6373 3750 **open** Fri–Wed 10–4, Sat 10–5
winemaker Peter Knights **production** 1500 **est.** 1985
product range ($12–19 CD) Sauvignon Blanc, Shiraz, Cabernet Sauvignon, Merlin Rouge, Lancelot's Liqueur, Round Table Tawny.
summary Sometimes called Knights Vines, although the wines are marketed under the Eurunderee Flats label. The 5 hectares of vineyards produce white wines of variable quality, and rather better dry red table wines.

knowland estate NR

Mount Vincent Road, Running Stream, NSW 2850 **region** Mudgee
phone (02) 6358 8420 **fax** (02) 6358 8423 **open** By appointment
winemaker Peter Knowland **production** 250 **est.** 1990
product range ($12.50–18 CD) Mt Vincent Sauvignon Blanc, Orange Pinot Noir, Mt Vincent Pinot Noir, Wellington Cabernet.
summary The former Mount Vincent Winery, which sells much of its grape production from the 3.5 hectares of vineyards to other makers but proposes to increase production under its own label.

kominos ★★★

New England Highway, Severnlea, Qld 4352 **region** Granite Belt
phone (07) 4683 4311 **fax** (07) 4683 4291 **open** 7 days 9–5
winemaker Tony Comino **production** 4000 **est.** 1976
product range ($10–13 CD) Riesling, Sauvignon Blanc, Chardonnay, Vin Doux, White Shiraz, Nouveau, Shiraz, Cabernet Merlot, Cabernet Sauvignon.
summary Tony Comino is a dedicated viticulturist and winemaker and, together with his father, he has battled hard to prevent ACI obtaining a monopoly on glass production in Australia, foreseeing many of the things which have in fact occurred. However, Kominos keeps a very low profile, selling all of its wine through cellar door and mailing list. No recent tastings.

kongwak hills winery NR

1030 Korumburra–Wonthaggi Road, Kongwak, Vic 3951 **region** Gippsland
phone (03) 5657 3267 **fax** (03) 5657 3267 **open** Weekends and public holidays 10–5
winemaker Peter Kimmer **production** 600 **est.** 1989
product range ($10–25 CD) Riesling, Pinot Noir, Shiraz, Cabernet Malbec.
summary Peter and Jenny Kimmer started the development of their vineyard in 1989 and now have 0.5 hectare each of cabernet sauvignon, shiraz and pinot noir, together with lesser quantities of malbec, merlot and riesling. Most of the wines are sold at cellar door, with limited distribution in Melbourne through Woods Wines Pty Ltd of Fitzroy.

koppamurra wines ★★★☆

Joanna, via Naracoorte, SA 5271 **region** Wrattonbully
phone (08) 8357 9533 **fax** (08) 8271 0726 **open** By appointment
winemaker John Greenshields **production** 4000 **est.** 1973
product range ($9–19.50 ML) Riesling, Chardonnay, Late Harvest Riesling, Dry Red, Pinot Meunier, Shiraz, Cabernet Merlot, Merlot, Cabernet Sauvignon, Two Cabernets, McLaren Vale Muscat.
summary Which Hollywood actress was it who said, 'I don't care what they say about me, as long as they spell my name right'? This might be the motto for Koppamurra Wines, which became embroiled in a bitter argument over the use of the name Koppamurra for the region in which its vineyards are situated and which, through what seems to be sheer bloodymindedness by various of the parties involved, is now known as Wrattonbully. The wines have limited retail distribution in the eastern States, and are exported to the US.

kopparossa estate ★★★☆

Bells Road, Naracoorte, SA 5271 **region** Wrattonbully
phone 1800 620 936 **fax** (08) 8762 0937 **open** Not
winemaker Gavin Hogg, Mike Press **production** 3500 **est.** 1996
product range ($15–25 CD) Chardonnay, Shiraz.
summary Industry veteran winemakers Mike Press and Gavin Hogg have formed a partnership to establish a 68-hectare vineyard with 34 hectares of cabernet sauvignon, 19 hectares of shiraz, 13 hectares of merlot and 2 hectares of petit verdot. They have put their money on the proposition that Wrattonbully is a red-wine region, but are not averse to taking advantage of the ready supply of locally grown chardonnay.

Kopparossa Estate Coonawarra Unwooded Chardonnay

YYYY **2000** Light green-yellow; the light and fresh bouquet has a mix of melon and a touch of mineral, the palate clean, light and fresh; one of those no-fault, no-particular-virtue wines so typical of unwooded Chardonnay. **rating:** 83

best drinking Now–2003 **best vintages** NA **drink with** Creamy pasta • $15

Kopparossa Estate Coonawarra Shiraz

YYYY **1998** Medium red-purple; the bouquet is clean, with quite pronounced oak dancing around sweet, dark berry/cherry fruit. The medium-bodied palate has a similar mix of sweet berry and vanilla oak (American, as ever, dominating the French), finishing with soft tannins. An easily approached and enjoyable mouthful. **rating:** 85

best drinking Now–2006 **best vintages** NA **drink with** Rib of beef • $25

kraanwood NR

8 Woodies Place, Richmond, Tas 7025 **region** Southern Tasmania
phone (03) 6260 2540 **open** Not
winemaker Frank van der Kraan **production** 150 **est.** 1994
product range ($16.20 ML) Schonburger, Montage, Unwooded Chardonnay, Pinot Noir.
summary Frank van der Kraan and wife Barbara established their 0.5-hectare vineyard Kraanwood between 1994 and 1995, with approximately equal plantings of pinot noir, chardonnay and cabernet sauvignon. Frank van der Kraan also manages the 1-hectare Pembroke Vineyard, and procures from it small quantities of schonberger, chardonnay, riesling and sauvignon blanc.

kulkunbulla 

Broke Road, Pokolbin, NSW 2320 **region** Lower Hunter Valley
phone (02) 4998 7358 **fax** (02) 9898 0200 **open** By appointment
winemaker Rhys Eather, Gavin Lennard **production** 5000 **est.** 1996
product range ($13.50–31 ML) Hunter Valley Semillon, Orion's Gate Semillon, The Glandore Semillon, Hunter Valley Chardonnay, Nullarbor Chardonnay, Orion's Gate Chardonnay, The Brokenback Chardonnay, Botrytis Semillon, Shiraz.
summary Kulkunbulla is owned by a relatively small Sydney-based company headed by Gavin Lennard and which has purchased part of the Brokenback Estate in the Hunter Valley formerly owned by Rothbury. For the time being all Kulkunbulla's wines are sold by mail order with a sophisticated brochure entitled Vinsight. Retail distribution in Victoria and Queensland.

Kulkunbulla Orion's Gate Semillon

2000 Light to medium yellow-green; the fresh, crisp bouquet is predominantly in the herb/mineral spectrum, with a faint touch of spice in the background. The smooth and flowing palate has clean lemon and citrus fruit, then crisp acid on the finish. **rating:** 89
best drinking 2002–2008 **best vintages** '00 **drink with** Fresh asparagus with finely chopped prosciutto • $13.50

Kulkunbulla The Glandore Semillon

2000 Light green-yellow; a spotlessly clean and fresh bouquet with hints of lemon/lemon tree leaves is followed by a fine, tight and well-balanced palate, with ultra-correct lemon and mineral flavours. **rating:** 91
best drinking 2003–2009 **best vintages** '98, '99, '00 **drink with** Balmain bugs • $25.50

Kulkunbulla Orion's Gate Chardonnay

1999 Medium to full yellow-green; the toasty/buttery bouquet is starting to show bottle-development, with the oak also contributing to the aromas. The palate has quite good depth and intensity to the stonefruit flavours; the oak is evident but not excessive, the wine finishing with good acidity. **rating:** 87
best drinking Now **best vintages** NA **drink with** Sautéed chicken • $14.50

Kulkunbulla Botrytis Semillon

1999 Glowing golden; strong botrytis shows in the cumquat/apricot aromas of the bouquet, with the French oak evident but restrained. The palate is intense and rich, with all the components well balanced to produce a quite lovely wine. **rating:** 94
best drinking Now–2006 **best vintages** '99 **drink with** Very rich cream-based desserts • NA

kyeema estate 

43 Shumack Street, Weetangera, ACT 2614 **region** Canberra District
phone (02) 6254 7557 (ah) **fax** (02) 6254 7536 **open** Not
winemaker Andrew McEwin **production** 750 **est.** 1986
product range ($22 ML) Chardonnay, Shiraz, Merlot, Cabernet Merlot.
summary Part-time winemaker, part-time wine critic (with *Winewise* magazine) Andrew McEwin produces wines full of flavour and character; every wine released under the Kyeema Estate label has won a show award of some description. Limited retail distribution in Brisbane and exports to California (The Grateful Palate).

laanecoorie ★★★

Bendigo Road, Betley, Vic 3472 **region** Pyrenees
phone (03) 5468 7260 **fax** (03) 5468 7388 **open** Not
winemaker John Ellis (Contract) **production** 1500 **est.** 1982
product range ($20 R) A single Bordeaux-blend dry red of Cabernet Franc, Cabernet Sauvignon and Merlot in roughly equal proportions.
summary John McQuilten's 7.5-hectare vineyard produces grapes of consistently high quality, and competent contract-winemaking by John Ellis at Hanging Rock has done the rest.

la cantina king valley NR

Honey's Lane, RMB 9460, King Valley, Vic 3678 **region** King Valley
phone (03) 5729 3615 **fax** (03) 5729 3613 **open** Weekends and holidays 10–5 and by appointment
winemaker Gino Corsini **production** 2000 **est.** 1996
product range ($10–14 CD) Riesling, Dry Red, Shiraz, Merlot, Cabernet Sauvignon.
summary Gino and Peter Corsini have 22 hectares of riesling, chardonnay, shiraz, merlot and cabernet sauvignon, selling most but making a small amount on site in a winery 'made of Glenrowan granite stone in traditional Tuscan style'. The wines are made without the use of sulphur dioxide (they are organic).

ladbroke grove NR

Coonawarra Road, Penola, SA 5277 **region** Coonawarra
phone (08) 8737 2082 **fax** (08) 8762 3236 **open** 7 days 10–4
winemaker Ken Ward **production** 800 **est.** 1982
product range ($8–14 CD) Riesling, Late Picked Riesling, Shiraz, Premium Shiraz.
summary Relaunched with both standard and Premium Shiraz after a hiatus; wine quality has been variable, but it does have 2 hectares of hand-pruned shiraz planted by John Redman in the 1960s upon which to draw.

lake barrington estate ★★★☆

1133–1136 West Kentish Road, West Kentish, Tas 7306 **region** Northern Tasmania
phone (03) 6491 1249 **fax** (03) 6334 2892 **open** Tues–Sun 10–5 (Nov–Apr)
winemaker Steve Lubiana (Sparkling), Andrew Hood (Table), both Contract **production** 500 **est.** 1986
product range ($18–33 CD) Riesling, Chardonnay, Pinot Noir, Alexandra Méthode Traditionelle, Alexandra Méthode Champenoise.
summary Lake Barrington Estate is owned by the vivacious and energetic Maree Taylor and takes its name from the adjacent Lake Barrington, 30 kilometres south of Devonport, on the northern coast of Tasmania. There are picnic facilities at the vineyard and, needless to say, the scenery is very beautiful.

lake breeze wines 

Step Road, Langhorne Creek, SA 5255 **region** Langhorne Creek
phone (08) 8537 3017 **fax** (08) 8537 3267 **open** 7 days 10–5
winemaker Greg Follett **production** 10 000 **est.** 1987
product range ($10–37 CD) Chardonnay, White Frontignac, Grenache, Cabernet Sauvignon, Bernoota (Cabernet Shiraz), Tawny Port. The premium Winemaker's Selection range was introduced in 1996 with Shiraz and Cabernet Sauvignon.
summary The Folletts have been farmers at Langhorne Creek since 1880, grape-growers since the 1930s. Since 1987 a small proportion of their grapes has been made into wine, and a cellar-door sales facility was opened in early 1991. The quality of the releases has been exemplary, the new Winemaker's Selection red wines particularly striking. Retail distribution in Victoria, New South Wales and Queensland is now augmented by exports to the US, the UK and Switzerland.

Lake Breeze Bernoota

ΨΨΨΨ **1999** Medium to full red-purple; the bouquet offers a mix of spice, berry, leaf and earth aromas; good tannins run throughout the dark chocolate, earth and berry-flavoured palate, with subtle oak adding to the complex, sustained finish. **rating:** 88

best drinking 2004–2009 **best vintages** '87, '88, '90, '92, '98 **drink with** Braised beef • $20

Lake Breeze Cabernet Sauvignon

YYYY **1998** Medium to full red-purple; abundant, sweet cassis fruit is accompanied by slightly dusty oak on the bouquet; the palate is powerful, but that dusty oak introduces a slightly jangly note. There is enough fruit there for the wine to settle down with time. **rating:** 88

best drinking 2003–2008 **best vintages** '87, '88, '90, '95, '96, '98 **drink with** Smoked kangaroo fillet • $23

lake george winery ★★★

Federal Highway, Collector, NSW 2581 **region** Canberra District
phone (02) 4848 0039 **fax** (02) 4848 0039 **open** Not
winemaker Angus Campbell **production** 750 **est.** 1971
product range ($28.50–49.50 R) Chardonnay, Semillon, Sauternes, Pinot Noir, Cabernet Sauvignon, Merlot, Fortifieds.
summary Dr Edgar Riek was an inquisitive, iconoclastic winemaker who was not content with his role as Godfather and founder of the Canberra district, forever experimenting and innovating. His fortified wines, vintaged in northeastern Victoria but matured at Lake George, were very good. He has sold the winery but for the time being continues as a consultant.

lake moodemere vineyard NR

McDonalds Road, Rutherglen, Vic 3685 **region** Rutherglen
phone (02) 6032 9449 **fax** (02) 6032 9449 **open** Fri–Mon 10–5
winemaker Michael Chambers **production** 3000 **est.** 1995
product range ($13.50–16 CD) Riesling, Chardonnay, Late Harvest Biancone, Shiraz, Cabernet Sauvignon.
summary Michael, Belinda, Peter and Helen are all members of the famous Chambers family of Rutherglen. They have 17 hectares of vineyards (tended by Peter), and Lake Moodemere Homestead is in its thirteenth year as a B&B facility.

lake's folly ★★★★★

Broke Road, Pokolbin, NSW 2321 **region** Lower Hunter Valley
phone (02) 4998 7507 **fax** (02) 4998 7322 **open** Mon–Sat 10–4
winemaker Rodney Kemp, Stephen Lake (Consultant) **production** 4500 **est.** 1963
product range ($37 CD) Simplicity itself: Chardonnay and Cabernets.
summary The first of the weekend wineries to produce wines for commercial sale, long revered for its Cabernet Sauvignon and thereafter its Chardonnay. Very properly, terroir and climate produce a distinct regional influence and thereby a distinctive wine style. Some find this attractive, others are less tolerant. The winery continues to enjoy an incredibly loyal clientele, with much of each year's wine selling out quickly by mail order. A little of the wine finds its way to the UK. Lake's Folly has been sold, but Stephen Lake continues as a consultant. The winery was purchased by Perth businessman Peter Fogarty, whose family company previously established the Millbrook Winery in the Perth Hills, so is no stranger to the joys and agonies of running a small winery.

Lake's Folly Chardonnay

YYYYY **1999** Brilliant yellow-green; the bouquet offers a complex yet subtle interplay between fruit, oak and malolactic fermentation, with no one character dominant. The palate is intense and much tighter than most, if not all, Hunter Valley Chardonnays, with the same seamless integration of all of its components. **rating:** 94

best drinking 2002–2007 **best vintages** '81, '82, '83, '84, '86, '89, '92, '96, '97, '99 **drink with** Sweetbreads • NA

Lake's Folly Cabernets

YYYY½ **1999** Medium red-purple; the bouquet is sweet and ripe, with a distinctive mix of small, dark berry fruit and earth. The palate opens with ripe, soft, fleshy fruit before distinctly regional savoury/earthy characters take over towards the finish; the parts need time to come together. **rating:** 90

best drinking 2004–2010 **best vintages** '69, '75, '81, '87, '89, '91, '97, '98 **drink with** Rabbit, hare • NA

lamont wines 

85 Bisdee Road, Millendon, WA 6056 **region** Swan District
phone (08) 9296 4485 **fax** (08) 9296 1663 **open** Wed–Sun 10–5

winemaker Mark Warren **production** 7000 **est.** 1978
product range ($9–25 CD) Riesling, Verdelho, Chenin Blanc, Barrel Fermented Semillon, Chardonnay, Barrel Fermented Chardonnay, Quartet, Sweet White, Light Red Cabernet, Shiraz, Merlot, Cabernet Merlot, Cabernet Sauvignon, Family Reserve; Fortifieds, including Flor Fino, Amontillado and Reserve Sherry (Oloroso style).
summary Corin Lamont is the daughter of the late Jack Mann, and makes her wines in the image of those her father used to make, resplendent in their generosity. Lamont also boasts a superb restaurant, with a gallery for the sale and promotion of local arts. The wines are going from strength to strength, utilising both estate-grown and contract-grown (from southern regions) grapes.

Lamont Riesling

🍷🍷🍷🍷🍷 **1999** Medium yellow-green; there are already pleasant bottle-developed toast and lime aromas to the bouquet; the flavour-packed palate has abundant character although it seems to have galloped along, and is already very toasty. The 2000 vintage promises to be even better. **rating:** 90
best drinking Now–2003 **best vintages** '99 **drink with** Bruschetta • $20

Lamont Barrel Fermented Semillon

🍷🍷🍷🍷🍷 **2000** Light to medium yellow-green; intense, rich citrus/grassy/lemon fruit is nicely married with gentle oak. The palate has good length and intensity; there is abundant fruit richness to carry the barrel-ferment-induced oak, and the overall result is totally harmonious. **rating:** 94
best drinking Now–2007 **best vintages** '00 **drink with** Trout pâté • $17

Lamont Verdelho

🍷🍷🍷🍷 **2000** Light to medium green-yellow; the bouquet is fresh, with obvious cool-ferment influences aiding the passionfruit of the bouquet. The light- to medium-bodied palate is, once again, fresh with fruit salad and passionfruit flavours. Clever winemaking. **rating:** 85
best drinking Now **best vintages** NA **drink with** Smoked chicken • $13

langanook wines NR

Faraday Road RSD 181, Castlemaine, Vic 3450 **region** Bendigo
phone (03) 5474 8250 **open** Weekends 11–5
winemaker Matt Hunter **production** 750 **est.** 1985
product range ($17.50–31 ML) Chardonnay, Cabernet Sauvignon, Reserve Cabernet Sauvignon Blend.
summary The Langanook vineyard was established back in 1985 (the first wines coming much later), at an altitude of 450 metres on the slopes of Mount Alexander.

Langanook Reserve Cabernet Sauvignon

🍷🍷🍷🍷 **1998** Medium red-purple; the complex bouquet is not overly intense, but does range through leathery/savoury/earthy/plum/prune aromas. The palate, similarly, is long rather than heavy, in a slippery/earthy/savoury mode; good acidity on a lingering finish; subtle oak handling throughout. **rating:** 84
best drinking 2002–2007 **best vintages** NA **drink with** Marinated lamb • $30.85

langbrook estate vineyard NR

65 Summerhill Road, Yarra Junction, Vic 3797 **region** Yarra Valley
phone (03) 5967 1320 **fax** (03) 5967 1182 **open** By appointment
winemaker Martin Williams **production** 500 **est.** 1996
product range ($18 R) Sauvignon Blanc.
summary Langbrook Estate has 3 hectares each of sauvignon blanc, chardonnay, pinot noir and merlot planted, which will provide the base for a substantial output in future years, although the only wine available as at March 2001 was Sauvignon Blanc. A cottage and studio joins the many wine-linked B&B operations in the Yarra Valley.

Langbrook Estate Sauvignon Blanc

🍷🍷🍷🍷 **2000** Light to medium yellow-green; a clean, relatively light mix of herb and a hint of passionfruit on the bouquet is followed by a somewhat unusual array of flavours on the palate, running through pear, apple and passionfruit. Attractive but somewhat atypical. **rating:** 85
best drinking Now **best vintages** NA **drink with** Smoked trout • $18

langmeil winery ★★★☆

Cnr Para and Langmeil Roads, Tanunda, SA 5352 **region** Barossa Valley
phone (08) 8563 2595 **fax** (08) 8563 3622 **open** 7 days 11–4.30
winemaker Paul Lindner **production** 10 000 **est.** 1996
product range ($12.50–48 CD) White Frontignac, Barossa Riesling, Semillon, Chardonnay, Bella Rouge Cabernet Sauvignon (Rosé style), Shiraz, The Freedom Shiraz, Barossa Grenache, Selwin's Lot (Cabernet blend), Cabernet Sauvignon, Ondenc (sparkling), Fortifieds.
summary Vines were first planted at Langmeil in the 1840s, and the first winery on the site, known as Paradale Wines, opened in 1932. In 1996 cousins Carl and Richard Lindner, along with brother-in-law Chris Bitter, formed a partnership to acquire and refurbish the winery and its 5-hectare vineyard planted to shiraz, including 2 hectares planted in 1846. This vineyard has now been supplemented by another vineyard acquired in 1998, taking total plantings to 14.5 hectares and including cabernet sauvignon and grenache. Distribution in New South Wales and Victoria; exports to Canada, France, Holland, Malaysia, Taiwan and the US.

Langmeil The Freedom Shiraz

YYYYY **1998** Full red-purple; the bouquet makes an immediate impact, with its complex, balanced and integrated play of dark fruit aromas and oak. The palate is lusciously rich, full and complex, with ripe berry, cherry and chocolate flavours supported by perfectly judged oak. Amazingly, the wine is bottled direct ex barrel, unfined and unfiltered, something that will provide extraordinary appeal for the Luddite sectors of the American market.
rating: 94

best drinking 2003–2013 **best vintages** '98 **drink with** Smoked Barossa sausage • $48

Langmeil Cabernet Sauvignon

YYYY **1999** Medium red-purple; solid dark berry fruit, a reasonable amount of chocolate and a lot of vanilla is followed by a palate with pleasant currant and chocolate flavours; the milky/vanilla oak tannins do clutter up the finish slightly. **rating:** 84

best drinking 2002–2007 **best vintages** NA **drink with** Barbecued sausages • $19.50

lark hill 

RMB 281 Bungendore Road, Bungendore, NSW 2621 **region** Canberra District
phone (02) 6238 1393 **fax** (02) 6238 1393 **open** Wed–Mon 10–5
winemaker Dr David Carpenter, Sue Carpenter **production** 3500 **est.** 1978
product range ($14–40 R) Riesling, Sauvignon Blanc, Chardonnay, Late Harvest (dessert wine), Pinot Noir, Shiraz, Cabernet Merlot, Exultation Cabernet, The Canberra Fizz.
summary The Lark Hill vineyard is situated at an altitude of 860 metres, level with the observation deck on Black Mountain Tower, and offers splendid views of the Lake George Escarpment. Right from the outset, the Carpenters have made wines of real quality, style and elegance but have defied all the odds (and conventional thinking) with the quality of their Pinot Noirs, the high quality of the other wines coming as no surprise.

Lark Hill Pinot Noir

YYYYY **1999** Light to medium red-purple; a very complex bouquet with a mix of plum/berry characters on the one side, and more savoury/earthy/spicy/foresty characters on the other, all adding up to the right result. The palate is similarly stylish and elegant; it travels to the edge with its savoury, foresty characters, but it is these very characters that invest the wine with style and length. Topped a high-class field with some major names at the 2001 Small Vigneron Awards. **rating:** 95

best drinking 2002–2008 **best vintages** '96, '97, '99 **drink with** Venison • $26

Lark Hill Cabernet Merlot

YYYY **1999** Quite strong red-purple; the clean and firm bouquet has pleasantly ripened small berry fruit, the palate with well-handled oak and tannin extract levels. The cedary/savoury edges to the berry fruit add a degree of elegance to the wine. **rating:** 85

best drinking 2003–2008 **best vintages** '88, '91, '92, '93, '94 '95, '97 **drink with** Rabbit, hare • $26

lashmar NR

c/o 24 Lindsay Terrace, Belair, SA 5052 **region** Warehouse
phone (08) 8278 3669 **fax** (08) 8278 3998 **open** Not
winemaker Colin Cooter, Contract **production** 500 **est.** 1996

product range ($40 R) Three Valleys Shiraz, Kangaroo Island Cabernet Sauvignon sourced from various regions in South Australia including Kangaroo Island, McLaren Vale and the Eden and Clare Valleys.
summary Colin and Bronwyn Cooter (who are also part of the Lengs & Cooter business) are the driving force behind Antechamber Bay Wines. The wines are in fact labelled and branded Lashmar; the Kangaroo Island Cabernet Sauvignon comes from vines planted in 1991 on the Lashmar family property situated on the extreme eastern end of Kangaroo Island overlooking Antechamber Bay. The first commercial wines were made in 1999 and released in October 2000. To give the business added volume, a second wine known as Three Valleys Shiraz, and coming from mainland regions of Eden Valley, Clare Valley and McLaren Vale, is also made.

Lashmar Three Valleys Shiraz

1999 Medium red-purple; the moderately intense bouquet has attractive peppery/spicy/earthy fruit with a slice of vanilla oak on top. The palate has solid cherry and vanilla flavours in a medium-bodied frame, with the oak again to the fore. Should come together with time, but will always be at the oaky end of the spectrum, I suspect.
rating: 86

best drinking 2003–2009 **best vintages** NA **drink with** Spiced beef • $40

Lashmar Kangaroo Island Cabernet

1999 Medium red-purple; the bouquet is clean, with moderately ripe spicy/savoury berry fruit and evident French oak. The palate has a mix of cedary/earthy/savoury flavours, with a fractionally bitter finish that may well soften and sweeten up with time in bottle. **rating:** 84

best drinking 2002–2007 **best vintages** NA **drink with** Kangaroo fillet • $40

latara NR

Cnr McDonalds and Deaseys Roads, Pokolbin, NSW 2320 **region** Lower Hunter Valley
phone (02) 4998 7320 **open** Sat 9–5, Sun 9–4
winemaker Iain Riggs (Contract) **production** 250 **est.** 1979
product range ($9.50–11 CD) Semillon, Cabernet Sauvignon, Shiraz.
summary The bulk of the grapes produced on the 5-hectare Latara vineyard, which was planted in 1979, are sold to Brokenwood. A small quantity is vinified for Latara and sold under its label. As one would expect, the wines are very competently made, and are of show-medal standard.

laurel bank ★★★★

130 Black Snake Lane, Granton, Tas 7030 **region** Southern Tasmania
phone (03) 6263 5977 **fax** (03) 6263 3117 **open** By appointment
winemaker Andrew Hood (Contract) **production** 800 **est.** 1987
product range ($17–18 R) Sauvignon Blanc, Pinot Noir, Cabernet Sauvignon Merlot.
summary Laurel (hence Laurel Bank) and Kerry Carland began planting their 3-hectare vineyard in 1986. They delayed the first release of their wines for some years and (by virtue of the number of entries they were able to make) won the trophy for Most Successful Exhibitor at the 1995 Royal Hobart Wine Show. Things have settled down since; wine quality is solid and reliable.

Laurel Bank Cabernet Sauvignon Merlot

1999 Medium red-purple; the bouquet has unusual and attractive but pronounced chocolate aromas, perhaps partly coming from oak. The palate has a mixture of more chocolate, vanilla and red berry fruit, finishing with soft tannins. Not up to the outstanding '98, but a pretty useful wine, nonetheless. **rating:** 89

best drinking 2003–2010 **best vintages** '98 **drink with** Sautéed lamb fillets • $18

lauren brook

Eedle Terrace, Bridgetown, WA 6255 **region** Blackwood Valley
phone (08) 9761 2676 **fax** (08) 9761 1879 **open** Weekends and school holidays 11–4
winemaker Stephen Bullied **production** 400 **est.** 1993
product range ($17–23 CD) Riesling, Unwooded Chardonnay, Bridgetown Classic, Cabernet Sauvignon.
summary Lauren Brook is established on the banks of the beautiful Blackwood River, and is the only commercial winery in the Bridgetown subregion of Mount Barker. An 80-year-old barn on the property has been renovated to contain a micro-winery and a small gallery. There is 1 hectare of estate chardonnay, supplemented by grapes purchased locally.

Lauren Brook Bridgetown Classic

YYYY 2000 Very pale straw-green; the bouquet is clean, with very delicate mineral/tropical/passionfruit aromas. The palate is similarly light, but clean, well balanced and well made. **rating:** 84

best drinking Now **best vintages** NA **drink with** Light seafood • $17

lavender bay NR

39 Paringa Road, Red Hill South, Vic 3937 **region** Mornington Peninsula
phone (03) 9869 4405 **fax** (03) 9869 4423 **open** Not
winemaker Garry Crittenden (Contract) **production** NA **est.** 1988
product range ($NA) Chardonnay, Pinot Noir.
summary Marketing consultant Kevin Luscombe established Lavender Bay in 1988 on a spectacular 4-hectare property in Red Hill South, with its view of the Bay to Phillip Island. Tiny quantities of the first three vintages were progressively released onto the market in mid-1997, distributed through Flinders Wholesale Wines. No recent sightings, however.

lawrence victor estate NR

Penola Road, Naracoorte, SA 5271 **region** Wrattonbully
phone (08) 8739 7276 **fax** (08) 8739 7344 **open** Not
winemaker Neil Dodderidge (Contract) **production** 1600 **est.** 1994
product range ($18–30 R) Shiraz, Cabernet Sauvignon.
summary Lawrence Victor Estate is part of a large South Australian company principally engaged in the harvesting and transportation of soft-wood plantation logging. The company was established by Lawrence Victor Dohnt in 1932, and the estate has been named in his honour by the third generation of the family. Although a small part of the group's activities, the plantings (principally contracted to Southcorp) are substantial, with 11 hectares of shiraz and 20 hectares of cabernet sauvignon established between 1994 and 1999. An additional 12 hectares of cabernet sauvignon and 6 hectares of pinot noir were planted in 2000.

lawson's hill ★★★

Henry Lawson Drive, Eurunderee, Mudgee, NSW 2850 **region** Mudgee
phone (02) 6373 3953 **fax** (02) 6373 3948 **open** Mon, Thurs, Fri, Sat 10–4.30, Sun 10–4
winemaker Various Contract and José Grace **production** 3500 **est.** 1985
product range ($11–39 CD) Chardonnay, Verdelho, Sauvignon Blanc, Riesling, Traminer Riesling, Louisa Rosé, Cabernet Merlot, Pinot Noir Gamay, Reserve Dryland Cabernet Sauvignon, Port.
summary Former music director and arranger (for musical acts in Sydney clubs) José Grace and wife June run a strongly tourist-oriented operation nextdoor to the Henry Lawson Memorial. It offers a kaleidoscopic array of wines produced from 8 hectares of vineyard and made under contract. The red wines are richly representative of the deeply coloured, flavoursome Mudgee style.

leasingham ★★★★★

7 Dominic Street, Clare, SA 5453 **region** Clare Valley
phone (08) 8842 2555 **fax** (08) 8842 3293 **open** Mon–Fri 8.30–5.30, weekends 10–4
winemaker Kerri Thompson **production** 95 000 **est.** 1893
product range ($12–37 R) Classic Clare Riesling, Shiraz, Sparkling Shiraz and Cabernet Sauvignon at the top end; mid-range Bin 7 Riesling, Bin 37 Chardonnay, Bin 23 Semillon, Bin 56 Cabernet Malbec, Bin 61 Shiraz; low-priced Hutt Creek Riesling, Sauvignon Blanc, Shiraz Cabernet; also Bastion Shiraz Cabernet.
summary Successive big-company ownerships and various peregrinations in labelling and branding have not resulted in any permanent loss of identity or quality. With a core of high-quality, aged vineyards to draw on, Leasingham is in fact going from strength to strength under BRL Hardy's direction. The stentorian red wines take no prisoners, compacting densely rich fruit and layer-upon-layer of oak into every long-lived bottle, the Bin 7 Riesling sweeping all before it in 2000.

Leasingham Bin 7 Riesling

YYYYY 2000 Light green-yellow; the powerful bouquet offers a perfect balance between lime, mineral and spice, with flowery overtones. The palate is intense, fine and long, delivering everything promised by the bouquet, finishing with perfect minerally acidity. Glorious now, in five years or in in ten. **rating:** 96

best drinking Now–2007 **best vintages** '97, '00 **drink with** Vegetable terrine • $14

Leasingham Bin 61 Shiraz

ҮҮҮҮ♀ **1999** Dense red-purple; a typically concentrated and powerful earthy, dark berry bouquet is followed by a palate that is so rich, powerful and concentrated, it feels almost thick. Will have a long life, and needs it; prior history is reassuring. **rating:** 90

best drinking 2004–2014 **best vintages** '88, '90, '91, '93, '94, '96, '99 **drink with** Spiced lamb kebabs • $22

Leasingham Classic Clare Shiraz

ҮҮҮҮҮ **1998** Medium to full red-purple; a concentrated and complex bouquet lavishly oaked, but with the fruit to ultimately sustain that oak. The palate is precisely as the bouquet promises, with lashings of deep, dark fruit, oak and tannins. A twenty-first anniversary wine for those born in 1998. **rating:** 94

ҮҮҮҮҮ **1997** Medium to full red-purple; announces its presence from the first whiff that greets you as the wine is poured into the glass and before you have even begun to lift it, so powerful, rich and sweet is it. Undoubtedly in the battleship class, but you cannot fault the abundance of ripe berry and chocolate fruit, sumptuous tannins and the controlled use of the American oak cannon. Two trophies at the National Wine Show 1999. **rating:** 94

best drinking 2008–2019 **best vintages** '88, '90, '91, '92, '94, '95, '96, '97 **drink with** Kangaroo, strong red meat, strong cheese • $37

Leasingham Bastion Clare Valley Shiraz Cabernet

ҮҮҮҮ **1999** Medium to full red-purple; there is plenty of weight to the blackberry fruit on the bouquet, and even more to the palate. Here the overall structure, tannins and depth contribute to a wine that will age well, is fruit-driven, and represents astonishing value. For those who are looking for the elusive $10 wine to cellar, this is it. **rating:** 85

best drinking 2002–2010 **best vintages** '99 **drink with** Roast saltbush lamb • $10

Leasingham Bin 56 Cabernet Malbec

ҮҮҮҮ **1999** Medium to full red-purple; the bouquet is rich and ripe, with succulent dark berry fruit and reasonably restrained oak. A very full-bodied wine with imposing, drying tannins, begging for time. **rating:** 89

best drinking 2006–2012 **best vintages** '88, '90, '91, '94, '95, '96, '97 **drink with** Jugged hare • $22

Leasingham Classic Clare Cabernet Sauvignon

ҮҮҮҮ **1998** Medium to full red-purple; savoury dark berry, dark chocolate and varietal earth aromas introduce a quite austere and distinctly restrained palate, again showing earthy rather than lush cabernet fruit; controlled tannin and oak extract. **rating:** 89

best drinking 2005–2015 **best vintages** '88, '90, '91, '92, '93, '96 **drink with** Rich red-meat dishes • $37

leconfield ★★★☆

Penola Road, Coonawarra, SA 5263 **region** Coonawarra

phone (08) 8737 2326 **fax** (08) 8737 2285 **open** 7 days 10–5

winemaker Phillipa Treadwell **production** 15 000 **est.** 1974

product range ($17.95–30.95 CD) Riesling, Old Vines Riesling, Noble Riesling, Chardonnay (Wooded and Unwooded), Merlot, Shiraz, Cabernet.

summary A distinguished estate with a proud, even if relatively short, history. Long renowned for its Cabernet Sauvignon, its repertoire has steadily grown with the emphasis on single varietal wines. The style overall is fruit-rather than oak-driven. Exports to Canada, the US, Asia, the UK and Europe.

Leconfield Old Vines Riesling

ҮҮҮ♀ **2000** Light to medium yellow-green; light mineral and spice aromas to the bouquet are followed by a palate of medium length, with delicate mineral and apple flavours. **rating:** 84

best drinking Now–2004 **best vintages** NA **drink with** Seafood salad • $17.95

Leconfield Chardonnay

ҮҮҮҮ **1999** Glowing yellow-green; a clean, smooth, bouquet with ripe yellow peach and a touch of honey leads into a similarly ripe, peachy palate with subliminal oak. **rating:** 86

best drinking Now **best vintages** '98 **drink with** Chicken pasta • $17.95

Leconfield Shiraz

ҮҮҮ♀ **1999** The colour suggests slightly elevated pH; a range of leafy/minty/gamey aromas leads into a fairly light palate with more spicy/savoury/leafy flavours. **rating:** 84

best drinking Now–2003 **best vintages** '88, '90, '91, '94, '95, '96 **drink with** Beef casserole • $28.95

Leconfield Cabernets

TTTT **1998** Light to medium red-purple; the bouquet is fresh, with aromas of mint and leaf, and minimal oak; the palate is elegant, but pretty light on for a '98. Gold medal at Concours Mondiale Brussels. **rating:** 86

best drinking Now–2004 **best vintages** '80, '82, '88, '90, '95 **drink with** Yearling steak, mild cheddar • $30.95

leeuwin estate ★★★★★

Stevens Road, Margaret River, WA 6285 **region** Margaret River
phone (08) 9757 6253 **fax** (08) 9757 6364 **open** 7 days 10–4.30
winemaker Bob Cartwright **production** 60 000 **est.** 1974
product range ($13–75 CD) Art Series Riesling, Sauvignon Blanc, Chardonnay, Pinot Noir, Cabernet Sauvignon; Prelude Classic Dry White, Chardonnay, Cabernet Merlot and Siblings Sauvignon Blanc Semillon are lower-priced alternatives.
summary Leeuwin Estate's Chardonnay is, in my opinion, Australia's finest example based on the wines of the last 18 years, and it is this wine alone that demands a five-star rating for the winery. The Cabernet Sauvignon can be an excellent wine with great style and character in warmer vintages. Almost inevitably, the other wines in the portfolio are not in the same Olympian class, although the Prelude Chardonnay and Sauvignon Blanc are impressive at their lower price level.

Leeuwin Estate Art Series Riesling

TTTT **2000** Light to medium straw-green; a strongly aromatic bouquet with a mix of passionfruit and lime leads into a lively and fresh palate with apple and passionfruit flavours. **rating:** 87

best drinking Now–2004 **best vintages** '99 **drink with** Margaret River marron • $14.80

Leeuwin Estate Art Series Sauvignon Blanc

TTTTY **1999** Pale green-yellow; the bouquet is highly aromatic, with a mix of passionfruit and other tropical fruit characters. The palate is lively, crisp, fresh and long, carrying all the fruit of the bouquet balanced by excellent acidity. A quite lovely wine underlining the ability of the Margaret River region to produce top-flight Sauvignon Blanc if the conditions are right. **rating:** 93

best drinking Now **best vintages** '95, '97, '99 **drink with** Asian • $30.43

Leeuwin Estate Siblings Sauvignon Blanc Semillon

TTTTY **2000** Very pale green-yellow; the bouquet is of light to medium intensity, with aromatic passionfruit, apple and spice; the crisp and delicate palate is not particularly intense, but is clean and refreshing. **rating:** 90

best drinking Now **best vintages** '00 **drink with** Vichyssoise • $21

Leeuwin Estate Prelude Classic Dry White

TTTT **1999** Light yellow-green; aromatic passionfruit and herb aromas are followed by a lively, fresh and crisp palate. It is not as intense as the Art Series Sauvignon Blanc, but still has plenty of character and, of course, is less expensive. **rating:** 87

best drinking Now **best vintages** NA **drink with** Scampi • $18.10

Leeuwin Estate Art Series Chardonnay

TTTTT **1998** Light to medium green-yellow; toasty barrel-ferment oak mingles with nectarine and grapefruit in a manner very reminiscent of the '97 when it was first released; the palate has tight grapefruit and melon together with a touch of cashew, with excellent length and acid balance. Yet another great wine from Leeuwin. **rating:** 94

best drinking Now–2010 **best vintages** '80, '81, '82, '83, '85, '87, '89, '90, '92, '94, '95, '96, '97, '98 **drink with** Veal saltimbocca • $75

Leeuwin Estate Prelude Chardonnay

TTTT **1999** Light green-yellow; the bouquet is clean and fruit driven, with melon and touches of citrus and mineral; the palate has good length, although is not particularly concentrated; the oak impact is negligible. **rating:** 85

best drinking Now–2003 **best vintages** '95, '96 **drink with** Sashimi • $29.60

Leeuwin Estate Art Series Cabernet Sauvignon

1997 Medium red, with just some purple remaining; the wine has the typical earthy/leafy/austere aromas of the label, the palate in the same rather austere mode with a mix of earthy/blackberry/leafy/bitter chocolate flavours, finishing with fine but persistent tannins. **rating:** 85

best drinking 2003–2010 **best vintages** '79, '86, '87, '89, '90, '92, '93 **drink with** Eye fillet of lamb • $38.50

lefroy brook NR

Glauder Road, Pemberton, WA 6260 **region** Pemberton
phone (08) 9386 8385 **open** Not
winemaker Peter Fimmel (Contract) **production** 350 **est.** 1982
product range ($21.95 R) Chardonnay, Pinot Noir.
summary Owned by Perth residents Pat and Barbara Holt, the former a graduate in biochemistry and microbiology working in medical research but with a passion for Burgundy. The 1.5 hectares of vines are now both netted and fenced with steel mesh, producing wines that, on tastings to date, are outside the mainstream.

legana vineyard NR

24 Vale Street, Prospect Vale, Tas 7250 **region** Tasmania
phone (03) 6344 8030 **fax** (03) 6343 2937 **open** By appointment
winemaker Richard Richardson (Contract) **production** NA **est.** 1994
product range ($21–23 R) Pinot Noir, Cabernet Sauvignon.
summary The Legana vineyard was the first established in the Tamar Valley, planted in 1966 by Graham Wiltshire, and provided the first Heemskerk wines. In 1983 Heemskerk moved to the Pipers River region, and Steven Hyde (Rotherhythe) leased the Legana vineyard until 1994. In May of that year Kurt and Kaye Beyer acquired the vineyard and began its rehabilitation, with rich dividends now being paid.

leland estate 

PO Lenswood, SA 5240 **region** Adelaide Hills
phone (08) 8389 6928 **open** Not
winemaker Robb Cootes **production** 1200 **est.** 1986
product range ($13.50–18.50 CD) Sauvignon Blanc, Pinot Noir, Adele (Sparkling).
summary Former Yalumba senior winemaker Robb Cootes, with a Master of Science degree, deliberately opted out of mainstream life when he established Leland Estate, living in a split-level, one-roomed house built from timber salvaged from trees killed in the Ash Wednesday bushfires. The Sauvignon Blanc is usually good. Retail distribution in Victoria, New South Wales and Queensland via Prime Wines; exports to Malaysia, Singapore and Hong Kong.

Leland Estate Sauvignon Blanc

2000 Light to medium green-yellow; a gently fragrant bouquet with passionfruit and gooseberry aromas, and no sign of reduction, is followed by a similarly delicately poised palate, featuring the same flavours, and finishing with crisp acidity. Delicious wine. **rating:** 90

best drinking Now **best vintages** '00 **drink with** Angel hair pasta and salmon • $13.46

Leland Estate Adele

1997 Light to medium yellow-green; the bouquet is quite complex with citrus and touches of yeast/bread, then a well-balanced creamy/citrus palate, with slight phenolics on the finish. **rating:** 84

best drinking Now–2004 **best vintages** NA **drink with** Hors d'oeuvres • $18.10

Leland Estate Pinot Noir

1999 Light to medium red-purple; a light, leafy, savoury bouquet with touches of spice leads into a clean palate with a gently savoury edge to the light plum and spice fruit flavours. **rating:** 84

best drinking Now **best vintages** NA **drink with** Asian • $15.83

le 'mins winery NR

40 Lemins Road, Waurn Ponds, Vic 3216 **region** Geelong
phone (03) 5241 8168 **open** Not
winemaker Steve Jones **production** 70 **est.** 1994
product range ($12 R) Pinot Noir.
summary Steve Jones presides over 0.5 hectare of pinot noir planted in 1998 to the MV6 clone, and 0.25 hectare of the same variety planted four years earlier to Burgundy clone 111. The tiny production is made for Le 'Mins at Prince Albert Vineyard, and the wine is basically sold by word of mouth.

lengs & cooter ★★★☆

24 Lindsay Terrace, Belair, SA 5042 **region** Warehouse
phone (08) 8278 3998 **fax** (08) 8278 3998 **open** Not
winemaker Contract **production** 2700 **est.** 1993
product range ($15–55 R) Watervale Riesling, Clare Valley Semillon, Clare Valley Old Vines Shiraz, Reserve Shiraz, Victor (Grenache Shiraz), Swinton (Cabernet blend).
summary Carel Lengs and Colin Cooter began making wine as a hobby in the early 1980s. Each had (and has) a full-time occupation outside the wine industry, and it was all strictly for fun. One thing has led to another, and although they still possess neither vineyards nor what might truly be described as a winery, the wines have graduated to big-boy status, winning gold medals at national wine shows and receiving critical acclaim from writers across Australia. Exports to the UK, France, Sweden, Canada and Singapore.

Lengs & Cooter Clare Valley Semillon

TTT♀ **2000** A rim of gas on the edge of the glass is confirmed by the palate, where the high level of carbon dioxide interferes at this juncture. Behind the carbon dioxide, a fuller style, with some good varietal aromas and flavours. Should merit significantly higher points once the gas dissipates with time. **rating:** 82
best drinking 2003–2008 **best vintages** NA **drink with** Leave it in the cellar • $15

Lengs & Cooter Clare Valley Old Vines Shiraz

TTTT **1999** Medium purple-red; the bouquet is flooded with ripe, juicy black cherry fruit with varietally derived gamey overtones. The youthful palate has luscious cherry, berry and mint flavours, and is not too tannic; indeed, it could do with just a little more structure. Still, an excellent outcome for the vintage. **rating:** 89
best drinking 2003–2008 **best vintages** '96, '99 **drink with** Rib of beef • $29

lenton brae wines ★★★★

Willyabrup Valley, Margaret River, WA 6285 **region** Margaret River
phone (08) 9755 6255 **fax** (08) 9755 6268 **open** 7 days 10–6
winemaker Edward Tomlinson **production** 8000 **est.** 1983
product range ($15–30 CD) Semillon Sauvignon Blanc, Sauvignon Blanc, Chardonnay, Late Harvest Semillon, Shiraz (Fergusson Valley), Margaret River (Cabernet Sauvignon), Cabernet Merlot.
summary Former architect, town-planner and political wine activist Bruce Tomlinson built a strikingly beautiful winery but would not stand for criticism of his wines or politics. Son Edward is more relaxed, and is in fact making wines that require no criticism. Retail distribution through all States, and exports to the UK, Singapore and Canada.

Lenton Brae Semillon Sauvignon Blanc

TTTT♀ **2000** Pale yellow-green, with a fair degree of carbon dioxide still present. The bouquet is crisp, light and clean, gently aromatic, and flowing into a crisp, clean, delicate palate with a mix of lemony and gooseberry fruit flavours. A trophy winner at the 2000 Adelaide Wine Show. **rating:** 90
best drinking Now–2003 **best vintages** '94, '95, '00 **drink with** Asian dishes • $18.50

Lenton Brae Margaret River

TTTTT **1998** Medium red-purple; a fine, fragrant, cedary bouquet with gently sweet berry aromas is followed by an elegant palate with sweet, cedary oak, soft, fine tannins and a gentle core of perfectly ripened berry fruit. A well-deserved gold-medal winner at the 2000 Wine Show of Western Australia. **rating:** 94
best drinking 2002–2012 **best vintages** '98 **drink with** Grilled beef • $30

leo buring ★★★★

Tanunda Road, Nuriootpa, SA 5355 **region** Barossa Valley
phone (08) 8560 9408 **fax** (08) 8563 2804 **open** Mon–Sat 10–5, Sun 1–5
winemaker Geoff Henriks (previous) **production** 25 000 **est.** 1931
product range ($10–31 R) A very much simplified range of Clare Valley Riesling, Late Picked Clare Valley Riesling, Clare Valley Chardonnay, Clare Valley Semillon, Clare Valley Shiraz, Clare Valley Shiraz Grenache and Barossa Valley Coonawarra Cabernet Sauvignon, all under the split label introduced in 1996; the Aged Show Releases are now under the Leonay Eden Valley label and Leo Buring Eden Valley Riesling.
summary Earns its high rating by virtue of being Australia's foremost producer of Rieslings over a 30-year period, with a rich legacy left by former winemaker John Vickery. But it also has the disconcerting habit of bobbing up here and there with very good wines made from other varieties, even if not so consistently. It will be interesting to see what the future holds for the wines (other than the Riesling) in the wake of the Southcorp/Rosemount merger.

Leo Buring Clare Valley Riesling

YYYY **2000** Light green-yellow; the bouquet is firm, fresh and clean, predominantly mineral, but with touches of herb and lime. The palate has plenty of life, and attractive zesty, minerally acidity; guaranteed to cellar well.
rating: 88

best drinking Now–2007 **best vintages** NA **drink with** South Australian whiting • $12

Leo Buring Clare Valley Semillon

YYYY **2000** Light to medium green-yellow; firm lemon, herb and mineral aromas precede a palate with plenty of weight and flavour, particularly on the rich mid-palate. A relatively early-developing example running counter to the norm for the label. **rating:** 88

best drinking Now–2004 **best vintages** '96 **drink with** Veal in white wine sauce • NA

leura glen estate NR

260 Green Gully Road, Glenlyon, Vic 3461 **region** Macedon Ranges
phone (03) 5348 7785 **fax** (03) 5348 4077 **open** Weekends and public holidays 11–5 or by appointment
winemaker Graham Ellender **production** 950 **est.** 1996
product range ($14–18 CD) Sauvignon Blanc, Mystique Rosé, Shiraz; also Glenlyon Vintners label.
summary Formerly a senior lecturer in dental science at the University of Melbourne, Graham Ellender moved to Daylesford with wife Jenny with the twofold purpose of escaping academia and starting a vineyard and winery, and simultaneously establishing dental practices at Daylesford and East Ivanhoe. The Ellenders have established 4 hectares of pinot noir, chardonnay, sauvignon blanc and pinot gris, which were expected to produce a significant crop in 2001. In the meantime they are acquiring shiraz and sauvignon blanc from Cowra, cabernet sauvignon from Harcourt, cabernet franc from Macedon and pinot noir from Narre Warren; these wines are made by Graham Ellender, and are released under the Glenlyon Vintners label. The estate-grown products will be released under the Leura Glen Estate label.

Glenlyon Vintners Shiraz

YYYY **1999** Medium to full red-purple; the bouquet is solid and ripe, with abundant dark fruit aromas and slightly dusty American oak. A super-rich, ripe, blackcurrant and chocolate-flavoured palate finishes with soft tannins and a significant kick from the 14.5° alcohol. A top-drawer Henry VIII style. **rating:** 87

best drinking Now–2006 **best vintages** NA **drink with** Thick-cut rump steak • $18

liebich wein 

Steingarten Road, Rowland Flat, SA 5352 **region** Barossa Valley
phone (08) 8524 4543 **fax** (08) 8524 4543 **open** Weekends 11–5, Mon–Fri by appointment
winemaker Ron Liebich **production** 2000 **est.** 1992
product range ($9–26 CD) Riesling of the Valleys (a blend of Barossa and Clare Valley Riesling), Semillon, Cameo Spätlese, Fortified Semillon, Bush Vine Grenache, Leveret Shiraz, The Darkie Shiraz, The Potter's Merlot, The Lofty Cabernet Sauvignon, Classic Old Barossa Tawny Port, Benno Port, Muscat; bulk Port constitutes major sales.
summary Liebich Wein is Barossa Deutsch for 'Love I wine'. The Liebich family have been grape-growers and winemakers at Rowland Flat since 1919, with C W 'Darky' Liebich one of the great local characters. His nephew Ron Liebich commenced making wine in 1969, but it was not until 1992 that he and his wife Janet began selling wine under the Liebich Wein label.

Liebich Wein Leveret Shiraz

YYYY **1999** Medium to full red-purple; attractive dark berry and chocolate fruit aromas are followed by a very ripe palate, with a mix of berry, jam and prune flavours, finishing with slightly prickly tannins. Obviously, deliberately late-picked. **rating:** 86

best drinking 2004–2009 **best vintages** NA **drink with** Jugged hare • $16.95

Liebich Wein The Darkie Shiraz

YYYY **1999** Dense red-purple; a rich, very ripe and powerful bouquet with dark chocolate and berry aromas is followed by an equivalently rich, ripe and dense palate. Here chewy prune and chocolate fruit has soaked up the oak, but not the 15° alcohol. **rating:** 89

best drinking 2005–2012 **best vintages** NA **drink with** Char-grilled rump • $26

Liebich Wein The Potter's Merlot

YYYY **1999** Medium red; the bouquet is quite fragrant, with savoury/spicy/leafy/minty nuances that flow through into the palate, joined by some chocolate characters, and finishing with fine tannins. **rating:** 87

best drinking 2003–2007 **best vintages** NA **drink with** Roast veal • $19

lilac hill estate NR

55 Benara Road, Caversham, WA 6055 **region** Swan District

phone (08) 9378 9945 **fax** (08) 9378 9946 **open** Tues–Sun 10.30–5

winemaker Stephen Murfit **production** 6500 **est.** 1998

product range ($12–16 R) Chenin Blanc, Verdelho, Chardonnay Verdelho, Chardonnay, Late Picked Frontignan, Zinfandel, Shiraz, Cabernet Merlot, Old Tawny Port.

summary Lilac Hill Estate is part of the renaissance sweeping the Swan Valley. Just when it seemed it would die a lingering death, supported only by Houghton, Sandalford and the remnants of the once Yugoslav-dominated cellar-door trade, wine tourism has changed the entire scene. Thus Lilac Hill Estate, drawing in part upon 4 hectares of estate vineyards, has already built a substantial business, relying on cellar-door trade and limited retail distribution in Perth.

lillydale vineyards ★★★★

45 Davross Court, Seville, Vic 3139 **region** Yarra Valley

phone (03) 5964 2016 **fax** (03) 5964 3009 **open** 7 days 11–5

winemaker Jim Brayne, Max McWilliam **production** NFP **est.** 1975

product range ($14–21.50 R) Gewurztraminer, Sauvignon Blanc, Chardonnay, Pinot Noir, Cabernet Merlot.

summary Acquired by McWilliam's Wines in 1994, with Max McWilliam in charge of the business. With a number of other major developments, notably Coonawarra and Barwang, on its plate, McWilliam's has adopted a softly, softly approach to Lillydale Vineyards; a winery restaurant opened in February 1997.

Lillydale Sauvignon Blanc

YYYY **2000** Very light yellow-green; the bouquet and the palate are immaculately clean, crisp and light, but lack fruit depth and varietal character. **rating:** 83

best drinking Now **best vintages** '98, '99 **drink with** Delicate fish dishes • $17.50

Lillydale Chardonnay

YYYY **1999** Light to medium yellow-green; the bouquet is not particularly intense, but is subtle, with gentle melon and nectarine fruit that is no way threatened by the subtle oak; the palate flows along smoothly in the same channel, with skilfully balanced and integrated fruit and oak. A gold-medal and trophy winner Best Victorian Dry White Wine at 1999 Melbourne Wine Show (I would guess before it was bottled). **rating:** 87

best drinking Now–2004 **best vintages** '86, '88, '90, '91, '97, '98 **drink with** Avocado • $17.50

Lillydale Vineyards Cabernet Merlot

YYYY **1999** Light to medium red-purple; a light, leafy, spicy/cedary bouquet is followed by a palate with attractive raspberry and redcurrant fruit at its core. A very impressive outcome for the vintage. Two gold medals in 2000 at Rutherlgen and Melbourne Wine Shows. **rating:** 89

best drinking 2002–2007 **best vintages** NA **drink with** Young veal • $21.50

lillypilly estate ★★★☆

Lillypilly Road, Leeton, NSW 2705 **region** Riverina
phone (02) 6953 4069 **fax** (02) 6953 4980 **open** Mon–Sat 10–5.30, Sun by appointment
winemaker Robert Fiumara **production** 8000 **est.** 1982
product range ($10–22.50 CD) Semillon, Sauvignon Blanc, Chardonnay, Tramillon® (Traminer Semillon), Spätlese Lexia, Noble Harvest, Noble Muscat of Alexandria, Red Velvet® (medium sweet red), Shiraz, Cabernet Sauvignon, Tawny Port.
summary Apart from occasional Vintage Ports the best wines by far are the botrytised white wines, with the Noble Muscat of Alexandria unique to the winery; these wines have both style and intensity of flavour and can age well. The Noble Semillon and Noble Traminer add strings to the bow. Exports to the US and Canada.

lindemans (coonawarra) ★★★★☆

Main Penola–Naracoorte Road, Coonawarra, SA 5263 **region** Coonawarra
phone (08) 8736 2222 **fax** (08) 8736 3202 **open** 7 days 10–5
winemaker Phillip John, Greg Clayfield **production** 15 000 **est.** 1908
product range ($42–50 R) Under the new Coonawarra Vineyard label: Riesling, Sauvignon Blanc, Coonawarra Limestone Ridge Shiraz Cabernet; then come the premium red trio: Pyrus (Cabernet blend), Limestone Ridge (Shiraz Cabernet), St George (Cabernet Sauvignon).
summary Lindemans is clearly the strongest brand other than Penfolds (and perhaps Rosemount) in the Southcorp Group, with some great vineyards and a great history. The Coonawarra vineyards are of ever-increasing significance because of the move towards regional identity in the all-important export markets, which has led to the emergence of a new range of regional/varietal labels. Whether the fullest potential of the vineyards (from a viticultural viewpoint) is being realised is a matter of debate. Worldwide distribution.

Lindemans Limestone Ridge

YYYYY **1998** Medium to full red-purple; clean, ripe black cherry and berry fruit with spicy overtones and well-managed oak on the bouquet foreshadow a quite delicious palate, with a core of sweet, black cherry fruit surrounded by fine tannins and positive oak. **rating:** 95
best drinking 2003–2013 **best vintages** '86, '88, '90, '91, '93, '94, '96, '97, '98 **drink with** Beef casserole • NA

Lindemans Pyrus

YYYYY **1998** Medium to full red-purple; luscious, deep, dark berry/blackcurrant aromas flow into a blackcurrant- and cassis-flavoured palate. The wine has good structure thanks to clearly defined but ripe tannins, and will (by the standards of Pyrus) be long lived. **rating:** 94
YYYY **1997** Medium to full red-purple; a complex, scented bouquet with quite spicy/savoury berry fruits and a nice touch of French oak leads into a well-weighted palate. Here the quite concentrated red berry, raspberry and blackberry fruit are augmented by positive tannins and a touch of smoky French oak. **rating:** 90
best drinking 2003–2013 **best vintages** '88, '90, '91, '96, '97, '98 **drink with** Entrecôte of beef • $35

Lindemans St George

YYYYY **1998** Medium to full red-purple; while the varietal character is clearly defined in a strong, blackcurrant/cassis mode, the bouquet is distinctively elegant, a character that enhances the tightly knit palate. There are no surprises with the flavours of blackberry and blackcurrant, nor the lingering tannins on the finish. **rating:** 94
best drinking 2003–2013 **best vintages** '86, '88, '90, '91, '96, '97, '98 **drink with** Shoulder of lamb • NA

lindemans (hunter valley) ★★★★

McDonalds Road, Pokolbin, NSW 2320 **region** Lower Hunter Valley
phone (02) 4998 7684 **fax** (02) 4998 7682 **open** Mon–Fri 9–4.30, weekends and public holidays 10–4.30 except Good Friday and Christmas Day
winemaker Patrick Auld **production** 12 000 **est.** 1843
product range ($8–38 R) Standard wines under annually changing Bin numbers of Semillon, Chablis, Sauvignon Blanc, White Burgundy, Semillon Chardonnay, Chardonnay, Shiraz, Cabernet Sauvignon, Hermitage; deluxe releases under Reserve Bin label, individual vineyard label (e.g. Steven); revitalised older Classic Release label and Hunter Valley Semillon, Shiraz and Reserve Semillon.

summary One way or another, I have intersected with the Hunter Valley in general and Lindemans in particular for over 45 years. Where it will head in the wake of the Rosemount Estate merger is far from clear, with any number of outcomes possible.

Lindemans Hunter River Reserve Semillon

YYYYY 1996 Bin 8850. Excellent, bright green-yellow; developing very well, with classic lemon, herb and a touch of toast to the aromas. A powerful wine on the palate, with lots of presence and character, now three-quarters of the way through its development phase, and will kick on from here. **rating:** 90

best drinking Now–2011 **best vintages** '96 **drink with** Sautéed veal Swiss style • $22

Lindemans Hunter Valley Semillon

YYYY 1999 Bin 9455. Light green-yellow. A spotlessly clean and classic bouquet with intense lemon and herb fruit is followed by a crisp, tight, youthful palate that is well balanced and has good length. All the wine needs is lots and lots of time in the bottle. **rating:** 89

best drinking 2004–2009 **best vintages** '63, '65, '68, '70, '79, '86, '87, '91, '93, '94, '98, '99 **drink with** Yabbies • $16

Lindemans Steven Vineyard Shiraz

YYYY 1998 Medium red-purple; the moderately intense bouquet is clean, quite fragrant and with savoury regional fruit characters; the light-to medium-bodied palate goes down much the same track; it is quite fresh, but not particularly complex. **rating:** 85

best drinking 2003–2008 **best vintages** '79, '83, '86, '87, '90, '91, '96, '97 **drink with** Mild mature cheese • $23

lindemans (karadoc) ★★★☆

Edey Road, Karadoc, via Mildura, Vic 3496 **region** Murray Darling
phone (03) 5051 3333 **fax** (03) 5051 3390 **open** 7 days 10–4.30
winemaker Phillip John (Chief) **production** 10 million **est.** 1974
product range ($7–51 R) Bin 23 Riesling, Bin 65 Chardonnay (one of the largest-selling Chardonnay brands in the world), Bin 95 Sauvignon Blanc, Bin 99 Pinot Noir, Bin 45 Cabernet Sauvignon, Bin 50 Shiraz, Bin 60 Merlot are the most important in terms of volume; Cawarra range of Colombard Chardonnay, Classic Dry White, Traminer Riesling, Shiraz Cabernet and Merlot; also Nyrang Semillon and Shiraz. Karadoc also produces the great fortified wines, including the premium Fino, Amontillado and Oloroso Sherries, Old Liqueur Muscat, Tokay, Madeira and fine Tawny Ports.
summary Now the production centre for all of the Lindemans and Leo Buring wines, with the exception of special lines made in the Coonawarra and Hunter wineries. The biggest and most modern single facility in Australia, allowing all-important economies of scale, and the major processing centre for the beverage wine sector (casks, flagons and low-priced bottles) of the Southcorp empire. Its achievement in making several million cases of Bin 65 Chardonnay a year is extraordinary given the quality and consistency of the wines. Worldwide distribution.

Lindemans Bin 95 Sauvignon Blanc

YYYY 1999 Light to medium green-yellow; the bouquet is clean and soft, with faint gooseberry aromas, the palate medium bodied, with some grass and mineral characters; quite well balanced, but not a flavour bomb, which may be all to the good for some. **rating:** 81

best drinking Now **best vintages** NA **drink with** Seafood • $8.50

Lindemans Bin 65 Chardonnay

YYYY 2000 Light to medium yellow-green; the moderately intense bouquet has a nutty edge from subtle oak influence to the melon and spice fruit; the light- to medium-bodied palate is clean, with light melon fruit and just a hint of oak influence. You have to admire the craft behind the wine. **rating:** 85

best drinking Now **best vintages** NA **drink with** Virtually anything you choose • $10

Lindemans Bin 99 Pinot Noir

YYYY 1999 Youthful colour; the bouquet shows fresh cherry with a touch of oak. The palate is light and simple, dominated by cherry fruit; the structure and mouthfeel are appropriate, even though there is not a lot of complexity or varietal character. **rating:** 83

best drinking Now **best vintages** NA **drink with** Pizza or pasta • $8.50

Lindemans Bin 50 Shiraz

▼▼▼▽ **1998** Light to medium red-purple; the moderately intense bouquet is clean, smooth, with straightforward berry fruit and minimal oak. The light- to medium-bodied palate is smooth, clean and unpretentious. Good value. **rating:** 82

best drinking Now **best vintages** NA **drink with** Pasta with meat sauce • $8.50

Lindemans Bin 45 Cabernet Sauvignon

▼▼▼▽ **1999** Light to medium red; the light fresh bouquet offers simple berry aromas and the barest twist of oak. The palate is light, but fresh and sweet; structurally very simple, but that only adds to the ease of everyday drinking. **rating:** 81

best drinking Now **best vintages** NA **drink with** Shepherd's pie • $9

Lindemans Classic Release Show Reserve Oloroso Z273

▼▼▼▼▽ **NV** Golden-brown; a complex, biscuity rancio bouquet is followed by a powerful and complex palate, long and biscuity, rather like a pumped-up Amontillado, with an off-dry, but not sweet, finish. A living testament to the fact that Australia is the only country in the world to produce sherry of the same quality and style as Spain. **rating:** 91

best drinking Now–2010 **best vintages** NA **drink with** Raisins • $51

lindemans (padthaway) ★★★★

Naracoorte Road, Padthaway, SA 5271 **region** Padthaway
phone (08) 8765 5155 **fax** (08) 8765 5073 **open** Not
winemaker Phillip John, Greg Clayfield **production** 68 000 **est.** 1908
product range ($11–17 R) Lindemans Padthaway Vineyard Sauvignon Blanc, Verdelho, Chardonnay, Pinot Noir, Cabernet Merlot and Botrytis Riesling; also Winemakers Reserve Chardonnay, Limestone Coast Chardonnay, Limestone Coast Shiraz and Padthaway Merlot.
summary Lindemans Padthaway Chardonnay is one of the best-performed premium Chardonnays on the market in Australia, with an exceptional capacity to age. However, all of the wines under the Padthaway label offer consistent quality and value for money.

Lindemans Padthaway Chardonnay

▼▼▼▼ **1999** Light to medium yellow-green; the bouquet is quite restrained, with markedly less oak than in previous vintages. The palate has fresh melon and white peach fruit supported by subtle oak; not particularly rich, but given the track record of this distinguished line will certainly improve with bottle age. **rating:** 85

best drinking Now–2005 **best vintages** '84, '85, '90, '94, '97 **drink with** Roast chicken • $14

Lindemans Padthaway Pinot Noir

▼▼▼▽ **1999** Medium red-purple; the moderately intense bouquet has plum and spice fruit, but without clear varietal definition; the medium-bodied palate really has more to do with generic dry red than Pinot Noir, though pleasant enough as such. The limitations lie in the vineyard, not in the winery. **rating:** 83

best drinking Now **best vintages** NA **drink with** Quail • $17

Lindemans Limestone Coast Shiraz

▼▼▼▽ **2000** Vivid purple-red; ripe black cherry and plum fruit aromas leap from the glass, the palate powerful and strong in a head and shoulders fashion, tapering off on the finish, and generally appearing somewhat underworked. On the other hand, impressive value at the price, and may well improve with a year or two in bottle. **rating:** 84

best drinking Now–2003 **best vintages** NA **drink with** Char-grilled lamb • $12

lirralirra estate 

Paynes Road, Lilydale, Vic 3140 **region** Yarra Valley
phone (03) 9735 0224 **fax** (03) 9735 0224 **open** Weekends and holidays 10–6, Jan 7 days
winemaker Alan Smith **production** 300 **est.** 1981
product range ($9–21 CD) Semillon, Wooded Semillon, Semillon Sauvignon Blanc, Sauvignon Blanc, Pinot Noir, Yarra Valley Cabernets.
summary Twenty years ago I wrote that the Yarra Valley was a viticultural Garden of Eden; little did I know. The trials and tribulations of Lirralirra over the past ten years have been awesome, yet Alan Smith retains a sense of proportion and faith in the future. All I can say is he deserves every success that comes his way.

Lirralirra Pinot Noir

🍷🍷🍷🍷 **1999** Light red-tawny; the bouquet has quite intense spicy/sappy/stalky/tomato vine varietal character, the lengthy palate proceeding along precisely the same lines. It is one of those Pinots that will utterly polarise opinion; my points are an attempt to find the middle ground. **rating:** 85

best drinking Now–2003 **best vintages** NA **drink with** Smoked quail • $19

little river wines NR

Cnr West Swan and Forest Roads, Henley Brook, WA 6055 **region** Swan District
phone (08) 9296 4462 **fax** (08) 9296 1022 **open** Fri–Wed 10–5
winemaker Bruno de Tastes **production** 4000 **est.** 1934
product range ($15.50–28 CD) Chenin Blanc, Viognier, Chardonnay, Old Vines Shiraz, Cabernet Sauvignon Merlot, Vin Doux Late Harvest, Noble Classic.
summary Following several quick changes of ownership (and of consultant winemakers) the former Glenalwyn now has as its winemaker the eponymously named Count Bruno de Tastes. I, however, have had no recent tastes.

little's winery ★★★☆

Lot 3 Palmers Lane, Pokolbin, NSW 2321 **region** Lower Hunter Valley
phone (02) 4998 7626 **fax** (02) 4998 7867 **open** 7 days 10–4.30
winemaker Ian Little, Suzanne Little **production** 12 000 **est.** 1984
product range ($15–34.50 R) Premium Hunter Valley range of Gewurztraminer, Semillon Chardonnay, Pinot Noir Shiraz, Cabernet Shiraz Merlot; Reserve range of Semillon, Chardonnay and Shiraz.
summary A successful cellar-door operation with friendly service and friendly wines: aromatic, fresh and sometimes slightly sweet white wines and light, inoffensive red wines in the premium range, and fuller, more structured wines in the Reserve range. Has grown steadily, with 37 hectares of estate vineyards. The wines are exported to the US, Canada, the UK, Japan, Hong Kong and New Zealand.

logan wines ★★★

Ground Floor, 160 Sailor's Bay Road, Northbridge, NSW 2063 **region** Orange
phone (02) 9958 6844 **fax** (02) 9958 1258 **open** Not
winemaker Peter Logan, Simon Gilbert (Contract) **production** 17 000 **est.** 1997
product range ($15–28 R) Riesling, Ripe White (Chardonnay), Chardonnay, Reserve Chardonnay, Shiraz, Ripe Red (Shiraz Grenache), Orange Cabernet Sauvignon.
summary Logan wines is a family operation, founded by businessman Mal Logan and assisted by three of his children: Peter, an oenology graduate from the University of Adelaide, Greg (advertising) and Kylie (office administrator). Retail distribution in all States; exports to the UK, the US and Hong Kong.

Logan Shiraz

🍷🍷🍷½ **1998** Light to medium red-purple; gently savoury, spicy fruit on the bouquet is mirrored by distinctly savoury, almost lemony fruit characters on the palate, finishing with soft, fine tannins. Seems radically different from the '97 vintage. **rating:** 83

best drinking 2002–2005 **best vintages** '97 **drink with** Game • $27.95

Logan Ripe Shiraz Grenache

🍷🍷🍷🍷 **1998** Light to medium red-purple; fresh, juicy berry aromas lead into a fresh, tangy palate with plum and spice flavours, soft tannins and minimal oak. **rating:** 85

best drinking Now **best vintages** NA **drink with** Takeaway • $14.95

london lodge estate NR

Muswellbrook Road, Gungal, NSW 2333 **region** Upper Hunter Valley
phone (02) 6547 6122 **fax** (02) 6547 6122 **open** 7 days 10–9
winemaker Gary Reed **production** NA **est.** 1988
product range NA
summary The 16-hectare vineyard of Stephen and Joanne Horner is planted to chardonnay, pinot noir, shiraz and cabernet sauvignon, and the wines sold through a cellar door (and restaurant) with a full array of tourist attractions, including arts and crafts.

long gully estate ★★★☆

Long Gully Road, Healesville, Vic 3777 **region** Yarra Valley
phone (03) 9510 5798 **fax** (03) 9510 9859 **open** 7 days 11–5
winemaker Peter Florance **production** 25 000 **est.** 1982
product range ($9–30 CD) Riesling, Victoria Collection Chardonnay, Chardonnay, Sauvignon Blanc, Sauvignon Blanc Semillon, Pinot Noir, Shiraz, Merlot, Irma's Cabernet, Victoria Collection Cabernet Sauvignon; Reserve Ice Riesling, Reserve Merlot.
summary One of the larger (but by no means largest) of the Yarra Valley producers to have successfully established a number of export markets over recent years. Wine quality is consistent rather than exhilarating; it is able to offer a range of wines with two to three years' bottle age. Recent vineyard extensions underline the commercial success of Long Gully.

Long Gully Estate Pinot Noir

YYYY **1999** Medium red; the bouquet is quite fragrant, with a mix of cherry and a hint of green, almost citrussy, characters. The palate has authentic Pinot Noir flavour, but the tannins are grippy and slightly green; overall, a very good result for a difficult vintage. **rating:** 85
best drinking Now–2003 **best vintages** NA **drink with** Asian • $16

Long Gully Estate Shiraz

YYYY **1998** Medium red-purple; the bouquet is clean and fresh, the palate with a mix of spicy, foresty and dark cherry flavours supported by subtle oak. The finish is clean, with a low tannin profile. **rating:** 85
best drinking 2002–2006 **best vintages** '97 **drink with** Civet of venison • $16

Long Gully Estate Reserve Merlot

YYYY **1998** Medium red-purple; the earthy/savoury bouquet offers a mix of olive and spice, characters that come through with high fidelity on the savoury/earthy/olive palate, finishing with lingering tannins. **rating:** 85
best drinking 2002–2007 **best vintages** NA **drink with** Braised veal • $20.85

Long Gully Estate Irma's Cabernet

YYYY **1998** The colour is slightly hazy, strongly suggesting the wine was not filtered. The bouquet is solid and briary, with some notes of sweet cassis that come through strongly, together with mulberry and a touch of chocolate, on the palate. A wine with real flavour and character, well-handled oak and tannins. **rating:** 89
best drinking 2003–2010 **best vintages** '97, '98 **drink with** Yarra Valley venison • $17

longleat ★★★☆

Old Weir Road, Murchison, Vic 3610 **region** Goulburn Valley
phone (03) 5826 2294 **fax** (03) 5826 2510 **open** Thurs–Mon 10–5
winemaker David Traeger (Contract) **production** 7000 **est.** 1975
product range ($13–17 CD) Riesling, Semillon, Chardonnay, Shiraz, Cabernet Sauvignon.
summary Longleat has long had a working relationship with Chateau Tahbilk, which makes the Longleat wines under contract, and buys significant quantities of grapes surplus to Longleat's requirements. The wines are always honest and full-flavoured, and have been given a striking new label design which, if nothing else, catches the eye. News of a change of ownership came as this book was going to print.

longview creek vineyard NR

150 Palmer Road, Sunbury, Vic 3429 **region** Sunbury
phone (03) 9744 1050 **fax** (03) 9744 1050 **open** Sunday 11–5
winemaker David Hodgson **production** 350 **est.** 1988
product range ($18–22 CD) Chardonnay, Chenin Blanc, Pinot Noir, Tarrango, Shiraz.
summary A relatively new arrival in the Sunbury subdistrict of the Macedon region, owned by Ron and Joan Parker. A total of 3.3 hectares of chardonnay, pinot noir and chenin blanc are in production, with an additional 2 hectares of shiraz coming into bearing.

lost lake vineyard & winery NR

Lot 3 Vasse Highway, Pemberton, WA 6260 **region** Pemberton
phone (08) 9776 1251 **fax** (08) 9776 1251 **open** 7 days 11–4
winemaker Michael Fogarty **production** 5000 **est.** 1990
product range ($16–27 CD) Sauvignon Blanc, Semillon Chardonnay, Chardonnay, Pinot Noir, Shiraz.
summary Previously known as Eastbrook Estate, this winery's origins go back to 1990 and to the acquisition of an 80-hectare farming property which was subdivided into three portions: 16 hectares, now known as Picardy, were acquired by Dr Bill Pannell; 18 hectares became the base for Lost Lake; and the remainder was sold. The initial plantings in 1990 were of pinot noir and chardonnay, followed by shiraz, sauvignon blanc, merlot and cabernet sauvignon between 1996 and 1998. Just under 8 hectares are now planted. A jarrah-pole and cedar winery with a crush capacity of 300 tonnes was built in 1995, together with a restaurant that seats 150 people; it is open six days a week for lunch, and for dinner on Friday and Saturday nights. In 1999 the business was acquired by four Perth investors, and Michael Fogarty, an Honours graduate from the University of Adelaide Roseworthy Campus, and with both Australian and French winemaking experience, has been installed as winemaker.

Lost Lake Pinot Noir

TTTT **1999** Medium red-purple; the bouquet is indubitably complex, but very oaky and foresty. The palate is a carbon copy, with plenty of oaky power, but not a lot of vinosity. Scores on character, and did win a silver medal at the 2000 Wine Show of Western Australia. **rating:** 85

best drinking Now **best vintages** NA **drink with** Smoked quail • $25

lost valley winery ★★★☆

Strath Creek, Vic 3658 **region** Central Victorian Mountain Country
phone (03) 9592 3531 **fax** (03) 9592 6396 **open** Not
winemaker Alex White (Contract) **production** 1000 **est.** 1995
product range ($23–28 ML) Verdelho, Shiraz, Merlot, Cortese.
summary Dr Robert Ippaso planted the Lost Valley vineyard at an elevation of 450 metres on the slopes of Mount Tallarook, with 1.25 hectares of shiraz and 0.85 hectare each of merlot, verdelho and cortese, the last the only such planting in Australia. It pays homage to Dr Ippaso's birthplace in Savoie in the Franco-Italian Alps, where cortese flourishes.

Lost Valley Cortese

TTTT **2000** Light green-yellow; the bouquet is bright and fresh, with a mix of mineral, green apple and pear aromas, the palate with bright, fresh green-apple flavours and attractive mouthfeel. Flawless winemaking. Only 1500 bottles produced. **rating:** 88

best drinking Now–2006 **best vintages** NA **drink with** Light seafood • $28

Lost Valley Verdelho

TTTT **2000** Bright, light green-yellow; the bouquet is fresh and lively, with crisp fruit-salad aromas, moving more to lemon/citrus on the palate, with bright, fresh acidity. Smart stuff for a pretty ordinary grape variety. **rating:** 86

best drinking Now–2003 **best vintages** NA **drink with** Stuffed pancakes • $23

louis-laval wines NR

160 Cobcroft Road, Broke, NSW 2330 **region** Lower Hunter Valley
phone (02) 6579 1105 **fax** (02) 6579 1105 **open** By appointment
winemaker Roy Meyer **production** 600 **est.** 1987
product range ($25 CD) Shiraz, Cabernet Sauvignon.
summary It is ironic that the winery name should have associations with Alfa Laval, the giant Swiss food and wine-machinery firm. Roy Meyer runs an organic vineyard (using only sulphur and copper sprays) and is proud of the fact that the winery has no refrigeration and no stainless steel. The wines produced from the 2.5-hectare vineyard are fermented in open barrels or cement tanks, and maturation is handled entirely in oak. At its first entry into the Hunter Valley Small Winemakers Show, the 1998 Cabernet Sauvignon won a silver medal, and the 1998 Shiraz a bronze medal.

lovegrove vineyard and winery ★★★☆

1420 Heidelberg–Kinglake Road, Cottles Bridge, Vic 3099 **region** Yarra Valley
phone (03) 9718 1569 **fax** (03) 9718 1028 **open** Weekends and public holidays 11–6, weekdays by appointment
winemaker Stephen Bennett, Karen Coulston **production** 1200 **est.** 1983
product range ($15–27.50 CD) Sauvignon Blanc, Chardonnay, Paradis, Petillant Methode Champenoise, Pinot Noir, Merlot, Cabernet Merlot.
summary Lovegrove is in fact a long-established winery in the Diamond Valley subregion, and while production is limited, offers the visitor much to enjoy, with picturesque gardens overlooking the Kinglake Ranges; antipasto, soup and cheese lunch; barbecue and picnic tables; and live music on the second Sunday of the month. Intermittent art exhibitions are staged, and the winery caters for private functions. The wines are produced from a little over 3 hectares of estate plantings, which are now fully mature, and a range of vintages spanning 1995 through 2000 is available.

lovey's estate NR

1548 Melba Highway, Yarra Glen, Vic 3775 **region** Yarra Valley
phone (03) 5965 2444 **fax** (03) 5965 2460 **open** Wed–Sun 12–5
winemaker Brian Love **production** 1000 **est.** 1989
product range ($25.50–27.50 CD) Sauvignon Blanc, Chardonnay, Pinot Noir, Cabernet Sauvignon.
summary Lovey's Estate is part of a restaurant and accommodation complex situated prominently on the Melba Highway, just on the far side of Yarra Glen. The majority of the production from the 11-hectare vineyard is sold; part is made under contract at Tarrawarra and is available through cellar door and the restaurant.

lowe family wines ★★★☆

c/o Peppers Creek Winery, cnr Broke and Ekerts Roads, Pokolbin, NSW 2325 **region** Mudgee
phone (02) 4998 7121 **fax** (02) 4998 7121 **open** Wed–Sun 9–5
winemaker David Lowe, Jane Wilson **production** 4000 **est.** 1987
product range ($18–25 ML) Semillon, Peacock Hill Chardonnay, Lawless Chardonnay, Peacock Hill Shiraz.
summary Former Rothbury winemaker David Lowe and Jane Wilson make the Lowe Family Wines at the Oakvale Winery, drawing upon 15 hectares of family-owned vineyards in Mudgee, supplemented by purchases from Orange and the Hunter Valley. Interestingly, the plantings include sangiovese, barbera and zinfandel. David and Jane also run an increasingly important contract-winemaking business.

Lowe Family Semillon

1999 Light green-yellow; the bouquet is light, with crisp herb and mineral aromas but with a slightly blurred background. The palate is minerally, with some notes of herb and lemon. Likely in a transition phase; needs time to sort itself out. **rating:** 83
best drinking 2003–2007 **best vintages** NA **drink with** Fried chicken • $21

Lowe Family Botrytis Semillon

1999 Glowing golden colour; the complex bouquet shows pronounced botrytis influence, with apricot to the fore, and honey and mead thereafter. The palate is as rich as the bouquet promises, with apricot and cumquat flavours; the intense sweetness by acidity. **rating:** 90
best drinking Now–2003 **best vintages** '99 **drink with** Fruit tart and King Island cream • $25

Lowe Family Shiraz

1998 Medium red-purple; the bouquet is clean and smooth, with nicely balanced fruit and oak inputs. A well-balanced, stylish and quite elegant palate with plummy fruit and cedary oak flavours; fine tannins and appropriate acidity complete the picture. **rating:** 87
best drinking 2003–2008 **best vintages** NA **drink with** Cheese • $25

lyre bird hill ★★★

Inverloch Road, Koonwarra, Vic 3954 **region** Gippsland
phone (03) 5664 3204 **fax** (03) 5664 3206 **open** Weekends and public holidays 10–5 or by appointment
winemaker Owen Schmidt **production** 2000 **est.** 1986

product range ($12–35 CD) Riesling, Traminer, Sauvignon Blanc, Bowers Bouquet (white blend), Chardonnay, Pinot Noir, Pinot Noir Cellar Reserve, Shiraz, Cabernet Sauvignon, Salut! (Cabernet Sauvignon Shiraz Merlot), Rhapsody (Sparkling), Phantasy (Sparkling).
summary Former Melbourne professionals Owen and Robyn Schmidt make small quantities of estate-grown wine (the vineyard is 2.4 hectares in size), offering accommodation for three couples (RACV four-star rating) in their spacious guest house and self-contained cottage. Frost in September 1999 decimated the yield, and led to the acquisition of fruit both from other Gippsland growers, and also an increased range of grapes from the Yarra Valley.

Lyre Bird Hill Pinot Noir Cellar Reserve

🍷🍷🍷🍷 **1999** Light to medium red-tawny; the bouquet is light, with aromas in the savoury/foresty/stemmy/ spicy spectrum, characters that flow through directly to the palate. The wine shows varietal character, has length, but really needs more sweet fruit at its core, for experience shows the woody/stemmy characters become more dominant as the wine matures. **rating:** 83

best drinking Now–2003 **best vintages** NA **drink with** Pot-roasted quail • $30

mcalister vineyards NR

Golden Beach Road, Longford, Vic 3851 **region** Gippsland
phone (03) 5149 7229 **fax** (03) 5149 7229 **open** By appointment
winemaker Peter Edwards **production** 550 **est.** 1975
product range A single wine, The McAlister, a blend of Cabernet Sauvignon, Cabernet Franc and Merlot.
summary The McAlister Vineyards actively shun publicity or exposure which, on the basis of prior tastings, is a pity.

macaw creek wines ★★★☆

Macaw Creek Road, Riverton, SA 5412 **region** Mount Lofty Ranges Zone
phone (08) 8847 2237 **fax** (08) 8847 2237 **open** Sun and public holidays 11–4
winemaker Rodney Hooper, Miriam Hooper **production** 2000 **est.** 1992
product range ($13–29 CD) Riesling, Yoolang Preservative Free Shiraz, Reserve Shiraz Cabernet, Grenache Shiraz Mourvedre.
summary The property on which Macaw Creek Wines is established has been owned by the Hooper family since the 1850s, but development of the estate vineyards did not begin until 1995; 10 hectares have been planted since that time, with a further 20 hectares in the winter/spring of 1999. Rodney and Miriam Hooper established the Macaw Creek brand previously (in 1992) with wines made from grapes from other regions, including the Preservative-Free Yoolang Cabernet Shiraz. Rodney Hooper is a highly qualified and skilled winemaker with experience in many parts of Australia and internationally in Germany, France and the US.

Macaw Creek Riesling

🍷🍷🍷🍷🍷 **1998** Medium to full yellow-green; a full, bottle-developed bouquet with traditional lime-accented fruit is followed by a palate with abundant character, concentration and power, with lime/citrus leading the way. **rating:** 91

best drinking Now–2006 **best vintages** NA **drink with** Lebanese dips • $14

Macaw Creek Yoolang Shiraz

🍷🍷🍷🍷 **2000** Dense, inky purple, similar to Chambourcin; the powerful bouquet has a mix of blackberry jam and chocolate aromas, which are largely repeated on the soft, fleshy, juicy palate. **rating:** 85

best drinking Now **best vintages** NA **drink with** Strong red meat • $15.50

Macaw Creek Wines Grenache Shiraz

🍷🍷🍷🍷 **1999** Medium red-purple; the bouquet is clean, with the grenache component at the lighter, sweeter end of the spectrum; the palate, likewise, is smooth, light-bodied and distinctly fruity, without the interposition of significant tannins or oak. **rating:** 85

best drinking Now **best vintages** NA **drink with** Takeaway • $14

mcgee wines NR

1710 Wattlevale Road, Nagambie, Vic 3608 **region** Goulburn Valley
phone (03) 5794 1530 **fax** (03) 5794 1530 **open** By appointment
winemaker Don Lewis (Contract) **production** 750 **est.** 1995
product range ($15.95 R) Chardonnay, Shiraz, Cabernet Sauvignon.

summary Andrew McGee and partner Kerry Smith (the viticulturist) have established 12 hectares of vines on the banks of the Goulburn River, the majority planted to shiraz, with lesser quantities of grenache, viognier and mourvedre. Currently, 95 per cent of the production is sold to Mitchelton, where the McGee wines are presently made, but the plan is for the partners to make the wine for themselves in the future, and to increase production. The wines are distributed through Woods Wines, 35 Greeves Street, Fitzroy.

mcguigan wines ★★★★

PO Box 300, Cessnock, NSW 2335 **region** Lower Hunter Valley
phone (02) 4998 7700 **fax** (02) 4998 7401 **open** 7 days 10–5
winemaker Brian McGuigan, Peter Hall, Thomas Jung, Brod Vallance **production** 825 000 **est.** 1992
product range ($9.50–36 R) The wines are sold in several price brackets: at the bottom, Harvest Range First Harvest, Night Harvest and Autumn Harvest; the Black Label range of Verdelho Chardonnay, Chardonnay, Traminer Riesling and Black Label Red; Vineyard Selection Gewurztraminer and Petite Verdot; then the Bin range of 2000 Shiraz, 3000 Merlot, 4000 Cabernet Sauvignon, 5000 Malbec, 6000 Verdelho, 7000 Chardonnay, 8000 Sauvignon Blanc, 9000 Semillon; finally Shareholder Reserve range and Personal Reserve range.
summary A public-listed company which is the ultimate logical expression of Brian McGuigan's marketing drive and vision, on a par with that of Wolf Blass in his heyday. Highly successful in its chosen niche market notwithstanding exceedingly garish labels. Has been particularly active in export markets, notably the US and more recently in China. The current range of wines spanning the 1998–2000 vintages commands respect.

McGuigan Bin 9000 Semillon

🍷🍷🍷🍷 **2000** Pale straw-green; the bouquet is clean, quite intense and stylish, with lemony fruit; the palate is elegant, well balanced, unforced, yet shows above-average flavour for a young Semillon. **rating:** 87
best drinking Now–2005 **best vintages** '00 **drink with** Balmain bugs • $12.95

McGuigan Limited Release Bin 8000 Sauvignon Blanc

🍷🍷🍷🍷 **2000** Light green-yellow; the bouquet is clean, correct and fresh, with a mix of mineral and passionfruit leading into a similarly fresh, light palate with good length, and an attractive balance of mineral and more tropical flavours. **rating:** 87
best drinking Now **best vintages** NA **drink with** Trout mousse • $13.50

McGuigan Bin 7000 Chardonnay

🍷🍷🍷🍷🍷 **2000** Medium yellow-green; the bouquet is clean and smooth, with attractive white peach fruit, subliminal oak and just a hint of creaminess from the mlf. The palate is very well balanced, with gentle peach and nectarine flavour, hints of cashew, and subtle oak. Won top gold medal in both the Hunter Valley and Cowra Wine Shows 2000, gold medal at the Perth Wine Show 2000, and silver at the Adelaide Wine Show 2000. **rating:** 90
best drinking Now–2003 **best vintages** '00 **drink with** Breast of chicken • $13.50

McGuigan Personal Reserve Mistletoe Lane Chardonnay

🍷🍷🍷🍷 **1998** Medium yellow-green; the solid bouquet showing some bottle development and obvious oak inputs onto the peach and honey fruit. A very generous wine on the palate, showing regional bottle-developed characters and, as with the bouquet, obvious oak inputs. **rating:** 88
best drinking Now **best vintages** NA **drink with** Lemon chicken • $26

McGuigan Personal Reserve Sandy Hollow Chardonnay

🍷🍷🍷🍷 **1998** Glowing yellow-green; a rich buttery/nutty/oaky bouquet is followed by a flavoursome and complex palate in which the fruit and oak components have been well integrated by bottle age. **rating:** 86
best drinking Now **best vintages** NA **drink with** Pan-fried veal • $26

McGuigan Personal Reserve Vine Vale Shiraz

🍷🍷🍷🍷🍷 **1998** Medium to full red-purple; the bouquet has rich dark fruit/black cherry/berry aromas that flow through on a palate with plenty of power, finishing with savoury tannins and well-handled oak. **rating:** 90
best drinking 2003–2008 **best vintages** NA **drink with** Crown roast of beef • $36

McGuigan Bin 3000 Merlot

🍷🍷🍷🍷 **2000** Medium purple-red; the bouquet is fresh but slightly callow with juicy berry aromas and a touch of leaf. The palate is quite supple and juicy, with fine tannins and subliminal oak. Not too callow. Won a gold medal at the New Zealand Liquorland Wine Show and silver at the Adelaide Wine Show 2000. **rating:** 86
best drinking Now **best vintages** NA **drink with** Roast chicken • $13.50

McGuigan Personal Reserve Vine Vale Cabernet Sauvignon

ΥΥΥΥ **1998** Medium red-purple; the bouquet has ripe plum and blackberry fruit supported by subtle oak, the palate is dense and chewy, with plum, blackberry and chocolate flavours together with persistent tannins. **rating:** 88

best drinking 2003–2010 **best vintages** '98 **drink with** Braised oxtail • $36

mcivor creek NR

Costerfield Road, Heathcote, Vic 3523 **region** Heathcote
phone (03) 5433 3000 **fax** (03) 5433 3456 **open** 7 days 10–5.30
winemaker Peter Turley **production** 5000 **est.** 1973
product range ($9.95–14.95 CD) Riesling, Auslese Riesling, Shiraz, Cabernet Shiraz, Fine Old Tawny Port.
summary The beautifully situated McIvor Creek winery is well worth a visit and does offer wines in diverse styles, of which the red are the most regional. Peter Turley has 5 hectares of cabernet sauvignon together with 2.5 hectares of cabernet franc and merlot, and supplements his intake with grapes from other growers. No recent tastings.

mclaren vale iii associates NR

130 Main Road, McLaren Vale, SA 5171 **region** McLaren Vale
phone 1800 501 513 **fax** (08) 8323 7422 **open** Mon–Fri 9–5, tasting by appointment
winemaker Brian Light **production** 12 000 **est.** 1999
product range ($15–20 R) Semillon Sauvignon Blanc, Chenin Blanc, Chardonnay, The Third Degree, Shiraz, Indent Cabernet, Indent Shiraz.
summary This is the type of name that gives editors and indexers nightmares, but then life wasn't meant to be easy. The three associates in question all have a decade or more of wine-industry experience; Mary Greer is managing partner, Reginald Wymond chairing partner, and Christopher Fox partner. The partnership owns 25 hectares of vines spanning two vineyards, one owned by Mary and John Greer, the other by Reg and Sue Wymond. Nineteen of the 25 hectares are planted to mainstream red varieties, with shiraz leading the way. The label was first introduced in 1999, the aim being to produce affordable quality wine. Rutherglen Wine and Spirits is a distributor in Queensland, New South Wales and Victoria, and Empire Liquor in South Australia.

McLaren Vale III Associates The Third Degree

ΥΥΥΥ **1999** Medium red-purple; light, berryish grenache aromas (and anonymous oak) are followed by a berry, jam and chocolate palate with subliminal tannins. Easy, early-drinking style. **rating:** 84

best drinking Now **best vintages** NA **drink with** Adelaide pie floater • NA

mcmanus NR

Rogers Road, Yenda, NSW 2681 **region** Riverina
phone (02) 6968 1064 **open** 7 days 9–5
winemaker Dr David McManus **production** 500 **est.** 1972
product range ($4–8 CD) Chardonnay, Chardonnay Semillon, Malbec, Merlot, Shiraz, Pinot Malbec Shiraz; many named after family members.
summary An extremely idiosyncratic winery run by Griffith GP Dr David McManus, his sister and other family members. Natural winemaking methods lead to considerable variation in quality, but the prices are from another era, and some of the vintages likewise.

mcpherson wines ★★☆

PO Box 529, Artarmon, NSW 2570 **region** Goulburn Valley
phone (02) 9436 1644 **fax** (02) 9436 3144 **open** Not
winemaker Leigh Clarnette, Andrew Dean, Andrew McPherson **production** 1 million **est.** 1993
product range ($7–10 R) Semillon Chardonnay, Chardonnay, Shiraz.
summary McPherson Wines is little known in Australia but is, by any standards, a substantial business. Its wines are almost entirely produced for the export market, with Dan Murphy being the sole (and exclusive) retail source in Australia. The wines are made at various locations from contract-grown grapes and represent good value at their price point. For the record, McPherson Wines is a joint venture between Andrew McPherson and Alister Purbrick of Tahbilk. Both have had a lifetime of experience in the industry.

mcwilliam's ★★★★☆

Jack McWilliam Road, Hanwood, NSW 2680 **region** Riverina
phone (02) 6963 0001 **fax** (02) 6963 0002 **open** Mon–Sat 9–5
winemaker Jim Brayne, Simon Crook **production** NFP **est.** 1916
product range ($6–50 R) A disciplined and easy-to-follow product range (all varietally identified) commencing with Hillside casks; Inheritance Range; Hanwood; Charles King; JJ McWilliams (first released 1996); Winemaker's Reserve Chardonnay and Cabernet Shiraz; and Regional Collection Limited Release Hunter Valley Chardonnay, Eden Valley Riesling and JJ McWilliam Riverina Botrytis Semillon. Also superb fortified wines including MCW11 Liqueur Muscat and 10-Year-Old Hanwood Tawny Port heading a much larger range of Sherries that still form an important part of the business.
summary The best wines to emanate from the Hanwood winery are from other regions, notably the Barwang Vineyard at Hilltops in New South Wales, Coonawarra and Eden Valley; as McWilliam's viticultural resources have expanded, so have they been able to produce regional blends from across southeastern Australia under the Hanwood label that, in the last few years, have been startlingly good. Exports to many countries, the most important being the UK and the US, via a major distribution joint venture with Paterno Home, Germany and New Zealand.

McWilliam's Eden Valley Riesling

🍷🍷🍷🍷 **1996** Glowing yellow-green; rich, complex lime and toast aromas suggest a far older wine, but so what. There is an interesting mix of lime, herb and cut-grass flavours on the palate but nothing to be gained from cellaring. **rating:** 89

best drinking Now–2003 **best vintages** NA **drink with** Rich fish dishes • $15

McWilliam's Hunter Semillon

🍷🍷🍷🍷½ **2000** Light green-yellow; the bouquet is quite intense, with herb, mineral, lemon rind/zest aromas, the palate clean, fresh and harmonious, with good length, but not quite the same degree of power as the bouquet suggests. **rating:** 90

best drinking Now–2006 **best vintages** '00 **drink with** Blue-eye cod • $17

McWilliam's Hanwood Semillon Chardonnay

🍷🍷🍷🍷 **1999** Light to medium yellow-green; the bouquet is clean, light and at two years of age still quite fresh, with a gentle hint of creamy oak. The palate is elegant and, like the bouquet, retaining freshness, with a mix of melon and nutty flavours, finishing crisply. Has improved continuously over 2000; a winner of three gold medals at national and regional Australian wine shows. **rating:** 87

best drinking Now **best vintages** NA **drink with** Pasta • $9.95

McWilliam's Hanwood Chardonnay

🍷🍷🍷🍷 **2000** Light to medium yellow-green; sophisticated nutty/cashew overtones to the melon fruit of the bouquet, plus just a hint of oak, are followed by a light but quite complex palate with a nice balance between the melon fruit and more cashew/creamy characters. **rating:** 89

best drinking Now **best vintages** '99, '00 **drink with** Fresh pasta • $9.95

McWilliam's Winemaker's Reserve Chardonnay

🍷🍷🍷🍷½ **1999** Medium yellow-green; the moderately intense bouquet shows melon, fig and oak aromas seamlessly woven together; the palate is at the cutting edge of the development of Australian Chardonnay style, elegant, intense, fine and long, yet not at all flashy nor even obviously complex; you have to get under the skin of the wine to find this, and it is sure to repay cellaring. **rating:** 91

best drinking 2002–2007 **best vintages** NA **drink with** Sautéed scallops • $49.95

McWilliam's Barossa Shiraz

🍷🍷🍷🍷 **1998** Dark red-purple; a clean, rich bouquet with masses of dark cherry fruit and quite obvious American oak is followed by a palate filled with flavour. Here dark cherry and blackberry fruit are balanced by substantial tannins and vanillin oak. **rating:** 88

best drinking 2002–2008 **best vintages** NA **drink with** Rare fillet steak • $15

McWilliam's Hanwood Merlot

🍷🍷🍷½ **2000** Medium red-purple; there is quite distinct leafy/gamey varietal character on the bouquet, the palate light to medium bodied with fresh, quite sweet, small berry flavours and gentle tannins on the finish. **rating:** 83

best drinking Now **best vintages** NA **drink with** Takeaway • $9.95

McWilliam's McLaren Vale Grenache

YYYY **1999** Medium red-purple; some slightly jammy varietal aromas mix with savoury, spice and old-glass cupboard scents. The intensity of the varietal fruit flavour picks up on the medium-bodied palate, with the fruit in a similar taste spectrum to that promised by the bouquet. **rating:** 85

best drinking Now **best vintages** NA **drink with** Spiced beef kebabs • $15

McWilliam's Winemaker's Reserve Cabernet Shiraz

YYYYY **1998** Medium to full red-purple; the complexity of the bouquet is immediately obvious, ranging through blackberry, plum, spice and more savoury aromas. The mouthfilling, rich and complex palate has abundant blackberry/blackcurrant/plum fruit married with rounded tannins and oak. **rating:** 94

best drinking 2003–2013 **best vintages** '98 **drink with** Aged fillet of beef • $49.95

McWilliam's Coonawarra Cabernet Sauvignon

YYYY **1998** Medium red, with just a touch of purple; the light to moderately intense bouquet is clean, smooth and just a fraction plain. On the palate, savoury/chocolate/briary/berry flavours mark a medium-bodied wine with pleasant tannin structure. **rating:** 86

best drinking Now–2004 **best vintages** NA **drink with** Lamb shanks on risotto • $15

McWilliam's Hanwood Cabernet Sauvignon

YYYY **2000** Medium purple-red; fresh red berry fruit and just a hint of oak flows through into the fresh, redcurrant/berry palate, with modest but evident tannin structure to close. **rating:** 84

best drinking Now **best vintages** NA **drink with** Pizza • $9.95

mcwilliam's mount pleasant ★★★★★

Marrowbone Road, Pokolbin, NSW 2320 **region** Lower Hunter Valley
phone (02) 4998 7505 **fax** (02) 4998 7761 **open** 7 days 10–5
winemaker Phillip Ryan, Scott Stephens **production** NFP **est.** 1921
product range ($10–45 R) Much simplified and rationalised over the past year. The base range now comprises Mount Pleasant Elizabeth, Philip, Late Harvest Dessert Wine, Semillon Sauvignon Blanc, Verdelho, Chardonnay, Unwooded Chardonnay, Pinot Chardonnay, Sparkling Pinot Noir, Merlot; then individual vineyard wines, Rosehill Shiraz, Old Paddock & Old Hill Shiraz, Lovedale Semillon (previously known as Anne), then Maurice O'Shea Chardonnay, Shiraz; finally Museum releases of Elizabeth, Lovedale Semillon, Late Harvest Reserve.
summary McWilliam's Elizabeth and the glorious Lovedale Semillon are generally commercially available with many years of bottle age and are undervalued and underpriced treasures with a consistently superb show record. The three individual vineyard wines, together with the Maurice O'Shea memorial wines, add to the lustre of this proud name. Exports to many countries, the most important being the UK, the US, Germany and New Zealand.

McWilliam's Mount Pleasant Elizabeth

YYYYY **1997** Glowing yellow-green; a powerful bouquet, with a mix of toast and honey on the one hand, and lime and herb on the other. Yet again, the wine has flavour, length and grip, with good acidity; still remarkably fresh. It alone has won two gold medals and three silver medals in a limited show career to date. **rating:** 93

best drinking Now–2011 **best vintages** '75, '81, '82, '83, '86, '89, '90, '91, '93, '94, '95, '96, '97 **drink with** Pan-fried veal • $17

McWilliam's Mount Pleasant Lovedale Semillon

YYYYY **1995** Medium to full yellow-green, quite developed; the bouquet is powerful, intense and complex; both it and the palate show aromas of herb, lemon and honey but as yet no toast and, indeed, may never do so. Has excellent mouthfeel and weight, very much in the tradition of Lovedale. The one question was the dodgy-looking cork. **rating:** 94

best drinking Now–2015 **best vintages** '69, '72, '74, '75, '79, '84, '86, '95 **drink with** Fine fish dishes • NA

McWilliam's Mount Pleasant Hunter Valley Chardonnay

YYYYY **1998** Glowing yellow-green; a rich, toasty, honeyed, buttery bouquet leads into a palate with mouthfilling flavour of ripe melon, honey, citrus and fig, all in turn interplaying with touches of barrel-ferment oak. Good acidity provides the essential balance for a wine that won a trophy and gold medal at the Hunter Valley Wine Show in 1998 as the Best Commercial Dry White. **rating:** 90

best drinking Now–2004 **best vintages** '98 **drink with** Char-grilled calamari • $14

McWilliam's Mount Pleasant O'Shea Chardonnay

🍷🍷🍷🍷🍷 **1998** Medium yellow-green; the bouquet is concentrated and quite rich, with clean nectarine fruit, the powerful and concentrated palate offering more of the same nectarine/peach fruit, supported by excellent acidity and nicely controlled oak. **rating:** 92

best drinking Now–2003 **best vintages** '98 **drink with** Roast pork • $31.95

McWilliam's Mount Pleasant O'Shea Shiraz

🍷🍷🍷🍷 **1997** Medium red-purple; a restrained, earthy, regional bouquet is followed by a palate with rather more sweet berry fruit, classy, fine-grained tannins, and subtle oak. A wine at the very start of its life, and may blossom with further bottle age. **rating:** 88

best drinking 2003–2013 **best vintages** NA **drink with** Roast veal • $32.95

madew wines NR

Westering, Federal Highway, Lake George, NSW 2581 **region** Canberra District
phone (02) 4848 0026 **open** Weekends, public holidays 11–5
winemaker David Madew **production** 2500 **est.** 1984
product range ($13–20 CD) Riesling, Reserve Riesling, Semillon, Chardonnay, Phoenix (Botrytis Chardonnay), Dry Red, Merlot, Cabernets.
summary Madew Wines bowed to the urban pressure of Queanbeyan and purchased the Westering Vineyard from Captain G P Hood some years ago. Plantings there have now increased to 9.5 hectares, with 1 hectare each of shiraz and pinot gris coming into bearing.

maglieri ★★★★

Douglas Gully Road, McLaren Flat, SA 5171 **region** McLaren Vale
phone (08) 8383 0177 **fax** (08) 8383 0735 **open** Mon–Sat 9–4, Sun 12–4
winemaker Charles Hargrave **production** NFP **est.** 1972
product range ($18–34.99 R) While still billing itself as the 'House of Lambrusco', and still producing a range of Italian-derived styles for specialty markets within Australia, this winery is increasingly known for the quality of its varietal table wines, spearheaded by Semillon, Chardonnay, Cabernet Sauvignon and Shiraz, the last released in two guises: as a simple varietal, and the top-end Steve Maglieri. Typically, several vintages available at any one time.
summary One of the better-kept secrets among the wine cognoscenti but not among the many customers who drink thousands of cases of white and red Lambrusco every year, an example of niche marketing at its profitable best. It was a formula that proved irresistible to Beringer Blass, which acquired Maglieri in 1999. Its dry red wines are invariably generously proportioned and full of character, the Shiraz particularly so.

Maglieri Semillon

🍷🍷🍷🍷 **2000** Light straw-green; slightly smoky overtones to crisp grassy/lemony fruit on the bouquet give a particularly promising start. The palate does not disappoint, with light oak and the crisp, lively varietal fruit not compromised. A singularly rare achievement for either McLaren Vale or the Barossa. **rating:** 89

best drinking Now–2006 **best vintages** '00 **drink with** Smoked eel • $14

Maglieri Chardonnay

🍷🍷🍷🍷 **2000** Light to medium green-yellow; a lemony citrussy, stone fruit bouquet with just a hint of oak is followed by a palate which is really quite delicate, with citrus and melon fruit, and the same subtle oak. Looks lighter than 13.5° alcohol. **rating:** 84

best drinking Now **best vintages** NA **drink with** Fresh fish • $14

Maglieri Shiraz

🍷🍷🍷🍷 **1999** Medium red-purple; spicy, vanilla American oak is dominant on the bouquet; cherry and plum is to be found on the palate, but overall the oak is dominant, and the flavour dips on the back palate, with a short finish. Simply not in the class of previous vintages. **rating:** 86

best drinking 2003–2007 **best vintages** '90, '91, '93, '95, '96, '97, '98 **drink with** Ravioli • $20

main ridge estate ★★★★☆

80 William Road, Red Hill, Vic 3937 **region** Mornington Peninsula
phone (03) 5989 2686 **fax** (03) 5931 0000 **open** Mon–Fri 12–4, weekends 12–5
winemaker Nat White **production** 1000 **est.** 1975

product range ($30–42 CD) Chardonnay, Pinot Noir, Half Acre Pinot Noir.
summary Nat White gives meticulous attention to every aspect of his viticulture and winemaking, doing annual battle with one of the coolest sites on the Peninsula. The same attention to detail extends to the winery and the winemaking. Minuscule production; sales through cellar door and mail order, exports to Singapore.

Main Ridge Chardonnay

ΨΨΨΨΥ **1999** Medium yellow-green; the bouquet is of moderate to full intensity, with ripe stonefruit aromas supported by subtle malolactic and oak influences. The palate is rich and mouthfilling, with peach and stonefruit coupled with more nutty characters, then finishing with subtle oak and nicely balanced acidity. From a very low-yielding vintage at a little over 1.5 tonnes to the acre. **rating:** 90
best drinking Now–2006 **best vintages** '91, '92, '94, '96, '97 '98, '99 **drink with** Sweetbreads • $39

Main Ridge Half Acre Pinot Noir

ΨΨΨΨΥ **1999** Full red-purple; much riper than usual, with dark forest and plum aromas, the palate with a cascade of dark plum, cherry, briar and forest flavours; subtle oak and soft tannins round off an excellent wine. **rating:** 93
best drinking Now–2006 **best vintages** '97, '99 **drink with** Grilled salmon • $42

maiolo wines NR

Bussell Highway, Carbunup River, WA 6282 **region** Margaret River
phone (08) 9755 1060 **fax** (08) 9755 1060 **open** 7 days 10–5
winemaker Charles Maiolo **production** 2500 **est.** 1999
product range ($13–17 CD) Semillon Sauvignon Blanc, Chardonnay, Pinot Noir, Shiraz.
summary Charles Maiolo has established a 26-hectare vineyard planted to semillon, sauvignon blanc, chardonnay, pinot noir, shiraz, merlot and cabernet sauvignon in blocks ranging from 1.4 to 6.5 hectares in size. He has completed the wine science degree at the Charles Sturt University, and presides over a winery with a capacity of 250 to 300 tonnes. As the vines are still coming into bearing, production will increase from the present level of around 50 tonnes to over 200 tonnes, with the option of selling surplus grapes. The red wines, in particular, show great promise, with Shiraz and Cabernet Sauvignon to the fore. The wines are distributed in Western Australia by Helen and Ken McGovern, and through Vintage Wine Exports.

Maiolo Shiraz

ΨΨΨΨ **1999** Bright red-purple; attractive spicy, leafy red berry fruit aromas are supported by subtle oak on the bouquet, the palate showing clear varietal character, with spicy red berry fruit, a touch of licorice, nicely handled oak and soft tannins. **rating:** 87
best drinking 2002–2007 **best vintages** NA **drink with** Lamb shanks • $19.80

majella ★★★★☆

Lynn Road, Coonawarra, SA 5263 **region** Coonawarra
phone (08) 8736 3055 **fax** (08) 8736 3057 **open** 7 days 10–4.30
winemaker Bruce Gregory **production** 9000 **est.** 1969
product range ($28–50 CD) Riesling, Shiraz, The Malleea Shiraz Cabernet, Cabernet Sauvignon, Sparkling Shiraz.
summary Majella is one of the more important contract grape-growers in Coonawarra, with 55 hectares of vineyard, principally shiraz and cabernet sauvignon, and with a little riesling and merlot in production and now fully mature. Common gossip has it that part finds its way into the Wynns John Riddoch Cabernet Sauvignon and Michael Shiraz, or their equivalent within the Southcorp Group. Production under the Majella label is increasing as long-term supply contracts expire, over the past few years rising from 2000 to 9000 cases; exports to the UK, the US, Singapore and Hong Kong.

malcolm creek ★★★★

Bonython Road, Kersbrook, SA 5231 **region** Adelaide Hills
phone (08) 8389 3235 **fax** (08) 8389 3235 **open** Weekends, public holidays 11–5
winemaker Reg Tolley **production** 650 **est.** 1982
product range ($19–22 R) Chardonnay, Cabernet Sauvignon.
summary Malcolm Creek is the retirement venture of Reg Tolley, and keeps a low profile. However, the wines are invariably well made and develop gracefully; they are worth seeking out, and are usually available with some extra bottle age at a very modest price.

maling family estate NR

Waverley-Honour, Palmers Lane, Pokolbin, NSW 2320 **region** Lower Hunter Valley
phone (02) 4998 7953 **fax** (02) 4998 7952 **open** 7 days 10–5
winemaker Gary Reed (Contract) **production** 4500 **est.** 1989
product range ($35–72 CD) Waverley Estate Semillon, Chardonnay, Sparkling, Hermitage, Cabernet Sauvignon.
summary The word 'unique' is, like 'passion', grossly overused. Nonetheless, unique is the only word to describe the Maling Family Estate operation, which dates back at the very least to 1989 and arguably to 1971 when the core of the existing vineyard was planted. In 1989 Terry Maling and family acquired the vineyard, which has since been increased to 21.5 hectares of shiraz, semillon, chardonnay and cabernet sauvignon. The large house-cum-cellar door/restaurant/B&B complex was constructed with materials from heritage buildings damaged in the 1989 Newcastle earthquake, including huge grey sandstone blocks, some blazed with convict tally markings; the big doors and roof trusses came from Newcastle bond stores built circa 1860. As well as the year of the earthquake, 1989 was also the first vintage of Maling Estate Wines; wines which, from that year onwards, have been made by Gary Reed. Remarkably, none of the wines were offered for sale until the end of 1999; since 2000, a range of vintages spanning every year between 1989 and 1995 have been on sale.

Maling Family Waverley Estate Semillon

1990 Glowing golden yellow-green; archetypal honey on buttered toast aromas lead into a richly flavoured palate replicating the bouquet but, best of all, having good acidity on the finish. **rating:** 92
best drinking Now–2004 **best vintages** '90 **drink with** Grilled spatchcock • NA

Maling Family Estate Hermitage

1995 Medium red-tawny; smooth, gently earthy, regional-accented varietal character comes through on the bouquet, the palate with sweet, chocolatey/berry flavours supported by sweet, ripe tannins. Warm and welcoming, rather than challenging. **rating:** 87
best drinking Now–2005 **best vintages** NA **drink with** Osso bucco • NA

malmsbury estate vineyard NR

Calder Highway, Malmsbury, Vic 3446 **region** Macedon Ranges
phone 0417 325 773 **fax** (03) 5423 2243 **open** Not
winemaker David Watson (former) **production** 550 **est.** 1989
product range ($15–19 R) Under the Lord Malmsbury label: Chardonnay, Pinot Noir, Classic Red.
summary David Rush and family planted 2 hectares in total of chardonnay, pinot noir, malbec, merlot, cabernet franc, shiraz and cabernet sauvignon in 1989. The vineyard is not irrigated, and has taken some time to come into commercial bearing, although the first experimental wine was made back in 1993.

Lord Malmsbury Chardonnay

2000 Medium yellow-green; subtle melon and citrus fruit on a fresh and clean bouquet are repeated on the lively, fresh palate featuring the same flavours. If any oak has been used in making the wine, it is not evident. **rating:** 83
best drinking Now–2003 **best vintages** NA **drink with** Light fish • $17.50

mandurang valley wines NR

77 Fadersons Lane, Mandurang, Vic 3551 **region** Bendigo
phone (03) 5439 5367 **fax** (03) 5439 3850 **open** Weekends 11–5
winemaker Wes Vine **production** 1200 **est.** 1994
product range ($13–18 CD) Riesling, Pinot Noir, Shiraz, Cabernet Sauvignon.
summary The eponymously named Wes and Pamela Vine have slowly built Mandurang Valley Wines, utilising 2.5 hectares of estate vines and a further 6 hectares of estate-grown grapes. As from Easter 2001 they have been offering café lunches to complement the existing outdoor seating and barbecue facilities. The wines are chiefly sold cellar door and by mailing list, with limited Melbourne distribution through Bacchus Wines, Armadale.

mann NR

105 Memorial Avenue, Baskerville, WA 6056 **region** Swan District
phone (08) 9296 4348 **fax** (08) 9296 4348 **open** Weekends 10–5 and by appointment from Aug 1 until sold out
winemaker Dorham Mann **production** 550 **est.** 1988
product range ($16 CD) Méthode Champenoise.

summary Industry veteran Dorham Mann has established a one-wine label for what must be Australia's most unusual wine: it is dry, only faintly pink, sparkling, and made exclusively from cabernet sauvignon grown on the 2.4-hectare estate surrounding the cellar door. Dorham Mann explains, 'Our family has made and enjoyed the style for more than 30 years, although just in a private capacity until recently.'

mansfield wines NR

204 Eurunderee Road, Mudgee, NSW 2856 **region** Mudgee
phone (02) 6373 3871 **fax** (02) 6373 3708 **open** 7 days 10–5
winemaker Bob Heslop **production** 3300 **est.** 1975
product range ($7–20 CD) Sauvignon Blanc, Chardonnay, Spectabilis White (semi-sweet), Sparkling Muscat, Shiraz Cabernet, Touriga, Zinfandel, Entertainer (non-vintage soft red), Cabernet Sauvignon Merlot, and a selection of fortified wines.
summary Mansfield Wines is one of the old-style wineries, offering a mix of varietal and generic table wines at low prices, and an even larger range of miscellaneous fortified wines, not all of which are locally produced. Distribution is through cellar door and various regional outlets.

mantons creek vineyard NR

Tucks Road, Main Ridge, Vic 3928 **region** Mornington Peninsula
phone (03) 5989 6264 **fax** (03) 5959 6060 **open** 7 days 10–5
winemaker Alex White (Contract) **production** 5000 **est.** 1998
product range ($15–25 CD) Sauvignon Blanc, Muscat, Pinot Gris, Chardonnay, Tempranillo, Pinot Noir.
summary The substantial Mantons Creek Vineyard was in fact established in the early 1990s, with the grapes from the first five years' production being sold to other makers. Since that time events have moved quickly: the label was launched in 1998 and a restaurant-cum-tasting room was opened in December 1998, boasting two chefs with impeccable credentials. The 14-hectare vineyard includes 3 hectares of tempranillo, which John Williams says grows well in the cool climate of the Mornington Peninsula, making a very rich style of wine with great flavour. I am yet to taste it.

margan family winegrowers ★★★★

1238 Milbrodale Road, Broke, NSW 2330 **region** Lower Hunter Valley
phone (02) 6579 1317 **fax** (02) 6579 1317 **open** Mon–Fri 9–5
winemaker Andrew Margan **production** 30 000 **est.** 1989
product range ($16.50–20.50 R) Semillon, Verdelho, Chardonnay, Botrytis Semillon, Merlot, Shiraz, Cabernet Sauvignon.
summary Andrew Margan followed in his father's footsteps by entering the wine industry 20 years ago and has covered a great deal of territory since, working as a Flying Winemaker in Europe, then for Tyrrell's, first as a winemaker then as marketing manager. His wife Lisa, too, has had many years of experience in restaurants and marketing. They now have 10 hectares of fully yielding vines at their 50-hectare Ceres Hill homestead property at Broke and lease the nearby 13-hectare Vere Vineyard. The first stage of a 700-tonne on-site winery was completed in 1998, the first wines having been made elsewhere in 1997. Wine quality (and the packaging) is consistently good.

Margan Family Semillon

ΥΥΥΥ **2000** Light to medium green-yellow; the intense and stylish bouquet has archetypal grass and lemon varietal aroma. The palate is tight and lively, with considerable power and length sustained by good acidity. Remarkably, the wine carries its unusually high (for Semillon, that is) alcohol of 13° with ease. **rating:** 88

best drinking Now–2008 **best vintages** '99, '00 **drink with** Rich seafood • $13

Margan Family Chardonnay

ΥΥΥΥ **1999** Medium yellow-green; attractive melon and nectarine fruit on the bouquet leads into a palate with plenty of flavour and richness; well balanced, with a good finish aided by a nice touch of acidity. The oak adds more texture than flavour, which is no bad thing. **rating:** 87

best drinking Now **best vintages** '98 **drink with** Breast of chicken • $16

Margan Family Shiraz

ΥΥΥΥΥ **1999** Medium purple-red; the bouquet has pronounced varietal and regional characteristics represented by the earthy overtones to the firm berry fruit. The palate has abundant power, structure and concentration, with a plum and cherry fruit core surrounded by soft tannins. It is a wine that will add levels of complexity as it softens and ages. **rating:** 91

best drinking 2004–2014 **best vintages** '99 **drink with** Braised lamb shanks • $18

Margan Family Cabernet Sauvignon

YYYY 1999 Medium red-purple; the bouquet is clean, with a mix of aromas predominantly in a savoury/earthy/leafy spectrum, more austere than the '98. The palate follows down the same track, showing some astringency, but well within the bounds of the variety. The oak input has been nicely controlled, and the wine will unquestionably repay cellaring. **rating:** 84

best drinking 2005–2011 **best vintages** NA **drink with** Braised ox cheek • $18

marienberg ★★★

2 Chalk Hill Road, McLaren Vale, SA 5171 **region** McLaren Vale
phone (08) 8323 9666 **fax** (08) 8323 9600 **open** 7 days 10–5
winemaker Grant Burge (Contract) **production** 30 000 **est.** 1966
product range ($9.95–24.95 R) Cottage Classic range of Riesling, Sauvignon Blanc Semillon, Unwooded Chardonnay, Cabernet Grenache Mourvedre; Reserve Chardonnay, Shiraz and Cabernet Sauvignon; Limeburner's Chardonnay, Botrytis Semillon, Cabernet Sauvignon; also Late Picked Frontignac, Nicolle Méthode Champenoise and Tawny Port.
summary The Marienberg brand was purchased by the Hill International group of companies in late 1991 following the retirement of Ursula Pridham. Releases under the new regime have been honest, if unashamedly commercial, wines. The Reserve wines do offer a significant lift in quality above the basic range. The wines are exported to the UK, the US, Canada, Hong Kong, Germany, the Netherlands, New Zealand, the Philippines, Switzerland and Thailand.

mariners rest NR

Jamakarri Farm, Roberts Road, Denmark, WA 6333 **region** Great Southern
phone (08) 9840 9324 **fax** (08) 9840 9324 **open** 7 days 11–5
winemaker Brenden Smith **production** 550 **est.** 1996
product range ($15–22.50 R) Chardonnay, Southern White, Autumn Gold, Autumn Red, Southern Red, Pinot Noir, Nelson's Blood (Tawny Port).
summary Mariners Rest is the reincarnation of the now defunct Golden Rise winery. A new 2.5-hectare vineyard was planted in 1997, and a slightly odd selection of replacement wines is being marketed.

Mariners Rest Autumn Gold

YYYYY 2000 0Light green-yellow; a lime/spice bouquet with little or no botrytis evident is followed by a quite stylish palate, well balanced, with a mix of lime, spice and grape flavours; barely sweet, but has considerable length. **rating:** 92

best drinking Now–2006 **best vintages** '00 **drink with** Prosciutto and melon • $14.75

marion's vineyard ★★★☆

Foreshore Drive, Deviot, Tas 7275 **region** Northern Tasmania
phone (03) 6394 7434 **fax** (03) 6394 7434 **open** 7 days 10–5
winemaker Mark Semmens, Marion Semmens **production** 2000 **est.** 1980
product range ($15–30 ML) Chardonnay, Müller Thurgau, Pinot Noir, Cabernet Sauvignon.
summary The irrepressible Mark Semmens and indefatigable wife Marion have one of the most beautifully situated vineyards and wineries in Australia, on the banks of the Tamar River. As well as an outdoor restaurant and accommodation, there is a jetty and a stage; indeed, life is a stage for Mark Semmens.

maritime estate NR

Tucks Road, Red Hill, Vic 3937 **region** Mornington Peninsula
phone (03) 9848 2926 **fax** (03) 9882 8325 **open** Weekends and public holidays 11–5, 7 days Dec 27–Jan 26
winemaker T'Gallant (Contract) **production** 1000 **est.** 1988
product range ($17–26 CD) Unwooded Chardonnay, Chardonnay, Pinot Gris, Pinot Noir, Cabernet Sauvignon.
summary John and Linda Ruljancich have enjoyed great success since their first vintage in 1994, no doubt due in part to skilled contract-winemaking but also to the situation of their vineyard, looking across the hills and valleys of the Red Hill subregion.

markwood estate NR

Morris Lane, Markwood, Vic 3678 **region** King Valley
phone (03) 5727 0361 **fax** (03) 5727 0361 **open** 7 days 9–5
winemaker Rick Morris **production** 300 **est.** 1971
product range ($15–30 CD) Rhine Riesling, Cabernet Sauvignon, White Port, Vintage Port, Old Tawny Port.
summary A member of the famous Morris family, Rick Morris shuns publicity and relies virtually exclusively on cellar-door sales for what is a small output. Of a range of table and fortified wines tasted several years ago, the Old Tawny Port (a cross between Port and Muscat, showing more of the character of the latter than the former) and a White Port (seemingly made from Muscadelle) were the best.

marribrook ★★★

Albany Highway, Kendenup, WA 6323 **region** Great Southern
phone (08) 9851 4651 **fax** (08) 9851 4652 **open** Wed–Sun 10.30–4.30
winemaker Gavin Berry **production** 2000 **est.** 1990
product range ($14–19 CD) Semillon Sauvignon Blanc, Stirling White (Semillon), Botanica Chardonnay, Reserve Chardonnay, Marsanne, Cabernet Merlot, Cabernet Malbec Merlot.
summary The Brooks family purchased the former Marron View vineyard (5.6 hectares) from Kim Hart in 1994 and renamed the venture Marribrook Wines. Those wines are now made by Gavin Berry at Plantagenet, having been made at Alkoomi up to 1994. The Brooks have purchased an additional property on the Albany Highway north of Mount Barker and immediately south of Gilbert's Wines. Cellar-door sales have moved to this location, and a dedicated cellar-door sales building with a small restaurant and gallery was completed in 2000, with great views out to the Stirling Range. Retail distribution in Victoria, New South Wales and South Australia; exports to the UK.

marsh estate 

Deasey Road, Pokolbin, NSW 2321 **region** Lower Hunter Valley
phone (02) 4998 7587 **fax** (02) 4998 7884 **open** Mon–Fri 10–4.30, weekends 10–5
winemaker Peter Marsh **production** 4000 **est.** 1971
product range ($18–25 CD) Semillon, Private Bin Semillon, Chardonnay (oaked and unoaked), Semillon Sauternes, Shiraz (Private Bin, Vat S and Vat R), Cabernet Sauvignon, Champagne Brut, Andrew IV Vintage Port.
summary Through sheer consistency, value-for-money product and unrelenting hard work, the Marsh family (who purchased the former Quentin Estate in 1978) has built up a sufficiently loyal cellar-door and mailing list clientele to allow all of the considerable production to be sold direct. Wine style is always direct, with oak playing a minimal role, and prolonged cellaring paying handsome dividends. No recent tastings.

martins hill wines NR

Sydney Road, Mudgee, NSW 2850 **region** Mudgee
phone (02) 6373 1248 **fax** (02) 6373 1248 **open** Not
winemaker Pieter Van Gent (Contract) **production** 700 **est.** 1985
product range ($13–16 R) Sauvignon Blanc, Pinot Noir.
summary Janette Kenworthy and Michael Sweeny are committed organic grape-growers and members of the Organic Vignerons Association. Theirs is a tiny operation at the moment, with only 0.5 hectare each of sauvignon blanc and pinot noir in production, but with an additional hectare of cabernet sauvignon that was due to produce its first grapes in the year 2000, and 1.5 hectares of shiraz in 2001. While there is no cellar door (only a mailing list), organic vineyard tours and talks can be arranged by appointment.

Martins Hill Sauvignon Blanc

YYYY **2000** Light straw-green; the bouquet is clean and crisp, minerally rather than fruity; while the varietal character is far from exuberant, the wine is well balanced and has pleasant mouthfeel. **rating:** 87
best drinking Now **best vintages** NA **drink with** Asparagus terrine • $16

marybrook vineyards NR

Vasse–Yallingup Road, Marybrook, WA 6280 **region** Margaret River
phone (08) 9755 1143 **fax** (08) 9755 1112 **open** Fri–Mon 10–5, 7 days 10–5 school holidays
winemaker Aub House **production** 2000 **est.** 1986

product range ($11–26.50 CD) Verdelho, Chardonnay, Classic White, Nectosia (sweet), Grenache, Cabernets, Cabernet Franc, Temptation (sweet red), Ruby Jetty Port, Liqueur Muscat.
summary Not to be confused with Marybrook Estate, Marybrook Vineyards is a separate operation owned by Aub and Jan House with 7 hectares of vineyards in production; back-vintages are usually available.

massoni wines ★★★★

32 Brasser Avenue, Dromana, Vic 3936 **region** Mornington Peninsula
phone (03) 5981 8008 **fax** (03) 5981 8015 **open** By appointment
winemaker Ian Home, Sam Tyrrell **production** 6000 **est.** 1984
product range ($17–35 R) Chardonnay, Pinot Noir, Lectus Cuvée are the top wines; also Homes Chardonnay, Pinot Noir, Shiraz, Merlot and Cabernet Merlot.
summary The changes have continued to flow after Ian Home (best known as the founder of Yellowglen) acquired the remaining 50 per cent of Massoni from former restaurateur Leon Massoni. There are now two ranges of wines, and (quite sensibly) the Shiraz and Cabernet Merlot releases are in whole or in part sourced from outside the Mornington Peninsula (from Langhorne Creek). The flagships continue to be the Chardonnay, Pinot Noir and Lectus Cuvée. Exports to the US.

matilda's meadow

Eladon Brook Estate, RMB 654 Hamilton Road, Denmark, WA 6333 **region** Great Southern
phone (08) 9848 1951 **fax** (08) 9848 1957 **open** Wed–Mon 10–5
winemaker Brenden Smith **production** 1200 **est.** 1990
product range ($13–25 CD) Semillon Sauvignon Blanc, Unwooded Chardonnay, Late Picked Riesling, Autumn Amethyst (light red), Pinot Noir, Cabernet Sauvignon Shiraz, Cabernet Sauvignon Cabernet Franc, Tawny Port Muscat blend.
summary Former hotelier Don Turnbull and oil-industry executive Pamela Meldrum have quickly established a thriving business at Matilda's Meadow, based on 6 hectares of estate plantings and with a restaurant offering morning and afternoon teas and lunches every day.

Matilda's Meadow Cabernet Sauvignon Cabernet Franc

▼▼▼▼▽ **1999** Medium red-purple; a lively, clean and fresh berry-accented bouquet is followed by a firm palate, with flavours ranging from ripe cassis berry through to a touch of herb, the latter adding rather than detracting. Subtle oak influence throughout. **rating:** 90
best drinking 2004–2009 **best vintages** '95, '98 **drink with** Beef sirloin • $19

Matilda's Meadow Cabernet Sauvignon Shiraz

▼▼▼▼ **1999** Light to medium red-purple; the bouquet is quite light, with distinct pepper/spice/leaf characters presumably coming from the shiraz. A nicely balanced wine on the palate in flavour terms, but the tannins are a little raspy. **rating:** 86
best drinking 2003–2007 **best vintages** NA **drink with** Devilled kidneys • $18

mawarra NR

69 Short Road, Gisborne, Vic 3437 **region** Macedon Ranges
phone (03) 5428 2228 **fax** (03) 9621 1413 **open** 7 days
winemaker John Ellis (Contract) **production** 1000 **est.** 1978
product range Semillon, Chardonnay, Pinot Noir.
summary Bob Nixon has a little under 3 hectares of semillon, chardonnay and pinot noir, and the wines are made for him by Macedon specialist, John Ellis (of Hanging Rock).

mawson ridge NR

24–28 Main Road, Hahndorf, SA 5066 **region** Adelaide Hills
phone (08) 8362 7826 **fax** (08) 8362 7588 **open** By appointment
winemaker Nepenthe (Contract) **production** 400 **est.** 1998
product range ($18–30 R) Sauvignon Blanc, Chardonnay, Pinot Noir.
summary You might be forgiven for thinking the winery name carries the cool-climate association a little bit too far. In fact, Sir Douglas Mawson, also a conservationist and forester, arrived in the Lenswood region in the early

1930s, harvesting the native stringy-barks for hardwood and replanting the cleared land with pine trees. A hut that Mawson built on the property still stands today on Mawson Road, the road to which the vineyard fronts. Here Raymond and Madeline Marin have established 3.5 hectares of vines, with contract-winemaking by Peter Leske of Nepenthe Vineyards.

maxwell wines ★★★★

Olivers Road, McLaren Vale, SA 5171 **region** McLaren Vale
phone (08) 8323 8200 **fax** (08) 8323 8900 **open** 7 days 10–5
winemaker Mark Day **production** 14 000 **est.** 1979
product range ($8–39 R) Under the Maxwell Wines brand, Semillon, Verdelho, Chardonnay, Grenache, Cabernet Merlot, Reserve Shiraz; Ellen Street Shiraz, Lime Cave Cabernet Sauvignon; and excellent Honey Mead, Spiced Mead and Liqueur Mead.
summary Maxwell Wines has come a long way since opening for business in 1979 using an amazing array of Heath Robinson equipment in cramped surroundings. A state-of-the-art and infinitely larger winery was built on a new site in time for the 1997 vintage, appropriate for a brand that has produced some excellent white and red wines in recent years. Exports to the US, Canada, the UK, Switzerland, Austria, Hong Kong, Germany, Belgium, Singapore, Thailand and New Zealand.

Maxwell Semillon

YYYY **2000** Light to medium green-yellow; a quite fragrant bouquet with a mix of spice and wild herb aromas leads into a palate with positive flavours of lemon, herb and an echo of spice from the bouquet, then moving on to a clean, crisp finish. **rating:** 87

best drinking Now–2005 **best vintages** NA **drink with** Blue swimmer crab • $8

Maxwell Ellen Street Shiraz

YYYY **1998** Medium red-purple; the moderately intense bouquet has red berry and spice fruit supported by subtle oak, the palate with sweet red berry fruit and chocolate; the wine has good tannin management and overall extract. **rating:** 88

best drinking 2003–2008 **best vintages** '82, '88, '91, '92, '94, '98 **drink with** Kangaroo • $20

Maxwell Reserve Shiraz

YYYYY **1998** Medium to full red-purple; the bouquet opens with ripe earthy/berry fruit, followed by licorice and chocolate; an archetypal powerhouse McLaren Vale style on the palate with inky fruit and ladles of black chocolate. Needless to say, 14° alcohol. **rating:** 93

best drinking 2003–2013 **best vintages** '95, '98 **drink with** Char-grilled rump • $39

Maxwell Lime Cave Cabernet Sauvignon

YYYY **1999** Medium to full red-purple; abundant, sweet and ripe cassis/blackberry fruit on the bouquet has touches of earth and chocolate; the concentrated, rich and ripe palate is fairly tannic and needs patience. **rating:** 87

best drinking 2004–2009 **best vintages** NA **drink with** Leave it in the cellar • $30

m. chapoutier australia ★★★★

PO Box 437 Robe, SA 5276 **region** Mount Benson
phone (08) 8768 5076 **fax** (08) 8768 5073 **open** Not
winemaker Jean Philippe Archambaud **production** 6000 **est.** 1998
product range ($25–28 R) Shiraz.
summary This is one of several winemaking ventures the famous Rhône Valley firm of M. Chapoutier is establishing in Australia. A large vineyard comprising 18 hectares of shiraz, 10 hectares of cabernet sauvignon, 4 hectares each of marsanne and viognier, and 2 hectares of sauvignon blanc is in the course of establishment using biodynamic farming methods. The only wine so far released is the very elegant Shiraz, but the range will be extended to include the other varieties in the not-too-distant future. For the time being winemaker Jean Philippe Archambaud makes the wines at nearby Cape Jaffa; exports to Europe and Asia through M. Chapoutier, to New Zealand through Eurowine and in the US through Paterno. Australian distribution through David Ridge Wines and Aria Wine Co.

M. Chapoutier Australia Mount Benson Shiraz

▼▼▼▼ **1999** Strong, deep purple-red; the fresh and powerful aromas of the bouquet centre on red and black cherry, with just a little oak support. The palate, likewise, has abundant fresh cherry fruit, touches of mint and fine tannins. The oak is barely visible. A significant advance on the much lighter '98. **rating:** 88

best drinking 2002–2009 **best vintages** '99 **drink with** Osso bucco • $28

meadowbank wines ★★★★☆

699 Richmond Road, Cambridge, Tas 7170 **region** Southern Tasmania
phone (03) 6248 4484 **fax** (03) 6248 4485 **open** 7 days 11–5
winemaker Andrew Hood (Contract) **production** 4000 **est.** 1974
product range ($21–32 CD) Riesling, Sauvignon Blanc, Unwooded Chardonnay, Grace Elizabeth Chardonnay, Pinot Noir, Henry James Pinot Noir, Cabernet Sauvignon, Mardi Methode Champenoise.
summary Now an important part of the Ellis family business on what was once (but is no more) a large grazing property on the banks of the Derwent. Increased plantings are being established under contract to BRL Hardy, and a splendid new winery has been built to handle the increased production.

Meadowbank Riesling

▼▼▼▼▽ **2000** Medium yellow-green; the complex but clean bouquet ranges through herb, grass, mineral and citrus, aromas that are reflected to a lesser or greater degree in the light, lively, fresh and elegant palate, neatly balanced by closing acidity. **rating:** 90

best drinking Now–2018 **best vintages** '99, '00 **drink with** Asparagus • $21

Meadowbank Henry James Pinot Noir

▼▼▼▼▽ **1999** Medium red, showing some development; there is positive varietal character in a typically cool-grown savoury/foresty/sappy spectrum on the bouquet. More of the same follows on the savoury/plummy/foresty palate, which finishes with good acidity; subtle oak. **rating:** 90

best drinking Now–2003 **best vintages** '94, '98, '99 **drink with** Ragout of duck • $30

Meadowbank Cabernet Sauvignon

▼▼▼▼▼ **1999** Medium to full red-purple; clean blackberry and blackcurrant fruit on the bouquet is supported by positive but not overwhelming oak; luscious, sweet blackcurrant fruit on the palate is supplemented by tannins and the distinctly sexy use of oak. **rating:** 94

▼▼▼▼▼ **1998** In 2000 this wine seemed bound by tannin chains. It is still quite tannic, but the fruit has burst free in impressive fashion. Deep purple-red, it has concentrated blackberry/blackcurrant aromas, albeit with an edge of austerity, leading into a powerful blackberry palate with imposing tannins, but not so imposing as to deprive it of top gold-medal status at the 2001 Tasmanian Wines Show. **rating:** 94

best drinking 2003–2010 **best vintages** '99 **drink with** Barbecued steak • $24

meerea park 

Lot 3, Palmers Lane, Pokolbin, NSW 2320 **region** Lower Hunter Valley
phone (02) 4998 7474 **fax** (02) 4930 7100 **open** At The Boutique Wine Centre, Broke Road, Pokolbin 9–5
winemaker Rhys Eather **production** 10 000 **est.** 1991
product range ($16.50–45 CD) Semillon, Sauvignon Blanc Semillon, Lindsay Hill Verdelho, Viognier, Unoaked Chardonnay, Forefathers Chardonnay, Alexander Munro Chardonnay, Late Harvest Traminer, The Aunts Shiraz, Alexander Munro Shiraz, Art Label Cabernet Merlot, Cabernet Merlot.
summary An interesting operation, selling its substantial production primarily through The Boutique Wine Centre and by mailing list. All of the wines are produced from grapes purchased from growers, primarily in the Broke/Fordwich region, but also from as far afield as McLaren Vale, the Barossa Valley, Mudgee and Orange. It is the brainchild of Rhys Eather, great-grandson of Alexander Munro (a leading mid-nineteenth century vigneron), who makes the wine in Simon Gilbert's contract winery. Retail distribution through the principal States, and the wines are exported to the UK, the US and Asia.

Meerea Park Alexander Munro Shiraz

▼▼▼▼ **1998** Medium red, with some purple. There is strong fruit on the bouquet, in typical Hunter mode, with a mix of dark berry, earth and leather. A powerful, concentrated and youthful palate, with lingering tannins, and the oak in restraint. Has much improvement and many years in front of it. **rating:** 88

best drinking 2003–2013 **best vintages** '97, '98 **drink with** Braised beef • $45

melaleuca grove NR

8 Melaleuca Court, Rowville, Vic 3178 **region** Central Victorian Mountain Country
phone (03) 9752 7928 **fax** (03) 9752 7928 **open** Not
winemaker Jeff Wright **production** 350 **est.** 1999
product range ($18 R) Chardonnay, Shiraz.
summary Jeff and Anne Wright are both Honours graduates in biochemistry who have succumbed to the lure of winemaking after lengthy careers elsewhere, in the case of Jeff, 20 years in research and hospital science. He commenced his winemaking apprenticeship in 1997 at Green Vineyards, backed up by further vintage work in 1999 and 2000 at Bianchet and Yarra Valley Hills, both in the Yarra Valley. At the same time he began the external Bachelor of Applied Science (Wine Science) course at Charles Sturt University, while continuing to work in biochemistry in the public hospital system. In both 1999 and 2000 the Wrights purchased grapes from Thomson's Vineyard at Limestone (near Yea) in the Central Victorian Mountain Country region, releasing their first two wines from the 1999 vintage. They are available through one or two local outlets and by mailing list.

merrebee estate 

Lot 3339 St Werburghs Road, Mount Barker, WA 6234 **region** Great Southern
phone (08) 9851 2424 **fax** (08) 9851 2425 **open** By appointment
winemaker Brenden Smith (Contract) **production** 3000 **est.** 1986
product range ($15–23 CD) Riesling, Giles Point Sauvignon Blanc Chardonnay, Chardonnay, Giles Point Unwooded Chardonnay, Mount Barker Chardonnay, Shiraz.
summary Planting of the Merrebee Estate vineyards commenced in 1986 and there is now a little under 9 hectares. The wines are available from selected retailers in Western Australia and from Rathdowne Cellars, Melbourne, and Ultimo Wine Centre, Sydney; exports to the US, Canada and Sweden.

Merrebee Estate Riesling

🍷🍷🍷🍷 **2000** Pale straw-green; the bouquet opens with clean, firm mineral characters, then displaying riper notes underneath, notes that drive the generously flavoured and quite soft palate. Well balanced, but fractionally short. **rating:** 89

best drinking Now–2004 **best vintages** '00 **drink with** Vegetable terrine • $19.50

Merrebee Estate Mount Barker Chardonnay

🍷🍷🍷½ **2000** Light to medium yellow-green; delicate but fresh stonefruit/melon/citrus fruit aromas have an appropriately subtle oak background, the clean and fresh palate providing a replay of the bouquet; not concentrated, but easy to enjoy. **rating:** 84

best drinking Now–2003 **best vintages** NA **drink with** Chinese prawns • $21

Merrebee Estate Mount Barker Shiraz

🍷🍷🍷🍷 **1999** Medium to full red-purple; fresh red berry and mint with background oak on the bouquet is followed by a fresh, red berry palate plus touches of chocolate and mint, finishing with quite fine tannins. **rating:** 85

best drinking 2002–2006 **best vintages** NA **drink with** Veal chops • $23

merricks estate 

Thompsons Lane, Merricks, Vic 3916 **region** Mornington Peninsula
phone (03) 5989 8416 **fax** (03) 9645 5474 **open** First weekend of each month in Jan and public holiday weekends 12–5
winemaker Michael Zitzlaff **production** 2500 **est.** 1977
product range ($20–25 CD) Chardonnay, Pinot Noir, Shiraz, Cabernet Sauvignon.
summary Melbourne solicitor George Kefford, together with wife Jacquie, runs Merricks Estate as a weekend and holiday enterprise as a relief from professional practice. Right from the outset it has produced distinctive, spicy, cool-climate Shiraz which has accumulated an impressive array of show trophies and gold medals.

merrivale wines 

Olivers Road, McLaren Vale, SA 5171 **region** McLaren Vale
phone (08) 8323 9196 **fax** (08) 8323 9746 **open** 7 days 11–5
winemaker Contract **production** 10 000 **est.** 1971

product range ($10–18 CD) Under the Tapestry label: Riesling, Chardonnay, Tapestry Spaetlese, Tapestry Shiraz, Tapestry Cabernet Shiraz, Tapestry Cabernet Sauvignon, Muscat of Alexandria, Old Tawny Port, Brian Light Reserve Shiraz.
summary After a relatively brief period of ownership by Brian Light and family, was then acquired by the Gerard family, former owners of Chapel Hill.

merum ★★★★☆

Hillbrook Road, Quinninup, WA 6258 **region** Pemberton
phone (08) 9776 6011 **fax** (08) 9776 6022 **open** By appointment
winemaker Maria Melsom **production** 500 **est.** 1996
product range ($22–28 ML) Semillon, Shiraz.
summary Merum is owned by Maria Melsom (formerly winemaker at Driftwood Estate) and Michael Melsom (former vineyard manager for Voyager Estate, both in the Margaret River region). The first 6.3 hectares of vineyard (3.3 hectares of shiraz, 2 hectares of semillon, 1 hectare of chardonnay) were planted in 1996, and the first wine made in 1999. An additional 2.6 hectares equally split between merlot and cabernet sauvignon were planted in the year 2000. The quality of the wines so far released has been truly excellent.

Merum Semillon

TTTT **2000** Light green-yellow; the bouquet is fragrant with a mix of passionfruit and tropical aromas, not unlike a ripe Sauvignon Blanc, and just the faintest hint of oak spice. The palate is spotlessly clean and well balanced, with some flavours of ripe apple as well as passionfruit. **rating:** 88
best drinking Now–2005 **best vintages** NA **drink with** Eggplant terrine • $22

Merum Shiraz

TTTTT **1999** Strong, deep red-purple; there is an altogether surprising concentration of dark cherry and plum fruit on the bouquet, the promise being fulfilled by the palate, which has lovely weight, texture and concentration, with abundant dark fruit flavours and perfectly integrated oak. **rating:** 94
best drinking 2003–2010 **best vintages** '99 **drink with** Braised beef in red wine • $25

métier wines ★★★★☆

Tarraford Vineyard, 440 Healesville Road, Yarra Glen, Vic 3775 **region** Yarra Valley
phone (03) 5962 2461 **fax** (03) 5962 2194 **open** Not
winemaker Martin Williams **production** 1400 **est.** 1995
product range ($29.50–32 R) Tarraford Vineyard Chardonnay, Schoolhouse Vineyard Chardonnay, Tarraford Vineyard Pinot Noir.
summary Métier is the French word for craft, trade or profession; the business is that of Yarra Valley-based winemaker Martin Williams, MW, who has notched up an array of degrees and winemaking stints in France, California and Australia which are, not to put too fine a word on it, extraordinary. The focus of Métier will be to produce individual vineyard wines, initially based on grapes from the Tarraford and Schoolhouse Vineyards, both in the Yarra Valley. The quality of the initial releases of Pinot Noir and Chardonnay is extremely high.

miceli

60 Main Creek Road, Arthurs Seat, Vic 3936 **region** Mornington Peninsula
phone (03) 5989 2755 **fax** (03) 5989 2755 **open** First weekend each month 12–5, public holidays, and also every weekend and by appointment in Jan
winemaker Anthony Miceli **production** 1250 **est.** 1991
product range ($17–30 CD) Chardonnay (unoaked), Olivia's Chardonnay, Iolanda Pinot Grigio, Olivia Pinot Noir, Lucy's Choice Pinot Noir, Reserve Pinot Noir.
summary It may be a part-time labour of love for general practitioner Dr Anthony Miceli, but this hasn't prevented him taking the whole venture very seriously. He acquired the property in 1989 specifically for the purpose of establishing a vineyard, carrying out the first plantings of 1.8 hectares in November 1991, followed by a further hectare of Pinot Gris in 1997. Ultimately the vineyard will be increased to 5 hectares, with a projected production of 2500–3000 cases a year. Between 1991 and 1997 Dr Miceli enrolled in and thereafter graduated from the Wine Science course at Charles Sturt University, and thus manages both vineyard and winery. Retail distribution through fine wine outlets and restaurants in Melbourne.

Miceli Iolanda Pinot Grigio

🍷🍷🍷🍷 **2000** Light to medium green-yellow; a highly floral bouquet with apple blossom and touches of leaf and spice leads into a crisp, lively minerally palate with good balance and length. **rating:** 89

best drinking Now–2004 **best vintages** NA **drink with** Shellfish • $19

Miceli Olivia's Chardonnay

🍷🍷🍷🍷🍷 **1999** Very good medium green-yellow, bright and vibrant; the clean bouquet has subtle barrel-ferment characters surrounding the core of citrus and melon fruit; the delicate but intense palate is driven by stonefruit and peach that flows along the tongue. Very smooth and stylish, and not hit by mlf or oak. **rating:** 94

best drinking Now–2005 **best vintages** '99 **drink with** Grilled fish • $17

michelini wines NR

Great Alpine Road, Myrtleford, Vic 3737 **region** Alpine Valleys
phone (03) 5751 1990 **fax** (03) 5751 1410 **open** 7 days 10–5 (except Christmas Day and New Year's Day)
winemaker Greg O'Keefe (Contract) **production** 6000 **est.** 1982
product range ($13.50–20 CD) Riesling, Unwooded Chardonnay, Chardonnay, Pinot Noir, Marzemino, Merlot, Shiraz, Cabernet Sauvignon, Fragolino.
summary The Michelini family are among the best known grape-growers in the Buckland Valley of northeast Victoria. Having migrated from Italy in 1949, they originally grew tobacco, diversifying into vineyards in 1982. A little over 42 hectares of vineyard have been established on terra rossa soil at an altitude of 300 metres, mostly with frontage to the Buckland River. The major part of the production is sold (to Orlando and others), but since 1996 an on-site winery has permitted the Michelinis to vinify part of their production. The winery in fact has capacity to handle 1000 tonnes of fruit, thereby eliminating the problem of moving grapes out of a declared phylloxera area. The quality of the initial releases was modest, but the area does have the potential to produce pleasant wine, and doubtless better things are in store.

Michelini Merlot

🍷🍷🍷🍷 **1999** Medium red-purple; the bouquet has spice, cedar and savoury fruit aromas nicely supported by oak. There is plenty of flavour to the medium-bodied palate, although vanilla oak is more evident here than on the bouquet; finishes with pleasant, soft tannins. **rating:** 85

best drinking Now–2004 **best vintages** NA **drink with** Veal scallopine • $20

middlebrook NR

RSD 43, Sand Road, McLaren Vale, SA 5171 **region** McLaren Vale
phone (08) 8383 0600 **fax** (08) 8383 0557 **open** Mon–Fri 9–5, weekends 10–5
winemaker Joseph Cogno **production** 12 000 **est.** 1947
product range ($14–20 CD) At the top: Middlebrook Pinot Chardonnay, Unwooded Semillon, Sauvignon Blanc, Chardonnay, Frontignac, Shiraz and Cabernet Sauvignon; then cheaper wines under the Cogno label.
summary After a brief period of ownership by industry veteran Bill Clappis (who renovated and reopened the winery), ownership has now passed to the Cogno Brothers Family, which has been winemaking at Cobbity, near Camden, New South Wales, since 1964. Through Middlebrook the family has become one of the largest producers of Lambrusco in Australia, available nationwide through Liquorland stores. Many other wines (18 in all) are produced under the Cogno Brothers label, while the Middlebrook cask hall has been given over to production of the Medlow chocolate range. The top wines are still sold under the Middlebrook label.

Middlebrook Vineyard Selection Unwooded Semillon

🍷🍷🍷½ **2000** Light green-yellow; the bouquet is quite rich, with lemon/lime aromatics, the palate clean and solid, with some weight, but not by any stretch of the imagination intense or long. **rating:** 83

best drinking Now–2004 **best vintages** NA **drink with** King George whiting • $14.50

Middlebrook Vineyard Selection Chardonnay

🍷🍷🍷🍷 **1999** Light to medium yellow-green; a clean, smooth bouquet has considerable complexity, with good fruit and oak integration. The palate is not intense, but the winemaking complexity gives an excellent outcome, with light melon and cashew flavours in a well-balanced and harmonious whole. **rating:** 87

best drinking Now–2004 **best vintages** NA **drink with** Pan-fried chicken • $15.50

Middlebrook Vineyard Selection Shiraz

🍷🍷🍷🍷 **1999** Medium to full red-purple; there is lots of vanilla oak, and some berry and chocolate on the bouquet; a big, quite powerful palate with mint and berry fruit, vanilla oak but very little tannin structure, no surprise for the yield of 4–5 tonnes to the acre, particularly if closer to the latter than the former. **rating:** 84

best drinking 2002–2006 **best vintages** NA **drink with** Spaghetti bolognaise • $20

middleton estate NR

Flagstaff Hill Road, Middleton, SA 5213 **region** Currency Creek
phone (08) 8555 4136 **fax** (08) 8555 4108 **open** Fri–Sun 11–5
winemaker Nigel Catt **production** 3000 **est.** 1979
product range ($9–16 CD) Riesling, Sauvignon Blanc, Semillon Sauvignon Blanc, Cabernet Hermitage.
summary Nigel Catt has demonstrated his winemaking skills at Andrew Garrett and elsewhere, so wine quality should be good. But despite its decade of production, I have never seen or tasted its wines. A winery restaurant helps the business turnover.

milburn park ★★★

Campbell Avenue, Irymple, Vic 3498 **region** Murray Darling
phone (03) 5024 6800 **fax** (03) 5024 6605 **open** Mon–Sat 10–4.30
winemaker Krister Jonsson, Gary Magilton **production** 2 million **est.** 1977
product range ($4–15 R) Top-end wines under the Milburn Park label are Chardonnay, Pinot Noir Chardonnay, Shiraz and Cabernet Sauvignon; then comes the standard Salisbury Estate range of Riesling Dry, Sauvignon Blanc, Chardonnay, Shiraz, Grenache, Cabernet Sauvignon, Cabernet Merlot; then the Castle Ridge range consisting of Colombard Chardonnay, Shiraz Malbec Mourvedre; Acacia Ridge non-vintage generics bring up the rear, with two wines in the Tennyson Vineyard off to one side.
summary Part of a widespread group of companies owned by Cranswick Premium Wines Limited, with a strong export focus.

mildara (murray darling) ★★★

Wentworth Road, Merbein, Vic 3505 **region** Murray Darling
phone (03) 5021 9319 **fax** (03) 5021 1300 **open** Mon–Fri 9–5, weekends 10–4
winemaker David Tierney **production** NFP **est.** 1888
product range ($10–25 R) Under the Mildara label are Chardonnay, Shiraz; Half Mile Creek Chardonnay, Verdelho, Cabernet Merlot, Shiraz; Church Hill Chardonnay and Dry Red; also makes fine Sherries (Chestnut Teal, George and Supreme) and superb Pot Still Brandy.
summary A somewhat antiquated Merbein facility remains the overall group production centre, although all of its premium wines are sourced from and made at Coonawarra.

milford vineyard ★★★★

Tasman Highway, Cambridge, Tas 7170 **region** Southern Tasmania
phone (03) 6248 5029 **fax** (03) 6224 2331 **open** Not
winemaker Andrew Hood (Contract) **production** 200 **est.** 1984
product range ($21.75 R) Pinot Noir.
summary Given the tiny production, Milford is understandably not open to the public, the excellent Pinot Noir being quickly sold by word of mouth. The 150-hectare grazing property (the oldest Southdown sheep stud in Australia) has been in Charlie Lewis's family since 1830. Only 15 minutes from Hobart and, with an absolute water frontage to the tidal estuary of the Coal River, it is a striking site. The vineyard is established on a patch of 5-foot-deep sand over a clay base with lots of lime impregnation.

milimani estate NR

92 The Forest Road, Bungendore, NSW 2621 **region** Canberra District
phone (02) 6238 1421 **fax** (02) 6238 1424 **open** Weekends and public holidays 10–4
winemaker Lark Hill (Contract) **production** 700 **est.** 1989
product range ($12.50–17 ML) Sauvignon Blanc, Chardonnay, Pinot Noir, Cabernet Franc Merlot.
summary The Preston family (Mary, David and Rosemary) have established a 4-hectare vineyard at Bungendore planted to sauvignon blanc, chardonnay, pinot noir, merlot and cabernet franc. Contract-winemaking at Lark Hill should guarantee the quality of the wine.

millers samphire NR

Cnr Watts Gully and Robertson Roads, Kersbrook, SA 5231 **region** Adelaide Hills
phone (08) 8389 3183 **fax** (03) 8389 3183 **open** 7 days 9–5 by appointment
winemaker Tom Miller **production** 70 **est.** 1982
product range ($9 CD) Riesling.
summary Next after Scarp Valley, one of the smallest wineries in Australia offering wine for sale; pottery also helps. Tom Miller has one of the more interesting and diverse CVs, with an early interest in matters alcoholic leading to the premature but happy death of a laboratory rat at Adelaide University and his enforced switch from biochemistry to mechanical engineering. The Riesling is a high-flavoured wine with crushed herb and lime aromas and flavours.

millfield

Lot 341, Mount View Road, Millfield, NSW 2325 **region** Lower Hunter Valley
phone (02) 4998 1571 **fax** (02) 4998 0172 **open** Fri–Sat 10–4 or by appointment
winemaker David Fatches **production** 4500 **est.** 1997
product range ($16–22 CD) Semillon, Chardonnay, Rose, Shiraz.
summary Situated on the picturesque Mount View Road, Millfield made its market debut in June 2000. With ten years of experience gained in the Hunter Valley Bordeaux, winemaker and partner David Fatches clearly knows not only how to select high-quality grapes, but also how to gain the maximum from these. The neatly labelled and packaged wines have won gold medals and trophies right from the first vintage in 1998, and high praise from wine-writers and critics both in Australia and the UK. The wines are sold both through the cellar door and mailing list, and through a limited number of fine-wine retailers and top-quality restaurants. All in all, a thoroughly impressive newcomer. Exports to the UK through Corney & Barrow.

Millfield Semillon

▼▼▼▼▽ **1999** Light to medium green-yellow; the bouquet is spotlessly clean, moderately intense, with quite ripe citrus fruit, and (unusually) a hint of nectarine. The wine has good mid-palate flavour, with ripe citrus and herb flavours, and an excellent flow through to the finish. Gold medal winner at the Cowra Wine Show 2000. **rating:** 90

best drinking 2002–2009 **best vintages** '99 **drink with** Fresh asparagus with hollandaise sauce • $19.50

Millfield Chardonnay

▼▼▼▼▽ **1998** Medium yellow-green; the bouquet is quite intense, with good varietal character in a nectarine/melon spectrum, with nice smoky oak overtones. In the mouth, gentle and understated, with excellent balance and subtle oak. This is sophisticated winemaking. Gold medal at the 1999 Hunter Valley Wine Show. **rating:** 90

best drinking Now–2003 **best vintages** NA **drink with** Sweetbreads • $22

Millfield Shiraz

▼▼▼▽ **1999** Medium red-purple; the bouquet is of light to medium intensity, with traditional, regional earthy/leathery regional aromas; the palate is of light to medium body, with some minty notes and dusty/spicy tannins. Overall, the wine gives the impression of marginal ripeness to the flavour, but may develop attractive characters with further bottle age. **rating:** 82

best drinking 2002–2003 **best vintages** NA **drink with** Beef stroganoff • $20

millinup estate

RMB 1280 Porongurup Road, Porongurup, WA 6324 **region** Great Southern
phone (08) 9853 1105 **fax** (08) 9853 1105 **open** Weekends 10–5
winemaker Rob Lee (Contract) **production** 200 **est.** 1989
product range ($14–20 CD) Twin Peaks Riesling, Old Cottage Riesling, Cabernet Sauvignon Merlot, Cabernet Sauvignon Cabernet Franc Merlot.
summary The Millinup Estate vineyard was planted in 1978, when it was called Point Creek. Owners Peter and Lesley Thorn purchased it in 1989, renaming it and having the limited production (from 0.5 hectare of riesling, supplemented by purchased red grapes) vinified at Plantagenet.

minot vineyard NR

PO Box 683 Margaret River, WA 6285 **region** Margaret River
phone (08) 9757 3579 **fax** (08) 9757 2361 **open** By appointment
winemaker Various Contract **production** 1000 **est.** 1986
product range ($13–20 ML) Semillon Sauvignon Blanc, Cabernet Sauvignon.
summary Minot, which takes its name from a small chateau in the Loire Valley in France, is the husband-and-wife venture of the Miles family, producing just two wines from the 4.2-hectare plantings of semillon, sauvignon blanc and cabernet sauvignon.

mintaro wines ★★★☆

Leasingham Road, Mintaro, SA 5415 **region** Clare Valley
phone (08) 8843 9046 **fax** (08) 8843 9050 **open** 7 days 9–5
winemaker Peter Houldsworth **production** 5000 **est.** 1984
product range ($16–24 CD) Riesling, Semillon Chardonnay, Late Picked Riesling, Anastasias Sparkling Cabernet Shiraz, Shiraz, Reserve Shiraz, Cabernet Sauvignon, Cabernet.
summary Has produced some very good Riesling over the years, developing well in bottle. The red wines are formidable, massive in body and extract, built for the long haul.

Mintaro Shiraz

🍷🍷🍷🍷🍷 **1999** Medium to full red-purple; potent blackberry, plum and prune aromas lead into a full-bodied palate, which has all of the fruit promised by the bouquet together with vanilla oak; good extract and tannin management. **rating:** 91

best drinking 2004–2009 **best vintages** '94, '95, '99 **drink with** Leave it in the cellar • NA

miramar 

Henry Lawson Drive, Mudgee, NSW 2850 **region** Mudgee
phone (02) 6373 3874 **fax** (02) 6373 3854 **open** 7 days 9–5
winemaker Ian MacRae **production** 8000 **est.** 1977
product range ($11–35 CD) Riesling, Semillon, Sauvignon Blanc, Chardonnay, Fumé Blanc, Eurunderee Rosé, Shiraz, Cabernet Sauvignon; Doux Blanc (sweet white), Encore and Encore Rouge (Sparkling).
summary Industry veteran Ian MacRae has demonstrated his skill with every type of winε over the decades, ranging through Rosé to Chardonnay to full-bodied reds. All have shone under the Miramar label at one time or another, although the Ides of March are pointing more to the red than the white wines these days. A substantial part of the production from the 33 hectares of estate vineyard is sold to others, the best being retained for Miramar's own use.

Miramar Doux Blanc 375 ml

🍷🍷🍷🍷 **1999** Light to medium green-yellow; there is intense lime fruit on the bouquet, notwithstanding the obvious botrytis influence; the palate has piercing sweet lime juice flavours and acidity which are nonetheless well balanced. **rating:** 89

best drinking Now–2004 **best vintages** NA **drink with** Fruit tart • $15

Miramar Eurunderee Rosé

🍷🍷🍷🍷 **2000** Light red; the bouquet is clean and fresh, with a light touch of strawberry, the palate a logical follow-on, finishing with pleasing dryness. **rating:** 84

best drinking Now **best vintages** NA **drink with** Anything Asian • $11

Miramar Shiraz

🍷🍷🍷🍷 **1999** Strong purple-red; deep, clean, strong dark cherry aromas, then a decidedly youthful cherry-flavoured palate with subtle oak and good acidity; slightly unformed, but should develop with bottle age. **rating:** 87

best drinking 2003–2008 **best vintages** '86, '90, '94, '95, '97 **drink with** Braised oxtail or, better still, the ox • $17

Miramar Cabernet Sauvignon

🍷🍷🍷🍷🍷 **1999** Bright red-purple; a moderately intense bouquet offers a mix of cassis, berry and earth, the palate with very fresh and flavoursome cassis fruit, fine tannins and subtle oak. Has fulfilled the promise it showed as a young wine. **rating:** 90

best drinking 2004–2009 **best vintages** '86, '90, '91, '99 **drink with** Veal chops • $20

miranda wines (barossa) ★★★☆

Barossa Highway, Rowland Flat, SA 5352 **region** Barossa Valley
phone (08) 8524 4537 **fax** (08) 8524 4066 **open** Mon–Fri 10–4.30, weekends 11–4
winemaker Gary Wall, Mark Murray **production** NFP **est.** 1919
product range ($9–70 CD) Premium Late Harvest Riesling; the Grey Series of Riesling, Semillon, Sauvignon Blanc, Chardonnay, Shiraz, Bush Vine Grenache and Cabernet Sauvignon; followed by Show Reserve range of Chardonnay, Old Vine Shiraz and Shiraz Cabernet; The Drainings (Shiraz Cabernet blend).
summary Increasingly absorbed into the Miranda Wine Group since its acquisition, drawing on grapes produced both in the Barossa Valley and throughout other parts of southeast Australia. The accent is on value for money, with consistent show success underlining the quality. Exports to the UK.

Miranda Rovalley Estate Eden Valley Riesling

TTTT **2000** Light to medium green-yellow; the bouquet offers a solid mix of spice and lime, with a touch of mineral; there is plenty of weight and flavour to the palate, with a nice lemony/minerally finish. **rating:** 88
best drinking Now–2005 **best vintages** NA **drink with** Salmon roulade • NA

Miranda Eden Valley Shiraz Cabernet

TTTT **1997** Medium red-purple; the bouquet has pleasant, bottle-developed, gently leathery aromas, followed by a soft palate with sweet berry, leather and spice flavours; fine tannins to close. Winner of four silver medals. **rating:** 86
best drinking Now–2005 **best vintages** NA **drink with** Roast veal • NA

Miranda The Drainings

TTTTY **1996** Medium red-purple; there is a nice balance and integration of fruit and oak, with notes of spice and cedar; the smooth, ripe palate has a mix of dark chocolate and sweet berry fruit, supported by soft tannins and gentle oak. A lovely wine maturing well. **rating:** 92
best drinking 2002–2010 **best vintages** '96 **drink with** Rack of lamb • $70

Miranda Rovalley Ridge Cabernet Sauvignon

TTTT **1998** Medium red-purple; light spicy/berry aromas come through on the palate which is, however, quite complex thanks to the addition of earthy/chocolate characters. Soft but ripe tannins and appropriate oak round the wine off. **rating:** 85
best drinking 2003–2007 **best vintages** NA **drink with** Lasagne • NA

miranda wines (griffith) ★★★

57 Jondaryan Avenue, Griffith, NSW 2680 **region** Riverina
phone (02) 6960 3000 **fax** (02) 6962 6944 **open** 7 days 9–5
winemaker Gary Wall, Sam Miranda Jnr **production** NFP **est.** 1939
product range ($6–25 R) Top of the range is Show Reserve Chardonnay, Old Vine Shiraz, Shiraz Cabernet; Golden Botrytis; followed by the High Country series (from the King Valley) of Riesling, Chardonnay, Merlot, Shiraz and Cabernet; Mirool Creek Dry White, Chardonnay and Cabernet Shiraz; Somerton Riesling Traminer, Semillon Chardonnay and Shiraz Cabernet; also lower-priced Christy's Land and assorted varietals, generics, sparkling and ports.
summary Miranda Wines continues its aggressive and successful growth strategy, having opened a new winery in the King Valley in 1998 and previously expanded winemaking operations into the Barossa Valley. A veritable cascade of wines now appears under the various brand names, the majority representing good value for money. Exports to Europe, the UK, Canada and Illinois.

Miranda Mirool Creek Semillon Sauvignon Blanc

TTTY **2000** Light to medium green-yellow; a spotlessly clean, crisp and correct bouquet is followed by a light, fresh and lively palate, with just a touch of gooseberry and apple fruit to add interest. **rating:** 83
best drinking Now **best vintages** NA **drink with** Light seafood • NA

Miranda Golden Botrytis

TTTTY **1999** Golden green-yellow; a complex bouquet with a cascade of honey, cumquat and lime marmalade aromas is followed by a palate with identical flavours and nicely balanced acidity. In the groove; very nearly as reliable as Noble One. **rating:** 91
best drinking Now–2004 **best vintages** '93, '94, '96, '97, '00 **drink with** Fruit ice-cream, sweet pastries • NA

Miranda The Pioneers Raisined Muscat

YYYY **2000** Light yellow-green; a fresh, grapey/raisiny bouquet is followed by a palate with intense grapey flavours offset by long, piercing acidity. **rating:** 87

best drinking Now **best vintages** NA **drink with** Fresh fruit • NA

Miranda Show Reserve Old Vine Shiraz

YYYY **1997** Medium red-purple; the bouquet is of light to medium intensity, with earth, chocolate and berry aromas supported by some, but not excessive, vanilla oak. The palate is pleasant, light to medium bodied, but overall the wine lacks the concentration expected of old vines. **rating:** 84

best drinking Now–2006 **best vintages** NA **drink with** Lasagne • $24.85

miranda wines (king valley) ★★★

Cnr Snow and Whitfield Roads, Oxley, Vic 3768 **region** King Valley
phone (02) 6960 3016 **fax** (02) 6964 4135 **open** 7 days 10–5
winemaker Luis F Simian Snr, Luis F Simian, Gary Wall **production** NFP **est.** 1998
product range ($9.95–24 R) The High Country series of Riesling, High Country Chardonnay, High Country Merlot, Shiraz, Cabernet Sauvignon, Dark Horse Cabernet Franc Malbec.
summary Miranda now has three quite separate winemaking entities: the original (and largest) in Griffith; the next in the Barossa Valley; and the most recent in the King Valley. It is at the latter winery that the High Country range is made, using 35 hectares of estate vineyards, supplemented by grapes purchased from elsewhere, including the Kiewa. Exports to the UK.

Miranda High Country Riesling

YYYY **2000** Light green-yellow; a spicy, minerally bouquet has some lemon and herb notes; the medium-weight palate is clean, quite well balanced, but low on fruit intensity. **rating:** 84

best drinking Now–2004 **best vintages** NA **drink with** Light seafood • NA

mistletoe wines 

771 Hermitage Road, Pokolbin, NSW 2335 **region** Lower Hunter Valley
phone (02) 4998 7770 **fax** (02) 4998 7792 **open** Mon–Fri 10–6 or by appointment
winemaker Contract **production** 3000 **est.** 1967
product range ($16–20 CD) Semillon, Silvereye Semillon, Barrel Fermented Chardonnay, The Rose, Shiraz.
summary Mistletoe Wines, owned by Ken and Gwen Sloan, can trace its history back to 1909, when a substantial vineyard was planted on what was then called Mistletoe Farm. The Mistletoe Farm brand made a brief appearance in the late 1970s and has now been revived under the Mistletoe Wines label by the Sloans, with contract-winemaking. No retail distribution, but worldwide delivery service available ex winery.

mitchell 

Hughes Park Road, Sevenhill, via Clare, SA 5453 **region** Clare Valley
phone (08) 8843 4258 **fax** (08) 8843 4340 **open** 7 days 10–4
winemaker Andrew Mitchell **production** 30 000 **est.** 1975
product range ($17–25 CD) Watervale Riesling, The Growers Semillon, The Growers Grenache, Peppertree Vineyard Shiraz, Sevenhill Cabernet Sauvignon.
summary For long one of the stalwarts of the Clare Valley, producing long-lived Rieslings and Cabernet Sauvignons in classic regional style but having extended the range with very creditable Semillon and Shiraz. A lovely old stone apple shed provides the cellar door and upper section of the compact winery. Production has increased by 50 per cent over the past few years and as well as national retail distribution, the wines are exported to the UK, the US, Canada, New Zealand, Switzerland and Hong Kong.

Mitchell Watervale Riesling

YYYYY **2000** Light to medium green-yellow; a mix of mineral, slate and herb aromas on the bouquet lead into a tight, intense, mineral and herb palate, driven by great length and persistence of flavour. An unequivocal return to form, ironically in a difficult vintage. **rating:** 93

best drinking Now–2010 **best vintages** '78, '84, '90, '92, '93, '94, '95, '00 **drink with** Grilled fish • $17

Mitchell The Growers Semillon

1999 Glowing yellow-green, quite advanced for its age. Strong, spicy/charry oak which is said to be French dominates the bouquet. A very big wine on the palate with lots of fruit and oak; notwithstanding the depth of the fruit, might have been better with a touch less oak. **rating:** 83

best drinking Now **best vintages** NA **drink with** Sugar-cured tuna • $15

Mitchell Peppertree Vineyard Shiraz

1999 Medium purple-red; the bouquet is clean and smooth, with gently ripe plum, spice and a touch of cedar; the palate offers an excellent marriage of fruit, oak and tannins, underpinned by ripe, black cherry fruit. Smooth and harmonious, more elegance than power, and an outstanding success. **rating:** 94

best drinking 2002–2010 **best vintages** '84, '86, '87, '94, '95, '96, '99 **drink with** Devilled kidneys • $25

Mitchell The Growers Grenache

1999 Light to medium red-purple; the bouquet is very typical, light and distinctly jammy. The palate, however, has far more to offer, with quite intense spicy fruit and soft tannins. Minimal oak input. The best to date. **rating:** 85

best drinking Now–2004 **best vintages** NA **drink with** Game pie • $15

Mitchell Sevenhill Cabernet Sauvignon

1998 Medium to full red-purple; a sweet and smooth bouquet with blackberry/currant fruit and gentle oak; the palate shows moderately ripe varietal character, with particularly appealing tannin structure and balance, the oak just where it should be in the background. **rating:** 89

best drinking 2003–2009 **best vintages** '78, '80, '84, '86, '90, '92, '94, '96, '98 **drink with** Roast lamb • $25

mitchelton ★★★★

Mitchellstown, via Nagambie, Vic 3608 **region** Goulburn Valley
phone (03) 5794 2710 **fax** (03) 5794 2615 **open** 7 days 10–5
winemaker Don Lewis **production** 200 000 **est.** 1969
product range ($12.95–42.95 CD) Top of the range is Print Label Red; then come Chardonnay, Cabernet Sauvignon, Marsanne; next Mitchelton III wines, White (Marsanne, Grenache, Viognier), Red (Shiraz, Grenache, Mourvedre); Chinaman's Bridge Merlot, Blackwood Park Riesling. Preece Chardonnay, Sauvignon Blanc, Merlot and Cabernet Sauvignon are volume sellers; Goulburn Valley Shiraz introduced in 1996. Finally, intermittent aged classic releases.
summary Acquired by Petaluma in 1994, having already put the runs on the board in no uncertain fashion with gifted winemaker Don Lewis. Boasts an impressive array of wines across a broad spectrum of style and price, but each carefully aimed at a market niche. The wines are exported to 19 countries throughout the UK, Europe, Asia and the US.

Mitchelton Blackwood Park Riesling

2000 An enduring classic, delicious when young but with an enviable show record as it moves into maturity at five years age or more. Fragrance and delicacy are the hallmarks of the aroma now, the palate lively and crisp, with excellent balance and structure; passionfruit, lime/citrus and herbs are all there. **rating:** 91

best drinking Now–2010 **best vintages** '85, '90, '91, '92, '94, '95, '96, '98, '99, '00 **drink with** Sashimi • $15.50

Mitchelton Viognier Roussanne

1998 Glowing yellow-green; the bouquet is rich, with some honeyed, bottle-developed aromatics, the palate with masses of weight and texture, featuring honey set against a background of mineral (the latter coming from the Roussanne, I suspect). Oak has contributed to texture rather than flavour; sophisticated winemaking, although I am not so certain about the subliminal touch of sweetness which seems to make the alcohol appear higher than it in fact is (at 13.5°). **rating:** 88

best drinking Now–2005 **best vintages** NA **drink with** Chicken casserole • $26

Mitchelton Airstrip Marsanne

1998 Glowing yellow-green; an exceptionally complex peach, butterscotch and nut aroma is followed by an extraordinarily powerful palate in Alsace Vendage Tardive style. The alcohol really does sear the palate, and I am left to wonder why the wine was fermented dry. **rating:** 84

best drinking Now–2008 **best vintages** NA **drink with** Rich pasta • $26.60

Mitchelton Preece Chardonnay

▼▼▼▽ **1999** Medium yellow-green; solid, yellow peach fruit on the bouquet leads into a solid, four-square palate, with plenty of flavour though not a great deal of finesse. An honest son of the sun. **rating:** 81

best drinking Now **best vintages** NA **drink with** Multicultural dishes • $16.60

Mitchelton Blackwood Park Botrytis Riesling

▼▼▼▼ **2000** Medium yellow-green; the bouquet is rich, with abundant tropical fruit and some grapefruit/lime undertones. The generously flavoured palate follows down the same track, with a hint of grapefruit marmalade, and well-balanced acidity. **rating:** 87

best drinking Now–2006 **best vintages** NA **drink with** Scallops in bechamel sauce • $14.40

Mitchelton Shiraz

▼▼▼▽ **1998** Medium red-purple; the aromas are predominantly of red cherry, with touches of spice and leather. The medium-bodied palate reflects American (rather than French) oak, with soft red berry fruit; a generous, but no-frills, style. **rating:** 84

best drinking Now–2005 **best vintages** NA **drink with** Braised duck • $15.50

Mitchelton Mourvedre Grenache

▼▼▼▼ **1998** Medium red, with a touch of purple; the spicy/savoury/earthy aromas (from the Mourvedre) are set against cherry and strawberry (from the Grenache). The palate has the same mix of light, sweet and spicy characters with more savoury notes. I can't help but think that using some Shiraz to join the parts would have been worthwhile. **rating:** 85

best drinking Now–2004 **best vintages** NA **drink with** Pizza • $26

---

molly morgan vineyard ★★★★

Talga Road, Lovedale, NSW 2321 **region** Lower Hunter Valley
phone (02) 9816 4088 **fax** (02) 9816 2680 **open** By appointment
winemaker Rhys Eather (Contract) **production** 3000 **est.** 1963
product range ($19–25.50 CD) Joe's Block Semillon, Old Vines Semillon, Chardonnay, Shiraz.
summary Molly Morgan has been acquired by Andrew and Hady Simon (who established the Camperdown Cellars Group in 1971, becoming the largest retailer in Australia before passing on to other pursuits), and John Baker (one of Australia's best-known fine-wine retailers, who owned or managed Quaffers, Double Bay Cellars, the Newport Bottler and Grape Fellas in Epping at various times). The property is planted to 5.5 hectares of 25-year-old unirrigated semillon (which goes to make the Old Vines Semillon), 0.8 hectare for Joe's Block Semillon, 2.5 hectares of chardonnay and 1.2 hectares of shiraz. The wines are contract-made (as has always been the case, in fact) but to a high standard. Exports to the US.

Molly Morgan Joe's Block Semillon

▼▼▼▼▽ **2000** Light green-yellow; a quite powerful bouquet with aromatic notes of lemon and herb; the palate is already mouthfilling, but not at all phenolic, with flavours bordering on the tropical, yet no botrytis. Early-drinking style. **rating:** 91

best drinking Now–2004 **best vintages** '99, '00 **drink with** Seafood • $19

Molly Morgan Old Vines Semillon

▼▼▼▼▽ **2000** Light green-yellow; more minerally and closed than Joe's Block, seemingly with higher sulphur dioxide. The palate opens up to lots of lemony/lemon zest flavour, and a crisp finish. More conventional. **rating:** 90

best drinking 2005–2010 **best vintages** '98, '99, '00 **drink with** Calamari • $19

---

monbulk winery 

Macclesfield Road, Monbulk, Vic 3793 **region** Yarra Valley
phone (03) 9756 6965 **fax** (03) 9756 6965 **open** Weekends and public holidays 12–5, or by appointment
winemaker Paul Jabornik **production** 800 **est.** 1984
product range ($10–15 CD) Chardonnay, Riesling, Pinot Noir, Cabernet Sauvignon, Shiraz; also Kiwifruit wines.
summary Originally concentrated on kiwifruit wines but now extending to table wines; the very cool Monbulk subregion should be capable of producing wines of distinctive style, but the table wines are (unfortunately) not of the same standard as the kiwifruit wines, which are quite delicious.

monichino wines ★★★

1820 Berrys Road, Katunga, Vic 3640 **region** Goulburn Valley
phone (03) 5864 6452 **fax** (03) 5864 6538 **open** Mon–Sat 9–5, Sun 10–5
winemaker Carlo Monichino, Terry Monichino **production** 14 000 **est.** 1962
product range ($10–25 CD) Riesling, Semillon Sauvignon Blanc, Sauvignon Blanc, Chardonnay, Botrytis Semillon, Orange Muscat, Golden Lexia, Rose Petals Spätlese, Shiraz, Merlot, Malbec, Carlo's Pressings, Rosso Doce, Cabernet Sauvignon, Italian Stubby; various Ports and Fortifieds; bulk sales also available.
summary A winery that has quietly made some clean, fresh wines in which the fruit character is carefully preserved.

Monichino Orange Muscat

🍷🍷🍷🍷 **1999** Light green-yellow; the bouquet is fresh and crisp, with strong orange-blossom aromas; the palate is well balanced, offsetting orange/lime pastille flavours of spätlese sweetness with clean acidity on the finish. Silver medal at the Victorian Wines Show. **rating:** 87

best drinking Now **best vintages** NA **drink with** Aperitif • $15

Monichino Botrytis Semillon

🍷🍷🍷🍷 **1996** Deep yellow-gold; complex cumquat and caramelised sugar/toffee aromas are followed by a pungently sweet palate; apricot/cumquat fruit flavours are offset by lingering acidity. **rating:** 89

best drinking Now–2003 **best vintages** NA **drink with** Rich desserts • $15

Monichino Liqueur Muscat

🍷🍷🍷🍷 **NV** Youthful tawny-red; vibrant raisiny fruit aromas lead into a palate of liquid raisins, and a slightly biscuity aftertaste. **rating:** 84

best drinking Now **best vintages** NA **drink with** Cake and black coffee • $25

montagne view estate NR

555 Hermitage Road, Pokolbin, NSW 2335 **region** Lower Hunter Valley
phone (02) 4998 7822 **fax** (02) 6574 7276 **open** 7 days 10–5
winemaker Greg Silkman (Contract) **production** 500 **est.** 1993
product range ($20–25 CD) Edith Margaret Chardonnay, Vivian Laurie Merlot.
summary The major investment and principal business of Montagne View is the eight-studio-suite guesthouse sitting among the 5 hectares of vines. There is also a high-quality restaurant (Brents) offering the prospect of all-inclusive gourmet weekends for around $550 per couple. The estate wines are sold through the restaurant and cellar door, with other local wines available in the restaurant.

montalto vineyards NR

33 Shoreham Road, Red Hill South, Vic 3937 **region** Mornington Peninsula
phone (03) 5983 5789 **fax** (03) 9826 9484 **open** 7 days 12–5
winemaker Daniel Green **production** 2000 **est.** 1998
product range ($18–27.50 CD) Riesling, Chardonnay, Pinot Noir.
summary John Mitchell and family established Montalto Vineyards in 1998, although the core of the vineyard goes back to 1986. There are 5 hectares of chardonnay and 4 hectares of pinot noir, with 0.5 hectare each of semillon, riesling and pinot meunier. Intensive vineyard work opens up the canopy, with yields ranging between 1.5 and 2.5 tonnes per acre, with the majority of the fruit hand-harvested. Wines are released under two labels, Montalto and Pennon, the latter effectively a lower-priced, second label. The first Montalto Pinot Noir (from 1999) won a silver medal at the Cowra Wine Show 2000, while the 1999 Chardonnay did even better, winning a gold medal at the 2000 Cool Climate Wine Show.

montara ★★★☆

Chalambar Road, Ararat, Vic 3377 **region** Grampians
phone (03) 5352 3868 **fax** (03) 5352 4968 **open** Mon–Sat 10–5, Sun 12–4
winemaker Mike McRae **production** NFP **est.** 1970
product range ($13.50–22 CD) Riesling, Chardonnay, Pinot Noir, Shiraz, Cabernet Sauvignon; 'M' range of Chardonnay, Pinot Noir, Pinot Noir Shiraz.

summary Achieved considerable attention for its Pinot Noirs during the 1980s, but other regions (and other makers) have come along since. It continues to produce wines of distinctive style, and smart new label designs do help. Limited national distribution; exports to the UK, Switzerland, Canada and Hong Kong.

Montara Riesling

🍷🍷🍷🍷 **2000** Light green-yellow; the bouquet is quite fragrant, with a mix of lime, herb and apple aromas, the light- to medium-bodied palate is gentle and appealing, but does shorten off on the finish. **rating:** 84

best drinking Now–2004 **best vintages** NA **drink with** Ginger prawns • $17.95

Montara M Pinot Shiraz

🍷🍷🍷🍷 **1998** Red, with a tawny rim; a very smoky/tangy/smoked bacon bouquet is followed by a palate with more of those smoky/tangy/foresty flavours in a silky texture; a thoroughly interesting wine. **rating:** 84

best drinking Now–2004 **best vintages** NA **drink with** Smoked quail • $17

Montara Shiraz

🍷🍷🍷🍷 **1998** Medium red-purple; a fragrant, high-toned spicy/tangy bouquet in typical winery style leads into a palate with spicy/tangy flavours, a hint of stem and low tannins. Another pointed and interesting wine.

rating: 85

best drinking Now–2005 **best vintages** NA **drink with** Char-grilled lamb • $24

montgomery's hill NR

Hassell Highway, Upper Kalgan, Albany, WA 6330 **region** Great Southern
phone (08) 9844 3715 **fax** (08) 9844 1104 **open** By appointment
winemaker Robert Lee (Porongurup Winery), John Wade (Consultant) **production** 2000 **est.** 1996
product range ($16.50–22.50 R) Unwooded Chardonnay, Cabernet Franc, Cabernets.
summary Montgomery's Hill is situated 16 kilometres northeast of Albany on a north-facing slope on the banks of the Kalgan River. The vineyard is situated on an area which was previously an apple orchard and is a diversification for the third generation of the Montgomery family which owns the property. Chardonnay, cabernet sauvignon and cabernet franc were planted in 1996, followed by sauvignon blanc, shiraz and merlot in 1997. The 1998 wines were contract-made by Brenden Smith at West Cape Howe Wines, but since 1999 Montgomery's Hill has been made at the new Porongurup Winery. The newly constructed cellar door was due to open in May 2001.

monument vineyard NR

Cnr Escort Way and Manildra Road, Cudal, NSW 2864 **region** Central Ranges Zone
phone (02) 6364 2294 **fax** (02) 6364 2069 **open** Due to open February 2002
winemaker Alison Eisermann **production** 900 **est.** 1998
product range Semillon, Chardonnay, Marsanne, Pinot Noir, Shiraz, Merlot, Sangiovese, Cabernet Sauvignon
summary In the early 1990s five mature-age students at Charles Sturt University, successful in their own professions, decided to form a partnership to develop a substantial vineyard and winery development on a scale that they could not individually afford. After a lengthy search, a large property at Cudal was identified, with ideal terra rossa basalt-derived soil over a limestone base. The property now has 108 hectares under vine, as a result of planting in the spring of 1998 and 1999. A non-commercial vintage was produced in 2000, and a small commercial crop was expected from 2001.

moondah brook ★★★★

c/o Houghton, Dale Road, Middle Swan, WA 6056 **region** Swan District
phone (08) 9274 5372 **fax** (08) 9274 5372 **open** Not
winemaker Larry Cherubino **production** 90 000 **est.** 1968
product range ($10–19 R) Chardonnay, Chenin Blanc, Verdelho, Sauvignon Blanc, Shiraz, Cabernet Sauvignon, Maritime (Sparkling); also occasional Show Reserve releases of Chenin Blanc and Verdelho.
summary Part of the BRL Hardy wine group, it has its own special character as it draws part of its fruit from the large Gingin vineyard, 70 kilometres north of the Swan Valley, and part from the Margaret River and Great Southern. In recent times this winery has excelled even its own reputation for reliability with some quite lovely wines, in particular honeyed, aged Chenin Blanc and finely structured Cabernet Sauvignon.

Moondah Brook Verdelho

ΨΨΨΨ **2000** Water white; a highly aromatic bouquet redolent of passionfruit and fruit salad is followed by a palate that fails to deliver all of the promise of the bouquet, but is a distinctive varietal alternative to Chardonnay. **rating:** 85

best drinking Now–2003 **best vintages** '90, '91, '93, '00 **drink with** Sugar-cured tuna • $14.99

Moondah Brook Cabernet Sauvignon

ΨΨΨΨ **1998** Medium red-purple; the bouquet is quite fragrant and sweet, with fresh red berry fruit and nicely controlled oak. The black cherry and chocolate flavours of the palate are likewise matched with sympathetic oak. Excellent value for money. Trophy winner in the large-volume commercial red wine class at the 1999 National Wine Show. **rating:** 88

best drinking Now–2008 **best vintages** '82, '88, '91, '93, '94, '96, '97, '98 **drink with** Veal chops Italian-style • $18.99

moondarra NR

Browns Road, Moondarra, Vic 3825 **region** Gippsland
phone (03) 9598 3049 **fax** (03) 9598 3049 **open** Not
winemaker Neil Prentice **production** NA **est.** 1991
product range ($90 R) Samba Side Pinot Noir, Conception Pinot Noir.
summary In 1991 Neil Prentice and family established their Moondarra vineyard in Gippsland, planted eleven low-yielding clones of pinot noir. The vines are not irrigated, and vineyard management is predicated on the minimum use of any sprays with the aim of ultimately moving to Biodynamic/Pagan farming methods. The winemaking techniques are strongly influenced by the practices of controversial Lebanese-born Burgundy consultant Guy Accad, with ten days pre-fermentation maceration and whole bunches added prior to fermentation.The wines are distributed in Melbourne and Sydney by Select Vineyards, go to Japan via Village Cellars, and to the US with John Larchet's Australian Premium Wine Collection. And yes, the $90 a bottle (or $1000 per dozen) is indeed the price.

moonshine valley winery NR

374 Mons Road, Forest Glen, Buderim, Qld 4556 **region** Queensland Zone
phone (07) 5445 1198 **fax** (07) 5445 1799 **open** Mon–Fri 10–4, weekends 10–5
winemaker Tom Weidmann **production** 3000 **est.** 1985
product range ($10–30 CD) A kaleidoscopic array of basically fruit-based wines, including White Moon, Red Moon, Chardonnay, Shiraz, Shiraz Cabernet Merlot. Liqueurs are Limoncello, Almondo, Espresso; Old Buderim Ginger, Strawberry Port, Old Ned (spirit), Porto Rubino, Ruby Moon Port (Shiraz Durif Sangiovese).
summary Frederick Houweling brings a European background to his making of these fruit-based wines. The winery is situated on a large property among natural lakes and forest, and also offers a restaurant, cafeteria and souvenir shop.

moorebank vineyard NR

Palmers Lane, Pokolbin, NSW 2320 **region** Lower Hunter Valley
phone (02) 4998 7610 **fax** (02) 4998 7367 **open** Fri–Mon 10–5 or by appointment
winemaker Iain Riggs (Contract) **production** 2000 **est.** 1977
product range ($19.50–24.50 CD) Chardonnay, Summar Semillon, Gewurztraminer, Merlot, now sold in the narrow 500-ml Italian glass bottle known as Bellissima.
summary Ian Burgess and Debra Moore own a mature 5.5-hectare vineyard with a small cellar-door operation offering immaculately packaged wines in avant-garde style. The peachy Chardonnay has been a medal-winner at Hunter Valley Wine Shows.

moorilla estate ★★★★☆

655 Main Road, Berriedale, Tas 7011 **region** Southern Tasmania
phone (03) 6277 9900 **fax** (03) 6249 4093 **open** 7 days 10–5
winemaker Michael Glover **production** 15 000 **est.** 1958

product range ($9–48 ML) Riesling, Gewurztraminer, White Label Chardonnay, Black Label Chardonnay, Botrytis Riesling, Black Label Pinot Noir, White Label Pinot Noir, Cabernet Sauvignon, Millennium Cuvée 2, Vintage Brut; Reserve wines include Pinot Noir, Syrah and Cabernet Sauvignon.

summary Moorilla Estate is an icon in the Tasmanian wine industry and is thriving. Previous winemaker Alain Rousseau was exceptionally gifted, producing better wines than previously came from Moorilla (particularly Pinot Noir), while the opening of the museum in the marvellous Alcorso house designed by Sir Roy Grounds adds even more attraction for visitors to the estate, a mere 15–20 minutes from Hobart. Five-star self-contained chalets are available, with a restaurant open for lunch 7 days a week.

Moorilla Estate Riesling

2000 Light green-yellow; the bouquet is not particularly aromatic; there are some unsettling off-flavours on both the bouquet and palate, and the wine presently has excess carbon dioxide. **rating:** 89

best drinking 2004–2010 **best vintages** '81, '82, '90, '91, '93, '94, '95, '97, '98, '99 **drink with** Asparagus • $23

Moorilla Estate Black Label Chardonnay

1999 Medium yellow-green; distinct barrel-ferment aromas and flavours seem capable of various interpretations; however, has very good fruit on the palate which provides both mid-palate weight and length of flavour. For those looking for an alternative style. **rating:** 93

best drinking Now–2005 **best vintages** '99 **drink with** Grilled spatchcock • $21.55

Moorilla Estate White Label Chardonnay

1999 Light green-yellow; the light citrus and melon fruit is slightly muffled on the bouquet, perhaps by the oak, but the wine comes alive on the typically intense palate with citrus and melon fruit, and crisp, tingling acidity. **rating:** 88

best drinking Now–2006 **best vintages** '99 **drink with** Lobster • $26.80

Moorilla Estate Black Label Pinot Noir

2000 Medium to full purple-red; a potent, stemmy/briary/foresty bouquet leads into a powerful palate, with lots of fruit intensity, and significant development in front of it. **rating:** 87

best drinking Now–2005 **best vintages** '00 **drink with** Game, of course • NA

Moorilla Estate Reserve Pinot Noir

1999 Medium red-purple; a complex bouquet with an intriguing mix of spicy/foresty/sappy overtones to small, dark berry/strawberry fruit is followed by a long, tangy, strawberry/cherry/plum-flavoured palate. A stylish and harmonious wine which won a gold medal at the 2001 Tasmanian Wines Show. **rating:** 94

best drinking Now–2006 **best vintages** '96, '97, '99 **drink with** Venison • $48

Moorilla Estate Reserve Cabernet Merlot

1998 Excellent red-purple; savoury dark berry aromas foreshadow a most attractive palate with sweet berry fruit, a touch of chocolate, and fine but ripe tannins. **rating:** 94

best drinking 2003–2008 **best vintages** NA **drink with** Leg of lamb • NA

Moorilla Estate Reserve Cabernet Sauvignon

1997 Medium red-purple; a firm, clean bouquet ranges through mint and berry, the clean, firm berry-accented palate finishing with attractive, dry but ripe tannins. **rating:** 93

best drinking 2002–2007 **best vintages** NA **drink with** Venison • NA

moorooduc estate ★★★★☆

501 Derril Road, Moorooduc, Vic 3936 **region** Mornington Peninsula

phone (03) 9696 4130 **fax** (03) 9696 2841 **open** First weekend each month 12–5

winemaker Dr Richard McIntyre **production** 7000 **est.** 1983

product range ($19–45 R) Sauvignon Blanc, Chardonnay, Pinot Noir, Cabernet; also Devil Bend Creek Chardonnay and Pinot Noir.

summary Dr Richard McIntyre regularly produces one of the richest and most complex Chardonnays in the region, with grapefruit/peach fruit set against sumptuous spicy oak, and that hallmark soft nutty/creamy/ regional texture. As well as retail distribution, the wines are exported to Japan.

morgan simpson ★★★☆

PO Box 241, Stepney, SA 5069 **region** McLaren Vale
phone (08) 8362 3128 **fax** (08) 8362 3128 **open** Not
winemaker Richard Simpson **production** 1000 **est.** 1998
product range ($9.50–13.50 ML) Chardonnay, Shiraz, Cabernet Sauvignon.
summary Morgan Simpson is a joint venture between South Australian businessman George Morgan and winemaker Richard Simpson, who is a wine science graduate from Charles Sturt University. Their grapes are sourced from the Clos Robert Vineyard (where the wine is made) established by Robert Alan Simpson in 1972. The partners say, 'As we gain knowledge and experience of winemaking we intend to increase both the range and quality of our products. Our current plan is to provide drinkable wines at a reasonable price.' They have succeeded admirably with the small quantities of wine so far released, and intend to limit production to its present level of around 20 tonnes/1000 cases per year.

Morgan Simpson Shiraz

🍷🍷🍷🍷 **1999** Medium red-purple; the moderately intense bouquet has pleasant plum/spice/cherry fruit with immediate appeal. The palate is soft, with plum and cherry-flavoured fruit, with savoury/earthy nuances and a harmonious finish. Like the Chardonnay, excellent value. **rating:** 84
best drinking Now–2004 **best vintages** NA **drink with** Italian sausages • $12

Morgan Simpson Cabernet Sauvignon

🍷🍷🍷🍷 **1999** Medium red-purple; the bouquet is soft, with gently earthy/savoury fruit joined with hints of regional chocolate characters. The palate is a mirror image of the bouquet; a no-nonsense, well-priced wine. A silver medal at the 2000 Royal Adelaide Wine Show suggests my points are somewhat miserable. **rating:** 83
best drinking Now–2003 **best vintages** NA **drink with** Braised ox cheek • $13.50

morning cloud wines NR

15 Ocean View Avenue, Red Hill South, Vic 3937 **region** Mornington Peninsula
phone (03) 5989 2762 **fax** (03) 5989 2700 **open** By appointment
winemaker Lindsay McCall (Contract) **production** 300 **est.** 1983
product range ($18 R) Chardonnay, Cabernet Sauvignon.
summary Morning Cloud Wines (previously Cloud Valley) is a joint venture between Kathy and Bill Allen and Peter and Judy Maxwell. Each family has its own vineyard at Red Hill South, and the grapes are pooled and the wine made under contract at Stonier's Winery. The Cabernet Sauvignon tends to be very leafy in Chinon-style; the Chardonnay, medium bodied, crisp and citrus-tinged.

morningside wines ★★★★

711 Middle Tea Tree Road, Tea Tree, Tas 7017 **region** Southern Tasmania
phone (03) 6268 1748 **fax** (03) 6268 1748 **open** By appointment
winemaker Peter Bosworth **production** 500 **est.** 1980
product range ($17–22 ML) Riesling, Chardonnay, Pinot Noir, Cabernet Sauvignon.
summary The name 'Morningside' was given to the old property on which the vineyard stands because it gets the morning sun first; the property on the other side of the valley was known as 'Eveningside'. Consistently with the observation of the early settlers, the Morningside grapes achieve full maturity with good colour and varietal flavour. Production is as yet tiny but will increase as the 2-hectare vineyard matures. Retail distribution through Sutherland Cellars, Melbourne and Tasmanian Wine Centre.

Morningside Chardonnay

🍷🍷🍷🍷🍷 **1999** Medium yellow-green; quite rich and developed nectarine and melon fruit together with subtle oak on the bouquet flows into a smooth palate with nicely ripened nectarine and melon flavours. Fruit-driven. **rating:** 90
best drinking Now–2003 **best vintages** '97, '99 **drink with** Tasmanian lobster • $22

Morningside Pinot Noir

🍷🍷🍷🍷🍷 **1999** Medium to full red-purple; a complex, powerful, ripe, multi-layered bouquet is replicated on the palate with a quite spectacular mix of plum, spice, stem and forest, all adding up to an emphatic presence. Tails off ever so slightly on the finish however. **rating:** 90
best drinking 2002–2007 **best vintages** '99 **drink with** Hare • $22

mornington vineyards estate 

c/o Dromana Estate, Harrison's and Bittern–Dromana Roads, Dromana, Vic 3936 **region** Mornington Peninsula
phone (03) 5987 3800 **fax** (03) 5981 0714 **open** at Dromana Estate 7 days 11–4
winemaker Gary Crittenden **production** 2000 **est.** 1989
product range ($17–28 CD) Chardonnay, Sauvignon Blanc, Pinot Noir, Shiraz.
summary As with so many Mornington Peninsula vineyards, a high degree of viticultural expertise, care and attention is needed to get to first base. With a little over 20 hectares in production, this is one of the larger vineyards on the Peninsula and is an important part of the public-listed Dromana Estate group.

morris 

Mia Mia Road, Rutherglen, Vic 3685 **region** Rutherglen
phone (02) 6026 7303 **fax** (02) 6026 7445 **open** Mon–Sat 9–5, Sun 10–5
winemaker David Morris **production** NFP **est.** 1859
product range ($12.95–45 R) A limited range of table wines sparingly distributed, the most important of which is the red wine Durif, and also Shiraz; then fortified wines comprising Mick Morris Old Tawny Port, Liqueur Tokay, Old Premium Liqueur Tokay, Mick Morris Muscat, Old Premium Liqueur Muscat, Mick Morris Commemorative Liqueur Muscat; Old Premium Liqueur Muscat at the top end of the range; tiny quantities of Show Reserve are released from time to time, mainly ex winery; Blue Imperial Cinsaut.
summary One of the greatest of the fortified winemakers, some would say the greatest. If you wish to test that view, try the Old Premium Muscat and Old Premium Tokay, which are absolute bargains given their age and quality and which give rise to the winery rating. The table wines are dependable, the white wines all being made by owner Orlando.

Morris Durif

1998 Dense, inky purple-red; a dark, blackberry/earthy bouquet runs into a palate with massive concentration and tannins. They really don't come any bigger than this, but history shows these wines do develop given enough time in bottle. **rating:** 92

best drinking 2008–2018 **best vintages** '70, '72, '74, '80, '83, '86, '88, '90, '92, '94, '96, '97, '98 **drink with** Biltong • $20

Morris Blue Imperial Cinsaut

1998 Medium purple-red, bright and clear. The bouquet is clean and fresh, with small berry fruits and the barest touch of oak. The palate is surprisingly elegant, with similar fruit flavours to those of the bouquet augmented by touches of sweet chocolate, and finishing with fine tannins. **rating:** 87

best drinking Now–2005 **best vintages** '98 **drink with** Mediterranean food • $18

Morris Liqueur Tokay

NV Light to medium golden-brown; a fragrant bouquet with fresh tea-leaf varietal aroma. There is masses of flavour on the palate, yet the wine is quite fresh with archetypal cold-tea and butterscotch flavours, with the mid-palate sweetness followed by a cleansing, crisp finish. **rating:** 90

best drinking Now–2010 **best vintages** NA **drink with** Aperitif or at the end of the meal • NA

Morris Liqueur Muscat

NV Light to medium red-brown; clearly articulated, lively, raisiny muscat varietal aromas. In the mouth you can literally taste the grapes, as if one were chewing on an explosively rich raisin; great length and perfect balance. **rating:** 91

best drinking Now–2010 **best vintages** NA **drink with** Aperitif or digestif • NA

Morris Old Premium Liqueur Muscat

NV Medium to full tawny, with a hint of olive on the rim; a rich bouquet with complex caramel, toffee and coffee aromas intermingling with the raisins. The palate shows more of the raisiny varietal fruit, although the complexity of the bouquet does repeat itself. A great example of blending. **rating:** 95

best drinking Now **best vintages** NA **drink with** Coffee, petits fours • NA

---

moss brothers ★★★★

Caves Road, Willyabrup, WA 6280 **region** Margaret River
phone (08) 9755 6270 **fax** (08) 9755 6298 **open** 7 days 10–5
winemaker Jane Moss, David Moss **production** 15 000 **est.** 1984
product range ($14–35 R) Semillon, Sauvignon Blanc, Verdelho, Wooded Chardonnay, Unwooded Chardonnay, Premium Chardonnay, Moses Rock White, NV Maggies Creek Pinot Noir, Shiraz, Cabernet Merlot, Cellar Door Red, Moses Rock Red (the last two unusual blends, Moses Rock including Merlot, Pinot Noir, Grenache and Cabernet Franc); Bona Vista Ruby.
summary Established by long-term viticulturist Jeff Moss and his family, notably sons Peter and David and Roseworthy-graduate daughter Jane. A 100-tonne rammed-earth winery was constructed in 1992 and draws upon both estate-grown and purchased grapes. Wine quality has improved dramatically, first the white wines, and more recently the reds. National wholesale distribution; exports to the UK, Singapore, Malaysia, the Philippines, Denmark, Sweden and Belgium.

Moss Brothers Semillon

YYYY **2000** Light to medium green-yellow; the bouquet is bright and brisk, strongly herbal/herbaceous, the palate commensurately tangy and lively, with a crisp finish. **rating:** 89
best drinking 2002–2006 **best vintages** '98, '99 **drink with** Fried chicken • $18

Moss Brothers Sauvignon Blanc

YYYY **2000** Light green-yellow; the bouquet has a mix of tropical fruit and a faint touch of flint, the palate ripe, tropical and flavoursome, but with a slightly phenolic finish. Other vintages have been better. **rating:** 85
best drinking Now–2003 **best vintages** '99 **drink with** Calamari • $18

Moss Brothers Semillon Sauvignon Blanc

YYYY **2000** Light green-yellow; a fresh, lively bouquet with a faint touch of reductive flint/burnt match as is the case with the Sauvignon Blanc. The fresh and lively palate dips slightly towards the finish. **rating:** 86
best drinking Now **best vintages** NA **drink with** Shellfish • NA

Moss Brothers Shiraz

YYYY **1999** Medium to full red-purple; a clean and rich bouquet with ripe dark cherry fruit and gentle oak is followed by a palate with solid dark cherry fruit and quite persistent tannins. **rating:** 89
best drinking 2003–2009 **best vintages** '99 **drink with** Game pie • $26.95

Moss Brothers Cellar Door Red

YYYY **1998** Medium red-purple; sweet, clean berry fruit and minimal oak on the bouquet is followed by a pleasant wine with lots of straightforward fruit flavour; unforced and uncomplicated. **rating:** 86
best drinking 2002–2005 **best vintages** NA **drink with** Barbecued spare ribs • $25.95

Moss Brothers Cabernet Sauvignon Merlot

YYYYY **1998** Medium to full purple-red; a fragrant and complex bouquet with spicy, red berry fruit and a nice dollop of oak is followed by a sophisticated, medium-bodied palate with good length, style and balance, effectively repeating the flavours promised by the bouquet. **rating:** 94
best drinking 2003–2008 **best vintages** '98 **drink with** Beef Wellington • $34.95

moss wood ★★★★★

Metricup Road, Willyabrup, WA 6280 **region** Margaret River
phone (08) 9755 6266 **fax** (08) 9755 6303 **open** By appointment
winemaker Keith Mugford **production** 6000 **est.** 1969
product range ($25–77 R) Semillon, Chardonnay, Lefroy Brook Vineyard Chardonnay, Pinot Noir, Cabernet Sauvignon, Glenmore Vineyard Cabernet Sauvignon.
summary Widely regarded as one of the best wineries in the region, capable of producing glorious Semillon (the best outside the Hunter Valley) in both oaked and unoaked forms, unctuous Chardonnay and elegant, gently herbaceous, superfine Cabernet Sauvignon that lives for many years. Exports to the UK, the US, Switzerland, Germany, Denmark, Belgium, France, Japan, Hong Kong, Indonesia, Malaysia, Singapore and New Zealand.

Moss Wood Semillon

YYYY 2000 Light green-yellow; the bouquet is clean and despite the power from 14° alcohol is not particularly aromatic; the power really comes through on the rich, mouth-coating mid-palate, and the dry but long finish.
rating: 87

best drinking Now–2005 **best vintages** '81, '82, '83, '84, '86, '87, '92, '94, '95, '97, '98, '99 **drink with** Crab, lobster • $25.30

Moss Wood Chardonnay

YYYYy 2000 Light to medium yellow-green; the oak is immediately obvious on the bouquet, and yet to settle down and integrate; however, the palate leaves no doubt this will happen, for it has lovely texture, weight and feel. Melon, a touch of citrus and a hint of fig show through strongly, the oak doing no more than partnering the fruit.
rating: 92

YYYY 1999 Medium yellow-green; the bouquet is complex, but still quite tight, with controlled oak. The palate has lots of structure, with chewy cashew flavours, the varietal fruit still imprisoned. Will undoubtedly develop with bottle age. **rating:** 87

best drinking 2002–2007 **best vintages** '90, '91, '95, '98, '99, '00 **drink with** Smoked chicken • $44

Moss Wood Cabernet Sauvignon

YYYYY 1998 Full, deep red-purple; a dense, ripe bouquet offers blackberry, chocolate, gentle spice and nice oak; the palate has equally attractive texture and depth, the tannins and oak woven through a range of savoury/blackberry/blackcurrant flavour. **rating:** 94

best drinking 2003–2013 **best vintages** '85, '90, '91, '95, '96, '98 **drink with** Beef with olives • $77

Moss Wood Glenmore Vineyard Cabernet Sauvignon

YYYY 1999 Medium red-purple; sweet red berry fruit with distinct touches of earth on the bouquet is followed by a classic Margaret River palate with red berry fruit on the mid-palate, but overall quite earthy/ savoury, and finishing with lingering tannins. **rating:** 89

best drinking 2003–2010 **best vintages** '99 **drink with** Roast venison • $31.80

---

mountadam ★★★★☆

High Eden Road, High Eden Ridge, SA 5235 **region** Eden Valley
phone (08) 8564 1101 **fax** (08) 8361 3400 **open** 7 days 11–4
winemaker Adam Wynn, Andrew Ewart **production** 35 000 **est.** 1972
product range ($13–60 CD) Premium Mountadam label: Chardonnay, Pinot Noir, The Red (50 per cent Merlot, 50 per cent Cabernet), Merlot, Cabernet Sauvignon, Pinot Noir Chardonnay; David Wynn label: Riesling, Sauvignon Blanc, Chardonnay, Pinot Noir, Shiraz, Patriarch Shiraz, Cabernet Sauvignon; organically grown Eden Ridge label: Sauvignon Blanc, Cabernet Sauvignon; also Ratafia Chardonnay and Pinot Noir.
summary One of the leading small wineries, founded by David Wynn and run by winemaker son Adam Wynn, initially offering only the Mountadam range at relatively high prices. The subsequent development of the three ranges of wines has been very successful, judged both by the winemaking and marketing viewpoint. Mountadam has built up an extensive export network over many years, with the US, Canada, Hong Kong, Japan and the UK being the major markets, but extending across the breadth of Europe and most Asian markets. This will doubtless be strengthened following the acquisition of Mountadam by Cape Mentelle in 2000.

Mountadam Chardonnay

YYYYy 1998 Bright green-yellow; the bouquet has complex bottle-developed aromas fusing fruit, oak, melon and cashew, the balanced, elegant palate providing plenty of flavour in the same seamless flow. **rating:** 90

best drinking Now–2005 **best vintages** '86, '89, '90, '91, '92, '93, '94, '97, '98 **drink with** Salmon terrine • $30.50

Mountadam Merlot

YYYYy 1998 Light to medium red; a fragrant bouquet with a mix of savoury, spicy and redcurrant aromas leads into a light- to medium-bodied palate, with lively, sappy, savoury flavours with enough red fruit running through to satisfy. A nicely balanced wine. **rating:** 90

best drinking 2002–2007 **best vintages** '97, '98 **drink with** Roast veal • $60

---

mount alexander vineyard ★★

Calder Highway, North Harcourt, Vic 3453 **region** Bendigo
phone (03) 5474 2262 **fax** (03) 5474 2553 **open** 7 days 10–5.30
winemaker Keith Walkden **production** 6000 **est.** 1984
product range ($10–14 CD) A wide range of various table wines, sparkling, fortifieds, meads and liqueurs.
summary A substantial operation with 17 hectares planted to all the right varieties. It is several years since I have tasted the wines, but a recent report gives me no reason to suppose they have changed much.

mount anakie wines ★★☆

Staughton Vale Road, Anakie, Vic 3221 **region** Geelong
phone (03) 5284 1452 **fax** (03) 5284 1405 **open** Tues–Sun 11–6
winemaker Otto Zambelli **production** 6000 **est.** 1968
product range ($10–18 R) Biancone, Riesling, Semillon, Chardonnay, Dolcetto, Shiraz, Cabernet Franc, Cabernet Sauvignon.
summary Also known as Zambelli Estate and once produced some excellent wines (under its various ownerships and winemakers), all distinguished by their depth and intensity of flavour. No recent tastings; prior to that, the wines tasted were but a shadow of their former quality. The level of activity seems relatively low.

mount avoca vineyard ★★★☆

Moates Lane, Avoca, Vic 3467 **region** Pyrenees
phone (03) 5465 3282 **fax** (03) 5465 3544 **open** Mon–Fri 9–5, weekends 10–5
winemaker Matthew Barry **production** 18 000 **est.** 1970
product range ($11–45 R) Sauvignon Blanc, Chardonnay, Rhapsody, Trioss White, Trioss Red, Shiraz, Cabernet; Reserve range of Noble Semillon, Merlot, Shiraz, Cabernet, Cabernet Franc, Arda's Choice (Cabernet Sauvignon Cabernet Franc Merlot), Millennium.
summary A substantial winery which has for long been one of the stalwarts of the Pyrenees region, and is steadily growing, with 23.7 hectares of vineyards. There has been a significant refinement in the style and flavour of the red wines over the past few years. I suspect a lot of worthwhile work has gone into barrel selection and maintenance.

Mount Avoca Shiraz

YYY𝑌 **1999** Medium red-purple; a solid bouquet, with a mix of earthy/chocolatey/berry aromas leads into a light, savoury palate which, like the bouquet, is clean, but not particularly dense. **rating:** 83
best drinking 2002–2005 **best vintages** NA **drink with** Marinated beef • $17

Mount Avoca Reserve Merlot

YYYY **1998** Medium to full red-purple; the bouquet is distinctly earthy/leafy, but the palate heads off in the opposite direction, with quite sweet, spicy red berry and plum fruit flavours; controlled oak and tannins.
rating: 85
best drinking 2002–2007 **best vintages** NA **drink with** Wood-fired pizza • $28

Mount Avoca Cabernet

YYYY **1998** Medium red-purple; a complex bouquet with mint and blackberry (conventional) and a hint of hay (less so); a big wine in the mouth, with lots of dark berry/blackcurrant fruit, and nice tannins to balance the finish.
rating: 87
best drinking 2003–2008 **best vintages** '88, '90, '91, '92, '93, '95, '97 **drink with** Char-grilled steak • $18

mount beckworth ★★★☆

RMB 915 Learmonth Road, Tourello, via Ballarat, Vic 3363 **region** Ballarat
phone (03) 5343 4207 **fax** (03) 5343 4207 **open** Weekends 10–6 or by appointment
winemaker Paul Lesock **production** 1000 **est.** 1984
product range ($15–18 CD) Unwooded Chardonnay, Pinot Noir, Shiraz, Cabernet Merlot, Cabernets.
summary The 4-hectare Mount Beckworth vineyard was planted between 1984 and 1985, but it was not until 1995 that the full range of wines under the Mount Beckworth label appeared. Until that time much of the production was sold to Seppelt Great Western for sparkling wine use. It is owned and managed by Paul Lesock, who studied viticulture at Charles Sturt University, and his wife Jane. The wines reflect the very cool climate. Limited Victorian retail distribution.

Mount Beckworth Pinot Noir

1999 Medium to full red-tawny; a strange mix of ripe prune, mint and plum on the bouquet comes together better on the palate with quite intense and long plummy fruit. Nonetheless, not up to previous vintages.
rating: 84

best drinking Now **best vintages** '96, '98 **drink with** Venison ragout • $18

mount broke wines NR

Adams Peak Road, Broke, NSW 2330 **region** Lower Hunter Valley
phone (02) 6579 1313 **fax** (02) 6579 1313 **open** Weekends and public holidays 10–4
winemaker Contract **production** 520 **est.** 1997
product range ($17–23 CD) River Bank Verdelho, River Bank Shiraz, Black Pine Ridge Merlot.
summary Phil and Jo McNamara began planting the 9-hectare vineyard to shiraz, merlot, verdelho, barbera, semillon and cabernet sauvignon in 1997 on the west side of Woollamai Brook. It is early days, but they have already established a wine club and have opened The Cow Cafe, with wine-tasting and wine-function capacity.

Mount Broke Wines River Bank Shiraz

1999 Medium to full red-purple; ultra-ripe plummy, shoe leather, licorice aromas flow straight through to an equally ripe and luscious palate showing masses of plummy fruit, soft tannins and oak almost inevitably in the background. A cool 14.8° alcohol, but actually does carry the alcohol reasonably well. **rating:** 88

best drinking 2004–2010 **best vintages** '99 **drink with** Barbecued rump • $23

mount charlie winery NR

228 Mount Charlie Road, Riddells Creek, Vic 3431 **region** Macedon Ranges
phone (03) 5428 6946 **fax** (03) 5428 6946 **open** Weekends by appointment
winemaker Trefor Morgan **production** 400 **est.** 1991
product range ($20 CD) Sauvignon Blanc, Chardonnay, Red (Cabernet Shiraz Merlot blend).
summary Mount Charlie's wines are sold principally through mail order and selected restaurants. A futures programme encourages mailing list sales with a discount of over 25 per cent on the ultimate release price. Owner/winemaker Trefor Morgan is perhaps better known as Professor of Physiology at Melbourne University.

Mount Charlie Sauvignon Blanc

2000 Light green-yellow; the clean, brisk, minerally bouquet is replicated on the fresh and lively palate; no fault of any description, but not a great deal of varietal fruit character either. **rating:** 83

best drinking Now **best vintages** NA **drink with** Light seafood • $20

mount cotton estate

850–938 Mount Cotton Road, Mount Cotton, Qld 4165 **region** Queensland Coastal
phone (07) 3206 2999 **fax** (07) 3206 0900 **open** 7 days 10–5
winemaker Adam Chapman **production** NA **est.** 1998
product range ($10–25 CD) Moreton Bay Harvest White, Chardonnay, Chardonnay Semillon Sauvignon Blanc, Stradbroke Semillon Sauvignon Blanc, Stradbroke Chardonnay, Reserve Chardonnay, Stradbroke Pinot Chardonnay, Reserve Pinot Chardonnay, Stradbroke Shiraz, Grenache Shiraz, Reserve Shiraz, Stradbroke Teewah, Moreton Bay Cabernet Sauvignon.
summary This is an unambiguously ambitious venture, with the professed aim of creating Queensland's premier winery. The Morris family (founders of Sirromet Wines, which owns Mount Cotton Estate) had a leading architect design the striking state-of-the-art winery which has a 75,000-case production capacity; the State's foremost viticultural consultant plant the three major vineyards which total 100 hectares; and Adam Chapman, the most skilled winemaker practising in Queensland, make the wine. It has a 200-seat restaurant and a wine club offering all sorts of benefits to its members, and is firmly aimed at the domestic and international tourist market, taking advantage of its situation halfway between Brisbane and the Gold Coast. The intention is to move to a predominantly estate-based operation as quickly as the vineyards (planted to 14 varieties) come into production. Both the quality of the first releases and their modest pricing bodes well for the future.

Mount Cotton Estate Stradbroke Chardonnay

YYYY **2000** Medium yellow-green; the bouquet is quite complex and stylish, with tangy fruit and well-integrated oak. The palate is on the light side (young vines, no doubt) but has pleasant melon fruit, and all in all shows clever winemaking with such a delicate base. **rating:** 85

best drinking Now–2003 **best vintages** NA **drink with** Fillet of bream • $16

Mount Cotton Estate Stradbroke Teewah

YYYY **2000** Bright red-purple; fresh, clean, red berry aromas lead into a sweet, fresh red berry palate with minimal tannins and subtle oak. Very clever winemaking. **rating:** 86

best drinking Now–2004 **best vintages** NA **drink with** Duck neck sausage • $18

mount duneed 

Feehan's Road, Mount Duneed, Vic 3216 **region** Geelong

phone (03) 5264 1281 **fax** (03) 5264 1281 **open** Public holidays and weekends 11–5 or by appointment

winemaker Ken Campbell, John Darling **production** 1000 **est.** 1970

product range ($10–18 CD) Semillon, Sauvignon Blanc, Riesling, Botrytis Semillon, Malbec, Cabernet Malbec, Cabernet Sauvignon.

summary Rather idiosyncratic wines are the order of the day, some of which can develop surprisingly well in bottle; the Botrytis Noble Rot Semillon has, from time to time, been of very high quality. A significant part of the production from the 7.5 hectares of vineyards is sold to others.

mount eliza estate NR

Cnr Sunnyside Road and Nepean Highway, Mount Eliza, Vic 3930 **region** Mornington Peninsula

phone (03) 9787 0663 **fax** (03) 9781 2106 **open** 7 days 11–5

winemaker Scott Ireland (Contract) **production** 1500 **est.** 1997

product range ($16–19 CD) Riesling, Sauvignon Blanc, Pinot Noir, Shiraz.

summary Robert and Jenny Thurley planted the 15-hectare vineyard at Mount Eliza Estate in 1997; the varieties are riesling, chardonnay, sauvignon blanc, shiraz, pinot noir and cabernet sauvignon. Son James, presently studying viticulture, has worked at the vineyard since day one under the direction of viticulturist Graeme Harrip, making the business a family affair. The cellar door, which has great views across Port Phillip Bay to the Melbourne city skyline, was opened in November 2000. The contract winemaker is Scott Ireland, of Provenance, who has had many years' experience in making wines from the Port Phillip Zone.

mount eyre vineyard 

1325 Broke Road, Broke, NSW 2330 **region** Lower Hunter Valley

phone 0427 494 528 **fax** (02) 6842 3330 **open** By appointment

winemaker Stephen Hagan (Contract) **production** 9000 **est.** 1996

product range ($14–35 CD) Released under three labels: Mount Eyre Semillon, Semillon Chardonnay, Unwooded Chardonnay; Three Ponds Semillon and Chardonnay, Shiraz; and Neptune (sparkling Semillon).

summary Dr Aniello Inannuzzi's 24-hectare estate at Broke is planted to semillon, chardonnay, shiraz, cabernet franc and cabernet sauvignon, the wines being contract-made off site.

Mount Eyre Vineyard Semillon

YYYY **2000** Light green-yellow; the bouquet is quite complex, with strong herb overtones to the mineral base. The palate is clean and crisp, but does seem to dip somewhat on the back palate. **rating:** 85

best drinking 2003–2008 **best vintages** NA **drink with** Seafood consomme • $14

Mount Eyre Vineyard Three Ponds Semillon

YYYY **2000** Very pale straw-green; a clean, crisp, very youthful and minerally bouquet is followed by a restrained, tight and long palate, with little more than mineral showing at this juncture. Rating wines such as this comes down to an article of faith. **rating:** 88

best drinking 2004–2010 **best vintages** NA **drink with** Leave it in the cellar • $20

Mount Eyre Vineyard Unwooded Chardonnay

YYYY **2000** Light to medium yellow-green; the lees complexity is clearly evident on the bouquet and palate, as are some minerally notes on the bouquet; the palate has above-average structure and grip, with attractive citrus/grapefruit flavours and above-average length for unwooded Chardonnay. **rating:** 88

best drinking Now–2003 **best vintages** '00 **drink with** Pan-fried whiting • $18

Mount Eyre Vineyard Three Ponds Shiraz

YYYY **2000** Medium to full purple-red; youthful black cherry and blackberry aromas are the leaders, with some oak in the background. An attractive young Shiraz, with nice cherry/berry fruit flavours and soft tannins. **rating:** 86

best drinking 2004–2009 **best vintages** NA **drink with** Barbecued porterhouse • $35

mountford NR

Bamess Road, West Pemberton, WA 6260 **region** Pemberton
phone (08) 9776 1345 **fax** (08) 9776 1345 **open** 7 days 10–4
winemaker Andrew Mountford, Saxon Mountford **production** 3000 **est.** 1987
product range ($16.50–28.50 R) Sauvignon Blanc, Chardonnay, Blanc de Noir, Pinot Noir, Merlot Cabernet Sauvignon.
summary English-born and trained Andrew Mountford and wife Sue migrated to Australia in 1983, first endeavouring to set up a winery at Mudgee and thereafter moving to Pemberton with far greater success. Their strikingly packaged wines (complete with beeswax and paper seals) have been well received in eastern Australian markets, being produced from 6 hectares of permanently netted, dry-grown vineyards. Exports to the UK.

mount gisborne wines NR

83 Waterson Road, Gisborne, Vic 3437 **region** Macedon Ranges
phone (03) 5428 2834 **fax** (03) 5428 2834 **open** By appointment
winemaker Stuart Anderson **production** 1200 **est.** 1986
product range ($25–40 CD) Chardonnay, Pinot Noir, Pinot Noir Limited Release.
summary Mount Gisborne Wines is very much a weekend and holiday occupation for proprietor David Ell, who makes the wines from the 7-hectare vineyard under the watchful and skilled eye of industry veteran Stuart Anderson, now living in semi-retirement high in the Macedon Hills.

mount horrocks ★★★★

The Old Railway Station, Curling Street, Auburn, SA 5451 **region** Clare Valley
phone (08) 8849 2243 **fax** (08) 8849 2265 **open** Weekends and public holidays 10–5
winemaker Stephanie Toole **production** 4500 **est.** 1982
product range ($23–36 R) Watervale Riesling, Semillon, Chardonnay, Cordon Cut Riesling, Cabernet Merlot, Shiraz.
summary Mount Horrocks has well and truly established its own identity in recent years, aided by positive marketing and, equally importantly, wine quality which has resulted in both show success and critical acclaim. Exports to New Zealand, the UK, the US, Belgium, Germany, Switzerland and Japan. Lunches available weekends.

Mount Horrocks Semillon

YYYYY **1999** Bright green-yellow; the bouquet is complex, with grassy and mineral notes set off against riper characters and a touch of honey ex the oak. The palate is rich and full, the barrel-ferment component adding layers to the structure and by no means dominating the flavour. **rating:** 90

best drinking Now–2006 **best vintages** '97, '99 **drink with** Pan-fried fish • $24

Mount Horrocks Cordon Cut Riesling

YYYYY **2000** Golden-green; rich, honey/honeycomb/lime aromas lead into a remarkably rich and viscous palate with flavours in the same spectrum, balanced by good acidity. **rating:** 90

best drinking Now–2005 **best vintages** '00 **drink with** Pavlova • $29.95

Mount Horrocks Shiraz

🍷🍷🍷🍷 **1998** Medium to full red-purple; the bouquet abounds with rich, ripe black cherry fruit and flashes of vanilla oak. The palate follows logically: full, luscious and ripe with nice, soft tannins. As generous as they come.

rating: 89

best drinking 2002–2008 **best vintages** '98 **drink with** Steak and kidney pie • $36

Mount Horrocks Cabernet Merlot

🍷🍷🍷 **1998** Medium red-purple; the bouquet has those slightly leafy/savoury aromas that seem endemic in Australian Cabernet Merlot blends. The flavours are sweeter, with a mix of berry and mint, followed by what I can only describe as milky tannins on the finish.

rating: 84

best drinking 2002–2007 **best vintages** NA **drink with** Ragout of veal • $33.95

mount ida ★★★★

Northern Highway, Heathcote, Vic 3253 **region** Heathcote
phone NA **open** Not
winemaker Matt Steel **production** NFP **est.** 1978
product range ($35 R) Shiraz.
summary Established by the famous artist Leonard French and Dr James Munro but purchased by Tisdall after the 1987 bushfires and thereafter by Beringer Blass when it acquired Tisdall. Up to the time of the fires, wonderfully smooth, rich red wines with almost voluptuous sweet, minty fruit were the hallmark. After a brief period during which the name was used as a simple brand (with various wines released), has returned to a single estate-grown wine.

Mount Ida Shiraz

🍷🍷🍷🍷🍷 **1998** Dense red-purple; the promise of the concentrated, dark chocolate/blackberry/cherry-filled bouquet is confirmed by the luscious palate, replete with beautifully concentrated fruit, fine tannins, subtle oak and good acidity. You can't ask for much more.

rating: 94

best drinking 2003–2013 **best vintages** '98 **drink with** Australian parmesan • $35

mountilford NR

Mount Vincent Road, Ilford, NSW 2850 **region** Mudgee
phone (02) 6358 8544 **fax** (02) 6358 8544 **open** 7 days 10–4
winemaker Don Cumming **production** NFP **est.** 1985
product range ($11–22 CD) Riesling, Chardonnay, Highland White, Windamere, Sylvaner, Pinot Shiraz, Cabernet Shiraz, Jubilation Cabernet Shiraz, Sir Alexander Port, Lady Alex.
summary Surprisingly large cellar-door operation which has grown significantly over the past few years. I have not, however, had the opportunity of tasting the wines.

mount langi ghiran vineyards ★★★★★

Warrak Road, Buangor, Vic 3375 **region** Grampians
phone (03) 5354 3207 **fax** (03) 5354 3277 **open** Mon–Fri 9–5, weekends 12–5
winemaker Trevor Mast, Andrew McLoughney **production** 35 000 **est.** 1969
product range ($12–52 ML) Riesling, Pinot Gris, Chardonnay, Joanna Cabernet Sauvignon; under Langi label, Shiraz and Cabernet Merlot.
summary A maker of outstanding cool-climate peppery Shiraz crammed with flavour and vinosity, and very good Cabernet Sauvignon. The Shiraz points the way for cool-climate examples of the variety, for weight, texture and fruit richness all accompany the vibrant pepper-spice aroma and flavour. Now partly owned by Trevor Mast, and partly by German wine entrepreneur Riquet Hess; the most tangible sign of the partnership has been the erection of a totally new, state-of-the-art winery, not to mention the expansion of the estate vineyards to over 70 hectares and the establishment of an export network throughout the US, the UK, Asia, Europe, New Zealand and Canada.

Mount Langi Ghiran Langi Riesling

🍷🍷🍷🍷 **2000** Light straw-green; the bouquet is clean, not particularly aromatic, with subdued mineral and apple aromas. The palate has plenty of structural strength, firm and dry, with continuation of the restrained fruit character of the bouquet. Likely to be durable.

rating: 86

best drinking 2002–2007 **best vintages** NA **drink with** Steamed asparagus • $17

Mount Langi Ghiran Pinot Gris

🍷🍷🍷🍷 **2000** Medium yellow-green; the bouquet is clean and floral, with some pear and apple along with more minerally characters. The palate tracks the bouquet, and is well balanced, but I am once again reminded of the analogy of painting a picture with white paint. **rating:** 84

best drinking Now–2005 **best vintages** NA **drink with** Antipasto • $22

Langi Shiraz

🍷🍷🍷🍷🍷 **1999** Medium to full red-purple; has an archetypal Langi bouquet, offering a mix of spice, black cherry, licorice and leather. The palate has lively, sweet fruit woven through the more spicy characters of the bouquet, but slightly sharp acidity on the finish needs to integrate. **rating:** 93

🍷🍷🍷🍷🍷 **1998** There is a special conjunction of climate and soil (the French call it terroir) that gives this wine such special character. Lively berry/spice/earth/black cherry aromas introduce a soft, sweet and supple palate with cherry, berry, plum and spice and an elegant end palate and finish. **rating:** 95

best drinking 2004–2009 **best vintages** '86, '88, '90, '92, '93, '94, '96, '97, '98, '99 **drink with** Game • $52

Langi Cabernet Merlot

🍷🍷🍷🍷🍷 **1998** Medium to full red-purple; a solid, smooth bouquet with dark berry and chocolate supported by gently sweet oak, characters repeated on the palate which has plenty of fruit weight and sweetness offset by fine tannins and subtle oak. Top vintage. **rating:** 90

best drinking 2003–2010 **best vintages** '97, '98 **drink with** Rare fillet of beef • $38

mount lofty ranges vineyard ★★★★

Harris Road, Lenswood, SA 5240 **region** Adelaide Hills
phone (08) 8389 8339 **fax** (08) 8389 8349 **open** Weekends 11–5
winemaker Nepenthe (Contract) **production** 800 **est.** 1992
product range ($14–22 CD) Five Vines Riesling, Chardonnay, Old Pump Shed Pinot Noir.
summary Mount Lofty Ranges is owned by Alan Herath and Jan Reed, who have been involved from the outset in planting, training and nurturing the 4.5-hectare vineyard. Both have professional careers but are intending to become full-time vignerons in the not-too-distant future. Skilled winemaking by Peter Leske at Nepenthe has already brought rewards and recognition to the vineyard.

Mount Lofty Five Vines Riesling

🍷🍷🍷🍷 **2000** Pale straw-green; the bouquet has very pronounced dried-herb aromas, together with splashes of spice, talc and slate; the medium-weight palate follows the bouquet, with good acidity on the finish. **rating:** 89

best drinking 2003–2008 **best vintages** '99 **drink with** Vegetable terrine • $14

Mount Lofty Old Pump Shed Pinot Noir

🍷🍷🍷🍷 **1999** Medium red-purple; quite solid plum and briar aromas lead into a ripe, powerful plummy palate, which does have positive varietal character and length from good acidity; subtle oak. **rating:** 87

best drinking Now–2006 **best vintages** '98 **drink with** Braised ox cheek • $20

mount macedon NR

Bawden Road, Mount Macedon, Vic 3441 **region** Macedon Ranges
phone (03) 5427 2735 **fax** (03) 5427 1071 **open** 7 days 10–5
winemaker Ian Deacon **production** 4500 **est.** 1989
product range ($16–25 CD) Unwooded Chardonnay, Chardonnay, Winemaker's Reserve Chardonnay, Pinot Noir Saignee Rosé, Pinot Noir, Shiraz, Cabernet Merlot.
summary Don and Pam Ludbey have established a substantial operation at Mount Macedon drawing upon two separate vineyards, Mount Macedon and Hay Hill. In all, they have a little over 11 hectares under vine. Ian Deacon has made wine in the Yarra Valley and surrounding cool regions for many years; his experience shows through in the wines which, while not particularly rich or full, have a touch of elegance.

mount majura wines ★★★★

RMB 314 Majura Road, Majura, ACT 2609 **region** Canberra District
phone 0403 355 682 **fax** (02) 6262 4288 **open** Not
winemaker Dr Frank van de Loo, Dr Roger Harris (Consultant) **production** 700 **est.** 1988

product range ($20–25 R) Chardonnay, Pinot Noir, Cabernet Franc Merlot.

summary The first vines were planted in 1988 by Dinny Killen on her family property on a site that had been especially recommended by Dr Edgar Riek; its attractions were red soil of volcanic origin over limestone, the reasonably steep east and northeast slopes providing an element of frost protection. The 1-hectare vineyard was planted to pinot noir, chardonnay and merlot in equal quantities; the pinot noir grapes were sold to Lark Hill and used in their award-winning Pinot Noir, while the chardonnay and merlot were made for Mount Majura by Lark Hill, both wines enjoying show success. In 1999 a private syndicate purchased the property and retained Roger Harris of Brindabella Hills as winemaker and consultant. The vineyard has been expanded to 8.4 hectares, but the 1999 vintage was decimated due to frost; the tiny quantities made in non-commercial volumes were, however, quite excellent. Tank samples of the 2000 Chardonnay and Pinot Noir fully justify the winery's four-star rating.

mount mary ★★★★★

Coldstream West Road, Lilydale, Vic 3140 **region** Yarra Valley

phone (03) 9739 1761 **fax** (03) 9739 0137 **open** Not

winemaker Dr John Middleton, Mac Forbes **production** 3000 **est.** 1971

product range ($32–60 ML) Chardonnay, Triolet (Sauvignon Blanc, Semillon, Muscadelle), Pinot Noir, Cabernets Quintet (Bordeaux-blend).

summary Superbly refined, elegant and intense Cabernets and usually outstanding and long-lived Pinot Noirs fully justify Mount Mary's exalted reputation. The Triolet blend is very good, more recent vintages of Chardonnay likewise. Limited quantities of the wines are sold through the wholesale/retail distribution system in Victoria, New South Wales, Queensland and South Australia.

Mount Mary Chardonnay

🍷🍷🍷🍷🍷 **1999** Bright, light green-yellow; a clean, reserved bouquet with a minerally underlay to the melon fruit; the oak is barely perceptible. The palate is fresh, clean and tight; elegant but reserved and understated, still waiting to flower.

rating: 91

best drinking 2004–2009 **best vintages** NA **drink with** Lobster • NA

Mount Mary Cabernets Quintet

🍷🍷🍷🍷🍷 **1998** Medium purple-red; the bouquet offers a mix of ripe cassis, blackberry and raspberry aromas with subtle but evident oak. The long, even palate has near-identical cassis and blackberry flavours, supported by fine, lingering tannins and subtle oak. Reflects the 1998 vintage; by the standards of Mount Mary, quite full.

rating: 94

best drinking 2003–2013 **best vintages** '78, '79, '84, '88, '90, '91, '94, '98 **drink with** Boned loin of lamb • NA

mount panorama winery NR

117 Mountain Straight, Mount Panorama, Bathurst, NSW 2795 **region** Southern New South Wales Zone

phone (02) 6331 5368 **fax** (02) 6331 5368 **open** By appointment

winemaker Bill Stuart, Deborah Stuart **production** 600 **est.** 1991

product range ($11.50–20 CD) Forrest Elbow Riesling, Chase Chardonnay, Hell Corner Shiraz, The Esses Cabernet Sauvignon, The Cutting (Cabernet blend), Thunder Mountain Port.

summary For all the obvious reasons, Mount Panorama Winery makes full use of its setting on Mountain Straight after the 'Hell Corner' on the inside of the famous motor-racing circuit. Bill and Deborah Stuart are wholly responsible for the production of the wine, from picking and using the hand-operated basket press through to bottling, labelling, etc. They are gradually extending both the size and scope of the cellar-door facilities to take advantage of the tourist opportunities of the site.

mount prior vineyard ★★★

Gooramadda Road, Rutherglen, Vic 3685 **region** Rutherglen

phone (02) 6026 5591 **fax** (02) 6026 5590 **open** 7 days 9–5

winemaker Tony Lacy **production** 15 000 **est.** 1860

product range ($11–25 CD) Chardonnay, Chenin Blanc, Classic Ibis White, Semillon Chardonnay, Late Picked Riesling, Noble Gold, Classic Ibis Dry Red, Cabernet Merlot, Shiraz, Durif, Sparkling Shiraz Durif, Brut Cuvée, Port, Muscat, Tokay.

summary A full-scale tourist facility, with yet more in the pipeline: full accommodation packages at the historic Mount Prior House; a restaurant operating weekends under the direction of Trish Hennessy, with four consecutive

Age Good Food Guide awards to its credit; picnic and barbecue facilities; and a California-style gift shop. The wines are basically sold through cellar door and an active mailing list. The already substantial 40 hectares of vineyards were expanded by a further 5 hectares of durif planted in 1998, a mark both of the success of Mount Prior and of the interest in Durif.

Mount Prior Sparkling Shiraz Durif

YYYY **NV** Dense red-purple; a massive berry and chocolate bouquet is followed by an equally huge chocolate, prune and plum palate, with relatively low gas levels. Totally idiosyncratic, but works well. **rating:** 89

best drinking 2003–2010 **best vintages** NA **drink with** Borscht • NA

Mount Prior Shiraz

YYYY **1999** Medium red-purple; the bouquet is solid, initially showing earthy/briary notes, and then some plum. It is the sweet, spicy/plummy fruit that comes to the fore on the palate; good control of extract and tannins. **rating:** 86

best drinking 2004–2009 **best vintages** NA **drink with** Barbecued beef • NA

mount tamborine winery NR

32 Hartley Road, Mount Tamborine, Qld 4272 **region** Queensland Zone
phone (07) 5545 3981 **fax** (07) 5545 3311 **open** 7 days 10–4
winemaker Brett Hetherington **production** 22 000 **est.** 1993
product range ($9.50–32 ML) Sauvignon Blanc Chardonnay, Semillon, Sauvignon Blanc Semillon, Cedar Ridge Chardonnay, Merlot Emily Cuvée de Rouge, Cedar Ridge Blanc de Blanc, Flaxton Nouveau Shiraz, Tehembrin Merlot, Shiraz Cabernet Merlot, Mountain Muscat, Bush Turkey (Port).
summary Mount Tamborine Winery draws upon 3 hectares of estate plantings adjacent to the winery, 30 hectares in Stanthorpe, and also purchases wine from the King Valley, Cowra and the Riverland to produce a wide range of wine styles. The Chardonnay and Merlot have both had success in Queensland wine shows and competitions, and the wines are sold both locally and exported to Southeast Asia.

mount trio vineyard ★★★☆

Cnr Castle Rock and Porongurup Roads, Porongurup WA 6324 **region** Great Southern
phone (08) 9853 1136 **fax** (08) 9853 1120 **open** By appointment
winemaker Gavin Berry **production** 3000 **est.** 1989
product range ($14–19 R) Sauvignon Blanc, Chardonnay, Pinot Noir, Cabernet Merlot.
summary Mount Trio was established by Gavin Berry and Gill Graham shortly after they moved to the Mount Barker district in late 1988. Gavin Berry was assistant winemaker to John Wade, and Gill Graham managed the cellar-door sales. Gavin is now senior winemaker and managing director of Plantagenet, and Gill is the mother of two young children. In the meantime they have slowly built up the Mount Trio business, based in part upon estate plantings of 2 hectares of pinot noir and 0.5 hectare of chardonnay and in part on purchased grapes. An additional 6 hectares was planted in the spring of 1999, and plans are to ultimately increase production to around 5000 cases.

mount view estate

Mount View Road, Mount View, NSW 2325 **region** Lower Hunter Valley
phone (02) 4990 3307 **fax** (02) 4991 1289 **open** Mon–Fri 10–4, weekends, holidays 10–5
winemaker Andrew Thomas **production** 3500 **est.** 1971
product range ($14–24 CD) Reserve Semillon, Verdelho, Reserve Verdelho, Chardonnay Verdelho Sauvignon Blanc, Kester Chardonnay, Reserve Chardonnay, Pinot Noir, Kester Shiraz, Reserve Shiraz, Merlot, Cabernet Sauvignon, Shiraz Port, Liqueur Verdelho, Trophy Muscat.
summary The Tulloch family no longer owns nor has any interest in Mount View Estate following its sudden sale in 2000, but winemaking has passed to the capable hands of former Tyrrell's winemaker Andrew Thomas.

Mount View Estate Reserve Chardonnay

YYYY **2000** Light green-yellow; light, fresh and crisp citrus/melon fruit aromas are followed by a nicely textured palate with good weight, the sweetness coming mainly from mid-palate fruit. It seems that rather more old than new French oak was used. **rating:** 87

best drinking Now–2004 **best vintages** NA **drink with** Poached chicken • $18

Mount View Estate Verdelho

🍷🍷🍷🍷 **2000** Light green-yellow; potent, high-toned lemon/pastille/frangipani aromas flow into a palate with well-above-average flavour, the sweetness coming from both high alcohol and, it appears, some residual sugar. A cellar-door special if ever there was one. **rating:** 84

best drinking Now **best vintages** '98 **drink with** Takeaway • $14

mountview wines ★★★

Mount Stirling Road, Glen Aplin, Qld 4381 **region** Granite Belt

phone (07) 4683 4316 **fax** (07) 4683 4111 **open** Fri–Mon 9.30–4.30, 7 days school and public holidays

winemaker Phillipa Hambleton **production** 1250 **est.** 1990

product range ($10–18 CD) Chardonnay Semillon Sauvignon Blanc, First Pick (Chardonnay blend), Emu Swamp White, Chardonnay Royal (sparkling), Bianco Bubbles (sparkling), Blanc de Blancs, Sparkling Perry, Short Flat White (dessert), Cerise (light red), Short Flat Red (light red), Shiraz, Merlot, Cabernet Merlot, Shiraz Royal (sparkling).

summary Mountview Wines has changed hands and is now owned by Pauline Stewart. I have no reason to suppose the quality of the Shiraz (in particular) has diminished.

mount vincent mead NR

Common Road, Mudgee, NSW 2850 **region** Mudgee

phone (02) 6372 3184 **fax** (02) 6372 3184 **open** Mon–Sat 10–5, Sun 10–4

winemaker Jane Nevell **production** 2000 **est.** 1972

product range ($12–32 CD) Honey Nectar, Napunya Dry Mead, Napunya Medium Sweet, Stringy Bark Medium Sweet, Napunya Sweet Metheglin, Yellow Box Liqueur Mead and Red Hot Devil (spiced). Each of these is vintage-dated.

summary Jane Nevell has ceased making table wine, instead concentrating on the meads, which can be absolutely outstanding, dramatically reflecting the impact of the different plants from which the bees have collected their nectar. Self-contained accommodation is available.

mount william winery NR

Mount William Road, Tantaraboo, Vic 3764 **region** Macedon Ranges

phone (03) 5429 1595 **fax** (03) 5429 1998 **open** 7 days 11–5

winemaker Murray Cousins, John Ellis (Hanging Rock) **production** 2000 **est.** 1987

product range ($15–28 CD) Bedbur's Riesling, Chardonnay, Macedon Sparkling Chardonnay, Pinot Noir, Cabernets, Blanc de Blanc, Louis Clare Sparkling Red.

summary Adrienne and Murray Cousins established 7 hectares of vineyards between 1987 and 1999, planted to pinot noir, cabernet franc, merlot, semillon and chardonnay. The wines are made under contract (Hanging Rock) and are sold through a stone tasting-room/cellar-door facility and also through a number of fine-wine retailers around Melbourne.

Mount William Bedbur's Riesling

🍷🍷🍷🍷 **2000** Light green-yellow; the bouquet is clean and crisp, opening with strong herbal aromas, then moving to mineral; much of the same occurs on the fresh, direct palate, which could do with a touch more mid-palate fruit, although time in bottle may help. **rating:** 84

best drinking Now–2007 **best vintages** NA **drink with** Fresh asparagus • $15

Mount William Chardonnay

🍷🍷🍷🍷 **1998** Light to medium yellow-green; gentle nectarine, together with touches of passionfruit and citrus on the bouquet, are followed by a palate with citrussy/grapefruit flavours, a hint of cashew/butterscotch, and overall giving the impression it will age well. **rating:** 84

best drinking Now–2006 **best vintages** NA **drink with** Delicate seafood • $20

mudgee wines NR

Henry Lawson Drive, Mudgee, NSW 2850 **region** Mudgee

phone (02) 6372 2258 **open** Thur–Mon 10–5, holidays 7 days

winemaker Jennifer Meek **production** 1000 **est.** 1963

product range ($9–15 CD) Chardonnay, Gewurztraminer, Crouchen, Riesling, Rosé, Shiraz, Pinot Noir, Cabernet Sauvignon.

summary All of the wines are naturally fermented with wild yeasts and made without the addition of any chemicals or substances, including sulphur dioxide; a very demanding route, particularly with white wines. For some consumers, any shortcoming in quality will be quite acceptable.

mulyan ★★★☆

North Logan Road, Cowra, NSW 2794 **region** Cowra
phone (02) 6342 1289 **fax** (02) 6341 1015 **open** Sat–Mon and public holidays 10–5 or by appointment
winemaker Simon Gilbert (Contract) **production** 3200 **est.** 1994
product range ($14–16 R) Chardonnay, Bushrangers Bounty Chardonnay, Shiraz, Bushrangers Bounty Shiraz.
summary Mulyan is a 1350-hectare grazing property purchased by the Fagan family in 1886 from Dr William Redfern, a leading nineteenth-century figure in Australian history. The current-generation owners Peter and Jenni Fagan began the establishment of 45 hectares of shiraz in 1994, and intend increasing the vineyard area to 100 hectares. Presently there are 28.8 hectares of shiraz and 14.8 hectares of chardonnay, with an experimental plot of sangiovese. The label features a statue of the Roman God Mercury which has stood in the Mulyan homestead garden since being brought back from Italy in 1912 by Peter Fagan's grandmother. The wines have limited Sydney retail distribution and are also available through the Quarry Cellars in Cowra.

Mulyan Cowra Chardonnay

1998 Medium yellow-green; the bouquet is solid, with yellow peach fruit and subtle oak. There is a quite rich opening and mid-palate fruit weight and flavour, but the wine then finishes rather short. **rating:** 84
best drinking Now **best vintages** NA **drink with** Creamy pasta • $15.99

munari wines ★★★★

1129 Northern Highway, Heathcote, Vic 3523 **region** Bendigo
phone (03) 5433 3366 **fax** (03) 5433 3095 **open** 7 days 10–5
winemaker Adrian Munari, Deborah Munari **production** 1000 **est.** 1993
product range ($22–25 CD) Ladys Creek Vineyard Chardonnay, Shiraz, Schoolhouse Red, Reserve Merlot, Reserve Malbec.
summary Adrian and Deborah Munari made a singularly impressive entry into the winemaking scene, with both their initial vintages winning an impressive array of show medals, and have carried on in similar vein since then. With a little over 6.8 hectares of estate vines, production will be limited, but the wines are well worth seeking out.

Munari Ladys Creek Vineyard Chardonnay

2000 Medium yellow-green; toasty, smoky barrel-ferment aromas join stonefruit on the bouquet, but on the palate the fruit comes into balance, with a mix of stonefruit and grapefruit; good structure and length. **rating:** 89
best drinking Now–2004 **best vintages** '98 **drink with** Barbecued yabbies • NA

Munari Shiraz

1999 Full red-purple; there is lots of toasty/charry oak alongside the dark berry fruit on the bouquet; dark, savoury berry fruit is supported by powerful but tight (and not coarse) tannins which provide a lingering finish to the palate. The suggestion on the back label that it is appropriate for short-term cellaring only is the reverse of the usual hype. **rating:** 90
best drinking 2004–2009 **best vintages** '99 **drink with** Barbecued lamb • NA

mundrakoona estate NR

Sir Charles Moses Lane, Old Hume Highway, Woodlands, via Mittagong, NSW 2575 **region** Southern New South Wales Zone
phone (02) 4872 1311 **fax** (02) 4872 1322 **open** Weekends and public holidays 9–6
winemaker Anton Balog **production** 1800 **est.** 1997
product range ($18–32 CD) Riesling, Sauvignon Blanc, Reserve Chardonnay, Nouveau Rouge, Reserve Cabernet Sauvignon Merlot.
summary During 1998 and 1999 Anton Balog progressively planted 3.2 hectares of pinot noir, sauvignon blanc and tempranillo at an altitude of 680 metres. He is using wild yeast ferments, hand-plunging and other 'natural' winemaking techniques with the aim of producing Burgundian-style Pinot and Chardonnay and Bordeaux-style Sauvignon Blanc and Cabernet Sauvignon. For the foreseeable future, estate production will be supplemented by grapes grown from local Southern Highlands vineyards.

Mundrakoona Estate Reserve Cabernet Sauvignon Merlot
YYYY 1999 Medium to full red-purple; there is solid berry fruit on the bouquet together with touches of earth and vanilla. The palate, likewise, shows ripe, sweet berry fruit with good depth. Slightly dusty oak is yet to integrate, and the wine is a little unformed. Time may see the disparate parts come together. **rating:** 84

best drinking 2004–2009 **best vintages** '99 **drink with** Roast venison • $32

murdoch hill NR

Mappinga Road, Woodside, SA 5244 **region** Adelaide Hills
phone (08) 8389 7081 **fax** (08) 8389 7991 **open** By appointment
winemaker Brian Light (Contract) **production** 1500 **est.** 1998
product range ($19.95–24.95 R) Sauvignon Blanc, Cabernet Sauvignon.
summary A little over 21 hectares of vines have been established on the undulating, gum-studded countryside of the Erinka property, owned by the Downer family, 4 kilometres east of Oakbank. In descending order of importance the varieties established are sauvignon blanc, shiraz, cabernet sauvignon and chardonnay. The wines are distributed by Australian Prestige Wines in Melbourne and Sydney.

murray robson wines NR

'Bellona', Old North Road, Rothbury, NSW 2335 **region** Lower Hunter Valley
phone (02) 4938 3577 **fax** (02) 4938 3577 **open** 7 days 9–5
winemaker Murray Robson **production** 10 000 **est.** 1970
product range ($18–24 CD) Traminer, Semillon, Chardonnay, Shiraz, Merlot Cabernet, Cabernet Sauvignon.
summary Like a phoenix from the ashes, Murray Robson Wines rose once again when it reopened in a new location in February 1997. Four hectares of estate plantings are supplemented by grapes purchased from other growers in the valley; the initial releases from 1996 were all produced in tiny quantities of 150 cases or less, produced and packaged with the irrepressible flair of Murray Robson and using the same label that appeared back in the early 1970s, each one hand-signed, as ever, by Murray Robson. Exports to the US, the UK and New Zealand.

murrindindi ★★★★

Cummins Lane, Murrindindi, Vic 3717 **region** Central Victorian Mountain Country
phone (03) 5797 8217 **fax** (03) 5797 8422 **open** Not
winemaker Alan Cuthbertson, Hugh Cuthbertson **production** 2000 **est.** 1979
product range ($23 R) Chardonnay, Cabernets Merlot.
summary Situated in an unequivocally cool climate, which means that special care has to be taken with the viticulture to produce ripe fruit flavours. In more recent vintages, Murrindindi has succeeded handsomely in so doing. Limited Sydney and Melbourne distribution through Wine Source.

Murrindindi Chardonnay
YYYY 1998 Medium yellow-green; the moderately intense bouquet shows well-balanced and integrated oak with melon fruit. The melon, cashew and subtle oak flavours of the palate are neatly balanced, but the wine lacks the intensity and persistence of the best vintages. **rating:** 85

best drinking Now–2006 **best vintages** '84, '90, '91, '92, '93, '96, '97 **drink with** Mussels • $23

murrumbateman winery NR

Barton Highway, Murrumbateman, NSW 2582 **region** Canberra District
phone (02) 6227 5584 **open** Thur–Mon 10–5
winemaker Duncan Leslie **production** 1650 **est.** 1972
product range ($12–30 CD) Sauvignon Blanc, Chardonnay, Sally's Sweet White, Rosé, Cabernet Merlot, Cabernet Sauvignon, Mead, Fortifieds and Sparkling.
summary Revived after an ownership change, this winery draws upon 4.5 hectares of vineyards, and also incorporates an à la carte restaurant and function room together with picnic and barbecue areas.

nandroya estate NR

262 Sandfly Road, Margate, Tas 7054 **region** Southern Tasmania
phone (03) 6267 2377 **open** By appointment
winemaker Andrew Hood (Contract) **production** 200 **est.** 1995
product range ($18–25 CD) Sauvignon Blanc, Pinot Noir.
summary John Rees and family have established 0.5 hectare each of sauvignon blanc and pinot noir, the wines being sold through the cellar door and to one or two local restaurants. The Reeses regard this as a holiday and retirement project and modestly wonder whether they deserve inclusion in this kind of work. They certainly do, for wineries of this size are an indispensable part of the Tasmanian fabric.

narkoojee ★★★★

1110 Francis Road, Glengarry, Vic 3854 **region** Gippsland
phone (03) 5192 4257 **fax** (03) 5192 4257 **open** By appointment
winemaker Harry Friend, Axel Friend **production** 1000 **est.** 1981
product range ($12–30 CD) Chardonnay, The Rose, The Athelstan Merlot, Cabernets.
summary Narkoojee Vineyard is within easy reach of the old goldmining town of Walhalla and looks out over the Strzelecki Ranges. The wines are produced from a little over 4 hectares of estate vineyards. Harry Friend was an amateur winemaker of note before turning to commercial winemaking with Narkoojee, his skills showing through with all the wines.

Narkoojee Chardonnay

🍷🍷🍷🍷🍷 **1999** Medium yellow-green; the bouquet shows sophisticated fruit and oak balance and integration, the mark of skilled winemaking. The palate is well balanced with an interplay of melon and cashew, again with the benefit of subtle but synergistic oak. **rating:** 90

best drinking Now–2003 **best vintages** '87, '89, '92, '93, '94, '97, '99 **drink with** Salmon pizza • $22

nashdale wines NR

Borenore Lane, Nashdale, NSW 2800 **region** Orange
phone (02) 6365 2463 **fax** (02) 6361 4495 **open** Weekends 2–6
winemaker Mark Davidson (Contract) **production** 1000 **est.** 1990
product range ($10–25 CD) Riesling, Sauvignon Blanc, Chardonnay, Pinot Noir, Cabernet Sauvignon.
summary Orange solicitor Edward Fardell commenced establishing the 10-hectare Nashdale Vineyard in 1990. At an elevation of 1000 metres, it offers panoramic views of Mount Canobolas and the Lidster Valley, with a restaurant-café open on weekends.

neagles rock vineyards NR

Lots 1 and 2 Main North Road, Clare, SA 5453 **region** Clare Valley
phone (08) 8843 4020 **fax** (08) 8843 4021 **open** Thur–Tues 10–5
winemaker Neil Pike (Contract), Steve Wiblin **production** 4000 **est.** 1997
product range ($15–22.50 CD) Riesling, Semillon, Chardonnay Pinot Noir Cuvée, Sweet Dorothy Botrytis Riesling, Shiraz, Grenache Shiraz, Cabernet Sauvignon, Richard Lincoln Liqueur Tawny Port.
summary Owner-partners Jane Willson and Steve Wiblin have taken the plunge in a major way, simultaneously raising a young family, resuscitating two old vineyards and, for good measure, stripping a dilapidated house to the barest of bones and turning it into an airy, first-rate restaurant-cum-cellar door (which I wholeheartedly recommend from personal experience). They bring 35 years of industry experience to Neagles Rock. Jane Willson held a senior marketing position with Southcorp before heading up Negociants Australia's Sales and Marketing team in a 15-year career that brought her unqualified respect. Steve Wiblin's 20-year career spanned Guinness to Grange, public companies to small ones, marketing to finance. Exports to the US, Belgium, Holland and Luxembourg.

Neagles Rock Riesling

🍷🍷🍷🍷 **1999** Light green-yellow; the spotlessly clean bouquet is starting to show the first signs of bottle development, and offering a mix of lime and toast. The palate flows on logically, with gentle lime flavours in a welcoming medium-weight mode. **rating:** 87

best drinking Now–2005 **best vintages** NA **drink with** Salad niçoise • $18

Neagles Rock Barrel Nurtured Semillon

YYYY **2000** Light to medium green-yellow; sophisticated, smoky barrel-ferment characters intermingle with tangy fruit on the bouquet. The palate continues the clever winemaking indicators, with good fruit and oak balance and integration in a wine that avoids the excessive phenolics of some South Australian oak-influenced Semillon. **rating:** 86

best drinking Now–2003 **best vintages** NA **drink with** Smoked chicken • $15

Neagles Rock Vineyards Sweet Dorothy Botrytis Riesling

YYYYY **1999** Golden-yellow; the bouquet is quite complex, with a tangy citrus and honey mix; the tangy, citrussy palate has a lingering finish bolstered by excellent acidity; you can see the botrytis at work. **rating:** 91

best drinking Now–2004 **best vintages** '99 **drink with** Fruit flan • $15

Neagles Rock Shiraz

YYYY **1999** Medium to full purple-red; bright, clean, firm dark cherry fruit and subtle oak on the bouquet herald a firm, youthful but well-balanced palate, with the guaranteed development of complexity as it ages. **rating:** 87

best drinking 2004–2009 **best vintages** NA **drink with** Patience • $22.50

Neagles Rock Grenache

YYYY **1999** Medium red-purple; mint, earth, blackberry and leather aromas are followed by a ripe but not jammy palate; savoury/earthy plum and blackberry flavours flow through to fine tannins on the finish. **rating:** 86

best drinking Now–2004 **best vintages** NA **drink with** Clare hare • NA

Neagles Rock Cabernet Sauvignon

YYYY **1999** Medium red-purple; the bouquet has savoury/spicy/leathery edges to berry fruit, the palate with a smooth core of sweet berry fruit, then touches of mint and spice. **rating:** 85

best drinking 2003–2008 **best vintages** NA **drink with** Lamb shanks • $22.50

needham estate wines NR

Ingoldby Road, McLaren Flat, SA 5171 **region** McLaren Vale
phone (08) 8383 0301 **fax** (08) 8383 0301 **open** Not
winemaker Contract **production** 2800 **est.** 1997
product range ($17–25 R) Albertus Shiraz, White House Shiraz.
summary Clive Needham has two vineyards; the first, of 4 hectares, is newly planted and will come into full production in 2001. The second has less than 0.5 hectare of 100-year-old shiraz vines, which go to produce the White House Shiraz, with an annual production of only 120 cases.

nepenthe vineyards ★★★★☆

Vickers Road, Lenswood, SA 5240 **region** Adelaide Hills
phone (08) 8431 7588 **fax** (08) 8431 7688 **open** By appointment
winemaker Peter Leske **production** 23 000 **est.** 1994
product range ($18–42 R) Riesling, Sauvignon Blanc, Unwooded Chardonnay, Chardonnay, Pinot Gris, Pinot Noir, Zinfandel, Fugue (Cabernet Merlot).
summary The Tweddell family established 21 hectares of close-planted vineyards at Lenswood between 1994 and 1997, with an exotic array of varieties reflected in the wines. In late 1996 it obtained the second licence to build a winery in the Adelaide Hills, Petaluma being the only other successful applicant back in 1978. A 500-tonne winery has been constructed, with Peter Leske in charge of winemaking. Nepenthe has quickly established itself as one of the most exciting new wineries in Australia. Distribution through most States, and exports to the UK, the US, Switzerland, Japan and Hong Kong.

Nepenthe Vineyards Lenswood Riesling

YYYYY **2000** Light green-yellow; the aromatic bouquet ranges through lime, passionfruit, apple and mineral, the palate lively and expressive, with apple and passionfruit flavours, and a brisk, clean finish. **rating:** 91

best drinking 2004–2010 **best vintages** '98, '99, '00 **drink with** Sashimi • $20

Nepenthe Vineyards Semillon

🍷🍷🍷🍷 **1999** Medium yellow-green; the bouquet is clean and soft, with incipient honey/toast aromas; the palate is quite soft, perhaps starting to go through the transition phase, with some herb and lemon, but also some riper fruit flavours. Shows its 14° alcohol. **rating:** 86

best drinking Now–2003 **best vintages** '97 **drink with** Sautéed veal • $22

Nepenthe Vineyards Pinot Gris

🍷🍷🍷🍷 **2000** Light straw-green; the bouquet is on the light side, but does have some spicy apple varietal character; the fruit weight and flavour on the mid-palate is not convincing, but crisp acidity on the finish does help. **rating:** 85

best drinking Now–2003 **best vintages** NA **drink with** Abalone • $18

Nepenthe Vineyards Chardonnay

🍷🍷🍷🍷 **1999** Medium yellow-green; the bouquet is clean, with tangy melon and nectarine fruit supported by subtle French oak. The palate, likewise, is elegant, with a similar play of melon/nectarine fruit, subtle oak, and a hint of cashew; good balance and length. **rating:** 89

best drinking Now–2005 **best vintages** '99 **drink with** Chinese steamed fish • $25

Nepenthe Vineyards Pinot Noir

🍷🍷🍷🍷🍷 **1999** Medium to full red, with a touch of purple; spice and plum aromas have a solid forest underlay; a very powerful wine in the mouth, still locked in on itself, and should age well, although it trembles on the brink of dry red. **rating:** 90

best drinking 2002–2006 **best vintages** '99 **drink with** Confit of duck • $28

Nepenthe Zinfandel

🍷🍷🍷🍷 **1999** Medium red, with some purple; the fruit aromas of the bouquet are complex, with a mix of mint, stewed cherry and warm spice, amplified by the palate which ranges through warm plum, spice, chocolate and prune. A fruit-driven wine that just carries its alcohol (Californian Zinfandels are typically this high) and hard to rate using a conventional judging approach. **rating:** 88

best drinking Now–2004 **best vintages** NA **drink with** Wild duck • $42

Nepenthe Vineyards The Fugue

🍷🍷🍷🍷🍷 **1998** Bright purple-red; the fragrant, spotlessly clean, fruit-driven bouquet has glorious cassis aromas, the palate likewise. Fine tannins and gentle oak; a true claret style, like a junior Grosset Gaia. **rating:** 94

best drinking Now–2009 **best vintages** '98 **drink with** Kangaroo fillet • $28

newstead winerny NR

Tivey Street, Newstead, Vic 3462 **region** Bendigo
phone (03) 5476 2733 **fax** (03) 5476 2536 **open** Weekends and public holidays 10–5
winemaker Ron Snep, Cliff Stubbs **production** 1500 **est.** 1994
product range ($15–16 CD) Welshman's Reef Semillon, Barrel Fermented Semillon, Unwooded Chardonnay, Cabernet Sauvignon; Burnt Acre Riesling, Shiraz.
summary Newstead Winery is established in the old Newstead Butter Factory, drawing upon two distinct vineyards at Welshman's Reef (near Maldon) and Burnt Acre Vineyard at Marong, west of Bendigo. Vineyard designations are used for each of the wines.

nicholson river ★★★★

Liddells Road, Nicholson, Vic 3882 **region** Gippsland
phone (03) 5156 8241 **fax** (03) 5156 8433 **open** 7 days 10–4 for sales, tastings only during holidays
winemaker Ken Eckersley **production** 2500 **est.** 1978
product range ($19–45 CD) Sauvignon Blanc Semillon, Chardonnay, Montview Chardonnay, Botrytis Semillon, Cuvée (Pinot Noir Chardonnay), Sparkling Red (Pinot Shiraz), Sparkling Chardonnay, Pinot Noir, Montview Pinot Noir, Shiraz Merlot, Merlot, Montview Cabernet Merlot.
summary The fierce commitment to quality in the face of the temperamental Gippsland climate and the frustratingly small production has been handsomely repaid by some stupendous Chardonnays, mostly sold through cellar door; a little is exported to the UK and the US. Ken Eckersley does not refer to his Chardonnays as white wines but as gold wines, and lists them accordingly in his newsletter.

Nicholson River Sauvignon Blanc Semillon

🍷🍷🍷🍷 **2000** Medium yellow-green; the bouquet is rich, with a mix of honey, toast and mead; a typically full-bodied, uncompromisingly dry wine with a slightly bitter finish that needs food in much the same way as Italian red wines do. **rating:** 85

best drinking Now–2004 **best vintages** NA **drink with** Roast pork • $27

Nicholson River Chardonnay

🍷🍷🍷🍷 **1999** Medium to full yellow; strong toasty/cashew barrel-ferment aromas lead into a wine with positively massive frame and texture, the fruit presently hiding under the toasty barrel-ferment oak characters. **rating:** 88

best drinking Now–2005 **best vintages** '86, '87, '92, '94, '97 **drink with** Pheasant with truffles • $45

Nicholson River Pinot Noir

🍷🍷🍷🍷 **1998** Dark, dense red; the bouquet is big, powerful and dry-reddish in style. The palate opens with massive, plummy fruit then moves through to slightly squeaky acid on the finish. Totally idiosyncratic, and rated as a dry red, rather than a Pinot Noir. **rating:** 86

best drinking 2002–2008 **best vintages** NA **drink with** Game • $45

nightingale wines ★★★

1239 Milbrodale Road, Broke, NSW 2330 **region** Lower Hunter Valley
phone (02) 6579 1499 **fax** (02) 6579 1477 **open** Wed–Sun 10–4
winemaker Andrew Margan (Contract) **production** 2400 **est.** 1997
product range ($17–19 CD) Semillon, Verdelho, Unwooded Chardonnay, Chardonnay, Sparkling, Botrytis Semillon, Shiraz, Cabernet Sauvignon, Port.
summary Paul and Gail Nightingale have wasted no time since establishing their business in 1997. They have planted 3 hectares each of verdelho and merlot, 2 hectares of shiraz, 1.5 hectares each of chardonnay and cabernet sauvignon, and 1 hectare of chambourcin. The wines are contract-made by Andrew Margan, and are sold only through the cellar door and the actively promoted wine club, and to selected local restaurants.

Nightingale Verdelho

🍷🍷🍷½ **2000** Medium yellow-green; quite powerful and complex, with deep tropical aromas, followed by a palate with masses of flavour, suggesting the possibility of skin contact, and certainly encouraging early consumption. **rating:** 84

best drinking Now **best vintages** NA **drink with** Pasta • $17

Nightingale Unwooded Chardonnay

🍷🍷🍷½ **2000** Medium yellow-green; as with the Verdelho, some weight and power to the bouquet, running from mineral to riper nectarine/peach. The palate delivers more of the same, with plenty of ripe peachy fruit in a big, drink-now style. **rating:** 84

best drinking Now **best vintages** NA **drink with** Grilled spatchcock • $17

Nightingale Shiraz

🍷🍷🍷🍷 **1999** Medium to full red-purple; there is good depth to the ripe plummy fruit of the bouquet that flows through to a palate with abundant plum, cherry and mint fruit; subtle American oak; good wine. **rating:** 89

best drinking 2003–2010 **best vintages** NA **drink with** Grilled rib of beef • $19

ninth island ★★★★

Baxter's Road, Pipers River, Tas 7252 **region** Northern Tasmania
phone (03) 6382 7122 **fax** (03) 6382 7231 **open** 7 days 10–5
winemaker Andrew Pirie **production** 14 000 **est.** 1999
product range ($18.14–23.09 R) Riesling, Chardonnay, Sauvignon Blanc, Straits Dry White, Botrytis Riesling, Pinot Noir, Cuvée Tasmania, Tamar Cabernets.
summary This is the former Rochecombe Vineyard, the Rochecombe brand having been discontinued. There is a sharing of vineyards and of winery facilities within the Pipers Brook Group; the Ninth Island Wines, however, have their own identity.

Ninth Island Pinot Grigio

ꝩꝩꝩ 2000 Pale straw; the bouquet is quite fragrant, with a mix of light spice and touches of ripe apple. Light, crisp apple flavours are the main strength of the palate, but the wine has a slightly skinsy finish. **rating:** 84

best drinking Now–2003 **best vintages** NA **drink with** Carpaccio of salmon • $19.50

Ninth Island Chardonnay

ꝩꝩꝩ 1999 Light green-yellow; the bouquet has fresh citrus/grapefruit/melon fruit; the citrussy palate crisp, light and lively, but not complex nor particularly intense. **rating:** 83

best drinking Now **best vintages** '92, '93, '94, '96, '97 **drink with** Crab, shellfish • $22

Ninth Island Pinot Noir

ꝩꝩꝩꝩ 2000 Strong red-purple, quite vivid and the best to date by far; there is ripe, plummy fruit in abundance on the bouquet, and the barest hint of oak; the palate, likewise, is full of cherry and plum fruit, so much so that there is a sneaking suspicion a bit more oak work could have produced a wine too good for the Ninth Island label. As it is, you get seriously good value for the money. **rating:** 89

best drinking Now–2004 **best vintages** '00 **drink with** Osso bucco • $23.60

no regrets vineyard NR

40 Dillons Hill Road, Glaziers Bay, Tas 7109 **region** Tasmania
phone (03) 6295 1509 **fax** (03) 6295 1509 **open** By appointment
winemaker Andrew Hood (Contract), Eric Phillips **production** 300 **est.** 2000
product range ($15–25 R) Riesling, Traminer, Sylvaner, Chardonnay, Sparkling Miss Otis, Pinot Noir.
summary Having sold Elsewhere Vineyard, Eric and Jette Phillips have turned around and planted another vineyard almost next door. No Regrets is their 'retirement' vineyard; they will be producing only one wine from the 1 hectare of newly planted pinot noir. They anticipate the first vintage in 2002. In the meantime they are selling the residual Elsewhere stock; the last wine from the old venture will be the 2000 Riesling, to be sold late 2001. The wines are also available most Saturdays at Hobart's Salamanca Market, stall 80.

noon winery ★★★★

Rifle Range Road, McLaren Vale, SA 5171 **region** McLaren Vale
phone (08) 8323 8290 **fax** (08) 8323 8290 **open** Weekends and public holidays 10–5 while stock available
winemaker Drew Noon **production** 2000 **est.** 1976
product range ($12.50–23 CD) One Night (Rosé), Solaire Reserve Grenache, Eclipse (Grenache Shiraz), Reserve Shiraz, Reserve Cabernet Sauvignon, Vintage Port.
summary Drew Noon has returned to McLaren Vale and purchased Noon Winery from his parents (though father David still keeps an eye on things), having spent many years as a consultant oenologist and viticulturist in Victoria, thereafter as winemaker at Cassegrain. Some spectacular and unusual wines have followed, such as the 17.9° alcohol Solaire Grenache, styled like an Italian Amarone. In 1998 Drew Noon gained the coveted Master of Wine (MW) award. Exports to the UK, the US, Germany, Switzerland and New Zealand.

Noon Reserve Shiraz

ꝩꝩꝩꝩ 1999 Dense red-purple; a massive, voluminous bouquet with concentrated earth, dark berry and alcohol aromas that is inevitably followed by an equally massive palate with dark berry, chocolate and earth flavours. 15.2° alcohol; 600 cases made. **rating:** 85

best drinking 2004–2009 **best vintages** NA **drink with** Don't • $19.50

Noon Eclipse

ꝩꝩꝩ 1999 Medium to full red-purple; the high alcohol (14.9°) is immediately obvious, but so are the cherry/spicy/earthy fruit aromas; the palate shows similar strongly accented fruit driven by the level of alcohol. It's a style; love it or leave it. **rating:** 84

best drinking 2003–2009 **best vintages** '97 **drink with** Venison • $17

Noon Solaire Reserve Grenache

ꝩꝩꝩ 1999 Dark red-purple; bramble, prune, plum and earth aromas lead into a palate that is almost impossible to describe, the sweetness coming from alcohol and (it would seem) a touch of unfermented sugar, which makes one wonder just what the baumé level of the grapes were when they were finally picked. This is a port by any other name, even though it is not fortified. **rating:** 84

best drinking 2004–2014 **best vintages** NA **drink with** You tell me • $21

Noon Reserve Cabernet Sauvignon

YYYY 1999 Medium red-purple; the bouquet is fragrant and high-toned in the typical Noon style; the palate offers ultra-ripe cassis/berry fruit, a touch of oak, and a decided twitch of alcohol (14.6°). **rating:** 84

best drinking 2003–2008 **best vintages** NA **drink with** Rich game • $19.50

Noon Vintage Port

YYYY 1999 Medium to full red-purple; rich blackberry/blackcurrant fruit with touches of chocolate and penetrating brandy spirit is followed by a powerful, dense palate with good tannin balance and extract. **rating:** 86

best drinking 2003–2013 **best vintages** NA **drink with** Panforte • $18

normans ★★★★

Grant's Gully Road, Clarendon, SA 5157 **region** McLaren Vale
phone (08) 8383 6138 **fax** (08) 8383 6089 **open** Wed–Sat 10–5, Sun and public holidays 11–5
winemaker Peter Fraser, Rebecca Kennedy **production** 1.1 million **est.** 1853

product range ($6.95–40 R) A spread of wines starting with the Riverland-sourced Lone Gum range of Chardonnay, Shiraz Cabernet, Merlot, Brut Reserve; Chandlers Hill Chardonnay Semillon, Chenin Blanc, Shiraz; Tarlina Strathbogie Ranges Chardonnay, Coonawarra Cabernet; then the White Label series of Riesling, Bin number-identified Chardonnay, Unwooded Chardonnay, Pinot Noir, Unfiltered Grenache, Merlot, Shiraz, Cabernet Sauvignon, NV Brut; Old Vine Shiraz, Old Vine Grenache; Regional Series of Adelaide Hills Chardonnay, Riverina Botrytis Semillon, Coonawarra Cabernet Sauvignon, Langhorne Creek Cabernets; and at the top of the scale Chais Clarendon Chardonnay, Shiraz, Cabernet Sauvignon; also kosher Chardonnay, Shiraz (mainly for export) under the Teal Lake label.

summary In late 1994 Normans raised $6 million in new share capital, the issue reflecting the success Normans has enjoyed in recent years in establishing its brand both in domestic and export markets. It has since expanded its viticultural base by purchasing vineyards in various parts of Australia, and disposing of others. The quality of the Chais Clarendon range is exemplary. Exports to the UK, much of Europe, the US, Canada, Japan, Southeast Asia and New Zealand.

Normans White Label Strathbogie Vineyard Riesling

YYYY 1999 Medium yellow-green; there are distinct tropical overtones to the citrus, lime/mandarin aromas of the bouquet. The medium-bodied palate offers pleasant, easy drinking; there seems to be a touch of botrytis at work here, and the wine falls into the 'drink now' category. **rating:** 80

best drinking Now **best vintages** NA **drink with** Vietnamese dishes • $12.95

Normans Adelaide Hills Chardonnay

YYYY 1999 Medium yellow-green; the barrel-ferment characters are quite strong, but there is high-quality citrus and melon fruit under the barrel-ferment inputs to the bouquet. A well-made wine on the palate, but the fruit seems to lack the intensity needed for this price range. **rating:** 85

best drinking Now–2004 **best vintages** NA **drink with** Braised pork neck • $25

Normans Riverina Botrytis Semillon 500 ml

YYYY 1999 Medium to full yellow-green; the moderately intense bouquet has a slightly fusty edge to the botrytis characters. The palate, however, is well balanced, aided by limey acidity on the finish, which adds to the length. It has to be said the wine is expensive, particularly given its 500 ml package. **rating:** 84

best drinking Now–2003 **best vintages** NA **drink with** Crème brûlée • $25.50

Normans Chais Clarendon Shiraz

YYYYY 1997 Medium red-purple; the bouquet has complex, moderately intense fruit with berry, spice and leather aromas and an abundance of American oak. The palate is medium-bodied, elegant, with spicy/tangy fruit all sitting in an armchair of American oak. **rating:** 90

best drinking Now–2007 **best vintages** '82, '86, '90, '91, '92, '94, '95, '96, '97 **drink with** Shoulder of lamb • $39.95

Normans Old Vine Shiraz

YYYY 1999 Medium to full red-purple; has a quite rich bouquet with a mix of dark berry and chocolate plus a touch of oak; the palate is solidly constructed, with dark berry, plum and chocolate supported by good tannins and neat oak. **rating:** 88

🍷🍷🍷🍷🍷 **1998** Medium to full red-purple; the bouquet is quite rich, with a mix of black cherry and chocolate fruit, a hint of earth, and attractive oak. The palate is fruit-driven, with abundant, supple, sweet berry fruit together with a touch of mint, the latter no doubt coming from the Barossa Valley component. **rating:** 90

best drinking 2003–2010 **best vintages** '98 **drink with** Spaghetti bolognaise • $20

Normans White Label Merlot

🍷🍷🍷🍷 **1998** Medium red-purple; the bouquet is clean, with smooth, ripe, sweet aromatic berry fruits. The palate offers similar sweet fruit flavours and soft tannins. Perhaps says a little less about Merlot than one would wish, but it is a very nice red wine for early consumption. **rating:** 86

best drinking Now–2003 **best vintages** NA **drink with** Braised Chinese duck • $15.50

Normans Old Vine Grenache

🍷🍷🍷🍷 **1999** Medium purple-red; clear, jammy/juicy varietal fruit on the bouquet is followed by a palate that shows good varietal character throughout, but with the rich, full fruit nicely balanced by tannins to prevent the cordial effect. **rating:** 88

best drinking 2002–2005 **best vintages** NA **drink with** Rich meat pie • $20

Normans Chais Clarendon Cabernet Sauvignon

🍷🍷🍷🍷🍷 **1998** Medium purple-red; clean, fragrant blackcurrant aromas lead into a palate with excellent flavour, structure and balance; cassis, mint, berry and cedary oak flow together in complete harmony. **rating:** 94

best drinking Now–2010 **best vintages** '82, '86, '90, '91, '92, '93, '95, '98 **drink with** Fillet of beef with bone marrow • $39.95

nuggetty vineyard NR

280 Maldon–Shelbourne Road, Nuggetty, Vic 3463 **region** Bendigo
phone (03) 5475 1347 **fax** (03) 5475 1647 **open** Weekends and public holidays 10–4 or by appointment
winemaker Greg Dedman, Jackie Dedman **production** 1000 **est.** 1993
product range ($15–30 CD) Semillon, Shiraz, Barrel Club Shiraz; Reef Series Shot of Gold Chardonnay, Nil Desperandum Shiraz.
summary Draws upon 6.5 hectares of estate plantings, with mailing list and cellar-door sales available while stocks last.

o'shea & murphy rosebery hill vineyard NR

Rosebery Hill, Pastoria Road, Pipers Creek, Vic 3444 **region** Macedon Ranges
phone (03) 5423 5253 **fax** (03) 5424 5253 **open** By appointment
winemaker Barry Murphy, John O'Shea **production** 1250 **est.** 1984
product range ($22 R) Cabernet Sauvignon Cabernet Franc Merlot.
summary Planting of the 8-hectare vineyard began in 1984 on a north-facing slope of red basalt soil that runs between the 600- and 875-metre elevation line; it is believed the hill was the site of a volcanic eruption 7 million years ago. The vines were established without the aid of irrigation (and remain unirrigated), and produced the first small crop in 1990. No grapes were produced between 1993 and 1995 owing to mildew. Murphy and O'Shea say, 'We tried to produce fruit with no sprays at all, and learned the hard way.' Part of the current production is made for the O'Shea & Murphy Roseberry Hill label, and part sold to others, all of whom attest to the quality of the fruit.

O'Shea & Murphy Rosebery Hill Vineyard Cabernet Sauvignon Cabernet Franc Merlot

🍷🍷🍷🍷 **1997** Medium red-purple; the bouquet is still firm and youthful, more herbal than sweet, but avoids outright herbaceousness. The palate has some delicate berry fruit, and, like the bouquet, is still remarkably youthful, with obvious time in front of it. A bronze-medal winner at the 2000 Macedon Ranges Wine Exhibition. **rating:** 84

best drinking 2002–2007 **best vintages** NA **drink with** Rib of beef • $22

oakridge estate ★★★☆

864 Maroondah Highway, Coldstream, Vic 3770 **region** Yarra Valley
phone (03) 9739 1920 **fax** (03) 9739 1923 **open** 7 days 10–5
winemaker Michael Zitzlaff, Paul Evans **production** 24 000 **est.** 1982

product range ($18–25 R) Riesling, Sauvignon Blanc, Chardonnay, Rosé, Double Fermented Pinot Noir, Shiraz, Merlot, Cabernet Merlot, Cabernet Sauvignon; Reserve Chardonnay, Merlot and Cabernet Sauvignon.
summary The 1997 capital-raising by Oakridge Vineyards Limited was successful, and a new winery was built and officially opened in 1998. Production of the Oakridge Estate wines is projected to increase in leaps and bounds in the first few years of the new millennium. Exports to the US, the UK, Switzerland and Sweden.

Oakridge Estate Double Fermented Pinot Noir

1999 Medium red-purple; the bouquet has some spice and forest characters, but the fruit is repressed. The wine is certainly there to be noticed in the mouth, but is at odds with the normal silky feel of Pinot Noir. **rating:** 83

best drinking Now–2003 **best vintages** NA **drink with** Smoked duck • $23

Oakridge Estate Victorian Shiraz

1999 Medium red-purple; clean, smooth dark plum fruit and subtle oak on the bouquet are followed by a palate with more sweet plum and chocolate fruit; the tannins and the oak are both gentle. **rating:** 86

best drinking Now–2005 **best vintages** '98 **drink with** Lasagne • $25

Oakridge Estate Yarra Valley Merlot

1999 Medium red with some purple; the bouquet is cedary, spicy and savoury, with slightly diminished red berry fruit; the palate is likewise savoury, the good tannin management being a feature. What is most astonishing about the wine is the back label reference to the 'outstanding quality of the vintage'. Whatever the vintage was on the southern side of the Yarra Valley, it was not outstanding. That said, Oakridge did a pretty good job. **rating:** 85

best drinking 2002–2006 **best vintages** '98 **drink with** Roast veal • $25

Oakridge Estate Cabernet Merlot

1998 Medium red-purple; a range of cedary/savoury/dusty/earthy/gamey aromas lead into a palate with similar underlying fruit aided by a hint of mocha from gently sweet oak, finishing with soft tannins. **rating:** 84

best drinking Now–2005 **best vintages** NA **drink with** Marinated lamb shanks • $20

Oakridge Estate Cabernet Sauvignon

1999 Medium red-purple; the moderately intense bouquet has some leafy astringency surrounding the red fruit, the modest red and blackberry fruit of the palate finishing with slippery/rubbery tannins. **rating:** 84

best drinking Now–2005 **best vintages** NA **drink with** Pizza • $25

oakvale ★★★☆

Broke Road, Pokolbin, NSW 2320 **region** Lower Hunter Valley
phone (02) 4998 7520 **fax** (02) 4998 7077 **open** 7 days 9–6
winemaker Michael Glover **production** 15 000 **est.** 1893
product range ($19.50–49 CD) There are three ranges: Oakvale Classic, Peach Tree Reserve and Peppercorn Reserve; also Milbrovale Owens Family.
summary All of the literature and promotional material emphasises the fact that Oakvale has been family-owned since 1893. What it does not mention is that three quite unrelated families have been the owners: first, and for much of the time, the Elliott family; then former Sydney solicitor Barry Shields; and, since 1999, Richard and Mary Owens, who also own the separately-run Milbrovale winery at Broke. Be that as it may, the original slab-hut homestead of the Elliott family which is now a museum, and the atmospheric Oakvale winery, are in the 'must-visit' category. The winery complex offers a delicatessen, espresso coffee shop, bookshop and picnic and playground facilities. Live entertainment 11 am to 3 pm each weekend.

Oakvale Reserve Peach Tree Semillon

1999 Light to medium green-yellow; the bouquet is quite intense, with some old-fashioned hay/wet hay aromas; the palate, however, has no problems, with intense herbal/mineral flavours running through to a long finish. The price, it must be said, is ambitious. **rating:** 86

best drinking 2003–2009 **best vintages** NA **drink with** Mediterranean vegetarian • $29.50

Oakvale Classic Verdelho

1999 Light to medium green-yellow; a clean and smooth bouquet with tropical fruit-salad aromas is followed by a palate with good fruit weight and intensity, and not reliant on residual sugar. This is pretty close to Verdelho at its (modest) best. **rating:** 85

best drinking Now–2004 **best vintages** NA **drink with** Pasta • $19.50

Oakvale Classic Unwooded Chardonnay

TTTT **1999** Light yellow-green; the bouquet is clean, moderately intense, with stonefruit/nectarine and a touch of citrus. The palate has quite good length and intensity, in particular helped by the crisp acidity of 7.5 grams per litre. **rating:** 86

best drinking Now **best vintages** NA **drink with** Creamy pasta • $19.50

Oakvale Classic French Oaked Chardonnay

TTTY **1999** Medium yellow-green; peach, fig, honey and nectarine on the bouquet followed by a medium-bodied and smooth palate, with a reasonably long finish. The strange thing about the wine is that the oak impact is minimal; no bad thing, but I really wonder where the (new French) oak went. **rating:** 84

best drinking Now–2003 **best vintages** NA **drink with** Trout • $19.50

Oakvale Peach Tree Reserve Chardonnay

TTTT **1999** Medium yellow-green; a solid bottle-developed bouquet with a touch of oak and melon/peach fruit leads into a smooth, slightly nutty, ripe peach palate. Nice enough but, once again, the price is ambitious. **rating:** 85

best drinking Now–2003 **best vintages** NA **drink with** Smoked salmon risotto • $29.50

Oakvale Classic Shiraz

TTTT **1999** Medium purple-red; clean, fresh dark cherry fruit and subtle oak on the bouquet lead into a palate that opens with abundant plum and dark cherry fruit, before being unsettled by acidity poking through abruptly on the finish. A very low pH and high acidity fall into place. **rating:** 87

best drinking 2004–2009 **best vintages** NA **drink with** Hard cheese • $19.50

Oakvale Peppercorn Reserve Shiraz

TTTT **1999** Medium purple-red; the bouquet offers an attractive mix of berry, spice, earth and French oak; the palate is fresh, with squeaky-clean red berry fruit and subservient oak. The same question on the acidity comes up as with the Classic Shiraz, all pointing to late, and a little over-enthusiastic, adjustment. **rating:** 89

best drinking 2004–2009 **best vintages** NA **drink with** Teppanyaki beef • $29.50

old caves NR

New England Highway, Stanthorpe, Qld 4380 **region** Granite Belt
phone (07) 4681 1494 **fax** (07) 4681 2722 **open** Mon–Sat 9–5, Sun 10–5
winemaker David Zanatta **production** 2200 **est.** 1980
product range ($7.50–13.50 CD) Chardonnay, Classic Dry White, Light Red, Shiraz, Cabernet Sauvignon and a range of generic wines in both bottle and flagon, including fortifieds.
summary Has a relatively uncritical and evidently loyal clientele.

old kent river ★★★☆

Turpin Road, Rocky Gully, WA 6397 **region** Great Southern
phone (08) 9855 1589 **fax** (08) 9855 1660 **open** At South Coast Highway, Kent River Wed–Sun 9–5 (extended hours during tourist season)
winemaker Alkoomi (Contract), Michael Staniford **production** 3000 **est.** 1985
product range ($15–30 CD) Chardonnay, Pinot Noir, Shiraz, Diamontina (Sparkling).
summary Mark and Debbie Noack have done it tough all of their relatively young lives but have earned respect from their neighbours and from the other producers to whom they sell more than half the production from the 10-hectare vineyard established on their sheep property. 'Grapes,' they used to say, 'saved us from bankruptcy.' Exports to Canada, the UK, the Netherlands and Hong Kong.

Old Kent River Chardonnay

TTTT **2000** Light to medium green-yellow; the highly fragrant bouquet has stonefruit and citrus associated with some slightly reductive characters that will offend some, but not others. The lively, crisp, citrussy palate has considerable length and again aromatic fruit. **rating:** 85

best drinking Now–2004 **best vintages** '92, '95 **drink with** Lemon chicken • $20

Old Kent River Pinot Noir

YYYY **1999** Medium red, with just a touch of purple; a foresty, spicy bouquet is followed by a palate with considerable flavour and complexity, running through briar, forest and spice. Will always be a deeper wine than the pretty 2000 vintage. **rating:** 87

best drinking Now–2004 **best vintages** '99 **drink with** Pasta, cheese • $25

old loddon wines NR

5 Serpentine Road, Bridgewater, Vic 3516 **region** Bendigo
phone (03) 5437 3197 **fax** (03) 5437 3201 **open** Weekends 10–5, Mon–Fri by appointment
winemaker Russell Burdett **production** 5000 **est.** 1995
product range ($12–15 CD) Merlot Shiraz, Merlot Cabernet Franc, Cabernet Franc, Cabernet Sauvignon.
summary Russell and Jill Burdett began planting 3 hectares of cabernet franc, merlot, cabernet sauvignon and shiraz in 1987 on the banks of the Loddon River at Bridgewater. Until 1995 all of the grapes were sold to other makers (including Passing Clouds). But in that year the Burdetts began to vinify part of the production and have since steadily increased their own wine production with the assistance of their daughters Brooke and Lisa. All of the wine is sold through cellar door and mailing list, and since September 2000 wines (predominantly Merlot and Cabernet Franc blends) from the 1996, 1997 and 1998 vintages were available at thoroughly old-fashioned prices.

old station vineyard ★★★★

St Vincent Street, Watervale, SA 5452 **region** Clare Valley
phone 0414 441 925 **fax** (02) 9144 1925 **open** Not
winemaker Quelltaler (Contract) **production** 2000 **est.** 1926
product range ($12–20 R) Watervale Riesling, Watervale Free Run Rosé, Grenache Shiraz, Shiraz.
summary When Bill and Noel Ireland decided to retire from the Sydney retail scene in 1996 to go all the way up (or down) the production stream and become grape-growers and winemakers, they did not muck around. In 1995 they had purchased a 6-hectare, 70-year-old vineyard at Watervale and formed an even significantly larger joint venture in the Margaret River region, which has given birth to Flinders Bay wines. In their first year of shows the Old Station Vineyard wines won two gold, three silver and eight bronze medals, a reflection of the strength of old vines and the skills of contract-winemaking at Quelltaler. Now, I just wonder what Bill Ireland feels about retailers who slash and burn the theoretical retail price of his wines.

Old Station Vineyard Shiraz

YYYY **1998** Dense, inky purple-red; a powerful bouquet with dark berry fruit and a suspicion of some oak-derived volatility which, however, makes no impact on the massive palate with its huge extract and tannins. Do not contemplate drinking the wine within ten years. **rating:** 87

best drinking 2010–2020 **best vintages** NA **drink with** Leave it in the cellar • $20

Old Station Vineyard Grenache Shiraz

YYYY **1999** Strong purple-red; luscious, minty/jammy/berry flows throughout both the bouquet and palate. Uncompromising varietal character, but it works. **rating:** 87

best drinking Now–2005 **best vintages** '98, '99 **drink with** Game casserole • $18

olive farm ★★★

77 Great Eastern Highway, South Guildford, WA 6055 **region** Swan District
phone (08) 9277 2989 **fax** (08) 9277 6828 **open** 7 days 10–5.30 cellar sales, 11.30–2.30 café
winemaker Ian Yurisich **production** 3500 **est.** 1829
product range ($11.50–31 CD) Gewurztraminer, Semillon, Sauvignon Blanc Semillon, Chenin Blanc, Classic White, Verdelho, Unwooded Chardonnay, Chardonnay, Sauterne Style, Pinot Noir, Shiraz, Merlot, Cabernet Sauvignon, Cabernet Shiraz Merlot, Fortifieds, Sparkling.
summary The oldest winery in Australia in use today, and arguably the least communicative. The ultra-low profile in no way inhibits flourishing cellar-door sales. The wines come from 14 hectares of estate plantings of 11 different varieties.

Olive Farm Sauvignon Blanc Semillon

ＹＹＹＹ 2000 Light green-yellow; the bouquet is rich, and quite tropical, but lacks varietal character. A clean, well-balanced, user-friendly palate is similarly shaped. **rating:** 83

best drinking 2002–2002 **best vintages** NA **drink with** Fried fish • $15.50

Olive Farm Unwooded Chardonnay

ＹＹＹＹ 2000 Light to medium yellow-green; the clean, moderately intense bouquet offers melon and stonefruit, the palate moving to stonefruit and fruit salad, finishing with brisk acidity. **rating:** 84

best drinking Now **best vintages** NA **drink with** Marron • $16.50

oliverhill NR

Seaview Road, McLaren Vale, SA 5171 **region** McLaren Vale
phone (08) 8323 8922 **open** 7 days 10–5
winemaker Stuart Miller **production** 1300 **est.** 1973
product range ($5–11 CD) Great Outdoors White and Red, Chardonnay, Shiraz Cabernet, Port, Muscat.
summary Oliverhill has changed hands but otherwise continues an operation aimed almost entirely at the local tourist trade.

olssens of watervale NR

Government Road, Watervale, SA 5452 **region** Clare Valley
phone (08) 8843 0065 **fax** (08) 8843 0065 **open** Fri–Mon and public holidays 11–5 or by appointment
winemaker Contract **production** 1000 **est.** 1994
product range ($13–19 CD) Riesling, Semillon, Botrytised Riesling, Cabernet Sauvignon Cabernet Franc Merlot.
summary Kevin and Helen Olssen first visited the Clare Valley in December 1986. Within two weeks they and their family decided to sell their Adelaide home and purchased a property in a small, isolated valley 3 kilometres north of the township of Watervale. Between 1987 and 1993 production from the 5-hectare vineyard was sold to other makers, but in 1993 the decision was taken to produce wine under the Olssen label.

Olssens of Watervale Riesling

ＹＹＹＹ 2000 Medium to full yellow-green; the bouquet is clean, of moderate to full intensity, with ripe lime and passionfruit, and even a touch of stonefruit. A big, generous fast-developing style for early enjoyment. **rating:** 87

best drinking Now–2003 **best vintages** NA **drink with** Chicken salad • $15.50

Olssens of Watervale Botrytised Riesling

ＹＹＹＹ 1999 Medium to full yellow-green; the bouquet shows substantial botrytis impact, with a slight musk overlay, followed by an intense apricot/musk palate, the sweetness balanced by lingering acidity. A slightly surprising winner of the Sweet White Wine Class at the 2001 Small Vigneron Awards. **rating:** 89

best drinking Now–2003 **best vintages** NA **drink with** Rich fruit-based pastry • $19

orani vineyard NR

Arthur Highway, Sorrel, Tas 7172 **region** Southern Tasmania
phone (03) 6225 0330 **fax** (03) 6225 0330 **open** Weekends and public holidays 9.30–6.30
winemaker Various Contract **production** NA **est.** 1986
product range ($15.60–18.35 R) Riesling, Chardonnay, Pinot Noir.
summary The first commercial release from Orani was of a 1992 Pinot Noir, with Chardonnay and Riesling following in the years thereafter. Since that time Orani has continued to do well with its Pinot Noirs, including a ripe, plummy, highly flavoured wine from the 1999 vintage. Owned by Tony and Angela McDermott, the latter the president of the Royal Hobart Wine Show.

orlando ★★★★☆

Barossa Valley Way, Rowland Flat, SA 5352 **region** Barossa Valley
phone (08) 8521 3111 **fax** (08) 8521 3100 **open** Mon–Fri 10–5, weekends 10–4
winemaker Philip Laffer **production** NFP **est.** 1847

product range ($8–60 R) The table wines are sold in four ranges: first the national and international best-selling Jacobs Creek Semillon Sauvignon Blanc, Chardonnay, Riesling, Shiraz Cabernet and Grenache Shiraz and special Limited Releases; then the Gramp's range of Chardonnay, Botrytis Semillon, Grenache, Cabernet Merlot; next the Saint range, St Helga Eden Valley Riesling, St Hilary Padthaway Chardonnay, St Hugo Coonawarra Cabernet Sauvignon; finally the premium range of Steingarten Riesling, Jacaranda Ridge Cabernet Sauvignon and Lawsons Padthaway Shiraz. Also Russet Ridge Coonawarra Chardonnay and Cabernet Shiraz Merlot off to one side; sparkling wines under the Trilogy and Carrington labels.

summary Jacob's Creek is one of the largest-selling brands in the world and is almost exclusively responsible for driving the fortunes of this French-owned (Pernod Ricard) company. A colossus in the export game, chiefly to the UK and Europe, but also to the US and Asia. In the latter part of the 1990s (and into 2000) wine quality across the full spectrum from Jacob's Creek upwards has been exemplary.

Orlando Jacob's Creek Riesling

YYYYY **2000** Light straw-green; a fine, fragrant bouquet with a spicy introduction to lime, herb, mineral and toast aromas is followed by an elegant and tight palate with a mix of mineral, herb, spice and lime flavours; very good balance and style. **rating:** 94

best drinking Now–2004 **best vintages** NA **drink with** Salads, seafood • $8

Orlando Steingarten Riesling

YYYY **2000** Light green-yellow; fresh, gentle lime aromas have a touch of tropical fruit; the clean, bright, fresh and crisp palate has good length and balancing acidity, with its future development assured. **rating:** 88

best drinking 2003–2008 **best vintages** '98 **drink with** Sautéed prawns • $25

Orlando Gramp's Barossa Semillon

YYYY **1999** Medium yellow-green; there are gentle toasty aromas on the bouquet, but it is the palate that really shines, with finesse, structure, length and grip. Not phenolic, not overtly oaked, and not typical Barossa. No surprise to see it win gold medals at Cowra and Melbourne. **rating:** 86

best drinking Now–2004 **best vintages** NA **drink with** Chicken pasta • $15

Orlando Jacob's Creek Chardonnay

YYYY **2000** Why is Jacob's Creek a major world brand? Why does the Australian export juggernaut keep rolling along? This wine is one answer, with clean, fresh, melon and citrus fruit, a subliminal hint of oak, and surprising length and balance. Year in, year out, a model of consistency. **rating:** 86

best drinking Now **best vintages** '00 **drink with** Takeaway • $8.95

Orlando Jacob's Creek Limited Release Chardonnay

YYYYY **1998** Medium to full yellow-green; the complex and rich bouquet has abundant nectarine/peach fruit and pronounced nutty oak. The palate flows logically from the bouquet, with similar flavours and some creamy textural notes from the partial malolactic fermentation. All of its gold medals (five) and its trophy were won in overseas competitions; it has won a string of silver and bronze medals in Australia. 2000 cases made. **rating:** 91

best drinking Now **best vintages** '96, '98 **drink with** Breast of guinea fowl • $24.95

Orlando St Hilary Padthaway Chardonnay

YYYY **1999** Bright green-yellow; the moderately intense bouquet has attractive melon/citrus fruit and subtle oak; the palate is nicely restrained, not particularly intense, but then not phenolic or oaky either; has good length and acidity. **rating:** 85

best drinking Now–2003 **best vintages** '96, '99 **drink with** Veal • $18

Orlando Trilogy Cuvée Brut

YYYY **NV** Light green-yellow; the clean and fresh bouquet has attractive lemon aromas, the palate following down the same track, with fresh, lively lemony/citrussy tangy fruit; a slightly hard finish the only possible criticism. **rating:** 87

best drinking Now **best vintages** NA **drink with** Steamed fish • $14

Orlando Jacob's Creek Reserve Shiraz

YYYYY **1998** A toss-up between this wine and its equally impressive brother, the Reserve Cabernet Sauvignon; both are most impressive newcomers. There is an attractive spicy edge to the earthy/berry fruit of the bouquet, complexed by positive oak; the medium- to full-bodied black cherry and chocolate palate likewise enjoys good oak. **rating:** 90

best drinking 2003–2008 **best vintages** '98 **drink with** Rare roast beef • $14.95

Orlando Jacob's Creek Limited Release Shiraz Cabernet

🍷🍷🍷🍷🍷 **1996** Six trophies and innumerable gold medals do this wine justice without flattering it. Sophisticated winemaking provides a stylish and complex bouquet with sweet berry fruit matched by positive oak, but the outstanding texture and structure of the palate is the feature of the wine, with long, fine-grained tannins.

rating: 95

best drinking Now–2011 **best vintages** '94, '96 **drink with** Illabo lamb • $60

Orlando Russet Ridge Coonawarra Cabernet Shiraz Merlot

🍷🍷🍷🍷 **1998** Strong red-purple; rich, ripe blackberry/blackcurrant/mulberry fruit aromas are repeated on the rich and powerful palate which is replete with all the tannin one could wish for in bold 1998 style. **rating:** 89

best drinking 2003–2010 **best vintages** '91, '92, '98 **drink with** Beef with olives • $16

Orlando Trilogy

🍷🍷🍷🍷🍷 **1998** The only wine to appear in consecutive Top 100s, its top gold medal at the 2000 Adelaide Wine Show confirming it is even better this year than last. The ripe, sweet blackcurrant, blackberry and dark chocolate fruit is there in abundance on both bouquet and palate, finishing with supple tannins. **rating:** 92

best drinking Now–2008 **best vintages** '98 **drink with** Roast shoulder of lamb • $14

Orlando Gramp's Cabernet Merlot

🍷🍷🍷🍷🍷 **1998** Strong bright colour and sweet blackberry/blackcurrant run through the bouquet, followed by a ripe, luscious palate with ample depth of fruit and spot-on oak. **rating:** 91

best drinking Now–2005 **best vintages** '98 **drink with** Butterfly leg of lamb • $15

Orlando Jacob's Creek Reserve Cabernet Sauvignon

🍷🍷🍷🍷 **1998** Medium to full red-purple; the bouquet is smooth, with ripe blackberry and chocolate fruit supported by subtle oak. There is more of the same on the palate, with attractive, ripe blackberry/blackcurrant fruit; good oak, good tannins. Gold medal winner at the 2000 Royal Adelaide Wine Show. **rating:** 89

best drinking 2002–2007 **best vintages** '98 **drink with** Braised oxtail • $14.95

Orlando St Hugo Cabernet Sauvignon

🍷🍷🍷🍷🍷 **1998** Medium red-purple; appealing, supple blackcurrant/cassis and nicely controlled oak on the bouquet foreshadow a quite delicious wine on the palate, with similar fruit flavours supported by gentle cedar/ vanilla oak and fine tannins.

rating: 94

best drinking 2002–2012 **best vintages** '86, '88, '90, '91, '92, '94, '96, '98 **drink with** Mixed grill • $32

osborns ★★★★

RMB 5935 Foxeys Road, Merricks North, Vic 3926 **region** Mornington Peninsula
phone (03) 5989 7417 **fax** (03) 5989 7510 **open** By appointment
winemaker Richard McIntyre (Consultant) **production** 1500 **est.** 1988
product range ($21.50–25 CD) Chardonnay, Pinot Noir, Cabernet Merlot, 'Sticky' (Botrytis Semillon Chardonnay blend).
summary Frank and Pamela Osborn are now Mornington Peninsula veterans, having purchased the vineyard land in Ellerina Road in 1988 and (with help from son Guy) planted the vineyard over the following four years. The first release of wines in 1997 offered six vintages each of Chardonnay and Pinot Noir and five vintages of Cabernet Sauvignon, quite a debut. Part of the production from the 5.5 hectares of vineyards is sold to others, but increasing amounts are made and marketed under the Osborns label.

oyster cove vineyard NR

134 Manuka Road, Oyster Cove, Tas 7150 **region** Tasmania
phone (03) 6267 4512 **fax** (03) 6267 4635 **open** By appointment
winemaker Andrew Hood **production** 90 **est.** 1994
product range ($15–20 CD) Chardonnay, Pinot Noir.
summary The striking label of Oyster Cove, with a yacht reflected in mirror-calm water, is wholly appropriate, for Jean and Rod Ledingham have been quietly growing tiny quantities of grapes from the 1 hectare of chardonnay and pinot noir since 1994.

padthaway estate

Keith–Naracoorte Road, Padthaway, SA 5271 **region** Padthaway
phone (08) 8765 5039 **fax** (08) 8765 5097 **open** 7 days 10–4
winemaker Nigel Catt, Ulrich Grey-Smith **production** 6000 **est.** 1980
product range ($14.95–22 R) Eliza Pinot Chardonnay Cuvée, Eliza Pinot Noir Brut, Eliza Sparkling Burgundy, Eliza Chardonnay (wooded and unwooded); Chardonnay, Unwooded Chardonnay, Cabernet Sauvignon.
summary For many years, until the opening of Stonehaven, the only functioning winery in Padthaway, set in the superb grounds of the Estate in a large and gracious old stone woolshed; the homestead is in the Relais et Chateaux mould, offering luxurious accommodation and fine food. Sparkling wines are the specialty of the Estate. Padthaway Estate also acts as a tasting centre for other Padthaway-region wines. National retail distribution; exports to the UK.

Padthaway Estate Eliza Pinot Chardonnay

1998 Light green-yellow; the bouquet is crisp and tight, with minerally aromas but not a great deal of complexity; the palate is similarly very tight and restrained, all in all suggesting that a longer period on lees might have led to some softening and complexity gain. **rating:** 84
best drinking Now **best vintages** NA **drink with** Aperitif • $25

Padthaway Estate Cabernet Sauvignon

1999 Medium red-purple; gently cedary oak is woven through quite spicy fruit on the bouquet; red berry fruit expresses itself more on the palate, albeit with some of those slightly stewy characters that are so much the marker of the 1999 vintage. **rating:** 85
best drinking 2002–2008 **best vintages** NA **drink with** Beef roulade • $18.95

palandri wines

NR

Bussell Highway, Cowaramup, WA 6284 **region** Margaret River
phone (08) 9216 7000 **fax** (08) 9216 7001 **open** 7 days 10–5
winemaker Tony Carapetis **production** 55 000 **est.** 2000
product range ($15–25 R) Under the lower-priced Aurora label: Semillon Sauvignon Blanc, Chardonnay, Shiraz, Cabernet Sauvignon; the flagship Palandri range: Chardonnay, Sauvignon Blanc, Shiraz, Cabernet Merlot, Cabernet Sauvignon.
summary The initial offerings from Palandri come in three ranges: at the bottom end, Aurora; in the middle Amadou; and, at the top, the recently acquired Baldivis Estate Wines. However, as Palandri's own vineyards come into production, the brands and the product mix will change significantly. A state-of-the-art winery completed just prior to the 2000 vintage now has a capacity of 2500 tonnes. The vineyards scheduled to supply Palandri Wines with 50 per cent of its intake are situated in the Frankland River subregion of the Great Southern. In September 1999 150 hectares of vines were planted at Frankland River; the major varieties are shiraz, merlot, cabernet sauvignon, riesling, chardonnay and sauvignon blanc. A further 60 hectares were planted in early September 2000, making this the largest single vineyard developed in Western Australia to this point of time. A second block has been purchased south of the Frankland River vineyard, and a further 140 hectares are being developed there. It has also acquired Baldivis Estate, Rosabrook Estate and a 51 per cent interest in Amberley Estate.

Palandri Aurora Semillon Sauvignon Blanc

2000 Light green-yellow; a clean bouquet with gentle passionfruit/tropical aromas and no sign of reduction. The palate is tighter, crisper and more minerally than the bouquet suggests, but not to the point of upsetting an attractive wine, which has good length and lemony acidity to close. **rating:** 90
best drinking Now **best vintages** '00 **drink with** Lightly spiced seafood • NA

Palandri Aurora Chardonnay

2000 Light to medium yellow-green; fresh and fragrant melon/grapefruit aromas are joined by a touch of oak on the bouquet; the palate is fruit-driven, with good weight and length the only problem being a fractionally firm finish. **rating:** 88
best drinking Now–2004 **best vintages** NA **drink with** Chinese stir-fried chicken • NA

Palandri Aurora Shiraz

2000 Medium to full red-purple; smooth, sweet dark plum, black cherry and vanilla aromas on the bouquet are followed by a medium- to full-bodied palate with plenty of flavour, although one would wish for a little more varietal definition. The oak and tannins have not been overplayed. **rating:** 86

best drinking 2002–2005 **best vintages** NA **drink with** Lamb kebabs • NA

Palandri Aurora Cabernet Merlot

2000 Medium to full red-purple; clean, sweet, blackberry fruit is married with well-integrated oak on the bouquet. The palate is a pleasant light-bodied style, with touches of blackberry and chocolate; a smooth, easy-drinking commercial red. **rating:** 84

best drinking 2002–2007 **best vintages** NA **drink with** Wood-fired oven pizza • NA

palmara

1314 Richmond Road, Richmond, Tas 7025 **region** Southern Tasmania
phone (03) 6260 2462 **fax** (03) 6260 2462 **open** 7 days 12–6 Sep–May
winemaker Allan Bird **production** 280 **est.** 1985
product range ($14.50–32.50 CD) Riesling, Chardonnay, Semillon Ehrenfeltzer, Exotica (Siegerrebe), Pinot Noir, Cabernet Sauvignon.
summary Allan Bird makes the Palmara wines in tiny quantities. (The vineyard is slightly less than 1 hectare in total.) The Pinot Noir has performed consistently well since 1990. The Exotica Siegerrebe blend is unchallenged as Australia's most exotic and unusual wine, with amazing jujube/lanolin aromas and flavours.

Palmara Exotica

1999 Light green-yellow; the bouquet has intense lanolin, jujube and spice aromas which are followed by a palate that is indeed dry, but has lots of flavour. I do find the recommended food choices on the label somewhat strange, however. **rating:** 84

best drinking Now **best vintages** NA **drink with** Prosciutto and melon • $15.50

palmer wines

Caves Road, Willyabrup, WA 6280 **region** Margaret River
phone (08) 9797 1881 **fax** (08) 9755 4107 **open** By appointment
winemaker Eddie Price, Amberley Estate (Contract) **production** 6000 **est.** 1977
product range ($12–36 R) Sauvignon Blanc, Semillon, Classic White, Chardonnay, Merlot, Shiraz Cabernet, Cabernet Sauvignon, Cabernet Merlot.
summary Stephen and Helen Palmer planted their first hectare of vines way back in 1977, but a series of events (including a cyclone and grasshopper plagues) caused them to lose interest and instead turn to thoroughbred horses. But with encouragement from Dr Michael Peterkin of Pierro, and after a gap of almost ten years, they again turned to viticulture and now have 15 hectares planted to the classic varieties.

Palmer Semillon Sauvignon Blanc

2000 Pale straw-green; the bouquet is crisp and tight, with a mix of minerally and herb aromas; the medium-weight palate has the same mix plus an element of tropical fruit on a clean finish. **rating:** 86

best drinking Now–2003 **best vintages** NA **drink with** Richer fish dishes • NA

Palmer Wines Shiraz

1999 Dense red-purple; the bouquet is at the big end of town, with lusciously ripe blackberry/blackcurrant fruit that cascades through into the lusciously rich palate. If it loses its puppy fat and keeps its shape, might develop into something quite special. **rating:** 93

best drinking 2005–2015 **best vintages** '99 **drink with** Marinated beef • $36

Palmer Shiraz Cabernet

1998 Medium red-purple; a complex bouquet with a range of leathery/savoury/earthy/licorice aromas, then a palate with berry and chocolate fruit, fair oak and masses of tannins. **rating:** 87

best drinking 2003–2008 **best vintages** NA **drink with** Marinated beef • NA

Palmer Merlot

1999 Dense red-purple, almost impenetrable; a ripe, sweet, concentrated bouquet with a mix of sweet oak and sweet fruit leads into a powerful and concentrated palate; this is a full-throated, full-bodied wine with not a great deal to do with Merlot as it is traditionally understood. **rating:** 87

best drinking 2003–2009 **best vintages** NA **drink with** Rump steak • NA

pankhurst NR

Old Woodgrove, Woodgrove Road, Hall, NSW 2618 **region** Canberra District
phone (02) 6230 2592 **fax** (02) 6230 2592 **open** Sun, public holidays and by appointment
winemaker Sue Carpenter (Contract) **production** 4000 **est.** 1986
product range ($14–25 CD) Sauvignon Blanc Semillon, Chardonnay, Pinot Noir, Cabernet Merlot.
summary Agricultural scientist and consultant Allan Pankhurst and wife Christine (with a degree in pharmaceutical science) have established a 5.7-hectare split-canopy vineyard. Tastings of the first wines produced showed considerable promise. In recent years Pankhurst has shared success with Lark Hill in the production of surprisingly good Pinot Noir considering the climatic limitations. Christine Pankhurst says it is the result of 'good viticulture here and great winemaking at Lark Hill', and she may well be right.

Pankhurst Sauvignon Blanc Semillon

2000 Light straw-green; a crisp, fresh, herb and mineral bouquet is followed by a crisp, brisk, fresh well-balanced palate giving the impression that the most has been made of a limited fruit base. **rating:** 85

best drinking Now **best vintages** NA **drink with** Light seafood • $14

Pankhurst Chardonnay

2000 Light green-yellow; the clean bouquet offers a subtle interplay between melon, cashew and oak. The palate, likewise, is long, clean and fresh, driven by citrus and melon fruit with just a touch of oak. Reflects the reputation of the vintage. **rating:** 90

best drinking Now–2004 **best vintages** '00 **drink with** Steamed mud crab • $18

Pankhurst Pinot Noir

2000 Medium to full red-purple; sweet, stylish, spicy plummy fruit promises much, but the palate comes as a minor disappointment, with slightly hard, salty edges. **rating:** 86

best drinking Now–2003 **best vintages** '96, '97, '98 **drink with** Tea-smoked duck • $25

panorama 

RSD 297 Lower Wattle Grove, Cradoc, Tas 7109 **region** Southern Tasmania
phone (03) 6266 3409 **fax** (03) 6266 3409 **open** 6 days 10–5
winemaker Michael Vishacki **production** 250 **est.** 1974
product range ($10–30 CD) Chardonnay, Sauvignon Blanc, Pinot Noir, Cabernet Sauvignon.
summary Michael and Sharon Vishacki purchased Panorama from Steve Ferencz two years ago, and have since spent considerable sums in building a brand new winery, an attractive cellar-door sales outlet, and in trebling the vineyard size.

paracombe wines 

Main Road, Paracombe, SA 5132 **region** Adelaide Hills
phone (08) 8380 5058 **fax** (03) 8380 5488 **open** Not
winemaker Paul Drogemuller (Overseeing Contract) **production** 2000 **est.** 1983
product range ($19–65 R) Sauvignon Blanc, Chardonnay, Pinot Chardonnay Méthode Champenoise, Sparkling Shiraz, Shiraz, Somerville Shiraz Limited Release, Cabernet Franc, Cabernet Sauvignon.
summary The Drogemuller family has established 12 hectares of vineyards at Paracombe, reviving a famous name in South Australian wine history. The wines are in fact contract-made at Petaluma and are sold by mail order and through retailers in South Australia. Exports to the US, Spain, Malaysia, Singapore and Hong Kong.

Paracombe Sauvignon Blanc

2000 Pale straw-green; the bouquet is clean and fresh, with light herb and asparagus aromas that are repeated on the palate; fair length. **rating:** 84

best drinking Now **best vintages** '95, '96, '97 **drink with** Trout mousse • $19

Paracombe Shiraz

🍷🍷🍷🍷 **1998** Medium purple-red; bright, fresh cherry fruit, a touch of spice and a dusting of oak on the bouquet is followed by a palate with plenty of ripe, gently sweet cherry fruit, touched with spice; good depth. **rating:** 89

best drinking 2003–2008 **best vintages** '98 **drink with** Moroccan lamb • $25

Paracombe Somerville Shiraz

🍷🍷🍷🍷🍷 **1997** Medium to full red-purple; a clean, spicy berry bouquet, with just a touch of oak, is followed by a palate with an attractive mix of berry, dark chocolate, vanilla and some more savoury characters to add another dimension of complexity; fine tannins; carries its massive 15.9° alcohol remarkably easily. **rating:** 90

best drinking 2002–2012 **best vintages** '97 **drink with** Rich game • $65

Paracombe Cabernet Franc

🍷🍷🍷🍷 **1999** Medium red-purple; there are typical olive, leaf and spice overtones to the berry fruit; the palate continues with dark berry, spice and a touch of olive supported by soft tannins; all in all, shows individual varietal character. **rating:** 87

best drinking 2002–2007 **best vintages** NA **drink with** Pastrami • $23

paradise enough NR

Stewarts Road, Kongwak, Vic 3951 **region** Gippsland

phone (03) 5657 4241 **fax** (03) 5657 4229 **open** Sun, public holidays 12–5

winemaker John Bell, Sue Armstrong **production** 600 **est.** 1987

product range ($13–25 CD) Chardonnay, Reserve Chardonnay, Pinot Noir, Cabernet Merlot, Pinot Chardonnay.

summary Phillip Jones of Bass Phillip persuaded John Bell and Sue Armstrong to establish their small vineyard on a substantial dairy and beef cattle property.

Paradise Enough Chardonnay

🍷🍷🍷🍷 **1997** Light to medium yellow-green; the bouquet is clean and surprisingly undeveloped, with some barrel-ferment oak characters. The powerful palate is smooth and very youthful, with the nectarine/citrus fruit sustained by acidity. **rating:** 87

best drinking Now–2007 **best vintages** NA **drink with** Rich seafood • NA

Paradise Enough Reserve Chardonnay

🍷🍷🍷🍷 **1997** Medium yellow-green; the bouquet is youthful, with a slice of barrel-ferment oak behind the nectarine and citrus fruit that leads the intense, youthful and slightly more concentrated palate. **rating:** 88

best drinking Now–2007 **best vintages** NA **drink with** Sweetbreads • NA

paringa estate ★★★★★

44 Paringa Road, Red Hill South, Vic 3937 **region** Mornington Peninsula

phone (03) 5989 2669 **fax** (03) 5931 0135 **open** 7 days 11–5

winemaker Lindsay McCall **production** 4000 **est.** 1985

product range ($20–45 R) Chardonnay, White Pinot, Pinot Noir, Shiraz, Cabernet Sauvignon; PE Chardonnay, PE Pinot Noir.

summary No longer a rising star but a star shining more brightly in the Mornington Peninsula firmament than any other. As recent vintages have emphasised, the Mornington Peninsula region is sensitive to growing-season conditions, with problems in 1995 and 1996, but having a succession of warm, dry vintages since. Paringa shines most brightly in the warmer years. The restaurant is open seven days 10–3.

Paringa Estate Pinot Noir

🍷🍷🍷🍷🍷 **1999** Medium red-purple; typically high-toned, fragrant sappy/foresty/spicy fruit aromas are supported by charry oak on the bouquet. A powerful palate with the Paringa mix of spice, plum, forest, wood and sap. More conventional than the '98, and a very good wine, particularly for the vintage. **rating:** 93

best drinking Now–2006 **best vintages** '88, '90, '91, '92, '93, '95, '97, '99 **drink with** Wild duck, game • $45

park wines NR

RMB 6291, Sanatorium Road, Allan's Flat, Yackandandah, Vic 3691 **region** Alpine Valleys

phone (02) 6027 1564 **fax** (02) 6027 1561 **open** Weekends and public holidays 10–5

winemaker Rod Park, Julia Park **production** NA **est.** 1995

product range ($16–17 CD) Chardonnay, Cabernet Sauvignon.

summary Rod and Julia Park have a 6-hectare vineyard of riesling, chardonnay, merlot, cabernet franc and cabernet sauvignon, set in the beautiful hill country of the Ovens Valley. Part of the vineyard is still coming into bearing, and the business is still in its infancy.

parker coonawarra estate ★★★★

Riddoch Highway, Coonawarra, SA 5263 **region** Coonawarra
phone (08) 8737 3525 **fax** (08) 8737 3527 **open** 7 days 10–4
winemaker Chris Cameron **production** 5000 **est.** 1985

product range ($30–75 R) Cabernet Sauvignon under two labels, Parker Coonawarra Estate First Growth and Parker Coonawarra Estate Terra Rossa, Terra Rossa Merlot.

summary Parker Coonawarra Estate is now a 50:50 joint venture between founder John Parker and family and James Fairfax. It is by this mechanism that Pepper Tree in the Hunter Valley (controlled by James Fairfax) has its Coonawarra stake. It has also led to the highly regarded wines being made by Pepper Tree winemaker Chris Cameron, albeit using the Balnaves winery in Coonawarra to do so. Exports to the UK, Switzerland, Germany, Japan, Taiwan, Hong Kong, Singapore, Malaysia and Indonesia.

Parker Coonawarra Estate Terra Rossa Merlot

YYYY **1998** Medium red-purple; a pungent bouquet with savoury/leathery/earthy fruit sweetened up by vanilla oak leads into a flavoursome palate, where the oak, led by American, tends to dominate. **rating:** 89

best drinking 2002–2007 **best vintages** NA **drink with** Spiced veal • $39.50

Parker Coonawarra Estate First Growth

YYYYY **1998** Medium to full red, with some purple tinges; a rich, quite sweet bouquet with a complex amalgam of fruit and positive oak. The palate is rich, at the top end of the oak town, but with lots of sweet, concentrated berry fruit to justify the oak. **rating:** 93

best drinking 2003–2013 **best vintages** '98 **drink with** Prime rib of beef • $69.95

Parker Coonawarra Estate Terra Rossa Cabernet Sauvignon

YYYY **1998** Medium red-purple; smoky/pencilly oak threatens the fruit on both the bouquet and palate; the cassis/blackberry fruit underneath needs time to express its innate quality. **rating:** 86

best drinking 2002–2006 **best vintages** NA **drink with** Beef in black bean sauce • $29.50

passing clouds ★★★★

RMB 440 Kurting Road, Kingower, Vic 3517 **region** Bendigo
phone (03) 5438 8257 **fax** (03) 5438 8246 **open** Weekends 12–5, Mon–Fri by appointment
winemaker Graeme Leith **production** 4000 **est.** 1974

product range ($15–30 CD) Red wine specialist; principal wines include Pinot Noir, Grenache, Shiraz, Shiraz Cabernet, Merlot, Graeme's Blend (Shiraz Cabernet), Angel Blend (Cabernet); also Ondine (Sparkling Shiraz Cabernet); Chardonnay and Sauvignon Blanc from the Goulburn Valley.

summary Graeme Leith is one of the great personalities of the industry. He has a superb sense of humour and makes lovely regional reds with cassis, berry and mint fruit. His smiling, bearded face adorned the front cover of many of the Victorian Tourist Bureau's excellent tourist publications for several years. The cellar in which he is seen dispensing wine was not his, incidentally; it is that of Tahbilk. Exports to the US and Japan.

Passing Clouds Graeme's Blend Shiraz Cabernet

YYYY **1999** Medium to full red-purple; the bouquet is ripe, with a mix of faintly jammy berry fruit and mint, characters repeated on the palate, plus a touch of chocolate. Earthy tannins are still to resolve and lead to a slightly jagged finish at the moment, but prior history reassures that the wine will come together with a few years bottle age. **rating:** 87

best drinking 2004–2008 **best vintages** '81, '82, '86, '90, '91, '92, '94, '97, '98 **drink with** Yearling steak or veal • $23

paternoster NR

17 Paternoster Road, Emerald, Vic 3782 **region** Yarra Valley
phone (03) 5968 3197 **open** Weekends 10.30–5.30

winemaker Philip Hession **production** 600 **est.** 1985
product range ($12–30 CD) Semillon, Chardonnay, Pinot Noir, Shiraz, Cabernets, Vintage Port.
summary The densely planted, non-irrigated vines (at a density of 5000 vines to the hectare) cascade down a steep hillside at Emerald in one of the coolest parts of the Yarra Valley. Pinot Noir is the specialty of the winery, producing intensely flavoured wines with a strong eucalypt mint overlay reminiscent of the wines of Delatite. No recent tastings; there also seems to be some dispute as to whether Paternoster falls within the Yarra Valley.

patrick creek vineyard NR

Springfield Park, North Down, Tas 7307 **region** Northern Tasmania
phone (03) 6424 6979 **fax** (03) 6424 6380 **open** By appointment
winemaker Andrew Hood (Contract) **production** 350 **est.** 1990
product range ($15 CD) Semillon, Chardonnay, Classic Dry White, Pinot Noir.
summary Patrick Creek Vineyard came into being in 1990 when Pat and Kay Walker established high-density plantings of chardonnay, pinot noir, semillon and sauvignon blanc in a 1-hectare vineyard.

patritti wines ★★☆

13–23 Clacton Road, Dover Gardens, SA 5048 **region** Adelaide Zone
phone (08) 8296 8261 **fax** (08) 8296 5088 **open** Mon–Sat 9–6
winemaker G Patritti, J Patritti **production** 100 000 **est.** 1926
product range ($3–9 CD) A kaleidoscopic array of table, sparkling, fortified and flavoured wines (and spirits) offered in bottle and flagon. The table wines are sold under the Blewitt Springs Estate, Patritti and Billabong Wines brands.
summary A traditional, family-owned business offering wines at modest prices, but with impressive vineyard holdings of 10 hectares of shiraz in Blewitt Springs and 6 hectares of grenache at Aldinga North.

pattersons 

St Werburghs Road, Mount Barker, WA 6234 **region** Great Southern
phone (08) 9851 2063 **fax** (08) 9851 2063 **open** Sat–Wed 10–5
winemaker Plantagenet (Contract) **production** 2000 **est.** 1982
product range ($15–27 CD) Chardonnay, Unwooded Chardonnay, Pattersons Curse White, Pinot Noir, Shiraz, Pattersons Curse Red, Sparkling Shiraz.
summary Schoolteachers Sue and Arthur Patterson have grown chardonnay, shiraz and pinot noir and grazed cattle as a weekend relaxation for a decade. The cellar door is in a recently completed and very beautiful rammed-earth house, and a number of vintages are on sale at any one time. Good Chardonnay and Shiraz have been complemented by the occasional spectacular Pinot Noir. Retail distribution in New South Wales, Western Australia; exports to the UK.

Pattersons Shiraz

YYYY **1997** A quite fragrant bouquet with a typical estate array of savoury/earthy/spicy aromas leads into a light- to medium-bodied palate with pleasantly sweet fruit surrounded by the aromas of the bouquet. **rating:** 89
best drinking Now–2005 **best vintages** '90, '93, '94, '96, '97 **drink with** Duck casserole • NA

paul conti ★★★☆

529 Wanneroo Road, Woodvale, WA 6026 **region** Greater Perth Zone
phone (08) 9409 9160 **fax** (08) 9309 1634 **open** Mon–Sat 9.30–5.30, Sun by appointment
winemaker Paul Conti, Jason Conti **production** 8000 **est.** 1948
product range ($12–27 CD) Chenin Blanc, Tuart Grove Chardonnay, Carabooda Chardonnay, Late Harvest Muscat Fronti, Medici Ridge Pinot Noir, Grenache Shiraz, Medici Ridge Shiraz, Mariginiup Shiraz, Cabernet Sauvignon, White Port, Reserve Port, Nero Sparkling Shiraz.
summary Third-generation winemaker Jason Conti has now assumed day-to-day control of winemaking, although father Paul (who had succeeded his father in 1968) remains interested and involved in the business. Over the years Paul Conti challenged and redefined industry perceptions and standards; the challenge for Jason Conti will be to achieve the same degree of success in a relentlessly and increasingly competitive market environment. Exports to the UK and Japan.

Paul Conti Tuart Grove Chardonnay

▼▼▼▽ **1999** Medium yellow-green; the moderately intense bouquet is clean, with subtle oak and some malolactic cashew characters. The palate is even more delicate and subtle than the bouquet, crisp, but needing a bit more punch. **rating:** 84

best drinking Now–2003 **best vintages** NA **drink with** Calamari • $19.95

Paul Conti Medici Ridge Pinot Noir

▼▼▼▼ **1999** Strong red-purple; the bouquet has clean, ripe, dark plum fruit with plenty of concentration; the palate, likewise, has impressive weight, with lots of dark plum/cherry fruit with development potential. The only discordant note is the oak, which seems heavy at this point, and I really wonder about the choice of oak type. **rating:** 89

best drinking Now–2006 **best vintages** '99 **drink with** Rich game dishes • $24

Paul Conti Mariginiup Shiraz

▼▼▼▼▽ **1998** Medium to full red-purple; a clean and smooth bouquet with gently ripe black cherry fruit and correspondingly gentle oak is followed by a generous, ripe and rich palate, offering black cherry, chocolate and soft tannins, again complemented by attractive oak. **rating:** 92

best drinking Now–2010 **best vintages** '88, '89, '91, '93, '94, '98 **drink with** Grilled steak • $26.69

paul osicka ★★★★

Majors Creek Vineyard at Graytown, Vic 3608 **region** Heathcote
phone (03) 5794 9235 **fax** (03) 5794 9288 **open** Mon–Sat 10–5, Sun 12–5
winemaker Paul Osicka **production** NFP **est.** 1955
product range ($14–25 CD) Chardonnay, Riesling, Cabernet Sauvignon, Shiraz.
summary A low-profile producer but reliable, particularly when it comes to the smooth but rich Shiraz. The wines are distributed in Melbourne and Sydney by Australian Prestige Wines, with exports to the UK, Hong Kong and Japan.

paulett ★★★★

Polish Hill Road, Polish Hill River, SA 5453 **region** Clare Valley
phone (08) 8843 4328 **fax** (08) 8843 4202 **open** 7 days 10–5
winemaker Neil Paulett **production** 14 000 **est.** 1983
product range ($16–25CD) Riesling, Sauvignon Blanc, Chardonnay, Late Harvest Riesling, The Quarry Mourvedre, Shiraz, Cabernet Merlot, Trillians (Sparkling Riesling), Polish Hill River Riesling.
summary The completion of the winery and cellar-door sales facility in 1992 marked the end of a development project that began back in 1982 when Neil and Alison Paulett purchased a 47-hectare property with a small patch of old vines (now extended to 14.4. hectares) and a house in a grove of trees (which were almost immediately burnt by the 1983 bushfires). The beautifully situated winery is one of the features of the scenic Polish Hill River region, as is its Riesling and Cabernet Merlot. Exports to New Zealand, the UK and Thailand.

Paulett Polish Hill River Riesling

▼▼▼▼▽ **2000** Light to medium yellow-green; the bouquet is clean, aromatic and quite elegant, with gentle passionfruit nuances. The palate is fresh, lively and flavoursome, tracking the bouquet, and finishing with good acidity. **rating:** 92

best drinking Now–2005 **best vintages** '84, '90, '92, '93, '95, '96, '98, '00 **drink with** Quiche Lorraine • $18.10

Paulett Polish Hill River Sauvignon Blanc

▼▼▼▼ **2000** Light straw-green; the bouquet is clean, firm, with some depth but not much piquancy. The palate has far more presence and attack, with sweet citrus fruit, good balance and length. **rating:** 88

▼▼▼▽ **1999** Medium yellow-green; the bouquet is clean, tending neutral, with some minerally aspects. The palate is much better, with lemon and grass flavours, and good grip, length and acidity. **rating:** 84

best drinking Now–2003 **best vintages** '00 **drink with** Shellfish • $18.10

Paulett Cabernet Merlot

▼▼▼▼▽ **1998** Medium red-purple; the bouquet has a mix of savoury/earthy/berry fruit, some cassis, and gentle oak. The palate is riper than the bouquet suggests, with that cassis character coming through strongly; ripe tannins and a gentle touch of French oak round off the wine. **rating:** 90

best drinking 2003–2010 **best vintages** '98 **drink with** Beef shashlik • $22.10

paxton wines NR

Sand Road, McLaren Vale, SA 5171 **region** McLaren Vale
phone (08) 8323 8645 **fax** (08) 8323 8903 **open** Not
winemaker Contract **production** 600 **est.** 1997
product range ($30 ML) Shiraz.
summary David Paxton is one of Australia's best-known viticulturists and consultants. He founded Paxton Vineyards in McLaren Vale with his family in 1979, and has since been involved in various capacities in the establishment and management of vineyards in the Adelaide Hills, Coonawarra, Clare Valley, Yarra Valley, Margaret River and Great Southern. The family vineyards in McLaren Vale remain the centre of attention, and are still contract-growers for others. However, as a means of promoting the quality of the grapes produced by the vineyards, Paxton Wines has ventured into small-scale winemaking (via contract) with an initial release of Shiraz. There are plans to increase the range in the future, but the volume of production of each wine will remain small. Exports to the US.

Paxton McLaren Vale Shiraz

TTTT **1998** Truly excellent red-purple; the bouquet is complex, with dark berry, chocolate and a hint of game, the palate very powerful and youthful, with brooding dark berry fruit and firm tannins. Needs time; rather daunting at this stage. **rating:** 86

best drinking 2003–2008 **best vintages** '98 **drink with** Roast lamb • $30

peacock hill vineyard NR

Cnr Branxton Road and Palmers Lane, Pokolbin, NSW 2320 **region** Lower Hunter Valley
phone (02) 4998 7661 **fax** (02) 4998 7661 **open** Fri–Mon, public and school holidays, 10–5, or by appointment
winemaker Bill Sneddon, Steve Langham **production** 1800 **est.** 1969
product range ($13.50–28 CD) Absent Friends Chardonnay, Reserve Chardonnay, Untamed Chardonnay, Jaan Shiraz, Cabernet Sauvignon.
summary The Peacock Hill Vineyard was first planted in 1969 as part of the Rothbury Estate, originally being owned by a separate syndicate but then moving under the direct control and ownership of Rothbury. After several further changes of ownership as Rothbury sold many of its vineyards, George Tsiros and Silvi Laumets acquired the 8-hectare property in October 1995. Since that time they have rejuvenated the vineyard and built a small but attractive accommodation lodge for two people, and have a tennis court and petanque rink for their exclusive enjoyment. Over the years, Peacock Hill has been a consistent medal-winner at local wine shows.

pearson vineyards NR

Main North Road, Penwortham, SA 5453 **region** Clare Valley
phone (08) 8843 4234 **fax** (08) 8843 4141 **open** Mon–Fri 11–5, weekends 10–5
winemaker Jim Pearson **production** 800 **est.** 1993
product range ($13–18 CD) Riesling, Late Harvest Riesling, Cabernet Franc, Cabernet Sauvignon.
summary Jim Pearson makes the Pearson Vineyard wines at Mintaro Cellars. The 1.5-hectare estate vineyards surround the beautiful little stone house that acts as a cellar door and which appears on the cover of my book, *The Wines, The History, The Vignerons of the Clare Valley*.

peel estate ★★★★

Fletcher Road, Baldivis, WA 6171 **region** South West Coast
phone (08) 9524 1221 **fax** (08) 9524 1625 **open** 7 days 10–5
winemaker Will Nairn **production** 8000 **est.** 1974
product range ($13.50–34 R) Chardonnay, Wood Matured Chenin Blanc, Medium Dry Chenin Blanc, Unwooded Chardonnay, Classic White, Verdelho, Shiraz, Zinfandel, Cabernet Sauvignon.
summary The winery rating is given for its Shiraz, a wine of considerable finesse and with a remarkably consistent track record. Every year Will Nairn holds a Great Shiraz tasting for six-year-old Australian Shirazes, and pits Peel Estate (in a blind tasting attended by 60 or so people) against Australia's best. It is never disgraced. The white wines are workmanlike, the wood-matured Chenin Blanc another winery specialty, although not achieving the excellence of the Shiraz. At five years of age it will typically show well, with black cherry and chocolate flavours, a strong dash of American oak, and surprising youth. There is limited retail distribution through each Australian State, and exports to Ireland.

Peel Estate Chardonnay

🍷🍷🍷🍷 **1998** Light to medium yellow-green; the bouquet is clean, with somewhat muted aromatics; light melon is the main player. The wine has nice, round, soft mouthfeel, and carries its generous alcohol surprisingly well. **rating:** 88

best drinking Now **best vintages** '98 **drink with** Seafood pasta • $21

Peel Estate Shiraz

🍷🍷🍷🍷🍷 **1996** Medium red-purple; the wine is quite fragrant, with a mix of cedary/dusty/spicy aromas. On the palate lively cherry, spice and vanilla flavours are offset by slightly hot alcohol on the finish; the tannins are soft, and the alcohol will not be so evident with food. **rating:** 92

best drinking Now–2006 **best vintages** '93, '94, '96 **drink with** Leg of lamb • $34

Peel Estate Cabernet Sauvignon

🍷🍷🍷🍷 **1997** Medium red; the bouquet is very developed, with cedary/savoury aromas, but the palate reassures, with a mix of cedar, chocolate, spice, vanilla and berry flavours supported by the estate's hallmark fine tannins. **rating:** 86

best drinking Now–2007 **best vintages** '97 **drink with** Herbed rack of lamb • $29

peerick vineyard NR

Wild Dog Track, Moonambel, Vic 3478 **region** Pyrenees
phone (03) 9817 1611 **fax** (03) 9817 1611 **open** Weekends 11–4
winemaker Contract **production** 1300 **est.** 1990
product range ($12.75–19.50 CD) Sauvignon Blanc, Semillon Sauvignon Blanc, Shiraz, Cabernet Sauvignon.
summary Peerick is the venture of Melbourne lawyer Chris Jessup and wife Meryl. They have mildly trimmed their Joseph's coat vineyard by increasing the plantings to 5.95 hectares and eliminating the malbec and semillon, but still manage to grow cabernet sauvignon, shiraz, cabernet franc, merlot, sauvignon blanc and viognier. Don't ask me where the semillon for the Semillon Sauvignon Blanc blend comes from; I don't know.

pembroke NR

Richmond Road, Cambridge, Tas 7170 **region** Southern Tasmania
phone (03) 6248 5139 **fax** (03) 6234 5481 **open** Not
winemaker Andrew Hood (Contract) **production** 100 **est.** 1980
product range ($18.75–20 ML) Pinot Noir.
summary The 1-hectare Pembroke vineyard was established in 1980 by the McKay and Hawker families and is still owned by them. It is predominantly planted to pinot noir, with tiny quantities of chardonnay, riesling and sauvignon blanc.

Pembroke Pinot Noir

🍷🍷🍷🍷 **1999** Medium red-purple; a very ripe, spicy, slightly pruney bouquet gives way to a palate with attractive sweet plummy fruit which is not overripe, contributing to good weight and mouthfeel. **rating:** 88

🍷🍷🍷🍷🍷 **1998** Medium red; complex bottle-developed aromas are starting to appear giving a spicy/savoury note to a wine that has abundant cherry and plum sweetness at its heart, and wonderful length. **rating:** 94

best drinking Now–2004 **best vintages** '98 **drink with** Squab • NA

pendarves estate ★★★☆

110 Old North Road, Belford, NSW 2335 **region** Lower Hunter Valley
phone (02) 6574 7222 **fax** (02) 9970 6152 **open** Weekends 11–5, Mon–Fri by appointment
winemaker Greg Silkman (Contract) **production** 10 000 **est.** 1986
product range ($16–20 CD) An unusual portfolio of Verdelho, Sauvignon Blanc, Semillon, Chardonnay, Pinot Noir, Chambourcin, Shiraz, Merlot Malbec Cabernet.
summary The perpetual-motion general practitioner and founder of the Australian Medical Friends of Wine, Dr Philip Norrie, is a born communicator and marketer as well as a wine historian of note. He also happens to be a passionate advocate of the virtues of Verdelho, inspired in part by the high regard held for that variety by vignerons around the turn of the century. His ambassadorship for the cause of wine and health in both Australia and overseas has no doubt indirectly contributed to the significant rise in production, and to the establishment of export markets in Singapore, the UK, Germany, China and Malyasia, as well as national distribution.

penfolds ★★★★★

Tanunda Road, Nuriootpa, SA 5355 **region** Barossa Valley
phone (08) 8568 9493 **fax** (08) 8568 9290 **open** Mon–Fri 10–5, weekends and public holidays 11–5
winemaker John Duval **production** 1.4 million **est.** 1844
product range ($9–300 R) Kalimna Bin 28 Shiraz, 128 Coonawarra Shiraz, 389 Cabernet Shiraz, 407 Cabernet Sauvignon, 707 Cabernet Sauvignon and Special Show Bin reds. Brands include Minchinbury Sparkling; Rawson's Retreat Chardonnay, Semillon Chardonnay and Cabernet Shiraz; Penfolds The Valleys Chardonnay, Old Vine Barossa Valley Semillon and Old Vine Barossa Valley Shiraz Grenache Mourvedre; Koonunga Hill Shiraz Cabernet, Semillon Sauvignon Blanc and Chardonnay; Magill Estate; Clare Estate Chardonnay; Clare Valley Reserve Aged Riesling, Eden Valley Riesling, Adelaide Hills Chardonnay, Adelaide Hills Semillon, Barossa Valley Semillon Chardonnay, RWT Barossa Valley Shiraz, Trial Bins Semillon; St Henri Cabernet Shiraz; Yattarna, Grange. Also various export-only labels. Finally, Grandfather Port and Great Grandfather Port.
summary Senior among the numerous wine companies or stand-alone brands in Southcorp Wines and undoubtedly one of the top wine companies in the world in terms of quality, product range and exports. The consistency of the quality of the red wines and their value for money is recognised worldwide, and – headed by the development of the ultra-premium Yattarna Chardonnay – it has steadily raised the quality of its white wines. Following the acquisition of Rosemount Estate by Southcorp in 2001, there will be even greater focus on the three leading brands of Penfolds, Lindemans and Rosemount, and it would not be surprising to see the sale of some lesser brands and the deletion of others.

Penfolds Clare Valley Reserve Aged Riesling

🍷🍷🍷🍷 **1997** Glowing yellow-green; a very toasty bouquet with some bottle-developed kerosene aromas is followed by a palate with much more lime fruit than the bouquet suggests, although the toasty characters are still there.
rating: 89
best drinking Now–2004 **best vintages** NA **drink with** Smoked fish • $25

Penfolds Trial Bin Adelaide Hills McLaren Vale Semillon

🍷🍷🍷🍷🍷 (half) **1994** Medium to full yellow-green; a powerful, rich and complex bouquet with toasty, almost charry, overtones leads into a palate that is every bit as complex and powerful, but which has some lovely fruit in the middle. The charry characters are, it must be said, slightly distracting. **rating:** 91
best drinking Now–2005 **best vintages** '94 **drink with** Rich seafood or veal • $25

Penfolds Yattarna Chardonnay

🍷🍷🍷🍷🍷 **1997** Without question, this has already developed into the best of the three vintages so far released, and has its best years in front of it. Fragrant, tangy fruit and oak coalesce throughout both bouquet and palate; the strength of the wine comes from its structure, balance and persistence of flavour and aftertaste. **rating:** 97
best drinking Now–2012 **best vintages** '95, '96, '97 **drink with** Rack of veal • $100

Penfolds Bin 128 Coonawarra Shiraz

🍷🍷🍷🍷🍷 (half) **1998** Medium to full red-purple; the bouquet is clean, with abundant, ripe dark plum fruit which has soaked up the oak; the palate is powerful, with much more concentration than usual, and in particular, tannins; has a very long life in front of it. **rating:** 92
best drinking 2003–2013 **best vintages** '63, '66, '80, '86, '89, '90, '91, '93, '94, '96, '98 **drink with** Veal; mild cheddar • $23

Penfolds Grange

🍷🍷🍷🍷🍷 **1996** Medium to full red-purple, still bright after five years, vibrant cherry and plum fruit aromas more than handle the oak on the bouquet; the palate is sumptuous, but not heavy, the cherry and plum flavours tracking the bouquet. The wine has a very long finish, with fine, integrated tannins. Destined to become one of the great Granges. **rating:** 97
best drinking 2006–2026 **best vintages** '52, '53, '55, '62, '66, '67, '71, '76, '78, '80, '83, '86, '90, '91, '92, '94, '96 **drink with** Aged fillet mignon • $300

Penfolds Kalimna Bin 28 Shiraz

🍷🍷🍷🍷🍷 (half) **1998** Full red-purple; the smooth, dark cherry and spice fruit together with a touch of vanilla oak on the bouquet lead into a strongly structured and concentrated palate. Here dark berry, plum and some more savoury characters are bound up with lingering tannins; patience will be richly rewarded. **rating:** 93
best drinking 2003–2020 **best vintages** '64, '66, '71, '80, '81, '83, '86, '90, '91, '94, '95, '96, '98 **drink with** Lamb or beef casserole • $23

Penfolds RWT Shiraz

ҮҮҮҮҮ **1997** Medium red-purple; the very elegant bouquet has savoury/spicy overtones to the cherry/plum fruit, supported by subtle French oak. The palate is no less elegant, with savoury/chocolate/berry flavours supported by fine tannins and similarly classy oak. **rating:** 94

best drinking 2002–2017 **best vintages** '97 **drink with** Roast veal • $80

Penfolds St Henri Shiraz

ҮҮҮҮ **1997** Medium red-purple; a moderately intense, clean bouquet has a range of savoury blackberry fruit aromas supported by the typically subtle oak. An elegant, medium-bodied palate with chocolate/savoury/berry flavours, the oak balanced and integrated, the tannins correct. Not the least bit flashy; in a curious way, a wholly appropriate fortieth anniversary wine. **rating:** 89

ҮҮҮҮҮ **1996** I am singularly unconvinced that St Henri should be one-sixth of the price of Grange, particularly with a classic vintage such as this. Piquantly ripe and fragrant, it is fruit-driven from start to finish (still matured in large, old oak vats), with a smooth and supple fresh berry palate and plush tannins. **rating:** 95

best drinking 2004–2014 **best vintages** '66, '67, '76, '82, '85, '88, '90, '91, '93, '94, '96 **drink with** Braised lamb • $50

Penfolds Old Vine Barossa Valley Bin 138 Shiraz Mourvedre Grenache

ҮҮҮҮ♀ **1998** Medium to full red-purple; a ripe, complex mix of savoury/spicy/berry aromas foreshadow a palate that first shows the mint latent in the bouquet allied with that special fruit sweetness that grenache bestows, and that is still evident through the considerable tannins on the finish. **rating:** 91

best drinking 2003–2013 **best vintages** '98 **drink with** Rich stews • $23

Penfolds Koonunga Hill Shiraz Cabernet

ҮҮҮҮ **1999** Medium red, with just a touch of purple; the bouquet is solid, with dark berry fruit and touches of chocolate and earth; the medium-bodied palate is well balanced; a supremely honest wine with skilled oak and tannin management in an average year. **rating:** 86

best drinking 2002–2006 **best vintages** '82, '87, '90, '91, '92, '94, '96, '98 **drink with** Jugged hare • $12

Penfolds Bin 389 Cabernet Shiraz

ҮҮҮҮҮ **1998** Full red-purple; dense, dark berry, dark chocolate, and savoury/spicy aromas are a backdrop for a palate full of cassis, blackberry and chocolate supported by a great depth of ripe tannins. Needs a decade to really start strutting its stuff, but will undoubtedly do so. **rating:** 94

best drinking 2008–2020 **best vintages** '66, '70, '71, '86, '90, '93, '94, '96, '98 **drink with** Double lamb loin chops • $35

Penfolds Bin 407 Cabernet Sauvignon

ҮҮҮҮҮ **1998** Medium to full red-purple; the bouquet leads with blackberry and cassis, with lesser notes of spice and cedar. The wine then shifts more into blackberry and bitter chocolate flavours on the long palate, sustained by lingering tannins. More elegant than the Bin 389, but will also be very long lived. **rating:** 94

best drinking 2005–2015 **best vintages** '90, '91, '92, '93, '94, '96, '98 **drink with** Venison, kangaroo fillet • $28

penley estate ★★★★

McLeans Road, Coonawarra, SA 5263 **region** Coonawarra

phone (08) 8736 3211 **fax** (08) 8736 3124 **open** Cellar door opening late 2001

winemaker Kym Tolley **production** 20 000 **est.** 1988

product range ($18–65 R) Chardonnay, Hyland Shiraz, Ausvetia Shiraz, Shiraz Cabernet Sauvignon, Merlot, Merlot, Reserve Cabernet Sauvignon, Phoenix Cabernet Sauvignon, Traditional Method Pinot Noir Chardonnay.

summary Owner winemaker Kym Tolley describes himself as a fifth-generation winemaker, the family tree involving both the Penfolds and the Tolleys. He worked 17 years in the industry before establishing Penley Estate and has made every post a winner since, producing a succession of rich, complex, full-bodied red wines and stylish Chardonnays. Now ranks as one of the best wineries in Coonawarra, drawing upon 91 precious hectares of estate plantings. Exports to the UK, Switzerland, Austria, Luxembourg, California, Canada, Malaysia, Singapore and Hong Kong.

Penley Estate Chardonnay

ΥΥΥΥ **1999** Glowing yellow-green; a big, full bouquet with ripe peachy fruit and some bottle-developed aromas is followed by a full, soft, peachy palate. **rating:** 85

best drinking Now **best vintages** NA **drink with** Pasta • $18

Penley Estate Pinot Chardonnay

ΥΥΥΥ **1994** Light green-yellow; an exceptionally tight and youthful bouquet is reflected in the palate, with amazing youth and freshness. It is hard to imagine how or why it has not developed more depth and complexity, but it is all the more interesting for that. **rating:** 85

best drinking Now–2005 **best vintages** NA **drink with** Shellfish • $32

Penley Estate Hyland Shiraz

ΥΥΥΥ **1999** Medium red-purple; smooth, sweet berry fruit and warm vanilla oak is a welcoming start, but the palate has slightly tart fruit and unexpected tannins. Needs time, but is, I fancy, intended as an early-drinking style. **rating:** 86

best drinking 2003–2007 **best vintages** '98 **drink with** Fillet mignon • $18

Penley Estate Shiraz Cabernet Sauvignon

ΥΥΥΥΥ **1998** Medium to full red-purple; the bouquet offers a mix of ripe raspberry, mulberry and blackberry fruit, some chocolate joining the mix on the luscious, fruit-driven palate. The barrel-ferment oak characters contribute as much to the texture as they do to the flavour. **rating:** 90

best drinking 2003–2008 **best vintages** '88, '90, '91, '92, '94, '96, '98 **drink with** Soft ripened cheese • $29

Penley Estate Merlot

ΥΥΥΥ **1999** Medium red-purple; a gently savoury/spicy bouquet with earth and olive aromas moves through to a rather riper palate, with red and black berry fruit. Overall, somewhat saturated with French oak. **rating:** 86

best drinking 2002–2006 **best vintages** '96 **drink with** Fillet of beef • $29

Penley Estate Phoenix Cabernet Sauvignon

ΥΥΥΥ **1999** Medium red-purple; a cedary/earthy bouquet with some spice is followed by a palate with redcurrant and blackberry fruit, fine tannins and just a hint of oak. **rating:** 87

best drinking 2003–2008 **best vintages** '98 **drink with** Aged parmesan cheese • $20

Penley Estate Reserve Cabernet Sauvignon

ΥΥΥΥ **1997** Medium red-purple; the bouquet has pronounced savoury/cedary aromas with some spice and berry fruit. The palate, likewise, most attractive cedary overtones to the restrained berry fruit and fine tannins. **rating:** 89

best drinking 2002–2012 **best vintages** '89, '90, '91, '92, '94, '96, '97 **drink with** Rare beef • NA

penny's hill vineyards NR

Main Road, McLaren Vale, SA 5171 **region** McLaren Vale
phone (08) 8362 1077 **fax** (08) 8362 2766 **open** By appointment
winemaker Ben Riggs (Contract) **production** 4300 **est.** 1988
product range ($23–27 R) Chardonnay, Shiraz, Specialized (Shiraz Cabernet Merlot).
summary Penny's Hill is a major new vineyard and winery operation in McLaren Vale owned by Adelaide advertising agency businessman Tony Parkinson and wife Susie. The Penny's Hill vineyard is 25 hectares and, unusually for McLaren Vale, is close-planted with a thin vertical trellis/thin vertical canopy, the work of consultant viticulturist David Paxton. The innovative red dot packaging was the inspiration of Tony Parkinson, recalling the red dot sold sign on pictures in an art gallery.

Penny's Hill Shiraz

ΥΥΥΥΥ **1998** Medium to full red-purple; the aromas of the bouquet are predominantly of dark berry and chocolate, but there are more spicy/savoury elements to add interest. The palate is succulent and smooth, with strong regional berry and chocolate fruit flavours supported by excellent oak and tannin handling. **rating:** 92

best drinking 2002–2012 **best vintages** '97, '98 **drink with** Roast ox kidney • $27

Penny's Hill Specialized

YYYY 1998 Medium purple-red; aromatic, sweet berry fruit aromas lead into a palate with berry, chocolate and spicy, dusty tannins; the green characters sometimes associated with a blend such as this are absent. **rating:** 85

best drinking 2002–2007 **best vintages** '98 **drink with** Veal shanks • $24

pennyweight winery NR

Pennyweight Lane, Beechworth, Vic 3747 **region** Beechworth
phone (03) 5728 1747 **fax** (03) 5728 1704 **open** Thur–Tues 10–5
winemaker Stephen Newton Morris **production** 1000 **est.** 1982

product range ($14–30 CD) The table wines include Beechworth Riesling, Semillon Sauvignon Blanc, Pinot Gamay (light red), Beechworth Pinot Noir, Beechworth Shiraz, Beechworth Cabernet and Vintage (sweet fortified); also important is the range of Oloroso, Fino and Amontillado Sherries and a range of Ports from Old Tawny to Ruby, Vintage Port, White Port and Muscat.

summary Pennyweight was established by Stephen Morris, great-grandson of the founder of Morris Wines, G F Morris. The 3 hectares of vines are not irrigated and are organically grown. The business is run by Stephen, together with his wife Elizabeth, and assisted by their three sons. According to Elizabeth Morris, 'It's a perfect world,' which would suggest that they are more than happy with their lot in life at Pennyweight.

Pennyweight Beechworth Shiraz

YYYY 1999 Medium red-purple; the moderately intense spicy/leafy/briary/berry bouquet is logically followed by a medium-bodied palate, with an attractive range of cherry/spicy/savoury flavours. The tannins are soft, the oak incidental. **rating:** 85

best drinking 2002–2009 **best vintages** NA **drink with** Free-range duck • $22

penwortham wines NR

Government Road, Penwortham, SA 5453 **region** Clare Valley
phone (08) 8843 4345 **open** Sat 10–5, Sun and holidays 10–4
winemaker Richard Hughes **production** 1000 **est.** 1985

product range ($13–16 CD) Riesling, Cabernet Sauvignon, Shiraz.

summary Richard Hughes has progressively established 12 hectares of riesling, semillon, verdelho, shiraz and cabernet sauvignon, selling most of the grapes and making restricted quantities of wine from the remainder.

pepper tree ★★★☆

Halls Road, Pokolbin, NSW 2321 **region** Lower Hunter Valley
phone (02) 4998 7539 **fax** (02) 4998 7746 **open** Mon–Fri 9–5, weekends 9.30–5
winemaker Chris Cameron **production** 90 000 **est.** 1993

product range ($10–70 CD) Sundial White and Red; Chardonnay, Shiraz, Cabernet Franc; Reserve range of Semillon, Chardonnay, Sauvignon Blanc, Traminer, Verdelho, Muscat, Malbec, Coonawarra Merlot and Cabernet Sauvignon.

summary The Pepper Tree winery is situated in the same complex as The Convent guesthouse and Roberts Restaurant. The company that now owns Pepper Tree made a decisive move in 1996, formalising the acquisition of a major interest in the Parker (Coonawarra) Estate vineyards, having previously purchased some of the fruit from those vineyards. Pepper Tree has made a determined, and quite successful, effort to establish its reputation as one of Australia's leading producers of Merlot. The new Audrey Wilkinson winery is in the same ownership.

Pepper Tree Reserve Semillon

YYY Y **2000** Light green-yellow; pronounced herbaceous/grassy aromas are a blast from the styles of 30 years ago, the palate having a flavour akin to chewing grass stems. **rating:** 83

best drinking Now–2003 **best vintages** NA **drink with** Marinated octopus • $20

Pepper Tree Reserve Chardonnay

YYYY 1999 Medium yellow-green; the clean, smooth bouquet is of light to medium intensity, with gentle fruit and subtle oak; the palate delivers more of the same in a clean, soft, correct mode; good length, but not much complexity. **rating:** 85

best drinking Now **best vintages** NA **drink with** Crab • $22

Pepper Tree Reserve Shiraz

🍷🍷🍷🍷 **1998** Medium to full red; the bouquet has dark berry fruit with touches of mint and leaf; there is ripe berry fruit in the core of the palate, sustained by utilitarian American oak. **rating:** 84

best drinking 2002–2006 **best vintages** NA **drink with** Takeway • NA

Pepper Tree Reserve Cabernet Franc

🍷🍷🍷🍷 **1999** Medium red-purple; the bouquet has aromas of crushed, dried gum leaf together with some red berry, the palate a strange mix of mint and sweet berry fruit. **rating:** 84

best drinking 2002–2005 **best vintages** NA **drink with** Vegetarian • $25

Pepper Tree Reserve Coonawarra Merlot

🍷🍷🍷🍷 **1998** Medium to full red-purple; the bouquet is complex and rich, but seriously dominated by oak; on the palate, some earthy red berry fruit comes through, and the structure is quite good. Perhaps it is my hypersensitivity to oak, but surely less of this would have made a significantly better wine. **rating:** 87

best drinking 2002–2008 **best vintages** '96 **drink with** Smoked lamb • $70

Pepper Tree Reserve Coonawarra Cabernet Sauvignon

🍷🍷🍷🍷🍷 **1998** Medium red-purple; fragrant cassis/mulberry fruit is augmented by oak on the bouquet; the same oak is present on the palate, but it is well integrated into a beautifully balanced wine that is a celebration of Cabernet Sauvignon varietal character. Blackberry and cassis flow along the tongue, lingering long after the wine is swallowed. **rating:** 96

best drinking 2003–2008 **best vintages** NA **drink with** Fillet steak • $60

peppers creek NR

Broke Road, Pokolbin, NSW 2321 **region** Lower Hunter Valley
phone (02) 4998 7532 **fax** (02) 4998 7531 **open** Wed–Sun 10–5
winemaker Peter Ireland **production** 700 **est.** 1987
product range ($20–25 CD) Enzo Bianco, Enzo Rosé, Semillon, Unwooded Chardonnay, Chardonnay, Enzo Rosso, Merlot, Yacht Squadron Port.
summary A combined winery and antique shop that sells all its wine through the cellar door and runs the Cafe Enzo. The red wines previously tasted were clean and full flavoured, the Merlot coming from the hectare of estate vineyards. No recent tastings.

perrini estate ★★★

Bower Road, Meadows, SA 5201 **region** Adelaide Hills
phone (08) 8388 3210 **fax** (08) 8388 3210 **open** Wed–Sun and public holidays 10–5
winemaker Antonio Perrini **production** 3500 **est.** 1997
product range ($13–21.50 CD) Semillon Sauvignon Blanc, Unwooded Chardonnay, Merlot, Shiraz, Cabernet Sauvignon, Tony's Blend, Tawny Port.
summary Perrini Estate is very much a family affair; Tony and Connie Perrini had spent their working life in the retail food business, and Tony purchased the land in 1988 as a hobby farm and retirement home (or so Tony told Connie). In 1990 Tony planted his first few grapevines, began to read everything he could about making wine, and thereafter obtained vintage experience at a local winery. Next came highly successful entries into amateur winemaker competitions, and that was that. Together the family established the 6 hectares of vineyard and built the winery and cellar door, culminating in the first commercial releases of the 1997 vintage, and steadily increasing production thereafter. Exports to the US and Asia.

Perrini Estate Shiraz

🍷🍷🍷🍷 **1999** Medium red-purple; the moderately intense bouquet has earthy/dark plum shiraz varietal character and an appropriate touch of oak. The medium-bodied palate opens with dark berry fruit, then some American oak influence, followed by savoury tannins on the finish. **rating:** 85

best drinking 2003–2008 **best vintages** NA **drink with** Grilled lamb chops • $21.50

Perrini Estate Merlot

🍷🍷🍷🍷 **1999** Medium purple-red; a spicy/savoury/cedary bouquet with rather a lot of oak is redeemed by the palate, with smooth berry and plum fruit; very fine tannins result in a well-structured wine. **rating:** 86

best drinking 2002–2007 **best vintages** NA **drink with** Ravioli • $21

pertaringa ★★★★

Cnr Hunt and Rifle Range Roads, McLaren Vale, SA 5171 **region** McLaren Vale
phone (08) 8323 8125 **fax** (08) 8323 7766 **open** Mon–Fri and public holidays 10–4
winemaker Geoff Hardy, Ben Riggs **production** 5000 **est.** 1980
product range ($14–28 R) Barrel Fermented Semillon, Sauvignon Blanc, Shiraz, Cabernet Sauvignon, Liqueur Frontignac.
summary The Pertaringa wines are made from part of the grapes grown by leading viticulturists Geoff Hardy and Ian Leask. The Pertaringa vineyard of 31 hectares was acquired in 1980 and rejuvenated. Establishment of the ultra-cool Kuitpo vineyard in the Adelaide Hills began in 1987; it now supplies leading makers such as Southcorp, Petaluma and Shaw & Smith. Retail distribution through South Australia, New South Wales, Victoria and Queensland; exports to the UK, the US, Canada, Denmark, Hong Kong and New Zealand.

Pertaringa Barrel Fermented Semillon

YYYY **1999** Medium yellow-green; the bouquet is full, showing ripe fruit, the oak obvious but integrated. A powerful wine in the mouth, with a mix of lemon, stonefruit and vanilla flavours, but is not excessively extractive or heavy. **rating:** 86
best drinking Now–2004 **best vintages** '94, '96 **drink with** Grilled eel • $18

Pertaringa Sauvignon Blanc

YYYY **2000** Medium yellow-green; the bouquet is soft, with herb and lemon aromas predominant, together with a touch of spice. The palate has an attractive flavour spectrum running through nectarine and gooseberry, balanced by good acidity. **rating:** 89
best drinking Now **best vintages** NA **drink with** Sashimi • $14

Pertaringa Shiraz

YYYYY **1999** Medium to full red, with the purple already starting to subside; solid dark berry/cherry/dark chocolate fruit aromas are balanced by vanilla oak on the bouquet; the palate has good richness, sweet and plump, ripe but not overripe; well-handled oak also a feature. **rating:** 90
best drinking 2004–2009 **best vintages** '97, '98, '99 **drink with** Beef casserole • $28

Pertaringa Cabernet Sauvignon

YYYY **1999** Medium red-purple; the aromas of the bouquet are in the savoury/earthy/leathery/herbaceous spectrum, which reappear on the medium-bodied palate that is, however, sweetened up by oak and also a touch of regional chocolate. The tannins need time to soften. **rating:** 84
best drinking 2003–2008 **best vintages** '89, '90, '91, '98 **drink with** Boned leg of lamb • $24

peschar's ★★★☆

179 Wambo Road, Bulga, NSW 2330 **region** Lower Hunter Valley
phone (02) 4927 1588 **fax** (02) 4927 1589 **open** Not
winemaker Tyrrell's (Contract) **production** 8000 **est.** 1995
product range ($14–18.50 ML) Chardonnay, Shiraz, Cabernet Merlot.
summary In 1995 John and Mary Peschar purchased the historic Meerea Park property which had been in the ownership of the Eather family, the name of which continues to be used by the Eathers for a quite separate winemaking operation. The property acquired by the Peschars is situated at the foot of the Wollemi National Park which rises steeply behind the vineyard, the latter being planted on sandy alluvial soils. There are 16 hectares of chardonnay, the wine being contract-made by Tyrrell's. While the focus is on Chardonnay, the Peschars have sourced 6 hectares of vines in the Limestone Coast Zone of South Australia for the production of Shiraz and Cabernet Merlot.

Peschar's Chardonnay

YYYY **1999** Light to medium yellow-green; the bouquet is of light to medium intensity, with good fruit and oak balance and integration. The palate doesn't appear to have the weight or complexity of the '98, but is clean and smooth, and the wine may well have development potential given the performance of the '98. **rating:** 82
YYYY **1998** Excellent light green-yellow; the bouquet is smooth, with ripe melon and nectarine fruit, although the oak is very slightly pencilly. The wine smooths out on the medium-bodied palate, with more of the nectarine and peach fruit of the bouquet, the oak subtle, and with good mouthfeel and balance. **rating:** 87
best drinking Now–2003 **best vintages** '98 **drink with** Pasta • $13.90

petaluma ★★★★★

Spring Gully Road, Piccadilly, SA 5151 **region** Adelaide Hills
phone (08) 8339 4122 **fax** (08) 8339 5253 **open** At Bridgewater Mill
winemaker Brian Croser **production** 30 000 **est.** 1976
product range ($19–90 R) Riesling, Viognier, Chardonnay, Merlot, Coonawarra (Cabernet Blend), Croser (Sparkling); second label, Sharefarmers White and Red; Bridgewater Mill is another label (see separate entry).
summary The Petaluma empire continues to flourish, now taking in Knappstein Wines, Mitchelton, Stonier and Smithbrook. While running a public-listed group, Brian Croser has never compromised his fierce commitment to quality, and doubtless never will. The Riesling is almost monotonously good; the Chardonnay is the big mover, going from strength to strength; the Merlot another marvellously succulent wine to buy without hesitation. The wines are exported to the UK and the US.

Petaluma Riesling

▼▼▼▼▽ **2000** Wow, Petaluma has taken a sharp knife to the pricing of this wine, putting it firmly into the 'must-buy' category. The bouquet is quite powerful, ranging through spice, apple, passionfruit, mineral and even a hint of toast starting to appear, the crisp, long palate more disciplined, its best before it. **rating:** 92

best drinking Now–2010 **best vintages** '80, '85, '86, '88, '90, '92, '93, '94, '95, '97, '98, '99, '00 **drink with** Blue swimmer crab • $20

Petaluma Viognier

▼▼▼▼▼ **1999** The second vintage (and the better) from a vineyard on the western escarpment of the Adelaide Hills specifically chosen for this variety. A more aromatic wine than the Yalumba Virgilius, with tropical fruit and dried-flower scents, and lots of mouthfilling flavour. Good acidity counterbalances the inevitable alcohol. **rating:** 94

best drinking Now–2003 **best vintages** '99 **drink with** Stuffed pig's trotter • $30

Petaluma Tiers Chardonnay

▼▼▼▼▼ **1997** Glowing yellow-green; a potent, complex and rich bouquet with strong barrel-ferment characters is followed by a palate with more elegance than the bouquet suggests. Intense, yet complex, it has an almost feathery texture, with an excellent fine, lingering finish. **rating:** 94

best drinking Now–2005 **best vintages** '97 **drink with** Slow-roasted salmon • $90

Petaluma Croser

▼▼▼▼▽ **1998** Pale straw-green; the bouquet is crisp and clean, with a mix of mineral and citrus aromas, the palate no less fresh, bright and pure; long in flavour, but really strikingly simple. This is minimalism of the highest order. **rating:** 90

best drinking Now–2003 **best vintages** '90, '92, '94, '96, '97, '98 **drink with** Oysters • $34

▼▼▼▼▽ **1991** Strong mousse; the bouquet is, as one would expect, very complex, with pronounced bready/biscuity autolysis characters. The palate is very dry, with relatively high acidity, suggesting either a very low or zero dosage. Extraordinarily restrained given its long time on lees. **rating:** 90

best drinking Now **best vintages** NA **drink with** Aperitif • $45

Petaluma Sharefarmers Red

▼▼▼▼▽ **1998** Strong red-purple; the bouquet is sweet, clean and ripe with a mix of plum, blackberry and blackcurrant fruit. An excellent palate, with complex sweet berry fruit, fresh and flavoursome, with well-balanced and integrated tannins and oak. By far the best Sharefarmers Red to date. **rating:** 91

best drinking Now–2011 **best vintages** NA **drink with** Lamb shanks • $18

Petaluma Merlot

▼▼▼▼▽ **1997** Medium red-purple; the bouquet is clean and fresh, with excellent fruit and oak balance and integration, something missing from so many Merlots. The palate is fine, supple, elegant and long, with a mix of savoury/earthy and cassis fruit, finishing with persistent tannins that do dry out the finish ever so slightly. **rating:** 92

best drinking 2002–2012 **best vintages** '94, '95, '96, '97 **drink with** Veal • $49

peter lehmann ★★★★☆

Para Road, Tanunda, SA 5352 **region** Barossa Valley
phone (08) 8563 2500 **fax** (08) 8563 3402 **open** Mon–Fri 9.30–5, weekends and public holidays 10.30–4.30
winemaker Peter Lehmann, Andrew Wigan, Peter Scholz, Leonie Lange, Ian Hongell **production** 200 000
est. 1979

product range ($11–55 CD) Barossa/Eden Valley Riesling, Blue Eden Riesling, Barossa Semillon, Chenin Blanc, Semillon Chardonnay, Chardonnay, Clancy's Classic Dry White, Late Harvest Frontignac, Noble Semillon, Pinot Noir Cuvée, Grenache, Merlot, Seven Surveys Dry Red, Barossa Shiraz, Cabernet Sauvignon, Clancy's Red, Bin AD 2015 Vintage Port, Old Tawny, Liqueur Muscat. Premium wines are Reserve Riesling, Reserve Chardonnay, Mentor, Stonewell Shiraz, Eight Songs Shiraz, Black Queen Sparkling Shiraz.

summary Public listing on the stock exchange has not altered the essential nature of the company, resolutely and single-mindedly focused on Peter Lehmann's beloved Barossa Valley. Some of the top-of-the-range wines are seriously good, the base range highly rated by the *Wine Spectator* and the International Wine and Spirit Competition. Exports to the UK through its own subsidiary; also to New Zealand, Asia, the South Pacific and the US.

Peter Lehmann Riesling

TTTT **2000** Light to medium yellow-green; a clean, moderately intense bouquet with lime and spice supported by a touch of mineral; a clean, well-balanced wine with plenty of mid-palate flavour and subliminal sweetness. **rating:** 85

best drinking Now–2004 **best vintages** NA **drink with** Dim sims • $11.95

Peter Lehmann Blue Eden Riesling

TTTT **2000** Medium yellow-green, showing some early development; a full, ripe, rich and strongly fruity bouquet is followed by a ripe, generous, full-flavoured, fruity and rich palate; a bold, early-developing style. **rating:** 87

best drinking Now–2004 **best vintages** NA **drink with** Sashimi • $20

Peter Lehmann Eden Valley Reserve Riesling

TTTTT **1996** Glowing yellow-green; complex bottle-developed lime-on-toast aromas are followed by an equally powerful and complex palate, with lime/toast flavours and perfect balancing acidity. A worthy successor to the great 1993 wine. **rating:** 94

best drinking Now–2006 **best vintages** '93, '96 **drink with** Prosciutto and melon • $24

Peter Lehmann Clancy's Classic Dry White

TTTT **2000** Very pale straw-green; the bouquet is crisp and clean, but has plenty of presence, the aromas predominantly in a mineral/herb spectrum. The palate likewise has plenty of fresh, crisp and lively flavour, in a dry seafood-friendly style. **rating:** 85

best drinking Now **best vintages** NA **drink with** Seafood pasta • $11.95

Peter Lehmann Black Queen Sparkling Shiraz

TTTTY **1994** Medium to full red; black cherry, blackberry and hints of spice and bread on the bouquet are followed by a mouthfilling, but not heavy, blackberry and spice palate. I just wonder whether a slightly lower dosage could have been used, but this is a class wine. **rating:** 90

best drinking Now–2006 **best vintages** NA **drink with** Pâté de foie gras; rich antipasto • $35

Peter Lehmann NV Black Queen Sparkling Shiraz

TTTTY **NV** Medium to full red-purple; the aromas are clean, with strong, blackberry/plum spicy fruit, the palate flowing on with ripe, black cherry and luscious plum flavours, yet nicely balanced, and does not cloy. **rating:** 90

best drinking Now–2005 **best vintages** NA **drink with** Rich consommé • $35

Peter Lehmann Eight Songs Shiraz

TTTTY **1998** Medium red-purple; ripe, intense dark cherry/plum fruit does the singing on the bouquet, subtle oak providing the harmony. On the palate, powerful dark berry, blackberry and plum provides the tenor, but it is the rumbling bass of the tannins that make up the loudest part of the wine at the present time. **rating:** 91

best drinking 2003–2013 **best vintages** '96, '97, '98 **drink with** Four and twenty pie • $50

Peter Lehmann Stonewell Shiraz

TTTTT **1996** Strong red-purple; a fragrant and exuberantly sweet cherry/cherry jam bouquet logically leads into a lusciously sweet cherry-flavoured palate, which is not overripe or jammy, and is neatly offset by oak and soft tannins. An absolutely delicious wine. **rating:** 94

best drinking Now–2006 **best vintages** '80, '89, '91, '92, '93, '94, '96 **drink with** Kangaroo fillet • $55

Peter Lehmann The Mentor

1997 Medium red-purple; a fragrant and elegant bouquet with spicy, berry and cedar aromas is followed by an intense but quite harmonious palate, where the highly attractive oak does not overshadow the fruit, and finishes with fine, ripe tannins. **rating:** 93

best drinking Now–2007 **best vintages** '80, '89, '91, '93, '94, '95, '96, '97 **drink with** Spiced beef • $40

peterson champagne house NR

Cnr Broke and Branxton Roads, Pokolbin, NSW 2320 **region** Lower Hunter Valley
phone (02) 4998 7881 **fax** (02) 4998 7882 **open** 7 days 9–5
winemaker Gary Reed **production** 10 000 **est.** 1994
product range ($14–28 CD) Sparkling whites include First Creek, Sparkling Ambrosia, Chardonnay Pinot Noir, Semillon Pinot, Chardonnay Blanc de Blanc Millennium, Pinot Noir Chardonnay Meunier; sparkling reds, Sparkling Shiraz, Sparkling Chambourcin, Rouge Ambrosia and Sparkling Merlot; also table wine Chardonnay and Pinot Noir.
summary Prominently and provocatively situated on the corner of Broke and Branxton Roads as one enters the main vineyard and winery district in the Lower Hunter Valley. It is an extension of the Peterson family empire and, no doubt, very deliberately aimed at the tourist. While the dreaded word 'Champagne' has been retained in the business name, the wine labels now simply say Peterson House, which is a big step in the right direction. Almost all of the wine is sold through cellar door and through the wine club mailing list.

petersons 

Mount View Road, Mount View, NSW 2325 **region** Lower Hunter Valley
phone (02) 4990 1704 **fax** (02) 4991 1344 **open** Mon–Sat 9–5, Sun 10–5
winemaker Colin Peterson **production** 15 000 **est.** 1971
product range ($15–40 CD) Semillon, Shirley Chardonnay, Verdelho, Back Block Pinot Noir, Back Block Shiraz, Cabernet Sauvignon, Botrytis Semillon, Muscat, Vintage Port, Sparkling; Back Block Cabernet Sauvignon, Ian's Selection Cabernet Sauvignon and Viognier are top of the range.
summary Has a distinctly lower profile these days; no doubt the booming Hunter Valley wine tourism industry soaks up much of the wine at cellar door. No recent tastings, but no reason to suppose the quality has slipped.

pewsey vale 

PO Box 10, Angaston, SA 5353 **region** Eden Valley
phone (08) 8561 3200 **fax** (08) 8561 3393 **open** At Yalumba
winemaker Louisa Rose **production** 25 000 **est.** 1961
product range ($15–25 R) Riesling, The Contour Riesling, Cabernet Sauvignon.
summary Pewsey Vale was a famous vineyard established in 1847 by Joseph Gilbert, and it was appropriate that when S Smith & Son (Yalumba) began the renaissance of the high Adelaide Hills plantings in 1961, they should do so by purchasing Pewsey Vale and establishing 59 hectares of riesling and cabernet sauvignon. Once famous for its Riesling, recent vintages have not been inspiring, tending to be somewhat dilute and unfocused. Perhaps the '99 is a sign of better things to come. Exports to all major markets.

Pewsey Vale Riesling

2000 A gold medal in the 2000 Royal Adelaide Wine Show underlines the fact that this is the best Pewsey Vale for many years. Decidedly aromatic and spicy, with bright, fresh, herb, green apple and lime fruit, augmented by steely/slatey acidity and grip to the finish. **rating:** 92

best drinking Now–2007 **best vintages** '69, '99, '00 **drink with** Vegetable terrine • $12.99

Pewsey Vale The Contour Riesling

1995 Medium yellow-green; a spotlessly clean and very fresh mix of lime, toast and mineral on the bouquet leads into a palate that is at once fresh, yet mature, with seductively intense lime juice and toast flavours. **rating:** 95

best drinking Now–2010 **best vintages** '95 **drink with** Pan-fried flathead • $24.95

Pewsey Vale Cabernet Sauvignon

TTTT **1998** Medium to full red-purple; rich, ripe dark berry (blackberry/mulberry) and chocolate aromas lead into a palate with dark berry fruit, a touch of austerity and moderately persistent tannins; hangs together well. Good wine. **rating:** 85

best drinking 2002–2008 **best vintages** '88, '92, '94, '98 **drink with** Wild mushroom risotto • $18.99

pfeiffer ★★★

Distillery Road, Wahgunyah, Vic 3687 **region** Rutherglen
phone (02) 6033 2805 **fax** (02) 6033 3158 **open** Mon–Sat 9–5, Sun 11–4
winemaker Christopher Pfeiffer **production** 27 500 **est.** 1984
product range ($11.50–46.50 R) Under the Pfeiffer label: Riesling, Chardonnay Semillon, Chardonnay, Frontignac, Auslese Tokay, Ensemble (light Rosé-style), Gamay, Pinot Noir, Shiraz, Merlot, Cabernet Sauvignon, Christopher's Vintage Port, Old Distillery Tawny, Old Distillery Classic Tokay, Old Distillery Classic Muscat, Old Distillery Liqueur Gold (all cellar door only); Vintage Reserve range: Chardonnay, Sparkling Brut, Sparkling Pinot Noir, The Piper; also the Carlyle range: Riesling, Chardonnay, Marsanne, Late Harvest Riesling, Shiraz, Cabernet Sauvignon and Classic Rutherglen Muscat, sold through retail and export.
summary Ex-Lindeman fortified winemaker Chris Pfeiffer occupies one of the historic wineries (built in 1880) that abound in northeast Victoria and which is worth a visit on this score alone. The fortified wines are good, and the table wines have improved considerably over recent vintages, drawing upon 32 hectares of estate plantings. The winery offers barbecue facilities, children's playground, gourmet picnic hampers, and dinners (by arrangement). Exports to the UK, Canada, Singapore and Taiwan (under the Carlyle label).

pfitzner ★★★★

Spring Gully Road, Piccadilly, SA 5151 **region** Adelaide Hills
phone (08) 8267 5404 **fax** (08) 8267 5404 **open** Not
winemaker Petaluma (Contract) **production** 1500 **est.** 1996
product range ($17.95 R) Sauvignon Blanc, Chardonnay, Pinot Noir, Merlot.
summary The subtitle to the Pfitzner name is Eric's Vineyard. The late Eric Pfitzner purchased and aggregated a number of small, subdivided farmlets to protect the beauty of the Piccadilly Valley from ugly rural development. His three sons inherited the vision, with a little under 6 hectares of vineyard planted principally to chardonnay and pinot noir, plus small amounts of sauvignon blanc and merlot. Half the total property has been planted, the remainder preserving the natural eucalypt forest. The wines are made by Brian Croser at Petaluma, and roughly half the production is sold in the UK. The remainder is sold through single retail outlets in Adelaide, Sydney, Melbourne and Perth.

Pfitzner Sauvignon Blanc

TTTT **1999** Light to medium green-yellow; the bouquet has plenty of weight and intensity, with fragrant tropical/gooseberry fruit. The palate has good structure, with a mix of mineral, tropical and herb/nettle flavours, with a squeaky-clean finish and good acidity. **rating:** 87

best drinking Now **best vintages** NA **drink with** Shellfish • $17.95

Pfitzner Chardonnay

TTTTY **1998** Light to medium green-yellow; the clean bouquet has gently sweet melon and nectarine fruit supported by subtle oak. The palate is still fresh, smooth and delicate, with melon flavours and subtle creamy/nutty oak and mlf inputs. Slow-developing, with good length. **rating:** 90

best drinking Now–2004 **best vintages** '99 **drink with** Terrine of scallops • $17.95

Pfitzner Pinot Noir

TTTY **1998** Medium red; the bouquet is clean, with some savoury/foresty characters, but, overall, quite subdued fruit aromatics. The palate is pleasant, with some plum and cherry fruit together with the more foresty characters, but falls away slightly on the finish. **rating:** 84

best drinking Now–2003 **best vintages** NA **drink with** Smoked quail • $17.95

phaedrus estate NR

220 Mornington–Tyabb Road, Moorooduc, Vic 3933 **region** Mornington Peninsula
phone (03) 5978 8134 **fax** (03) 5978 8134 **open** Weekends and public holidays 11–5
winemaker Ewan Campbell, Maitena Zantvoort **production** 600 **est.** 1997
product range ($14–18 R) Semillon Sauvignon Blanc, Chardonnay, Pinot Noir, Shiraz.
summary Ewan Campbell and Maitena Zantvoort established Phaedrus Estate in 1997. At that time both had already had winemaking experience with large wine companies, and were at the point of finishing their wine science degrees at Adelaide University. They decided they wished to (in their words) 'produce ultra-premium wine with distinctive and unique varietal flavours, which offers serious (and lighthearted) wine drinkers an alternative to mainstream commercial styles'. Campbell and Zantvoort believe that quality winemaking involves both art and science, and I don't have any argument with that.

Phaedrus Estate Semillon Sauvignon Blanc

1998 Medium yellow-green; the bouquet is still relatively neutral, with some mineral notes. The palate is solid, with mineral and some herb flavours; lacks fruit zip, but is well balanced. **rating:** 83
best drinking Now–2003 **best vintages** NA **drink with** Steamed fish • $14

Phaedrus Estate Pinot Noir

1999 Medium red-purple; very ripe fruit on the bouquet has some unusual spicy overtones, but far from unpleasant. The palate is quite powerful, with a mix of spicy/foresty/savoury flavours, all consistent with the winemaking techniques employed. **rating:** 85
best drinking Now–2003 **best vintages** NA **drink with** Smoked quail • $18

phillip island vineyard ★★★★☆

Berrys Beach Road, Phillip Island, Vic **region** Gippsland
phone (03) 5956 8465 **fax** (03) 5956 8465 **open** 7 days 11–7 (Nov–March) 11–5 (April–Oct)
winemaker David Lance, James Lance **production** 3500 **est.** 1993
product range ($17–35 CD) Sea Spray (Sparkling), Sauvignon Blanc, Cape Woolamai (Semillon Sauvignon Blanc), Summerland (Chardonnay), Newhaven (Riesling Traminer), Botrytis Chardonnay, The Nobbies (Pinot Noir), Merlot, Berry's Beach (Cabernet Sauvignon), Western Port, Pyramid Rock.
summary A separate operation of Diamond Valley Vineyards, now coming into full flower. 1997 marked the first harvest from the 2.5 hectares of the Phillip Island vineyard, which is totally enclosed in the permanent silon net that acts both as a windbreak and protection against birds. The quality of the wines across the board must be especially pleasing to the Lance family; this is definitely not a tourist-trap cellar door, rather a serious producer of quality wine. Exports to Southeast Asia.

Phillip Island Sauvignon Blanc

2000 Light green-yellow; a fragrant bouquet with gooseberry, passionfruit and sundry tropical aromas leads into a delicate, well-balanced palate which caresses rather than threatens. **rating:** 91
best drinking Now **best vintages** '97, '99, '00 **drink with** Fresh crab • $29.60

Phillip Island Vineyard Botrytis Chardonnay

1999 Light green-gold; the bouquet has a gentle citrus overlay on underlying peachy varietal fruit; the palate is very clean, with peachy flavours and well-balanced acidity; far from luscious, more towards Auslese in weight and sweetness. **rating:** 86
best drinking Now–2004 **best vintages** NA **drink with** Fresh fruit • $20

Phillip Island Vineyard The Nobbies

1999 Medium red, with just a touch of purple; the moderately intense bouquet is clean, with gentle strawberry and plum fruit aromas, the palate, likewise, light to medium bodied, with spicy plum and strawberry flavours; could do with a tad more intensity. **rating:** 87
best drinking Now–2003 **best vintages** '96, '98 **drink with** Smoked quail • $27.30

piano gully NR

Piano Gully Road, Manjimup, WA 6258 **region** Pemberton
phone (08) 9772 3140 **fax** (08) 9316 0336 **open** By appointment
winemaker Michael Staniford **production** 6000 **est.** 1987
product range ($15–25 R) Chardonnay Sauvignon Blanc, Chardonnay, Pinot Noir, Cabernet Sauvignon Shiraz, Cabernet Sauvignon.
summary The 4-hectare vineyard was established in 1987 on rich Karri loam, 10 kilometres south of Manjimup, with the first wine made from the 1991 vintage. A change of ownership and winemaker should hopefully see a lift in wine quality. For the record, the name of the road (and hence the winery) commemorates the shipping of a piano from England by one of the first settlers in the region. The horse and cart carrying the piano on the last leg of the long journey were within sight of their destination when the piano fell from the cart and was destroyed.

Piano Gully Chardonnay

YYYYY **1999** Medium yellow-green; the bouquet is tangy, with distinct cool-climate/vegetal notes with a hint of oak in the background. The light- to medium-bodied palate is quite elegant, with cool-climate citrus and melon fruit, again with judiciously handled oak. **rating:** 91
best drinking Now–2003 **best vintages** '99 **drink with** Marron • $23.95

pibbin NR

Greenhill Road, Balhannah, SA 5242 **region** Adelaide Hills
phone (08) 8388 4794 **fax** (08) 8398 0015 **open** Weekends 11–5.30
winemaker Roger Salkeld **production** 1500 **est.** 1991
product range ($15–22 CD) Pinot Noir, Rosé Pinot Noir, White Pinot, Sparkling Pinot.
summary The 7-hectare Pibbin vineyard, near Verdun, is managed on organic principles; owners Roger and Lindy Salkeld explain that the name 'Pibbin' is a corruption of a negro-spiritual word for heaven, adding that while the wines may not have achieved that lofty status yet, the vineyard has. Pibbin has made a name for itself for producing massive, dense Pinot Noir in a style radically different from that of the rest of the Adelaide Hills.

picardy ★★★★

Cnr Vasse Highway and Eastbrook Road, Pemberton, WA 6260 **region** Pemberton
phone (08) 9776 0036 **fax** (08) 9776 0245 **open** By appointment
winemaker Bill Pannell, Dan Pannell **production** 5000 **est.** 1993
product range ($25 CD) Chardonnay, Pinot Noir, Shiraz, Cabernet Merlot.
summary Picardy is owned by Dr Bill Pannell and his wife Sandra, who were the founders of Moss Wood winery in the Margaret River region (in 1969). Picardy reflects Bill Pannell's view that the Pemberton area will prove to be one of the best regions in Australia for Pinot Noir and Chardonnay, but it is perhaps significant that the wines to be released include a Shiraz, and a Bordeaux-blend of 50 per cent Merlot, 25 per cent Cabernet Franc and 25 per cent Cabernet Sauvignon. Time will tell whether Pemberton has more Burgundy, Rhône or Bordeaux in its veins. It has lost no time in setting up national distribution, and exports to the UK, the US, Japan, Singapore, Malaysia, Indonesia and Hong Kong.

Picardy Chardonnay

YYYY **1999** Light straw-green; a very cool-grown style, with light citrus fruit which, on the palate, looks rather like a Chardonnay Sauvignon Blanc cross. It is at least fresh and lively. **rating:** 82
best drinking Now **best vintages** NA **drink with** Light seafood • $25

picarus NR

Winetrust Estate, Caves Road, Naracoorte, SA 5271 **region** Limestone Coast
phone (02) 9816 4088 **fax** (02) 9816 2680 **open** Not
winemaker John Baruzzi **production** 5000 **est.** 1998
product range ($25–80 R) Limestone Coast Chardonnay, Limestone Coast Shiraz, Reserve A Padthaway Shiraz, Limestone Coast Cabernet Sauvignon, Reserve 1 Coonawarra Cabernet Sauvignon.
summary Picarus is a partnership between Hunter winemaker John Baruzzi and long-term marketer Mark Arnold. They have established 12 hectares of vineyards (4 hectares each of chardonnay, shiraz and cabernet sauvignon) in the Limestone Coast region and supplement the production from these vineyards with contract-

grown grapes in Coonawarra and Padthaway. The wines are distributed nationally through the National Liquor Company in Sydney and Melbourne.

Picarus Limestone Coast Chardonnay

1999 Light to medium yellow-green; the moderately intense bouquet is clean and smooth, with attractive melon and citrus varietal character. The palate is particularly impressive, with considerable length and crystal-clear varietal feel and flavour. **rating:** 93

best drinking Now–2004 **best vintages** '99 **drink with** Grilled fish • NA

Picarus Reserve A Padthaway Shiraz

1998 Medium to full red-purple; a quite rich and complex dark plum and berry bouquet, then a powerful, intense and somewhat underworked palate, which seems to have been taken to bottle before it was ready. On the other hand, has stacks of flavour and varietal character, and will improve from here. **rating:** 87

best drinking 2003–2008 **best vintages** '98 **drink with** Steak and kidney pie • NA

piccadilly fields NR

185 Piccadilly Road, Piccadilly, SA 5151 **region** Adelaide Hills
phone (08) 8370 8800 **fax** (08) 8232 5395 **open** Not
winemaker Sam Virgara **production** 3000 **est.** 1989
product range ($17.95 ML) Chardonnay, Merlot Cabernet Franc Cabernet Sauvignon.
summary Piccadilly Fields draws upon a very substantial vineyard, with much of the production being sold to Petaluma. The plantings include 10 hectares of pinot meunier, 8 hectares of pinot noir, 5 hectares each of chardonnay, merlot and sauvignon blanc, 2 hectares of cabernet franc and 1 hectare of cabernet sauvignon.

pierro

Caves Road, Willyabrup, via Cowaramup, WA 6284 **region** Margaret River
phone (08) 9755 6220 **fax** (08) 9755 6308 **open** 7 days 10–5
winemaker Dr Michael Peterkin **production** 7500 **est.** 1979
product range ($20–53 R) Chardonnay, Semillon Sauvignon Blanc LTC, Pinot Noir, Cabernets, Cabernet Merlot; also Fire Gully Semillon Sauvignon Blanc, Cabernet Sauvignon Merlot.
summary Dr Michael Peterkin is another of the legion of Margaret River medical practitioners who, for good measure, married into the Cullen family. Pierro is renowned for its stylish white wines, which often exhibit tremendous complexity. The Chardonnay can be monumental in its weight and complexity. The wines are exported to the UK, the US, Japan and Indonesia.

Pierro Fire Gully Semillon

2000 Light green-yellow; the bouquet is clean, quite intense, with herbaceous varietal character. A long, clean, crisp palate with firm acidity and some minerally notes will develop given time, and the slightly grippy finish should soften. **rating:** 90

best drinking 2003–2010 **best vintages** NA **drink with** Marinated baby octopus • $20.80

Pierro Semillon Sauvignon Blanc LTC

2000 Light to medium yellow-green; quite powerful and complex, with toasty overtones; the palate is likewise structured and powerful, with a mix of herb, mineral and toast. **rating:** 87

best drinking Now–2004 **best vintages** '87, '89, '90, '94, '95, '97 **drink with** Veal cutlets • $20.80

Pierro Fire Gully Semillon Sauvignon Blanc

2000 Light green-yellow; the bouquet is quite potent, with pronounced herbaceous/grassy aromas that, paradoxically, are ripe, not green. Latent passionfruit and gooseberry comes through strongly on a refreshing palate, which happily retains some delicacy. **rating:** 91

best drinking Now–2003 **best vintages** '00 **drink with** Coquilles St Jacques • $18.80

Pierro Chardonnay

1999 Medium yellow-green; soft, ripe peach fruit and relatively restrained oak on the bouquet give little hint of the massive impact of the powerful palate, with creamy/nutty mlf influences, finishing with soft acidity. The alcohol seems higher than the 14° stipulated. **rating:** 89

best drinking Now–2003 **best vintages** '86, '87, '89, '90, '92, '94, '95, '96 **drink with** Seafood pasta • $52.80

Pierro Cabernet Merlot

🍷🍷🍷🍷🍷 **1998** Light to medium red-purple; the bouquet is clean, firm and fresh, featuring bright berry fruit with minimal oak influence. The wine opens up further on the palate with sweet, dark berry fruit and positive oak; good moderating tannins to balance the wine on the finish. **rating:** 93

best drinking 2003–2008 **best vintages** '98 **drink with** Lamb shoulder • $46.80

Pierro Fire Gully Cabernet Sauvignon Merlot

🍷🍷🍷🍷 **1999** Medium purple-red; a sappy/foresty/earthy bouquet is followed by a palate with more sweet fruit than anticipated, but which then sharpens off with a somewhat acidic finish. **rating:** 84

best drinking 2002–2006 **best vintages** NA **drink with** Yearling beef • $26.80

piesse brook NR

226 Aldersyde Road, Bickley, WA 6076 **region** Perth Hills

phone (08) 9293 3309 **fax** (08) 9293 3309 **open** Sat 1–5, Sun, public holidays 10–5 and by appointment

winemaker Di Bray, Ray Boyanich (Michael Davies Consultant) **production** 1200 **est.** 1974

product range ($10–17.50 CD) Chardonnay, Shiraz, Brian Murphy Reserve Shiraz, Merlot, Cabernet Sauvignon, Cabernet Merlot, Cabernet Shiraz, Cabernova (early-drinking style).

summary Surprisingly good red wines made in tiny quantities, and which have received consistent accolades over the years. The first Chardonnay was made in 1993; a trophy-winning Shiraz was produced in 1995. Now has 4 hectares of chardonnay, shiraz, merlot and cabernet sauvignon under vine.

pieter van gent ★★★

Black Springs Road, Mudgee, NSW 2850 **region** Mudgee

phone (02) 6373 3807 **fax** (02) 6373 3910 **open** Mon–Sat 9–5, Sun 11–4

winemaker Pieter van Gent, Philip van Gent **production** 15 000 **est.** 1978

product range ($11.50–24 CD) The dry wines are the Verdelho, Chardonnay, Müller Thurgau, Shiraz, Shiraz Cabernet and Cabernet Sauvignon; the Flower of Florence, Angelic White and Sundance Soft Red all have varying degrees of sweetness; fortified wines are the specialty, including Pipeclay Port, Mudgee White Port, Cornelius Port, Mudgee Oloroso, Mistella, Pipeclay Vermouth.

summary Many years ago Pieter van Gent worked for Lindemans, before joining Craigmoor then moving to his own winery in 1979, where he and his family have forged a strong reputation and following for his fortified wines in particular, although the range extends far wider. The wines are seldom seen outside cellar door.

Pieter van Gent Unwooded Chardonnay

🍷🍷🍷🍷 **2000** Very pale straw-green; light lemon and melon varietal fruit on the bouquet is followed by a light-bodied but clean palate, with lemony/citrussy overtones to the fruit. **rating:** 82

best drinking Now **best vintages** NA **drink with** Crab • $14

Pieter van Gent Chardonnay

🍷🍷🍷🍷 **1999** Very obvious smoky/tangy barrel-ferment oak inputs lead the bouquet and the complex palate; oak challenges the fruit throughout the wine, but there is certainly plenty happening here. **rating:** 86

best drinking Now–2003 **best vintages** NA **drink with** Spiced chicken • $17.50

piggs peake NR

697 Hermitage Road, Pokolbin, NSW 2321 **region** Lower Hunter Valley

phone (02) 6574 7000 **fax** (02) 6574 7070 **open** Mon–Sat 10–4, Sun 10–3

winemaker Steve Dodd, Lesley Minter **production** 5000 **est.** 1998

product range ($14–20 CD) Pokolbin Semillon, Lovedale Semillon, Pokolbin Verdelho, Rylstone Chardonnay, Lovedale Premium Chardonnay, Mudgee Botrytis Semillon, Hunter Valley Shiraz, Hunter Valley Merlot, Mudgee Tempranillo Cabernet.

summary The derivation of the name remains a mystery to me, and if it is a local landmark, I have not heard of it. Certain it is that it is one of the newest wineries to be constructed in the Hunter Valley, sourcing most of its grapes from other growers to complement the 1 hectare of estate plantings.

pikes ★★★★

Polish Hill River Road, Sevenhill, SA 5453 **region** Clare Valley
phone (08) 8843 4370 **fax** (08) 8843 4353 **open** 7 days 10–4
winemaker Neil Pike, John Trotter **production** 35 000 **est.** 1984
product range ($15–28 R) Riesling, Reserve Riesling, Sauvignon Blanc, Sauvignon Blanc Semillon, Chardonnay, Shiraz, Shiraz Grenache Mourvedre, Cabernet Sauvignon.
summary Owned by the Pike brothers, one of whom (Andrew) was for many years the senior viticulturist with Southcorp, the other (Neil) a former winemaker at Mitchells. Pikes now has its own winery, with Neil Pike presiding. Generously constructed and flavoured wines are the order of the day. The wines are exported to the UK, the US, Canada, Japan, Switzerland, Germany, New Zealand, Malaysia, Singapore and Belgium.

Pikes Riesling

YYYY **2000** Light green-yellow; a firm bouquet with clean, bright herb and mineral aromas is followed by a palate in similar mould, with considerable grip and length; a died-in-the-wool stayer. **rating:** 89
best drinking 2002–2012 **best vintages** '86, '90, '92, '93, '95, '97, '00 **drink with** Lightly spiced chicken salad • $16.99

Pikes Shiraz

YYYY **1998** Medium red, with some purple hues. The bouquet is of moderate to full intensity, clean, with berry fruit (but no spice) and subtle oak. The full-flavoured palate is in an open, honest style, with blackberry and bitter chocolate fruit flavours supplemented by substantial tannins. **rating:** 89
best drinking 2003–2013 **best vintages** '85, '86, '90, '91, '93, '98 **drink with** Char-grilled rump • $25

Pikes Shiraz Grenache Mourvedre

YYYY **1999** Light to medium red-purple; the bouquet is quite fragrant and spicy, the light- to medium-bodied palate opening with similar spicy/berry fruit, a touch of mint and then sweet vanilla oak before finishing with soft, supple tannins. Nice wine. **rating:** 89
best drinking Now–2004 **best vintages** '98 **drink with** Kangaroo fillet • $20

Pikes Cabernet Sauvignon

YYYY **1998** Medium to full red-purple; the bouquet offers a mix of berry, blackberry and plum in a moderately intense mode. The palate is firm, fresh and tight, with a touch of mint, and still needing to soften and open up. When it does, will merit higher points. **rating:** 86
best drinking 2004–2009 **best vintages** NA **drink with** Roast beef • $28

---

pinelli NR

30 Bennett Street, Caversham, WA 6055 **region** Swan District
phone (08) 9279 6818 **fax** (08) 9377 4259 **open** 7 days 10–6
winemaker Robert Pinelli **production** 7000 **est.** 1979
product range ($5–16 CD) Limited table wine range centred on Chenin Blanc, Chardonnay, Shiraz and Cabernet Sauvignon, and an extensive range of fortified wines, including Cabernet-based Vintage Port. The wines have won a number of medals at the Perth Show in recent years.
summary Dominic Pinelli and son Robert (a Roseworthy Agricultural College graduate) sell 75 per cent of their production in flagons but are seeking to place more emphasis on bottled-wine sales in the wake of recent show successes with Chenin Blanc.

pipers brook vineyard ★★★★★

1216 Pipers Brook Road, Pipers Brook, Tas 7254 **region** Northern Tasmania
phone (03) 6382 7527 **fax** (03) 6382 7226 **open** 7 days 10–5
winemaker Andrew Pirie **production** 60 000 **est.** 1974
product range ($22–55 R) Riesling, Gewurztraminer, Pinot Gris, Chardonnay, Reserve Chardonnay, Museum Chardonnay, Reserve Pinot Noir, Opimium (Cabernets), Summit Vineyard Chardonnay, Pirie Cuvée Vintage Sparkling; also Estate range of Riesling, Gewurztraminer, Pinot Gris, Pinot Noir.
summary The Pipers Brook Tasmanian empire has continued to grow apace. It now has over 220 hectares of vineyard supporting the Pipers Brook and Ninth Island labels (see separate entry for Ninth Island), with the major focus, of course, being on Pipers Brook. As ever, fastidious viticulture and winemaking, immaculate packaging and

enterprising marketing constitute a potent and effective blend. Piper Brook operates three cellar-door outlets, one at headquarters, one at Strathlyn (phone 03 6330 2388), the third at Ninth Island. The wines are exported to the UK, the US, Japan, Canada and Singapore, and are distributed throughout Australia by S Smith and Son. However, a considerable part of its sales are to its shareholders, who receive a substantial discount, and who have supported the company through to its public status on the Australian Stock Exchange.

Pipers Brook Vineyard Estate Riesling

YYYYY **2000** Brand managers take note: a label revamp that is so subtle you would barely know it has taken place, as stylish as the wine. Pristine, spotless passionfruit and lime fruit runs through a delicate but intense and long palate, with fine minerally acidity. Great Tasmanian vintage, great wine. **rating:** 93

best drinking Now–2012 **best vintages** '82, '91, '92, '93, '94, '98, '99, '00 **drink with** Pan-fried scallops • $22.50

Pipers Brook Gewurztraminer

YYYYY **2000** Light green-yellow; the delicate and flowery bouquet has aromas of rose petal and spice, the super-elegant palate being similarly crisp and delicate until the very finish, where there is just a little varietal grip. **rating:** 90

best drinking Now–2004 **best vintages** '99, '00 **drink with** Duck liver pâté • $28

Pipers Brook Pinot Gris

YYYYY **2000** Distinct straw/pink tinges to the bouquet are an indicator of the variety, and not of any oxidation problems. Aromatic ripe pear, apple and a touch of spice aromas flow through to the palate, with spice and pear fruit; the 13.9°alcohol becomes apparent only on the aftertaste. **rating:** 90

best drinking Now **best vintages** '00 **drink with** Steamed fish, Chinese style • $22.50

Pipers Brook Vineyard Estate Chardonnay

YYYYY **1999** The second of three consecutive outstanding vintages for Tasmania, coupled with the impact of fully mature vines, has helped build a great wine. Fresh, elegant citrus and melon fruit, a hint of cashew and subtle oak are the preamble; the palate is stylish and long, and not overly acidic. **rating:** 95

best drinking Now–2009 **best vintages** '82, '88, '91, '92, '93, '94, '97, '98, '99 **drink with** Tasmanian lobster • $34.95

Pipers Brook Pirie Cuvée

YYYYY **1996** The first release (1995) was an outstanding success, and this carries on the same style. Very elegant, the offsets to the naturally high Tasmanian acidity are a high percentage of pinot noir and barrel ageing of a portion of the base wines. Intense, with some bready autolysis, it has great mid-palate flavour and persistence. **rating:** 95

best drinking Now **best vintages** '95, '96 **drink with** Tasmanian oysters • $55

Pipers Brook Vineyard Estate Pinot Noir

YYYY **1999** Medium red-purple; the bouquet offers cherry, raspberry and plum, in a moderately intense frame, with touches of savoury/foresty characters, and some lift. The palate moves more to ripe fruit flavours with a touch of mint; a slightly hard, glossy edge needs to soften. **rating:** 89

best drinking 2002–2007 **best vintages** '99 **drink with** NA • $34.95

piromit wines NR

113 Hanwood Avenue, Hanwood, NSW 2680 **region** Riverina
phone (02) 6963 0200 **fax** (02) 6963 0277 **open** Mon–Fri 9–5
winemaker Dom Piromalli, Pat Mittiga **production** 60 000 **est.** 1998
product range ($8–17 CD) Semillon, Old Briggie Semillon Chardonnay, Colombard Chardonnay, Chardonnay, Botrytis Semillon, Shiraz, Old Briggie Shiraz Cabernet, Cabernet Merlot, Cabernet Sauvignon.
summary I simply cannot resist quoting directly from the background information kindly supplied to me. 'Piromit Wines is a relatively new boutique winery situated in Hanwood, New South Wales. The winery complex, which crushed 1000 tonnes this season, was built for the 1999 vintage on a 14-acre site which was until recently used as a drive-in. Previous to this, wines were made on our 100-acre vineyard. The winery site is being developed into an innovative tourist attraction complete with an Italian restaurant and landscaped formal gardens.' It is safe to say this extends the concept of a boutique winery into new territory, but then it is a big country. It is a family business run by Pat Mittiga, Dom Piromalli and Paul Hudson.

pirramimma ★★★★

Johnston Road, McLaren Vale, SA 5171 **region** McLaren Vale
phone (08) 8323 8205 **fax** (08) 8323 9224 **open** Mon–Fri 9–5, Sat 11–5, Sun, public holidays 11.30–4
winemaker Geoff Johnston **production** 30 000 **est.** 1892
product range ($10–21.50 R) Stocks Hill Semillon Chardonnay, Adelaide Hills Semillon, McLaren Vale Semillon, Hillsview Chardonnay, Stocks Hill Shiraz, Petit Verdot, Hillsview Cabernet Merlot, Cabernet Sauvignon, Ports.
summary An operation with large vineyard holdings of very high quality and a winery that devotes much of its considerable capacity to contract-processing of fruit for others. In terms of the brand, has been a consistent under-performer during the 1990s. The marketing of the brand does scant justice to the very considerable resources available to it, notably its gold medal Petit Verdot and fine, elegant Chardonnay. Exports to the UK, New Zealand, Germany, Switzerland and the US.

Pirramimma Stocks Hill Shiraz

YYYY **1998** Medium to full red-purple; the bouquet is quite fragrant, with smooth, dark cherry fruit and distinct touches of spice. The savoury/chocolate/dark cherry fruit flavours of the palate are supported by a deft touch of vanilla oak and gentle tannins. Carries its 14° with ease. **rating:** 87
best drinking 2003–2008 **best vintages** '98 **drink with** Devilled kidneys • $20

Pirramimma Hillsview Cabernet Merlot

YYYY **1998** Medium to full red-purple; the bouquet is quite powerful, with a mix of blackberry/blackcurrant and chocolate; the palate is slightly rustic, but oozing rich, regional fruit character, reflecting the excellent vintage. **rating:** 87
best drinking 2003–2010 **best vintages** NA **drink with** Braised ox cheek • $21.35

Pirramimma Cabernet Sauvignon

YYYY **1997** Medium red-purple; the bouquet has an array of smoky, earthy, chocolatey, savoury aromas all within the cabernet varietal spectrum. There is lots of sweet, ripe, dusty/chocolatey cabernet fruit on the palate, with nicely balanced tannins. Any oak is incidental. **rating:** 89
best drinking Now–2007 **best vintages** NA **drink with** Braised ox cheek • $14.90

---

pizzini ★★★

King Valley Road, Wangaratta, Vic 3768 **region** King Valley
phone (03) 5729 8278 **fax** (03) 5729 8495 **open** 7 days 12–5
winemaker Alfred Pizzini, Joel Pizzini, Mark Walpole **production** 8000 **est.** 1980
product range ($12–40 CD) Riesling, Sauvingon Blanc, Alfred Pizzini Chardonnay, Sangiovese, Nebbiolo, Alfred Pizzini Shiraz Cabernet, Cabernet, Shiraz.
summary Fred and Katrina Pizzini have been grape-growers in the King Valley for over 20 years with 66 hectares of vineyard. Grape-growing (rather than winemaking) still continues to be the major focus of activity, but their move into winemaking has been particularly successful, and I can personally vouch for their Italian cooking skills. It is not surprising, then, that their wines should span both Italian and traditional varieties.

plantagenet ★★★★

Albany Highway, Mount Barker, WA 6324 **region** Great Southern
phone (08) 9851 2150 **fax** (08) 9851 1839 **open** Mon–Fri 9–5, weekends 10–4
winemaker Gavin Berry **production** 55 000 **est.** 1974
product range ($16–35 CD) Riesling, Omrah Sauvignon Blanc, Omrah Chardonnay (unoaked), Mount Barker Chardonnay, Fronti, Fine White, Fine Red, Pinot Noir, Shiraz, Henry II, Cabernet Sauvignon, Mount Barker Brut; Breakaway Fine White and Fine Red.
summary The senior winery in the Mount Barker region, making superb wines across the full spectrum of variety and style: highly aromatic Riesling, tangy citrus-tinged Chardonnay, glorious Rhône-style Shiraz, ultra-stylish Cabernet Sauvignon and an occasional inspiring Pinot Noir. Exports to the US, the UK, Germany, Austria, Singapore, Japan, Switzerland and Hong Kong.

Plantagenet Omrah Sauvignon Blanc

YYYY **2000** Light green-yellow; the bouquet is quite fragrant, with a mix of passionfruit and gooseberry aromas which are most appealing. The palate, while lively, fresh and crisp, doesn't quite live up to the promise of the bouquet, but still provides plenty of action. **rating:** 87

best drinking Now **best vintages** '00 **drink with** Shellfish • $16

Plantagenet Mount Barker Chardonnay

YYYY **1999** Medium yellow-green; the bouquet is quite pungent, with citrus/melon fruit and some funky lees characters. The palate is likewise complex and tangy, again showing some offbeat, quasi-Burgundian characters. No shortage of character. **rating:** 85

best drinking Now **best vintages** '81, '83, '86, '92, '94, '95 **drink with** Breast of chicken • $17

Plantagenet Mount Barker Shiraz

YYYYY **1998** Medium to full red-purple; a clean, lively, fresh bouquet with sweet red berry and cherry fruit picks up pace and complexity on the palate, with a core of red berry/cherry fruit surrounded by lovely splashes of spice and tannin; very good flavour and structure. Trophy winner 2000 Qantas Wine Show of Western Australia. **rating:** 95

best drinking 2003–2013 **best vintages** '82, '83, '85, '88, '89, '90, '91, '93, '94, '96, '98 **drink with** Hare, squab • $35

Plantagenet Omrah Shiraz

YYYYY **1999** Youthful purple-red; there is a complex savoury edge to ripe plum and cherry shiraz fruit on the bouquet; the palate has good flavour and texture, with soft, ripe tannins and nicely balanced oak. **rating:** 90

best drinking 2003–2008 **best vintages** '90 **drink with** Lamb shashlik • $19.50

Plantagenet Omrah Merlot Cabernet

YYYY **1999** Medium to full red-purple; the bouquet is quite fragrant, with a mix of juicy berry, spice and earth. The palate is as yet somewhat disjointed; the spicy berry fruit is quite stylish, but the oak a little dusty and the wine still a little callow. Needs some time to get its act together, but should do so. **rating:** 88

best drinking 2003–2009 **best vintages** '99 **drink with** Pizza • $17

Plantagenet Mount Barker Cabernet Sauvignon

YYYYY **1998** Medium red-purple; clean berry and blackcurrant aromas, together with a touch of oak, are followed by a delicious palate, with pristine cassis/blackcurrant fruit, a touch of chocolate, ripe tannins and subtle oak. **rating:** 90

best drinking 2003–2008 **best vintages** '81, '83, '85, '86, '90, '91, '94, '98 **drink with** Rack of lamb • $28

platt's NR

Mudgee Road, Gulgong, NSW 2852 **region** Mudgee

phone (02) 6374 1700 **fax** (02) 6372 1055 **open** 7 days 9–5

winemaker Barry Platt **production** 4000 **est.** 1983

product range ($9–12 CD) Chardonnay, Semillon, Gewurztraminer, Cabernet Sauvignon.

summary No recent tastings; problems with oak handling marked the last wines tasted some years ago.

plunkett ★★★

Lambing Gully Road, Avenel, Vic 3664 **region** Central Victorian Mountain Country

phone (03) 5796 2150 **fax** (03) 5796 2147 **open** 7 days 11–5

winemaker Sam Plunkett **production** 10 000 **est.** 1980

product range ($15–34 CD) The top-of-the-range wines are released under the Strathbogie Ranges label with Riesling, Chardonnay, Reserve Shiraz, Merlot, Cabernet Merlot, Sparkling Chardonnay Pinot; standard wines under the Blackwood Ridge brand of Gewurztraminer, Semillon, Sauvignon Blanc Semillon, Unwooded Chardonnay, Botrytis Gewurztraminer, Pinot Noir, Shiraz.

summary The Plunkett family first planted grapes way back in 1968, establishing 3 acres with 25 experimental varieties. Commercial plantings commenced in 1980, with 100 hectares now under vine. While holding a vigneron's licence since 1985, the Plunketts did not commence serious marketing of the wines until 1992 and have now settled down into producing an array of wines that are pleasant and well-priced. Wholesale distribution to all States; exports to Malaysia, Canada and Hong Kong.

Plunkett Blackwood Ridge Gewurztraminer

🍷🍷🍷🍷 **2000** Light green-yellow; the bouquet is quite aromatic and flowery, with delicate spicy varietal character; the light- to medium-bodied palate has nice spice and lime flavours, but does move through to a slightly congested finish, always a trap with this variety. **rating:** 84

best drinking Now **best vintages** NA **drink with** Asian • $15

Plunkett Chardonnay Pinot

🍷🍷🍷🍷 **1997** Light straw-green; the bouquet is quite complex, with slight charry overtones to the autolysis/ bready aromas. The palate is fresh and lively, with citrussy fruit, and cleansing acidity on the finish. **rating:** 87

best drinking Now–2004 **best vintages** NA **drink with** Aperitif • $25

Plunkett Blackwood Ridge Pinot Noir

🍷🍷🍷🍷 **1999** Medium to full red-purple; a clean bouquet, with some sweet plum and spice; the palate has above-average varietal character for the Strathbogie Ranges region, pleasantly plummy, and a nice spicy edge. **rating:** 85

best drinking 2002–2005 **best vintages** NA **drink with** Wild-mushroom risotto • $16

poet's corner wines ★★★☆

Craigmoor Road, Mudgee, NSW 2850 **region** Mudgee
phone (02) 6372 2208 **fax** (02) 6372 4464 **open** Mon–Fri 10-4.30, weekends and public holidays 10–4
winemaker James Manners **production** NFP **est.** 1858
product range ($9–22 R) Semillon Sauvignon Blanc Chardonnay, Unwooded Chardonnay, Shiraz Cabernet Sauvignon Cabernet Franc; Poet's Corner PC range of Chardonnay, Merlot, Pinot Chardonnay; Henry Lawson range of Semillon, Chardonnay, Shiraz, Cabernet Sauvignon; also home to the Craigmoor and Montrose labels.
summary Poet's Corner is located in one of the oldest wineries in Australia to remain in more or less continuous production: Craigmoor (as it was previously known) was built by Adam Roth in 1858/1860, and his grandson, Jack Roth, ran the winery until the early 1960s. Notwithstanding the change of name, both Craigmoor and Poet's Corner are produced.

Henry Lawson Semillon

🍷🍷🍷🍷🍷 **2000** Light green-yellow; the bouquet is intense, with excellent grassy/lemony varietal character, the palate delicate, fresh and lively with crisp lemon-tingle flavours due to the touch of carbon dioxide in the wine that will help it age well. Poet's Corner regards 2000 as the best white wine vintage in Mudgee for over a decade. Great value. **rating:** 92

best drinking Now–2010 **best vintages** '00 **drink with** Tempura • $15

Montrose Stony Creek Chardonnay

🍷🍷🍷🍷 **1999** Light to medium yellow-green; the bouquet is clean and fresh, with citrus and melon fruit supported by a light touch of oak; the palate is a replay of the bouquet, with above-average length. **rating:** 86

best drinking Now–2004 **best vintages** NA **drink with** Veal fricassee • $16

Henry Lawson Shiraz

🍷🍷🍷🍷🍷 **1998** Medium red-purple; a quite complex bouquet, with spicy berry fruit and a dusting of vanilla oak; the palate has abundant dark cherry and chocolate fruit, plus a touch of spice; a fruit-driven style, though the tannins and oak are there in good balance. **rating:** 90

best drinking 2003–2008 **best vintages** '97, '98 **drink with** Osso bucco • $18

Poet's Corner Shiraz Cabernet Sauvignon Cabernet Franc

🍷🍷🍷🍷 **1999** Bright red-purple; striking raspberry fruit (and subtle oak) on the bouquet is reflected in the luscious, sweet berry fruit on the palate. The oak balance and integration is good, as are the soft tannins. Full flavoured but easy on the gums. **rating:** 87

best drinking 2002–2007 **best vintages** NA **drink with** Beef in red wine sauce • $8.99

Montrose Sangiovese

🍷🍷🍷🍷 **1998** Light to medium red; light, savoury, spicy, earthy aromas and flavours are typical of the variety; the palate has some length, but the tannin profile is low. Given the age of the vines, one has to conclude that this is not a distinguished clone. **rating:** 84

best drinking 2002–2006 **best vintages** NA **drink with** Vitello tonnata • $22

Craigmoor Cabernet Sauvignon

🍷🍷🍷🍷🍷 **1996** Quite dark red; sweet, dark berry fruit has whispers of chocolate, spice and vanilla on the bouquet. The palate has rich chocolate and dark berry fruit, with excellently balanced and integrated oak. An excellent Mudgee red, totally delicious now but with time in front of it. **rating:** 92

best drinking Now–2006 **best vintages** '96 **drink with** Shoulder of lamb • $14

Henry Lawson Cabernet Sauvignon

🍷🍷🍷🍷 **1998** Medium red-purple; dusty vanilla oak surrounds the quite solid fruit of the bouquet, and on the palate blackberry/currant fruit struggles with persistent, chewy tannins on the one hand, and lots of vanilla oak on the other. A lumbering heavyweight, perhaps, but does pack a lethal punch. **rating:** 86

best drinking 2003–2010 **best vintages** NA **drink with** Rump steak • $18

pokolbin estate ★★☆

McDonalds Road, Pokolbin, NSW 2321 **region** Lower Hunter Valley
phone (02) 4998 7524 **fax** (02) 4998 7765 **open** 7 days 10–6
winemaker Contract **production** 2500 **est.** 1980
product range ($15–40 CD) Riesling, Semillon, Chardonnay, Show Reserve Chardonnay, Late Picked Riesling, Dessert Verdelho, Shiraz; Port.

summary An unusual outlet, offering its own-label wines made under contract by Trevor Drayton, together with the wines of Lake's Folly, Peacock Hill and Pothana, and with cheap varietal 'cleanskins'. Wine quality under the Pokolbin Estate label has been very modest, although the 1997 Hunter Riesling (perversely, true Riesling, not Semillon) won a silver medal and was the top-pointed wine in its class at the 1997 Hunter Valley Wine Show. No recent news.

poole's rock ★★★☆

Lot 41 Wollombi Road, Broke, NSW 2330 **region** Lower Hunter Valley
phone (02) 9667 1622 **fax** (02) 9667 1442 **open** Not
winemaker Philip Ryan (Contract) **production** 4000 **est.** 1988
product range ($23.50 R) Chardonnay.

summary Sydney merchant banker David Clarke has had a long involvement with the wine industry, including a directorship of McGuigan Brothers Limited. The 18-hectare Poole's Rock vineyard, planted purely to chardonnay, is his personal venture, the resource recently bolstered by the acquisition of the larger, adjoining Simon Whitlam Vineyard. The wine has retail distribution throughout Australia and is exported to the UK and the US.

pooley wines NR

Cooinda Vale Vineyard, Barton Vale Road, Campania, Tas 7026 **region** Southern Tasmania
phone (03) 6224 3591 **fax** (03) 6224 3591 **open** Wed–Sun 10–5
winemaker Mat Pooley, Andrew Hood (Contract) **production** 1000 **est.** 1985
product range ($15–24 CD) Cooinda Vale Riesling, Coal River Riesling, Coal River Chardonnay, Nellies Nest Pinot Noir, Cooinda Vale Pinot Noir; Reserve Range of Cooinda Vale Riesling, Cooinda Vale Pinot Noir.

summary Three generations of the Pooley family have been involved in the development of the Cooinda Vale Estate; it was indeed under the Cooinda Vale label that the winery was previously known. After a tentative start on a small scale, plantings have now reached 8 hectares on a property that covers both sides of the Coal River in a region which is substantially warmer and drier than most people realise. The wines have limited retail distribution in Victoria (Southern Fine Wines) and of course in Tasmania.

Pooley Wines Coal River Riesling

🍷🍷🍷🍷 **2000** Medium yellow-green; a big, rich, full-on lime, earth and spice bouquet is followed by a powerful palate, with a touch of relatively high acidity on the finish. **rating:** 84

best drinking Now–2004 **best vintages** NA **drink with** Trout mousse • $20

Pooley Wines Cooinda Vale Riesling

🍷🍷🍷🍷 **2000** Light to medium green-yellow; clean but very reserved fruit, in a radically different style from the Coal River wine. The palate is in similarly contrasting style: gentle, pretty, clean and soft. **rating:** 83

best drinking Now–2004 **best vintages** NA **drink with** Cold seafood • $18

Pooley Coal River Chardonnay

🍷🍷🍷🍷 **2000** Medium green-yellow; the bouquet is quite complex, with good fruit and oak balance and integration, moving into a pleasant, ripe and quite round melon-fruited palate. Does finish slightly short, however.

rating: 85

best drinking Now–2003 **best vintages** NA **drink with** Breast of chicken • $22

poplar bend NR

RMB 8655 Main Creek Road, Main Ridge, Vic 3928 **region** Mornington Peninsula
phone (03) 5989 6046 **fax** (03) 5989 6460 **open** Weekends and public holidays 10–5 and by appointment
winemaker David Briggs **production** 350 **est.** 1988
product range ($16–28 ML) Pineau Chloe, Cabernet Chloe, Sparkling Chloe, Pinot Noir, Cellar Reserve Pinot Noir, Cabernet Shiraz.
summary Poplar Bend was the child of Melbourne journalist, author and raconteur Keith Dunstan and wife, Marie, who moved into full-scale retirement in 1997, selling Poplar Bend to David Briggs. The changes are few; the label still depicts Chloe in all her glory, which could be calculated to send the worthy inhabitants of the Bureau of Alcohol, Tobacco and Firearms (of the US) into a state of cataleptic shock.

port phillip estate ★★★★☆

261 Red Hill Road, Red Hill, Vic 3937 **region** Mornington Peninsula
phone (03) 5989 2708 **fax** (03) 5989 2708 **open** Weekends and public holidays 12–5
winemaker Lindsay McCall (Contract) **production** 4000 **est.** 1987
product range ($18–35 R) Sauvignon Blanc, Chardonnay, Pinot Noir, Reserve Pinot Noir, Reserve Shiraz, Shiraz.
summary Established by leading Melbourne QC Jeffrey Sher, who, after some prevarication, sold the estate to Giorgio and Dianne Gjergja in February 2000. The Gjergjas are rightly more than content with the quality and style of the wines; the main change is enhanced cellar-door facilities.

Port Phillip Estate Pinot Noir Reserve

🍷🍷🍷🍷🍷 **1999** Medium red-purple; an intense and fragrant bouquet with sappy/savoury fruit and charry oak leads into a long, lively, slippery/sappy/savoury/foresty palate with strong varietal character, but less ripe fruit than the Paringa.

rating: 90

best drinking Now–2005 **best vintages** '97, '98, '99 **drink with** Duck • $35

port stephens wines NR

69 Nelson Bay Road, Bobs Farm, NSW 2316 **region** Northern Rivers Zone
phone (02) 4982 6411 **fax** (02) 4982 6766 **open** 7 days 10–5
winemaker Contract **production** 3500 **est.** 1984
product range ($10–21.50 CD) Chardonnay, Tri-Blend, Tomaree White, Late Harvest, Golden Sands, Shiraz, Cabernet Merlot, Cabernet Sauvignon, Sparkling and Fortifieds.
summary Planting of the quite substantial Port Stephens Wines vineyard began in 1984, and there are now 4 hectares of vines in production. The wines are made under contract by John Baruzzi at Wilderness Estate in the Hunter Valley but are sold through an attractive, dedicated cellar-door sales outlet on site.

portree ★★★☆

72 Powells Track, via Mount William Road, Lancefield, Vic 3455 **region** Macedon Ranges
phone (03) 5429 1422 **fax** (03) 5429 2205 **open** Weekends and public holidays 11–5
winemaker Ken Murchison **production** 800 **est.** 1983
product range ($15–35 CD) Chardonnay, Greenstone Chardonnay (unoaked), Macedon (Blanc de Blanc), Pinot Noir, Damask (Cabernet Franc Rosé), Quarry Red (Cabernet Franc Merlot).
summary Owner Ken Murchison selected his 4-hectare Macedon vineyard after studying viticulture at Charles Sturt University and being strongly influenced by Dr Andrew Pirie's doctoral thesis. All of the wines show distinct cool-climate characteristics, the Quarry Red having clear similarities to the wines of Chinon in the Loire Valley. However, it is with Chardonnay that Portree has done best and which is its principal wine (in terms of volume). As from the 1998 vintage the wines have been made at an on-site winery.

Portree Macedon Ranges Chardonnay

ΨΨΨΨΥ **1998** Glowing yellow-green; smooth stonefruit and citrus aromas announce a wine that is still tightly knit, with good length and lemony acidity. The oak handling throughout has been well judged. **rating:** 90

best drinking Now–2004 **best vintages** '91, '93, '97, '98 **drink with** Fish terrine • $24

Portree Pinot Noir

ΨΨΨΥ **1999** Attractive red-purple colour; the bouquet is clean, with direct plummy fruit and some fragrance. The palate takes the fruit characters of the bouquet through to a fresh, clean finish. A little simple as yet, but will likely develop in bottle. **rating:** 84

best drinking Now–2004 **best vintages** NA **drink with** Slow-cooked Tasmanian salmon • $24

potters clay vineyards ★★★

Main Road, Willunga, SA 5172 **region** McLaren Vale
phone (08) 8556 2799 **fax** (08) 8556 2922 **open** Not
winemaker John Bruschi **production** 900 **est.** 1994
product range ($15.90–16.90 R) Chardonnay, Shiraz, Merlot Cabernet Franc.
summary John and Donna Bruschi are second-generation grape-growers who assumed full ownership of the 16-hectare Potters Clay Vineyard in 1994 with the aim of establishing their own winery and label. In 1999 construction of stage one of a two-stage boutique winery was completed. Stage one is a winery-production facility, stage two (at some future date) is to be cellar door, restaurant and garden/picnic area. At least this is in the correct order; all too often it is the cellar door and restaurant which come first. The first and second vintages (1998 and 1999) were made off site by John Bruschi, but future operations will be centralised. The clever packaging and high-quality promotional literature should do much to enhance sales.

powercourt vineyard NR

2 McEwans Road, Legana, Tas 7277 **region** Northern Tasmania
phone (03) 6330 1225 **fax** (03) 6330 2161 **open** By appointment
winemaker Ralph Power **production** 1000 **est.** 1972
product range ($18 CD) Pinot Noir, Cabernet Pinot, Cabernet Sauvignon.
summary A long-established but ultra-low-profile winery with a mostly local clientele, also retail distribution in Canberra.

prentice NR

30 Brasser Avenue, Dromana, Vic 3936 **region** South East Australia Zone
phone (03) 5989 9063 **fax** (03) 5989 9068 **open** Not
winemaker Daniel Green, Neil Prentice **production** 2500 **est.** 1996
product range ($15–27 R) Victoria Chardonnay, Whitfield Pinot Gris, Pinot Grigio, Pinot Noir, Nebbiolo.
summary The Prentice brand is owned by a group of Melbourne businessmen, headed by its founder, Neil Prentice. Both restaurateur and vigneron, Neil Prentice has been making and marketing wine since 1985 under the quite separate Moondarra label. Prentice sources contract-grown grapes from various parts of southeast Australia, primarily the King Valley in Victoria, but also Coonawarra and the Barossa Valley. Up until the 2000 vintage the wines were made at Rochford Winery by David Creed; they are now made at Tuck's Ridge at Mornington Peninsula by Daniel Green. The wines are all well made and competitively priced. Distribution is through Nelson Wine Company Victoria, Young and Rashleigh New South Wales, and Select Vineyards, Queensland.

Prentice Whitfield Pinot Gris

ΨΨΨΥ **2000** Very pale straw-green; a clean, flinty/minerally bouquet without much fruit is followed by a delicate, fresh, faintly spicy palate. The wine is well enough made but lacks fruit intensity, unless you like northern Italian Pinot Grigio, of course. **rating:** 84

best drinking Now–2004 **best vintages** NA **drink with** Fresh crab • $18

Prentice Victoria Chardonnay

ΨΨΨΨ **1998** Light green-yellow; a fresh, clean bouquet with gentle nectarine and a touch of cashew is followed by a nicely balanced, fresh palate with nectarine and melon fruit, and little or no oak. **rating:** 85

best drinking Now–2004 **best vintages** NA **drink with** Creamy pasta • $19

Prentice Whitlands Pinot Noir

🍷🍷🍷 1998 Medium red, with just a touch of purple; the savoury/foresty bouquet is of light to medium intensity, the palate has some length, but seems to be starting to drop the sweeter end of the fruit spectrum of flavour, suggesting it is quickly moving past its best. **rating:** 81

best drinking Now **best vintages** NA **drink with** Smoked chicken • $27

preston peak NR

31 Preston Peak Lane, Toowoomba, Qld 4352 **region** Granite Belt
phone (07) 4630 9499 **fax** (07) 4630 9499 **open** Wed–Fri 11–3, weekends 10–5
winemaker Philippa Hambleton, Rod MacPherson **production** 5500 **est.** 1994
product range ($11–26 CD) Code Flag White, Reserve Chardonnay, Leaf Series Chardonnay, Code Flag Red, Wild Flower White, Wild Flower Red, Venus, Leaf Series Shiraz, Cabernet Merlot, Cabernets, sparkling and fortified.
summary The ambitious growth plans of dentist owners Ashley Smith and Kym Thumpkin have seemingly slowed to a more realistic level; winemaking continues at Wyberba, with the proposed winery at Toowoomba on hold, but cellar-door sales take place there.

Preston Peak Leaf Series Chardonnay

🍷🍷🍷 1999 Light green-yellow; the bouquet is clean, with citrus and melon fruit aromas, and no oak contribution evident. The light- to medium-bodied palate has gentle mouthfeel; there is not much happening, but what there is, is pleasant. **rating:** 81

best drinking Now **best vintages** NA **drink with** Crabmeat cannelone • $19

Preston Peak Cabernet Franc Cabernet Sauvignon Merlot Shiraz

🍷🍷🍷 1999 Medium purple-red; the bouquet is fairly and squarely in a herbal/leafy/minty spectrum, suggesting lack of physiological ripeness. The same flavours prevail on the palate, which is just a little rough around the edges. **rating:** 80

best drinking 2002–2005 **best vintages** NA **drink with** Marinated beef • $26

primo estate ★★★★★

Old Port Wakefield Road, Virginia, SA 5120 **region** Adelaide Plains
phone (08) 8380 9442 **fax** (08) 8380 9696 **open** June–Aug Mon–Sat 10–4, Sep–May Mon–Fri 10–4
winemaker Joseph Grilli **production** 20 000 **est.** 1979
product range ($13–50 R) La Biondina Colombard, Joseph La Magia Botrytis Riesling, Il Briccone Shiraz Sangiovese, Joseph Moda Amarone Cabernet Merlot, Joseph The Fronti, Joseph Sparkling Red.
summary Roseworthy dux Joe Grilli has risen way above the constraints of the hot Adelaide Plains to produce an innovative and always excellent range of wines. The biennial release of the Joseph Sparkling Red (in its tall Italian glass bottle) is eagerly awaited, the wine immediately selling out. Also unusual and highly regarded are the vintage-dated extra virgin olive oils. However, the core lies with the zingy, fresh Colombard, the velvet-smooth Adelaide Shiraz and the distinguished, complex Joseph Cabernet Merlot. National distribution through Negociants; exports to the UK, Asia, Europe and Japan.

Primo Estate La Biondina Colombard

🍷🍷🍷🍷 2000 As ever, a Sauvignon Blanc look-alike, with a fresh, crisp, zingy bouquet, and a palate to match, with excellent flavour, mouthfeel and length; cleansing acid to close. **rating:** 90

best drinking Now **best vintages** '99, '00 **drink with** Shellfish • $14

Primo Estate Il Briccone Shiraz Sangiovese

🍷🍷🍷 1999 Light red, with tinges of purple. Both the bouquet and palate are very light-bodied, with aromas and flavours in a minty spectrum that does not strike me as being particularly varietal. All in all, more interest in the label than in the bottle. **rating:** 82

best drinking Now **best vintages** NA **drink with** Bruschetta • $20

Primo Estate Joseph The Fronti

🍷🍷🍷🍷 NV IV. Mahogany brown, bright and clear; there is attractive raisin/Christmas-cake fruit on the bouquet, with subtle spirit; the palate has bell-clear raisin muscat fruit in a much lighter frame than one usually encounters, truly with Madeira overtones. **rating:** 88

best drinking Now **best vintages** NA **drink with** Biscotti and espresso • $40

prince albert ★★★★☆

100 Lemins Road, Waurn Ponds, Vic 3216 **region** Geelong
phone (03) 5241 8091 **fax** (03) 5241 8091 **open** By appointment
winemaker Bruce Hyett **production** 500 **est.** 1975
product range ($29 ML) Pinot Noir.
summary Australia's true Pinot Noir specialist (it has only ever made the one wine), which also made much of the early running with the variety: the wines always show good varietal character and have rebounded after a dull patch in the second half of the 1980s. In 1998 the vineyard and winery was certified organic by OVAA Inc. Apart from the mailing list, the wine is sold through fine-wine retailers in Sydney and Melbourne, with a little finding its way to the UK.

Prince Albert Pinot Noir

YYYYY **2000** Very good red-purple; the bouquet is rich, opulent and ripe, with blood plum, cherry and spice fruit aromas in abundance. There is considerable depth to the flavour of the palate, again in a ripe, plummy spectrum, finishing with subtle oak. Fully reflects an excellent vintage. **rating:** 92

best drinking 2002–2006 **best vintages** '97, '98, '00 **drink with** Game pie • $29

provenance wines ★★★☆

PO Box 74, Bannockburn, Vic 3331 **region** Port Phillip Zone
phone (03) 5281 7477 **fax** (03) 5281 7377 **open** Not
winemaker Scott Ireland **production** 1200 **est.** 1995
product range ($22–27 R) Pinot Gris, Chardonnay, Pinot Noir, Merlot, Shiraz.
summary Provenance is the reborn Melbourne Wine Company, with Scott Ireland its principal and sole winemaker. All of the wine will be sourced from the Geelong region.

Provenance Pinot Gris

YYYY **1999** Light bronze-pink, the colour due to the variety and not to any technical winemaking shortcoming; apple and a range of spice aromas on the bouquet introduce a palate with presence and length, with more of the spicy apple characters of the bouquet. Good acidity and a clean finish. **rating:** 86

best drinking Now–2004 **best vintages** NA **drink with** Antipasto • $22.35

Provenance Geelong Chardonnay

YYYY **1999** Light to medium yellow-green; the bouquet is quite complex, with a touch of smoky oak and a hint of solids fermentation which is a net contributor. Sweet nectarine and fig fruit and a touch of oak move through to a quite firm finish. **rating:** 86

best drinking Now–2005 **best vintages** NA **drink with** Char-grilled calamari • $22.35

Provenance Geelong Pinot Noir

YYYY **1999** Strong purple-red; ripe, spicy/plummy fruit on the bouquet is followed by a firm, fresh and youthful palate with considerable length; has obvious development potential. **rating:** 87

best drinking Now–2005 **best vintages** '99 **drink with** Smoked duck • $27.10

providence vineyards ★★★★☆

236 Lalla Road, Lalla, Tas 7267 **region** Northern Tasmania
phone (03) 6395 1290 **fax** (03) 6395 1290 **open** 7 days 10–5
winemaker Andrew Hood (Contract) **production** 600 **est.** 1956
product range ($18.50–24.95 CD) Riesling, Semillon, Botrytis Semillon, Chardonnay, Pinot Noir; in exceptional years may be released under the Miguet label.
summary Providence incorporates the pioneer vineyard of Frenchman Jean Miguet, now owned by the Bryce family, which purchased it in 1980. The original 1.3-hectare vineyard has been expanded to a little over 3 hectares, as well as grafting over unsuitable grenache and cabernet (left from the original plantings) to chardonnay, pinot noir and semillon. Miguet in fact called the vineyard 'La Provence', reminding him of the part of France from whence he came, but after 40 years the French authorities forced a name change to Providence.

Providence Vineyards Riesling

YYYY **2000** Medium yellow-green; the bouquet is clean, quite intense, with tropical lime aromas, the palate with good weight and concentration, rounded off with a firm finish. **rating:** 87

best drinking Now–2007 **best vintages** NA **drink with** Antipasto • NA

Providence Chardonnay

2000 Light to medium yellow-green; ripe, sweet melon and nectarine fruit on both the bouquet and palate reflect the warm 2000 vintage. The wine has excellent length and intensity, the oak being a backdrop and no more; finishes with good acidity. **rating:** 94

1999 Light to medium yellow-green; the bouquet is of moderate to full intensity, with cashew, mineral and lees/malolactic component adding complexity. A nicely balanced wine on the palate with more texture than usual and good length. I gave this wine gold medal points on my score sheet at the 2000 Tasmanian Wines Show. Retasted January 2001, once again scoring gold medal points on my sheet for its complexity, otherwise, very similar tasting notes to 12 months ago. **rating:** 91

best drinking Now–2004 **best vintages** '99, '00 **drink with** Fresh abalone • NA

Providence Miguet Reserve Pinot Noir

1999 Medium red-purple; the bouquet is both complex and potent, with spice, licorice and a hint of game; the palate is at once very complex yet elegant, the complexity coming from the plum, spice and ripe fruit flavours; the elegance from the silky texture and fine tannin finish. **rating:** 97

best drinking Now–2006 **best vintages** '99 **drink with** Breast of duck • NA

punters corner

Cnr Riddoch Highway and Racecourse Road, Coonawarra, SA 5263 **region** Coonawarra
phone (08) 8737 2007 **fax** (08) 8737 3138 **open** 7 days 10–5
winemaker Peter Bissell (Contract) **production** 10 000 **est.** 1988
product range ($12–24 CD) Riesling, Chardonnay, Shiraz, Spartacus Reserve Shiraz, Cabernet Merlot, Cabernet Sauvignon.

summary The quaintly named Punters Corner started off life in 1975 as James Haselgrove but in 1992 was acquired by a group of investors who quite evidently had few delusions about the uncertainties of viticulture and winemaking, even in a district as distinguished as Coonawarra. The arrival of Peter Bissell as winemaker at Balnaves paid immediate (and continuing) dividends. Sophisticated packaging and label design add to the appeal of the wines. National retail distribution; exports to the US, Canada, Malaysia, Singapore, Japan, New Zealand, Belgium, Switzerland, Italy and Holland.

queen adelaide

Sturt Highway, Waikerie, SA 5330 **region** Barossa Valley
phone (08) 8541 2588 **fax** (08) 8541 3877 **open** Not
winemaker Peter Gajewski, Sue Franke **production** 800 000 **est.** 1858
product range ($6–7 R) Rhine Riesling, Chenin Blanc, Semillon Chardonnay, Chardonnay, Spätlese Lexia, Sauvignon Blanc, Regency Red, Shiraz, Grenache Pinot Noir.

summary The famous brand established by Woodley Wines and some years ago subsumed into the Seppelt and now Southcorp Group. It is a pure brand, without any particular home either in terms of winemaking or fruit sources, but is hugely successful; Queen Adelaide Chardonnay is and has for some time been the largest-selling bottled white wine in Australia. The move away from agglomerate to synthetic corks should end the glue-taint problems of prior years.

Queen Adelaide Chardonnay

2000 Light green-yellow; the bouquet is light and fresh, with a slightly herbaceous caste to the melon fruit. The palate is light, with more herbaceous melon fruit and a slightly short finish. **rating:** 79

best drinking Now **best vintages** NA **drink with** Takeaway • $6

raleigh winery

NR

Queen Street, Raleigh, NSW 2454 **region** Northern Rivers Zone
phone (02) 6655 4388 **fax** (02) 6655 4265 **open** 7 days 10–5
winemaker Lavinia Dingle **production** 1000 **est.** 1982
product range ($13–25 CD) Semillon Chardonnay, Traminer Riesling, Rouge (Rosé), Late Harvest, Shiraz Cabernet Merlot, Port.

summary Raleigh Winery lays claim to being Australia's most easterly vineyard. The vineyard was initiated in 1982 and was purchased by Lavinia and Neil Dingle in 1989, with the wine produced in part from 1 hectare of vines planted to no less than six varieties. The wines have won bronze medals at the Griffith Wine Show.

ralph fowler wines ★★★★

Limestone Coast Road, Mount Benson, SA 5265 **region** Mount Benson and Robe
phone (08) 8365 6968 **fax** (08) 8365 2516 **open** Mon–Fri 9–5
winemaker Ralph Fowler **production** 6500 **est.** 1999
product range ($18–38 R) Limestone Coast Sauvignon Blanc, Limestone Coast Shiraz, Limestone Coast Cabernet Sauvignon.
summary Established in February 1999 by the Fowler family, headed by well-known winemaker Ralph Fowler, with wife Deborah and children Sarah (currently studying Wine Science) and James all involved in the 40-hectare vineyard property at Mount Benson. Ralph Fowler began his winemaking career at Tyrrell's, moving to the position of chief winemaker before moving to Hungerford Hill, and then to the Hamilton/Leconfield group. He thus brings great experience to the venture, and has interestingly planted two varieties to provide the flagship wines: shiraz and viognier.

ramsay's vin rose NR

30 St Helier Road, The Gurdies, Vic 3984 **region** Gippsland
phone (03) 5997 6531 **fax** (03) 5997 6158 **open** Wed–Mon 12–5
winemaker Dianne Ramsay, Roger Cutler **production** 220 **est.** 1995
product range ($8–18 CD) Riesling, Satin Rosé (dry), Satin Rosé (sweet), Cabernet Sauvignon.
summary The slightly curious name (which looks decidedly strange in conjunction with Riesling and Cabernet Sauvignon) stems from the original intention of Alan and Dianne Ramsay to grow roses on a commercial scale on their property. Frank Cutler at Western Port Winery persuaded them to plant wine grapes instead, and they established the first 2 hectares of vines in 1995. They opened their micro-winery in 1999, and have four two-bedroom self-contained units set around their 800-bush rose garden. The pinot noir and chardonnay are sold to Diamond Valley, so for the time being the range of wines released is limited to Riesling, a Cabernet Franc-based Rosé and Cabernet Sauvignon, with a Merlot maturing in barrel. Ultimately, the Ramsays hope to use all of the estate grapes for their wines.

Ramsay's Vin Rosé Cabernet Sauvignon

YYYY **1999** Medium red-purple; an earthy, savoury bouquet is followed by a light- to medium-bodied palate, with pleasant red berry fruit, subtle oak and just a light dusting of tannin. **rating:** 85
best drinking 2002–2006 **best vintages** NA **drink with** Veal chops • $18

ravenswood lane ★★★★☆

Ravenswood Lane, Hahndorf, SA 5245 **region** Adelaide Hills
phone (08) 8388 1250 **fax** (08) 8388 7233 **open** Not
winemaker Robert Mann, Stephen Pannell (Red), Glenn James (White) at Hardys **production** 12 800 **est.** 1993
product range ($18–50 R) The Gathering Sauvignon Blanc, Beginning Chardonnay, Reunion Shiraz; Starvedog Lane Sauvignon Blanc, Chardonnay, Shiraz, Cabernet Sauvignon, Sparkling.
summary With their sales and marketing background, John and Helen Edwards opted for a major lifestyle change when they began the establishment of the first of the present 28.1 hectares of vineyards in 1993. Initially, part of the production was sold to BRL Hardy, but now some of the wine is made for release under the Ravenswood Lane label. A joint venture with BRL Hardy is Starvedog Lane, producing wines from a patchwork of vineyards throughout the Adelaide Hills. Exports to the UK and Singapore.

Ravenswood Lane The Gathering Sauvignon Blanc

YYYY♈ **2000** Light straw-green; the bouquet is complex and quite intense, with smoky gunflint aromas; the palate is crisp, crunchy and minerally, with herb and spice, and imperceptible oak. Finishes with crisp acidity. **rating:** 90
best drinking Now **best vintages** '99, '00 **drink with** Coquilles St Jacques • $27

Ravenswood Lane Beginning Chardonnay

YYYY♈ **2000** Light to medium yellow-green; a fragrant and stylish bouquet, with subtle barrel-ferment French oak over a melon and stonefruit base, then a delicate, fruit-driven palate where stonefruit with a touch of citrus run through to a long finish with good acidity. Clear development potential. **rating:** 90

▼▼▼▼▽ **1999** Medium to full yellow-green; a complex mix of gently spicy oak, cashew and figgy fruit on the bouquet foreshadows a quite restrained and elegant palate, the fruit ranging through citrus, melon and fig, oak doing no more than providing a cushion. **rating:** 91

best drinking Now–2005 **best vintages** '97, '99, '00 **drink with** Sweetbreads • $37

Starvedog Lane Chardonnay

▼▼▼▼ **2000** Medium yellow-green; ghetto-blaster charry/toasty barrel ferment jumps out of the glass; there is lots happening on the palate, too, with good texture and the fruit able to wave the flag from underneath the oak. **rating:** 89

best drinking 2002–2005 **best vintages** '98, '99 **drink with** Barbecued chicken • $27

Ravenswood Lane Reunion Shiraz

▼▼▼▼▼ **1998** This is cool-climate Shiraz, a far cry from the traditional Barossa/South Australian flavour profile. A highly perfumed, intense bouquet with black cherry, anise and licorice in classic Rhône Valley style is matched by a palate with spectacular fruit complemented by oak and fine, silky tannins. **rating:** 95

best drinking 2003–2013 **best vintages** '97, '98 **drink with** Beef Bourgignon • $49.99

Starvedog Lane Cabernet Sauvignon

▼▼▼▼▼ **1998** Medium to full red-purple; the bouquet is clean and rich, flooded with cassis and blackberry fruit. The palate, likewise, is rich and ripe, with masses of cassis supported by very good oak handling; an emphatically classy wine. **rating:** 94

best drinking 2003–2013 **best vintages** NA **drink with** Steak Diane • $25

ray-monde NR

250 Dalrymple Road, Sunbury, Vic 3429 **region** Sunbury
phone (03) 5428 2657 **fax** (03) 5428 3390 **open** Sundays or by appointment
winemaker John Lakey **production** 700 **est.** 1988
product range ($25–27 CD) Pinot Noir.
summary The Lakey family has established 5 hectares of pinot noir on their 230-hectare grazing property at an altitude of 400 metres. Initially the grapes were sold to Domaine Chandon, but in 1994 son John Lakey (with experience at Tarrawarra, Rochford, Virgin Hills and Coonawarra plus a vintage in Burgundy) commenced making the wine – and very competently.

reads ★★

Evans Lane, Oxley, Vic 3678 **region** King Valley
phone (03) 5727 3386 **fax** (03) 5727 3559 **open** Mon–Sat 9–5, Sun 10–6
winemaker Kenneth Read **production** 1900 **est.** 1972
product range ($7.50–13 CD) Riesling, Chardonnay, Sauvignon Blanc, Crouchen, Cabernet Shiraz, Cabernet Sauvignon, Port.
summary Limited tastings have not impressed, but there may be a jewel lurking somewhere, such as the medal-winning though long-gone 1990 Sauvignon Blanc.

redbank winery ★★★★

Sunraysia Highway, Redbank, Vic 3467 **region** Pyrenees
phone (03) 5467 7255 **fax** (03) 5467 7248 **open** Mon–Sat 9–5, Sun 10–5
winemaker Neill Robb **production** 58 000 **est.** 1973
product range ($12–50 R) The range centres on a series of evocatively named red wines, with Sally's Paddock the flagship; then Rising Chardonnay, Sunday Morning Pinot Gris, Frenchman's Pinot Noir, Fighting Flat Shiraz and Percydale Cabernet Merlot. Long Paddock Shiraz Cabernet, Long Paddock Chardonnay and Emily Pinot Chardonnay Brut Cuvée are cheaper, larger-volume second labels.
summary Neill Robb makes very concentrated wines, full of character; the levels of volatile acidity can sometimes be intrusive but are probably of more concern to technical tasters than to the general public. Sally's Paddock is the star, a single vineyard block with an esoteric mix of cabernet, shiraz and malbec and which over the years has produced many great wines.

Redbank Sunday Morning Pinot Gris

ΥΥΥΥ **2000** Light straw-green; a crisp bouquet with a slightly smoky/flinty edge, no doubt from the barrel-ferment component, is followed by a palate with nice texture and structure although, as ever, positive varietal character is a little hard to find. **rating:** 85

best drinking Now **best vintages** NA **drink with** Antipasto • $19.95

Redbank Fighting Flat Shiraz

ΥΥΥΥ **1999** Medium purple-red, bright and clear; the clean, moderately intense bouquet provides a neat marriage between fruit and cedary oak, the palate following down the same well-balanced track; savoury, spicy berry fruit and supple tannins complete the picture. **rating:** 86

best drinking 2002–2005 **best vintages** NA **drink with** Designer hamburger • $19.95

Redbank Sally's Paddock

ΥΥΥΥ **1999** Medium red, with some purple, curiously with a distinctly less bright hue than the Fighting Flat Shiraz this year. The bouquet is savoury, spicy and scented, the palate with red berry and cassis on entry, then quite potent savoury flavours and tannins to close. **rating:** 89

best drinking 2003–2009 **best vintages** '79, '80, '81, '86, '88, '91, '93, '98 **drink with** Venison • $49.95

Redbank Percydale Cabernet Merlot

ΥΥΥΥ **1999** Once again, the colour is distinctly better than Sally's Paddock this year. Fresh blackberry/mulberry fruit on the bouquet is followed by a palate that is still in its primary phase, slightly hard and tannic. You get the feeling this wine may have spent as much time in stainless steel as it did in barrel. **rating:** 86

best drinking 2004–2008 **best vintages** NA **drink with** Marinated lamb • $19.95

---

red clay estate NR

269 Henry Lawson Drive, Mudgee, NSW 2850 **region** Mudgee

phone (02) 6372 4569 **fax** (02) 6372 4596 **open** Jan–Sept 7 days 10–5, Oct–Dec Mon–Fri 10–5 or by appointment

winemaker Ken Heslop **production** NA **est.** 1997

product range NA

summary Ken Heslop and Annette Bailey are among the recent arrivals in Mudgee, with a 2.5-hectare vineyard planted to a diverse range of varieties. The wines are exclusively sold through cellar door and by mail order.

red edge ★★★★★

Golden Gully Road, Heathcote, Vic 3523 **region** Bendigo

phone (03) 9337 5695 **fax** (03) 9337 7550 **open** By appointment

winemaker Peter Dredge, Judy Dredge **production** 500 **est.** 1971

product range ($29–35 R) Shiraz, Cabernet Sauvignon.

summary Red Edge is a new name on the scene, but the vineyard dates back to 1971, at the renaissance of the Victorian wine industry. In the early 1980s it produced the wonderful wines of Flynn & Williams and has now been rehabilitated by Peter and Judy Dredge, producing two quite lovely wines in their inaugural 1997 vintage. For the time being, at least, Peter Dredge continues to keep body and soul together by making the wines at Wildwood and at Witchmount Estate, Rockbank. Trying to eke a living out of 500 cases of what in these days are moderately priced wines is simply not possible.

Red Edge Shiraz

ΥΥΥΥΥ **1999** Dense purple-red, almost black; the bouquet is immensely concentrated, with sweet earth, spice and dark black fruit aromas, the palate commensurately powerful, concentrated and chewy. One of those wines where fining and/or filtering may have been a good thing, but perhaps age will do the work. **rating:** 91

best drinking 2005–2015 **best vintages** '97, '98, '99 **drink with** Beef stroganoff • $35

Red Edge Cabernet Sauvignon

ΥΥΥΥΥ **1999** Dense purple-red; the bouquet is crammed with rich, ripe, luscious cassis/blackberry fruit, the palate with awesome concentration and power. Flavour and texture go hand-in-hand through to a long, slightly grippy finish that will soften given time. **rating:** 90

best drinking 2004–2014 **best vintages** '97, '98, '99 **drink with** Roast lamb • $32

---

redgate ★★★★

Boodjidup Road, Margaret River, WA 6285 **region** Margaret River
phone (08) 9757 6488 **fax** (08) 9757 6308 **open** 7 days 10–5
winemaker Andrew Forsell **production** 14 000 **est.** 1977
product range ($14–32.50 CD) Sauvignon Blanc Reserve, Chardonnay, OFS Semillon, Chenin, Late Harvest Riesling, Pinot Noir, Cabernet Franc, Cabernet Sauvignon, White Port.
summary Twenty hectares of vineyard provide the base for a substantial winery that probably has a lower profile than it deserves. The wines do have limited distribution in the eastern States, and export markets in Singapore, Hong Kong, Canada, Japan, Denmark, Switzerland and the UK have been established.

Redgate Semillon

YYYY **1999** Medium yellow-green; a complex bouquet with the fruit showing tropical overtones and obvious barrel-fermentation inputs. The palate is full flavoured, with tangy, ripe, citrus and stonefruit flavours well beyond those normally associated with Semillon. The oak has not been overplayed. **rating:** 85

best drinking Now–2004 **best vintages** '99 **drink with** Rich fish dishes • $21

Redgate OFS Semillon

YYYYy **2000** Very light straw-green; an intensely aromatic bouquet has distinct and slightly unusual (for Semillon) passionfruit characters. The palate moves more towards conventional varietal character, retaining the freshness and aromaticity of the bouquet, the positive flavour with some grapefruit. **rating:** 90

best drinking Now–2003 **best vintages** '00 **drink with** Salmon mousse • $21

Redgate Sauvignon Blanc Reserve

YYYYy **1999** Medium yellow-green; the bouquet is complex, with tropical, tangy fruit and similar oak handling to the Semillon. A substantial and rich food-style palate, with tangy, ripe gooseberry and tropical fruit flavours. **rating:** 90

best drinking Now–2003 **best vintages** '99 **drink with** Creamy seafood pasta • $20

Redgate Chardonnay

YYYy **1999** Light green-yellow; a potent, toasty, citrus/grapefruit-accented bouquet has a touch of reductive matchstick character. The palate is no less potent, with citrus and melon fruit in a somewhat idiosyncratic style. **rating:** 84

best drinking 2002–2005 **best vintages** NA **drink with** Pan-fried veal • $21

Redgate Pinot Noir

YYYYy **1999** Medium red, with a touch of purple; a complex, slightly funky, carbonic/charry oak bouquet moves through uncertainly to gamey/plummy fruit, signalling plenty of activity to come on the palate. Here complex flavour, structure and texture repeat the plum/briary/savoury characters of the bouquet, with a touch of gamey character (which may or may not have a bacterial origin) to add further piquancy to the wine. Tasted in the shadow of influenza; I wish I was sure about my note, but I can't change the points. **rating:** 93

best drinking 2002–2006 **best vintages** NA **drink with** Well-hung game • NA

Redgate Cabernet Franc

YYYY **1998** Medium red-purple; the bouquet is firm, with some slightly astringent earthy/charry characters that resolve themselves on a complex, multiflavoured palate which has both good length and good structure. **rating:** 88

best drinking 2003–2008 **best vintages** NA **drink with** Braised beef • NA

red hill estate ★★★★

53 Redhill–Shoreham Road, Red Hill South, Vic 3937 **region** Mornington Peninsula
phone (03) 5989 2838 **fax** (03) 5989 2855 **open** 7 days 11–5
winemaker Michael Kyberd **production** 20 000 **est.** 1989
product range ($15–36 CD) Particular emphasis on Méthode Champenoise, but also producing Unoaked Chardonnay, Chardonnay, Riesling, Sauvignon Blanc, Hill Block Pinot (Rosé), Pinot Noir and Cabernet Sauvignon; also Muscat (from Rutherglen material) available through cellar door only.
summary Sir Peter Derham and family completed the construction of an on-site winery in time for the 1993 vintage, ending a period in which the wines were made at various wineries under contract arrangements. The 10-hectare vineyard is one of the larger plantings on the Mornington Peninsula, and the tasting room and restaurant have a superb view across the vineyard to Westernport Bay and Phillip Island. Production continues to surge, and the winery goes from strength to strength.

redman ★★★★

Riddoch Highway, Coonawarra, SA 5253 **region** Coonawarra
phone (08) 8736 3331 **fax** (08) 8736 3013 **open** Mon–Fri 9–5, weekends 10–4
winemaker Bruce Redman, Malcolm Redman **production** 18 000 **est.** 1966
product range ($13–28 R) Shiraz, Cabernet Sauvignon Merlot, Cabernet Sauvignon.
summary After a prolonged period of mediocrity, the Redman wines are showing sporadic signs of improvement, partly through the introduction of modest amounts of new oak, even if principally American. It would be nice to say the wines now reflect the full potential of the vineyard, but there is still some way to go.

Redman Cabernet Sauvignon Merlot

YYYY **1997** Medium red-purple; juicy blackberry fruit plus spicy oak on the bouquet are followed by a light- to medium-bodied palate, with unexpectedly sweet fruit for the vintage, in turn augmented by nicely integrated and balanced sweet oak; lingering tannins on the finish. **rating:** 87
best drinking 2003–2007 **best vintages** '93, '94, '96, '97 **drink with** Shoulder of lamb • $28

Redman Cabernet Sauvignon

YYYYY **1998** Strong red-purple; the bouquet is powerful, with concentrated earthy cabernet fruit dominant. The palate confirms the bouquet; by far the richest and most concentrated wine to come from Redman since the 1960s, replete with soft, chewy tannins and just a touch of oak. **rating:** 92
best drinking 2003–2013 **best vintages** '90, '92, '93, '98 **drink with** Stuffed capsicum • $22.95

red rock winery NR

Red Rock Reserve Road, Alvie, Vic 3249 **region** Geelong
phone (03) 5234 8382 **open** Not
winemaker Rohan Little **production** 5000 **est.** 1981
product range ($15–25 R) Semillon Sauvignon, Chardonnay, Pinot Noir, Shiraz, also MC (Methode Champenoise).
summary The former Barongvale Estate, with 8 hectares of sauvignon blanc, semillon, pinot noir, and shiraz. A part-time occupation for Rohan Little, with wines sold under both the Red Rock and Otway Vineyards labels. A cellar door and café is planned for December 2001.

reedy creek vineyard NR

Reedy Creek, via Tenterfield, NSW 2372 **region** Northern Slopes Zone
phone (02) 6737 5221 **fax** (02) 6737 5200 **open** 7 days 9–5
winemaker Bruce Humphery-Smith (Contract) **production** 2800 **est.** 1971
product range ($13–17 CD) Bianco Alpino, Chardonnay, Unwooded Chardonnay, Rosso Alpino, Shiraz Mourvedre, Old Vine Shiraz, Merlot, Durif, Liqueur Muscat, Red Deer Port.
summary Like so many Italian settlers in the Australian countryside, the De Stefani family has been growing grapes and making wine for its own consumption for over 30 years at its Reedy Creek property near Tenterfield, in the far north of New South Wales. What is more, like their compatriots in the King Valley, the family's principal activity until 1993 was growing tobacco, but the continued rationalisation of the tobacco industry prompted the De Stefanis to turn a hobby into a commercial exercise. The vineyard has now been expanded to 6.1 hectares, and the first commercial vintage of Shiraz was made in 1995, with Chardonnay following in 1998. The wines are made by the incredibly industrious Bruce Humphery-Smith at Rimfire Vineyards at MacLagan and are sold cellar door from the maturation cellar opened in 1997.

reg drayton wines ★★★☆

Cnr Pokolbin Mountain and McDonalds Roads, Pokolbin, NSW 2321 **region** Lower Hunter Valley
phone (02) 4998 7523 **fax** (02) 4998 7523 **open** 7 days 10–5
winemaker James Estate (Contract) **production** 4000 **est.** 1989
product range ($17–28 CD) Lambkin Semillon, Lambkin Verdelho, Pokolbin Hills Chardonnay, Pokolbin Hills Chardonnay Semillon, Pamela Robyn Sparkling Chardonnay, Three Sons Shiraz, Pokolbin Hills Shiraz, Pokolbin Hills Cabernet Shiraz, Port.

summary Reg and Pam Drayton were among the victims of the Seaview/Lord Howe Island air crash in October 1984, having established Reg Drayton Wines after selling their interest in the long-established Drayton Family Winery. Their daughter Robyn (a fifth-generation Drayton and billed as the Hunter's first female vigneron) and husband Craig continue the business, which draws chiefly upon the Pokolbin Hills Estate but also takes fruit from the historic Lambkin Estate vineyard. The wines are made for them at James Estate.

reilly's wines NR

Cnr Hill and Burra Streets, Mintaro, SA 5415 **region** Clare Valley
phone (08) 8843 9013 **fax** (08) 8843 9013 **open** 7 days 10–5
winemaker Justin Ardill **production** 5000 **est.** 1994
product range ($12–40 CD) Watervale Riesling, Semillon, St Clare Semillon, Chardonnay, Sparkling Grenache, Late Picked Riesling, Old Bushvine Grenache, Block 1919 Grenache Shiraz, Clare Valley Shiraz, Dry Land Shiraz, Cabernet Sauvignon, Port.
summary Justin and Julie Ardill are relative newcomers in the Clare Valley, with half a dozen or so vintages under their belt. An unusual sideline of Reilly's Cottage is the production of an Extra Virgin Olive Oil; unusual in that it is made from wild olives found in the Mintaro district of the Clare Valley. Exports to the US, Ireland, Malaysia and Singapore.

Reilly's Semillon

ΥΥΥΥ **1999** Medium to full yellow-green; the bouquet is quite intense, with lemon, a hint of stonefruit and a dash of mineral. The palate has a similar range of positive flavours, but does dip a little towards the finish. **rating:** 84
best drinking Now–2004 **best vintages** NA **drink with** Rich fish soup • $14

Reilly's 1919 Grenache

ΥΥΥΥ **1999** Medium red, with just a touch of purple; the bouquet has strong stewy/jammy/spicy grenache varietal character in a mode that appeals to some and not others. The same somewhat jammy/stewy fruit comes through on the palate, together with some cedary characters. An interesting wine which points cannot do justice to. **rating:** 80
best drinking Now–2004 **best vintages** NA **drink with** Greek stifado • $17

Reilly's Cabernet Sauvignon

ΥΥΥΥ **1998** Medium red-purple; the bouquet has distinctly earthy/rustic/charry overtones to the blackberry fruit, and both it and the palate show some signs of bottle development. The palate is quite rich and chocolatey, with ripe tannins, and the overall impact of the wine is pleasant if, as I say, a little rustic. **rating:** 87
best drinking Now–2006 **best vintages** NA **drink with** Game pie • $30

reynell ★★★★

Reynell Road, Reynella, SA 5161 **region** McLaren Vale
phone (08) 8392 2222 **fax** (08) 8392 2202 **open** 7 days 10–4, except public holidays
winemaker Stephen Pannell **production** NFP **est.** 1838
product range ($40 R) Basket Pressed Shiraz, Basket Pressed Merlot, Basket Pressed Cabernet Sauvignon.
summary Reynell is the name under which all wines from the historic Reynella winery (once called Chateau Reynella) are released. What is more, the range of wines was compressed and taken into the super-premium category with the introduction of the Basket Pressed range in 1997.

Reynell Basket Pressed Shiraz

ΥΥΥΥ **1997** Medium to full red-purple; a complex mix of dark berry fruit, spice and charry vanilla oak on the bouquet leads into a wine with impressive extract and body; all it needs is a decade or two. **rating:** 89
best drinking 2007–2017 **best vintages** '94, '95, '96 **drink with** Barbecued rump steak • $40

Reynell Basket Pressed Cabernet Sauvignon

ΥΥΥΥ **1997** Medium to full red-purple; powerful, earthy cabernet fruit aromas thread their way through a forest of toasty/charry oak; the palate is big, dense, chewy and extractive; a massive wine that needs a lengthy term of imprisonment before being released. **rating:** 88
best drinking 2007–2017 **best vintages** '94, '95 **drink with** Leave it in the cellar • $40

reynolds NR

'Quondong', Cargo Road, Cudal, NSW 2864 **region** Orange
phone (02) 6930 7900 **fax** (02) 6364 2388 **open** Cellar door planned for late 2001
winemaker Jon Reynolds, Nic Millichip, Tony Cosgriff **production** 50 000 **est.** 1967
product range ($15–25 CD) From the Hunter Valley: Semillon, White Cypress Chardonnay, Late Harvest, Red Cyprus Shiraz; from Orange: Sauvignon Blanc, Chardonnay, Merlot, Cabernet Sauvignon, and the Portrait series of MoonShadow Chardonnay, Marble Man Merlot and The Jezebel Cabernet Sauvignon; Handpicked Sauvignon Blanc Semillon and Handpicked Triple Blend are blends from both South Australia and Victoria.
summary In 2000 the Reynolds brand was aquired by Cabonne Limited. Later that year Cabonne Limited, which joined the stock market in 1999, announced a global alliance with Trinchero's Family Estates of the US, best known as the owner of America's biggest brand, Sutter Home. Cabonne is the ninth largest vineyard operator in Australia with 900 hectares of vineyards at Molong near Orange. Its 20 000-tonne winery should place it among the top 20 companies in Australia (by volume) in 2001. As a result, volumes will be lifted 175 000 cases in the first year of the US distribution, with a target of 500 000 cases per annum within five years. The Reynolds Yarraman label is being phased out in consequence.

Reynolds Hunter Valley Semillon

YYYYY **2000** Bright, light green-yellow; the bouquet is clean, quite crisp, with grass and lemon aromatics, the palate full of promise, showing good varietal character, length and intensity, finishing with brisk acidity. **rating:** 91
best drinking 2003–2010 **best vintages** '91, '92, '96, '98, '00 **drink with** Mussels • $15

Reynolds Orange Merlot

YYYY **1999** Medium to full red-purple; generous, dark berry fruit with touches of spice and prune on the bouquet are followed by a palate with considerable depth and substance to its dark berry flavour and structure. An excellent red wine; perhaps not such a great Merlot. **rating:** 87
best drinking 2003–2008 **best vintages** '98 **drink with** Braised veal • $24

Reynolds Orange Cabernet Sauvignon

YYYY **1999** Medium red-purple; the moderately intense, smooth bouquet has olive, earth and berry aromas supported by subtle oak. The palate has excellent texture and structure to the savoury blackberry fruit; supple tannins run through the length of the palate. **rating:** 88
best drinking 2004–2009 **best vintages** '96 **drink with** Beef stroganoff • $24

ribbon vale estate ★★★☆

Lot 5 Caves Road, Willyabrup, via Cowaramup, WA 6284 **region** Margaret River
phone (08) 9755 6272 **fax** (08) 9755 6337 **open** 7 days 10–4
winemaker Keith Mugford **production** 5000 **est.** 1977
product range ($17.50–23 CD) Semillon, Semillon Sauvignon Blanc, Sauvignon Blanc, Merlot, Cabernet Sauvignon Merlot, Cabernet Sauvignon.
summary Made crisp, herbaceous Semillon and Sauvignon Blanc (and blends), ideal seafood wines, and austere, very firm Cabernets all in mainstream regional style. Retail distribution in Western Australia, New South Wales and Victoria. For the time being, at least, Moss Wood is maintaining the full product range from Ribbon Vale, doubtless to help relieve pressure on the core Moss Wood brand products.

Ribbon Vale Semillon

YYYY **2000** Medium yellow-green; a complex, rich and concentrated bouquet with the suggestion of some barrel ferment is followed by a palate with typical Margaret River richness and weight, the fruit ripe to the point of almost being tropical, and once again hints of spice suggestive of some barrel ferment. **rating:** 89
best drinking Now–2005 **best vintages** '85, '88, '92, '93, '94 **drink with** Vichyssoise • $19.50

Ribbon Vale Sauvignon Blanc

YYYY **2000** Light green-yellow; the bouquet is firm and crisp, with a mix of mineral, grass, gooseberry and apple aromas. The palate is much lighter than the Semillon of the same year, but has pleasant gooseberry/apple flavours, and well-balanced acidity. **rating:** 86
best drinking Now–2003 **best vintages** NA **drink with** Avocado and seafood salad • $19.50

Ribbon Vale Merlot

TTTT **1999** Medium to full red-purple; a clean, slightly subdued bouquet has small, dark berry fruit aromas, and minimal oak. The medium-bodied palate ranges through savoury/olive/currant flavours; good length, but a very slightly green finish. **rating:** 85

best drinking 2003–2008 **best vintages** NA **drink with** Char-grilled veal chops • $23

richfield vineyard NR

Bruxner Highway, Tenterfield, NSW 2372 **region** Northern Slopes Zone
phone (02) 6737 5588 **fax** (02) 6737 5598 **open** Not
winemaker Contract **production** NA **est.** 1997
product range Chardonnay, Shiraz, Merlot, Cabernet Sauvignon, with the first release unlikely before the end of the decade.
summary Richfield Vineyard points to the tyranny of State boundaries. Established at the instigation of Denis Parsons of Bald Mountain vineyards in the Granite Belt (Queensland), Richfield is little more than 30 kilometres south of Bald Mountain vineyards as the crow flies. A little over 11 hectares were planted in 1997. All of the indications are that the Tenterfield–Granite Belt area will become a very significant cross-border wine-growing region.

richmond grove ★★★★☆

Para Road, Tanunda, SA 5352 **region** Barossa Valley
phone (08) 8563 2184 **fax** (08) 8563 2804 **open** Mon–Fri 10–5, weekends 10–4
winemaker John Vickery **production** NFP **est.** 1977
product range ($9.95–19.95 R) Eden Valley Traminer Riesling, Watervale Riesling, Barossa Riesling, Hunter Valley Semillon, Marlborough Sauvignon Blanc, Hunter Valley Classic Dry White, Cowra Chardonnay, Cowra Verdelho, French Cask Chardonnay, McLaren Vale Chardonnay, Barossa Shiraz, Cabernet Merlot, Coonawarra Cabernet Sauvignon.
summary Richmond Grove now has two homes, including one in the Barossa Valley where John Vickery presides. It is owned by Orlando Wyndham and draws its grapes from diverse sources. The Richmond Grove Barossa Valley and Watervale Rieslings made by John Vickery represent excellent value for money (for Riesling) year in, year out. If these were the only wines produced by Richmond Grove, it would have five-star rating. Exports to the UK.

Richmond Grove Barossa Riesling

TTTT **2000** Light to medium yellow-green; the bouquet is clean, quite ripe, with tropical fruit aromas. There is abundant mid-palate fruit giving overall richness and an element of grip. **rating:** 87

best drinking Now–2004 **best vintages** '94, '95, '96, '97, '99 **drink with** Pasta, white-meat dishes • $15

Richmond Grove Watervale Riesling

TTTTY **2000** Made by Australia's doyen of Riesling craftsmen, John Vickery, is also in the vanguard of the renaissance of the Stelvin screw-cap closure (used with this wine). The moderately intense bouquet has attractive, sweet lime aromas; the wine flows evenly across the palate with gentle lime and equally gentle acidity. **rating:** 90

best drinking Now–2010 **best vintages** '94, '96, '97, '98, '99, '00 **drink with** Steamed fish, Chinese-style • $15

Richmond Grove Hunter Valley Semillon

TTTTY **2000** Light green-yellow; distinct herbal/wild herb aromas precede a palate with good flavour intensity and acidity, all providing plenty of structure for the wine to build on as it ages. Fully reflects an excellent vintage. **rating:** 90

best drinking 2004–2010 **best vintages** '00 **drink with** Chicken breast • NA

Richmond Grove Marlborough Sauvignon Blanc

TTTTY **1999** Light to medium yellow-green; the fragrant bouquet has lifted aromas of passionfruit, gooseberry and peach suggesting that the palate may be a little over the top. In fact it is not; it is clean and crisp, with good length, the restraint a nice counterbalance to the bouquet. **rating:** 90

best drinking Now **best vintages** '98, '99 **drink with** Shellfish • $14.50

Richmond Grove McLaren Vale Chardonnay

1999 Medium yellow-green; the moderately intense bouquet is clean with light melon and white peach fruit supported by subtle oak. The palate is likewise clean and pleasant; at the end of the day, it is as hard to criticise the wine as it is to praise it. Simply a nice, no-nonsense drink. **rating:** 84

best drinking Now **best vintages** NA **drink with** Creamy pasta • $15

Richmond Grove Barossa Shiraz

1998 Densely coloured, it exudes striking, luscious, rich and ripe dark plum and berry fruit aromas, the palate similarly flooded with luscious rich fruit. All in all, will be better still once it has shed its puppy fat. **rating:** 91

best drinking 2003–2013 **best vintages** '98 **drink with** Marinated game • $18

Richmond Grove Coonawarra Cabernet Sauvignon

1998 Medium red-purple; spicy/smoky/vanilla overtones to a core of blackberry fruit on the bouquet are followed by a palate with plenty of red and blackberry fruit, supported by quite powerful tannins. The oak use is controlled. **rating:** 88

best drinking 2003–2008 **best vintages** '94, '96, '98 **drink with** Lamb cutlets • NA

richmond park vineyard NR

Logie Road, Richmond, Tas 7025 **region** Southern Tasmania
phone (03) 6265 2949 **fax** (03) 6265 3166 **open** Not
winemaker Andrew Hood (Contract) **production** 600 **est.** 1989
product range ($9–15 ML) Chardonnay, Pinot Noir.
summary A small vineyard owned by Tony Park, which gives the clue to the clever name.

Richmond Park Chardonnay

2000 Medium green-yellow; the bouquet is clean, with smooth citrus/melon fruit, the palate fresh, clean and citrussy, with just a touch of oak. Slightly simple, perhaps, but well priced. **rating:** 82

best drinking Now–2004 **best vintages** NA **drink with** Seafood takeaway • NA

rimfire vineyards ★★★

Bismarck Street, MacLagan, Qld 4352 **region** Darling Downs
phone (07) 4692 1129 **fax** (07) 4692 1260 **open** 7 days 10–5
winemaker Tony Connellan **production** 6000 **est.** 1991
product range ($10–16 CD) Verdelho, Chardonnay, Marsanne Chardonnay, Pioneer White, Ruby Cabernet, Country Rose, Shiraz; Fortifieds.
summary The Connellan family (parents Margaret and Tony and children Michelle, Peter and Louise) began planting the 12-hectare, 14-variety Rimfire Vineyards in 1991 as a means of diversification of their very large (1500-hectare) cattle stud in the foothills of the Bunya Mountains, 45 minutes drive northeast of Toowoomba. Increasingly producing a kaleidoscopic array of all manner of wines, the majority without any regional claim of origin. The Black Bull Café is open daily 10–5, blackboard menu and wine by the glass. Annual Jazz on the Lawn concert each spring.

Rimfire Shiraz

2000 Medium red-purple; a moderately intense, clean bouquet with smooth dark berry and chocolate fruit is followed by a clean, easy-drinking style that has not been bulked up with oak chips. **rating:** 83

best drinking 2002–2005 **best vintages** '95 **drink with** Grilled steak • $16

rivendell 

Lot 328 Wildwood Road, Yallingup, WA 6282 **region** Margaret River
phone (08) 9755 2235 **fax** (08) 9755 2295 **open** 7 days 10–5
winemaker Mike Davies, Jan Davies (Contract) **production** 2750 **est.** 1987
product range ($12.50–14.50 CD) Semillon Sauvignon Blanc, Honeysuckle Late Harvest Semillon, Verdelho, Shiraz Cabernet.
summary With 13.5 hectares of vineyards coming into bearing, production for Rivendell will increase significantly over the coming years. The cellar-door sales facility is in a garden setting, complete with restaurant. An unusual sideline is the sale of 50 types of preserves, jams and chutneys. No recent tastings.

riverbank estate NR

126 Hamersley Road, Caversham, WA 6055 **region** Swan District
phone (08) 9377 1805 **fax** (08) 9377 2168 **open** Weekends and public holidays 10–5
winemaker Robert James Bond **production** 3500 **est.** 1993
product range ($12–16 CD) Semillon, Verdelho, Chenin, Chardonnay, Cabernet.
summary Robert Bond, a graduate of Charles Sturt University and a Swan Valley viticulturist for 20 years, established RiverBank Estate in 1993. He draws upon 11 hectares of estate plantings and, in his words, 'The wines are unashamedly full-bodied, produced from ripe grapes in what is recognised as a hot grape-growing region.'

riverina estate ★★★☆

700 Kidman Way, Griffith, NSW 2680 **region** Riverina
phone (02) 6962 4122 **fax** (02) 6962 4628 **open** 7 days 9–5.30
winemaker Sam Trimboli **production** 3 million **est.** 1969
product range ($4–27 CD) An extensive range of varietal wines with Warburn Estate Semillon, Verdelho, Chardonnay, Shiraz, Durif, Merlot, Cabernet Merlot; Ridgewood Estate Chardonnay, Grenache Mataro; Ballingal Estate Traminer, Semillon, Semillon of the Riverina, Semillon Chardonnay, Sauvignon Blanc, Marsanne, Chardonnay, Shiraz, Merlot, Barbera, Cabernet Sauvignon; 1164 Semillon, Shiraz; Nonno Guiseppi Semillon Verdelho, Cabernet Durif Merlot; 3 Corners and Lizard Ridge ranges with Semillon Sauvignon Blanc, Semillon Chardonnay, Chardonnay, Shiraz, Shiraz Cabernet, Merlot; Bushmans Gully Bin 157 Crisp Dry White, Bin 158 Soft Dry Red, Semillon Chardonnay, Shiraz Cabernet; Montello Classic Dry White, Botrytis Semillon, Botrytis Sauvignon Blanc. There is also a range of sparkling wines and fortifieds in both bottle and cask.
summary One of the large producers of the region, drawing upon 1100 hectares of estate plantings. While much of the wine is sold in bulk to other producers, selected parcels of the best of the grapes are made into table wines, with quite spectacular success. At the 1997 National Wine Show, Riverina Wines won an astonishing six gold medals, topping no less than four classes. That success has, it seems, given rise to the introduction of the Show Reserve wines, and while the 1997 success has not been equalled since, the Show Reserve wines continue to justify their label. Exports to the UK and Canada.

Ballingal Estate Semillon

🍷🍷🍷🍷 **1999** Glowing yellow-green; a massive bouquet with lots of spicy oak the driving force, is followed by a palate with some fruit intensity and lemony length, but which urgently needs drinking before the phenolics take over. For all that, offers exceptional value. **rating:** 84

best drinking Now **best vintages** '99 **drink with** Pasta marinara • $9.50

Ballingal Estate Semillon Chardonnay

🍷🍷🍷🍷 **1999** Glowing yellow-green; the bouquet is big, rich and complex, with powerful oak influence. The palate has masses of flavour, but is already showing signs of breaking up and really should have been drunk a year ago, when it would have rated higher points. However, you still get a lot of wine for your dollar. **rating:** 82

best drinking Now **best vintages** '99 **drink with** KFC • $9.50

Warburn Estate Show Reserve Chardonnay

🍷🍷🍷🍷 **1999** Deep, glowing yellow-gold; quite powerful peachy fruit is complemented by relatively subtle oak on the bouquet. There is plenty of palate flavour and length, and, all in all, the wine is hanging together well. **rating:** 86

best drinking Now **best vintages** '98 **drink with** KFC • $18

Riverina Late Picked Botrytis Sauvignon Blanc 375 ml

🍷🍷🍷🍷 **1997** Deep gold; there is a mix of interesting honey, mead and cumquat aromas on the bouquet; the palate flavours are of mandarin, orange peel and honey, but lack intensity and bite. It is impossible to see varietal character behind the botrytis, and I suspect this wine was better still 12 months ago. **rating:** 88

best drinking Now **best vintages** '97 **drink with** Home-made ice-cream • $11.95

Warburn Estate Show Reserve Shiraz

🍷🍷🍷🍷 **1999** Medium red-purple; the bouquet is quite rich, with good fruit and oak balance, but the palate comes as a qualified disappointment, with less mid-palate fruit and strong, raspy tannins. The total flavour is adequate enough, and the wine may fill out and settle down with a few years in bottle. **rating:** 83

best drinking 2002–2006 **best vintages** NA **drink with** Devilled kidneys • $21

Warburn Estate Show Reserve Durif

1999 Medium to full purple-red; the bouquet opens with sweet, ripe, dark prune fruit, then American oak takes over. The palate is a replay, with spicy, luscious prune progressively encased in a coffin of toasty American oak. **rating:** 84

best drinking 2002–2007 **best vintages** NA **drink with** Barbecued meat • NA

Warburn Estate Show Reserve Merlot

1999 Dark red-purple; lusciously ripe fruit is once again swathed in masses of oak on the bouquet; however, the full-bodied palate has fleshy, ripe dark berry fruit and quite pronounced tannins that more than cope with the oak, but leave little or no clue as to the varietal composition of the wine. Rated as a red wine, rather than as a Merlot. **rating:** 86

best drinking 2002–2006 **best vintages** '98 **drink with** Lamb shanks • $16.95

Warburn Estate Show Reserve Cabernet Merlot

1999 Dense red-purple; strong dark berry fruit and sweet vanilla oak flood the bouquet; the rich, full-bodied palate has good dark berry fruit, and oak under some control; the tannins are noticeably dry, and hopefully time will soften these. **rating:** 85

best drinking 2003–2008 **best vintages** NA **drink with** Strong game • NA

riversands vineyards NR

Whytes Road, St George, Qld 4487 **region** Queensland Zone
phone (07) 4625 3643 **fax** (07) 4625 5043 **open** Mon–Sat 8–6, Sunday 9–4
winemaker Ballandean Estate (Contract) **production** 3500 **est.** 1990
product range ($11–20 CD) Sauvignon Blanc Semillon, Explorers Chardonnay, Major Mitchell White, Three Rivers Red, Dr Seidel's Soft Red, Ellen Meacle Merlot, Golden Liqueur Muscat, Gaolhouse Port.
summary Riversands is situated on the banks of the Balonne River near St George in the southwest corner of Queensland. It is a mixed wine grape and table grape business, acquired by present owners Alison and David Blacket in 1996. The wines are very competently made under contract at Ballandean Estate and have already accumulated a number of silver and bronze medals. The Chardonnay is particularly meritorious.

roberts estate wines

Game Street, Merbein, Vic 3505 **region** Murray Darling
phone (03) 5024 2944 **fax** (03) 5024 2877 **open** Not
winemaker Ian McElhinney **production** 80 000 **est.** 1998
product range ($8–10 R) Chardonnay, Merlot, Shiraz, Cabernet Sauvignon; under the Denbeigh label Chardonnay, Semillon Chardonnay, Colombard Chardonnay, Shiraz, Cabernet Sauvignon, Shiraz Cabernet.
summary A very large winery acting as a processing point for grapes grown up and down the Murray River. Over 10 000 tonnes are crushed each vintage; much of the wine is sold in bulk to others, but some is exported under the Denbeigh and Kombacy labels.

robinsons family vineyards

Curtin Road, Ballandean, Qld 4382 **region** Granite Belt
phone (07) 4684 1216 **fax** (07) 4684 1216 **open** 7 days 9–5
winemaker Craig Robinson **production** 3000 **est.** 1969
product range ($14–25 CD) Sauvignon Blanc Semillon, Chardonnay, Unwooded Chardonnay, Lyra Dry White, Traminer, Late Harvest Traminer, Shiraz, Shiraz Cabernet, Cabernet Sauvignon, Sparkling.
summary The conjunction of a picture of a hibiscus and 'cool climate' in a prominent typeface on the labels is a strange one, but then that has always been the nature of Robinsons Family Vineyards. The red wines can be very good, particularly when not overly extracted and tannic.

Robinsons Family Cabernet Sauvignon

1999 Medium to full red-purple; powerful, earthy cabernet aromas on the bouquet are a pure expression of the grape; however, the very powerful, austere and terrifyingly tannic palate is absolutely daunting. It is fair to point out that the wine won the Queensland Sheraton Wine Award Best Red Wine Trophy in 2000. **rating:** 84

best drinking 2005–2015 **best vintages** NA **drink with** Roast beef • $25

robinvale ★★★

Sea Lake Road, Robinvale, Vic 3549 **region** Murray Darling
phone (03) 5026 3955 **fax** (03) 5026 1123 **open** Mon–Fri 9–6, Sun 1–6
winemaker Bill Caracatsanoudis **production** 15 000 **est.** 1976
product range ($8.50–20 CD) A unique offering of white, red and fortified wines, the majority estate-grown under the internationally recognised Bio-Dynamic Demeter Grade A requirements, the highest level. In addition, a number are Kosher wines, and all are certified free of any genetically modified organisms.
summary Robinvale was one of the first Australian wineries to be fully accredited with the Biodynamic Agricultural Association of Australia. Most, but not all, of the wines are produced from organically grown grapes, with certain of the wines made preservative-free. Production has increased dramatically, no doubt reflecting the interest in organic and biodynamic viticulture and winemaking. Exports to the UK and Japan.

Robinvale Kosher Sterling Vineyards Chardonnay

🍷🍷🍷🍸 **1999** Medium to full yellow-green; a clean, toasty, ripe melon and peach bouquet is followed by a full, ripe, rich, soft and flavoursome peachy palate which does, however, lack acidity. **rating:** 82
best drinking Now **best vintages** NA **drink with** Your choice • $12

Robinvale Oak Barrel Organic Chardonnay

🍷🍷🍷🍸 **1998** Full yellow-green; a strong, toasty/oaky bouquet is followed by a ripe, rich, peach and toast-flavoured palate ready for immediate drinking. **rating:** 83
best drinking Now **best vintages** NA **drink with** Your choice • $18

Robinvale Organic Origins Chardonnay

🍷🍷🍷🍸 **1998** Medium yellow-green; a toasty/peachy bouquet and palate are very similar to the Oak Barrel Organic Chardonnay; the only slight difference may be a little more sweetness in this wine. **rating:** 83
best drinking Now **best vintages** NA **drink with** Your choice • NA

Robinvale Cabernets

🍷🍷🍷🍸 **1998** Medium red-purple; a light, spicy/berry bouquet, with touches of cedar, leads into a light- to medium-bodied palate which has gentle spicy/cedary flavour. **rating:** 84
best drinking Now–2003 **best vintages** NA **drink with** Your choice • $10

rochford ★★★★

Romsey Park, Rochford, Vic 3442 **region** Macedon Ranges
phone (03) 5429 1428 **fax** (03) 5429 2356 **open** 7 days 10–4
winemaker David Creed **production** 6000 **est.** 1983
product range ($13–35 R) Riesling, Chardonnay, Macedon Blanc de Blancs, Pinot Noir, Cabernet Sauvignon; Romsey Park label includes Riesling, Pinot Grigio, Chardonnay, Pinot Noir, Merlot, Cabernet Sauvignon.
summary Since acquiring Rochford in early 1998, Helmut Konecsny and Yvonne Lodoco-Konecsny have made a substantial investment in the estate vineyards, but have been more than content to leave the style unchanged, with David Creed continuing as winemaker. The emphasis is on Chardonnay and Pinot Noir, and as the new plantings come into bearing, so will production increase.

Rochford Chardonnay

🍷🍷🍷🍷🍸 **1999** Light to medium green-yellow; clean, melon, citrus and pear fruit aromas lead the bouquet, the palate with gently delicate melon fruit, harmoniously balanced with the malolactic and oak influences. The ultimate sotto voce style, but it works. **rating:** 90
best drinking 2002–2007 **best vintages** '99 **drink with** Fresh abalone • $20

Rochford Pinot Noir

🍷🍷🍷🍷🍸 **1999** Medium red-purple; fragrant spice and plum aromas together with hints of more stemmy/green aromas are followed by a lively, fresh palate with flavours of plum, mint and spice. Developing slowly and impressively. **rating:** 90
best drinking Now–2005 **best vintages** '91, '92, '93, '95, '96, '98, '99 **drink with** Jugged hare • $35

rockfield estate vineyard NR

Rosa Glen Road, Margaret River, WA 6285 **region** Margaret River
phone (08) 9757 5092 **fax** (08) 9757 5092 **open** 7 days 10–5
winemaker Mike Lemmes **production** 2000 **est.** 1997
product range ($16–18 CD) Semillon, Semillon Sauvignon Blanc, Autumn Harvest Semillon, Rosa (Rosé), Cabernet Shiraz, Reserve Cabernet.
summary Rockfield Estate Vineyard is very much a family affair. Dr Andrew Gaman wears the hats of chief executive officer, assistant winemaker and co-marketing manager; wife Anne Gaman is a director; Alex Gaman and Nick McPherson are viticulturists, Andrew Gaman Jnr is also an assistant winemaker and Anna Walter (née Gaman) helps Dr Andrew Gaman with the marketing. The Chapman Brook meanders through the property, the vines running from its banks up to the wooded slopes above the valley floor, and the winery offers light refreshments and food from the café throughout the day.

Rockfield Estate Rosa

2000 Very light red; light spicy/strawberry aromas are replicated on the palate, finishing with a hint of sweetness; cleverly made. **rating:** 83
best drinking Now **best vintages** NA **drink with** Summer salad • $16

rockford ★★★★

Krondorf Road, Tanunda, SA 5352 **region** Barossa Valley
phone (08) 8563 2720 **fax** (08) 8563 3787 **open** Mon–Sat 11–5
winemaker Robert O'Callaghan, Chris Ringland **production** 19 000 **est.** 1984
product range ($10.50–45 CD) Eden Valley Riesling, Local Growers Semillon, Alicante Bouchet, White Frontignac, Basket Press Shiraz, Sparkling Black Shiraz, Dry Country Grenache, Cabernet Sauvignon, Tawny Port.
summary The wines are sold through Adelaide retailers only (and cellar door) and are unknown to most eastern Australian wine-drinkers, which is a great pity because these are some of the most individual, spectacularly flavoured wines made in the Barossa today, with an emphasis on old, low-yielding dry-land vineyards. This South Australian slur on the palates of Victoria and New South Wales is exacerbated by the fact that the wines are exported to Switzerland, the UK and New Zealand; it all goes to show we need proper authority to protect our living treasures.

Rockford Black Shiraz

NV Dark red, but with some brick hues evident. There is an attractive mix of spice and earth aromas on the bouquet, but the palate is something else, with that fine, faintly spicy, faintly earthy taste of mature Shiraz of the old Great Western style. It is neither heavy nor sweet, and has tremendous balance and length. **rating:** 94
best drinking Now **best vintages** NA **drink with** Needs no accompaniment • NA

roehr NR

Roehr Road, Ebenezer near Nuriootpa, SA 5355 **region** Barossa Valley
phone (08) 8565 6242 **fax** (08) 8565 6242 **open** Not
winemaker Contract **production** 300 **est.** 1995
product range Elmor's Ebenezer Old Vine Shiraz.
summary Karl Wilhelm Roehr arrived in Australia in 1841, and was amongst the earliest settlers at Ebenezer in the northern end of the Barossa Valley. His great, great grandson Elmor Roehr is the custodian of 20 hectares of shiraz, grenache, mataro and chardonnay on a vineyard passed down through the generations. In 1995 he decided to venture into winemaking and produced a Shiraz from 80-year-old vines which typically crop at less than 1.5 tonnes to the acre. It, together with the 1996 Old Vine Shiraz, which has already been released, will be sold exclusively in Germany and the US.

romavilla NR

Northern Road, Roma, Qld 4455 **region** Queensland Zone
phone (07) 4622 1822 **fax** (07) 4622 1822 **open** Mon–Fri 8–5, Sat 9–12, 2–4
winemaker David Wall, Richard Wall **production** 2500 **est.** 1863
product range ($12–40 CD) An extensive range of varietal and generic table wines including Rhine Riesling, Crouchen, Chenin Blanc, Reserve Chenin Blanc, Viognier, Reserve Chardonnay, Rosé, Maranoa Shiraz, Cellarman's

Shiraz and fortified wine styles including Madeira and Tawny Port are on sale at the winery; the Very Old Tawny Port is made from a blend of material ranging in age from ten to 25 years.

summary An amazing historic relic, seemingly untouched since its nineteenth-century heyday, producing conventional table wines but still providing some extraordinary fortifieds, including a truly stylish Madeira made from Riesling and Syrian (the latter variety originating in Persia). David Wall has now been joined by son Richard in the business, which will hopefully ensure continuity for this important part of Australian wine history.

rosabrook estate ★★★★☆

Rosa Brook Road, Margaret River, WA 6285 **region** Margaret River
phone (08) 9757 2286 **fax** (08) 9757 3634 **open** 7 days 10–4
winemaker Simon Keall **production** 4000 **est.** 1980
product range ($15–25 CD) Semillon Sauvignon Blanc, Chardonnay, Autumn Harvest Riesling, Botrytis Riesling, Shiraz, Cabernet Merlot.

summary The 14-hectare Rosabrook Estate vineyards have been established progressively since 1980, with seven varieties planted. The cellar-door facility is housed in what was Margaret River's first commercial abattoir, built in the early 1930s, with a new winery constructed in 1993. It has been acquired by the rapidly expanding Palandri Wines, which should find the quality of the Rosabrook wines very useful.

Rosabrook Estate Shiraz

🍷🍷🍷🍷🍷 **1999** Medium to full red-purple; the bouquet is extremely complex, with many aromatic qualities, spicy black cherry fruit on the one side, and more savoury, earthy, oaky characters on the other. The palate has arrestingly piquant tangy cherry-pip fruit, oak and lingering tannins. **rating:** 92

best drinking 2003–2010 **best vintages** '99 **drink with** Osso bucco • NA

Rosabrook Estate Cabernet Merlot

🍷🍷🍷🍷🍷 **1999** Medium to full red-purple; the bouquet has concentrated cassis/berry fruit with slightly raw oak. The palate is powerful, pure and concentrated with slightly austere dark berry fruit, and long, lingering tannins. Patience will be rewarded. **rating:** 90

🍷🍷🍷🍷🍷 **1998** Medium purple-red; the clean and smooth bouquet has moderately ripe but sweet red berry fruit cushioned with well-handled French oak. The palate is riper, richer and sweeter still, with the fruit matched by powerful yet well-balanced and integrated oak. **rating:** 94

best drinking 2005–2010 **best vintages** '91, '92, '98 **drink with** Rump steak • $25

rosemount estate (hunter valley) ★★★★★

Rosemount Road, Denman, NSW 2328 **region** Upper Hunter Valley
phone (02) 6549 6400 **fax** (02) 6549 6499 **open** 7 days 10–4
winemaker Philip Shaw **production** Over 2 million **est.** 1969
product range ($8.99–55.99 R) A very large range of wines that in almost all instances are varietally identified, sometimes with the conjunction of vineyards at the top end of the range, and which in the case of the lower-priced volume varietals increasingly come from all parts of southeast Australia. Names and label designs change regularly but the emphasis remains on the classic varietals. Roxburgh Chardonnay is the white flagbearer; Mountain Blue Shiraz Cabernet the real leader. Chardonnay, Shiraz and Cabernet Sauvignon under the standard labels consistently excellent at the price. In 1997 a Yarra Valley Chardonnay was added to the regional range, which also encompasses Coonawarra, Orange and Mudgee (Hill of Gold).

summary Rosemount Estate has achieved a miraculous balancing act over the past years maintaining, indeed increasing, wine quality while presiding over an ever-expanding empire and dramatically increasing production. The wines are consistently of excellent value; all have real character and individuality; not a few are startlingly good. The outcome was the merger with Southcorp in March 2001; while in financial terms Southcorp was the acquirer, most of the key management positions within the merged group are held by Rosemount executives. Exports to the UK and the US.

Rosemount Estate Diamond Label Semillon

🍷🍷🍷🍷 **2000** Light to medium yellow-green; the clean and crisp bouquet has fresh, youthful varietal grass and citrus aromas; a well-made and composed palate follows, crisp, clean and minerally, with excellent acidity to carry and lengthen the finish. **rating:** 88

best drinking Now–2005 **best vintages** '00 **drink with** Fried fish • $12.95

Rosemount Estate Show Reserve Semillon

TTTT **2000** Light green-yellow; a firm, clean and crisp bouquet with herb and lemon aromas leads into a similarly flavoured and nicely balanced palate which has good length and persistence. **rating:** 89

best drinking Now–2007 **best vintages** '98, '00 **drink with** Breast of turkey • $25

Rosemount Estate Rose Label Orange Vineyard Chardonnay

TTTTY **1999** Light green-yellow; the bouquet is clean, fresh and lively with melon, a touch of apple and subtle oak; the palate is delicious and unforced, with flavours of apple, melon and a touch of cashew. **rating:** 93

best drinking Now–2005 **best vintages** '92, '95, '96, '97, '99 **drink with** Oyster soup • $25

Rosemount Estate Roxburgh Chardonnay

TTTY **1998** Light to medium yellow-green; the bouquet shows strong barrel-ferment oak characters, the oak being slightly pencilly, and the palate, while undoubtedly having good fruit, once again shows a surprising lack of oak integration. The wine spent 18 months in bottle prior to release, and I am unable to understand why the oak is as it is. A major disappointment after the excellent '97 vintage of this wine. **rating:** 84

best drinking Now–2004 **best vintages** '86, '87, '89, '91, '92, '93, '95, '97 **drink with** Veal, pork • NA

Rosemount Estate Show Reserve Chardonnay

TTTT **1999** Medium yellow-green; the bouquet is quite complex, with some nutty oak, soft, not intense; the palate is clean with gentle cashew flavours alongside stonefruit and gentle oak to close. Another pleasant wine under this label. **rating:** 88

best drinking Now–2004 **best vintages** '97, '99 **drink with** Pan-fried veal • $25

Rosemount Estate Diamond Label Shiraz

TTTT **1999** A merely excellent price/quality ratio after the explosive start of the first two red wines, and shouldn't be ignored. Clean, fresh, moderately intense dark cherry fruit and subtle oak aromas; then a palate with considerable substance, with dark cherry fruit and nicely worked and integrated tannins and oak. **rating:** 87

best drinking Now–2003 **best vintages** '88, '90, '91, '92, '94, '96, '98, '99 **drink with** Lamb shanks • $12.95

Rosemount Estate Rose Label Orange Vineyard Shiraz

TTTTY **1997** Medium to full red-purple; the bouquet is much riper and richer than many '97 vintage wines, with luscious/spicy berry aromas. The supple palate has flavours of cherry, berry and mint cleverly framed by a nice touch of sweet oak. **rating:** 93

best drinking 2002–2010 **best vintages** '97 **drink with** Moroccan lamb • $36

Rosemount Estate Shiraz Cabernet

TTTT **2000** Light to medium red-purple; the bouquet is clean, fresh, light and fairly simple, with earthy fruit. The palate, however, offers rather more, with sweet berry fruit verging on the confection, but appropriate nonetheless for immediate summer drinking. Subtle oak. Won a gold medal at Cowra 2000. **rating:** 86

best drinking Now **best vintages** '96, '98, '99 **drink with** Lasagne • $10

Rosemount Estate Mountain Blue Shiraz Cabernet

TTTTY **1998** Medium to full red-purple; the aromas of the bouquet open with elegant, red berry fruit, followed by some savoury, spicy notes and a gentle skein of oak. Red berry and chocolate fruit flavours on the palate are backed by persistent, slightly chewy tannins. **rating:** 91

best drinking 2003–2010 **best vintages** '95, '96, '97, '98 **drink with** Barbecued beef • $53

Rosemount Estate Rose Label Orange Vineyard Cabernet Sauvignon

TTTTY **1997** Medium purple-red; a firm but attractive bouquet with a spicy edge to the restrained dark fruit aromas and subtle oak is followed by a palate with a real touch of elegance and sophistication; shows it is cool-grown, but is not green. **rating:** 92

best drinking 2002–2007 **best vintages** '96, '97 **drink with** Roast lamb shoulder • $25

rosemount estate (mclaren vale) ★★★★★

Ingoldby Road, McLaren Vale, SA 5171 **region** McLaren Vale
phone (08) 8383 0001 **fax** (08) 8383 0456 **open** Mon–Fri 10–4.30, weekends and public holidays 11–4.30
winemaker Charles Whish **production** 1 million **est.** 1888
product range ($20–69.99 CD) Ryecroft Unwooded Chardonnay, Balmoral Syrah, Show Reserve Shiraz, GSM (Grenache Shiraz Mourvedre blend), Traditional (Cabernet blend), Ryecroft Cabernet Shiraz.
summary The specialist red-wine arm of Rosemount Estate, responsible for its prestigious Balmoral Syrah, Show Reserve Shiraz and GSM, as well as most of the other McLaren Vale-based Rosemount brands.

Rosemount Estate Show Reserve Shiraz

YYYY **1997** Medium to full red-purple; the bouquet offers well-balanced and integrated fruit and oak of moderate to full intensity. The ripe, soft chocolate and vanilla flavours of the palate are very pleasant, but the wine lacks the fruit intensity of the best vintages such as '95. **rating:** 87

best drinking 2002–2010 **best vintages** '90, '91, '93, '94, '95 **drink with** Marinated beef • $28

Rosemount Estate Balmoral Syrah

YYYYY **1998** Medium to full red-purple; a potent, powerful and intense bouquet redolent of spicy black cherry leads into a palate with layer-upon-layer of black cherry, licorice, leather, tannins and oak. Approach with extreme caution for the next eight years or so. **rating:** 95

best drinking 2008–2018 **best vintages** '86, '87, '88, '89, '91, '93, '95, '96, '97, '98 **drink with** Char-grilled rump • $68

Rosemount Estate GSM

YYYY **1998** Medium to full red-purple; fully ripe, indeed bordering on jammy, spicy/berry fruit on the bouquet leads into a lusciously ripe palate with berry and prune flavours which seem to have strayed just a little bit too far into super-ripe territory. The wine has appeal, but is fractionally disappointing given the vintage. **rating:** 89

best drinking 2003–2010 **best vintages** '94, '95, '96 **drink with** Beef with olives • $27.50

Rosemount Estate Traditional

YYYYY **1998** Medium to full red-purple; the bouquet is quite powerful, with a complex array of dark, foresty, chocolate and berry aromas, characters that flow through precisely into the rich, concentrated palate. **rating:** 92

best drinking 2003–2012 **best vintages** '91, '94, '95, '96, '97, '98 **drink with** Char-grilled beef • $25

rosevears estate 

1a Waldhorn Drive, Rosevears, Tas 7277 **region** Northern Tasmania
phone (03) 6330 1800 **fax** (03) 6330 1810 **open** 7 days 10–4
winemaker James Chatto (Consultant) **production** 10 000 **est.** 1999
product range ($18–24 CD) Riesling, Sauvignon Blanc, Unwooded Chardonnay, Rosé, Pinot Noir, Cabernet Sauvignon, Notley Gorge Cabernet Sauvignon.
summary The multi-million-dollar Rosevears Estate winery and restaurant complex was opened by the Tasmanian premier in November 1999. Built on a steep hillside overlooking the Tamar River, it is certain to make a lasting and important contribution to the Tasmanian wine industry. It is owned by a syndicate of investors headed by Dr Mike Beamish and incorporates both Notley Gorge and Ironpot Bay. The inaugural winemaker was the youthful Jim Chatto (now a consultant), who brought with him large winery experience gained in the Hunter Valley and an extremely acute palate.

Rosevears Estate Unwooded Chardonnay

YYYY **2000** Light green-yellow; a tangy, citrussy, grapefruity bouquet leads into a light, elegant wine with good length. **rating:** 85

best drinking Now–2003 **best vintages** NA **drink with** Cold seafood • NA

Rosevears Estate Pinot Noir

YYYY **1999** Medium red-purple; fresh, spicy strawberry and plum fruit on both the bouquet and palate is surrounded by a forest of oak. A controversial wine because of that oak, the points representing something of a compromise. **rating:** 86

best drinking 2002–2007 **best vintages** NA **drink with** Braised venison • NA

Rosevears Estate Cabernet Sauvignon
YYYY **1999** Medium to full red, with the purple starting to change; the bouquet is of light to medium intensity, offering dark berry and a touch of chocolate; the palate, too, has an interesting touch of dark chocolate and licorice with the berry fruit, finishing with light tannins. **rating:** 87
best drinking 2002–2007 **best vintages** NA **drink with** Rack of lamb • NA

Rosevears Estate Notley Gorge Cabernet Sauvignon
YYYY **1999** Medium to full red-purple; the wine has excellent blackberry fruit, but that fruit is seriously threatened by masses of new oak on both bouquet and palate. If it does settle down with time, and it well may, those judges who gave it gold-medal points at the 2001 Tasmanian Wines Show will be vindicated, even though the outcome at the show was only a strong silver. **rating:** 87
best drinking 2004–2009 **best vintages** NA **drink with** Rare eye fillet • NA

rosewhite vineyards NR

Happy Valley Road, Rosewhite, via Myrtleford, Vic 3737 **region** Alpine Valleys
phone (03) 5752 1077 **open** Weekends and public holidays 10–5, 7 days Jan
winemaker Joan Mullett **production** 700 **est.** 1983
product range ($10 CD) Traminer, Chardonnay, Pinot Noir, Shiraz, Cabernet Sauvignon, Tawny Port.
summary After careers with the Victorian Department of Agriculture, agricultural scientists Ron and Joan Mullett began the establishment of Rosewhite in 1983 and now have a little over 2 hectares of vineyards at an altitude of 300 metres.

rosily vineyard NR

Yelveton Road, Willyabrup, WA 6284 **region** Margaret River
phone (08) 9755 6336 **fax** (08) 9485 0772 **open** By appointment
winemaker Mike Lemmes, Dan Pannell (Consultant) **production** 7000 **est.** 1994
product range ($16–20 ML) Semillon, Semillon Sauvignon Blanc, Sauvignon Blanc, Chardonnay.
summary The partnership of Mike and Barb Scott and Ken and Dot Allan acquired the Rosily Vineyard site in 1994. Under the direction of consultant Dan Pannell (of the Pannell family) 12 hectares of vineyard were planted over the next three years: first up sauvignon blanc, semillon, chardonnay and cabernet sauvignon, and thereafter merlot, shiraz and a little grenache and cabernet franc. The first crops were sold to other makers in the region, but in 1999 Rosily built a winery with a 120-tonne capacity, and is now moving to fully utilise that capacity. The initial releases are well crafted and stylish, and very reasonably priced.

Rosily Vineyard Semillon
YYYY **2000** Light green-yellow; obvious oak is the first impression on the bouquet; on the palate citrus, cashew and spicy oak are all to be found, but less oak would have been far better. This is easy to say, but far more difficult to achieve with such minuscule production. **rating:** 84
best drinking Now–2004 **best vintages** NA **drink with** Swordfish • $18

Rosily Vineyard Sauvignon Blanc
YYYY **2000** Very pale straw-green; the bouquet is clean and crisp, but quite intense, with a mix of mineral, herb and lemon aromas. The palate, likewise, is delicate yet intense; there is an edge to the flavour that comes either from the fruit or the oak, and which will hopefully soften over the next six months. **rating:** 85
best drinking Now **best vintages** NA **drink with** Fresh crab • $16

Rosily Vineyard Semillon Sauvignon Blanc
YYYY **2000** Light green-yellow; the bouquet is quite complex, with mineral and herb fruit complemented by a touch of French oak. The palate shows similar characters to the Sauvignon Blanc, a trifle tart, but certainly fresh and lively, and the oak is subtle. **rating:** 85
best drinking Now **best vintages** NA **drink with** Chinese steamed fish with ginger • $18

Rosily Vineyard Chardonnay
YYYY **2000** Light green-yellow; a very light, citrussy bouquet; paradoxically, the oak influence is much more delicate than in the case of the Semillon. The palate is fresh and lively, akin to a cross between Sauvignon Blanc and Chardonnay, with citrussy, minerally flavours, and a touch of oak on the finish. **rating:** 85
best drinking Now–2004 **best vintages** NA **drink with** Smoked turkey • $20

ross estate wines ★★★☆

Barossa Valley Way, Lyndoch, SA 5351 **region** Barossa Valley
phone (08) 8524 4033 **fax** (08) 8524 4533 **open** Tues–Sat 10–5, Sun 1–5
winemaker Rod Chapman **production** 10 000 **est.** 1999
product range ($13–26 CD) Riesling, Semillon, Semillon Sauvignon Blanc, Sauvignon Blanc Semillon, Chardonnay, Beekeeper's Blend (Late Harvest), Shiraz, Tempranillo Graciano, Old Vine Grenache, Merlot, Cabernet Sauvignon Cabernet Franc Merlot, Cabernet Sauvignon.
summary Darius and Pauline Ross laid the foundation for Ross Estate Wines when they purchased 43 hectares of vines that included two blocks of 75- and 90-year-old grenache. Also included were blocks of 30-year-old riesling and semillon, and 13-year-old merlot. The remaining vines were removed and chardonnay, sauvignon blanc, cabernet sauvignon, cabernet franc and shiraz were planted, which are now seven years old. A winery was built in time for the 1998 vintage, and a tasting room was opened in 1999. The immensely experienced Rod Chapman, with 38 vintages under his belt, including 18 years as red winemaker with Southcorp/Penfolds, is in charge of winemaking. Production is rising rapidly, with over 30 000 cases by 2002 as other family vineyards come into full production. Exports to the US.

Ross Estate Sauvignon Blanc Semillon

▼▼▼▽ **2000** Medium yellow-green; the bouquet is solid, with plenty of weight, the aromas running through mineral, herb and lemon; the palate replicates the flavour and weight of the bouquet, but does thicken somewhat on the finish. **rating:** 83

best drinking Now **best vintages** NA **drink with** Smoked eel • $16

Ross Estate Shiraz

▼▼▼▼ **1999** Medium to full red-purple; a dense, dark, black cherry and blackberry-accented bouquet is followed by a powerful palate, with the berry fruit managing to carry the pervasive vanillin oak. Winner of the Leslie Kemeny Trophy for Best 1999 Dry Red at the 2001 Sydney Wine Show. **rating:** 86

best drinking 2002–2007 **best vintages** NA **drink with** Braised beef • $26

Ross Estate Tempranillo Graciano

▼▼▼▽ **NV** Medium red with a touch of purple; the bouquet offers an unusual array of tobacco, hay and more herbal characters, the palate with interesting flavours distinctly reminiscent of Rioja and/or La Mancha. One might have expected a touch more tannin; perhaps this will come as the vines age. **rating:** 84

best drinking Now–2003 **best vintages** NA **drink with** Baby lamb • NA

Ross Estate Merlot

▼▼▼▼ **1999** Medium to full red-purple; the high-toned aromatics veer between minty, spiky and sweet redcurrant, introducing a palate with lots of high-toned fruit and slightly milky oak tannins. An unusual wine which nonetheless has appeal. **rating:** 85

best drinking Now–2005 **best vintages** NA **drink with** Lasagne • $25

rossetto

Farm 576 Rossetto Road, Beelbangera, NSW 2686 **region** Riverina
phone (02) 6966 0200 **fax** (02) 6966 0298 **open** Mon–Sat 8.30–5.30
winemaker Belinda Morandin **production** 400 000 **est.** 1930
product range ($5.75–20.85 R) Several ranges, the commercial Wattle Glen series ($5.75), the Mirror Lake range ($8.30), the Silky Oak range ($8.35–$9.90), the Promenade Range of Semillon, Semillon Riverina, Chardonnay, Botrytis Semillon, Shiraz, Cabernet Merlot ($13–$20.85) and Mitchell Brooke Limited Release Shiraz (McLaren Vale); also fortifieds and sparkling.
summary Another family-owned and run Riverina winery endeavouring to lift the profile of its wines, although not having the same spectacular success as Riverina Wines. Rossetto does have distributors in each State and exports to New Zealand, Asia and Europe, but much of the total production is sold in bulk to other makers.

rothbury estate ★★★☆

Broke Road, Pokolbin, NSW 2321 **region** Lower Hunter Valley
phone (02) 4998 7363 **fax** (02) 4993 3559 **open** 7 days 9.30–4.30
winemaker Neil McGuigan **production** NFP **est.** 1968

product range ($8.90–28 R) At the top comes the Individual Vineyard range of Hunter Valley Semillon, Chardonnay and Shiraz; next the Hunter Valley range of varietals; finally, varietals from Mudgee and Cowra.

summary Rothbury celebrated its 30th birthday in 1998, albeit not quite in the fashion that founder and previous chief executive Len Evans would have wished. After a protracted and at times bitter takeover battle, it became part of the Beringer Blass empire. It remains to be seen what impact the surprise retention of Neil McGuigan as winemaker will have; one would expect a significant lift in quality.

Rothbury Estate Hunter Valley Semillon

🍷🍷🍷🍷🍷 **2000** Light green-yellow; the bouquet ranges through citrus, herb, earth, mineral and lemon, the powerful and long palate tangy and quite rich, with ripe citrussy/lemony characters and flavours. **rating:** 90

best drinking 2004–2014 **best vintages** '72, '73, '74, '76, '79, '94, '97, '98, '00 **drink with** Smoked eel • NA

Rothbury Estate Verdelho

🍷🍷🍷🍷 **2000** Light green-yellow; the bouquet is clean, crisp, neutral and pleasant, the palate likewise. The wine has no fault, but I cannot imagine how it could win two trophies at the Royal Perth Wine Show 2000, including a trophy for Best Current Vintage Dry White. I simply have to be missing something. **rating:** 83

best drinking Now **best vintages** NA **drink with** Pasta • $12

Rothbury Estate Brokenback Shiraz

🍷🍷🍷🍷 **1999** Medium red-purple; a clean, moderately intense bouquet has gently earthy regional shiraz aromas. A pleasant, light- to medium-bodied palate, but nothing remarkable, and a long way from my concept of a gold medal. **rating:** 85

best drinking 2002–2005 **best vintages** NA **drink with** Shepherd's pie • $28

rothbury ridge NR

Talga Road, Rothbury, NSW 2320 **region** Lower Hunter Valley
phone (02) 4930 7122 **fax** (02) 4930 7198 **open** Mon–Sat 9–5, Sun 10–5
winemaker Peter Jorgensen **production** 10 000 **est.** 1988

product range ($15–28 ML) Stanleigh Park Reserve Semillon, Mary FDW Chablis Style, Anne Chardonnay Semillon, Steven FBW Chardonnay, Mount Royal Reserve Durif, Early Release Chambourcin, Edgar Chambourcin, James Shiraz Chambourcin, Mount Royal Reserve Chambourcin, Joye Cabernet Sauvignon, Mount Royal Methode Champenoise.

summary Rothbury Ridge has an extraordinarily eclectic choice of varieties planted, with 1.2–2.4 hectares each of chardonnay, semillon, verdelho, chambourcin, durif, shiraz and cabernet sauvignon.

rotherhythe ★★★★

Hendersons Lane, Gravelly Beach, Exeter, Tas 7251 **region** Northern Tasmania
phone (03) 6394 4869 **open** By appointment
winemaker Steven Hyde **production** 1600 **est.** 1976

product range ($16–26.95 CD) Chardonnay, Pinot Noir, Cabernet Sauvignon, Pinot Chardonnay.

summary At the 1996 Tasmanian Wines Show Rotherhythe swept all before it, winning trophies galore. Ironically, two days later Dr Steven Hyde sold the vineyard, although he has retained all of the existing wine stocks and will remain involved in the winemaking for some time to come. In both 1997 and again in 1998 Rotherhythe was awarded the trophy for Most Successful Exhibitor at the Tasmanian Wines Show. Since then the pace has slowed.

rothvale vineyard ★★★★☆

Deasy's Road, Pokolbin NSW 2321 **region** Lower Hunter Valley
phone (02) 4998 7290 **fax** (02) 4998 7290 **open** 7 days 10–5
winemaker Max Patton, Luke Patton **production** 5000 **est.** 1978

product range ($18–35 CD) Vat 8 Semillon, Barrel Fermented Semillon, Angus's Semillon Chardonnay, Unwooded Chardonnay, Lightly Oaked Chardonnay, Reserve Chardonnay A (American Oak), Reserve Chardonnay F (French Oak), Annie's Dry Red, Tilda's Shiraz, Luke's Shiraz, Cabernet Sauvignon.

summary Owned and operated by the Patton family, and headed by Max Patton who has the fascinating academic qualifications of BVSc, MSc London, BA Hons Cantab, the scientific part of which has no doubt come in use for his winemaking. The wines are sold only through cellar door and direct to an imposing list of restaurants in the Hunter Valley and Sydney. Rothvale also has four vineyard cottages available for B&B accommodation. The wines have already accumulated an impressive array of medals. Numerous new samples arrived as this book was going to print.

Rothvale Vineyard Cabernet Sauvignon

YYYYY **1998** Medium to full red-purple; blackberry/blackcurrant/cassis fruit is married with lots of high toast, charry oak on the bouquet; the palate has perfectly ripened cabernet fruit that carries the American oak far better than one might expect. The extract has not been forced, and the tannins are fine but ripe. **rating:** 93

best drinking 2003–2010 **best vintages** '98 **drink with** Rump steak • $30

rouge homme ★★★☆

Riddoch Highway, Coonawarra, SA 5263 **region** Coonawarra
phone (08) 8736 3205 **fax** (08) 8736 3250 **open** 7 days 10–5
winemaker Paul Gordon, Brett Sharpe **production** 64 000 **est.** 1954
product range ($11–17 R) Semillon, Chardonnay, Unoaked Chardonnay, Pinot Noir, Reserve Pinot Noir, Shiraz Cabernet, Cabernet Merlot, Cabernet Sauvignon.
summary From time to time I have described Rouge Homme as the warrior brand of the Lindeman Group Coonawarra operations. In recent times it has proved a formidable warrior, particularly with its Cabernet and Cabernet blend wines benefiting from the 1996 and 1998 vintages.

Rouge Homme Chardonnay

YYYY **1999** Light green-yellow; the bouquet offers cashew, mineral and melon supported by subtle oak, the palate with the same suite of flavours, well enough balanced, but lacking concentration. Not up to the usual standard. **rating:** 84

best drinking Now–2003 **best vintages** '94, '96, '97 **drink with** Richly sauced white-meat dishes • NA

Rouge Homme Cabernet Merlot

YYYY **1998** Medium to full red-purple; the bouquet is distinctly richer, riper and sweeter than any of the preceding vintages, the palate responding with attractive blackberry/blackcurrant and cassis fruit offset by a touch of slightly earthy tannins; subtle oak. **rating:** 89

best drinking 2003–2008 **best vintages** '98 **drink with** Braised lamb • $17

Rouge Homme Cabernet Sauvignon

YYYYY **1998** Strong red-purple; a full mulberry/blackcurrant/cassis bouquet leads into a full-bodied palate with blackcurrant, plum and cassis flavours beautifully complemented by oak and tannins. A top outcome for a very good vintage, and a great bargain. **rating:** 92

best drinking 2003–2013 **best vintages** '88, '90, '91, '94, '96, '98 **drink with** Roast leg of lamb • $17

ruker wines NR

Barton Highway, Dickson, ACT 2602 **region** Canberra District
phone (02) 6230 2310 **fax** (02) 6230 2818 **open** Weekends, public holidays 10–5
winemaker Richard Ruker **production** 500 **est.** 1991
product range ($15 CD) Riesling, Gewurztraminer.
summary Barbara and Richard Ruker, with the assistance of eldest daughter Niki, planted 2 hectares of riesling and traminer in 1984. The cellar door-cum-winery is a farmshed subsequently converted to an office and then to its present function of winery and restaurant; it is finished with heavy wooden beams salvaged from a railway bridge near Tarago and clad with the remains of an old slab hut, while the tables are made from huge red and yellow box trees that were cut down when the vineyard was planted.

rumbalara 

Fletcher Road, Fletcher, Qld 4381 **region** Granite Belt
phone (07) 4684 1206 **fax** (07) 4684 1299 **open** 7 days 9–5
winemaker Bob Gray **production** 1500 **est.** 1974
product range ($11.50–19.50 CD) Barrel Fermented Semillon, Granitegolde, Light Shiraz, Cabernet Sauvignon, Pinot Noir, Cabernet Shiraz and a range of Fortified wines, Cider and Vermouth.
summary Has produced some of the Granite Belt's finest honeyed Semillon and silky, red-berry Cabernet Sauvignon, but quality does vary. The winery incorporates a spacious restaurant, and there are also barbecue and picnic facilities. No recent tastings.

rumball sparkling wines NR

55 Charles Street, Norwood, SA 5067 **region** Warehouse
phone (08) 8332 2761 **fax** (08) 8364 0188 **open** Mon–Fri 9–5
winemaker Peter Rumball **production** 8000 **est.** 1988
product range ($20 R) Sparkling Shiraz (also available in half bottles, magnums and jeroboams).
summary Peter Rumball has been making and selling sparkling wine for as long as I can remember, but has led a somewhat peripatetic life, starting in the Clare Valley but now operating what I can only describe as a 'warehouse winery' operation, with neither vineyards nor winery of his own. The grapes are purchased and the wines made at various places under the supervision of Peter Rumball. His particular specialty has always been Sparkling Shiraz, and was so long before it became 'flavour of the month'. National retail distribution through Tucker Seabrook, and exports to Japan and the US.

ryland river NR

RMB 8945 Main Creek Road, Main Ridge, Vic 3928 **region** Mornington Peninsula
phone (03) 5989 6098 **fax** (03) 9899 0184 **open** Weekends and public holidays 10–5 or by appointment
winemaker John W Bray **production** 2000 **est.** 1986
product range ($15–30 CD) Semillon Sauvignon Blanc, Chardonnay, Cabernet Sauvignon, Jack's Delight Tawny Port and Muscat.
summary John Bray has been operating Ryland River at Main Ridge on the Mornington Peninsula for a number of years, but not without a degree of controversy over the distinction between Ryland River wines produced from Mornington Peninsula grapes and those produced from grapes purchased from other regions. A large lake with catch-your-own trout and a cheese house are general tourist attractions.

rymill

The Riddoch Run Vineyards, Riddoch Highway, Coonawarra, SA 5263 **region** Coonawarra
phone (08) 8736 5001 **fax** (08) 8736 5040 **open** 7 days 10–5
winemaker John Innes **production** 50 000 **est.** 1970
product range ($12–28 R) March Traminer, Sauvignon Blanc, Chardonnay, June Traminer Late Harvest, Shiraz, MC2 (Merlot Cabernet Sauvignon Cabernet Franc), Cabernet Sauvignon and Sparkling.
summary The Rymills are descendants of John Riddoch and have long owned some of the finest Coonawarra soil, upon which they have grown grapes since 1970, with present plantings of 165 hectares. Peter Rymill made a small amount of Cabernet Sauvignon in 1987 but has long since plunged headlong into commercial production, with winemaker John Innes presiding over the striking winery portrayed on the label. Australian distribution is through Negociants Australia; exports go to all of the major markets in Europe, North America and Asia.

Rymill Sauvignon Blanc

TTTT **2000** Light straw-green; the bouquet is crisp, clean and fresh, with grassy/lemony aromas, the palate similarly fresh and clean but showing sweeter tropical fruit flavours partially derived from that skin contact; an easy, early-drinking style. **rating:** 85

best drinking Now **best vintages** NA **drink with** Yabbies • $14.50

Rymill Shiraz

TTTT **1998** Medium red-purple; the bouquet is moderately intense, with spicy, savoury and sweet leather aromas together with vanilla oak. The palate really comes alive, with attractive, dark cherry fruit, positive oak and soft tannins. **rating:** 89

best drinking Now–2008 **best vintages** '90, '91, '92, '95, '97, '98 **drink with** Stuffed eggplant • $20

Rymill MC2

TTTT **1999** Medium to full red-purple; ripe blackberry/blackcurrant aromas, with underlying hints of leaf and spice, lead into a quite solid palate with blackcurrant-driven fruit; good balance, weight, length and integrated oak. Much better than its predecessors. **rating:** 89

best drinking 2003–2008 **best vintages** '99 **drink with** Marinated beef • $19

Rymill Cabernet Sauvignon

TTTTY **1998** Medium to full red-purple; solid, dark berry/blackberry/earthy varietal fruit on the bouquet is repeated on the powerful palate, joined by touches of dark chocolate. Has good length and sufficient tannins to guarantee a long life. **rating:** 90

best drinking 2003–2013 **best vintages** '90, '93, '98 **drink with** Mushroom risotto • $28

saddlers creek ★★★☆

Marrowbone Road, Pokolbin, NSW 2320 **region** Lower Hunter Valley
phone (02) 4991 1770 **fax** (02) 4991 2482 **open** 7 days 9–5
winemaker John Johnstone **production** 15 000 **est.** 1989
product range ($18–46 CD) Marrowbone Chardonnay, Pinot Noir, Bluegrass Cabernet Sauvignon; Equus Shiraz; Verdelho, Classic Hunter Semillon, Reserve Selection Sauvignon Blanc, Botrytis Semillon, Classical Gas (Methode Champenoise), Single Vineyard Hunter Shiraz, Reserve Selection Merlot, Langhorne Reserve Cabernet; Liqueur Muscat.
summary Made an impressive entrance to the district with consistently full-flavoured and rich wines. Marrowbone Chardonnay and Equus Hunter Shiraz are its best. Limited retail distribution in New South Wales, Queensland and Victoria.

Saddlers Creek Classic Hunter Semillon

TTTT **2000** Pale straw-green; the bouquet is light, with relatively little other than minerally notes showing yet. The light-bodied palate has nice mouthfeel, good balance and touches of citrus to add interest and underline the potential of the wine. **rating:** 87

best drinking 2004–2010 **best vintages** 2000 **drink with** Shellfish • $17.50

Saddlers Creek Marrowbone Chardonnay

TTTT **1999** Light to medium yellow-green, bright and clear; the bouquet is clean and fresh, with light melon fruit and subtle, smoky oak, the palate likewise having clean, gentle melon, cashew and smoky oak flavours; closes with pleasant acidity. **rating:** 86

best drinking Now–2003 **best vintages** '95, '97 **drink with** Bone marrow in brioche • $25

Saddlers Creek Equus Shiraz

TTTT **1999** Medium red, with a touch of purple; abundant earthy/oaky/savoury aromas move into the medium-bodied palate where chocolate and berry join the fray; good tannin management, likewise oak. **rating:** 86

best drinking 2004–2009 **best vintages** NA **drink with** Braised oxtail • NA

Saddlers Creek Reserve Merlot

TTTY **1999** Medium red-purple; the bouquet is relatively light, with savoury, earthy berry characters, the oak influence being significantly more powerful on the slightly overworked palate, with tannins starting to grab on the finish. Does not have the silky texture of Merlot, however much flavour it presents. **rating:** 84

best drinking 2004–2008 **best vintages** NA **drink with** Designer hamburger • $40

Saddlers Creek Bluegrass Cabernet Sauvignon

TTTY **1999** Medium red; the bouquet is driven by dusty American oak, without a lot of varietal character or fruit inputs, but the palate offers rather more, with an easygoing blend of chocolate, berry and vanilla. **rating:** 84

best drinking 2003–2007 **best vintages** NA **drink with** Smoked lamb • $26

st gregory's NR

Bringalbert South Road, Bringalbert South, via Apsley, Vic 3319 **region** Henty
phone (03) 5586 5225 **open** By appointment
winemaker Gregory Flynn **production** NFP **est.** 1983
product range ($14 ML) Port.
summary Unique Port-only operation selling its limited production direct to enthusiasts (by mailing list).

st hallett ★★★★

St Hallett's Road, Tanunda, SA 5352 **region** Barossa Valley
phone (08) 8563 7000 **fax** (08) 8563 7001 **open** Mon–Sat 9–5, Sun and public holidays 10–5
winemaker Stuart Blackwell, Cathy Spratt, Di Ferguson **production** 65 000 **est.** 1944
product range ($10–149 CD) Poacher's Blend (White), Eden Valley Riesling, Semillon Sauvignon Blanc, Semillon Select, Sweet Meredith, The Garden Chardonnay, Gamekeeper's Reserve (Red), Faith Shiraz, Blackwell Shiraz, Cabernet Merlot, Old Block Shiraz, Cabernet Sauvignon, The Reward Cabernet Sauvignon, Cabernet Reserve, Fortifieds.
summary Nothing succeeds like success. St Hallett has now merged with Tatachilla to form Banksia Wines, which will provide significant economics of scale while keeping the character and identity of the brands separate. St Hallett understandably continues to ride the Shiraz fashion wave, but all its wines are honest and well priced. It has established its own distribution network in the UK, and actively exports to Europe, North America and Asia.

St Hallett Barossa Sauvignon Blanc Semillon

YYYY **1999** Medium yellow-green; the moderately intense bouquet is politically correct with mineral, herb and grass aromas. The palate has good balance and flavour, again showing exemplary varietal characters with a citrus/mineral mix; good length. **rating:** 85
best drinking Now **best vintages** NA **drink with** Fish and chips • $13.95

St Hallett Faith Shiraz

YYYY **1999** Vivid purple-red; youthful cherry, plum and spice aromas, with a touch of earth, and followed by a quite chunky palate, with rich plummy fruit; slightly furry oak blurs the finish. **rating:** 87
best drinking 2003–2009 **best vintages** NA **drink with** Italian • $18.95

St Hallett Cabernet Sauvignon

YYYY **1998** Medium red-purple; the bouquet is quite fragrant, with spicy overtones to the savoury berry fruit; those leafy/savoury characters tend to come through a little assertively on the palate. **rating:** 85
best drinking Now–2006 **best vintages** NA **drink with** Parmesan cheese • $18.95

St Hallett The Reward Cabernet Sauvignon

YYYYY **1996** Medium red-purple; the bouquet is clean, smooth and still fresh, with a mix of berry, cedar, spice and earth. Mint is added to the roster on the palate adding to a fine, elegant, mature wine. **rating:** 90
best drinking Now–2006 **best vintages** NA **drink with** Rack of veal • $44.95

st huberts ★★★★

Maroondah Highway, Coldstream, Vic 3770 **region** Yarra Valley
phone (03) 9739 1118 **fax** (03) 9739 1096 **open** Mon–Fri 9–5, weekends 10.30–5.30
winemaker Matt Steel **production** NFP **est.** 1966
product range ($20–35 R) Roussanne, Chardonnay, Pinot Noir, Cabernet Sauvignon, Cabernet Merlot; under the second label Rowan Sauvignon Blanc, Chardonnay, Shiraz, Pinot Noir, Cabernet Merlot.
summary The changes have come thick and fast at St Huberts, which is now part of the Beringer Blass Group. It has produced some quite lovely wines, notably Chardonnay and Cabernet Sauvignon, but the brand is slowly but surely losing its direction and meaning.

St Huberts Roussanne

YYYY **2000** Light green-yellow; a clean and crisp bouquet with lemon-blossom aromatics is followed by a delicate palate with orange and lemon-peel/zest/blossom flavours dancing in the background; nice length and mouthfeel. Wisely, no oak. **rating:** 89
best drinking Now–2004 **best vintages** '94, '98, '00 **drink with** Pork with apple or peach • $25

St Huberts Chardonnay

YYYY **2000** Light straw-green; the bouquet shows quite pronounced, slightly pencilly oak that also comes through on the palate; needs time to settle down and integrate. **rating:** 84
best drinking Now **best vintages** '88, '90, '91, '92, '93, '94, '95, '97 **drink with** Yabbies • $20

St Huberts Pinot Noir

🍷🍷🍷🍷 **1999** Medium red, with just a touch of purple; there are unusual meaty/gum-leaf aromas to the bouquet; the palate is quite sappy, with cherry and mint flavours; varietal character is present, but in left-field mode. **rating:** 85

best drinking Now **best vintages** '96, '97 **drink with** Strong red-meat dishes • $22

St Huberts Cabernet Merlot

🍷🍷🍷½ **1997** Medium red-purple; the bouquet is clean, still fresh, with light redcurrant fruit and a touch of spice. The palate is light bodied, with attractive and fresh flavour and feel. **rating:** 84

best drinking Now–2003 **best vintages** NA **drink with** Lamb kebabs • $20

St Huberts Reserve Cabernet Sauvignon

🍷🍷🍷🍷½ **1998** Excellent red-purple; the bouquet shows clean cabernet varietal fruit ranging through earth, mint, leaf and cassis. The palate picks up on the sweet berry/cassis/raspberry notes of the bouquet, complemented by attractive oak; faintly milky tannins. **rating:** 91

best drinking 2003–2010 **best vintages** '98 **drink with** Ragout of beef • $35

st ignatius vineyard NR

Sunraysia Highway, Avoca, Vic 3467 **region** Pyrenees
phone (03) 5465 3542 **fax** (03) 5465 3542 **open** 7 days 10–5
winemaker Enrique Diaz **production** 700 **est.** 1992
product range ($18–22 CD) Released under the Djarmbee label are Graveyard Hill Chardonnay, Australian Pyrenees Shiraz, Hangmans Gully Cabernet Sauvignon.
summary Silvia and husband Enrique Diaz began the establishment of their vineyard, winery and restaurant complex in 1992. They have established shiraz (the major planting at 3.2 hectares), chardonnay (1.6 hectares), cabernet sauvignon (1 hectare) and sauvignon blanc (0.4 hectare) in bearing, with merlot (1.6 hectares) and sangiovese (0.2 hectare) planted but not yet in production. The vineyard has already received three primary production awards, and all of the wine is made on site by Enrique Diaz.

Djarmbee Australian Pyrenees Shiraz

🍷🍷🍷½ **1999** Dense, deep purple-red; very youthful, callow, dark fruits on the bouquet; a massively concentrated and underworked palate that needed much more time and work in barrel to soften out the hard edges, tannin and extract. **rating:** 84

🍷🍷🍷🍷 **1998** Medium to full red-purple; an interesting mix of plum, Christmas cake, cedar and spice on the bouquet is followed by a powerful and quite long palate, radically different in style from the '99 vintage, finishing with savoury, fine tannins. **rating:** 85

best drinking 2004–2009 **best vintages** NA **drink with** Smoked beef • NA

Djarmbee Hangman's Gully Cabernet Sauvignon

🍷🍷🍷🍷 **1998** Medium red-purple; a quite aromatic mix of savoury, cedary, spicy and brambly characters on the bouquet is followed by a palate with similar structure to the '98 Shiraz; red berry fruit and slippery tannins and mouthfeel. **rating:** 85

best drinking 2002–2007 **best vintages** NA **drink with** Baby lamb • $18

st leonards ★★★☆

Wahgunyah, Vic 3687 **region** Rutherglen
phone (02) 6033 1004 **fax** (02) 6033 3636 **open** 7 days 11–5
winemaker Peter Brown **production** NFP **est.** 1860
product range ($13.50–24 CD) Muscadello, Semillon, Chenin Blanc, Sauvignon Blanc, Chardonnay, Orange Muscat, Pinot Noir, Shiraz, Classic Rutherglen Muscat.
summary An old favourite, relaunched in late 1997 with a range of three premium wines cleverly marketed through a singularly attractive cellar door and bistro at the historic winery on the banks of the Murray. All Saints and St Leonards are now wholly owned by Peter Brown; the vast majority of the wines are sold through cellar door and by mailing list.

St Leonards Sauvignon Blanc

YYYY **2000** Light green-yellow; the bouquet has some complexity, with minerally characters supported by a touch of oak, but the palate doesn't kick on, simply producing a pleasant commercial style at a fair price. **rating:** 82

best drinking Now **best vintages** NA **drink with** Chicken pasta • $13.50

St Leonards Orange Muscat

YYYY **2000** Light green-yellow; a clean, floral, lemon-blossom bouquet is followed by a tangy, lemony/citrussy palate with a pleasantly dry finish and balancing acidity. **rating:** 84

best drinking Now **best vintages** NA **drink with** Pancakes • $13.50

st mary's ★★★★

V & A Lane, via Coonawarra, SA 5277 **region** Limestone Coast Zone
phone (08) 8736 6070 **fax** (08) 8736 6045 **open** 7 days 10–4
winemaker Barry Mulligan **production** 4000 **est.** 1986
product range ($12–22 CD) Riesling, Chardonnay, Shiraz, House Block Cabernet Sauvignon.
summary Established by the Mulligan and Hooper families in 1986, but with Tyrrell's Vineyards purchasing the Hooper interest in the vineyards (though not the brand name St Mary's) in 1995. The winemaking operation continues as a separate entity, now wholly owned by the Mulligans. National distribution through agents in each State; exports to the US, Canada and the UK.

st matthias 

113 Rosevears Drive, Rosevears, Tas 7277 **region** Northern Tasmania
phone (03) 6330 1700 **fax** (03) 6330 1975 **open** 7 days 10–5
winemaker Michael Glover **production** 4000 **est.** 1983
product range ($9.35–18.50 CD) Riesling, Chardonnay, Pinot Noir.
summary After an uncomfortable period in the wilderness following the sale of the vineyard to Moorilla Estate, and the disposal of the wine made by the previous owners under the St Matthias label, Moorilla has re-introduced the label, and markets a full range of competitively priced wines which are in fact made at Moorilla Estate.

St Matthias Riesling

YYYY **2000** Quite deep in colour, but the hue is good; the bouquet is firm and smooth, with some tropical notes, but not particularly aromatic. The palate is quite rich, with friendly tutti-frutti flavour. **rating:** 87

best drinking Now–2003 **best vintages** '97, '99 **drink with** Gravlax • NA

st peters edenhope wines NR

Whitton Stock Route, Yenda, NSW 2681 **region** Riverina
phone (02) 4285 3180 **fax** (02) 4285 3180 **open** Mon–Fri 9–5
winemaker Contract **production** 10 000 **est.** 1977
product range ($8–20 CD) A wide variety of wines under the St Peters, Edenhope, Yenda Vineyards and Wilton Estate labels.
summary Draws grapes and wine from various parts of southern Australia and New South Wales for its dry table wines, most of which are sold overseas through Australian Prestige Wines.

salem bridge wines NR

Salem Bridge Road, Lower Hermitage, SA 5131 **region** Adelaide Hills
phone (08) 8380 5240 **fax** (08) 8380 5240 **open** Not
winemaker Barry Miller **production** 300 **est.** 1989
product range ($19 R) Cabernet Franc.
summary Barry Miller acquired the 45-hectare Salem Bridge property in the Adelaide Hills in 1988. A little under 2 hectares of cabernet franc were planted in 1989, and cabernet franc has been the only commercial release prior to 1999. However, a further 14 hectares have been planted to cabernet sauvignon, shiraz and merlot, with a Shiraz and Cabernet Sauvignon release in the pipeline. The wine is made off site by contract-winemaking, with input from Barry Miller.

Salem Bridge Cabernet Franc

▼▼▼▼▽ **1998** Medium red-purple; the bouquet has lively, fresh small berry fruit aromas with just a hint of olive; the smooth, sweet berry fruit provides the opening stanza of the palate, with pleasant, if slightly dusty, tannins and well-controlled oak cutting on the back palate and finish. **rating:** 90

best drinking Now–2005 **best vintages** '98 **drink with** Veal chops • $19

salitage ★★★★

Vasse Highway, Pemberton, WA 6260 **region** Pemberton
phone (08) 9776 1771 **fax** (08) 9776 1772 **open** 7 days 10–4
winemaker Patrick Coutts **production** 20 000 **est.** 1989
product range ($16–35 R) Chardonnay, Unwooded Chardonnay, Pinot Noir, Pemberton (Cabernet blend); Treehouse range Chardonnay Verdelho, Pinot Noir, Shiraz and Cabernets.
summary Salitage is the showpiece of Pemberton. If it had failed to live up to expectations, it is a fair bet the same fate would have befallen the whole of the Pemberton region. The quality and style of Salitage has varied substantially, presumably in response to vintage conditions and yields. It still remains the key producer in the Pemberton region but the variability is a little unsettling, as is the propensity to age quickly. Key retail distribution in all States, and exports to New Zealand, Taiwan, Singapore, Japan, Hong Kong, the Philippines, Malaysia, Germany, Switzerland, Canada, Denmark, Korea and the Netherlands.

Salitage Unwooded Chardonnay

▼▼▼▼ **2000** Medium to full yellow-green; the bouquet is clean, running through melon/citrus/mineral/nectarine, the alcohol (14°) investing the rich and powerful palate with some sweetness that adds to the overall impact. **rating:** 86

best drinking Now–2003 **best vintages** '97 **drink with** Vegetarian dishes • $17

Salitage Pinot Noir

▼▼▼▼▽ **1999** Medium to full red-purple; the bouquet has abundant sweet, plummy fruit together with some spice; a very substantial wine on the palate with plenty of power and depth to the complex, plummy fruit. Perhaps verging on dry red in style, but, on the other hand, the best Salitage Pinot Noir to date. Top gold medal winner Wine Show of Western Australia 2000. **rating:** 92

best drinking Now–2004 **best vintages** '93, '94, '99 **drink with** Barbecued quail • $35

Salitage Treehouse Pinot Noir

▼▼▼▼▽ **1999** Medium red-purple; the bouquet has modest cherry and plum fruit, with some fragrance and varietal character; the medium-bodied palate shows a mix of ripe plum and more savoury flavours; the oak is subtle, the length good. Gold medal winner at the 2000 Wine Show of Western Australia. **rating:** 91

best drinking Now–2003 **best vintages** '99 **drink with** Salt-roasted salmon • $20

saltram 

Salters Gully, Nuriootpa, SA 5355 **region** Barossa Valley
phone (08) 8564 3355 **fax** (08) 8564 2209 **open** 7 days 10–5
winemaker Nigel Dolan **production** NFP **est.** 1859
product range ($10–49.95 R) At the top is No. 1 Shiraz; then Mamre Brook, now 100 per cent Barossa and comprising Chardonnay, Shiraz and Cabernet Sauvignon; Metala Black Label and White Label; and the Saltram Classic range sourced from southeast Australia; also Pepperjack range with Shiraz and Cabernet Sauvignon.
summary There is no doubt that Saltram has taken giant strides towards regaining the reputation it held 30 or so years ago. Under Nigel Dolan's stewardship, grape-sourcing has come back to the Barossa Valley for the flagship wines, a fact of which he is rightly proud. The red wines in particular have enjoyed great show success over the past few years, with No. 1 Shiraz, Mamre Brook and Metala leading the charge.

Saltram Metala Black Label Shiraz

▼▼▼▼▽ **1998** Medium red-purple; the clean, quite intense and fragrant bouquet has an enticing mix of fruit, oak and spice. The palate carries on the story, with excellent texture and weight; cherry, berry and chocolate flavours are supported by fine tannins and well-handled oak. **rating:** 92

best drinking 2003–2010 **best vintages** '96, '98 **drink with** Stewed venison • $32

Saltram No. 1 Reserve Shiraz

▼▼▼▼ **1997** Medium red-purple; the moderately intense bouquet is clean and elegant, with the aromas in the savoury/earthy end of the spectrum. The palate follows down a near-identical track, with spicy notes in addition; the oak handling is assured. Has won three gold medals, including a gold medal at the National Wine Show in 1999. **rating:** 89

best drinking 2002–2007 **best vintages** '96, '97 **drink with** Richly sauced casserole • $37.50

Mamre Brook Cabernet Sauvignon

▼▼▼▼▽ **1998** Quite simply the best Mamre Brook for decades, a celebration of the great 1998 vintage. The bouquet has a mix of gently sweet cassis and mulberry fruit, which easily carries the positive oak input; there is more of the same on the seductively rich and smooth palate. Delicious. **rating:** 93

best drinking Now–2011 **best vintages** '96, '98 **drink with** Roast kid • $19.50

Pepperjack Barossa Cabernet Sauvignon

▼▼▼▼ **1998** Medium red-purple; obvious charry/toasty oak dominates the bouquet, but there is a major role-reversal on the palate, where strong red berry/blackberry/cassis fruit is the driving force; good length and tannins. **rating:** 87

best drinking 2003–2010 **best vintages** NA **drink with** Smoked beef • $20

sandalford ★★★★

West Swan Road, Caversham, WA 6055 **region** Swan District

phone (08) 9374 9374 **fax** (08) 9274 2154 **open** 7 days 10–5

winemaker Peter Gambetta, Richard Moore **production** 80 000 **est.** 1840

product range ($12.95–35 R) At the bottom end under the Caversham label, Chenin Verdelho, Late Harvest Cabernet Shiraz; then the 1840 Collection of Semillon Sauvignon Blanc, Chardonnay and Cabernet Merlot; under the premium range, Margaret River Mount Barker Riesling, Margaret River Verdelho, Mount Barker Margaret River Chardonnay, Mount Barker Margaret River Shiraz, Mount Barker Margaret River Cabernet Sauvignon; also excellent fortifieds, notably Sandalera; also the new Element brand including Chenin Verdelho, Chardonnay and Cabernet Shiraz.

summary The installation of a new winemaking team headed by the highly experienced Peter Gambetta, and continuing winery upgrading has meant that wine quality has improved year by year, with Chenin Blanc and Chardonnay leading the way. The quality of the labelling and packaging has also taken a giant leap forwards. Exports to the UK, Switzerland, the US, Japan Singapore and Hong Kong.

Sandalford Semillon

▼▼▼▼ **2000** Light to medium yellow-green; a complex bouquet with slightly spicy notes from the oak integrated with tangy fruit. The palate is quite crisp, avoiding excess phenolics; citrus flavours predominate in a wine with good length, focus and balance. **rating:** 89

best drinking Now–2005 **best vintages** NA **drink with** Scallops • $22.80

Sandalford Sauvignon Blanc

▼▼▼▼ **2000** Very pale straw-green; the aromas show a faintly reduced character alongside the quite intense passionfruit and gooseberry aromas; the palate is flavoursome, with similar characters; the question is how do you react to that faint reduction character? **rating:** 87

best drinking Now **best vintages** NA **drink with** Shellfish • $20.80

Sandalford Merlot

▼▼▼▼ **1999** Medium red-purple; the bouquet features very ripe, sweet fruit coupled with attractively sweet oak; the palate provides more of the same, with enticing sweet, red fruit flavours, a touch of mocha, and well-handled tannins and oak. Very well handled; would have received even higher points had it shown more varietal character. **rating:** 87

best drinking Now–2006 **best vintages** NA **drink with** Mushroom risotto • $25.30

Sandalford Founders Reserve Liqueur Port

▼▼▼▼ **NV** Red-brown; the bouquet is quite complex, with strong dried-fig aromas; dried fig and nutty characters dominate the medium-bodied palate, which finishes clean and relatively dry. **rating:** 86

best drinking Now **best vintages** NA **drink with** Dried fruits • $23.60

sandalyn wilderness estate NR

Wilderness Road, Rothbury, NSW 2321 **region** Lower Hunter Valley
phone (02) 4930 7611 **fax** (02) 4930 7611 **open** 7 days 10–5
winemaker Adrian Sheridan (Contract) **production** 4000 **est.** 1988
product range ($16–22 CD) Semillon, Verdelho, Semillon Verdelho, Chardonnay, Semillon Late Harvest, Pinot Noir, Conservatory Shiraz, Sparkling.
summary Sandra and Lindsay Whaling preside over the picturesque cellar-door building of Sandalyn on the evocatively named Wilderness Road, where you will find a one-hole golf range and views to the Wattagan, Brokenback and Molly Morgan ranges. The estate has 8.85 hectares of vineyards.

sand hills vineyard ★★☆

Sandhills Road, Forbes, NSW 2871 **region** Lachlan Valley
phone (02) 6852 1437 **fax** (02) 6852 4401 **open** Mon–Sat 9–5, Sun 12–5
winemaker Jill Lindsay **production** 1000 **est.** 1920
product range ($9–18 CD) Classic Dry White, Chardonnay, Colombard Semillon, Banderra The White, Vat 1 Dry Red, Dry Red, Pinot Noir, Shiraz Cabernet, Cabernet Shiraz, Banderra The Red, Oloroso Cream Sherry, Lucien Tawny Port.
summary Having purchased Sand Hills from long-term owner Jacques Genet, the Saleh family has replanted the vineyard, with over 6 hectares of premium varieties having been established. Winemaking is carried out by Jill Lindsay of Woodonga Hill.

Sand Hills Vineyard Banderra The Red

▼▼▼▽ **1999** Medium red; the bouquet is of light to medium intensity, with earthy/berry fruit and minimal oak; there are some minty notes on the palate to go with the berry aromas of the bouquet, and the wine finishes with soft tannins. The best from Sand Hills Vineyard to date. **rating:** 83
best drinking Now–2003 **best vintages** NA **drink with** Pasta • $17.80

sandhurst ridge 

156 Forest Drive, Marong, Vic 3515 **region** Bendigo
phone (03) 5435 2534 **fax** (03) 5435 2548 **open** Weekends 1–5 and by appointment
winemaker Paul Greblo, George Greblo **production** 2000 **est.** 1990
product range ($17–20 CD) Sauvignon Blanc, Chardonnay, Shiraz, Cabernet Sauvignon.
summary The four Greblo brothers, with combined experience in business, agriculture, science and construction and development, began the establishment of Sandhurst Ridge in 1990 with the planting of the first 2 hectares of shiraz and cabernet sauvignon. Those plantings have now been increased to over 6 hectares, principally cabernet and shiraz, but with small amounts of merlot, sauvignon blanc and chardonnay. The fully equipped winery was completed in 1996 with a cellar capacity of 400 barriques. The white wines are not up to standard, but there is no problem with the reds.

Sandhurst Ridge Shiraz

▼▼▼▽ **1999** Full red-purple; the bouquet has solid, dark berry fruit aromas with some slightly savoury edges, the palate with dark berry, plum and chocolate; the oak is subtle but the tannins are persistent, and the wine needs time to soften. **rating:** 84
best drinking 2004–2009 **best vintages** NA **drink with** Char-grilled rib of beef • $20

sandstone 

PO Box 558 Busselton, WA 6280 **region** Margaret River
phone (08) 9755 6271 **fax** (08) 9755 6292 **open** By appointment
winemaker Mike Davies, Jan Davies **production** 3000 **est.** 1988
product range ($19–25 ML) Semillon, Cabernet Sauvignon.
summary The family operation of consultant-winemakers Mike and Jan Davies, who also operate very successful mobile bottling plants.

sandy farm vineyard NR

RMB 3734 Sandy Farm Road, Denver, via Daylesford, Vic 3641 **region** Macedon Ranges
phone (03) 5348 7610 **open** Weekends 10–5 or by appointment
winemaker Peter Comisel **production** 800 **est.** 1988
product range ($15–20 CD) Pinot Noir, Merlot, Cabernet Sauvignon.
summary Peter Covell has a small, basic winery in which he makes preservative-free Cabernet Sauvignon, Merlot and Pinot Noir, attracting a loyal local following.

sarsfield estate NR

345 Duncan Road, Sarsfield, Vic 3875 **region** Gippsland
phone (03) 5156 8962 **fax** (03) 5156 8970 **open** By appointment
winemaker Dr Suzanne Rutschmann **production** 1000 **est.** 1995
product range ($17.50–20 CD) Pinot Noir, Cabernets Shiraz Merlot.
summary The property is owned by Suzanne Rutschmann (who has a PhD in Chemistry, a Diploma in Horticulture and a BSc (Wine Science) from Charles Sturt University) and Swiss-born Peter Albrecht, a civil and structural engineer who has also undertaken various courses in agriculture and viticulture. For a part-time occupation, these are exceptionally impressive credentials. Their 2-hectare vineyard was planted between 1991 and 1998; the first vintage made at the winery was 1998, the grapes being sold to others in previous years.

Sarsfield Estate Cabernets Shiraz Merlot

ΨΨΨY **1999** Medium red-purple; there are some lifted notes on the leafy/minty/berry bouquet; the palate is at the austere end of the spectrum, with savoury/earthy fruit, but is quite long, and the tannins have been well managed.
rating: 83

best drinking 2003–2007 **best vintages** NA **drink with** Shoulder of lamb • $17.50

scarborough ★★★★

Gillards Road, Pokolbin, NSW 2321 **region** Lower Hunter Valley
phone (02) 4998 7563 **fax** (02) 4998 7786 **open** 7 days 9–5
winemaker Ian Scarborough **production** 10 000 **est.** 1985
product range ($18.50–30 CD) Semillon, Chardonnay, Pinot Noir.
summary Ian Scarborough put his white-winemaking skills beyond doubt during his years as a consultant, and his exceptionally complex and stylish Chardonnay is no disappointment. Vintage conditions permitting, Ian Scarborough makes two styles: a rich, traditional, buttery White Burgundy version for the Australian market (exemplified by the 1995 with its mustard-gold label) and a lighter, more elegant Chablis style (under a blue-silver label) for the export market. Exports to the UK, the US and New Zealand.

Scarborough Semillon

ΨΨΨΨ **2000** Light to medium green-yellow; a clean, very ripe bouquet moving into the ripe citrus spectrum. The mouthfilling and powerful palate has more in common with the Adelaide Hills style than traditional Hunter Valley; it will be interesting to see how the wine develops in bottle. In the absence of any other indication, I would drink it sooner rather than later.
rating: 87

best drinking Now–2004 **best vintages** NA **drink with** Rich fish dishes • NA

scarpantoni estate ★★★☆

Scarpantoni Drive, McLaren Flat, SA 5171 **region** McLaren Vale
phone (08) 8383 0186 **fax** (08) 8383 0490 **open** Mon–Fri 10–5, weekends 11–5
winemaker Michael Scarpantoni, Filippo Scarpantoni **production** 15 000 **est.** 1979
product range ($5.50–26 CD) Block 1 Riesling, Sauvignon Blanc, Unwooded Chardonnay, Chardonnay, Fleurieu Brut, Black Tempest (sparkling), Botrytis Riesling, Gamay, Fiori, School Block (Cabernet Shiraz Merlot), Block 3 Shiraz, Cabernet Sauvignon, Tawny Port, Vintage Port.
summary While an erratic producer at times, and not helped by the earlier use of agglomerate corks, has made some excellent wines in recent years which, if repeated, would earn the winery an even higher rating.

Scarpantoni Estate Sauvignon Blanc

🍷🍷🍷🍷 **1999** Light green-yellow; some passionfruit aromatics are set against a faintly reductive background. The crisp, lemony palate likewise has that shadow of reduction, a commonly encountered character with Sauvignon Blanc. **rating:** 82

best drinking Now **best vintages** NA **drink with** Light seafood • $16

Scarpantoni Estate Black Tempest

🍷🍷🍷🍷 **NV** Strong red-purple; complex licorice, spice and berry aromas and flavours attest to the quality of the base wine; in recognition of that quality, the dosage has been kept low, which is sensible. **rating:** 85

best drinking Now–2006 **best vintages** NA **drink with** Pâté de foie gras • $26

Scarpantoni Estate Block 3 Shiraz

🍷🍷🍷🍷 **1999** Medium red-purple; the moderately intense, clean bouquet has an array of cherry, mint and earth aromas that sustain the solid palate; not a lot of complexity or character, perhaps, but then you don't get 1998 quality every year. **rating:** 84

🍷🍷🍷🍷🍷 **1998** Full red-purple; the bouquet is rich, with plum, cherry and chocolate fruit. The palate is similarly rich, dense and mouthfilling, with plum, chocolate and vanilla flavours; well-managed tannins and oak. **rating:** 90

best drinking 2002–2006 **best vintages** '96, '97, '98 **drink with** Seared kangaroo fillet • $20

Scarpantoni Estate School Block

🍷🍷🍷🍷 **1998** Medium red-purple; the quite complex bouquet reflects the varietal mix, with a mix of savoury, leathery, spicy aromatics. A firm palate has plenty of dark berry fruit flavours supported by soft tannins and subtle oak. Excellent value for money. **rating:** 85

best drinking 2002–2007 **best vintages** NA **drink with** Osso bucco • $16

Scarpantoni Estate Cabernet Sauvignon

🍷🍷🍷🍷 **1999** Medium red-purple; the bouquet is of light to medium intensity, with some leaf and berry aromas, the palate correspondingly light to medium bodied in a plain, no-frills style offering some varietal character, but not a lot of richness. **rating:** 83

best drinking 2002–2006 **best vintages** NA **drink with** Leg of lamb • $20

scarp valley vineyard ★★★

8 Robertson Road, Gooseberry Hill, WA 6076 **region** Perth Hills

phone (08) 9454 5748 **open** By appointment

winemaker Hainault (Contract) **production** 24 **est.** 1978

product range ($17 ML) Darling Range Hermitage.

summary Owner Robert Duncan presides over what has to be one of the smallest producers in Australia, with one-quarter acre of shiraz and 30 cabernet sauvignon vines producing a single cask of wine each year if the birds do not get the grapes first. The property, which has views all the way to the city of Perth, and cannot be built out, was offered for sale in March 2001.

Scarp Valley Darling Range Hermitage

🍷🍷🍷🍷 **1999** Medium purple-red; a bouquet of ripe, black cherry fruit and touches of earth; the palate has plenty of red cherry fruit, again with some earthy tones and tannins that are wholly varietal. **rating:** 86

best drinking 2003–2007 **best vintages** '98 **drink with** Fillet steak • $17

schild estate wines ★★★☆

Cnr Barossa Valley Way and Lyndoch Valley Road, Lyndoch, SA 5351 **region** Barossa Valley

phone (08) 8524 5560 **fax** (08) 8524 4333 **open** Mon–Fri 11–5, weekends and public holidays 10–5

winemaker Rod Chapman (Contract) **production** 3500 **est.** 1998

product range ($11–23 ML) Barossa Valley Riesling, Eden Valley Riesling, Semillon, Chardonnay, Shiraz, Cabernet Sauvignon.

summary Ed Schild has been a Barossa Valley grape-grower who first planted a small vineyard at Rowland Flat in 1952, steadily increasing his vineyard holdings over the past 40 years to their present level of 130 hectares. Currently only 10 per cent of the production from these vineyards is used to produce Schild Estate Wines, but the plans are to steadily increase this percentage. The flagship wine will be made from 150-year-old shiraz vines on the Moorooroo Block, due for release late 2002. The cellar door is situated in what was the old ANZ Bank at Lyndoch, and provides the sort of ambience that can only be found in the Barossa Valley.

Schild Estate Barossa Valley Riesling

YYYY 2000 Light to medium green-yellow; the floral bouquet has soft lime and lemon fruit aromas, the palate pleasant, falling away slightly on the mid-palate before coming again on the finish. Technically well-made; early-developing style. **rating:** 84

best drinking Now–2004 **best vintages** NA **drink with** Stuffed eggplant • $15

Schild Estate Eden Valley Riesling

YYYY 2000 Light straw-green; a tangy bouquet with a mix of citrus, herb and a touch of mineral leads into a crisp, long and lively citrus and herb palate, which finishes with good acidity. **rating:** 87

best drinking 2003–2009 **best vintages** NA **drink with** Caesar salad • $16

Schild Estate Chardonnay

YYYY 2000 Medium to full yellow-green; the bouquet has plenty of richness and weight with its ripe peach fruit flowing through into the full-flavoured palate. Probably derives this weight from a period of skin contact, and is an emphatic drink-now style. **rating:** 84

best drinking Now **best vintages** NA **drink with** Takeaway • $11

Schild Estate Shiraz

YYYY 1999 Medium to full red-purple; a ripe, solid bouquet with a mix of chocolate, berry and earth supported by subtle oak is followed by a well-constructed palate. Here sweet, ripe chocolatey fruit is supported by soft, ripe tannins on the finish. **rating:** 88

best drinking 2003–2009 **best vintages** NA **drink with** Barossa sausage • $23

Schild Estate Cabernet Sauvignon

YYYYY 1999 Medium to full red-purple; clean blackcurrant/cassis/blackberry fruit and gentle oak are followed by a rich, full palate with abundant cassis fruit and fine tannins on the finish. **rating:** 92

best drinking 2003–2009 **best vintages** '99 **drink with** Roast lamb • $23

schmidts tarchalice ★★★

Research Road, Vine Vale, via Tanunda, SA 5352 **region** Barossa Valley
phone (08) 8563 3005 **fax** (08) 8563 0667 **open** Mon–Sat 10–5, Sun 12–5
winemaker Christopher Schmidt **production** 1500 **est.** 1984
product range ($8.50–19.75 CD) Barossa Riesling, Eden Valley Riesling, Barossa Chardonnay, Barossa Semillon, Auslese Riesling, Shiraz Cabernet/Cabernet Franc, Magna Carta Shiraz, Carta's Choice Shiraz Cabernet, four different Ports and Old Liqueur Frontignac.
summary Typically has a range of fully mature wines at low prices available at cellar door.

Schmidts Tarchalice Magna Carta Shiraz

YYYY 1997 Medium red-purple; the clean, moderately intense bouquet has sweet leather overtones, the palate very smooth, with pleasantly sweet cherry, plum, berry fruit; fine tannins and subtle oak. **rating:** 85

best drinking Now–2005 **best vintages** NA **drink with** Grilled bratwurst • NA

Schmidts Tarchalice Carta's Choice Shiraz Cabernet

YYYY 1996 Medium red-purple, with some traces of purple remaining. A mix of plum and more savoury/ earthy aromas on the bouquet are followed by ripe, sweet plum, earth and cedar flavours on the palate; well-balanced tannins. **rating:** 84

best drinking Now–2006 **best vintages** NA **drink with** Roast beef • NA

scotchmans hill ★★★☆

190 Scotchmans Road, Drysdale, Vic 3222 **region** Geelong
phone (03) 5251 3176 **fax** (03) 5253 1743 **open** 7 days 10.30–4.30
winemaker Robin Brockett **production** 30 000 **est.** 1982

product range ($15.50–26.50 R) Sauvignon Blanc, Chardonnay, Pinot Noir, Cabernet Sauvignon Merlot; the Swan Bay range of Sauvignon Blanc Semillon, Chardonnay Sauvignon Blanc Chardonnay and Pinot Noir replaces the former Spray Farm label.

summary Situated on the Bellarine Peninsula, southeast of Geelong, with a well-equipped winery and first-class vineyards. It is a consistent performer with its Pinot Noir and has a strong following in both Melbourne and Sydney for its astutely priced, competently made wines. A doubling in production has seen the establishment of export markets to the UK and the Netherlands. The second label of Spray Farm takes its name from a National Trust property with panoramic views of Port Phillip Bay and Melbourne, which has also been planted to vines by the Brown family and is run as a distinct vineyard and brand operation. The same four varieties are produced but at a lower price-point across the range.

Scotchmans Hill Chardonnay

YYYY 1999 Medium yellow-green; the clean bouquet has smooth, moderately ripe melon aromas, the palate precisely following down the same track, clean and soft, with a mix of melon and nectarine fruit, the oak influence throughout being reflected more in texture and structure than in flavour. **rating:** 86

best drinking Now–2003 **best vintages** '91, '92, '94, '97 **drink with** Smoked salmon • $26.50

scotts brook NR

Scotts Brook Road, Boyup Brook, WA 6244 **region** Blackwood Valley
phone (08) 9765 3014 **fax** (08) 9765 3015 **open** Weekends, school holidays 10–5 or by appointment
winemaker Aquila Estate (Contract) **production** 2000 **est.** 1987
product range ($11–19 CD) Riesling, Autumn Harvest White, Chardonnay, Cabernet Sauvignon.
summary The Scotts Brook winery at Boyup Brook (equidistant between the Margaret River and Great Southern regions) has been developed by local schoolteachers Brian Walker and wife Kerry (hence the opening hours during school holidays). There are 17.5 hectares of vineyards, but the majority of the production is sold to other winemakers, with limited quantities being made by contract.

sea winds vineyard NR

RMB 9020 Main Creek Road, Main Ridge, Vic 3928 **region** Mornington Peninsula
phone (03) 5989 6204 **fax** (03) 5989 6204 **open** Not
winemaker Kevin McCarthy (Contract) **production** NA **est.** 1990
product range NA
summary Ron Matson has developed 3 hectares of sauvignon blanc, chardonnay and pinot noir; the wines are made for him by Kevin McCarthy at T'Gallant.

seldom seen vineyard ★★★☆

Cnr Gulgong and Hill End Roads, Mudgee, NSW 2850 **region** Mudgee
phone (02) 6372 4482 **fax** (02) 6372 1055 **open** 7 days 9.30–5
winemaker Barry Platt, Marcus Platt **production** 3000 **est.** 1987
product range ($11–16 CD) Semillon (wooded and unwooded), Chardonnay Semillon, Chardonnay, Traminer.
summary A substantial grape-grower (with 18 hectares of vineyards) which reserves a proportion of its crop for making and release under its own label.

Seldom Seen Chardonnay

YYYY 1999 Medium yellow-green; a nice touch of spicy oak on both bouquet and palate nicely offsets the fresh fruit flavours. In a commercial mould, but seductively so. **rating:** 88

best drinking Now **best vintages** NA **drink with** Chicken lasagne • $16

seppelt ★★★★★

RSD Seppeltsfield, via Nuriootpa, SA 5355 **region** Barossa Valley
phone (08) 8568 6200 **fax** (08) 8562 8333 **open** Mon–Fri 10–5, Sat 10.30–4.30, Sun 11–4
winemaker James Godfrey **production** NFP **est.** 1851
product range ($8–500 R) The great wines of Seppeltsfield are first and foremost Para Liqueur Port (bottling 119), Para Liqueur 21 year old, Vintage Tawny, Show Tawny Port DP90, Rutherglen Show Muscat, Rutherglen Show Tokay, Mount Rufus Finest Tawny Port DP4, Trafford DP30, Seppeltsfield Fino Sherry, Show Amontillado

DP116, Show Fino DP117, Show Oloroso DP38, Seppelt Show Vintage Shiraz, Dorrien Cabernet Sauvignon. The other wines in the Seppelt portfolio are handled at Great Western. The 100 Year Old Para Liqueur Port is the $500 a bottle (375 ml) jewel in the crown, the current vintage being the 1901.

summary A multi-million-dollar expansion and renovation programme has seen the historic Seppeltsfield winery become the production centre for the Seppelt wines, adding another dimension to what was already the most historic and beautiful major winery in Australia. It is now home to some of the world's unique fortified wines, nurtured and protected by the passionate James Godfrey. Worldwide distribution.

Seppelt Dorrien Vineyard Cabernet Sauvignon

YYYYY **1996** The wine's two trophies and five gold medals do it scant justice. The bouquet is wonderfully fragrant, and starting to develop that mix of cedar and earth common to mature Bordeauxs, the palate with similar breed and elegance; seduction, not rape. **rating:** 96

best drinking Now–2016 **best vintages** '88, '89, '91, '92, '93, '94, '96 **drink with** Pink roast lamb • $53

Seppelt Rutherglen Show Tokay DP57

YYYYY **NV** Mahogany gold; complex, sweet and rich tea-leaf, raisin and plum-pudding aromas are followed by an equally complex, multiflavoured palate that leaves the mouth fresh, thanks to its perfect balance. **rating:** 94

best drinking Now–2019 **best vintages** NA **drink with** Fine, dark chocolate • NA

Seppelt Show Reserve Muscat DP63

YYYYY **NV** Deep mahogany brown, with a mix of gold and green on the rim. Rich, raisined, spicy plum-pudding aromas are lifted by perfectly balanced and integrated spirit. The powerful, complex and rich palate – plum pudding and Christmas cake – has a very long, lingering finish. **rating:** 96

best drinking Now **best vintages** NA **drink with** Dried fruits • NA

Seppelt Amontillado Sherry DP116

YYYYY **NV** Bright mid-gold; the bouquet has a lovely touch of honey over the bite of the rancio; the very elegant, very fresh palate finishes distinctly dry after the mellowness of the bouquet and mid-palate. This is as it should be. **rating:** 94

best drinking Now **best vintages** NA **drink with** A great winter aperitif • NA

Seppelt Show Fino Sherry DP117

YYYYY **NV** Brilliant green-yellow; the bouquet is strong and stylish, with that faintly nutty, faintly tangy cut that is the hallmark of Fino Sherry. The palate is intense and racy, the flavour lingering in the mouth long after the wine is swallowed, but not so long to stop you taking the next mouthful. **rating:** 96

best drinking Now **best vintages** NA **drink with** Olives, tapas • NA

Seppelt Show Oloroso Sherry DP38

YYYYY **NV** Golden-brown; nutty rancio complexity, with just a hint of sweetness, introduce a finely balanced palate with a constant interplay between nutty, honeyed sweetness and drier, rancio characters. **rating:** 95

best drinking Now **best vintages** NA **drink with** Sweet biscuits • NA

Seppelt Show Tawny Port DP90

YYYYY **NV** The tawny hues are rimmed with olive-green, immediately proclaiming the age of the wine; the bouquet is fine, fragrant and penetrating, much closer to the Tawny Ports of Portugal than most Australian wines. The palate offers flavours of spice, butterscotch and more nutty characters, but it is the length of flavour and finish that is absolutely remarkable. Given its age, arguably the most undervalued wine on the Australian market today. **rating:** 97

best drinking Now **best vintages** NA **drink with** Dried fruits and nuts • NA

Seppelt Para Liqueur Port

YYYYY **NV** Dark mahogany tinged with green; the bouquet is complex, and both richer and sweeter than DP90, with malt, butterscotch and strong rancio characters. The palate has complex structure and great power, yet paradoxically has an almost dry finish, and no biscuity aftertaste. **rating:** 94

best drinking Now **best vintages** NA **drink with** Coffee, chocolate • NA

seppelt great western ★★★★★

Moyston Road, Great Western, via Ararat, Vic 3377 **region** Grampians
phone (03) 5361 2222 **fax** (03) 5361 2200 **open** 7 days 10–5
winemaker Ian McKenzie (Chief) **production** 2 million **est.** 1865
product range ($6–60 R) Méthode Champenoise comprising (from the bottom up) Brut Reserve, Imperial Reserve, Grande Reserve, 2000 Brut Cuvée NV, M2 Chardonnay Pinot Noir, M2 Sparkling Shiraz, Sunday Creek Pinot Noir Chardonnay, Fleur de Lys, Harpers Range, Rhymney Sparkling Sauvignon Blanc, Original Sparkling Shiraz, Sparkling Shiraz Great Western Vineyard, Show Sparkling Reserve, Drumborg Vineyard Blanc de Blancs and Salinger; table wines include Moyston Unoaked Chardonnay and Cabernet Shiraz; Sheoak Spring Riesling; Terrain Series Chardonnay, Shiraz and Cabernet Sauvignon; Eden Valley Botrytis Gewurztraminer, Corella Ridge Chardonnay, Harpers Range Cabernet Sauvignon, Chalambar Shiraz, Sunday Creek Pinot Noir, Drumborg Vineyard Riesling, Partalunga Vineyard Adelaide Hills Chardonnay, Great Western Shiraz, Mornington Peninsula Pinot Gris and Drumborg Cabernet Sauvignon. Great Western Hermitage and Show Reserve Sparkling Burgundy are the flagbearers alongside Salinger.
summary Australia's best-known producer of sparkling wine, always immaculate in its given price range but also producing excellent Great Western-sourced table wines, especially long-lived Shiraz and Australia's best Sparkling Shirazes. Now the production centre for many Southcorp Group brands, with a vast new bottling plant and attendant warehouse facilities. Worldwide distribution.

Seppelt Fleur de Lys Méthode Champenoise

YYYY **1994** A multiple gold and silver medal winner. I'm glad I don't have to calculate the cost of selling a six-year-old vintage bottle-fermented sparkling wine at this price; Pinot Noir and Chardonnay, too, are the base wines. Has a great combination of lees and cork age giving complexity, but the lively palate is still fresh, with bright acidity. **rating:** 89

best drinking Now **best vintages** '93, '94 **drink with** Oysters or shellfish • $15

Seppelt Salinger Méthode Champenoise

YYYYY **1994** This is a truly ludicrous price for what, on any view, once was and still should be a market leader. Clean, supremely elegant and stylish, it has a gently bready/creamy/yeasty bouquet; the palate is equally elegant and harmonious, with fruit and yeast autolysis, still fine, and fresh as a daisy. Great aperitif. **rating:** 94

best drinking Now **best vintages** '88, '89, '90, '91, '93, '94 **drink with** Aperitif, oysters, shellfish • $23

Seppelt M2 Chardonnay Pinot Noir

YYYYY **1995** A special Cuvée made for (and lost in?) the Millennium celebrations from 100 per cent Drumborg base wines that spent four years on yeast lees. Intense citrus and stonefruit interwoven with fine, bready yeast autolysis on the bouquet lead into a gloriously fresh and lively citrus/melon-accented palate finishing with delectable acidity. **rating:** 95

best drinking Now–2005 **best vintages** '95 **drink with** Tempura oysters • $38

Seppelt Great Western Vineyard Sparkling Shiraz

YYYYY **1990** Medium red; the complex bouquet offers a mix of spice, leather, licorice and berry, followed by abundant sweet, red berry fruit on the mid-palate, which finishes fine and dry. **rating:** 94

best drinking Now–2010 **best vintages** '90 **drink with** Borscht • $60

Seppelt M2 Sparkling Show Shiraz

YYYYY **1993** Medium red; the bouquet is very complex, with spice, licorice and berry fruit aromas, the intense and long palate providing more of the above, most importantly neither sweet nor oaky. **rating:** 93

best drinking Now–2005 **best vintages** '93 **drink with** Chinese meat dishes • $38

Seppelt Original Sparkling Shiraz

YYYY **1996** Medium red-purple; pleasantly sweet plum and cherry fruit, with no evident oak on the bouquet, leads into a palate with gentle plum and cherry fruit; perfectly balanced, not too sweet, and not a hair out of place. **rating:** 87

best drinking Now–2006 **best vintages** '93, '95 **drink with** Pâté and game • $17

Seppelt Great Western Shiraz

YYYYY **1996** Medium to full red-purple; a voluminous, complex and rich bouquet with cascades of licorice, berry and blackberry flows into a powerful, rich, complex palate with a mix of the berry fruit of the bouquet and some savoury/earthy edges. Powerful but balanced tannins give the wine great structure. **rating:** 95

best drinking Now–2016 **best vintages** '54, '56, '60, '63, '71, '84, '85, '86, '91, '93, '95, '96 **drink with** Herbed rack of lamb • $37

Seppelt Drumborg Cabernet Sauvignon

YYYYY **1996** Medium red, still tinged with purple on the rim; the savoury/cedary/leafy bouquet has strong Bordeaux characters, the red berry/redcurrant palate with touches of mint and bitter chocolate that do not, however, take away from its supple texture; nicely controlled French oak rounds off a classy wine. **rating:** 91

best drinking Now–2011 **best vintages** '94, '96 **drink with** Marinated lamb • $42

serventy ★★☆

Valley Home Vineyard, Rocky Road, Forest Grove, WA 6286 **region** Margaret River
phone (08) 9757 7534 **fax** (08) 9757 7534 **open** Fri–Sun, holidays 10–4
winemaker Peter Serventy **production** 1500 **est.** 1984
product range ($15 CD) Chardonnay, Pinot Noir, Shiraz.
summary Peter Serventy is nephew of the famous naturalist Vincent Serventy and son of ornithologist Dominic Serventy. It is hardly surprising, then, that Serventy should practise strict organic viticulture, using neither herbicides nor pesticides. The wines, too, are made with a minimum of sulphur dioxide, added late in the piece and never exceeding 30 parts per million.

settlers ridge NR

54b Bussell Highway, Cowaramup, WA 6284 **region** Margaret River
phone (08) 9755 5388 **fax** (08) 9755 5388 **open** 7 days 10–5
winemaker Wayne Nobbs **production** NFP **est.** 1998
product range ($13–25 CD) Chenin Blanc, Chenin Sauvignon Blanc, Sauvignon Blanc, Shiraz, Shiraz Cabernet Sauvignon, Cabernet Sauvignon.
summary Wayne and Kaye Nobbs have established what they say is the only winery in Western Australia with organic certification and the only winery in Australia with dual classification from NASAA (National Association for Sustainable Agriculture Australia) and OVAA (Organic Vignerons Association of Australia Inc.). They have 6.4 hectares of vineyard in bearing, with an additional hectare of merlot coming into production. All of the wines are distributed direct from cellar door.

settlers rise montville NR

249 Western Avenue, Montville, Qld 4560 **region** Queensland Zone
phone (07) 5478 5558 **fax** (07) 5478 5655 **open** 7 days 10–5
winemaker Peter Scudamore-Smith (Contract) **production** 3000 **est.** 1998
product range ($14–20 CD) Queensland Classic White, Blackall Range White, Semillon Sauvignon Blanc Chardonnay, Chardonnay, Shiraz Cabernet Sauvignon, Tawny Port.
summary Settlers Rise is located in the beautiful highlands of the Blackall Range, 75 minutes' drive north of Brisbane and 20 minutes from the Sunshine Coast. A little over a hectare of chardonnay, verdelho, shiraz and cabernet sauvignon have been planted at an elevation of 450 metres on the deep basalt soils of the property. First settled in 1887, Montville has gradually become a tourist destination, with a substantial local arts and crafts industry and a flourishing B&B and lodge accommodation infrastructure.

sevenhill cellars ★★★★

College Road, Sevenhill, SA 5453 **region** Clare Valley
phone (08) 8843 4222 **fax** (08) 8843 4382 **open** Mon–Fri 9–4.30, Sat and public holidays 10–4
winemaker Brother John May, John Monten **production** 20 000 **est.** 1851
product range ($8–20 CD) Riesling, Gewurztraminer, Semillon, St Aloysius (Chenin Blanc, Chardonnay, Verdelho blend), College White, Verdelho, Botrytis Semillon, Shiraz, Shiraz Touriga Malbec, Merlot, Cabernet Sauvignon, St Ignatius (Cabernet Sauvignon Malbec Cabernet Franc Merlot blend), Fortifieds, Sacramental Wine.

summary One of the historical treasures of Australia; the oft-photographed stone wine cellars are the oldest in the Clare Valley, and winemaking is still carried out under the direction of the Jesuitical Manresa Society and in particular Brother John May. Quality is very good, particularly that of the powerful Shiraz, all the wines reflecting the estate-grown grapes from old vines. Extensive retail distribution throughout all States; exports to New Zealand, Switzerland, Germany and Ireland.

Sevenhill Cellars Riesling

ΥΥΥΥ **2000** The colour of the wine is very difficult to get around, with hints of brown that should not be there. The bouquet and palate, however, are a contradiction, with mineral, herb and spice aromas, and a palate with good intensity, length and balance. Very much the curate's egg. **rating:** 86

best drinking Now–2003 **best vintages** '87, '89, '91, '92, '94, '97 **drink with** Antipasto • $18

Sevenhill Cellars Semillon

ΥΥΥΥ **1999** Light to medium green-yellow; the bouquet is clean, quite intense, with very correct herb and grass varietal character. The palate offers similarly clear varietal character, with plenty of weight and flavour; seems to fall away fractionally on the finish. **rating:** 88

best drinking Now–2004 **best vintages** NA **drink with** Rich fish dishes • $12

Sevenhill Cellars Shiraz

ΥΥΥΥY **1999** Medium to full purple-red; a rich, concentrated bouquet with dark berry, mint and earth aromas flows through seamlessly into a palate with similar flavours, good tannins and good oak management. A superior outcome for the vintage. **rating:** 91

best drinking 2003–2009 **best vintages** '89, '91, '93, '94, '95, '99 **drink with** Barbecued beef • $18

severn brae estate NR

Lot 2 Back Creek Road (Mount Tully Road), Severnlea, Qld 4352 **region** Granite Belt
phone (07) 4683 5292 **fax** (07) 3391 3821 **open** Mon–Fri 12–3, weekends 10–5, or by appointment
winemaker Bruce Humphery-Smith **production** 1400 **est.** 1987
product range ($14–16 ML) Murray Grey White, Unwooded Chardonnay, Estate Chardonnay, Light Fruity Red, Merlot Sangiovese, Reserve Shiraz; Liqueur Muscat and Chardonnay.
summary Patrick and Bruce Humphery-Smith have established 5.5 hectares of chardonnay with relatively close spacing and trained on a high, two-tier trellis. Winery and cellar-door facilities were completed in time for the 1995 vintage. Prior to that time, the Chardonnay was made at Sundown Valley winery.

seville estate ★★★★☆

Linwood Road, Seville, Vic 3139 **region** Yarra Valley
phone (03) 5964 2622 **fax** (03) 5964 2633 **open** Weekends and public holidays 10–5
winemaker Iain Riggs **production** 5000 **est.** 1970
product range ($12–26 ML) Chardonnay Sauvignon Blanc, Chardonnay, Pinot Noir, Shiraz, Cabernet Sauvignon; new GP label of Chardonnay Semillon and Cabernet Sauvignon in honour of winery founder Dr Peter McMahon.
summary In February 1997 a controlling interest in Seville Estate was acquired by Brokenwood (of the Hunter Valley) and interests associated with Brokenwood. I was one of the founding partners of Brokenwood, and the acquisition meant that the wheel had turned full circle. This apart, Seville Estate will add significantly to the top end of the Brokenwood portfolio, without in any way competing with the existing styles.

Seville Estate Chardonnay

ΥΥΥΥY **1999** Medium yellow-green; obvious charry/smoky barrel-ferment characters drive the bouquet, but on the palate it is sweet, ripe peach and melon fruit to lead the way, the barrel-ferment/oak characters following through on the finish. Trophy winner at the 2000 Cowra Wine Show, gold medal winner at the Ballarat Wine Show 2000. **rating:** 91

best drinking Now–2005 **best vintages** '99 **drink with** Yabbies or marron • $26

Seville Estate Pinot Noir

ΥΥΥY **1999** Medium red with some tawny notes starting to develop; the bouquet is distinctly green/savoury/foresty, the moderately intense palate likewise at the green end of the spectrum. The wine does, however, have good structure and length. **rating:** 84

best drinking Now–2004 **best vintages** NA **drink with** Smoked quail • $26

shadowfax vineyard and winery ★★★★

K Road, Werribee, Vic 3030 **region** Geelong
phone (03) 9731 4420 **fax** (03) 9731 4421 **open** 7 days 11–5
winemaker Matt Harrop **production** 12 000 **est.** 2000
product range ($17–29 CD) Riesling, Sauvignon Blanc Semillon, Pinot Gris, Chardonnay, Shiraz.
summary Shadowfax is part of an awesome development at Werribee Park, a mere 20 minutes from Melbourne towards Geelong. The truly striking winery, designed by Wood Marsh Architects, was erected in time for the 2000 vintage crush, adjacent to the extraordinary 60-room private home built in the 1880s by the Chirnside family and known as The Mansion. It was then the centrepiece of a 40 000-hectare pastoral empire, and the appropriately magnificent gardens were part of the reason why the property was acquired by Parks Victoria in the early 1970s. The Mansion is now The Mansion Hotel, with 92 rooms and suites, and an emphasis on conference bookings during the week, and general tourism on the weekend. The striking packaging of the wines, and the quality of the first releases, all underline the thoroughly serious nature of this quite amazing venture.

Shadowfax Riesling

🍷🍷🍷🍷🍷 **2000** Light green-yellow; the bouquet has good fruit intensity with a mix of floral, lime/lime blossom aromatics. The palate is slightly less intense than the bouquet, but is elegant, fine and well balanced, and will undoubtedly develop greater weight and complexity with time in bottle. **rating:** 90
best drinking Now–2010 **best vintages** '00 **drink with** Light seafood • $18

Shadowfax Sauvignon Blanc Semillon

🍷🍷🍷🍷 **2000** Light green-yellow; a fresh, clean bouquet with a mix of herb and light tropical fruit is followed by a very light, clean, crisp and correct palate, pretty much straight up and down the line. **rating:** 85
best drinking Now–2004 **best vintages** NA **drink with** Seafood salad • $17

Shadowfax Pinot Gris

🍷🍷🍷🍷 **2000** Light straw-green; a voluminous bouquet with musk, spice, hay and straw aromas is followed by a palate that runs through a similar spectrum of flavours, with some dried fruit characters and a dry finish. Altogether idiosyncratic, but works well. **rating:** 87
best drinking Now–2003 **best vintages** NA **drink with** Mediterranean food • $20

Shadowfax Burong Vineyard Chardonnay

🍷🍷🍷🍷 **1999** Medium yellow-green; the bouquet is clean, with melon and citrus fruit, and just a hint of toasty oak and creamy mlf; the palate is surprisingly light and delicate, given the age of the vines and the planting density, with fine citrus and melon flavours, the oak input subtle. This may develop considerable character over the next few years. **rating:** 86
best drinking Now–2005 **best vintages** NA **drink with** Calamari • $24

shantell ★★★★

1974 Melba Highway, Dixons Creek, Vic 3775 **region** Yarra Valley
phone (03) 5965 2264 **fax** (03) 5965 2331 **open** Thur–Mon 10.30–5
winemaker Shan Shanmugam, Turid Shanmugam **production** 2000 **est.** 1980
product range ($15–32 CD) Semillon, Chardonnay, Glenlea Chardonnay, Pinot Noir, Shiraz, Cabernet Sauvignon, Sparkling.
summary The substantial and now fully mature Shantell vineyards provide the winery with a high-quality fruit source; part is sold to other Yarra Valley makers, the remainder vinified at Shantell. In January 1998 Shantell opened a new cellar door situated at 1974 Melba Highway, 50 metres along a service road from the highway proper. Chardonnay, Semillon and Cabernet Sauvignon are its benchmark wines, sturdily reliable, sometimes outstanding (witness the 1997 Chardonnay). Domestic and international distribution through Australian Prestige Wines.

Shantell Chardonnay

🍷🍷🍷🍷🍷 **1999** Glowing yellow-green; the bouquet offers clean, smooth white peach and melon fruit supported by subtle oak, the palate with luscious white peach and a touch of fig in a smooth, mouthfilling frame. A particularly good outcome for the vintage. **rating:** 90
best drinking Now–2005 **best vintages** '90, '92, '94, '97, '98, '99 **drink with** Yarra Valley smoked trout • $24

Shantell Cabernet Sauvignon

YYYY 1999 Medium to full red-purple; clean blackcurrant and raspberry fruit in a gently ripe mode on the bouquet leads into a palate with sweet cassis, raspberry and mulberry-flavoured palate; subtle oak and fine-grained tannins. **rating:** 88

best drinking 2003–2008 **best vintages** '90, '91, '92, '93, '95 **drink with** Shoulder of lamb • $24

sharmans ★★★☆

Glenbothy, 175 Glenwood Road, Relbia, Tas 7258 **region** Northern Tasmania
phone (03) 6343 0773 **fax** (03) 6343 0773 **open** Weekends by appointment
winemaker James Chatto, Rosevears Estate (Contract) **production** 1000 **est.** 1987
product range ($15–25 ML) Riesling, Sauvignon Blanc, Chardonnay, Noble Late Harvest, Pinot Noir, Cabernet Sauvignon.
summary Mike Sharman has very probably pioneered one of the more interesting wine regions of Tasmania, not far south of Launceston but with a distinctly warmer climate than (say) Pipers Brook. Ideal north-facing slopes are home to a vineyard now approaching 3 hectares, most still to come into bearing. The few wines produced in sufficient quantity to be sold promise much for the future.

Sharmans Noble Late Harvest

YYYY 1999 Medium to full yellow-green; rich, tropical canned fruit-salad and lime aromas lead into a palate that should have wide appeal, with its attractive fruit/sugar/acid balance making for immediate enjoyment. **rating:** 88

best drinking Now–2003 **best vintages** NA **drink with** Fruit tart • $15

Sharmans Cabernet Sauvignon

YYYY 1999 Inky purple-black colour; strong blackberry/cassis/earth aromas lead into a powerful, dense palate with immense flavour and extract. **rating:** 89

best drinking 2004–2009 **best vintages** NA **drink with** Leave it in the cellar • $15

shaw & smith ★★★★★

Lot 4 Jones Road, Balhannah, SA 5242 **region** Adelaide Hills
phone (08) 8398 0500 **fax** (08) 8398 0600 **open** By appointment
winemaker Martin Shaw, Willy Lunn **production** 22 000 **est.** 1989
product range ($21–35 R) Sauvignon Blanc, Unoaked Chardonnay, Reserve Chardonnay, Merlot; also Incognito Chardonnay and Merlot.
summary Has progressively moved from a contract grape-growing base to estate production with the development of a 40-hectare vineyard at Balhannah in the Adelaide Hills, followed by the erection prior to the 2000 vintage of a state-of-the-art, beautifully designed and executed winery at Balhannah, ending the long period of tenancy at Petaluma. While wine quality has been exemplary, the perfectionism of Martin Shaw will now receive full play. The wines have wide international distribution including the UK, Italy, Japan, the US, Canada, Hong Kong, Japan, Singapore and Malaysia.

Shaw & Smith Sauvignon Blanc

YYYYY 2000 The first wine made in their splendid new winery, and the result of rigorous fruit selection and declassification of lesser wine. Has the aromatics missing from the majority of eastern States wines, running through gooseberry and tropical notes, including passionfruit. The flavoursome palate precisely tracks the bouquet. **rating:** 93

best drinking Now **best vintages** '92, '93, '95, '97, '99, '00 **drink with** Poached mussels • $21

Shaw & Smith Unoaked Chardonnay

YYYYY 2000 Light to medium yellow-green; a highly aromatic bouquet with a mix of citrus, melon and tropical fruit, characters that carry on through the palate, perhaps with a little more grapefruit coming through. The length and intensity of the flavour put this wine well above any other unoaked Chardonnay from the 2000 vintage (or almost any vintage, for that matter). **rating:** 90

best drinking Now–2004 **best vintages** '00 **drink with** Pan-fried scallops • $21

Incognito Chardonnay

YYYYY 2000 Bright green-yellow; an elegant and sophisticated bouquet, with all of the components understated, rather than the reverse, but the nectarine and grapefruit flavours provide a sure foundation. **rating:** 90

best drinking 2002–2005 **best vintages** '00 **drink with** Pheasant or guinea fowl • $21

Shaw & Smith Reserve Chardonnay

ΥΥΥΥΥ **1999** Medium yellow-green; a stylish bouquet shows complex barrel-ferment characters mingling with ripe melon and apple fruit. The palate flows logically along the same tracks, with malolactic cashew characters adding a nice touch to the fruit; has good length, and won't overdevelop. **rating:** 92

best drinking 2002–2007 **best vintages** '92, '94, '95, '96, '97, '98, '99 **drink with** Slow-cooked Tasmanian salmon • $29

Shaw & Smith Merlot

ΥΥΥΥ **1999** Medium to full red-purple; the bouquet offers the seamless handling and balance of red berry fruit and oak, immaculately done and the best feature of the wine. I am not entirely convinced by the palate, with savoury/berry fruit and tannins building somewhat towards the finish. **rating:** 88

best drinking 2004–2009 **best vintages** NA **drink with** Veal saltimbocca • $35

Incognito Merlot

ΥΥΥΥ **1999** Medium red-purple; strange though it may seem, the 13.5° alcohol is actually the mark of an elegant and restrained bouquet, benefiting from French oak. The palate, likewise, is in radically different style from the usual for McLaren Vale, not the least bit heavy, and with bright berry fruit touched by spice. **rating:** 89

best drinking 2002–2006 **best vintages** '98 **drink with** All things Italian • NA

shottesbrooke ★★★★

Bagshaws Road, McLaren Flat, SA 5171 **region** McLaren Vale
phone (08) 8383 0002 **fax** (08) 8383 0222 **open** Mon–Fri 10–4.30, weekends and public holidays 11–5
winemaker Nick Holmes **production** 8000 **est.** 1984
product range ($15–35 CD) Fleurieu Sauvignon Blanc, Chardonnay, Shiraz, Eliza Reserve Shiraz, Merlot, Cabernet Merlot Malbec.

summary Now the full-time business of former Ryecroft winemaker Nick Holmes; the grapes grown on his vineyard at Myoponga, at their best, show clear berry fruit, subtle oak and a touch of elegance. A compact, handsome new winery was erected prior to the 1997 vintage. Exports to the UK, the US and Canada supplement distribution through all Australian States.

Shottesbrooke Chardonnay

ΥΥΥΥ **2000** Light green-yellow; the bouquet opens with obvious charry/smoky barrel-ferment characters on light fruit, but the roles are reversed on the palate, with lemony citrus fruit and a touch of creamy lees contact to the fore, and oak in the background. **rating:** 85

best drinking Now–2003 **best vintages** NA **drink with** King George whiting • $15.50

Shottesbrooke Eliza Shiraz

ΥΥΥΥΥ **1998** Medium red-purple; the bouquet is clean, with gentle dark berry fruit and touches of spice and vanilla; the palate has good structure, delivering sweet, dark berry/cherry fruit nicely supported by fine, soft, lingering tannins. **rating:** 90

best drinking 2002–2008 **best vintages** '98 **drink with** Roast leg of lamb • $35

silk hill NR

324 Motor Road, Deviot, Tas 7275 (postal) **region** Northern Tasmania
phone (03) 6394 7385 **fax** (03) 6326 2350 **open** Not
winemaker Gavin Scott **production** NA **est.** 1990
product range Pinot Noir.

summary Pharmacist Gavin Scott has been a weekend and holiday viticulturist for many years, having established the Glengarry Vineyard, which he sold, and then establishing the 0.5-hectare Silk Hill (formerly Silkwood Vineyard) in 1989, planted exclusively to pinot noir. Growing and making Pinot Noir and fishing will keep him occupied when he sells his pharmacy business.

silvan winery NR

Lilydale–Silvan Road, Silvan, Vic 3795 **region** Yarra Valley
phone (03) 9737 9392 **open** Weekends, public holidays 11–6

winemaker John Vigliaroni **production** 500 **est.** 1993
product range ($8 CD) Chardonnay, Pinot Noir, Cabernet, Cabernet Shiraz Merlot, Merlot.
summary One of the newer and smaller of the Yarra Valley wineries; tastings are held in the Vigliaronis' spacious Italian villa, being offered for sale by auction in March 2001.

simon gilbert wines ★★★☆

1220 Sydney Road, Mudgee, NSW 2850 **region** Mudgee
phone (02) 9958 1322 **fax** (02) 8920 1333 **open** From August 2001
winemaker Simon Gilbert, Drew Tuckwell **production** 70 000 **est.** 1993
product range ($14–50 R) Card Series Semillon Sauvignon Blanc, Verdelho, Chardonnay and Shiraz; Orange Pinot Noir, Wongalere McLaren Vale Shiraz, Mudgee Shiraz, McLaren Vale Grenache Shiraz Mourvedre, Central Ranges Cabernet Merlot, Abbaston Cabernet Sauvignon.
summary The transition from a converted butter factory at Muswellbrook to a spectacularly sited state-of-the-art $10-million winery at Mudgee represents the culmination of a family winemaking history that dates back to 1847; that is when forebear Captain Joseph Gilbert commenced the establishment of a splendid vineyard and winery at Pewsey Vale, in the East Barossa Ranges. Simon Gilbert Wines is now a significant public company listed on the stock exchange with a primary base of large-scale contract-winemaking for others, but with plans to rapidly develop a three-tiered range of proprietary wines sourced from grapes grown in premium regions around southeast Australia and, in the future, from the 40 hectares of hillside vineyards surrounding the winery. A spacious cellar door and restaurant overlooking the micro-valley in which the winery is situated was due to open in August 2001. Exports to the UK, the US and Canada.

Simon Gilbert Card Series Semillon Sauvignon Blanc

YYYY **2000** Light green-yellow; the bouquet is clean, with gently ripe citrus fruit from the Sauvignon Blanc component, and mineral from the Semillon. The palate provides more of the same, with particularly well-handled and balanced acidity adding to the length and style of the wine. **rating:** 87
best drinking Now–2003 **best vintages** NA **drink with** Steamed fish • $14

Simon Gilbert McLaren Vale Grenache Shiraz Mourvedre

YYYY **1998** Medium red-purple; sweet red berry and spice fruit on the bouquet is followed by a palate with sweet red berry fruit, a touch of mint and soft tannins. Attractive early-drinking style. **rating:** 86
best drinking Now–2004 **best vintages** '98 **drink with** Lasagne • $25

Simon Gilbert Wongalere McLaren Vale Shiraz

YYYY **1998** Medium to full red-purple; obvious vanilla oak straddles sweet berry fruit on the bouquet; the palate has plenty of similar juicy berry fruit but is still somewhat callow, and needs time to come together. **rating:** 85
best drinking 2003–2008 **best vintages** NA **drink with** Kangaroo fillet • $40

Simon Gilbert Central Ranges Cabernet Merlot

YYYY **1999** Medium to full red, with some purple tinges; the solid bouquet has dark berry, chocolate and a touch of earth, the oak in restraint. The palate flows smoothly, with berry, plum and raspberry flavours again complemented by a nice hint of oak. Won a gold medal at the 2000 Cowra Wine Show. **rating:** 86
best drinking 2003–2008 **best vintages** NA **drink with** Fettuccine with pesto • $25

simon hackett

Budgens Road, McLaren Vale, SA 5171 **region** McLaren Vale
phone (08) 8323 7712 **fax** (08) 8323 7713 **open** Wed–Sun 11–5
winemaker Simon Hackett **production** 14 000 **est.** 1981
product range ($12–35 R) Barossa Valley Semillon, Barossa Valley Chardonnay, McLaren Vale Shiraz, McLaren Vale Anthony's Shiraz, McLaren Vale Old Vine Grenache, McLaren Vale Cabernet Sauvignon, McLaren Vale Foggo Road Cabernet Sauvignon.
summary In 1998 Simon Hackett acquired the former Taranga winery in McLaren Vale, which has made his winemaking life a great deal easier. He also has 8 hectares of estate vines and has contract growers in McLaren Vale, the Adelaide Hills and the Barossa Valley, with another 32 hectares of vines.

sinclair wines NR

Graphite Road, Glenoran, WA 6258 **region** Pemberton
phone (08) 9421 1399 **fax** (08) 9421 1191 **open** By appointment
winemaker Brenden Smith **production** 2500 **est.** 1993
product range ($10–22 CD) Glenoran Sauvignon Blanc, Chardonnay, Unwooded Chardonnay, Glenoran Cabernet Sauvignon.
summary Sinclair Wines is the child of Darelle Sinclair, a science teacher, wine educator and graduate viticulturist from Charles Sturt University, and John Healy, a lawyer, traditional jazz musician and graduand wine-marketing student of Adelaide University, Roseworthy Campus. Five hectares of estate plantings are in production.

sittella wines NR

100 Barrett Road, Herne Hill, WA 6056 **region** Swan District
phone (08) 9296 2600 **fax** (08) 9473 0774 **open** Thurs–Sun and most public holidays 11–4
winemaker Julie White **production** 1000 **est.** 1998
product range ($11–19 CD) Chenin Blanc, Semillon, Verdelho, Chardonnay, Sparkling, Shiraz, Frontignac (Muscat), Tawny Port.
summary Perth couple Simon and Maaike Berns acquired a 7-hectare block at Herne Hill, making the first wine in February 1998 and opening the most attractive cellar-door facility later in the year. They also own the Wildberry Springs Estate vineyard in the Margaret River region, which commenced to provide grapes from the 1999 vintage.

s kidman wines NR

Riddoch Highway, Coonawarra, SA 5263 **region** Coonawarra
phone (08) 8736 5071 **fax** (08) 8736 5070 **open** 7 days 9–5
winemaker John Innes (Contract) **production** 8000 **est.** 1984
product range ($13–19 CD) Riesling, Sauvignon Blanc, Shiraz, Cabernet Sauvignon.
summary One of the district pioneers, with a 16-hectare estate vineyard which is now fully mature. No recent tastings; limited retail distribution in Melbourne and Adelaide.

skillogalee ★★★★

Off Hughes Park Road, Sevenhill, via Clare, SA 5453 **region** Clare Valley
phone (08) 8843 4311 **fax** (08) 8843 4343 **open** 7 days 10–5
winemaker Dave Palmer **production** 7000 **est.** 1970
product range ($13.50–27 CD) Riesling, Late Picked Riesling, Gewurztraminer, Chardonnay, Sparkling Riesling, Shiraz, The Cabernets, Fortifieds.
summary David and Diana Palmer purchased the small hillside stone winery from the George family at the end of the 1980s and have capitalised to the full on the exceptional fruit quality of the Skillogalee vineyards. The winery also has a well-patronised lunchtime restaurant. All of the wines are generous and full flavoured, particularly the reds.

Skillogalee Gewurztraminer

YYYY **1998** Green-gold; the bouquet is ripe, with spicy lychee and lime marmalade aromas. A powerful, solidly built palate demands a strong food background. **rating:** 86
best drinking Now **best vintages** NA **drink with** Highly spiced Asian • $15

Skillogalee Shiraz

YYYY **1998** Medium to full red-purple; the bouquet opens with lots of dusty American oak, with plum and mint fruit traipsing along in the background, but the mint, plum, chocolate and cherry fruit comes through more strongly on the palate, supported by soft tannins. **rating:** 88
best drinking 2002–2008 **best vintages** '97, '98 **drink with** Rich game • $27

Skillogalee The Cabernets

YYYYY **1998** Medium to full red-purple; the spotlessly clean bouquet with ripe cassis berry fruit and subtle oak is followed by a palate with loads of succulent cassis berry fruit; abundant tannins round off a full-blooded, full-bodied wine not to be trifled with. **rating:** 93
best drinking 2003–2013 **best vintages** '84, '87, '90, '93, '96, '97, '98 **drink with** Yearling steak • $27

smithbrook ★★★☆

Smith Brook Road, Middlesex, via Manjimup, WA 6258 **region** Pemberton
phone (08) 9772 3557 **fax** (08) 9772 3579 **open** By appointment
winemaker Michael Symons **production** 10 000 **est.** 1988
product range ($15–23.50 R) Sauvignon Blanc, Chardonnay, Merlot, Cabernet Merlot, Cabernet Sauvignon.
summary Smithbrook is a major player in the Pemberton region, with 60 hectares of vines in production. A majority interest was acquired by Petaluma in 1997 but will continue its role as a contract-grower for other companies, as well as supplying Petaluma's needs and making relatively small amounts of wine under its own label. Perhaps the most significant change has been the removal of Pinot Noir from the current range of products, and the introduction of Merlot. National distribution through Negociants; exports to the UK and Japan.

Smithbrook Sauvignon Blanc

🍷🍷🍷☐ **2000** Water-white; quite intense smoky/passionfruit aromas on the cusp of that armpit character that seems part and parcel of Sauvignon Blanc are followed by a pleasant palate, albeit with less fruit intensity than the bouquet suggests. Well priced. **rating:** 84
best drinking Now **best vintages** NA **drink with** Sashimi • $15

Smithbrook Chardonnay

🍷🍷🍷🍷 **1999** Light green-yellow; an aromatic bouquet with scented nectarine fruit is followed by a lively, fresh and crisp nectarine and citrus palate that has soaked up the oak. The wine must have had considerable acidity prior to the malolactic fermentation. **rating:** 89
best drinking 2002–2005 **best vintages** '92, '94, '96 **drink with** Fresh Atlantic salmon • $19.50

Smithbrook Merlot

🍷🍷🍷🍷 **1999** Medium red-purple; the firm bouquet offers strong varietal character in an olive/herb/earth/briar spectrum, the palate moving more to small red berry fruit flavours surrounded by the characters of the bouquet. The wine has soft but persistent tannins that provide it with good texture. **rating:** 87
best drinking 2003–2009 **best vintages** '99 **drink with** Milk-fed veal • $23

Smithbrook Cabernet Merlot

🍷🍷🍷🍷 **1998** Medium red-purple; the aromas are soft, with quite sweet blackcurrant fruit and a touch of oak. The fruit flavours of the palate faithfully reproduce the bouquet in a medium-bodied frame; subtle oak. **rating:** 85
best drinking Now–2006 **best vintages** NA **drink with** Braised veal • $23

smithleigh vineyard NR

53 Osborne Road, Lane Cove, NSW 2066 (postal) **region** Lower Hunter Valley
phone 0418 411 382 **fax** (02) 9420 2014 **open** Not
winemaker Andrew Margan (Contract) **production** 4000 **est.** 1997
product range ($11.50–14 ML) Old Vine Hunter Semillon, Verdelho, Chardonnay, Shiraz.
summary As the name suggests, a partnership between Rod and Ivija Smith and John and Jan Leigh, who purchased the long-established vineyard from Southcorp in 1996. A lot of work in the vineyard and skilled contract-winemaking by Andrew Margan brought immediate results with the 1998 Old Vine Semillon, which won a silver medal at both the Hunter Valley and Cowra Wine Shows, demonstrating considerable power and flavour.

snowy river winery NR

Rockwell Road, Berridale, NSW 2628 **region** Southern New South Wales Zone
phone (02) 6456 5041 **fax** (02) 6456 5005 **open** 7 days 10–5
winemaker Contract **production** 2500 **est.** 1984
product range ($10–20 CD) Alpine Dry White, Semillon, Sauvignon Blanc, Semillon Chardonnay, Müller Thurgau Sylvaner, Sieger Rebe [sic], Rhine Riesling Auslese, Snow Bruska, Port.
summary Claimed the only Eiswein to have been made in Australia, picked on 8 June 1990 after a frost of minus eight degrees Celsius. Also makes a Trocken Beeren Auslese [sic] picked mid-May from the vineyard situated on the banks of the Snowy River, one hour from Mount Kosciusko. One suspects many of the wines are purchased from other makers.

somerset hill wines ★★★☆

891 McLeod Road, Denmark, WA 6333 **region** Great Southern
phone (08) 9840 9388 **fax** (08) 9840 9394 **open** 7 days 11–5
winemaker Brenden Smith (Contract) **production** 3000 **est.** 1995
product range ($17.50–35 CD) Semillon, Sauvignon Blanc, Chardonnay (Unwooded), Harmony (Chardonnay Semillon Sauvignon Blanc), Methode Champenoise, Pinot Noir.
summary Graham Upson commenced planting 10 hectares of pinot noir, chardonnay, semillon, merlot and sauvignon blanc in 1995, and Somerset Hill Wines duly opened its limestone cellar-door sales area with sweeping views out over the ocean. Limited retail distribution in Melbourne and Sydney; also exported to the UK.

Somerset Hill Semillon

🍷🍷🍷🍸 **2000** Medium yellow-green; a rich and aromatic bouquet with an exotic spectrum of ripe citrus, grass, herbs and green bean is followed by a palate that has significant fruit sweetness, softening somewhat on the finish. **rating:** 84

best drinking Now–2004 **best vintages** NA **drink with** Stuffed capsicum • $19.50

Somerset Hill Sauvignon Blanc

🍷🍷🍷🍷 **2000** Light green-yellow; a crisp bouquet ranging through capsicum, herb, grass and passionfruit is followed by a palate with good flavour, balance and length, essentially tracking the characters of the bouquet. **rating:** 87

best drinking Now **best vintages** NA **drink with** Spicy calamari • $19.50

Somerset Hill Harmony

🍷🍷🍷🍷 **2000** Medium yellow-green; the bouquet seems significantly riper and sweeter than either the Semillon or the Sauvignon Blanc, with strong tropical aromas. The palate is quite fleshy with stonefruit and citrus flavours, balanced and cut by acidity on the finish. **rating:** 85

best drinking Now–2003 **best vintages** NA **drink with** Barbecued prawns • $17.50

Somerset Hill Unwooded Chardonnay

🍷🍷🍷🍸 **2000** Light green-yellow; the bouquet is firm, with some citrus and herbaceous characters, the palate likewise, with a fair degree of flavour, but some suggestion of slow-ferment characters. **rating:** 84

best drinking Now **best vintages** NA **drink with** Vegetable terrine • $19.50

sorrenberg NR

Alma Road, Beechworth, Vic 3747 **region** Beechworth
phone (03) 5728 2278 **fax** (03) 5728 2278 **open** Mon–Fri by appointment, most weekends 1–5 (phone first)
winemaker Barry Morey **production** 1500 **est.** 1986
product range ($20–32 CD) Sauvignon Blanc Semillon, Chardonnay, Gamay, Cabernet Sauvignon, Havelock Hills Shiraz, Cabernet Merlot Franc.
summary Barry and Jan Morey made their first wines in 1989 from the 2.5-hectare vineyard situated on the outskirts of Beechworth. No recent tastings, but the wines have a good reputation and loyal clientele.

spring vale vineyards ★★★★

Spring Vale, Swansea, Tas 7190 **region** Southern Tasmania
phone (03) 6257 8208 **fax** (03) 6257 8598 **open** Weekends, holidays 10–5
winemaker Andrew Hood (Contract) **production** 3000 **est.** 1986
product range ($19.50–29.50 CD) Gewurztraminer, Chardonnay, Pinot Gris, Pinot Noir.
summary Rodney Lyne has progressively established 1.5 hectares each of pinot noir and chardonnay and then added 0.5 hectare each of gewurztraminer and pinot gris; the latter produced a first crop in 1998. After frost problems, Spring Vale was enjoying the fruits of excellent vintages from 1997 to 2000 before frost returned to devastate 2001.

Spring Vale Gewurztraminer

🍷🍷🍷🍷 **2000** Light green-yellow; the bouquet shows some varietal character, but it does tend more to lime than spice; the palate has attractive soft, sweet fruit, again with as much lime as spice, and strongly appealed to several of the judges. **rating:** 89

best drinking Now–2004 **best vintages** NA **drink with** Stir-fried shrimp • NA

Spring Vale Pinot Gris

🍷🍷🍷🍷 **2000** Medium yellow-green; the bouquet is quite rich, with honeyed characters, the palate powerful and mouthfilling, almost Viognier-like. Altogether striking. **rating:** 86

best drinking Now–2004 **best vintages** NA **drink with** Honey prawns • NA

Spring Vale Chardonnay

🍷🍷🍷🍷🍷 **1999** Medium green-yellow; the bouquet is subdued, with some mineral and cashew notes, but the wine flowers on the elegant and harmonious palate with nectarine, citrus and cashew supported by subtle oak. **rating:** 90

best drinking Now–2005 **best vintages** '97, '99 **drink with** Veal or pork • NA

Spring Vale Pinot Noir

🍷🍷🍷🍷 **1999** Medium red-purple; a spicy, tangy bouquet with some maceration characters adding complexity is followed by an elegant palate with considerable style and good length; for some the wine seems a little stemmy/minty, but I like it. **rating:** 89

best drinking Now–2006 **best vintages** NA **drink with** Roast duck • NA

springviews wine NR

Woodlands Road, Porongurup, WA 6324 **region** Great Southern
phone (08) 9853 2088 **fax** (08) 9853 2098 **open** 7 days 10–5
winemaker Howard Park (Contract) **production** 420 **est.** 1994
product range ($16–20 CD) Riesling, Chardonnay, Cabernet Sauvignon.
summary Andy and Alice Colquhoun planted their 5-hectare vineyard (2 hectares each of chardonnay and cabernet sauvignon and 1 hectare of riesling) in 1994. The wine is contract-made and is sold through the cellar door and mailing list.

Springviews Riesling

🍷🍷🍷🍷🍷 **2000** Pale straw-green; a very powerful, even idiosyncratic, wine from start to finish with an almost Alsatian-like intensity. The palate has great weight, with considerable grip to the long finish. **rating:** 90

best drinking 2003–2009 **best vintages** '00 **drink with** Braised pork neck • $20

stanley brothers ★★★

Barossa Valley Way, Tanunda, SA 5352 **region** Barossa Valley
phone (08) 8563 3375 **fax** (08) 8563 3758 **open** 7 days 9–5
winemaker Lindsay Stanley **production** 10 000 **est.** 1994
product range ($11–25 CD) Sylvaner, Full Sister Semillon, Chardonnay Pristine, John Hancock Shiraz, Thoroughbred Cabernet Sauvignon, Cabernet Shiraz, Late Harvest Sylvaner; NV Black Sheep; Sparkling, Fortifieds.
summary Former Anglesey winemaker and industry veteran Lindsay Stanley established his own business in the Barossa Valley when he purchased (and renamed) the former Kroemer Estate in late 1994. As one would expect, the wines are competently made. Twenty-one hectares of estate plantings have provided virtually all of the grapes for the business. Exports to Canada, France, Hong Kong, Singapore and the US.

stanthorpe wine co NR

Granite Belt Drive, Thulimbah, Qld 4377 **region** Granite Belt
phone (07) 4683 2011 **fax** (07) 4683 2600 **open** 7 days 9–5
winemaker Contract **production** 1200 **est.** 1997
product range ($11–19 CD) Semillon Chardonnay, Sweet White, Pinot Bubbly, Emily Rose, Shiraz Cabernet, Tawny Port; also fruit wines and liqueurs.
summary The Stanthorpe Wine Co does a bit of everything. Its ten partners are mainly professional people who work in Brisbane, but who share a love of wine. They decided to establish a business that would offer wine education, sell other wines of the region, and have wines contract-made for the centre's own label. The partners have also established a vineyard with 3 hectares of shiraz and 1 hectare each of merlot, petit verdot, tempranillo and cabernet sauvignon, and plan to set up a small, specialised winemaking facility to make the wine from this vineyard under the Summit Estate label.

stanton & killeen wines ★★★★★

Jacks Road, Murray Valley Highway, Rutherglen, Vic 3685 **region** Rutherglen
phone (02) 6032 9457 **fax** (02) 6032 8018 **open** Mon–Sat 9–5, Sun 10–5
winemaker Chris Killeen **production** 15 000 **est.** 1875
product range ($10.50–55 CD) A red wine and fortified wine specialist, though offering Chardonnay, Riesling, White Frontignac and Dry White as well as Dry Red, Cabernet Sauvignon Cabernet Franc Shiraz, Cabernet Franc Merlot, Cabernet Shiraz, Shiraz, Durif; fortifieds in 500 ml bottles are Classic Range Port, Tokay, Muscat; Auslese Tokay, Grand Muscat, Vintage Port.
summary Chris Killeen has skilfully expanded the portfolio of Stanton & Killeen but without in any way compromising its reputation as a traditional maker of smooth, rich reds, some of Australia's best Vintage Ports, and attractive, fruity Muscats and Tokays. All in all, deserves far greater recognition.

Stanton & Killeen Durif

🍷🍷🍷🍷🍷 **1999** Medium to full red-purple; a powerful, dark berry, blackberry, cedar and briar bouquet leads into a full-bodied, rich and sweet palate with voluptuous berry flavours and feel neatly counterbalanced by tannin and oak. **rating:** 91
best drinking 2005–2015 **best vintages** '97, '98, '99 **drink with** Two-inch-thick rump steak • $23.50

Stanton & Killeen Cabernet Sauvignon Cabernet Franc Merlot

🍷🍷🍷🍷🍷 **1998** Medium to full red-purple; the bouquet is quite powerful, with lively, earthy characters to the fore, together with touches of blackberry and mint, the oak making a positive contribution. The palate is rich and ripe, with lots of blackberry flavour, but too extractive. There is clever use of oak throughout the wine, and good tannin management. **rating:** 92
best drinking 2003–2013 **best vintages** NA **drink with** Yearling steak • $25

Stanton & Killeen Tawny Port

🍷🍷🍷🍷🍷 **NV** Medium red-tawny; the bouquet is clean with nice butterscotch overtones and, like the palate, shows positive but not aggressive rancio. **rating:** 93
best drinking Now **best vintages** NA **drink with** Aperitif or coffee • NA

Stanton & Killeen Vintage Port

🍷🍷🍷🍷🍷 **1995** Medium to full red-purple; the complex, spicy fruit of the bouquet has clean spirit, the palate again complex, with spicy licorice and blackberry flavours; drier than most Australian Vintage Ports, perhaps due not only to lower residual sugar, but also to that extra period in old wood prior to bottling. **rating:** 94
best drinking 2005–2015 **best vintages** '92, '93, '95 **drink with** Walnuts • $23.50

staughton vale vineyard NR

20 Staughton Vale Road, Anakie, Vic 3221 **region** Geelong
phone (03) 5284 1477 **fax** (03) 5284 1229 **open** Fri–Mon and public holidays 10–5 or by appointment
winemaker Paul Chambers **production** 2000 **est.** 1986
product range ($14–20 ML) Rhine Riesling, Pinot Noir, Staughton (Merlot blend), Tawny Port, Liqueur Shiraz.
summary Paul Chambers has 6 hectares of grapes, with the accent on the classic Bordeaux mix of cabernet sauvignon, merlot, cabernet franc and petit verdot, although chardonnay and pinot noir are also planted. Weekend lunches available at the Staughton Cottage Restaurant.

steels creek estate NR

1 Sewell Road, Steels Creek, Vic 3775 **region** Yarra Valley
phone (03) 5965 2448 **fax** (03) 5965 2448 **open** Weekends and public holidays 10–6 or by appointment
winemaker Simon Peirce **production** 400 **est.** 1981
product range ($15–22 CD) Colombard, Chardonnay, Shiraz, Cabernet Sauvignon.
summary Established by brother-and-sister team Simon and Kerri Peirce. While only a tiny operation, with 1.7 hectares of vineyard planted at various times between 1981 and 1994, Steels Creek Estate has an on-site winery where the wines are made with assistance from consultants, but increasingly by Simon Peirce, who has completed his associate diploma in Applied Science (Winegrowing) at Charles Sturt University.

Steels Creek Estate Colombard

ΨΨΨΥ **2000** Light straw-green; there are some flowery aromatics, though not in the Sauvignon Blanc spectrum, and the light- to medium-bodied palate is clean and well made, but really lacking any identifiable varietal markers. **rating:** 81

best drinking Now **best vintages** NA **drink with** Light seafood pasta • $15

Steels Creek Estate Cabernet Sauvignon

ΨΨΨΥ **1997** Medium to full red, with just a touch of purple; the bouquet is clean, not particularly aromatic, but does have nice varietal character and subtle oak. The powerful palate does show some fractionally gamey/canopy cabernet characters which, in the cooler parts of the Yarra Valley, are very hard to avoid. **rating:** 84

best drinking 2002–2007 **best vintages** NA **drink with** Braised lamb • $22

stefano lubiana ★★★★

60 Rowbottoms Road, Granton, Tas 7030 **region** Southern Tasmania
phone (03) 6263 7457 **fax** (03) 6263 7430 **open** 7 days 10–5 (closed public holidays)
winemaker Steve Lubiana **production** 8000 **est.** 1990
product range ($25–49 R) Riesling, Sauvignon Blanc, Sur Lie Chardonnay, Chardonnay, Pinot Grigio, Pinot Noir, Non Vintage Brut, Vintage Brut; also Primavera Pinot Noir.
summary Steve Lubiana has moved from one extreme to the other, having run Lubiana Wines at Moorook in the South Australian Riverland for many years before moving to Granton to set up a substantial winery. The estate-produced Stefano Lubiano wines come from 7.7 hectares of beautifully located vineyards sloping down to the Derwent River. Exports to the UK and the US.

Stefano Lubiana Riesling

ΨΨΨΨ **2000** Light green-yellow; the bouquet has pronounced passionfruit and lime aromatics, with more intensity than most other Southern Tasmanian Rieslings at a comparable stage of development. The palate is delicate, fresh and lively, and shows no sign of phenolics from the increased pressings blended back into the wine. **rating:** 89

best drinking Now–2006 **best vintages** '00 **drink with** Tempura • $26

Stefano Lubiana Sauvignon Blanc

ΨΨΨΥ **2000** Very pale straw-green; the bouquet is clean, crisp and has grassy overtones, the palate with similar flavours and slightly edgy acidity. Picked early, and I am not convinced the very early picking, designed to subdue the tropical flavours, has worked. **rating:** 83

best drinking Now **best vintages** NA **drink with** Smoked salmon • $25

Stefano Lubiana Chardonnay

ΨΨΨΨ **1999** Light green-yellow; a clean, crisp and tangy bouquet with a mix of melon, honeydew and citrus is followed by a light, elegant wine, with some creamy/cashew characters from the malolactic fermentation; very well made, with perfect acidity, but very pricey. **rating:** 89

best drinking Now–2006 **best vintages** NA **drink with** Chinese prawns • $40

Stefano Lubiana NV Brut

ΨΨΨΨ **NV** Light straw-green; the bouquet is clean, bright and fresh, with crisp lemon and apple aromas, the palate harmonious, with touches of cashew, apple, lemon and strawberry; good mouthfeel and balance. **rating:** 89

best drinking Now–2003 **best vintages** NA **drink with** Fresh oysters • $33

Stefano Lubiana Vintage Brut

ΨΨΨΨ **1995** Pale straw-bronze; there is an obvious Pinot Noir influence on the powerful bouquet and likewise on the palate, which has masses of character and flavour in a Bollinger-esque style. Appealed to me far more than it did to other judges at the 2001 Tasmanian Wines Show. **rating:** 87

best drinking Now–2003 **best vintages** NA **drink with** Smoked roe • $49

Stefano Lubiana Pinot Noir

ΨΨΨΨΥ **1999** Light to medium red-purple; a pleasantly fragrant bouquet offering cherry and a touch of plum is followed by a palate, which while light bodied, has much more complexity than the bouquet suggests. Intense plum and spice fruit is neatly braced by a subtle hint of oak. **rating:** 93

best drinking Now–2004 **best vintages** '98, '99 **drink with** Jugged hare • $40

steins ★★★☆

Pipeclay Lane, Mudgee, NSW 2850 **region** Mudgee
phone (02) 6373 3991 **fax** (02) 6373 3709 **open** 7 days 10–4.30
winemaker Robert Stein, Michael Slater **production** 6000 **est.** 1976
product range ($10–16.50 CD) Riesling, Gewurztraminer, Semillon, Semillon Chardonnay, Chardonnay, Late Harvest Gewurztraminer, Rosé, Mt Buckaroo Dry Red, Shiraz, Reserve Shiraz, Cabernet Sauvignon and a range of Muscats and Ports; Robert Stein range of Semillon, Chardonnay, Shiraz, Cabernet Shiraz, Cabernet Sauvignon.
summary The sweeping panorama from the winery is its own reward for cellar-door visitors. Right from the outset Steins has been a substantial operation but has managed to sell the greater part of its production direct from the winery by mail order and cellar door, with limited retail distribution in Sydney, Victoria and South Australia. Wine quality has been very good from time to time, with the Shiraz and Chardonnay variously coming out on top.

Steins Robert Stein Semillon

YYYY **2000** Light green-yellow; the bouquet is clean, and quite crisp, with a mix of lemon/lemongrass and mineral aromas, the crisp and fresh palate finishing with lemony/minerally acidity. **rating:** 89
best drinking 2003–2010 **best vintages** NA **drink with** Shellfish • NA

stellar ridge estate ★★★★

Clews Road, Cowaramup, WA 6284 **region** Margaret River
phone (08) 9755 5635 **fax** (08) 9755 5636 **open** 7 days 10–5
winemaker Bernie Abbott **production** 1000 **est.** 1994
product range ($19.50–29.50 CD) Sauvignon Blanc, Verdelho, Unwooded Chardonnay, Shiraz, Cabernet Sauvignon; also estate-grown varietally identified olive oil (Pendolino, Leccino, Frantolo, WA Mission).
summary Colin and Helene Hellier acquired a 49-hectare grazing property at Cowaramup in 1993 which included 2.5 hectares of chardonnay and sauvignon blanc planted in 1987. A large dam was constructed in 1994, and the following year 11 hectares of new vineyards and 4 hectares of olive trees were planted; 1.6 hectares of zinfandel followed in 1996, bringing total plantings to 15.1 hectares. The majority of the 100-tonne grape production is sold to other local wineries, with 14 to 15 tonnes being retained for the Stellar Ridge label. The wines are sold exclusively through cellar door and mailing list, and are well worth seeking out.

Stellar Ridge Estate Verdelho

YYYY **2000** Water-white; a highly aromatic bouquet with intense tropical aromas of pineapple, passionfruit and nectarine seems almost too much of a good thing. However, the palate has controlled extract, with good passionfruit and nectarine flavour; pretty impressive. **rating:** 85
best drinking Now–2003 **best vintages** '00 **drink with** Prosciutto and melon • $19.50

Stellar Ridge Estate Shiraz

YYY **1999** Medium red-purple; there is a quite complex web of moderately intense cedary/spicy/savoury/gamey aromas that lead into a light- to medium-bodied palate with black cherry fruit at the core, and some gamey, cool-climate characteristics; low tannins. **rating:** 84
best drinking 2002–2006 **best vintages** NA **drink with** Lamb shanks • $29.50

Stellar Ridge Estate Cabernet Sauvignon

YYYY **1999** Medium to full red-purple; the bouquet is clean, with attractive blackberry/blackcurrant fruit; the palate is remarkably complex given the youth of the wine, with more perfectly poised cabernet fruit and positive oak inputs. All it needs is time. **rating:** 87
best drinking 2004–2009 **best vintages** NA **drink with** Barbecued lamb • $29.50

stephen john wines ★★★

Government Road, Watervale, SA 5452 **region** Clare Valley
phone (08) 8843 0105 **fax** (08) 8843 0105 **open** 7 days 11–5
winemaker Stephen John **production** 5000 **est.** 1994
product range ($10–40 CD) Watervale Riesling, Watervale Pedro Ximinez, Chardonnay, Clare Valley Shiraz, Estate Reserve Shiraz, Merlot, Clare Valley Cabernet Sauvignon, Estate Reserve Cabernet Sauvingon, Traugott Cuvée Sparkling Burgundy.

summary The John family is one of the best-known names in the Barossa Valley, with branches running Australia's best cooperage (AP John & Sons) and providing the chief winemaker of Lindemans (Philip John) and the former chief winemaker of Quelltaler (Stephen John). Stephen and Rita John have now formed their own family business in the Clare Valley, based on a 6-hectare vineyard overlooking the town of Watervale and supplemented by modest intake from a few local growers. The cellar-door sales area is housed in an 80-year-old stable which has been renovated and is full of rustic charm. The significantly increased production has led to the appointment of distributors in each of the eastern States, and to limited exports to the US.

Stephen John Clare Valley Cabernet Sauvignon

1998 Medium red-purple; there are some slightly astringent/earthy overtones to the bouquet, but the palate has powerful blackberry fruit at its core which sustains the overall rusticity of the wine. Patience may well be rewarded. **rating:** 81

best drinking 2003–2008 **best vintages** NA **drink with** Braised beef • $40

sterling heights NR

Faulkners Road, Winkleigh, Tas 7275 **region** Northern Tasmania
phone (03) 6396 3214 **fax** (03) 6396 3214 **open** By appointment
winemaker Moorilla Estate (Contract) **production** 400 **est.** 1988
product range ($14–16 CD) Riesling, Chardonnay, Breton Rosé, Pinot Noir.
summary With 2 hectares of vines, Sterling Heights will always be a small fish in a small pond. However, the early releases had considerable success in wine shows, and the quality was all one could expect. The wines are also available through Hartzview Wine Centre. No recent tastings.

stonehaven ★★★★

Stonehaven Winery, Riddoch Highway, Padthaway, SA 5271 **region** Padthaway
phone (08) 8765 6140 **fax** (08) 8765 6137 **open** 7 days 10–4
winemaker Tom Newton, Duncan McGillivray, Robert Mann **production** NFP **est.** 1998
product range ($15–35 R) Padthaway Unwooded Chardonnay, Cabernet Merlot, Chardonnay, Limestone Coast Chardonnay, Shiraz, Limestone Coast Shiraz, Padthaway Cabernet Sauvignon, Limited Release Chardonnay.
summary It is, to say the least, strange that it should have taken 30 years for a substantial winery to be built at Padthaway. However, when BRL Hardy took the decision, it was no half measure: $20 million has been invested in what is the largest greenfields winery built in Australia for more than 20 years.

Stonehaven Limited Release Chardonnay

1999 Light to medium yellow-green; a complex bouquet, with slightly charry barrel-ferment oak merging with nectarine and grapefruit on the bouquet. The palate is long in flavour and very youthful, with the components still coming together, a process that will be completed over the next year or so. **rating:** 90

best drinking Now–2005 **best vintages** '99 **drink with** Braised neck of pork • $26.99

Stonehaven Limestone Coast Shiraz

1998 Medium red-purple; the bouquet is quite complex, with a range of savoury/spicy/liquorice/gamey/red berry characters, all strongly varietal. The medium-bodied palate offers a similar range of Rhône-like characters, with great mid-palate flavour; there is just a faint touch of bitterness on the finish. Still, a very interesting wine at the price. **rating:** 89

best drinking 2003–2008 **best vintages** '98 **drink with** Traditional Aussie meat pie • $15.99

stonemont NR

421 Rochford Road, Rochford, Vic 3442 **region** Macedon Ranges
phone (03) 5429 1540 **fax** (03) 5429 1878 **open** By appointment
winemaker Contract **production** 500 **est.** 1997
product range ($18 R) Chardonnay, Sparkling Macedon, Pinot Noir.
summary Ray and Gail Hicks began the establishment of their vineyard in 1993, extending plantings to a total of 1.5 hectares each of chardonnay and pinot noir in 1996. The tiny production of Chardonnay, Pinot Noir and Sparkling Macedon is contract-made by various Macedon Ranges winemakers, and the wines are sold by mail order and (by appointment) through the cellar door, which is situated in a heritage stone barn on the vineyard site.

Stonemont Chardonnay

🍷🍷🍷🍷 **1999** Medium yellow-green; the bouquet is still firm, with melon-accented fruit and subtle oak. The palate is light, elegant, well balanced but not particularly generous, and with a long life in front of it during which time it should build greater complexity. Well made, and the oak has been held in appropriate restraint. **rating:** 83

🍷🍷🍷🍷 **1997** Medium yellow-green; the bouquet is clean and smooth, with distinctive regional melon and mineral fruit aromas. The palate is pleasant, smooth, not particularly complex, but with good length and the promise of further development. **rating:** 85

best drinking Now–2007 **best vintages** NA **drink with** Fish terrine • $18

stone ridge ★★★

Limberlost Road, Glen Aplin, Qld 4381 **region** Granite Belt
phone (07) 4683 4211 **fax** (07) 4683 4211 **open** 7 days 10–5
winemaker Jim Lawrie, Anne Kennedy **production** 1950 **est.** 1981
product range ($10–40 CD) Under the Stone Ridge label Semillon, Chardonnay, Shiraz, Cabernet Malbec; under the Mount Sterling label Dry Red Shiraz.
summary Spicy Shiraz is the specialty of this doll's-house-sized winery, but the portfolio has progressively expanded over recent years to include two whites and the only Stanthorpe region Cabernet Malbec (and occasionally a straight varietal Malbec). No recent tastings.

stonier wines ★★★★☆

362 Frankston–Flinders Road, Merricks, Vic 3916 **region** Mornington Peninsula
phone (03) 5989 8300 **fax** (03) 5989 8709 **open** 7 days 12–5 (summer 11–5) (except Christmas Day)
winemaker Tod Dexter, Geraldine McFaul **production** 25 000 **est.** 1978
product range ($18–39 CD) Chardonnay, Reserve Chardonnay, Pinot Noir, Reserve Pinot Noir, Cabernet Sauvignon.
summary Looked at across the range, Stonier is now the pre-eminent winery in the Mornington Peninsula; its standing is in turn based more or less equally on its Chardonnay and Pinot Noir under the Reserve label. The acquisition of a 70 per cent interest by Petaluma in 1998 has given both Stoniers (and the Mornington Peninsula as a whole) even greater credibility than hitherto. Exports to the UK, Canada, Belgium, Germany, Italy, New Zealand, Singapore and Japan.

Stonier Chardonnay

🍷🍷🍷🍷 **1999** Light green-yellow; the bouquet is light and minerally, with touches of stone fruit and citrus, the palate quite crisp and dry, but notably lacking fruit depth. **rating:** 84

best drinking Now–2003 **best vintages** '91, '93, '94, '97, '98 **drink with** Pasta, rich seafood • $19

Stonier Reserve Chardonnay

🍷🍷🍷🍷🍷 **1999** Light to medium yellow-green; the sophisticated bouquet of melon, cashew and a touch of oak is logically followed by a nicely balanced, harmonious and attractive palate; here, cashew, melon and a touch of barrel ferment are seamlessly integrated. **rating:** 92

best drinking Now–2005 **best vintages** '86, '88, '91, '93, '94, '95, '96, '97, '98, '99 **drink with** Milk-fed veal • $36

Stonier Pinot Noir

🍷🍷🍷🍷 **1999** Light to medium red-purple; the bouquet is clean, with strawberry and cherry aromas dominant, together with a touch of the mint that often seems part of the Stonier Pinot make-up. The palate is lively, fresh and quite long, but is structurally a little simple. Good outcome for a difficult vintage. **rating:** 84

best drinking Now **best vintages** '92, '94, '95, '97 **drink with** Game of any kind • $23

Stonier Reserve Pinot Noir

🍷🍷🍷🍷 **1999** Light to medium purple-red, still with brightness to the hue; the bouquet is bright and fresh, with lively cherry and a hint of mint; the palate is similarly lively and fruity, with subtle oak, but still needing to build texture and structure. **rating:** 89

best drinking 2002–2006 **best vintages** '90, '91, '92, '94, '95, '97, '99 **drink with** Coq au vin • $39

stratherne vale estate NR

Campbell Street, Caballing, WA 6312 **region** Central Western Australia Zone
phone (08) 9881 2148 **fax** (08) 9881 3129 **open** Not
winemaker James Pennington (Contract) **production** 600 **est.** 1980
product range A single red wine made from a blend of Cabernet Sauvignon, Zinfandel, Merlot and Shiraz.
summary Stratherne Vale Estate stretches the viticultural map of Australia yet further. It is situated near Narrogin, which is north of the Great Southern region and south of the most generous extension of the Darling Ranges. The closest viticultural region of note is at Wandering, to the northeast.

strathkellar NR

Murray Valley Highway, Cobram, Vic 3644 **region** Goulburn Valley
phone (03) 5873 5274 **fax** (03) 5873 5270 **open** 7 days 10–6
winemaker Chateau Tahbilk (Contract) **production** 2000 **est.** 1990
product range ($9–15 CD) Chenin Blanc, Chardonnay, Late Picked Chenin Blanc, Shiraz, Muscat, Tokay, Putters Port, Sparkling.
summary Dick Parkes planted his 5.5-hectare vineyard to chardonnay, shiraz and chenin blanc in 1990, and has the wine contract-made at Chateau Tahbilk by Alister Purbrick. The fact that the wines are made at Chateau Tahbilk is a sure guarantee of quality, and the prices are modest.

straws lane 

Cnr Mount Macedon Road and Straws Lane, Hesket, Vic 3442 **region** Macedon Ranges
phone (03) 9654 9380 **fax** (03) 9663 6300 **open** Not
winemaker Stuart Anderson, John Ellis **production** 1000 **est.** 1987
product range ($23.50–40 R) Gewurztraminer, Macedon Blanc de Noir, Pinot Noir.
summary The Straws Lane vineyard was planted 12 years ago, but the Straws Lane label is a relatively new arrival on the scene; after a highly successful 1995 vintage, adverse weather in 1996 and 1997 meant that little or no wine was made in those years, but the pace picked up again with subsequent vintages. Stuart Anderson guides the making of the Pinot Noir, Hanging Rock Winery handles the Gewurztraminer and the sparkling wine base, and Cope-Williams looks after the tiraging and maturation of the sparkling wine. It's good to have co-operative neighbours.

Straws Lane Gewurztraminer

YYYY **1999** Light straw-green; the bouquet is quite aromatic, with lychee, rose-petal and spice aromas, but the palate is still surprisingly firm and closed, needing time to show its full potential. **rating:** 84
best drinking Now–2005 **best vintages** NA **drink with** Chinese prawns • $23.50

Straws Lane Blanc de Noir

YYYY **1996** Strong straw-gold colour; the bouquet has masses of bready/biscuity pinot noir varietal character, the palate likewise big and rich, the only downside being its faintly tough finish. **rating:** 85
best drinking Now–2004 **best vintages** NA **drink with** Fresh salmon • $40

Straws Lane Pinot Noir

YYYY **1998** Light to medium red-purple; a quite fragrant bouquet has a stylish mix of spicy/slippery/foresty varietal characters. There is plenty of power, character and structure to the palate, basically in the foresty spectrum, but with an ample core of sweet cherry/plum fruit. **rating:** 88
best drinking Now–2004 **best vintages** '98 **drink with** Ragout of veal • $31

---

stringy brae 

Sawmill Road, Sevenhill, SA 5453 **region** Clare Valley
phone (08) 8843 4313 **fax** (08) 8843 4319 **open** Weekends and public holidays 10–5, weekdays refer to road sign
winemaker Contract (Mitchell) **production** 1500 **est.** 1991
product range ($14–48 CD) Riesling, Sparkling Riesling, Shiraz, Black Knight Shiraz, Mote Hill, Cabernet Sauvignon.

summary Donald and Sally Willson have established over 9 hectares of vineyards that since the 1996 vintage have produced all the grapes for their wines. (Previously grapes from Langhorne Creek were used.) The Australian domestic market is serviced direct by mail order, but the wines are exported to the UK, Singapore and the US.

Stringy Brae Riesling

YYYY **2000** Light straw-green; a clean bouquet ranging through spice, lime and mineral is followed by an apple and lime-flavoured palate, with the grip and intensity typical of the 2000 vintage in the Clare Valley. **rating:** 88

best drinking 2004–2010 **best vintages** NA **drink with** Asparagus • $15

Stringy Brae Cabernet Sauvignon

YYYy **1999** Medium red-purple; the bouquet is clean, of light to moderate intensity, and just a little plain. The palate has rather more happening, with chocolate, earthy and berry fruit, supported by appropriately modest oak. **rating:** 83

best drinking 2002–2007 **best vintages** NA **drink with** Chump chops • $21

stuart range estates ★★★☆

67 William Street, Kingaroy, Qld 4610 **region** South Burnett
phone (07) 4162 3711 **fax** (07) 4162 4811 **open** 7 days 9–5
winemaker Charles Pregenzer **production** 7500 **est.** 1997
product range ($8–18 CD) Chardonnay, Goodger Chardonnay, South Burnett Chardonnay, Goodger Reserve Chardonnay, Range White and Range Red (both semi-sweet), Goodger Shiraz, Shiraz (unwooded), Cabernet Merlot, Blue Moon Liqueur, Explorer Tawny Port.
summary Stuart Range Estates is a prime example of the extent and pace of change in the Queensland wine industry, coming from nowhere in 1997 to crushing just under 120 tonnes of grapes in its inaugural vintage in 1998. The grapes are supplied by up to seven growers in the South Burnett Valley, with 52 hectares planted by 1996. A state-of-the-art winery has been established within an old butter factory building. The barrel-fermented Chardonnay won the trophy for the Best Queensland White Wine in the annual *Courier-Mail* Top 100 Wine Competition.

Stuart Range Estates Chardonnay

YYYy **2000** Medium yellow-green; an unusual combination of pungent fruit and spicy oak is followed by a high-toned, almost floral, palate with a mix of lemon, citrus and melon flavours; lots happening. Excellent value. **rating:** 83

best drinking Now **best vintages** NA **drink with** Spicy Thai • $12

Stuart Range Estates Goodger Chardonnay

YYYY **2000** Light to medium green-yellow; obvious, tangy barrel-ferment aromas mingle with the citrus fruit of both the bouquet and surprisingly elegant palate. Here melon flavour also comes to the fore, and the oak is not overdone. **rating:** 86

best drinking Now **best vintages** NA **drink with** Char-grilled salmon • $15

Stuart Range Estates Goodger Shiraz

YYYY **2000** Medium purple-red; the bouquet has good fruit and oak balance, with positive dark cherry fruit and vanilla oak overtones. The palate is powerful and youthful, inevitably slightly undermade/callow, but you cannot complain at the price. **rating:** 85

best drinking 2002–2006 **best vintages** NA **drink with** Barbecued beef • $15

stumpy gully ★★★

1247 Stumpy Gully Road, Moorooduc, Vic 3933 **region** Mornington Peninsula
phone (03) 5978 8429 **fax** (03) 5978 8419 **open** Weekends 11–5
winemaker Wendy Zantvoort, Maïtèna Zantvoort, Ewan Campbell **production** 4600 **est.** 1988
product range ($15–30 CD) Riesling, Sauvignon Blanc, Marsanne, Chardonnay, Encore Chardonnay, Pinot Grigio, Sparkling Pinot Chardonnay, Botrytis Riesling, Pinot Noir, Sangiovese, Merlot Cabernet, Cabernet Sauvignon; also Peninsula Panorama Chardonnay and Pinot Noir.
summary When Frank and Wendy Zantvoort began planting their first vineyard in 1989 there were no winemakers in the family; now there are three, plus two viticulturists. Mother Wendy was first to obtain her degree from Charles Sturt University, followed by daughter Maïtèna, who then married Ewan Campbell, another

winemaker. Father Frank and son Michael look after the vineyards. The original vineyard has 9 hectares of vines, but in establishing the new 20-hectare Moorooduc vineyard (first harvest 2001) the Zantvoorts have deliberately gone against prevailing thinking, planting it solely to red varieties, predominately cabernet sauvignon, merlot and shiraz. They believe they have one of the warmest sites on the Peninsula, and that ripening will in fact present no problems. In all they now have ten varieties planted, producing a dozen different wines.

Stumpy Gully Sauvignon Blanc

ŢŢŢŢ **2000** Light straw-green; a herbaceous/minerally bouquet leads into a crisp, crunchy palate with herb and mineral flavours; gentle acidity to close. **rating:** 85

best drinking Now **best vintages** NA **drink with** Steamed mussels • $15

Stumpy Gully Pinot Grigio

ŢŢŢŢ **2000** Very light straw-bronze; the bouquet is clean, with aromas ranging from green apple through to baked apple and spice, characters that are repeated on the pleasing palate, which has plenty of character and mouthfeel. **rating:** 85

best drinking Now–2003 **best vintages** NA **drink with** Antipasto • $16

suckfizzle augusta ★★★★☆

Lot 14 Kalkarrie Drive, Augusta, WA 6290 (PO Box 570, Margaret River, WA 6285) **region** Margaret River
phone (08) 9758 0303 **fax** (08) 9758 0304 **open** Not
winemaker Stuart Pym **production** 1500 **est.** 1997
product range ($30–40 R) Semillon Sauvignon Blanc, Cabernet Sauvignon.
summary First things first. The back label explains: 'the name Suckfizzle has been snaffled from the fourteenth century monk and medico-turned-writer Rabelais and his infamous character the great lord Suckfizzle'. Suckfizzle is the joint venture of two well-known Margaret River winemakers who, in deference to their employers, do not identify themselves on any of the background material or the striking front and back labels of the wines.

Suckfizzle Augusta Semillon Sauvignon Blanc

ŢŢŢŢŢ **1998** Medium straw-yellow; as with the first release, an opulent and rich bouquet with spicy nutmeg French oak quite evident on both bouquet and palate, but with a strong base of sweet fruit to carry the oak. Mouthfilling and enticing. **rating:** 92

best drinking Now–2008 **best vintages** '97, '98 **drink with** Marron • NA

Suckfizzle Augusta Cabernet Sauvignon

ŢŢŢŢ **1997** Medium red-purple; savoury/earthy aromas in secondary mode are followed by a palate that is definitely on the lean, earthy side of the Bordeaux fence; needs more sweet fruit to convince. **rating:** 86

best drinking 2002–2006 **best vintages** NA **drink with** Braised beef • $38

summerfield ★★★★

Main Road, Moonambel, Vic 3478 **region** Pyrenees
phone (03) 5467 2264 **fax** (03) 5467 2380 **open** 7 days 9–6
winemaker Ian Summerfield, Mark Summerfield **production** 3500 **est.** 1979
product range ($10–31 CD) Sauvignon Blanc, Trebbiano, Shiraz, Reserve Shiraz, Cabernet Sauvignon, Reserve Cabernet.
summary A specialist red-wine producer, the particular forte of which is Shiraz. The wines since 1988 have been consistently excellent, luscious and full bodied and fruit-driven but with a slice of vanillin oak to top them off.

Summerfield Shiraz

ŢŢŢŢ **1999** Medium red-purple; the solid bouquet is of moderate to full intensity, offering dark berry, plum and mint, the palate with lively minty fruit and largely incidental oak. **rating:** 86

best drinking 2002–2007 **best vintages** '88, '90, '91, '92, '93, '94, '96, '97 **drink with** Beef stew • $23

Summerfield Reserve Shiraz

ŢŢŢŢŢ **1999** Medium red-purple; a clean and smooth bouquet with touches of spice and earth leads into a smooth, gently ripe, medium- to full-bodied palate with ripe plum fruit and subtle vanilla oak. **rating:** 90

best drinking 2003–2009 **best vintages** '98, '99 **drink with** Venison pie • $31

Summerfield Reserve Cabernet

TTTT **1999** Medium to full red-purple; in total contrast to the varietal wine, abundant oak dominates the bouquet, but on the palate dark berry and chocolate accompanies the vanilla oak and pulls the wine back into balance. **rating:** 86

best drinking 2003–2008 **best vintages** NA **drink with** Osso bucco • $31

surveyor's hill winery NR

215 Brooklands Road, Wallaroo, NSW 2618 **region** Canberra District
phone (02) 6230 2046 **fax** (02) 6230 2048 **open** Weekends and public holidays or by appointment
winemaker Hardys (Contract) **production** 1000 **est.** 1986
product range ($13–25 R) Riesling, Estate Dry White, Alexandra's Block Chardonnay, Touriga Dry Red, Shiraz, Cabernet Sauvignon.
summary Surveyor's Hill has 7.5 hectares of vineyard, but most of the grapes are sold to Hardys, which vinifies the remainder for Surveyor's Hill – which should guarantee the quality of the wines sold.

sutherland smith wines NR

Cnr Falkners Road and Murray Valley Highway, Rutherglen, Vic 3685 **region** Rutherglen
phone (03) 6032 8177 **fax** (03) 6032 8177 **open** Weekends 10–5 or by appointment
winemaker George Sutherland-Smith **production** 1000 **est.** 1993
product range ($10.90–16.50 CD) Riesling, Josephine (Riesling Traminer), Chardonnay, Merlot, Cabernet Shiraz, Port.
summary George Sutherland-Smith, for decades managing director and winemaker at All Saints, has opened up his own small business at Rutherglen, making wine in the refurbished Emu Plains winery, originally constructed in the 1850s. He draws upon fruit grown in a leased vineyard at Glenrowan and also from grapes grown in the King Valley.

sylvan springs estates ★★★★

Blythmans Road, McLaren Flat, SA 5171 **region** McLaren Vale
phone (08) 8383 0500 **fax** (08) 8383 0499 **open** Not
winemaker Brian Light (Consultant) **production** 1000 **est.** 1974
product range ($13–22 R) Chardonnay, Shiraz, Cabernet Sauvignon.
summary The Pridmore family has been involved in grape-growing and winemaking in McLaren Vale for four generations spanning over 100 years. The pioneer was Cyril Pridmore who established The Wattles Winery in 1896, purchasing Sylvan Park, one of the original homesteads in the area, in 1901. The original family land in the township of McLaren Vale was sold in 1978, but not before third generation Digby Pridmore had established new vineyards (in 1974) near Blewitt Springs. When he retired in 1990, his son David purchased the 45-hectare vineyard (planted to 11 different varieties) and, with sister Sally, ventured into winemaking in 1996, with Brian Light as consultant winemaker.

Sylvan Springs Estates Shiraz

TTTY **1999** Dark red-purple; a highly aromatic bouquet with spice, leaf and berry is followed by ripe, sweet dark plum, prune and chocolate flavours on the palate. The oak is subtle, which allows the sweet fruit free rein, perhaps a little too much so. **rating:** 84

best drinking 2003–2008 **best vintages** NA **drink with** Steak and kidney pie • $22

Sylvan Springs Estates Cabernet Sauvignon

TTTT **1998** Medium to full red-purple; a solid, ripe bouquet with a mix of blackberry/blackcurrant and dark chocolate fruit is largely replicated on the palate, with similar fruit flavours, gentle tannins and subtle oak. **rating:** 87

best drinking 2003–2008 **best vintages** NA **drink with** Braised beef • $22

symphonia wines ★★★★

Boggy Creek Road, Myrrhee, Vic 3732 **region** King Valley
phone (03) 5729 7579 **fax** (03) 5729 7519 **open** By appointment

winemaker Peter Read **production** 400 **est.** 1998
product range ($12–18.50 CD) Chardonnay Plus Viognier & Petit Manseng, Pinot Grigio, Quintus, Tempranillo Plus Cabernet & Merlot, Merlot, Cabernet Plus Tannat & Merlot, Merlot Plus Cabernet & Merlot, Pinot Chardonnay Methode Champenoise, Portuguese style Port.
summary Peter Read and his family are veterans of the King Valley, having commenced the development of their vineyard in 1981 to supply Brown Brothers. As a result of extensive trips to both Western and Eastern Europe, Peter Read embarked on an ambitious project to trial a series of grape varieties little known in this country. The process of evaluation and experimentation continues, but Symphonia released the first small quantities of wines in mid-1998 and will slowly build on that start. A number of the wines have great interest and no less merit. Did particularly well at the 2001 Winewise Competition.

Symphonia Quintus

🍷🍷🍷🍷🍷 **1999** Dark red-purple; solid, dark, briary berry fruit on the bouquet leads into a powerful, quite chewy palate with lingering tannins and a mix of sweet dark fruit and more savoury characters, doubtless attesting to the multiple varietal inputs. **rating:** 91

best drinking 2003–2009 **best vintages** '99 **drink with** Pasta with meat sauce • $17.60

Symphonia King Valley Merlot

🍷🍷🍷🍷🍷 **1999** Excellent purple-red; the bouquet has quite firm, fresh and ripe redcurrant aromas that flow into the attractively red fruit-driven palate, finishing with nice tannins. Seductively framed, ready for early drinking. **rating:** 92

best drinking Now–2004 **best vintages** '99 **drink with** Light Italian • $17.60

tahbilk ★★★★☆

Goulburn Valley Highway, Tabilk, Vic 3608 **region** Goulburn Valley
phone (03) 5794 2555 **fax** (03) 5794 2360 **open** Mon–Sat 9–5, Sun 11–5
winemaker Alister Purbrick, Neil Larson, Alan George **production** 95 000 **est.** 1860
product range ($7.95–115 R) Riesling, Marsanne, Roussanne, Viognier, Sauvignon Blanc, Semillon, Verdelho, Chardonnay, Lexia (sweet white), Dulcet (sweet white), Grenache, Cabernet Franc, Malbec, Merlot, Cabernet Merlot, Shiraz, Cabernet Sauvignon; 1860 Vines Shiraz is rare flagship, with a Reserve red released from each vintage; Fortifieds, Sparkling.
summary A winery steeped in tradition (with high National Trust classification), which should be visited at least once by every wine-conscious Australian, and which makes wines – particularly red wines – utterly in keeping with that tradition. The essence of that heritage comes in the form of the tiny quantities of Shiraz made entirely from vines planted in 1860. Its releases on the market in 2001 are all excellent, as if to commemorate the dropping of Chateau from the winery name. As well as Australian national distribution through Tucker Seabrook, Tahbilk has agents in every principal wine market, including the UK, Europe, Asia and North America.

Tahbilk Riesling

🍷🍷🍷🍷🍷 **2000** Light green-yellow; a powerful wine, with a mix of spicy characters allied with fruit ranging from lime to apple to mineral; an ultra-powerful palate with lime, green apple, herb and spice flavours, and considerable grip. Covered itself in glory at the 2000 National Wine Show (winning two trophies) and was also a gold medal winner at the 2000 Adelaide Wine Show. **rating:** 90

best drinking Now–2005 **best vintages** '86, '90, '92, '94, '99, '00 **drink with** Seafood salad • $13.95

Tahbilk Viognier

🍷🍷🍷🍷 **2000** A gold medal at Melbourne followed by a silver medal in Adelaide is a remarkable debut for a first-up vintage. Clean and quite rich, with honey, honeysuckle and spice, it has genuine varietal style and mouthfeel; great promise for the future. **rating:** 88

best drinking Now **best vintages** '00 **drink with** Stacked eggplant • $14

Tahbilk Marsanne

🍷🍷🍷🍷 **1999** Light to medium yellow-green; the complex bouquet opens with minerally/earthy aromas, followed by a touch of toast, and then herb, grass and lemon; the palate has crisp lemon and grass flavours, complemented by an attractive acid cut on the finish; all it needs is time. **rating:** 87

best drinking Now–2005 **best vintages** '53, '74, '79, '81, '84, '85, '87, '88, '91, '92, '93, '95, '96, '98, '99 **drink with** Lighter Italian or Asian dishes • $12.95

Tahbilk Shiraz

TTTT **1998** Medium red-purple; clean, fresh cherry fruit with faint spice/savoury nuances on the bouquet leads into an attractive, fresh, lively, mid-weight palate, with cherry berry fruit, soft tannins and subtle oak. The best Tahbilk Shiraz for many years. **rating:** 89

best drinking Now–2008 **best vintages** '61, '62, '65, '68, '71, '74, '76, '78, '81, '84, '85, '86, '91, '98 **drink with** Barbecued T-bone steak • $20.55

Tahbilk 1860 Vines Shiraz

TTTTY **1995** Medium red-purple; the solid bouquet is stacked with ripe plum fruit together with touches of chocolate and vanilla flowing into a powerful, concentrated, rich and sweet palate with a mix of plum, berry and mint, supported by lingering tannins through the mid- to back palate. The best 1860s Vines wine for years. 290 dozen made. **rating:** 90

best drinking Now–2015 **best vintages** '82, '84, '86, '91, '92, '95 **drink with** Marinated venison • $115

Tahbilk Reserve Shiraz

TTTTY **1994** Medium red-purple; the bouquet, while fine and elegant, is quite intense, with intriguing spicy/sappy overtones. The palate is more powerful than the bouquet, but not distressingly so; here berry, mint, chocolate and spice flavours intermingle with a gentle touch of French oak. **rating:** 90

best drinking Now–2014 **best vintages** '94 **drink with** Lamb Provençale • $65

Tahbilk Cabernet Sauvignon

TTTT **1998** Medium red-purple; the bouquet is clean, with sweet, fresh berry fruit, soft yet quite rich, and is followed by a nicely balanced, fresh redcurrant palate with subtle oak and soft tannins. Like the Shiraz, the best for years. **rating:** 89

best drinking 2002–2008 **best vintages** '65, '71, '72, '75, '76, '78, '79, '86, '90, '92, '97, '98 **drink with** Strong mature cheddar, stilton • $20.55

Tahbilk Reserve Cabernet Sauvignon

TTTTY **1994** Medium to full red-purple; there are pronounced earthy bottle-developed cabernet aromas on the bouquet, with slightly dusty oak. In the mouth, powerful tannins run through an austere, savoury wine in traditional style. I would just like to see a touch more sweet berry fruit. **rating:** 90

best drinking Now–2011 **best vintages** '62, '65, '68, '71, '75, '76, '80, '81, '82, '84, '85 **drink with** Rich red-meat dishes • $65

tait wines NR

Yaldara Drive, Lyndoch, SA 5351 **region** Barossa Valley
phone (08) 8524 5000 **fax** (08) 8524 5220 **open** Weekends 10–5 and by appointment
winemaker Contract **production** 500 **est.** 1994
product range ($12–18 CD) Chardonnay, Bush Vine Grenache, Shiraz, Cabernet Sauvignon.
summary The Tait family has been involved in the wine industry in the Barossa for over 100 years, making not wine but barrels. Their recent venture into winemaking was immediately successful; retail distribution through single outlets in Melbourne, Adelaide and Sydney.

talijancich NR

26 Hyem Road, Herne Hill, WA 6056 **region** Swan District
phone (08) 9296 4289 **fax** (08) 9296 1762 **open** Sun–Fri 11–5
winemaker James Talijancich **production** 10 000 **est.** 1932
product range ($17–135 CD) Verdelho, Voices Dry White, Grenache, Shiraz, Julian James White Liqueur, Julian James Red Liqueur, Liqueur Tokay 375 ml.
summary A former fortified-wine specialist (with old Liqueur Tokay) now making a broad range of table wines, with particular emphasis on Verdelho: on the third Saturday of August each year there is a tasting of fine three-year-old Verdelho table wines from both Australia and overseas. Also runs an active wine club and exports to China, Japan and Hong Kong.

Talijancich Shiraz

1999 Medium red-purple; there is a solid array of plum, berry, earth and chocolate on the bouquet, and plenty of substance and structure to the berry and chocolate fruit-driven palate, finishing with ample, ripe tannins. **rating:** 89

best drinking 2004–2009 **best vintages** NA **drink with** Beef casserole • NA

taliondal NR

Old North Road, Rothbury, NSW 2320 **region** Lower Hunter Valley
phone (02) 9427 6812 **fax** (02) 9427 6812 **open** Not
winemaker Frank Brady **production** 240 **est.** 1974
product range ($8–15 ML) Traminer, Cab Fizz, Cabernet Sauvignon.
summary The Brady Bunch, headed by Frank Brady, acquired Taliondal in 1974 as a family hideaway. Says Frank Brady, 'When in the Hunter do as the Hunter does,' so 1 hectare of cabernet sauvignon was planted in 1974, and 1.5 hectares of traminer the following year. For many years the family was content to sell the grapes to local vignerons, but now take a small portion of the production and make wine on the property. The Cabernet Sauvignon has been a consistent medal-winner at Hunter shows, the 1998 winning the trophy for Open Vintage Reds at the 1999 Boutique Winemakers Show. This has led to a decision to concentrate on red winemaking, and while some Traminer remains for sale, future production will be of the Cabernet Sauvignon only.

tallarook

Ennis Road, Tallarook, Vic 3659 **region** Central Victorian Mountain Country
phone (03) 9818 3455 **fax** (03) 9818 3646 **open** Not
winemaker Martin Williams **production** 2000 **est.** 1987
product range ($23–25 ML) Chardonnay, Marsanne, Pinot Noir, with Shiraz, Viognier and Rousanne on the way.
summary TallarooK has been established on a property between Broadford and Seymour at an elevation of 200–300 metres. Since 1987 10.7 hectares of vines have been planted, the three principal varieties being chardonnay, shiraz and pinot noir. The retainer of Martin Williams as winemaker in the 1998 vintage brought a substantial change in emphasis, and the subsequent release of an impressive Chardonnay. The wine is mainly sold by mail order; also retail distribution in Melbourne and exports to the UK.

TallarooK Chardonnay

1999 Medium to full yellow-green; rich, complex, toasty, nutty barrel-ferment oak accompanies stonefruit, fig and cashew on both bouquet and palate. Here figgy/cashew flavours lead through to a quite dry finish. **rating:** 90

best drinking Now–2005 **best vintages** '99 **drink with** Pan-fried veal • $25

TallarooK Pinot Noir

1999 Medium red-purple; a distinctly complex bouquet with spice, plum, forest and good oak lead into a savoury palate showing clever winemaking. However, the overall profile and texture lacks mid-palate fruit, investing the wine with a slightly hard profile. **rating:** 86

best drinking Now–2004 **best vintages** NA **drink with** Pot-roasted quail • $25

taltarni

Taltarni Road, Moonambel, Vic 3478 **region** Pyrenees
phone (03) 5467 2218 **fax** (03) 5467 2306 **open** 7 days 10–5
winemaker Shane Clohesy, Chris Markell, David Crawford **production** 80 000 **est.** 1972
product range ($11.90–33 R) Sauvignon Blanc, Lalla Gully Chardonnay, Rosé, Merlot Cabernet, Shiraz, Cabernet Sauvignon, Merlot; Fiddleback red and white; Cuvée Brut, Brut Tache.
summary In the shadow of the departure (on the best of terms) of long-serving winemaker and chief executive Dominique Portet, Taltarni seems to have backed off the high levels of tannin and extract evident in the older vintage wines, which, after a brief period of uncertainty, seems to be paying off. Exports to all the major markets, including the UK, the US, Canada, Japan, Hong Kong, Switzerland, Sweden and extensively thoughout Southeast Asia and Western Europe.

Taltarni Sauvignon Blanc

▼▼▼▼ **2000** Very pale straw-green; the bouquet is clean and fresh, with mineral, asparagus and gooseberry aromas all evident; the medium-bodied palate is clean, crisp and unforced. **rating:** 87

best drinking Now **best vintages** '96, '97, '98 **drink with** Calamari • $19.50

Taltarni Shiraz

▼▼▼▼▽ **1998** Medium to full red-purple; a solid bouquet with plum and dark, briary aromas is followed by a rich, ripe and full palate, showing as much extract as ever, but not excessively tannic and with a core of deliciously sweet fruit. One of the best vintages for many years for Taltarni. **rating:** 90

best drinking 2003–2010 **best vintages** '84, '88, '90, '91, '92, '96, '98 **drink with** Gippsland blue cheese • $18

Taltarni Cabernet Sauvignon

▼▼▼▽ **1997** Medium red, with just a touch of purple; the bouquet is savoury, with some slightly gamey/vegetal canopy aromas, the palate with similar earthy/savoury fruit, a touch of chocolate, and finishing with moderate tannins. **rating:** 83

best drinking 2002–2007 **best vintages** NA **drink with** Ox cheek • $28

talunga NR

Adelaide to Mannum Road (PO Box 134), Gumeracha, SA 5233 **region** Adelaide Hills

phone (08) 8389 1222 **fax** (08) 8389 1233 **open** Wed–Sun and public holidays 10.30–5

winemaker Vince Scaffidi **production** 4000 **est.** 1994

product range ($11–24.50 CD) Sauvignon Blanc, Semillon, Chardonnay, Yearling Blend, Shiraz, Sangiovese Merlot, Cabernet Merlot, High Block Cabernet Sauvignon, Cabernet Sauvignon.

summary Talunga owners Vince and Tina Scaffidi have a one-third share of the 62-hectare Gumeracha Vineyards, and it is from these vineyards that the Talunga wines are sourced.

tamar ridge ★★★★☆

Auburn Road, Kayena, Tas 7270 **region** Northern Tasmania

phone (03) 6394 7000 **fax** (03) 6334 6050 **open** 7 days 10–5

winemaker Julian Alcorso **production** 25 000 **est.** 1994

product range ($15–25 CD) Riesling, Josef Chromy Selection Riesling, Sauvignon Blanc, Chardonnay, Pinot Noir, Cabernet Sauvignon, RV (Sparkling); second label Devil's Corner Dry White, Riesling, Chardonnay, Dry Red, Pinot Noir.

summary Tamar Ridge is the most recent venture into wine production of grass-fed-beef magnate Joe Chromy. When he sold Heemskerk and Rochecombe to Pipers Brook in 1998, he retained a substantial vineyard in the Tamar Valley, which presently has over 50 hectares in bearing and which is to be increased to 70 hectares over the next two to three years. The new winery, situated on the edge of a large dam (or lake, for that is what it looks like), is a striking piece of architecture, and a large restaurant is in the plans for the future. The quality of the early releases is impressive; led by consistently superb Rieslings. Exports to Canada, Japan and Singapore.

Tamar Ridge Riesling

▼▼▼▼▼ **2000** Light to medium green-yellow; a floral nose, with a mix of spicy, almost bready, mineral and lime aromas transfers to a rich, powerful palate with spicy overtones to the intense juicy, cool-grown fruit; very intense and very long. **rating:** 94

▼▼▼▼▼ **1998** Medium yellow-green; a powerful, scented and complex bouquet of lime and toast, and the first signs of kerosene/mineral development starting to show. A classic bottle-developed palate with lovely richness and length, and, in particular, a great mid-palate with lime and apple fruit flavours. Going from strength to strength. **rating:** 95

best drinking Now–2007 **best vintages** '98, '99, '00 **drink with** Sashimi • $18

Tamar Ridge Josef Chromy Selection Riesling

▼▼▼▼▼ **1999** Medium yellow-green; an intensely fragrant and powerful bouquet with lime juice and a hint of tropical fruit possibly ex botrytis. The palate is equally magnificently rich, complex and powerful, again with some tropical overlay, but with the acidity to balance. **rating:** 97

best drinking Now–2007 **best vintages** '99 **drink with** Cold smoked salmon • NA

Tamar Ridge Sauvignon Blanc

ⲯⲯⲯⲯ **2000** Light green-yellow; the bouquet is clean, crisp and quite positive in character, with grassy/herb characters, the palate fresh, bracing and crisp, albeit with fairly penetrating acidity. **rating:** 86

best drinking Now **best vintages** NA **drink with** Shellfish • $18.50

Tamar Ridge Chardonnay

ⲯⲯⲯⲯ **1999** Medium yellow-green; a clean, smooth, fruit-driven nectarine and melon bouquet is followed by an elegant and fresh palate showing precisely the same flavours; the oak influence is subliminal at best, but definitely adds to the structure of the wine. **rating:** 87

best drinking Now–2003 **best vintages** '98 **drink with** Stir-fried abalone • $20

Tamar Ridge Devil's Corner Chardonnay

ⲯⲯⲯⲯ **2000** Medium yellow-green; clean melon and nectarine fruit on the bouquet is followed by a palate with plenty of fruit, good balance and length, and soft acidity. In the top echelon of unwooded Chardonnay from Australia, the best from Devil's Corner to date. **rating:** 90

best drinking Now–2004 **best vintages** '00 **drink with** Crayfish • $15

Tamar Ridge RV

ⲯⲯⲯⲯⲯ **1995** Light to medium green-yellow; the bouquet is clean, with some bready/autolysis notes coming in over the citrus-tinged fruit of the bouquet. The palate has length and intensity, with a bright, clean finish. **rating:** 94

best drinking Now–2004 **best vintages** '95 **drink with** Shellfish • $21

Tamar Ridge Pinot Noir

ⲯⲯⲯⲯ **1999** Light to medium red-purple; the clean and fresh bouquet offers plum, cherry and a hint of mint, the light- to medium-bodied palate with clean, plummy fruit and subtle oak. The wine has good varietal character even if it is a fraction simple, simplicity that is easy to accept at the price. **rating:** 85

best drinking Now–2003 **best vintages** NA **drink with** Spiced quail • $20

Tamar Ridge Cabernet Sauvignon

ⲯⲯⲯⲯ **1998** Medium red; the bouquet has a mix of raspberry and blackcurrant fruit, with neatly handled oak and tannins to add structure to and sweeten up the palate, which doesn't quite match the fruit of the bouquet. **rating:** 87

best drinking 2003–2008 **best vintages** NA **drink with** Grass-fed beef • $25

Tamar Ridge Josef Chromy Selection Cabernet Sauvignon

ⲯⲯⲯⲯ **1998** Medium red-purple; the moderately intense bouquet is fragrant, with attractively sweet berry aromas that translate into sweet berry fruit on the palate, neatly married with a deft touch of spicy oak. **rating:** 88

best drinking 2003–2008 **best vintages** NA **drink with** Leave it in the cellar • NA

tamburlaine ★★★☆

McDonalds Road, Pokolbin, NSW 2321 **region** Lower Hunter Valley

phone (02) 4998 7570 **fax** (02) 4998 7763 **open** 7 days 9.30–5

winemaker Mark Davidson **production** 50 000 **est.** 1966

product range ($18–22 CD) Highland Riesling, Semillon, Verdelho, Highland Sauvignon Blanc, Highland Chardonnay, The Chapel Reserve Chardonnay, Cabernet Merlot Malbec, The Chapel Reserve Red.

summary A thriving business that, notwithstanding the fact it has doubled its already substantial production in recent years, sells over 90 per cent of its wine through cellar door and by mailing list (with an active tasting club members' cellar programme offering wines that are held and matured at Tamburlaine). Unashamedly and deliberately focused on the tourist trade (and, of course, its club members).

Tamburlaine Semillon

ⲯⲯⲯⲯ **2000** Pale straw-green; clean, fine, elegant and delicate aromatics presage a very dry herb and mineral-flavoured palate, considerably lengthened by the acidity. Leave alone for five years. **rating:** 90

best drinking 2005–2010 **best vintages** '86, '89, '91, '93, '94, '00 **drink with** Leave it in the cellar • $18

Tamburlaine Verdelho

ⲯⲯⲯ **2000** Light to medium yellow-green; the bouquet has fruit-salad and citrus aromas, the palate fresh and zesty, but not as ferociously acid as the analysis would suggest. Interesting. **rating:** 84

best drinking Now–2003 **best vintages** NA **drink with** Japanese • $18

tanglewood downs NR

Bulldog Creek Road, Merricks North, Vic 3926 **region** Mornington Peninsula
phone (03) 5974 3325 **fax** (03) 5974 4170 **open** Sun–Mon 12–5
winemaker Ken Bilham, Wendy Bilham **production** 1200 **est.** 1984
product range ($25 CD) Riesling, Gewurztraminer, Chardonnay, Pinot Noir, Cabernet Sauvignon, Cabernet Franc Merlot.
summary One of the smaller and lower-profile wineries on the Mornington Peninsula, with Ken Bilham quietly doing his own thing on 2.5 hectares of estate plantings. Winery lunches and dinners are available by arrangement.

tannery lane vineyard NR

174 Tannery Lane, Mandurang, Vic 3551 **region** Bendigo
phone (03) 5439 3227 **open** By appointment
winemaker Lindsay Ross (Contract) **production** NA **est.** 1990
product range ($15–23 CD) Sangiovese, Shiraz, Merlot, Cabernet Merlot.
summary In 1990 planting began of the present total of 2 hectares of shiraz, cabernet sauvignon, cabernet franc, sangiovese, merlot and nebbiolo. Their Sangiovese is the only such wine coming from the Bendigo region at the present time. The micro-production is sold through cellar door only and then only while stocks last, which typically is not for very long.

tantemaggie NR

Kemp Road, Pemberton, WA 6260 **region** Pemberton
phone (08) 9776 1164 **fax** (08) 9776 1810 **open** By appointment
winemaker Contract **production** 600 **est.** 1987
product range ($20–25 CD) Verdelho, Cabernet Sauvignon.
summary Tantemaggie was established by the Pottinger family with the help of a bequest from a deceased aunt named Maggie. It is part of a mixed farming operation, and by far the greatest part of the 20 hectares is under long-term contract to Houghton. The bulk of the plantings are cabernet sauvignon and verdelho, the former producing the light-bodied style favoured by the Pottingers.

tarrawarra estate 

Healesville Road, Yarra Glen, Vic 3775 **region** Yarra Valley
phone (03) 5962 3311 **fax** (03) 5962 3887 **open** 7 days 10.30–4.30
winemaker Clare Halloran, Damian North **production** 20 000 **est.** 1983
product range ($22–48 R) Chardonnay and Pinot Noir each released under the Tarrawarra Estate and second label Tin Cows (formerly Tunnel Hill). Tin Cows also includes Shiraz and Merlot; also Kidron Chardonnay (kosher).
summary Slowly evolving Chardonnay of great structure and complexity is the winery specialty; robust Pinot Noir also needs time and evolves impressively if given it. The second label Tin Cows (formerly Tunnel Hill) wines are more accessible when young, and better value for those who do not wish to wait for the Tarrawarra wines to evolve. National retail distribution; exports to the UK, Switzerland, Belgium, Singapore, Hong Kong and the US.

Tarrawarra Tin Cows Pinot Noir

YYYY **2000** Medium to full red, with some purple tinges; the bouquet has abundant character, with strong spicy nutmeg aromas over the top of plummy fruit. The palate provides the same play between powerful plum and spice in full-on Tarrawarra style. **rating:** 89

best drinking 2002–2006 **best vintages** '91, '92, '94, '96, '97, '00 **drink with** Game pie • $25

tarwin ridge NR

Wintles Road, Leongatha South, Vic 3953 **region** Gippsland
phone (03) 5664 3211 **fax** (03) 5664 3211 **open** Weekends and holidays 10–5
winemaker Brian Anstee **production** 700 **est.** 1983
product range ($16–27 CD) Sauvignon Blanc, White Merlot, Pinot Noir, Pinot Noir Premium, Cabernet Merlot.
summary For the time being Brian Anstee is making his wines at Nicholson River under the gaze of fellow social worker Ken Eckersley; the wines come from 2 hectares of estate pinot and 0.5 hectare each of cabernet and sauvignon blanc.

tatachilla ★★★★☆

151 Main Road, McLaren Vale, SA 5171 **region** McLaren Vale
phone (08) 8323 8656 **fax** (08) 8323 9096 **open** Mon–Sat 10–5, Sun and public holidays 11–5
winemaker Michael Fragos, Justin McNamee **production** 229 000 **est.** 1901
product range ($11.95–45 R) Adelaide Hills Sauvignon Blanc, Growers (Chenin Blanc Semillon Sauvignon Blanc), Adelaide Hills Chardonnay, McLaren Vale Chardonnay, Padthaway Chardonnay, Pinot Noir NV, Sparkling Malbec, Foundation Shiraz, McLaren Vale Shiraz, McLaren Vale Merlot, Clarendon Merlot, Keystone (Grenache Shiraz), Adelaide Hills Cabernet Merlot, Partners (Cabernet Sauvignon Shiraz), McLaren Vale Cabernet Sauvignon, Padthaway Cabernet Sauvignon, Tawny Port.
summary Tatachilla was reborn in 1995 but has an at times tumultuous history going back to 1901. For most of the time between 1901 and 1961 the winery was owned by Penfolds but was closed in 1961 then reopened in 1965 as the Southern Vales Co-operative. In the late 1980s it was purchased and renamed The Vales but did not flourish, and in 1993 it was purchased by local grower Vic Zerella and former Kaiser Stuhl chief executive Keith Smith. After extensive renovations, the winery was officially reopened in 1995 and won a number of tourist awards and accolades. The star turns are Keystone (Grenache Shiraz) and Foundation Shiraz, bursting with vibrant fruit. Late in 2000 it merged with St Hallett to form the public-listed Banksia Wines; the group has worldwide distribution.

Tatachilla McLaren Vale Chardonnay

🍷🍷🍷🍷 **2000** Medium yellow-green; soft, slightly fuzzy melon fruit with some nutty barrel-ferment aromas on the bouquet lead into a complex palate with nutty melon flavours and a splash of oak. The fruit just staggers across the line. **rating:** 86

best drinking Now–2004 **best vintages** NA **drink with** Pasta • $15.90

Tatachilla Foundation Shiraz

🍷🍷🍷🍷½ **1998** Dark, deep red; there is typically abundant blood plum, cherry and spice fruit married with vanilla oak on the bouquet; the palate is rich and concentrated, with plum, chocolate and vanilla flavours supported by persistent tannins. Will improve with further bottle age. **rating:** 90

best drinking 2003–2013 **best vintages** '95, '97, '98 **drink with** Kangaroo fillet • $45

Tatachilla McLaren Vale Shiraz

🍷🍷🍷🍷 **1999** Medium to full red-purple; a powerful bouquet with strong, dark berry fruit and heaps of oak is followed by a palate with masses of ripe berry fruit and chocolate; big but smooth, and carries the oak well. **rating:** 89

best drinking 2004–2009 **best vintages** '98, '99 **drink with** Rump steak • $22.95

Tatachilla McLaren Vale Merlot

🍷🍷🍷🍷½ **1999** Medium red-purple; a powerful and complex bouquet is followed by a palate stacked with rich, ripe berry, spice and chocolate-flavoured fruit, with lovely tannin and oak structure. Won a gold medal at both Melbourne and Adelaide 2000. The only comment is that the wine is a lovely medium-bodied dry red, and not so much a Merlot. **rating:** 93

best drinking 2002–2007 **best vintages** '96, '97, '98, '99 **drink with** Rare rump steak • $22.95

Tatachilla Adelaide Hills Cabernet Merlot

🍷🍷🍷🍷½ **1998** Medium to full red-purple; cherry-kernel, vanilla and spice aromas lead into a palate with lovely sweet black cherry and blackcurrant fruit, with just the right amount of oak and pleasantly soft tannins. **rating:** 90

best drinking Now–2006 **best vintages** '98 **drink with** Rare roast beef • $25

Tatachilla Partners Cabernet Sauvignon Shiraz

🍷🍷🍷🍷 **2000** Medium to full red-purple; a typical strongly fruit bouquet, quite dense, is followed by a sweet, ripe, chewy palate with nicely handled tannins. A good outcome for the vintage. **rating:** 86

best drinking Now–2005 **best vintages** '96, '97, '98 **drink with** Marinated beef • $14.50

Tatachilla McLaren Vale Cabernet Sauvignon

🍷🍷🍷🍷🍷 **1998** Medium to full purple-red; the exceptional quality of this wine comes from the perfectly and precisely articulated cabernet varietal character on both bouquet and palate. It achieves a magic balance of the slight austerity that all great young Cabernet has, and yet a core of cassis and blackberry fruit that gives the wine immediate appeal. The tannin and oak management is impeccable, doing no more than providing a frame for the wonderful fruit. **rating:** 97

best drinking 2003–2013 **best vintages** '97, '98 **drink with** Rare roast baby lamb • $22.95

tawonga vineyard NR

2 Drummond Street, Tawonga, Vic 3697 **region** Alpine Valleys
phone (03) 5754 4945 **fax** (03) 5754 4925 **open** By appointment
winemaker John Adams **production** 500 **est.** 1994
product range ($12.50–13.75 CD) Verdelho, Pinot Noir, Shiraz.
summary Diz and John Adams made their first wine in 1995, but it was not until 1998 that they finally received their producer's licence entitling them to sell the wine they had made. With a planned maximum production of 10 tonnes in 2001, Tawonga has been able to take advantage of the small-business tax exemption. In the meantime the price for their handcrafted wines (virtually all of which have won show medals) remains at a magically low $12.50 to $13.75.

taylors ★★★★

Taylors Road, Auburn, SA 5451 **region** Clare Valley
phone (08) 8849 2008 **fax** (08) 8849 2240 **open** Mon–Fri 9–5, Sat and public holidays 10–5, Sun 10–4
winemaker Adam Eggins, Graig Grafton **production** 200 000 **est.** 1972
product range ($8.50–50 R) At the top come the super-premium St Andrews releases of Chardonnay, Shiraz and Cabernet Sauvignon, then the premium range, which consists of Chardonnay, Clare Riesling, Gewurztraminer, White Clare, Promised Land Unwooded Chardonnay, Pinot Noir, Merlot, Shiraz and Cabernet Sauvignon; the lower-priced Clare Valley range consists of Dry White, Sweet White and Dry Red.
summary Taylors continues to flourish and expand, with yet further extensions to its vineyards, now totalling almost 500 hectares, by far the largest holding in Clare Valley. There have also been substantial changes on the winemaking front, both in terms of the winemaking team and in terms of the wine style, the latter moving to fresher, earlier-release wines. After an initial period of adjustment, wine quality has increased significantly. Widespread national distribution, with exports to New Zealand, Germany, Northern Ireland, the US, Thailand, Fiji, Hong Kong, China, Malaysia and Singapore.

Taylors Clare Riesling

YYYY **1999** Medium yellow-green; the bouquet is full and soft, with ripe lime fruit plus tropical overtones. The palate has a big impact, with abundant, rounded though not sweet, citrus and toast flavour. Quite exceptional at the price and ready now. **rating:** 87
best drinking Now–2003 **best vintages** '82, '87, '92, '93, '94, '96, '99 **drink with** Avocado • $8.89

Taylors St Andrews Shiraz

YYYY **1997** Medium red-purple; big, dark plum/cherry/leather aromas introduce a powerful palate with tremendous depth of fruit, if a slightly rustic texture. Strong silver medal winner at the 2000 Clare Valley Wine Show. **rating:** 87
best drinking 2002–2012 **best vintages** NA **drink with** Steak Dianne • $50

Taylors Merlot

YYYYY **1999** Medium red, with some purple; the bouquet is fragrant, with sweet, small berry fruit aromas and nice savoury touches; positive oak also plays a part. Soft, sweet, textured fruit gives the feel of Merlot more than the flavour, but on the other hand, there really isn't a clear standard for the variety in Australia. **rating:** 94
best drinking 2002–2009 **best vintages** NA **drink with** Veal saltimbocca • $16

Taylors Cabernet Sauvignon

YYYY **1999** Medium to full red-purple; there is lots going on here, with slightly aggressive berry/earth fruit and some oak contribution. A powerful, youthful wine on the palate, with earthy/blackberry fruit and somewhat tough tannins. Very young, and should settle down with bottle age, offering excellent value when it does. An element of prospectivity in the points and vintage rating. **rating:** 86
best drinking 2003–2009 **best vintages** '86, '89, '90, '92, '94, '99 **drink with** Mixed grill • $16

temple bruer ★★★☆

Milang Road, Strathalbyn, SA 5255 **region** Langhorne Creek
phone (08) 8537 0203 **fax** (08) 8537 0131 **open** Mon–Fri 9.30–4.30
winemaker Nick Bruer **production** 14 000 **est.** 1980
product range ($12.80–23.70 R) Riesling, Verdelho, Viognier, Chenin Blanc, Botrytis Riesling, Cornucopia Grenache, Cabernet Merlot, Reserve Merlot, Shiraz Malbec, Sparkling Cabernet Merlot.

summary Always known for its eclectic range of wines, Temple Bruer (which also carries on a substantial business as a vine-propagation nursery) has seen a sharp lift in wine quality. Clean, modern, redesigned labels add to the appeal of a stimulatingly different range of red wines. Part of the production from the 24 hectares of estate vineyards is sold to others, the remainder being made under the Temple Bruer label. All of the 24-hectare vineyard is now certified organic.

templer's mill NR

The University of Sydney, Leeds Parade, Orange, NSW 2800 **region** Orange
phone (02) 6360 5509 **fax** (02) 6360 5698 **open** Mon–Fri 9–4.30 or by appointment
winemaker Jon Reynolds **production** 5000 **est.** 1997
product range ($14–17 CD) Chardonnay, Shiraz, Cabernet Sauvignon.
summary Templer's Mill is the outcome of a joint venture between winemaker Jon Reynolds, entrepreneur-cum-vigneron Gary Blom (of Barrington Estate in the Upper Hunter Valley) and the Orange campus of the University of Sydney. There were plans to erect a substantial winery, but these have now been abandoned for a number of reasons. For the time being, at least, the label continues, utilising just under 20 hectares of vines grown on the university's property.

Templer's Mill Chardonnay

▼▼▼▼ **1999** Medium yellow-green; a clean and smooth bouquet with gentle nectarine and light oak is followed by a clean palate with some grip to the finish, but not a lot of flesh in the middle. Still, nicely put together. **rating:** 85
best drinking Now–2003 **best vintages** NA **drink with** Marinated octopus • $14

Templer's Mill Cabernet Sauvignon

▼▼▼▽ **1999** Medium red-purple; the cedary/leafy/berry bouquet is quite fragrant, the palate elegant and light with a mix of berry and leaf; the tannin balance is correct, but, like the Chardonnay, is short on mid-palate fruit. **rating:** 84
best drinking Now–2004 **best vintages** NA **drink with** Pork spare ribs • $17

tempus two wines ★★★☆

Hermitage Road, Pokolbin, NSW 2321 **region** Lower Hunter Valley
phone (02) 9818 7222 **fax** (02) 9818 7333 **open** 7 days 10–5
winemaker Peter Hall **production** 30 000 **est.** 1997
product range ($14–35 R) Varietal range of Verdelho, Semillon Sauvignon Blanc, Cowra Chardonnay, Angle Vale Shiraz, Hunter Shiraz, Merlot, Cabernet Shiraz; Heart range of Broke Chardonnay, Sparkling Chardonnay, Sparkling Shiraz, Mudgee Merlot, Hollydene Cabernet Sauvignon, Vine Vale Shiraz; Reserve range of Clare Riesling, Cabernet Merlot and Botrytis Semillon.
summary Tempus Two is the new name for Hermitage Road Wines, a piece of doggerel akin to that of Rouge Homme, except that it is not Franglais, but a mix of Latin (Tempus means time) and English. I should not be too critical, however; the change was forced on the winery by the EU Wine Agreement and the prohibition of the use of the word 'hermitage' on Australian wine labels. Nor should the fracas over the labels disguise the fact that some very attractive wines have appeared so far, and will do so in the future, no doubt.

Tempus Two Somerset Vineyard Verdelho

▼▼▼▽ **2000** Light to medium green-yellow; light fruit-salad aromas are tinged with citrus, the clean, bright, crisp and fresh palate having a degree of focus and elegance not often encountered with Verdelho. **rating:** 84
best drinking Now **best vintages** NA **drink with** Takeaway • $14

terrace vale

Deasey's Lane, Pokolbin, NSW 2321 **region** Lower Hunter Valley
phone (02) 4998 7517 **fax** (02) 4998 7814 **open** 7 days 10–4
winemaker Alain Leprince **production** 8000 **est.** 1971
product range ($14.50–19 CD) Bin 1 Semillon, Bin 2 Chardonnay, Semillon Chardonnay, Gewurztraminer, Elizabeth Sauvignon Blanc, Sauvignon Blanc Semillon, Fine Hunter White, Pinot Noir, Bin 6 Shiraz, Fine Hunter Red, Cabernet Merlot, Bin 7 Cabernet Sauvignon, Sparkling, Vintage Port.
summary Sold shortly before this book went to print; no details yet about the intention of the purchaser.

t'gallant ★★★★

Mornington Road, Red Hill, Vic 3937 **region** Mornington Peninsula
phone (03) 5989 6565 **fax** (03) 5989 6577 **open** 7 days 10–5
winemaker Kathleen Quealy, Kevin McCarthy **production** 18 000 **est.** 1990
product range ($18–60 R) An ever-changing list of names (and avant-garde label designs) but with Unwooded Chardonnay and Pinot Gris at the centre. Labels include Chardonnay, Lot 2 Chardonnay, The T'Gallant Chardonnay, Pinot Grigio, Tribute Pinot Gris, Imogen Pinot Gris, Celia's White Pinot, Cape Schanck Pinot Grigio Chardonnay, Triumph Late Harvest Pinot Gris, Holystone, Single Vineyard Pinot Noir, Pinot Noir and a range of wines under the Lyncroft label.
summary Husband-and-wife consultant-winemakers Kathleen Quealy and Kevin McCarthy are starting to carve out an important niche market for T'Gallant, noted for its innovative label designs and names. The acquisition of a 15-hectare property, and the planting of 10 hectares of pinot gris gives the business a firm geographic base, as well as providing increased resources for its signature wine. The yearly parade of new (usually beautiful and striking, it is true) labels designed by Ken Cato do not make my life at all easy. No sooner is the database built up than it is discarded for next year's rash of labels. La Baracca Trattoria is open seven days for lunch and for specially booked evening events. Watch for the single vineyard Gainsborough Park and Lyncroft Pinots from 2000 due for release in the second half of 2001. Exports to the UK.

T'Gallant Celia's White Pinot

YYYY 2000 Pale pink-straw; the bouquet is clean, with touches of strawberry and mineral, the palate fresh, light and pleasant in a pleasingly dry style, albeit otherwise unremarkable. **rating:** 83
best drinking Now **best vintages** NA **drink with** Antipasto • $23

T'Gallant Pinot Grigio

YYYY 2000 Light green-yellow; the bouquet has quite attractive varietal character, with apple and pear aromas; the palate is clean, pleasant and easy drinking, not particularly striking, but no fault. 12.5° alcohol may be no bad thing. **rating:** 86
best drinking Now **best vintages** NA **drink with** Smoked salmon • $19.80

T'Gallant Pinot Noir

YYYY 2000 Light to medium purple-red; the bouquet is clean, moderately intense, with aromas of plum, cherry and a hint of spice; the palate offers gentle fruit in a nicely balanced medium-bodied style, with plum and cherry fruit running through a silky, soft palate, which is just a fraction short. **rating:** 87
best drinking Now–2004 **best vintages** '00 **drink with** Breast of duck • $35

thalgara estate NR

De Beyers Road, Pokolbin, NSW 2321 **region** Lower Hunter Valley
phone (02) 4998 7717 **fax** (02) 4998 7774 **open** 7 days 10–5
winemaker Steve Lamb **production** 3000 **est.** 1985
product range ($15–30 CD) Chardonnay, Show Reserve Chardonnay, Semillon Chardonnay, Shiraz, Show Reserve Shiraz, Shiraz Cabernet.
summary A low-profile winery which had its moment of glory at the 1997 Hunter Valley Wine Show when it won the Doug Seabrook Memorial Trophy for Best Dry Red of Show with its 1995 Show Reserve Shiraz.

the blok estate NR

Riddoch Highway, Coonawarra, SA 5263 **region** Coonawarra
phone (08) 8737 2734 **fax** (08) 8737 2994 **open** 7 days 10–4
winemaker Contract **production** 1200 **est.** 1999
product range ($16–28 CD) Riesling, Chardonnay, Pinot Chardonnay, Shiraz, Cabernet Sauvignon.
summary Di and John Blok have owned a tiny vineyard planted to cabernet sauvignon for the past five years. They have now decided to take the production from this and from contract-grown grapes elsewhere in Coonawarra for release under their own label. The cellar door is situated in an old stone home which has recently been renovated and surrounded by newly landscaped gardens.

the fleurieu NR

Main Road, McLaren Vale, SA 5171 **region** McLaren Vale
phone (08) 8323 8999 **fax** (08) 8323 9332 **open** 7 days 9–5
winemaker Mike Farmilo **production** 3500 **est.** 1994
product range ($18–35 R) Shiraz, released under the Fleurieu and Stump Hill labels.
summary A specialist Shiraz producer, with 6.5 hectares of estate vineyards and contract winemaking by the former long-serving Seaview/Edwards & Chaffey winemaker Mike Farmilo. Exports to the UK, the US, Singapore, Hong Kong, Japan, the Philippines and Canada.

The Fleurieu Shiraz

🍷🍷🍷🍷🍷 **1998** Medium to full red-purple; the bouquet is succulent and smooth, with rich, dark chocolate, berry and earth fruit cocooned in high-quality oak, the powerful palate providing a seamless train of fruit, oak and tannins. **rating:** 94
best drinking 2003–2013 **best vintages** '98 **drink with** Kangaroo fillet • $35

the gap ★★★☆

Pomonal Road, Halls Gap, Vic 3381 **region** Grampians
phone (03) 5356 4252 **fax** (03) 5356 4645 **open** Wed–Sun 10–5, 7 days during school holidays
winemaker Trevor Mast, Andrew McLoughney **production** 1600 **est.** 1969
product range ($16–30 CD) Chardonnay, Late Harvest Riesling, Shiraz Cabernet Sauvignon; Four Sisters Sauvingon Blanc Semillon; Billi Billi Creek Shiraz Cabernet, Four Sisters Shiraz.
summary The Gap is the reincarnation of Boroka, a spectacularly situated vineyard 5 kilometres east of Halls Gap, with the slopes of the Mount William Range forming a backdrop. The vineyard was planted in 1969 but following its acquisition by Mount Langi Ghiran has been rehabilitated, and extensive renovations have been made to the cellar-door sales area which offers estate-grown 'The Gap' wines and a selection of Mount Langi Ghiran and Four Sisters wines.

Four Sisters Sauvignon Blanc Semillon

🍷🍷🍷🍷 **2000** Light green-yellow; the bouquet is tangy, with correct varietal grass/herb/citrus aromas, the spotlessly clean palate moderately intense and nicely balanced, with a pleasingly delicate finish. Good value. **rating:** 85
best drinking Now **best vintages** NA **drink with** Shellfish • $13.50

Four Sisters Shiraz

🍷🍷🍷🍷 **1999** Medium red-purple; the gently spicy bouquet is moderately intense, with a quite complex mix of savoury and red berry fruit characters supported by subtle oak. The medium-bodied palate displays pleasant black cherry/berry fruit in a non-threatening style. **rating:** 85
best drinking Now–2005 **best vintages** NA **drink with** Roast beef • $13.95

the green vineyards ★★★★

1 Alber Road, Upper Beaconsfield, Vic 3808 **region** Yarra Valley
phone (03) 5944 4599 **fax** (03) 5944 4599 **open** Weekends by appointment
winemaker Sergio Carlei **production** 2000 **est.** 1994
product range ($12–25 CD) Yarra Valley Riesling, Mornington Sauvignon Blanc, Yarra Valley Chardonnay, Sunbury Pinot Noir, Heathcote Shiraz, Yarra Valley Cabernets.
summary The Green Vineyards has come a long way in a little time, with Sergio Carlei graduating from home winemaking in a suburban garage to his own (real) winery in Upper Beaconsfield, which happens to fall just within the boundaries of the Yarra Valley. As the product range attests, many of the wines come from grapes grown by others for Green Vineyards, but Carlei does have 2.25 hectares of pinot noir and his preferred source is the Yarra Valley. He has already produced a number of remarkably stylish wines, with more in the pipeline.

the gurdies NR

St Helier Road, The Gurdies, Vic 3984 **region** Gippsland
phone (03) 5997 6208 **fax** (03) 5997 6511 **open** 7 days 10–5 or by appointment
winemaker Peter Kozik **production** 1500 **est.** 1991

product range ($18–25 CD) Riesling, Gurdies Hill White (Chardonnay), Pinot Noir, Reserve Pinot Noir, Shiraz, Merlot, Cabernet Merlot, Gurdies Hill Red (Cabernet Sauvignon Shiraz), Cabernet Sauvignon.
summary The only winery in the southwest Gippsland region, established on the slopes of The Gurdies hills overlooking Westernport Bay and French Island. Plantings of the 3.5-hectare vineyard commenced in 1981, but no fruit was harvested until 1991 owing to bird attack. A winery has been partially completed, and it is intended to increase the vineyards to 25 hectares and ultimately build a restaurant on site.

the mews NR

84 Gibson Street, Kings Meadows, Tas 7249 **region** Northern Tasmania
phone (03) 6344 2780 **fax** (03) 6343 2076 **open** Not
winemaker Graham Wiltshire **production** 300 **est.** 1984
product range Chardonnay.
summary Robin and Anne Holyman have established 0.4 hectare of pinot noir and 9.2 hectares of chardonnay at Kings Meadows, only 4 kilometres from the centre of Launceston. Industry veteran Graham Wiltshire acts as winemaker, and the wines are sold by direct contact with the Holymans.

the minya winery NR

Minya Lane, Connewarre, Vic 3227 **region** Geelong
phone (03) 5264 1397 **fax** (03) 5264 1097 **open** Public holidays and by appointment
winemaker Susan Dans **production** 330 **est.** 1974
product range ($14.50–20 CD) Gewurztraminer, Unwooded Chardonnay, Shiraz, Grenache, Cabernet Sauvignon Shiraz Merlot.
summary Geoff Dans first planted vines in 1974 on his family's dairy farm, followed by further plantings in 1982 and 1988. I have not tasted any of the wines.

the silos estate NR

Princes Highway, Jaspers Brush, NSW 2535 **region** Shoalhaven
phone (02) 4448 6082 **fax** (02) 4448 6246 **open** Wed–Sun 10–5
winemaker Gaynor Sims, Kate Khoury **production** 1000 **est.** 1985
product range ($13–18 CD) Traminer Riesling, Semillon, Chardonnay, Sauvignon Blanc, Wileys Creek Brut, Mostly Malbec, Softly Shiraz, Tawny Port, Liqueur Muscat.
summary Since 1995, Gaynor Sims and Kate Khoury, together with viticulturist Jovica Zecevic, have worked hard to improve the quality of the wine, starting with the 5 hectares of estate vineyards but also in the winery. The winery continues to rely on the tourist trade, however, and the wines do not appear in normal retail channels.

the warren vineyard NR

Conte Road, Pemberton, WA 6260 **region** Pemberton
phone (08) 9776 1115 **fax** (08) 9776 1115 **open** 7 days 11–5
winemaker Bernard Abbott **production** 600 **est.** 1985
product range ($15–25 CD) Riesling, Chardonnay, Cabernet Merlot, Cabernet Sauvignon, Cabernet Blanc.
summary The 1.5-hectare vineyard was established in 1985 and is one of the smallest in the Pemberton region, coming to public notice when its 1991 Cabernet Sauvignon won the award for the Best Red Table Wine from the Pemberton Region at the 1992 SGIO Western Australia Winemakers Exhibition.

the willows vineyard ★★★

Light Pass Road, Light Pass, Barossa Valley, SA 5355 **region** Barossa Valley
phone (08) 8562 1080 **fax** (08) 8562 3447 **open** 7 days 10.30–4.30
winemaker Peter Scholz, Michael Scholz **production** 6000 **est.** 1989
product range ($12–22.50 R) Riesling, Semillon, Shiraz, Cabernet Sauvignon.
summary The Scholz family have been grape-growers for generations and have a little over 30 hectares of vineyards, selling part and retaining part of the crop. Current generation winemakers Peter and Michael Scholz could not resist the temptation to make smooth, well-balanced and flavoursome wines under their own label. These are all marketed with some years' bottle age.

the yarrahill ★★★★

10 St Huberts Road, Coldstream, Vic 3770 **region** Yarra Valley
phone (03) 9739 0666 **fax** (03) 9739 0633 **open** 7 days 10–5.30
winemaker Rob Dolan, Kate Goodman **production** 6000 **est.** 1999
product range ($18–23 R) Semillon, Sauvignon Blanc, Chardonnay, Shiraz, Merlot, Cabernet Sauvignon.
summary The YarraHill brings together a syndicate headed by Rob Dolan (as winemaker) and Malcolm Fell (as viticulturist). The venture has been in the pipeline for several years, the wines having been made (under contract) at Yarra Ridge, where Rob Dolan was chief winemaker for a decade. The venture controls three vineyards, the home vineyard of The YarraHill (45 hectares), Napoleone (39 hectares) and Briarty Hill (15 hectares). A new winery has been established on St Huberts Road, which processed the 2001 vintage; the cellar door is part of the same complex.

The YarraHill Merlot

2000 Medium to full red-purple; the bouquet is clean, deep and solid, with red berry and a touch of plum; the palate is clean, fruit-driven, with solid red berry and plum fruit, exuding potential. **rating:** 89
best drinking 2003–2008 **best vintages** '00 **drink with** Pot-roasted lamb rump • NA

The YarraHill Cabernet Sauvignon

2000 Medium to full purple-red; a clean, youthful palate with blackcurrant and a touch of mint; a ripe, sweet, luscious blackberry/currant palate with oak in the background. **rating:** 90
best drinking 2004–2009 **best vintages** '00 **drink with** Kangaroo fillet • $23

thistle hill ★★★☆

McDonalds Road, Mudgee, NSW 2850 **region** Mudgee
phone (02) 6373 3546 **fax** (02) 6373 3540 **open** 7 days 9–5
winemaker David Robertson **production** 4000 **est.** 1976
product range ($13–22 CD) Riesling, Semillon, Chardonnay, Pinot Noir, Cabernet Sauvignon, Muscat.
summary David and Leslie Robertson produce supremely honest wines, always full of flavour and appropriately reflecting the climate and terroir. Some may be a little short on finesse but never on character. Chardonnay and Cabernet Sauvignon lead the way and age well.

Thistle Hill Semillon

1997 Medium to full yellow-green; the bouquet is clean, quite full, and still in its primary citrus/lemon stage of development. The palate is rich, full and generous; unoaked, doesn't cloy, and is a dead-set food style. **rating:** 85
best drinking Now–2005 **best vintages** NA **drink with** Rich fish or chicken dishes • $15

Thistle Hill Cabernet Sauvignon

1997 Medium to full red-purple; the solid bouquet offers ripe, dark berry, chocolate and sweet earth aromas that flow through into the rich, ripe palate with its pleasantly chewy tannins. A sturdy, honest, slightly old-fashioned style which is all the more appealing, and which will obviously repay extended cellaring. **rating:** 88
best drinking 2002–2010 **best vintages** '85, '86, '88, '89, '90, '97 **drink with** Barbecued meat • $19

thomas NR

23–24 Crowd Road, Gelorup, WA 6230 **region** Geographe
phone (08) 9795 7925 **open** By appointment
winemaker Gill Thomas **production** 600 **est.** 1976
product range ($4.50–25 CD) Pinot Noir, Cabernet Sauvignon.
summary I have not tasted the elegant wines of Bunbury pharmacist Gill Thomas for several years; they are only sold to a local clientele.

thornhill/the berry farm NR

Bessel Road, Rosa Glen, WA 6285 **region** Margaret River
phone (08) 9757 5054 **fax** (08) 9757 5116 **open** 7 days 10–4.30
winemaker Eion Lindsay **production** NFP **est.** 1990

product range ($11.50–25 CD) Under the Thornhill label: Classic Dry Semillon, Sauvignon Blanc, Cabernet Sauvignon, Tickled Pink (Sparkling Cabernet Sauvignon), Still Tickled Pink (Light Cabernet Sauvignon). Under The Berry Farm label: a range of fruit-based wines, including Sparkling Strawberry and Plum Port.
summary Although I have not enjoyed the Thornhill table wines, the fruit wines under The Berry Farm label are extraordinarily good. The sparkling strawberry wine has intense strawberry flavour; the plum port likewise, carrying its 16° alcohol with remarkable ease.

three moon creek NR

Waratah Vineyard, Mungungo, via Monto, Qld 4630 **region** South Burnett
phone (07) 3876 9666 **fax** (07) 3876 9311 **open** 7 days 10–5
winemaker Peter Scudamore-Smith (Contract) **production** 500 **est.** 1998
product range ($15–20 CD) Queensland White, Queensland Shiraz Cabernet Sauvignon.
summary David Bray is one of the doyens of wine journalism in Brisbane, and, indeed, Australia. After decades of writing about wine, he and wife Pamela have joined Max Lindsay (Pamela's brother) and partner Lynne Tucker in establishing the Waratah Vineyard and Winery joint venture at Mungungo, near Monto, at the top of the Burnett Valley. The wines are principally sourced from the 4-hectare Waratah Vineyard with 3.2 hectares of vineyard planted to chardonnay, verdelho, semillon, marsanne, viognier, shiraz, merlot and petit verdot, an exotic mix if ever there was one, supplemented by grapes grown at Inglewood and Murgon. The wines are made by the energetic Peter Scudamore-Smith MW.

tilba valley NR

Glen Eden Vineyard, 947 Old Highway, Corunna Lake, NSW 2546 **region** South Coast Zone
phone (02) 4473 7308 **fax** (02) 4476 1693 **open** Mon–Sat 10–5, Sun 11–5
winemaker Barry Field **production** 12 000 **est.** 1978
product range ($15–16.50 CD) Traminer Riesling, Semillon, Semillon Chardonnay, Cabernet Shiraz, Tawny Port.
summary A strongly tourist-oriented operation, serving a ploughman's lunch daily from noon to 2 pm. Has 8 hectares of estate vineyards; no recent tastings.

tim adams ★★★★

Warenda Road, Clare, SA 5453 **region** Clare Valley
phone (08) 8842 2429 **fax** (08) 8842 3550 **open** Mon–Fri 10.30–5, weekends 11–5
winemaker Tim Adams **production** 15 000 **est.** 1986
product range ($14–45 CD) Riesling, Semillon, Botrytis Semillon, Botrytis Reisling, The Fergus (Grenache), Shiraz, Aberfeldy Shiraz, Cabernet.
summary Tim and Pam Adams have built a first-class business since Tim Adams left his position as winemaker at Leasingham in 1985. The 11 hectares of estate vineyards increasingly provide the wine for the business, supplemented by grapes from local growers. Tim Adams has consistently produced wines of exceptional depth of flavour and he also makes significant quantities of wine under contract for others in the district. Extensive distribution through all Australian States; exports to the UK and the US.

Tim Adams Riesling

🍷🍷🍷🍷 **2000** Light to medium yellow-green; in typical style, the bouquet is ripe and powerful, with citrus/lime aromas, the palate firm and minerally, with some citrus and then firm acidity providing grip to the finish. As ever, demands time. **rating:** 86

best drinking 2005–2010 **best vintages** NA **drink with** Seafood salad • NA

Tim Adams Shiraz

🍷🍷🍷🍷 **1999** Medium to full red-purple; a very high-toned and aromatic bouquet with violets and crushed-ant aromas; a similarly powerful if not confrontational palate, with plenty of high-toast American oak adding to the impact. **rating:** 86

best drinking 2004–2009 **best vintages** '86, '88, '90, '92, '93, '96 **drink with** Spit-roasted lamb • NA

Tim Adams Aberfeldy Shiraz

🍷🍷🍷🍷🍷 **1998** Medium to full red-purple; the rich bouquet has dense, ripe dark cherry fruit married with well-handled American oak. The very concentrated, ripe, juicy berry fruit of the palate is girdled by firm yet fine tannins on the finish. An in-your-face style, perhaps, but the quality is there. **rating:** 91

best drinking 2003–2013 **best vintages** '97, '98 **drink with** Char-grilled rump • $45

Tim Adams Cabernet

🍷🍷🍷🍷 **1999** Medium red-purple; the bouquet is strong, with complex cassis and mint aromas, and quite assertive oak. The palate does not have the juicy fruit of the '98 vintage, but has all of the tannin and extract one could wish for. **rating:** 87

best drinking 2004–2009 **best vintages** '86, '88, '90, '92, '94, '98 **drink with** Char-grilled rump steak • NA

tim gramp ★★★☆

Mintaro Road, Watervale, SA 5452 **region** Clare Valley
phone (08) 8431 3338 **fax** (08) 8431 3229 **open** Weekends and holidays 10.30–4.30
winemaker Tim Gramp **production** 5000 **est.** 1990
product range ($16.50–30 R) Watervale Riesling, McLaren Vale Shiraz, Watervale Cabernet Sauvignon.
summary Tim Gramp has quietly built up a very successful business with a limited product range, and – by keeping overheads to a minimum – provides good wines at modest prices. The operation is supported by 2 hectares of cabernet sauvignon around the cellar door. Exports to the UK and the US.

Tim Gramp Watervale Riesling

🍷🍷🍷🍷 **2000** Light to medium straw; the bouquet is unequivocally in the mineral/talc/dusty/slatey spectrum, the palate following down the same track, but has good length and good acidity. An austere style which, were it not for the faintest question mark about that colour, be labelled as a cellaring certainty. **rating:** 85

best drinking Now–2007 **best vintages** '97, '98 **drink with** Bouillabaisse • $15.50

tinderbox vineyard NR

Tinderbox, Tas 7054 **region** Southern Tasmania
phone (03) 6229 2994 **fax** (03) 6229 2994 **open** By appointment
winemaker Andrew Hood (Contract) **production** 175 **est.** 1994
product range ($25 CD) Pinot Noir.
summary Liz McGown is a Hobart nurse who has established her 1-hectare vineyard on the slope beneath her house, overlooking the entrance to the Derwent River and the D'Entrecasteaux Channel. The attractive label was designed by Barry Tucker, who was so charmed by Liz McGown's request that he waived his usual (substantial) fee.

Tinderbox Vineyard Pinot Noir

🍷🍷🍷🍷🍷 **1999** Medium to full purple-red; a complex dark briary/plummy bouquet is followed by a complex and rich palate with plum, spice and briar flavours, the oak in balance. Some judges have seen aldehydes in the wine; I didn't. **rating:** 90

best drinking Now–2006 **best vintages** '99 **drink with** Braised quail • NA

tingle-wood ★★★★

Glenrowan Road, Denmark, WA 6333 **region** Great Southern
phone (08) 9840 9218 **fax** (08) 9840 9218 **open** 7 days 9–5
winemaker Brenden Smith (Contract) **production** 1000 **est.** 1976
product range ($15–30 CD) Yellow Tingle Riesling, Tree Top Walk (late harvest), Red Tingle Cabernet Sauvignon Shiraz, Ruby Tingle (Port-style).
summary An intermittent producer of Riesling of extraordinary quality, although birds and other disasters do intervene and prevent production in some years.

Tingle-Wood Yellow Tingle Riesling

🍷🍷🍷🍷 **2000** Light green-yellow; both the bouquet and palate run through apple, pear, lime and passionfruit, characters that invest the palate with lots of soft fruit flavour balanced by good acidity on the finish. Great to see the wine back again. **rating:** 88

best drinking Now–2008 **best vintages** '90, '91, '00 **drink with** Sashimi, fuller-flavoured fish • $15

tinklers vineyard NR

Pokolbin Mountains Road, Pokolbin, NSW 2330 **region** Lower Hunter Valley
phone (02) 4998 7435 **fax** (02) 4998 7529 **open** 7 days 10–4
winemaker Ian Tinkler **production** 1000 **est.** 1997
product range ($10–20 CD) Semillon, Semillon Verdelho, Verdelho, Chardonnay, Volcanic Ash (sweet white), Merlot, Shiraz, Cabernet Sauvignon, Muscat.
summary Ian and Usher Tinkler own a large (32-hectare) vineyard on the slopes of the Pokolbin Mountain Road; most of the production is sold, a small amount being contract-made for cellar-door sales.

tinlins NR

Kangarilla Road, McLaren Flat, SA 5171 **region** McLaren Vale
phone (08) 8323 8649 **fax** (08) 8323 9747 **open** 7 days 9–5
winemaker Warren Randall **production** 30 000 **est.** 1977
product range ($1.50–3.40 CD) Generic table, fortified and flavoured wines sold for $1.50 for table wines and $3.40 for fortified wines.
summary A very interesting operation run by former Seppelt sparkling winemaker Warren Randall, drawing upon 100 hectares of estate vineyards; specialises in bulk-wine sales to the major Australian wine companies. A small proportion of the production is sold direct through the cellar door at mouthwateringly low prices to customers who provide their own containers and purchase by the litre. McLaren Vale's only bulk-wine specialist.

tinonee vineyard NR

Milbrodale Road, Broke, NSW 2330 **region** Lower Hunter Valley
phone (02) 6579 1308 **fax** (02) 6579 1146 **open** Weekends and public holidays 11–4
winemaker Andrew Margan, Ray Merger (Contract) **production** 1000 **est.** 1997
product range ($15–18 CD) Chardonnay, Chardonnay Semillon, Verdelho, Merlot, Shiraz.
summary Ian Craig has established 14 hectares of vineyards on a mix of red volcanic and river-flat soils at Broke. Part are in production, with the remainder coming into bearing last decade, ultimately producing 5000 cases of wine per year.

tintilla wines NR

725 Hermitage Road, Pokolbin, NSW 2335 **region** Lower Hunter Valley
phone 0411 214 478 **fax** (02) 9767 6894 **open** By appointment
winemaker Jon Reynolds (Contract) **production** 3000 **est.** 1993
product range ($15–30 CD) Semillon, Sangiovese, Sangiovese Merlot, Shiraz, Reserve Shiraz, Merlot.
summary The Lusby family has established a 7.5-hectare vineyard (including 1 hectare of sangiovese) on their northeast-facing vineyard, with its red clay and limestone soil. They have also established an olive grove producing four different types of olive, which are cured and sold on the estate.

tipperary hill estate NR

Alma–Bowendale Road, Alma, via Maryborough, Vic 3465 **region** Bendigo
phone (03) 5461 3312 **fax** (03) 5461 3312 **open** Weekends 10–5 or by appointment
winemaker Paul Flowers **production** 300 **est.** 1986
product range ($16–24 CD) Shiraz, Pinot Noir, Cabernets.
summary All of the wine is sold through the cellar door and on site restaurant, open on Sundays. Production depends 'on the frost, wind and birds' says Paul Flowers, which perhaps explains why this is very much a part-time venture. Situated 7 kilometres west of the city of Maryborough, Tipperary Hill Estate is the only winery operating in the Central Goldfields Shire. Winemaker Paul Flowers built the rough-cut pine winery and the bluestone residential cottage next-door with the help of friends. Together with wife Margaret he also operates a restaurant.

tizzana winery ★★☆

518 Tizzana Road, Ebenezer, NSW 2756 **region** South Coast Zone
phone (02) 4579 1150 **fax** (02) 4579 1216 **open** Weekends, holidays 12–6, other times by appointment
winemaker Peter Auld **production** 300 **est.** 1887

product range ($11.50–17 CD) From Tizzana vineyards Rosso di Tizzana (a light, dry Cabernet Sauvignon), Waterloo Shiraz, Sackville Tawny, Vintage Port, Old Liqueur Sweet White and Mrs Fiaschi's Old Sweet Red; the Tizzana Selection from other regions of Traminer Riesling, White Port, Sherry (the latter two from Stanton & Killeen) and then two wines from South Australia under the Hawkesbury History Heritage 2001 Committee (a strange combination), including Federation Semillon Chardonnay and Federation Tawny Port.
summary Tizzana has been a weekend and holiday occupation for Peter Auld for many years now, operating in one of the great historic wineries built (in 1887) by Australia's true renaissance man, Dr Thomas Fiaschi. The wines may not be great, but the ambience is.

tollana ★★★★

Tanunda Road, Nuriootpa, SA 5355 **region** Barossa Valley
phone (08) 8560 9408 **fax** (08) 8562 2494 **open** Mon–Sat 10–5, Sun 1–5
winemaker Neville Falkenberg (Previous) **production** 30 000 **est.** 1888
product range ($12–29 R) Bay F2 Reserve Eden Valley Riesling, Eden Valley Riesling, Adelaide Hills Sauvignon Blanc, Eden Valley Chardonnay, Eden Valley Adelaide Hills Chardonnay, Coonawarra Botrytis Riesling, Hermitage, Shiraz Bin TR16, Show Reserve Shiraz, Eden Valley Shiraz, Cabernet Sauvignon Bin TR222.
summary As the Southcorp Wine Group moves to establish regional identity for its wines, Tollana is emphasising its Eden Valley base. Seemingly as a by-product of Penfolds' development ofYattarna and related wines, the Tollana Chardonnay style has become more elegant, now standing comfortably alongside the flavoursome Riesling and Shiraz. However, the Rosemount merger suggests one should watch this space.

Tollana Bay F2 Reserve Eden Valley Riesling

1994 Medium yellow-green; a complex, toasty, bottle-developed bouquet with a mix of honey, toast and solidly sweet lime leads into a powerfully constructed, rich palate with a mix of honey, toast and lime. My initial take on this wine halfway through was, quite simply, wrong. **rating:** 93
best drinking Now–2006 **best vintages** '94 **drink with** Rich fish dishes • $29

Tollana Eden Valley Riesling

2000 Light to medium yellow-green; a full bouquet, with abundant lime fruit the first impression, and undertones of herb and mineral; a very powerful wine, with considerable persistence and body in an uncompromising food style. **rating:** 89
best drinking Now–2006 **best vintages** '86, '87, '90, '92, '93, '97 **drink with** Seafood salad • $12

Tollana Bin TR16 Shiraz

1998 Medium red-purple; firm, dark berry fruit and a generous but not daunting dollop of oak on the bouquet are followed by a palate that has even more richness and sweetness, with attractive cherry/berry fruit and nice, fine tannins. Controlled oak another plus. **rating:** 88
best drinking Now–2008 **best vintages** NA **drink with** Lamb Provençale • $19

tom's waterhole wines NR

Felton, Longs Corner Road, Canowindra, NSW 2804 **region** Cowra
phone (02) 6344 1819 **fax** (02) 6344 2172 **open** Weekends 10–5
winemaker Graham Kerr **production** 500 **est.** 1997
product range ($10–12 ML) Semillon, Chardonnay, Vat 7 Shiraz.
summary Graham Timms and Graham Kerr started the development of Tom's Waterhole Wines in 1997, progressively establishing 2 hectares of shiraz and 2 hectares each of cabernet sauvignon and semillon, the planting programme completed in 2000. A decision has been taken to bypass the use of irrigation, and the yields will be low, with an expectation that the small on-site winery will crush around 20 tonnes per year.

toorak estate NR

Toorak Road, Leeton, NSW 2705 **region** Riverina
phone (02) 6953 2333 **fax** (02) 6953 4454 **open** Mon–Sat 9–5
winemaker Robert Bruno **production** 30 000 **est.** 1965
product range ($4–32 CD) Willandra Leeton Selection range of Traminer Riesling, Semillon Chardonnay, Shiraz, Soft Shiraz, Cabernet Shiraz, Cabernet Merlot; Willandra Estate range of Semillon, Chardonnay, Botrytis Semillon, Shiraz, Cabernet Sauvignon, Muscat of Alexandria; Toorak Varietal range of Traminer Riesling,

Semillon Chardonnay; Amesbury Estate range of Classic Dry White, Semillon Sauvignon Blanc, Classic Dry Red, Grenache Shiraz; Frank Bruno Red Lambrusco; Sparkling; Fortifieds.
summary A traditional, long-established Riverina producer with a strong Italian-based clientele around Australia. Production has been increasing significantly, utilising 80 hectares of estate plantings and grapes purchased from other growers.

torbreck vintners ★★★★★

Roennfeldt Road, Marananga, SA 5352 **region** Barossa Valley
phone (08) 8562 4155 **fax** (08) 8562 4195 **open** Not
winemaker David Powell **production** 7000 **est.** 1994
product range ($29.25–107.50 ML) Marsanne Viognier Rousanne, The Steading (Grenache Shiraz), RunRig (Shiraz Viognier,) Juveniles (Grenache, Mataro, Shiraz), Descendant (Shiraz Viognier), The Factor (Shiraz).
summary Torbreck has made a major impact since its first releases in 1997 of a 1995 RunRig and 1996 The Steading. David Powell's family has assembled small patches of old-vine shiraz, grenache and mourvedre in the Barossa Valley, which they are sharefarming, complementing a small vineyard of their own. Each succeeding vintage has added to an extraordinary cult following for the wines, the flames fanned by fulsome praise from Robert Parker and bottles sold at auction in New York for $US1000 each. Powell, however, is keeping a level head, knowing this fever will abate sooner or later. The wines are also exported to Germany, Switzerland, New Zealand and Singapore.

Torbreck The Factor

YYYYY **1998** Deep, intense red-purple, yet still bright; the bouquet offers a powerful mix of dark cherry and plum fruit together with a gentle touch of vanilla oak. A massive, mouthfilling wine with concentrated black cherry, plum, spice, leather and vanilla flavours complexed by moderately full tannins. **rating:** 94
best drinking 2005–2015 **best vintages** '98 **drink with** Braised ox cheek • $55

Torbreck The Descendant

YYYY **1999** Striking, deep purple-red; the bouquet is distinctly gamey and very complex, with a core of dark berry fruits. The powerful palate is even more tannic than the RunRig (at least in relation to its fruit depth, and requires equal patience). **rating:** 88
best drinking 2007–2014 **best vintages** NA **drink with** Leave it in the cellar • $55

Torbreck The Juveniles

YYYY **2000** Medium purple-red; the bouquet is clean, quite fresh and spicy, with some gamey varietal character, a character that is often (incorrectly) attributed to brettanomyces. Sweet, soft berry fruit and ripe tannins run through the palate which inevitably shows the absence of oak maturation, but overall works well enough. **rating:** 85
best drinking Now–2005 **best vintages** NA **drink with** Rich pasta • $29.25

Torbreck The RunRig

YYYYY **1998** Dense red-purple; a clean and rich bouquet oozes blackberry, black cherry fruit and spice, foreshadowing a massively concentrated and quite tannic palate, laden with black fruits. Leave for ten years at least, and rated in part as an article of faith. **rating:** 95
YYYYY **1997** Dense red-purple; a powerful wine with black fruits and abundant oak on the bouquet. The concentrated and youthful palate has an array of dark cherry, redcurrant and minty fruit flavours; these flavours and the oak are still coming together. **rating:** 92
best drinking 2008–2018 **best vintages** '96, '97, '98 **drink with** Game • $107.50

Torbreck The Steading

YYYYY **1999** Medium to full red-purple; the potent, voluminous dark berry, leather, spice and blackberry aromas of the bouquet lead into a rich, mouthfilling wine on the palate, with very ripe (14.5°) fruit nicely offset with gently chewy tannins and subtle oak. **rating:** 92
best drinking 2003–2009 **best vintages** '97, '98, '99 **drink with** Lamb Provençale • $32.50

tower estate

Cnr Broke and Hall Roads, Pokolbin, NSW 2320 **region** Lower Hunter Valley
phone (02) 4998 7989 **fax** (02) 4998 7919 **open** 7 days 10–5
winemaker Dan Dineen **production** 8000 **est.** 1999

product range ($19–35 CD) Clare Valley Riesling, Hunter Valley Semillon, Adelaide Hills Sauvignon Blanc, Hunter Valley Verdelho, Hunter Valley Chardonnay, Hunter Valley Shiraz, Barossa Valley Shiraz, Muscat.
summary Tower Estate is a joint venture headed by Len Evans, featuring a luxury conference centre and accommodation. It draws upon varieties and regions that have a particular synergy, coupled with the enormous knowledge of Len Evans and the winemaking skills of Dan Dineen.

Tower Estate Clare Riesling

YYYY **2000** Medium to full yellow-green, showing considerable development; a very powerful, potent bouquet, an essence of the 2000 vintage character, is followed by a full, rich palate which, unsurprisingly, lacks the finesse of the '99. Very much the product of a highly stressed, low-yielding vintage. 874 cases made. **rating:** 86
best drinking Now–2003 **best vintages** '99 **drink with** Antipasto • $22

Tower Estate Hunter Valley Semillon

YYYYY **2000** Light to medium yellow-green; a heady bouquet with lemon zest, citrus, herb and mineral aromas is followed by a bright, fresh, well-balanced but generously flavoured palate. A riper style than 1999, but should develop well over the long term. 1000 cases made. **rating:** 90
best drinking 2005–2015 **best vintages** '99, '00 **drink with** Fine seafood • $22

Tower Estate Adelaide Hills Sauvignon Blanc

YYYYY **2000** Medium yellow-green; the bouquet is clean and quite firm, at the mineral/herbaceous end of the spectrum, although there are hints of sweetness. Those hints appear on the palate, where there is sweet gooseberry fruit as well as the herbal components; stylish but restrained. **rating:** 90
best drinking Now **best vintages** '99 **drink with** Pan-fried calamari • $26

Tower Estate Barossa Shiraz

YYYYY **1999** Medium to full red-purple; the bouquet is elegant, with spice and leaf overtones to the berry fruit; positive oak. The palate is fresh, with a very interesting texture and flavour, utterly belying its 14.5° alcohol; excellent oak and tannin management. **rating:** 91
best drinking 2003–2013 **best vintages** '99 **drink with** Barbecued rump steak • $35

Tower Estate Hunter Valley Shiraz

YYYYY **1999** Medium to full red-purple; dark berry fruit, sweet earth and chocolate aromas are followed by a powerful wine, with concentrated fruit on the mid-palate; very different in structure from the Barossa Shiraz, but of equal quality. **rating:** 91
best drinking 2004–2010 **best vintages** '99 **drink with** Rare roast beef • $28

trafford hill vineyard NR

Lot 1 Bower Road, Normanville, SA 5204 **region** Fleurieu Zone
phone (08) 8558 3595 **open** Thurs–Mon and holidays 10.30–5
winemaker John Sanderson, Allan Dyson (Consultant) **production** 350 **est.** 1996
product range ($5.50–19 ML) Riesling, Isabella Family Reserve Blend, Tawny Port, Parsons Ghost Liqueur Tawny Port.
summary Irene and John Sanderson have established 2 hectares of vineyard at Normanville, on the coast of the Fleurieu Peninsula near to its southern extremity. Irene carries out all the viticulture, and John Sanderson makes the wine with help from district veteran Allan Dyson. Distribution is through local restaurants, the remainder through mail order and cellar door.

tranquil vale NR

325 Pywells Road, Luskintyre, NSW 2321 **region** Lower Hunter Valley
phone (02) 4930 6100 **fax** (02) 4930 6105 **open** Fri–Mon 10–4 or by appointment
winemaker Andrew Margan, David Hook **production** 2250 **est.** 1998
product range ($16–20 ML) Semillon, Chardonnay, Shiraz, Cabernet Shiraz.
summary Phil and Lucy Griffiths purchased the property site-unseen from a description in an old copy of the *Australian Weekend* found in the High Commission Office in London. The vineyard they established is situated on the banks of the Hunter River, opposite Wyndham Estate, on relatively fertile, sandy, clay loam. Irrigation has been installed, and what is known as VSP trellising. Within the blink of an eye, they have become experts, and find themselves 'in the amusing position that people ask us our opinion!' The three luxury, self-contained cottages on

site offer the extras of a swimming pool, tennis court, gymnasium, etc. and sleep a family or two couples each. Finally, competent contract-winemaking has resulted in the production of good wines, some of which have already had show success. The 2000 Semillon (83 points) is a ripe, early-developing style, the 2000 Shiraz (85 points) is impressively rich and powerful, but really needed more barrel work to bring out its full potential.

treehouse vineyard & wine centre ★★★★

257 Richmond Road, Cambridge, Tas 7170 **region** Southern Tasmania
phone (03) 6248 5367 **fax** (03) 6248 4175 **open** Wed–Sun 12–5
winemaker Andrew Hood (Contract) **production** 500 **est.** 1991
product range ($17–23 CD) Riesling, Chardonnay, Pinot Noir, Cabernet Merlot.
summary Gradon and Margaret Johnstone established Treehouse in 1991 with the planting of their first grapes. Restaurant meals and casual food are available at the Treehouse Wine Centre, and all of the wines are sold through the cellar door and by mail order. Treehouse was purchased by Gillian Christian and her husband Todd Goebel in 1999.

treen ridge estate NR

Packer Road, Pemberton, WA 6260 **region** Pemberton
phone (08) 9776 1131 **fax** (08) 9776 0442 **open** Wed–Fri 11–5, weekends 10–5
winemaker Andrew Mountford (Contract) **production** 600 **est.** 1992
product range ($15–25 CD) Riesling, Sauvignon Blanc, Springfield Shiraz, Shiraz, Sparkling Shiraz.
summary The Treen Ridge vineyard and three-room accommodation is set between the Treen Brook State Forest and The Warren National Park and is operated by Mollie and Barry Scotman.

treeton estate 

North Treeton Road, Cowaramup, WA 6284 **region** Margaret River
phone (08) 9755 5481 **fax** (08) 9755 5051 **open** 7 days 10–6
winemaker David McGowan **production** 3000 **est.** 1984
product range ($15–17 R) Chardonnay, Riesling, Estate White, Petit Rouge, Shiraz, Liqueur Muscat.
summary In 1982 David McGowan and wife Corinne purchased the 30-hectare property upon which Treeton Estate is established, beginning to plant the vines two years later. David has done just about everything in his life, and in the early years was working in Perth, which led to various setbacks for the vineyard. The wines are light and fresh, sometimes rather too much so.

trentham estate ★★★☆

Sturt Highway, Trentham Cliffs, NSW 2738 **region** Murray Darling
phone (03) 5024 8888 **fax** (03) 5024 8800 **open** Mon–Fri 8.30–5, weekends 9.30–5
winemaker Anthony Murphy, Shane Kerr **production** 45 000 **est.** 1988
product range ($8.50–18 R) Riesling, Murphy's Lore Semillon Chardonnay, Sauvignon Blanc, Viognier, Chardonnay, Spätlese Lexia, Noble Taminga, Autumn Red, Sparkling Ruby, Pinot Noir, Merlot, Shiraz, Murphy's Lore Shiraz Cabernet, Ruby Cabernet, Cabernet Sauvignon Merlot, Vintage Port, Burke & Wills Tawny Port.
summary Remarkably consistent tasting notes across all wine styles from all vintages since 1989 attest to the expertise of ex-Mildara winemaker Tony Murphy, now making the Trentham wines from his family vineyards. Indeed, Trentham seems to be going from strength to strength with each succeeding vintage. The winery restaurant is also recommended. National retail distribution; exports to the US, Canada, Asia and Europe.

Trentham Estate Viognier

YYYY **2000** Medium yellow-green; soft, ripe, gently peachy fruit on both bouquet and palate provides a very pleasant wine, with some velvety texture to the mouthfeel, finishing with soft acidity. Won a gold medal at the 2000 Melbourne Wine Show, and a silver medal in Adelaide. **rating:** 86

best drinking Now **best vintages** NA **drink with** Creamy pasta • $18

Trentham Estate Chardonnay

YYYY **1999** Glowing green-yellow; the bouquet is unexpectedly complex, with soft nectarine and melon fruit supported by subtle French oak. That nectarine fruit comes through on the medium-bodied palate, which has above-average balance and length. A bargain at the price. **rating:** 86

best drinking Now **best vintages** '89, '90, '92, '95, '98, '99 **drink with** Stir-fried abalone • $14

Trentham Estate Noble Taminga

YYYY **1999** Deep gold; soft, tropical spice, peach and apricot aromas lead into a ripe palate with spicy fruit vaguely reminiscent of late harvest traminer. **rating:** 87

best drinking Now **best vintages** NA **drink with** Fruit flan • $10

trevelen farm ★★★★

Weir Road, Cranbrook, WA 6321 **region** Great Southern
phone (08) 9826 1052 **fax** (08) 9826 1209 **open** Thur–Mon 10–4.30 or by appointment
winemaker Michael Staniford (Contract) **production** 3000 **est.** 1993
product range ($14–17 CD) Riesling, Sauvignon Blanc, Chardonnay, Cabernet Merlot.

summary John and Katie Sprigg, together with their family, operate a 1300-hectare wool, meat and grain-producing farm, run on environmental principles with sustainable agriculture at its heart. As a minor, but highly successful, diversification they established 5 hectares of sauvignon blanc, riesling, chardonnay, cabernet sauvignon and merlot in 1993, adding 1.5 hectares of shiraz in 2000. Vines, it seems, are in the genes, for John Sprigg's great-great-grandparents established 20 hectares of vines at Happy Valley, South Australia, in the 1870s. The quality of the wines is as consistent as the prices are modest, and visitors to the cellar door have the added attraction of both garden and forest walks, the latter among 130 hectares of remnant bush that harbours many different orchids which flower from May to December.

Trevelen Farm Riesling

YYYYY **2000** Light straw-green, slightly suspect; the bouquet is very spicy, with some herb, slate and citrus, the wine having moderate length only. Was strongly supported by one or two judges at the Riesling Challenge, but not by others. Possibly some random oxidation problems here. **rating:** 90

best drinking Now–2006 **best vintages** NA **drink with** Fresh asparagus • NA

Trevelen Farm Sauvignon Blanc

YYYYY **2000** Pale green-yellow; the bouquet is highly aromatic, with a potent mix of passionfruit, herb and lime. The medium-bodied palate has fine varietal definition in a gently sweet tropical/passionfruit mode, and has good balance. **rating:** 94

best drinking Now **best vintages** '00 **drink with** Smoked eel • NA

trevor jones ★★★★

Barossa Valley Highway, Lyndoch, SA 5351 **region** Barossa Valley
phone (08) 8524 4303 **fax** (08) 8524 4880 **open** 7 days 9–6
winemaker Trevor Jones **production** 2000 **est.** 1996
product range ($15–36.50 CD) Riesling, Virgin Chardonnay, Dry Grown Shiraz, Cabernet Merlot.

summary Trevor Jones is an industry veteran, with vast experience in handling fruit from the Barossa Valley, Eden Valley and Adelaide Hills. He has finally taken the step of introducing his own strikingly designed label, using grapes purchased from various contract growers, with the first wines going on sale in 1996. Exports to the US and Japan.

Trevor Jones Dry Grown Shiraz

YYYY **1996** Medium red-purple; the bouquet has pleasant bottle-developed earth and spice aromas with some residual berry fruit. The medium-bodied palate has attractive sweet berry fruit and chocolate, sustained by fine tannins. Minimal input from new oak. **rating:** 89

best drinking Now–2006 **best vintages** '95, '96 **drink with** Beef Wellington • $36.50

Trevor Jones Cabernet Merlot

YYYY **1995** Medium red; strong French oak sits on top of dark berry fruit on the bouquet, but rich, sweet fruit comes through on the palate, married with the oak and supported by soft, fine tannins. All in all, a pretty nice wine. **rating:** 88

best drinking Now–2005 **best vintages** '94 **drink with** Osso bucco • $32

tuck's ridge ★★★★

37 Shoreham Road, Red Hill South, Vic 3937 **region** Mornington Peninsula
phone (03) 5989 8660 **fax** (03) 5989 8579 **open** 7 days 12–5
winemaker Daniel Greene **production** 12 000 **est.** 1988

product range ($14–45 CD) Riesling, Chardonnay, Pinot Noir, Altera Pinot Noir, Callanans Road Pinot Noir, A Trial Selection Pinot Noir, Reserve Pinot Noir, Merlot.
summary After an initial burst of frenetic activity following its launch in July 1993, Tuck's Ridge has slowed down a little. Nonetheless, plantings have been increased to a little over 25 hectares, making it one of the largest vineyards in production on the Mornington Peninsula, with wine quality to match.

Tuck's Ridge A Trial Selection Pinot Noir

YYYY **1998** Medium red-purple; the bouquet is of light to medium intensity; the range of spicy/leafy/sappy/savoury aromas flow into a palate that lacks mid-palate flesh and structure, but has bell-clear varietal character. **rating:** 85

best drinking Now **best vintages** NA **drink with** Pastrami • $35

Tuck's Ridge Callanans Road Pinot Noir

YYYY **2000** Strong red-purple; the bouquet has full, dark plum fruit and some spice, the palate with soft, sweet plummy fruit, not particularly long, but with a silky-soft feel. Great present drinking. **rating:** 87

best drinking Now **best vintages** NA **drink with** Guinea fowl or pheasant • NA

tulloch ★★★☆

'Glen Elgin', De Beyers Road, Pokolbin, NSW 2321 **region** Lower Hunter Valley
phone (02) 4998 7503 **fax** (02) 4998 7682 **open** Mon–Fri 9–4.30, weekends and public holidays 10–4.30
winemaker Greg Jarratt, Briony Seaton **production** 20 000 **est.** 1895
product range ($12–16 R) Unoaked Chardonnay, Classic Hunter White, Semillon Chardonnay, Verdelho, Justina (Fruity White), Cuvée Brut, Classic Rich Red, Cabernets, Hector of Glen Elgin (Hermitage), Fortifieds.
summary A once-great name and reputation that suffered enormously under multiple ownership changes with a loss of identity and direction. In production terms at least, it has found its feet, for it is now the centre of winemaking activities in the Hunter Valley for the Lindemans, Hungerford Hill and Tulloch brands, the last suckling at the breast of the Verdelho, and doing very nicely. How long this state of affairs will continue in the wake of the Southcorp/Rosemount merger remains to be seen.

Tulloch Verdelho

YYYY **2000** Light green-yellow; the clean and fresh bouquet offers a mix of moderately intense fruit-salad and mineral aromas, the fresh and lively fruit carrying through the palate in gentle but pleasing fashion. Good varietal character. Won a gold medal at Brisbane 2000. **rating:** 85

best drinking Now **best vintages** NA **drink with** Asian, pasta or white meat dishes • $12

tumbarumba wine cellars NR

Sunnyside, Albury Close, Tumbarumba, NSW 2653 **region** Tumbarumba
phone (02) 6948 3055 **fax** (02) 6948 3055 **open** Weekends and public holidays or by appointment
winemaker Charles Sturt University (Contract) **production** 600 **est.** 1990
product range ($15–25) Chardonnay, Pinot Noir and Pinot Chardonnay sparkling wines under the Black Range label, with further individual labels likely for the future.
summary Tumbarumba Cellars has taken over the former George Martins Winery (itself established in 1990) to provide an outlet for wines made from Tumbarumba-region grapes. It is essentially a co-operative venture, involving local growers and businessmen, and with modest aspirations to growth.

tumbarumba wine estates NR

Maragle Valley, via Tumbarumba, NSW 2653 **region** Tumbarumba
phone (02) 6948 4457 **fax** (02) 6948 4457 **open** Not
winemaker Charles Sturt University (Contract) **production** NA **est.** 1995
product range Chardonnay, Pinot Chardonnay Sparkling.
summary Having established his vineyards progressively since 1982, Frank Minutello decided to seek to add value (and interest) to the enterprise by having a small proportion of his production vinified at Charles Sturt University, commencing with the 1995 vintage. The wines are sold by mail order and from The Elms Restaurant in Tumbarumba.

turkey flat ★★★★☆

Bethany Road, Tanunda, SA 5352 **region** Barossa Valley
phone (08) 8563 2851 **fax** (08) 8563 3610 **open** 7 days 11–5
winemaker Peter Schell **production** 12 000 **est.** 1990
product range ($11.99–42 R) Semillon, Rosé, Grenache Noir, Butchers Block, Shiraz, Cabernet Sauvignon.
summary The establishment date of Turkey Flat is given as 1990 but it might equally well have been 1870 (or thereabouts), when the Schulz family purchased the Turkey Flat vineyard, or 1847, when the vineyard was first planted to the very shiraz that still grows today. In addition there are 8 hectares of very old grenache and 8 hectares of much younger semillon and cabernet sauvignon, together with a total of 7.3 hectares of mourvedre, dolcetto and (a recent arrival) marsanne. An on-site winery completed just prior to the 2001 vintage will give Turkey Flat even greater control over its wine production. Retail distribution in Adelaide, Melbourne and Sydney; exports to the US, the UK, Belgium and Switzerland.

Turkey Flat Semillon

YYYY **1999** Medium yellow-green; the toasty bouquet has touches of honey and citrus, the palate with a corresponding mix of toast and grass flavours. Quite rich, but almost inevitably doesn't have the finesse required for ageing. **rating:** 85
best drinking Now **best vintages** NA **drink with** Pasta • $19

Turkey Flat Rosé

YYYYY **2000** Vivid fuschia-purple; the bouquet has strong cherry and plum fruit, the palate with soft, smooth, sweet cherry fruit and gentle acidity. **rating:** 90
best drinking Now **best vintages** '99, '00 **drink with** Nothing or anything • $19

Turkey Flat Butchers Block

YYYY **1998** Light to medium red-purple; a light but fragrant mix of earth, cinnamon spice and strawberry aromas is followed by a palate with a slightly curious light-bodied style that nonetheless comes from very old grenache vines. I readily accept that others will regard my points as miserable. **rating:** 87
best drinking Now–2005 **best vintages** NA **drink with** Mushroom risotto • $30

Turkey Flat Grenache Noir

YYYY **1999** Medium purple-red; clean, but lacks the intensity of the very best examples; the palate comes through with pleasant fruit, but, consistently with the bouquet, is just a fraction simple. **rating:** 86
best drinking Now–2005 **best vintages** '91, '92, '93, '96, '98 **drink with** Maggie Beer's game pie • $25

turramurra estate ★★★★

RMB 4327 Wallaces Road, Dromana Vic 3926 **region** Mornington Peninsula
phone (03) 5987 1146 **fax** (03) 5987 1286 **open** 12–5 first weekend of the month or by appointment
winemaker David Leslie **production** 7000 **est.** 1989
product range ($26–40 CD) Sauvignon Blanc, Chardonnay, Pinot Noir, Shiraz, Cabernet Sauvignon.
summary Dr David Leslie gave up his job as a medical practitioner after completing the Bachelor of Applied Science (Wine Science) at Charles Sturt University to concentrate on developing the family's 10-hectare estate at Dromana. Wife Paula is the viticulturist. Limited retail distribution in Melbourne and Sydney; exports to the UK.

Turramurra Estate Chardonnay

YYYY **1999** Medium yellow-green; a complex bouquet offering cashew, melon, vanilla and toffee flows into a palate with soft, filigreed texture, wandering through cashew, cream and melon in typical Mornington Peninsula style. **rating:** 88
best drinking Now–2005 **best vintages** NA **drink with** Brains in black butter sauce • $29

12 acres 

Nagambie–Rushworth Road, Bailieston, Vic 3608 **region** Goulburn Valley
phone (03) 5794 2020 **fax** (03) 5794 2020 **open** Thurs–Mon 10–6, July weekends only
winemaker Peter Prygodicz, Jana Prygodicz **production** 700 **est.** 1994
product range ($16 CD) Shiraz, Merlot, Grenache, Cabernet Sauvignon.

summary The charmingly named 12 Acres is a red wine specialist, with Peter and Jana Prygodicz making the wines on site in a tiny set-up. The wines could benefit from renewal of the oak in which they are matured, but the underlying fruit is good.

12 Acres Shiraz

ŸŸŸ▽ **1997** Medium red, with some tawny on the rim; a mix of earthy/foresty/briary aromas on the one side, and sweet berry and chocolate on the other, leads into a smooth, bottle-developed palate with earthy/berry flavours and soft oak. A nice wine at the price. **rating:** 83

best drinking 2002–2007 **best vintages** NA **drink with** Rack of lamb • $16

twin bays NR

Lot 1 Martin Road, Yankalilla, SA 5203 **region** Fleurieu Zone
phone (08) 8267 2844 **fax** (08) 8239 0877 **open** Weekends and holidays
winemaker Bruno Giorgio, Alan Dyson **production** 1000 **est.** 1989
product range ($10.50–21 CD) Riesling, Aged Riesling, Rosado, Wild Grenache, Shiraz, Cabernet Sauvignon, Fortifieds.

summary Twin Bays operates the first winery in the Yankalilla district, one hour's drive south of Adelaide on the Fleurieu Peninsula. Two hectares of estate plantings have been established, but until these and future plantings come into bearing, the wines are being made by district veteran Alan Dyson and Adelaide doctor and specialist Bruno Giorgio from grapes partly estate-grown and partly purchased from McLaren Vale. Retail distribution in Sydney, Melbourne and Adelaide.

Twin Bays Fleurieu Wild Grenache

ŸŸŸŸ **1999** Medium red-purple; the quite fragrant and lively bouquet of spice, leaf and berry leads into a light, pleasant and cheerful early-drinking style with nice fruit. **rating:** 85

best drinking Now–2003 **best vintages** NA **drink with** Meat-based pasta • $18

twin valley estate NR

Hoffnungsthal Road, Lyndoch, SA 5351 **region** Barossa Valley
phone (08) 8524 4584 **fax** (08) 8524 4978 **open** Weekends 10–5
winemaker Fernando Martin, Kay Martin **production** 3500 **est.** 1990
product range ($9–18 CD) Traminer, Frontignac Spätlese, Eden Valley Rhine Riesling, Semillon Chardonnay, Cabernet Sauvignon Franc, Classic Burgundy, Pinot Cabernet, White Port, Martin's Mead.

summary While Fernando Martin has always had his sights set firmly on the tourist trade, the Twin Valley Estate wines are more than acceptable; the spicy, limey Frontignac Spätlese is a particularly good example of its kind.

2 bud spur NR

Postal address: Unit 2, 8 Binney Court, Sandy Bay, Tas 7005 **region** Southern Tasmania
phone (03) 6225 0711 **fax** (03) 6233 3477 **open** Not
winemaker Michael Vishacki **production** 300 **est.** 1996
product range ($20 ML) Sauvignon Blanc, Chardonnay, Pinot Noir.

summary Phil Barker and Anne Lasala commenced establishing 2.2 hectares of vineyard in 1996. Phil Barker has the most extraordinary qualifications, having worked as a chef for over ten years after acquiring a PhD in botany, and is now a botanist with the Tasmanian Parks and Wildlife Department. There is still much agonising about the name; originally called Latitude, it has now become 2 Bud Spur, a term viticulturists are very familiar with, but which will completely confuse the average wine drinker.

tyrrell's ★★★★★

Broke Road, Pokolbin, NSW 2321 **region** Lower Hunter Valley
phone (02) 4993 7000 **fax** (02) 4998 7723 **open** Mon–Sat 8–5
winemaker Andrew Spinaze, Mark Richardson **production** 850 000 **est.** 1858
product range ($7–50 R) At the bottom end the large-volume Long Flat White, Chardonnay and Red; next in price is Traditional Range of Traminer Riesling, Twin Wells Chardonnay, Blanquette, Shiraz Cabernet, Twin Wells Shiraz Cabernet; then Old Winery Semillon, Chardonnay, Chardonnay Semillon, Sauvignon Blanc Semillon,

Verdelho, Pinot Noir, Shiraz, Cabernet Merlot; Rufus Stone Shiraz; next the Individual Vineyard range of wines including Stevens Semillon, Lost Block Semillon, Shee-Oak Chardonnay, Moon Mountain Chardonnay, Eclipse Pinot Noir, Brokenback Shiraz, Stevens Shiraz; at the very top Vat 1 Semillon, Vat 91 Chardonnay, Vat 8 Shiraz Cabernet, Vat 9 Shiraz, Vat 47 Pinot Chardonnay. Also Sparklings, Fortifieds.

summary A quite extraordinary family winery that has grown up from an insignificant base in 1960 to become one of the most influential mid-sized companies, successfully competing with wines running all the way from cheap, volume-driven Long Flat White up to the super-premium Vat 47 Chardonnay, which is one of Australia's best. There is a similar range of price and style with the red wines, and in recent years Tyrrell's has simply never faltered within the parameters of price and style. Exports to all of the major markets throughout North America, Europe and Southeast Asia.

Tyrrell's Lost Block Semillon

YYYYY 2000 Bright, light green-yellow; the bouquet has intense and precise varietal character, with excellent lemon/citrus fruit. The palate has remarkable power, intensity, depth and length, but looks as if it will be a relatively early-developing wine. Gold medal Brisbane 2000. **rating:** 94

best drinking Now–2006 **best vintages** '93, '94, '96, '97, '99, '00 **drink with** Calamari • $20

Tyrrell's Stevens Reserve Semillon

YYYYY **1997** Glowing light to medium yellow-green; a very complex, toasty bouquet which, if tasted blind, would leave you in no doubt that some barrel fermentation was involved. In fact there is none. The palate is still very tight and focused, with intense citrus and lemon flavours, lingering acidity, and a long finish. **rating:** 93

best drinking 2002–2010 **best vintages** '96, '97 **drink with** Balmain bugs • $25

Tyrrell's Moon Mountain Chardonnay

YYYY 2000 Light to medium yellow-green; there is a light touch of smoky oak surrounding the stonefruit and white peach aromas of the bouquet; the fresh, light and lively palate has quite delicate white peach fruit, with just a touch of creaminess before a crisp finish. A consistent performer for Tyrrell's. **rating:** 88

best drinking Now **best vintages** '97, '98 **drink with** Salmon pizza • $22

Tyrrell's Vat 47 Pinot Chardonnay

YYYYY 1999 Light to medium yellow-green; the bouquet is elegant yet complex, with particularly harmonious oak integration through the melon and nectarine fruit. The palate has that extra dimension and length that immediately sets this wine apart from all its peers. Retasted October 2000 with similar notes; more cashew evident. **rating:** 95

best drinking Now **best vintages** '82, '84, '85, '89, '91, '94, '95, '96, '97, '98, '99 **drink with** Fresh, slow-cooked salmon • $50

Tyrrell's Old Winery Shiraz

YYYY 1998 Medium purple-red; the bouquet is clean, fresh with primary cherry fruit and a touch of more earthy varietal character; subtle oak. The palate is firm, quite concentrated, with some impressive base material that could have been of the highest quality if given a bit more oak and barrel work. Time in bottle will help soften the wine. **rating:** 86

best drinking Now–2006 **best vintages** '81, '83, '87, '91, '92 **drink with** Smoked cheese • $14

Tyrrell's Rufus Stone Shiraz

YYYYY **1998** Heathcote. Medium to full red-purple; a rich, ripe bouquet stacked with blackberry and dark cherry fruit together with some American oak leads into a richly fleshy palate with excellent mouthfeel; the tannins are fine, despite all that flavour, and the sweet fruit carries right through to the finish. Received a double gold medal at the Sydney International Wine Competition 2000. **rating:** 93

best drinking Now–2010 **best vintages** '96, '97, '98 **drink with** Pot-roasted quail • $22

Tyrrell's Rufus Stone McLaren Vale Merlot

YYYYY **1999** Medium to full red-purple; the bouquet offers a powerful mix of savoury/dark berry/game/leather aromas, leading into an opulent palate with chunky, savoury, chocolatey flavours, which says much more about red wine than Merlot, but which is of undoubted quality. Won two golds within months of release, and the trophy at 2000 National Wine Show for Best Dry Red 1999 Vintage. **rating:** 90

best drinking 2004–2009 **best vintages** '99 **drink with** Braised beef • $21.95

Tyrrell's Old Winery Cabernet Merlot

YYYY **2000** Medium purple-red; fresh, clean and lively berry fruit aromas are supported by subtle oak on the bouquet; the blackcurrant and blackberry flavours of the palate are similarly fresh and lively; back to its best.

rating: 88

best drinking Now–2004 **best vintages** '89, '90, '91, '92, '93, '94, '99, '00 **drink with** Grilled kidneys • $13.50

uleybury wines NR

Uley Road, Uleybury, SA 5114 **region** Mount Lofty Ranges Zone
phone (08) 8280 7335 **fax** (08) 8280 7925 **open** Not
winemaker Tony Pipicella **production** 2000 **est.** 1995
product range ($15–19.50 R) Semillon, Uley Chapel Shiraz, Grenache Shiraz.
summary The Pipicella family, headed by Italian-born Tony, has established over 40 hectares of vineyard near the township of One Tree Hill in the Mt Lofty Ranges. Ten varieties have been planted, with more planned. Daughter Natalie Pipicella, who has completed the wine-marketing course at the University of South Australia, was responsible for overseeing the design of labels, the promotion and advertising, and the creation of the website. The wines are currently being made off site under the direction of Tony Pipicella, but the family has plans to construct a winery and cellar door on the property.

Uleybury Semillon

YYYY **2000** Medium yellow-green; a powerful bouquet, typical of the Adelaide Hills, and with the intensity reminiscent of well-made white Bordeaux followed by a solid, flavoursome palate, with a faintly grippy finish.

rating: 85

best drinking Now–2006 **best vintages** NA **drink with** Antipasto • $15

undercliff NR

Yango Creek Road, Wollombi, NSW 2325 **region** Lower Hunter Valley
phone (02) 4998 3322 **fax** (02) 4998 3322 **open** Weekends 10–4 or by appointment
winemaker David Carrick **production** 1400 **est.** 1990
product range ($15–20 CD) Semillon, Shiraz, Sparkling Shiraz.
summary Peter and Lesley Chase now own Undercliff, but it continues to function as both winery cellar door and art gallery. The wines, produced from 2.5 hectares of estate vineyards, have won a number of awards in recent years at the Hunter Valley Wine Show and the Hunter Valley Small Winemakers Show. All of the wine is sold through cellar door.

upper reach vineyard NR

77 Memorial Avenue, Baskerville, WA 6056 **region** Swan District
phone (08) 9296 0078 **fax** (08) 9296 0278 **open** Weekends and public holidays 11–5
winemaker Derek Pearse, Dorham Mann **production** 1000 **est.** 1996
product range ($13–18 CD) Unwooded Chardonnay, Reserve Chardonnay, Shiraz, Cabernet Sauvignon.
summary The 10-hectare property, situated on the banks of the upper reaches of the Swan River, was purchased by Laura Rowe and Derek Pearse in 1996. Four hectares of 12-year-old chardonnay made up the original vineyard, being expanded with 1.5 hectares of shiraz and 1 hectare of cabernet sauvignon, with plans for trials of merlot, zinfandel and barbera in the pipeline. The partners also own 4 hectares of vineyard in the Margaret River region planted to shiraz, cabernet sauvignon, merlot and semillon, but the releases so far have been drawn from the Swan Valley vineyards. The fish on the label, incidentally, is black bream, which can be found in the pools of the Swan River during the summer months.

vale view wines NR

5 Berrys Road, Vale View, Qld 4352 **region** Queensland Zone
phone (07) 4696 2282 **fax** (07) 4696 2282 **open** Weekends and public holidays 10–6 or by appointment
winemaker Giovanni Chersini, Matthew Chersini, Hazel Chersini **production** 600 **est.** 1999
product range ($9–17 CD) Semillon, Chardonnay, Shiraz, Cabernet Sauvignon, Fruit Wines.
summary Giovanni (John) Chersini was born in Valle d'Isria (then in Italy but now part of Croatia) in a wine-growing region. Visits by John, wife Hazel and son Matthew to John's birthplace inspired the planting of a few

experimental vines in 1991, and to the subsequent expansion of the vineyard to its present 2.4 hectares of cabernet sauvignon, shiraz, chardonnay, semillon and frontignac. A family affair it may be, but it is also a multicultural one in the fullest sense of the word: both Hazel and Matthew are nearing completion of the external course in wine science at Charles Sturt University, while John prefers to adhere to the philosophies and practices inherited from his forebears.

van de scheur NR

O'Connors Lane, Pokolbin, NSW 2321 **region** Lower Hunter Valley
phone (02) 4998 7789 **fax** (02) 4998 7789 **open** Weekends 10–5
winemaker Kees Van De Scheur **production** 2000 **est.** 1995
product range ($16.50 CD) Semillon, Chardonnay, Shiraz.
summary Kees Van De Scheur is a Hunter Valley veteran, having spent the last 25 years in the Hunter Valley, first with the Robson Vineyard and then Briar Ridge, before leaving in November 1993 to establish his own winery and label. He has purchased part of the historic Ingleside property established by vigneron Frederick Ingle in 1872. After a hiatus of 60 years, vines have returned, with an initial planting of a little over 1 hectare (semillon, chardonnay and shiraz) since increased to 4 hectares.

varrenti wines NR

Glenheather, Blackwood Road, Dunkeld, Vic 3294 **region** Grampians
phone (03) 5577 2368 **fax** (03) 5577 2367 **open** 7 days 12–3
winemaker Ettore Varrenti **production** NA **est.** 1999
product range ($12–14.99 R) Grenache, Grenache Shiraz, Cabernet Shiraz.
summary Ettore Varrenti has established 4 hectares of pinot noir, malbec, shiraz and cabernet sauvignon at the extreme southern end of the Grampians National Park. It is remote from any other winery, and appears to fall just outside the Grampians region.

vasse felix ★★★★☆

Cnr Caves Road and Harmans Road South, Willyabrup, WA 6284 **region** Margaret River
phone (08) 9756 5000 **fax** (08) 9755 5425 **open** 7 days 10–5
winemaker Clive Otto, Will Shields **production** 100 000 **est.** 1967
product range ($12–57 R) Classic Dry White, Theatre White and Red, Semillon, Chardonnay, Heytesbury Chardonnay, Sparkling Brut, Noble Riesling, Classic Dry Red, Shiraz, Cabernet Merlot, Cabernet Sauvignon.
summary In 1999 the production of Vasse Felix wines moved to a new 2000-tonne winery; the old winery is dedicated entirely to the restaurant and tasting rooms. A relatively new 140-hectare vineyard at Jindong in the north of the Margaret River supplies a large part of the increased fruit intake. National Australian distribution; exports to the UK, the US, Canada, Switzerland, Germany, Austria, Sweden, France, Singapore, New Zealand, Indonesia, Fiji, Hong Kong and Japan.

Vasse Felix Semillon

YYYY **2000** Light green-yellow; the bouquet is complex, with very obvious tangy/smoky barrel-ferment inputs. A powerful and complex palate follows, but the oak is a little too intrusive for my personal taste. **rating:** 88
best drinking Now–2004 **best vintages** '92, '93, '95, '96, '99 **drink with** Coquilles St Jacques • $22.50

Vasse Felix Chardonnay

YYYYY **1999** Medium yellow-green; clean nectarine and citrus fruit drives the bouquet; the palate opens with gentle nectarine fruit, but then expands, much in the way of a top Pinot Noir towards the back palate and finish; a marvellously polished, fruit-driven wine with good acidity, length and grip. **rating:** 94
best drinking Now–2005 **best vintages** '99 **drink with** Pork chops • $22.50

Vasse Felix Heytesbury Chardonnay

YYYYY **1999** Light to medium yellow-green; the bouquet is clean, with light cashew aromas and minimal oak. The palate is much more intense, with a mix of cashew, fig and melon flavours, soft and stylish. Restrained oak-use is a distinct class. **rating:** 90
best drinking Now–2006 **best vintages** '97, '98, '99 **drink with** Rich seafood • $35

Vasse Felix Noble Riesling 375 ml

🍷🍷🍷🍷 **1999** Light green-yellow; the lime juice and mandarin aromas of the bouquet are slightly marred by just a touch of reductive burnt-match character. The intense palate has strong, lime juice flavours and excellent length. If it throws off that touch of reduction, it could develop superbly. **rating:** 88

best drinking Now–2005 **best vintages** '98 **drink with** Fresh fruit • $19

Vasse Felix Shiraz

🍷🍷🍷🍷🍷 **1999** Dark, dense red-purple; lashings of rich, full dark cherry/berry fruit on the bouquet is followed by a palate with masses of velvety dark cherry and plum fruit, with a smooth whipping of vanilla oak. Superbly balanced and constructed. **rating:** 96

best drinking 2004–2019 **best vintages** '83, '85, '88, '90, '91, '92, '94, '96, '99 **drink with** Rich casseroles • $35

Vasse Felix Heytesbury

🍷🍷🍷🍷🍷 **1998** Medium to full red-purple; a wonderfully complex and satisfying bouquet with fruit intermingling with sweet, cedary oak. The soft, rich and ripe palate is multitextured and multilayered in terms of flavour. The oak is plentiful, but so is the fruit. Top end of the town. **rating:** 94

best drinking 2003–2008 **best vintages** '95, '96, '97, '98 **drink with** Beef Bordelaise • $57

Vasse Felix Cabernet Merlot

🍷🍷🍷🍷 **1999** Medium red-purple; the dark berry/chocolate/savoury fruit is complemented by positive oak input on the bouquet, the palate with ripe, smooth dark berry/dark currant fruit and soft tannins. **rating:** 88

best drinking 2004–2009 **best vintages** NA **drink with** Braised beef • $22.50

Vasse Felix Cabernet Sauvignon

🍷🍷🍷🍷 **1999** Medium to full red-purple; the bouquet has clean, smooth berry fruit and well-integrated oak; the medium-bodied palate is no less smooth, with gently ripe berry fruit and oak flowing evenly across the tongue. **rating:** 89

best drinking 2004–2009 **best vintages** '85, '88, '90, '91, '94, '95, '96, '99 **drink with** Lamb cutlets • $30

vasse river wines NR

Bussell Highway, Carbunup, WA 6280 **region** Margaret River
phone (08) 9755 1111 **fax** (08) 9755 1111 **open** 7 days 10–5
winemaker Robert Credaro, Bernie Stanlake **production** 3500 **est.** 1993
product range ($14–20 CD) Semillon Sauvignon Blanc, Verdelho, Chardonnay, Shiraz, Ruby Red, Cabernet Merlot.
summary This is a major and rapidly growing business owned by the Credaro family. Their 45 hectares of chardonnay, semillon, verdelho, sauvignon blanc, cabernet sauvignon, merlot and shiraz have been established on the typical gravelly red loam soils of the region. These plantings will be in full production by 2005, and it is intended to build a new winery and cellar-door sales area prior to that time.

veritas 

94 Langmeil Road, Tanunda, SA 5352 **region** Barossa Valley
phone (08) 8563 2330 **fax** (08) 8563 3158 **open** Mon–Fri 9–5, weekends 11–5
winemaker Rolf Binder, Christa Deans **production** 14 000 **est.** 1955
product range ($10–30 CD) Riesling, Semillon, Chardonnay, Cabernet Shiraz, Cabernet Merlot, Binder's Bull's Blood, Shiraz Mourvedre Pressings, Fortifieds.
summary The Hungarian influence is obvious in the naming of some of the wines, but Australian technology is paramount in shaping the generally very good quality. Veritas has 28 hectares of estate vineyards to draw on. A near-doubling of production has coincided with the establishment of export markets to the UK, Germany, Switzerland, Belgium, the Netherlands and the US.

verona vineyard NR

Small Winemakers Centre, McDonalds Road, Pokolbin, NSW 2321 **region** Lower Hunter Valley
phone (02) 4998 7668 **fax** (02) 4998 7430 **open** 7 days 10–5

winemaker Greg Silkman, Gary Reed (Contract) **production** NA **est.** 1972
product range ($15–18.50 CD) Under the Verona label: Verdelho, Semillon and Shiraz; also Tallamurra Verdelho, Chardonnay and Shiraz.
summary Verona has had a chequered history, and is still a significant business acting as a sales point for a number of other Hunter Valley winemakers from its premises in McDonalds Road, directly opposite Brokenwood. The Verona wines come from 22 hectares at Muswellbrook, and 5 hectares surrounding the winery.

vicarys NR

Northern Road, Luddenham, NSW 2745 **region** South Coast Zone
phone (02) 4773 4161 **fax** (02) 4773 4411 **open** Mon–Fri 9–5, weekends 10–5
winemaker Chris Niccol **production** 1700 **est.** 1923
product range ($12–36 CD) Chardonnay, Semillon, Riesling, Gewurztraminer, Fumé Blanc, Cabernet Sauvignon, Shiraz Cabernet Merlot, Sparkling, Fortifieds.
summary Vicarys justifiably claims to be the Sydney region's oldest continuously operating winery, having been established in a very attractive, large stone shearing shed built about 1890. Most of the wines come from other parts of Australia, but the winery does draw upon 1 hectare of estate traminer and 3 hectares of chardonnay for those wines, and has produced some good wines of all styles over the years.

vico NR

Farm 1687 Beelbangera Road, Griffith, NSW 2680 **region** Riverina
phone (02) 6962 2849 **open** Mon–Fri 9–5
winemaker Ray Vico **production** 1200 **est.** 1973
product range ($5–15 CD) Semillon, Late Harvest Semillon, Barbera, Cabernet Sauvignon, Liqueur Muscat.
summary Ray Vico has been growing grapes for many years. He has 9 hectares of vines and more recently has decided to bottle and sell part of the production under the Vico label. At $60–70 a dozen for the table wines and $15 per bottle for the 1984 Liqueur Muscat, the prices are positively mouthwatering.

villa primavera NR

Mornington–Flinders Road, Red Hill, Vic 3937 **region** Mornington Peninsula
phone (03) 5989 2129 **fax** (03) 5931 0045 **open** Weekends, public holidays 10–5, 7 days Dec 26–Jan 31.
winemaker Gennaro Mazzella **production** 300 **est.** 1984
product range ($18–30 CD) Chardonnay, Pinot Noir, Limoncello, Méthode Champenoise.
summary A most unusual operation, which is in reality an Italian-style family restaurant at which the wine is principally sold and served, and which offers something totally different on the Mornington Peninsula. A consistent winner of tourism and food awards, it is praised by all who go there, particularly for the concerts staged throughout January each year.

vinden estate NR

17 Gillards Road, Pokolbin, NSW 2320 **region** Lower Hunter Valley
phone (02) 4998 7410 **fax** (02) 4998 7421 **open** Fri–Mon and public holidays 10–5 or by appointment
winemaker Guy Vinden, John Baruzzi (Consultant) **production** 750 **est.** 1998
product range ($19–21 CD) Semillon, Chardonnay, Shiraz.
summary Sandra and Guy Vinden have bought their dream home with landscaped gardens in the foreground and 6 hectares of vineyard with the Brokenback mountain range in the distance. Much of the winemaking is now done on site, and increasingly drawn from the estate vineyards. The wines are available through the cellar door and also via a wine club that offers buying advantages to members.

Vinden Estate Semillon

YYYY **2000** Light to medium yellow-green; a big style, with quite ripe, slightly broad fruit on the bouquet, although the palate is somewhat tighter, with positive citrus and grass flavours. Will be fairly quick-developing by normal Semillon standards. **rating:** 85
best drinking Now–2005 **best vintages** NA **drink with** Rich fish dishes • $19

vinifera wines NR

194 Henry Lawson Drive, Mudgee, NSW 2850 **region** Mudgee
phone (02) 6372 2461 **fax** (02) 6372 6731 **open** 7 days 10–5.30
winemaker Steve Dodd **production** 800 **est.** 1997
product range ($12–19 CD) Riesling, Semillon, Chardonnay, Tempranillo, Cabernet Sauvignon.
summary Tony and Debbie McKendry have much in common with Dave and Leslie Robertson of Thistle Hill, the latter another Mudgee winery. Dave Robertson lost a leg in a motorcycle accident, and used the compensation proceeds to establish Thistle Hill, turning adversity into good fortune. The McKendrys tell a similar tale. Having lived in Mudgee for 15 years, Tony McKendry (a regional medical superintendent) and Debbie succumbed to the lure, and planted and tended their small (1.5-hectare) vineyard in 1995. In Debbie's words, 'Tony, in his spare two minutes per day, also decided to start studying wine science at Charles Sturt University in 1992.' She continues, 'His trying to live 27 hours per day (plus with our four kids!) fell to pieces when he was involved in a severe car smash in 1997. Two months in hospital stopped full-time medical work, and the winery dreams became inevitable.' Here, too, financial compensation finally came through and the little winery was built.

Vinifera Chardonnay

1999 Medium yellow-green; the bouquet is clean, offering a mix of melon and more mineral fruit aromas. The medium-bodied and smooth palate is not especially complex, but does have smooth-flowing melon fruit, with no oak influence evident. **rating:** 88

best drinking Now–2003 **best vintages** NA **drink with** Smoked pork • $16

vintina estate NR

1282 Nepean Highway, Mount Eliza, Vic 3930 **region** Mornington Peninsula
phone (03) 9787 8166 **fax** (03) 9775 2035 **open** 7 days 9–5
winemaker Jim Filippone, Kevin McCarthy (Consultant) **production** 400 **est.** 1985
product range ($12–14 CD) Chardonnay, Semillon, Pinot Gris, Pinot Noir, Cabernet Sauvignon.
summary The initial releases of Vintina (the only wines tasted to date) were mediocre. With competent contract-winemaking, improvement can be expected. However, no recent tastings.

violet cane vineyard NR

PO Box 409 Buddina, Qld 4557 **region** Granite Belt
phone 0418 739 257 **fax** (07) 3829 9605 **open** Not
winemaker Adam Chapman **production** 80 **est.** 1994
product range ($23.50 ML) Merlot.
summary The intriguingly named Violet Cane Vineyard, and no less startlingly labelled wine, is the tiny personal business of former Ballandean winemaker Adam Chapman, who manages to fit in three winemaking lives: one at Mount Cotton, one for Clovely and for Violet Cane.

virage 

13B Georgette Road, Gracetown, WA 6284 **region** Margaret River
phone (08) 9755 5318 **fax** (08) 9755 5318 **open** Not
winemaker Bernard Abbott **production** 1000 **est.** 1990
product range ($13–20 R) Sauvignon Blanc, Semillon Chardonnay, Traminer Riesling, Cabernet Shiraz Zinfandel, Cabernet Merlot.
summary Former Vasse Felix winemaker Bernard Abbott, together with wife Pascale, acquired (under long-term lease) the former government research station vineyard at Bramley Estate in 1990. Bernard Abbott makes the wines at a local Margaret River winery and sells them by mailing list and direct to retailers and restaurants in Perth, Melbourne and Sydney.

virgin hills 

Salisbury Road, Lauriston West, via Kyneton, Vic 3444 **region** Macedon Ranges
phone (03) 5422 7444 **fax** (03) 5422 7400 **open** By appointment
winemaker Peter Howland, Chris Smales **production** 2500 **est.** 1968

product range ($39.95 R) A single Cabernet Sauvignon Shiraz Merlot blend called Virgin Hills; occasional limited Reserve releases.

summary Virgin Hills has passed through several ownership changes in a short period of time. It is now owned by Michael Hope, who also presides over the fast-growing Hope Estate in the Hunter Valley. While there have been one or two raised eyebrows at some of the events that occurred in the Hunter Valley several years ago, the quality of the wines currently being made by Peter Howland at Hope Estate cannot be questioned, any more than the quality of the 1998 Virgin Hills. So, after some prevarication, the five-star rating remains in place. Exports to the UK and the US.

Virgin Hills

▼▼▼▼▽ **1998** Medium red-purple, the hue reassuringly bright; the clean and smooth bouquet shows a pleasantly ripe and complex mix of berry fruits. The elegant, bright and lively palate has a slight minty backdrop to the predominant red berries, finishing with fine tannins and subtle oak. **rating:** 92

best drinking 2003–2010 **best vintages** '74, '75, '76, '80, '82, '85, '88, '90, '91, '92, '95, '98 **drink with** Duck • NA

voyager estate ★★★★☆

Lot 1 Stevens Road, Margaret River, WA 6285 **region** Margaret River
phone (08) 9757 6354 **fax** (08) 9757 6494 **open** 7 days 10–5
winemaker Cliffe Royal **production** 30 000 **est.** 1978

product range ($20–48 R) Semillon, Sauvignon Blanc Semillon, Tom Price Sauvignon Blanc Semillon, Tom Price Semillon Sauvignon Blanc, Marsanne, Chardonnay, Shiraz Grenache, Cabernet Sauvignon Merlot, Tom Price Cabernet Merlot.

summary Voyager Estate has come a long way since it was acquired by Michael Wright (of the mining family) in May 1991. It now has an important, high-quality, 63-hectare vineyard that puts Voyager Estate in the position of being able to select only the best parcels of fruit for its own label, and to supply surplus (but high-quality) wine to others. The Cape Dutch-style tasting room and vast rose garden are a major tourist attraction, although the winery itself remains in strictly utilitarian form.

Voyager Estate Semillon

▼▼▼▼ **1999** Light straw-green; a clean, crisp, lemon and herb bouquet is followed by a surprisingly light and crisp palate, which looks much like a cross between Hunter Valley and Margaret River Semillon. Given the reputation of the vintage, the delicacy is surprising; likewise, the oak influence is not at all obvious. **rating:** 86

best drinking 2002–2006 **best vintages** '95, '96 **drink with** Chicken • $25

Voyager Estate Sauvignon Blanc Semillon

▼▼▼▼ **2000** Light green-yellow; a clean mix of herb and riper fruit provides a dense yet not particularly aromatic bouquet. The unoaked palate has good length, with gentle tropical-fruit flavours and a fresh finish. **rating:** 89

best drinking Now–2005 **best vintages** '95, '97 **drink with** Marinated octopus • $20

Voyager Estate Tom Price Semillon Sauvignon Blanc

▼▼▼▼ **1997** Glowing yellow-green; by far the most dominant feature of both bouquet and palate is the strong barrel-ferment oak; there is quite ripe bottle-developed fruit and balancing acidity, but it is clasped in the fist of all that oak. Reaction to the wine will vary widely, some will love it, others will not. **rating:** 87

best drinking Now–2006 **best vintages** NA **drink with** Rich seafood • $48

Voyager Estate Chardonnay

▼▼▼▼▼ **1999** Medium green-yellow; in typical Voyager fashion, the oak is quite assertive on the bouquet, but is of high quality, and the fruit is there to sustain that oak. The complex palate puts to rest any doubts, with intense nectarine, fig and melon fruit; good length, balance and style. **rating:** 94

▼▼▼▼▽ **1998** Strong green-yellow; the complex and intense bouquet has citrus, melon and peach fruit surrounded by nicely controlled barrel-ferment characters. The tight, youthful but powerful palate again shows exemplary barrel-ferment oak handling, giving the fruit pleasantly nutty overtones. Malolactic fermentation no doubt also plays a role here. **rating:** 93

best drinking Now–2008 **best vintages** '92, '93, '95, '96, '97, '98, '99 **drink with** Braised pork neck • $34

Voyager Estate Shiraz

ŸŸŸŸŸ **1999** Dense red-purple; the bouquet is clean, rich and full, with ripe, black cherry fruit. The palate is more complex than the bouquet, with black cherry and licorice fruit supported by well-handled oak; an altogether impressive debut. **rating:** 94

best drinking 2003–2012 **best vintages** '99 **drink with** Barbecued leg of lamb • $28

Voyager Estate Cabernet Sauvignon Merlot

ŸŸŸŸŸ **1998** Deep red-purple; the typically complex and powerful bouquet ranges through dark berry, cassis, a touch of chocolate and a savoury edge. The elegant and harmonious palate has superbly balanced and integrated fruit, and oak and fine tannins running through a sweet, lingering finish. Won top gold medal in a very strong class at the 2000 Wine Show of Western Australia, and very nearly a major trophy winner. **rating:** 96

best drinking 2003–2018 **best vintages** '91, '93, '97, '98 **drink with** Beef in red wine sauce • $40

Voyager Estate Tom Price Cabernet Merlot

ŸŸŸŸ **1994** Medium purple-red; a powerful, earthy savoury/grainy bouquet is followed by a wine with monumental extract and tannins. I cannot see how the tannins will soften before the fruit dies. **rating:** 85

best drinking 2004–2010 **best vintages** '92 **drink with** Grain-fed beef • NA

wa-de-lock ★★★

76 Tyers Street, Stratford, Vic 3862 **region** Gippsland
phone (03) 5145 7050 **fax** (03) 5145 7030 **open** 7 days 10–6, summer weekends 10–8
winemaker Graeme Little **production** 2000 **est.** 1987
product range ($10–28.50 R) Chardonnay, Reserve Chardonnay, Sauvignon Blanc, Pinot Noir, EGL Cabernet Sauvignon, Avon Valley Tawny Port, Noble Sauvignon Blanc.

summary The initial plantings of pinot noir, cabernet sauvignon and sauvignon blanc in 1987 have been progressively expanded by increases in those varieties and the addition of chardonnay, nebbiolo, shiraz, merlot and durif, with 12 hectares under vine, some of it still coming into production. The quality of the wines has improved steadily as Graeme Little's handling of oak has become more assured, and the range of wines has increased. The wines have distributors in Victoria, Tasmania and Queensland.

Wa-De-Lock Noble Sauvignon Blanc

ŸŸŸY **1999** Deep golden-bronze; the bouquet is tropical, but vestiges of sauvignon blanc varietal character come through on both the bouquet and the palate. The acidity is fairly high in the context of the moderate sweetness of the wine, but, once again, does allow the sauvignon blanc character to express itself. **rating:** 82

best drinking Now–2003 **best vintages** '96, '97 **drink with** Prosciutto and melon • $16.85

Wa-De-Lock Pinot Noir

ŸŸŸŸ **1999** Light to medium red, with some tawny hue on the rim; the bouquet is distinctive, with stemmy/foresty/carbonic maceration characters all giving an intense tomato-vine overlay; the powerful stemmy/foresty/maceration palate flavours are all in the savoury spectrum, with red fruits nowhere to be seen, but nonetheless a wine of plenty of length and presence. **rating:** 86

best drinking 2002–2006 **best vintages** '93, '95, '97 **drink with** Risotto • $18.75

Wa-De-Lock EGL Cabernet Sauvignon

ŸŸŸY **1999** Medium red-purple; the herbaceous, savoury bouquet is on the borderline of ripeness; the savoury, blackberry, almost lemony, flavours of the palate again test the ripeness limits, but the tannins are fine and the oak subtle. **rating:** 83

best drinking 2003–2008 **best vintages** NA **drink with** Beef in black bean sauce • $28.50

wadjekanup river estate NR

Flatrocks Road, Broomehill, WA 6318 **region** Great Southern
phone (08) 9825 3080 **fax** (08) 9825 3007 **open** By appointment
winemaker Michael Staniford (Alkoomi Contract) **production** 400 **est.** 1995
product range ($16–18 CD) Sauvignon Blanc, Shiraz.

summary The Witham family (Scott and Sue, Jim and Ann) began the development of Wadjekanup River Estate in 1995 as a minor diversification for a 3000-hectare wool, prime lamb, beef and cereal cropping enterprise worked by the family. They began with 1.2 hectares of shiraz and sauvignon blanc, since extended to 8 hectares that include a 1-hectare block of merlot with its first production in 2001. The aims for the future include a purpose-built cellar for storage and sales, with a possibility of farm-stay accommodation also being considered. The present wine range of Sauvignon Blanc and Shiraz will be extended with a varietal Merlot, and the possibility of a Semillon or other white somewhere down the track.

wallington wines NR

Nyrang Creek Vineyard, Canowindra, NSW 2904 **region** Cowra
phone (02) 6344 7153 **fax** (02) 6344 7153 **open** By appointment
winemaker Blair Duncan, Murray Smith (Contract) **production** 2000 **est.** 1992
product range ($14–20 CD) Chardonnay, Shiraz, Cabernet Sauvignon.
summary Anthony and Margaret Wallington commenced the development of their Nyrang Creek Vineyard with a little over 2 hectares of cabernet sauvignon in 1992, followed by 7 hectares of chardonnay in 1994, then shiraz (2.5 hectares) and semillon (0.75 hectare) in 1995 and ultimately 0.75 hectare each of cabernet franc and pinot noir in 1998. Most of the production is sold, but Blair Duncan at Arrowfield makes the Wallington Chardonnay and Murray Smith of Canobolas-Smith Wines at Orange makes the Cabernet Sauvignon and Shiraz. The quality of the wines is such that exports to the US have already commenced.

walsh family wines NR

90 Walnut Road Bickley, WA 6076 **region** Perth Hills
phone (08) 9291 7341 **fax** (08) 9291 7341 **open** 7 days 9–5
winemaker Rob Marshall (Contract) **production** 450 **est.** 1995
product range ($15–18 CD) Gewurztraminer, Shiraz.
summary Walsh Family Wines is aptly named: it is a partnership of the Walshes and their eight children. One of those children is establishing a vineyard near Bridgetown in the Great Southern, the grapes from which will ultimately form part of the Walsh Family winery intake.

wandering brook estate NR

PO Box 32 Wandering, WA 6308 **region** Greater Perth Zone
phone (08) 9884 1064 **fax** (08) 9884 1064 **open** Weekends 9.30–6
winemaker Steve Radikovich **production** 2000 **est.** 1989
product range ($10–14.95 CD) Verdelho, Chardonnay, Unwooded Chardonnay, Soft Red and White, Cabernet Sauvignon, Sparkling Verdelho, Port.
summary Laurie and Margaret White have planted 10 hectares of vines on their 130-year-old family property in a move to diversify. Up to 1994 the wines were made at Goundrey, currently at Jadran. Renamed Wandering Brook Estate late in 1994; up until then known as Redhill Estate.

wandin valley estate ★★★★

Wilderness Road, Lovedale, NSW 2320 **region** Lower Hunter Valley
phone (02) 4930 7317 **fax** (02) 4930 7814 **open** 7 days 10–5
winemaker Sarah-Kate Wilson, Karl Stockhausen (Consultant) **production** 10 000 **est.** 1973
product range ($10–25 R) Pavilion Range Dry White, Rosé and Dry Red; Estate Range of Semillon, Verdehlo, Chardonnay, Cabernets Merlot, Cabernet Sauvignon and Muscat; top of the range Sparkling Semillon, Reserve Chardonnay, Bridie's Shiraz and Reserve Cabernet Sauvignon.
summary The former Millstone vineyard, now owned by the producer of Australian TV classic 'A Country Practice'. Rapidly developing Chardonnays have been the focal point of Wandin Valley's considerable show success. The estate also boasts a Cope-Williams-type village cricket oval and extensive cottage accommodation. Exports to Canada, Malaysia and Japan.

waninga ★★★★

Hughes Park Road, Sevenhill, via Clare, SA 5453 **region** Clare Valley
phone (08) 8843 4395 **fax** (08) 8843 4395 **open** 7 days 10–5
winemaker Tim Adams, Jeffrey Grosset (Contract) **production** 1500 **est.** 1989

product range ($13–19 CD) Skilly Hills Riesling, Chenin Blanc, Ninnes, Shiraz, Cabernet Sauvignon, Hilary Port.
summary The large vineyards (36.3 hectares) owned by Waninga were established in 1974, but it was not until 1989 that a portion of the grapes was withheld from sale and vinified for the owners. Since that time, Waninga has produced some quite lovely wines, having wisely opted for very competent contract-winemaking. Exports to the US.

Waninga Shiraz

YYYYY **1998** Medium red-purple; the bouquet is an exciting ride through a range of slightly stewy, gamey, spicy, leathery aromas, all varietal but equally all on the brink. However, the palate gets it all together with lots of ripe licorice/game/berry flavours, excellent oak and tannin handling, and a surprisingly harmonious mouthfeel thanks to the excellent structure. **rating:** 94

best drinking 2002–2010 **best vintages** '89, '91, '96, '98 **drink with** Steak and kidney pie • $19

Waninga Cabernet Sauvignon

YYYY **1998** Medium to full red-purple; the bouquet has a few errant characters, possibly slightly aldehydic; a powerful, extractive palate with some dark chocolate fruit, and an echo of the bouquet in a faintly bitter finish. However, has great depth of flavour, and may settle down and soften with more time in bottle. **rating:** 83

best drinking 2003–2008 **best vintages** '91, '92, '93, '94 **drink with** Rump steak • $19

wansbrough wines NR

Richards Road, Ferguson, WA 6236 **region** Geographe
phone (08) 9728 3091 **fax** (08) 9728 3091 **open** Weekends 10–5
winemaker Willespie Wines (Contract) **production** 250 **est.** 1986
product range ($12–18 CD) Riesling, Semillon, Sauvignon Blanc, Constantia (late-picked Semillon), Shiraz Cabernet, Port.
summary Situated east of Dardanup in the picturesque Ferguson Valley, Wansbrough enjoys views of the distant Geographe Bay and the nearer State forest, with the Bibblemun Track running along its northern and eastern borders. To taste the wine you need either to order by mail or visit the Wansbrough restaurant on weekends.

wantirna estate NR

Bushy Park Lane, Wantirna South, Vic 3152 **region** Yarra Valley
phone (03) 9801 2367 **fax** (03) 9887 0225 **open** Not
winemaker Reg Egan, Maryann Egan **production** 1000 **est.** 1963
product range ($35–42 CD) Isabella Chardonnay, Lily Pinot Noir, Amelia Cabernet Sauvignon Merlot.
summary Situated well within the boundaries of the Melbourne metropolitan area, Wantirna Estate is part of a nature reserve. The only retail outlet for the wine is Richmond Hill Cellars; all the remainder is sold through mail order to selected restaurants and to a few overseas customers. In deference to Reg Egan's very firmly held views on the subject, neither the winery nor the wines are rated.

Wantirna Estate Isabella Chardonnay

1999 Medium yellow-green; toasty cashew, vanilla and melon aromas on the bouquet are followed by a palate with very sweet fruit and mouthfeel, reflecting the substantial alcohol.

best drinking Now–2004 **best vintages** '91, '92, '93, '94 **drink with** Pan-fried trout in black butter • $35

Wantirna Estate Lily Pinot Noir

1999 Light to medium purple-red; a firm mix of plum, leaf and spice, with minimal oak input; there is plenty of ripe, plummy fruit on the palate, should evolve well over the next few years.

best drinking Now–2005 **best vintages** '91, '92, '94, '96, '97 **drink with** Peking duck • $42

Wantirna Estate Amelia Cabernet Sauvignon Merlot

1998 Medium red-purple; clean, sweet, redcurrant fruit and subtle oak on the bouquet followed by a quite delicious palate, with ripe cassis, redcurrant and mulberry fruit supported by long, fine tannins.

best drinking 2003–2008 **best vintages** '90, '91, '92, '93, '98 **drink with** Roast veal • $42

wards gateway ★★☆

Barossa Valley Highway, Lyndoch, SA 5351 **region** Barossa Valley
phone (08) 8524 4138 **open** 7 days 9–5.30
winemaker Ray Ward (plus Contract) **production** 800 **est.** 1979
product range ($7.50–17 CD) Riesling, Frontignac, Chardonnay, Frontignac Spätlese, Barossa Shiraz, Cabernet Sauvignon, Port.
summary The very old vines surrounding the winery produce the best wines, which are made without frills or new oak and sold without ostentation.

warrabilla NR

Murray Valley Highway, Rutherglen, Vic 3685 **region** Rutherglen
phone (02) 6035 7242 **fax** (02) 6035 7242 **open** 7 days 10–5
winemaker Andrew Sutherland Smith **production** 6000 **est.** 1986
product range ($15–24 CD) Chardonnay, KV Brut Rosé, Brimin Shiraz, Reserve Shiraz, Merlot, Reserve Durif, Vintage Port, Liqueur Muscat.
summary Former All Saints winemaker Andrew Sutherland Smith has leased a small winery at Corowa to make the Warrabilla wines from a 4-hectare vineyard he has developed with Carol Smith in the Indigo Valley. Exports to the US.

warramate 

27 Maddens Lane, Gruyere, Vic 3770 **region** Yarra Valley
phone (03) 5964 9219 **fax** (03) 5964 9219 **open** 7 days 10–6
winemaker David Church **production** 900 **est.** 1970
product range ($18–30 CD) Riesling, Shiraz, Cabernet Sauvignon.
summary Wine quality has been variable in recent years; it would seem that the oak in some of the older barrels is questionable. At their best, the wines reflect the distinguished site on which the vineyard sits. The 2000/2001 extension of the 30-year-old vineyard will lead to greater production in the years ahead.

warraroong estate NR

Wilderness Road, Lovedale, NSW 2321 **region** Lower Hunter Valley
phone (02) 4930 7594 **fax** (02) 4930 7199 **open** 7 days 10–5
winemaker Andrew Thomas **production** 3000 **est.** 1988
product range ($15–25 CD) Semillon, Sauvignon Blanc, Chenin Blanc, Chardonnay, Shiraz, Malbec.
summary Warraroong Estate was formerly Fraser Vineyard and adopted its new name after it changed hands in 1997. The name 'Warraroong' is an Aboriginal word for hillside, reflecting the southwesterly aspect of the property looking back towards the Brokenback Range and Watagan Mountains. The label design is from a painting by local Aboriginal artist Kia Kiro who, while coming from the Northern Territory, is living and working in the Hunter Valley.

warrenmang vineyard resort 

Mountain Creek Road, Moonambel, Vic 3478 **region** Pyrenees
phone (03) 5467 2233 **fax** (03) 5467 2309 **open** 7 days 10–5
winemaker Luigi Bazzani, Simon Clayfield **production** 17 000 **est.** 1974
product range ($13–80 CD) The wines are released in two ranges: the lower-priced Bazzani white and red blends, Methode Champenoise and Vintage Port; then a subtly differing range of wines under the Warrenmang label, predominantly estate-grown and including Sauvignon Blanc, Chardonnay, Grand Pyrenees, Shiraz, Cabernet Sauvignon, Late Harvest Traminer; and, at the top, a flagship wine that varies from time to time.
summary Warrenmang is now the focus of a superb accommodation and restaurant complex created by former restaurateur Luigi Bazzani and wife Athalie. It is in much demand as a conference centre as well as for weekend tourism. The striking black Bazzani label is gradually overtaking the Warrenmang label in importance, and is responsible for the growth in the volume of production. It is partially sourced from contract-growers; the estate wines are, as their name suggests, estate-grown.

Warrenmang Sauvignon Blanc

▼▼▼▼ **1999** Light green-yellow; the bouquet is clean and crisp, with the neutral fruit aromas in the mineral spectrum. The wine has nice mouthfeel and balance, with a subtle hint of French oak; a very easy style and well made, although not a lot of varietal character. **rating:** 86

best drinking Now **best vintages** NA **drink with** Seafood • $27

Warrenmang Estate Chardonnay

▼▼▼▼ **1999** Medium yellow-green; solid, ripe melon fruit and subtle oak on the bouquet lead into a wine with plenty of mouthfeel and weight; melon and white peach meld with vanilla/cashew malolactic and oak inputs on the palate. **rating:** 86

best drinking Now–2003 **best vintages** NA **drink with** Pasta • $30

Warrenmang Black Puma Shiraz

▼▼▼▼▽ **1998** Medium to full red-purple; the bouquet has sweet, dark plum fruit, a hint of prune, and attractive oak; the rich and concentrated palate follows down the same track, with dark plum, chocolate and prune flavours; the oak and ripe tannins are nicely controlled. **rating:** 90

best drinking 2003–2010 **best vintages** '98 **drink with** Venison • $51.60

Warrenmang 10th Anniversary

▼▼▼▼ **1997** Medium to full red-purple; the complex bouquet offers a range of ripe blackberry, raspberry and cedar aromas, followed by a surprisingly juicy cherry and raspberry-flavoured palate, with soft tannins and a gentle touch of oak. The Warrenmang style is usually much more muscular than this, which is no way intended as a criticism. **rating:** 87

best drinking Now–2007 **best vintages** '97 **drink with** Braised quail • $55

Warrenmang Grand Pyrenees

▼▼▼▼ **1997** Medium red-purple; the moderately intense bouquet is strongly influenced by the Merlot component, with cedary/leafy aromas. Mint, leaf and cedar flavours are sustained by soft, fine tannins on the palate. A polar opposite in style to the Shiraz, but of similar quality. **rating:** 86

best drinking 2002–2007 **best vintages** '97 **drink with** Aged rump • $45

warrina wines NR

Back Road, Kootingal, NSW 2352 **region** Northern Slopes Zone
phone (02) 6760 3985 **fax** (02) 6765 5746 **open** Not
winemaker David Nicholls **production** 100 **est.** 1989
product range ($5–12 ML) Sauvignon Blanc, Semillon, Chardonnay, Shiraz, Cabernet Sauvignon.
summary David Nicholls has progressively established a total of 2 hectares of sauvignon blanc, semillon, chardonnay, shiraz and cabernet sauvignon at his vineyard 15 kilometres northeast of Tamworth. Wine prices are low, but the production has see-sawed wildly over the years.

water wheel ★★★☆

Bridgewater-on-Loddon, Bridgewater, Vic 3516 **region** Bendigo
phone (03) 5437 3060 **fax** (03) 5437 3082 **open** Oct–Apr 7 days 11–5, May–Sept Mon–Fri 11–5, weekends and public holidays 1–4
winemaker Peter Cumming, Bill Trevaskis **production** 30 000 **est.** 1972
product range ($14–18 R) Bendigo Sauvignon Blanc, Chardonnay, Shiraz, Cabernet Sauvignon.
summary Peter Cumming gained great respect as a winemaker during his four-year stint with Hickinbotham Winemakers, and his 1989 purchase of Water Wheel was greeted with enthusiasm by followers of his work. Recent releases have been of consistent quality and modest price, being distributed throughout Australia and with export markets in New Zealand, Asia, the UK, Switzerland, Austria, the US and Canada.

Water Wheel Bendigo Sauvignon Blanc

▼▼▼▼ **2000** Light green-yellow; the bouquet is clean and crisp, tending to a little neutral, and with more mineral than fruit. The palate picks up a little with good length, and there is a pleasant minerally grip to the finish. **rating:** 85

best drinking Now **best vintages** '00 **drink with** Asian seafood • $14

Water Wheel Chardonnay

🍷🍷🍷 2000 Medium yellow-green; there is solid, ripe fruit, but there is a slightly distracting character coming from what I take to be oak on the bouquet. The palate is solid, ripe, flavoursome and fruit-driven, offering honest value. **rating:** 84

best drinking Now **best vintages** NA **drink with** Roast pork • $14

Water Wheel Bendigo Shiraz

🍷🍷🍷🍷 1999 Medium to full purple-red; a clean bouquet with rich, dark plum and black cherry fruit is followed by a concentrated, full, fruit-driven palate with excellent varietal character, finishing with soft tannins. **rating:** 89

best drinking 2002–2007 **best vintages** '94, '96, '97, '98, '99 **drink with** Rich meat dishes • $17

waybourne NR

60 Lemins Road, Waurn Ponds, Vic 3221 **region** Geelong
phone (03) 5241 8477 **fax** (03) 5241 8477 **open** By appointment
winemaker David Cowburn (Contract) **production** 730 **est.** 1980
product range ($12–16 ML) Riesling, Trebbiano, Pinot Gris, Cabernet Sauvignon.
summary Owned by Tony and Kay Volpato, who have relied upon external consultants to assist with the winemaking. No recent tastings.

wayne thomas wines ★★★★

26 Kangarilla Road, McLaren Vale, SA 5171 **region** McLaren Vale
phone (08) 8323 9737 **fax** (08) 8323 9737 **open** 7 days 12–5
winemaker Wayne Thomas **production** 4500 **est.** 1994
product range ($14–30 ML) Shiraz, Cabernet Sauvignon, Premium Brut, Sparkling Cabernet Franc.
summary Wayne Thomas is a McLaren Vale veteran, having commenced his winemaking career in 1961, working for Stonyfell, Ryecroft and Saltram before establishing Fern Hill with his wife Pat in 1975. When they sold Fern Hill in April 1994 they started again, launching the Wayne Thomas Wines label, using contract-grown grapes sourced from throughout McLaren Vale. The wines are exported to the US, as well as enjoying limited retail distribution through all Australian States except Western Australia.

Wayne Thomas McLaren Vale Shiraz

🍷🍷🍷🍷🍷 1999 Medium to full purple-red; ripe, earthy, solid dark berry/plum/chocolate fruit on the bouquet leads into a remarkably rich and concentrated palate, with lots of regional dark chocolate-accented fruit supported by nicely controlled vanilla oak and soft, ripe tannins. An altogether impressive wine, and the best by far to have been released under the Wayne Thomas label so far. **rating:** 90

best drinking 2003–2010 **best vintages** '99 **drink with** Wafu beef • $29

Wayne Thomas McLaren Vale Cabernet Sauvignon

🍷🍷🍷🍷🍷 1999 Medium red-purple; cassis and blackberry fruit, with a touch of chocolate, is supported by gently sweet oak on the bouquet. A succulent palate offers plum, cassis and chocolate flavours, once again supported by nicely judged oak and soft tannins. **rating:** 90

best drinking 2003–2010 **best vintages** '99 **drink with** Kangaroo fillet • $29.30

wedgetail estate ★★★★☆

40 Hildebrand Road, Cottles Bridge, Vic 3099 **region** Yarra Valley
phone (03) 9714 8661 **fax** (03) 9714 8661 **open** Weekends and public holidays 10–5 or by appointment
winemaker Guy Lamothe **production** 1200 **est.** 1994
product range ($17–55 CD) Chardonnay, Pinot Noir, Pinot Reserve, Cabernet Blend.
summary Canadian-born photographer Guy Lamothe and partner Dena Ashbolt started making wine in the basement of their Melbourne home in the 1980s. Insidiously, the idea of their own vineyard started to take hold, and the search for a property began. Then, in their words, 'One Sunday, when we were just out for a drive, we drove past our current home. The slopes are amazing, true goat terrain, and it's on these steep slopes that in 1994 we planted our first block of pinot noir.' While the vines were growing – they now have 5.5 hectares in total – Lamothe enrolled in the wine-growing course at Charles Sturt University, having already gained practical experience working at Tarrawarra in the Yarra Valley, Mornington Peninsula and Meursault. The net result is truly excellent wine.

Wedgetail Estate Chardonnay

TTTT **1999** Medium yellow-green; the bouquet is soft, with ripe peach and melon fruit, subtle oak, and a hint of nutty complexity, possibly from malolactic fermentation. The palate has an attractive depth of ripe peach/nectarine flavour, balanced by good acidity. An impressive outcome for a dodgy vintage. **rating:** 89

best drinking Now–2004 **best vintages** NA **drink with** Sweetbreads • $27

Wedgetail Estate Pinot Noir

TTTTY **1999** Light to medium purple-red, deeper than the Par 3 (below). The bouquet has a mix of savoury, plum, cherry and some strawberry aromas; the palate has excellent length, flowing from the second it enters the mouth, and a long, persistent finish. This is not a heavyweight wine: there isn't an abundance of fruit, but what there is is very good indeed. **rating:** 90

best drinking Now–2004 **best vintages** '98, '99 **drink with** Quail • $26

Wedgetail Estate Par 3 Pinot Noir

TTTY **1999** Light red; a light, clean bouquet with a mix of strawberry and more savoury aromas is followed by a clean, light and fresh palate with attractive flavours but relatively simple structure. **rating:** 83

best drinking Now **best vintages** '99 **drink with** Cold lightly smoked meat • $17

Wedgetail Estate Reserve Pinot Noir

TTTTT **1999** Medium to full red-purple, darker in turn than the varietal. There are riper, darker fruit aromas, with forest and plum, and a touch of new oak evident. The palate has far more concentration and complexity to the flavour, with ripe plummy fruit and good tannins. **rating:** 94

best drinking 2002–2007 **best vintages** '99 **drink with** Squab • $55

wellington ★★★★☆

Cnr Richmond and Denholms Roads, Cambridge, Tas 7170 **region** Southern Tasmania
phone (03) 6248 5844 **fax** (03) 6248 5855 **open** By appointment
winemaker Andrew Hood **production** 3000 **est.** 1990
product range ($18–24 R) Riesling, Iced Riesling 375 ml, Chardonnay, Pinot Noir, Ruby Port.
summary Consultant-winemaker Andrew Hood (ex-Charles Sturt University) and wife Jenny have constructed a state-of-the-art winery on land leased from the University of Tasmania. The 2000-case production of Wellington is dwarfed by the 4500 cases contract-made for others, but the wines are always flawlessly crafted, particularly the Chardonnay.

Wellington Riesling

TTTT **2000** Medium to full yellow-green; the bouquet has masses of ripe citrus and pineapple fruit, the palate with generous, mouthfilling sweet citrus-fruit flavours, typical of the 2000 vintage. **rating:** 88

best drinking Now–2006 **best vintages** '96, '97, '98, '99 **drink with** Sautéed prawns • NA

Wellington Chardonnay

TTTTT **1999** Good when first tasted 12 months ago, but has developed superbly, seeming to pick up power and concentration in the bottle, with a mix of citrus and more tropical fruit now emerging in a powerful frame. Received top gold medal at the 2001 Tasmanian Wines Show. **rating:** 95

best drinking Now–2006 **best vintages** '92, '95, '96, '97, '98, '99 **drink with** Gravlax • NA

Wellington Pinot Noir

TTTT **1999** Medium red-purple; a stylish and fragrant bouquet with spicy, savoury aromas is followed by an elegant palate with a mix of similar spicy savoury characters to those of the bouquet supported by plum; there seems to be some whole-bunch character here when, so far as I know, the fruit is totally crushed. Interesting. Subtle oak. **rating:** 88

best drinking Now–2003 **best vintages** '94, '98, '99 **drink with** Tasmanian salmon • $24

wells parish wines NR

Benerin Estate, Sydney Road, Kandos, NSW 2848 **region** Mudgee
phone (02) 6379 4168 **fax** (02) 6379 4996 **open** By appointment
winemaker Pieter Van Gent **production** 500 **est.** 1995
product range ($17–18 CD) Chardonnay, Cabernet Sauvignon, Strayleaves Vintage Port.

summary Richard and Rachel Trounson, with help from father Barry Trounson, have established 16 hectares of vineyards at Benerin Estate since 1995. Most of the grapes are sold to Southcorp, but small quantities of wine are made for sale under the Wells Parish label. The vineyards are situated at the eastern extremity of the Mudgee region, near Rylstone, and both the soils and climate are distinctly different from those of the traditional Mudgee area.

Wells Parish Chardonnay

YYYYY **1999** Medium yellow-green; the bouquet is quite complex, with some lifted barrel-ferment aromas; abundant peach/melon/grapefruit flavours flood the rich, full palate, which has good length. What seems to be fairly high alcohol is the only possible thing that is questionable. **rating:** 94

best drinking Now–2003 **best vintages** '99 **drink with** Roast chicken • $15

wendouree ★★★★★

Wendouree Road, Clare, SA 5453 **region** Clare Valley
phone (08) 8842 2896 **open** By appointment
winemaker Tony Brady **production** 2500 **est.** 1895
product range ($15–36 ML) Shiraz, Shiraz Malbec, Shiraz Mataro, Cabernet Malbec, Cabernet Sauvignon, Muscat of Alexandria.

summary The iron fist in a velvet glove best describes these extraordinary wines. They are fashioned with passion and yet precision from the very old vineyard with its unique terroir by Tony and Lita Brady, who rightly see themselves as custodians of a priceless treasure. The 100-year-old stone winery is virtually unchanged from the day it was built; this is in every sense a treasure beyond price.

Wendouree Shiraz Malbec

YYYYY **1998** Dense, vivid red-purple; an exceptionally powerful bouquet with deep, black fruits and slightly earthy overtones leads into an almost impossibly powerful palate with massive black fruit and tannins. You don't describe it; it describes you. Requires an absolute minimum of 20 years. The points are largely irrelevant. **rating:** 95

best drinking 2013–2028 **best vintages** '96, '98 **drink with** Leave it in the cellar • NA

Wendouree Cabernet Malbec

YYYYY **1998** Medium to full purple-red; the bouquet has high-toned edges to the blackberry, earth and spice; the massive, mouthfilling blackberry/blackcurrant palate has all-pervasive tannins running through its length, yet is still in balance. **rating:** 94

best drinking 2013–2028 **best vintages** '83, '86, '89, '90, '91, '92, '94, '95, '96, '98 **drink with** Leave it in the cellar • NA

west cape howe wines NR

PO Box 548 Denmark, WA 6333 **region** Great Southern
phone (08) 9848 2959 **fax** (08) 9848 2903 **open** 7 days 10–5
winemaker Brenden Smith, Dave Cleary **production** 7000 **est.** 1997
product range ($11.75–22 CD) Semillon Sauvignon Blanc, Unwooded Chardonnay, Chardonnay, Late Picked Riesling, Shiraz, Cabernet Merlot, Muscat.

summary Brenden Smith was senior winemaker at Goundrey Wines for many years and has branched into business on his own with a contract-winemaking facility for growers throughout the Great Southern region. West Cape Howe wines are exported to the UK.

West Cape Howe Chardonnay

YYYY **2000** Medium yellow-green; the bouquet is complex, with strong, charry barrel-ferment inputs; the fairly light melon fruit on the palate staggers somewhat under the load of the oak. **rating:** 84

best drinking Now–2003 **best vintages** '99 **drink with** Roast pork • $19

West Cape Howe Shiraz

YYYY **1999** Light to medium purple-red; the moderately intense bouquet is clean and fresh, with bright cherry fruit and subtle oak, the medium-bodied palate delivering exactly what the bouquet promises, finishing with fine tannins. Very enjoyable. **rating:** 88

best drinking 2002–2007 **best vintages** NA **drink with** Lamb fillets • $21

westend estate wines ★★★☆

1283 Brayne Road, Griffith, NSW 2680 **region** Riverina
phone (02) 6964 1506 **fax** (02) 6962 1673 **open** Mon–Fri 8.30–5, Sat 9.30–4
winemaker William Calabria, James Ceccato **production** 142 500 **est.** 1945
product range ($8–20 CD) Outback Traminer Riesling, Semillon Sauvignon Blanc, Classic Dry Red, Shiraz; Richland Chardonnay, Sauvignon Blanc, Shiraz, Merlot, Cabernet Merlot, Cabernet Sauvignon; Port and Liqueur Muscat; followed by 3 Bridges range: Chardonnay, Shiraz, Cabernet Sauvignon, Golden Mist Botrytis Semillon.
summary Along with a number of Riverina producers, Westend is making a concerted move to lift both the quality and the packaging of its wines, spearheaded by the 3 Bridges range, which has an impressive array of gold medals to its credit since being first released in April 1997. It has also ventured into the export market, with distribution in the UK, the US and Switzerland.

Westend 3 Bridges Golden Mist Botrytis Semillon

▼▼▼▼▽ **1999** Deep gold; a complex and intense bouquet is redolent of botrytis-induced cumquat and apricot aromas; some lemony notes tighten up the palate nicely, also adding to the complexity and contributing to the long finish. **rating:** 90
best drinking Now–2003 **best vintages** '96, '99 **drink with** Fruit tart • $19.95

westfield

Cnr Memorial Ave and Great Northern Highway, Baskerville, WA 6056 **region** Swan District
phone (08) 9296 4356 **fax** (08) 9296 4356 **open** 7 days 10–5.30
winemaker John Kosovich **production** 11 000 **est.** 1922
product range ($17–22 CD) Verdelho, Sauvignon Blanc, Unwooded Chardonnay, Chardonnay, Bronze Wing Chardonnay, Chenin Blanc, Semillon, Riesling, Verdelho, Bronze Wing Verdelho, Bronze Wing Merlot, Shiraz, Cabernet Sauvignon, Vintage Port, Liqueur Muscat, Sparkling.
summary Consistent producer of a surprisingly elegant and complex Chardonnay; the other wines are more variable, but from time to time there has been an attractive Verdelho and excellent Cabernet Sauvignon. 1998 saw the first release of wines partly or wholly coming from the family's new planting at Pemberton, those being Swan/Pemberton blends released under the Bronze Wing label. Limited retail distribution in Perth, Melbourne and Sydney.

wetherall

Naracoorte Road, Coonawarra, SA 5263 **region** Coonawarra
phone (08) 8737 2104 **fax** (08) 8737 2105 **open** 7 days 10–4
winemaker Michael Wetherall **production** 1500 **est.** 1991
product range ($20–25 CD) Shiraz, Cabernet Sauvignon, Sparkling Cabernet.
summary The Wetherall family has been growing grapes in Coonawarra for more than 30 years, and Michael Wetherall (a Roseworthy graduate) has been responsible for overseeing wine production since Wetherall extended its operations into winemaking in 1991.

Wetherall Shiraz

▼▼▼▽ **1999** Medium purple-red; there is plenty of dark fruit, but even more oak, on both the bouquet and palate; the oak seriously dominates the quite good underlying fruit. I simply do not know whether time in bottle will restore the balance. **rating:** 82
best drinking 2003–2009 **best vintages** NA **drink with** Smoked meat • $20

Wetherall Cabernet Sauvignon

▼▼▼▼ **1999** Medium to full red-purple; a quite potent bouquet has a complex range of savoury/earthy/leathery/spicy and gamey aromas, becoming more focused on the palate where powerful blackberry and mulberry fruit is expressed. Lots going on here. **rating:** 85
best drinking 2004–2009 **best vintages** NA **drink with** Roast beef • $22

wharncliffe NR

Summerleas Road, Kingston, Tas 7050 **region** Southern Tasmania
phone (03) 6229 7147 **fax** (03) 6229 2298 **open** Not
winemaker Andrew Hood (Contract) **production** 115 **est.** 1990
product range ($20 ML) Chardonnay.
summary With total plantings of 0.75 hectare, Wharncliffe could not exist without the type of contract-winemaking service Andrew Hood offers, which would be a pity, because the vineyard is beautifully situated on the doorstep of Mount Wellington, the Huon Valley and the Channel regions of southern Tasmania.

Wharncliffe Chardonnay

YYYY **2000** Light green-yellow; the bouquet is light and fragrant, with a mix of citrus and passionfruit, showing faintly reduced characters. The palate follows down the same track, an intense, cool-grown wine that looks for all the world like a Chardonnay Sauvignon Blanc cross, although, needless to say, it is not. **rating:** 85
best drinking Now–2004 **best vintages** NA **drink with** Shellfish • $20

whiskey gully wines NR

Beverley Road, Severnlea, Qld 4352 **region** Granite Belt
phone (07) 4683 5100 **fax** (07) 4683 5155 **open** 7 days 8.30–5
winemaker Philippa Hambleton, Rod MacPherson **production** 500 **est.** 1997
product range ($12–30 CD) Beverley Chardonnay, Republic Red, Shiraz, Cabernet Sauvignon.
summary Close inspection of the winery letterhead discloses that The Media Mill Pty Ltd trades as Whiskey Gully Wines. It is no surprise, then, to find proprietor John Arlidge saying, 'Wine and politics are a heady mix; I have already registered the 2000 Republic Red as a voter in 26 marginal electorates and we are considering nominating it for Liberal Party pre-selection in Bennelong.' Wit to one side, Arlidge has big plans for Whiskey Gully Wines, in the long range to establish 40 hectares of vineyards, extending the varietal range with petit verdot, malbec, merlot, semillon and sauvignon blanc. At present the wines are made off site, but as production increases (to over 1600 cases within four years) on-site winemaking will be progressively introduced.

whispering hills NR

54 Gibbs Road, Majorca, Vic 3465 **region** Bendigo
phone (03) 5964 6070 **fax** (03) 5964 6231 **open** Not
winemaker Murray Lyons, Ron Snep **production** 500 **est.** 1994
product range ($22 ML) Chardonnay, Cabernet Sauvignon.
summary The minuscule production of Whispering Hills is limited to two wines that are sold by mail order and word of mouth.

whisson lake NR

PO Box 91 Uraidla, SA 5142 **region** Adelaide Hills
phone (08) 8390 1303 **fax** (08) 8390 3822 **open** By appointment
winemaker Roman Bratasiuk (Contract) **production** 300 **est.** 1985
product range ($27.50–31.50 CD) Pinot Noir.
summary Mark Whisson is primarily a grape-grower, with 4.5 hectares of close-planted, steep-sloped north-facing vineyard. A small quantity of the production is made for the Whisson Lake label by Roman Bratasiuk, best known as the owner/winemaker of Clarendon Hills. Tiny quantities are exported to the US and the UK.

whitehorse wine NR

4 Reid Park Road, Mount Clear, Vic 3350 **region** Ballarat
phone (03) 5330 1719 **fax** (03) 5330 1288 **open** Weekends 11–5
winemaker Noel Myers **production** 900 **est.** 1981
product range ($10–18 CD) Riesling, Riesling Müller Thurgau, Chardonnay, Pinot Noir, Cabernet Shiraz.
summary The Myers family has moved from grape-growing to winemaking, utilising the attractive site on its sloping hillside south of Ballarat. Four hectares of vines are in production, with pinot noir and chardonnay the principal varieties.

wignalls wines ★★★☆

Chester Pass Road (Highway 1), Albany, WA 6330 **region** Great Southern
phone (08) 9841 2848 **fax** (08) 9842 9003 **open** 7 days 12–4
winemaker Bill Wignall **production** 5000 **est.** 1982
product range ($12–32 R) Chardonnay, Sauvignon Blanc, Late Harvest Frontignac, Pinot Noir, Reserve Pinot Noir, Cabernet Sauvignon, Tawny Port, White Port.
summary A noted producer of Pinot Noir, Wignalls has extended the map for the variety in Australia. The Pinots have tremendous style and flair, but do age fairly quickly. The white wines are elegant, and show the cool climate to good advantage. A new winery was constructed and opened for the 1998 vintage, utilising the production from the 16 hectares of estate plantings.

Wignalls Pinot Noir

🍷🍷🍷🍷 **1999** Light to medium red, with just a touch of purple; the bouquet initially opened with fresh, clean, light, relatively simple aromas but then a certain degree of tangy complexity came up. The palate stayed on the left side of the tracks, with a mix of vegetal/tangy/savoury/minty characters that offered plenty of action, but which really needed more ripe fruit, and ended up light. **rating:** 82

best drinking Now–2004 **best vintages** '85, '86, '88, '91, '93, '95, '97 **drink with** Seared Tasmanian salmon • NA

wild dog NR

South Road, Warragul, Vic 3820 **region** Gippsland
phone (03) 5623 1117 **fax** (03) 5623 6402 **open** 7 days 10–5
winemaker John Farrington **production** 3000 **est.** 1982
product range ($12–18 CD) Riesling, Chardonnay, Rosé, Pinot Noir, Shiraz, Cabernet Sauvignon.
summary An aptly named winery that produces somewhat rustic wines from the 12 hectares of estate vineyards; even the Farringtons say that the Shiraz comes 'with a bite', also pointing out that there is minimal handling, fining and filtration. Be warned.

Wild Dog Shiraz

🍷🍷🍷🍷 **1998** Medium red; a mix of earthy, spicy, oaky aromas are only moderately enticing, but the palate is altogether different, with abundant, rich plum and cherry fruit, and just a touch of mint. Soft tannins; well-handled extract. **rating:** 87

best drinking 2002–2007 **best vintages** NA **drink with** Braised beef in red wine • $18

wild duck creek estate NR

Spring Flat Road, Heathcote, Vic 3523 **region** Heathcote
phone (03) 5433 3133 **fax** (03) 5433 3133 **open** By appointment
winemaker David Anderson **production** 4000 **est.** 1980
product range ($25–75 CD) Springflat Shiraz, Alan's Cabernets, Alan's Cabernets Pressings, The Blend, Duck Muck, Cabernet Sauvignon Reserve, Sparkling Duck 2.
summary The first release of Wild Duck Creek Estate from the 1991 vintage marks the end of 12 years of effort by David and Diana Anderson. They commenced planting the 4.5-hectare vineyard in 1980, made their first tiny quantities of wine in 1986, the first commercial quantities of wine in 1991, and built their winery and cellar-door facility in 1993. Exports to the US (where Duck Muck has become a cult wine), the UK, Belgium, Germany and Singapore.

wilderness estate NR

Branxton Road, Pokolbin, NSW 2321 **region** Lower Hunter Valley
phone (02) 4998 7755 **fax** (02) 4998 7750 **open** 7 days 9–5
winemaker Josef Lesnik **production** 31 000 **est.** 1986
product range ($11.50–18.50 R) The premium varietal range, Wilderness Estate label: Unwooded Semillon, Individual Block Semillon, Unwooded Chardonnay, Reserve Chardonnay, Shiraz, Cabernet Merlot, Merlot; the second range of lower-priced varietals, Black Creek label: Traminer Riesling, Semillon, Verdelho, Chardonnay, Sparkling Brut, Pinot Noir, Shiraz.

summary Long-term Wyndham Estate winemaker John Baruzzi has formed a 50:50 joint venture with Joe Lesnik, resulting in the former Lesnik Family Winery being renamed Wilderness Estate. The Lesnik label will be phased out, with all wines from the '95 vintage being released either under the Wilderness Estate label or under the Black Creek label. National distribution through Normans is supplemented by exports to the US, Canada and the UK. As this book was going to print Wilderness Estate was being offered for sale by auction.

wildwood ★★★★☆

St John's Lane, Wildwood, Bulla, Vic 3428 **region** Sunbury
phone (03) 9307 1118 **fax** (03) 9331 1590 **open** 7 days 10–6
winemaker Dr Wayne Stott, Peter Dredge **production** 1500 **est.** 1983
product range ($20–32 CD) Chardonnay, Pinot Noir, Shiraz, Cabernets, Merlot Cabernet Franc.
summary Wildwood is situated just 4 kilometres past Melbourne airport. The vineyard and cellar door are situated at an altitude of 130 metres in the Oaklands Valley, which provides unexpected views back to Port Phillip Bay and the Melbourne skyline. Plastic surgeon Wayne Stott has taken what is very much a part-time activity rather more seriously than most by completing the wine science degree at Charles Sturt University. The rating is given for the red wines; it has to be said the white wines are less impressive.

Wildwood Pinot Noir

🍷🍷🍷🍷 **1999** The colour is quite developed, which, as is so often the case with Pinot Noir, is no reliable guide; the bouquet is complex, with a mix of spicy/briary/forest/stemmy varietal aromas; there are sweet spicy characters, almost into nutmeg, which lift the palate, possibly coming from the astute use of oak. **rating:** 89

best drinking Now **best vintages** '98 **drink with** Duck breast • $25

Wildwood Shiraz

🍷🍷🍷🍷🍷 **1999** Dense red-purple; a strong, powerful and concentrated bouquet with plum and earth is followed by a palate where pronounced chocolate and spice are added to the plum mix. Avoids the excess extract/tannin trap on the finish. Won trophy for Best Regional Wine at the 2000 Ballarat Wine Show. **rating:** 91

best drinking 2003–2009 **best vintages** '97, '98, '99 **drink with** Coq au vin • $32

Wildwood Cabernets

🍷🍷🍷🍷 **1999** Medium red-purple; the bouquet offers a mix of soft raspberry/blueberry/earthy aromas, with more sweetness and ripeness on the supple blackberry-flavoured palate. Nice wine. **rating:** 87

best drinking 2002–2007 **best vintages** '93, '97, '98 **drink with** Oxtail • $30

---

wildwood of yallingup NR

Caves Road, Yallingup, WA 6282 **region** Margaret River
phone (08) 9755 2544 **fax** (08) 9755 2644 **open** 7 days 10–4
winemaker James Pennington, Gary Baldwin (Consultant) **production** 5000 **est.** 1984
product range ($14.50–30 CD) Chardonnay, Semillon, Sauvignon Blanc, Chenin Blanc, Shiraz, Cabernet Merlot.
summary Wildwood is part of the spectacularly expanding Hotham Valley Estate empire, which now includes a 33-hectare property at Chapman Brook with 5 hectares under vine; the Bridgeland Vineyard, a 207-hectare property with 97 hectares under vine; and Wildwood, with 56 hectares and featuring a restaurant, cellar door and accommodation, with 6 hectares under vine – all in the Margaret River region. These complement the original property at Wandering, which has 15 hectares and a state-of-the-art winery completed in 1993. All of this will see current production of 5000 cases skyrocket to 100 000 cases in the years ahead, with Wildwood providing the principal cellar-door sales outlet.

willespie ★★★☆

Harmans Mill Road, Willyabrup, via Cowaramup, WA 6284 **region** Margaret River
phone (08) 9755 6248 **fax** (08) 9755 6210 **open** 7 days 10.30–5
winemaker Michael Lemmes **production** 4000 **est.** 1976
product range ($15–35 R) Sauvignon Blanc, Semillon Sauvignon Blanc, Verdelho, Riesling, Shiraz, Cabernet Sauvignon, Merlot; Harmans Mill White and Harmans Mill Red are cheaper second-label wines.
summary Willespie has produced many attractive white wines over the years, typically in brisk, herbaceous Margaret River style. All are fruit- rather than oak-driven; the newer Merlot also shows promise. The wines have had such success that the Squance family (which founded and owns Willespie) has announced plans to substantially increase winery capacity, drawing upon an additional 25 hectares of estate vineyards.

willow bridge estate ★★★★

Gardin Court Drive, Dardanup, WA 6236 **region** Geographe
phone (08) 9728 0055 **fax** (08) 9728 0066 **open** By appointment
winemaker Rob Bowen **production** 24 000 **est.** 1997
product range ($14–25 R) Sauvignon Blanc, Sauvignon Blanc Semillon, Semillon Sauvignon Blanc, Chenin Blanc, Chardonnay, Shiraz, Cabernet Sauvignon.
summary The Dewar family has followed a fast track in developing Willow Bridge Estate since acquiring their spectacular 180-hectare hillside property in the Ferguson Valley in 1996. They have already planted 60 hectares of chardonnay, semillon, sauvignon blanc, shiraz and cabernet sauvignon, with tempranillo added in the spring of 2000, and another 10 hectares due to be planted over the next year or two. A state-of-the-art winery has been constructed which will be capable of handling the 1200 to 1500 tonnes expected from the estate plantings by 2004. Winemaker Rob Bowen has had a long and distinguished career, first as winemaker at Plantagenet and thereafter at Capel Vale.

Willow Bridge Estate Sauvignon Blanc

▼▼▼▼ **2000** Light green-yellow; a highly aromatic and intense bouquet with a mix of tropical and passionfruit aromas changes direction somewhat on the more minerally, restrained palate; something of a rollercoaster ride, perhaps. **rating:** 86

best drinking Now **best vintages** NA **drink with** Poached scallops • NA

Willow Bridge Estate Sauvignon Blanc Semillon

▼▼▼▼▽ **2000** Light green-yellow; a clean bouquet, with gentle tropical gooseberry fruit leads into a palate with good balance, intensity and length, showing an appealing mix of tropical and more herbaceous flavours running through to a lingering finish. **rating:** 93

best drinking Now–2003 **best vintages** '00 **drink with** Fresh abalone • NA

Willow Bridge Estate Chenin Blanc

▼▼▼▽ **2000** Light green-yellow; the pleasant and clean bouquet has gentle fruit-salad characters with faint tropical overtones, the palate following languidly down the same track. Inoffensive but unremarkable. **rating:** 84

best drinking Now–2003 **best vintages** NA **drink with** Pasta • NA

Willow Bridge Estate Chardonnay

▼▼▼▽ **1999** Medium yellow-green; a clean, soft bouquet with the hallmark gentle fruit that seems to be the mark of all of these wines, with nectarine and peach; the palate is similar, with soft nectarine fruit, but lacks concentration. **rating:** 84

best drinking Now **best vintages** NA **drink with** Crumbed brains • NA

Willow Bridge Estate Cabernet Sauvignon

▼▼▼▼ **1999** Medium red-purple; an interesting bouquet with blackberry aromas, but then a range of spicy/savoury/earthy/licorice notes akin to shiraz; the palate has good, sweet, ripe fruit on entry and running into the middle, which carries the evident oak; does tail off slightly on the finish. **rating:** 87

best drinking Now–2005 **best vintages** NA **drink with** Seared beef • NA

willow creek ★★★★

166 Balnarring Road, Merricks North, Vic 3926 **region** Mornington Peninsula
phone (03) 5989 7448 **fax** (03) 5989 7584 **open** 7 days 10–5
winemaker Simon Black **production** 14 000 **est.** 1989
product range ($15–27 R) Sauvignon Blanc, Unoaked Chardonnay, Tulum Chardonnay, Pinot Noir, Shiraz, Cabernet Sauvignon, Sparkling Cuvée.
summary Yet another significant player in the Mornington Peninsula area, with 15 hectares of vines planted to cabernet sauvignon, chardonnay and pinot noir. Expansion of the cellar door was completed by January 1998, with a winery constructed for the 1998 vintage. The restaurant is open for lunch 7 days and Friday and Saturday nights for dinner. The wines are exported to Singapore, the US and the UK.

Willow Creek Sauvignon Blanc

YYYY **2000** Light green-yellow; the bouquet is quite aromatic, with herb and gooseberry fruit touched with more tropical passionfruit characters. The palate veers more towards the tighter end of the spectrum, with crisp, mineral and herb flavours sustained by neatly balanced acidity. **rating:** 87

best drinking Now **best vintages** '00 **drink with** Asparagus and salmon terrine • $20

Willow Creek Unwooded Chardonnay

YYYY **2000** Light green-yellow; the bouquet is fresh with some passionfruit fragrance, quite possibly an attractive overhang of yeast-fermentation character. The palate is light, fresh and crisp, with a mix of melon and citrus fruit; a good summer lunch wine for immediate drinking. **rating:** 85

best drinking Now **best vintages** NA **drink with** Vegetable terrine • $16

Willow Creek Tulum Chardonnay

YYYY **1999** Medium yellow-green; the bouquet is clean, with a mix of melon and mineral aromas; the light- to medium-bodied palate has the same melon-mineral mix, with moderate length and subtle oak. **rating:** 84

best drinking Now **best vintages** '98 **drink with** Pan-fried flathead fillets • $25

Willow Creek Pinot Noir

YYYY **1999** Light to medium red-purple; the bouquet is quite aromatic with a mix of spicy cherry and plum fruit and some savoury overtones. The palate is lively, with cherry and plum fruit the major component, but with a touch of mint that detracts; it should not be part of Pinot Noir. **rating:** 85

best drinking Now **best vintages** '91, '94, '95, '97, '98 **drink with** Gently spiced Asian food • $25

willow vale estate NR

11 Willow Vale Road, Gerringong, NSW 2534 **region** South Coast Zone
phone (02) 4234 0975 **fax** (02) 4234 4477 **open** Not
winemaker Bevan Wilson **production** NA **est.** 1998
product range Arneis, Verdelho, Chardonnay, Shiraz, Sangiovese, Chambourcin, Cabernet Sauvignon.
summary With 13.5 hectares of vineyard planted to chardonnay, verdelho, arneis, shiraz, cabernet sauvignon, merlot, ruby cabernet, sangiovese and chambourcin, Willow Vale has the largest vineyard on the New South Wales South Coast. Production is expected to increase to 10 000 cases by 2003, as a winery is being constructed on site. Cellar-door sales, craft shop and café opened in early 2001.

willowvale wines NR

Black Swamp Road, Tenterfield, NSW 2372 **region** Northern Slopes Zone
phone (02) 6736 3589 **fax** (02) 6736 3753 **open** 7 days 10–5
winemaker John Morley **production** 1200 **est.** 1994
product range ($14–25 CD) Federation Classic White, Ambrosia, Late Harvest Riesling, Cabernet Merlot, Cabernet Sauvignon, Bushranger Musket, Centenary of Federation Port.
summary John Morley commenced establishing 1.8 hectares of vineyard of equal portions of chardonnay, merlot and cabernet sauvignon in 1994 with further planting in 1999 and 2000. The vineyard is at an altitude of 940 metres and was the first in the growing Tenterfield region. Advanced vineyard climatic monitoring systems have been installed, and a new winery building was constructed and equipped in time for the 2000 vintage.

will taylor wines ★★★★

1B Victoria Avenue, Unley Park, SA 5061 **region** Warehouse
phone (08) 8271 6122 **fax** (08) 8271 6122 **open** By appointment
winemaker Various Contract **production** 1300 **est.** 1997
product range ($20 R) Clare Valley Riesling, Hunter Valley Semillon, Adelaide Hills Sauvignon Blanc, Geelong/Yarra Valley Pinot Noir.
summary Will Taylor is a partner in the leading Adelaide law firm Finlaysons and specialises in wine law. Together with Suzanne Taylor, he has established a classic negociant wine business, having wines contract-made to his specification. Moreover, he chooses what he considers to be the best regions for each variety and added a Geelong/Yarra Valley Pinot Noir in 2000. Most of the wine is sold to restaurants, with small volumes sold to a select group of fine-wine stores and mail order. Exports to the US.

Will Taylor Clare Valley Riesling

ΥΥΥΥΥ **2000** Light to medium yellow-green; the firm, intense bouquet has quite herbaceous overtones to the underlying lime and apple fruit of the bouquet. The palate is similarly intense and full-flavoured, with lime, apple and herb; good length and balance. 358 cases made. **rating:** 90

best drinking 2002–2007 **best vintages** '00 **drink with** Char-grilled octopus salad • $20.45

Will Taylor Hunter Valley Semillon

ΥΥΥΥ **2000** Pale straw-green; the clean, crisp and fresh bouquet is so far showing little other than hints of lemon; the palate is lively, fresh and well balanced, crying out for time to develop the latent fruit character and complexity. Well made. **rating:** 87

best drinking 2003–2010 **best vintages** NA **drink with** Light pasta • $20.50

Will Taylor Adelaide Hills Sauvignon Blanc

ΥΥΥΥΥ **2000** Light to medium yellow-green; the bouquet is clean, with a nice balance between herbaceous and riper, more tropical, fruit aromas. An identical mix of flavours manifests itself on the palate; delicate, but has flavour and length. 412 cases made. **rating:** 90

best drinking Now–2003 **best vintages** '00 **drink with** Oysters • $20.45

wilmot hills vineyard NR

407 Back Road, Wilmot, Tas 7310 **region** Northern Tasmania
phone (03) 6492 1193 **fax** (03) 6492 1193 **open** 7 days 9–7
winemaker John Cole, Ruth Cole **production** NA **est.** 1991
product range ($15–18 CD) Muller Thürgau, Pinot Noir, El Nino Pinot Noir, fruit wines and ciders.
summary The beautiful Wilmot Hills Vineyard is situated on the western side of Lake Barrington, not far from the Cradle Mountain road, with marvellous views to Mount Roland and the adjacent peaks. It is very much a family affair, established by John and Ruth Cole, and produces both wine and cider. John Cole spent 18 years in Melbourne participating in engineering design and some graphic art, Ruth working in the hospitality industry for ten years and making fruit wines for 20 years. The neat on-site winery was both designed and built by the Coles, as was much of the wine and cider-making equipment.

wilson vineyard ★★★★

Polish Hill River, Sevenhill, via Clare, SA 5453 **region** Clare Valley
phone (08) 8843 4310 **open** Weekends May–Oct 10–4
winemaker John Wilson, Daniel Wilson **production** 4000 **est.** 1974
product range ($13–26 CD) Gallery Series Riesling, Semillon, Leucothea (sweet), Bin 95 Hippocrene Sparkling Burgundy.
summary Dr John Wilson is a tireless ambassador for the Clare Valley and for wine (and its beneficial effect on health) in general. His wines were made using techniques and philosophies garnered early in his wine career and can occasionally be idiosyncratic but in recent years have been most impressive. The winemaking mantle has now passed to his son, Daniel. The wines are sold through cellar door and retail in Sydney, Melbourne, Brisbane and Adelaide; no mailing list.

wimbaliri wines NR

Barton Highway, Murrumbateman, NSW 2582 **region** Canberra District
phone (02) 6227 5921 **fax** (02) 6227 5921 **open** Weekends 11–5 and by appointment
winemaker John Andersen **production** 550 **est.** 1988
product range ($16–19 CD) Chardonnay, Pinot Noir, Cabernet Merlot.
summary John and Margaret Andersen moved to the Canberra district in 1987 and started to establish their vineyard at Murrumbateman in 1988; the property borders the highly regarded Canberra producers Doonkuna and Clonakilla. The vineyard is close-planted with a vertical trellis system, with a total of 2.2 hectares planted to chardonnay, pinot noir, shiraz, cabernet sauvignon and merlot (plus a few vines of cabernet franc).

windarra NR

De Beyers Road, Pokolbin, NSW 2321 **region** Lower Hunter Valley
phone (02) 4998 7648 **fax** (02) 4998 7648 **open** Tues–Sun 10–5
winemaker Tom Andresen **production** NA **est.** 1985

product range ($9–23.50 CD) Semillon, Chardonnay, Limited Edition Reserve Chardonnay, Chardonnay Semillon, Rose, Shiraz, White Liqueur Port, Tawny Port, Mead, Gold Wine (Mead, with 22-carat gold flakes).
summary The Andresen family has 6 hectares of semillon, chardonnay and shiraz; the wines are contract-made.

windermere wines NR

Lot 3, Watters Road, Ballandean, Qld 4382 **region** Granite Belt
phone (07) 4684 1353 **fax** (07) 4684 1353 **open** 7 days 9.30–5
winemaker Wayne Beecham, Kate Beecham **production** 500 **est.** 1995
product range ($11–17 CD) Chardonnay, Lilybrook DW Chardonnay Semillon, Sangiovese Merlot Cabernet, Millroad DR Cabernet Merlot, Shiraz, Liqueur Muscat; a selection of liqueurs and fruit wines.
summary After spending three years travelling in Europe between 1983 and 1986, Wayne Beecham returned to Australia to take up a position with what was then Thomas Hardy Wines, and specifically to establish the RhineCastle wine distribution in Queensland. During the next seven and a half years he studied wine marketing at Roseworthy while working for Hardys, but in 1993 he, wife Julie and daughter Kate decided to move to the Granite Belt to establish Windermere Wines from the ground up. His long service with Hardys stood him in good stead, landing him a cellar position at Hardys Tintara in the 1994 vintage, working with winemaker David O'Leary. In typical Australian fashion, Wayne Beecham says they decided on the Granite Belt because 'if we were to succeed, we might as well do it in the toughest new region in the industry'.

Windermere Chardonnay

🍷🍷🍷🍷 **1999** Light green-yellow; the bouquet has light but clean fruit, the palate similarly fresh, light and not forced. The smoky vanilla oak has not been overplayed, which would have been all too easy with a wine of this weight. Winner of two bronze medals. **rating:** 81

best drinking Now **best vintages** NA **drink with** Pasta • $16

windowrie estate NR

Windowrie, Canowindra, NSW 2804 **region** Cowra
phone (02) 6344 3234 **fax** (02) 6344 3227 **open** 7 days 10–6 at The Mill, Vaux Street, Cowra
winemaker Rodney Hooper, Stephen Craig **production** 24 000 **est.** 1988
product range ($12–21 ML) Chardonnay, Botrytis Sauvignon Blanc, Shiraz; The Mill range of Traminer Riesling, Sauvignon Blanc, Chardonnay, Shiraz and Cabernet Sauvignon Merlot Cabernet Franc.
summary Windowrie Estate was established in 1988 on a substantial grazing property at Canowindra, 30 kilometres north of Cowra and in the same viticultural region. Most of the grapes from the 230-hectare vineyard are sold to other makers, with increasing quantities being made for the Windowrie Estate and The Mill labels, the Chardonnays enjoying show success. The cellar door is situated in a flour mill built in 1861 from local granite. It ceased operations in 1905 and lay unoccupied for 91 years until restored by the O'Dea family.

windy ridge vineyard & winery NR

Foster–Fish Creek Road, Foster, Vic 3960 **region** Gippsland
phone (03) 5682 2035 **open** Holiday weekends 10–5
winemaker Graeme Wilson **production** 350 **est.** 1978
product range ($15–35 CD) Traminer, Pinot Noir, Cabernet Sauvignon Malbec, Malbec Cabernet Sauvignon, Vintage Port, Georgia's Liqueur Pinot Noir, Graeme's Late Bottled Vintage Port.
summary The 2.8-hectare Windy Ridge Vineyard was planted between 1978 and 1986, with the first vintage not taking place until 1988. Winemaker Graeme Wilson favours prolonged maturation, part in stainless steel and part in oak, before bottling his wines, typically giving the Pinot Noir three years and the Cabernet two years before bottling. No recent tastings.

winewood NR

Sundown Road, Ballandean, Qld 4382 **region** Granite Belt
phone (07) 4684 1187 **fax** (07) 4684 1187 **open** Weekends, public holidays 9–5
winemaker Ian Davis **production** 1000 **est.** 1984
product range ($15–20 CD) Chardonnay, Chardonnay Marsanne, Shiraz Marsanne, MacKenzies Run (Cabernet blend), Muscat.
summary A weekend and holiday activity for schoolteacher Ian Davis and town-planner wife Jeanette; the tiny winery is a model of neatness and precision planning. The use of marsanne with chardonnay and semillon shows an interesting change in direction. Has a little over 3 hectares of estate plantings. All wine sold through cellar door.

winstead ★★★★☆

75 Winstead Road, Bagdad, Tas 7030 **region** Southern Tasmania
phone (03) 6268 6417 **fax** (03) 6268 6417 **open** By appointment
winemaker Andrew Hood (Contract), Neil Snare **production** 750 **est.** 1989
product range ($19–24 CD) Riesling, Ensnared Riesling, Pinot Noir.
summary The good news about Winstead is the outstanding quality of its extremely generous and rich Pinot Noirs, rivalling those of Freycinet for the abundance of their fruit flavour without any sacrifice of varietal character. The bad news is that production is so limited, with only half a hectare each of riesling and pinot noir being tended by fly-fishing devotee Neil Snare and wife Julieanne. Retail distribution in Melbourne.

Winstead Ensnared Riesling

YYYY **2000** Strong green-yellow; the bouquet is rich, with ever-so-slightly burnt sugar aromatics; rights itself on the powerful, intense mandarin/lime juice palate. **rating:** 88
best drinking 2002–2005 **best vintages** '99 **drink with** Poached fruit • $19

Winstead Pinot Noir

YYYYY **1999** Medium to full red-purple; a wonderfully complex and aromatic bouquet has a stemmy/woodsy/briary/spicy/plummy serenade of aromas, then magically changing into a sweet palate that flows smoothly across the tongue, with an overwhelming impression of elegance. **rating:** 94
best drinking 2002–2007 **best vintages** '96, '97, '98, '99 **drink with** Saddle of hare • $24

wirilda creek ★★★

RSD91 McMurtrie Road, McLaren Vale, SA 5171 **region** McLaren Vale
phone (08) 8323 9688 **fax** (08) 8323 9260 **open** 7 days 10–5
winemaker Kerry Flanagan **production** 1500 **est.** 1993
product range ($13–25 CD) Grape Pickers (Riesling Chardonnay Semillon), Sauvignon Blanc, Verdelho, Shiraz, Shiraz Rare, Cabernet Merlot, Vine Pruners Cabernet Blend, Cabernet Sauvignon Rare, Evening Shadow (Sparkling Shiraz), Fortifieds.
summary Wirilda Creek may be one of the newer arrivals in McLaren Vale but it offers the lot: wine, lunch every day (Pickers Platters with local produce) and accommodation (four rooms opening onto a private garden courtyard). Co-owner Kerry Flanagan (with partner Karen Shertock) has had great experience in the wine and hospitality industries: a Roseworthy graduate (1980) he has inter alia worked at Penfolds, Coriole and Wirra Wirra, and also owned the famous Old Salopian Inn for a period of time. A little under 4 hectares of McLaren Vale estate vineyards have now been joined with a little over 3 hectares of vineyards planted at Antechamber Bay, Kangaroo Island. Limited retail distribution in New South Wales and South Australia; exports to the US.

Wirilda Creek Cabernet Sauvignon Merlot

YYYY **1998** Medium purple-red; there is quite sweet fruit on the bouquet, with nice touches of mint and vanilla; the palate continues in a pleasant easy style with sweet berry and chocolate fruit flavours, rounded up by soft tannins. Nice wine. **rating:** 86
best drinking 2002–2007 **best vintages** NA **drink with** Hot pot • $18

wirra wirra ★★★★☆

McMurtie Road, McLaren Vale, SA 5171 **region** McLaren Vale
phone (08) 8323 8414 **fax** (08) 8323 8596 **open** Mon–Sat 10–5, Sun 11–5
winemaker Ben Riggs, Samantha Connen **production** 80 000 **est.** 1969
product range ($14–69 R) The Cousins (Sparkling), Hand Picked Riesling, Late Picked Riesling, Semillon Sauvignon Blanc Chardonnay, Scrubby Rise Semillon, Sauvignon Blanc, Chardonnay, Sexton's Acre Unwooded Chardonnay, RSW Shiraz, Allawah Vineyard Barossa Grenache, Original Blend (Grenache Shiraz), Merlot, The Angelus Cabernet Sauvignon, Church Block (Cabernet Shiraz Merlot), Fortifieds.
summary Long-respected for the consistency of its white wines, Wirra Wirra has now established an equally formidable reputation for its reds. Right across the board, the wines are of exemplary character, quality and style, The Angelus Cabernet Sauvignon and RSW Shiraz battling with each other for supremacy. Long may the battle continue under the direction of the highly respected Tim James, lured from his senior position at BRL Hardy late in 2000. The wines are exported to the US, the UK, Switzerland, Germany, the Netherlands, New Zealand, Hong Kong and Singapore.

Wirra Wirra Sauvignon Blanc

ΨΨΨΨ **2000** Light green-yellow; the very grassy/herbaceous bouquet is slightly old-fashioned, the palate crisp, with quite a deal of flavour, but, as with the bouquet, more in yesterday's style than today's. **rating:** 86

best drinking Now **best vintages** '91, '92, '94, '96, '97 **drink with** Blue swimmer crab • $16

Wirra Wirra Chardonnay

ΨΨΨΨ **1999** Light to medium yellow-green; the bouquet is clean but slightly diffuse, with a mix of melon, fig and peach fruit; the palate is soft, with sweet, slightly spongy fruit, redeemed in part by clever oak handling. **rating:** 87

best drinking Now–2003 **best vintages** '82, '89, '91, '92, '94, '96, '97 **drink with** Wiener schnitzel • $25

Wirra Wirra RSW Shiraz

ΨΨΨΨΨ **1998** Medium to full red-purple; an excellent range of varietal aromas running through spice, berry and chocolate, with lesser hints of earth and oak. The palate has lovely, sweet cherry/berry flavour, and manages to carry its 14.5° alcohol far better than one might imagine; the tannin control is equally good. **rating:** 94

best drinking 2003–2013 **best vintages** '94, '95, '97, '98 **drink with** Smoked beef • $41

Wirra Wirra Merlot

ΨΨΨΨΨ **1998** Medium red-purple; the bouquet is clean, aromatic and intense, with positive, ripe varietal character and attractive oak. The wine has excellent structure, with finely delineated, gently sweet red berry varietal fruit, and equally attractive fine tannins and gentle oak. Spot on. **rating:** 94

best drinking 2002–2010 **best vintages** '98 **drink with** Milk-fed lamb • $41

Wirra Wirra Allawah Vineyard Barossa Grenache

ΨΨΨΨΨ **1997** One of a series of singularly impressive small-batch (250 dozen) wines from Wirra Wirra. Grenache doesn't come much better than this, with gently ripe, juicy but not jammy berry aromas, and a quite lovely palate: supple, round and smooth, the sweet, spicy fruit encapsulated in excellent oak. **rating:** 95

best drinking Now–2007 **best vintages** '97 **drink with** Cassoulet • $43

Wirra Wirra Church Block Cabernet Shiraz Merlot

ΨΨΨΨ **1999** Medium to full red-purple; the bouquet is clean, the red berry fruit showing touches of spice and earth; a pleasant, well-balanced commercial red wine with nice fruit and gentle oak, but a far cry from the exciting wine it once was. **rating:** 86

best drinking 2002–2006 **best vintages** '90, '91, '94, '98 **drink with** Pasta bolognaise • $18.50

Wirra Wirra The Angelus Cabernet Sauvignon

ΨΨΨΨΨ **1998** The trophy for Best Cabernet Sauvignon in a class of 163 wines at the 2000 Royal Adelaide Wine Show was justice for this pristine, powerful example of the variety. Potent savoury, earthy berry fruit marks both the bouquet and the great length of the palate, sustained by fine-grained but persistent tannins. **rating:** 95

best drinking 2003–2023 **best vintages** '86, '90, '91, '92, '95, '96, '97, '98 **drink with** Spring lamb • $41

wise wines NR

Lot 4 Eagle Bay Road, Dunsborough, WA 6281 **region** Margaret River
phone (08) 9756 8627 **fax** (08) 9756 8770 **open** 7 days 10.30–4.30
winemaker Siobhan Lynch **production** 36 000 **est.** 1986
product range ($17–35 R) Sauvignon Blanc Semillon, Aquercus Chardonnay (Unwooded), Leaf Chardonnay, Classic White, Late Harvest (Chenin Blanc, Semillon, Muscat), Pinot Noir, Classic Soft Red, Eagle Bay Shiraz, Shiraz Merlot, Cabernet Sauvignon, Tawny Port.
summary Wise Wines, headed by Perth entrepreneur Ron Wise, brings together the 20.5-hectare Eagle Bay Vineyard at Meelup, the 10.3-hectare Donnybrook Valley Vineyard at Donnybrook and the 4-hectare Bramley Estate Vineyard at Margaret River. The appointment of Siobhan Lynch, formerly winemaker at Chatsfield, has coincided with a sharp increase in production, and exports to the US.

witchmount estate NR

557 Leakes Road, Rockbank, Vic 3335 **region** Sunbury
phone (03) 9747 1047 **open** Wed–Sun
winemaker Peter Dredge **production** 2000 **est.** 1991
product range ($10–30 CD) Semillon, Sauvignon Blanc, Chardonnay, Nebbiolo, Shiraz, Cabernet Sauvignon.

summary Gaye and Matt Ramunno operate Witchmount Estate along with its on site Italian restaurant and function rooms, which are open from Wednesday to Sunday inclusive for lunch and dinner. In 1991 12 hectares of vines were established; a further 9 hectares are currently being planted. Varieties include nebbiolo and the rare northern Italian white grape picolit. Another variety new to the region will be tempranillo.

wolf blass ★★★★☆

Bilyara Vineyards, Sturt Highway, Nuriootpa, SA 5355 **region** Barossa Valley
phone (08) 8562 1955 **fax** (08) 8562 4181 **open** Mon–Fri 9.15–4.30, weekends 10–4.30
winemaker John Glaetzer (Chief), Wendy Stuckey (White), Caroline Dunn (Red) **production** NFP **est.** 1966
product range ($11–100 R) White wines under White, Yellow, Green and Gold labels, with emphasis on Riesling and blended Classic Dry White, Gold Label Riesling; red wines under Red, Yellow, Brown, Grey and Black labels with emphasis on Cabernet Sauvignon, Shiraz and blends of these, Brown Label Classic Shiraz, Grey Label Cabernet Sauvignon Shiraz, Green Label Shiraz. Also sparkling and fortified wines. The Eaglehawk now roosts here, too: Eaglehawk Chardonnay, Eaglehawk Riesling, Eaglehawk Sauvignon Blanc, Eaglehawk Semillon Sauvignon Blanc, Traminer Riesling, Grenache Shiraz. The Blass range, with its red, minimalist labels in stark contrast to the usual baroque designs so loved by Wolf, is a relatively recent addition: Vintage Brut, Pinot Chardonnay Brut, Clare Valley Red Label Riesling, Semillon Sauvignon Blanc, Chardonnay.
summary Although merged with Mildara and now under the giant umbrella of Beringer Blass, the brands (as expected) have been left largely intact. The white wines (made by Wendy Stuckey) are particularly impressive, none more so than the Gold Label Riesling. After a short pause, the red wines have improved out of all recognition thanks to the sure touch (and top palate) of Caroline Dunn. Worldwide distribution.

Blass Clare Valley Red Label Riesling

YYYY **2000** Glowing yellow-green, surprisingly developed; a rich, ripe bouquet with abundant tropical/lime fruit is followed by a very full-flavoured, rich palate with masses of sweet lime juice fruit. Utterly atypical, but will give pleasure over the next 12 months. **rating:** 89

best drinking Now **best vintages** NA **drink with** Crab mornay • NA

Wolf Blass Gold Label Riesling

YYYYY **2000** Bright, light green-yellow; intense, clean, lime blossom and passionfruit aromas lead into a beautifully balanced, fresh and quite tight palate, with lots of lime and mineral fruit power, yet not heavy; flows across the tongue. **rating:** 94

best drinking Now–2007 **best vintages** '90, '92, '95, '96, '97, '98, '00 **drink with** Salad Niçoise • $16

Blass Barossa Shiraz

YYYY **1998** Medium purple-red; obvious but not excessive oak joins fresh berry and plum fruit on the bouquet. The palate opens with sweet, minty fruit, but closes with a slightly tart finish; the suspicion is of last-minute acid adjustment, but this may be unjust. **rating:** 86

best drinking 2002–2007 **best vintages** NA **drink with** Braised beef • $17

Wolf Blass Brown Label Classic Shiraz

YYYY½ **1998** Medium to full red-purple; the bouquet is clean and smooth, with good fruit and oak balance and integration. The medium-bodied palate has abundant dark cherry and plum fruit; sweet oak is there, but controlled; good weight and richness. **rating:** 90

best drinking 2003–2008 **best vintages** '87, '88, '90, '91, '93, '96, '97, '98 **drink with** Spaghetti bolognaise • $25

Blass Cabernet Merlot

YYYY½ **1998** Caroline Dunn has an excellent palate and is a talented winemaker: this is sophisticated winemaking, every component precisely calibrated. A nicely ripened red berry fruit bouquet is set within high-quality, well-integrated French oak, and the attractive palate offers the same polished balance of red berry fruit and oak. **rating:** 93

best drinking Now–2008 **best vintages** '98 **drink with** Rare roast beef • $17

Wolf Blass Black Label Cabernet Sauvignon Shiraz

YYYYY **1998** Medium to full purple-red; the bouquet is literally bursting with intense and sweet cassis/berry/plum fruit. The palate is likewise extremely rich, flooded with cassis, berry and plum; subtle oak and soft tannins. A major change in style is evident here. Due for release at the end of 2001. **rating:** 94

🍷🍷🍷🍷🍷 **1997** Medium red-purple; a savoury, spicy, toasty, oaky bouquet, radically different from that of the '98. The palate is complex and full flavoured, with lots of oak but also plenty of chocolate and berry fruit, finishing with lingering, soft tannins. **rating:** 92

🍷🍷🍷🍷🍷 **1996** Luscious, ripe red and black berry fruit aromas on the bouquet flow into the palate, where there is an additional slice of mint; nicely controlled oak, and a wine that is absolutely ready to roll. Multiple gold medals underline its seductive qualities. **rating:** 91

best drinking 2003–2010 **best vintages** '86, '88, '90, '91, '95, '96, '97, '98 **drink with** Steak with wild mushrooms • $90

Wolf Blass Grey Label Cabernet Sauvignon Shiraz

🍷🍷🍷🍷🍷 **1997** Medium red-purple; the bouquet has a complex and quite savoury fusion of oak and fruit. The fruit depth and power come through on a highly structured palate, supported by ample tannins. **rating:** 91

best drinking 2002–2007 **best vintages** '97 **drink with** Beef bordelaise • NA

Blass Barossa Cabernet Sauvignon

🍷🍷🍷🍷🍷 **1996** Medium to full red-purple; the bouquet offers an amalgam of rich, cassis berry fruit and vanilla (American) oak; the finely structured palate ranges through cassis, blackberry and a touch of chocolate, seamlessly integrated with vanillin oak and fine tannins. Surprisingly elegant. Winner of two trophies and seven gold medals. **rating:** 94

best drinking 2002–2010 **best vintages** '96 **drink with** Kangaroo fillet • NA

Wolf Blass Yellow Label Cabernet Sauvignon

🍷🍷🍷🍷🍷 **1998** Medium to full red-purple; a quite concentrated dark berry/blackcurrant bouquet with well-integrated oak flows through into ample, sweet dark berry fruit on the palate, with good concentration and well-balanced and integrated oak; good tannins. **rating:** 90

best drinking 2003–2008 **best vintages** '98 **drink with** Steak and kidney pie • $15

---

woodend winery NR

82 Mahoneys Road, Woodend, Vic 3442 **region** Macedon Ranges
phone (03) 5427 2183 **fax** (03) 5427 4007 **open** Not
winemaker Howard Bradfield **production** 400 **est.** 1983
product range ($15–30 CD) Unwooded Chardonnay, Pinot Noir, Cabernet Franc.
summary Woodend Winery (for a while known as Bluestone Bridge, a name that had to be relinquished due to trademark problems) draws upon 2.5 hectares of vines established way back in 1983, although the winemaking is of much more recent origin. The wines are distributed through wholesaler Australian Prestige Wines.

woodlands NR

Cnr Caves and Metricup Roads, Willyabrup, via Cowaramup, WA 6284 **region** Margaret River
phone (08) 9755 6226 **fax** (08) 9481 1700 **open** Weekends by appointment
winemaker David Watson, Mark Lane, Dorham Mann (Consultant) **production** 1000 **est.** 1973
product range ($40–45 CD) Chloe Chardonnay, St Clare Cabernet Sauvignon.
summary The production (and visibility) of Woodlands have varied over the years, the core of the business lying with 6.8 hectares of cabernet sauvignon, more recently joined by merlot (1.2 hectares), malbec (0.8 hectare), cabernet franc (0.2 hectare), pinot noir (0.2 hectare) and chardonnay (0.8 hectare), all now in bearing. The 2000 Chloe Chardonnay (84 points) is a nice wine with good flavour, and the ability of the vineyard to produce high-quality cabernet sauvignon has long since been proved.

woodonga hill NR

Cowra Road, Young, NSW 2594 **region** Hilltops
phone (02) 6382 2972 **fax** (02) 6382 2972 **open** 7 days 9–5
winemaker Jill Lindsay **production** 4000 **est.** 1986
product range ($12.50–21 CD) Dry Rhine Riesling, Sauvignon, Chardonnay, Botrytis Semillon, Auslese Gewurztraminer, Meunier, Shiraz, Vintage Port, Cherry Liqueur Port.
summary Early problems with white-wine quality appear to have been surmounted. The wines have won bronze or silver medals at regional wine shows in New South Wales and Canberra, and Jill Lindsay is also a successful contract-winemaker for other small producers.

wood park NR

RMB 1139 Bobinawarrah–Whorouly Road, Milawa, Vic 3678 **region** King Valley
phone (03) 5727 3367 **fax** (03) 5727 3682 **open** By appointment
winemaker John Stokes, Rick Kinzbrunner **production** 1800 **est.** 1989
product range ($15–30 CD) Meadow Creek Chardonnay, Shiraz Cabernet.
summary The first vines were planted at Wood Park in 1989 by John Stokes as part of a diversification programme for his property at Bobinawarrah in the hills of the Lower King Valley to the east of Milawa. The bulk of the 8-hectare production is sold to Brown Brothers, with a further 8 hectares of vineyard being established for Southcorp. In an unusual twist, Stokes acquires his chardonnay from cousin John Leviny, one of the King Valley pioneers, who has his vineyard at Meadow Creek. To complicate matters further, all four vintages of Chardonnay ('95–'98) were made by Rick Kinzbrunner.

woodsmoke estate NR

Lot 2 Kemp Road, Pemberton, WA 6260 **region** Pemberton
phone (08) 9776 0225 **fax** (08) 9776 0225 **open** By appointment
winemaker Julie White **production** 1500 **est.** 1992
product range ($18–25 CD) Sauvignon Blanc, Semillon, Cabernet blend.
summary The former Jimlee Estate was acquired by the Liebeck family in July 1998 and renamed to WoodSmoke Estate. The current plantings of a little over 2 hectares of semillon, sauvignon blanc, cabernet franc and cabernet sauvignon were expanded with a further 2.4 hectares of cabernet franc and merlot planted in 2000.

woodstock winery & coterie ★★★★

Douglas Gully Road, McLaren Flat, SA 5171 **region** McLaren Vale
phone (08) 8383 0156 **fax** (08) 8383 0437 **open** Mon–Fri 9–5, weekends and holidays 12–5
winemaker Scott Collett **production** 30 000 **est.** 1974
product range ($9.95–50 CD) Riesling, Semillon, Douglas Gully Semillon Sauvignon Blanc, Verdelho, Chardonnay, Botrytis Sweet White, Five Feet (Dry Red), Shiraz, Grenache, Douglas Gully Malbec Cabernet Sauvignon Petit Verdot, Cabernet Sauvignon, Vintage Port, Tawny Port and Muscat. The Stocks Shiraz is a recently introduced flagship.
summary One of the stalwarts of McLaren Vale, producing archetypal, invariably reliable, full-bodied red wines and showing versatility with spectacular botrytis sweet whites and high-quality (14-year-old) Tawny Port. Also offers a totally charming reception-cum-restaurant, which understandably does a roaring trade with wedding receptions. Has supplemented its 18 hectares of McLaren Vale vineyards with 10 hectares at its Wirrega Vineyard near Bordertown in the Limestone Coast Zone. The wines are exported to the UK, Switzerland, the US, Canada, New Zealand, the Philippines, Malaysia, Singapore and Taiwan.

woody nook ★★★★

Metricup Road, Busselton, WA 6280 **region** Margaret River
phone (08) 9755 7547 **fax** (08) 9755 7007 **open** 7 days 10–4.30
winemaker Neil Gallagher **production** 4000 **est.** 1982
product range ($16.50–26 R) Chenin Blanc, Sauvignon Blanc, Classic Dry White, Classique, Late Harvest, Velvet Rose, Nooky Delight, Shiraz, Merlot, Cabernet Sauvignon; Gallagher's Choice Cabernet Sauvignon is top of the range.
summary This improbably named and not terribly fashionable winery has produced some truly excellent wines in recent years, with its Classic Dry White and Cabernet Sauvignon both starring at the various *Winewise* Smallmakers Competitions, having put in a similar performance at prior *Winewise* competitions, and likewise at the West Australian Wines Shows. Exports to the US and Hong Kong.

wyanga park NR

Baades Road, Lakes Entrance, Vic 3909 **region** Gippsland
phone (03) 5155 1508 **fax** (03) 5155 1443 **open** 7 days 9–5
winemaker Graeme Little **production** 5000 **est.** 1970

product range ($8–20 CD) Riesling Traminer, Estate Grown Sauvignon Blanc, Colombard, Estate Grown Chardonnay, Miriam's Fancy Chardonnay, Rosé, Boobialla (medium-sweet white), Shiraz, Shiraz Cabernet Sauvignon, Fortifieds.
summary Offers a broad range of wines of diverse provenance directed at the tourist trade; one of the Chardonnays and the Cabernet Sauvignon are estate-grown. Winery cruises up the north arm of the Gippsland Lake to Wyanga Park are scheduled four days a week throughout the entire year.

wyldcroft estates NR

98 Stanleys Road, Red Hill South, Vic 3937 **region** Mornington Peninsula
phone (03) 5989 2646 **fax** (03) 5989 2646 **open** Weekends and public holidays 10–5
winemaker Philip Jones (Contract) **production** 700 **est.** 1987
product range ($18–21 CD) Chardonnay, Unwooded Chardonnay, Pinot Noir, Cabernet Sauvignon.
summary Richard Condon and Sharon Stone commenced planting Wyldcroft Estates in 1987, extending the plantings in 1993 and 1996 to the present total of just over 3 hectares, constructing a mudbrick winery and cellar door in 1995.

wyndham estate ★★★☆

Dalwood Road, Dalwood, NSW 2335 **region** Lower Hunter Valley
phone (02) 4938 3444 **fax** (02) 4938 3422 **open** Mon–Fri 9.30–5, weekends 10–4
winemaker Brett McKinnon **production** NFP **est.** 1828
product range ($6.95–45 R) In ascending order: Bin TR2 Select White and Select Red; Semillon Sauvignon Blanc, Oak Cask Chardonnay; Bin 777 Semillon, Bin 111 Verdelho, Bin 222 Chardonnay, Bin 333 Pinot Noir, Bin 555 Shiraz, Bin 444 Cabernet Sauvignon, Bin 888 Cabernet Merlot; Show Reserve range of Semillon, Chardonnay, Shiraz, Cabernet Merlot, Mudgee Cabernet Sauvignon; 1828 range of Semillon Sauvignon Blanc, Semillon Chardonnay, Unwooded Chardonnay and Cabernet Sauvignon Shiraz Ruby Cabernet; Vintage Brut Cuvée, Vintage Chardonnay (sparkling).
summary Has risen to the challenge in recent years, its varietal wines smoothly dependable, the Show Reserves usually justifying their name (and price).

Wyndham Estate Semillon Sauvignon Blanc

🍷🍷🍷🍷(3.5) **2000** Light green-yellow; a scented, floral, but not particularly varietal bouquet is followed by a crisp, clean, lemony/herbaceous and well-balanced palate that does come as a pleasant surprise after the bouquet. **rating:** 84
best drinking Now **best vintages** NA **drink with** Seafood takeaway • $9

Wyndham Estate Show Reserve Chardonnay

🍷🍷🍷🍷 **1999** Medium to full yellow-green; the bouquet has charry oak, with ripe peach and melon fruit; the palate has plenty of flavour, but the oak flexes its muscles more than is needed. Less would have been better. **rating:** 86
best drinking Now **best vintages** NA **drink with** Smoked chicken • $20

Wyndham Estate Bin 333 Pinot Noir

🍷🍷🍷🍷 **2000** Medium red-purple; some foresty notes on the bouquet made me open my eyes (and nostrils); the palate came as a major shock, with some real varietal character and style. The best low-priced Pinot on the market today. **rating:** 85
best drinking Now **best vintages** NA **drink with** Light meat dishes • $10

Wyndham Estate Bin 444 Cabernet Sauvignon

🍷🍷🍷🍷(3.5) **1998** Medium red-purple; the moderately intense bouquet is clean, but relatively plain; on the palate there is rather more happening, with clean, fresh berry fruit plus touches of tannin and oak. Pretty well-composed, all things considered. **rating:** 84
best drinking 2002–2006 **best vintages** NA **drink with** Braised beef • $12.99

wynns coonawarra estate ★★★★★

Memorial Drive, Coonawarra, SA 5263 **region** Coonawarra
phone (08) 8736 3266 **fax** (08) 8736 3202 **open** 7 days 10–5
winemaker Sue Hodder, Sarah Pidgeon **production** 380 000 **est.** 1891

product range ($11–87 R) Wynns Coonawarra Estate Riesling, Chardonnay, Shiraz, Cabernet Shiraz Merlot, Cabernet Sauvignon, Black Label Cabernet Sauvignon; Michael Shiraz, John Riddoch Cabernet Sauvignon; also Ovens Valley Shiraz (not sourced from Coonawarra).

summary The large-scale production has in no way prevented Wynns from producing excellent wines covering the full price spectrum from bargain-basement Riesling and Shiraz through to deluxe John Riddoch Cabernet Sauvignon and Michael Shiraz. Even with steady price increases, Wynns offers extraordinary value for money.

Wynns Coonawarra Estate Riesling

ΥΥΥΥ **2000** One might wonder why one should waste precious Coonawarra terroir on riesling, or, more to the point, on an $11 wine. A gift horse, to be sure. Crisp apple, mineral, herb and lime aromas announce a powerful mineral/slate/herb palate with a clean, dry finish and heaps of development potential. **rating:** 89

best drinking Now–2010 **best vintages** '90, '91, '93, '95, '96, '98, '99, '00 **drink with** King George whiting • $11

Wynns Coonawarra Estate Chardonnay

ΥΥΥΥ **2000** Light to medium yellow-green; a typically complex bouquet with nutty/cashew/melon aromas is followed by a palate that is elegant, light and, in a sense, understated, yet also invested with complexity. **rating:** 87

best drinking Now–2003 **best vintages** '92, '93, '94, '96, '97, '98, '99 **drink with** Robe lobster • $15

Wynns Coonawarra Estate Shiraz

ΥΥΥΥ **1999** Medium to full red-purple; clean, smooth, cherry and plum fruit with a touch of vanilla oak is followed by a medium-bodied palate with good balance, weight and extract. A very good outcome for the vintage. **rating:** 89

best drinking 2002–2006 **best vintages** '54, '55, '62, '65, '70, '85, '86, '89, '90, '91, '93, '94, '96, '98 **drink with** Spiced lamb • $18

Wynns Coonawarra Estate Michael Shiraz

ΥΥΥΥΥ **1998** Dark red-purple; the bouquet exudes oak from every pore as only Michael can; powerful, sweet black cherry and plum fruit on the palate demands to be heard behind the fanfare of oak trumpets; prior history makes it a near certainty the wine will sort itself out, however improbable that may seem right now. **rating:** 94

ΥΥΥΥ **1997** Medium red-purple; that satin-smooth and sweet bouquet with abundant berry fruit and plenty of sexy oak leads into a palate with a similarly silky, smooth texture; here licorice and chocolate join the sweet berry, encased in sweet oak and lingering, faintly milky, tannins. **rating:** 92

best drinking 2008–2015 **best vintages** '90, '91, '93, '94, '96, '98 **drink with** Leave it in the cellar • $86

Wynns Coonawarra Estate Cabernet Shiraz Merlot

ΥΥΥΥ **1998** Medium red-purple; the bouquet offers a sweet mix of fruit, vanilla and earth, the palate powerful and quite chewy; seems much more oaky than previous releases, and will doubtless please traditionalists. **rating:** 85

best drinking 2003–2008 **best vintages** '86, '88, '90, '91, '92, '96 **drink with** Yearling beef • $19

Wynns Coonawarra Estate Black Label Cabernet Sauvignon

ΥΥΥΥΥ **1998** Medium to full red-purple; sweet and ripe cassis/blackberry/raspberry fruit aromas are followed by a full-bodied, fruit-driven style, with oak and tannins playing a nicely judged support role; smooth and supple; every bit as good as the vintage reputation would suggest. **rating:** 94

best drinking 2003–2013 **best vintages** '53, '57, '58, '62, '82, '86, '88, '90, '91, '94, '95, '96, '97, '98 **drink with** Roast beef • $29

Wynns Coonawarra Estate John Riddoch Cabernet Sauvignon

ΥΥΥΥΥ **1998** Impenetrable purple-red; blackberry/cassis/blackcurrant fruit has largely soaked up the oak on the bouquet; likewise, intense and powerful cassis/blackcurrant/blackberry fruit drives the palate, with oak well integrated and balanced. An exceptionally powerful wine, but the balance is already there to be seen. A major success for John Riddoch. **rating:** 96

best drinking 2008–2023 **best vintages** '82, '85, '86, '88, '90, '91, '94, '96, '97, '98 **drink with** Leave it in the cellar • NA

---

xanadu wines ★★★★

Boodjidup Road, Margaret River, WA 6285 **region** Margaret River
phone (08) 9757 2581 **fax** (08) 9757 3389 **open** 7 days 10–5
winemaker Jürg Muggli **production** 65 000 **est.** 1977
product range ($14–56 R) Semillon, Lagan Estate Semillon, Semillon Sauvignon Blanc, Secession Semillon Chardonnay, Chardonnay, Secession White (Semillon Sauvignon Blanc Chenin Blanc), Noble Semillon, Secession Rosé of Cabernet, Secession Red, Shiraz, Merlot, Cabernet Franc, Cabernet Sauvignon, Lagan Estate Cabernet Reserve.
summary Samuel Taylor Coleridge would thoroughly approve of the labels on the Xanadu wines and, one imagines, would be equally pleased with wine quality (which can be excitingly variable, but is more often good than not). In the wake of a substantial raising of capital from the public in 1999, Xanadu now has 130 hectares of vines spread across three vineyards, and production has soared to 65 000 cases.

Xanadu Semillon

🍷🍷🍷🍷 **1999** Light green-yellow; the firm bouquet initially shows distinctly herbal notes, then come the hints of barrel-ferment oak and malolactic fermentation. The palate is firm, with a particularly complex structure reflecting the winemaking inputs. This is a somewhat idiosyncratic but thoroughly legitimate style of Semillon. **rating:** 89
best drinking Now–2007 **best vintages** '96, '97, '98, '99 **drink with** Richer fish dishes • $19

Xanadu Semillon Sauvignon Blanc

🍷🍷🍷🍷 **2000** Light green-yellow; the bouquet is clean, with a mix of lemon/lemongrass and mineral aromatics; the palate is long, crisp and lingering thanks to lemony acidity; it is not until you get to the very end that the texture imparted by the barrel fermentation comes into play, but does so effectively. **rating:** 88
best drinking Now–2004 **best vintages** '99, '00 **drink with** Pan-fried scallops • $16

Xanadu Secession Semillon Chardonnay

🍷🍷🍷🍷 **1999** Light green-yellow; the bouquet is crisp, with aromas of mineral, herb and grass. The palate is quite intense, but the faintly bitter finish is disappointing after a good start. **rating:** 85
best drinking Now **best vintages** NA **drink with** Crab • $14

Xanadu Secession

🍷🍷🍷½ **2000** Light green-yellow; a crisp and clean bouquet with a nice minerally bite is followed by a palate with plenty of flavour across a spectrum of fruit characters, and well balanced. Could have been rated significantly higher were it not for a slightly short finish. **rating:** 84
best drinking Now **best vintages** '85, '87, '90, '92, '93 **drink with** Crab • $14

Xanadu Chardonnay

🍷🍷🍷🍷½ **1999** Light to medium yellow-green; the bouquet is clean, quite intense, with stonefruit and citrus together with some barrel-ferment characters; the palate is fresh, long and elegant; another Margaret River Chardonnay with an enticing cellaring future. **rating:** 90
best drinking Now–2007 **best vintages** '99 **drink with** White-fleshed fish • $23

Xanadu Noble Semillon

🍷🍷🍷🍷½ **1999** Full golden-orange; the complex and powerful bouquet with rich cumquat and mandarin aromas is followed by a long, rich and concentrated palate with varietal character obscured by the intense botrytis; the oak has been nearly entirely absorbed by the fruit. Impressive winemaking. **rating:** 92
best drinking Now–2004 **best vintages** NA **drink with** Rich desserts • $25

Xanadu Merlot

🍷🍷🍷🍷½ **1998** Medium purple-red; a moderately fragrant and savoury bouquet has a mix of spice and leather aromas which are varietal, supported by good oak handling. The palate has lots of flavour, with sweet vanilla and cedar oak coming through just a little assertively. Pretty good stuff, though. **rating:** 91
best drinking 2002–2007 **best vintages** '98 **drink with** Smoked beef • $40

Xanadu Reserve Cabernet Sauvignon

🍷🍷🍷🍷 **1998** Medium red-purple; the bouquet is quite fragrant, with cedar, cigar box and earthy cabernet varietal character. The palate contains no surprises, reflecting a considerable time in oak, and finishing with some slightly dusty tannins. Quite classically proportioned. **rating:** 88
best drinking 2003–2008 **best vintages** '83, '84, '86, '90, '91, '93, '94 **drink with** Roast lamb • $56

yaldara wines ★★★★

Gomersal Road, Lyndoch, SA 5351 **region** Barossa Valley
phone (08) 8524 4200 **fax** (08) 8524 4678 **open** 7 days 9–5
winemaker Matt Tydeman **production** 500 000 **est.** 1947
product range ($10–45 R) A full range of wines under (in ascending order) the Lakewood, Earth's Portrait, Julians and the super-premium The Farms label.
summary Two days before Christmas 1999 Yaldara was purchased by the publicly listed Simeon Wines, who embarked on a $10 million upgrade of the winery with the intention of allowing it to bottle 2 million cases of wine per year. Only part of the wine will be premium Barossa, the rest coming through from the parent Simeon. As expected the quality of the wines has taken a sharp lift upwards, partly through selection and blending of vintages prior to 2000, and the promise of even better things in store.

Yaldara Earth's Portrait Eden Valley Riesling

YYYY **2000** Light to medium yellow-green; the bouquet shows good regional/varietal character, with solid lime juice aromas. The palate has quite good length, crisp and limey, together with minerally acidity on the finish. **rating:** 85

best drinking Now–2005 **best vintages** NA **drink with** Seafood salad • $15

Yaldara Julian's Chardonnay

YYYY **1998** Light to medium yellow-green, remarkably undeveloped for its age. The bouquet, likewise, is still developing, offering melon and citrus supported by a touch of nutty oak. The medium-weight palate has nice melon and stonefruit flavour, and just a hint of oak to add complexity. **rating:** 86

best drinking Now–2003 **best vintages** NA **drink with** Breast of chicken • $20

Yaldara The Farms Yarra Valley Chardonnay

YYYYY **1999** Medium yellow-green; the bouquet is complex, with both barrel-ferment and mlf influences which do not overimpose themselves on the underlying fruit. The stylish palate has citrus and stonefruit, with excellent length and assured winemaking inputs. **rating:** 92

best drinking Now–2005 **best vintages** '99 **drink with** Lobster • $30

Yaldara The Farms Barossa Valley Shiraz

YYYYY **1998** Medium to full red, with some purple hues remaining. The bouquet is rich and savoury, with chocolatey berry fruit and gentle oak. An altogether serious wine on the palate, with a complex array of dark berry fruit, chocolate and spice allied with excellent tannin management and overall concentration. Gold medal winner at the London International Wine Challenge 2000. **rating:** 94

best drinking 2003–2010 **best vintages** '97, '98 **drink with** Venison • $45

Yaldara The Farms Show Liqueur Tawny Port

YYYYY **NV** Strong tawny colour; the aromatic bouquet has excellent spice, spirit and rancio characters; the palate is intense, with high rancio character and an excellent long, dry finish. **rating:** 93

best drinking Now **best vintages** NA **drink with** Walnuts, dried fruit • NA

yalumba ★★★★☆

Eden Valley Road, Angaston, SA 5353 **region** Barossa Valley
phone (08) 8561 3200 **fax** (08) 8561 3393 **open** Mon–Fri 8.30–5, Sat 10–5, Sun 12–5
winemaker Brian Walsh, Alan Hoey, Louisa Rose **production** 750 000 **est.** 1849
product range ($8–90 R) A clearly structured portfolio arranged by price point, from the bottom, Oxford Landing, then Christobel's, Unwooded Chardonnay and Galway Vintage Shiraz; next varietal wines under the Yalumba Barossa umbrella; then Eden Valley and The Virgilius Viognier; Clare Valley Shiraz and Cabernet Sauvignon; then at the top of the dry table wines, Mawsons Coonawarra Cabernet Shiraz Merlot, The Menzies Coonawarra Cabernet Sauvignon, The Signature Barossa Shiraz and The Octavius Old Vine Barossa Shiraz; a newly added trio of Noble Pick sweet wines and the Yalumba D sparkling wines and fortifieds.
summary Family-owned and run by Robert Hill-Smith; much of its prosperity in the late 1980s and early 1990s turned on the great success of Angas Brut in export markets, but the company has always had a commitment to quality and shown great vision in its selection of vineyard sites and brands. In particular, it has always been a serious player at the top end of full-bodied (and full-blooded) Australian reds. Exports to all major markets.

Yalumba Barossa Semillon

ΥΥΥΥ **2000** Medium yellow-green; the moderately intense bouquet has herb and lemon fruit aromas, supported by subtle oak. On the palate excellent oak handling adds as much to the texture as it does to the flavour, which has a hint of nectarine to accompany the herb and lemon. Nonetheless, drink now while it has the attractive freshness of youth. **rating:** 86

best drinking Now **best vintages** NA **drink with** Barossa yabbies • $14.95

Yalumba Christobels Dry White

ΥΥΥΥ **2000** Light green-straw; the bouquet is light and crisp, with a nice herbaceous cut, the palate lemony and lively; spot-on for a wine of this style and price. **rating:** 85

best drinking Now **best vintages** '94, '99 **drink with** Light seafood • $12

Yalumba The Virgilius

ΥΥΥΥΥ **1999** Full yellow-straw; rich, ripe dried-apricot and spice aromas on the bouquet lead into a super-powerful palate driven by 14.5° alcohol but undeniably viognier. A gold medal at the 2000 Adelaide Wine Show is a testament to that power. **rating:** 92

best drinking Now–2003 **best vintages** '99 **drink with** Pork neck • $43.95

Yalumba Barossa Chardonnay

ΥΥΥΥ **2000** Medium to full yellow-green; big, rich and ripe yellow peach fruit has a hint of French oak on the bouquet. The palate is big, lush and mouthfilling, with masses of yellow peach flavour and hints of cashew and oak in a ripe, take-me-now style. It has to be said, a cut above the average Barossa Chardonnay. **rating:** 86

best drinking Now **best vintages** NA **drink with** Cassoulet (unfermented) • NA

Yalumba D

ΥΥΥΥΥ **1997** Cuvee 97-1. Light straw-green; an extremely complex bouquet shows all sorts of inputs ranging from wet socks to bread to aldehyde and mlf, which may sound unattractive, but is in fact appealing. The long, persistent and dry palate carries on the good work, looking suspiciously like the real thing. **rating:** 91

best drinking Now–2004 **best vintages** '90, '91, '93, '95, '96, '97 **drink with** Richer seafood dishes • $27.99

Jansz

ΥΥΥΥΥ **1996** Light to medium yellow-green; the bouquet offers an intense mix of citrus peel, bread and a touch of the old socks to be found in the Yalumba D. Fruit comes to the fore on the palate, with citrussy stonefruit flavours on the tip of the tongue, and providing fruit sweetness (not dosage) through to the finish of the wine. **rating:** 92

best drinking Now–2004 **best vintages** '96 **drink with** Shellfish • $32.99

Jansz Cuvée

ΥΥΥΥ **NV** Medium yellow-green; the bouquet is clean, with quite intense citrus/melon fruit; attractive, tangy, citrussy fruit on the palate has some creamy notes offset by brisk acidity. **rating:** 88

best drinking Now **best vintages** NA **drink with** Aperitif • $19.99

Yalumba Noble Pick Riesling

ΥΥΥΥΥ **1999** Glowing yellow-green; intense lime and mandarin aromas leave no doubt about the botrytis; the palate is full-on, with a mix of sweet mandarin, lime and spice, holding just enough acidity for balance. 1650 dozen (375 ml bottles) made. **rating:** 90

best drinking Now–2004 **best vintages** '99 **drink with** Rich cream-based desserts • NA

Yalumba Noble Pick Semillon

ΥΥΥΥΥ **1999** Glowing yellow-green; intense peach, honey, spice and apricot aromas foreshadow a palate that has the most texture and mouthfeel of the three Noble Pick releases, though not the most intense fruit. **rating:** 91

best drinking Now–2004 **best vintages** NA **drink with** Rich cream-based desserts • NA

Yalumba Noble Pick Viognier

ΥΥΥΥΥ **1998** Light to medium green-yellow; the bouquet has true viognier varietal aromas: a mix of pastille, candy and apple blossom. The palate is long, with honeysuckle and fruit pastille flavours, with perfectly balanced acidity. A surprisingly large 2000 dozen (375 ml bottles) were made. **rating:** 92

best drinking Now–2004 **best vintages** '98 **drink with** Fresh fruit • NA

Yalumba Barossa Shiraz

YYYY **1999** Light to medium red-purple; the bouquet is clean, moderately intense, with cool-climate mint and leaf characteristics entirely at odds with its Barossa origin and the vintage. The palate shows more slightly herbaceous/green fruit, helped by vanilla American oak. The wine won a gold medal at the San Francisco Wine Fair and topped its under $15 Class 14 at the 2000 Royal Adelaide Wine Show. Yes, under $15. **rating:** 87

best drinking Now–2006 **best vintages** NA **drink with** Guinea fowl • $16.95

Yalumba Octavius Shiraz

YYYY **1997** Medium to full red-purple; as ever, powerful American oak makes a major impact on both bouquet and palate. On the other side of the forest, dense and powerful dark cherry/small black fruits show their strength, the two parts united by tannins. A meal in itself. **rating:** 89

best drinking 2007–2017 **best vintages** '88, '90, '92, '93, '95, '96 **drink with** The biggest steak imaginable • NA

Yalumba Mawsons Coonawarra Cabernet Sauvignon Shiraz Merlot

YYYY **1998** Medium red-purple; the moderately intense bouquet has aromas of cedar, leaf and earth dominant, but the palate offers far riper fruit with a mix of blackberry, blackcurrant and mulberry supported by soft French oak and nice tannins. **rating:** 89

best drinking 2002–2008 **best vintages** '98 **drink with** Rib of beef • $18.95

Yalumba Signature Cabernet Shiraz

YYYYY **1997** Medium to full red-purple; rich, ripe, dark berry fruit is accompanied by strongly accented vanilla oak on the complex bouquet. The palate carries on in much the same vein, with rich, luscious dark berry and dark chocolate fruit supported by ripe tannins. An outstanding achievement for the '97 vintage. **rating:** 93

best drinking 2003–2013 **best vintages** '62, '66, '75, '81, '85, '88, '90, '91, '92, '93, '95, '96, '97 **drink with** Rare roast beef • NA

Yalumba The Menzies Cabernet Sauvignon

YYYYY **1998** Medium to full red-purple; the bouquet is clean and ripe, with a mix of blackberry/savoury/ earthy varietal aromas. There is masses of fruit power and considerable extract on the long palate. A vivid demonstration of the quality of the '98 vintage. **rating:** 91

best drinking 2003–2010 **best vintages** '90, '91, '94, '96, '98 **drink with** Topside steak • NA

yandoit hill vineyard NR

Nevens Road, Yandoit Creek, Vic 3461 **region** Bendigo

phone (03) 9379 1763 **fax** (03) 9379 1763 **open** By appointment (special open days for mailing list customers)

winemaker Colin Mitchell **production** 300 **est.** 1988

product range ($18–21 CD) Arneis, Cabernets, Nebbiolo Cabernet Sauvignon.

summary Colin and Rosa Mitchell commenced the development of Yandoit Hill with the first plantings in 1988 with merlot, and a little under a hectare each of cabernet franc and cabernet sauvignon followed by 0.5 hectare each of arneis (the first planting in Australia), and nebbiolo in 1995. The vineyard is situated 20 kilometres north of Daylesford and, although situated on the north-facing slope of Yandoit Hill, is in an uncompromisingly cool climate. Colin Mitchell has already discovered that nebbiolo won't ripen to his satisfaction in most years but in vintages like 1988 makes a successful wine. The Cabernet Franc blends made between 1994 and the first commercial vintage in 1998 all show pronounced cool-climate characteristics.

Yandoit Hill Arneis

YYYY **2000** Light to medium yellow-green; the light, clean bouquet has a mix of blossom and spice, and no hint of phenolics. The palate is similarly clean, well made and with good mouthfeel, but it is hard work trying to find distinctive varietal fruit flavours. **rating:** 84

best drinking Now–2004 **best vintages** NA **drink with** Shellfish • $21

yarrabank ★★★★★

42 Melba Highway, Yarra Glen, Vic 3775 **region** Yarra Valley
phone (03) 9730 2188 **fax** (03) 9730 2189 **open** 7 days 10–5
winemaker Claude Thibaut, Tom Carson, Darren Rathbone **production** 2000 **est.** 1993
product range ($35 R) Thibaut & Gillet Cuvée Brut, Cuvée Rosée, Brut Cuvée.
summary The 1997 vintage saw the opening of the majestic new winery established as part of a joint venture between the French Champagne house Devaux and Yering Station, and which adds another major dimension to the Yarra Valley. Until 1997 the Yarrabank Cuvée Brut was made under Claude Thibaut's direction at Domaine Chandon, but henceforth the entire operation will be conducted at Yarrabank. Four hectares of dedicated 'estate' vineyards have been established at Yering Station; the balance of the intake comes from other growers in the Yarra Valley and southern Victoria. Wine quality has been quite outstanding, the wines having a delicacy unmatched by any other Australian sparkling wines.

Yarrabank Brut Cuvée

🍷🍷🍷🍷🍷 **1997** A polar opposite to the Domaine Chandon, an aperitif as opposed to food style. As usual, the aromas are fine, elegant and restrained, yet quite intense, exactly mirrored by the minerally/citrussy flavours of the palate, which has a sustained, lingering and crystal-fresh finish. **rating:** 94

best drinking Now **best vintages** '93, '94, '95, '97 **drink with** Aperitif, shellfish • $35

---

yarra burn ★★★★

Settlement Road, Yarra Junction, Vic 3797 **region** Yarra Valley
phone (03) 5967 1428 **fax** (03) 5967 1146 **open** 7 days 10–5
winemaker Tom Newton, Ed Carr, Stephen Pannell **production** 4500 **est.** 1975
product range ($18–45 R) Sauvignon Blanc Semillon, Chardonnay, Pinot Noir, Chardonnay Pinot Noir, Shiraz, Cabernet Sauvignon, Sparkling Pinot, Chardonnay Pinot; Bastard Hill Chardonnay, Bastard Hill Pinot Noir.
summary Acquired by BRL Hardy in 1995 and for the time being the headquarters of Hardy's substantial Yarra Valley operations, the latter centring on the 1000-tonne production from its Hoddles Creek vineyards. The new brand direction is slowly taking shape; the Bastard Hill Reserve wines are among the signs of change.

Yarra Burn Chardonnay

🍷🍷🍷🍷 **1998** Medium yellow-green; the bouquet is complex and tangy, with good barrel-ferment characters; the palate is moderately intense, with tangy stonefruit and melon flavours, subtle oak and attractive acidity. **rating:** 88

best drinking Now–2005 **best vintages** '97, '98 **drink with** Grilled scampi • $19.99

Yarra Burn Pinot Noir Chardonnay

🍷🍷🍷🍷🍷 **1999** Light straw-green; the bouquet is fresh and crisp, with spicy/bready aromas; the palate is very lively, with a fresh, citrussy finish making it an excellent aperitif style. **rating:** 90

best drinking Now–2003 **best vintages** '96, '97, '98, '99 **drink with** Sunshine • $20

Yarra Burn Pinot Noir

🍷🍷🍷🍷 **1999** Medium purple-red; a fragrant bouquet, underpinned by some toasty oak, has a mix of plum, forest and more savoury characters. There is plummy fruit on entry to the mouth, but the palate then moves to a slightly hard, savoury finish. Overall, a creditable effort for a difficult vintage. **rating:** 85

best drinking Now–2003 **best vintages** '97 **drink with** Ragout of venison • $23.99

Yarra Burn Cabernet Sauvignon

🍷🍷🍷🍷🍷 **1998** Medium to full red-purple; fully ripe, sweet blackberry/cassis fruit, with no green characters at all, drives both the bouquet and palate, the latter supported by gentle, albeit positive, oak, and lingering tannins. **rating:** 91

best drinking 2003–2008 **best vintages** '98 **drink with** Marinated beef • $23.99

---

yarra edge ★★★☆

PO Box 390 Yarra Glen, Vic 3775 **region** Yarra Valley
phone (03) 9730 1107 **fax** (03) 9739 0135 **open** At Yering Station
winemaker Tom Carson, Darren Rathbone **production** 2000 **est.** 1984
product range ($27.50–28.50 CD) Chardonnay, Cabernets.
summary Now leased to Yering Station, which makes the wines but continues to use the Yarra Edge brand for grapes from this estate. Tom Carson, Yering Station winemaker, was briefly winemaker/manager at Yarra Edge and knows the property intimately, so the rich style can be expected to continue.

Yarra Edge

YYYY **1996** The colour in this Cabernet Sauvignon, Merlot, Malbec and Cabernet Franc blend is showing some development, the bouquet with a light, savoury, faintly gamey/spicy character. The palate provides more of the same, with some vestigial sweet fruit, in a smooth, soft, low-tannin, subtle-oak mode. **rating:** 86
best drinking Now–2005 **best vintages** NA **drink with** Diced lamb • $28.50

yarra ridge ★★★★

Glenview Road, Yarra Glen, Vic 3755 **region** Yarra Valley
phone (03) 9730 1022 **fax** (03) 9730 1131 **open** 7 days 10–5
winemaker Matt Steel **production** NFP **est.** 1983
product range ($16–45 R) Chardonnay, Sauvignon Blanc, Botrytis Semillon, Pinot Noir, Reserve Pinot Noir, Merlot, Shiraz, Cabernet Sauvignon; Mount Tanglefoot has been introduced as a second range expressly made from grapes grown in regions other than the Yarra Valley.
summary Under the sole ownership and control of Beringer Blass, with a winery that is strained to its limits. Recent vineyard plantings in the Yarra Valley, and continued purchasing of Yarra Valley grapes, mean that the majority of the wines will continue to be Yarra Valley-sourced. Sometimes it is not easy to tell which are and which aren't, even if one has a master's degree in label reading and interpretation.

Yarra Ridge Sauvignon Blanc

YYYY **2000** Light green-yellow; the bouquet is crisp, minerally and not particularly varietal, the palate fresh, light, crisp and well balanced, but far from intense. A bizarre winner of the top gold medal in the aromatic class 1 at the Sydney Royal Wine Show 2001. **rating:** 85
best drinking Now **best vintages** NA **drink with** Fish and chips • $18.50

Yarra Ridge Chardonnay

YYYY **2000** Light to medium yellow-green; a clean and smooth bouquet with a mix of melon and stonefruit flows through into a crisp, lemony palate with an almost minerally finish; sensitive oak handling. **rating:** 87
best drinking Now–2003 **best vintages** '90, '92, '93, '94, '96 **drink with** Scallops, mussels • $18.50

Yarra Ridge Reserve Pinot Noir

YYYY **1998** Medium to full red, a ripe, full bouquet with primary plummy fruit, then hints of game and forest; the palate is very ripe, with opulent plum/prune fruit, then some tannins on a slightly choppy finish. **rating:** 87
best drinking Now–2004 **best vintages** '94, '96, '97 **drink with** Game, jugged hare • $45

Yarra Ridge Cabernet Sauvignon

YYYY **1998** Medium red-purple; the moderately intense bouquet has savoury/earthy overtones to the red berry fruit and oak; nicely weighted red berry and more savoury fruit on the palate is supported by well-integrated oak and gentle tannins, all contributing to good length. **rating:** 87
best drinking 2003–2008 **best vintages** NA **drink with** Rolled shoulder of lamb • $23

Yarra Ridge Reserve Cabernet

YYYYY **1997** Medium red-purple; a clean, attractive, red berry bouquet with nicely integrated oak leads into a long, lingering cassis/red berry palate with excellent tannins on a long finish. **rating:** 92
best drinking 2002–2007 **best vintages** '97 **drink with** Lamb fillet • $45

yarra track wines ★★★★

Viggers Vineyard, 518 Old Healesville Road, Yarra Glen, Vic 3775 **region** Yarra Valley
phone (03) 9730 1349 **fax** (03) 9730 1910 **open** Weekends and public holidays 10–5.30
winemaker Martin Williams (Contract) **production** 400 **est.** 1989
product range ($23–25 CD) Chardonnay, Pinot Noir.
summary Jim and Diana Viggers began establishing their vineyard back in 1989; it now has 3.1 hectares of chardonnay and 3.4 hectares of pinot noir. The Viggers have chosen very competent winemakers (Tom Carson 1997, 1998 and Martin Williams from 1999) and intend to increase wine production progressively while selling part of the grape production in the meantime. The wine is sold only through cellar door and local restaurants.

Yarra Track Chardonnay

🍷🍷🍷 **1999** Medium yellow-green; the bouquet has pleasant, albeit light, melon and nectarine fruit with minimal oak influence. The palate is clean, light to medium bodied, well-balanced, but not particularly concentrated; perhaps elegance is a better perspective. **rating:** 84

best drinking Now–2004 **best vintages** NA **drink with** Pan-fried veal • $23

yarra valley hills NR

c/o Dromana Estate, Harrison's and Bittern–Dromana Roads, Dromana, Vic 3936 **region** Yarra Valley
phone (03) 5987 3800 **fax** (03) 5981 0714 **open** At Dromana Estate 7 days 11–4
winemaker Garry Crittenden **production** 10 000 **est.** 1989
product range ($18–27 CD) Warranwood Riesling, Warranwood Pinot Noir, Log Creek Sauvignon Blanc, Kiah Yallambee Chardonnay, Log Creek Pinot Noir, Log Creek Cabernet Sauvignon, Log Creek Sauvignon Blanc Semillon.
summary The business of Yarra Valley Hills was acquired by Dromana Estate in 2000. Dromana has kept the Yarra Valley Hills brand, but sold the winery to a syndicate headed by Martin Williams, who will use it to both provide custom crush-and-make facilities for other Yarra Valley wineries and (in the case of Martin Williams) to make his own Métier brand.

yarra yarra ★★★★★

239 Hunts Lane, Steels Creek, Vic 3775 **region** Yarra Valley
phone (03) 5965 2380 **fax** (03) 9830 4180 **open** By appointment
winemaker Ian Maclean **production** NFP **est.** 1979
product range ($30–45 CD) Semillon Sauvignon Blanc, Merlot, Cabernets, Reserve Cabernet Merlot.
summary Notwithstanding its tiny production, the wines of Yarra Yarra have found their way onto a veritable who's who listing of Melbourne's best restaurants. This encouraged Ian Maclean to increase the estate plantings from 2 hectares to over 7 hectares during the 1996 and 1997 seasons. The demand for the wines will only be intensified by the quality of the current releases.

Yarra Yarra Semillon Sauvignon Blanc

🍷🍷🍷🍷 **1998** Light to medium yellow-green; that typically rich, powerful and complex mix of tangy fruit and a hint of spicy oak is followed by a quite fleshy palate, much fatter than the usual style, no doubt thanks to the relentless heat of the '98 vintage. Spicy nutmeg oak does help the finish. **rating:** 87

best drinking Now–2004 **best vintages** '97 **drink with** Wiener schnitzel • $30

Yarra Yarra Reserve Cabernet Sauvignon

🍷🍷🍷🍷🍷 **1998** Medium red, with tinges of purple on the rim; the bouquet is fragrant and elegant, with cedary, savoury aromas, the palate similarly elegant and cedary, with a gentle core of red berry fruit and an almost delicate finish. All about finesse, not power. **rating:** 91

best drinking 2002–2010 **best vintages** '97 **drink with** Braised beef • $45

yarra yering ★★★★★

Briarty Road, Coldstream, Vic 3770 **region** Yarra Valley
phone (03) 5964 9267 **fax** (03) 5964 9239 **open** Sat 10–5, Sun 12–5
winemaker Bailey Carrodus **production** 6000 **est.** 1969

product range ($65–135 CD) Dry White No 1 (Sauvignon Blanc Semillon), Chardonnay, Pinot Noir, Dry Red No 1 (Bordeaux blend), Dry Red No 2 (Rhône blend), Merlot (tiny quantities at $100 a bottle), Underhill Shiraz, Underhill 3 Year Cask Shiraz, Portsorts. The portfolio continues to expand, with Dry Red No 3, Sangiovese and Viognier all making an appearance from the 1998 and/or '99 vintages.

summary Dr Bailey Carrodus makes extremely powerful, occasionally idiosyncratic wines from his 30-year-old, low-yielding, unirrigated vineyards. Both red and white wines have an exceptional depth of flavour and richness, although my preference for what I believe to be his great red wines is well known. As he has expanded the size of his vineyards, so has the range of wines become ever more eclectic, none more so than the only Vintage Port being produced in the Yarra Valley. The wines are exported to the UK, the US, Switzerland, Germany, Hong Kong, Japan, Malaysia and Singapore.

Yarra Yering Pinot Noir

▼▼▼▼ **1999** A slightly dull red, suggesting colour change will come fairly quickly; a complex bouquet offers cinnamon, nutmeg and brandied plum aromas, with a background hint of forest floor. The flavoursome, medium-bodied palate is unmistakably varietal, with spice and plum flavours; finishes slightly short. **rating:** 89

best drinking 2003–2008 **best vintages** '97, '98 **drink with** Squab • NA

Yarra Yering Underhill Shiraz

▼▼▼▼ **1999** Medium red, showing some signs of early development; the bouquet is quite powerful, with a range of licorice, spice and black cherry; the smooth, almost creamy, texture of the palate, with red and black cherry fruit, has a spicy backdrop and soft tannins. **rating:** 89

best drinking 2003–2009 **best vintages** '91, '92, '93, '97 **drink with** Victorian Parmesan cheese • NA

Yarra Yering Dry Red No 2

▼▼▼▼▽ **1999** The colour is much better than that of the Underhill of the same vintage: more vibrant; the clean and smooth bouquet has perfectly balanced and integrated oak running through red and black cherry fruit, the supple texture of the palate showcasing the smooth cherry fruit and perfectly integrated and balanced oak. **rating:** 90

best drinking 2004–2011 **best vintages** '80, '81, '86, '89, '90, '91, '92, '93, '96, '97, '98 **drink with** Beef bourguignon • NA

Yarra Yering Merlot

▼▼▼▼▽ **1999** The colour is of medium depth, showing some early signs of development. Distinct toasty French oak opens the bouquet, with sappy/olive aromas underneath. The palate has considerable length, with a mix of olive and more savoury flavours, sustained by fine-grained tannins. Lingers in the mouth long after it is swallowed; a compelling wine. **rating:** 92

best drinking 2004–2009 **best vintages** NA **drink with** Braised veal • $135

Yarra Yering Dry Red No 1

▼▼▼▼▽ **1999** The best colour of all of the '99 wines from Yarra Yering, strong red-purple; the aromatic bouquet has distinctive earthy/leafy/olive overtones, strongly reminiscent of Bordeaux. The palate has good structure and texture, with blackberry/blackcurrant fruit, fine tannins, and positive but balanced oak. A major success for an ordinary vintage. **rating:** 93

best drinking 2004–2014 **best vintages** '80, '81, '86, '89, '90, '91, '93, '94, '96, '97, '98, '99 **drink with** Roast leg of lamb • NA

Yarra Yering Portsorts

▼▼▼▼▼ **1999** Dark red-purple; a fragrant, spicy, licorice, cedary/cigar box bouquet is followed by a fascinating palate, with every flavour imaginable running from chocolate to allspice to cinnamon to blackberries. I am always blown away by this wine in its youth. **rating:** 94

best drinking 2002–2022 **best vintages** '96, '97, '98, '99 **drink with** As many friends as possible • NA

yass valley wines NR

9 Crisps Lane, Murrumbateman, NSW 2582 **region** Canberra District

phone (02) 6227 5592 **fax** (02) 6227 5592 **open** Wed–Sun and public holidays 11–5 or by appointment

winemaker Michael Withers **production** 500 **est.** 1979

product range ($15–33 CD) Riesling, Rieselle, Semillon, Chardonnay, Allegro (white blend), Barbera, Merlot, Cabernet Sauvignon.

summary Michael Withers and Anne Hillier purchased Yass Valley in January 1991 and have subsequently rehabilitated the existing run-down vineyards and extended the plantings. Mick Withers is a chemist by profession and has completed a Wine Science degree at Charles Sturt University; Anne is a registered psychologist and has completed a viticulture diploma at Charles Sturt. No recent tastings.

yaxley estate ★★★☆

31 Dransfield Road, Copping, Tas 7174 **region** Southern Tasmania
phone (03) 6253 5222 **fax** (03) 6253 5222 **open** 7 days 10–6.30
winemaker Andrew Hood (Contract) **production** 333 **est.** 1991
product range ($19.80–22 CD) Pinot Gris, Sauvignon Blanc, Chardonnay, Pinot Noir.
summary While Yaxley Estate was established back in 1991, it was not until 1998 that it offered each of the four wines from its vineyard plantings, which total 1.7 hectares. Once again, the small-batch handling skills (and patience) of contract-winemaker Andrew Hood have made the venture possible.

Yaxley Estate Pinot Gris

🍷🍷🍷🍷 **2000** Light to medium straw-green; the fruit aromas are in the dried flower/dried fruit spectrum, slightly subdued; the palate has good fruit depth and has the balance missing from the '99. **rating:** 87
best drinking Now–2004 **best vintages** NA **drink with** Summer salads • $22

Yaxley Estate Chardonnay

🍷🍷🍷½ **2000** Light green-yellow; crisp, clean, light citrus, melon and apple aromas and flavours provide a fresh, crisp wine for immediate consumption. **rating:** 82
best drinking Now **best vintages** NA **drink with** Cold seafood • $19.80

yellowglen ★★★☆

Whites Road, Smythesdale, Vic 3351 **region** Ballarat
phone (03) 5342 8617 **fax** (03) 5333 7102 **open** Mon–Fri 10–5, weekends 11–5
winemaker Charles Hargraves **production** NFP **est.** 1975
product range ($10–25 R) Brut Cremant, Brut Pinot Chardonnay, Brut Rosé, Vintage Cuvée Victoria, Vintage Pinot Chardonnay, Y, Yellow, Yellow Chardonnay, Grande Cuvée.
summary Just as the overall quality of Australian sparkling wine has improved out of all recognition over the past ten years, so has that of Yellowglen. Initially the quality lift was apparent at the top end of the range but now extends right to the non-vintage commercial releases.

Yellowglen Grande Cuvée Pinot Noir

🍷🍷🍷½ **NV** Light straw-yellow; the bouquet has distinct minerally/bready/biscuity pinot noir varietal character, that same varietal character expressing itself with particular clarity on the back palate and finish. A neat achievement. **rating:** 84
best drinking Now **best vintages** NA **drink with** Finger food • $18

Yellowglen Vintage Cuvée Victoria

🍷🍷🍷🍷 **1996** Light straw-green; the bouquet has fresh apple with touches of bready/yeast aromas, the palate in crisp, restrained style, again with lively apple and mineral flavours. **rating:** 88
best drinking Now **best vintages** '90, '91, '92, '95, '96 **drink with** Aperitif • NA

Yellowglen Vintage Brut

🍷🍷🍷🍷 **1997** Light straw-green; a tight minerally/citrussy bouquet with a hint of spice is followed by a crisp, clean and elegant palate, fairly light bodied but with quite good length. **rating:** 87
best drinking Now **best vintages** '88, '90, '92, '94 **drink with** Aperitif or oysters • NA

yeringberg ★★★★★

Maroondah Highway, Coldstream, Vic 3770 **region** Yarra Valley
phone (03) 9739 1453 **fax** (03) 9739 0048 **open** By appointment
winemaker Guill de Pury **production** 1100 **est.** 1863
product range ($30–45 CD) Chardonnay, Marsanne/Roussanne, Pinot Noir, Yeringberg (Cabernet blend).

summary Makes wines for the new millennium from the low-yielding vines re-established on the heart of what was one of the most famous (and infinitely larger) vineyards of the nineteenth century. In the riper years, the red wines have a velvety generosity of flavour that is rarely encountered, yet never lose varietal character, while the Yeringberg White takes students of history back to Yeringberg's fame in the nineteenth century. The wines are exported to the UK, the US, Switzerland and Germany.

yering farm NR

St Huberts Road, Yering, Vic 3770 **region** Yarra Valley
phone (03) 9739 0461 **fax** (03) 9735 4012 **open** 7 days 10–5
winemaker Alan Johns **production** 3000 **est.** 1989
product range ($18–25 ML) Chardonnay, Pinot Noir, Merlot, Cabernet Sauvignon.
summary Alan and Louise Johns established their 12-hectare vineyard in 1989 on the site of the original Yeringa winery built by the Deschamps family in the last century. Between 1992 and 1998 the wines were made by Alan Johns, and since then at Yarra Ridge, which purchases much of the production from the vineyard.

yering range vineyard NR

14 McIntyre Lane, Coldstream, Vic 3770 **region** Yarra Valley
phone (03) 9739 1172 **fax** (03) 9739 1172 **open** By appointment
winemaker Kevin Ryan, Margaret Ryan **production** 300 **est.** 1989
product range ($18 CD) Cabernet Sauvignon.
summary Yering Range has 2 hectares of cabernet sauvignon under vine, part being sold and part made under the Yering Range label by John Ellis at Hanging Rock. The tiny production is sold through a mailing list. The 1999 Cabernet Sauvignon is a light, elegant wine, with just a touch of green fruit.

yering station ★★★★☆

Melba Highway, Yering, Vic 3770 **region** Yarra Valley
phone (03) 9730 1107 **fax** (03) 9739 0135 **open** Thur–Sun 10–5
winemaker Tom Carson, Dan Buckle, Darren Rathbone **production** 45 000 **est.** 1988
product range ($12.50–45 CD) Baraks Bridge Chardonnay, Pinot Noir, Shiraz, Cabernet Sauvignon, Botrytis Semillon; Yering Station Sauvignon Blanc, Chardonnay, Pinot Noir Rosé ED, Pinot Noir, Cabernet Merlot; Reserve range of Chardonnay, Pinot Noir and Shiraz; also Verjuice in 375 ml bottles.
summary The historic Yering Station (or at least the portion of the property on which the cellar door and vineyard are established) was purchased by the Rathbone family in January 1996 and is now the site of a joint venture with the French Champagne house Devaux. A spectacular and very large winery has been erected which handles the Yarrabank sparkling wines and the Yering Station and Yarra Edge table wines. Immediately became one of the focal points of the Yarra Valley, particularly with the historic Chateau Yering next door, where luxury accommodation and fine dining is available. Exports to the UK, the US, Sweden, Malayisa and Japan.

Yering Station Sauvignon Blanc

YYYY 2000 Light green-yellow; the bouquet is light, with a grass, herb and mineral backdrop. The palate is light, clean and crisp, but without much power or length. **rating:** 84

best drinking Now **best vintages** NA **drink with** Shellfish • $18

Yering Station Pinot Noir Rosé 2000 ED

YYYY **2000** Salmon pink; the lively bouquet offers a mix of spice, earth, forest and stem, the palate dry and spicy, with distinctive pinot varietal character. **rating:** 86

best drinking Now **best vintages** NA **drink with** Seafood, Singapore noodles, you name it • $18

Yering Station Pinot Noir

YYYY **1999** Light to medium red; the bouquet is fragrant but in a sappy/foresty/earthy spectrum; the palate is tangy, but light, the savoury/earthy overtones to the fruit reflecting the vintage. **rating:** 87

best drinking Now–2003 **best vintages** '91, '94, '96, '97 **drink with** Smoked quail • $23

Yering Station Reserve Shiraz

YYYYY **1998** Medium red, with some purple. The elegant, aromatic bouquet has cherry, spice and a touch of game; the intense but fine palate has a core of dark cherry fruit supported by subtle oak, and then fine tannins and neatly balanced acidity on the finish. **rating:** 94

best drinking 2002–2012 **best vintages** '97, '98 **drink with** Venison • $45

yunbar estate ★★★☆

Light Pass Road, Vine Vale, SA 5352 **region** Barossa Valley
phone (08) 8563 1371 **fax** (08) 8563 1571 **open** By appointment
winemaker Vicky-Louise Bartier **production** 1800 **est.** 1998
product range ($18–25 CD) Eden Riesling, Bushvines Semillon, Chaste Chardonnay, Sinners Shiraz, Miracle Merlot, Craig's Cabernet.
summary The intriguingly named Sinners Shiraz, the Merlot, Semillon and Chardonnay are produced from a total of 8 hectares of estate-grown grapes; the Eden Riesling is made from contract-grown grapes. Exports to the US.

Yunbar Estate Eden Riesling

🍷🍷🍷🍷🍷 **2000** Light to medium yellow-green; the fragrant bouquet has a mix of lime juice and mineral, the fresh, lively and crisp palate already showing considerable length, but needing time to fully express itself. **rating:** 90
best drinking 2004–2009 **best vintages** NA **drink with** Leave it in the cellar • $18

Yunbar Estate Chaste Chardonnay

🍷🍷🍷🍷 **2000** Medium to full yellow-green; the bouquet is quite complex, with nicely judged French oak supporting rather than overwhelming the melon and stonefruit aromas. The light- to medium-bodied palate is tangy, lively, and has good length. Excellent value; 300 cases produced. **rating:** 87
best drinking 2002–2006 **best vintages** '00 **drink with** Fresh Atlantic salmon • $18

Yunbar Estate Miracle Merlot

🍷🍷🍷🍷 **2000** Medium red-purple; the bouquet has some distinctive olive and herb varietal aromas, and the palate is likewise soft and silky, as befits the variety. Pretty light bodied, but nicely done as an early-drinking style. **rating:** 84
best drinking Now–2004 **best vintages** NA **drink with** Pasta • $18

yungarra estate NR

Yungarra Drive, Dunsborough, WA 6281 **region** Margaret River
phone (08) 9755 2153 **fax** (08) 9755 2310 **open** 7 days 10–5
winemaker Erland Happ (Contract) **production** 1450 **est.** 1988
product range ($10.50–12 CD) Semillon, Sauvignon Blanc, Quartet (Semillon, Sauvignon Blanc, Chenin Blanc, Verdelho), Chenin Blanc Verdelho, Pink Opal (sweet red table wine made from Cabernet and Merlot), Springtime (sweet Sauvignon Blanc, Verdelho), Cabernet Sauvignon, Cabernet Merlot, Royale.
summary Yungarra Estate is a combined tourist lodge and cellar-door facility set on a 40-hectare property overlooking Geographe Bay. The 9-hectare vineyard was first planted in 1988, producing its first wines in 1992, contract-made by Erland Happ. Cellar-door sales commenced in 1993; there are five B&B cottages on the Yungarra Estate property.

zappacosta estate wines NR

301 Kidman Way, Hanwood, NSW 2680 **region** Riverina
phone (02) 6963 0278 **fax** (02) 6963 0278 **open** By appointment
winemaker Dino Zappacosta **production** 40 000 **est.** 1996
product range ($12 CD) Riesling, Semillon, Dry White, Shiraz.
summary Zappacosta Estate, briefly known as Hanwood Village Wines, is a relatively new business, with the first release from the 1996 vintage.

zarephath wines ★★★☆

Moorialup Road, East Porongurup, WA 6324 **region** Great Southern
phone (08) 9853 1152 **fax** (08) 9841 8124 **open** Wed–Sun 10–4
winemaker Brenden Smith **production** 2000 **est.** 1994
product range ($16.50–24 CD) Riesling, Chardonnay, Pinot Noir, Cabernet Sauvignon.
summary The 9-hectare Zarephath vineyard is owned and operated by Brothers and Sisters of The Christ Circle, a Benedictine community. They say the most outstanding feature of the location is the feeling of peace and tranquillity that permeates it, something I can well believe on the basis of numerous visits to the Porongurups.

Zarephath Riesling

TTTTY **2000** Light to medium straw-green; a highly fragrant and aromatic bouquet with a mix of citrus and bath powder moves into an intensely fruity, lime and passionfruit-flavoured palate in ultra-typical regional mould.

rating: 90

best drinking Now–2005 **best vintages** '00 **drink with** Chinese prawns • $22.09

Zarephath Pinot Noir

TTTT **1999** Medium red-purple; the bouquet is clean and fresh, with some cherry fruit; the palate follows down the same track, without overmuch varietal character, and a slightly grippy finish. Still, better than many. **rating:** 85

best drinking Now–2003 **best vintages** NA **drink with** Roast duck • $23.79

zema estate 

Riddoch Highway, Coonawarra, SA 5263 **region** Coonawarra
phone (08) 8736 3219 **fax** (08) 8736 3280 **open** 7 days 9–5
winemaker Tom Simons **production** 12 000 **est.** 1982
product range ($15–40 CD) Sauvignon Blanc, Shiraz, Cabernet Sauvignon, Family Selection Cabernet Sauvignon, Cluny (Cabernet blend).
summary Zema is one of the last outposts of hand-pruning in Coonawarra, the various members of the Zema family tending a 40-hectare vineyard progressively planted between 1982 and 1994 in the heart of Coonawarra's terra rossa soil. Winemaking practices are straightforward; if ever there was an example of great wines being made in the vineyard, this is it. Exports to the UK, France, Germany, Malaysia, Thailand, Hong Kong and New Zealand.

Zema Estate Cluny

TTTTY **1998** Medium to full purple-red; the ripe aromas of the bouquet range through blackberry, cassis and plum; subtle oak. In the mouth, the richest and ripest of all of the Clunys to date, with lashings of ripe, small berry red fruits and fine tannins.

rating: 93

best drinking 2002–2012 **best vintages** '96, '97, '98 **drink with** Braised lamb • $23.95

Zema Estate Cabernet Sauvignon

TTTTT **1998** If you hand-prune Coonawarra cabernet sauvignon, and don't seek to embellish it in the winery with masses of oak, this is what you get. Rich, complex, dark berry spice and chocolate, tinged with more savoury aromas, lead into a concentrated, tongue-coating blackberry-flavoured palate and great tannins. **rating:** 95

best drinking 2003–2018 **best vintages** '84, '86, '88, '92, '93, '96, '97, '98 **drink with** Barbecued leg of lamb • $23.95

ziebarth wines NR

Foleys Road, Goodger, Qld 4610 **region** South Burnett
phone (07) 4162 3089 **fax** (07) 4162 3084 **open** 7 days 10–5
winemaker John Crane (Contract) **production** 420 **est.** 1998
product range ($13.50–14.50 CD) Semillon, Fairview White, Rosé, Shiraz Cabernet Franc.
summary The 4-hectare vineyard (with 1 hectare each of semillon, cabernet sauvignon, merlot and chardonnay, together with 0.25 hectare of chambourcin) is a minor diversification on a beef-cattle property set on the edge of the Stuart Range, and which enjoys superb views. It is a small family operation with the aim of providing a wine experience for visitors, the wines being made for Ziebarth by John Crane at Crane Winery.

zuber estate NR

Northern Highway, Heathcote, Vic 3523 **region** Heathcote
phone (03) 5433 2142 **open** 7 days 9–6
winemaker A Zuber **production** 450 **est.** 1971
product range ($10–12 CD) Chardonnay, Pinot Noir, Shiraz, Cabernet Sauvignon.
summary A somewhat erratic winery that is capable of producing the style of Shiraz for which Bendigo is famous but does not always do so. No recent tastings.

new zealand

wineries and wines

akarangi NR

River Road, Havelock North, Hawke's Bay **region** Hawke's Bay
phone (06) 877 8228 **fax** (06) 877 2200 **open** Weekends, public holidays and summer 9–5
winemaker Morton Osborne **production** 800 **est.** 1988
product range ($12–18 CD) Sauvignon Blanc, Riesling Late Harvest, Chardonnay, Cabernet Merlot.
summary Former contract grape-growers now making and selling tiny quantities cellar door and through one or two local shops. Morton and Vivien Osborne have 5 hectares of vineyards and operate the cellar-door sales through a century-old Presbyterian church moved onto the property.

alana estate ★★★★

Puruatanga Road, Martinborough **region** Wairarapa
phone (06) 306 9784 **fax** (06) 306 9784 **open** Mon–Thurs 1–3, Fri–Sun 11–5
winemaker John Kavanagh **production** 10 000 **est.** 1995
product range ($17–36 CD) Riesling, Sauvignon Blanc, Chardonnay, Pinot Noir.
summary Ian and Alana Smart acquired their prime vineyard site, between Dry River and Te Kairanga, in 1995, which was no mean feat given the scarcity of such sites on the Martinborough terraces. It came after a decade of living in London and travelling incessantly, and is now their permanent home. Between 1995 and 2000 they established 22 hectares of vineyard. A completed stage one of a gravity-fed winery has been built into the side of a hill, and production is projected to increase to about 12 000–15 000 cases by 2002. Winemaker John Kavanagh has joined Alana Estate from Palliser Estate, bringing both industry and local knowledge with him. Exports to the UK, the US, Asia and France.

Alana Estate Pinot Noir

🍷🍷🍷🍷 **1999** Bright red-purple; the bouquet is ripe, with pleasant, ripe plummy aromas of moderate intensity. The medium-bodied palate moves on logically from the bouquet, with pleasant plummy fruit and tannins, but does seem to dip fractionally on the back palate and finish. **rating:** 86
best drinking Now–2004 **best vintages** '98 **drink with** Ragout of venison • $36

---

alan mccorkindale ★★★★★

PO Box 29338, Christchurch **region** Waipara
phone (03) 351 4924 **fax** (03) 351 4925 **open** By appointment
winemaker Alan McCorkindale **production** 4000 **est.** 1996
product range ($19.90–29.90 R) Dry Riesling, Gewurztraminer, Sauvignon Blanc, Chardonnay, Brut, Pinot Noir.
summary Alan McCorkindale established a reputation as one of New Zealand's finest winemakers during his ten-year stint as Corbans (and Stoneleigh) winemaker before deciding to do his own thing in 1996. During his time with Corbans, he had begun the development of a small, close-planted vineyard in Waipara, North Canterbury, planted to specially selected clones of pinot noir, chardonnay and meunier. This vineyard provides the base wine for the Millennium Brut; the riesling, sauvignon blanc, chardonnay and pinot noir all come from Marlborough. Exports to Spain and the Netherlands.

Alan McCorkindale Marlborough Chardonnay

🍷🍷🍷🍷 **1999** Medium yellow-green; the bouquet is moderately intense, with well-judged barrel-ferment and malolactic-ferment inputs to the citrus and melon fruit. The wine has nice mouthfeel in a restrained, sophisticated style, with some melon flavour. I just wish there were a few more horsepower under the bonnet. **rating:** 85
best drinking Now–2004 **best vintages** NA **drink with** Milk-fed veal • $24.80

---

alexander vineyard NR

Dublin Street Extension, Martinborough (PO Box 87) **region** Wairarapa
phone (06) 306 9389 **open** Not
winemaker Elise Montgomery **production** 500 **est.** 1991
product range ($15–30 ML) Dusty Road Dry Red, Pinot Noir, Alexander Cabernet Sauvignon Merlot.
summary The Alexanders share with Benfield & Delamere the conviction that Martinborough is best-suited to the Bordeaux varieties of cabernet sauvignon, cabernet franc and merlot, which they have planted on a high-density, low-trellis, guyot-pruned configuration. The first small vintage was in 1994; an on-site winery was built for the 1996 vintage.

alexandra wine company NR

176 Airport Road, RD1, Alexandra **region** Central Otago
phone (03) 448 8466 **fax** (03) 448 8466 **open** By appointment
winemaker Matt Dicey **production** 1000 **est.** 1997
product range ($14–22 R) Riesling, Gewurztraminer, Chardonnay, Pinot Noir.
summary This venture brings together two separately owned vineyards: Crag an Oir, situated just north of Alexandra and owned by Murray and Chris Bell, and the Davishon Vineyard of David and Shona Garry, situated on the Dunstan Flats. When the grapes of both vineyards are combined, the wine is given the brand name Ferauds, a link to Jean Feraud, who planted the first vines in Otago on the Dunstan Flats in the 1860s. Varietals produced from one or other of the vineyards are then labelled under that vineyard name, Crag an Oir (being Gaelic for 'hill of gold'). The Pinot Noir, in particular, has been very well received.

Alexandra Crag an Oir Riesling

TTTT **2000** Medium yellow-green; a powerful bouquet with quite developed tropical tones is logically replayed on the palate, which has masses of flavour ranging through lime to tropical, giving an overall impression of some sweetness. **rating:** 85
best drinking Now **best vintages** NA **drink with** Guacamole • $15

alexia

PO Box 5473, Wellington **region** Nelson
phone (02) 549 4272 **fax** (04) 385 1402 **open** Not
winemaker Jane Cooper **production** 700 **est.** 2000
product range ($17–20 R) Nelson Sauvignon Blanc, Nelson Chardonnay.
summary Jane Cooper has been making wine in Nelson since 1993; between then and 1996 she was winemaker at Seifried Estate, and in the following year did three vintages: the first in the Hunter Valley, the second at Nelson, and the third in Northern Italy. Since that time she has continued to make wine for various wineries in Nelson, currently for Te Mania Estate, Richmond Plains and Kaimira Estate, all three at the Kaimira Estate Winery. It is here that Jane Cooper has commenced to make her Alexia wines, using grapes provided by three contract vineyards on the Waimea Plains.

Alexia Sauvignon Blanc

TTTTY **2000** Very pale straw-green; an intense, herbaceous/grassy bouquet, slightly old-fashioned, perhaps, but full of character, is followed by a lively, fresh palate with gooseberry and apple flavours joining the herbs of the bouquet; excellent balance. **rating:** 93
best drinking Now **best vintages** '00 **drink with** Shellfish • $17.95

Alexia Chardonnay

TTTY **2000** Light straw-green; the bouquet is clean and light, with citrus/melon fruit and little or no oak evident; a pleasant, light, fresh palate, again fruit-driven; overall slightly simple. **rating:** 84
best drinking Now–2003 **best vintages** NA **drink with** Grilled fish • $19.95

allan scott wines

Jacksons Road, RD3, Blenheim **region** Marlborough
phone (03) 572 9054 **fax** (03) 572 9053 **open** 7 days 9.30–4.30
winemaker Greg Trought **production** 45 000 **est.** 1990
product range ($14–30 R) Marlborough Riesling, Marlborough Sauvignon Blanc, Chardonnay, Methode Traditionelle, Autumn Riesling, Merlot; Prestige range of Chardonnay, Cabernet Sauvignon.
summary The collapse of Vintech in 1995 accelerated former Corbans' chief viticulturist Allan Scott's plans for his own winery and full-time winemaker (previously the wines were contract-made at Vintech). Thus from 1996 a winery joined the attractive cellar-door sales and restaurant (open seven days from noon to 4 pm), utilising 61 hectares of estate vineyards. Wine quality is all one could ask for. Exports to the UK, the US, Germany and Australia.

Allan Scott Marlborough Riesling

🍷🍷🍷🍷🍷 **2000** Light green-yellow; the fine, bright and zesty bouquet has floral lime blossom, herb and mineral aromatics. The palate, likewise, is crisp, with a touch of passionfruit coming through; the lower than usual residual sugar (4 grams per litre rather than the normal 7) tends to accentuate the minerally acidity, but not to the point where the wine is unbalanced. Will repay cellaring. **rating:** 90

best drinking 2002–2009 **best vintages** '92, '93, '97, '99, '00 **drink with** Fresh asparagus • $16

Allan Scott Marlborough Sauvignon Blanc

🍷🍷🍷🍷🍷 **2000** Light green-yellow; the bouquet is crisp and minerally with a passing illusion of a hint of oak, before lemon and passionfruit kicks in. The palate is bright and lively, with a tight yet juicy feel running through to a crystal clear finish. Very much a food style. **rating:** 90

best drinking Now **best vintages** '92, '94, '97, '98 **drink with** Sugar-cured tuna • $18

Allan Scott Prestige Chardonnay

🍷🍷🍷🍷🍷 **1999** Medium yellow-green; the bouquet has considerably more complexity and intensity than the varietal version, with a combination of citrus, melon and a sweet, almost creamy, finish and aftertaste. **rating:** 92

best drinking Now–2004 **best vintages** '99 **drink with** Pan-fried schnapper • $30

Allan Scott Merlot

🍷🍷🍷🍷🍷 **1999** Medium red-purple; the moderately intense bouquet has a savoury/minty spectrum that is less convincing than the palate. This really does have the texture and mouthfeel of Merlot, with a mix of gently savoury and red berry fruits, supported by fine tannins. Understated and elegant. **rating:** 91

best drinking 2002–2007 **best vintages** NA **drink with** Ragout of veal • $24

alpha domus ★★★★

1829 Maraekakaho Road, RD1, Bridge Pa, Hastings **region** Hawke's Bay

phone (06) 879 6752 **fax** (06) 879 6952 **open** Mon–Fri 10–4, summer 7 days 10–5

winemaker Evert Nijzink **production** 12 000 **est.** 1996

product range ($14–45 CD) Chardonnay, Semillon Sauvignon Blanc, Sauvignon Blanc, Leonarda Late Harvest Semillon, Rosé, Pinot Noir, Cabernet Merlot, The Navigator (Cabernet Merlot); AD Selection Barrel Fermented Semillon, Barrel Fermented Chardonnay, Noble Selection, Cabernet Merlot Malbec Franc.

summary An estate-based operation drawing upon 16 hectares of vineyards and enjoying significant growth in production. The wines have attracted considerable favourable comment in New Zealand, with export markets in the Netherlands and the UK.

Alpha Domus The Navigator Cabernet Merlot

🍷🍷🍷🍷🍷 **1999** Medium red-purple; a fine, aromatic, cedary, savoury bouquet is followed by an elegant and fine palate; here gentle red berry fruit is supported by spicy/cedary notes, partly fruit-derived, partly oak-derived. A strong gold medal at the Royal Easter Wine Show 2001. **rating:** 91

best drinking 2003–2009 **best vintages** NA **drink with** Venison sausage • $30

amor-bendall wines ★★★★

145 Wairere Road, Gisborne **region** Gisborne

phone (06) 868 0925 **fax** (06) 868 0926 **open** By appointment 7 days

winemaker Noel Amor **production** 1500 **est.** 1998

product range ($12–28 R) Gewurztraminer, Chardonnay Unoaked, Chardonnay Reserve, Summer Red.

summary Former food technologist and process engineer Noel Amor, together with partner Alison Bendall, has designed and built an ultra-sophisticated micro-winery that is fully equipped to tackle the technically difficult task of making small quantities of white wines, which, incidentally, have been well received. They have no vineyards of their own, relying on the abundance of contract-grown grapes in the region.

Amor-Bendall Reserve Chardonnay

🍷🍷🍷🍷🍷 **2000** Light green-yellow; a fine, discreet and elegant bouquet with barrel-ferment and malolactic-ferment influences plain to see. The wine has excellent balance on the complex but quite delicate palate. **rating:** 92

best drinking Now–2004 **best vintages** '00 **drink with** Milk-fed veal • $28

anapai river ★★★☆

Couts Island Road, Christchurch **region** Christchurch
phone NA **open** Not
winemaker Alan McCorkindale **production** NA **est.** NA
product range Marlborough Sauvignon Blanc, Canterbury Pinot Noir.
summary A negociant business, using the skills of Alan McCorkindale to produce wines from contract-grown grapes initially aimed at the export markets of the UK and Australia.

arahura vineyard NR

Ness Valley Road, Clevedon, RD5, Papakura **region** Auckland Area
phone (09) 292 8749 **fax** (09) 292 8743 **open** Weekends 9–7 or by appointment
winemaker Tim Mason **production** 1000 **est.** 1991
product range ($15–30 CD) Arahura Merlot Cabernet Sauvignon and Malbec Cabernet Franc are the leaders; the Ness Valley Cabernet Sauvignon Merlot and Merlot Cabernet Sauvignon are on a lower price level.
summary Retired judge Ken Mason and wife Dianne are following in the footsteps of Tony Molloy QC by venturing into a new viticultural area and specialising in a single Bordeaux-style red (the plantings also include a little cabernet franc and merlot). A micro-winery was built in 1997 to handle the production from the 2 hectares of vineyards. The initial releases from 1998 and 1999 were favourably reviewed.

artisan wines NR

225 Henderson Valley Road, Henderson, Waitakere City **region** Auckland Area
phone (09) 836 4949 **fax** (09) 836 4950 **open** 7 days 10–5
winemaker Greg Foster (Contract, Matariki) **production** 1100 **est.** 1999
product range ($8.50–19.95 R) Gewurztraminer, Chardonnay, Pinot Noir.
summary A new venture bringing together the vineyards of three grape-growing families in Marlborough, Gisborne and Auckland: Sunde, Kennedy and Gaw. The largest plantings are at Gisborne, with 19 hectares under vine, the other two shareholders contributing another 5 hectares. As well as estate-grown grapes, the plan is to supplement the crush with contract-grown fruit. With this viticultural resource, production can be expected to rise significantly in the years ahead.

ascension vineyard NR

480 Matakana Road, Matakana **region** Northland and Matakana
phone (09) 422 9601 **fax** (09) 422 9602 **open** 7 days 10–5
winemaker Darryl Soljan **production** 2000 **est.** 1996
product range ($15–29 CD) Riesling, Chardonnay, The Ascent Chardonnay, Pinotage, The Ascent Cabernet Merlot Malbec.
summary Darryl Soljan is a fifth-generation grape-grower and winemaker. In 1996 he began the planting of 3.6 hectares of vineyard, and has built a cellar door, café and winery on site using architecture inspired by the Spanish missions of California. The vines are planted on a steep hillside, and the intended focus is on high-quality, flavoursome styles.

ashwell vineyards ★★★★

Kitchener Street, Martinborough **region** Wairarapa
phone (04) 472 0519 **fax** (04) 389 8748 **open** Not
winemaker John Phipps **production** 500 **est.** 1989
product range ($17.50–28 R) Sauvignon Blanc, Chardonnay, Pinot Noir, Cabernet Merlot.
summary Vivienne and John Phipps planted 2 hectares of vines in 1989, which were only to suffer severe frost damage in 1991. Undaunted, they doubled plantings in 1994 and were appropriately rewarded with show medals and wine writers' praise for their Pinot Noirs.

Ashwell Vineyards Pinot Noir

YYYYY **1999** Good, youthful red-purple; a fragrant, tangy, smoky and stylish bouquet flows through to a long and quite intense palate with hints of raspberry and cherry. Excellent acid and tannin management provide a good aftertaste. **rating:** 92

best drinking Now–2004 **best vintages** '99 **drink with** Wild pork • $28

askerne NR

267 Te Mata–Mangateretere Road, Havelock North **region** Hawke's Bay
phone (06) 877 6085 **fax** (06) 877 2089 **open** Sat 10–5, Sun 10.30–4.30 or 10–5 in summer
winemaker Sorrelle Pearson, Jenny Dobson (Consultant) **production** 1500 **est.** 1993
product range ($15.50–25 CD) Riesling, Semillon, Semillon Sauvignon Blanc, Sauvignon Blanc, Chardonnay, Botrytised Riesling.
summary Askerne is the venture of John Loughlin (son of Dr John Loughlin of Waimarama Estate) who has named his vineyard after the Yorkshire town which was his wife's birthplace. It runs counter to conventional Hawke's Bay wisdom by having its 5.6-hectare vineyard planted entirely to white varieties: in descending order sauvignon blanc, riesling, semillon, chardonnay, gewurztraminer and optima.

ata rangi ★★★★★

Puruatanga Road, Martinborough **region** Wairarapa
phone (06) 306 9570 **fax** (06) 306 9523 **open** 7 days Oct–Mar, 1–3 midweek, 11–5 weekends
winemaker Clive Paton, Oliver Masters **production** 6000 **est.** 1980
product range ($16–45 CD) Craighall Chardonnay, Petrie Chardonnay, Dalnagairn Chardonnay (Hawke's Bay), Summer Rosé, Pinot Noir, Celebre (Cabernet, Syrah, Merlot blend).
summary Consistently ranks among the best wineries in New Zealand, let alone Martinborough. Both the Pinot Noir and Celebre are remarkable for their depth of colour and sweetness of fruit, showing the impact of full physiological ripeness. A new winery was commissioned for the 1996 vintage, handling the grapes from the 19 hectares of estate plantings as well as the grapes purchased from other regions. The wines are exported to Australia, the UK and the US.

Ata Rangi Pinot Noir

TTTTT **1999** Typically deeply coloured; potent plum, black cherry and spice aromas flood the bouquet; ravishly sweet but not jammy dark berry, plum, cherry and spice flavours on the palate swell to a crescendo on the finish, the tannins in much better balance than they were in 1998. **rating:** 95

best drinking 2002–2010 **best vintages** '86, '88, '89, '90, '91, '92, '93, '94, '96, '97, '99 **drink with** New Zealand venison • $45

babich ★★★★

Babich Road, Henderson **region** Auckland Area
phone (09) 833 7859 **fax** (09) 833 9929 **open** Mon–Fri 9–5, Sat 9–6, Sun 11–5
winemaker Neill Culley **production** 80 000 **est.** 1916
product range ($10–33.50 R) The Patriarch Chardonnay, Cabernet Sauvignon; Irongate Chardonnay, Cabernet Merlot; Mara Estate Chardonnay, Sauvignon, Merlot, Cabernet Sauvignon, Syrah; also varietal/regional wines such as Marlborough Sauvignon Blanc, Hawke's Bay Sauvignon Blanc, East Coast Chardonnay.
summary Continues to uphold the reputation it gained in the 1960s, but has moved with the times in radically changing its fruit sources and wine styles. Particularly given the volume of production, quality is admirably consistent, with the expanded Mara Estate range leading the way, and strong support from Irongate Chardonnay. It now has 114 hectares of estate vineyards, with 57 hectares in the Gimblett Road region of Hawke's Bay, 42 hectares in the Awatere Valley of Marlborough and the remainder around the Henderson winery. Wines are exported throughout Europe, Asia and North America.

Babich Marlborough Riesling

TTTT **2000** Medium yellow-green; the moderately intense and quite complex bouquet has generous tropical/lime aromatics that provide the wine with plenty of mid-palate weight, again in a lime/tropical spectrum, and which (together with the acidity) carry the sweetness left in the wine. **rating:** 89

best drinking Now–2004 **best vintages** NA **drink with** Chinese • $16

Babich Winemaker's Reserve Sauvignon Blanc

TTTT **2000** Medium yellow-green; a solid, ripe and quite complex bouquet with no herbaceous or especially distinctive varietal fruit character is reflected in a complex palate with understated varietal character; excellent balance and moderate length, but I wonder whether taming the beast is such a good thing. **rating:** 88

best drinking Now **best vintages** '99 **drink with** Seafood paella • $19

banks peninsula wines NR

French Farm Valley Road, RD2, French Farm **region** Canterbury
phone (03) 304 5870 **fax** (30) 304 5870 **open** Not
winemaker Mark Leonard **production** 1000 **est.** 1996
product range ($15–20 R) Akaroa Harbour brand: Riesling, Chardonnay, Pinot Noir and Merlot.
summary To quote from a small leaflet of Banks Peninsula Wines: '150 years ago French settlers grew grapes at French Farm. In 1991 a small vineyard called Sunnybrae was established on the western side of Akaroa Harbour. Sunnybrae Vineyard overlooks the beautiful bay and valley of French Farm.' Thus we have Sunnybrae, French Farm, Akaroa Harbour and Banks Peninsula all co-existing as place names, and another winery called French Farm which started out life as a winery, then became a restaurant and subsequently reverted to a winery. In any event, you can sort the mystery out by visiting the Banks Peninsula.

bannockburn heights NR

Cairnmuir Road, RD2, Cromwell, Bannockburn **region** Central Otago
phone (03) 445 3211 **fax** (03) 445 0887 **open** 7 days 10–6
winemaker Steve Davies **production** 4000 **est.** 1999
product range ($18–32 R) Pinot Gris, Chardonnay, Pinot Noir.
summary Sir Clifford Skeggs began planting the 50-hectare vineyard in 1995, and constructed an on site 500-tonne winery in 1999; it is expected to produce 26 000 cases of wine a year by 2004. Winemaker Steve Davies has had considerable experience as a flying winemaker and the first releases (from 1999) of Akarua Chardonnay and Pinot Noir have been very well reviewed. It hardly needs be said this venture will be a major force in the rapidly growing Otago region in the years ahead.

beach house wines NR

c/o Roosters Brewhouse, 1470 Omahu Road, Hastings **region** Hawke's Bay
phone (06) 879 4127 **fax** (06) 879 7410 **open** Mon–Fri 10–7
winemaker Chris Harrison, Jill Harrison **production** 750 **est.** 1997
product range ($12.90–16.90CD) Riesling, Sauvignon Blanc, Chardonnay, Cabernet Merlot.
summary Chris and Jill Harrison are both graduates of the Roseworthy campus of the University of Adelaide, and had extensive experience in making wine in both France and New Zealand before turning their hand to making beer. Their Hastings brewery has been so successful they have been able to establish Beach House Wines as a sideline, bringing the wheel full circle.

bell hill vineyard NR

Old Weka Pass Road, Waikari, North Canterbury **region** Canterbury
phone (03) 379 4374 **fax** (03) 379 4374 **open** By appointment
winemaker Marcel Giesen, Sherwyn Veldhuizen **production** 150 **est.** 1997
product range ($35 ML) Old Weka Pass Road Pinot Noir.
summary Marcel Giesen and partner Sherwyn Veldhuizen have ventured into new territory, finding limestone soil and a climate that closely resembles that of Burgundy. They have planted 1 hectare of ultra-high-density pinot noir and chardonnay, and the first wine (from 18-month-old vines) is a brilliant achievement, with enormous promise for the future.

Bell Hill Vineyard Old Weka Pass Road Pinot Noir

1999 Vivid purple-red; a very pure expression of varietal character on the bouquet is still evolving; the palate is remarkably long and intense, with dark plum, bramble and a touch of spice. The wine has soaked up the French oak. **rating:** 93

best drinking 2002–2006 **best vintages** NA **drink with** Duck breast • $35

benfield & delamare NR

Cambridge Road, Martinborough **region** Wairarapa
phone (06) 306 9926 **fax** (06) 306 9926 **open** Summer weekends 1–5 or by appointment
winemaker Bill Benfield **production** NA **est.** 1987
product range ($47.50 CD) 'Martinborough', a single Cabernet Sauvignon Merlot Cabernet Franc blend.

summary Wellington architect Bill Benfield and partner, librarian Sue Delamere, have single-mindedly set about recreating Bordeaux, with an ultra-high-density, very low-trellised vineyard and utilising 'conservative' techniques of the kind favoured by the Bordelaise. All of the tiny production is sold by mailing list and limited exports to the UK and the US.

bentwood wines NR

Akaroa Highway, Tai Tapu, Canterbury **region** Canterbury
phone (03) 329 6191 **fax** (03) 329 6192 **open** By appointment
winemaker Grant Whelan **production** 500 **est.** 1991
product range ($14–17 CD) Riesling, Gewurztraminer, Pinot Blanc, Pinot Noir.
summary Ray Watson has established a 2-hectare vineyard on the Banks Peninsula, his interest in wine fired after a 12-month sojourn living on a vineyard in France. The first wines were released from the 1995 vintage; the Pinot Blanc is already a silver medal winner.

bilancia 

2396 State Highway 50 (PO Box 2508, Stortford Lodge), Hastings **region** Hawke's Bay
phone (06) 877 8288 **fax** (06) 877 8288 **open** Not
winemaker Warren Gibson, Lorraine Leheny **production** 1000 **est.** 1997
product range ($24–30 R) Pinot Grigio, Pinot Grigio Reserve, Chardonnay, Merlot.
summary Warren Gibson and Lorraine Leheny are winemakers at Trinity Hill and in 1997 made their first wines under the Bilancia label, using the Trinity Hill facilities to do so. (John Hancock is a very broadminded and generous employer.) So far Bilancia has relied on purchased grapes (again with John Hancock's good graces) but in 1998 began establishing their own close-planted steep-hillside vineyard.

black ridge 

Conroys Road, Earnscleugh, Alexandra **region** Central Otago
phone (03) 449 2059 **fax** (03) 449 2597 **open** 7 days 10–5
winemaker Tim Wardell **production** 3000 **est.** 1981
product range ($12.50–35 R) Otago Gold, Riesling, Chardonnay, Gewurztraminer, Pinot Noir, Cabernet Sauvignon.
summary The formidable, rocky vineyard site at Black Ridge is legendary even in New Zealand where toughness is taken for granted. The 8-hectare vineyard will always be low-producing, but the wines produced to date have all had clear and bracing varietal character. The outstanding Pinot Noir is a particularly good example of what the site can produce. Exports to the UK and the US.

bladen 

Conders Bend Road, Renwick, Marlborough **region** Marlborough
phone (03) 572 9417 **fax** (03) 572 9217 **open** 7 days 11–5 Labour weekend–Easter weekend or by appointment
winemaker Simon Waghorn (Contract) **production** 2000 **est.** 1997
product range ($16–20 ML) Riesling, Gewurztraminer, Pinot Gris, Sauvignon Blanc.
summary The McDonald family began establishing the Bladen vineyard in 1989, inspired by travels through Europe in the mid-1980s. The name has two derivations: the burial place of Sir Winston Churchill, and a combination of the names of the McDonald children, Blair and Deni. Initially all of the grapes were sold to Grove Mill, but since 1997 part of the 6-hectare vineyard production has been vinified by contract-winemaker Simon Waghorn. Exports to the UK and the US.

Bladen Marlborough Riesling

ΨΨΨΨ **2000** Brilliant light green-yellow; a clean bouquet with a mix of floral lime, lemon, apple and mineral leads into a palate that opens with lively, lemony fruit, the residual sugar clicking in a fraction too soon. It is obviously the style Bladen desires, but a little less sweetness would be so much better. **rating:** 88

best drinking 2002–2005 **best vintages** '00 **drink with** Pasta marinara • $16

Bladen Gewurztraminer

YYYY 2000 Light to medium green-yellow; the moderately intense bouquet is clean and smooth, with tropical overtones, but not a lot of varietal character. The palate is soft, and a little flabby, propped up by residual sugar.
rating: 83

best drinking Now **best vintages** '99 **drink with** Fresh fruit • $20

Bladen Sauvignon Blanc

YYYYY 2000 Light green-yellow; the floral bouquet is clean and moderately intense, offering a mix of fresh apple and gooseberry aromas. The lively and fresh palate has crisp lemony/citrus/gooseberry flavours, and a balanced, dry finish. **rating:** 90

best drinking Now **best vintages** '00 **drink with** Shellfish • $16

Bladen Pinot Gris

YYYYY 2000 Light straw-green; the quite delicate and crisp bouquet with herb, blossom and mineral is followed by a long, lively palate, adding a hint of stonefruit to the flavours promised by the bouquet. Consistently with prior releases, a pleasantly dry finish. **rating:** 90

best drinking Now–2003 **best vintages** '99, '00 **drink with** Crab salad • $20

borthwick estate NR

Dakins Road, Wairarapa **region** Wairarapa
phone (06) 372 7512 **fax** (06) 372 7513 **open** By appointment
winemaker Paddy Borthwick **production** 2300 **est.** 1999
product range ($16–32 R) Riesling, Sauvignon Blanc, Chardonnay, Pinot Noir, Cabernet Sauvignon Merlot Malbec, Sangiovese.
summary Paddy Borthwick, with a degree in oenology from Roseworthy College/University of Adelaide, seven years as a flying winemaker between the Northern and Southern hemispheres, and five years at Allan Scott Wines, is as experienced as they come. In 1997 he began planting his vineyards on the newly exploited Ruanahunga Terraces; the first wines were made in 1999 using the facilities at the nearby Mebus Estate. As one might expect, wine quality is good, particularly given the youth of the wines.

bradshaw estate NR

291 Te Mata Road, Havelock North **region** Hawke's Bay
phone (06) 877 8017 **fax** (06) 876 5494 **open** 7 days 10–5
winemaker Wayne Bradshaw, Murray McGill **production** 2500 **est.** 1994
product range ($16–29.95 CD) Sauvignon Blanc, Non-wooded Chardonnay, Merlot Cabernet.
summary Wayne and Judy Bradshaw established their operation on the historic Vidal's No. 1 Vineyard and Homestead and in 1996 opened a new winery with an attendant restaurant on the vineyard. The winery restaurant is open Friday to Sunday and every day throughout January.

briar vale estate NR

Kelliher Lane, Alexandra, Central Otago **region** Central Otago
phone (03) 448 8221 **fax** (03) 448 8221 **open** Weekends and public holidays 12–4.30 at Alexandra Boutique Wines, Centennial Avenue, Alexandra
winemaker John Currie, Judy Currie **production** 200 **est.** 1990
product range ($15–30 R) Riesling, Chardonnay, Late Harvest Riesling, Pinot Blanc, Pinot Noir.
summary Alsace was the inspiration for the varieties chosen by John and Judy Currie when they established their 1.78-hectare vineyard on a steep, north-facing slope above their cherry orchard. The cool climate carries the threat of spring frosts, however, and until the installation of frost protection (via overhead sprinklers) the crops were significantly reduced; better things are now on the way.

brick bay NR

PO Box 28270, Remuera, Auckland **region** Auckland Area
phone (09) 524 2831 **fax** (09) 524 2831 **open** Not
winemaker Anthony Ivicevich of West Brook (Contract) **production** 400 **est.** 1998

product range ($22 ML) Pinot Gris.

summary A new producer that made a dramatic entrance with its gold medal winning Pinot Gris, which was the first wine from 0.75 hectare of bearing vineyard. However, a further 2 hectares of cabernet sauvignon, cabernet franc, merlot and malbec have been planted by proprietors Christine and Richard Didsbury, with a 2000 vintage red due for release late 2001.

brightwater vineyards ★★★★

546 Main Road, RD1, Brightwater, Nelson **region** Nelson
phone (03) 544 1066 **fax** (03) 544 1066 **open** By appointment
winemaker Sam Weaver (Consultant), Garry Neale **production** 1500 **est.** 1999
product range ($15.95–19.95 R) Riesling, Sauvignon Blanc, Chardonnay, Merlot.

summary Garry Neale and wife Valley returned to Nelson in 1992 after working overseas. They purchased an 8-hectare property at Brightwater, and commenced establishment of their vineyard the following year. Until 1999 they sold the grapes to others, but from that year onwards have retained part of the production, making the wine at the nearby Greenhough Winery, using Sam Weaver as a consultant. They have had outstanding success with their first releases, and despite a professed dislike of the brash styles that succeed in wine shows, have managed two gold medals already. The wine is currently sold through a mailing list, to local retailers and some Christchurch restaurants and fine-wine outlets. The plan is to build production slowly to 6000 cases.

Brightwater Neslon Riesling

2000 Light to medium yellow-green; rich, lime aromatics come up and up each time you swirl the glass. The palate has most attractive lime/lemon flavours, with very good length and grip; threshold residual sugar is perfectly balanced against the acidity. **rating:** 93

best drinking Now–2005 **best vintages** '00 **drink with** Fish terrine • $17

Brightwater Sauvignon Blanc

2000 Medium yellow-green; the fragrant bouquet ranges through gooseberry, passionfruit and lemon; once again, the issue of whether or not reduction is a bad thing is raised. The palate has very good mouthfeel, delicate and lively, with quite lovely fruit and acid balance, the passionfruit of the bouquet coming through to add to an already very appealing wine. **rating:** 94

best drinking Now **best vintages** '00 **drink with** Artichoke with hollandaise sauce • $16

Brightwater Nelson Chardonnay

1999 Medium yellow-green; melon, nectarine and apple aromas are followed by a light- to medium-bodied palate with melon, a hint of cashew, barely perceptible oak, and a quite creamy mouthfeel thanks to relatively soft acidity. Easy on the gums. **rating:** 87

best drinking Now **best vintages** '99 **drink with** Breast of chicken • $18

brookfields vineyards ★★★★

Brookfields Road, Meeanee, Napier **region** Hawke's Bay
phone (06) 834 4615 **fax** (06) 834 4622 **open** 7 days 10.30–4.30
winemaker Peter Robertson **production** 10 000 **est.** 1937
product range ($16–48 R) Chardonnay, Reserve Chardonnay, Gewurztraminer, Barrel Fermented Sauvignon Blanc, Fumé Blanc, Pinot Gris, Cabernet Sauvignon, Reserve Cabernet Merlot.

summary Peter Robertson has worked hard since acquiring Brookfields in 1977, producing stylish Sauvignon Blanc, lightly oaked, understated Chardonnay and, best of all, the powerful, structured Gold Label Cabernet Merlot, now his highly regarded top-of-the-range release. A particular feature of his wines is their ability to age with grace. Exports to Brazil, Japan, Singapore and Canada.

Brookfields Gewurztraminer

2000 Light green-yellow; the bouquet is clean, fresh and spicy, the palate showing more of the typical full, mouthfilling flavour of the Brookfield style, with touches of lychee and tropical fruit. A touch more acidity might have lifted it into the highest class. **rating:** 86

best drinking Now **best vintages** NA **drink with** Asian cuisine • $19

Brookfields Chardonnay

TTTT **1999** Medium yellow-green; full, ripe citrus and peach fruit is offset by a twitch of lemony oak on the bouquet; the palate is tighter and more restrained, with lemony citrus flavours and moderate length. **rating:** 86

best drinking Now **best vintages** NA **drink with** Grilled chicken • $18

Brookfields Cabernet Sauvignon

TTTT **1999** Medium red-purple; a clean, fairly leafy/herbaceous bouquet with just a touch of oak is followed by a light- to medium-bodied palate with delicate red berry fruit, a touch of herb, and finishing with fine tannins. **rating:** 86

best drinking 2003–2007 **best vintages** NA **drink with** Prime rib of beef • $18

cairnbrae wines ★★★★

Jacksons Road, RD3, Blenheim **region** Marlborough
phone (03) 572 8048 **fax** (03) 572 7018 **open** 7 days 9–5
winemaker Matt Thomson, Kim Crawford (Consultant) **production** 14 000 **est.** 1981
product range ($17–25 R) Riesling, Reserve Riesling, Old River Riesling, Noble Riesling, Semillon, Sauvignon Blanc, Barrel Fermented Sauvignon Blanc, Pinot Gris, Chardonnay, Reserve Chardonnay.
summary The Brown family (Daphne, Murray and Dion) established 18 hectares of vineyard progressively from 1981, selling the grapes to Corbans until 1992, when part of the production was made for them by Kim Crawford, and the label was launched with immediate success. A fast-growing one to watch, with Pinot Noir and Pinot Gris now added. Exports to Australia, the US, Hong Kong, the Netherlands, Denmark and Canada.

Cairnbrae Marlborough Old River Riesling

TTTT **2000** Light green-yellow; the bouquet has immediately appealing lime/tropical aromas that come through very strongly on the palate, with abundant, ripe lime tropical fruit, the sweetness offset by some carbon dioxide and nicely handled acidity. The most interesting question is whether you drink the wine now, or rely on the carbon dioxide and acidity to keep it fresh. **rating:** 86

best drinking Now–2004 **best vintages** '98, '99 **drink with** Vegetarian • $17

Cairnbrae The Stones Sauvignon Blanc

TTTT **2000** Light green-yellow; a complex bouquet, with the passionfruit and gooseberry that comes through in many of the 2000 vintage wines, introducing additional flavours of ripe apple and herb on the palate. A crisp and lively finish rounds off a very nice wine. **rating:** 87

best drinking Now **best vintages** '93, '94, '97, '00 **drink with** Grilled flounder • $18

camana farm NR

Orapiu Road, Te Matuku Bay, RD1, Waiheke Island **region** Waiheke Island
phone (09) 372 7757 **fax** (09) 372 7257 **open** Winter Sat–Sun and holidays 10–4, summer Tues–Sun 10–4
winemaker David Evans-Gander **production** 420 **est.** 1998
product range ($16–30 R) Unoaked Chardonnay, Forte (Cabernet Franc Merlot Cabernet Sauvignon blend).
summary David Evans-Gander is a graduate of Roseworthy College/University of Adelaide, and his Swiss wife Veronika also has a winemaking background. They have planted 4 hectares of vines on the 16-hectare property at the far eastern end of Waiheke Island (including some viognier in 1999) and can plant as much again. The two vintages of Forte (1998, 1999) are very much in the style one expects from Waiheke Island.

canadoro NR

New York Street, Martinborough **region** Wairarapa
phone (04) 387 9761 **fax** (04) 387 9761 **open** Via The Grape Vine
winemaker Chris Lintz, Greg Robins **production** 400 **est.** 1993
product range ($25–28 CD) Chardonnay, Cabernet Sauvignon.
summary A weekend operation for Wellington residents Greg and Lesley Robins. The 1.25-hectare vineyard is planted to cabernet sauvignon and chardonnay but is due to be expanded over the next few years; Greg Robins makes the wine with assistance from Chris Lintz.

canterbury house vineyards ★★★

780 Glasnevin Road, RD3, Amberley **region** Waipara
phone (03) 314 6700 **fax** (03) 314 6905 **open** 7 days 10–4
winemaker Mark Rattray **production** 17 500 **est.** 1994
product range ($16.90–23.90 CD) Riesling, Sauvignon Blanc, Chardonnay, Pinot Gris, Pinot Noir, Merlot, Cabernet Sauvignon.
summary Californian Michael Reid (and his wife) came to New Zealand for a vacation and are now engaged in a most ambitious vineyard and winery development in the Waipara region. The first of five planned stages of winery construction was completed in time for the 1998 vintage; when the final phase is completed it will have a production capacity of 150 000 cases. The first 60 hectares of vineyard have been established, with more due to be planted over the coming years. If that is not the most expensive vacation ever taken, I don't know what is. Exports to the UK, the US and Australia.

cellier le brun ★★★★

Terrace Road, Renwick **region** Marlborough
phone (03) 572 8859 **fax** (03) 572 8814 **open** 7 days 9–5
winemaker Allan McWilliams **production** 18 000 **est.** 1985
product range ($16–37 CD) Méthode Champenoise specialist with a large range of both vintage and non-vintage wines, including the Daniel Le Brun range of Brut, Brut Taché, Vintage, and Blanc de Blancs. Small quantities of Sauvignon Blanc, Chardonnay, Classic Brut and Pinot Noir table wine also made and sold under the Terrace Road label.
summary For almost a decade has produced some of New Zealand's highly rated sparkling wines, initially somewhat erratic but now much more consistent in style, and less baroque than it once was. The restaurant is open seven days for evening dining. A doubling of production over the past few years bears eloquent testimony to the quality of the wines, which are also exported to the UK and the US.

Cellier Le Brun Terrace Road Classic Brut

YYYY **NV** Light yellow-straw; a restrained bouquet with secondary aromas and a high malolactic-fermentation input is followed by a lively palate with quite crisp acidity. **rating:** 84
best drinking Now **best vintages** NA **drink with** Aperitif • $19

central hawke's bay wines NR

Takapau, RD3, Central Hawke's Bay **region** Hawke's Bay
phone (06) 855 8318 **open** Not
winemaker Evert Nijnk **production** NA **est.** 1996
product range ($10.50–22 R) Three Sisters Chenin Blanc, Riesling, Gewurztraminer, Pinot Noir; Richard Harrison Sauvignon Blanc, Chardonnay Chenin and Pinot Noir.
summary A most interesting small-scale operation that combines the output from five small vineyards, the wines being released under the Richard Harrison and Three Sisters labels. Sir Richard Harrison heads the consortium, overseeing the making of wines in a relatively austere, European style.

chancellor wines of waipara 

133 Mount Cass Road, Waipara **region** Waipara
phone (03) 347 6727 **fax** (03) 347 6579 **open** By appointment
winemaker Kym Rayner **production** 7600 **est.** 1982
product range ($16–25 R) Mount Cass Waipara Riesling, Sauvignon, Chardonnay and Cabernet Sauvignon; Nor'Wester Marlborough Chardonnay, Marlborough Cabernet Merlot; The Hanmer Junction Marlborough Chardonnay.
summary Having been grape-growers for 15 years the Willy family took the plunge and established the Chancellor Wines brand in 1995, also trebling the estate plantings to 18.4 hectares; Pinot Noir will be added to the portfolio in the near future, and others have come in as financial partners. A winery, cellar door and restaurant are all planned. Wines are exported to the UK, the US, Canada and Hong Kong.

Chancellor Mount Cass Road Waipara Riesling

ΥΥΥΥ **2000** Light green-yellow; mineral and lime aromas and flavours are present on both bouquet and palate, the latter quite intense and long. **rating:** 87

best drinking 2002–2006 **best vintages** '00 **drink with** Grilled white-fleshed fish • $17

Chancellor The Hanmer Junction Marlborough Chardonnay

ΥΥΥΥ 1999 Medium yellow-green; tangy grapefruit and melon fruit aromas drive the bouquet; the palate provides more of the same, with good length and intensity. The winemaker's thumbprints have been kept off the wine. **rating:** 87

best drinking Now **best vintages** NA **drink with** Fresh Atlantic salmon • NA

chard farm ★★★★☆

Chard Road, RD1, Gibbston **region** Central Otago

phone (03) 442 6110 **fax** (03) 441 8400 **open** 7 days 11–5

winemaker Duncan Forsyth, Rob Hay **production** 21 000 **est.** 1987

product range ($18–39 R) Riesling, Gewurztraminer, Sauvignon Blanc, Pinot Gris Sur Lie, Judge and Jury Chardonnay, Closeburn Chardonnay, Southern Lakes Chardonnay, River Run Pinot Noir, Finla Mor Pinot Noir, Bragato Pinot Noir, Arcadia Special Cuvée Brut, Perrelle Grand Cuvée.

summary Perched precariously between sheer cliffs and the fast-flowing waters of the Kawarau River, Chard Farm is a tribute to the vision and courage of Rob and Gregory Hay. At a latitude of 45°, viticulture will never be easy, but Chard Farm has made every post a winner to date, supplementing production from the 20-hectare vineyard with grapes purchased from Marlborough, and increasingly from new vineyards in the Otago area managed and partly owned by the Hays. The Chardonnay and Pinot Noir are superb, especially the intermittent prestige releases.

Chard Farm Finla Mor Pinot Noir

ΥΥΥΥΥ **1999** Light to medium red, with a touch of purple; a fragrant bouquet with cherry, strawberry and smoky oak aromas leads into a medium-bodied palate with excellent texture; here there are flavours of cherry, plum and strawberry supported by spicy oak and finishing with fine tannins. A wine that grows on you as you retaste it. **rating:** 90

best drinking 2002–2005 **best vintages** '99 **drink with** Grilled quail • $34

charles wiffen ★★★☆

1639 Parnassus Road, Cheviot, North Canterbury **region** Marlborough

phone (03) 319 2826 **fax** (03) 319 2829 **open** Not

winemaker Anthony Ivicevich **production** 3000 **est.** 1997

product range ($17–35 R) Riesling, Sauvignon Blanc, Chardonnay, Late Harvest Riesling, Reserve Merlot.

summary The Wiffen family conducts farming operations both in Marlborough (since 1907) and in North Canterbury, the latter being the principal base. The Marlborough vineyard, with 16 hectares of sauvignon blanc, 4 hectares of riesling, 8 hectares of chardonnay and 2 hectares of merlot, was established in 1980, but it was not until 1997 that the Wiffens moved from grape-growing to winemaking, with immediate and continued success.

Charles Wiffen Riesling

ΥΥΥΥ **2000** Medium yellow-green; lifted, floral, ripe fruit aromas are followed by a high-toned, rich palate, ready to roll. **rating:** 84

best drinking Now **best vintages** NA **drink with** Chinese fish • $15

Charles Wiffen Sauvignon Blanc

ΥΥΥΥ **2000** Medium to full yellow-green; a big, ripe, full-on bouquet ranging through gooseberry, pineapple and honey makes you wonder what is coming on the palate. Happily, it is more restrained, with good length and balance, and a gently dry finish. **rating:** 88

best drinking Now **best vintages** '99, '00 **drink with** Bouillabaisse • $17.95

Charles Wiffen Chardonnay

🍷🍷🍷🍷 **2000** Medium yellow-green; melon and citrus fruit is married with nicely balanced and integrated oak on the bouquet. The palate is smooth, with sweet melon fruit and subtle oak; not especially complex, but has some length. **rating:** 86

best drinking Now **best vintages** NA **drink with** Pasta carbonara • $21

Charles Wiffen Reserve Merlot

🍷🍷🍷½ **2000** Medium to full red-purple; there is surprising complexity and ripeness to the bouquet, with a mix of forest, plum, spice and blackberry. However, the palate comes to a jarring halt, with that typical undermade callow character, and the tannins needing to soften. The base material appears to be good, but has not been given a chance by being rushed to bottle. **rating:** 84

best drinking 2003–2006 **best vintages** NA **drink with** Give it a chance • $35

chateau waimarama NR

PO Box 8638, Havelock North **region** Hawke's Bay
phone (06) 877 4822 **fax** (06) 877 2980 **open** Not
winemaker Elise Montgomery (Consultant) **production** 3000 **est.** 1988
product range ($NA) Syrah, Cabernet Sauvignon, Cabernet Merlot, Dessert Cabernet; Undercliffe is the second label.
summary Waimarama Estate was purchased by a Japanese company in 1999, and virtually all of the wine produced now goes to that company in Japan.

Chateau Waimarama Hawke's Bay Merlot Cabernet

🍷🍷🍷🍷½ **1998** Medium purple-red; sweet, deep cassis/berry is followed by a fully ripe palate with all the flavour and sweetness even the most one-eyed Australian could hope for, emphatically underscoring the character of the vintage. **rating:** 92

best drinking 2003–2010 **best vintages** NA **drink with** Beef teriyaki • NA

christina estate NR

Puruatanga Road, Martinborough, Wairarapa **region** Wairarapa
phone (06) 306 9615 **fax** (06) 306 9615 **open** Not
winemaker Christina Eagen, Chris Buring (Contract) **production** NA **est.** 1988
product range ($14.50–22 CD) Riesling, Rosé.
summary The Walker family (Liz, Brendan and son James) established what they believed to be a two-variety vineyard, riesling and shiraz, in 1988. Until 1993 the grapes were sold to other Martinborough winemakers, but since that time have been vinified under the Walker Estate label. The intriguingly named Notre Vigne (our vine) stems from the fact that the vines thought to be shiraz are in fact of an as-yet unidentified variety, with DNA testing failing to reveal the answer. The wines made from the mystery grape are extremely powerful, densely coloured and most unusual.

church road winery ★★★★★

150 Church Road, Taradale **region** Hawke's Bay
phone (06) 844 2053 **fax** (06) 844 3378 **open** 7 days 9–5
winemaker Tony Prichard **production** NFP **est.** 1897
product range ($18.35–79 R) Church Road Sauvignon Blanc, Chardonnay, Noble Semillon, Cabernet Sauvignon Merlot; Church Road Reserve Chardonnay, Merlot, Cabernet Sauvignon Merlot; Twin Rivers Cuvée Brut; Tom, a super-deluxe Cabernet Cuvée was released in 1997.
summary Montana's acquisition of the historic McDonald Winery in 1989 and its investment of $2 million on refurbishment, followed by the announcement of the Cordier joint venture together with the acquisition of premium Hawke's Bay vineyards, signalled Montana's determination to enter the top end of the market with high-quality Chardonnay and Cabernet Sauvignon. Legal squabbles (since terminated) forced the adoption of the Church Road name for the wine label. Exports to the UK and Australia.

Church Road Reserve Chardonnay

🍷🍷🍷🍷🍷 **1999** Light to medium yellow-green; complex, spicy oak is integrated with aromatic peach/nectarine fruit on the bouquet. The palate is powerful but smooth and round, with ripe stone fruit flavours before good acidity tightens up the finish. **rating:** 94

best drinking Now–2004 **best vintages** '94, '95, '96, '99 **drink with** Stir-fried prawns • $33

Tom

🍷🍷🍷🍷🍷 **1998** Deep red-purple; a more concentrated and rich bouquet, with luscious blackberry and chocolate fruit; a supple and sumptuous palate, rich and ripe, but not jammy, with excellent tannins and length. Like the '96, has soaked up the oak. **rating:** 97

🍷🍷🍷🍷🍷 **1996** Light to medium red-purple; a fragrant and elegant bouquet with a mix of cedar and blackberry leads into a similarly styled and shaped palate, the flavours basically in the savoury spectrum thanks in part to fine, persistent, ripe tannins. The aftertaste is particularly impressive. **rating:** 94

best drinking 2003–2013 **best vintages** '96, '98 **drink with** Rack of lamb • $79

Church Road Reserve Cabernet Sauvignon Merlot

🍷🍷🍷🍷🍷 **1999** Medium red-purple; blackberry and blackcurrant fruit aromas are integrated in a controlled fashion with dark spice and oak in the background. The palate, likewise, is in a restrained/controlled mode, with good structure and texture derived from the fine-grained, slightly savoury tannins. **rating:** 93

best drinking 2004–2009 **best vintages** '99 **drink with** Rare beef • $21

churton NR

PO Box 25, Renwick, Marlborough **region** Marlborough
phone (03) 572 4007 **fax** (03) 572 4007 **open** Not
winemaker Sam Weaver **production** 1400 **est.** 1997
product range Sauvignon Blanc, Pinot Noir.
summary Churton is the private winemaking business of Sam Weaver and wife Amanda. Weaver wears many hats, the principal one being Corbans winemaker (now part of Montana) at Marlborough. He has an active consultancy to Waimea, Greenhough and Brightwater in Nelson, but has also started his own export-oriented business, utilising contract-grown grapes and the Lawsons Dry Hills winemaking facilities. His grandfather's home was called Churton (both Weaver and his wife are English), and all the wine is exported to the UK.

c j pask winery ★★★★☆

1133 Omahu Road, Hastings **region** Hawke's Bay
phone (06) 879 7906 **fax** (06) 879 6428 **open** Mon–Fri 9–5, Sat and public holidays 10–5, Sun 11–4
winemaker Kate Radburnd **production** 35 000 **est.** 1985
product range ($14.50–50 R) Sauvignon Blanc, Chenin Blanc, Chardonnay, Reserve Chardonnay, Pinot Noir, Merlot, Reserve Merlot, Cabernet Merlot, Cabernet Sauvignon, Reserve Cabernet Sauvignon, Reserve Cabernet Sauvignon Malbec Merlot; second label of Roy's Hill White and Red.
summary Ex-cropduster pilot Chris Pask became one of the most highly regarded grape-growers in Hawke's Bay; his coup in securing former Vidal winemaker Kate Radburnd (née Marris) has paid the expected dividends. Production has increased rapidly, and the wines have had significant and consistent success in New Zealand and international wine shows thanks to the complexity of the Chardonnays and the supple, sweet fruit of its Cabernet Merlots and Reserve Cabernet Sauvignons. The wines find their way to Australia, Canada, the US, Japan, Thailand, the UK and the Netherlands.

C J Pask Winery Gimblett Road Chardonnay

🍷🍷🍷🍷 **1997** Medium yellow-green; rich, ripe peach and nectarine fruit on the bouquet is supported by well-controlled oak; the wine is ageing remarkably well by New Zealand standards, with plenty of flavour, and sustained by fresh acidity. The zero mlf policy pays big dividends here. **rating:** 89

best drinking Now **best vintages** NA **drink with** Grilled spatchcock • NA

C J Pask Gimblett Road Merlot

🍷🍷🍷🍷 **1999** Medium red-purple; there is a complex array of sweet fruit, spice and vanilla oak on the bouquet, a mix that is replayed on the seductively round and soft palate; has length, and finishes with supple, spicy tannins together with an echo of oak. **rating:** 88

best drinking 2002–2008 **best vintages** '95, '98 **drink with** Devilled kidneys • $28

C J Pask Reserve Merlot

🍷🍷🍷🍷🍷 **1999** Dense red-purple; the bouquet is highly aromatic and quite vibrant, with a mix of raspberry fruit and high-toned vanilla and spice oak. There is a similar high-toned fragrant mix of raspberry and blackberry fruit that starts to stray across the line from Merlot to Cabernet in character; on the other hand, the wine is not overly tannic. As with any mix of French and American oak, it is the American oak that stares into your face, and a very good wine would have been even better with some old French replacing the new American. **rating:** 92

best drinking 2002–2006 **best vintages** '97, '98 **drink with** Grilled calf's liver • $35

C J Pask Reserve Cabernet Sauvignon Malbec Merlot

🍷🍷🍷🍷 **1999** Light to medium purple-red; a very fragrant and lively bouquet with dancing red fruits trying to find a way through the American oak; the palate, too, is fragrant, with brisk acidity, but yet again the American oak (or both oak types, it really doesn't matter) dominate. **rating:** 88

best drinking 2004–2009 **best vintages** NA **drink with** Smoked lamb • $50

C J Pask Reserve Cabernet Sauvignon

🍷🍷🍷🍷 **1998** Medium red, starting to show the first signs of development; the bouquet is high-toned and fragrant, but dominated by the American oak. The palate, likewise, has nice texture and mouthfeel, but overly influenced by the American oak which seems to work even less well with Cabernet Sauvignon than the other Pask varieties. **rating:** 89

best drinking 2002–2007 **best vintages** '91, '94, '95, '98 **drink with** Smoked beef • $50

claddagh vineyards NR

Puruatanga Road, Martinborough **region** Wairarapa
phone (06) 306 9264 **fax** (06) 306 9264 **open** By appointment
winemaker Russell Pearless **production** 300 **est.** 1991
product range ($14.95–25 R) Pinot Noir, Cabernet Sauvignon.
summary Presently a weekend and holiday occupation for computer-industry executives Russell and Suzanne Pearless, but when the 4-hectare vineyard (also planted to chardonnay and sauvignon blanc) comes into full bearing, the level of involvement will doubtless increase.

clearview estate ★★★★★

Clifton Road, RD2, Te Awanga **region** Hawke's Bay
phone (06) 875 0150 **fax** (06) 875 1258 **open** 7 days Labour weekend–Easter, winter Fri–Sun 10–5
winemaker Tim Turvey **production** 4000 **est.** 1989
product range ($12–75 CD) Black Reef Riesling, Te Awanga Sauvignon Blanc, Reserve Te Awanga Sauvignon Blanc, Beach Head Chardonnay, Reserve Chardonnay, Reserve Merlot, Reserve Cabernet Franc, Reserve Old Olive Block (Cabernet Sauvignon Merlot), Basket Press Cabernet Merlot, Blush, Sea Red (red dessert wine), Noble 51 (botrytised Chardonnay).
summary Clearview Estate is situated on a shingly site first planted by Anthony Vidal in 1916 on the coast of Te Awanga; it has been replanted since 1988 with chardonnay, semillon, sauvignon blanc, malbec, cabernet sauvignon, cabernet franc and merlot, with grapes also coming from a neighbouring vineyard. All of the wines to date have been of exceptional quality, especially the magically concentrated and complex Chardonnay. The icing on the cake is an outstanding restaurant, once rated by Bob Campbell as Hawke's Bay's best; together with cellar door, it accounts for most of Clearview's wine sales.

Clearview Estate Reserve Chardonnay

🍷🍷🍷🍷🍷 **1999** Medium to full yellow-green; an exceedingly complex and rich bouquet is typical of the style, the rich, ripe and full palate, crammed with peach and nectarine fruit likewise. Oak, of course, plays a major part in the structure of the wine, as does alcohol (in this instance 14.6°). If such things turn you off, this wine is not for you; if you like them, walk a crooked mile to find it. **rating:** 93

best drinking Now–2003 **best vintages** '94, '95, '96, '98, '99 **drink with** Sweetbreads • $30

clifford bay estate ★★★★☆

26 Rapaura Road, Blenheim **region** Marlborough
phone (03) 572 7148 **fax** (03) 572 7138 **open** 7 days 9–5
winemaker Glen Thomas (Vavasour Wines, Contract) **production** 10 500 **est.** 1994

product range ($14.95–18.95 R) Single Vineyard Riesling, Sauvignon Blanc, Single Vineyard Chardonnay.

summary Clifford Bay made the most spectacular entry onto the scene imaginable, winning two gold medals (Air New Zealand Wine Awards and Christchurch Show) with its first wine, a 1997 Sauvignon Blanc, and hasn't looked back since. It is the venture of Eric and Beverley Bowers, Graham and Thelma Cains and Chris Wilson. Viticultural advice has come from Richard Bowling, and the wine is made by the masterful Glen Thomas. There are 20 hectares of sauvignon blanc, chardonnay and riesling under vine. The wines are exported to Australia, the UK and the US.

Clifford Bay Single Vineyard Riesling

🍷🍷🍷🍷🍷 **2000** Light green-yellow; the bouquet is light and floral, with a mix of lime and apple blossom aromas; the palate offers a mix of attractive apple and citrus fruit; well balanced, quite dry and good length. **rating:** 90

best drinking Now–2005 **best vintages** '99, '00 **drink with** Asparagus • $15.95

Clifford Bay Sauvignon Blanc

🍷🍷🍷🍷🍷 **2000** Light green-yellow; the aromatic bouquet is fresh and clean, showing enticing gooseberry, apple and more tropical notes. The palate lives up to the beguiling bouquet, with very harmonious flavour and balance. **rating:** 92

best drinking Now **best vintages** '97, '99, '00 **drink with** Sugar-cured tuna • $17

Clifford Bay Single Vineyard Chardonnay

🍷🍷🍷🍷 **1999** Medium yellow-green; the bouquet is smooth, with fig, cashew and hazelnut, melon, and integrated spicy oak; the lively palate has melon, cashew, toasty oak and some acidity to tighten things up on the finish. **rating:** 89

best drinking Now **best vintages** '99 **drink with** Brains in black butter • $18.95

cloudy bay ★★★★★

Jacksons Road, Blenheim **region** Marlborough

phone (03) 520 9140 **fax** (03) 520 9040 **open** 7 days 10–4.30, except Christmas Day and Easter Sunday

winemaker Kevin Judd **production** 100 000 **est.** 1985

product range ($24.95–42 R) Sauvignon Blanc, Chardonnay, Pinot Noir, Pelorus NV and Pelorus Vintage (sparkling); also Te Koko (barrel-fermented, bottle-aged Sauvignon Blanc).

summary The other arm of Cape Mentelle, masterminded by David Hohnen and realised by Kevin Judd, his trusted lieutenant from day one. A marketing tour de force, it became a world-recognised brand in only a few years, but the wine quality and style should not be underestimated: Hohnen and Judd may share a great sense of humour, but they are perfectionists in every way and the wines are consistently great. A warped New World view, perhaps, but I rate the Sauvignon Blanc the best in the world, all vintages taken into account. Kevin Judd, incidentally, could as easily earn a living as a photographer; he has a rare talent. The wines are available in Australia, Asia, the Virgin Islands, South Africa, the UK and most parts of Europe.

Cloudy Bay Sauvignon Blanc

🍷🍷🍷🍷🍷 **2000** Light green-yellow; the bouquet is clean but complex, with a multiplicity of aromas covering the full spectrum of varietal fruit ripeness. The palate offers more of the same, running from mineral, grass and herb through to tropical, yet without any one character or flavour dominating. Excellent dry and cleansing but persistent finish. **rating:** 94

best drinking Now–2003 **best vintages** '92, '94, '96, '98, '99, '00 **drink with** Virtually any seafood dish • $21.50

Cloudy Bay Te Koko

🍷🍷🍷🍷🍷 **1997** Glowing yellow-green; extremely complex toasty/nutty aromas are followed by a palate with wonderfully integrated mouthfeel and texture, in some ways vaguely reminiscent of a high-quality, aged, wood-matured (Australian) Semillon. In rating the wine you have to ignore the varietal origin. **rating:** 94

best drinking Now–2004 **best vintages** '97 **drink with** Pan-fried veal • $34

Cloudy Bay Chardonnay

🍷🍷🍷🍷🍷 **1999** Medium to full yellow-green; the usual complex inputs from barrel and malolactic fermentation provide toasty/smoky/cashew overtones to the tangy melon fruit of the bouquet. The palate is rich, with melon, nectarine and white peach offset by the softening effects of the malolactic cashew characters. **rating:** 91

best drinking 2002 - 2004 **best vintages** '87, '91, '93, '94, '95, '97, '98, '99 **drink with** Sweetbreads • $32.50

Cloudy Bay Pelorus Vintage

1996 Medium yellow-green; very complex, with strong wet-dog, autolysis and aldehyde aromas; the palate is massively concentrated for a sparkling wine, but is less quirky than the bouquet. The ultimate food style.
rating: 90

best drinking Now–2003 **best vintages** NA **drink with** Discretion • $35.70

Cloudy Bay Late Harvest Reserve Riesling 375 ml

1999 Glowing yellow-green; the bouquet is strangely reserved at first, but opens up to display a mix of tropical cumquat, apricot and lime. Having lost the plot a little on the bouquet, the lively and expressive palate more than makes amends, with intense lime juice flavour and varietal character, finishing with perfectly balanced acidity.
rating: 92

best drinking Now–2004 **best vintages** '99 **drink with** Fruit tart • $24

Cloudy Bay Pinot Noir

1999 Good, bright red-purple; a particularly complex and fragrant bouquet has 'sous bois' and exotic small berry fruit aromas; the palate is voluptuous, with ripe, spicy berries, showing excellent structure and length sustained by super-fine tannins.
rating: 94

best drinking Now–2006 **best vintages** '97, '99 **drink with** Venison • $34

collards

303 Lincoln Road, Henderson, Auckland **region** Auckland Area
phone (09) 838 8341 **fax** (09) 837 5840 **open** Mon–Sat 9–5, Sun 11–5
winemaker Bruce Collard, Geoff Collard **production** 20 000 **est.** 1910
product range ($7.70–25 CD) Queen Charlotte Riesling, Old Vines Semillon, Sauvignon Blanc (Rothesay, Marlborough), Viognier, Chenin Blanc, Chardonnay (Rothesay, Hawke's Bay, Blakes Mill), Chenin Semillon Chardonnay, Late Harvest Riesling, Botrytised Riesling, Queen Charlotte Marlborough Pinot Noir, Marlborough Syrah, Hawke's Bay Merlot, Rothesay Cabernet Sauvignon, Cabernet Merlot, Tawny Port.
summary A family-owned and run business which is a bastion of conservatism, adopting a low promotional profile but consistently produces fastidiously crafted wines of excellent quality. Has moved with the times in developing new wines and labels. Exports to Singapore, Japan, the UK, Germany, Holland, Denmark, Canada and Australia.

coopers creek

State Highway 16, Huapai **region** Auckland Area
phone (09) 412 8560 **fax** (09) 412 8375 **open** Mon–Fri 9–5.30, weekends 10.30–5.30
winemaker Simon Nunns **production** 60 000 **est.** 1980
product range ($11–36 CD) Hawke's Bay Riesling, Chardonnay, Pinot Noir, Merlot, Cabernet Sauvignon Franc; Sour Puss Semillon, East Coast Semillon Chardonnay, First Edition, Marlborough Sauvignon Blanc, Fat Cat Chardonnay, Gisborne Chardonnay, East Coast Pinot Noir, Tom Cat Merlot, Huapai Cabernet Merlot; the Reserve Range of Hawke's Bay Reserve Riesling, Reserve Oak Aged Sauvignon Blanc, Marlborough Reserve Sauvignon Blanc, Swamp Reserve Chardonnay, Wild Ferment Chardonnay, Late Harvest Riesling, Late Harvest Semillon, Hawke's Bay Reserve Pinot Noir, Hawke's Bay Reserve Merlot, Huapai Reserve Merlot The Gardner, Hawke's Bay Reserve Merlot Cabernet Franc, Hawke's Bay Reserve Cabernet Merlot, Hawke's Bay Reserve Cabernet Sauvignon.
summary A long-term producer of stylish white wines sourced from Gisborne, Hawke's Bay and Marlborough, respectively. They are full of character and flavour but avoid the heavy, coarse phenolics that were once so much part of the white-wine scene in New Zealand.

Coopers Creek Marlborough Sauvignon Blanc

2000 Light yellow-green; the moderately intense bouquet is crisp, clean and vibrant, the palate picking up the pace even more with passionfruit and stonefruit flavours which, perhaps improbably, are delicate and clearly focused.
rating: 88

best drinking Now **best vintages** '91, '94, '96, '97, '00 **drink with** Sushi • $14.95

corbans ★★★★

320 Ti Rakau Drive, East Tamaki, Auckland **region** Auckland Area
phone (09) 273 4800 **fax** (09) 273 4844 **open** Not
winemaker Michael Kluczko (previous) **production** 1.5 million **est.** 1902
product range ($11–36 R) The Corbans wines are now marketed under five sub-brands, each with their separate price range: Cottage Block ($25–36), Private Bin ($20–26); Select ($14–16), Estate ($12–14) and White Label ($8–10); also Amadeus and Verde (sparkling). There are then the quasi-independent and stand-alone brands of Longridge (Hawke's Bay) and Stoneleigh (Marlborough) which have their own entries.
summary Was New Zealand's second largest wine group (500 hectares of estate vineyards and 500 hectares of contracted vineyards) with a turnover exceeding $NZ100 million. In 2000 it was acquired by Montana, the two companies controlling half of New Zealand's production and 60 per cent of its exports. Wine quality is exemplary, setting the pace for others. The wines are exported to Europe, Asia, the US, Canada and Iceland.

Corbans Private Bin Marlborough Riesling

YYYY **1999** Medium green-yellow; the bouquet is rich and full with abundant lime juice aromas, the palate offering a flavoursome mix of lime and kerosene characters; while quite Germanic in style, it is developing with disconcerting rapidity. **rating:** 85

best drinking Now **best vintages** NA **drink with** Rich seafood • $25

Corbans Cottage Block Marlborough Sauvignon Blanc

YYYY **1999** Light yellow-green; the bouquet is highly aromatic with voluminous fruit and a slightly reductive, burnt-match background. A huge wine on the palate in a most unusual style. Strictly for those who love Sauvignon Blanc. **rating:** 83

best drinking Now **best vintages** '97 **drink with** Rich fish • $25.95

Corbans Private Bin Marlborough Sauvignon Blanc

YYYY **1999** Light green-yellow; a powerful bouquet with many things going on, including the suspicion of reduction, but may be just the oak and malolactic-fermentation influence. The palate, too, is somewhat like the curate's egg, good in parts. It may be I am unduly harsh; others will appreciate it far more. **rating:** 81

best drinking Now **best vintages** '97 **drink with** Deep-fried calamari • $25

Corbans Cottage Block Hawke's Bay Cabernet Sauvignon Cabernet Franc Merlot

YYYY **1998** Medium to full red-purple; the bouquet has abundant bright berry fruit which is still very fresh; earthy touches and gentle oak are all to the good. The structure of the palate has the firmness of a young Bordeaux; it needs time, and will be very elegant in its maturity. **rating:** 89

best drinking 2002–2007 **best vintages** '98 **drink with** Roast lamb • $35.95

Corbans Private Bin Hawke's Bay Cabernet Sauvignon Cabernet Franc Merlot

YYYY **1998** Medium purple-red; the high-toned and fragrant bouquet has pronounced spicy/earthy aromas radically different from its Australian counterparts. The palate is powerful and concentrated, with plenty of tannins and structure; while there is dark berry and earth varietal fruit, it is quite austere for a super-premium wine from the '98 vintage. Time will surely help. **rating:** 89

best drinking 2003–2010 **best vintages** NA **drink with** Venison • $25

cottle hill winery NR

Cnr State Highway 10 and Cottle Hill Drive, Kerikeri **region** Northland and Matakana
phone (09) 407 5203 **fax** (09) 407 6808 **open** 7 days 10–5
winemaker Mike Webb **production** 1000 **est.** 1997
product range ($14–29 CD) Sauvignon Blanc, Chardonnay, Bay Breeze (Sauvignon Blanc Chardonnay), Pinotage, Cabernet Sauvignon.
summary Michael and Barbara Webb are fugitives from 'the southern California rat-race'. They first arrived in the Bay of Islands on their yacht in 1992 and have now returned to establish Cottle Hill Winery.

covell estate NR

Troutbeck Road, Galatea, RD1, Murupara **region** Waikato and Bay of Plenty
phone (07) 366 4827 **fax** (07) 366 4071 **open** 7 days 10–4 by appointment
winemaker Bob Covell, Robert Covell Jnr, Norm Iles **production** 1000 **est.** NA
product range ($12–20 CD) Riesling, Chardonnay, Pinot Noir, Rata (Cabernet Merlot).
summary Owners Bob and Desarei Covell have established this vineyard using strict biodynamic organic standards; they mature their wines for extended periods in oak, and give them further time in bottle.

crab farm ★★★★

125 Main Road, Bay View, Hawke's Bay **region** Hawke's Bay
phone (06) 836 6678 **open** 7 days 10–5
winemaker Hamish Jardine **production** 3900 **est.** 1989
product range ($10–17 CD) Gewurztraminer, Sauvignon Blanc, Chardonnay, Pinot Noir, Merlot, Cabernet Sauvignon.
summary Hamish Jardine has worked at both Chateau Reynella and Matawhero. The family vineyards were planted in 1980 and are now mature, so given the equable Hawke's Bay climate there is no reason why the wines should not succeed. A seafood restaurant has recently been added, open from the end of October to Easter seven days a week 11.30–3. Exports to the UK, Taipai and the US. The 1998 Merlot is a superb wine, the 1999 Cabernet Sauvignon in much the same class, winning at the 2001 *Winewise* competition in Australia.

Crab Farm Top End Chardonnay

ΨΨΨΨ **1999** Medium to full yellow-green; the bouquet is complex, with distinct Burgundian characters giving depth and texture, and while the barrel-ferment characters come through, the oak is not aggressive; the palate is likewise complex but rich, with good structure and texture, some cashew lees flavours and nicely married fruit and oak. **rating:** 89

best drinking Now–2004 **best vintages** NA **drink with** Turkey • NA

craggy range vineyards ★★★★☆

The Tin Shed, 18 Napier Road, Havelock North **region** Hawke's Bay
phone 0508 CRAGGY **fax** (06) 877 7141 **open** Not
winemaker Steve Smith MW, Douglas Wisor **production** 15 000 **est.** 1998
product range ($18–34 R) Rapaura Road Vineyard Marlborough Riesling, Old Renwick Vineyard Marlborough Sauvignon Blanc, Apley Road Vineyard Hawkes Bay Chardonnay, Strugglers Flat Vineyard Marlborough Pinot Noir, Seven Poplars Vineyard Merlot.
summary A major arrival on the scene in New Zealand, with vineyard developments hinged around a 40-hectare site on Gimblett Road and a 70-hectare site in Martinborough. A spectacular winery has been designed for the Hawke's Bay site, with a circular red-wine-fermentation cellar and underground barrel hall, wine and culinary school, guest house and restaurant; the winery will be completed by March 2002, which will coincide with the first vintages from the estate vineyards. In the meantime, single vineyard wines (a cornerstone of the winery's philosophy) have been made from selected sites in Marlborough, Martinborough and Hawke's Bay.

Craggy Range Riesling

ΨΨΨΨ **1999** Medium yellow-green, showing obvious development. An aromatic and ripe bouquet with peachy/pineapple aromas is followed by a soft, toasty palate with more of those very ripe, tropical/canned-fruit flavours. **rating:** 87

best drinking Now **best vintages** NA **drink with** Summer salad • $19

Craggy Range Old Renwick Vineyard Sauvignon Blanc

ΨΨΨΨΨ **2000** Light straw-green; the bouquet is spotlessly clean, but not overly aromatic, with mid-range fruit ripeness. The palate, similarly, is tight, crisp and intense, with a very long, clean, bracing finish; no single fruit component dominates a complex, food-style wine. **rating:** 92

best drinking Now–2003 **best vintages** '00 **drink with** Richer fish • $20

Craggy Range Seven Poplars Vineyard Chardonnay

🍷🍷🍷🍷🍷 **2000** Light to medium yellow-green; subtle and particularly complex barrel-ferment characters are perfectly integrated with melon and cashew on the bouquet, the highly sculptured palate offering more of the same in a complex, new generation-style New Zealand Chardonnay, certain to age well. **rating:** 94

best drinking Now–2005 **best vintages** '00 **drink with** Pan-fried veal • $34

Craggy Range Seven Poplars Vineyard Merlot

🍷🍷🍷🍷 **1999** Medium red-purple; the spicy, savoury bouquet presents hints of olive and leaf to the core of red berry fruit. The palate is distinctly savoury, albeit fruit-driven, with spicy/tangy flavour and feel. Fine tannins, gentle oak. **rating:** 88

best drinking 2003–2008 **best vintages** NA **drink with** Wild mushroom risotto • NA

cross roads winery NR

State Highway 50, Korokipo Road, Fernhill, Napier **region** Hawke's Bay
phone (06) 879 9737 **fax** (06) 879 6068 **open** 7 days 10–5
winemaker Malcolm Reeves, Andrea Paterson **production** 8500 **est.** 1990
product range ($10–35 CD) Gewürztraminer, Dry Riesling, Late Harvest Riesling, Chardonnay, Reserve Chardonnay, Oak Aged Sauvignon, Sauvignon, Rosé, Reserve Pinot Noir, Syrah, Cabernet Merlot, Reserve Cabernet Merlot, Talisman, Stormy Ports, Shiraz.
summary In September 2000 a Wellington-based investment company acquired Cross Roads from its founders Lester O'Brien and Malcom Reeves. It simultaneously purchased 60 hectares of land on Kereru Road, and announced plans to invest several million dollars in increasing winery capacity to between 800 and 900 tonnes. It also proposes to refocus wine production and branding.

Cross Roads Gimblett Road Syrah

🍷🍷🍷🍷🍷 **1999** Medium purple-red; a clean, fresh and brightly fruited bouquet with cherry and a hint of citrus is an enticing introduction. There are similar bright fruit flavours to the palate, ranging through plum, cherry and blackberry, with good weight and mouthfeel. Strangely, the American oak doesn't dominate a quite lovely wine. **rating:** 95

best drinking 2003–2009 **best vintages** '99 **drink with** Fillet of venison • NA

daniel schuster ★★★★☆

192 Reeces Road, Omihi Valley, RD3, Amberley **region** Waipara
phone (03) 314 5901 **fax** (03) 314 5902 **open** By appointment
winemaker Danny Schuster **production** 7000 **est.** 1986
product range ($19–40 R) Mount Nelson Sauvignon Blanc, Canterbury Chardonnay, Petrie Vineyard Selection Chardonnay, Canterbury Pinot Noir, Omihi Hills Selection Pinot Noir.
summary Austrian-born, German-trained Danny Schuster must now rank as one of the leading consultant viticulturists in the world, his clients ranging from Stag's Leap, Neibaum Coppola, Moraga and Spotswoode in the Napa Valley to Antinori in Tuscany. The mix is all the more fascinating when one considers that the Napa Valley makers are all producing powerful and dense Cabernet-based red wines; that the climate of Tuscany is as far removed from that of Canterbury as one could imagine; and that at home Danny Schuster is known for his pioneering work in the production of Pinot Noir from the Canterbury/Waipara region. Truly a man for all seasons, producing wines of equally variable (seasonal) quality, at times exhilarating, at times depressing. Exports to Australia, Italy, Japan, the US and Canada.

Mount Nelson Sauvignon Blanc

🍷🍷🍷🍷🍷 **2000** Light green-yellow; a clean, classic bouquet with a mix of gooseberry, herb and mineral, and not tropical; a powerful, long and intense palate in a beautifully disciplined and restrained mould. A wine that invites the second glass. **rating:** 94

best drinking Now–2004 **best vintages** '99, '00 **drink with** Antipasto • $25.60

Daniel Schuster Petrie Vineyard Selection Chardonnay

🍷🍷🍷🍷🍷 **1999** Excellent, light green-yellow; the bouquet is crisp, with a mix of citrus and nectarine fruit, and a faint touch of burnt-match reduction. The crisp, lively palate throws off any slight problem with the bouquet, tangy and youthful, with crisp acid and subtle oak. A rare beast indeed in the normally fast-developing New Zealand scene. **rating:** 91

best drinking Now–2005 **best vintages** '96, '97, '98 **drink with** Fresh abalone • $30.10

darjon vineyards NR

North Eyre Road, Swannanoa, North Canterbury **region** Canterbury
phone (03) 312 6045 **fax** (03) 312 6544 **open** Weekends and most public holidays 12–5
winemaker John Baker **production** NA **est.** 1992
product range ($14 CD) The minute estate-produced range of Pinot Noir and Riesling is supplemented by wines from Marlborough and from other New Zealand and Australian boutique producers.
summary A new arrival on the Christchurch scene, run by former amateur winemaker John Baker and his wife Michelle. The restaurant was opened on site in 1994, coinciding with the first production from the 2 hectares of estate plantings of riesling and pinot noir, and all of the Darjon wine will be sold through the restaurant, mail list and cellar door. Due to seasonal conditions, no wine was made in 2000 or 2001.

de gyffarde NR

Giffords Road, Rapaura, RD3, Blenheim **region** Marlborough
phone (03) 572 8189 **fax** (03) 572 8178 **open** At Marlborough Vintners, Rapaura Road, Blenheim
winemaker Graeme Paul **production** 5000 **est.** 1995
product range ($16–18 CD) Sauvignon Blanc, Unoaked Chardonnay under de Gyffarde and Lofthouse labels.
summary English-born owners Di and Rod Lofthouse were 20-year veterans of the film and television industry before establishing their 6-hectare vineyard in 1989 and moving into winemaking from 1995. They have now taken the process one step further by becoming part-owners of Marlborough Vintners Limited. This operates the new winery, commissioned for the 1998 vintage, which makes the wine for de Gyffarde and three other similar-sized Marlborough wineries. The wines are now sold in New Zealand under the Lofthouse label, which is also used for some exports along with de Gyffarde. Exports to the UK and the US.

Lofthouse Sauvignon Blanc

YYYY **2000** Light to medium yellow-green; a powerful, complex bouquet has a slightly edgy/grassy lift, but the palate settles down, continuing crisp and with some grassy/herbal characters, then a nicely balanced, dry finish.

rating: 88

best drinking Now **best vintages** NA **drink with** Oysters • $16

delegat's wine estate

Hepburn Road, Henderson **region** Auckland Area
phone (09) 836 0129 **fax** (09) 836 3282 **open** Mon–Fri 10–5, weekends 10–6
winemaker Michael Ivicevich **production** NFP **est.** 1947
product range ($18.50–25 R) Estate label of Chardonnay, Sauvignon Blanc and Cabernet Merlot; top-of-the-range Reserve Hawke's Bay label of Chardonnay, Fumé Blanc, Cabernet Sauvignon and Merlot. Also vineyard-designated Chardonnay from Hawke's Bay, Oyster Bay Chardonnay and Sauvignon Blanc, and Sauvignon Blanc from Marlborough.
summary Delegat's now sources most of its grapes from Hawke's Bay, utilising its own vineyards there and contract growers. The quality of the wines is seldom less than good, with a number of excellent wines, conspicuously the Chardonnay. In July 1999 Delegat's successfully floated a new company, Oyster Bay Marlborough Vineyards Limited, to continue the development of the Oyster Bay label. Delegat's owns 30 per cent of that company.

denton winery

Awa Awa Road, Ruby Bay, Nelson **region** Nelson
phone (03) 540 3555 **fax** (03) 540 3555 **open** 7 days 11–5 Sep–Apr
winemaker Richard Denton **production** 2000 **est.** 1995
product range ($15–35 CD) Riesling, Sauvignon Blanc, Chardonnay, Reserve Chardonnay, Pinot Noir, Reserve Pinot Noir, Merlot, Folly (a super-premium Merlot Cabernet).
summary Richard Denton and wife Alexandra discovered Nelson while on a world tour and some years later moved from their native England to purchase the property in 1995. The first 2 hectares of vines were planted, and a winery with the seemingly obligatory café and art gallery appeared in time for the 1997 vintage. Richard Denton was an amateur brewer for many years and graduated to amateur winemaking before taking the final plunge into commercial winemaking. A further 3 hectares of vineyard are to be planted; increased production will follow.

Denton Riesling

🍷🍷🍷🍷 **1998** Medium to full yellow-green; quite pronounced bottle-developed aromas have started to appear, with a mix of tropical and lime fruit suggestive of a touch of botrytis; the palate is soft, rich and (for a Riesling) full-bodied, with a moderately dry finish. **rating:** 83

best drinking Now **best vintages** NA **drink with** Avocado salad • $16

Denton Folly

🍷🍷🍷🍷🍷 **1998** Medium to full red-purple; the ripe and stylish bouquet has a pleasing mix of small red berry fruits and more savoury/olive. The palate brings no surprises, with attractively ripe fruit, good oak balance and integration, and ripe tannins to round the wine off. A really attractive wine, the best I tasted in a trip through Nelson in 2001. **rating:** 90

best drinking 2002–2008 **best vintages** '98 **drink with** Fillet of beef • $35

de redcliffe estates NR

Lyons Road, Mangatawhiri Valley, Bombay Hills, near Auckland **region** Waikato and Bay of Plenty
phone (09) 302 3325 **fax** (09) 303 3726 **open** 7 days 9.30–5
winemaker Mark Compton, Brett Dunnett (Assistant) **production** 45 000 **est.** 1976
product range ($14.95 R) Mangatawhiri Chardonnay, Estates Chardonnay, Semillon Chardonnay, Hawke's Bay Estates Cabernet Merlot, Hawke's Bay Cabernet Merlot Franc, Marlborough Estates Riesling, Marlborough Estates Sauvignon Blanc, Estates Tawny Port.
summary The lavish development at De Redcliffe was funded by the Japanese company Otaka, which owned the Hyatt hotel in Auckland and built the Hotel du Vin at De Redcliffe. Having sold the Hyatt, the rationale for the investment in De Redcliffe disappeared, and the business is now in two parts. Winemaking is now being carried out by the newly created and independent Firstland group, which is also reviewed in this book, and the future of De Redcliffe and the Hotel du Vin will presumably be decided by the purchaser of those assets.

domaine georges michel NR

Vintage Lane, RD3, Blenheim **region** Marlborough
phone (03) 572 7230 **fax** (03) 572 7231 **open** By appointment
winemaker Guy Brac de la Pi, John McGinlay **production** NA **est.** 1998
product range ($16.50–24 CD) Sauvignon Blanc, La Reserve Chardonnay, Petit Pinot Noir.
summary Domaine Georges Michel is the new incarnation of Merlen Estate. Georges Michel, a French native of the Island of Réunion, has widespread business interests, including a chateau in Beaujolais. Michel has invested several million dollars in upgrading and expanding the winery and in the acquisition of additional vineyards, with the aim of increasing production to 20 000 cases.

Domaine Georges Michel La Reserve Chardonnay

🍷🍷🍷🍷 **1999** Medium to full yellow-green; the bouquet is quite complex, with grapefruit and stonefruit aromas, the palate solid, with a mix of grapefruit and stonefruit together with positive spicy oak, tailing off ever-so-slightly on the finish. **rating:** 88

best drinking Now–2003 **best vintages** NA **drink with** Caesar salad • $24

drewerys wineshed NR

Cossars Road, Taitapu, RD2, Christchurch **region** Canterbury
phone (03) 329 6940 **fax** (03) 329 6168 **open** 7 days 11–6
winemaker Peter Gatehouse (Contract) **production** 140 **est.** 1999
product range ($17.95 R) Riesling, Chardonnay.
summary The rather curious name becomes clearer when you find that Graeme and Anette Drewery have established a combined 3-hectare vineyard, restaurant and two-couple home-stay accommodation near Christchurch. The restaurant is open for lunch every day throughout summer and for dinner Thursday to Sunday. Although the operation is micro in size, there are plans for the development of an on-site winery.

dry gully vineyard NR

Earnscleugh Road, RD1, Alexandra **region** Central Otago
phone (03) 449 2030 **fax** (03) 449 2030 **open** By appointment
winemaker Dean Shaw (Contract) **production** 150 **est.** 1997
product range ($29 R) Pinot Noir.
summary Sibylla and Bill Moffitt purchased what was then an apricot orchard in the late 1970s. The trees were old and unproductive, so they were removed and a little over 1.5 hectares of pinot noir was planted. The first commercial vintage was 1997, and the wine was rewarded with a gold medal, a dream start. The Moffitts have since acquired more land and planted it with new Dijon clones that started to come into bearing in 2001.

drylands estate winery ★★★★☆

Hammerichs Road, Rapaura **region** Marlborough
phone (03) 570 5252 **fax** (03) 570 5272 **open** Mon–Sun 10–5
winemaker Darryl Woolley **production** NFP **est.** 1934
product range ($9–35 CD) Selaks Drylands Marlborough label: Riesling, Sauvignon Blanc, Chardonnay; Selaks Premium Selection label: Riesling, Sauvignon Blanc, Chardonnay; Selaks Founders Reserve Sauvignon Blanc, Chardonnay, Merlot. Also a Riesling Gewurztraminer Ice Wine.
summary In 1998 Nobilo acquired Selaks, and in so doing acquired the state-of-the-art winery then recently built by Selaks at its Rapaura vineyard. Like the little old lady who swallowed a fly, Nobilo was in turn promptly acquired by BRL Hardy of Australia. The Drylands Winery is now the sole production facility for the Drylands brand, the Selaks brand and also Nobilo.

Drylands Estate Dry Riesling

🍷🍷🍷🍷🍷 **2000** Light green-yellow; intense, cool-grown herb, lime, spice and mineral aromas flow into a powerful, intense palate with above-average length and intensity, neatly sustained by crisp acidity and subliminal residual sugar. **rating:** 94

best drinking Now–2006 **best vintages** '99, '00 **drink with** Asian seafood • $17

Selaks Premium Selection Sauvignon Blanc

🍷🍷🍷🍷🍷 **2000** Light to medium yellow-green; an enticingly rich, tropical bouquet with a bright cross-cut of herb and mineral is followed by a palate with brilliant length, balance and varietal definition. **rating:** 95

best drinking Now **best vintages** '00 **drink with** Bouillabaisse • $15

Drylands Estate Winemakers Reserve Sauvignon Blanc

🍷🍷🍷🍷🍷 **2000** Light green-yellow; the bouquet is first and foremost complex, with a mix of ripe gooseberry and herb, and a background hint of other characters. The palate is well balanced and smooth, with a long fruit travel falling between melon and gooseberry. Complex stuff. **rating:** 94

best drinking Now–2003 **best vintages** '00 **drink with** Green-lipped mussels • $21

Drylands Estate Chardonnay

🍷🍷🍷🍷🍸 **2000** Light to medium yellow-green; the bouquet has obvious charry barrel-ferment aromas, but there is ample fruit both on the bouquet and palate to carry that oak; nectarine and citrus flavours run through to a long finish. **rating:** 91

best drinking Now–2003 **best vintages** '00 **drink with** Whitebait fritters • $17

Drylands Estate Pinot Noir

🍷🍷🍷🍸 **1999** Light to medium red-purple; a light, fresh, strawberry-accented bouquet is followed by a pleasant, smooth and sweet strawberry/cherry-flavoured palate with easy, non-cerebral appeal. Drink now for lunch. **rating:** 84

best drinking Now **best vintages** NA **drink with** Sugar-cured tuna • $17

Drylands Estate Marlborough Merlot

🍷🍷🍷🍷🍸 **1999** Medium purple-red; the moderately intense bouquet offers roughly equal amounts of plum, spice and oak; it is on the palate that the seductive oak handling of sweet berry fruit really takes hold. The sort of wine the occasional red-wine drinker would go for in a big way. **rating:** 92

best drinking 2002–2006 **best vintages** NA **drink with** Italian • $23

Selaks Founders Reserve Merlot

🍷🍷🍷🍷 **1999** Medium purple-red; the clean, fresh bouquet with ripe berry/plum fruit and just a hint of oak is followed by an attractively soft palate, with lush fruit and ripe tannins in a quite delicious early-drinking style.

rating: 89

best drinking Now–2006 **best vintages** '99 **drink with** Steak and kidney pie • $23

dry river ★★★★★

Puruatanga Road, Martinborough **region** Wairarapa
phone (06) 306 9388 **fax** (06) 306 9275 **open** Not
winemaker Neil McCallum **production** 3000 **est.** 1979
product range ($21.50–55 CD) Craighall Riesling, Estate Gewurztraminer, Estate Sauvignon Blanc, Amaranth Chardonnay, Estate Pinot Gris, Botrytis Late Pick Riesling, Late Harvest Riesling, Botrytis Berry Selection Chardonnay, Amaranth Pinot Noir, Arapoff Syrah.
summary Winemaker/owner Neil McCallum is a research scientist with a doctorate from Oxford University, with winemaking very much a part-time occupation. He has justifiably gained an international reputation for the exceptional quality of his wines, which he jealously protects. Each is made in tiny quantities and sells out immediately on release, but minuscule quantities are now making their way to Australia. Some rate Dry River as New Zealand's best winery, and I'm not sure I would disagree. Limited exports to the UK and Australia.

Dry River Amaranth Chardonnay

🍷🍷🍷🍷½ **1999** Glowing yellow-green; the intense and complex bouquet has well-balanced and integrated barrel-ferment and fruit characters; the light- to medium-bodied, elegant and understated palate, with melon and stonefruit flavours, has excellent mouthfeel.

rating: 92

best drinking Now–2004 **best vintages** '90, '92, '94, '95, '96, '97, '99 **drink with** Milk-fed veal • $33

Dry River Botrytis Selection Riesling

🍷🍷🍷🍷🍷 **2000** Glowing yellow-green; intense botrytis on the bouquet results in great complexity, with peach, lime, pineapple and melon apparent on both bouquet and palate, the latter with perfect acidity and great length.

rating: 94

best drinking Now–2004 **best vintages** '96, '00 **drink with** Fruit tart • $29

Dry River Amaranth Pinot Noir

For many observers, New Zealand's finest Pinot Noir and certainly its most sought after. Immaculately crafted, as are all of Neil McCallum's wines, but with all of the robust fruit of Martinborough at its best.

🍷🍷🍷🍷½ **1999** Deep red-purple; an immensely concentrated and powerful bouquet with dark plum and black cherry fruit leads into a similarly massively concentrated palate, reminiscent of the famous Burgundy producer, Leroy.

rating: 93

best drinking Now–2006 **best vintages** '89, '90, '91, '93, '94, '96, '97, '99 **drink with** Coq au vin • $55

edbrooke vineyard NR

339 Gordon's Road, Half Moon Bay, Waiheke Island **region** Waiheke Island
phone (09) 372 9556 **fax** (09) 372 9556 **open** Not
winemaker Jeremy Edbrooke **production** 100 **est.** 1998
product range ($NA) Merlot, Bordeaux blend.
summary Jeremy Edbrooke and Vyvean Oakley have established a 3.5-hectare vineyard to the Bordeaux varieties of cabernet sauvignon, merlot and cabernet franc. Merlot was produced in 2000, the Bordeaux blend to come in subsequent vintages.

edgewater estate NR

455 Glenbrook Beach Road, RD1, Waiuku **region** Greater Auckland Area
phone (09) 235 3351 **fax** (09) 235 3351 **open** Not
winemaker Peter Stiffe **production** 400 **est.** 1998
product range ($15.95–19.95 R) Pinot Noir; Bordeaux blend of Merlot, Cabernet Sauvignon, Cabernet Franc.
summary Vodaphone manager Peter Stiffe and Catherine Young have planted 2 hectares of vines that will be gradually extended, the property being 8 hectares in extent. It is akin to home winemaking, the entire production being made and bottled on site.

ellesmere NR

150 Old Tai Tapu Road (Days Road RD4), Christchurch **region** Canterbury
phone (03) 329 5311 **open** Not
winemaker Grant Whelan (Contract) **production** 100 **est.** 1998
product range ($NA) Pinot Noir, Rosé, Gewurztraminer.
summary Pam Smith named her vineyard after Lake Ellesmere, not far distant. She has established 0.75 hectare on a diversified farmlet of 6 hectares, her other activities being growing chestnuts and farming cattle. The wines, made by Grant Whelan at Rossendale Winery, are sold through local restaurants.

eskdale winegrowers NR

Main Road, Eskdale **region** Hawke's Bay
phone (06) 836 6302 **open** Mon–Sat 9–5
winemaker Kim Salonius **production** 1500 **est.** 1973
product range ($25 R) Gewurztraminer, Chardonnay, Cabernet Merlot.
summary Having gained winemaking experience at McWilliam's, Canadian-born Kim Salonius and family have established a small 4-hectare estate operation, making wines in very small quantities that are sold cellar door, and which have gained a strong reputation for consistency of style; the Chardonnay is barrel-aged for two years and bottle-aged for a further three years, the Cabernet Merlot oak-aged for three years.

esk valley estate ★★★★☆

745 Main Road, Bay View, Napier **region** Hawke's Bay
phone (06) 836 6411 **fax** (06) 836 6413 **open** 7 days 9–5.30 summer, 9–5 winter
winemaker Gordon Russell **production** 30 000 **est.** 1933
product range ($15.50–75 CD) Black Label Riesling, Sauvignon Blanc, Chenin Blanc, Chardonnay, Merlot Cabernet, Merlot Malbec Cabernet Sauvignon Cabernet Franc; Reserve Chardonnay, Late Harvest Chenin Blanc, Merlot Rosé, Reserve Merlot Malbec Cabernet Sauvignon Cabernet Franc; also The Terraces, a super-premium single-estate vineyard Bordeaux-blend sold by mail order only, when two years old.
summary The little brother in the Villa Maria-Vidal family, but with the ultra-premium The Terraces standing boldly in the top echelon of New Zealand reds and making the winery rating difficult. Which is not to say that some of the other wines in the portfolio aren't impressive; they are. Exports to the UK, Ireland, Canada, Hong Kong, Thailand and Singapore.

Esk Valley Reserve Chardonnay

▼▼▼▼▽ **1999** Medium to full yellow-green; a very complex bouquet with spicy barrel-ferment oak and ripe citrus/melon fruit. The palate is similarly rich and mouthfilling, with layer-upon-layer of flavour. Great with food; daunting without. **rating:** 90

best drinking Now **best vintages** '94, '95, '96, '98, '99 **drink with** Roast spatchcock • $30

Esk Valley Reserve Merlot Malbec Cabernet Sauvignon

▼▼▼▼ **1999** Medium to full purple-red; massive, dark blackberry/blackcurrant fruit and oak fill the bouquet and the entry to the mouth; thereafter it becomes a battle with the extract and powerful, drying tannins. Almost routinely awarded a gold medal at the Royal Easter Wine Show 2001, but not by me. **rating:** 89

best drinking 2009–2015 **best vintages** '96, '98 **drink with** Aged beef • $40

Esk Valley Estate Black Label Merlot Cabernet Sauvignon

▼▼▼▼ **1998** Medium to full red-purple; the bouquet has sweet red berry fruit at its core, supported by spicy/vanilla oak. The palate is noticeably ripe, soft and fleshy, almost to the point of being slightly squashy. **rating:** 85

best drinking 2002–2007 **best vintages** NA **drink with** Game pie • $19.95

fairhall downs estate

814 Wrekin Road, RD2, Brancott Valley, Marlborough **region** Marlborough
phone (03) 572 8356 **fax** (03) 572 8357 **open** By appointment
winemaker Ken Small, John Forrest (Contract) **production** 10 000 **est.** 1996
product range ($16.95–29.95 R) Sauvignon Blanc, Pinot Gris, Chardonnay.

summary Ken Small and Stuart Smith have been grape-growers in Marlborough since 1982, supplying Montana and Villa Maria from their 23.5-hectare vineyard at the top of the Brancott Valley Road. In 1996 they launched their own label, with John Forrest as contract-winemaker and using the Forrest Estate winery facility. Instant success followed, and has continued unabated. The wines are exported to Australia, the UK, Belgium, the US, Canada, Brazil and Hong Kong.

Fairhall Downs Sauvignon Blanc

🍷🍷🍷🍷🍷 **2000** Light green-yellow; a clean, moderately intense bouquet has a mix of fruit aromatics encompassing passionfruit, citrus and stonefruit, but no one of them dominant. The bouquet is elegant and clean, with gentle passionfruit and gooseberry flavours flowing through to a smooth finish. **rating:** 90

best drinking Now **best vintages** '98, '99, '00 **drink with** Tempura • $17

Fairhall Downs Pinot Gris

🍷🍷🍷🍷🍷 **2000** Light to medium yellow-green; the bouquet is firm, with distinctly herbal/grassy notes over a minerally base. A crisp, well-balanced palate, adding apple to the flavour mix, has good length, and a pleasingly dry finish. **rating:** 92

best drinking Now–2003 **best vintages** '00 **drink with** Antipasto • $22

Fairhall Downs Chardonnay

🍷🍷🍷🍷 **2000** Light to medium yellow-green; very strong charry/smoky barrel-ferment aromas dominate the bouquet and make themselves present on the palate. There is some light nectarine and melon fruit there; the wine was tasted early in its life, and its track record suggests it will rate more highly by the end of 2001. **rating:** 84

best drinking Now–2003 **best vintages** '97, '99 **drink with** Wok-fried king prawns • $19

fairmont estate NR

Gladstone Road, RD2, Gladstone, Wairarapa **region** Wairarapa
phone (06) 379 8498 **fax** (06) 379 5498 **open** 7 days 9–5
winemaker Jon McNab **production** 2000 **est.** 1996
product range ($10–30 CD) Riesling, Sauvignon Blanc, Chardonnay, Young Vines Pinot Noir, Old Vines Pinot Noir.
summary Jon McNab started his career at Martinborough Vineyard 'as a general dogsbody'. He worked for Larry McKenna for two years before becoming an assistant-winemaker in Germany. Thereafter he commuted between Germany and Martinborough Vineyard for several years before coming back to Fairmont Estate and its first on site vintage in 1997. (The initial vintage was made off site by Chris Lintz at Lintz Estate.) Fairmont is in the Gladstone subregion of Wairarapa, situated on the free-draining alluvial Ruamahanga River terrace.

felton road ★★★★★

Bannockburn, RD, Central Otago **region** Central Otago
phone (03) 445 0885 **fax** (03) 445 0881 **open** 7 days 11–5 Nov–Apr, Mon–Fri 11–5 May–Oct
winemaker Blair Walter **production** 6500 **est.** 1991
product range ($22–55 CD) Dry Riesling, Riesling, Chardonnay, Barrel Fermented Chardonnay, Pinot Noir, Pinot Noir Block 3, Pinot Noir Block 5.
summary The fairytale story of Felton Road began in 1997 when grape-grower Stuart Elms decided to discontinue selling his grapes to Gibbston Valley and build a winery. He secured the services of a young but immensely well-credentialled flying winemaker, Blair Walter, who designed and oversaw the construction of a compact 200-tonne winery. The wines he made were of an exceptionally high standard, and when the Pinot Noir Block 3 made its appearance, Felton Road was firmly established as one of the half-dozen icon wines in New Zealand, with a near-frenetic following there, in Australia and in the UK. And thereby hangs a tale: an English connoisseur, Nigel Greening, managed to get his name onto the mailing list, and was so taken with the wines he purchased land nearby and began developing a vineyard. It was only then that he heard that Stuart Elms was considering selling Felton Road; Greening caught the next plane to New Zealand, resolving not to leave until he had acquired Felton Road, which he duly did. And the very last thing Greening wishes to see happen is the departure of Blair Walter, who remains an integral part of the whole project.

Felton Road Dry Riesling

ỲỲỲỲỲ **2000** Light to medium yellow-green; a tightly knit bouquet with perfectly ripened lime and lemon fruit moves through into an exceptionally smoothly flowing palate, with admirably balanced acidity and residual sugar providing a seamless, lingering finish. **rating:** 96

best drinking Now–2011 **best vintages** '99, '00 **drink with** Leave it in the cellar • $22

Felton Road Wines Barrel Fermented Chardonnay

ỲỲỲỲY **1999** Medium yellow-green; the bouquet is complex, with strong, tangy, toasty barrel-ferment oak inputs; not unexpectedly, the elegant, citrus/melon fruit is outmuscled on the palate by the oak at this juncture, but there is still enough there to give confidence for the future of what is a pretty smart wine. **rating:** 92

best drinking Now–2005 **best vintages** '99 **drink with** Milk-fed veal • $45

Felton Road Pinot Noir

ỲỲỲỲY **1999** Good purple-red; the sheer class of the wine is apparent from the first whisper of the bouquet, moving into top gear on the silky smooth, incredibly long palate with black cherry, spice and herb ripples of flavour. **rating:** 93

best drinking 2002–2008 **best vintages** '98, '99 **drink with** Jugged hare • $50

Felton Road Pinot Noir Block 3

ỲỲỲỲỲ **1999** Significantly deeper colour; the wine is built in much the same way as the varietal, except that it is more intense, more savoury, longer and finer, with absolutely perfect extract and tannin management. **rating:** 95

best drinking 2002–2010 **best vintages** '98, '99 **drink with** Rare breast of squab • $47

Felton Road Pinot Noir Block 5

ỲỲỲỲỲ **1999** More colour, even richer and more voluptuously plummy fruit and even more complexity than the Block 3, but I really need to sit down to a prolonged comparative tasting before I am prepared to award higher points to one or the other. **rating:** 95

best drinking 2002–2010 **best vintages** '99 **drink with** Rare breast of squab • $55

fenton estate ★★★★★

56 Korora Road, Oneroa, Waiheke Island **region** Waiheke Island
phone (09) 372 2441 **fax** (09) 372 2441 **open** By appointment
winemaker John Hancock, Stephen White, Kim Crawford **production** 600 **est.** 1989
product range ($30–50 R) Premium release Fenton Cabernet Merlot; second label The Red (only produced in lesser vintages).

summary Despite its tiny size (2 hectares) Fenton has already made its contribution to the international reputation enjoyed by Waiheke Island; the 1994 Stonyridge Airfield Cabernet Merlot, which won the trophy for Best New Zealand Cabernet Merlot Blend at the Air New Zealand Wine Awards, was made from Twin Bays grapes. Since 1998 the wine has been made by John Hancock at Trinity Hill; not surprisingly, the '98 was a wonderful wine.

fiddler's green ★★★☆

Georges Road, Waipara **region** Waipara
phone (03) 314 6979 **fax** (03) 314 6978 **open** Mon–Sat 11.30–5
winemaker Petter Evans (Contract) **production** 2700 **est.** 1994
product range ($15–16 CD) Riesling, Sauvignon Blanc.

summary Fiddler's Green has been established by Christchurch lawyer Barry Johns and his wife Jenny; 30 hectares have been established with 20 hectares of vines (5 hectares each of sauvignon blanc and semillon, 4 hectares each of riesling and pinot noir, and 2 hectares of chardonnay). New Burgundian clones of both chardonnay and pinot noir have been chosen, but the best results to date have come from the Sauvignon Blanc and the Riesling.

Fiddler's Green Waipara Riesling

ỲỲỲỲ **2000** Light green-yellow; the shy bouquet is clean and fresh, with lime aromas gradually appearing; the well-balanced palate has a gentle mix of lime and tropical fruit, with a pleasantly dry finish. **rating:** 85

best drinking 2002–2006 **best vintages** '99 **drink with** Seafood antipasto • $16

firstland vineyards ★★★★

PO Box 7063, Wellesly Street, Auckland **region** Hawke's Bay
phone (09) 302 3325 **fax** (09) 303 3726 **open** Not
winemaker Mark Compton, Brent Dunnet **production** 15 000 **est.** 1994
product range ($20–35 R) Riesling, Sauvignon Blanc, Chardonnay, Reserve Chardonnay, Pinot Noir, Cabernet Merlot, Reserve Cabernet.
summary Firstland was created following the decision of Otaka of Japan to withdraw from at least some of its New Zealand investments, notably the de Redcliffe and Hotel du Vin, but also from lesser investments in the Forrest (Marlborough) and Pask (Hawke's Bay) Wineries. It's a complicated scene, with de Redcliffe general manager and winemaker Mark Compton running Firstland until new investors are put in place. Regardless of this, Firstland will continue drawing upon 15 hectares of vines in Hawke's Bay and Marlborough's Waiharau Valley. Distributed in New Zealand by Advintage; exports to the Netherlands and Japan.

Firstland Marlborough Riesling

🍷🍷🍷🍸 **2000** Light green-yellow; the bouquet is light, fresh and elegant, with gentle lime aromas. The palate is a logical extension, light, but well balanced and, all things considered, quite long. It may surprise with bottle age, but I wouldn't bet on it. **rating:** 83

best drinking Now **best vintages** NA **drink with** Light seafood • $18

Firstland Marlborough Sauvignon Blanc

🍷🍷🍷🍷🍸 **2000** Light to medium yellow-green; the bouquet has the enticing pungent passionfruit/gooseberry tropical aromatics of the vintage (and the maker) without any hint of reduction. The palate is quite weighty, with gently ripe tropical fruit, and well-above-average length. Closes with good acidity. **rating:** 92

best drinking Now **best vintages** '00 **drink with** Mussels in white wine sauce • $18

Firstland Reserve Cabernet Sauvignon Merlot

🍷🍷🍷🍷🍸 **1998** Medium red-purple; ripe, dark foresty/berry aromas and a touch of spice are followed by a powerful palate with potent dark berry fruit and lashings of tannins. The fruit should prove to have sufficient power for the tannins to soften first. **rating:** 90

best drinking 2003–2008 **best vintages** '98 **drink with** Barbecued marinated lamb kebabs • NA

floating mountain NR

418 Omihi Road, Waipara **region** Canterbury
phone (03) 314 6710 **fax** (03) 314 6710 **open** Weekends by appointment
winemaker Mark Rattray **production** 3000 **est.** 1992
product range ($39 R) Pinot Noir.
summary The Maori name for Mount Grey, the peak of which rises above the winter mists, is Maukatere; the English translation of that name is Floating Mountain. It is the poetic new name for the previous prosaically named Mark Rattray Vineyards.

Floating Mountain Pinot Noir

🍷🍷🍷🍷 **1999** Deeply coloured; the powerful bouquet is in the foresty/spicy/dark berry spectrum, but the palate shifts up another gear, in a very big, ultra-ripe plummy mode, with strong tannins on the finish. I have no idea whether time will sort the wine out; one can but hope. **rating:** 86

best drinking 2003–2008 **best vintages** '98 **drink with** Strong game • $39

forrest estate ★★★★★

Blicks Road, Renwick, Marlborough **region** Marlborough
phone (03) 572 9084 **fax** (03) 572 9086 **open** 7 days 10–5
winemaker John Forrest **production** 30 000 **est.** 1988
product range ($15–25 ML) Riesling, Estate Dry Riesling, Vineyard Selection Riesling, Semillon, Sauvignon Blanc, Marlborough Chardonnay, Indian Summer Late Harvest, Botrytis Riesling, Botrytised Semillon Sauvignon Blanc, Pinot Noir, Gibsons Creek Merlot.

summary Former biochemist and genetic engineer John Forrest has had considerable success since his first vintage in 1990, relying initially on purchased grapes but now with a 63-hectare vineyard. Wine quality has been exemplary right across the range, perhaps reflecting John Forrest's strong grounding in chemistry. Exports to the US, Australia, the UK, Denmark, Germany and Canada.

Forrest Estate Dry Riesling

ΥΥΥΥΥ **2000** Very pale; a crisp bouquet with a mix of mineral, herb and apple is precisely mirrored in the similarly flavoured palate; well balanced and long, distinctly in the drier end of the spectrum; a cerebral Riesling. **rating:** 91

best drinking 2003–2008 **best vintages** '90, '91, '92, '99, '00 **drink with** Summer salad • $19

Forrest Estate Sauvignon Blanc

ΥΥΥΥΥ **2000** Light yellow-green; an intensely aromatic and tangy bouquet has gooseberry, grapefruit and passionfruit which some may see as faintly reductive. The palate has exceptional length and intensity, with tangy/limey/gooseberry flavours. Ironically, it was a Sauvignon Blanc made by Forrest for Cardmember in very similar style that won the trophy for Best Wine of Show at the Royal Easter Wine Show 2001. **rating:** 96

best drinking Now **best vintages** '91, '92, '94, '95, '97, '98, '99, '00 **drink with** Fresh schnapper • $15

Forrest Estate Botrytis Riesling 375 ml

ΥΥΥΥΥ **2000** Light to medium green-yellow; a fine, fresh and fragrant bouquet with admirably pure lime juice varietal character is followed by a no less elegant and pure palate, with just a touch of apricot making its appearance alongside the lime; long and well balanced, like a German Beerenauslese. **rating:** 93

best drinking Now–2004 **best vintages** '98, '00 **drink with** Baked apples • $24

Forrest Estate Marlborough Pinot Noir

ΥΥΥΥ **1999** Medium red-purple; very unusual, lifted, spicy/mint/garden mint aromas of the bouquet happily don't come through on the palate, which has good intensity and mouthfeel, with fine, slippery tannins and a clean aftertaste.= **rating:** 89

best drinking Now–2004 **best vintages** NA **drink with** Asian • $22

foxes island wines ★★★★☆

PO Box 1039, Blenheim **region** Marlborough
phone (03) 578 6221 **fax** (03) 578 4482 **open** 7 days 10–5 at Wairau River Wine Shop
winemaker John Belsham **production** 3500 **est.** 1992
product range ($33–35 R) Chardonnay, Pinot Noir.

summary Former Hunter's winemaker John Belsham runs Rapaura Vintners contract-winemaking business (formerly Vintech), but since 1992 has made small quantities of wine under the Foxes Island label. He has established an 8.3-hectare vineyard planted to chardonnay and pinot noir, giving the wines an estate base. Exports to Japan, Europe, Hong Kong and the US.

Foxes Island Chardonnay

ΥΥΥΥΥ **1999** Bright green-yellow; the bouquet ranges through melon, citrus and stonefruit, with contrasting hints of mineral and cashew; as ever, the palate is intense but tight, with stonefruit and citrus to the fore, the malolactic and oak influences under tight control, good acidity providing the seal to a first-class act. **rating:** 94

best drinking Now–2005 **best vintages** '94, '96, '97, '98, '99 **drink with** Blanquette of veal • $32.95

Foxes Island Pinot Noir

ΥΥΥΥΥ **1999** Medium red-purple; there are complex, spicy, savoury edges to soft, plummy fruit on the bouquet; the palate has excellent texture and structure, with sweet, spicy plummy fruit supported by soft tannins. By far the best Pinot yet from Foxes Island. **rating:** 92

best drinking 2002–2006 **best vintages** '99 **drink with** Quail • $34.95

framingham ★★★★☆

Conders Bend Road, Marlborough **region** Marlborough
phone (03) 572 8884 **fax** (03) 572 9884 **open** 7 days 11–5
winemaker Ant Mackenzie **production** 17 000 **est.** 1982

product range ($16–28 CD) Classic Riesling, Dry Riesling, Gewurztraminer, Sauvignon Blanc, Pinot Gris, Chardonnay, Methode Traditionelle, Reserve Late Harvest Riesling, Noble Selection, Pinot Noir, Merlot.

summary Rex and Paula Brooke-Taylor established their 13-hectare vineyard in 1981, being content to sell the grapes in the intervening years to various makers, most conspicuously Grove Mill and Corbans. Since 1994 most of their grape production has been vinified under the Framingham label, with exports to Australia, the UK, Germany, Denmark, Holland, Ireland, Switzerland, Canada and the US.

Framingham Classic Riesling

YYYY **2000** Medium yellow-green; a powerful bouquet, slightly diffuse, with some tropical notes leads into a generous palate, quite soft and round, with a complex, lingering aftertaste that has a great deal more to say than simple residual sugar. **rating:** 89

best drinking Now **best vintages** NA **drink with** Summer salad • $17

Framingham Dry Riesling

YYYYY **2000** Light green-yellow; a crisp apple-blossom/apple/lime bouquet leads into a wine that is tighter, more powerful and intense than the Classic, with fine acidity producing a drier, longer finish. **rating:** 93

best drinking 2002–2008 **best vintages** '00 **drink with** Asparagus • $20

Framingham Gewurztraminer

YYYYY **2000** Light green-yellow; a classic, light to moderately intense bouquet with rose petal, lychee and a touch of spice leads into a crisp palate that is nicely balanced, has fruit power, is dry, and avoids phenolics on the finish. **rating:** 90

best drinking Now–2004 **best vintages** '99, '00 **drink with** Light Thai dishes • $20

Framingham Sauvignon Blanc

YYYY **2000** Light green-yellow; the moderately intense bouquet has an attractive array of blossom, passionfruit, apple, melon and herb characters that sustain the wine through to its crisp, firm, dry finish. In a relatively austere style overall, but many would say all the better for that. **rating:** 89

best drinking Now **best vintages** '00 **drink with** Fried oysters • $17

Framingham Pinot Gris

YYYYY **2000** Medium yellow-green; highly scented, floral apple-blossom aromas are followed by a lively palate, ranging through green apple, spice and lemon flavours. **rating:** 93

best drinking Now–2003 **best vintages** '00 **drink with** Vegetarian • $22

fraser river estate NR

280 Earnscleugh Road, Alexandra **region** Central Otago

phone (03) 449 2690 **fax** (03) 449 2200 **open** Not

winemaker Steve Davies (Contract) **production** 100 **est.** 1997

product range ($20 R) Chardonnay, Cabernet Merlot.

summary Karen and Shayne Hitchcock established 0.5 hectare of chardonnay and 0.5 hectare of cabernet sauvignon and merlot (thereafter pinot noir) on a rough, rocky hillside that was covered in thyme before the vines were planted. The northern aspect allows the low-yielding vines to produce fully ripe grapes (provided they are not cabernet sauvignon).

french farm vineyards NR

12 Winery Road, French Farm, Akaroa Harbour **region** Canterbury

phone (03) 304 5784 **fax** (03) 304 5785 **open** 7 days 10–5

winemaker Mark Leonard **production** NA **est.** 1998

product range ($18–24 R) Chardonnay, Rosé, Pinot Noir.

summary Has had a short but complicated history, which seems par for the course on the Banks Peninsula. Established as a winery-cum-restaurant, later becoming a restaurant only (leasing out the winery portion) before once again venturing back into winemaking (in 1998) and building an outdoor pizza and barbecue facility for good measure.

fromm winery ★★★★★

Godfrey Road, RD2, Blenheim **region** Marlborough
phone (03) 572 9355 **fax** (03) 572 9366 **open** Sat 11–5, summer holidays Tues–Sat 11–5
winemaker Hatsch Kalberer, George Fromm **production** 6000 **est.** 1992
product range ($15–53 R) The labelling of the Fromm wines has been very difficult to unravel, thanks both to subtlety and changes from one year to the next. For the time being the super-premium wines will be released under the Fromm La Strada Fromm Vineyard label (replacing the previous reserve range), with the varietal wines under the La Strada name. Don't ask me why there is a 1999 Reserve Chardonnay; I can't tell you.
summary Swiss-born and resident George Fromm, wife Ruth, and former Matawhero winemaker Hatsch Kalberer have formed a dynamic team to produce exceptionally full-flavoured wines, with the emphasis on reds. Fromm has 21 hectares of estate vineyards and, while the emphasis remains on Pinot Noir, produces an utterly eclectic range of wines, with Sangiovese in the pipeline. Exports to Australia, the UK, the US and (of course) Switzerland.

Fromm La Strada Chardonnay

YYYY **1999** Light to medium yellow-green; the bouquet immediately tells you this is no ordinary Marlborough Chardonnay: it is nutty, creamy and has understated fruit. The palate tracks the same way, with some edgy nutty characters, a slightly softening buttery edge and a creamy cast from the full malolactic fermentation; notwithstanding all this, finishes with brisk acidity. **rating:** 88

best drinking Now–2005 **best vintages** NA **drink with** Brains in black butter • $29

Fromm La Strada Fromm Vineyard Chardonnay

YYYY½ **1999** Light to medium yellow-green; the bouquet is decidedly more complex than the standard wine, with more oak evident; the same play occurs on the palate, with some sweet honey/nutty/buttery notes balanced by that firm acidity on the finish. **rating:** 91

best drinking Now–2006 **best vintages** NA **drink with** Roast chicken • $24

Fromm La Strada Riesling Auslese

YYYY½ **2000** Light green-yellow; the bouquet is intense and highly aromatic, with lime juice and pineapple fruit; the palate provides a similar register of flavours, long and well-balanced. **rating:** 92

best drinking Now–2010 **best vintages** '00 **drink with** Fresh fruit • $35

Fromm La Strada Riesling Trockenbeerenauslese

YYYYY **1998** A glorious wine with unbelievable intensity and fantastic length, the lusciousness equivalent to that of a Tokay Essence, perfectly balanced by acidity. No one has bothered to try to analyse the wine for anything more than sugar; why should they? **rating:** 98

best drinking **best vintages** '98 **drink with** NA • NA

Fromm La Strada Pinot Noir

YYYY½ **1999** Medium to full purple-red; the bouquet is, of course, concentrated with plum and cherry fruit; the palate is charged with fruit and power, but the wine is already in good balance, and far more accessible than the Fromm Vineyard wine. Nonetheless, patience is still recommended. **rating:** 92

best drinking 2004–2009 **best vintages** NA **drink with** Wild boar • $35

Fromm La Strada Fromm Vineyard Pinot Noir

YYYYY **1999** Medium to full red-purple; the bouquet is powerful and dense with dark small berry, forest, plum and spice aromas that move into a massively structured and tannic palate with some plush fruit surrounded by the extract. It is almost impossible to come up with a conventional rating for such an unconventional wine, which would surely score 100 points from Robert Parker. **rating:** 94

best drinking 2005–2015 **best vintages** '99 **drink with** Leave it in the cellar • $53

Fromm La Strada Fromm Vineyard Syrah

YYYYY **1999** Dense, impenetrable colour; the bouquet is flooded with dark, small berry fruits, licorice and tar. The inevitably concentrated and powerful palate has the same fruit characters, but does not finish with the extractive tannins one fears. **rating:** 95

best drinking 2004–2014 **best vintages** '99 **drink with** Leave it in the cellar • $36

Fromm La Strada Merlot Malbec

▼▼▼▼▽ **1999** Deep red-purple; the spice from the malbec is immediately obvious, woven through a mix of the ripe berry and dark savoury contribution from the merlot; the palate is far more accessible a style than any of the other Fromm red wines, with nice fruit and subtle and fine, lingering tannins. **rating:** 90

best drinking 2003–2008 **best vintages** NA **drink with** Venison pie • $19.50

gatehouse wines NR

Jowers Road, RD6, Christchurch **region** Canterbury
phone (03) 342 9682 **fax** (03) 342 9682 **open** Mon–Sat 10–5 Nov–Feb, Sat 10–5 Mar–Oct
winemaker Peter Gatehouse **production** 500 **est.** 1989
product range Chardonnay, Gewurztraminer, Riesling, Pinot Noir, Merlot, Cabernet Sauvignon.
summary The Gatehouse family made its first wines in 1989 from estate plantings commenced in the early 1980s. The initial release was under the Makariri label, but subsequent releases have been under the Gatehouse label.

gibbston valley ★★★★★

State Highway 6, Gibbston, RD1, Queenstown **region** Central Otago
phone (03) 442 6910 **fax** (03) 442 6909 **open** 7 days 10–5.30
winemaker Grant Taylor **production** 15 000 **est.** 1989
product range ($19–55 R) Riesling, Marlborough Sauvignon Blanc, Pinot Gris, Greenstone (unoaked Chardonnay), Reserve Chardonnay, Blanc de Pinot Noir, Pinot Noir, Reserve Pinot Noir, Merlot.
summary A highly professional and attractive winery, restaurant and cellar-door sales facility situated near Queenstown that has been an outstanding success since the day it opened. The rapid expansion of the Central Otago area, and the development of vineyards in a range of meso-climates, has allowed Gibbston Valley to both lift production and simultaneously lift the quality of its wines, and particularly Pinot Noir, to the highest level. The role of winemaker Grant Taylor, a pinotphile, has also been pivotal. The wines are distributed throughout Australia by Negociants.

Gibbston Valley Central Otago Riesling

▼▼▼▼▽ **2000** Light green-yellow; the moderately intense and spotlessly clean bouquet has lime/lime pastille aromas, the palate a joyous celebration of riesling varietal character with pure lime juice, the acidity rather than the residual sugar coming through on the finish. **rating:** 90

best drinking Now–2007 **best vintages** '93, '94, '96, '00 **drink with** Fresh asparagus • $20

Gibbston Valley Marlborough Sauvignon Blanc

▼▼▼▼▽ **2000** Light to medium green-yellow; the fragrant and intense bouquet has touches of passionfruit to the underlying citrus/gooseberry; the light- to medium-bodied palate is elegant, with nicely balanced citrus/passionfruit flavours and finishing acidity. **rating:** 90

best drinking Now **best vintages** '92, '94, '96, '97, '98, '00 **drink with** Seafood salad • $19

Gibbston Valley Central Otago Pinot Gris

▼▼▼▼ **2000** Medium yellow-green; a strongly aromatic and fruity bouquet has ripe apple and pear in abundance, the palate with positive flavours ranging through apple, fruit salad and mandarin. This is much more than a picture painted with white paint. **rating:** 87

best drinking Now–2006 **best vintages** '99 **drink with** Salmon risotto • $22

Gibbston Valley Reserve Chardonnay

▼▼▼▼ **1999** Light to medium yellow-green; the bouquet is fragrant, with ripe melon, well-integrated oak and subtle cashew notes from the mlf. The palate is smooth and rounded, with those cashew/nutty characters woven through the melon fruit. Good acidity tightens up the finish. **rating:** 88

best drinking Now–2004 **best vintages** '99 **drink with** Sautéed scallops • $30

Gibbston Valley Pinot Noir

▼▼▼▼▽ **1999** Good, bright and deep colour; the bouquet is fragrant, with a complex mix of spice, plum and forest; the palate is very much in a lighter style, but has all the elegance and the fine, linear, intense fruit one looks for in Pinot Noir. A wine that has in no way been forced to be something it is not. **rating:** 93

best drinking Now–2004 **best vintages** '94, '96, '97, '98, '99 **drink with** Spiced quail • $30

Gibbston Valley Reserve Pinot Noir

🍷🍷🍷🍷🍷 **1999** Strong purple-red; the bouquet is even more complex, and certainly more powerful than the varietal release of the same year, which is as one would expect. The fruit is riper, with abundant cherry and plum with a fine cross-cut of more savoury/foresty/oaky characters. Great wine. **rating:** 96

best drinking 2002–2006 **best vintages** '96, '97, '98, '99 **drink with** Venison • $48

giesen estate ★★★★★

Burnham School Road, Burnham **region** Canterbury
phone (03) 347 6729 **fax** (03) 347 6450 **open** Mon–Sat 10–4
winemaker Andrew Blake **production** 100 000 **est.** 1981
product range ($14–35 CD) Riesling, Reserve Riesling, Sauvignon Blanc, Chardonnay, Reserve Chardonnay, Late Harvest Riesling, Pinot Noir, Reserve Pinot Noir, Voyage Methode Traditionelle.
summary Determination, skill and marketing flair have seen Giesen grow from obscurity to one of the largest family-owned and run wineries in New Zealand, with no sign of the growth slowing. Given the Giesens' Rhine Valley origins it is not surprising that they have done so well with aromatic, non-wooded white wines, but they have also gained acclaim for impressive Chardonnay and Pinot Noir. The ever-increasing production has allowed distribution throughout Europe, the US, Canada, and the Pacific including Australia through Negociants.

Giesen Marlborough Sauvignon Blanc

🍷🍷🍷🍷🍷 **2000** Light green-yellow; the bouquet is clean, with relatively gentle, tropical melon and passionfruit aromas; the flavour fills the mouth with lots of upfront, immediate tropical fruit, but the finish is attractively controlled, with a crisp, lively acid finish. **rating:** 92

best drinking Now **best vintages** '97, '98, '99, '00 **drink with** Full-flavoured Asian seafood • $14

Giesen Reserve Barrel Selection Marlborough Chardonnay

🍷🍷🍷🍷🍷 **1999** Excellent green-yellow; strong, charry barrel-ferment oak influences come through powerfully on both bouquet and palate, the malolactic influence rather less assertively. However, the tangy melon/citrus fruit is also remarkably powerful, and the palate has length. **rating:** 90

best drinking Now–2003 **best vintages** '94, '97, '98 **drink with** Calamari • $22

Giesen Canterbury Pinot Noir Reserve Barrel Selection

🍷🍷🍷🍷🍷 **1999** Light to medium red-purple; a hallmark bouquet of fragrant smoky/gamey/briary/foresty/ plummy aromatics. The palate is fine and long, with pointed accents and a lingering aftertaste. The oak is certainly evident, but the fruit carries the oak. The first vintage to include clone 115, and hand-sorting of bunches in the winery. **rating:** 94

best drinking Now–2005 **best vintages** '94, '96, '98, '99 **drink with** Peking duck • $33

gillan estate wines ★★★☆

454B Rapaura Road, Blenheim, Marlborough **region** Marlborough
phone (03) 572 9979 **fax** (03) 572 9980 **open** 7 days 10.30–5 spring, summer and autumn; by appointment in winter
winemaker Sam Weaver, Ian Marchant **production** 2500 **est.** 1992
product range ($15.95–27.95 CD) Eastfields Sauvignon Blanc, Single Vineyard Chardonnay, Merlot, Brut Reserve.
summary Gillan Wines is a partnership between English-born Toni and Terry Gillan and local vignerons Hamish and Anne Young. A white, Mediterranean-style wine cellar and restaurant (serving tapas-style food) opened in 1996. While being Mediterranean in style, architect Neil Charles-Jones believes it is also a building 'which belongs in the Marlborough landscape while quietly alluding to the great Champagne cellars of France'. That is quite an achievement. Exports to the UK and Germany.

gladstone vineyard ★★★★☆

Gladstone Road, RD2, Carterton, Wairarapa **region** Wairarapa
phone (06) 379 8563 **fax** (06) 379 8563 **open** Tues–Sun 11–5
winemaker Christine Kernohan **production** 2000 **est.** 1987
product range ($11–30 CD) Riesling, Sauvignon Blanc, Pinot Gris, Chardonnay, Cabernet Merlot; occasional releases of Reserve Merlot and Late Harvest Riesling. Red Label and Cafe Red are cheaper second labels.

summary Gladstone Vineyard was acquired from founder Dennis Roberts by Christine and David Kernahan in February 1996, with Christine now in charge of winemaking. That the transition has been without pain is handsomely demonstrated by the quality of the always brilliant Sauvignon Blanc.

glenmark wines ★★☆

Mackenzies Road, Waipara **region** Waipara
phone (03) 314 6828 **fax** (03) 314 6828 **open** 7 days 11–5
winemaker Kym Rayner (Consultant) **production** 2000 **est.** 1981
product range ($11–25 CD) Waipara White, Triple Peaks Dry, Triple Peaks Medium, Riesling Dry, Riesling Medium, Weka Plains Riesling, Gewurztraminer, Sauvignon Blanc, Chardonnay, Waipara Red, Pinot Noir, Port.
summary Much of the wine is sold cellar door, with the Weka Plains Wine Garden offering a full restaurant service and wine by the glass from October through to April. Bookings are essential. Owner John McCaskey has put the property on the market, and it may well be sold by the time you read these words.

glover's vineyard ★★★☆

Gardner Valley Road, Upper Moutere **region** Nelson
phone (03) 543 2698 **open** 7 days 10–6
winemaker David Glover **production** 1900 **est.** 1984
product range ($15–28 CD) Sauvignon Blanc, Riesling, Late Harvest Riesling, Nelson Pinot Noir, Moutere Pinot Noir Back Block, Moutere Pinot Noir Front Block, Springgrove Shiraz, Cabernet Sauvignon.
summary David Glover studied winemaking and viticulture at Charles Sturt University in southern New South Wales during a 17-year stay in Australia, adding to his PhD in algebra. He and his wife Penny returned to establish their own vineyard in 1984, struggling with birds and other predators before producing their first wines in 1989.

Glover's Late Harvest Riesling

YYYY☐ **1997** Brilliant green-yellow; scented, floral, lime-blossom and lemon aromas are precursors to a wine that has strong Germanic flavours on the palate, with a lively and intense entry, and lovely balancing acidity on the finish. **rating:** 90

best drinking 2002–2005 **best vintages** '97 **drink with** Prosciutto and melon • $24

Glover's Moutere Pinot Noir Front Block

YYYY **1999** Light to medium red-purple; the bouquet is clean, offering sweeter fruit than many of the Glover's wines. The palate, likewise, has a mix of raspberry, strawberry, plum and mint; the tannins are there, but not awesome. **rating:** 87

best drinking 2002–2006 **best vintages** '99 **drink with** Char-grilled venison • $38

Glover's Moutere Pinot Noir Back Block

YYY☐ **1999** Medium to full red-purple; ripe, sweet plum and chocolate aromas flow into the opening of a huge palate before the trademark tannins coat all corners of the mouth. Not yet released. **rating** 84

best drinking 2003–2008 **best vintages** NA **drink with** Leave it in the cellar • NA

golden slope NR

1121 Back Ormond Road, RD1, Gisborne **region** Gisborne
phone (06) 868 9142 **fax** (06) 868 6199 **open** Not
winemaker John Thorpe, Kim Crawford **production** 1000 **est.** 1998
product range ($26 R) TW Chardonnay.
summary Golden Slope, an oblique reference to Burgundy's Côte d'Or, is a joint venture between Gisborne grape-growers Geordie Witters and Paul Tietjen, who decided to have a small part of their joint grape production vinified under the TW label.

Golden Slope TW Chardonnay

YYYY **1999** Medium to full yellow-green; gentle barrel-ferment and malolactic-ferment influences on the bouquet give nice cashew and melon aromas, the palate bigger, richer and fuller, but all coming together convincingly on the finish. **rating:** 88

best drinking Now **best vintages** NA **drink with** Yakitori chicken • $26

goldwater estate ★★★★★

18 Causeway Road, Putiki Bay, Waiheke Island **region** Waiheke Island
phone (09) 372 7493 **fax** (09) 372 6827 **open** 7 days 11–4 summer while stocks last
winemaker Kim Goldwater, Nicholai St George **production** 26 000 **est.** 1978
product range ($19.95–90 R) Marlborough Roseland Chardonnay, Zel Waiheke Island Chardonnay, Dog Point Marlborough Sauvignon Blanc, Waiheke Island Esslin Merlot, Waiheke Island Cabernet Sauvignon Merlot.
summary Goldwater Estate goes from strength to strength. Having initially forged a reputation for its Waiheke Island Cabernet Merlot Franc, it has built on that with its superb Waiheke Island Esslin Merlot and a range of beautifully crafted wines made from Marlborough grapes, with the limited volume Waiheke Island-sourced Delamore Chardonnay providing additional support. The wines come from 13 precious hectares on Waiheke Island and 35 hectares in Marlborough. The wines are exported to Australia (DWS), the US, the UK, Europe, Brazil, Singapore, Israel, the Philippines, and half a dozen other countries.

greenhough vineyard ★★★★

Patons Road, RD1, Richmond, Nelson **region** Nelson
phone (03) 542 3868 **fax** (03) 542 3462 **open** Mon–Sat 10–5 Dec–Mar
winemaker Andrew Greenhough **production** 2000 **est.** 1991
product range ($16–32 CD) Nelson Riesling, Sauvignon Blanc, Chardonnay, Nelson Pinot Noir, Hope Vineyard Pinot Noir.
summary Yet another name change for what was initially Ranzau, then Pelorus and now Greenhough – the last change a sensible one, dictated by the confusion with the Pelorus Méthode Champenoise of Cloudy Bay. Under whatever name, the personable and highly regarded Andrew Greenhough makes appealing wines, notably the Sauvignon Blanc and Riesling. As his vineyard holdings increase, so will the reputation of his wines.

Greenhough Vineyard Nelson Sauvignon Blanc

🍷🍷🍷🍷 **2000** Light to medium yellow-green; a very rich and ripe bouquet has tropical fruit merging into stonefruit, well away from the more traditional style. The palate delivers exactly what the bouquet promises, its flavour coming from fruit, rather than residual sugar. **rating:** 88

best drinking Now **best vintages** '00 **drink with** Rich seafood pasta • $16

Greenhough Nelson Chardonnay

🍷🍷🍷🍷 **1999** Light to medium yellow-green; tangy melon and subtle oak on the bouquet lead into a classic, cool-grown style with melon/grapefruit flavours and gently rounded mouthfeel. **rating:** 87

best drinking Now–2003 **best vintages** NA **drink with** Medium-weight seafood • $19

Greenhough Vineyard Hope Vineyard Pinot Noir

🍷🍷🍷🍷🍷 **1999** Deeply coloured; the potent, powerful and complex bouquet has a mix of darl plum, berry and herb; the palate is flooded with rich fruit in a big, bold style, with abundant ripe tannins on the finish justified by all of that plush fruit. Very reminiscent of the Tarrawarra (Yarra Valley) style at its best. **rating:** 92

best drinking 2003–2009 **best vintages** '97, '99 **drink with** Braised duck • $32

---

greenstone point NR

Weedons Ross Road, RD5, Christchurch **region** Canterbury
phone (03) 347 9060 **fax** (03) 347 8225 **open** Not
winemaker Dayne Sherwood **production** NA **est.** 1999
product range Marlborough Sauvignon Blanc, Chardonnay, Pinot Noir.
summary Greenstone Point owns three vineyards situated in the Rapaura region of the Wairau Valley in Marlborough. The wine, however, is made by Dayne Sherwood at his Christchurch Winery.

grove mill ★★★★☆

Waihopai Valley Road, Marlborough **region** Marlborough
phone (03) 572 8200 **fax** (03) 572 8211 **open** 7 days 11–5
winemaker David Pearce, Sarah Hennessy **production** 60 000 **est.** 1988
product range ($12.95–30 R) Marlborough Sauvignon Blanc, Chardonnay, Riesling and Pinot Noir; Winemakers Reserve Pinot Noir, Merlot; Lansdowne Chardonnay; also lower-priced Sanctuary Sauvignon Blanc, Chardonnay and Pinotage.

summary Has firmly established itself as a producer of wines of consistently high quality in substantial volumes. Its success in wine shows both in New Zealand and elsewhere (particularly Australia) underlines the continuing achievements of the winemaking team headed by David Pearce. The wines are now distributed through New Zealand by Eurowine, Australia by Fesq & Co, and are also found in Hong Kong, the US, Canada, Singapore, Japan, the UK and the Netherlands.

Grove Mill Marlborough Riesling

YYYY **1999** Medium yellow-green; a toasty, bready bouquet with a whisker of the matchstick reduction that was apparent when the wine was young; there is lots of flavour on the palate, but the structure is loose. **rating:** 84

best drinking Now–2010 **best vintages** '91, '92, '93, '94, '96, '98, '99 **drink with** Salad of snow peas • NA

Grove Mill Marlborough Chardonnay

YYYYY **1999** Light green-yellow; fresh, attractive nectarine and white peach fruit is supported by subtle oak on the bouquet. The light- to medium-bodied palate is developing well, still elegant and stylish. An emphatic return to top form by Grove Mill. Won a gold medal at the Royal Easter Wine Show 2001. **rating:** 94

best drinking Now–2003 **best vintages** '99 **drink with** Slow-cooked salmon • $20

Grove Mill Marlborough Pinot Noir

YYYY **1999** Medium to full red-purple; a potent bouquet with gamey/savoury overtones to rich dark plum fruit starts well, but the palate has rather too much tannin and extract, giving a discontinuous feel to the palate. **rating:** 84

best drinking 2002–2005 **best vintages** NA **drink with** Strong game • $28

gunn estate NR

85 Ohiti Road, RD9, Hastings **region** Hawke's Bay
phone (06) 874 3250 **fax** (06) 874 3256 **open** By appointment
winemaker Denis Gunn **production** 2000 **est.** 1994
product range ($18–25 R) As from the 1998 vintage, only two wines will be produced: Skeetfield Chardonnay and Woolshed Merlot Cabernet Sauvignon.
summary Denis and Alan Gunn have been contract grape-growers since 1982, with 15 hectares of vines providing grapes for many of the best-known names in the Hawke's Bay region. In the interim, Denis Gunn graduated from Roseworthy College, Australia, and became assistant-winemaker at Villa Maria in 1993, moving to Kemblefield in 1995, where the 1995 Gunn Estate wines were made. Subsequently, production moved to Sacred Hill. Exports to the UK, the US and Singapore.

Gunn Estate Woolshed Merlot Cabernet Sauvignon

YYYY **1998** Medium red-purple; not a heavyweight by any stretch of imagination, but with an appealing array of spicy/earthy/berry aromas and flavours. The oak is nicely integrated, the tannins soft. **rating:** 83

best drinking 2002–2006 **best vintages** NA **drink with** Yearling steak • $21

harrier rise vineyard ★★★★

748 Waitakere Road, Kumeu **region** Auckland Area
phone (09) 412 7256 **fax** (09) 412 7256 **open** Weekends 12–6
winemaker Tim Harris **production** 3700 **est.** 1986
product range ($18–35 CD) Cabernet Franc, Uppercase Merlot, Bigney Coigne Kumea Merlot.
summary The project of Auckland lawyer and wine-writer Tim Harris and wife Alix. The resolution of some complicated vineyard ownership arrangements in 1996 led to the change of name from Waitakere Road to Harrier Rise, and to the Harrises acquiring full ownership of the 7-hectare Harrier Rise Vineyard, replete with 15-year-old cabernet sauvignon, merlot and cabernet franc. Wine quality is impressive in better vintages, with ripe flavours and tannins. Exports to Australia, the US, Hong Kong and Malaysia.

Harrier Rise Bigney Coigne Merlot

YYYY **1998** Medium purple-red; the bouquet is clean, with direct fresh berry, mint, leaf and other savoury aromas, the palate in a savoury/foresty varietal spectrum, with fine, lingering tannins. Gentle oak handling throughout. **rating:** 85

best drinking Now–2005 **best vintages** NA **drink with** Braised ox tail • $35

Harrier Rise Uppercase Merlot

🍷🍷🍷🍷 **1999** Medium red-purple; in typical Harrier Rise style, the bouquet is of light to medium intensity, with an earthy/cedary/spicy fruit spectrum; the light- to medium-bodied palate following down the same foresty/savoury/earthy path. May not sound too attractive, but this is a legitimate manifestation of Merlot which winemakers in St Emilion would understand. **rating:** 84

best drinking 2002–2006 **best vintages** NA **drink with** Spiced lamb • $22

hawkdun rise NR

241 Letts Gully Road, Alexandra **region** Central Otago
phone (03) 448 7782 **fax** (03) 448 7752 **open** By appointment
winemaker Alan Brady **production** 300 **est.** 1998
product range ($30 R) Redbarnais Pinot Noir.
summary Roy and Judy Faris have established a 2-hectare vineyard planted to pinot noir and are running an executive vineyard B&B operation (two queen-size bedrooms, one double bedroom). The plan is to double the size of the vineyard in 2002, and to continue having the wine made for them by Alan Brady at his Mount Edward Winery. The Pinot Noirs so far released have received enthusiastic ratings.

hawkesbridge wines ★★★★

Hawkesbury Road, Renwick, Marlborough **region** Marlborough
phone (03) 572 8024 **fax** (03) 572 9489 **open** 7 days 10.30–4.30 Dec–Apr
winemaker Contract (Neudorf) **production** 3500 **est.** 1991
product range ($17–28 R) Willowbank Vineyard Sauvignon Blanc, Sophie's Vineyard Chardonnay, Sophie's Vineyard Chardonnay Reserve, Pinot Noir, Cabernet Merlot, Merlot.
summary Hawkesbridge Wines and Estates (to give it its full name) is presently chiefly a contract grape-grower, but export demand for its wines is likely to see half the production from its 16 hectares of vines vinified under the Hawkesbridge label. Exports to Australia, the US, France, the Netherlands and the UK.

Hawkesbridge Willowbank Vineyard Sauvignon Blanc

🍷🍷🍷🍷🍷 **2000** Light to medium green-yellow; the bouquet has an elegant mix of gently tropical and gooseberry-accented fruit. The palate has intense fruit, ranging through passionfruit to gooseberry, and well-above-average length. **rating:** 92

best drinking Now **best vintages** '94, '96, '97, '99, '00 **drink with** Seafood • $20

hay's lake vineyard NR

PO Box 1304, Queenstown **region** Central Otago
phone (03) 489 1008 **fax** (03) 489 1003 **open** Not
winemaker Rudi Bauer **production** 2400 **est.** 1998
product range ($18.95–28.95 R) Sauvignon Blanc, Chardonnay, Pinot Noir.
summary Rodney and Michelle Johnson began the establishment of Hay's Lake with a 3.8-hectare vineyard at Lake Hayes, followed by the progressive establishment of 8 hectares in the Gibbston Valley subregion, and finally 33 hectares (planted in 1999) at Lowburn. Their house is situated on the Lake Hayes property, and the proposed winery will ultimately be constructed at Lowburn. Pinot noir has the lion's share of the plantings, supported by lesser amounts of chardonnay, pinot gris, sauvignon blanc, riesling and gewurztraminer.

heron's flight NR

Sharp Road, Matakana **region** Northland and Matakana
phone (09) 422 7915 **fax** (09) 422 7915 **open** 7 days 10–6
winemaker David Hoskins **production** 1500 **est.** 1987
product range ($17–50 CD) La Volée (Unoaked Chardonnay), Barrique Fermented Matakana Chardonnay, Sangiovese, Montepulciano.
summary Having established a small vineyard in 1987, David Hoskins and Mary Evans leased the defunct Antipodean Winery that was the scene of so much marketing hype and excitement in the mid-1980s. (The Antipodean has built a new winery since.) The first Heron's Flight wine (a densely coloured and flavoured Cabernet Sauvignon) was produced from the 1991 vintage and was a gold medal winner. Quality has bounced around since, partly due to the vagaries of climate.

herzog 

81 Jeffries Road, RD3, Blenheim, Marlborough **region** Marlborough
phone (03) 572 8770 **fax** (03) 572 8730 **open** By appointment
winemaker Hans Herzog **production** 2500 **est.** 1996
product range ($24–65 CD) Riesling, Pinot Gris, Chardonnay, Pinot Noir, Spirit of Marlborough Merlot Cabernet Sauvignon, Montepulciano.
summary Hans and Therese Herzog are part of a mini-migration of Swiss winemakers to New Zealand and Tasmania. Hans Herzog graduated from the Wine University of Wadenswil in Switzerland, and until the end of 1999 owned a prominent winery near Zurich. The Herzogs purchased the Blenheim property in 1994, and planted it over the 1996–1998 planting seasons, with 17 hectares now under organic management. If this were not enough, Therese Herzog owned the Michelin-starred restaurant Taggenberg, and has been joined in New Zealand by her staff and chef. Michelin doesn't allow stars to be transported, but the restaurant (Herzog's on Jeffries) brings another dimension to the New Zealand food scene.

Herzog Riesling

YYYY **2000** Pale straw-green; the bouquet is clean and fine, with a mix of herb, lime, mineral and slate. The palate, however, is painfully dry and has relatively little fruit or varietal character left in the wake of the malolactic fermentation. Will appeal to those who like old-style, cold-climate wines. Ageing in bottle will add something, but, in my view, not enough. **rating:** 83

best drinking Now–2007 **best vintages** NA **drink with** Shellfish • $27

Herzog Marlborough Pinot Gris

YYYY **1999** Light to medium yellow-green; the bouquet is clean, crisp and fresh, with a mix of mineral, spice and apple aromas. The power of the wine is immediately evident on the potent palate, which reflects the 14° alcohol, but which (mercifully) finishes dry, such sweetness as there is deriving from the alcohol. 100 cases made. **rating:** 88

best drinking Now–2004 **best vintages** NA **drink with** Antipasto • $28

Herzog Pinot Noir

YYYYY **2000** Bright, light red-purple; highly fragrant cherry aromas, with predictably little oak influence, lead through to a restrained, fine but tangy palate with lovely fresh cherry fruit. Guaranteed to repay cellaring. **rating:** 91

best drinking 2002–2007 **best vintages** NA **drink with** Quail casserole • $38

Herzog Marlborough Montepulciano

YYYYY **1998** Medium to full red-purple; the bouquet is complex, with ripe, faintly gamey fruit supported by spicy, cedary oak. The palate has abundant black cherry fruit, almost running into licorice and prune, with lingering tannins and positive oak handling. A wine that absolutely fulfils the promise of the 1998 vintage. **rating:** 92

best drinking 2003–2008 **best vintages** '98 **drink with** Marinated venison • $65

Herzog Spirit of Marlborough Merlot Cabernet Sauvignon

YYYYY **1999** Full red-purple; a spotlessly clean and refined bouquet with a lovely mix of cedar, blackcurrant and blackberry leads into a concentrated wine with excellent texture and structure; the fruit is still austere and a long way from opening up, but will do so. **rating:** 90

YYYY **1998** Medium red-purple; the fragrant and elegant bouquet has plenty of ripe cassis fruit supported by subtle oak. The palate, likewise, has ripe cassis fruit flavours together with dusty/silky tannins. The wine still seems slightly unformed, although given its pedigree, this should resolve with further time in bottle. **rating:** 89

best drinking 2004–2014 **best vintages** '98 **drink with** Rack of lamb • $65

hidden valley vineyard NR

Moiki, RD1, Greytown **region** Wairarapa
phone (06) 306 9287 **fax** (06) 306 8315 **open** By appointment
winemaker James Francis, Clare Kennet **production** NA **est.** 1997
product range ($18–22 R) Semillon, Chardonnay, Shiraz.
summary James Francis and Clare Kennet have established 1 hectare of vines in an out-of-the-way spot near Martinborough, so out of the way that Hidden Valley seemed the logical name. To add further spice, the tiny winery has been constructed out of straw bales.

highfield estate ★★★★

Brookby Road, RD2, Blenheim **region** Marlborough
phone (03) 572 8592 **fax** (03) 572 9257 **open** 7 days 10–5
winemaker Alistair Soper **production** 25 000 **est.** 1990
product range ($13.95–53 CD) Under the Highfield label are Riesling, Sauvignon Blanc, Chardonnay and Merlot; under the Elstree range: Vintage Cuvée and Millennium Brut.
summary Highfield Estate was purchased by an international partnership in late 1991, the English and Japanese limbs of which are associated with the French Champagne house Drappier. The ornate Tuscan-style winery that has since been built is Marlborough's answer to some of the more bizarre edifices of the Napa Valley. After a period of winemaking and marketing uncertainty, has returned to an even keel. Exports to Australia, the UK, Japan and the US.

Highfield Estate Marlborough Chardonnay

YYYY **1999** Medium yellow-green; the bouquet shows obvious nutty barrel-ferment characters allied with cashew and fig; the palate is stylishly smooth and clean, in a nicely restrained style, and excellent balance on the finish. **rating:** 89

best drinking Now–2003 **best vintages** '91, '93, '94 **drink with** Rich seafood • $33

Highfield Estate Pinot Noir

YYYYY **1999** Medium red-purple; the bouquet is quite savoury, with some oak, and a backdrop of dark fruit. The palate has a similar mix of savoury and stemmy characters on the one hand, and attractive small berry fruits on the other; overall, it is round, concentrated and has length. **rating:** 91

best drinking Now–2005 **best vintages** '99 **drink with** Braised duck • $42

Highfield Estate Merlot

YYYY **1998** Medium to full red-purple; a complex bouquet with solid, dark plum fruit, then a massive palate with lots of extract and dark plum fruit; just stays within the limits. **rating:** 86

best drinking 2003–2008 **best vintages** '90, '91, '94 **drink with** Game • NA

himmelsfeld moutere vineyard NR

Gardner Valley Road, RD1, Upper Moutere, Nelson **region** Nelson
phone (03) 543 2223 **fax** (03) 543 2223 **open** Labour Weekend, March or by appointment
winemaker Daniel Schwarzenbach (Contract) **production** 500 **est.** 1997
product range ($15–28 R) Sauvignon Blanc, Chardonnay, Cabernet Sauvignon.
summary Beth Eggers established her tiny 1.5-hectare vineyard, the name of which means heaven's field, after cycling around vineyards in Germany and Switzerland. Her family has lived in the Nelson area for generations. The wines are made at Seifried and most are exported to Germany.

huia ★★★★

Rapaura Road, RD3, Blenheim **region** Marlborough
phone (03) 572 8326 **fax** (03) 572 8331 **open** Summer 7 days 10–4.30, other times by appointment
winemaker Claire Allan, Mike Allan **production** 12 000 **est.** 1996
product range ($22–38 CD) Riesling, Gewurztraminer, Sauvignon Blanc, Chardonnay, Pinot Gris, Pinot Noir, Marlborough Brut.
summary Owners Claire and Mike Allan bring a wealth of experience to Huia. Both are winemakers and both have had outstanding careers in Marlborough, variously working at Cloudy Bay, Corbans Marlborough, Rapaura Vintners, Lawsons Dry Hills and Vavasour Wines – as well as working an 'extended stage' in Champagne, France. They acquired their vineyard in Rapaura Road in late 1990 and have now planted 24.6 hectares of vines, with new Dijon (Burgundy) clones of pinot noir and chardonnay which came into full production in 1999. Exports to Australia, the UK, the US, Hong Kong and Japan.

Huia Chardonnay

YYYYY **1999** Light to medium yellow-green; a clean and complex bouquet has a range of nutty aromatics, together with touches of honey and citrus. The fresh and lively palate is driven by tangy, citrussy fruit, enriched with a faint touch of cashew, and finishes with sustaining acidity. **rating:** 90

best drinking Now–2004 **best vintages** '97, '98, '99 **drink with** Full-flavoured fish • $26

Huia Marlborough Pinot Noir

ΥΥΥΥΥ **1999** Deeply coloured for Pinot Noir; the bouquet is both dense and intense, with an attractive mix of dark plum, ripe cherry and spice. The palate has great mouthfeel, round and plush, with plum, a hint of mint, and an underlying touch of game. The tannins are balanced, but the wine really needs time to fully evolve. **rating:** 92

best drinking 2003–2008 **best vintages** NA **drink with** Wild duck • $29

hunter's wines ★★★★★

Rapaura Road, Blenheim **region** Marlborough

phone (03) 572 8489 **fax** (03) 572 8457 **open** 7 days 9.30–4.30

winemaker Gary Duke **production** 40 000 **est.** 1980

product range ($15.95–32 R) Riesling, Gewurztraminer, Sauvignon Blanc, Oak Aged Sauvignon Blanc, Single Vineyard Sauvginon Blanc, Winemaker's Selection Sauvignon Blanc, Chardonnay, Pinot Noir, Merlot, Brut, Miru Miru Brut; Spring Creek is a newly-introduced second label.

summary Hunter's has long been a producer of consistently excellent wines with tremendous varietal character. Given the quantity and quality of its production it is a winery of world standing, and certainly among the top 20 in Australasia: it is hard to choose between its long-lived Riesling, Sauvignon Blanc, Oak Aged Sauvignon Blanc (a tour de force) and subtly complex Chardonnay. Exports to the UK, Switzerland, Denmark, Hong Kong, Japan, Brazil, the US and Australia.

Hunter's Riesling

ΥΥΥΥΥ **2000** Light green-yellow; a firm, minerally bouquet with subdued fruit leads through to a relatively austere palate, although all the makings are there. A wine which demands to be cellared for several years yet to begin to show its true colours. **rating:** 90

best drinking 2003–2008 **best vintages** '90, '91, '94, '99, '00 **drink with** Asparagus with hollandaise sauce • $16

Hunter's Gewurztraminer

ΥΥΥΥ **2000** Light green-yellow; a very tight and closed bouquet, with little escaping at this juncture; the palate is fine and delicate, without a hint of phenolics, but vividly reflecting the difficulty of striking a balance between flavour and excessive phenolics on the one hand, and extreme delicacy on the other. Still, an all-purpose wine which will never offend. **rating:** 85

best drinking Now–2003 **best vintages** NA **drink with** Chinese • $17

Hunter's Sauvignon Blanc

ΥΥΥΥΥ **2000** Very pale straw-green; a clean bouquet with a mix of predominantly gently tropical fruit and more minerally/gooseberry characters is followed by an intense but not aggressive palate with crystal clear varietal character and flawless balance, moving through to a clear, bright finish. **rating:** 94

best drinking Now–2003 **best vintages** '88, '89, '91, '92, '94, '96, '99, '00 **drink with** All seafood • $16.50

Hunter's Single Vineyard Sauvignon Blanc

ΥΥΥΥΥ **2000** Light green-yellow; the bouquet is fragrant and crisp, with a mix of mineral and gooseberry; it is on the piercingly intense and long palate that the character of the wine comes through, although, even here, the fruit flavours are still to fully express themselves. **rating:** 93

best drinking Now–2004 **best vintages** '00 **drink with** Fresh asparagus • $20

Hunter's Chardonnay

ΥΥΥΥ **1998** Light to medium yellow-green; soft, toasty barrel-ferment and malolactic-ferment characters are based on nectarine fruit; the light- to medium-bodied palate has the same range of flavours, and is ageing slowly and reassuringly. **rating:** 87

best drinking Now–2004 **best vintages** '90, '91, '92, '94, '95, '96, '97 **drink with** Honey prawns • $20

Hunter's Brut

ΥΥΥΥΥ **1996** Medium yellow-green; has much fuller bouquet than Miru Miru, rich, with some biscuity/bready characters. While still fine, has richer mouthfeel and weight, with some attractive bready notes. Retasted February 2001 and still in great condition. **rating:** 92

best drinking 2000–2000 **best vintages** '96 **drink with** Bluff oysters • NA

Hunter's Pinot Noir

ŸŸŸŸ **1999** Light to medium red-purple; spicy/foresty/stemmy aromas from the bouquet are in the Hunter's mainstream, the light- to medium-bodied palate with sappy cherry and spice flavours, and more length than I have previously encountered. **rating:** 87

best drinking Now–2004 **best vintages** NA **drink with** Saddle of hare • $23.45

huthlee estate NR

Montana Road, RD5, Hastings, Hawke's Bay **region** Hawke's Bay
phone (06) 879 6234 **fax** (06) 879 6234 **open** Mon–Sat 10–5, Sun 11–4
winemaker Devon Lee **production** 3000 **est.** 1991
product range ($13–28 ML) Pinot Gris, Sauvignon Blanc, Rosé, Kaweka Red, Cabernet Franc, Reserve Cabernet Franc, Merlot, Cabernet Sauvignon Merlot.
summary Devon and Estelle Lee commenced planting their 10.5-hectare vineyard in 1984 and established an on site cellar door in 1992. The majority of the grapes are sold to other producers; the best is reserved for their own label, almost all of which is sold in an ultra-low-ley fashion through cellar door.

Huthlee Estate Merlot

ŸŸŸŸ **1999** Medium red-purple; very ripe, sweet plum and berry fruit is in the mainstream of the Huthlee style; there is a similar play of very ripe, spicy fruit to the palate, replaying some of the characters of the '98 vintage, with an underlying hint of sweet and sour characters. **rating:** 87

best drinking Now–2003 **best vintages** NA **drink with** Venison casserole • $28

hyperion wines NR

Tongue Farm Road, Matakana, North Auckland **region** Northland and Matakana
phone (09) 422 9375 **fax** (09) 422 9375 **open** Weekends and holidays 10–5
winemaker John Crone **production** 1500 **est.** 1994
product range ($13.50–27 CD) Helios Chardonnay, Selene Chardonnay Pinot Gris, Phoebe Pinot Gris, Eos Pinot Noir, Gaia Merlot, Kronos Cabernet Merlot, Millennios Cabernet Sauvignon.
summary Jill and John Crone were enthusiastic wine drinkers for many years before they began the establishment of Hyperion Wines in 1994 by planting vines on a site near the Providence Vineyard. In 1996 they purchased part of the renowned Antipodean Farm (of the warring Vuletic family). The Crones now live on the vineyard at Matakana.

Hyperion Gaia Merlot

ŸŸŸŸ **1999** Medium purple-red; there is a youthful mix of juicy berry and more savoury/earthy aromas followed by a palate with quite complex fruit flavour and structure, finishing with fine but sustained tannins. Not in the fruity end of the spectrum, but nonetheless a u eful wine. **rating:** 87

best drinking Now–2004 **best vintages** '98 **drink with** Smoked beef • $27

inverness estate NR

Ness Valley Road, Clevedon, Manukau City **region** Auckland Area
phone (09) 292 8710 **fax** (09) 292 8714 **open** By appointment
winemaker Anthony Ivicevich **production** 500 **est.** 1993
product range ($18–24 R) Ness Valley Chardonnay, Cabernet Franc, Reserve Cabernet Franc.
summary Yo and John Robinson purchased the 35-hectare property on which Inverness Estate is established in 1993. Situated in the Ness Valley, grape-growing is but part of a larger hospitality complex that features an Andalusian horse stud and equestrian activities, and native and exotic forests complete with a stream that meanders through the garden surrounding the house (which offers four double rooms, each with an en-suite). The 2.8-hectare vineyard is planted to cabernet franc, chardonnay and semillon, and the first wines were released in 1999. With the skill of Anthony Ivicevich as contract-winemaker, quality should be assured.

isabel estate 

Hawkesbury Road, Renwick, Marlborough **region** Marlborough
phone (03) 572 8300 **fax** (03) 572 8383 **open** By appointment
winemaker Jeff Sinnott **production** 22 000 **est.** 1982

product range ($18.95–28.95 R) Marlborough Sauvignon Blanc, Marlborough Chardonnay, Isabel Estate Noble Sauvage Late Harvest Sauvignon Blanc, Marlborough Pinot Noir.

summary The 54-hectare Isabel Estate vineyard was planted in 1982 and until 1994 was purely and simply a grape-growing enterprise (and the largest external supplier to Cloudy Bay). In that time it built up a considerable reputation for the quality of its grapes and in 1994 introduced the Isabel Estate label. It has now taken a further critical step, constructing a 300-tonne winery, which was commissioned for the 1998 vintage, and employing a dedicated and highly skilled winemaker. Stage 2 has seen the completion (in 2001) of the construction of an underground cellar for 500 barrels. Wine quality across the range is immaculate. The wines are exported to Australia, Canada, Japan, Hong Kong, the US, the UK and the Netherlands.

Isabel Estate Marlborough Riesling

YYYYY 2000 Light green-yellow; the bouquet offers gentle lime and apple aromas, with just a subliminal touch of spice and mineral. The exceptionally well-balanced palate has the same spectrum of flavours in a fine, stylish and apparently dry mode; good length. **rating:** 92

best drinking 2002–2007 **best vintages** NA **drink with** Delicate Chinese steamed fish • $23

Isabel Estate Marlborough Sauvignon Blanc

YYYYY 2000 Light green-yellow; a very fragrant bouquet with a riotous array of gooseberry, melon, passionfruit and sundry other characters is followed by a flavour-packed palate in rollercoaster style, ultimately finishing with mix of ripe fruit and minerally acidity. As sophisticated as ever. **rating:** 94

best drinking Now **best vintages** '94, '97, '98, '99, '00 **drink with** Sugar-cured tuna • $23

Isabel Estate Marlborough Pinot Gris

YYYYY 2000 Light straw-green; a typical, very clean, somewhat neutral bouquet with green apple and pear aromas is followed by a medium-bodied palate, with distinct mid-palate flesh, but not offering (nor seeking to offer) any high-toned fruit. The wine is all about texture and subtlety. **rating:** 90

best drinking Now–2004 **best vintages** NA **drink with** Antipasto • $23

Isabel Estate Noble Sauvage Late Harvest Sauvignon Blanc

YYYYY 1999 Medium yellow-green; a very complex, concentrated bouquet with cumquat, tropical and apricot fruit aromas is followed by a palate with similar flavours in a rich honey/honeysuckle cradle, finishing with relatively gentle, non-abrasive acidity. **rating:** 90

best drinking Now–2003 **best vintages** '99 **drink with** Fruit tart • NA

jackson estate ★★★★☆

Jacksons Road, Blenheim **region** Marlborough

phone (03) 572 8287 **fax** (03) 572 9500 **open** At Jackson Estate shop, Blenheim airport 9–7.30 or by appointment

winemaker Martin Shaw (Consultant) **production** 22 000 **est.** 1988

product range ($10.55–30 ML) Riesling, Dry Riesling, Sauvignon Blanc, Reserve Chardonnay, Botrytis Riesling, Methode Traditionelle, Pinot Noir, Jackson 2000. A top-line maker of Sauvignon Blanc and Chardonnay.

summary Long-term major grape-growers John and Warwick Stichbury, with leading viticulturist Richard Bowling in charge, own substantial vineyards in the Marlborough area and have now established their own winery and brand. The wines are exported to Australia, the UK, the US, Canada and Japan.

Jackson Estate Sauvignon Blanc

YYYYY 2000 Medium yellow-green; a pungent, powerful, almost savoury mix of herb, citrus, mineral and passionfruit aromas come together with remarkable harmony on the gently ripe palate which flows through to a long finish. **rating:** 94

best drinking Now **best vintages** '91, '92, '93, '94, '97, '99, '00 **drink with** Calamari • $17

Jackson Estate Pinot Noir

YYYYY 1999 Light to medium red-purple; a spicy, foresty aromatic bouquet is followed by an extremely stylish palate, with that silky smooth, almost slippery, mouthfeel, and a complex array of spice and cherry/plum flavours. **rating:** 90

best drinking Now–2003 **best vintages** '99 **drink with** Rare breast of duck • $30

johanneshof cellars NR

State Highway 1, Koromiko, RD3, Blenheim **region** Marlborough
phone (03) 573 7035 **fax** (03) 573 7034 **open** Tues–Sun 10–4
winemaker Edel Everling, Warwick Foley **production** 4000 **est.** 1991
product range ($15–33.50 R) Riesling, Sauvignon Blanc, Sauvignon Blanc Reserve, Pinot Gris, Chardonnay, Noble Late Harvest, Emmi Méthode Traditionnelle, Summer Pinot Noir (Rosé style), Pinot Noir.
summary Marlborough district winemaker Warwick Foley met his wife-to-be Edel Everling in New Zealand and followed her back to Germany (where her family has a winemaking history) to spend five years studying and working, inter alia at Geisenheim. The couple have returned to New Zealand to make European-style wines in an underground cellar blasted into a hillside between Blenheim and Picton, the surrounding vineyard on slopes as steep as those of the Rhine Valley. Remote from any other winery, but on a major tourist trail. The wines are exported, naturally, to Germany.

Johanneshof Sauvignon Blanc

YYYY **2000** Light green-yellow; the bouquet is ripe and soft, with some faintly nutty/creamy edges; the palate is infinitely tighter and more severe than the bouquet, with minerally/grassy flavours and crisp, crunchy acidity on the finish. **rating:** 86

best drinking Now–2003 **best vintages** NA **drink with** Shellfish • $17.50

Johanneshof Pinot Gris

YYYYY **2000** Light to medium yellow-green; a strong, riveting bouquet with strong overtones of Alsace, slightly oily (but in the best sense); followed by a power-laden palate that carries all of its components (fruit, alcohol, acid) with ease. Terrific stuff. **rating:** 95

best drinking Now–2005 **best vintages** '00 **drink with** Pork neck in white wine • $24

Johanneshof Marlborough Chardonnay

YYYY **1997** Medium yellow-green; barrel-ferment and oak characters dominate the palate, with some cashew from what I take to be malolactic fermentation. Against the odds, I quite like the texture, structure and mouthfeel that focuses on fig and cashew, with a good finish and aftertaste. The most remarkable feature of the wine is its youth. **rating:** 87

best drinking Now–2004 **best vintages** NA **drink with** Shellfish • $20

Johanneshof Pinot Noir

YYYY **2000** Light to medium red-purple; as one might expect, a youthful bouquet, as yet slightly unformed, with some spice and an earthy tang. The palate is light, with flickers of style, and tangy small berry fruit flavours. **rating:** 83

best drinking Now **best vintages** NA **drink with** Fresh salmon • $19.95

johner & schubert NR

57 Cambridge Road, Martinborough **region** Wairarapa
phone (06) 306 8505 **fax** (06) 306 8506 **open** Not
winemaker Karl-Heinz Johner **production** NA **est.** 2001
product range Pinot Noir.
summary Karl-Heinz Johner and Kai Schubert (the latter the viticulturist) have established a pinot noir vineyard at East Taratahi, south of Masterton and near Gladstone Winery. Their shop-front is in the main part of town, and the first vintage was made in 2001. Most of the production will be exported to Germany.

john mellars of great barrier island NR

Okupu Beach, Great Barrier Island **region** Northland and Matakana
phone (09) 429 0361 **fax** (09) 429 0370 **open** By appointment
winemaker John Mellars **production** 100 **est.** 1990
product range ($35 R) Great Barrier Cabernet.
summary The winery's hectare of vines is planted on a steep, stony slope facing the nearby sea, and is the only planting on the island. Output is tiny and likely to remain so, perhaps fortunate given that access to the cellar door is either a ten-minute beach and track walk or by dinghy from a boat. Judging by the newsletter, those who make the effort will be rewarded by a delightfully eccentric and humorous John Mellars in person.

kahurangi estate NR

Sunrise Road, RD1, Upper Moutere **region** Nelson
phone (03) 543 2980 **fax** (03) 543 2981 **open** 7 days 10.30–5, September 1–April 30
winemaker Saralinda MacMillan **production** 7000 **est.** 1998
product range ($17–21 CD) Dry Riesling, Gewurztraminer, Sauvignon Blanc, Unwooded Chardonnay, Chardonnay, Pinot Noir.
summary Greg and Amanda Day purchased the vineyard and winery which is now Kahurangi Estate in 1998. It had been planted in the early 1970s by district veterans Agnes and Hermann Seifried, who had long since outgrown the property and built a new winery elsewhere. There are 10 hectares of vineyard planted to riesling, chardonnay, pinot noir, sauvignon blanc and gewurztraminer, together with a substantial winery, cellar-door sales and café area, and a fully refurbished self-contained two-bedroom cottage available for hire. Roseworthy graduates Saralinda MacMillan (winemaker) and Frank Foreman (viticulturist) run the grape-growing and winemaking.

Kahurangi Estate Moutere Dry Riesling

YYYY **1999** Light yellow-green; a clean and crisp bouquet with touches of lime and herb picks up weight on the palate with similar flavours and a lengthy, dry finish. **rating:** 86

best drinking Now–2004 **best vintages** NA **drink with** Summer salad • $17.95

Kahurangi Estate Gewurztraminer

YYYY **2000** Light yellow-green; attractive spicy floral/rose-petal aromas introduce a palate in classic cellar-door style, with neatly balanced sweetness and acidity, but without losing the varietal character shown on the bouquet. **rating:** 85

best drinking Now–2002 **best vintages** NA **drink with** Lightly spiced Asian • $17.95

Kahurangi Estate Sauvignon Blanc

YYYY **1999** Light straw-green; the bouquet has gentle but quite pronounced tropical and gooseberry aromas, the light- to medium-bodied palate following in the same path, crisp and lively throughout. **rating:** 87

best drinking Now **best vintages** NA **drink with** Deep-fried calamari • $17.95

Kahurangi Estate Pinot Noir

YYYY **1999** Light red-purple; a bright and fresh bouquet with light plum and cherry fruit, complexed by a hint of spice, leads through to a palate that puts some sappy/savoury touches around the red berry fruits of the bouquet; subtle oak and good length. **rating:** 88

best drinking Now–2003 **best vintages** NA **drink with** Yakitori chicken • $20.95

kaikoura wine company ★★★★

140 State Highway 1, Kaikoura **region** Kaikoura
phone (03) 319 4440 **fax** (03) 319 4441 **open** 7 days 10–5.30
winemaker Mike Just, Jo-Anne Logan (Assistant) **production** 1650 **est.** 1998
product range ($12–25 CD) Reisling, Gewurztraminer, Sauvignon Blanc, Chardonnay (unoaked), Rosé, Pinot Noir, Méthode Champenoise.
summary Conceived and founded by Kaikoura-born Ross Lawson, a direct descendant of Luke and Anne Abraham, the first Europeans to settle at Kaikoura (halfway between Blenheim and Christchurch). The brand-new 150-tonne winery, with 5 hectares of surrounding vineyard, is situated on a limestone bluff with views of snow-capped mountain ranges on one side and the Pacific ocean on the other. Its six shareholders are all involved in various aspects of the business, which is buying grapes from Marlborough until its own vineyards and local contract-growers fill the breach.

Kaikoura Riesling

YYYY **2000** Light green-yellow; a moderately intense mix of tropical pineapple and lime with splashes of herb lead into a full-flavoured palate, spurred on by easily perceived residual sugar. **rating:** 84

best drinking Now **best vintages** '99 **drink with** Chinese pork • $16

Kaikoura Méthode Champenoise

YYYY **NV** Light straw-green; the bouquet has aromas of wheat, hay, nuts and some aldehyde; the textured palate has creamy/nutty flavours before moving through to a complex but dry finish. **rating:** 85

best drinking Now **best vintages** NA **drink with** Aperitif • $25

kaimira estate winery 

121 River Terrace Road, RD1, Bridgewater, Nelson **region** Nelson
phone (03) 542 3431 **fax** (03) 542 3431 **open** By appointment
winemaker Jane Cooper **production** 4000 **est.** 1997
product range ($16–24 R) Riesling, Dry Riesling, Sauvignon Blanc, Pinot Gris, Golden Bay Chardonnay, Golden Bay Pinot Noir, Brightwater Pinot Noir.
summary The husband-and-wife team of Ian Miller and June Hamilton planted the Kaimira Estate vineyard in 1997 and built a 12 000-case winery in time for the 1999 vintage. Kaimira Estate will act as a contract winemaker until such time as its own 6.5-hectare vineyard comes into full bearing, and is supplementing its own label production with limited amounts of contract-grown grapes from the Nelson area.

Kaimira Estate Nelson Sauvignon Blanc

▼▼▼▼ **2000** Light yellow-green; the bouquet is soft, with a mix of gooseberry and gentle tropical fruit aromas, characters that come through in identical fashion on the light- to medium-bodied palate. No one could dislike a wine such as this. **rating:** 85

best drinking Now **best vintages** NA **drink with** Soft-shell crab • $16.50

Kaimira Estate Brightwater Pinot Noir

▼▼▼▼ **1999** Medium red-purple; distinctive, sweet plummy fruit with a nice touch of spice and French oak; the palate has appealing, fresh plummy fruit, spicy overtones, good extract and particularly appealing slippery tannins on the finish. **rating:** 89

best drinking Now–2004 **best vintages** '99 **drink with** Smoked duck • $24

---

kaituna valley 

230 Kaituna Valley Road, RD2, Christchurch **region** Canterbury
phone (03) 329 0110 **fax** (03) 329 0113 **open** Not
winemaker Grant Whelan, Helen Whelan **production** 1000 **est.** 1993
product range ($17–30 R) Awatere Vineyard Sauvignon Blanc, Pinot Noir.
summary Grant and Helen Whelan bring considerable skills to this tiny venture: Grant Whelan was a tutor in wine science and viticulture at Lincoln University before becoming winemaker for Rossendale Wines in Christchurch, while Helen has a PhD in plant pathology. The vineyard is established on the Banks Peninsula on a north-facing, non-irrigated slope. Extensive canopy work paid dramatic dividends with the first vintage (1993), and subsequent vintages have proved that the early success was no fluke. Regrettably, no recent tastings; if there had been, I suspect the winery would receive a higher rating.

kanuka forest wines NR

Moore Road, Thornton, RD2, Whakatane **region** Waikato and Bay of Plenty
phone (07) 304 9963 **fax** (07) 304 9963 **open** Weekends 10–6, Tues–Fri 3–6
winemaker Tony Hassall **production** 500 **est.** 1992
product range ($12.50–20 CD) Rangitaiki River Sauvignon Blanc, Whale Island Cabernet Sauvignon Merlot.
summary The Hassalls established the 3-hectare vineyard in 1992, selling it to Gerrit and Will Kruithoed in 1997. The tiny amount of wine that comes from the vineyard has been made at Ohinemuri Estate, but plans are afoot to equip a small winery on the property.

kawarau estate 

Rapid number 927, Cromwell–Wanaka Highway, SH6, Cromwell **region** Central Otago
phone (03) 445 1315 **fax** (03) 215 9356 **open** By appointment
winemaker Dean Shaw (Contract) **production** 1400 **est.** 1992
product range ($17–31.90 CD) Sauvignon Blanc, Chardonnay, Reserve Chardonnay, Pinot Noir, Reserve Pinot Noir.
summary Kawarau Estate is owned by four partners: Wendy Hinton and Charles Finney, and Geoff Hinton and Nicola Sharp-Hinton; Geoff is the vineyard manager and Nicola the marketing and sales manager. The 8.5-hectare Dunstan Vineyard at Lowburn, 10 kilometres north of Cromwell, which is managed according to strict organic principles, has been the principal source of grapes. Exports to the UK and the US.

Kawarau Estate Sauvignon Blanc

YYYYY **2000** Light straw-green; an intensely fragrant passionfruit and grapefruit aroma has a reductive edge to it which the distinguished French researcher Dennis Dubourdieu says is part and parcel of such a wine. The same intense passionfruit/grapefruit flavours come through on the long, lingering palate. **rating:** 92

best drinking Now **best vintages** '00 **drink with** Ratatouille • $17

kemblefield estate ★★★★

Aorangi Road, RD1, Hastings **region** Hawke's Bay

phone (06) 874 9649 **fax** (06) 874 9457 **open** Mon–Fri 9–5, weekends 11–3

winemaker John Kemble **production** 16 000 **est.** 1993

product range ($16–36 CD) Gewürztraminer, Sauvignon Blanc, Reserve Sauvignon Blanc, Chardonnay, Merlot Cabernet, Merlot, Reserve Merlot; also Terrace View range of Sauvignon Blanc, Chardonnay and Cabernet Sauvignon Merlot.

summary With 8.6 hectares of sauvignon blanc, 15 hectares of chardonnay, 14.6 hectares of merlot and 8.3 hectares of cabernet sauvignon together with other varieties, lifting the total to 59 hectares, Kemblefield Estate has accelerated out of the blocks since it graduated from grape-growing to winemaking in 1994. John Kemble, incidentally, is a graduate of UC Davis, and worked in California for 15 years before moving to Hawke's Bay. Exports to the UK, the US, Switzerland, Sweden, Canada, Germany and Japan.

Kemblefield Estate Terrace View Sauvignon Blanc

YYYY **2000** Light to medium yellow-green; the bouquet is clean, with touches of citrus and lemon; the light- to medium-bodied palate is smooth, with well-balanced citrussy/lemony/herby fruit and soft acidity. **rating:** 85

best drinking Now **best vintages** NA **drink with** Takeaway • $17

Kemblefield Estate Reserve Merlot

YYYYY **1998** Medium to full red-purple; voluminous, dense, ripe fruit on the bouquet seems to say more about Cabernet than Merlot, and the palate is built in similar Battlestar class. Here, complex, ripe blackberry fruit has spice, and even a touch of anise; a very powerful wine. Whether seduction or rape, hard to deny its Winner Best Merlot or Merlot Blend at the 2001 Small Vigneron Awards. **rating:** 93

best drinking 2003–2008 **best vintages** '98 **drink with** Roast venison • $35.95

kenley vineyard NR

Earnscleugh Road, RD, Alexandra **region** Central Otago

phone (03) 449 2674 **fax** (03) 440 2064 **open** Not

winemaker Black Ridge (Contract) **production** 300 **est.** 1989

product range ($12–20 R) Riesling, Gewurztraminer, Sauvignon Blanc, Pinot Noir.

summary Ken and Bev Boddy have taken the slow boat in establishing their 1-hectare Kenley Vineyard. Ken Boddy became interested in the possibility of growing grapes in the Central Otago region in the mid-1960s during his time as a staff bacteriologist at the Oamaru Hospital. He corresponded with institutions around the world as well as New Zealand's Te Kauwhata Research Station, the latter giving him scant encouragement but eventually supplying him with grape cuttings that formed the nucleus of a back-garden nursery vineyard. Another 20 years were to pass before the Boddys acquired their present vineyard site (in 1989), planting 0.5 hectare of pinot noir and 0.5 hectare of gewurztraminer. They have 10 hectares available for planting, and Ken Boddy is currently evaluating the potential for scheurebe and viognier through trial plantings of each. Even after this long time, they appear to be in no great hurry.

kennedy point vineyard NR

44 Donald Bruce Road, Waiheke Island **region** Waiheke Island

phone (09) 372 5600 **fax** (09) 372 6205 **open** Weekends 11–4 or by appointment

winemaker Herb Friedli **production** 280 **est.** 1999

product range ($17–40 R) Marlborough Sauvignon Blanc, Waiheke Island Cabernet Sauvignon.

summary Susan McCarthy (who has traded one island, Hawaii, for another) and Neal Kunimura have established a combined olive plantation and vineyard on a narrow peninsula on the southern side of Waiheke Island. A micro-winery and tasting facility has been established, and a guesthouse with sea and vineyard views is available, sleeping up to six people. The first vintage of 1999 Waiheke Cabernet Sauvignon has been well received; a Marlborough-sourced Sauvignon Blanc has been added to the range, rather like Goldwater Estate.

kerr farm vineyard NR

48 Dysart Lane, Kumeu, Auckland **region** Auckland Area
phone (09) 412 7575 **fax** (09) 412 7575 **open** Sat 11–6 or by appointment
winemaker Brent Marris **production** 2800 **est.** 1989
product range ($14.95–23 CD) Semillon, Sauvignon Blanc, Chardonnay, Limited Release Kumeu Chardonnay, Pinotage, Cabernet Sauvignon.
summary Jason and Wendy Kerr have established 7.5 hectares of vines on the site of an old Corbans vineyard; their first wines were made in 1995.

kim crawford wines ★★★★☆

Clifton Road, Te Awanga, Hawke's Bay **region** Hawke's Bay
phone (09) 529 0804 **fax** (09) 529 0805 **open** Summer 7 days, winter Thur–Mon 11–6
winemaker Kim Crawford **production** 22 000 **est.** 1996
product range ($15–40 R) Marlborough Dry Riesling, Hawke's Bay Semillon, Marlborough Sauvignon Blanc, Awatere Sauvignon, Marlborough Unoaked Chardonnay, Tietjen Gisborne Chardonnay, Te Awanga Chardonnay, Boyzown Marlborough Pinot Gris, Brut Rory, Pinot Noir, Te Awanga Merlot, East Coast Merlot Cabernet Franc; Pia, Tané, Reka.
summary Kim Crawford first made his reputation as winemaker at Coopers Creek, then as consultant winemaker for a number of vineyards, and now as the producer of a number of very good wines under his own label (as well as wines made for others), sourced from vineyards in Marlborough, Hawke's Bay and Gisborne. Exports to Australia, the UK, the US and Europe. Wine sales and tastings at Clifton Road, RD2, Hastings, Hawke's Bay.

Kim Crawford Marlborough Dry Riesling

YYYYY **2000** Light green-yellow; a highly floral and rich bouquet with a mix of apple and lime leads into a palate with great power and intensity, high acidity balanced against some residual sugar and substantial alcohol. It is a balancing act that only Kim Crawford seems able to pull off. Gold medal winner at the Royal Easter Wine Show 2001. **rating:** 94

best drinking 2002–2007 **best vintages** '97, '98, '00 **drink with** Calamari • $17

Kim Crawford Marlborough Sauvignon Blanc

YYYYỲ **2000** Light green-yellow; a potent, pungent grass and herb bouquet is followed by a palate that is at once delicate yet complex, with excellent mouthfeel and balance, in many ways a complete contrast to the message of the bouquet. Together, it all works well. **rating:** 91

best drinking Now **best vintages** '97, '00 **drink with** Salmon terrine • $20

Kim Crawford Marlborough Unoaked Chardonnay

YYYY **2000** Light green-yellow; the bouquet is quite complex, with creamy characters alongside more minerally notes; however, the palate seems to have shed a lot of the varietal fruit flavour, making one wonder whether a less aggressive approach might not have produced a better wine. **rating:** 86

best drinking Now **best vintages** NA **drink with** Chinese prawns • $20

kingsley estate ★★★★★

PO Box 1100, Hastings **region** Hawke's Bay
phone (025) 454 780 **open** Not
winemaker Kingsley Tobin **production** 1400 **est.** 1991
product range ($39 ML) Merlot, Cabernet Sauvignon.
summary Kingsley Tobin has established a 5-hectare vineyard in Gimblett Road with certified Bio-Gro™ status. Most of the grapes are sold; a small but increasing portion is made at Trinity Hill, but Tobin does have plans to establish his own storage facility at the vineyard and to expand production. The superb but tiny production of Merlot and Cabernet Sauvignon is sold by mail order, with a few cases exported to Denmark and Malaysia.

Kingsley Estate Gimblett Road Merlot

YYYYY **1998** Medium red-purple; fragrant and intensely sweet small berry varietal fruit on the bouquet flows seamlessly into the almost satin-like medium-bodied palate, with seductive oak and fine-grained soft tannins. **rating:** 94

best drinking 2003–2008 **best vintages** '98 **drink with** Roast veal • $39

Kingsley Estate Gimblett Road Cabernet Sauvignon

YYYYY **1998** Medium to full red-purple; the spotlessly clean bouquet is redolent of blackberry and blackcurrant fruit augmented by a dash of spicy oak. The palate is positively luscious, with more of the blackberry and blackcurrant fruit of the bouquet, nice oak and soft tannins. **rating:** 94

best drinking 2003–2008 **best vintages** '98 **drink with** Shoulder of lamb • $39

konrad & conrad wines NR

706 Waihopai Valley Road, Renwick, Marlborough **region** Marlborough
phone (03) 572 4110 **fax** (03) 572 4113 **open** Not
winemaker Contract **production** 10 000 **est.** 1999
product range ($17.95–18.95 R) Marlborough Riesling, Dry Riesling, Sigrun Noble Riesling, Marlborough Sauvignon Blanc.
summary A father-and-son partnership that has established two vineyards at the extreme upper end of the Waihopai Valley. In total, 29 hectares have been planted, with 25 hectares of sauvignon blanc, together with 3 hectares of riesling and 4 hectares of pinot noir. Reflecting their Australian domicile, the partners are also marketed in Australia.

koura bay wines ★★★★

7 Nursery Road, Seddon **region** Marlborough
phone (03) 578 3882 **fax** (03) 578 3771 **open** By appointment
winemaker Simon Waghorn **production** 2000 **est.** 1997
product range ($16.95–19.95 R) Awatere Valley Riesling, Whalesback Sauvignon Blanc, Mount Fyffe Chardonnay, Sharkstooth Pinot Gris, Blue Duck Pinot Noir.
summary Geoff and Dianne Smith have established 17 hectares of vineyard; they initially sold their grapes to Nobilo and gained recognition for their quality when the 1996 Nobilo Grand Reserve Marlborough Sauvignon Blanc won a gold medal at the Braggato Awards (the medal went to the vineyard, not the winery). This no doubt prompted the Smiths to have part of their production vinified for sale under the Koura Bay label; since 1998 Whitehaven Wines has fulfilled that task. Exports to Australia, Ireland, Canada and the UK.

Koura Bay Awatere Valley Riesling

YYYY **2000** Light green-yellow; the bouquet is quite complex, with lime, lemon, mineral and herb aromas, the palate literally packed with flavour, the touch of sweetness justified by the power and depth of the fruit. **rating:** 80

best drinking 2002–2007 **best vintages** '00 **drink with** Vegetarian • $16.95

kumeu river wines ★★★★☆

550 Highway 16, Kumeu **region** Auckland Area
phone (09) 412 8415 **fax** (09) 412 7627 **open** Mon–Fri 9–5.30, Sat 11–5.30
winemaker Michael Brajkovich **production** 20 000 **est.** 1944
product range ($12–45 CD) At the top end: limited-production Maté Vineyard Chardonnay; then the Kumeu River range of Chardonnay, Pinot Gris, Pinot Noir and Melba (Merlot Malbec Cabernet Franc); the less-expensive Brajkovich Signature range: Sauvignon Blanc, Chardonnay, Pinot Noir, Merlot and Cabernet Franc.
summary The wines of Michael Brajkovich defy conventional classification, simply because the highly trained, highly skilled and highly intelligent Brajkovich does not observe convention in crafting them, preferring instead to follow his own French-influenced instincts and preferences. The wines enjoy strong export markets in the US, the UK, Hong Kong, Japan, Belgium, Denmark, France, Italy, Switzerland and Australia.

lake chalice wines ★★★★

Vintage Lane (Box 66), Renwick **region** Marlborough
phone (03) 572 9327 **fax** (03) 572 9327 **open** Mon–Sat 10.30–4.30
winemaker Matt Thomson, Chris Gambitsis **production** 10 000 **est.** 1989
product range ($16.95–24.50 R) The Black Label range of Marlborough Riesling, Marlborough Sauvignon Blanc, Marlborough Chardonnay, Marlborough Botrytised Riesling, Merlot; the Platinum range of Chardonnay, Merlot and Cabernet Sauvignon.
summary Lake Chalice Wines is a partnership of three long-time friends, Chris Gambitsis, Ron Wichman and Phil Binnie. In 1989 they purchased the 11.5-hectare Falcon Vineyard; the name of the winery comes from a

wilderness lake situated in the Richmond Range, which borders the northern side of Marlborough's Wairau Plain. Another 12 hectares have been acquired and planted to sauvignon blanc and pinot noir. The first wine release was in 1993; the first red wine was released in 1997. Exports to Australia and the US.

landmark estate wines NR

132 Bruce McLaren Road, Henderson, Auckland **region** Auckland Area
phone (09) 838 8459 **fax** (09) 837 4939 **open** Not
winemaker Zlatomir Vitasovich **production** NA **est.** 1937
product range ($12–30 R) Headed by the infrequently released Earls label; then Landmark Estate ($11–17) with Chardonnay and Gewurztraminer from Gisborne, Sauvignon Blanc, Chenin Blanc and Cabernet Sauvignon from Hawke's Bay; the Albatross Point label ($11–14) at the bottom with a series of blended and varietal wines.
summary One of the long-established Auckland wineries; has moved with the times and now sources almost all of its grapes from Gisborne and Hawke's Bay.

langdale estate NR

Langdale Road, West Melton, Christchurch **region** Canterbury
phone (03) 342 6266 **fax** (03) 342 4059 **open** Tues–Thur 11–5, Fri–Sat 11–late, Sun 11–6
winemaker Carol Bunn **production** 3000 **est.** 1989
product range ($12.95–31.95 R) Riesling, Marlborough Sauvignon Blanc, Pinot Gris, Chardonnay, Breidecker, Pinot Noir, Melton Hills Pinot Noir.
summary Based upon 4.5 hectares of estate vineyards planted to pinot noir, riesling, breidecker and pinot gris, with plantings commencing in 1989 and expanded since. Until 1998 the wines were made elsewhere, but in that year an on-site winery was constructed prior to the vintage. Most of the wine is sold through the cellar door and restaurant and wedding function centre on site.

Langdale Estate Riesling

🍷🍷🍷🍷 **2000** Light yellow-green; the bouquet is clean and intense, with lime and ripe apple aromatics; the quite powerful palate is distinguished by its crisp yet ripe fruit flavours, and the skilful offsetting of subliminal residual sugar against crisp acidity, all of which significantly enhance the length of the wine. **rating:** 89

best drinking 2002–2007 **best vintages** '00 **drink with** Warm scallop salad • $18

larcomb vineyard NR

Larcombs Road, RD5, Christchurch **region** Canterbury
phone (03) 347 8909 **open** Tues–Sun 11–5 Nov–March, Fri–Sun 11–5 Apr–Oct
winemaker Alan McCorkindale (Contract) **production** 1300 **est.** 1985
product range ($14–19 CD) Riesling, Breidecker, Gewurztraminer, Pinot Gris, Chardonnay, Pinot Noir.
summary Following its acquisition by Michelle and Warren Barnes in 1995, the winery has apparently obtained a reputation for itself as 'home of Rattle the Rafters Barn Dance', which, if nothing else, is something different.

lawson's dry hills ★★★★☆

Alabama Road, Blenheim **region** Marlborough
phone (03) 578 7674 **fax** (03) 578 7603 **open** 7 days 10–5
winemaker Mike Just **production** 25 000 **est.** 1992
product range ($17–25 R) Riesling, Gewurztraminer, Sauvignon Blanc, Chardonnay, Late Harvest Riesling, Pinot Noir.
summary Lawson's Dry Hills is situated on the Wither Hills, which in turn take their name from their parched midsummer look. It is part-owned by Barbara and Ross Lawson, recently joined by three shareholders who have contributed vineyards, giving a total of 22 hectares. The partners have all graduated from being grape-growers to winemakers with conspicuous success, and production is steadily rising. Exports to Australia, the UK, the US, Brazil, the Netherlands, Italy, Ireland, France, Denmark, Switzerland, Singapore and Hong Kong.

Lawson's Dry Hills Riesling

🍷🍷🍷🍷🍷 **2000** Light to medium yellow-green; a clean and pure bouquet with lime, mineral and apple aromatics flows into an equally crisp, clean and pure palate, with lingering lime flavours, and excellent balance and acidity. **rating:** 93

best drinking Now–2006 **best vintages** '94, '98, '00 **drink with** Asparagus with hollandaise sauce • $19

Lawson's Dry Hills Gewurztraminer

TTTTY **2000** Light green-yellow; powerful spice and lychee aromas flow into the V8 engine of the palate, reflecting the 14.5° alcohol. This is Gewurztraminer from the big end of town. **rating:** 92

TTTTY **1999** Medium yellow-green; scented, spice, lychee and rose-petal aromas are followed by a powerful palate, with more spice and lychee flavours, and (by New Zealand standards), a particularly firm and pleasantly dry finish. **rating:** 90

best drinking Now–2004 **best vintages** '98, 99, '00 **drink with** Delicate Asian seafood • $22

Lawson's Dry Hills Sauvignon Blanc

TTTTY **2000** Light to medium yellow-green; a pungently scented bouquet with masses of gooseberry and passionfruit, coupled with that faint touch of reduction that seems (almost) par for the course, then a power-packed palate with a mix of passionfruit, gooseberry, capsicum and mineral. **rating:** 92

best drinking Now **best vintages** '94, '97, '99, '00 **drink with** Crayfish • $20

Lawson's Dry Hills Chardonnay

TTTTY **1999** Medium yellow-green; the bouquet is complex, with a mix of tangy barrel-ferment and bottle-development aromatics. The palate, too, is complex, showing the various inputs of the bouquet, but has considerable fruit intensity. I like the outcome. **rating:** 92

best drinking Now–2003 **best vintages** '93, '94, '99 **drink with** Coquilles St Jacques • $25

leaning rock vineyard ★★★☆

Hillview Road, Alexandra **region** Central Otago
phone (03) 448 9169 **fax** (03) 448 9169 **open** By appointment
winemaker Mark Hesson, Dhana Pillai **production** 1000 **est.** 1991
product range ($18–28 CD) Riesling, Gewurztraminer, Chardonnay, Pinot Noir.
summary Notwithstanding bare gravel soils and a northerly slope, spring frosts proved a major problem for geologist owners Mark Hesson and Dhana Pillai, curtailing production until sprinklers were installed prior to the 1996 growing season. Small quantities of strongly flavoured wines were then produced, with gradually increasing quantities (particularly Pinot Noir) expected over coming vintages.

Leaning Rock Vineyard Rise and Shine Pinot Noir

TTTT **1999** Light to medium red-purple; the cherry-accented bouquet has aromatic spicy/foresty sidelights; the palate has nice balance and weight, with cherry and plum fruit, and a slight tannin twitch on the finish. **rating:** 88

best drinking 2002–2006 **best vintages** '97, '98 **drink with** Braised duck Chinese style • $30

le brun family estate ★★★★

169 Rapaura Road, Rapaura, RD3, Blenheim **region** Marlborough
phone (03) 572 9876 **fax** (03) 572 9875 **open** Summer 7 days 10–4.30, winter Mon–Fri 10–3
winemaker Daniel Le Brun **production** 2000 **est.** 1996
product range ($29-35) Daniel Le Brun Methode Traditionnelle, Blanc de Blancs
summary This is the new venture of Daniel and Adele Le Brun, and, like their former winery (Cellier Le Brun), is a sparkling wine specialist, drawing on 4 hectares of estate vineyards. The quality of the wines so far released is beyond reproach.

Daniel Le Brun Methode Traditionnelle

TTTT **NV** Light yellow-green; the bouquet has a nice balance of fruit and bready autolysis characters, the edge of aldehyde being within tolerance. The palate strikes off on a direction of its own: bright, clean and citrussy. **rating:** 89

best drinking Now **best vintages** NA **drink with** Shellfish • $29

Daniel Le Brun Blanc de Blancs

TTTTY **1996** Very good green-yellow; a clean, fresh and crisp bouquet with a nice mix of bready autolysis and citrus/melon fruit. The medium-weight palate is fresh, long and lively, with lingering nutty/citrussy flavours on the finish. **rating:** 90

best drinking Now–2004 **best vintages** '96 **drink with** Aperitif • $35

limeburners bay NR

112 Hobsonville Road, Hobsonville **region** Auckland Area
phone (09) 416 8844 **open** Mon–Sat 9–6
winemaker Alan Laurenson **production** 3500 **est.** 1978
product range ($7–19.95 CD) Müller Thurgau, Semillon Chardonnay, Sauvignon Blanc, Chardonnay, Cabernet Merlot, Cabernet Sauvignon.
summary Initially established a reputation for itself in the 1980s with some good Cabernet Sauvignon, but with more variable outcomes in the 1990s. No recent tastings.

lincoln vineyards ★★★

130 Lincoln Road, Henderson **region** Auckland Area
phone (09) 838 6944 **fax** (09) 838 6984 **open** Mon–Fri 9–5.30, weekends 10–6
winemaker Joseph Papesch **production** 35 000 **est.** 1937
product range ($11–57 CD) The wines are now labelled in three tiers: the top of the range President's Selection; then comes the Heritage Collection; and (quaintly) the Winemaker's Reserve Range at the cheapest end of the products. The usual varieties are incorporated, with a hefty reliance on Chardonnay.
summary A substantial family-owned operation drawing its grapes from Auckland, Gisborne and Hawke's Bay. The labels are avant-garde, but the wines have been variable, good at best but sometimes disappointing, even if the prices are competitive. However, recent moves to consolidate production with greater emphasis on quality reflect an attempt to iron out the variability problem. Exports to the UK, Taiwan, Japan, Thailand and Canada.

Lincoln Heritage Collection Chardonnay

YYYY **2000** Medium yellow-green; very obvious, slightly pencilly barrel-ferment oak on the bouquet carries through to the palate, where there is quite sweet peachy fruit. Precocious flavour; drink as soon as possible.
rating: 84

best drinking Now **best vintages** NA **drink with** Tempura • $18

Lincoln President's Selection Chardonnay

YYYY **2000** Medium yellow-green; subtle barrel-ferment and malolactic influences provide a seamless mix of cashew and melon on the bouquet; the palate has plenty of rich flavour, with quite a deal of oak, and gives the impression it will develop rapidly. **rating:** 87

best drinking Now **best vintages** NA **drink with** Crumbed brains • $25

linden estate NR

SH5 Napier–Taupo Road, Esk Valley, RD2, Napier, Hawke's Bay **region** Hawke's Bay
phone (06) 836 6806 **fax** (06) 836 6586 **open** 7 days 10–5
winemaker Nicholas Chan **production** 12 000 **est.** 1971
product range ($18–25 CD) Old Vine Gewurztraminer, Sauvignon Blanc, Chardonnay Esk Valley, Whole Bunch Press Chardonnay, Reserve Chardonnay, Caprice (dessert wine), Merlot Esk Valley, Dam Block Cabernet Merlot, Cabernet Esk Valley.
summary This is the project of retired civil engineer and long-term grape-grower Wim van der Linden and family, son John being a tutor in viticulture at the Polytechnic in Hawke's Bay. The estate vineyard was replanted in 1989 to 13 hectares of premium varieties, including a 2.5-hectare hillside planting producing a Reserve wine first released in 1996. The wines are distributed in New Zealand (Eurowine), and exported to the UK, Denmark, the Netherlands, Switzerland, Canada and the US.

lintz estate NR

Kitchener Street, Martinborough **region** Wairarapa
phone (06) 306 9174 **fax** (06) 306 9175 **open** By appointment while stocks last
winemaker Chris Lintz **production** 5800 **est.** 1989
product range ($15–65 CD) Fraters Rise Range of Waipipi Riesling, Sauvignon Blanc, Chenin Blanc, Golden Slope Chardonnay, Cabernet Sauvignon Merlot, Cabernet Sauvignon; Saint Anthony Riesling, Reserve Riesling, Chardonnay Barrique Ferment, Pinot Noir, Pinot Noir Barrique Selection, Moy Hall Pinot Noir, Cabernet Merlot #1, Franc Merlot, Renaissance, Vitesse Cabernet Sauvignon, Muscat, Optima Noble Selection.

summary New Zealand-born Chris Lintz comes from a German winemaking family and graduated from Geisenheim. The first stage of the Lintz winery, drawing grapes from the 9-hectare vineyard, was completed in 1991. Since 1996 Lintz Estate has enjoyed much show success, winning numerous gold medals across the full range of wines, both white and red, success that underpinned a public issue of shares in 1998. Exports to the UK and the US.

lombardi wines NR

298 Te Mata Road, Havelock North **region** Hawke's Bay
phone (06) 877 7985 **fax** (06) 877 7816 **open** 7 days 10–5
winemaker Tracy Haslam **production** 6000 **est.** 1948
product range ($11.95–30 CD) Barrel Fermented Sauvignon Blanc, Barrel Fermented Chardonnay, Methode Champenoise, Merlot Cabernet, Merlot Cabernet Reserve, Ports, Liqueurs.
summary Once the Australian Riverland transported to the unlikely environment of Hawke's Bay, with a half-Italian, half-English family concentrating on a kaleidoscopic array of Vermouths and sweet, flavoured fortified wines. A change of ownership at the end of 1994 shifted the focus to a product range more in keeping with Hawke's Bay, and with some success.

Lombardi Merlot Cabernet Reserve

TTTT **1998** Medium red-purple; a savoury red berry bouquet is followed by a palate with attractive red and blackcurrant fruit flavours, nicely resolved tannins and just the barest support of oak. **rating:** 89
best drinking 2003–2008 **best vintages** '98 **drink with** Rare T-bone steak • $30

longbush wines NR

State Highway 2, Manutuke, Gisborne **region** Gisborne
phone (06) 862 8577 **fax** (06) 867 8012 **open** Tues–Sun 10–5 Oct–Easter
winemaker John Thorpe **production** 15 000 **est.** 1992
product range ($10–20 R) Woodlands Gewurztraminer, Chardonnay, Merlot Cabernet Franc; the Longbush range of Chardonnay, Pinot Noir, Merlot; Nicks Head Sol Muscat Muller Thurgau, Chardonnay, Merlot.
summary Part of the ever-changing circus of winemaking and brand ventures of the Thorpe Brothers Group. Woodlands is the premium label; Longbush the principal (and mid-range) label; Nicks Head is the third and lowest priced.

longridge of hawke's bay ★★★☆

91 Thames Street, Napier **region** Hawke's Bay
phone (06) 835 4333 **fax** (06) 835 9791 **open** Not
winemaker Kirsty Walton **production** NA **est.** 1944
product range ($12–14 R) Gewurztraminer, Sauvignon Blanc, Chardonnay and Merlot Cabernet.
summary Longridge is the Hawke's Bay brand of Corbans, with its own distinct identity and price point, with all of the products line-priced.

Longridge of Hawke's Bay Sauvignon Blanc

TTTY **1999** Light to medium yellow-green; a big, rich bouquet with obvious bottle-development to the tangy fruit. The palate is similarly rich with gooseberry, pineapple, herb and a touch of spice from the barrel-ferment component; not particularly long, and I suspect would have been at its best in late 1999/early 2000. **rating:** 83
best drinking Now **best vintages** NA **drink with** Creamy goat's cheese • $14

Longridge of Hawke's Bay Cabernet Merlot

TTTY **1999** Medium red-purple; the bouquet is light, fresh and clean with red berry fruit and subliminal oak. On the palate sappy, green herbaceous characters come through in New Zealand style. **rating:** 80
best drinking Now **best vintages** NA **drink with** Spaghetti bolognaise • $14

longview estate NR

State Highway 1, Whangarei **region** Northland and Matakana
phone (09) 438 7227 **fax** (09) 438 7224 **open** Summer Mon–Sat 8.30–6; winter Sat 8.30–5.30, Sun 9–5
winemaker Mario Vuletich **production** 2800 **est.** 1969

product range ($12–27 CD) Unwooded Chardonnay, Barrique Chardonnay, Reserve Chardonnay, Gewurztraminer, Northern White, White Diamond, Scarecrow Cabernet Sauvignon, Mario's Merlot, Hawke's Bay Merlot, Gumdigger's Port, Golden Sherry, Dry Sherry.
summary Mario and Barbara Vuletich have been involved in viticulture and winemaking since 1969; they have replanted the 6-hectare vineyard on elevated slopes overlooking Whangarei Harbour with the four principal Bordeaux varieties (and shiraz) with the intention of making full-bodied dry reds. They have succeeded handsomely in doing so: both the Cabernet Sauvignon and the Merlot have received four stars in *Cuisine* magazine for the '93, '94 and '96 vintages; the Unwooded Chardonnay has also attracted praise.

loopline vineyard NR

Loopline Road, RD1, Masterton **region** Wairarapa
phone (06) 377 3353 **fax** (06) 378 8338 **open** 7 days 10–6
winemaker Frank Parker **production** 500 **est.** 1994
product range ($17.50–29.50 CD) Riesling, Sauvignon Blanc, Chenin Blanc, Pinot Noir, Merlot, Cabernet Merlot, Joseph's (Cabernet Sauvignon Merlot Cabernet Franc).
summary Frank and Bernice Parker are pioneer viticulturists on the Opaki Plains, 5 kilometres north of Masterton. They have established 1 hectare of riesling and 0.5 hectare of chasselas, supplementing their intake with limited quantities of grapes grown by other producers in the region.

Loopline Riesling

YYYY **2000** Light green-yellow; the bouquet is crisp and clean, with mainstream mineral/lime/apple/herb aromas. The palate has a crisp mix of mineral and herb, and seems barely off-dry. **rating:** 87
best drinking 2002–2006 **best vintages** '00 **drink with** Chinese stir-fried prawns • $19

lucknow estate winery NR

3764 State Highway 50, RD1, Maraekakaho, Hawke's Bay **region** Hawke's Bay
phone (06) 874 9007 **fax** (06) 874 9008 **open** 7 days 10.30–5.30
winemaker Bruce Nimon **production** 2000 **est.** 1998
product range ($14–18 CD) Waihopai Valley Riesling, Dunegen Road Merlot, Cabernet Sauvignon Cabernet Franc.
summary Bruce Nimon graduated with a degree in horticulture, and then left for Australia where he worked as a landscaper. Three years later he returned to New Zealand to a job with Lion Breweries. It was then he was bitten by the wine bug and deliberately sought employment with CJ Pask so he could work with Kate Radburnd, whose wines he particularly admired. He studied winemaking at night, doing a vintage in Oregon with Rex Hill Vineyards in 1995. After five years with Pask he moved to Kemblefield Estate for two years, and then finally realised his ambition of establishing his own business, specialising in Hawke's Bay reds. 'Far too many producers are trying to be everything to everyone; I hope to keep it simple,' he says.

lynskeys wairau peaks ★★★☆

36 Godfrey Road, RD2, Blenheim **region** Marlborough
phone (03) 572 7180 **fax** (03) 572 7181 **open** Summer weekends 10.30–4.30, winter by appointment
winemaker Graeme Paul (Contract) **production** 2000 **est.** 1998
product range ($18–35 CD) Gewurztraminer, Sauvignon Blanc, Chardonnay, Pinot Noir.
summary Ray and Kathy Lynskey bring diverse backgrounds to their newly established business. Kathy Lynskey has moved between Sydney and New Zealand at various times and established her first vineyard in 1989, providing contract-grown chardonnay. She now has a distribution business in Sydney (Lynskeys New Zealand Wine Cellars) selling not only the Lynskey wines but those of Lake Chalice, Le Grys and de Gyffarde. Ray Lynskey is an airline pilot based in Blenheim, flying gliders for relaxation so successfully that he won the world gliding championships at Omarama in 1995. Their 6-hectare vineyard is now in production; the wine is made at Marlborough Vintners. Exports to the US, Canada and Australia.

Lynskeys Wairau Peaks Marlborough Chardonnay

YYYYY **2000** Medium yellow-green; strong barrel-ferment oak drives the bouquet, but on the palate quite rich, ripe tropical fruit is also to be found, and there is good acidity to lengthen the finish. At the baroque end of the spectrum. **rating:** 90
best drinking Now **best vintages** '00 **drink with** Smoked salmon • $22

Lynskeys Wairau Peaks Pinot Noir

YYYY **1999** Quite strong colour; the bouquet is complex, with luscious, ripe plum and black cherry fruit which reappears on the palate; the oak is quite evident and does toughen up the wine a little. **rating:** 86

best drinking Now–2004 **best vintages** NA **drink with** Mushroom risotto • $35

mccashin's ★★★★

664 Main Road, Stoke, Nelson **region** Nelson
phone (03) 547 0205 **fax** (03) 547 6876 **open** 6 days 10–6
winemaker Craig Gass **production** 15 000 **est.** 1999
product range ($16–25 R) Waipara Riesling, Marlborough Sauvignon Blanc, Nelson Sauvignon Blanc, Marlborough Pinot Gris, Marlborough Chardonnay, Marlborough Nelson Pinot Noir, Hawke's Bay Merlot, Hawke's Bay Cabernet Sauvignon, Methode Traditionelle.
summary Normally, brewers and spirit merchants simply go out and acquire wineries created by others. In this instance, McCashin's has done it from scratch, harnessing the unstoppable energy of winemaker Craig Gass, aided by the purchase of a mature 41-hectare vineyard property (from Waimea Estate) prior to the 2000 vintage.

McCashin's Marlborough Sauvignon Blanc

YYYYY **2000** Light green-yellow; a clean, intense bouquet runs the full gamut of gooseberry, citrus, passionfruit and apple, without the slightest hint of reduction. The well-balanced palate simply extends the message of the bouquet, flowing on seamlessly through to the finish. **rating:** 90

best drinking Now **best vintages** '99 **drink with** New Zealand whitebait • $19

McCashin's Hawke's Bay Merlot

YYYY **2000** Youthful purple-red; a bright, fresh, fruit-driven bouquet with lively juicy fruit and just a hint of vanilla oak, then a similarly bright and fresh palate that has not been overworked and allows the sweet fruit full expression. **rating:** 86

best drinking 2002–2006 **best vintages** NA **drink with** Italian • $19.95

mahurangi estate winery NR

162 Hamilton Road, Warkworth **region** Northland and Matakana
phone (09) 425 0306 **fax** (09) 425 0307 **open** Summer weekends, public holidays 10–5 or by appointment
winemaker Various (Contract) **production** est. 1996
product range ($15–21 R) Moutere Riesling, Malborough Sauvignon Blanc, Gisborne Mendoza Chardonnay, Hawke's Bay Merlot Cabernet Sauvignon.
summary Mahurangi Estate was established in 1996 by Colin and Hamish McDonald. It is simultaneously developing two vineyards, with 11 hectares already planted at Matakana and 5.5 hectares on Gimblett Road in Hawke's Bay. The principal varieties are the Bordeaux group of cabernet sauvignon, merlot, cabernet franc and malbec; the Matakana plantings also include syrah, viognier and chardonnay. A winery and café are planned for 2002. In the meantime Mahurangi Estate is buying Mendoza-clone chardonnay from Gisborne, riesling from Nelson and sauvignon blanc from Marlborough to add to its Hawke's Bay Merlot Cabernet Sauvignon. These wines are contract-made by leading winemakers throughout New Zealand.

margrain vineyard ★★★★☆

Ponatahi Road (PO Box 97), Martinborough **region** Wairarapa
phone (06) 306 9292 **fax** (04) 569 2698 **open** Weekends, holidays 11–5
winemaker Strat Canning **production** 3000 **est.** 1992
product range ($16–34 CD) Riesling Dry, Riesling Proprietor's Reserve, Gewurztraminer, Chenin Blanc, Chardonnay, Botrytis Selection Riesling, Rosé, Pinot Noir, Merlot.
summary Graham and Daryl Margrain planted their first vines in 1992 and produced the first wine (Chardonnay) in 1994. The vineyard is now planted to a total of 11 hectares of chardonnay, pinot noir, merlot, gewurztraminer, chenin blanc and pinot gris; eight luxury accommodation villas have been built on an adjoining ridge, and a woolshed has been converted into a conference facility and tasting room. An underground cellar was constructed in 1994, and a winery (including a restaurant) was commissioned for the 1996 vintage, followed by the acquisition of Chifney in early 2000. And what did the Margrains do before they established Margrain Vineyard? They spent 25 years in the building industry, of course. Exports to the UK.

Margrain Proprietor's Selection Riesling

🍷🍷🍷🍷🍷 **2000** Light to medium yellow-green; vibrant and intense, fine lime/lemon aromas are followed by a palate with fantastic fruit intensity and length, showing the same lime and lemon flavours that well and truly balance the residual sugar. **rating:** 94

best drinking 2002–2008 **best vintages** '00 **drink with** Delicate seafood • $23

Margrain Botrytis Selection Riesling

🍷🍷🍷🍷🍷 **2000** Glowing yellow-green; the bouquet is fine, intense and fragrant, botrytis leaping out of the glass. The palate is exceptionally intense and lime-juicy, long and elegant. For me, goes into the highest plane (because the botrytis has not overwhelmed the Riesling varietal character). **rating:** 96

best drinking 2002–2007 **best vintages** '00 **drink with** Poached fruit • $24

Margrain Unfiltered Pinot Noir

🍷🍷🍷🍷🍷 **1999** Medium to full red-purple; a rich, full bouquet with a range of plum, prune, chocolate and spice aromas; the palate confirms the bouquet with a Joseph's coat array of ripe cherry, plum and even citrus flavours; the tannins, while evident, are balanced by all the fruit, and the wine has great length. **rating:** 94

best drinking 2002–2007 **best vintages** '99 **drink with** Ragout of venison • $34

mariri NR

Weka Road, RD2, Upper Moutere, Nelson **region** Nelson
phone (03) 526 6022 **fax** (03) 526 6022 **open** Not
winemaker Antony Heywood **production** NA **est.** 1998
product range ($18 R) Weka Road Block Riesling, Weka Road Block Sauvignon Blanc.
summary Antony Heywood is a graduate of Lincoln College, and makes the wines at Waimea Estate. The name of the vineyard means 'heavenly place', and the plans are to increase production in the years ahead.

martinborough vineyard ★★★★★

Princess Street, Martinborough **region** Wairarapa
phone (06) 306 9955 **fax** (06) 306 9217 **open** 7 days 11–5
winemaker Claire Mulholland **production** 10 000 **est.** 1980
product range ($19–70 R) Chardonnay, Pinot Noir, Pinot Noir Reserve.
summary After almost 15 years of devoted service to Martinborough Vineyards, during which time he lifted its profile to the highest level in both the domestic and international markets, Larry McKenna was effectively squeezed out and is actively developing his own vineyard and consultancy interests in both New Zealand and Australia. Incoming winemaker Claire Mulholland has big shoes to fill, but if she fails to do so, it won't be because of lack of commitment. And for the time being, the five-star rating remains. Exports to Australia, the UK, the US, Canada, Belgium, Germany and Singapore.

Martinborough Vineyard Reserve Pinot Noir

🍷🍷🍷🍷🍷 **1998** Medium to full red-purple; the bouquet has, as one would expect, very ripe plum and spice fruit that stops well short of being overripe or pruney, and a positive but not excessive hint of smoky oak. Again as one would expect, the wine has a full mid-palate, with excellent texture and balance, finishing with soft, ripe tannins. **rating:** 96

best drinking 2002–2008 **best vintages** '94, '96, '98 **drink with** New Zealand venison • $70

matariki wines ★★★★

Kirkwood Road, Hastings **region** Hawke's Bay
phone (06) 879 6226 **open** Mon–Fri 9–5 or by appointment
winemaker John O'Connor, Greg Foster **production** 2500 **est.** 1981
product range ($19.95–38 CD) Sauvignon Blanc, Chardonnay, Syrah, Anthology (Bordeaux-blend), Blanc de Blanc Methode, Late Harvest Riesling, Merlot.
summary John and Rosemary O'Connor purchased their Gimblett Road property in 1981 and are now the owners of the largest individual vineyard in that area, with 30 hectares (of a total 60 hectares) under vine. They have syrah and sauvignon blanc planted on pure shingle, and cabernet franc, cabernet sauvignon, malbec, merlot, semillon and chardonnay on terraces with a greater amount of soil. More recently they purchased a limestone terrace property below Te Mata Peak, which is cooler and has been planted to chardonnay. Currently they share

the Trinity Hill winery with John Hancock; it houses their own winemaking equipment, but they have plans for a large two-storey winery drawn up. The quality of the wines released to date has been impressive. Exports to the UK, the US and Ireland.

Matariki Chardonnay

🍷🍷🍷🍷🍷 **1999** Medium yellow-green; the bouquet shows obvious barrel-ferment characters, but in a complex skein of stonefruit, citrus and mineral. The elegant palate has excellent mouthfeel and length, the oak balanced and integrated. A thoroughly stylish wine. Won gold at the Air New Zealand Wine Awards 2000. **rating:** 92

best drinking Now–2004 **best vintages** '99 **drink with** Sweetbreads • $27.95

Matariki Pinot Noir

🍷🍷🍷🍷 **1999** Deeply coloured; the complex bouquet offers ultra-ripe prune, plum, leather and spice aromas; the texture and feel of the palate has more to do with Pinot Noir than the bouquet, with considerable length and grip, the tannins within bounds. **rating:** 86

best drinking 2002–2007 **best vintages** NA **drink with** Venison • $38

Matariki Hawke's Bay Syrah

🍷🍷🍷🍷🍷 **1999** Bright purple-red; clean black cherry and plum fruit with some leather and a little spice on the bouquet is supported by evident but not aggressive oak. The palate has good weight and richness, but is certainly not heavy or extractive, even having a touch of Pinot-feel. The oak and tannin support the berry/cherry fruit. Sets one of the benchmarks. **rating:** 92

best drinking 2003–2009 **best vintages** '99 **drink with** Beef and mushroom goulash • $30

Matariki Merlot

🍷🍷🍷🍷 **1999** Medium red-purple; the aromatic bouquet has a most attractive mix of very ripe plummy fruit and more savoury notes; subtle oak. The palate, likewise, provides fruit that is ripe and soft in the mouth, offset by savoury/chocolate notes, and finishing with fine but persistent tannins. **rating:** 87

best drinking 2003–2009 **best vintages** NA **drink with** Jugged hare • $29.95

matawhero wines ★★☆

Riverpoint Road, Matawhero **region** Gisborne
phone (06) 868 8366 **fax** (06) 867 9856 **open** Mon–Sat 9–5
winemaker Denis Irwin **production** 6000 **est.** 1975
product range ($15–25 CD) Gewurztraminer, Riesling, Chardonnay, Reserve Chardonnay, Sauvignon Blanc, Chenin, Pinot Noir, Syrah, Cabernet, Bridge Estate.
summary The wines have always been cast in the mould of Matawhero's unpredictable founder and owner, Denis Irwin: at their best, in the guise of the Gewurztraminer from a good vintage, they are quite superb, racy and powerful; at their worst, they are poor and exhibit marked fermentation problems.

matua valley ★★★★

Waikoukou Road, Waimauku **region** Auckland Area
phone (09) 411 8301 **fax** (09) 411 7982 **open** Mon–Fri 9–5, Sat 10–5, Sun 11–4.30
winemaker Mark Robertson, Corey Hall **production** 125 000 **est.** 1974
product range ($11–38 CD) At the bottom end of the market is the Settlers Series wines ($10.95); next is a regional series comprising Hawke's Bay Sauvignon Blanc, Eastern Bays Chardonnay and Cabernet Merlot ($13.95–14.95); then the Shingle Peak range ($13.95–17.95) with Riesling, Sauvignon Blanc, Chardonnay and Pinot Noir; then an estate series from the Matheson Vineyard in Hawke's Bay ($18.45) of Chardonnay, Reserve Sauvignon Blanc and Cabernet Merlot; next is the Innovator Series ($18.95–22.95) for experimental wines, currently including Hand Picked Judd Chardonnay, Alex Chardonnay, Wairarapa Pinot Noir and Matheson Grenache; and at the very top the intermittent releases from exceptional vintages of Ararimu Chardonnay and Merlot Cabernet Sauvignon ($37.95); Sparkling, Fortifieds.
summary One of the stalwarts of the New Zealand wine industry, producing a wide range of wines of good quality. The Shingle Peak label has been particularly successful, while the presentation of the Ararimu Chardonnay and Cabernet Sauvignon (not to mention the quality of the wines) set new standards of excellence for New Zealand. There are substantial exports to the UK, the US, Western Europe, Canada, Hong Kong, Japan and Australia.

Matua Valley Smith-Dartmoor Merlot

ᴛᴛᴛᴛ **2000** Medium to full red-purple; solid dark berry fruit drives the bouquet, moving to blackberry and plum on the clean palate. Oak is but a suggestion in the background. **rating:** 85

best drinking 2002–2006 **best vintages** '98 **drink with** Veal chops • $24

mazuran's vineyard NR

255 Lincoln Road, Henderson **region** Auckland Area
phone (09) 838 6945 **open** Mon–Sat 9–6
winemaker Rado Hladilo **production** 1400 **est.** 1938
product range ($12–350 CD) Sherries and Ports.
summary A Sherry and Port specialist, still surviving on the reputation built for its wines by George Mazuran, who died in 1980. The business is continued by his son and son-in-law. The $350, incidentally, is not a typographical error; it is the price of a 1942 Port.

mebus NR

Dakins Road, RD7, Wairarapa **region** Wairarapa
phone (06) 377 3696 **fax** (06) 377 2922 **open** Not
winemaker Michael Mebus, Hidde Mebus **production** 1000 **est.** 1995
product range ($16–24 R) Sauvignon Blanc, Cabernet Merlot; Chardonnay and Malbec Franc Merlot Cabernet blend scheduled for release late 2001, to be followed by a Pinot Noir in 2002.
summary Brothers Michael and Hidde Mebus have extended the boundaries of the Wairarapa region after a protracted search through various parts of New Zealand for suitable viticultural land. In 1995 they purchased 20 hectares, followed by a further 25 hectares the following year, adjacent to the Ruamahanga River. The stony, gravelly soil is free-draining and similar to that of Martinborough, and the valley situation may give some protection against the ever-present Wairarapa winds. A winery with underground cellars was erected shortly prior to the 2000 vintage; a winery extension allowing a gravity-feed system to be completed over 2001–2002, and, finally, a building 'beautification' is programmed for 2003 to dress up the 200 square-metre shed that presently constitutes the winery.

melness wines ★★★☆

1816 Cust Road, Cust, North Canterbury **region** Canterbury
phone (03) 312 5402 **fax** (03) 512 5466 **open** Summer 7 days 10–5, winter Thurs–Sun 10–4.30
winemaker Mathew Donaldson, Lynette Hudson **production** 1500 **est.** NA
product range ($18–30 CD) Riesling, Sauvignon Blanc, Chardonnay (spray free), Pinot Noir, Merlot Cabernet.
summary The Melness vineyards are run organically, which makes the utilisation of what is claimed to be the only Lyre Trellis system on the South Island all the more understandable (it maximises sunlight and wind penetration). Owners Colin and Norma Marshall have established the winery with a café in a garden setting.

Melness Pinot Noir

ᴛᴛᴛᴛ **1999** Medium red, with some purple hues; the clean, relatively light bouquet offers plum and spice, the attractive palate ranging through spice, plum and a hint of cherry, finishing with soft, fine tannins. All in all, a much lighter touch than was shown in the '98. **rating:** 88

best drinking 2002–2006 **best vintages** '98, '99 **drink with** Rich game • $30

mills reef winery ★★★★☆

Moffat Road, Bethlehem, Tauranga **region** Bay of Plenty
phone (07) 576 8800 **fax** (07) 576 8824 **open** 7 days 10–5
winemaker Paddy Preston, Tim Preston **production** 50 000 **est.** 1989
product range ($11–35 CD) Under the Mills Reef label: Riesling, Sauvignon Blanc, Chenin Chardonnay, Chardonnay, Rosé, Cooks Beach Pinot Noir and Merlot Cabernets; then comes the Reserve range: Riesling, Gewurztraminer, Chenin Blanc, Chardonnay Gisborne, Chardonnay Hawke's Bay, Botrytised Riesling, Merlot, Cabernet Merlot and Cabernet Sauvignon; at the top is the Elspeth range: Chardonnay, Pinot Noir, Syrah, Merlot, Cabernet Syrah Merlot, Cabernet Merlot and Cabernet Sauvignon; Traditional Method comprises Non Vintage and Vintage; Vintage Port.

summary Mills Reef has recently completed a new winery, situated on a 15-hectare vineyard within five minutes of Tauranga, incorporating wine tasting and display rooms, a restaurant and a conference/meeting room, together with usual winemaking facilities. The initial releases from Mills Reef were impressive, and after a wobbly period the flagship Elspeth range is among New Zealand's best. With its Hawke's Bay base, it is able to span Chardonnay, Cabernet-based reds and Méthode Champenoise with equal ease. Exports to the US, Australia, Hong Kong and Japan.

Mills Reef Reserve Riesling

ΨΨΨΨ **2000** Medium green-yellow; the rich and full bouquet has quite voluminous lime/tropical aromas that come through strongly on the full-flavoured, fractionally sweet but very easy-drinking palate. **rating:** 87

best drinking Now **best vintages** NA **drink with** Steamed calamari • $15

Mills Reef Moffat Road Sauvignon Blanc

ΨΨΨΨ **2000** Light to medium yellow-green; clean and vibrant gooseberry and citrus aromas flow through into a lively palate with good length. **rating:** 87

best drinking Now **best vintages** '00 **drink with** Shellfish • $12

Mills Reef Elspeth Syrah

ΨΨΨΨ **1999** Medium purple-red; it's not altogether easy to see just how much fruit there is on the bouquet and palate; it's certainly there, and is ripe, but you have to play hide and seek with it to penetrate the oak. Flavoursome, and will undoubtedly have market appeal. **rating:** 87

best drinking 2002–2006 **best vintages** NA **drink with** Braised beef • $35

Mills Reef Elspeth Merlot Cabernet Syrah

ΨΨΨΨΨ **1999** Medium red-purple; sweet, dark cassis/berry fruit, allied with some plum and cherry (it is a complex blend) has handled the new oak better on the palate than the bouquet. It is on the palate that the underlying concentration of the fruit comes through, with nicely judged tannins. Tasted at the same time as the '98 version, and, not surprisingly, the '98 ranked significantly higher (93 points). **rating:** 90

best drinking 2004–2009 **best vintages** '98 **drink with** Roasted stuffed porcini mushrooms • $35

miro NR

Browns Road, Waiheke Island **region** Waiheke Island
phone (09) 372 7854 **fax** (09) 372 7056 **open** By appointment
winemaker Stephen White, Barnett Bond **production** 500 **est.** 1994
product range ($20–70 R) Chardonnay, Archipelago (Bordeaux-blend second label) and Miro (super-premium Bordeaux-blend).

summary Dr Barnett Bond and wife Cate Vosper are the most recent arrivals on the beautiful Waiheke Island scene, planting their first vines in 1994 and extending the vineyard to 3 hectares in 1996. A luxury holiday cottage overlooking the steep, north-facing slopes of the vines and out to the Onetangi Bay is on site.

mission estate winery ★★★★☆

Church Road, Taradale **region** Hawke's Bay
phone (06) 844 2259 **fax** (06) 844 6023 **open** Mon–Sat 8.30–5.30, Sun 11–4
winemaker Paul Mooney **production** 74 000 **est.** 1851
product range ($11–30 CD) Mission Estate range: Gewurztraminer, Riesling, Pinot Gris, Sauvignon Blanc, Chardonnay, Rosé, Merlot, Cabernet Merlot, Cabernet Sauvignon, Botrytised Semillon and Ice Wine; Mission Reserve range: Riesling, Semillon, Pinot Gris, Sauvignon Blanc, Moteo Road Chardonnay, Gimblett Road Syrah, Cabernet Franc, Cabernet Sauvignon Merlot, Cabernet Sauvignon; premium Jewelstone Selection range: Chardonnay, Gimblett Road Syrah and Gimblett Road Cabernet Merlot; Fine Old Port

summary New Zealand's oldest winemaker, owned by the Society of Mary. Once content to make honest, basically unpretentious wines at modest prices, it has developed some top-end wines since 1992, notably the Jewelstone range, but the quality (and value for money) across the range is most impressive. Production has been increased by 50 per cent in recent years, partly reflecting the buoyancy of the New Zealand wine industry but also the quality (and value) of the wines. Exports to Japan and Germany.

Mission Chardonnay

🍷🍷🍷🍷🍷 **2000** Medium yellow-green; fragrant, tangy melon and grapefruit aromas precede an elegant, long, fruit-driven but well-balanced palate with touches of citrus and cashew. At no point did I see the wine as being sweet, nor did the other judges. Fantastic value. **rating:** 94

best drinking Now **best vintages** '89, '91, '92, '94, '95, '00 **drink with** Blue-lipped mussels • $14

Mission Estate Moteo Reserve Chardonnay

🍷🍷🍷🍷 **1999** Medium yellow-green; the bouquet is complex, with good barrel ferment and fruit balance. The palate is fresh and crisp, the fruit lively and the oak under control, but it is slightly hard on the finish. **rating:** 89

best drinking Now–2003 **best vintages** NA **drink with** Smoked chicken • $24

Mission Estate Reserve Cabernet Sauvignon Merlot

🍷🍷🍷🍷🍷 **1998** Very developed colour for its age; distinctly savoury/cedary/earthy aromas give strong Bordeaux overtones to the bouquet. The palate goes down the same track, complex, with secondary, chocolate/savoury/berry flavours supported by fine but persistent tannins. The oak is sympathetic and in balance. **rating:** 93

best drinking 2002–2007 **best vintages** '98 **drink with** Barbecued leg of lamb • $30

Mission Estate Gimblett Road Reserve Cabernet Sauvignon

🍷🍷🍷🍷 **1999** Medium red-purple; a moderately intense, clean and fragrant bouquet with red berry/cassis fruit leads into an elegant, medium-bodied and well-balanced palate that is not luscious, but that, on the other hand, has not been over-extracted. **rating:** 89

best drinking 2003–2008 **best vintages** NA **drink with** Rack of lamb • $25.95

monarch wines NR

79 Arcus Road, Te Horo, Otaki **region** West Coast
phone (06) 364 3033 **fax** (04) 922 1380 **open** Not
winemaker Alastair Pain (Contract) **production** NA **est.** 1999
product range Chardonnay, Bordeaux Blend, Sangiovese.
summary David and Anne Heath have established a 2.4-hectare vineyard on the old flood plain of the Otaki River, with deep-river gravels and sea breezes providing a terroir not unlike that of Marlborough. The wines are made at the nearby Te Horo Winery.

montana wines ★★★★☆

171 Pilkington Road, Glen Innes, Auckland **region** Auckland Area
phone (09) 570 8400 **fax** (09) 570 8440 **open** 7 days 9.30–5.30
winemaker Jeff Clarke (Chief) **production** 35 000 tonnes (2.25 million-case equivalent) **est.** 1977
product range ($9.95–29 R) A vast range headed by Marlborough Sauvignon Blanc, Riesling, Chardonnay, Pinot Noir, Cabernet Sauvignon; Renwick Estate Chardonnay, Timara Riesling, Brancott Estate Sauvignon Blanc, Fairhall Estate Cabernet Sauvignon, Saints Sauvignon Blanc (also all from Marlborough); Ormond Estate Chardonnay (Gisborne); important sparkling wines headed by Deutz Marlborough Cuvée (Brut and Blanc de Blanc) and Lindauer (Special Reserve Brut de Brut, Brut, Sec and Rosé); large volume Wohnsiedler Müller Thurgau, Blenheimer and Chablisse; Church Road Chardonnay and Cabernet Sauvignon are top of the range. The bright-blue bottle of Azure Bay was a colourful (and commercially significant) addition in 1996.
summary It has been a busy time for Montana recently. In 2000 it acquired the country's second-largest winery, Corbans, in so doing cementing its place as by far the largest producer in New Zealand, the group now accounting for 60 per cent of the total exports. Then, in the first few months of 2001, it fought off a determined takeover bid by the giant English liquor company Allied Domecq. Industry observers think that story is not yet finished, however. Montana has also taken steps to reinvent itself in much the same way as Gallo has done. Uncharacteristically, it has poured millions of dollars into its visitors centre at its Brancott Winery, and, even more surprisingly, by 2002 will be one of the largest producers of Pinot Noir in the world, with over 100 000 cases annually. Exports to every part of the globe, but most importantly the UK, Australia, the US and Japan.

Montana Reserve Riesling

ΥΥΥΥΥ **1998** Medium to full yellow-green, showing bottle development; the bouquet is rich and toasty, with some sweeter stonefruit and citrus aromas; the palate is rich and mouthfilling, with a similar suite of flavours to the bouquet, and particularly well balanced. **rating:** 94

best drinking Now–2004 **best vintages** '98 **drink with** Chinese prawns • $18

Montana Patutahi Gewurztraminer

ΥΥΥΥ **2000** Bright yellow-green; there is bell-clear and rich spice and lychee varietal character on the bouquet, and equally on the palate. The wine has 13.6° alcohol, and 11 grams per litre of residual sugar; taken together, these seem to introduce a degree of sweetness that may please the cellar door more than it does me. **rating:** 88

ΥΥΥΥΥ **1998** Glowing yellow-green; the bouquet is incredibly rich, almost essencey, with lychee/peach/ tropical fruit aromas. The palate is similarly exotically rich and power-packed, though not excessively. Not for the timorous. **rating:** 90

best drinking Now–2003 **best vintages** NA **drink with** Spicy Asian food • $25

Montana Gisborne Semillon

ΥΥΥΥΥ **2000** Light to medium yellow-green; the bouquet is quite fascinating, rich and full in the Margaret River/Adelaide Hills style. The palate is similarly rich and powerful, with lemony fruit and subtle oak; has masses of flavour, yet avoids phenolics. A Blue Gold winner at the 2001 Sydney International Wine Competition. **rating:** 91

best drinking Now–2004 **best vintages** '00 **drink with** Goat's cheese and rocket salad • $11.50

Montana Sauvignon Blanc

ΥΥΥΥ **2000** Light green-yellow; gooseberry and more herbal aromatics (the latter due to the UK demand) lead into a medium-bodied palate with a range of fruit characters in the mid-ripeness spectrum, moving from gooseberry to some herb and capsicum. **rating:** 87

best drinking Now **best vintages** '80, '81, '84, '85, '88, '89, '91, '94, '97, '00 **drink with** Shellfish • $12.95

Montana Marlborough Reserve Vineyard Selection Sauvignon Blanc

ΥΥΥΥΥ **2000** Light green-yellow; the bouquet has a range of gooseberry, melon and mineral aromas, with the faintest touch of passionfruit detectable. A richer, rounder, fuller wine in the mouth, with gooseberry and melon predominant. **rating:** 91

ΥΥΥΥΥ **1999** Light to medium green-yellow; the bouquet is clean, with a mix of passionfruit and herb aromas. The palate has good concentration and length of flavour, with harmonious mouthfeel and neatly balanced acidity. **rating:** 90

best drinking Now **best vintages** '97, '99, '00 **drink with** Stuffed capsicum • $19.95

Montana Gisborne Chardonnay

ΥΥΥΥ **2000** Medium yellow-green; there is good fruit and oak balance and integration on the bouquet, the palate as honest as they come: full flavoured, with a mix of peach, melon and citrus, and just a light dusting of oak. The Reserve version from the same vintage is more powerful and complex, but I prefer the varietal release given the price comparison ($16 for the Reserve). **rating:** 87

best drinking Now **best vintages** '00 **drink with** Avocado and roast pepper salad • $11.50

Montana Ormond Estate Chardonnay

ΥΥΥΥ **1998** Medium to full yellow-green; clean and smooth, with well-balanced and integrated oak. The palate carries on the good work, with fine, smooth, melon and peach fruit in a medium- to full-bodied frame. **rating:** 87

best drinking Now **best vintages** NA **drink with** Grilled pork chops • $26.95

Montana Reserve Barrique Fermented Marlborough Chardonnay

ΥΥΥΥ **1997** Bright yellow-gold in typical New Zealand fashion. The bouquet has clean, sweet nectarine fruit with subtle oak, and the palate comes as a great surprise, still tight and fresh, with peach/nectarine fruit, crisp acidity and some minerally characters. The oak, too, has integrated very well. **rating:** 89

best drinking Now–2003 **best vintages** NA **drink with** Pasta • $19.95

Montana Lindauer Special Reserve Brut

🍷🍷🍷🍷 **NV** Pale pink-straw; a fresh and lively bouquet is not, however, particularly complex in terms of autolysis/lees development. On the other hand, the palate is fresh and fruity, with a delicate appeal, and excellent acidity.

rating: 87

best drinking Now **best vintages** NA **drink with** Aperitif • $16

Deutz Marlborough Cuvée

🍷🍷🍷🍷 **NV** Very light straw-green; a spotlessly clean, fine, reserved and delicate bouquet, with lemon and apple as its base leads into a very fresh palate with mineral, citrus and apple running through to a long, lingering finish. There is little obvious yeast influence, but this in no way detracts from the wine. **rating:** 90

best drinking Now **best vintages** NA **drink with** Aperitif • $28

Montana Reserve Barrique Matured Pinot Noir

🍷🍷🍷🍷 **1999** Medium purple-red; a quite rich and ripe bouquet with spice and plum fruit and a nicely judged touch of oak. The palate lacks the texture of the very best New Zealand Pinots, but on the other hand the wine has some finesse, and the flavour and varietal character are there in abundance. **rating:** 90

best drinking Now–2004 **best vintages** '99 **drink with** Pot-roasted quail • $29

Montana Cabernet Sauvignon Merlot

🍷🍷🍷 **1998** Medium red-purple; the bouquet is clean, fresh and light with some small berry fruit aromas. The palate is fresh and youthful, and appears to have been handled mainly in tank. Neither rich nor complex, but an interesting alternative style reminiscent of Chinon Cabernet Franc from the Loire Valley, France. **rating:** 82

best drinking Now **best vintages** NA **drink with** Chicken salad • $14.95

morton estate ★★★★

State Highway 2, RD2, Kati Kati **region** Waikato and Bay of Plenty
phone (07) 552 0795 **fax** (07) 552 0651 **open** 7 days 10.30–5
winemaker Evan Ward, Chris Archer **production** 90 000 **est.** 1978
product range ($11.95–33 CD) At the top end, the Black Label range: Chardonnay, Pinot Noir, Merlot, Merlot Cabernet Sauvignon and Méthode Traditionelle; next, the Individual Vineyard range: Chardonnay made from Riverview, Sauvignon Blanc from Colefield (both in Hawke's Bay) and Sauvignon Blanc from Stone Creek in Marlborough. The White Label range features a Hawke's Bay range, including Chardonnay, Sauvignon Blanc, Pinot Gris, Syrah, Pinot Noir and a Bordeaux-blend called Mercure; and a Marlborough range of Chardonnay, Sauvignon Blanc, Riesling and Pinot Noir. At the lower-priced end is Mill Road.
summary Now owned by John Coney, with Evan Ward in charge of winemaking, long-term winemaker John Hancock having left to head up his new Hawke's Bay winery. It will be interesting to watch the development of wine style; it seems probable that the more restrained approach of recent years will continue. A key development for the future has been the construction of a winery in Hawke's Bay, which came on-stream in time for the 2001 vintage. Exports to the UK, the US, the Netherlands, Singapore, Fiji and Japan.

Morton Estate Riverview Chardonnay

🍷🍷🍷 **1998** Medium yellow-green; a clean, smooth, peachy bouquet leads into a nicely weighted peach and nectarine palate; the oak influence is present, but far from dominant, and the wine is a fraction simple, but pleasant. **rating:** 84

best drinking Now **best vintages** NA **drink with** Pasta • $25

morworth estate NR

Shands Road, Christchurch **region** Canterbury
phone (03) 349 5014 **fax** (03) 349 4419 **open** By appointment
winemaker Contract **production** 4000 **est.** 1995
product range ($9–17 CD) Riesling, Breidecker, Sauvignon Blanc, Pinot Noir.
summary Leonie and Chris Morkane have established 13 hectares of vines on the outskirts of Christchurch, predominantly planted to pinot noir (6 hectares) and riesling (3 hectares), with lesser quantities of breidecker, pinot gris and gewurztraminer. The Morkanes have erected a stylish 200-tonne winery-cum-art gallery and function centre on the property.

moteo terroire NR

100 Moteo Pa Road, RD3, Napier **region** Hawke's Bay
phone (06) 757 9074 **fax** (06) 758 1182 **open** Not
winemaker Grant Edmonds (Contract) **production** 400 **est.** 1998
product range ($21.95–24.95 R) Moko Reserve Chardonnay, Moteo Terroire Cabernets Merlot.
summary Alan Ross and Noel Cave have owned the Moteo Vineyard in Hawke's Bay for over a decade, selling the grapes to other wineries. A label surfaced some years ago, but then disappeared, to reappear again in 1998 with a different winemaking team. The Cabernets Merlot (a blend of 42 per cent Merlot, 32 per cent Cabernet Sauvignon and 26 per cent Cabernet Franc) has been very highly rated.

mt difficulty wines ★★★★

Felton Road, RD2, Bannockburn, Cromwell **region** Central Otago
phone (03) 445 1054 **fax** (03) 445 1052 **open** Not
winemaker Matt Dicey **production** 5000 **est.** 1998
product range ($19–33 R) Riesling, Sauvignon Blanc, Pinot Gris, Chardonnay, Pinot Noir.
summary Mt Difficulty is a rare beast in the wine world: a joint venture between four grape-growers who have banded together to have the wine made under a single brand, giving economies of scale otherwise impossible. The vineyards will produce the equivalent of 25 000 cases annually once they are in full production, which won't be too many years away. The difficulty comes from the 'my grapes are better than yours' syndrome which, whether true or not, tends to thwart ventures such as this. It is to their credit that the joint venturers have worked around the problem. The wines are made at the Longburn winery owned by the Dicey family, one of the four grape-grower partners. Exports to the UK.

Mt Difficulty Riesling

🍷🍷🍷🍷🍷 **2000** Medium yellow-green; while the bouquet has abundant, sweet lime aromas, it does not go over the top. There is a replay of the bouquet on the palate, crammed with fruit, and probably quick-developing, but retaining excellent balance amidst all of that fruit power and flavour. **rating:** 91
best drinking Now **best vintages** '00 **drink with** Rich fish dishes • $20

mount edward ★★★★

Coalpit Road, Gibbston, Queenstown **region** Central Otago
phone (03) 442 6113 **fax** (03) 442 9119 **open** By appointment
winemaker Alan Brady **production** 700 **est.** 1995
product range ($18–35 R) Riesling, Pinot Noir.
summary Alan Brady was the driving force behind the establishment and success of Gibbston Valley winery. In 1998 he retired as general manager of Gibbston Valley and commissioned Queenstown architect Michael Wyatt to design a new small winery on Brady's private vineyard in Coalpit Road. Here 1 hectare of riesling is planted, which he supplements with pinot noir (his continuing passion) purchased from growers in the Otago region. Tastings, and tutored tastings, are by appointment only and are always conducted by Alan Brady in person. Exports to the UK.

Mount Edward Pinot Noir

🍷🍷🍷🍷 **1999** Light to medium red-purple; fine cherry and plum fruit aromas are followed by a clean, fresh no-frills palate with similar flavours; however, it does lengthen considerably on the finish, with fine, slippery, supple tannins. **rating:** 88
best drinking Now–2004 **best vintages** '99 **drink with** Roast veal • $33

mountford vineyard NR

434 Omihi Road, Waipara, North Canterbury **region** Waipara
phone (03) 314 6819 **fax** (03) 314 6820 **open** By appointment
winemaker C P Lin (Consultant) **production** 1000 **est.** 1991
product range ($30–35 CD) Chardonnay, Pinot Noir.

summary Michael and Buffy Eaton have established 4 hectares of vines on an east-facing slope of the Waipara Valley, producing the first tiny vintage in 1996; full production began in 1999. An on-site winery has been constructed, as has a lodge with up-market accommodation. The wines have all been highly rated by Bob Campbell and Michael Cooper.

mount maude NR

Maungawera Valley, RD2, Wanaka, Central Otago **region** Central Otago
phone (03) 443 8398 **fax** (03) 443 1908 **open** By appointment
winemaker Dean Shaw **production** NA **est.** 1994
product range ($17.50 R) Riesling, Pinot Noir.
summary Dawn and Terry Wilson have established 4 hectares of steep hillside vineyard in the beautiful (what is not beautiful in Central Otago?) Maungawera Valley that runs down to Lake Wanaka. There are 1.5 hectares of pinot noir, 1 hectare each of riesling and chardonnay, and 0.75 hectare of gewurztraminer; chardonnay and gewurztraminer are sold to Gibbston Valley, the other grapes used for Mount Maude. Tastings are by appointment in the architect-designed mudbrick house, and there is also a pottery showroom.

Mount Maude Riesling

2000 Light green-yellow; the crisp and flinty bouquet offers a range of mineral and herbal aromas, the palate with lively, brisk acidity, showing striking similarities to many young Tasmanian Rieslings; well made, but seems to show some young vine character, not surprisingly. **rating:** 84
best drinking Now–2006 **best vintages** NA **drink with** Shellfish • $17.50

mount michael NR

McNab Road, RD2, Cromwell, Central Otago **region** Central Otago
phone (03) 445 1351 **open** 7 days 11–5 Oct–Apr
winemaker Matt Dicey **production** 150 **est.** 1998
product range Chardonnay, Pinot Noir.
summary Martin and Sue Anderson planted 3 hectares of pinot noir and chardonnay on an ancient river terrace in 1994, supplying the grapes to Chard Farm until 1999 when one tonne of each was contract-made by Matt Dicey of Mt Difficulty Wines.

mount riley ★★★★

Cnr Malthouse Road and State Highway 1, Blenheim **region** Marlborough
phone (09) 486 0286 **fax** (09) 486 0643 **open** By appointment
winemaker Bill 'Digger' Hennessy **production** 25 000 **est.** 1995
product range ($15–39 R) Riesling, Sauvignon Blanc, Semillon, Chardonnay, Seventeen Valley Chardonnay, Seventeen Valley Pinot Noir, Cabernet Merlot, Cabernet Sauvignon, Sparkling Sauvignon Blanc Savée.
summary Mount Riley is a joint venture between Auckland-based businessmen and wine enthusiasts Steve Hotchin and John Buchanan, and Marlborough vigneron and winemaker Allan Scott. Mount Riley owns three vineyards in the Wairau Valley and has developed a fourth vineyard in Seventeen Valley, 10 kilometres south of Blenheim, planted to clonally selected pinot noir. In all, Mount Riley owns 80 hectares of vineyards and is in no sense a second label of Allan Scott, even though it shares winemakers and wine facilities with Allan Scott Wines. If there were a value rating, Mount Riley would receive five stars. Exports to Australia, the UK, Germany, Canada, Scandinavia, Singapore and Hong Kong.

Mount Riley Sauvignon Blanc

2000 Light yellow-green; a lively, vibrant bouquet with a mix of gooseberry and lime is a promising start. That promise is fulfilled by the punchy/crisp palate with fresh citrus and redcurrant fruit flavours. **rating:** 92
best drinking Now **best vintages** '00 **drink with** Clams • $19

Mount Riley Chardonnay

2000 Light to medium yellow-green; the bouquet is clean and light, showing minimal oak influence. However, the wine comes alive on its fresh and long palate, showing melon and citrus fruit, the oak resting quietly in the background. **rating:** 90
best drinking Now–2003 **best vintages** '00 **drink with** Crab cakes • $18

moutere hills vineyard ★★★

Sunrise Valley, RD1, Upper Moutere, Nelson **region** Nelson
phone (03) 543 2288 **fax** (03) 543 2288 **open** October–Easter 11–6
winemaker Simon Thomas **production** 2500 **est.** 1996
product range ($14.50–18.50 CD) Nelson Riesling, Barrique Fermented Sauvignon Blanc, Chardonnay, Sunrise Valley Red (Rosé), Merlot, Cabernet Merlot.
summary Moutere Hills winery was established in an old shearing shed by owners Simon and Alison Thomas. Overlooking the Moutere Valley, it draws upon 3 hectares of estate vineyards supplemented by small quantities of grapes purchased from local growers. Wines are available by the glass, matched by light meals. The 2000 Sauvignon Blanc is an attractively crisp, minerally style with punchy acidity (82 points).

mudbrick vineyard NR

Church Bay Road, Oneroa, Waiheke Island **region** Waiheke Island
phone (09) 372 9050 **fax** (09) 372 9052 **open** 7 days summer, lunch and dinner (reduced hours in winter)
winemaker James Rowan **production** 1600 **est.** 1992
product range ($25–35 CD) Chardonnay, Cabernet Sauvignon Merlot Malbec Cabernet Franc, Croll Vineyard Cabernet Syrah.
summary The metamorphosis from accountancy to winemaking and restaurateurs/hoteliers is about as radical as they come, but Nick and Robyn Jones have accomplished it. Their 6-hectare vineyard is planted to chardonnay, cabernet sauvignon, syrah, cabernet franc, merlot and malbec. There is also a restaurant and accommodation.

muddy water ★★★☆

424 Omihi Road, Waipara **region** Waipara
phone (03) 377 7123 **fax** (03) 377 7130 **open** By appointment
winemaker Belinda Gould (Contract) **production** 4500 **est.** 1992
product range ($18–32 CD) Waipara Dry Riesling, Waipara Riesling, Waipara Chardonnay, Waipara Pinot Noir.
summary I must say, I don't think I could ever be persuaded to call my winery (least of all my wines) Muddy Water, even if it does happen to be the literal translation of the Maori word 'Waipara'. However, Michael East, a Christchurch doctor, and his wife Jane, who studied viticulture at Lincoln University, had different ideas when they established Muddy Water in 1992. They already have 7.49 hectares of vineyard planted, with another 4 hectares on the drawing board, and room for a total of 25 hectares. Exports to the UK, the US and Japan.

Muddy Water Waipara Pinot Noir

🍷🍷🍷🍷 **1999** Strong colour; both bouquet and palate are complex, with a range of foresty/gamey characters contrasted with more sappy/plummy notes. Slippery tannins on the finish are part of a wine with good style. **rating:** 85

best drinking Now–2004 **best vintages** '97 **drink with** Char-grilled salmon • $30

mud house ★★★★

197 Rapaura Road, Renwick, Marlborough **region** Marlborough
phone (03) 572 9490 **fax** (03) 572 9491 **open** 7 days 10–5
winemaker Matt Thomson (Winemaker Consultant) **production** 21 000 **est.** 1993
product range ($16–42 CD) Le Grys Sauvignon Blanc, Mudhouse Sauvignon Blanc, Le Grys Chardonnay, Mudhouse Chardonnay, Mudhouse Pinot Noir Black Swan Reserve, Le Grys Merlot, Mudhouse Merlot Black Swan Reserve.
summary Mud House marks the end of an odyssey dating back to 1066; Jennifer Joslin's family name (Le Grys) dates back to that time, and the Marlborough vineyard was purchased by John and Jennifer Joslin at the end of a six-year sailing trip around the world. A mudbrick guesthouse built in 1995 is ultimately to be followed by a mudbrick tasting room and cellar. Production has almost trebled over the past few years, and the wines are distributed (through separate agencies for Mud House and Le Grys respectively) in the UK, the US and Australia.

Le Grys Sauvignon Blanc

🍷🍷🍷🍷🍷 (half) **2000** Light green-yellow; the bouquet is clean and lively, showing surprisingly little impact from the complicated winemaking that lies behind it, offering a ripe mix of melon, stonefruit and a hint of passionfruit. The palate is fresh, crisp and lively, with a special brightness. Gold medal winner at the Royal Easter Wine Show 2001. **rating:** 90

best drinking Now **best vintages** '97, '99, '00 **drink with** Tortellini • $16

Le Grys Chardonnay
▼▼▼▽ **1999** Light green-yellow; a very reserved, tight, slow-developing bouquet with slightly lemony oak is followed by a palate with intensity derived from fairly high alcohol, but which is still closed and not particularly varietal, tending more to apple. **rating:** 84

best drinking Now–2004 **best vintages** '98 **drink with** Seafood pasta • $20.50

Mud House Marlborough Chardonnay
▼▼▼▼▽ **2000** Medium yellow-green; fresh nectarine and melon aromas, with just a hint of nutty oak, is followed by a fresh, fruit-driven palate with nectarine and melon fruit and good length. **rating:** 90

best drinking Now **best vintages** '00 **drink with** Stir-fried prawns • $21

Mud House Black Swan Reserve Pinot Noir
▼▼▼▼▼ **1999** Medium to full red, with some touches of purple; a powerful bouquet with obvious but not aggressive French oak merges with tangy plum, cherry and raspberry fruit aromas. The palate shows excellent varietal character in a rich mode, with plummy fruit offset by more spicy/savoury flavours; good extract, weight and tannins. **rating:** 94

best drinking Now–2005 **best vintages** '99 **drink with** Wild mushroom and duck ragout • $42

Mud House Black Swan Reserve Merlot
▼▼▼▼ **1999** Medium to full red-purple; the bouquet has some of the aromas associated with cooler climates in Australia, which give a slightly gamey cast to the aroma. The palate has fresh, tangy small berry fruit, minimal tannins and nicely judged oak. **rating:** 85

best drinking 2003–2007 **best vintages** NA **drink with** Marinated pork spare ribs • $28

muirlea rise

50 Princess Street, Martinborough **region** Wairarapa
phone (06) 306 9332 **fax** (06) 306 8510 **open** 7 days 10–6
winemaker Willie Brown **production** 1200 **est.** 1987
product range ($18–45 CD) Pinot Blush, Pinot Noir, Justa Red, Mareth, Apres Wine Liqueur, Apres Royale.
summary Former Auckland wine distributor Willie Brown has established a 2.25-hectare vineyard. Since the first wine release of a 1991 Pinot Noir, the accent has remained on that variety, but with an extraordinarily eclectic gaggle of other wines that are decidedly left-of-centre in style.

Muirlea Rise Pinot Noir
▼▼▼▼ **1999** Medium red-purple; a moderately intense, clean bouquet has quite complex tangy/savoury aromatics; the light- to medium-bodied palate is well balanced, particularly the gentle but persuasive tannins. **rating:** 87

best drinking Now–2004 **best vintages** '99 **drink with** Smoked pork • $40

murdoch james estate ★★★☆

c/o Barbara Turner, 15 Cologne Street, Martinborough **region** Wairarapa
phone (06) 306 9193 **fax** (06) 306 9120 **open** Not
winemaker Chris Buring **production** 2100 **est.** 1986
product range ($16–45 R) Unoaked Chardonnay, Pinot Noir, Blue Rock Reserve Pinot Noir, Cabernet Franc, Shiraz, Tres Amis Pinot Noir Cabernet Sauvignon Cabernet Franc.
summary The origin of Murdoch James Estate goes back to 1986 when Roger and Jill Fraser planted 2.5 hectares of shiraz and pinot noir. Their plans were interrupted in 1989 when Roger was transferred to Melbourne with work, and they decided to sell the grapes rather than make wine. Between 1993 and 1998 only tiny quantities of wine were made, but the estate then purchased Blue Rock Vineyard, giving 11 hectares of estate vines and triggering construction of underground barrel-storage tunnels and a new tasting room.

Murdoch James Blue Rock Reserve Pinot Noir
▼▼▼▼▽ **1999** Medium red-purple; the bouquet shows lifted, sweet aromatics, with most attractive cherry that is the dominant driver on the elegant and quite long palate; finishes with fine tannins. **rating:** 90

best drinking Now–2004 **best vintages** '99 **drink with** Herbed chicken • $45

mystery creek wines NR

277 Mystery Creek Road, RD1, Ohaupo **region** Waikato and Bay of Plenty
phone (07) 823 6464 **fax** (07) 823 6181 **open** By appointment
winemaker Garry Major **production** 2000 **est.** 1999
product range ($14.95–29.95 R) Unwooded Chardonnay, Chardonnay, Pinot Noir, Merlot.
summary Former Villa Maria employees Garry Major and Vicki Edwards have established a 2.5-hectare vineyard, with consultancy advice by viticulturist David Jordan.

nautilus wines ★★★★☆

12 Rapaura Road, Marlborough **region** Marlborough
phone (09) 572 9364 **fax** (09) 572 9374 **open** 7 days 10.30–4.30
winemaker Clive Jones **production** 50 000 **est.** 1985
product range ($19.95–35 R) Chardonnay, Reserve Chardonnay, Sauvignon, Pinot Noir, Cabernet Sauvignon Merlot, Riverbrook Reserve Cabernet Merlot, Cuvée Marlborough Brut, Marlborough Sauvignon, Marlborough Chardonnay; Twin Islands is the second label, sold only in NZ.
summary Nautilus is ultimately owned by Yalumba of Australia. Until 1996 the wines were made by Yalumba winemaker Alan Hoey at Matua Valley, but from that vintage most were made at Rapaura Vintners (of which Nautilus is now a part-owner) under the direction of former Brokenwood (Australia) winemaker Matt Harrop, now replaced by Clive Jones. In 2000 a single-purpose, ultimate state-of-the-art Pinot Noir winery was opened at the very end of Rapaura Road, which draws both upon 15.5 hectares of estate vineyards and contract-grown grapes, and is on the very brink of a five-star rating for the quality of all its wines. Given its parentage, with Yalumba itself having a major agency export business around the world, it is not surprising that Nautilus is exported through much of Europe, Asia, the Pacific Islands, the US and Canada.

Nautilus Marlborough Sauvignon

ŸŸŸŸY **2000** Light to medium green-yellow; a highly aromatic bouquet of passionfruit, gooseberry and nectarine is followed by a palate that has all of the characters of the bouquet plus lemony/minerally acidity on the finish. **rating:** 90

best drinking Now **best vintages** '89, '90, '91, '94, '99, '00 **drink with** Crayfish • $20

Nautilus Marlborough Chardonnay

ŸŸŸŸ **1999** Light to medium yellow-green; a fine, elegant bouquet with subtle oak and creamy/nutty aromatics that are repeated on the palate, where the malolactic fermentation has a marked influence on the structure without diminishing the length of the wine. Sophisticated stuff. **rating:** 89

best drinking Now–2005 **best vintages** '91, '94, '98 **drink with** Scallops in cream sauce • $24

Nautilus Cuvée Marlborough Brut

ŸŸŸŸY **NV** Light to medium yellow-green; as one would expect from the making, the aromas are quite savoury, a long way on from primary fruit, and there are distinct bready/yeasty characters. The palate is tight, with excellent structure, balance and length, the dosage low at 6 grams per litre, and the acidity long and fine. **rating:** 91

best drinking Now **best vintages** NA **drink with** Aperitif • $29.95

Nautilus Pinot Noir

ŸŸŸŸY **2000** Bright purple-red; attractive spicy, plummy aromatics, with the fruit, rather than the oak, leading the way is followed by a wine with excellent structure (attributed by winemaker Clive Jones to the 10/5 clone) is reflected in fine, plummy fruit and altogether finer tannins and mouthfeel. **rating:** 92

ŸŸŸŸ **1999** Excellent red-purple colour; a deep, savoury/plum bouquet with attractive wisps of smoky oak is followed by a powerfully structured palate with considerable weight and just a little more tannin on the finish than I would look for. 500 cases made. **rating:** 89

best drinking Now–2004 **best vintages** '00 **drink with** Braised duck • $34.95

Nautilus Cabernet Merlot

ŸŸŸŸŸ **1998** Medium to full red-purple; ripe cassis/blackcurrant/blackberry fruit is seamlessly married with subtle, spicy oak; the same truly ripe fruit is evident on the palate, with dark berry and a touch of chocolate; the wine has exceptional structure: Bordeaux-like, with fine, lingering tannins. An unhesitating gold medal from all concerned at the Royal Easter Wine Show 2001. **rating:** 94

best drinking 2003–2013 **best vintages** '98 **drink with** Lamb casserole • $24.95

Nautilus Riverbrook Reserve Cabernet Merlot

YYYYY **1998** Medium to full red-purple; potent, cassis/dark berry fruit is married with positive but not aggressive oak on the bouquet. The palate has fabulous structure: rich, full and ripe, with ripe but quite fine tannins. All in all, like a top Bordeaux from a top vintage. **rating:** 96

best drinking 2003–2005 **best vintages** '98 **drink with** Venison • $34.95

neudorf vineyards ★★★★★

Neudorf Road, Upper Moutere, Nelson **region** Nelson

phone (03) 543 2643 **fax** (03) 543 2955 **open** 7 days 10–5 September–May

winemaker Tim Finn, Mike Weersing **production** 7500 **est.** 1978

product range ($16.90–48 CD) The Moutere label is reserved for estate-grown wines, notably Riesling, Chardonnay and Pinot Noir; Nelson typically indicates a mix of estate-grown and locally purchased grapes from the Nelson region with Chardonnay and Pinot Noir; also Brightwater Riesling, Sauvignon Blanc and Blackbird Valley Cabernet.

summary Tim Finn has produced some of Australasia's most stunningly complex and rich Chardonnays, outstanding in any class. But his skills do not stop there, spanning all varieties consistently to show-medal standard. Indeed, the complex Neudorf Pinot Noir is seriously challenging the Chardonnay for top billing, with an even more exciting future as new clones from Burgundy come into production. Exports to Australia, the UK, the US, France, Denmark, Brazil, Japan, France and Singapore. The restaurant is open 27 December to 31 January.

Neudorf Brightwater Riesling

YYYYY **2000** Light yellow-green; a fragrant and floral bouquet with gentle lime, then a high-toned, fresh and lively palate with tangy/citrussy fruit. Presses all the right buttons for me. **rating:** 93

best drinking Now–2007 **best vintages** '00 **drink with** Summer salad • $17.80

Neudorf Moutere Riesling

YYYYY **2000** Light yellow-green; the bouquet is much fuller than that of the Brightwater, with pronounced herb and mineral characters. The palate, too, has a lot more to do with texture and structure, big and strong, but neither fat nor broad, simply denser. I know I am supposed to like this more than the Brightwater, but I prefer the simpler style. **rating:** 92

best drinking Now–2010 **best vintages** '91, '93, '94, '97, '00 **drink with** Marinated grilled octopus • $23.80

Neudorf Moutere Chardonnay

YYYYY **1999** Light to medium yellow-green; the bouquet is more intense than the Nelson Chardonnay, with citrus-edged melon fruit. The palate is substantial, yet has finesse, with cashew, fig and melon woven through spicy French oak. **rating:** 94

best drinking Now–2006 **best vintages** '91, '92, '93, '94, '96, '97, '98, '99 **drink with** Veal, pasta • $39

Neudorf Nelson Chardonnay

YYYYY **2000** Medium yellow-green; clean melon, nectarine and citrus fruit drives both the bouquet and the fresh, excellently structured palate. Not only is the oak influence subtle, so is that of the mlf, simply adding to the mouthfeel without detracting from the fruit. **rating:** 91

best drinking Now–2004 **best vintages** '99, '00 **drink with** Abalone • $23.80

Neudorf Moutere Pinot Noir

YYYYY **1999** Bright purple-red; a firm, bright but full bouquet of cherry and plum fruit is, like the palate, still very much in its primary fruit phase of development; the palate has all the balance and structure one could wish for, with very fine tannins and subtle oak. **rating:** 93

best drinking 2002–2007 **best vintages** '90, '91, '92, '94, '97, '98, '99 **drink with** New Zealand venison • $36

Neudorf Moutere Reserve Pinot Noir

YYYYY **1999** Deep red-purple; the bouquet is much deeper, richer and fuller than the varietal wine, the palate likewise lush, with full plummy fruit and a mix of oak and spice to enrich the structure of the finish. Like the varietal, still very much in the primary phase of its development. **rating:** 95

best drinking 2004–2009 **best vintages** '99 **drink with** Boned quail stuffed with chicken livers • $48

nevis bluff NR

PO Box 2012, Wakatipu, Queenstown **region** Central Otago
phone 0800-4-PINOT **fax** (03) 441 3287 **open** Not
winemaker Dean Shaw (Contract) **production** 2256 **est.** 1995
product range ($16–23.50 R) Pinot Gris, Chardonnay, Pinot Noir.
summary Yet another impressive Central Otago label. Owned by Dunedin chartered accountant Bill Dawson. Nevis Bluff presently has 7.5 hectares of estate vineyards that huddle in a mountain-flanked valley, sheltered by the spectacularly steep and jagged Nevis Bluff. Exports to the UK.

Nevis Bluff Pinot Noir

ΥΥΥΥ **1999** Medium red, with just a touch of purple; the fragrant bouquet has a range of aromas from plum and cherry through to more herby/savoury/woodsy. The light- to medium-bodied palate carries on with the herb flavours without supplanting the plum and cherry of the bouquet. Fair length. **rating:** 85

best drinking Now–2003 **best vintages** NA **drink with** Game terrine • $23.50

newton forrest estate ★★★★★

Cnr State Highway 50 and Gimblett Road, Hawke's Bay **region** Hawke's Bay
phone (06) 879 4416 **fax** (06) 876 6020 **open** At Forrest Estate, Blicks Road, Renwick
winemaker John Forrest (Contract) **production** 3300 **est.** 1988
product range ($34-50 ML) Under the Cornerstone Merlot, Cabernet Merlot and Cabernet Sauvignon.
summary Newton Forrest is a joint venture between Hawke's Bay grape-grower Bob Newton and the hugely talented Marlborough winemaker John Forrest of Forrest Estate. It has produced the super-premium Cornerstone Cabernet Merlot each year since 1994; more recently a small quantity of Cabernet Sauvignon has been made. The remainder of the production from the 30 hectares of vines is sold to the Villa Maria/Vidal/Esk Valley for their Reserve wines.

Newton Forrest Cornerstone Merlot

ΥΥΥΥΥ **1999** Medium purple-red; the bouquet offers clean, bright small-berry aromatics with positive but controlled oak. The palate has excellent structure, with dark berry fruit and spice, finishing with remarkably ripe tannins. You could say that it is a Merlot trying to look like a Cabernet, but it's so good, who cares? **rating:** 94

best drinking 2003–2008 **best vintages** '99 **drink with** Aged venison fillet • $50

Newton Forrest Cornerstone Cabernet Merlot

ΥΥΥΥΥ **1999** Full purple-red; a clean, fragrant bouquet has red berry and cassis fruit and gentle oak in support. The palate moves up another notch, with abundant ripe, fleshy fruit on the mid-palate, then moving through to a silky yet tannin-enriched finish. It emerged a clear second in the trophy taste-off for Best Wine of Show. Tasted on four occasions in February 2001, and each time was superb, gaining maximum points. **rating:** 96

best drinking 2004–2014 **best vintages** '99 **drink with** Char-grilled rump • $34

Newton Forrest Cornerstone Cabernet Sauvignon

ΥΥΥΥ **1998** Medium to full red-purple; pristine but ripe blackberry cabernet sauvignon aromas come first, then a slightly savoury twist. The same play occurs on the palate, opening with spotlessly clean and sweet berry fruit before moving through to persistent tannins on the finish. A cerebral wine. **rating:** 92

best drinking 2005–2012 **best vintages** '98 **drink with** Leave it in the cellar • $50

ngaruroro estate winery NR

5 Whakapirau Road, Hastings **region** Hawke's Bay
phone (06) 879 8842 **fax** (06) 879 5336 **open** Not
winemaker David Harley **production** 150 **est.** 1995
product range Cabernet Merlot.
summary David and Ros Harley started as home winemakers, and are still making their wines from purchased grapes. However, they have established a terraced vineyard rising above the Ngaruroro River and planted to merlot and shiraz; 2001 should provide the first estate-grown wine. Homestay accommodation is provided, with three double rooms at the property.

ngatarawa wines ★★★★

Ngatarawa Road, Bridge Pa, RD5, Hastings **region** Hawke's Bay
phone (06) 879 7603 **fax** (06) 879 6675 **open** 7 days 11–5
winemaker Alwyn Corban, Peter Gough **production** 35 000 **est.** 1981
product range ($12.95–60 R) The top wines under the Glazebrook label include Chardonnay and Cabernet Merlot; the lesser-priced Stables range comprises Chardonnay, Sauvignon Blanc, Classic White, Merlot and Cabernet Merlot. Also Alwyn Chardonnay, Noble Botrytis.
summary Alwyn Corban is a highly qualified and highly intelligent winemaker from a famous New Zealand wine family. He has elected to grow vines organically and make wines that sometimes (but certainly not always) fall outside the mainstream. Challenging and interesting, and not to be taken lightly. The wines are exported to the UK, Europe, Asia, the US, Canada and Australia.

Ngatarawa Stables Merlot

YYY▽ **1999** Medium red-purple; the bouquet is clean, with moderately ripe spicy/savoury fruit, the tannin in the same savoury/earthy spectrum, but avoiding harsh green flavours or tannins. **rating:** 82
best drinking Now **best vintages** NA **drink with** Takeaway • NA

Ngatarawa Glazebrook Cabernet Merlot

YYYY▽ **1999** Light to medium red-purple; a fragrant, lively and spicy bouquet, with a touch of leaf but no astringency, leads into a stylish, almost delicate palate with supple tannins and a nice touch of sweet oak. **rating:** 92
best drinking 2003–2009 **best vintages** '90, '91, '95, '96, '99 **drink with** Rib of veal • $23.95

nga waka vineyard ★★★★

Kitchener Street, Martinborough **region** Wairarapa
phone (06) 306 9832 **fax** (06) 306 9832 **open** Weekends 1–5 while stocks last
winemaker Roger Parkinson **production** 5000 **est.** 1988
product range ($22–40 R) Riesling, Sauvignon Blanc, Chardonnay, Pinot Noir.
summary Roseworthy-trained Roger Parkinson produces the Nga Waka wines from 10.5 hectares of estate plantings in the heart of the Martinborough Terraces. The early promise of the vineyard came into full flower in the unlikely environment of the 1995 vintage with the performance of the 1995 Sauvignon Blanc at the Air New Zealand Wine Awards of that year. Subsequent vintages have been good to very good. Exports to Australia, Europe, Japan and the US.

Nga Waka Riesling

YYY▽ **1999** Light to medium green-yellow; a very full, complex, tropical bouquet is suggestive of some botrytis at work; the powerful palate travels down the same track, with lemon/lime fruit underneath more tropical/honeyed characters. An in-your-face style. **rating:** 84
best drinking Now–2004 **best vintages** '98 **drink with** Mussels • $22

Nga Waka Sauvignon Blanc

YYYY **2000** Very pale straw-green; the bouquet is not overly intense, but is complex, offering a mix of ripe tropical fruit and more minerally characters; the palate is well balanced but the fruit seems to run out on the powdery/talcy finish. **rating:** 85
best drinking Now **best vintages** '94, '95 **drink with** Seafood pasta • $24

Nga Waka Chardonnay

YYYYY **1999** Medium yellow-green; the clean bouquet has excellent nectarine and melon fruit, with cashew oak a subtle backdrop. The palate is equally appealing, with abundant flavour and excellent mouthfeel and balance. Here nectarine, grapefruit and cashew are held together with sure oak handling. **rating:** 94
best drinking Now–2004 **best vintages** '99 **drink with** Milk-fed veal • $35

Nga Waka Pinot Noir

YYYY **1999** Deep purple-red; a powerful, dense dark plum bouquet heralds a super-powerful, dark plum-flavoured palate that is still quite chewy and seriously locked in on itself. Should by rights develop very well given time. **rating:** 89
best drinking 2002–2006 **best vintages** '99 **drink with** Jugged hare • $40

nobilo ★★★★

Station Road, Huapai **region** Auckland Area
phone (09) 412 6666 **fax** (09) 412 7124 **open** Mon–Fri 9–5, Sat 10–5, Sun 11–4
winemaker Darryl Woolley **production** 375 000 **est.** 1943
product range ($8.95–34.95 R) At the bottom the White Cloud range ($8.95–9.95); then Fernleaf Sauvignon Blanc, Chardonnay and Cabernet Sauvignon ($9.95); then Fall Harvest Sauvignon Blanc, Chardonnay, Cabernet Shiraz and Merlot ($11.95); next Marlborough Sauvignon Blanc, Poverty Bay Chardonnay and Marlborough Merlot ($15); then Icon Sauvignon Blanc, Riesling, Gewurztraminer and Chardonnay ($18); and finally Reserve Sauvignon Blanc ($22.95) and Reserve Chardonnay ($34.95).
summary One of the more energetic and effective wine marketers, with production heavily focused on white wines sourced from Gisborne, Hawke's Bay and Marlborough. Significantly increased the critical mass of its business with the acquisition of Selaks, giving it secure access to Marlborough. A long-time exponent of flamboyant label and packaging redesign, but the quality of the top-of-the-range Grand Reserve wines leaves nothing to be desired. In September 2000 BRL Hardy acquired full ownership of Nobilo (and through that acquisition, Selaks and that company's newly constructed Drylands Winery in Marlborough). There is no reason to suppose the quality of the wines will be in any way compromised, nor the innovative and energetic marketing of the products. Exports to the UK, much of Europe, North America and Singapore.

Nobilo Icon Sauvignon Blanc

YYYYY 2000 Light green-yellow; fragrant and clean passionfruit is the dominant fruit character on the bouquet. The excellent palate has the accessibility of the bouquet, with a long, easy-drinking mix of passionfruit and gooseberry, closing with balanced acidity. Won a gold medal at the Royal Easter Wine Show 2001. **rating:** 94
best drinking Now **best vintages** '97, '00 **drink with** Trout mousse • $18

Nobilo Marlborough Merlot

YYYY 1999 Medium red-purple; the bouquet is fragrant, with a mix of sweet and more savoury fruit, the palate light to medium bodied, but with the lingering savoury characters and fine tannins I see as part of true varietal character. **rating:** 89
best drinking 2002–2006 **best vintages** '99 **drink with** Veal chops • $15

obsidian NR

Te Makiri Road, Onetangi, Waiheke Island **region** Waiheke Island
phone (09) 372 6100 **fax** (09) 372 6100 **open** Summer 7 days 11–4, winter by appointment
winemaker Simon Nunns **production** 1500 **est.** 1993
product range ($26.50–45 R) Obsidian (Cabernet Sauvignon Merlot), Island Red (Merlot Cabernet)
summary Although still in its infancy (the first vintage was 1997), destined to be an important part of the Waiheke Island scene. A partnership between Andrew Hendy (owner of Coopers Creek), vigneron Chester Nicholls and businessman Lindsay Spilman, it has ambitious plans, which have in part come to fruition with its 1999 Cabernet Sauvignon Merlot (after lesser vintages in 1997 and 1998). The wine is initially offered en primeur by mailing list, and then to selected on-premise outlets on Waiheke Island. Exports to the UK via Farr Vintners.

odyssey wines NR

6D, 50 Keeling Road, Henderson **region** Auckland Area
phone (09) 837 5410 **fax** (09) 837 5409 **open** Not
winemaker Rebecca Salmond **production** 4500 **est.** 1994
product range ($16–28 R) Marlborough Sauvignon Blanc, Gisborne Pinot Gris, Gisborne Chardonnay, Hawke's Bay Reserve Cabernet Sauvignon. Within New Zealand the flagship wines carry the Reserve Illiad label.
summary Rebecca Salmond (formerly winemaker for Pleasant Valley) makes the wines for her Odyssey brand at Landmark. There are no cellar-door sales; the wines are sold via retail and mail order. Exports to Japan.

ohinemuri estate NR

Moresby Street, Karangahake **region** Waikato and Bay of Plenty
phone (07) 862 8874 **fax** (07) 862 8847 **open** 7 days 10–6
winemaker Horst Hillerich **production** 1000 **est.** 1989
product range ($15.50–20 CD) Riesling, Gewurztraminer, Chardonnay, Pinotage.

summary German-born, trained and qualified winemaker Horst Hillerich came to New Zealand in 1987, first working at Totara before establishing Ohinemuri Estate. An atmospheric restaurant was duly opened at the newly constructed winery in the Karangahake Gorge in 1993. Hillerich has produced some highly regarded Gewurztraminer and Sauvignon Blanc. All of the grapes, incidentally, are purchased from growers in Hawke's Bay, the Waikato and Gisborne.

okahu estate NR

Okahu Road, Kaitaia **region** Northland and Matakana
phone (09) 408 2066 **fax** (09) 408 2686 **open** 7 days 10–6 Oct–June, Mon–Fri July–Sept
winemaker Michael Bendit **production** 5000 **est.** 1984
product range ($16.95–45 CD) In more or less ascending order: Shipwreck Bay Riesling, Lightly Oaked Chardonnay, Red; Clifton Riesling and Chardonnay; Ninety Mile Semillon Chardonnay and Cabernet Merlot; Adelines Blanc de Blanc Methode Traditionelle; and at the top of the range Kaz Semillon, Shiraz and Cabernet; also sundry fortified and sweet wines.
summary The Ninety Mile wines (respectively blends of Chardonnay, Semillon and Arnsburger, and Cabernet Merlot, Pinotage and Pinot Noir) signal the location of Okahu Estate at the bottom end of New Zealand's well-known 90 Mile Beach. Recently the focus of the estate plantings of 2.5 hectares has switched to semillon and shiraz, which are said to show considerable promise; the plethora of other wines are made from grapes purchased from other regions.

olssen's of bannockburn ★★★☆

306 Felton Road, Bannockburn, Central Otago **region** Central Otago
phone (03) 445 1716 **fax** (03) 445 0050 **open** 7 days 10–4
winemaker Peter Bartle **production** 3500 **est.** 1989
product range ($17.95–43 CD) Riesling, Gewurztraminer, Sauvignon Blanc, Chardonnay, Pinot Noir, Slapjack Creek Reserve Pinot Noir, Robert the Bruce (Shiraz Pinotage Cabernet Sauvignon blend), Dessert Gold Late Harvest Riesling.
summary Heather McPherson and John Olssen began the establishment of their 10-hectare vineyard (and now 5 hectares of rural garden and outdoor eating sites) in 1989. For the first three years after the vineyard came into bearing the grapes were sold to Chard Farm, but in 1997 the first wines were made under the Olssen's of Bannockburn label. A new but substantial enterprise in the Central Otago scene. Exports to the UK.

Olssen's of Bannockburn Pinot Noir

ΥΥΥΥ **1999** Bright purple-red; the bouquet is quite light, but fresh, with cherry pip-kernel aromas and flavours. As was the case with the '98, the wine finishes with fairly brisk acidity, giving it a particular character which almost none of the other Central Otago wines have. **rating:** 86

best drinking 2002–2005 **best vintages** NA **drink with** Stuffed mushrooms • $38

omaka springs estate ★★★☆

Kennedys Road, RD2, Blenheim, Marlborough **region** Marlborough
phone (03) 572 9933 **fax** (03) 572 9934 **open** 7 days 12–5
winemaker Ian Marchant **production** 19 600 **est.** 1992
product range ($7.99–25 R) Riesling, Semillon, Sauvignon Blanc, Chardonnay, Pinot Noir, Merlot, Cabernet Merlot, Marlborough Riesling.
summary Omaka Springs is a substantial operation with their state-of-the-art winery, built at the end of 1994, now reaching capacity (20 000 cases) and drawing upon 60 hectares of estate vineyards. The reliable wines are particularly well-priced, and are exported to Australia, the UK, Sweden, the US, Canada, Hong Kong and Ireland.

Omaka Springs Marlborough Riesling

ΥΥΥY **2000** Very good green-yellow colour; a rich bouquet with a mix of lime, lemon and tropical aromas is followed by a palate with abundant fruit, but unnecessarily pronounced residual sugar which detracts from an otherwise excellent wine. **rating:** 83

best drinking Now **best vintages** NA **drink with** Eggplant salad • $13

Omaka Springs Sauvignon Blanc

TTTT **2000** Light green-yellow; a vibrant and fresh bouquet with sweet gooseberry aromas flows into a quite juicy palate, with the flavours almost headed to the nectarine of Chardonnay, yet without cloying. **rating:** 89

best drinking Now **best vintages** '94, '97, '99, '00 **drink with** Steamed crab • $17

Omaka Springs Marlborough Reserve Pinot Noir

TTTT **1999** Medium red-purple; ripe, dark glossy plum and spice aromatics, coupled with new oak, follow through into a powerful, multifaceted palate with plum/cherry/spice fruit; the extract and tannins are a little harsh at this juncture, but will hopefully soften with age, justifying a higher rating. **rating:** 87

best drinking 2002–2006 **best vintages** NA **drink with** Roast squab • $25

onetangi road vineyard NR

82 Onetangi Road, RD1, Waiheke Island **region** Waiheke Island
phone (09) 372 6130 **fax** (09) 372 6130 **open** By appointment
winemaker Simon Lampen **production** 900 **est.** 1998
product range ($18–40 R) Rosé, Merlot Cabernet, Reserve Cabernet Malbec Merlot.
summary Having established a 2-hectare vineyard, a micro-brewery and a self-contained cabin that sleeps two, in quick time John and Megan Wallace sold Onetangi Road to George Craddock in September 2000. In the meantime the wines they had made at Mudbrick Vineyard in 1998 and 1999 have shown themselves to be of the standard expected of Waiheke Island.

Onetangi Road Reserve Cabernet Malbec Merlot

TTTY **1999** Medium red-purple; there is abundant French oak on both the bouquet and palate currently doing a good job of suppressing the blackberry and plum fruit. The fairly brisk acidity should ensure the wine ages well, and one can always hope the oak will subside. **rating:** 83

best drinking 2003–2007 **best vintages** NA **drink with** Smoked beef • $40

opihi vineyard NR

Gould's Road, Opihi, Pleasant Point, South Canterbury **region** Canterbury
phone (03) 614 7232 **fax** (03) 614 7234 **open** Vineyard Cafe is open Tues–Sun 11–4.30, tel (03) 614 8308
winemaker Andrew Meggitt **production** 1200 **est.** 1991
product range ($10–27 CD) Riesling, Müller Thurgau, Chardonnay, Pinot Gris, Pinot Noir.
summary Plantings at Opihi Vineyard commenced in 1991; it now has 2.2 hectares of pinot noir, 2 hectares of pinot gris and 0.3 hectare each of chardonnay, riesling and müller thurgau. The vineyard is established on a north-facing slope of Timaru clay loam with superb views across to the snow-clad Two Thumb Range. The tiny production is chiefly sold by mail order, with limited South Canterbury regional distribution. Production has fluctuated, the 2000 vintage almost entirely destroyed by frost.

pacific vineyards ★★★

90 McLeod Road, Henderson **region** Auckland Area
phone (09) 838 9578 **fax** (09) 838 9578 **open** Mon–Sat 9–6
winemaker Steve Tubic **production** 8000 **est.** 1936
product range ($11.50–17 CD) Under the Phoenix label: Marlborough Riesling, Gisborne Gewurztraminer, Marlborough Sauvignon Blanc, Gisborne Chardonnay, Late Harvest Gewurztraminer, Cabernet Sauvignon Merlot; at the top of the range is Minnie's Merlot.
summary One of the more interesting New Zealand wineries, notwithstanding its low profile. It has at various times produced very large quantities of wine (sold in cask and bulk) but is now refocusing on its bottled wine production (in more limited quantities) utilising grapes from Marlborough, Hawke's Bay and Gisborne, and on the other side of the fence has ventured into beer brewing.

Pacific Phoenix Gisborne Chardonnay

TTTY **2000** Light yellow-green; a light, elegant bouquet with a subtle hint of cashew is followed by an easy-drinking palate with gentle melon fruit and a clean finish. **rating:** 83

best drinking Now **best vintages** NA **drink with** Takeaway • $16

packspur vineyard NR

Heaney Road, Lowburn, RD2, Cromwell, Central Otago **region** Central Otago
phone (03) 445 1638 **fax** (03) 445 1639 **open** By appointment
winemaker Anne McAuley, Laurie McAuley **production** 300 **est.** 1992
product range Sauvignon Blanc, Pinot Noir.
summary Anne and Laurie McAuley are feeling their way, content to sell most of their grape production to Gibbston Valley, and making tiny quantities of Sauvignon Blanc and Pinot Noir themselves on a semi-experimental basis. They expect to reach a more developed stage by 2001, and to gradually increase their own production from then on.

palliser estate ★★★★☆

Kitchener Street, Martinborough **region** Wairarapa
phone (06) 306 9019 **fax** (06) 306 9946 **open** 7 days 10–4
winemaker Allan Johnson, Sharon Goldsworthy (Assistant) **production** 20 000 **est.** 1989
product range ($18–35 CD) Riesling, Sauvignon Blanc, Chardonnay, Pinot Gris, Noble Riesling, Noble Chardonnay, Méthode Champenoise, Pinot Noir; Pencarrow Sauvignon Blanc, Chardonnay and Pinot Noir is the second label.
summary Palliser Estate has produced a series of highly regarded and highly awarded wines from its state-of-the-art winery, right from its first vintage in 1989. It has grown rapidly in recent years under the energetic direction of CEO Richard Riddiford. My tasting notes indicate high scores across the full range of the wines produced, with the perfumed silky Pinot Noir to the fore. The wines are distributed in Australia through Negociants; other exports to the UK, Denmark, Switzerland, Canada, Bermuda, Singapore, Hong Kong, Italy, Fiji, France, Germany and the US.

Palliser Estate Riesling

YYYY **2000** Light to medium yellow-green; a highly aromatic and lifted bouquet suggestive of some botrytis which may or may not be there; the palate is similarly full flavoured, intense and long, powering through to the finish. **rating:** 87

best drinking Now–2003 **best vintages** '93, '96, '97, '98 **drink with** Lightly poached asparagus • $20

Palliser Estate Pinot Noir

YYYY **1999** Medium red-purple; the ripe plum of the bouquet has powerful undertones of fresh earth; the complex, powerful and stylish palate provides a similar play until the very finish, where it grips a little uncomfortably. Needs time to soften. **rating:** 89

best drinking 2002–2005 **best vintages** '89, '91, '94, '96, '98 **drink with** Duck risotto • $35

parker mc NR

91 Banks Street, Gisborne **region** Gisborne
phone (06) 867 6967 **fax** (06) 867 6967 **open** 7 days 9.30–6
winemaker Phil Parker **production** 1000 **est.** 1987
product range ($15–32 R) Dry Flint, Classical Brut, Rosé Brut, Firstlight Red, Firstlight Fortified.
summary A Méthode Champenoise specialist that has caused much interest and comment. Firstlight Red is a blend of Merlot and Pinotage and is billed as being the world's first light red wine each year; unless it is picked on 1 January it is unlikely that claim will stand unchallenged. Has not entered the show ring and I have not tasted the wines. The winery also has a restaurant open for lunch and dinner every day of the week.

park estate winery NR

2087 Pakowhai Road, RD3, Napier **region** Hawke's Bay
phone (06) 844 8137 **fax** (06) 844 6800 **open** 7 days 10–5.30
winemaker Owen Park **production** 5000 **est.** 1992
product range ($9–25 CD) Riesling, Gewurztraminer, Sauvignon Blanc, Chardonnay, Merlot, Cabernet Sauvignon, Sparkling Sauvignon Cuvée, Late Harvest Muscat; Bell Tower is the cheaper second label.

summary Owen and Dianne Park run a thriving and varied enterprise offering both fruit- and grape-based wines (and 35 different types of fudge) from a large mission-style winery and restaurant. Wine production from grapes constitutes a modest part of the business. Exports to Australia, Singapore, Hong Kong, Japan, the Netherlands, Germany and the US.

pegasus bay ★★★★☆

Stockgrove Road, Waipara, RD2, Amberley **region** Waipara
phone (03) 314 6869 **fax** (03) 314 6869 **open** 7 days 10.30–5
winemaker Matthew Donaldson, Lynnette Hudson **production** 15 000 **est.** 1986
product range ($19.95–55 CD) Riesling, Sauvignon Blanc Semillon, Chardonnay, Aria (Reserve Riesling), Pinot Noir, Prima Donna Pinot Noir (unfiltered), Maestro (Bordeaux-blend), Finale (Reserve Noble Chardonnay); Main Divide is second label with Pinot Noir.
summary Leading wine judge Professor Ivan Donaldson (a neurologist) has, together with his wife and family, established the largest winery in Waipara, with 33 hectares of vineyards in bearing and a large and striking cathedral-like winery. Son Matthew is a Roseworthy graduate, and in every respect this is a serious operation. A winery restaurant adds to the attraction for visitors. Wine quality is consistently good, the wines with style and verve. Exports to Australia, the US, Japan, Singapore, Belgium, Denmark and even Luxembourg.

Pegasus Bay Riesling

TTTT **2000** Light green-yellow; a fragrant and flowery bouquet with intense lime and passionfruit aromas leads into a flavoursome, seductive, fruity style, let down on the finish to a degree by what seems to be unnecessary sweetness. **rating:** 89

best drinking Now–2004 **best vintages** '98 **drink with** Prosciutto and melon • $20

Pegasus Bay Sauvignon Semillon

TTTT **1999** Light to medium yellow-green; a potent, complex, smoky oak and ripe gooseberry bouquet is followed by a super-opulent and rich palate that cloys slightly on the finish. **rating:** 86

TTTY **1998** Glowing yellow-green; the bouquet is solid, clean, but not aromatic. There is very ripe fruit on the palate, but not at all varietal, presumably reflecting the unusually hot conditions of the 1998 vintage which caused so many problems for sauvignon blanc in New Zealand. **rating:** 84

best drinking Now–2003 **best vintages** NA **drink with** Fettuccine • $25

Pegasus Bay Canterbury Pinot Noir

TTTT **1999** Lighter in colour than the normal Pegasus Bay style, heralding a lighter than usual bouquet and palate (all things being relative, of course). Soft and subtle plum and cherry fruit swells the mid-palate, followed by balanced tannins on the finish. **rating:** 88

best drinking Now–2005 **best vintages** '93, '94, '95, '97, '98 **drink with** Rare breast of squab • $36

Pegasus Bay Prima Donna Pinot Noir

TTTTY **1999** Significantly deeper colour than the varietal release; strong aromas of plum, chocolate and a touch of smoky oak tinged with spice are followed by a magisterial palate, in the powerful mainstream of Pegasus Bay style. **rating:** 93

TTTT **1998** Medium to full purple-red; the bouquet is warm, spicy and scented; plum fruit is married with positive oak. An extremely rich and mouthfilling style with prodigious plum, oak and tannin flavours that are fractionally over the top. **rating:** 89

best drinking 2003–2008 **best vintages** '98 **drink with** Big game • $55

peninsula estate NR

52A Korora Road, Oneroa, Waiheke Island **region** Waiheke Island
phone (09) 372 7866 **fax** (09) 372 7840 **open** Weekends 1–4
winemaker Christopher Lush **production** 1400 **est.** 1986
product range ($13–35 CD) The top-of-the-line release is Peninsula Estate Cabernet Merlot; the intermittent second label is Oneroa Bay Cabernet Merlot. Both in fact include a small percentage of Cabernet Franc and Malbec. Since 1998 has also included Chardonnay and Syrah.
summary The Peninsula Estate Cabernet Merlot comes from a 5.5-hectare estate vineyard situated on a peninsula overlooking Oneroa Bay. The spectacular vineyard has produced some equally spectacular wines. The expansion to the range of wines came in the wake of forming a joint venture with its next-door neighbours, Robert and Emerald Gilmour, doubling the size of vineyards and making a little Chardonnay and rather more Syrah available. No recent tastings, however.

peregrine wines NR

c/o Wentworth Estate, RD1, Gibbston, Queenstown **region** Central Otago
phone (03) 442 4000 **fax** (03) 442 4038 **open** Mon–Sat 10–5
winemaker Rudi Bauer **production** 6000 **est.** 1998
product range ($19–30 R) Riesling, Gewurztraminer, Sauvignon Blanc, Pinot Gris, Pinot Noir.
summary Peregrine, a joint venture between Steve Smith (one of the world's first MW viticulturists), Greg Hay (also a viticulturist) and Adam Peren's Wentworth Estate, is on a fast track to success. From a standing start in 1998, production is expected to increase past the 1999 level of 6000 cases to 30 000 cases by 2004. Fifty hectares of vineyards are being planted, and the 1998 Sauvignon Blanc (from the first vintage under the Peregrine label) won the Air New Zealand Trophy at the Air New Zealand Wine Show of that year.

Peregrine Sauvignon Blanc

ŸŸŸŸ **1999** Medium green-yellow; the bouquet is clean, quite solid, with gooseberry and herb aromas. A similarly solid palate follows, with plenty of ripe fruit and length; overall, just a little soft. **rating:** 87
best drinking Now **best vintages** NA **drink with** Bluff oysters • $22

Peregrine Pinot Gris

ŸŸŸŸ **1999** Light green-yellow; the aromas are delicate, with rose-petal, flower and spice nuances. The palate is clean and crisp, with a mix of mineral and faint stonefruit; the wine has length, and has avoided the residual sugar trap. **rating:** 87
best drinking Now–2003 **best vintages** '99 **drink with** Poached fish • $25

perrelle lake hayes NR

c/o Chard Farm, Chard Road, RD1, Queenstown **region** Central Otago
phone (03) 442 6110 **fax** (03) 441 8400 **open** Not
winemaker Rob Hay, Duncan Forsyth **production** 3000 **est.** 1995
product range ($20–30 R) Cuvée de Prestige, Grand Cuvée Brut, Blanc de Blancs, Arcadia Lake Hayes Special Cuvée Brut.
summary Perrelle Lake Hayes is a specialist sparkling wine producer and a joint venture between John Derby (who is the general manager of the business) and Rob Hay, longtime Chard Farm owner-winemaker. Back in 1989 they identified an outstanding vineyard site at Gibbston, which was purchased and then subdivided and sold as vineyard lots. Part of the grapes for Perrelle come from these vineyards, but future growth will come from new plantings on the Amisfield Vineyard near Cromwell, where 120 hectares will be developed by 2004. Perrelle Lake Hayes has a major holding in this venture.

petrae estate NR

Cnr Regent Street and Paruatanga Road, Martinborough **region** Martinborough
phone (02) 148 4854 **fax** (06) 306 9626 **open** Not
winemaker Peter Jackson **production** 100 **est.** 2000
product range ($30 R) Pinot Noir.
summary Peter and Raewyn Jackson planted their 4-hectare vineyard ten years ago, the grapes being sold to Dry River up to and including 1999. In 2000 part of the production was made at Benfield and Delamare, and was due to be released in May 2001.

pleasant valley wines ★★★☆

322 Henderson Valley Road, Waitakere **region** Auckland Area
phone (09) 838 8857 **fax** (09) 838 8456 **open** Mon–Sat 9–6, Sun 11–6
winemaker Stephen Yelas **production** 10 000 **est.** 1902
product range ($9.80–21.95 CD) Gewurztraminer, Sauvignon Blanc, Chenin Chardonnay, Chardonnay, Riesling, Pinotage, together with a range of fortified wines, chiefly Sherries but also Port.
summary A former moribund fortified winemaker, revitalised in 1984 and now complementing its stocks of old fortified wines with well-made, well-priced table wines sourced from Hawke's Bay, Gisborne and Marlborough, supplementing a 7-hectare estate vineyard at Henderson. Exports to Japan.

pleiades vineyard NR

RD6, Blenheim **region** Marlborough
phone (03) 572 4841 **fax** (03) 572 4842 **open** Not
winemaker Winston Oliver **production** 300 **est.** 1993
product range ($28 R) Maia (Merlot Malbec blend).
summary Pleiades Vineyard has been established as a partnership between Maggie Dewar, a clinical psychologist in real life, and Winston Oliver, who has had ten years experience in the Marlborough wine industry, including the Marlborough viticultural course and practical winery experience at Cloudy Bay. The vineyard is situated in the Waihopai Valley (one of the offshoots of the Wairau Valley) with clay-rich loam over very deep gravels. Merlot, malbec and pinot gris are planted, with more pinot noir and pinot gris planned, which will lift the total plantings to 5 hectares. The 1998 Pleiades Maia was a brilliant debut for the winery.

ponder estate ★★★★

New Renwick Road, Blenheim **region** Marlborough
phone (03) 572 8642 **fax** (03) 572 9034 **open** 7 days 10–4.30
winemaker Graham Paul **production** 12 000 **est.** 1987
product range ($16.50–45 CD) Classic Riesling, Marlborough Sauvignon Blanc, Chardonnay; Artist's Reserve Chardonnay and Pinot Noir.
summary Well-known artist Mike Ponder and wife Diane began planting their vineyard and olive grove in 1987. With 25 hectares, Ponder Estate is primarily a grape-grower (supplying chardonnay, sauvignon blanc and riesling to Matua Valley for its Shingle Peak label) but is rapidly increasing the amount vinified for its own label (featuring a Mike Ponder illustration). It also has a press house for its own olive oil production. Exports to Australia, the UK and the US.

Ponder Estate Marlborough Sauvignon Blanc

🍷🍷🍷🍷 **2000** Very pale colour, almost white; the bouquet is fresh and clean with light tropical/passionfruit aromas as much Australian in character as Marlborough. The palate does not have a great deal of weight or intensity, but has good length, and the flavours are certainly very pleasant. **rating:** 87

best drinking Now **best vintages** '94, '97, '00 **drink with** Shellfish • $17.50

Ponder Estate Artist's Reserve Chardonnay

🍷🍷🍷🍷🍷 **1999** Light to medium green-yellow; the bouquet shows much more oak/barrel-ferment character than the varietal wine, adding to its complexity. Fig, nectarine and cashew flavours on the palate provide good mouthfeel and flow; better still, the oak doesn't come over the top. **rating:** 91

best drinking Now–2003 **best vintages** NA **drink with** Quiche Lorraine • NA

Ponder Estate Reserve Marlborough Pinot Noir

🍷🍷🍷🍷🍷 **1999** Medium red-purple; the bouquet is positively complex, with plum, a hint of game, and spice, the latter partly fruit-derived, partly oak-derived. The medium- to full-bodied palate has attractive sweet plummy fruit, gentle tannins and good length. **rating:** 92

best drinking Now–2004 **best vintages** '99 **drink with** Mushroom risotto • $44

porter's ★★★★

47 Kitchener Street, Martinborough **region** Martinborough
phone (06) 306 9013 **fax** (06) 306 8228 **open** By appointment
winemaker John Porter **production** 350 **est.** 1992
product range ($33–39 CD) Pinot Gris, Chardonnay, Pinot Noir.
summary John and Annabel Porter are Wellington lawyers with a long-standing interest in wine. That interest was intensified when John Porter went to France to play rugby, further reinforced by a sabbatical tour of the vineyards of Burgundy and Tuscany in the late 1980s. Returning to Martinborough they found wines on their own doorstep that captivated them with their intensity of flavour and quality. The establishment of a small vineyard was the inevitable next step. They have learned as they went and the vineyard is now 2 hectares, complemented by commercial plantings of olives and lavender. Pinot Noir is by far the most important wine in the portfolio, but the Porters have also developed a special interest in the small amount of Pinot Gris they make.

Porter's Pinot Gris

🍷🍷🍷 1999 Light green-yellow; a potent, intense bouquet with strong, dried-fruit aromas is followed by an uncompromisingly sweet palate that, to my taste, is overdone, simply because it overwhelms the fruit varietal character. But then, I am no admirer of most Alsace Vendange Tardive styles, so others will be far happier with the outcome. **rating:** 84

best drinking Now–2004 **best vintages** NA **drink with** Fresh foie gras • $33

Porter's Pinot Noir

🍷🍷🍷🍷 1999 Medium to full red-purple; very ripe, rich, glossy, plummy fruit with some forest and spice undertones on the bouquet is followed by a rich, full, luscious plum and dark briar-accented palate. In the full-frontal New Zealand style. **rating:** 90

best drinking Now–2004 **best vintages** '99 **drink with** Game • $39

pouparae park NR

Bushmere Road, Gisborne **region** Gisborne
phone (06) 867 7931 **fax** (06) 867 7909 **open** 7 days 10–6
winemaker Alec Cameron **production** 500 **est.** 1994
product range ($7.50–15 R) Riesling, Chardonnay, Solstice Blanc (Müller Thurgau, Dr Hogg Muscat blend), Pinotage.
summary Pouparae Park was established on the family's property by Alec and Rachel Cameron in 1994, surrounded by a much larger kiwi fruit orchard. 'Pouparae' means 'high vantage point'.

purple heights estate NR

Main West Coast Road, RD6, Christchurch **region** Canterbury
phone (03) 358 2080 **fax** (03) 325 3843 **open** Not
winemaker Dayne Sherwood (Contract) **production** NA **est.** 1996
product range Riesling, Noble Riesling.
summary Partners Delwyn and John Mathieson and David and Diana Jackson named their vineyard after the colour of the nearby foothills, planting 2 hectares to riesling. Having sold the grapes to other makers for many years, the partners ventured into winemaking (via contract at Sherwood Estate) in 1996. There are no sales to the public; all wine is sold wholesale to retailers and restaurants.

putiki bay vineyard NR

84 Vintage Lane, Te Whau Point, RD1, Waiheke Island **region** Waiheke Island
phone (09) 372 7322 **fax** (09) 372 8098 **open** Not
winemaker Chris Lush (Contract) **production** 950 **est.** 1997
product range ($45 R) Pinot Noir, Pinot Gris, Merlot, Malbec.
summary The 4.5-hectare Putiki Bay Vineyard has been established by a German businessman who is an absentee owner, still living in Germany, whence much of the production will ultimately head. The majority of the plantings are, somewhat eccentrically, pinot noir, which makes a predictably big, tannic red wine. Limited quantities of the three red wines will be offered by mail order within New Zealand.

quarry road estate NR

Waerenga Road, RD1, Te Kauwhata **region** Waikato and Bay of Plenty
phone (07) 826 3595 **fax** (07) 826 3595 **open** 7 days 8–6
winemaker Toby Cooper, Jenny Gander, Nikki Cooper **production** 3500 **est.** 1996
product range ($6.50–22 R) Grape juices, table wines, sparkling wines, fortified wines and liqueurs. Table wines: Sauvignon Blanc, Chardonnay, Cabernet Sauvignon Merlot. Wines also purchased in bulk from Bazzard Estate.
summary In 1996 (a nominal year of establishment) the former Aspen Ridge was acquired by the Cooper family and became Quarry Road Estate. With the aid of consultancy advice, they intend to move more towards the production of premium table wines and to expand the cellar-door facilities.

quartz reef ★★★★☆

McNulty Road, Lake Dustan Estate, Cromwell, Central Otago **region** Central Otago
phone (03) 445 3084 **fax** (03) 445 3086 **open** Mon–Fri 11–3 or by appointment
winemaker Rudi Bauer, Clotilde Chauvet **production** 5000 **est.** 1996
product range ($20–35 R) Pinot Gris, Pinot Noir, Chauvet Méthode Champenoise.
summary Quartz Reef is a joint venture between the effervescent, hyperactive Rudi Bauer and Clotilde Chauvet, both of whom were at one time or another Rippon winemakers. They also provide contract-winemaking services for an increasing number of Otago grape-growers. Three hectares have been planted to pinot noir and chardonnay, with plantings intended to extend to 10 hectares of pinot noir and 2 hectares of pinot gris. The wines are exported to the UK, Germany and Denmark.

Quartz Reef Pinot Noir

YYYYY **1999** Medium red-purple; a highly scented bouquet with a mix of spice, plum and cherry pip together with subtle oak is followed by a delicious palate with that distinctive vineyard cherry flavour, long and elegant.

rating: 94

best drinking Now **best vintages** '98, '99 **drink with** Wild boar • $35

rabbit ridge NR

407 Taylor Road, Waimauku **region** Auckland Area
phone (09) 411 8556 **fax** (09) 411 8556 **open** By appointment
winemaker Matua Valley (Contract) **production** 210 **est.** 1990
product range ($19.95 R) Burrow Cabernet Sauvignon Merlot.
summary Former architect and now leading New Zealand fine-wine wholesaler and importer Paul Mitchell (of Wine Direct Imports) is indulging in a little poaching at Rabbit Ridge. He established a 1-hectare vineyard 30 minutes from the centre of Auckland, with his house situated in the middle of the vineyard; it is sufficiently elevated for him to see rabbits feeding in the vineyard from the lounge. The wines are contract-made at Matua Valley, and Paul Mitchell has no intention of hopping into a fermenter at vintage time. However, he does concede there are plans to build a small cellar-door sales and barrel storage area; in the meantime the wines are available from Wine Direct or by mail order.

ransom wines NR

Valerie Close, Warkworth **region** Northland and Matakana
phone (09) 425 8862 **open** Weekends 10–6 summer, 11–5 winter, or by appointment
winemaker Robin Ransom **production** NA **est.** 1996
product range ($16–24 R) Gumfield Chardonnay, Barrique Chardonnay, Clos de Valerie Pinot Gris, Dark Summit Cabernet Sauvignon.
summary Robin and Marion Ransom are in the course of establishing a 6-hectare vineyard south of Warkworth with north-facing slopes and relatively free-draining soils. Their weekend and holiday relaxation through Ransom Wines was the result of a trip to Tuscany and some subsequent vintage experience in Nelson. For a self-taught winemaker, Robin Ransom is doing a remarkably good job with both white and red wines.

redmetal vineyards NR

2006 Maraekakaho Road, RD1, Bridge Pa, Hastings **region** Hawke's Bay
phone (06) 879 6567 **fax** (06) 879 6717 **open** Not
winemaker Grant Edmonds **production** 1500 **est.** 1992
product range ($24–90 R) Rosé, The Merlot, Basket Press Merlot Cabernet Franc, Merlot Cabernet Franc Cabernet Sauvignon.
summary A joint venture between the vastly experienced winemaker Grant Edmonds, wife Sue, and Diane and Gary Simpson, with initial plantings of 7 hectares on an alluvial silt over gravel soil known locally as red metal. The wines are exported to the UK. No recent tastings.

richmond plains NR

c/o The Grape Escape, McShane Road, RD1, Richmond, Nelson **region** Nelson
phone (03) 544 4230 **fax** (03) 544 4231 **open** Summer 7 days 10–5, winter Tues-Sun 10–4.30
winemaker Jane Cooper **production** 1300 **est.** 1995
product range ($15–28 R) Sauvignon Blanc, Organic Sauvignon Blanc, Chardonnay, Escapade White (a blend of German varieties), Escapade Red (a weird blend of eight varieties including Domina).
summary David Holmes has secured Bio-Gro certification for his 4.5-hectare Richmond Plains vineyard, and the quality of the grapes proves the worth of organic farming. The wines are sold at the eccentrically charming Grape Escape, which it shares with Te Mania (and also shares Te Mania's winemaker, Jane Cooper).

Richmond Plains Sauvignon Blanc

YYYY **2000** Light green-yellow; a powerful, ripe bouquet redolent of passionfruit and even a touch of melon is followed by a tangy palate, with more tropical/passionfruit flavours rounded up by crisp acidity on the finish.
rating: 87

best drinking Now **best vintages** NA **drink with** Seafood pasta • $17

richmond range estate NR

Jackson's Road, Rapaura, Blenheim **region** Marlborough
phone (03) 578 1937 **fax** (03) 578 1937 **open** By appointment
winemaker Greg Trought **production** 200 **est.** 1995
product range ($11–13.50 R) Sauvignon Blanc, Chardonnay.
summary Thomas and Nola Hurford are long-term grape-growers with just under 10 hectares of vines, the crop being sold to Allan Scott. However, the Hurfords retain a small proportion for release under the Richmond Range Estate label, which is sold principally through restaurants in Nelson and Christchurch. Wine quality is said to be good, and the wines can be purchased direct by appointment.

ridge view vineyards NR

Gordons Road, Austend, Waiheke Island **region** Waiheke Island
phone (09) 372 6220 **open** Not
winemaker Ushzula Musson, Rainer Eschenbruch (Consultant) **production** NA **est.** 1999
product range Bordeaux-blend.
summary Brian and Wendy Saward head a group of a dozen shareholder investors who have established a 5-hectare vineyard planted to Bordeaux varieties. The wines are made at Peninsula Estate.

rimu grove ★★★★☆

Bronte Road East, RD1, Upper Moutere, Mapua, Nelson **region** Nelson
phone (03) 540 2345 **fax** (03) 540 2345 **open** 7 days 10–5
winemaker Patrick Stowe **production** 700 **est.** 2000
product range Chardonnay, Pinot Noir.
summary Like Philip Jones (of Spencer Hill Estate), Patrick and Barbara Stowe left California (indeed the Napa Valley) to establish their 3-hectare vineyard at Nelson. Both have backgrounds in science, and currently work in Wellington, but have plans to move to the winery and to develop guest accommodation and other attractions. The wine will be both sold locally and exported to the US.

Rimu Grove Chardonnay

YYYYY **2000** Light to medium green-yellow; melon, cashew and spice together with some creamy malolactic nuances on the bouquet are followed by a truly stylish and elegant wine, showing skilled winemaking and handling in reaction to the fruit; melon, cashew and spice flavours run through a well-balanced, long palate. A nigh-on perfect debut.
rating: 93

best drinking Now–2004 **best vintages** NA **drink with** Abalone • NA

rippon vineyard & winery ★★★☆

Mount Aspiring Road, Lake Wanaka **region** Central Otago
phone (03) 443 8084 **fax** (03) 443 8084 **open** Dec–Apr 7 days 11–5, July–Nov 1.30–4.30, May–June by appointment
winemaker Russell Lake **production** 5000 **est.** 1975
product range ($14.50–35 CD) Riesling, Gewurztraminer, Sauvignon Blanc, Hotere White, Osteiner, Chardonnay, Gamay Rosé, Emma Rippon Sparkling, Pinot Noir.
summary Claimed, with some justification, to be the most beautifully sited vineyard in the world, situated on the edge of Lake Wanaka (which is responsible for the remarkable site climate) with the snow-clad New Zealand Alps painting a striking backdrop. Right across the range, Rippon has produced some outstanding wines, but its former flagbearer, Pinot Noir, has been overtaken by many other Otago wineries. In recent years Rippon has moved to Bio-Gro™ certified organic status. The wines are exported to Australia, the UK, the US, Hong Kong, Brazil and Japan.

riverline vineyard NR

State Highway 83, Georgetown, North Otago **region** Central Otago
phone (03) 431 1737 **fax** (03) 431 1737 **open** 7 days 12–6
winemaker Graeme Thorn **production** 8 **est.** 1994
product range ($15–20 CD) Riesling, Gewurztraminer, Pinot Noir.
summary Graeme and Pip Thorn preside over a micro-vineyard and winery in North Otago (the only winery in this region). Experimental plantings of 0.5 hectare of pinot noir and 0.25 hectare each of gewurztraminer and riesling produced 100 bottles of wine in 1999, sold through the shop on site, which also offers other New Zealand wines and beer. It also offers the only taxidermy showroom I have ever encountered as part of a winery cellar door.

riverside wines ★★★

Dartmoor Road, Puketapu, Napier **region** Hawke's Bay
phone (06) 844 4942 **fax** (06) 844 4671 **open** Summer 7 days 11–5, winter by appointment
winemaker Russell Wiggins **production** 12 000 **est.** 1989
product range ($12–28 CD) Dartmoor Sauvignon Blanc, Barrel Fermented Sauvignon Blanc, Dartmoor Chardonnay, Stirling Chardonnay, Reserve Chardonnay, Rosé, Merlot, Stirling Merlot Cabernet.
summary Ian and Rachel Cadwallader have established 14 hectares of vines on their farm, which are coming progressively into production. The wine is made on site in the small winery above the Dartmoor Valley. It has to be said that overall wine quality was far from exciting, but the arrival of Russell Wiggins as winemaker in late 1998 has improved matters. In the meantime, exports to the US and Thailand are underway.

Riverside Stirling Merlot Cabernet

YYYY **1998** Medium to full red-purple; the bouquet has plenty of ripe, sweet cassis and mint aromas; the palate with more of the same in a soft, mouthfilling mode, supported by attractive oak and tannins. **rating:** 89
best drinking 2003–2008 **best vintages** '98 **drink with** Beef in red wine sauce • $19

rongopai wines ★★★

Te Kauwhata Road, Te Kauwhata **region** Waikato and Bay of Plenty
phone (07) 826 3981 **fax** (07) 826 3462 **open** Mon–Fri 9–5, Sat 10–5, Sun 11–4
winemaker Tom van Dam **production** 15 000 **est.** 1985
product range ($11.50–35.50 R) Sauvignon Blanc, Sauvignon Blanc The Knoll, Sauvignon Blanc Vintage Reserve, Riesling, Chardonnay, Chardonnay Single Vineyard, Chardonnay Vintage Reserve, Chardonnay Swan Road, Pinot Noir, Merlot Cabernet and Botrytised Selection.
summary Now owned solely by Tom van Dam and wife Faith but going from strength to strength, it would seem. The reputation of Rongopai rests fairly and squarely upon its spectacular botrytised wines, which enjoyed equal quantities of show success and critical acclaim throughout most of the 1990s. Both Chardonnay and the more conventional Riesling are used in these wines; the minimal use of chemicals and herbicides in the vineyards promotes late-season botrytis, countered by vine-trimming, leaf-plucking and bunch-thinning for the conventional table wines. All grapes are hand-picked. No recent tastings

rosebank estate NR

Cnr Johns and Groynes Drives, Belfast, Christchurch **region** Canterbury
phone (03) 323 8539 **fax** (03) 323 8538 **open** 7 days 10–5
winemaker Kym Rayner (Contract) **production** 1200 **est.** 1993
product range ($6.95–15.95 CD) Riesling, Sauvignon Blanc, Waipara Chardonnay, Marlborough Chardonnay, Marlborough Riesling, Canterbury Chardonnay, Reserve Canterbury Chardonnay, Müller Thurgau, Directors' White, Sparkling Sekt, Pinot Noir, Cabernet Shiraz.
summary Situated only minutes from the city centre and six minutes from Christchurch airport, this is as much an entertainment centre as it is a winery, with a beautiful garden setting containing hundreds of roses, rhododendrons and camellias; lunch is served from the restaurant each day, and à la carte dinner from Wednesday to Sunday from 6 pm. Most of the grapes are being sourced from Marlborough. In 1996 a cricket ground was established at Rosebank in village-green style. No recent tastings.

rossendale wines NR

150 Old Tai Tapu Road, Christchurch **region** Canterbury
phone (03) 322 7780 **fax** (03) 332 9272 **open** 7 days 10–5
winemaker Grant Whelan **production** 6000 **est.** 1987
product range ($12–22 CD) Chardonnay, Barrel Selection Chardonnay, Riesling, Sauvignon Blanc, St Helena Pinot Noir, Reserve Pinot Noir.
summary Rossendale is the highly successful venture of beef exporter Brent Rawstron, who ventured into viticulture on his farm in 1987. A 120-year-old gatekeeper's lodge on the farm has been converted into a restaurant and sales area, nestling in a century-old forest. All this, and situated only 15 minutes from the centre of Christchurch, making it the closest winery to that city. Exports to the UK and Canada.

ruby bay winery NR

Korepo Road, RD1, Upper Moutere, Nelson **region** Nelson
phone (03) 540 2825 **fax** (03) 540 2105 **open** 7 days 11–6
winemaker Anita Ewart-Croy **production** 750 **est.** 1976
product range ($15–22.50 CD) Nelson Sauvignon Blanc, Marlborough Chardonnay, Nelson Pinot Noir.
summary The beautifully sited former Korepo winery, bought by the Moore family in 1989, is well known for its restaurant. The winery changed hands in 1999, and was back on the market in late 2000. No recent tastings.

ryan estate NR

Oak Avenue, RD5, Hastings **region** Hawke's Bay
phone (06) 879 9072 **fax** (06) 879 8675 **open** Not
winemaker Evert Nijsink **production** 500 **est.** 1998
product range ($18 R) Cabernet Sauvignon.
summary Kurt Ryan has a 10-hectare vineyard known as the Oero Farm, acquired from his family in 1992. Simply a grape-grower until 1998, he made a small quantity of Cabernet Sauvignon in that year, and when brother Adam returned from overseas, they formed a partnership to make a larger quantity of wine in 2000 (there was no 1999). The 2000 vintage was made at Alpha Domus, the likely facility in the future.

sacred hill ★★★★☆

Dartmoor Road, RD6, Napier **region** Hawke's Bay
phone (06) 844 0138 **fax** (06) 844 3271 **open** Summer 7 days 11–4
winemaker Tony Bish **production** 60 000 **est.** 1986
product range ($14–40 R) At the very top, intermittent releases of special selection wines, including Sauvage Sauvignon Blanc, Rifleman's Chardonnay, Brokenstone Merlot, Helsman Cabernet Sauvignon; then the Reserve range, although not necessarily carrying that word in the name (just to confuse the unwary, typically being described as barrel-fermented or basket press) with Sauvignon Blanc, Chardonnay and Merlot Cabernet; at the bottom, the Whitecliff Vineyards range of Sauvignon Blanc, Chardonnay and Merlot.
summary The Mason family are pastoralists-turned-grape-growers and thereafter winemakers (Mark Mason is a Roseworthy graduate). Sacred Hill has had its ups and downs since it was founded in 1986 but has steadied significantly since 1995. The top-of-the-range Rifleman's Chardonnay, Brokenstone Merlot and Basket Press Cabernet Sauvignon are high-quality wines. Exports to the UK and the US.

Sacred Hill Sauvage Sauvignon Blanc

YYYY **1998** Medium to full yellow-green; strong, toasty barrel-ferment characters on the bouquet and palate take the wine to the polar opposite in style to the Whitecliff wine (below). Interestingly, does not cloy on the finish, but I still prefer the Whitecliff version at half the price. **rating:** 85

best drinking Now–2004 **best vintages** NA **drink with** Guinea fowl • $30

Sacred Hill Whitecliff Vineyards Sauvignon Blanc

YYYY **2000** Light green-yellow; the bouquet is fresh and crisp, with passionfruit, lemon and lime aromatics, followed by a palate that is lively and intense yet quite delicate. Into the bargain, has good length. **rating:** 88

best drinking Now **best vintages** '97, '00 **drink with** Light seafood • $14

Sacred Hill Reserve Barrel Fermented Chardonnay

YYYYY **1999** Medium yellow-green; a complex bouquet with the generous use of barrel fermentation and malolactic fermentation to push the wine along. The palate is long and quite intense, with fig and cashew flavours, the fruit supporting the winemaking inputs. Retasted February 2001 and has developed impressively. **rating:** 91

best drinking Now **best vintages** '99 **drink with** Pasta carbonara • NA

Sacred Hill Rifleman's Chardonnay

YYYYY **1999** Medium to full yellow-green; the bouquet is complex, with well-balanced and integrated fruit and oak; the palate finds a similar balance, with mouthfilling peach/nectarine/citrus fruit, and the oak and mlf influences nicely restrained. Stylish and fruity, not oaky this vintage. **rating:** 94

best drinking Now **best vintages** '97, '98, '99 **drink with** Turkey • $39.95

Sacred Hill Whitecliff Vineyards Merlot

YYYYY **2000** Bright, youthful purple-red; fresh and clean sweet berry/currant aromas to the bouquet lead into an appealing, fresh and lively palate supported by gentle tannins. Continues the form of the '99. **rating:** 90

best drinking Now–2003 **best vintages** '99, '00 **drink with** Whatever takes your fancy • $15.95

Sacred Hill Helmsman Cabernet Sauvignon

YYYY **1998** Medium red-purple; the bouquet is quite fragrant, moderately intense, with fresh cassis berry fruit and toasty oak. The gentle, medium-bodied palate has cassis/berry fruit but slightly charry oak and some astringency shows through. **rating:** 87

best drinking 2003–2008 **best vintages** NA **drink with** Marinated beef • $20

saint clair estate ★★★★☆

156 New Renwick Road, RD2, Blenheim **region** Marlborough

phone (03) 578 8695 **fax** (03) 578 8696 **open** At Taste of Marlborough, Cnr Selmes and Rapaura Roads, Blenheim

winemaker Kim Crawford, Matt Thomson (Consultants) **production** 30 000 **est.** 1978

product range ($15–27 R) The Marlborough range: Riesling, Tuatara Bay Sauvignon Blanc, Sauvignon Blanc, Unoaked Chardonnay, Chardonnay, Merlot; the Reserve range: Fairhall Riesling, Awatere Sauvignon Blanc, Wairau Sauvignon Blanc, Omaka Chardonnay, Rapaura Road Merlot and Doctors Creek Noble Botrytis.

summary Neal and Judy Ibbotson followed the tried-and-true path of growing grapes for 15 or so years before venturing into wine production, which they did with spectacular success in 1994. Since that year, ever-increasing quantities of grapes from their 56 hectares have been vinified, with the exceptional skills of Kim Crawford leading to a cascade of show awards. The wines are exported to over 20 countries across Europe, North America, Asia and the Pacific Region, including Australia.

Saint Clair Estate Fairhall Reserve Riesling

YYYYY **2000** Light green-yellow; the bouquet is fine and quite delicate, taking time to open up. The class of the wine shows through on its long palate, with lime/lemon/apple flavours, and excellent balance between the fruit and acidity on the finish. **rating:** 91

best drinking 2004–2010 **best vintages** '00 **drink with** Salad niçoise • $19

Saint Clair Estate Marlborough Riesling

ΨΨΨΨ **2000** Light green-yellow; a quite aromatic and flowery bouquet ranging through lime and apple is followed by an extremely powerful, fleshy, high-toned palate with a riot of tropical flavour; the residual sugar is (largely) balanced by the depth of fruit and the acidity. Tasted several times and, I must admit, with differing impressions and points. This rating is something of a compromise. **rating:** 89

best drinking Now **best vintages** '99 **drink with** Fresh fruit • $16

Saint Clair Estate Marlborough Sauvignon Blanc

ΨΨΨΨ **2000** Light green-yellow; a clean, moderately intense bouquet offers passionfruit and a hint of lemongrass, the palate fresh and lively, with harmonious flavours, good intensity, length and finish. **rating:** 88

best drinking Now **best vintages** '94, '96, '97, '00 **drink with** Sashimi • $16

Saint Clair Estate Tuatara Bay Sauvignon Blanc

ΨΨΨΨ **2000** Light green-yellow; the bouquet is clean, fresh and crisp, with a mix of lemon/citrus and gooseberry; similar flavours run through the nicely balanced and weighted palate. **rating:** 87

best drinking Now **best vintages** '00 **drink with** Crab cakes • NA

Saint Clair Estate Wairau Reserve Sauvignon Blanc

ΨΨΨΨΨ **2000** Medium yellow-green; the intense but clean bouquet ranges through stonefruit, gooseberry and passionfruit, leading into a palate with well-above-average weight, depth and intensity; textured gooseberry, stonefruit and mineral flavours are singularly impressive. **rating:** 93

best drinking Now **best vintages** '00 **drink with** Calamari • $18.50

Saint Clair Estate Unoaked Chardonnay

ΨΨΨΨ **2000** Light green-yellow; a clean, fresh, light melon/citrus/smoky cashew bouquet is followed by a palate running through the same flavours, and some freshness to the aftertaste. **rating:** 83

best drinking Now **best vintages** NA **drink with** Takeaway • $16

Saint Clair Estate Marlborough Chardonnay

ΨΨΨΨΨ **2000** Medium yellow-green; a complex bouquet with melon, spicy oak and touches of cashew is followed by a fruit-driven palate with ripe nectarine and melon, and a touch of citrus powering the length and finish. A stylish wine in all respects. **rating:** 94

best drinking Now **best vintages** '99, '00 **drink with** Grilled fish • $17

Saint Clair Estate Omaka Valley Reserve Chardonnay

ΨΨΨΨΨ **1999** Medium yellow-green; the bouquet is exceedingly complex, with a heap of oak but, even more, powerful Burgundian characters. The palate provides even more of the same; like it or not, you cannot ignore a wine with as much personality as this has. **rating:** 91

best drinking Now–2004 **best vintages** '98, '99 **drink with** Roast veal • $25

Saint Clair Estate Marlborough Merlot

ΨΨΨΨΨ **2000** Youthful purple-red; a very ripe, plummy, almost Pinot-like bouquet is followed by a soft, fleshy, mouthfilling plum and berry-flavoured palate, with soft tannins and a hint of vanilla oak. **rating:** 92

best drinking 2002–2007 **best vintages** '98, '00 **drink with** Lamb fillets • $20

Saint Clair Estate Rapaura Road Reserve Merlot

ΨΨΨΨ **1999** Medium red-purple; bright, sweet, small berry fruit on the bouquet is offset by spice and vanilla notes from the oak. The wine is quite soft and sweet on the mid-palate, tightening up slightly on the finish. **rating:** 87

best drinking 2003–2008 **best vintages** '98 **drink with** Duck confit • $27

st francis wine company NR

c/o Valerie Close, SH1, Warkworth **region** Northland and Matakana
phone (02) 152 6736 **fax** (02) 169 7526 **open** Not
winemaker Simon Lampen **production** 1300 **est.** 1997
product range ($14.50–25 R) Riesling, Gewurztraminer, Chardonnay.

summary Simon Lampen is a graduate of Lincoln's post-graduate wine course (and also has a degree in commerce), having caught the wine bug while working as a sommelier. He and partner Penny Reekie are developing an 8-hectare vineyard in Marlborough, planted to riesling, gewurztraminer, pinot gris, pinot noir and sauvignon blanc, to yield its first vintage in 2001. All the wines to date have been made from grapes purchased from growers in Hawke's Bay and Marlborough.

st helena estate ★★★☆

Coutts Island Road, Christchurch **region** Canterbury
phone (03) 323 8202 **fax** (03) 323 8252 **open** Mon–Sat 10–4.30, Sun 12–5
winemaker Alan McCorkindale **production** 10 000 **est.** 1978
product range ($7.50–30 CD) Riesling, Canterbury Plains Müller Thurgau, Southern Alps Dry White, Chardonnay, Reserve Chardonnay, Noble Bacchus, Pinot Gris, Reserve Pinot Gris, Pinot Blanc, Pinot Noir, Reserve Pinot Noir, Port Hills Dry Red, Peers Port, Marlborough Chardonnay, Marlborough Sauvignon Blanc, Reserve Canterbury Chardonnay.
summary In its moments of success or otherwise, controversy has never been far from St Helena's door. After a spectacular debut for its Pinot Noir in 1982, it has been a roller-coaster ride since, but much work in the vineyard (and winery) is starting to pay dividends. The arrival of the talented Alan McCorkindale as winemaker has seen some lift in quality, but the limitations of the vigorous soil at the vineyard are still apparent, as the best wines come from Marlborough. The wines are exported to Australia, the UK and Canada.

St Helena Estate Canterbury Riesling

🍷🍷🍷🍸 **2000** Light green-yellow; both the bouquet and palate show above-average complexity and fruit intensity, aided by what appears to be an element of botrytis. The sweetness is evident, but no means unbalanced. **rating:** 84
best drinking Now–2006 **best vintages** NA **drink with** Smoked fish • $14

St Helena Marlborough Sauvignon Blanc

🍷🍷🍷🍷 **2000** Light straw-green; a spotlessly clean and crisp bouquet with asparagus/green bean/herb aromas is followed by a palate with pleasing mouthfeel, thanks to slightly sweeter fruit flavours. **rating:** 87
best drinking Now **best vintages** NA **drink with** Summer salad • $14

St Helena Estate Canterbury Reserve Pinot Gris

🍷🍷🍷🍸 **1999** Medium to full straw-yellow; the bouquet is complex, with hints of smoky/toasty oak and moderately intense fruit. The palate is even more complex, quite Alsace-like in style, with ripe pear and apple flavours, and just a hint of nuttiness. **rating:** 84
best drinking Now–2003 **best vintages** NA **drink with** Smoked eel • $19

St Helena Estate Marlborough Chardonnay

🍷🍷🍷🍷 **2000** Medium yellow-green; the complex bouquet ranges through melon, cashew, almond and subtle oak, logical forerunners of a sophisticated, gently understated palate. **rating:** 86
best drinking Now–2004 **best vintages** '99 **drink with** Sweetbreads • $17

St Helena Estate Canterbury Pinot Noir

🍷🍷🍷🍷 **1999** Light to medium red; a high-toned greenish/stemmy bouquet is followed by a lively, sappy palate that has many Burgundian hallmarks about it. Without question, an alternative style. **rating:** 88
best drinking Now **best vintages** '84, '91, '94, '95 **drink with** Asian • $19

st jerome wines NR

219 Metcalfe Road, Henderson **region** Auckland Area
phone (09) 833 6205 **fax** (09) 833 6205 **open** Mon–Sat 9–6, Sun 12–5
winemaker Davorin Ozich, Miro Ozich **production** 7000 **est.** 1968
product range ($14.50–36 CD) Riesling, Sauvignon Blanc, Chardonnay, Chablis, Gewurztraminer, Cabernet Merlot, Port.
summary The Cabernet Merlots made by Davorin Ozich reflect his Master of Science degree and practical training at Chateau Margaux and Chateau Cos d'Estournel in Bordeaux. They are hugely powerful wines that polarise opinion. The white wines are much less interesting.

st nesbit NR

Hingaia Road, RD1, Papakura **region** Auckland Area
phone (09) 379 0808 **fax** (09) 376 6956 **open** Not
winemaker Dr Tony Molloy QC **production** 800 **est.** 1980
product range ($37 CD) A single Cabernet Merlot (Cabernet Sauvignon, Cabernet Franc, Merlot, Malbec, Petit Verdot) Bordeaux-blend has been supplemented more recently by a Rosé, the result of indifferent vintages in 1992 and 1993 and of the effects of leaf-roll virus.
summary Tony Molloy is a leading tax lawyer with a weekend passion; his Bordeaux-blend is revered in New Zealand and well regarded elsewhere. His outstanding Cabernet Merlot is always produced in tiny quantities, but the last indication of the quality of the vineyard was in 1991. Since that time there has been a much troubled replanting of the 4-hectare vineyard, and the next wine is unlikely to be released much before 2004.

sanderson winery NR

41 Trotter Road, Twyford, Hastings **region** Hawke's Bay
phone (06) 879 8003 **fax** (06) 879 8003 **open** Not
winemaker Ken Sanderson **production** 650 **est.** 1999
product range ($20–30 R) Chardonnay, Methode Champenoise, Sangiovese, Syrah, and others to come.
summary Ken Sanderson is an industry veteran with a graduate degree in food technology from Massey University, and winemaking experience in France, Italy and Germany, as well as several years as winemaker at Crossroads. Together with two shareholders, he has built up a small contract-winemaking business in a shed which he leases on Trotter Road, relying on contract-grown grapes for the Sanderson label. In 1999 he began the development of a vineyard in Ngatarawa Road, planted to red varieties, with riesling (one of his passions acquired in Germany) part of the future planting plan.

sandihurst wines NR

Main West Coast Road, West Melton, Canterbury **region** Canterbury
phone (03) 347 8289 **fax** (03) 347 8289 **open** Weekends 11–5 or by appointment
winemaker Andrew Meggitt **production** 4200 **est.** 1992
product range ($12–17 ML) Riesling, Gewurztraminer, Pinot Gris, Pinot Gris Reserve, Chardonnay (unwooded), Premier Pinot Noir.
summary Yet another of the ever-expanding number of wineries in the Christchurch region. It is a substantial operation, with 16 hectares of vineyards in bearing. However production (and winemaking) has fluctuated, the best wines undoubtedly being the Pinot Noir and Pinot Gris. Exports to Australia and the UK.

seifried estate ★★★★

Cnr State Highway 60 and Redwood Road, Appleby, Nelson **region** Nelson
phone (03) 544 5599 **fax** (03) 544 5522 **open** 7 days 11–5
winemaker Hermann Seifried, Daniel Schwarzenbach **production** 80 000 **est.** 1973
product range ($9–30 R) Old Coach Road is the third, or lowest, tier ($9–14); then comes Siefried Estate in the middle ($13–20); and finally the Winemaker's Collection at the top ($17–30).
summary With 87 hectares of vineyards established progressively since 1973 and a crush well in excess of 1000 tonnes, Seifried Estate is by far the largest of the Nelson wineries. The production is heavily biased towards white wines, which are of wholly admirable consistency of style and quality. Just prior to vintage in 1996 Seifried moved to its new winery situated in its picturesque Appleby Vineyard. Exports to the UK, the US, Canada, Germany, Austria, Switzerland, Belgium, Thailand, Japan and Hong Kong.

Seifried Estate Winemaker's Collection Riesling

YYYYY **2000** Bright light to medium-green yellow, always a good sign. The intense bouquet has a mix of lime blossom, passionfruit and a controversial touch of reduction. There is no problem with the palate, however, which is fresh and lively, with masses of lime blossom and passionfruit running through to a lingering, slightly off-dry finish. **rating:** 90

best drinking Now–2004 **best vintages** '00 **drink with** Sitr-fried squid • $18.95

Seifried Estate Gewurztraminer Dry

🍷🍷🍷🍷 **1999** Light to medium yellow-green; strong, spicy, lychee varietal fruit has tropical overtones, the palate fleshy and mouthfilling, with good weight and varietal character. There is an underlying sweetness that is a desirable part of the wine. **rating:** 87

best drinking Now **best vintages** '99 **drink with** Chinese prawns • $14

Seifried Estate Winemaker's Collection Gewurztraminer

🍷🍷🍷🍷🍷 **2000** Light yellow-green; tropical fruit dominates the bouquet, but lychee certainly makes its presence felt. The wine expands markedly on the palate, with rich lychee/fruit-salad/tropical flavours well balanced by acidity that stops the wine cloying. **rating:** 90

best drinking Now–2003 **best vintages** '00 **drink with** Chinese prawns • $20

Seifried Estate Nelson Sauvignon Blanc

🍷🍷🍷🍷 **2000** Light green-yellow; a crisp, quite vibrant herb and grass bouquet is followed by a crisp lemony/minerally palate with bracing acidity on the finish. **rating:** 86

best drinking Now **best vintages** '91, '92, '93, '94, '96, '97 **drink with** Shellfish • $14.95

Seifried Estate Old Coach Road Sauvignon Blanc

🍷🍷🍷🍷🍷 **2000** Light to medium green-yellow; clean lemon rind and gooseberry aromas lead into a surprisingly concentrated and well-balanced palate with riper fruit flavours than the bouquet, heading towards passionfruit. Sauvignon Blanc that invites the second, and even the third, glass. **rating:** 90

best drinking Now **best vintages** '00 **drink with** Caesar salad • NA

Seifried Estate Ice Wine 375 ml

🍷🍷🍷🍷🍷 **2000** Light to medium yellow-green; the aromatic bouquet has lime and apricot blossom, the palate very intense, lemony/limey, with fantastic acidity on the finish. 11.2 grams per litre acid and 140 grams per litre of residual sugar tells it all. Ridiculously underpriced. **rating:** 94

best drinking 2003–2010 **best vintages** '00 **drink with** Fruit tart • $18

Seifried Estate Winemaker's Collection Pinot Noir

🍷🍷🍷🍷 **2000** Light to medium red-purple; cherry, plum and spice aromas on the bouquet feed into an appealing mix of plummy fruit and savoury/silky texture and tannins, rounded off with subtle oak. **rating:** 87

best drinking Now–2004 **best vintages** NA **drink with** Shabu shabu • $22.95

Seifried Estate Winemaker's Collection Cabernet Merlot

🍷🍷🍷🍷🍷 **1998** Medium red-purple; a clean and smooth bouquet, with moderately ripe red berry fruit and a hint of mocha; the palate provides more of the same, with some nice chocolate touches added, and nice ripe tannins to close. **rating:** 90

best drinking 2002–2007 **best vintages** NA **drink with** Crown roast of lamb • $25

seresin estate ★★★★★

Bedford Road, Renwick, Marlborough **region** Marlborough

phone (03) 572 9408 **fax** (03) 572 9850 **open** Summer 10–4.30

winemaker Brian Bicknell, Gordon Ritchie **production** 15 000 **est.** 1992

product range ($21.90–34 R) Riesling, Sauvignon Blanc, Pinot Gris, Estate Chardonnay, Reserve Chardonnay, Chardonnay, Pinot Noir.

summary Seresin has charged into the Marlborough scene since New Zealand filmmaker Michael Seresin purchased a little over 60 hectares of prime alluvial terrace land adjacent to the Wairau River. Forty hectares of vineyard have been established, and the state-of-the-art winery designed by Ian Athfield (of Te Mata Estate fame) constructed. Brian Bicknell, one of New Zealand's most experienced Flying Winemakers (he has worked in New Zealand, Hungary, France and for three years in Chile) has been installed as chief winemaker. The first vintage in 1996 immediately established Seresin as one of the star performers in the Marlborough scene. Exports to Australia, the UK, Denmark, Switzerland, Belgium, the Netherlands, Ireland, Canada and the US.

Seresin Estate Sauvignon Blanc

🍷🍷🍷🍷🍷 **2000** Light yellow-green; a complex web of gooseberry, ripe apple, herb and lemon aromas, then a palate that derives its strength from its texture, structure, intensity and length. Crisp and crunchy, no single fruit or other component stands out, the herbal and tropical characters in complete harmony. **rating:** 94

best drinking Now–2003 **best vintages** '99, '00 **drink with** Steamed crab • $22

Seresin Estate Pinot Gris

🍷🍷🍷🍷 **2000** Medium yellow-green; the bouquet is typically shy, with some low-level aromatic pear and spice characters. The bone-dry palate is tight, with a mix of mineral and apple, and is clearly destined to develop slowly. **rating:** 89

best drinking 2002–2006 **best vintages** '99 **drink with** Smoked white-fleshed fish • $23

Seresin Estate Chardonnay

🍷🍷🍷🍷🍷 **2000** Bright yellow-green; the bouquet has tight, lively citrus/melon fruit and gentle spicy oak aromas. An elegant and fine palate shows vibrant fresh fruit and the barest touch of cashew and oak; very good mouthfeel. This particular wine had lower malolactic fermentation and no new oak, a departure from the usual. **rating:** 92

best drinking Now–2004 **best vintages** '99, '00 **drink with** Steamed mussels • $21

Seresin Estate Pinot Noir

🍷🍷🍷🍷🍷 **1999** Medium red-purple; a wondrously complex savoury/spicy/plummy/dark fruit bouquet sets the bells ringing. The palate follows on in much the same vein, with very good texture, and sweet mid-palate fruit, then tannins that are gentle but ripe, running through a long, silky finish. **rating:** 94

best drinking Now–2005 **best vintages** '97, '99 **drink with** Game • $34

shalimar estate NR

Ngatapa Road, RD2, Gisborne **region** Gisborne
phone (06) 862 7776 **fax** (06) 862 7776 **open** 7 days 10–5
winemaker Alexander Stuart **production** 900 **est.** 1994
product range ($8–16 R) Sauvignon Blanc, Semillon, Chardonnay, Pinot Gris, Pinotage, Cabernet Merlot.
summary Having been grape-growers for 25 years, the Stuart family took the plunge into winemaking in 1994, drawing upon a recently established (and in Gisborne, rare) terraced hillside vineyard. Alexander Stuart believes greater flavour and character will follow the lower than normal yields. Most of the production from the 8-hectare vineyard is, once again, being sold to others, and the winery is up for sale.

sherwood estate ★★★☆

Weedons Ross Road, Christchurch **region** Canterbury
phone (03) 347 9060 **fax** (03) 347 8225 **open** 7 days 11–5
winemaker Dayne Sherwood **production** 17 000 **est.** 1987
product range ($12–28 R) Canterbury Riesling, Müller Thurgau, Sauvignon Blanc, Chardonnay, Unoaked Chardonnay, Reserve Chardonnay, Estate Pinot Noir, Reserve Pinot Noir, Single Vineyard Selection Rivendell Pinot Noir, Cabernet Franc.
summary Sherwood Estate produced its first wines in 1990; situated close to Christchurch (15 minutes' drive), it also offers a garden-setting tasting room with snacks and lunches available in the Vineyard Bar throughout summer. Production has risen significantly since the early days, making Sherwood Estate an important part of the Christchurch landscape. After a disappointing period, the quality of the wines has significantly improved. Exports to Australia, the UK, Europe, Asia and the US.

Sherwood Estate Reserve Pinot Noir

🍷🍷🍷🍷 **1998** Light red; the bouquet is clean and fresh, with light cherry fruit and a dash of charry oak. The palate is lively, fresh, relatively light bodied, and while it has fair length, does not have overmuch texture. Still, a nice light wine. **rating:** 85

best drinking Now–2003 **best vintages** NA **drink with** Coq au vin • $28

shingle peak wines ★★★☆

Cnr Rapaura Road and State Highway 6, Blenheim **region** Marlborough
phone (09) 411 8301 **fax** (09) 411 7982 **open** At Matua Valley
winemaker Mark Robertson **production** 25 000 **est.** 1990
product range ($14–19 R) Riesling, Sauvignon Blanc, Chardonnay, Pinot Gris, Botrytis Riesling, Pinot Noir, Merlot.
summary Shingle Peak is the stand-alone Marlborough brand for Matua Valley. The wines are made at Rapaura Vintners, in which Matua Valley has a significant shareholding, and consistently offer excellent value for money.

Matua Valley Sauvignon Blanc

▼▼▼▽ **1999** Light to medium green-yellow; strong, in-your-face, herb and grass aromas in a rather old-fashioned style that certainly announces its presence as you pick up the glass. The palate is consistent, with crisp herbaceous/mineral flavours, and a dry, slightly hard finish. Plenty of impact. **rating:** 84
best drinking Now **best vintages** NA **drink with** New Zealand whitebait • $15

sileni estates

Maraekakaho Road, Bridge Pa, Hastings **region** Hawke's Bay
phone (06) 879 8768 **fax** (06) 879 7187 **open** 7 days 10–5
winemaker Grant Edmonds, Nigel Davies, Eleanor Dodd **production** 15 000 **est.** 1997
product range ($26.50–40 R) Semillon, Chardonnay, Pourriture Noble (Semillon Botrytis), Merlot Cabernets, EV Merlot Cabernets.
summary Sileni Estates is poised to become a leading force in the Hawke's Bay region. The three partners are chief winemaker Grant Edmonds, Graeme Avery and Chris Cowper. Between them, they and their families have winemaking, management and marketing and financial backgrounds and skills. With just under 100 hectares of vines planted, production has increased in leaps and bounds, and the quality has indeed proved to be excellent. A striking state-of-the-art winery, top-end restaurant, café and spacious tasting-room facility constitute a major landmark in the region. Exports to the UK, France and the US through Louis Latour.

Sileni Semillon

▼▼▼▼ **2000** Light to medium yellow-green; a clean, subtle bouquet is presently in a holding pattern, the wine coming alive in the mouth, with sweet fruit on the mid-palate and hints of sage and herb, and a persuasively dry finish. **rating:** 89
best drinking Now–2006 **best vintages** NA **drink with** White-fleshed fish • $26.50

Sileni Chardonnay

▼▼▼▼▽ **2000** Light to medium green-yellow; the fragrant melon and citrus fruit of the bouquet has soaked up the oak. The lovely fresh citrus, melon and stonefruit flavours of the palate likewise carry the wine, which has particularly good length. **rating:** 93
best drinking Now–2005 **best vintages** '98, '00 **drink with** Grilled scampi • $32

Sileni Pourriture Noble

▼▼▼▼▽ **2000** Glowing yellow-gold; an exceptionally rich tropical/cumquat/apricot bouquet is the key to the palate, which has identical flavours, finishing with enough acidity to give the wine balance (and longevity). **rating:** 91
best drinking Now–2005 **best vintages** NA **drink with** Crème brûlée • $40

Sileni Merlot Cabernets

▼▼▼▼▽ **1999** Light to medium red-purple; fragrant and spotlessly clean red and black berry fruit aromas on the bouquet lead into to a no less spotlessly clean and beautifully modulated palate, with fine, ripe tannins and great balance. **rating:** 90
best drinking 2003–2009 **best vintages** '98 **drink with** Braised lamb • $35

sirocco wines NR

The Settlement (11 Methven–Barrhill Road), Rakai **region** Canterbury
phone (03) 302 7252 **fax** (03) 302 7252 **open** 7 days 10–5
winemaker Paul Phillips **production** 500 **est.** 1997

product range ($12–16 CD) Riesling, Chardonnay, Pinot Noir.

summary Paul and Helena Phillips run a small but surprisingly diverse business on their property on the famous salmon- and trout-fishing Rakaia River. They produce cut flowers (gentians) for the export market, and Helena teaches decorative painting on the property. Paul Phillips was brought up in the Swan Valley, which prompted their other development of vines and winemaking. The first experimental varieties were planted 12 years ago, there being no other local vineyards to point the way. In the outcome 2.5 hectares of chardonnay, riesling, sauvignon blanc and pinot noir have been taken to the point of commercial production, and all of the wines are made on site by Paul. The vineyard is moving towards Bio-Gro™ organic status, and the Phillipses are the Canterbury representatives for the New Zealand Grapevine Improvement Group.

soljans wines ★★★

263 Lincoln Road, Henderson **region** Auckland Area
phone (09) 838 8365 **fax** (09) 838 8366 **open** Mon–Sat 9–6, Sun 11–5
winemaker Matt Ussher **production** 25 000 **est.** 1937

product range ($9–20 CD) The Estate Range: Ivory, Hawke's Bay Müller Thurgau, Marlborough Riesling, Gisborne Gewurztraminer, Lynham Vineyard Sauvignon Blanc, Marlborough Sauvignon Blanc, Hawke's Bay Chardonnay, Ebony, Hawke's Bay Cabernet Merlot, Auckland Pinotage; the Barrique Reserve Range: Chardonnay, Merlot, Cabernet Merlot and Legacy (Méthode Traditionelle); also Momento (sparkling), Fusion (sparkling Muscat) and Sienna (red Méthode Traditionelle); Port, Muscat.

summary The traditional but immaculately maintained winery and vineyard constitute a major tourist attraction, and the well-made wines are sold at very modest prices. In 1993 Soljans made a heavy investment importing state-of-the-art sparkling winemaking equipment from France and is now a major contractor for New Zealand Méthode Traditionelle producers. Exports to the UK, the US, Japan, France, Belgium, Denmark and Poland (the latter a considerable achievement).

solstone estate NR

119 Solway Crescent, Masterton **region** Wairarapa
phone (06) 377 5505 **fax** (06) 337 7504 **open** Mon–Fri 8–5, weekends and public holidays 10.30–4.30
winemaker Luc des Bonnets **production** 3100 **est.** 1981

product range ($12–38 CD) Riesling, Rosé, Pinot Noir, Merlot, Cabernet Franc, Cabernet Merlot Franc.

summary Tiny quantities of the wines sold to date have been eagerly snapped up by the local clientele, but wines are now being distributed (sparingly) through Kitchener Wines. The wines draw upon 2 hectares of estate cabernet sauvignon and 1 hectare of pinot noir, sauvignon blanc, merlot and cabernet franc. Incidentally, Solstone is the former Bloomfield Estate.

Solstone Estate Pinot Noir

ΥΥΥΥ **1999** Light to medium red; the bouquet is fragrant, with some stem characters that flower on a light but elegantly sappy/spicy palate. **rating:** 87

best drinking Now–2004 **best vintages** NA **drink with** Guinea fowl • $34

spencer hill estate ★★★★

Best Road, RD1, Upper Moutere, Nelson **region** Nelson
phone (03) 543 2031 **fax** (03) 543 2031 **open** Thurs–Sat 12–4 Dec–Feb
winemaker Philip Jones, Matt Rutherford (Viticulturist) **production** 15 000 **est.** 1991

product range ($14–24 R) Spencer Hill is the top label from single-vineyard sources; Tasman Bay is the second but main label made in larger volume. Evan's Vineyard Riesling, Tasman Bay Nelson Riesling, Tasman Bay Marlborough Sauvignon Blanc, Tasman Bay Nelson Sauvignon Blanc, Tasman Bay Marlborough Pinot Gris, Tasman Bay Nelson Chardonnay, Tasman Bay Nelson Pinot Noir, Evan's Vineyard Pinotage, Evan's Vineyard Grand Vendange.

summary The urbane Philip Jones is a graduate in viticulture from UCLA Davis, California, and also undertook an oenology degree at Fresno State University. The ornately complex Spencer Hill Chardonnays have won a cascade of trophies and gold medals, joined by the Tasman Bay Chardonnay in 1997, in wine competitions from New Zealand to London. There can be no doubt that Philip Jones is a highly talented grape-grower and winemaker, and an equally accomplished marketer, with exports to Australia, the UK, Hong Kong and Japan.

Spencer Hill Evan's Vineyard Moutere Riesling

YYYY 2000 Light green-yellow; the bouquet is solid, with a mix of lime and tropical fruit, but not especially fragrant; the palate has lots of flavour in a big frame, again showing tropical fruit characters. Plenty happening here. **rating:** 87

best drinking Now–2006 **best vintages** NA **drink with** Salmon and asparagus terrine • $20

Spencer Hill Tasman Bay Marlborough Sauvignon Blanc

YYYY 2000 Light green-yellow; the moderately intense bouquet runs through mineral, herb and spice, the oak subliminal at best. The palate has good balance and intensity, still at the herbaceous end of the spectrum, but texturally enriched by the barrel age, mlf and high alcohol (13.5°) components. **rating:** 86

best drinking Now **best vintages** NA **drink with** Whitebait • NA

Spencer Hill Tasman Bay Nelson Sauvignon Blanc

YYYY 2000 Light to medium yellow-green; the bouquet is quite rich and ripe, with the oak no more than subliminal. The palate is much brighter and brisker than the bouquet suggests, with lively, lemony acidity and good mouthfeel. Excellent value. **rating:** 88

best drinking Now–2004 **best vintages** NA **drink with** Calamari • $13.95

Spencer Hill Tasman Bay Marlborough Pinot Gris

YYYYY 2000 Light but brilliant copper-straw; a highly aromatic bouquet with apple blossom and spice is followed by a palate with well-above-average sweet apple flavour, good length and good balance. Not surprisingly, the 800 cases made sold out in six weeks. **rating:** 91

best drinking Now–2004 **best vintages** '00 **drink with** Cocquilles St Jacques • $17

Spencer Hill Evan's Vineyard Moutere Pinot Noir

YYYYY 2000 Medium red-purple; strong, glossy plummy varietal fruit wafts from the glass, backed by subtle oak. The palate is rich and voluptuous, with abundant plummy fruit and fine tannins to close. **rating:** 94

best drinking Now–2004 **best vintages** '00 **drink with** Game • $21.95

Spencer Hill Tasman Bay Pinot Noir

YYYY 2000 Light to medium red-purple; the bouquet is light, with a mix of savoury/gamey/cherry/plummy aromas, the palate with a similar range of flavours, minimal tannins and subtle oak. This wine comes from the higher-yielding blocks in the vineyard. **rating:** 85

best drinking Now–2004 **best vintages** NA **drink with** Stuffed spatchcock • $21

springvale estate NR

Dunstan Road, Alexandra **region** Central Otago

phone (03) 449 2995 **fax** (03) 449 2331 **open** 7 days Dec 18–Apr, weekends and public holidays May–Dec

winemaker Dean Shaw (Contract), **production** 1000 **est.** 1989

product range ($16.50–26 CD) Gewurztraminer, Chardonnay (Oaked and Unoaked), Pinot Noir, Cabernet Sauvignon.

summary Tony and Jo-Anne Brun planted their first hectare of vines in 1989, gradually increasing the area to its present level of 10 hectares. The neat restaurant caters for all tastes from nibbles to functions. The 1998 Pinot Noir was a marvellous wine, deserving its gold medal at the 1999 Royal Easter Wine Show.

spy valley NR

Waihopai Valley Road, RD6, Marlborough **region** Marlborough

phone (03) 572 9840 **fax** (03) 572 9830 **open** By appointment

winemaker Alan McCorkindale **production** 14 000 **est.** 1995

product range ($16.50–28 R) Gewürztraminer, Sauvignon Blanc, Chardonnay, Pinot Noir, Merlot.

summary This is a major new venture in the Marlborough region. In 1995 130 hectares of land were purchased and over the next four years 104 hectares of vines were planted, with (inevitably) the major focus on sauvignon blanc, but also with significant plantings of chardonnay and pinot noir. Smaller amounts of riesling, pinot gris, gewurztraminer and merlot make up the roster. The first wine was not made until the 2000 vintage, and the major part of the grape production is currently being sold to Corbans Wines. The 2001 vintage is planned to produce 14 000 cases, but when it erects its own winery (to be called Johnston Estate) prior to the 2002 vintage, external grape sales will diminish, with a 2002 production target of 40 000 cases, and an end-point of 85 000 cases.

Spy Valley Gewurztraminer

🍷🍷🍷🍷🍷 **2000** Light straw-green; the bouquet has exemplary varietal character, with floral spice/lychee/rose-petal aromas, the palate flowing on seamlessly from the bouquet, delicate, well balanced and not too sweet. **rating:** 91

best drinking Now–2003 **best vintages** '00 **drink with** Lightly spiced seafood • $17.50

Spy Valley Sauvignon Blanc

🍷🍷🍷🍷 **2000** Pale straw-green; a clean, light and fresh bouquet, but not a lot of fruit or varietal expression; the palate providing more of the same in a crisp, clean, light style that certainly won't frighten the horses. **rating:** 86

best drinking Now **best vintages** NA **drink with** Light seafood • $16.50

staete landt ★★★★

275 Rapaura Road, RD3, Blenheim, Marlborough **region** Marlborough
phone (03) 572 4400 **fax** (03) 572 4433 **open** By appointment
winemaker Ruud Maasdam, Sam Weaver **production** 4600 **est.** 1998
product range ($21.50–32 ML) Sauvignon Blanc, Pinot Gris.

summary Ruud Maasdam and Dorien Vermaas emigrated from Holland with their two children with the specific intention of establishing a vineyard and winery in New Zealand. In 1998 they purchased a fruit orchard on Rapaura Road, pulled out the trees, and two years later had their first crop from the 20 hectares of vines they had established. The principal varieties planted are sauvignon blanc, chardonnay and pinot noir, with a tiny amount of pinot gris. The wines are made by Ruud Maasdam under the direction of consultant Sam Weaver using the Framingham Winery facilities. Incredibly, Staete Landt has already established distribution in Australia, Asia, the US and the EU, with only 13 per cent being allocated for sale in New Zealand.

Staete Landt Sauvignon Blanc

🍷🍷🍷🍷🍷 **2000** Light to medium yellow-green; the intense and complex bouquet puts the accent on ripe/tropical fruit with some gooseberry counterpoints, the nicely balanced and structured palate ripe, but not aggressive; subtle oak adds positively to the texture of the wine, without obscuring the lush varietal character. **rating:** 92

best drinking Now **best vintages** '00 **drink with** Slow-cooked Tasmanian salmon • NA

sterling lines vineyard NR

Torlesse Wines, 2 Loffhagen Drive, Waipara **region** Waipara
phone (03) 314 6099 **fax** (03) 314 6097 **open** Not
winemaker Gabrielle (Darby) Brunton, Kym Rayner (Consultant) **production** 300 **est.** 1999
product range Riesling.

summary Ash and Gabrielle Brunton came from an army background, deciding on a vineyard as a part-time retirement activity. The name comes from military 'lines' (referring to the military huts) and also to the proximity of the Weka Pass railway line. It's all rather obscure. Regardless, they began the planting of their 12-hectare vineyard in 1985, and now have sauvignon blanc, riesling, chardonnay and pinot noir in production. Most of the grapes are sold; so far the only wine made under the Sterling Lines vineyard is Riesling.

stonecroft vineyard NR

Mere Road, RD5, Hastings **region** Hawke's Bay
phone (06) 879 9610 **fax** (06) 879 9610 **open** Weekends, public holidays 11–5
winemaker Dr Alan Limmer **production** 2500 **est.** 1982
product range ($19–45 CD) Gewurztraminer, Sauvignon Blanc, Chardonnay, Ruhani, Crofter's Red, Syrah, Zinfandel.

summary Analytical chemist Dr Alan Limmer produces full-bodied, rich and ripe wines from his 6-hectare vineyard situated on free-draining, gravelly soils that promote early ripening. Most interesting is the almost unprocurable (mailing list only) Syrah, one of the first to achieve a reputation in New Zealand. His gewurztraminer is also remarkable, particularly with some bottle age. Not rated because there have been no tastings for several years. Exports to Australia, the UK, Japan and Brazil.

Stonecroft Gewurztraminer

🍷🍷🍷🍷🍷 **1998** Light to medium yellow-green; intense, voluminous and fragrant spice and lychee aromas leap from the glass. The wine has excellent depth to the mouthfeel and flavour, showing exemplary varietal character throughout. Truly outstanding. **rating:** 95

best drinking Now–2004 **best vintages** '98 **drink with** Nothing needed • NA

Stonecroft Syrah

ỲỲỲỲ **1999** Medium red-purple, quite developed; moderately intense and complex spice and game aromas flow into a light- to medium-bodied palate with an elegant mix of spice and game flavours, minimal tannins and subtle oak; not released at the time of tasting, but I really doubt that cellaring will be repaid. **rating:** 89

best drinking 2002–2004 **best vintages** NA **drink with** Yearling steak • $40

stonecutter vineyard ★★★☆

Todds Road, Martinborough **region** Wairarapa
phone (06) 306 9871 **fax** (06) 306 9871 **open** By appointment
winemaker Roger Pemberton **production** 500 **est.** 1995
product range ($18–25 ML) Pinot Gris, Topaz, Pinot Noir.
summary The Stonecutter Vineyard, which occupies 2.75 hectares of the 4-hectare site, was planted in 1995, with 1.5 hectares of pinot gris, 1 hectare of pinot noir and 0.25 hectare of gewurztraminer. It is established on the famed Martinborough Terrace, one of the most eagerly sought after viticultural terroirs in New Zealand, and almost completely developed. The present tiny production will peak at between 800 to 1000 cases, and the limitations of the vineyard size impose a permanent ceiling.

Stonecutter Vineyard Pinot Noir

ỲỲỲỲ **1999** Medium red-purple; a clean, rich and ripe bouquet with dark plum and (adopting Roger Pemberton's own description) brandied prunes, is followed by a similarly exotically flavoured ripe, sweet plum and blackberry palate. The texture is smooth, but some might see the wine as overripe. **rating:** 89

best drinking Now–2004 **best vintages** NA **drink with** Coq au vin • $25

stoneleigh vineyards ★★★★

Jacksons Road, RD3, Blenheim **region** Marlborough
phone (03) 572 8198 **fax** (03) 572 8199 **open** 7 days 10–4
winemaker Sam Weaver **production** NA **est.** 1988
product range ($11–36 R) Marlborough Riesling, Marlborough Sauvignon Blanc, Marlborough Chardonnay, Marlborough Pinot Noir.
summary Stoneleigh is the Marlborough brand of Corbans. Like Longridge, it has its own largely separate existence and brand identity and, what is more, is open to visitors. It has its own separate price-point, pitched above that of Longridge.

Stoneleigh Marlborough Sauvignon Blanc

ỲỲỲỲ **2000** Light to medium yellow-green; an intense and fragrant bouquet with passionfruit and tropical aromatics has the frequently encountered touch of reduction/burnt match. The powerful and intense palate has good length and grip, again with passionfruit/tropical flavours. **rating:** 89

best drinking Now **best vintages** '92, '94, '96, '98, '00 **drink with** Shellfish • $17.50

Stoneleigh Marlborough Pinot Noir

ỲỲỲỲ **1999** Light to medium red-purple; a light, savoury/sappy/earthy bouquet, very different in style from the Montana, is followed by a palate in similar vein, although the fruit does step up a level, with some cherry/cherry-pip flavours. **rating:** 86

best drinking Now **best vintages** NA **drink with** Cassoulet • $19

stony batter estate NR

c/o Man O'War Farms Ltd, RD1, Waiheke Island **region** Waiheke Island
phone (09) 372 7013 **fax** (09) 372 2799 **open** Not
winemaker Luc Desbonnets **production** 1700 **est.** 1996
product range Chardonnay, Sauvignon Blanc Semillon, Pinot Noir, Cabernet Merlot.
summary Paper magnate John Spencer has a total holding of 2200 hectares on Waiheke Island. Together with a small group of family investors, he has developed a number of vineyards ranging in size from 1 to 5 hectares, on favoured north-facing slopes in sheltered sites. In all, 28 hectares are under vine, the largest holding on Waiheke Island. The development has been leisurely, but the erection of an on-site winery is a further indication of the very serious nature of the investment. The first wine (from 1998) is due to be released sometime in 2001.

stonyridge vineyard ★★★★★

80 Onetangi Road, Waiheke Island **region** Waiheke Island
phone (09) 372 8822 **fax** (09) 372 8766 **open** 7 days 9–5
winemaker Stephen White **production** 1250 **est.** 1982
product range ($30–115 ML) The top label is Larose Cabernets; the second is Airfield Cabernets. Minuscule quantities of Que Sera Syrah are also grown, and Hawke's Bay Chardonnay, Row 10 Waiheke Island Chardonnay and Why Heke If You Don't Have To? Hawke's Bay Merlot has recently joined the band.
summary The winery that justifies the hype about Waiheke Island. Consistently great wines have been produced, albeit in minuscule quantities; small wonder it has established the highest ex-winery price of well over $50 en primeur, and $115 upon commercial release, with a limit of one bottle per customer! For many, patronising the winery restaurant will be the only means of tasting these exalted wines (open weekends 11.30–5 during winter and 7 days in summer subject to availability). Minuscule exports to the UK, the US, Australia, Japan, Malaysia, Belgium, Denmark, Germany, Brazil and Taiwan.

stratford wines of martinborough NR

115 New York Street, Martinborough **region** Wairarapa
phone (06) 306 9257 **fax** (06) 306 8257 **open** By appointment
winemaker Stratford Canning **production** 2000 **est.** 1993
product range ($16–28 CD) Riesling, Chardonnay, Pinot Noir.
summary Strat Canning has worked as a winemaker in the Martinborough region for a number of years and is now also producing his own wines from 1 hectare each of pinot noir, chardonnay and riesling.

sunset valley vineyard NR

Eggers Road, Sunrise Valley, RD1, Upper Moutere, Nelson **region** Nelson
phone (03) 543 2161 **fax** (03) 543 2161 **open** 7 days 11–5
winemaker Ian Newton **production** est. 1998
product range ($15–22 R) Sauvignon Blanc, Chardonnay, Pinot Noir, Cabernet Sauvignon.
summary Ian Newton has a post-graduate winemaking degree from Lincoln University, and practical experience as a winemaker gained in Switzerland and Provence, as well as at Martinborough Vineyard and Seifried. He purchased a 25-hectare rolling hill property in Upper Moutere with the specific intention of growing the grapes organically, and now has full Bio-Gro™ certification. Two hectares have been planted (predominantly to pinot noir, with lesser quantities of chardonnay, sauvignon blanc and cabernet sauvignon).

tai-ara-rau wines NR

Upper Stout Street, Gisborne **region** Gisborne
phone (06) 867 2010 **fax** (06) 867 2024 **open** 7 days 10–5
winemaker Mike Spivey **production** 1000 **est.** 1989
product range Estate Chardonnay and Merlot; Waimata Vineyard Chardonnay, Pinot Noir and Merlot.
summary Tairawhiti Polytechnic has followed in the footsteps of Australia's Charles Sturt University in making commercial quantities of wine as part of the wine industry certificate course that the institute offers. It is the only New Zealand institution to do so, drawing upon 3 hectares of chardonnay, merlot and sauvignon blanc.

te awa farm winery ★★★★☆

2375 Roys Hill Road, SH 50 RD5, Hastings **region** Hawke's Bay
phone (06) 879 7602 **fax** (06) 879 7756 **open** Mon–Fri 9–5, weekends 10–6
winemaker Jenny Dobson **production** 20 000 **est.** 1992
product range ($14.95–39.95 R) Longlands brand: Sauvignon Blanc, Chardonnay, Pinotage, Merlot, Cabernet Merlot; Reserve range: Frontier Sauvignon Blanc, Frontier Chardonnay, Boundary (a Bordeaux-blend); Zone 10 Cabernet Sauvignon.
summary The Lawson family is yet another to venture into winemaking after being contract grape-growers for over 15 years. Unusually, however, when Gus and Ian Lawson decided to do it, they started all over again: in 1992 they purchased a 173-hectare sheep property on Roys Hill Road and established 32 hectares of sauvignon blanc, chardonnay, merlot, cabernet franc, cabernet sauvignon and syrah. The first vintage from Te Awa Farm was in 1994

and an on-site production facility (incorporating a cellar-door sales area) was constructed in 1997. The peripatetic Jenny Dobson is now in charge of winemaking. The winery also boasts a fabulous restaurant with Rick Rutledge-Manning, New Zealand's best chef, in charge. Exports to the UK, Denmark, Singapore, Japan and the US.

Te Awa Farm Zone 10 Cabernet Sauvignon

YYYYY **1998** Medium red, with some development starting to show; the bouquet has a wonderful mix of savoury/berry/chocolate/olive aromas that lead the band on the savoury, chocolate and spice-flavoured palate. Very distinctive, with quite delicious texture and mouthfeel, particularly through the fine-grained, supple tannins.

rating: 95

best drinking 2003–2008 **best vintages** '98 **drink with** Braised lamb shanks • $39.95

te horo vineyards NR

State Highway 1, Te Horo **region** West Coast
phone (06) 364 3392 **fax** (06) 364 3392 **open** 7 days 11–late
winemaker Alastair Pain **production** 1200 **est.** 1985
product range ($9.95–19.95 CD) Chardonnay, Sauvignon Blanc, Riesling, Pinot Gris, Gewurztraminer, Merlot, Cabernet Sauvignon Cremant Méthode Traditionale; a selection of fruit wines.
summary Formerly called Grape Republic, a marketing and promotion tour-de-force using direct mail and wine club techniques. It once produced a vast array of flavoured wines and now does smaller quantities of more expensive table wines that are distinctly austere. An underground cellar and sales area was opened in 1995. Most of the wine is sold direct ex winery.

te kairanga wines ★★★★

Martins Road, Martinborough **region** Wairarapa
phone (06) 306 9122 **fax** (06) 306 9322 **open** 7 days 10–5
winemaker Peter Caldwell **production** 16 000 **est.** 1984
product range ($13–45 CD) At the top end, the Reserve range: Chardonnay, Pinot Noir; then the Premium range: Sauvignon Blanc, Chardonnay, Pinot Noir, Cabernet Sauvignon, Cabernet Merlot; at the bottom, the Castlepoint range: Müller Thurgau, Dry White, Dry Red, Cabernet Sauvignon.
summary Te Kairanga is an enigma. For a long time its wines were disappointing, then they took a distinct turn for the better. More recent tastings are less conclusive, so close and yet so far from the best of what is undoubtedly a great region. The appointment of Peter Caldwell, and the fact that it has over 30 hectares of mature vineyards, will help Te Kairanga realise its full potential. Winning the trophy for Best Wine of Show at the Royal Easter Wine Show 2000 with its Cabernet Sauvignon will also help, however much it may complicate plans to phase out the production of that variety. Exports to Australia and the US.

Te Kairanga Chardonnay

YYYYY **1997** Deep yellow, typical for New Zealand Chardonnay of this age; the bouquet is complex, with barrel-ferment characters running through melon and citrus fruit. The palate is long and sustained, with ripe fig and melon fruit together with some bottle-developed butterscotch characters. Good acidity. **rating:** 90

best drinking Now **best vintages** '90, '91, '94, '96, '97 **drink with** Veal fricassee • $24

Te Kairanga Reserve Chardonnay

YYYY **1999** Light to medium yellow-green; the bouquet has **winemaker** inputs all over it, with obvious barrel-ferment characters, dusty oak, and nutty malolactic-fermentation characters. The palate is light, with creamy/nutty flavours, not particularly intense and slightly short. Less mlf might have been a better option. **rating:** 84

best drinking Now **best vintages** '94, '95, '96 **drink with** Sweetbreads • $30

Te Kairanga Pinot Noir

YYYY **1999** Medium red, with a touch of purple; the potent bouquet has a mix of ripe cherry and plum on the one hand, and more savoury/spicy/foresty characters on the other, the latter predominating on the bouquet. The palate is currently in the primary fruit phase, with rich cherry and plum flavours and well-above-average depth.

rating: 88

best drinking 2002–2007 **best vintages** '91, '93, '94, '97, '99 **drink with** Baked smoked ham • $35

Te Kairanga Reserve Pinot Noir

YYYYY 1999 Very dense and deep purple-red, striking for a Pinot Noir; the bouquet oozes rich, ripe, dense plum fruit and almost inevitably subservient oak. The palate is similarly powerful and concentrated with dark plum and black cherry fruit; a wine that absolutely demands further time, and could be spectacular with age. **rating:** 93

best drinking 2002–2007 **best vintages** '98, '99 **drink with** Smoked quail • $45

te mania estate ★★★★

c/o The Grape Escape, McShanes Road, Richmond, Nelson **region** Nelson
phone (03) 544 4541 **fax** (03) 544 4541 **open** Mon–Fri summer, 10–5, winter 11–4
winemaker Jane Cooper **production** 4000 **est.** 1990
product range ($15–20 CD) Riesling, Late Harvest Riesling, Sauvignon Blanc, Home Block Sauvignon Blanc, Nelson Chardonnay, Pinot Noir, Merlot, Three Brothers.

summary Jon and Cheryl Harrey commenced development of their vineyard in 1990, planting 4.5 hectares in that year (which came into production in 1992), and expanded the plantings in 1994 and 1995 with an additional 4 hectares. They previously sold most of their grapes to other Nelson winemakers, but since 1995 have had Jane Cooper as winemaker. Together with another vineyard owner, the Harreys have purchased a property on which they have erected The Grape Escape, a cellar-door sales facility, café and arts and crafts centre. Has a rapidly growing reputation, particularly for Sauvignon Blanc. The wines are exported to Australia, the UK, Japan and the Netherlands.

Te Mania Estate Riesling

YYYY 2000 Light to medium yellow-green; the bouquet is finer, and more slatey/minerally than the '99; a fine, tangy, limey palate with good length and a pleasingly dry finish gives the wine balance and freshness. **rating:** 89

best drinking 2001–2006 **best vintages** NA **drink with** Vegetarian • $14.95

Te Mania Estate Sauvignon Blanc

YYYYY 2000 Light green-yellow; a pure, light and clean bouquet has a gentle mix of gooseberry, herb and celery; the clean, crisp, no-frills palate has a surprising amount of flavour, with gooseberry and redcurrant fruit before a dry, crunchy finish. **rating:** 90

best drinking Now **best vintages** '00 **drink with** Crab salad • $15.95

Te Mania Estate Nelson Chardonnay

YYYY 2000 Light to medium yellow-green; bright, fresh nectarine fruit has just a hint of oak .n support; the lively palate is driven by its citrus and melon fruit from a clonal mix in the vineyard. The oak beads used in the ferment are barely perceptible. Won a silver medal at the Air New Zealand Wine Awards 2000. **rating:** 86

best drinking Now **best vintages** '98 **drink with** Crab cakes • $18.95

Te Mania Estate Pinot Noir

YYYY 1999 Medium to full red-purple; a quite potent mix of dark plum, briar and spice gives a sweet overall impression to the bouquet. Soft, plummy fruit, gentle tannins and the barest lick of oak rounds the palate. **rating:** 89

best drinking Now–2004 **best vintages** NA **drink with** Japanese • $19.95

Te Mania Estate Three Brothers

YYYYY 1999 Medium purple-red; a lovely cascade of ripe, sweet cassis/Ribena/blackcurrant aromas on the bouquet are followed by a palate with more flavour diversity, sweetness from the Merlot and some olive/herb notes from the Cabernet Franc. Minty and supple; a very nice wine. **rating:** 92

best drinking 2002–2006 **best vintages** NA **drink with** Rack of lamb • $19.95

te mata estate ★★★★★

Te Mata Road, Havelock North **region** Hawke's Bay
phone (06) 877 4399 **fax** (06) 877 4397 **open** Mon–Fri 9–5, Sat 10–5, Sun 11–4
winemaker Peter Cowley **production** 30 000 **est.** 1896
product range ($11.50–66 CD) Oak Aged Dry White, Castle Hill Sauvignon Blanc, Cape Crest Sauvignon Blanc, Woodthorpe Terraces Viognier, Chardonnay, Elston Chardonnay, Rosé, Bullnose Syrah, Coleraine Cabernet Franc Merlot, Cabernet Merlot, Awatea Cabernet Merlot.

summary In the eyes of many, New Zealand's foremost producer of Cabernet Merlot, notwithstanding the consistency of the show success of the Vidal/Villa Maria group. The wines of Te Mata are made in a different style, restrained and elegant but always packed with fine fruit. Nor should the consistently stylish and varietally correct white wines be ignored: these too are of the highest quality. Initially only available via cellar door and mailing list, the wines are now conventionally distributed throughout New Zealand, and are exported to Australia, Belgium, France, Germany, Switzerland, Malyasia, Hong Kong, Singapore, the UK and the US.

Te Mata Estate Cape Crest Sauvignon Blanc

YYYY☐ **1999** Light to medium yellow-green; a complex mix of herb, mineral and redcurrant aromas lead into a complex, strongly structured wine in a white Bordeaux mould. One of the few New Zealand Sauvignon Blancs to offer cellaring potential. **rating:** 90

best drinking Now–2004 **best vintages** '91, '94, '95, '96, '99 **drink with** Quiche Lorraine • $30

Te Mata Estate Chardonnay

YYYY☐ **2000** Light to medium yellow-green; the complex and stylish bouquet offers a subtle interplay of melon, cashew and oak; the palate provides more of the same in the context of good length and structure. A major success. **rating:** 92

best drinking Now–2006 **best vintages** '00 **drink with** Whitebait • $19.85

Te Mata Estate Elston Chardonnay

YYYY☐ **1999** Medium yellow-green; the bouquet is complex and powerful, with a seamless integration of barrel-ferment oak and sweet melon fruit aromas. The palate marks a wine that stands apart from most New Zealand Chardonnays given the power and intensity of its fruit structure; it has excellent mouthfeel and balance to the citrussy fruit flavours. rating: 92

best drinking Now–2005 **best vintages** '93, '94, '95, '96, '97, '99 **drink with** Turkey • $43

Te Mata Estate Coleraine Cabernet Franc Merlot

YYYYY **1998** Medium to full red-purple; the complex and generous bouquet is swollen with blackcurrant, raspberry, cherry and (unexpectedly) licorice/game aromas. The palate is richer, deeper, and more powerful than the Awatea; the balance is excellent, the tannins powerful but not overpowering. A great wine with a great future. **rating:** 95

best drinking 2003–2018 **best vintages** '89, '91, '94, '95, '96, '97, '98 **drink with** New Zealand lamb • $66

Te Mata Estate Awatea Cabernet Merlot

YYYY☐ **1998** Medium to full red-purple; clean, perfectly ripened red berry fruit intermingles with subtle, cedary/spicy oak. The palate opens with ripe plum, redcurrant and blackberry fruit; what is really surprising is the strength and length of the tannins, which are soft and ripe. **rating:** 92

best drinking 2002–2012 **best vintages** '89, '91, '94, '95, '98 **drink with** New Zealand lamb • $43

te whare ra ★★★

Anglesea Street, Renwick, Marlborough **region** Marlborough
phone (03) 572 8581 **fax** (03) 572 8518 **open** 7 days 10.30–4.30 (reduced hours in winter)
winemaker Warwick Foley **production** 3500 **est.** 1979
product range ($16–25 CD) Premium range, Duke of Marlborough: Riesling, Gewurztraminer, Semillon, Chardonnay; also an unoaked Chardonnay and several botrytis wines, and Sarah Jennings (Cabernet blend).
summary Te Whare Ra was purchased from the founding Hogan family by Roger and Christine Smith in October 1997. The Smiths and winemaker Warwick Foley have done much to improve wine quality; the 1999 Duke of Marlborough Gewurztraminer was the gold medal winner and Champion Gewurztraminer at the 1999 Air New Zealand Wine Awards, and continues to be the best wine in the portfolio.

Te Whare Ra Duke of Marlborough Riesling

YYY☐ **2000** Light to medium yellow-green; the bouquet is quite aromatic, with plenty of lime and passionfruit promising much. Sadly, the sweetness on the palate has been overplayed (unless, of course, you happen to like overtly sweet Riesling). **rating:** 82

best drinking Now–2003 **best vintages** NA **drink with** Chinese barbecue pork • $16

Te Whare Ra Duke of Marlborough Chardonnay

ŸŸŸŸ **1999** The developed straw colour is not promising; however, there is lots happening on the complex hay/cashew/nut/straw/melon bouquet, and even more on the massively structured, high-alcohol but very complex palate. Silver-medal winner at the Bragato Wine Awards 2000. My rating may nonetheless be generous.

rating: 86

best drinking Now **best vintages** NA **drink with** KFC • $20

Te Whare Ra Noble Semillon

ŸŸŸŸ **1999** Medium to full yellow-green; the bouquet offers a cascade of tropical fruits ranging through pineapple, apricot, peach and citrus, the palate with ample flavour but distinctly soft. **rating:** 87

best drinking Now **best vintages** NA **drink with** Luscious dessert • NA

Te Whare Ra Sarah Jennings

ŸŸŸŸ **1999** Medium red-purple; the quite ripe bouquet has blackberry/currant/dark fruit aromas and a touch of spice; the palate shows the same good fruit character, but seems to have been underworked in barrel and/or taken to bottle a bit too early.

rating: 85

best drinking 2003–2007 **best vintages** NA **drink with** Venison sausages • NA

te whau vineyard ★★★★☆

218 Te Whau Drive, Waiheke Island **region** Waiheke Island
phone (09) 377 3119 **fax** (09) 307 2322 **open** 11–5 through summer months
winemaker Tony Forsyth, Herb Freidli **production** 550 **est.** 1993
product range ($38–48 CD) Te Whau Bay Chardonnay, The Point (Bordeaux-blend).
summary Tony Forsyth has established a little over 2 hectares of close-planted vines on a sheltered and steep (20°) north-facing slope. A second sheltered vineyard site has been planted with three clones of chardonnay, which produced 50 cases of Chardonnay in 1999. The first wines were made in 1999 at the on site gravity-feed winery, complete with fully underground barrel hall. Te Whau Bay Chardonnay and The Point (a four-variety Bordeaux-blend with 54 per cent Cabernet Sauvignon, 31 per cent Merlot, 10 per cent Cabernet Franc and 5 per cent Malbec) were released in November 2000.

Te Whau Chardonnay

ŸŸŸŸŸ **2000** Medium yellow-green; a fine, intense bouquet with nectarine and melon spun through a web of oak; the palate is textured and layered, with a mix of stonefruit and spicy oak, a creamy character adding to the length.

rating: 92

best drinking 2002–2005 **best vintages** NA **drink with** Fresh lobster • NA

thabo vineyard NR

72 Onetangi Road, Waiheke Island, Auckland **region** Waiheke Island
phone (09) 372 6450 **fax** (09) 372 6450 **open** By appointment
winemaker Michael John Cooper **production** NA **est.** 1994
product range ($20–50 CD) Rose.
summary Mike and Jo Cooper are Waiheke Island veterans, but have hastened slowly. Cooper (no relation to the noted New Zealand wine expert and author Michael Cooper) planted and managed Fenton's Twin Bay Vineyard between 1990 and 1999. In 1994 he and Jo purchased their own property on the Onetangi Strait, and slowly planted 3 hectares of cabernet sauvignon, merlot, malbec and cabernet franc. In 1999 they moved permanently onto their own property and began building a gravity-flow winery with underground wine cellars. A Cabernet Sauvignon Rose came on the market in November 2000; the first 'serious releases' of Cabernet Sauvignon and Merlot Cabernet were planned for November 2001.

thainstone wines NR

Giffords Road, RD3, Blenheim **region** Marlborough
phone (03) 572 8823 **fax** (03) 572 8623 **open** Not
winemaker Graeme Paul **production** 3000 **est.** 1990
product range ($11–16 ML) Cirrus Riesling, Sauvignon Blanc, Cirrus Sauvignon Blanc, Cirrus Chardonnay.

summary Jim and Viv Murray acquired their 6-hectare vineyard in 1990; already planted to sauvignon blanc, the decision was later taken to graft part over to chardonnay, which came into production in 1997. Until 1995 all the grapes were sold, but since that time the amounts of wine made have gradually increased. There are limited exports to Canada and the UK.

Thainstone Cirrus Riesling

YYYYY 2000 Light to medium yellow-green; the bouquet is very lively, floral and fruity, the palate having excellent length and persistence, easily handling the touch of residual sugar. **rating:** 91

best drinking 2002–2007 **best vintages** '00 **drink with** Char-grilled calamari • $15

the antipodean NR

PO Box 5, Matakana **region** Northland and Matakana
phone (09) 422 7957 **fax** (09) 422 7656 **open** Not
winemaker Michelle Chignell-Vuletic **production** 300 **est.** 1977
product range ($92–100 CD) The Antipodean (a blend of Cabernet Sauvignon, Merlot and Malbec), 'A' (Sauvignon Blanc and Semillon blend), The Iconoclast (Shiraz), Obiter (Cabernet Sauvignon).
summary More words have been written about this tiny winery than almost any other in New Zealand; almost certainly more words than bottles produced. As the range and prices testify, not your run-of-the-mill winery.

the millton vineyard ★★★★

119 Papatu Road, Manutuke, Gisborne **region** Gisborne
phone (06) 862 8680 **fax** (06) 862 8869 **open** By appointment
winemaker James Millton **production** 12 000 **est.** 1984
product range ($15–28 CD) Riesling Opou Vineyard, Gisborne Viognier Tietjen Vineyard, Te Arai Vineyard Chenin Blanc, Gisborne Vineyards Chardonnay, Chardonnay Opou Vineyard, Malbec Te Arai Vineyard, Merlot Cabernet Te Arai Vineyard, Gisborne Muskats @ Dawn.
summary The first of the increasing number of registered organic vineyards in New Zealand using biodynamic methods and banning insecticides and herbicides; winemaking methods are conventional but seek to limit the use of chemical additives wherever possible. The white wines, particularly botrytised, can be of the highest quality; the Germanic, lime-flavoured Riesling Opou Vineyard is almost always outstanding, while James Millton is doing some of the most exciting things with Chenin Blanc anywhere in the world outside the Loire Valley. Exports to Belgium, Hong Kong, the UK, Japan, Malaysia and the Philippines.

Millton Te Arai Vineyard Chenin Blanc

YYYYY 2000 Pale straw-gold; the clean bouquet has very attractive tropical fruit-salad aromas, the delicious palate with fresh-cut ripe pineapple and honey, before the finish where the acidity seems to have a touch of grapefruit. The oak plays a purely textural role. **rating:** 91

best drinking Now–2005 **best vintages** '92, '93, '94 **drink with** Seafood bisque • $20

the village winery NR

417 Mount Eden Road, Mount Eden, Auckland **region** Auckland Area
phone (09) 638 8780 **fax** (09) 638 9782 **open** Sun–Wed 10–9, Thurs–Sat 10–10
winemaker Ken Sanderson **production** 4500 **est.** 1994
product range ($7.50–28.95 R) Windmill Road range: Hawke's Bay Sauvignon Blanc, Hawke's Bay Chardonnay, Hawke's Bay Merlot, Cabernet Sauvignon Merlot Franc, Jean Method Traditional Vintage (Sparkling).
summary Enterprises such as this are not uncommon in California but it is the only one I know of in either Australia or New Zealand, with the winery established in the main street of suburban Mount Eden, which was (until owner Peter Schinckel found a loophole in the law) a 'dry' area. (New Zealand, like Australia, still has areas in which alcohol may not be sold.) The wines are made under the Windmill Road label, the winery-cum-shop stocking a broad range of wines from other producers as well as Windmill Road. Exports to Japan, Germany and Switzerland.

thornbury wines NR

29a Ocean Beach Road, Mt Maunganui **region** Hawke's Bay
phone (07) 572 2281 **open** Not
winemaker Steve Bird **production** NA **est.** 1998
product range ($17–25 R) Marlborough Sauvignon Blanc, Hawke's Bay Chardonnay, Hawke's Bay Merlot.
summary A most impressive newcomer, marking a partnership between Steve Bird, former Morton Estate winemaker, and Bruce and Sharon McCutcheon. The 1998 vintage relied on contract-grown grapes, with winemaking in rented space. In 1999 Thornbury acquired a vineyard of its own in Hawke's Bay but will continue to source sauvignon blanc from Marlborough.

tiritiri vineyard ★★★

Rural Bag 7417, Waimata Valley Road, Gisborne **region** Gisborne
phone (06) 867 0372 **fax** (06) 867 0372 **open** 7 days 9–5
winemaker John Thorpe (Contract) **production** 100 **est.** 1994
product range ($16–32 CD) Chardonnay, Reserve Chardonnay.
summary Duncan and Judy Smith purchased their 10-hectare property as part of the subdivision of a large sheep and cattle farm. It included the original homestead and six paddocks nestling at the foot of the Gisborne Ranges. Duncan Smith is a plant pathologist and a professional photographer with a 750 000-slide photo-library of horticultural, agricultural and wildlife subjects. In 1994 they took the plunge, having taken contrary advice ('don't try') from a viticultural expert, and planted 0.3 hectare each of mendoza and Clone 15 chardonnay with the intention of growing the grapes organically. Production is tiny, but the wines are well enough made, and the organic status of the vineyard means they sell out very quickly.

Tiritiri Vineyard Reserve Chardonnay

YYYY **1999** Light green-yellow; the bouquet is light, crisp, with some minerally characters, and fresher than the varietal or standard wine of the same vintage. The palate is in what might best be described as a European style: light, crisp and minerally, giving the promise of bottle development over a year or two. **rating:** 83
best drinking Now–2003 **best vintages** NA **drink with** Whitebait fritters • $32

tohu wines NR

72 Trafalgar Street, Nelson **region** Nelson
phone (03) 545 6838 **fax** (03) 548 4901 **open** Not
winemaker Simon Waghorn (Consultant) **production** 4000 **est.** 1998
product range ($15–28 ML) Sauvignon Blanc, Chardonnay, Reserve Chardonnay.
summary This is a joint venture between three Maori investment trusts with vast financial resources. The wines are made at Whitehaven Winery by Simon Waghorn from contract-grown grapes sourced primarily in Marlborough and Gisborne; some of the Gisborne chardonnay comes from one of the joint-venture partners' plantings. Exports to Australia, the US and the UK.

Tohu Gisborne Chardonnay

YYYY **2000** Light to medium yellow-green; the bouquet has highly aromatic and striking nectarine fruit; the palate is less intense than the bouquet, but still very interesting, with nectarine fruit and subtle oak. **rating:** 84
best drinking Now–2004 **best vintages** NA **drink with** Sun-dried tomato pasta • $19

torlesse

Waipara Village, Waipara, Canterbury **region** Waipara
phone (03) 314 6929 **fax** (03) 314 6867 **open** Fri–Sun 11–4 or by appointment
winemaker Kym Rayner **production** 5000 **est.** 1990
product range ($12.50–29.50 R) Riesling (Dry and Medium), Marlborough Gewurztraminer, Marlborough Sauvignon Blanc, Chardonnay Lightly Oaked, Chardonnay Waipara Reserve, Pinot Noir, Pinot Noir Selection, Cabernet Sauvignon, Cabernet Merlot Selection, Reserve Port, Waipara Riesling, South Island Chardonnay.
summary Torlesse was effectively reborn in 1990 when its existing shareholders purchased the business from a receiver. They include Dr David Jackson, author of several books on viticulture, and winemaker Kym Rayner; all have vineyards in the Canterbury region that supply Torlesse with grapes, supplemented by grapes purchased from the Stonier Vineyard in Marlborough. The plans are for production to increase to about 13 000 cases. Exports to Australia, Canada and the UK.

totara vineyards NR

Main Road, Thames **region** Waikato and Bay of Plenty
phone (07) 868 6798 **fax** (07) 868 8729 **open** 7 days 10–6 summer, 10–5.30 winter
winemaker Gilbert Chan **production** 10 000 **est.** 1950
product range ($7.95–19.95 R) Müller Thurgau, Chardonnay, Reserve Chardonnay, Sauvignon Blanc, Chenin Blanc, Cabernet Sauvignon.
summary A substantial operation that has had its share of problems, leading to a decision to remove all its vineyards in 1986 under the Vine Pull Scheme; it now relies on local growers to provide the grapes for its wines. Had its moment of glory in the 1992 Air New Zealand Wine Awards when the '90 Reserve Chardonnay won the Chardonnay Trophy.

trents estate vineyard NR

Trents Road, Templeton **region** Canterbury
phone (03) 349 6940 **fax** (03) 349 6940 **open** Thurs, Sun 11–4.30; Fri, Sat 11–late
winemaker Alan McCorkindale **production** 1000 **est.** 1995
product range ($21–25 R) Riesling, Chardonnay, Pinot Noir.
summary This combined vineyard and restaurant business takes its name from a property established by Edwin Trent in 1866. Trent ran a highly successful chicory growing and drying industry on the farm to supply chicory for blending with coffee essence, a concoction that remained popular in New Zealand until the arrival of instant coffee in the 1960s. The building that now houses the restaurant was used as a chicory drying kiln. One hectare each of chardonnay, riesling and pinot noir were planted in 1995, and the wines are contract-made by Alan McCorkindale. They are sold exclusively through the restaurant, but can be purchased for consumption off premise at a 10 per cent discount.

trinity hill ★★★★☆

2396 State Highway 50, RD5, Hastings **region** Hawke's Bay
phone (06) 879 7778 **fax** (06) 879 7770 **open** 7 days 10–5
winemaker John Hancock, Warren Gibson **production** 35 000 **est.** 1996
product range ($15–38 R) Cheaper Shepherds Croft brand: Sauvignon Blanc, Chardonnay, Merlot Cabernet Franc Syrah; Wairarapa Riesling; premium Gimblett Road label: Chardonnay, Syrah, Merlot, Cabernet Sauvignon Merlot, Cabernet Sauvignon.
summary A fast-rising star in the New Zealand firmament. A joint venture between former Morton Estate winemaker John Hancock, an Auckland businessman and a pair of London restaurateurs. The venture began with the establishment of a 15.5-hectare vineyard on a prime Gimblett Road site, followed by the erection of a state-of-the-art winery in 1996. All of the wines so far released have achieved great critical acclaim. An additional 60 hectares are under contract, and the wines are exported to Australia, Brazil, France, Hong Kong, Israel, Japan, the Netherlands, the Philippines, Singapore, the UK and the US.

Trinity Hill Gimblett Road Merlot

YYYYY **1999** Medium to full purple-red; a ripe, lush plummy/berry/spicy bouquet flows seductively into a ripe, lush, fleshy palate with sweet berry and plum flavours; oak is there, but in a support role, and the tannins are remarkably soft and ripe. A strong gold-medal performer at the Royal Easter Wine Show 2001. **rating:** 94
best drinking 2003–2009 **best vintages** NA **drink with** Veal goulash • $34

two paddocks NR

PO Box 369, Queenstown **region** Central Otago
phone (03) 442 5988 **fax** (03) 441 1123 **open** Not
winemaker Dean Shaw (Contract) **production** 650 **est.** 1997
product range ($31 R) Neill Pinot Noir.
summary Two Paddocks (only one is presently in production) is the venture of actor Sam Neill. By 2002 both the Gibbston Valley and Earnscleugh vineyards will be in production, producing two single-vineyard Pinots.

unison vineyard ★★★★☆

2163 Highway 50, RD5, Hastings **region** Hawke's Bay
phone (06) 879 7913 **fax** (06) 879 7915 **open** By appointment
winemaker Anna-Barbara and Bruce Helliwell **production** 2500 **est.** 1993
product range ($23.50–38 CD) Unison and Unison Selection (Merlot, Cabernet Sauvignon and Syrah blends).
summary Bruce Helliwell, a New Zealand winemaker with MSc Honours degree, met his German-born and trained viticulturist and winemaker wife Anna-Barbara while she was managing a small estate in Chianti Classico hill country. Between them they have winemaking and viticultural experience in New Zealand, Germany, California, Italy, Switzerland and France. The vines on the 6-hectare estate are close-planted at a density of 5000 vines per hectare, with the yield reduced to only 1 kilogram per vine. These are seriously good wines. Exports to Australia, the UK, the US, Germany, Belgium, Sweden and Switzerland.

Unison Selection

YYYYY **1999** Medium purple-red; a spotlessly clean bouquet with a melange of dark berries woven through perfectly balanced and integrated oak; blackberry, currant and plum fruit on the bouquet is lengthened by persistent but balanced tannins. An exceptionally good outcome for the vintage. **rating:** 94

best drinking 2004–2009 **best vintages** '98, '99 **drink with** Braised ox tail • $38

Unison

YYYY **1999** Medium red-purple; the bouquet is initially fragrant and fresh, with the oak evident but not excessive. Strangely, the oak tended to dominate more as the wine was aerated, not withstanding the obviously restricted oak inputs. A lively palate with a range of red fruits and what seems to be quite brisk acidity again has a minor Indian arm-wrestle with the oak. Because of its youth and the making methods, I am prepared to wager the fruit will win the day. **rating:** 88

best drinking 2004–2009 **best vintages** NA **drink with** Lamb chops • $29

valli NR

Coal Pit Road, Gibbston, Otago **region** Central Otago
phone (03) 442 6778 **open** Not
winemaker Grant Taylor **production** 200 **est.** NA
product range ($33 R) Pinot Noir.
summary This is the own-label venture of Gibbston Valley winemaker Grant Taylor, based on his own 4-hectare vineyard, and made not at Gibbston Valley, but at Mount Edward. The name comes from a distant relative and early migrant, Guiseppe Valli. The first vintages released were from grapes purchased from other growers while the estate plantings came into bearing. Predictably, the wines have been enthusiastically received.

van asch wines NR

Back Road, Gibbston **region** Central Otago
phone (02) 432 3203 **fax** (03) 442 7122 **open** Not
winemaker Grant Taylor **production** 350 **est.** 1999
product range ($29 R) Pinot Noir.
summary Henry van Asch was one of the co-founders of bungy jumping from the bridge that crosses the Kawarau River Gorge near Chard Farm. Watching the development of Chard Farm caused van Asch to develop his own 3-hectare vineyard in 1990. Until 1999 the crop was sold to other winemakers, but in that year he had part of the production made for him by Grant Taylor at Mount Edward Winery.

vavasour wines 

Redwood Pass Road, Awatere Valley, Marlborough **region** Marlborough
phone (03) 575 7481 **fax** (03) 575 7240 **open** Mon–Sat 10–5 April–Sept, 7 days 10–5 Oct–Mar
winemaker Glenn Thomas **production** 25 000 **est.** 1986
product range ($14.95–29 R) Top end, Vavasour Single Vineyard Sauvignon Blanc, Chardonnay; then Awatere Valley Reisling, Sauvignon Blanc, Chardonnay, Pinot Noir, Cabernet Sauvignon; then Dashwood Chardonnay, Sauvignon Blanc, Pinot Noir; also Stafford Brook Chardonnay, Cabernet.

summary Vavasour has established itself as one of the most reliable and best producers in the Marlborough region. The drier, slightly warmer climate of the Awatere Valley and the unique river-terrace stony soils on which the 12.5-hectare vineyard is established are producing grapes of great intensity of flavour, which are in turn being skilfully handled in the winery by Glenn Thomas. Exports to Australia, the UK, the US, France, Ireland, Switzerland and Spain.

Vavasour Awatere Valley Riesling

YYYY **2000** Light green-yellow; a firm, clean and crisp bouquet is uncompromisingly dry and minerally, the palate with good balance and length, touches of apple and mineral, and proclaiming its potential if given time in bottle. **rating:** 86

best drinking 2004–2009 **best vintages** NA **drink with** Leave it in the cellar • $20

Vavasour Sauvignon Blanc

YYYYY **1999** Light green-yellow; the bouquet is crisp, with a mix of herb, spice and mineral aromas, the lemony palate lively and fresh, with cleansing acidity. **rating:** 91

best drinking Now **best vintages** '99 **drink with** Bluff oysters • $23

Vavasour Awatere Valley Sauvignon Blanc

YYYY **2000** Light straw-green; the clean, crisp and minerally bouquet is moderately intense, with a twist of lemon, the palate following suit with a fresh, crisp and lively mouthfeel. One of those rare Sauvignon Blancs that actually needs time in bottle for the fruit expression to blossom. **rating:** 85

best drinking 2002–2004 **best vintages** '97 **drink with** Shellfish • $20

Vavasour Single Vineyard Sauvignon Blanc

YYYY **1999** Light to medium yellow-green; the tangy and twangy bouquet is lifted by the French oak, giving it nutty overtones. The palate highlights the fruit more with touches of gooseberry and citrus, reassuring the horses, and most certainly offering an alternative style. **rating:** 88

best drinking Now–2004 **best vintages** '89, '91, '94, '96, '99 **drink with** Char-grilled baby octopus • $29

Vavasour Awatere Valley Chardonnay

YYYYY **1999** Bright yellow-green; the bouquet is fresh and clean, with focused melon and nectarine fruit; the same attractive fruit runs through the palate, with some white peach joining the nectarine. Good acidity to close. Ageing nicely. **rating:** 90

best drinking Now–2003 **best vintages** NA **drink with** Gravlax • $25

Vavasour Pinot Noir

YYYY **1998** Light to medium red-purple; the bouquet is quite intense, with good fruit and oak balance and integration; touches of plum and forest. The savoury/plummy palate has good length with well-managed tannins and subtle oak. Shows the hallmark of an outstanding vintage in Marlborough. **rating:** 87

best drinking Now–2004 **best vintages** '94, '97, '98 **drink with** Braised duck • $28.95

vidal estate ★★★★☆

913 St Aubyns Street East, Hastings **region** Hawke's Bay
phone (06) 876 8105 **fax** (06) 876 5312 **open** Summer Mon–Sat 10–6, Sun 10–5; winter Sun–Fri 10–5, Sat 10–6
winemaker Rod McDonald **production** 45 000 **est.** 1905
product range ($14.50–40 CD) The product range has been slimmed down and simplified, with the usual varietal array of Sauvignon Blanc, Riesling, Chardonnay (Hawke's Bay and East Coast) and Pinot Noir; Reserve Gewurztraminer, Chardonnay, Cabernet Sauvignon Merlot, Cabernet Sauvignon and Methode Traditionelle Brut complete the range.
summary Together with Te Mata, Villa Maria and Esk Valley, consistently produces some of New Zealand's finest red wines; they have ripeness, richness and balance, a far cry from the reds of bygone years. Surprisingly, notwithstanding the success of Vidal year after year at the Sydney International Wine Competition, and notwithstanding that its wines are distributed in the UK, Canada, much of Asia and the Pacific, it has still not sought distribution in Australia. Surely it will be only a question of time, for production continues to increase, the quality immaculate. It also has a restaurant open seven days for lunch and dinner.

Vidal Estate Hawke's Bay Sauvignon Blanc

ŸŸŸŸ **2000** Light to medium yellow-green; quite intense lemon, herb and mineral aromas are followed by a medium-bodied, well-balanced and focused palate. **rating:** 89

best drinking Now **best vintages** '94, '96, '00 **drink with** Poached scallops • $15.50

Vidal Reserve Chardonnay

ŸŸŸŸŸ **1999** Medium to full yellow-green; a complex, powerful bouquet showing strong barrel-ferment characters (which also come through on the palate) supported by potent grapefruit aromas and flavours. An imperious wine, not to be taken lightly. **rating:** 95

best drinking Now **best vintages** '90, '91, '94, '96, '97, '98 **drink with** Veal fricassee • $30

Vidal Estate Pinot Noir

ŸŸŸŸY **1999** Medium red-purple; a fragrant and stylish bouquet offers a mix of spice, plum and cherry fruit, the oak in restraint; the palate is a logical follow-on, elegant and long, with vibrant cherry and plum fruit supported by fine tannins. **rating:** 93

best drinking Now–2004 **best vintages** '99 **drink with** Quail • $19

Vidal Estate Reserve Cabernet Sauvignon Merlot

ŸŸŸŸY **1999** Medium to full purple-red; the bouquet is quite fragrant, with black fruits balanced against varietal austerity. Tasted immediately after bottling, you could see the components, the Malbec and American oak providing sweetness and spice, the Cabernet and Merlot the blackberry concentration and tannins. Rated as it tasted, but very likely deserving of even higher points as it matures. **rating:** 91

ŸŸŸŸY **1998** Medium red, with some purple hues remaining. Blackberry and blackcurrant fruit aromas are the primary drivers of the complex bouquet, with light touches of earth and olive in the background. There is lots of sweet oak surrounding the fruit on the palate, showing touches of chocolate along with the red berries; the tannins are quite strong, but ripe, and it all comes together impressively. **rating:** 93

best drinking 2004–2009 **best vintages** '90, '91, '98, '99 **drink with** Grilled calf's liver • $32

Vidal Estate Reserve Cabernet Sauvignon

ŸŸŸŸŸ **1998** Bright red-purple; a complex bouquet with quite savoury/olive characters, the oak evident but not oppressive; the palate is rich and textured, with ripe blackberry and chocolate fruit flavours cradled by persistent, lingering tannins and well-judged oak. **rating:** 94

best drinking 2003–2008 **best vintages** '90, '91, '94, '95, '98 **drink with** Seared lamb fillet • $40

vilagrad wines NR

Rukuhia Road, RD2, Ohaupo **region** Waikato and Bay of Plenty
phone (07) 825 2893 **open** 7 days 10–5
winemaker Peter Nooyen **production** 3200 **est.** 1922
product range ($15–22 CD) Chardonnay Traminer, Mt Pirongia Chardonnay (unwooded), Chardonnay Reserve, Vesna Semi Sec (sparkling), Rukuhia Estate Red, Mt Pirongia Pinot Noir, Pinot Noir Reserve, Cabernet Merlot Malbec Reserve, Vintage Port, Tawny Port.
summary A low-profile operation making wines of modest but consistently acceptable quality that age surprisingly well. A winery restaurant is open on Sundays (and for functions at other times by arrangement).

villa maria ★★★★★

5 Kirkbride Road, Mangere, Auckland **region** Auckland Area
phone (09) 255 0660 **fax** (09) 255 0661 **open** 7 days 9–6
winemaker Michelle Richardson **production** 500 000 **est.** 1961
product range ($7.50–39.95 CD) A large range of wines under the Private Bin label, basically varietally identified, stands at the bottom end of the portfolio; next comes the Cellar Selection range of Chardonnay, Cabernet Merlot; at the top end the Reserve Bin range of Barrique Fermented Chardonnay, Gewurztraminer, Cabernet Merlot and Cabernet Sauvignon; also Keltern Chardonnay.
summary Whether viewed on the basis of its performances at the Sydney International Winemakers Competition or on any other show result over the last few years, Villa Maria has to be rated one of New Zealand's best large wineries. The quality of the wines, both white and red, is exemplary, the flavours magically full without going over the top. Not surprisingly, the wines are exported to Europe, North America and Asia, but (as is the case with Vidal) so far, not to Australia.

Villa Maria Reserve Riesling

2000 Light green-yellow; as one would expect from the background, an immensely powerful bouquet, with lots of complexity and depth including some spicy overtones. The power flows through to the deep, spicy palate which, magically, doesn't show any adverse signs of the high alcohol. **rating:** 91

best drinking 2002–2007 **best vintages** '00 **drink with** Lightly spiced Thai • $20

Villa Maria Keltern Chardonnay

2000 Medium to full yellow-green; the bouquet offers lots of opulent, spicy barrel-ferment oak, the palate more of the same, but with plenty of fruit power and richness. Definitely from the big end of town and almost certainly best over the next 12 months. **rating:** 92

best drinking Now **best vintages** '00 **drink with** Seafood risotto • NA

Villa Maria Cellar Selection Bacchus Pinot Noir

1999 Deep red; the moderately intense bouquet has very ripe gamey/plummy fruit, the palate with masses of sweet, ripe plum; the saving grace, as it were, is that it is not over-extracted or tannic. **rating:** 90

best drinking 2002–2006 **best vintages** '99 **drink with** Jugged hare • $24.50

Villa Maria Reserve Hawke's Bay Merlot

1999 Medium to full red-purple; a very concentrated bouquet with masses of dark berry, plum, quince and exotic spice translates directly to the lush blackberry/currant/plum palate, finishing with ample but not threatening tannins and high-quality oak. An immediate and unanimous gold at the Royal Easter Wine Show 2001. **rating:** 95

best drinking 2004–2009 **best vintages** '96, '98, '99 **drink with** Venison medallions • $38.50

Villa Maria Reserve Merlot Cabernet

1999 Medium to full red-purple; rich cassis berry aromas and nicely balanced and integrated oak lead into a palate with strong, pristine fruit, with the cabernet making a major statement; lovely sweetness and fine tannins. To my palate everything the Esk Valley of the same year is not. **rating:** 96

best drinking 2004–2011 **best vintages** '85, '87, '90, '91, '92, '94, '95, '98, '99 **drink with** Rich, soft ripened cheese • $34.50

villa maria (marlborough) ★★★★★

Cnr New Renwick and Paynters Roads, Blenheim **region** Marlborough
phone (03) 577 9530 **fax** (03) 577 9585 **open** 7 days 10–5
winemaker George Seris **production** NA **est.** 1999
product range ($NA) A varying roster which, in ascending order, normally includes Private Bin Sauvignon Blanc, Wairau Valley Reserve Sauvignon Blanc, and then the varietal Reserve Bin range of Marlborough Chardonnay, Sauvignon Blanc and Noble Riesling.
summary The Marlborough winery of Villa Maria serves the obvious purpose of reducing transport time from vineyard to the point of processing. Many of the wines from Villa Maria are, of course, regional blends, with fruit coming from Marlborough, Hawke's Bay and Gisborne. The quality of the wines is beyond reproach.

Villa Maria Cellar Selection Sauvignon Blanc

2000 Light to medium yellow-green; very rich, exotic, ripe, tropical fruit aromas are faithfully repeated on the soft, full-flavoured palate. Gold medal at the Royal Easter Wine Show 2001; rating it is a question of style rather than quality. **rating:** 89

best drinking Now **best vintages** '00 **drink with** Fish soup • $19

Villa Maria Private Bin Sauvignon Blanc

2000 Light green-yellow; a complex, powerful, minerally bouquet leads into a palate that provides rich, herbaceous/capsicum fruit flavours within a tight, minerally frame. I like the style of the wine. **rating:** 94

best drinking Now **best vintages** '00 **drink with** Gazpacho • $15

Villa Maria Reserve Clifford Bay Sauvignon Blanc

2000 Light to medium yellow-green; the bouquet is full, with intense passionfruit/tropical fruit aromatics which in turn provide the flavour for the palate; an easy, harmonious style that flows smoothly across the tongue. **rating:** 91

best drinking Now **best vintages** '97, '99, '00 **drink with** Prawn and avocado salad • $25.50

Villa Maria Wairau Valley Reserve Sauvignon Blanc

YYYYY **2000** Light to medium yellow-green; quite intense herb and mineral aromas with a spicy twitch, followed by an intense forepalate, again in the mineral and herb spectrum, then moving through to much riper gooseberry flavours on the back palate. **rating:** 90

best drinking Now **best vintages** '92, '94, '96, '97 **drink with** Smoked haddock • $23.95

Villa Maria Cellar Selection Marlborough Chardonnay

YYYYY **1999** Medium yellow-green; the bouquet offers a convincing mix of ripe stonefruit, melon, cashew and straw aromas. Then comes a particularly smooth palate, led by stonefruit and melon, and supported by subtle oak on a long finish. **rating:** 91

best drinking Now–2003 **best vintages** '99 **drink with** Creamy pasta • $19

Villa Maria Reserve Marlborough Chardonnay

YYYYY **1999** Full yellow-green; the bouquet is rich, with peach and more citrussy fruit harmoniously integrated with well-balanced oak; the palate has good length, and again finds an appropriate balance between the nectarine/citrus fruit and the spicy French oak. Gold medal at the Royal Easter Wine Show 2001. **rating:** 93

best drinking Now–2003 **best vintages** '94, '96, '97, '99 **drink with** Coquilles St Jacques • $30

Villa Maria Reserve Noble Riesling

YYYYY **1999** Medium to full yellow-green; the apricot and cumquat bouquet is essence-like in its extraordinary intensity, the palate no less decadently rich and lush, with the complex, concentrated botrytis fruit flavours balanced by long, lingering acidity. **rating:** 95

best drinking Now–2004 **best vintages** '91, '92, '93, '94, '96, '97, '98, '99 **drink with** Any rich dessert • $38.50

vin alto ★★★★

424 Creightons Road, RD2, Papakura, Clevedon **region** Auckland Area
phone (09) 292 8845 **fax** (09) 274 9542 **open** Not
winemaker Enzo Bettio **production** 2000 **est.** 1996
product range ($29–89 R) Semillon, Ordinario (Sangiovese, Corvina and Nebbiolo, with Cabernets and Merlot), Ritorno and Rettico.
summary Swiss-Italian Enzio Bettio came to New Zealand with his English wife, Margaret, in 1980 and before long had started what is now one of New Zealand's largest fine food and wine importing and distribution businesses, Delmaine. This has afforded him the opportunity of establishing Vin Alto, a steep hillside property with sweeping views across the Hauraki Gulf towards Waiheke Island. Here he has planted the largest selection of Italian varieties and clones in Australasia and set about producing red wine using the ancient methods of Valpolicello, and in particular Amarone (using, amongst other assistance, advice from Sandro Boscaini of Masi). What might have been a folly has been an unqualified success, even if you have to dig deep to taste the fruits of that success.

voss estate 

Puruatanga Road, Martinborough **region** Wairarapa
phone (06) 306 9668 **fax** (06) 306 9668 **open** 7 days 11–6 summer
winemaker Gary Voss **production** 2000 **est.** 1988
product range ($16–28 CD) Reserve Chardonnay, Sauvignon Blanc, Pinot Noir, Waihenga Cabernet Merlot Franc.
summary Voss Estate has been established by Annette Atkins, Gary Voss and Murray Voss, with 9.5 hectares of vineyards (5.5 hectares of pinot noir, 2 hectares chardonnay, 1 hectare of riesling and 0.5 hectare each of cabernet sauvignon, merlot and sauvignon blanc). Production is largely estate-based, with some grapes purchased from other Martinborough growers. Exports to Australia and Canada.

Voss Estate Pinot Noir

YYYY **1999** Medium red-purple; the bouquet has distinctly foresty/stemmy/savoury aromatics that are more or less precisely repeated on the stylish, though earthy, palate. A polar opposite of Ata Rangi or Dry River. **rating:** 87

best drinking Now–2004 **best vintages** NA **drink with** Baby lamb • $28

waiheke vineyards 

76 Onetangi Road, Onetangi, Waiheke Island **region** Waiheke Island
phone (09) 486 3859 **fax** (09) 486 2341 **open** Not

winemaker Paul Dunleavy, John Dunleavy **production** 1300 **est.** 1990
product range ($35–49 R) Te Motu Cabernet Merlot, Dunleavy Merlot Franc.
summary The venture of the Dunleavy family, headed by long-term, but now-retired, Wine Institute of New Zealand chief executive Terry Dunleavy. Produced outstanding wines in 1993 and 1994, providing yet further evidence (if any was needed) of the suitability of Waiheke Island for the production of ripe, full-bodied, Cabernets. Exports to the UK, Ireland, France and the US.

wai-iti river vineyard NR

Livingstone Road, Waimea West, Nelson **region** Nelson
phone (03) 542 3205 **fax** (03) 542 3205 **open** By appointment
winemaker Dave Glover (Contract) **production** 1000 **est.** 1993
product range ($17–30 CD) Riesling, Chardonnay, Pinot Noir, Cabernet Sauvignon.
summary Chan and Philip Woollaston planted their small (6-hectare) vineyard on the Waimea Plains near Nelson in the winter of 1993 on old riverbed gravels. The cellar-door sales and tastings opened in 1999.

Wai-iti River Chardonnay

ΥΥΥΥ **1997** Medium to full yellow-green; a big, full, broad, ripe melon and honey bouquet, with touches of spice is in stark contrast to the light- to medium-bodied palate. Far fresher and far more delicate than the bouquet would suggest, it has good acidity, and is chugging along nicely. **rating:** 85
best drinking Now **best vintages** NA **drink with** Chicken kebabs • $18

waimata wines NR

Rural Studios Unit, Stout Street, Gisborne **region** Gisborne
phone (06) 867 2010 **fax** (06) 867 2024 **open** Not
winemaker Mike Spivey **production** 3000 **est.** 1990
product range ($12–20 R) Chardonnay, Merlot.
summary Waimata Wines is part of the Tairawhiti Polytech, and is a working winery providing practical winemaking, viticultural, packaging and marketing experience to students in much the same way as the Charles Sturt University Winery does.

waimea estates ★★★★

148 Main Road, Hope, Nelson **region** Nelson
phone (03) 544 6385 **fax** (03) 544 6385 **open** 7 days Oct–Mar 10–6, Apr–Sept 10–5
winemaker Michael Brown **production** 15 000 **est.** 1997
product range ($15–45 R) Riesling, Classic Riesling, Sauvignon Blanc, Chardonnay, Noble Riesling, Rosé, Pinot Noir, Merlot Cabernet, Cabernet Merlot; Waimea Plains label: Nelson Riesling, Nelson Sauvignon Blanc.
summary Former orchardists Trevor and Robyn Bolitho diversified into viticulture in 1993 and by 2001 had 48 hectares of vineyard established. Part of the production is sold to other producers, but since 1997 Waimea Estates has produced wine under its own label. In 1998 a winery was built on site with an ultimate production capacity of 50 000 cases. The quality of the wines so far released has been consistently good. Exports to Australia, Japan and the US.

Waimea Plains Nelson Riesling

ΥΥΥΥΥ **2000** Light green-yellow; fine, lime, citrus and apple aromas are followed by a fresh, crisp, delicate and lingering palate. Won a silver medal at the Air New Zealand 2000 Wine Awards. **rating:** 90
best drinking Now–2007 **best vintages** '00 **drink with** Stuffed capsicum • $15

Waimea Plains Nelson Sauvignon Blanc

ΥΥΥΥ **2000** Light green-yellow; a quite pungent/grassy/gooseberry/capsicum-accented bouquet is followed by a lively, fresh, lemony palate, with some mid-palate texture and a good finish. **rating:** 88
best drinking Now **best vintages** '97, '99 **drink with** Calamari • $16

Waimea Estates Noble Riesling 375 ml

ΥΥΥΥΥ **2000** Golden yellow; voluminous and intense, rich apricot and cumquat aromas and flavours flood both the bouquet and palate thanks to the 200 grams per litre of residual sugar. Less than 500 litres made. **rating:** 94
best drinking Now–2010 **best vintages** NA **drink with** Rich fruit tart • $44.95

waipara downs NR

State Highway 7, Bains Road, RD3, Amberley **region** Waipara
phone (03) 314 6873 **fax** (03) 314 6873 **open** By appointment
winemaker François Crochet **production** 800 **est.** 1989
product range ($12–16 CD) Chardonnay, Pinot Noir, Cabernet Sauvignon, Port.
summary Six hectares of vines on a 320-hectare farm puts Waipara Downs into perspective, but does not diminish the enjoyment Ruth and Keith Berry derive from producing their wines from the limestone soils of the Waipara Valley. The wines have been consistent bronze and silver medal winners in New Zealand wine shows. The wines are distributed in Australia through Negociants.

waipara springs wines ★★★★

State Highway 1, Waipara, North Canterbury **region** Waipara
phone (03) 314 6777 **fax** (03) 314 6777 **open** 7 days 11–5
winemaker Stephanie Henderson-Grant **production** 10 000 **est.** 1990
product range ($15–28 CD) Riesling, Dry Riesling, Sauvignon Blanc, Chardonnay, Reserve Barrique Chardonnay, Botrytised Riesling 375 ml, Reserve Pinot Noir, Cabernet Sauvignon.
summary Owned by Bruce and Jill Moore and the Grant family, represented by Andrew Grant and Stephanie Henderson-Grant. The initial plantings of 4 hectares in 1982 have now risen to 20 hectares, providing all of the grapes for the significantly increased production. The wines have deservedly gained an excellent reputation; exports to Australia, the UK, the US and Canada.

Waipara Springs Sauvignon Blanc

2000 Light green-yellow; there are interesting passionfruit and lychee aromas, vaguely reminiscent of traminer, and at the tropical end of the spectrum. Similarly lush passionfruit and gooseberry flavours are to be found on the palate, which has good length, and buttoned up with crisp acidity on the finish. **rating:** 89
best drinking Now **best vintages** NA **drink with** Deep-fried calamari • $15

Waipara Springs Reserve Barrique Chardonnay

1999 Medium yellow-green; quite strong barrel-ferment aromas are offset by citrus and stonefruit aromas on the bouquet. The palate is tight, tangy and long, with similar citrus and stonefruit flavours dominant, the oak playing a pure support role. **rating:** 90
best drinking Now **best vintages** NA **drink with** Pan-fried fresh fish • $21

Waipara Springs Reserve Pinot Noir

1999 Medium red-purple; plum, spice and briar aromas are followed by a plummy/cherry/strawberry-flavoured palate, with good length and structure; gentle tannins and subtle oak. **rating:** 89
best drinking Now–2004 **best vintages** NA **drink with** Rabbit and mushroom casserole • $28

waipara west NR

376 Ram Paddock Road, Amberley, RD2, North Canterbury **region** Waipara
phone (03) 314 8699 **fax** (03) 314 8692 **open** By appointment 10–4 most week days
winemaker Petter Evans **production** 6000 **est.** 1989
product range ($12–35 CD) Riesling, Sauvignon Blanc, Chardonnay, Pinot Noir are the premium varietals; Ram Paddock Red and Two Terrace Red are second-label blends.
summary Waipara West is situated at the gorge of the Waipara River. The vineyard is surrounded by steep banks and planted on naturally sloping terraces that vary in height and aspect. Over 21 hectares of chardonnay, sauvignon blanc, riesling, merlot, cabernet sauvignon, cabernet franc and pinot noir have been planted, with the very experienced Petter Evans (ex St Helena) in charge of winemaking. Exports to the UK, Denmark, France, Holland, Norway, the US and Malaysia.

wairau river wines

Cnr Rapaura Road and State Highway 6, Blenheim **region** Marlborough
phone (03) 572 9800 **fax** (03) 572 9885 **open** 7 days 9–5
winemaker John Belsham **production** 20 000 **est.** 1978
product range ($17–40 CD) Riesling, Botrytised Riesling Reserve, Sauvignon Blanc, Sauvignon Blanc Reserve, Chardonnay, Chardonnay Reserve; Philip Rose Estate is the second label, introduced in 1995.

summary Phil and Chris Rose have been long-term grape-growers in the Marlborough region, having established 110 hectares of vineyard progressively since 1978. The first wines were made under the Wairau River label in 1991 by contract-winemaker John Belsham, and all of the vintages to date have been of exemplary quality, particularly the tropical-accented Sauvignon Blanc. Exports to Australia (all States), Canada, the US, the UK, Germany, Hong Kong, Singapore and Sweden.

Wairau River Sauvignon Blanc

TTTTY **2000** Light green-yellow; the clean bouquet has attractively ripened gooseberry and a touch of passionfruit; quite stylish. The light- to medium-bodied palate has a highly civilised even flow across the tongue, lifted by slightly lemony acidity on the finish. **rating:** 91

best drinking Now **best vintages** '91, '92, '93, '94, '96, '97, '98, '00 **drink with** Deep-fried calamari • $19

Wairau River Sauvignon Blanc Reserve

TTTTY **1999** Light to medium yellow-green; a powerful, concentrated and complex bouquet has bottle-developed and oak-influenced aromatics; the long and powerful palate provides more of the same, with the gently tropical fruit carrying through and expressing itself quite strongly on the aftertaste. **rating:** 90

best drinking Now–2003 **best vintages** '99 **drink with** Veal fricassee • $23

Wairau River Chardonnay Reserve

TTTTY **1997** Medium yellow-green; the smooth bouquet is led by fig, melon and cashew aromas, the barrel-ferment characters in second place. The same play occurs on the fresh and smooth palate; altogether elegant and unforced. **rating:** 90

best drinking Now–2005 **best vintages** '97 **drink with** Milk-fed veal • $28

waitiri creek wines NR

State Highway 6, Gibbston Valley RD, Queenstown **region** Central Otago
phone (09) 520 0572 **fax** (09) 520 0965 **open** By appointment
winemaker Dean Shaw **production** NA **est.** 1994
product range ($18–30 R) Gewurztraminer, Chardonnay, Pinot Noir.
summary In a move reminiscent of the relocation in 1965 of an 1840 stone jail to house the then Hordern's Wybong Estate Winery in the Upper Hunter of New South Wales, Waitiri Creek's cellar door is housed in a 110-year-old Rimu church that has been moved to the site and which opened in November 2000.

Waitiri Creek Pinot Noir

TTTY **1999** The colour is already showing some change from red-purple to reddish brick; the bouquet is stalky/sappy with quite pronounced charry, high-toast oak. The palate is rather light-on, presumably due to young vines, and a little simple in fruit terms, but overall has definite varietal character. **rating:** 83

best drinking Now **best vintages** NA **drink with** Grilled salmon • $28

waiwera estate ★★★☆

Rocklands Road, Takaka **region** Nelson
phone (03) 525 8059 **fax** (03) 525 9898 **open** Not
winemaker David Heraud **production** 200 **est.** 1991
product range ($25 R) Pinot Noir.
summary David Heraud planted 0.5 hectare of pinot noir a kilometre away from the historic Ellis & Sons winery, the first winery in Nelson established in 1868. Heraud makes the wine with help from Sam Weaver as consultant, and sells it to shops in Nelson and Christchurch.

Waiwera Estate Pinot Noir

TTTT **1999** Quite dark red, the hue suggesting elevated pH; a voluminous bouquet of very ripe fruit tending to pruney is followed by a commensurately opulent, powerful and rich palate, crammed with ripe fruit and some tannins. Time in bottle just might surprise. **rating:** 89

best drinking 2002–2006 **best vintages** NA **drink with** Big game • $25

walnut ridge ★★★★☆

159 Regent Street, Martinborough **region** Wairarapa
phone (06) 306 9323 **fax** (06) 306 9323 **open** Weekends 11–5 while stocks last
winemaker Bill Brink **production** 800 **est.** 1986
product range ($17–40 CD) Sauvignon Blanc, Botrytised Sauvignon Blanc, Pinot Noir, Cabernet Sauvignon.
summary While Bill Brink produces both Pinot Noir and Cabernet Sauvignon, he falls on the Pinot Noir side of the argument as far as Martinborough is concerned. That view, mind you, is not so surprising when you find that the first release from Walnut Ridge was the 1994 Pinot Noir, which was awarded a silver medal at the 1995 Air New Zealand Wine Awards. As to the rest, I should quote Bill Brink, who says that he 'came to New Zealand via the somewhat circuitous route of Samoa and the Peace Corps in 1973. After a number of years in public service and doing the Dominion crossword, and a change-of-pace year at Victoria University deliberating the obfuscatory logic of "existential deterrence", I came to Martinborough and began the development of what has become Walnut Ridge.' Exports to Australia and the UK.

Walnut Ridge Pinot Noir

🍷🍷🍷🍷 **1999** Medium to full red-purple; a clean, full bouquet with ripe, rich black cherry offset by a touch of forest; the powerful and serious palate has great texture and flavour, running through all manner of small berries and plums; just when it seems it might be over the top, fine tannins and good acidity round the wine off. **rating:** 93
best drinking 2002–2007 **best vintages** '96, '99 **drink with** Any wild game • $40

Walnut Ridge Cabernet Sauvignon

🍷🍷🍷🍷 **1998** Medium to full red-purple; rich and ripe blackberry and plum fruit together with appealing oak on the bouquet lead into a most attractive palate with excellent weight and richness, once again supported by the positive impact of high-quality French oak. **rating:** 93
best drinking 2003–2010 **best vintages** '98 **drink with** Saddle of lamb • NA

west brook winery ★★★☆

215 Ararimu Valley Road, Waimauku, Auckland **region** Auckland Area
phone (09) 411 9924 **fax** (09) 411 9925 **open** Mon–Sat 10–5, Sun 11–5
winemaker Anthony Ivicevich **production** 10 000 **est.** 1937
product range ($11.95–28.95 CD) Marlborough Riesling, Sauvignon Blanc, Barrique Fermented Chardonnay, Hawke's Bay Chenin Blanc, Hawke's Bay Merlot, Henderson Merlot, Henderson Cabernet Merlot; also under the Blue Ridge label are Marlborough Sauvignon Blanc, Marlborough Chardonnay, Late Harvest Marlborough Riesling, Henderson Cabernet Merlot.
summary West Brook made its last vintage at the old Henderson winery in 1999 and has now moved to a new winery in the Ararimu Valley. It is reasonable to expect that the already good range of wines will improve in the years ahead, bolstered by 3.5 hectares of estate vineyards at Hawke's Bay, with an additional 2 hectares still to be planted. Exports to the UK.

West Brook Marlborough Sauvignon Blanc

🍷🍷🍷🍷 **2000** Light to medium green-yellow; there is a cascade of tropical fruit/stonefruit/pineapple/passionfruit on the bouquet. The rich and fleshy mid-palate is offset by brisk acidity on the finish, but a skein of sweetness (in fruit terms) runs through a long and flavoursome wine. **rating:** 92
best drinking Now **best vintages** '00 **drink with** Pan-seared scallops • $14.95

West Brook Hawke's Bay Chenin Blanc

🍷🍷🍷🍷 **1999** Medium yellow-green; soft, spicy oak and equally soft butterscotch aromas are followed by a full-flavoured palate with pineapple, butterscotch and honey, the oak subliminal. **rating:** 87
best drinking Now **best vintages** NA **drink with** Roast pork • $13

West Brook Blue Ridge Late Harvest Marlborough Riesling

🍷🍷🍷🍷 **1999** Light to medium yellow-green; the bouquet has a mix of tropical, citrus, honey and peach aromas, the citrus/lime palate showing excellent varietal character, sustained in turn by good acid balance. Quite a classy wine. **rating:** 92
best drinking Now–2004 **best vintages** '00 **drink with** Crème brûlée • $28.95

West Brook Hawke's Bay Merlot

TTTT **1999** Medium to full red-purple; the bouquet is solid and quite smooth, albeit with slightly subdued aromatics. The palate is big and rich, with dark plum and berry fruit, and equally prominent tannins. A lighter touch on the press might have made an even better wine. **rating:** 86

best drinking 2004–2009 **best vintages** NA **drink with** Braised ox cheek • $18.95

weston reserve winery NR

25 Forresbank Avenue, Wakari, Dunedin **region** Central Otago
phone (03) 467 5544 **open** By appointment
winemaker Geoff Weston **production** 350 **est.** 1997
product range ($10–25 ML) Barrel One Chardonnay, Garden Block Chardonnay, Weston Reserve Chardonnay and Pinot Noir; also various fruit wines.
summary Geoff Weston is a man of many parts, who has graduated from making fruit-based wines on a hobby scale to small-scale commercial winemaking from grapes purchased from various parts of New Zealand. The location of the winery has been authenticated by the *Guinness Book of Records* as the world's most southern winery, a location (at 45°51' S) which means there can be no local vinifera grapes used, and which might be argued makes the location of the winery coincidental at best. However, Weston is a born marketer, and uses it and a number of other catchy gimmicks (including his own special wine stamps) as marketing tools. Into the bargain, the wines are all made using thoroughly non-interventionist techniques.

whitehaven wine company ★★★★☆

1 Dodson Street, Blenheim, Marlborough **region** Marlborough
phone (03) 577 8861 **fax** (03) 577 8868 **open** 7 days 9–5
winemaker Simon Waghorn **production** 18 000 **est.** 1993
product range ($13.50–21 CD) Riesling, Festival Riesling, Sauvignon Blanc, Barrel Fermented Sauvignon Blanc, Chardonnay, Pinot Noir; also Single Vineyard Reserve Riesling, Gewurztraminer, Sauvignon Blanc, Pinot Gris, Noble Riesling.
summary Whitehaven is a joint venture between Greg and Sue White and winemaker Simon Waghorn. Waghorn qualified as a winemaker at Roseworthy in Australia, first becoming assistant winemaker at Cooks Wines and thereafter spending five years as senior winemaker at Corbans' Gisborne winery, where he was responsible for production of a string of gold medal winning wines. A 200-tonne state-of-the-art winery has been built which includes a restaurant and wine shop as part of the complex. As one would expect, the initial releases under the Whitehaven label have had great show success. The business has grown dramatically, and the wines are now exported to the UK, Japan, the Netherlands, the US, Hong Kong and Australia.

Whitehaven Riesling

TTTT **2000** Light green-yellow; a fine, clean and crisp bouquet heralds an elegant, restrained palate, the sweetness so well balanced by the acidity it becomes simply part of the flavour-flow, and in no sense an add-on. **rating:** 89

best drinking Now–2004 **best vintages** '00 **drink with** Pan-fried tarakihi • $15

Whitehaven Single Vineyard Reserve Sauvignon Blanc

TTTTY **2000** Light to medium yellow-green; sits at the ripe end of the Sauvignon Blanc spectrum, with gooseberry and stonefruit aromas and flavours. The mouthfeel is excellent: full, round and soft, without cloying. The sort of wine that should melt the stoniest heart. **rating:** 92

best drinking Now **best vintages** '00 **drink with** Antipasto • $19

william hill winery NR

Dunstan Road, RD1, Alexandra **region** Central Otago
phone (03) 448 8436 **fax** (03) 448 8434 **open** Mon–Sun 10–4.30
winemaker Gerry Rowland, David Grant **production** 2000 **est.** 1982
product range ($17–28 CD) Riesling, Gewurztraminer, Chardonnay, Pinot Noir.
summary Notwithstanding that the William Hill vineyards extend to 9 hectares, production grew painfully slowly in the early years. A new winery was commissioned for 1995 (happily an exceptional vintage for Central Otago) that offers contract-winemaking services for other wineries in the region. It has recently acquired an additional 80 hectares of land, and planted 10 hectares of pinot noir in 2000. Exports to the US.

winslow wines ★★★★☆

Princess Street, Martinborough **region** Wairarapa
phone (06) 306 9648 **fax** (06) 306 9271 **open** 7 days 10–5.30 Aug–April, winter by appointment
winemaker Elise Montgomery, Steve Tarring **production** 625 **est.** 1985
product range ($19–36 CD) St Vincent Riesling, St Vincent Reserve Riesling, Rosetta Cabernet Rosé, Petra Cabernet Sauvignon and, at the pinnacle, Turakirae Reserve Cabernet Sauvignon Franc.
summary The Bio-Gro™-managed estate plantings of 2.2 hectares are planted to cabernet sauvignon (2 hectares) and cabernet franc (0.2 hectare). Owners Jennifer and Steve Tarring buy the remainder of the grapes for the small production from contract growers. It produced a quite brilliant and intense St Vincent Reserve Riesling in 1999, and a gold medal-winning 1998 Turakirae Reserve Cabernet Sauvignon Franc in 1998. It is a great pity production is so small.

wishart estate winery NR

728 Main North Road, Bay View, Napier **region** Hawke's Bay
phone (06) 836 6355 **fax** (06) 836 6375 **open** By appointment
winemaker Don Bird **production** 1700 **est.** 1999
product range ($17–29 R) Sauvignon Blanc, Chardonnay, Reserve Chardonnay, Cabernet Merlot Malbec, Reserve Merlot Malbec Cabernet.
summary This is a rapidly expanding partnership between the Bird family (previously owners of Esk Valley Winery before it was sold in 1986) and Alex Elton of Auckland. Two vineyards are either owned or leased, and plantings are to be expanded over the next three years, with merlot the main focus. The winery is not open for cellar-door sales because of objections of Transit New Zealand, but are available mail order and retail.

Wishart Estate Reserve Merlot Malbec Cabernet

1999 Medium to full red-purple; the bouquet is clean, with sweet, ripe cassis/blackcurrant fruit that manifests itself on the powerfully built but well-made palate; all the wine needs is a bit of time for the ever-so-slightly abrasive tannins on the finish to soften. **rating:** 93

best drinking 2004–2009 **best vintages** '99 **drink with** Char-grilled rump • $29

wither hills vineyards ★★★★☆

New Renwick Road, RD2, Blenheim **region** Marlborough
phone (09) 522 9684 **fax** (09) 522 9685 **open** Not
winemaker Brent Marris **production** 20 000 **est.** 1994
product range ($20–45 R) Sauvignon Blanc, Chardonnay, Pinot Noir.
summary The Marris family have been grape-growers in Marlborough for 12 years and now have 80 hectares under vine, with a further 35 hectares available for planting. Since Brent Marris left his position as chief winemaker for Delegat's, production of Wither Hills has increased rapidly, though part of the estate grapes are still sold. Having initially secured a reputation with the Sauvignon Blanc and Chardonnay, Brent Marris leapt to prominence with his 1998 Pinot Noir. Exports to Australia, the US, Singapore, Brazil, Indonesia, the UK, France, the Philippines and Japan.

Wither Hills Vineyards Pinot Noir

1999 Medium red-purple; a wonderfully fragrant and stylish bouquet blends sappy/spicy fruit with charry oak; the elegant, medium-bodied palate has long, sappy/cherry fruit, with convincing tannins on the finish. Great stuff. **rating:** 95

best drinking 2002–2006 **best vintages** '98, '99 **drink with** Breast of squab • $45

woodbourne estate NR

Rapaura Road, RD3, Blenheim **region** Marlborough
phone (03) 527 7133 **fax** (03) 572 7134 **open** 7 days 10–5
winemaker Bill Hennessy **production** 1300 **est.** 1998
product range ($NA) Sauvignon Blanc, Chardonnay, Pinot Noir, Blanc de Noir Methode Champenoise.

summary Rob and Ann Myers purchased an 11-hectare orchard in 1997, and immediately replanted it to vines. Until it comes into bearing they purchase grapes from contract growers and have their wines contract-made at Rapaura Vintners. In 1999 it opened a cellar-door and restaurant complex as a joint venture with Clifford Bay Estate.

Woodbourne Estate Marlborough Chardonnay

ҮҮҮҮ **2000** Light yellow-green; the bouquet is of light to medium intensity, with citrus and melon fruit, and minimal, if any, oak. The palate is clean, nicely balanced, with more of the citrus and melon flavours of the bouquet. Silver medal winner at the Royal Easter Wine Show 2001. **rating:** 86

best drinking Now **best vintages** NA **drink with** White-fleshed fish • $18

woodfield estate NR

57 Duncan Road, Hamilton **region** Waikato and Bay of Plenty
phone (07) 827 7170 **fax** (07) 827 7140 **open** Tues–Sun 10–5
winemaker Brian Mahoney **production** 500 **est.** 1994
product range ($14–25 CD) Chardonnay, Cabernet Merlot.
summary June and Brian Mahoney have established a small winery and cellar-door facility in an architect-designed farmhouse style, and use natural winemaking methods (minimal additives, minimal filtration, no stabilisation) in handling the Waikato-grown grapes they use to make their wines

index

Macedon Ranges

McLaren Vale

Manjimup

Margaret River

Marlborough

Wine Atlas of Australia and New Zealand

New revised edition

This new edition offers all the detail and research of the previous edition, and more. Including maps of Australia's new wine regions, profiles on Australia and New Zealand's top winemakers and wineries and stunning photographs, the *Wine Atlas of Australia and New Zealand* is an indispensable reference tool.

ISBN: 0 7322 6448 0

Collecting Wine: You and Your Cellar

a necessity for every wine enthusiast, this book contains valuable information on how to start and maintain a cellar, how to choose white and red wines for cellaring, the most efficient cellar racking systems and the problems a bottle may encounter during its life. It also provides Australian and imported wine vintage charts and recommends wine merchants, auction houses, societies and literature.

ISBN: 0 7322 6528 2